CIVITAS:
A Framework for Civic Education

Charles N. Quigley
Editorial Director

Charles F. Bahmueller, Ph.D.
General Editor

A collaborative project of the
Center for Civic Education
and the
Council for the Advancement of Citizenship
with support from
The Pew Charitable Trusts

National Council for the Social Studies Bulletin No. 86

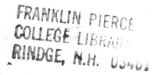
 Center for Civic Education, Calabasas, CA

CURR
JK
1764
.C57
1991

To

R. Freeman Butts

in recognition for his contributions to CIVITAS
and a lifetime of dedication to American education
and its civic misson.

Acknowledgments

Center for Civic Education
Charles N. Quigley, Executive Director
Charles F. Bahmueller, Project Director

Project Advisors
John Hale
Duane Smith

Copy Editors
Judith Matz
Jane Sure

Production Manager
Patricia Mathwig

Research Assistant
Daniel Wojcik

Council for the Advancement of Citizenship
John H. Buchanan, Jr., Executive Director
Nancy Warzer, Assistant Director

Framework Development Steering Committee
Margaret Stimmann Branson
R. Freeman Butts
Jack Hoar

Book Design and Production
Theresa M. Richard

Production Assistants
Rosalyn Danberg
Jan Ruyle

Editorial Director
Charles N. Quigley

General Editor
Charles F. Bahmueller

The Center for Civic Education wishes to thank the members of the Framework Development Committee, the National Review Council, and the National Teachers Advisory Committee for their invaluable advice, assistance, and support. In addition, the following individuals made contributions to the development of CIVITAS:

Dr. Ron Abler of the American Association of Geographers arranged for the initial production of the geography section and cooperated in reviewing the final draft; **Professor Benjamin Barber** of Rutgers University, lent his support for the project, recommended a contributor, and kindly reviewed a section of the mss.; **Professor David R. Berman** of the University of Arizona read and commented on a section of the mss.; **Debra Blackman** of the CCE greatly assisted the project director with her clerical skills; **Professor Thad L. Beyle** of the University of North Carolina at Chapel Hill read and commented on a section of the mss.; **Professor Harry Boyte** of the University of Minnesota read and made valuable comments on the Rationale; **Donald Bragaw** of East Carolina University gave the project his unfailing support and valuable advice; **Sharon Bravo** of the Center for Civic Education (CCE) kindly assisted with the final preparations of the mss.; **Diane Brooks** of the California Department of Education kindly arranged for the project's review and gave valuable advice for its improvement; the Hon. **John H. Buchanan, Jr.**, Executive Director of the Council for the Advancement of Citizenship (CAC), ably directed the CAC's involvement in all aspects of its cooperative effort; **Lonnie G. Bunch III** of the American History Museum of the Smithsonian Institution read parts of the manuscript and made important suggestions for its improvement; **Mark Cannon**, former Administrative Assistant to the Chief Justice of the U.S. Supreme Court, assisted in the editing of the Rationale, recommended contributors and gave the project his support. **Elaine Craig** of the CCE wrote articles to publicize the project and lent her support throughout its development; **Professor Juris Dreifelds** of Brock University, Ontario, Canada, revised and corrected the material on Canada and reviewed a portion of the manuscript; **Thomas Dunthorn** of the Florida Department of Education rendered valuable advice and support throughout the course of the project's development; **Diane Eisenberg**, former Executive Director of the CAC, lent the project her full support and directed the CAC's efforts during the first phases of the project's development; **John Ellington** of the North Carolina Department of Public Instruction gave his support and rendered valuable advice throughout the project's development; **Dr. John Fonte** of the U.S. Department of Education made extensive scholarly comments on successive drafts, suggested contributors, and offered invaluable advice and support both as scholar and as colleague at key moments of development; **Professor Paul Gagnon** of the Council for Basic Education Research made helpful, detailed comments on a draft of the mss. and lent his support for maintenance of the project's scholarship; **Louis Grigar** of the Texas Education Agency gave the project his full support as well as valuable advice throughout its development; **John Hale** of the CCE undertook administrative duties during the early phases of the project and lent it his advice and support; **Frances Haley**, Executive Director of the National Council for the Social Studies, agreed to the NCSS's distribution of the framework and undertook numerous administrative tasks for printing the mss. and for the project's successful launching. Her many kindnesses during the final phases of production were greatly appreciated; **David Hargrove** of the CCE kindly proofread sections of the final mss., correcting many errors and assisted editorially with the index; **Darlene Heninger** of the CCE lent her assistance to the project by carefully typing the index; **Jack Hoar**, Consultant, History and Social Studies, Long Beach Unified School District, carefully reviewed and made valuable, detailed commentary on the scope and sequence portion of the mss. and extended his support and advice throughout the project's development; **Professor James Horton** of George Washington University and the Smithsonian Institution contributed an initial draft for a section of the mss.; **Professor Ralph Ketcham** of Syracuse University contributed an initial draft of the Rationale and made a number of helpful comments and suggestions; **Katherine Kersten**, an attorney, read and made detailed comments on a section of the mss. and recommended a contributor; **Dr. John Kincaid**, Executive Director of the Advisory Commission on Intergovernmental Relations, read and commented on a portion of the mss., offered valuable advice on the project, and also agreed to coauthor a section of the mss. at very short notice; **Professor Dale Krane** of the University of Nebraska at Omaha, read and commented on a section of the of the mss.; **Professor James B. Lane** of the University of Indiana Northwest suggested the names of contributors and gave the project his support; **Neil Leavitt** kindly volunteered to assist in proofreading the final draft mss. and lent the project her constant support; **Professor Robert Meister** of the University of California at Santa Cruz volunteered his services to the project and offered helpful advice and support; **Professor David R. Morgan** of the University of Oklahoma read and commented on a portion of the mss.; **Suzanne Morse** of the Kettering Foundation ably carried out her duties as project evaluator and offered helpful suggestions and advice; **Professor James Nathan** of the University of Alabama, Montgomery, read portions of the mss. and repeatedly gave valuable, detailed advice for its improvement; **John Patrick** of the University of Indiana contributed much important advice and assistance and recommended a contributor at the eleventh hour; **Robert Pickus,** President of the World Without War Council, Berkeley, California, gave detailed advice for the improvement of the mss. even while recovering from a serious illness and patiently guided a distracted project director through the shoals of new terrain; **Brian Pallasch**, formerly of the CAC, kindly contributed an initial draft of a section of the mss.; **Ivor Pritchard** of the U.S. Department of Education made extensive, valuable comments for improving successive drafts of the mss.; **Kevin Quigley**, program officer for The Pew Charitable Trusts, patiently assisted the project at many points of development and lent his support for requests for vital deadline extensions; **Richard Remy** of Ohio State University made important suggestions and detailed comments on initial drafts of the mss. and gave the project his support; **Theresa Richard** of the CCE brought her considerable skills in book design and production to the project as well as unfailing professionalism, courtesy, and patience over a period of months. The trouble she took with the text was greatly appreciated; **Lorenca Rosal** of the CCE kindly supplied the name of a contributor and in other ways lent the project her constant support; **Howard Safier** of Fairfax High School, Los Angeles, contributed an initial draft of a section of the mss.; **Professor Stephen Schechter** of Russell Sage College read and commented on a section of the mss.; **Professor Donald O. Schneider**, past president of NCSS, of the University of Georgia commented on a draft of the mss. and made valuable suggestions for its strengthening; **Martha Sharma** adapted the geography section to the project's format and commented on a later draft; **Professor Peter Skerry** of the University of California at Los Angeles (UCLA) kindly arranged for a contributor to join the project; **Professor Duane Smith** of UCLA and the CCE read parts of the mss. and offered valuable advice for its improvement; **Juliet de Souza** of the CCE kindly aided the project with typing and other assistance; **Professor Joseph Stoltman** of Western Michigan University volunteered to make detailed revisions a section of the mss. and gave important advice for its improvement; **Dr. Ray Sumner**, of the Queensland University of Technology, Brisbane, Australia, read a portion of the mss. and made helpful comments for its improvement; **Tam Taylor** of the CCE undertook the complex task of publicizing the project's launch and gave the project her interest and support and kindly volunteered her assistance for final preparations of the mss.; **Dr. Ross Terrill**, author and Fellow of the East Asian Research Center, Harvard University, read a portion of the mss., made detailed suggestions for its refinement, and suggested a contributor; **Dr. Mary Jane Turner** of the Close Up Foundation participated in a development meeting for the project and offered valuable advice and support; **Professor Reed Ueda** of Tufts University gave his unfailing cooperation and helpful advice and support for the project; **Professor Richard Vetterley** of Brigham Young University contributed a draft mss. and commented on part of the mss.; **Professor Michael Walzer** of the Institute of Advanced Studies, Princeton, New Jersey, read and made detailed comments on sections of the mss. over a period of months and made indispensable suggestions for its improvement; **Nancy Warzer**, formerly of the CAC, performed many tasks as a stalwart staff member of the Council and deserves special thanks for her administrative contributions and unfailing kindness and support throughout the project's development; **Professor James Q. Wilson** of UCLA suggested the names of contributors and reviewers for portions of the mss.; **Professor Daniel Wojcik** of the University of Oregon lent his fine scholarship to several parts of the mss., copy edited several sections, and greatly assisted the final stages of the project.

Two individuals must be singled out for special recognition and gratitude. **Dr. Margaret Stimmann Branson**, Administrator, Division of Instructional Services, Office of Kern County Superintendent of Schools, made many key contributions as a member of the Framework Development Committee and its Steering Committee over the entire course of the project's development. Beyond these essential contributions, for three years she made numerous suggestions for the project's improvement and gave important advice. She read and made detailed comments on sections of the mss., which would otherwise have gravely suffered; in addition, she provided a considerable number of research materials to the project director that greatly assisted the project's development. Her personal support was invaluable. CIVITAS is greatly in her debt.

Professor R. Freeman Butts made a greater contribution to CIVITAS than any other single contributor and must be extended the special gratitude of the project. He made many journeys to meetings of the Framework Development Committee and its Steering Committee and contributed countless constructive suggestions during every phase of development. He was always available to assist the project director, who constantly relied upon his counsel and good judgment; he undertook to write substantial and difficult portions of the mss. and submitted his work in a timely manner. Whenever asked, he wrote small pieces to flesh out the text. He painstakingly proofread all drafts of his work; he spotted inconsistencies and infelicities in the mss. and suggested remedies; he critically reviewed sections of the mss., as requested, making numerous helpful suggestions. Throughout the complex and sometimes frustrating process of development he displayed unfailing civility and generosity of spirit and exemplified the ideal of a gentleman and a scholar. *Si monumentum requiris, circumspecie.*

Contributors

Charles F. Bahmueller. Civic Virtue (coauthor, Conceptual Perspective); Fundamental values and principles (coauthor, Conceptual Perspective, except as indicated); The nature of the state (except as indicated); Diversity (Contemporary Perspective); America and the international system (Change and continuity in international life; Canada; coauthor, Historical Perspective); Major types of government, (Conceptual Perspective); Major types of legal systems (Islamic law); Rationale (principal author, Part I); Role of the citizen (Conceptual Perspective); miscellaneous contributions. Center for Civic Education; Los Angeles, California

Mark Blitz. Conflicts among principles. The Hudson Institute; Washington, D.C.

Dom Bonafede. The press and the political process. Department of Communications, American University; Washington, D.C.

Harry Boyte. Civic and community action. The Humphrey Institute, University of Minnesota; Minneapolis, Minnesota

R. Freeman Butts. Political authority (Historical and Contemporary Perspectives); Human rights; Civic virtue (commentary); The public good; Separation of church and state; The state as educator and Religious toleration (in The nature of the state). William F. Russell Professor Emeritus in the Foundations of Education, Teachers College, Columbia University; Carmel, California

George Carey. The separation of powers. Department of Political Science, Georgetown University; Washington, D.C.

Erwin Chemerinsky. The American judicial system. The Law Center, University of Southern California; Los Angeles, California

John Fonte. American political philosophy (in The nature of the state). U.S. Department of Education; Washington, D.C.

Robert Fullinwider. Morality and politics. Institute for Philosophy and Public Policy, University of Maryland; College Park, Maryland

Curt Garbesi. International law. Loyola Law School; Los Angeles, California

Charles Haynes. Religion and public life. First Liberty Institute, George Mason University; Fairfax, Virginia.

Mark Hartman. Mexico (in America and the international system); Latin America (in The nature of the state). The Brookings Institution; Washington, D.C.

Richard Harwood. The citizen and the policy process. The Harwood Group; Bethesda, Maryland

John Immerwhar. Public opinion (coauthor). Department of Philosophy, Villanova University; Villanova, Pennsylvania

Katherine Isaac. Interest groups (Historical and Contemporary Perspectives); Politics and the environment (with Ralph Nader). The Center for Study of Responsive Law; Washington, D.C.

Michael James. Public choice theory. Centre for Independent Studies; Melbourne, Australia

Kathleen Hall Jamieson. Television and politics. Dean, Annenberg School for Communication, University of Pennsylvania; Philadelphia, Pennsylvania

Richard Jensen. Local political participation; Citizenship and military participation. Department of History, University of Illinois; Chicago, Illinois

Donald Kettl. Bureaucracy. Department of Political Science, University of Wisconsin; Madison, Wisconsin

John Kincaid. Federalism; State and local government (coauthor). Executive Director, U.S. Advisory Commission on Intergovernmental Relations; Washington, D.C.

Donald Leet. The American economic system. Department of Economics; Fresno State University, Fresno, California

Robert Meister. Law (Conceptual Perspective). Board of Politics, University of California; Santa Cruz, California

Keith Melder. National political participation. The Smithsonian Institution; Washington, D.C.

Ralph Nader. Interest groups (Historical and Contemporary Perspectives); Politics and the environmental; (with Katherine Isaac). The Center for Study of Responsive Law; Washington, D.C.

Teresa Nance. Public opinion (coauthor). Department of Communications, Villanova University; Villanova, Pennsylvania

James Nathan. America and the international system (Conceptual Perspective). Department of Political Science, Auburn University; Montgomery, Alabama

Fred Newmann. Rationale for participation; Participation (coauthor). Director, National Center on Effective Secondary Schools, University of Wisconsin; Madison, Wisconsin

Suzanne Ogden. China (in Conceptual and Historical Perspectives, The nature of the state). Department of Political Science, Northeastern University; Boston, Massachusetts

Norman Ornstein. Informal processes of Washington politics. American Enterprise Institute; Washington, D.C.

Robert Palmer. State and local government (coauthor). Department of Political Science, University of Maine; Orono, Maine

John Patrick. Individual rights. Social Studies Development Center, Indiana University; Bloomington, Indiana

Robert Pickus. Civil disobedience. World Without War Council; Berkeley, California

Gerald Pomper. Political parties and elections. Department of Political Science, Rutgers University; New Brunswick, New Jersey

Charles N. Quigley. Conceptual structure of the framework; Participation (coauthor); Scope and sequence; Civic virtue (coauthor, Conceptual Perspective); Fundamental values and principles (coauthor, Conceptual Perspective, except as indicated); miscellaneous contributions. Center for Civic Education, Los Angeles, California

Sherry Rockey. America and the international system (Historical Perspective (coauthor, 1945-1989); Contemporary Perspective). Director of International Relations, League of Women Voters; Washington, D.C.

Christopher Salter. Geography (coauthor). Department of Geography, University of Missouri; Columbia, Missouri

Christina Sommers. Gender Issues (part author). Department of Philosophy, Clark University; Worcester, Massachusetts

Ted J. Smith III. Propaganda. Department of Mass Communications, Virginia Commonwealth University; Richmond, Virginia

Joseph Stoltman. Geography (coauthor). Department of Geography, Western Michigan University; Kalamazoo, Michigan

Sandra Stotsky. Civic writing. Graduate School of Education, Harvard University; Cambridge, Massachusetts

Reed Ueda. Diversity (Conceptual and Historical Perspectives). Department of History; Tufts University, Medford, Massachusetts

David Vogler. Congress and the presidency. Department of Political Science, Wheaton College; Norton, Massachusetts

Daniel Wojcik. Major types of legal systems (Historical Perspective). Department of English, University of Oregon, Eugene, Oregon

Harmon Zeigler. Interest groups (Conceptual Perspective; Contemporary Perspective, part author). Department of Political Science, University of Puget Sound; Tacoma, Washington

Contents

Foreword

When the Soviets hurled a shiny, 184-pound satellite into space in 1957, America was stunned, our confidence shaken. This single event generated a tremendous national response, as we perceived that the very survival of our democracy was in danger. And as we sought to recapture our leadership and our pride, the path most vigorously pursued, and most revealing of our national character, was our renewed commitment to public education. In particular, we decided that mathematics and science education must be strengthened if we were to remain economic and technological leaders in the future.

Today in the United States, we continue to be told that we must have better schools and tougher mathematics and science standards within those schools to make the nation strong and competitive again. We're told that our work force must be better prepared. Yet in the drive to improve the schools, and to make students more proficient in mathematics and science, another urgent question has been neglected: How can we adequately educate our students to become good citizens and to make responsible decisions that will sustain our country and advance the quality of life, both nationally and internationally?

It was in response to this challenge that an impressive new project was undertaken. CIVITAS, a cooperative venture involving educators, scholars, public leaders, and national associations, has directly addressed our nation's civic literacy needs in this critical publication. CIVITAS: A Framework for Civic Education is designed to help students develop a rich and varied understanding of government, public policy, and citizenship in this country; and it should serve as a road map for strengthening civic education in the years ahead.

The publication of the CIVITAS framework comes at a time when the economic, technological, and human problems confronting our nation and, indeed, our world are growing quickly in complexity and magnitude. Since Sputnik made its solitary orbit, the number of human beings on Earth has dramatically increased, from about 2.8 billion people in 1957 to about 5.3 billion in 1990 with prospects of doubling again in less than forty years. In China, the world's most populated nation, forty-five babies are born every minute.

Today, the world's 165 independent nations and sixty-odd political units are interlocked. High interest rates in the United States hurt Common Market countries; bad harvests in the Soviet Union help Canadian farmers; a Middle East oil glut means less pressure in Brazil to aid capital-starved Africa;

unemployment in Germany sends ripples through Spain and Yugoslavia; a robotics breakthrough in Tokyo makes a difference in Detroit. Pretoria and Peoria are connected.

As conditions have changed both at home and abroad, our political agenda has come to include increasingly complicated questions. For example, how can we reduce our reliance on fossil fuels? Should we limit imports from other countries to protect our own industries? To what extent should human rights violations in other countries influence our foreign policy? How can we come to an agreement on international standards for atmospheric pollution? Even the metaphysical question of when a human life begins and ends has become a topic of political debate.

These fundamental issues, and many others, will continue to press in, shaping the public agenda and even the private lives of most Americans. And yet the information needed to think constructively about these issues seems increasingly beyond our grasp. To put it plainly, we are becoming civically illiterate as a nation. Unable to make informed judgments on complicated issues and debates, many Americans are tempted to turn to simple answers, to slogans, or to nostalgia for a world that never was. They succumb to the blandishments of glib electronic soothsayers, or simply withdraw, convinced that nothing can be done.

If public opinion surveys are to be believed, half of Americans do not believe that important national problems such as energy shortages, inflation, and crime can be solved through traditional American political institutions. Many argue that it is no longer possible to resolve complex public issues through the democratic process because citizens are not sufficiently informed to debate policy choices of consequence. Further, the proportion of citizens professing "great confidence" in the leaders of major social institutions has declined dramatically. A recent survey of college freshmen revealed that a significant percentage of these students distrust many of the nation's most basic social institutions. Confidence in the executive branch of government continues to go down, and roughly half of our citizens do not believe that the electoral process is the principal determinant of how the country is actually run.

For those contributing to the CIVITAS project, and all others who care about government "by the people," this increase in apathy and decline in public confidence cannot go unchallenged. In a world where human survival is at stake, cynicism and ignorance are not acceptable alternatives. The replacement of democratic government by a technocracy and the control of policy by special-interest groups cannot be tolerated.

Thus the need to help all students become intelligent and informed citizens is self-evident, and clear and intelligent guidelines for improving civic education like those proposed in the CIVITAS agenda must be vigorously pursued. If education cannot help students see beyond themselves and better understand issues of national and international significance, then each new generation will remain ignorant, and its capacity to live intelligently and responsibly will be diminished.

By heeding CIVITAS's recommendations, we have a great opportunity to increase the capacity of elementary and secondary school students and indeed, citizens of all ages to understand the meaning, the rights, and the responsibilities of citizenship in a democratic society. And at this crucial moment of transition, it is my hope that all who care about the quality of our civic life will consider carefully the framework proposed in this report.

The longer it goes, the more I am convinced that the destiny of this country may indeed be threatened not so much by weapons systems, but by the inclination of public officials to obscure the truth. And, further, I am convinced that if our students are to become responsible citizens for a new century, civic education must be concerned, above all, with the quality of communication. The work of democracy is carried on through thoughtful discourse through town meetings, city councils, study groups, informal conversations, and television screens. And citizenship training, if it means anything at all, means teaching students to think critically, listen with discernment, and communicate with power and precision. If students learn to listen, speak, read, and write more carefully, they will not only be civically empowered, but also they will know how to distinguish between the authentic and the fraudulent in human discourse. A better grounding in rhetoric and logic and in the techniques of discussion and debate would also help prepare them for responsible citizenship.

Second, civic education for a new century also must provide students with a core of basic knowledge about social issues and institutions, to allow them to put their understanding of democracy in perspective. Civic understanding means a study of history and literature. It means that students should encounter the classic political thinkers, from Plato, Hobbes, Locke, and Montesquieu to John Adams, James Madison, and John C. Calhoun. Equally important, it means they should study government today, not just by examining its theory and machinery, but also by exploring current public issues.

Third, I'm convinced that civic education means classrooms that are active, not passive, places. We must begin to recognize that students are already members of an institution, the school; and that they need to understand how this place works, and to participate in school decisions that affect their lives, just as they will be asked to do later on, in other institutions and in society at large. If we fail to give students these experiences while they're young, there is a high probability that they will be deferred for a lifetime.

In *Classroom Life as Civic Education*, David Bricker makes the essential point that much of what young people learn about citizenship comes to them "indirectly as they draw out ideas about how people should conduct themselves in public, from the ways their teachers manage classroom life." Clearly, citizenship is not something to be deferred; rather, it should be demonstrated in every institution in which the student is involved, especially at school.

Another point. Teaching about government today all too often has focused exclusively on textbooks, without involving students sufficiently in the process of decision making. The National Assessment of Educational Progress found that textbook readings were by far the most common method of instruction in civics classrooms. Other activities, such as writing papers and working on group projects, were less prevalent. When twelfth graders were asked how often they participated in mock trials, imitation elections, legislative hearings, or governmental bodies, more than half said they had never done so. And yet the national assessment reported that students exposed to such learning performed better than peers who had only occasionally or never participated in these activities.

I'm suggesting that for civic education to come to life, theories of government must be tested in the classroom. Students should become knowledgeable about contemporary issues and be asked to thoughtfully weigh the options. For example, each student might study a contested issue currently being considered by Congress, the Supreme Court a state legislature, or a local government body, reporting on the history of the problem, defining points of tension, and proposing plausible solutions. The classroom itself should become a town meeting, where ideas and views are exchanged.

Finally, education for citizenship means helping students make connections between what they learn and how they live. During our study of the American high school, we found too many young people who felt unwanted, unneeded, and unconnected to the larger world. Further, we found a serious gap between the young and the old in our society, an intergenerational separation in which youth and their elders are not seriously engaged in common discourse.

In response to this challenge, in our High School report, we proposed a new Carnegie unit: one based on service. The idea is that every student should be asked to volunteer his or her time at retirement villages, daycare centers, or youth camps, or to tutor other kids at school. But there's a caution here. While such projects can give students a sense of worth, they must be viewed as part of the educational experience and not just an after-school activity. Specifically, service projects should include a written evaluation by the student, and should be informed by and related to civic education as envisoned by CIVITAS.

I'm suggesting that as an essential part of civic education, students need to understand that learning is for living, and that education means developing the capacity to make judgments, form convictions, and act boldly on values held. We must help them understand that not all choices, in thought or in action, are equally valid. Such an education does not dictate solutions or suggest that there are simple answers for every complicated question. Rather, it means helping students develop responsible ways of thinking, believing, and acting.

On a related matter, it is becoming increasingly important in our diversified culture that students be encouraged to deal thoughtfully with our deepest differences. The harsh truth is that society today is characterized by such divisiveness that consensus often seems almost impossible, and this puts the nation's schools squarely in the middle. Indeed, teachers are often criticized if they try to examine sensitive issues in the classroom. Yet to ignore controversial issues is to offer students an incomplete education, an incapacity to think carefully about life's most important concerns.

I remain convinced that even in matters where society is sharply divided, schools have an especially important role to play, one that goes beyond silence or the extension of the status quo. If we hope to make progress toward resolving deep conflicts in the culture, we must encourage open and sensitive classroom discussion about choices, even in such controversial areas as sex, drugs, cultural differences, and religious beliefs. Finding a way to deal thoughtfully with our deepest differences is perhaps the greatest challenge citizenship education now confronts. And in the guidance of such inquiry, teachers must be trusted.

The focus of civic education must be extended beyond the American agenda to the world beyond our shores. That world may not yet be a global village, but surely our sense of neighborhood includes more people and cultures than ever before. Refugees flow from one country to another, but too many students can neither point to the locations of these great migrations on a map nor talk about the famines or wars or poverty that caused them. Philosophers, statesmen, inventors, and artists from around the world enrich our lives, and the contributions should be taught and celebrated.

Obviously, formal education cannot single-handedly deal with the massive challenge of civic education. Beyond the classroom, churches, libraries, youth groups, labor unions, senior citizen's organizations, and many other groups must become greater sources of civic education, though not to the exclusion of more direct political participation. The media—newspapers, journals, radio, and television—also have a powerful role to play. Still, the nation's schools have a special obligation to combat growing illiteracy about public issues. And it is here—in the nation's classrooms—that the CIVITAS framework has a particularly vital role to play. Schools and colleges simply must help students understand the process by which public policy is shaped and prepare them to make informed, discriminating judgments on questions that will affect their futures, as well as those of the nation and the world.

Ernest L. Boyer

A Personal Preface

The idea of CIVITAS was formally broached to the Pew Charitable Trusts in February 1987 by representatives of the Center for Civic Education and the Council for the Advancement of Citizenship. Our purpose was no less than to formulate a coherent and defensible conception of citizenship for American life that would be of use to those who were struggling to design more effective programs for the civic education of all American youth.

The product was to be a curriculum framework for the schools (kindergarten through grade 12) developed by scholars, professional educators, and public leaders who hold a broad range of political, economic, and social views. The goal was to establish a solid intellectual and scholarly grounding for civic education in the schools, propose a common core of knowledge, values, and skills desirable for all students in the nation to achieve, and outline a desirable school learning environment appropriate for students holding a diversity of beliefs and outlooks and reflecting an expanding plurality of ethnic, racial, linguistic, and religious communities in the United States.

The assumption was that the increasingly complex conditions and issues facing American citizens could best be resolved by informed and responsible participation by the citizenry, a kind of participation that is rooted not only in civic action but in an understanding of our commitment to basic democratic values, what the Founders called the civic virtue required of citizens in a republic.

These goals explain our use of the term "*civitas*," originating in Latin and now a perfectly good English word defined in Webster's New International Dictionary (Third Edition) and in the new Random House Dictionary. Civitas has two related meanings: the functioning body of persons and institutions constituting a politically organized community or state; and the concepts and values of citizenship that impart shared responsibility, common purpose, and sense of community among the citizens of the political order.

CIVITAS attempts to delineate both meanings as clearly and objectively as possible as they pertain to the United States. It attempts to promote a comprehensive national effort by the nation's schools and voluntary organizations to design substantive, effective, and vital programs of civic education. It seeks to outline the content and core of knowledge defining the values, concepts, and principles underlying the American politically organized community and democratic constitutional order. And it seeks to define the behavior of civility befitting

a citizen's competence, skills, and commitments to participate in the forming of judgments required for the public good of a democratic society.

We believe that education for citizenship is the primary reason for establishing universal education in the American Republic: i.e., the purpose to develop among all students, whether in private or in public schools, the virtues, sentiments, knowledge, and skills of good citizenship. Paramount to this general civic purpose is education that will develop in all students a commitment to the fundamental principles and values of the Constitution and the Bill of Rights and an understanding of the issues and controversies arising in their history and in their contemporary practice.

Generalized statements such as these are easy to come by in reports of public commissions and in the preambles to curriculum guides and textbooks. But CIVITAS takes them seriously and attempts to spell them out with scholarly care and detail for all who would read and think seriously about the principles of American democracy.

The immediate impetus for the project was a combination of a decade of ferment in a surprisingly long-lived educational reform movement and the approach of the five years of the bicentennial celebration of the U.S. Constitution and Bill of Rights (1987-1991). But little did we dream that those five years would culminate in an almost world-wide revolution for democracy and a convulsing war affecting much of the world.

Events have caught up with CIVITAS, far exceeding our original expectations. CIVITAS appears at just the right moment. Dare I say a "defining moment?" It is not hastily or precipitously thrown together to meet the urgencies of a post-war period or a new initiative from the governors or the White House. But it does respond remarkably well to the present stage of domestic educational reform as well as to the cravings to learn about democracy billowing up from many regions of the world—in Eastern Europe, the Soviet Union, Africa, the Americas, and perhaps even in the Middle East.

A few words about both movements. Education has risen to the top of everyone's stated list of domestic political priorities, Republican and Democratic, liberal and conservative, business and labor, urban and rural, majority and minority, federal, state, and local. At the same time, the decade-long educational reform movement has begun to focus on the common core of knowledge and curriculum content that should be taught and tested in all American schools, succinctly summarized in the phrase "what all students need to know and be able to do."

Notable efforts by several academic and professional associations have been made to formulate national standards of achievement for secondary school students in various subject matter fields: in mathematics, in science, in biology, in chemistry, in geography, in English, and in economics.

The two projects most directly related to civic education in purpose and in content were: (1) the Bradley Commission on History in the Schools (Kenneth T. Jackson of Columbia University, chair), whose eighteen members were history scholars in universities and history teachers in schools (succeeded by the National Council for History Education); and (2) the National Commission on Social Studies in the Schools, initiated by the American Historical Association (Arthur S. Link, president) and the National Council for the Social Studies (Donald H. Bragaw, president). Joined in sponsorship by the Carnegie Foundation for the Advancement of Teaching (Ernest L. Boyer, president) and the Organization of American Historians (Stanley N. Katz, president), these four presidents made up the executive committee of the Commission, which consisted of 46 members representing a broad spectrum of academic disciplines, professional organizations, and public bodies.

Prompted by similar concerns to develop common understandings in the curriculum but not confined to one subject matter field, CIVITAS focuses on the single most important purpose of American education: the preparation for citizenship in our constitutional democracy. CIVITAS draws upon the same high level of scholarly knowledge exemplified in the fields mentioned above, especially from history, political science and political philosophy, and other academic fields in the social sciences and humanities as well as from experienced professionals in education and public service.

CIVITAS arrives on the domestic scene at a particularly timely and urgent period of educational reform, when the combined efforts of the President, the Secretary of Education, and the fifty state governors are being exerted to formulate and implement national goals for American education.

In April 1991 President Bush announced that a decade of educational reform had ended and an educational revolution has begun. The time for issuing reports, making studies, and convening panels is past. The status quo is upended. It is time to transform America's schools. In Chester Finn's even more colorful and emphatic words: American education is dead in the water; we must cast aside everything we've thought about education in the past; erase everything; start from scratch; and invent.

The President's announcement was the culmination of the education summit held with the fifty governors in Charlottesville in October 1989. The introductory statement on national education goals adopted by the National Governors' Association in March 1990 refers to citizenship education several times:

> If the United States is to maintain a strong and responsible democracy and a prosperous and growing economy into the next century, it must be prepared to address and respond to major challenges at home and in the world. A well-educated population is the key to our future. Americans must be prepared to:....Participate knowledgeably in our democracy and our democratic institutions;...Function effectively in increasingly diverse communities and states and in a rapidly shrinking world....Today a new standard of an educated citizenry is required, one suitable for the next century....[All students] must understand and accept the responsibilities and obligations of citizenship.

CIVITAS not only agrees with these statements, it carries them out specifically in this detailed curriculum framework.

CIVITAS not only talks about citizenship; it does something about it. It outlines in detail the values fundamental to civic virtue, civic participation, and the civic knowledge and skills that are necessary to achieve the goals agreed upon by the governors' National Education Goals Panel, co-chaired by Democratic Gov. Roy Romer of Colorado and Republican Gov. Carroll A. Campbell, Jr. of South Carolina. Although drawn up independently and prior to the Panel's agreement on education goals, CIVITAS should be extremely useful to all parties now involved in discussions of national goals, national standards, and national assessments. CIVITAS will be useful in achieving those objectives of Goal #3 on Student Achievement that call for all students to be involved in "activities that promote and demonstrate good citizenship" and to be "knowledgeable about the cultural diversity of the nation and about the world community."

The document introduced in April 1991 by President Bush and by Secretary Alexander entitled *America 2000: An Education Strategy* outlines a strategy to achieve the six national education goals adopted by the president and the governors in 1990. Goal #3 on student achievement states:

> American students will leave grades four, eight, and twelve having demonstrated competency in challenging

subject matter including English, mathematics, science, history, and geography; and every school in America will ensure that all students learn to use their minds well, so that they may be prepared for responsible citizenship, further learning, and productive employment in our modern economy.

Similarly, Goal #5 on adult literacy alludes to the necessity of civic education: "Every adult American will be literate and will possess the knowledge and skills necessary to compete in a global economy and exercise the rights and responsibilities of citizenship."

Since the issuance of *America 2000*, public debate has continued about the desirability of setting national standards and devising national tests to assess student achievement toward such standards. CIVITAS does not take sides in these debates, but its threefold emphasis upon the goals of civic virtue, civic participation, and civic knowledge and skills is bound to be useful to all curriculum developers, textbook writers, and test makers who are genuinely dedicated to improving education for American citizenship.

Significantly, an increasing number of professional educators has been calling for national standards that stimulate achievement but do not infringe on the local autonomy of schools and teachers. For example, Marshall Smith, dean of the School of Education at Stanford University, argues that we must "think nationally." He has proposed that America needs not a national test but a widely accepted set of national curriculum goals, whose major themes are spelled out in depth and specificity but which allow maximum flexibility for local districts and local teachers to select those topics or issues they choose to deal with.

This is precisely what the CIVITAS framework has sought to do for the concepts, knowledge, and values inherent in American citizenship and in the subjects most germane to civic education.

Historically, professional educators from classroom teachers to administrators have been opposed to national curriculums and national tests. But the subject is less taboo than it once was. Albert Shanker, president of the American Federation of Teachers, Keith Geiger, president of the National Education Association, and other influential educators have joined the National Council on Education Standards and Testing to advise the National Education Goals Panel whether or not to proceed with formulating national standards and, if so, to propose ways to develop a new national assessment system to monitor student achievement. The Council consists of representatives from the Bush administration, Congress, the Goals Panel's Resource Group on Student Achievement, state legislatures, state and local school officials, teachers' organizations, higher education, and the public at large.

CIVITAS does not propose a national curriculum, but if national standards for such a curriculum (or national tests) should materialize, it is interesting to note that the CIVITAS framework actually performs in effect what the governors' National Education Goals Panel proposes for national goals and national standards with regard to civic education. It was designed and developed by clusters of representatives from a number of states who worked together as members of its Framework Development Committee, its National Review Council, and its National Teachers' Advisory Committee, whose members represented virtually all states. It set a pattern of collaboration not unlike that of a network of states and cities called The New Standards Project, headed by Lauren B. Resnick of the University of Pittsburgh.

In 1988 the Center for Civic Education analyzed more than forty state social studies frameworks dealing with civic education. Major findings included the following:

- The question of what citizenship means was seldom addressed.
- Little was said about the aims of citizenship education.
- Descriptions of civic education as a subject tend toward conceptual fuzziness and diffusion.
- In only a few instances could a specific rationale for civic education be found.

I cannot go into detail here about the usefulness of CIVITAS in the continuing wars over the best approach to civic education. But I would like to wager that CIVITAS will not only be useful but essential to be reckoned with by all the major disputants and ideologies.

In recent years, the most highly publicized disputes over the social studies have arisen over the role of history vis-a-vis the other social sciences, and the role of multiculturalism versus the Western cultural and political tradition as the core of study. Major examples of the public debate include the following:

The 1988 report of the Bradley Commission on History in Schools, *Building a History Curriculum: Guidelines for Teaching History in Schools*, argued that chronological history must be the core of the entire social studies curriculum. The principal investigator, Paul A. Gagnon of the University of Massachusetts at Boston, strongly stated the case that history is the indispensable study in the education of citizens in a democracy.

The 1989 report of the National Commission on Social Studies in the Schools, *Charting a Course: Social Studies for the 21st Century*, argued that history and geography should provide the matrix or framework for social studies, but that key concepts from political science, economics, and other social sciences should be integrated throughout the entire social studies curriculum. The report of the Commission's Curriculum Task Force (whose principal author was William H. McNeill of the University of Chicago) persuasively proposed that world and American history and geography should be integrated into a three-year chronological sequence with approximately equal attention being given to the United States and to principal world civilizations and societies. Both of these major commissions emphasized that their chief goal was education for citizenship; both reserved the special study of government to the twelfth grade.

Prior to the Bradley Commission report, the 1987 California *Framework in History/Social Science* had largely adopted the central role of history, and the New York State *Syllabuses in Social Studies* of 1988 had incorporated considerable emphasis on recurrent themes and concepts drawn from the several social sciences. The frameworks of both states have not only been praised as exemplary state curriculum frameworks in social studies but also have been targets of heated criticism in public as well as in academic discourse on the grounds that they overstressed Western values and European contributions to human civilization and neglected the contributions of non-European cultures to the United States and to the world.

CIVITAS takes no sides on the controversy over multiculturalism, but believes that its contents will be useful to all major approaches to the social studies, inasmuch as it features the major themes of citizenship, which all profess to be a goal. Every topic in CIVITAS incorporates a three-fold approach: a conceptual perspective, a historical perspective, and a contemporary perspective. It asserts the need for civic education to be content oriented, value oriented, and skills oriented. This is made clear in each of the three major sections of CIVITAS: Civic Virtue, Civic Participation, and Civic Knowledge and Skills.

CIVITAS provides major resources for those who would stress history, conceptual analysis, critical thinking, objective study of controversial contemporary public policy issues, or active political participation. CIVITAS should appeal to the broad spectrum of curriculum approaches and teaching methods that seek to improve civic education through any of the major curriculum components of the social studies. It seeks to strike a balance between the civic themes that compose the common core of democratic values and those that compose the values of cultural, religious, and ethnic diversity. As John Gardner put it in his keynote address at the centennial commencement at Stanford in May 1991, American citizenship seeks "wholeness incorporating diversity."

In contrast to proposals for national goals, national standards, and national assessment, the educational reform movement has also emphasized the need for restructuring schools, stressing the values of local school site-management, shared decision making, and autonomous curriculum-building by teachers, administrators, and parents. One widely heralded example is the Coalition of Essential Schools organized by Theodore R. Sizer of Brown University and admired by *America 2000*. The fifty collaborating schools extol the themes of diverse practice, commonly shared ideas, and the active role of students and teachers in helping adolescents to use their minds well, echoing basic tenets of progressive education.

Another well publicized example, but more structured in approach, is the Paideia Program organized in 1982 by Mortimer Adler at the Institute for Philosophical Research in Chicago and moved in 1990 to the National Center for the Paideia Program at the University of North Carolina-Chapel Hill under Dean Donald Stedman of the School of Education. Both the Essential Schools and the Paideia Schools agree that, if a political democracy is to flourish, schools must produce students who are knowledgeable and able to participate effectively in political discourse. Obviously, the structure and content of CIVITAS could be adapted for use in these types of schools as well as for the "effective schools" movement typified by the massive studies and subsequent coalition of schools undertaken by John Goodlad of the University of Washington.

Our logic regarding restructuring of schools is this: We believe that CIVITAS will be eminently useful to curriculum developers; if teachers in individual schools are to be their own curriculum developers, then CIVITAS will be useful for teachers in local schools as well as for curriculum developers in district and state school systems and in private schools. How else can proponents of local, decentralized, and loosely regulated approaches to educational reform achieve the common core of knowledge and skills envisioned by national goals and standards?

Another influential voice in the recent educational reform movement is the Educational Excellence Network, organized and headed by Diane Ravitch of Teachers College, Columbia University, and Chester E. Finn, Jr. of Vanderbilt University, both of whom have worked closely with Secretary Alexander. The aim of their increasingly popular monthly *Network News and Views* consisting of notes, comments, and reprints is to promote high academic standards through study of the major academic subjects in the liberal arts and sciences. A recurrent theme of the printed articles is the priority of the teaching of chronological history as the basic preparation for citizenship in preference to an undigested amalgam of social studies.

The Network joined with the American Federation of Teachers and Freedom House in sponsoring an Education for Democracy Project designed to elevate the role of schools in the purposeful imparting to students of an informed, reasoned allegiance to the ideals of a free and democratic society. In many respects, the project's *Statement of Principles* resonates well with the goals of CIVITAS as do Paul Gagnon's efforts to inject more attention to the fortunes of democratic values in textbooks on world history and United States history as portrayed in his *Democracy's Untold Story* and *Democracy's Half-Told Story*.

CIVITAS advances no position on the politically volatile issue of parental school choice. But the more headway choice makes, the more important it is that CIVITAS become a resource for private as well as public schools in order that they all provide a common set of guidelines for civic content in the schools of choice. Private as well as public schools should be evaluated and held accountable for achieving the goals of education for citizenship.

The same point could well be made with regard to the impending expansion of private effort in American schooling, both non-profit and for-profit. One example is the establishment in July 1991 of the non-profit New American Schools Development Corporation designed to elicit funds from corporate America to lend research support to 535 experimental schools (at least one in each congressional district) intended to become models of reform and innovation. The Corporation, headed by Thomas H. Kean, was introduced by President Bush and Secretary Alexander as an integral part of *America 2000*. The prime example of innovative schools for profit was announced in May 1991 by Chris Whittle, who plans to devote two to three billion dollars over the next five years to establish a chain of several hundred "new American schools" demonstrating ways the latest research could be used to redesign schooling. Experiments designed to elevate the role of private enterprise in American education should be held accountable, as is public education, with achievement in education for citizenship.

The educational reform movement has bubbled up in higher education as well as in elementary and secondary education. The respective roles to be played in the education of teachers by the academic subjects offered in departments of liberal arts and sciences and by professional studies offered in the schools of education continue to be debated. The stated function of CIVITAS is to improve civic education in the elementary and secondary schools from kindergarten through grade 12, but it is clear that it can be effective only if teachers grapple with its goals and content during their pre-service or in-service preparation. This requires the cooperative efforts of the liberal arts faculties, the professional education faculties, and the practitioners in schools.

Some notable efforts were made in the early 1980s to ignite a zeal for citizenship as a primary goal of liberal education. As soon as Ernest L. Boyer became president of the Carnegie Foundation for the Advancement of Teaching, he turned his attention to this effort. In 1981, his book with Fred M. Hechinger, *Higher Education in the Nation's Service*, repeatedly called for the advancement of civic learning as a prime goal of a new, integrated core of studies in liberal education. Under the auspices of the Carnegie Foundation, Frank Newman, president of the Education Commission of the States, sounded the tocsin in 1985 in *Higher Education and the Resurgence of America* in which he not only called for colleges to devote themselves to civic goals in the curriculum but to promote active service to the community and to the nation. As a result, a project called Campus Compact was formed as a coalition of well over 100 institutions to enlist undergraduate students in public service activities as an integral part of their college experience.

Meanwhile, the Kettering Foundation under the leadership of David Mathews as president was prodding and supporting several moves toward civic education in liberal arts colleges. The Association of American Colleges, with Mark H. Curtis as president, promoted the ideas in its periodical, *Liberal Education*, and issued a special commission report on *Integrity in the College Curriculum* in which the civic goals of liberal education were emphasized as few higher education commissions have done. And the Kettering Foundation kept up a steady drumbeat on the same themes through support of the quarterlies, *The Antaeus Report* and *The Civic Arts Review*, edited by Bernard Murchland.

Somehow, in the late 1980s, what seemed like promising movements to view the liberal arts as civic arts were overshadowed by acerbic laments over the decline of the core values of Western civilization in liberal education in the face of claims to highlight values rooted in race and ethnicity. Major voices were those of Allan Bloom in his *The Closing of the American Mind* and of William Bennett as Secretary of Education. These arose to a crescendo over multiculturalism in the early 1990s.

Then, in the summer of 1991 the claims for civic education were reemphasized when Kettering published a major collection of articles recalling universities to their civic goals. Entitled *Higher Education and the Practice of Democratic Politics; a Political Education Reader* and edited by Murchland, this book was addressed to "anyone concerned with the role of colleges and universities in preparing young Americans for political responsibility, civic competence, and public leadership." These goals for higher education clearly complement those of CIVITAS for elementary and secondary education and could help to recall liberal education to its civic role in preparing teachers.

In the mid-1980s the American Association of Colleges for Teacher Education and other professional education associations flirted with the idea of putting civic values at the core of their preparation of teachers. As a result of a national seminar held at the Hoover Institution in 1984, which was sponsored by twelve major academic and professional organizations, AACTE undertook a short-lived project on civic learning for teachers. But the Hoover proposals still await major implementation in liberal arts colleges and in schools of education. Perhaps CIVITAS could help ignite new and joint interest among those institutions that prepare teachers.

However, powerful voices have been attacking schools of education and their courses in pedagogy as unnecessary and even harmful for good teaching. William Bennett, for example, as Secretary of Education, endorsed alternatives to established teacher education programs, whereby mature persons from various fields of endeavor could be recruited directly into teaching, thus bypassing required courses in schools of education. This movement toward "alternative certification" has struck a responsive note among politicians and business leaders, including *America 2000*, and especially among those interested in promoting scientific and vocational studies that will enhance American competitiveness in world markets. Whether those teaching the social studies enter the profession through alternative certification or through traditional avenues, a thorough grounding in CIVITAS will benefit their efforts in the classroom.

Considerably at odds with temporary approaches to the selection and training of teachers is the National Board for Professional Teaching Standards, initially funded by the Carnegie Corporation's Forum on Education and the Economy. The Board's chairman is James B. Hunt, Jr., a former governor of North Carolina, and the president and chief executive officer is James A. Kelly, with headquarters in Detroit.

The National Board is in the process of developing high national standards for the certification of teachers beyond the usual certification requirements of the several states. Based on proposals made by a project headed by Lee Shulman at Stanford, the Board has developed policies for national certificates in all subject fields and at all levels from ages 3 through 18. Included in the subjects are "Social Studies/History." The Board has adopted the general national purpose to assess "what teachers should know and be able to do."

The Board has been roundly criticized in some quarters because it does not require course work in schools of education as a prerequisite for candidates to become Board Certified. Nevertheless, the Board is likely to have a significant influence on the education of teachers in the long term. CIVITAS could be a major resource when the Board develops its standards of assessment for highly qualified teachers of "Social Studies/History."

Other groups that are seeking to influence reform in teacher education and that should be alert to the importance of CIVITAS are the Holmes Group of education deans long headed by Judith E. Lanier, dean at Michigan State; the Teacher Corps run by the Department of Education; and such voluntary groups as Teach for America which stress recruiting liberal arts graduates with minimal preparation in professional education. All of these need the rich resources of civic education as set forth in CIVITAS.

Finally, several important initiatives are under way to respond to requests from governments and educators from other lands who are interested in developing their own programs of civic education for democracy. We do not assume that countries with little experience in democracy can simply be handed translations of *The Federalist Papers*, but CIVITAS could be enormously useful in aiding the efforts of new democratic governments that seek to reform the role of citizenship education in Eastern European nations and in the republics of the Soviet Union as well as in Africa and Latin America.

Just as the seven industrial nations opened their conference in London in early July 1991 to consider what aid could be given to a Soviet Russia in dire straits economically and politically, the president of Czechoslovakia, Vaclav Havel, again significantly argued, as he had in his address to Congress in February 1990, that

> ...it was in the interest of my country, of Europe and of the whole world to help make the Soviet Union a more free, more democratic and more stable place with the emphasis on democracy. The experience of the postwar period has shown us that no amount of economic assistance will make a

totalitarian country more prosperous unless it is also made more democratic.

There could not be a better definition of the potential role of CIVITAS in international education.

The Project for Democracy-International, sponsored by the American Federation of Teachers and the Educational Excellence Network, could find prime use for CIVITAS as it deals with educators in Eastern Europe and elsewhere. Similarly, as the Department of Education, the U.S. Peace Institute, Peace Corps, USAID, USIA, and the National Endowment for Democracy set about to design new programs of foreign assistance, CIVITAS could be an indispensable aid to them in translating the values of democratic citizenship as visualized and practiced in the United States.

With the stunning and successful conclusion of the military phase of the Persian Gulf War, attention returned to the role of schools in developing civic responsibility and civic participation in the United States itself, but now in a new and even more urgent context. In his Foreword to CIVITAS, Ernest Boyer reminds us that his studies of the high school a few years ago included proposals for a "new Carnegie unit" requiring civic participation and community service for high school graduation. Likewise, many plans for national service have recently been afoot in Congress.

In this regard, all future national service projects, whether voluntary or compulsory, whether military or civilian, could profit from a basic component of substantive content dealing with democratic values, knowledge, and skills as embodied in CIVITAS. The sense of self satisfaction or good feeling derived from participating in some kind of useful activity or service for others is undeniably important, but it is not sufficient as a component of good citizenship unless it knowingly contributes to the public good.

The Markle Commission on the Media and the Electorate, headed by Robert O'Neil, proclaims its purpose to develop "a national education program to improve citizens' understanding of their stake in the democratic process." In view of the dramatic demographic changes taking place in the American population, special review could well be made by the Immigration and Naturalization Service of the civic content available to and required of new immigrants who are coming into the United States in increasing numbers. CIVITAS could be an invaluable substantive source for designers of programs intended to help prepare new and recent immigrants not simply to be minimally "naturalized" but effectively "citizenized" American citizens.

Suddenly, in the spring of 1991, political alienation seemed to be overshadowed in the perceptions of the public by a new patriotism and national pride engendered by the Gulf War successes. What had preoccupied the nation during the elections of 1990 in the form of apathy, anger, or frustration with governing bodies and politicians was overtaken by a patriotic pride in country. What had been antipathy toward the sloth, ignorance, and unruly indiscipline of youth became adulation of their performance in the war. Could these be the same youth who could not locate the United States on a map of the world?

As of this writing, it is undoubtedly too soon to develop adequate perspectives on the meaning of the Persian Gulf War for citizenship education in the U.S., but it should be noted that CIVITAS tried to deal carefully with the meaning of patriotism long before the war was envisaged or started. It is an intriguing sequence of events whereby the election of November 6, 1990 was pasted up as an exercise in voters' alienation from government and their elected officials, only to be followed by the historic debates in Congress about declaring war. Quickly, Congress was revealed to be representing "us," not "them." The waves of patriotism evoked by the onset and conclusion of actual hostilities changed the atmosphere—at least for a time. In any case, the fundamental values set forth in the CIVITAS section on Civic Virtue, including patriotism, might well take on greater depth of meaning.

We cannot predict what the long range outcome of the Gulf War may be for America's sense of patriotism and sense of community. But there were clear and sharp divergences of opinion about the wisdom, morality, and outcomes of the war, both before its onset and after its conclusion, as expressed by politicians in the Congressional debates, by opposing views taken by military and political experts in the press and on television, by the differing views of responsible religious leaders, and by academic professionals on college campuses. The intensity of the national debate may actually serve to reinforce the view that the essence of patriotism as defined in CIVITAS is displayed not only by cheering the returning troops but also by adopting a well-developed sense of civic virtue bulwarked by substantive knowledge and participatory skills of citizenship.

The military victory in the Persian Gulf War revealed at least one immediate lesson of import for the public and for educators: American citizens can achieve a powerful sense of community when the cause is perceived to promote such values as the public good, freedom, justice, human rights, truth, and patriotism. The questions now before us are: How can American education sustain the values of the Constitution and Bill of Rights as the core of our common compact and promote the general welfare at home as well as a viable peace abroad as we approach the world of 2000? Can we heed the injunction of William James in *The Moral Equivalent of War* and find the means henceforward "to inflame the civic temper as past history has inflamed the military temper"? CIVITAS provides one clear answer to these questions.

For more than forty years I have been associated with a number of projects and movements designed specifically to improve education for citizenship. In the 1950s, the Citizenship Education Project at Teachers College, Columbia University supported by the Carnegie Corporation reached thousands of teachers in more than a thousand schools as well as personnel on military posts with the endorsement of General Dwight D. Eisenhower when he was commander of NATO. But, after the decade of the 1950s, the project did not gain sustaining support from the academic community or the public. In the late 1960s, the Center for Research and Education in American Liberties at Columbia attracted distinguished academic scholars in politics, education, law, and jurisprudence, but it was overtaken by the unrest and distractions of the Vietnam War on the college campuses. In the 1970s and 1980s, a coalition of public and professional organizations devoted to a variety of projects in law-related education made remarkable headway in promoting a series of excellent albeit partial approaches to education for citizenship. CIVITAS has greatly benefitted from these efforts, supported by various agencies of the federal government, by bar associations, and by such foundations as Danforth and Kettering.

Now, for more than a decade my most satisfying and fruitful associations have been with the Center for Civic Education and the Council for the Advancement of Citizenship. Together, they have produced CIVITAS, which I believe is by far the most comprehensive and coherent approach to civic education of those forty years. Together, in the effort to build on the past and break new ground, they and their associates have been able not only to mobilize the combined talents of scores of academic scholars and professional educators but also the leaders of more than ninety public spirited national organizations. I hope that they will be able to convince the educational reformers of the 1990s that competent achievement in the knowledge of civics and government is a core requirement for preparing all youth to become participating and responsible American citizens.

"One more time unto the breach, dear friends, one more time...."

R. Freeman Butts
July 4, 1991

INTRODUCTION

The ultimate goal of civic education in America is the widespread participation in the political process of citizens who are knowledgeable and committed to the realization of the fundamental values and principles of constitutional democracy. Those principles require that the citizen's decision to participate be freely made. Authoritarian regimes have often demanded their subjects' participation in order to establish "legitimacy" and penalized those who oppose them or in other ways failed to adhere to the standard model of obedient subject. But constitutional democracies must rely upon the willing participation of citizens who are entirely free to decline democracy's standing offer to enter the process of self-government. Education and example are among the few means at a democracy's disposal to inspire the voluntary participation of its members, a task that clearly indicates the central place of the civic mission of our schools.

The primary goal of **CIVITAS: A Framework for Civic Education** is to suggest guidelines for the development or enhancement of civic education instructional programs in public and private elementary and secondary schools in order to promote civic competence, civic responsibility, and the widespread participation of youth in the social and political life of their communities and the nation.

"Civic competence" is the capacity to participate effectively in the American political as well as social systems. "Civic responsibility" is the commitment to fulfilling the obligations of citizenship. Among these are the responsibility to study issues; to vote and otherwise influence government policy, particularly in ways that benefit the whole nation and future generations; to work to improve the quality of government functioning; to limit governments to their constitutional authority; and to help one's family, neighborhood, and community through voluntary service.

PRIMARY AUDIENCE AND USE

The CIVITAS curriculum framework is specifically designed as a model and resource for professional educators responsible for the development of such documents. Typically, this includes curriculum specialists in state departments of education, local educational agencies, and private schools.

OTHER USES

The framework may also serve as a resource for teacher trainers, textbook writers, and others responsible for implementing programs in civic education. Although not designed to meet the specific needs of teachers for instructional materials, many teachers may find it useful in planning instruction and selecting curricular materials.

Public officials, civic organizations (such as the Boy and Girl Scouts, Rotary Clubs, and American Legions), and business, labor, and professional associations that wish to plan and promote civic education both in and out of academic settings may also find the framework a useful resource.

ORGANIZATION OF THE FRAMEWORK

There are two major sections in the framework. These are
1. A **rationale** that explains the basic philosophy, purpose, and nature of the framework.

2. A statement of **goals and objectives** that civic education should foster. **Goals** are general statements of the ends of civic education. They outline capacities that should be developed and what students should be able to do as a result of civic education. **Objectives** are more specific statements of educational outcomes which must be attained in order to reach the goals of civic education.

The statement of goals and objectives provides the focus for the planning of instructional programs and experiences for students. It does **not** specify the means by which the goals and objectives are to be obtained, e.g., the methods to be used, experiences to be provided students. (Suggested means are contained, however, in the Model Scope and Sequence statements contained in parts II and III.) This section is divided into three parts.

Part I: Civic Virtue
> **Goal** — To foster among citizens **civic dispositions** and commitments to fundamental values and principles required for competent and responsible citizenship.

Part II: Civic Participation
> **Goal** — To develop among citizens the **participatory skills** required to monitor and influence the formulation, implementation, adjudication, and enforcement of public policy, as well as to participate in voluntary efforts to solve neighborhood and community problems.

Part III: Civic Knowledge and Intellectual Skills
> **Goal** — To provide citizens the **knowledge and intellectual skills** required to monitor and influence the formulation, implementation, adjudication, and enforcement of public policy, as well as to participate in voluntary efforts to solve neighborhood and community problems.

RATIONALE

I. A RATIONALE FOR CIVIC EDUCATION

If liberty and equality, as is thought by some, are chiefly to be found in democracy, they will be attained when all persons alike share in the government to the utmost.

Aristotle, *Politics* (c.340 B.C.)

Civic education in a democracy is education in self-government. Self-government means active participation in self-governance, not passive acquiescence in the actions of others. The words of Aristotle reflect the view that the ideals of democracy are most completely fulfilled when every member of the political community actively shares in government. Members of the political community are its citizens; citizenship in a democracy is **membership** in the sovereign body politic. Some contemporary political philosophers go beyond Aristotle, arguing that citizenship should be considered an **office of government** like any other, with its own responsibilities.

The first and primary reason for civic education in a constitutional democracy is that the health of the body politic requires the widest possible civic participation of its citizens consistent with the public good and the protection of individual rights. The aim of civic education is therefore not just any kind of participation by any kind of citizen; it is the participation of **informed** and **responsible** citizens, skilled in the arts of deliberation and effective action.

No one's civic potential can be fulfilled without forming and maintaining an intention to pursue the common good; to protect individuals from unconstitutional abuses by government and from attacks on their rights from any source, public or private; to seek the broad knowledge and wisdom that informs judgment of public affairs; and to develop the skill to use that knowledge effectively. Such values, perspectives, knowledge, and skill in civic matters make responsible and effective civic participation possible. Fostering these qualities constitutes the mission of civic education.

What should that education include? The late Sidney Hook once defined civic education as

> ...the intensive study and understanding of American political institutions, especially the system of self-government, its values, commitments, and assumptions; its relevant history, its problems, burdens, and opportunities; its challenges and alternatives, in short the theory and practice of free and open democratic society as it has devel-

oped in the United States (*The Humanities and Civic Learning*, [1984]).

To this formulation could be added a study of the purpose of government, the nature of law, the way private behavior affects the public order and the political system, and the international context of politics. Citizens need to recognize the growing importance for the preservation of American democracy of the political, economic, environmental, and social context of the world beyond our borders. International and global interdependence and connections demands raised horizons for effective citizenship. Finally, learning to develop and practice civic skills is essential to fulfill the promise of constitutional democracy.

How important is civic education?

The importance of civic education has been remarked upon since the early days of American independence. In 1786, three years before the framing of the Constitution, Benjamin Rush wrote that youth should be educated to "watch for the state as if its liberties depended on [their] vigilance alone." Other concerned voices from Thomas Jefferson to John Dewey to the present have insisted that enlightened citizens capable of following their own initiative are necessary for both the perpetuation and the continuous renewal of the republic.

Through virtually our entire history under the Constitution, however, many Americans have not participated in the processes of governance. Although at the outset not all were eligible to vote, not even a majority of those who were eligible bothered to vote for delegates to state conventions ratifying the Constitution. To those concerned about the threat of popular democracy, voices have sometimes been heard arguing that it is perfectly safe to allow the people to vote because most will not do so. The behavior of twentieth-century Americans might sometimes be said to confirm this estimate. Indeed recent levels of American voting are among the lowest of western democracies. And, although it is only one form of political participation, the voting rate serves as a barometer of popular involvement and tells us how many citizens feel a sufficient sense of civic responsibility and involvement in the political process to bestir themselves on polling days.

The failure of citizens to take part in elections at every level is just one indication—an easily measurable and therefore unmistakable one—of widespread disengagement of citizens from the responsibilities and rewards of involvement inherent in our constitutional system. And, perhaps because the political order does not collapse when many citizens fail to participate in public affairs, Americans have tended toward a lackadaisical acceptance of their own apathy and inertia. We tend to perceive the Constitution, in Michael Kammen's evocative phrase, as "a machine that would go of itself." Our constitution's very success has created indifference in many citizens to investing themselves in the political system that sustains their prosperity and well-being.

Some political scientists assert that non-participation indicates satisfaction with the state of things. Even if this were true for some individuals, America has a sufficiently broad and deep range of social problems to banish such complacency. It is a dangerous illusion to suppose that American democracy is like a self-perpetuating mechanism. Beneath the discernible operation of constitutional machinery, the American system is not mechanical but organic. It is like a plant whose visible portion remains healthy only as long as its hidden but vital roots are watered and nourished. It does not "go of itself" but requires careful attention and assiduous cultivation.

This reality is not easily perceived in temperate times when comparatively little discipline or sacrifice is demanded of citizens; but when crises occur, the commitment of any society to its own principles is tested. Even in more normal times, the words and deeds of both public officials and ordinary citizens constantly demonstrate whether the values and principles of democracy are generally understood and accepted and whether the skills and dispositions to carry them into effect are present.

It is a general truth that societies that neither understand nor practice their own principles are liable to find their institutions in decay or overthrown. This could be said of the ancient Roman Republic, of royal absolutism, including the *ancien régime* in France, and of communist states in the late twentieth century. The decline of institutions that follows the widespread disbelief or cynicism regarding the principles that underlie them is the political expression of the biblical proverb, "where there is no vision, the people perish."

What is the relationship between civic participation and constitutional democracy?

Whatever the long-term dangers may be, American government retains its immediate stability, and only the most insecure or alarmist would auger its fall in the foreseeable future. What, then, does it mean to say that constitutional democracy relies upon the participation of an enlightened citizenry? Constitutional democracy depends on the participation of an enlightened citizenry because government policies are in significant measure shaped and determined by the decisions of voters; and because limited government remains limited only by the vigilance of citizens who prevent or protest ethical and constitutional breaches. Moreover, only through thoughtful participation can the promise be achieved of the free and full development of the individual as an autonomous and morally responsible person—a self-governing adult.

Why must civic education be taught in the schools?

Just as there has been general agreement on the centrality of the role citizens play in a constitutional democracy, so most observers agree that the citizen's office is one that requires a specific education. What is acquired informally is inadequate training for citizenship, especially among the disadvantaged, for whom gaining the influence and political expertise to contribute to the common good and improve their lives poses the greatest difficulty. Birth may make us citizens in law; in practice, however, competent and responsible citizens are created through education in school, in the family, and in the larger community. It is in these settings that during youth the basis in knowledge, skills, and dispositions either is or is not formed that in adulthood can lead to a sense of civic membership and responsibility and political efficacy.

That common sense and ordinary experience alone do not constitute a sufficient civic education seems evident. The nature of American constitutional democracy and the responsibilities and opportunities of citizenship in it are not readily apparent. The philosophical, historical, and practical reasons for its organization and procedures as well as the rights it is designed to protect are often not obvious. Indeed, to the untutored observer, the apparent inefficiencies wrought by the complexities of our federal system, with its separated powers, its checks and balances, and its tedious pace, may be cause for alienation from it.

Moreover, many citizens lack an adequate understanding of the reasons for such fundamental features of the constitutional order as the protections extended to those accused of crimes or to those expressing unpopular or obnoxious views. Principles that are repeated simply as catechisms, rather than grounded in experience and understanding, rest upon weak foundations.

In summary, the citizen needs a deeper understanding of the American political system than is currently commonplace, both as a framework for judgment and as common ground for public discussion. It is true that events often vindicate the common sense and basic good judgment of the American electorate. Common sense is more reliable, however, when rooted in a firm understanding of basic principles and a solid commitment to constitutional goals.

What should the role of the schools be in civic education?

As there are many sources of education, there are many sources of civic education. Family, religion, community groups, government, business, labor, and communications media shape civic attitudes, convey civic knowledge, and to a greater or lesser extent, foster civic virtue. But historically Americans have assigned to the public schools the special mission of preparing the young for citizenship, whether they are native born or the children of the millions of immigrants who have chosen to become Americans. In the words of Horace Mann, "schoolhouses are the republican line of fortifications."

The responsibility of formal education in fostering civic virtue and a sense of citizenship is surely self-evident. Schools and other community groups should build upon a foundation laid in the child's earliest years. Some evidence suggests that this foundation is not very strong. Thus the role of the school in developing civic character is especially important, though it should not attempt to replace the functions of family, religion, and other institutions of society. In addition to their traditional and central role of imparting civic knowledge and skills, the schools must help students to see the relevance of a civic dimension for their lives.

Schools and community groups must, as R. Freeman Butts has argued, take seriously their "civic mission." This mission should extend beyond academic and vocational preparation, especially for the those with the least political power. Schools have a unique role, or at least a unique potential, in this regard, for only they can provide the thoughtful, sequential preparation needed to equip young people with the capacity to assume the responsibilities and enjoy the opportunities of adult citizenship.

What role can the family play in civic education?

A further consideration, the importance of involving students' families in their education, can hardly be overstated. While this involvement is true of all facets of education, special emphasis should be laid upon the role of the family in civic education. Research has shown that the family plays a substantial role in the formation of political attitudes in youth. The children of apathetic or alienated families may acquire similar attributes. Searching for means to enlist the family in the student's civic development should specially concern those seeking to strengthen civic education programs.

In many cases, schools will find a relative lack of family attention to political and civic matters. Imaginative educators

devise means to draw families more completely into the educational orbit. They might consider, for example, home visits by teachers to discuss educational issues and problems with parents. Aspects of civic learning could form part of the purpose of such visits. And students might discuss civic issues among family members as part of homework assignments. Students might also attend civic organization events with family—including extended family—members. However it is accomplished, family involvement should be considered a key component of any fully developed civic education program.

What is the purpose of the CIVITAS framework?

The goal of the **CIVITAS** curriculum framework is the development of fully participating, competent, and responsible citizens—citizens with a reasoned commitment to the fundamental values and principles of American constitutional democracy, who find satisfaction in employing those values and principles to serve others and fulfill their potential as effective public actors. **CIVITAS** seeks to foster commitment to constitutional principles and values, though not through some form of indoctrination. This goal is to be reached by imparting to young people civic knowledge and skills and providing them relevant experience, all linked to a disposition to look beyond their own particular interests and the social groups of which they are members and seek the **common** good both for the present and for generations to come. Thus instructional programs based upon the **CIVITAS** curricular framework should convey a profound understanding of the bases of American constitutional democracy. This understanding provides the most promising foundation for the citizen's development of a reasoned commitment to sustaining the institutions and furthering the ideals of American constitutional democracy.

II. A RATIONALE FOR CIVIC PARTICIPATION

Competent and responsible participation as a priority for civic education.

Democracy is self-government and self-government requires effective citizen participation. Effective participation in a modern, complex world is unlikely to occur without a concerted effort to create effective programs of civic education. For years public schools have issued broad statements of their intention to educate for responsible democratic citizenship. However sincere these statements may have been, systematic programs to educate for civic participation have yet to appear, and no more than a few students ever emerge from schools with the knowledge, skills, and dispositions to monitor and influence the public policies that affect their communities, the nation, and the world. This educational failure can be traced to two sources. First is the relative lack of commitment to the importance of civic education as it competes with many other goals of schooling, such as basic literacy. The second is an inadequate conception of civic participation which, even when pursued with commitment, fails to empower students to participate effectively.

The goal of effective civic participation is widely endorsed without being carefully defined. Rather than providing programmatic guidance, the goal functions more often like a conceptual sponge, absorbing diverse interpretations that mirror ideological contradictions in the society at large. Some civic educators, for example, see participation mainly as voting to select the governing elites to run existing political institutions. For others, effective participation entails nothing short of grass roots organizing to change the way existing political institutions conduct their business.

This Framework cannot resolve fundamental disagreement over the appropriate goals and forms of democratic participation. We must nevertheless articulate and justify the particular conception of participation that guides the Framework. Unless the knowledge, civic virtue, and skills of participation set forth in the statement of goals and objectives which follows all aim toward a carefully articulated and commonly understood goal of effective civic participation, the Framework is unlikely to advance the cause of democratic citizenship. It is important at the outset, therefore, to clarify in some detail what is meant by the Framework's ultimate goal: enabling all students when they become adult citizens to become competent and responsible participants in social and political life.

Competent and responsible civic participation refers not only to the frequency of citizens' activities, but more importantly to the quality of their efforts to monitor and influence public policy. To be competent, participation must be well-informed and well-directed influence on public policy. To be responsible, participation must be ethically justified in terms of its respect for the rights of the individual and its contribution to the common good, or the long range interests of the nation as a whole.

The quality and frequency of civic participation may be influenced by many factors, such as family values, economic opportunity, and the communications media, but the need to foster competent and responsible participation underscores the special contribution that education should make to democratic participation. It is not the proper role of the schools to indoctrinate students to participate but rather to develop competence and a democratic orientation that increase the likelihood of effective participation in self-government.

Common forms of political participation include—among others—voting, letter-writing to public officials and numerous other forms of civic writing, joining local or national groups seeking to influence public policy and actively supporting them, donating to political campaigns, organizing and participating in demonstrations for political issues, attending various kinds of public meetings, and becoming a governing representative in bodies from local schools boards to Congress. Self-governance in a large, complex society entails an enormous range of activity extending far beyond behaviors such as voting or letter-writing that have dominated conventional civics courses.

Students should be introduced to a wide range of forms of participation and given experience in their use. But, the student's decision to participate in any given activity with any particular frequency must be a matter of individual choice. The goal of the CIVITAS framework is to enhance the competence and opportunity of students to participate, while leaving choices as to where, when and how to participate up to the adult citizen.

Monitoring and Influencing Public Policy

Self-government is the essence of constitutional democracy. Self-government can be broadly interpreted, for example, by including such actions as choosing what clothes to wear, objecting to an employer's salary schedule, or formulating regulations for the disposal of nuclear waste. While self-government may pervade many aspects of human experience, it would be unrealistic and inappropriate to expect civic education to prepare students for all conceivable activities which may be considered self-government. Instead, the primary concern of civic education must be training in **political** self-government. Thus the ultimate goal of civic education should be to enable students to participate competently and responsibly in the monitoring and influencing of public policy.

What is public policy?

Public policies are embodied in the rules, decisions, and actions of the legislative, executive, and judicial branches of local, state, and national governments. But policies of the many other institutions and organizations also have a public character and a significant effect on the quality of citizens' lives. These include the wide arena of society at large, for example, policies of corporations, labor unions, and religious organizations, private social service agencies, all part of "civil society." Broadly interpreted, civic participation involves the monitoring and influencing of the policies of any organization that significantly affects individual rights and the common good.

We must add, however, that the foundations of American democracy are imperiled to the extent that citizens withdraw their attention and concern from political institutions in favor of exclusive involvement with the broader arena of civic activities in civil society. Thus neither sphere of participation—political institutions on the one hand and the wide domain of society at large on the other—should be ignored. And broadly conceived civic participation should not be taken as an adequate substitute for participation in the monitoring and influencing of government policy at all levels.

Although public policy is most commonly thought of as dealing with issues of national or international significance (wars, elections, inflation, pollution) which receive widespread media exposure, the CIVITAS definition of public policy broadens this focus to include countless political issues more local in character; for example, cyclists urging local government to establish bike trails or volunteer workers trying to change regulations of a public mental health clinic are attempting to influence public policy. The monitoring and influencing of local policy which usually escapes national attention offers a rich, almost unlimited agenda for civic participation.

Because government involvement and influence in contemporary life is so extensive, it is not always easy to discriminate between issues that may properly be considered to be related to public policy and those that fall solely within the private domain. For this reason, it may sometimes be difficult to identify the special terrain of civic education. Suppose, for example, that as part of an effort to protect the environment, students decide to boycott fast food restaurants to try to persuade them to use alternative containers. The project is clearly intended to enhance the public good, and a full-scale study of the problem could address public policies dealing with tax incentives, trade agreements, disposal of waste, or civil liberties. Although this particular campaign focuses on the "private" policies of vendors and the "private" choices of consumers, it clearly involves civic participation relevant to influencing policy by one or more levels of government.

Beginning with an interest in helping others or offering some service to the community, junior high students may wish to do volunteer service in an elementary school or a nursing home. Initially the students may not connect such "civic-minded" activities to issues of public policy. But volunteer service can make a major contribution to education for effective participation if student reflection extends beyond the technical challenge of how to help others on an individual basis. When students begin to raise questions about the quality of education and care their clients receive and how this might be improved, their volunteer service experience can bolster education in the monitoring, influencing, and shaping of government policy.

Volunteer service need not be confined to philanthropic activity, however. It is also very much a feature of democratic politics. All forms of participation by citizens is voluntary service. Political parties, interest groups, individual candidates, political campaigns, and the like all depend on voluntary assistance. Youth as well as adults can further their civic education by lending themselves to these forms of participation.

Monitoring public policy

In a representative democracy citizens participate in self-government not primarily by direct policy formulation and administration on a daily basis but instead by delegating this authority to democratically chosen leaders and then monitoring their performance. According to democratic theory, when government fails to meet the expectations of citizens, they attempt to influence policy either directly or by choosing new leaders. A fundamental task of self-government, therefore, is for citizens to make judgments about the extent to which existing policies adequately protect their rights and advance the public good.

This watchdog or monitoring process is complex and requires a fund of knowledge as well as the development of sophisticated intellectual and participatory skills. For instance, the effective monitoring of public policy requires understanding the ways in which government actions impinge upon one's own and others' lives; an ability to assess the extent to which existing policies or alternatives are more and less likely to achieve specific goals, and the capacity to evaluate public policy using a defensible set of values or criteria. In addition, since citizens seldom have the time to monitor more than a few aspects of public policy, they must have the capacity to make selective judgments about what issues are most important to follow. Presumably, conclusions resulting from this sort of monitoring will determine the issues on which citizens chooses to exert more active influence.

Influencing public policy

Influencing public policy also requires a fund of knowledge and sophisticated intellectual and participatory skills. The first step in influencing public policy relies heavily on conclusions from the monitoring process, that is, the clarification of long-range and short-range goals. If reducing poverty is the long-range goal, short-term goals might include electing a favored candidate, lobbying for an adult literacy campaign, or pressuring government to allocate more funds for shelters for the homeless. Achieving any of these goals will undoubtedly require even more specific intermediate objectives. Once one has chosen a course of action, the central challenge is to win sufficient support from relevant authorities and constituencies to achieve it.

Since most public issues involve persisting controversies over the allocation of scarce resources, the distribution of power among competing factions, or the affirmation of particular values, the process of exerting influence involves continuing negotiation and compromise. It is unlikely that a citizen's original goals will be achieved completely, and the process of winning support may often entail some modification of the goals themselves. Thus, exerting influence should not be seen simply as winning or getting one's general policy goals or values accepted. Instead, it should be construed as producing outcomes in a direction consistent with one's policy goals. In the example above, even if the candidate were to lose, the campaign might raise public consciousness on the issue that eventually would manifest itself in anti-poverty policy.

Since the difficulty of producing immediate results and of assessing the extent of one's influence can breed disillusionment among those citizens who try to make a difference, it is important for civic education programs to give serious attention to the possible rewards and frustrations of participation and to such dispositions as assertiveness, perseverance, patience, and even humor, that self-government requires. It is also fitting that civic education address the serious challenges that face American democracy.

PART ONE. CIVIC VIRTUE

MODEL FORMAT

Part Three. Civic knowledge and skills

THE NATURE OF POLITICS AND GOVERNMENT

TOPIC I. Political authority

> It was from America that...ideas long locked in the breast of solitary thinkers, and hidden among Latin folios, burst forth like a conqueror upon the world...and the principle gained ground, that a nation can never abandon its fate to an authority it cannot control.
>
> **Lord Acton** (1907)

As an essential basis for understanding the nature of politics and government the citizen should understand the nature of political authority, differing positions on the sources of its legitimacy, the difference between the legitimate use of authority and the use of power without authority, the history of the evolution of political authority, and contemporary events and issues related to authority.

Each of these sections includes a brief introductory statement of content and goals.

OBJECTIVES

The citizen should be able to

1. discriminate between the exercise of political authority and the use of power without authority.

2. take and justify (or evaluate) positions on proper sources of authority and whether the exercise of authority is legitimate.

3. explain the significance of limitations on authority.

4. explain why consent is a basis of authority.

5. distinguish between different forms of consent and explain the circumstances under which each form occurs.

contains statements of the intellectual skills required of citizens to be able to apply the knowledge specified in the frame of reference to historical and contemporary situations, events, and issues.

FRAME OF REFERENCE

Conceptual perspective

I.   **Political power and authority.** Power and authority are to be distinguished from each other.

   A.   Political power. Political power is the **capacity** to control, direct, or exert influence over something or someone, whether or not there is a right to do so.

   B.   Political authority. Political authority is the legitimized and institutionalized **right** to exercise power. Authority implies the right to exercise power, whether or not adequate means are available to carry out what those in authority decide. Some of the basic characteristics of political authority with which citizens should be familiar are the following...

contains a statement of fundamental concepts and other ideas related to the topic or subtopic which should form one part of the citizen's frame of reference.

Historical perspective

I.   **Political authority in the ancient world.** Concepts of political authority have undergone many changes from classical times to the present. Claims to authority were based upon claims to divine revelation or divine sanction, as in the case of Moses; authority for the rulers of Plato's *Republic* was...

contains brief statements of illustrative historical events, trends, issues, facts, figures, and scholarly and literary works related to the concepts and ideas which should form a second part of the citizen's frame of reference.

Contemporary perspective

I.   **Disputes of legitimacy.** The world today teems with contention over issues regarding the legitimacy of authority claimed over those subject to it; the proper source of authority is similarly disputed. Examples of the first issue include the Northern Ireland minority's rejection of the authority of the British crown and the similar rejection by West Bank and Gaza Strip... Israel's authority to rule them. In a different vein, in the spring of 1989 the Chinese students challenged the scope and...

contains brief statements of illustrative contemporary events, issues, and findings of social science research related to the concepts and ideas which should form the third part of the citizen's frame of reference.

PART ONE. CIVIC VIRTUE

Virtue is the principle of republican government...Virtue in a republic is love of one's country, that is, love of equality. It is not a moral virtue, not a Christian, but a public virtue.

Montesquieu (1748)

The aim of every political constitution is, or ought to be, first to obtain for rulers men who possess most wisdom to discern, and most virtue to pursue, the common good of the society; and in the next place, to take the most effectual precautions for keeping them virtuous whilst they continue to hold their public trust.

James Madison (1787)

Every government degenerates when trusted to the ruler of the people alone. The people themselves are its only safe depositories. And to render even them safe their minds must be improved to a certain degree. This indeed is not all that is necessary, though it be essentially necessary. An amendment of our constitution must come here in aid of the public education. The influence over government must be shared among all the people.

Thomas Jefferson (1785)

Traditionally, civic virtue has meant the willingness of the citizen to set aside private interests and personal concerns for the sake of the common good. CIVITAS broadens the traditional definition to include both the republican and liberal-democratic views of citizenship described in Part I. In the CIVITAS curriculum framework, **civic virtue** is described in terms of **civic dispositions** and **civic commitment**.

- **Civic dispositions** refer to those attitudes and habits of mind of the citizen that are conducive to the healthy functioning and common good of the democratic system.

- **Civic commitments** refer to the freely-given, reasoned commitments of the citizen to the fundamental values and principles of American constitutional democracy.

Civic virtue is distinct from those virtues that are relevant to our private or personal lives, such as courage and honesty, although there are areas in which these virtues overlap. In this section, those dispositions and commitments are outlined which, taken together, comprise civic virtue. These commitments and dispositions are imperative for two reasons:

- They enable the political process to work effectively to promote the common good.

- They contribute to the realization of the fundamental ideals of the American political system including protection of the rights of the individual.

CIVIC VIRTUE AS AN ULTIMATE GOAL

The ultimate goal of CIVITAS is to enable students equipped with the requisite civic knowledge and the skills of civic participation to make their own commitment to the civic values deemed necessary for the nurture and strengthening of the ideals of American democracy. We sum up this goal in the term "civic virtue." Despite its unfamiliarity in modern usage, we revive the term not only to call to mind one of the enduring traditional values underlying the founding experience of the American republic, but also to highlight those dispositions and commitments to the public good needed by American citizens as they confront an increasingly complex, fractious, and interdependent world.

A foundation of knowledge and skills should underlie commitment

In the following sections of this Framework, we set forth a core content of knowledge and of desirable experiential skills through which students may develop a reasoned and informed commitment to the ideals of constitutional democracy. They are ideals long denied by dictatorial regimes of both right and left but which have recently been reasserted in spectacular fashion by millions of people throughout the world. This democratic resurgence makes it all the more fitting that American education reaffirm these values to ensure the safety of democracy at home. It is not reassuring to witness the key role of students and intellectuals demanding free elections in the democratic revolutions abroad and then to realize how few American youth even bother to vote. It would be the ultimate irony of modern history if Americans gave themselves up to self-indulgence, corruption, apathy, or greed just as the rest of the world was clamoring for democracy and freedom in the idioms of Jefferson, Madison, and Lincoln.

In Part One of this Framework we outline those civic values that we believe should be studied with as much care as is devoted to acquiring knowledge of the nature of politics and government, the state, law, and the fundamental principles of a democratic constitutional order. The fostering of commitment, without command of relevant knowledge and without the skills of democratic participation, can lead to mindless subjection to tyranny, just as acquiring a mass of undigested, fragmented knowledge can lead to apathy; or as single-minded participation on behalf of some special interest can lead to the undermining of the public good.

Balancing the classical republican and liberal traditions

Drawing upon the classical republican tradition of politics, stemming from Aristotle and Cicero and coursing through Machiavelli, Montesquieu, and Rousseau, the Founders of the American republic used the term "public" or "civic virtue" to mean the willingness of citizens to subordinate their private interests and elevate their personal obligation to work on behalf of the public good. But the Founders of the American republic also drew upon another political tradition, arising especially in the seventeenth and eighteenth centuries in the vein of Hobbes and Locke, namely, traditional liberalism, which viewed the chief end of government to be the prime protector of the individual rights of citizens in a democratic republic.

Throughout American history, these two traditions have regularly vied for political power and at various times one or the other has dominated American thought and action by capturing the loyalties of majorities of American citizens; but both have persisted at various levels of intensity throughout our history. Neither one has existed in pristine form for any considerable length of time. We believe that both the classical republican tradition and the traditional liberal view of citizenship are legitimate elements in the historical spectrum of American civic values and that both have a place in our broadened view of civic virtue for the future.

We seek to achieve a workable balance or dynamic equilibrium among these values as we enter the third century of the American democratic republic. We challenge oncoming generations to engage in the rigorous intellectual and political process of grappling with those public issues and the underlying values that have confronted American citizens since the founding two hundred years ago. Sometimes, the balance has tipped toward values weighted with the public good, most easily recognizable in great crises of war, calamitous economic depression, or unexpected natural disasters. At other times, the scales dip toward the values of individual rights, as in the efforts to protect the freedoms of religion, speech, assembly, and due process against infringement by the government or by aggressive majorities in the states or local communities.

We view the citizen committed to civic virtue as one who watches both sets of values—those of the public good and those of freedom, diversity, and individual rights—and who acts on the basis of the best informed judgment that serious study and active participation can provide. We believe that civic virtue embraces thinking and acting in such a way that individual rights are viewed in light of the public good and that the public good includes the basic protection of individual rights. Whether one prefers to stress balance, equilibrium, or tension between these traditions, or views them as a blend, mixture, or tapestry, we believe that the effort to identify and understand their ingredients is the first major step toward the practice of civic virtue and that the ultimate goal is reasoned commitment to all of them.

TOPIC 1. CIVIC DISPOSITIONS

[A purpose of government is] to inbreed and cherish in a great people the seeds of virtu, and public civility.

John Milton (1641)

I must purchase by civility that regard which I had expected to enforce by insolence.

Dr. Samuel Johnson (1752)

All I want of you is a little seevility, and that of the commonest goddamnedest kind.

A whaler's ship's mate to his ill-humored captain (c. 1850)

...I often wonder whether we do not rest our hopes too much upon constitutions, upon laws and courts. These are false hopes; believe me, these are false hopes. Liberty lies in the hearts of men; when it dies there, no constitution, no law, no court can save it....

Judge Learned Hand (1941)

Civic dispositions refers to those attitudes and ingrained habits of mind that are conducive to behavior that leads to the healthy functioning and common good of the democratic system. These dispositions also enhance the individual's ability to participate competently and responsibly in the political system.

OBJECTIVES

Citizens should understand those dispositions which are conducive to behavior that will

1. enhance their effectiveness in monitoring and influencing public policy.

2. lead to the healthy functioning of American constitutional democracy.

FRAME OF REFERENCE
Conceptual Perspective

Dispositions of the citizen conducive to the healthy functioning of the American constitutional democracy include the following:

I. **Civility**. In its civic context, civility has the following characteristics:

   A. **Respect**. Civility includes treating others with respect and as individuals inherently worthy of regard whether or not one agrees with their positions.

   B. **Civil discourse**. Civility includes a disposition to take part in public debate and in doing so to adhere to commonly accepted standards of discourse such as:

      1. **Addressing the issue.** Debate should be based on the substance of opponents' arguments or positions on the issue and not on personal attacks on their character.

      2. **Respecting the right of others to be heard.** Disruptive tactics that undermine debate in a public forum should be avoided. However, when people are unjustly denied their right to express their views, disruptive tactics such as civil disobedience and similar non-violent activities can be justified.

II. **Individual responsibility**. Citizens should be disposed to care for and take responsibility for themselves and their actions.

III. **Self-discipline**. Virtuous citizens freely adhere to the fundamental rules required for the maintenance of the American system of constitutional government without requiring the imposition of external authority.

IV. **Civic-mindedness**. Thoughtful citizens recognize that there is often a tension between private interest and the common good. Citizens should understand that there are times when they should place the common good above their personal interests.

V. **Open-mindedness**. The disposition to be receptive to different ideas and arguments includes the following attributes.

   A. **Openness**. Citizens should be open to considering opposing positions and changing or modifying their own positions. Openness to opposing positions and arguments, however, does not mean that all views are of equal value or validity.

   B. **Skepticism**. A healthy skepticism is an appropriate response of the citizen to unsupported generalizations and dogmatism.

   C. **Recognition of ambiguity**. Citizens should recognize that actions and situations are sometimes capable of more than one interpretation and that the character of political and social reality is therefore sometimes ambiguous. It may therefore be difficult to achieve full understanding or certainty.

VI. **Compromise**. A disposition to compromise when appropriate should be based upon an understanding that the alternative may be political stalemate, indecision, or, in extreme cases, violence. Compromise is aided by understanding the following ideas.

   A. **Conflict of principles.** Citizens should understand that principles and values important to themselves and to various groups may sometimes conflict and compromise may be needed to attain an acceptable solution.

   B. **Limits to compromise.** Citizens should be able to distinguish between matters fit for compromise and matters that are unfit because they involve basic values or principles of constitutional democracy whose compromise imperils its continued existence.

VII. **Toleration of diversity.** The disposition to tolerate, appreciate, and support diversity includes respect for the right of others to differ in ideas, ways of life, customs, and beliefs. Support for diversity in everyday life should be based upon an understanding of the benefits of having people of diverse beliefs and ethnic and racial backgrounds as a part of the community.

VIII. **Patience and persistence.** Citizens should understand that forming or changing public policy usually requires a great deal of time and persistent effort. They should not be dissuaded from seeking desirable goals by this fact or by the inevitable delays and failures that result when trying to exert influence on governmental decision making.

IX. **Compassion**. Compassion is the disposition to empathize with others and show concern for their welfare, an essential attribute of citizens in a society devoted to the common good.

X. **Generosity**. Generosity means the disposition to expend time, effort, and resources in a civic context for the benefit of others. The virtuous citizen shows generosity to others and to the community at large.

XI. **Loyalty to the nation and its principles**. Citizens should habitually act in accord with the fundamental values and principles of the American constitutional system and be committed to narrowing the gap between those values and principles and actual practice.

COMMENTARY

Engendering civic dispositions

The dispositions to civic virtue identified above enhance the capacity of the individual to participate effectively in the American political system. They also contribute to the healthy functioning of that system. While some of these qualities undoubtedly characterize certain members of our society, it can hardly be denied that the dispositions that collectively constitute civic virtue are not as pervasive in either breadth or depth as they should be.

Traditionally, many of these dispositions are fostered by families, schools, churches, and communities. Daily life under these influences can habituate the young to such virtuous dispositions as tolerance, compassion, respect for the rights of others, open-mindedness, and other aspects of civility. On the other hand, it is just as evident that various environments and powerful strands of contemporary culture tend to foster self-indulgence, a lack of self-restraint and therefore may undermine the very virtues sought by school, family, and church.

Whatever one's view of the present-day bearing of home, church, and community on fostering the disposition to civic virtue, it is evident that the school must play a significant role in providing an environment conducive to developing these virtues. Within the school, the responsibility of furthering these dispositions must not be confined solely to classes devoted to civic education. The advance of civic dispositions should instead be a responsibility that pervades the entire school atmosphere. Teachers and other adults should model these dispositions, and the expectations, norms, and rules of the school should require and reinforce their development.

Moreover, the role of these civic dispositions should be a matter of deliberate study and discussion rather than left to haphazard assimilation. Classes in language arts and history, for example, might include literary and historical figures exemplifying the dispositions of civic virtue.

A variety of distractions has often conspired to prevent schools from adequately placing a priority on consciously and systematically fostering these dispositions. It is vital that this omission be rectified wherever it has occurred. The CIVITAS framework should prove useful in promoting the attention to this important responsibility that it deserves.

TOPIC 2. CIVIC COMMITMENTS

[T]here are other ways to teach loyalty and patriotism, which are the sources of national unity, than by compelling the pupil to affirm that which he does not believe....Without recourse to such compulsion the state is free to compel attendance at school and require teaching by instruction and study of...our history and...the structure and organization of our government, including the guaranties of civil liberty which tend to inspire patriotism and love of country.
Justice Harlan Fiske Stone (1940)

The understanding and experience gained by the student from a careful study of the history and principles of American constitutional democracy should foster among citizens a freely-given, reasoned commitment to those fundamental values and principles essential to the preservation and improvement of the constitutional order.

OBJECTIVE

The citizen should demonstrate a reasoned commitment to those fundamental values and principles essential to the preservation and improvement of American constitutional democracy.

FRAME OF REFERENCE
Conceptual Perspective

Commitments of the citizen to the fundamental values and principles necessary for the preservation and improvement of American constitutional democracy include the following:

Fundamental principles of American constitutional democracy

I. **Popular sovereignty.** The citizenry is collectively the sovereign of the state and holds ultimate authority over public officials and their policies. Within constitutional limits majorities should have the right to make political decisions.

II. **Constitutional government.** In order to protect the basic rights of the people, government should be limited both in its scope and in its methods. By consenting to the Constitution, the sovereign people agrees to the limitations of its own powers as it agrees to limit the powers of government. The principle of constitutional government includes the following related principles:

A. **The rule of law**. Both government and the governed should be subject to the law. Government decisions and actions should be made according to established laws rather than by arbitrary actions and decrees.

B. **Separation of powers**. Legislative, executive, and judicial powers should be exercised by different institutions in order to maintain the limitations placed upon them.

C. **Checks and balances**. The powers given to the different branches of government should be balanced, that is roughly equal, so that no branch can completely dominate the others. Branches of government are also given powers to check the power of other branches.

D. **Minority rights**. Decisions made by majorities should not unreasonably and unfairly infringe upon the rights of minorities. Constitutionally-guaranteed rights should be placed out of the reach of legislative majorities.

E. **Civilian control of the military**. Civilian authority should control the military in order to preserve constitutional government.

F. **Separation of church and state**. Church and state should be separated in order to preserve liberty of conscience and belief.

G. **Power of the purse**. All federal laws for raising revenue must originate in the legislative house closest to the people (the House of Representatives) as well as be approved by the Congress as a whole.

H. **Federalism**. Power is shared between two sets of governmental institutions, those of the states and those of the central or federal authorities, as stipulated by the Constitution. Although federal law is the supreme law of the land, it does not cover certain subjects of governance, which are the province of state or local authority.

For commentary on these principles see appropriate items in Part III, Civic Knowledge.

Fundamental values of American constitutional democracy

I. **The public or common good**. The citizen should attempt to determine the public good and seek to promote it.

II. **Individual rights**. Individual rights may be divided into the three forms stated in the Declaration of Independence.

A. **Life**. The individual's right to life should be considered inviolable except in certain highly restricted and extreme circumstances, such as the use of deadly force to protect one's own or others' lives.

B. **Liberty**. The right to liberty should be considered an unalterable aspect of the human condition. This right includes the following.

1. **Personal freedom**. Individuals should be free from arbitrary arrest and detention and secure in their persons, homes, papers, and effects against unreasonable searches and seizures. There should be a private realm in which the individual is free to act and which government cannot legitimately invade. This realm includes, for example, the individual's rights to freedom of conscience and belief, to freedom of association and expression, and the right to be let alone.

2. **Political freedom**. Citizens should have the right to participate freely in the political process, to choose and remove public officials, to be governed under a rule of law, and to participate in the creation of their laws. This process requires the free flow of information and ideas, open debate, and the right of assembly.

3. **Economic freedom**. Citizens should have the right to acquire, use, transfer, and dispose of private property without unreasonable governmental interference. This right includes the right, for example, to seek employment wherever one pleases; to change employment at will; and to engage in any lawful economic activity either by oneself or in combination with others in units such as business partnerships and corporations or labor unions.

C. **The pursuit of happiness**. It is the right of citizens in the American constitutional democracy to attempt to attain—to "pursue"—happiness in their own way, so long as they do not infringe upon rights of others. The idea of the "pursuit of happiness" as a right denies the legitimacy of paternalism on the part of government, that is, it denies the legitimacy of the government to define what happiness one ought to seek.

III. **Justice**. People should be treated fairly in the distribution of the benefits and burdens of society, correction of wrongs and injuries, and gathering of information and making of decisions.

IV. **Equality**. The idea of equality may be divided into various kinds of equality.

    A. **Political equality**. All citizens who attain the status of adulthood should have equal political rights. No one is to be denied these rights unless by due process of law.

    B. **Legal equality**. All people should be treated as equals before the law, without favoritism toward any individual or group.

    C. **Social equality.** There should be no class hierarchy sanctioned by law, e.g., no nobility in which individuals, by virtue of their membership, have certain privileges and duties that others do not have.

    D. **Economic equality**. Economic equality tends to strengthen political and social equality; extreme economic inequality tends to undermine all other forms of equality and should therefore be avoided.

V. **Diversity.** Variety in cultural and ethnic background, race, lifestyle, and belief is not only permissible but desirable and beneficial in a pluralist society.

VI. **Truth.** Citizens can legitimately demand that truth-telling as refraining from lying and full disclosure by government be the rule, since trust in the veracity of government constitutes an essential element of the bond between governors and governed. Citizens should not always expect complete or immediate truth-telling by government, however, since legitimate interests of state may be fatally compromised by premature admission and disclosure.

VII. **Patriotism.** Virtuous citizens display a devotion to their country, including devotion to the fundamental values and principles upon which it depends.

COMMENTARY

Fundamental values of American constitutional democracy

I.   The public good

The obligation to promote the public good

However it may be defined in specific circumstances, the public or common good requires that individual citizens have the commitment and motivation—that they accept their obligation—to promote the welfare of the community and to work together with other members for the greater benefit of all. This commitment may mean subordinating the citizen's personal interests to the more inclusive benefits of the whole, even at times sacrificing one's own well-being or safety.

Acceptance of a personal obligation to serve the welfare of the various groups to which citizens belong (family, religion, kinship, work place) is necessary to sustain the common life of the group. This is no less true of the civic obligation to ensure the stability and very existence of the political community. The habits and virtues of self-discipline, compassion, and devotion to duty are especially important in a democratic society that honors the diversity of pluralist groups as well as the fundamental principles of a constitutional order.

Voluntarism and the public good

Most citizens can recognize war or the threat of war as a time when their individual lives, security, and freedom are directly bound up with the larger welfare of the nation and can clearly see their obligation to contribute to the common good. But there are other occasions when the individual's obligation to the public good is less obvious, but just as necessary. A devastating hurricane on the East Coast, a sudden earthquake on the West Coast, and violent tornadoes in between dramatize the necessity of urgent help for those directly affected. Voluntary efforts by private individuals to help fellow citizens meet their immediate needs for food, shelter, and clothing are exemplary models of the role of voluntarism on behalf of the public good.

Public and private sector responsibility

Such disasters also illustrate the need for careful organization by professionals in humanitarian private organizations and in all levels of government. The value of well-trained and committed officers in public service careers is never more visible and welcome: police, fire, and emergency services; medics, paramedics, and nurses; social workers, mental health workers; and, not least, teachers. After immediate emergency needs are met, long-range questions arise concerning the relative responsibility of private and governmental agencies in paying for relief efforts and for rebuilding private property as well as restoring the infrastructure of highways, bridges, water and power resources, schools and hospitals, and all else necessary for promoting the public good.

The need to foster commitment to the public good

The occasions for addressing issues of the public good are by no means limited to the dramatic events of natural disasters, domestic upheavals, or grave international crises. All communities at one time or another face decisions on tax levies for schools, libraries, public highways and transportation, medical care and hospitals, and community projects for child care, mental health, the chronic homeless, senior housing, and teen centers. Are these matters to be undertaken by government and therefore financed by taxes, or are they best left to private effort and voluntarism? How is the public good to be served?

Similar questions arise in issues concerning armaments, environmental pollution, drugs, crime, and poverty. We do not argue that matters of such cosmic proportion can be settled by the school curriculum, but we do argue that the welfare of the American political community depends upon a growing sense of obligation for the common good among American citizens. The school curriculum must be enlisted in this task.

II. Individual rights

Nothing could be more stunning than the eruption of demands for individual rights against Communist statism by the Chinese in their aborted efforts to establish a free democratic order in the spring of 1989, by East Europeans in the fall of 1989, and even by republics of the Soviet Union in 1990-1991 seething with discontent, seeking independence and equality, demanding freedom and rights for the peoples of all nationalities, and threatening the break up of the Soviet Union itself. The revolutionary words of Thomas Jefferson were at last resonating among the citizens of Communist countries, as they had in the independence movements of the colonial peoples of the Third World after World War II (see the section Human Rights, below).

It had long been clear that when polities experimenting with liberal democracy went so far in the direction of pluralist diversity that their very existence was threatened, they needed to achieve a greater sense of cohesive common good

(as when the thirteen American colonies moved from confederation to union). Similarly, it was clearer than ever that when the cohesive instruments of force and compulsion in statist polities became unbearable, the enforcing structures of party and government—as symbolized by the Berlin Wall—began to crack and tumble.

What may have seemed to American students as "dry" U.S. and world history could now be refreshed by the flooding events of the late 1980s and early 1990s. Millions in the Communist world were discovering (the young generations discovering for the first time) those values of freedom, justice, equality, and consent of the governed in the rule of law that have been the ideals of liberal constitutional democracy for two centuries.

However dramatic and spectacular these events may be to adults who have seen freedom crushed by dictatorships of the right and left in the twentieth century, it is still necessary to arouse the interest and attention of American students. They can hardly be expected to realize how the battles to achieve and protect individual rights even in a highly developed liberal democracy must constantly be waged—that they are never waged once and for all.

Issues of individual rights that directly affect educational policy, teachers, and the students themselves could be used as beginning points for study and discussion, as a means of developing in students a commitment to the underlying values of individual rights. These values include personal freedoms, public freedoms, and economic freedoms. All are fundamental elements of the dispositions and commitments of virtuous citizens. (They are described at length in slightly different form in the section on Civic Knowledge).

Life. The right to life may be considered the most basic and fundamental of all, since without it other rights amount to little. Liberal democracy does not require that one give up one's life to the polity for use as the state determines. Such a requirement is thoroughly inimical to American constitutional democracy, under which one's right to life is inviolable under all ordinary circumstances. Only when citizens turn against the community in violent crime that threatens others' lives may the community protect itself by threatening the life of the criminal. One circumstance in which the political community can rightly require citizens' to place their lives in jeopardy, however, is in defense of the republic. But this is not an obligation to die. Even here, the laws of war as well as conscientious objection to fighting limit the community's legitimate powers.

Liberty. Personal, political, and economic liberty may be distinguished from each other:

Private (Personal) freedom. Personal freedom includes the right, the opportunity, and the ability of everyone to live his or her life in dignity and security and to seek self-fulfillment as an individual or as a member of a chosen group without arbitrary constraint by government or by others in the community. It is well to remember that when James Madison made his original proposals for amendments to the Constitution, he argued that the bill of rights would protect individuals from government abuse as well as that the government itself would act to protect individuals from abuses of their liberties by others in the community, especially by domineering majorities.

In recent years, the right to **privacy** has become one of the most important and controversial issues in the field of individual rights. The right to privacy is generally considered to be the right of individuals to be left alone to decide for themselves what their private actions should be and what information about themselves and their private conduct should be communicated to others or made public.

Infringement of the right of privacy was one of the most inflammatory of the practices of the British in the American colonies. It led to the Third Amendment of the Constitution, protecting citizens against the quartering of troops in their households during peacetime, and the Fourth Amendment's guarantee that the people shall be secure in their persons, houses, papers, and effects against unreasonable searches and seizures. The revelations that the CIA and FBI had tapped telephones and spied on American citizens during the Vietnam War and the scandals of Watergate redoubled concerns about protection of privacy from government intrusion.

The right of privacy has moved beyond what personal matters should be inviolable against technological surveillance by public or private agencies (including credit raters). While the word "privacy" does not appear in the Bill of Rights, the Supreme Court has interpreted the freedoms of the First, Fifth, and Fourteenth Amendments to prohibit legislation regulating such intimate and private matters as birth control methods and abortion. The now famous case of *Roe v. Wade* in 1973 legalizing abortion and its subsequent limitation in *Webster v. Reproductive Health Services* in 1989 set off nationwide political campaigns of almost unprecedented turmoil that promised to last well into the 1990s. Whatever views a concerned citizen may take on these matters, the constitutional issues of personal freedom and privacy are likely to be debated again and again in elections and in the nation's legislatures and courtrooms. Confrontations on these issues will profoundly test citizens' commitment to civic virtue.

Public (political) freedom. Public freedoms are those intellectual and political rights of individuals that inhere in the common good of the democratic political community and that the liberal state is obligated actively to protect from infringement by coercive majorities, by despotic minorities, or by government itself. The First, Fifth, and Fourteenth Amendments outline the general principles of freedom of speech, press, assembly, and petition that are indispensable for democratic public decision making. These are the first rights to be suppressed when dictators overthrow democratic regimes and the first to be demanded when the people seek to recover their liberties. Political freedom is the most obvious form of public freedom. It includes the right, the opportunity, and the ability of all citizens to have a genuine part in shaping the institutions and laws under which they live and to do this by making uncoerced choices and by participating in public affairs in cooperation with fellow citizens. (The various aspects of political freedom are spelled out in the Framework section on Civic Knowledge.)

An equally important form of political freedom is intellectual and academic freedom. It includes the right of citizens to speak, read, inquire, think, express, learn, and teach without arbitrary constraint. This freedom is the safest means by which citizens can make rational political choices among real alternatives on the basis of valid and reliable knowledge. The genius of American democracy is that the Bill of Rights protects the intellectual and religious freedom of individuals against infringement even by popular majorities arrived at through the political process of free and fair elections.

Economic Freedom. We deal with property rights as an aspect of individual freedom to underline the concept of private property as a fundamental element in the American constitutional order and to recognize some of the major changes in this element that have taken place in the past two hundred years. It is not that citizens must become economists but that the ownership of property should be looked upon in a democratic society as a fundamental right carrying with it responsibilities. This right should be viewed in relation to the public good, justice, equality, and the other values of civic virtue.

Throughout much of the American colonial period the ideas of property and liberty went hand in hand. Indeed, government in early America was often looked upon as a means to protect individuals from one another and to protect their property. The bitter defense of property rights against British regulation and taxation is well-known, but following the Revolutionary War the independent states nevertheless intruded into traditional private realms through their own taxation, coinage of money, and restraints on trade among states and with foreign powers. It was the intrusive interventions by state legislatures that seemed to threaten the security of property, money, credit, and liberty of the newly independent individuals.

The federal Constitution was designed in large part to free persons and property from interventions by populist state legislatures but at the same time to protect commerce and promote a stable currency, reasonable taxation, respect for contracts, and the security of a stronger union. The new federal government would provide still greater protection for property rights than did the Articles of Confederation. In the nineteenth century, the values of individual achievement were deftly woven together with the ideal of a free market system operating as the best guarantor of national development and prosperity.

The American economic dream that combined the virtues of individual rights and the common good beckoned millions of immigrants to America and motivated millions more to strive for it. The dream was not realized for vast numbers in the decades of rapid social and economic change, including economic depressions. But this dream is a potent force still alive in America and elsewhere in the world.

There are also those who argue that in the interests of justice and equality, "property" should be redefined to include the social benefits and entitlements (including education) that have emerged since the New Deal. According to this view, welfare state benefits such as social security, medicare, and unemployment insurance are not simply governmental largesse, but a new kind of economic or property rights that cannot be withdrawn or withheld without due process of law.

There is, of course, bitter and continuing controversy over such a broadening of the meaning of property rights. This issue also provides grounds to judge how far we have come since the compromises of the Constitution that regarded black slaves as three-fifths of a person and the *Dred Scott* decision that regarded them as non-persons, as tangible and exchangeable property, the ultimate corruption of property rights as a privilege of individual rights. The story of the long and tenacious efforts to replace the corrupted view of individual rights with the fundamental ideals of personal liberty, justice, and political equality is a required ingredient for building the commitment to civic virtue.

III. Justice

The earliest known written rules or laws of justice were apparently based on practices developed among tribal societies. They were first codified in the civilizations of the Middle East some 4000 years ago. As early as 2100 B.C., the Sumerian codes (or cuneiform laws) set a pattern for the succeeding Babylonian and Assyrian empires of the Mesopotamian region. They proclaimed punishments considered to be just as recompense for such wrongs as bodily injury and the flight of slaves as well as regulations governing marriage, property, and contracts.

The most famous of these formulations was the Code of Hammurabi who ruled Babylonia during the first half of the eighteenth century B.C. The code consisted of 282 legal cases determining what were considered to be the just relationships among individuals in what we would now call property law, family law, civil law (slavery and debt), and criminal law (theft, assault, and homicide). Punishments for infractions of the code varied according to the status of the offender and the victim. There was no principle of social or political equality in traditional views of justice. The primary principle of punishment was the *lex talionis* (the law of retribution) in which the punishment was designed to correspond in kind and degree to the offense inflicted by the wrongdoer.

The surviving tablets show Hammurabi praying to the God of Justice, illustrating an age-old reliance of secular law upon divine support for its legitimacy. To the Western world, the best known instance of the traditional principle of retribution or rectification, common to the Sumerian and Semitic traditions, is the Mosaic law of justice summarized in the phrase "an eye for an eye." According to views generally accepted by Jews and Christians alike, who believe in the words of the Old Testament, Moses received the Ten Commandments and the laws governing justice among individuals as the divine revelation on Mt. Sinai in the thirteenth century B.C.

They included laws governing the just treatment of servants, family, property, and personal behavior, and just punishments for injuries inflicted by one person upon another: "But if there is serious injury, you are to take life for life, eye for eye, tooth for tooth, hand for hand, foot for foot, burn for burn, wound for wound, bruise for bruise." (*Exodus*, 21:23)

Many centuries later on the Arabian peninsula, when traditional Islamic law was codified by Mohammed and his successors from the seventh and ninth centuries, the law of retribution was central to the principles of justice, duty, and personal conduct that bound the faithful Muslim in his submission to the will of Allah.

Traditional Islamic law, known as the Shari'ah, sets forth the offenses that were punishable by specified forms of retaliation; e.g., death for highway robbery and apostasy; amputation of the hand for theft; death by stoning for extra-marital sexual relations; and a specified number of lashes for other sexual offenses and for drinking alcoholic beverages. These rigid rules of justice were interpreted somewhat differently by the different branches of Islam and in different regions of the world, but they were gradually modified in some regions, especially through the influence of the West in the nineteenth and twentieth centuries. Debates still rage in the United States over the humaneness of capital punishment and whether the death penalty is ever morally justified or whether it is "cruel and unusual punishment."

Other ancient and traditional codes of conduct embodying just rules of personal behavior as fundamental stabilizers of social order were developed, especially by Buddha in India and China, Confucius in China, and in Palestine by Jesus of Nazareth whose gospel of mercy, forgiveness, and love did much to modify conceptions of retaliatory justice as it spread from the Middle East to Europe and subsequently throughout much of the world.

These great codes of conduct had enormous influence for centuries, but by and large they were moral rules set out authoritatively to be obeyed by the virtuous person in ways that were suitable to his or her station in life. They did not specifically emphasize theoretical speculation or political philosophy analyzing the purpose of the political state, how justice should be thought about, or what the civic obligation of the person as citizen should be. This phase of political philosophy arose principally in Greece, Rome, and Western Europe, as the following sections of this Framework will describe in some detail (see The Nature of the State).

Originating in Greece in the fourth century B.C., Plato's *Republic* is widely considered to be a probing inquiry into the meaning of political justice. Plato sets forth persuasively the argument of Thrasymachus that justice is what the most powerful persons say it is ("Justice is the interest of the stronger," or "might makes right."), but Plato argues through Socrates that justice in the ideal republic rests on the obligation of each person to do what he is best fitted by nature to do: the wise and well-educated to rule; the brave and courageous warriors to fight for and defend the state; and the obedient workers to till the soil, produce and distribute the goods necessary for the welfare of the state. Plato's meritocracy, legitimizing the rule of the best and the brightest and rewarding each person according to what each naturally deserves, has affected conceptions of justice ever since.

Similarly, Aristotle exerted, if anything, an even more profound influence upon Western conceptions of justice. While he recognized the principle of retribution or rectification in his conception of justice in his *Ethics*, Aristotle added the idea of proportionality, a sense of moderation or fairness in which there is a balance among extremes. Punishments should not be too harsh or too soft. Just governments are based upon law in order to ensure the fair treatment of different citizens for the sake of each other and for the sake of the common good and the happiness of the political society. Unjust governments ignore the law and serve the private interests of the rulers, whether they may be one, or few, or many. In economic transactions, fairness requires exchange of things that are equal or equivalent in value, and awards should be made on the basis or merit or just desert.

Neither Plato nor Aristotle arrived at a conception of justice based upon social or political equality, but they did lay a basis for arguing that certain natural laws of human nature are antecedent to the laws of the state and thus should be observed in the practice of legal justice. Various views of natural law were developed by Christian thinkers of the Middle Ages from St. Augustine to St. Thomas Aquinas and by secular political philosophers culminating in the works of John Locke and Jean-Jacques Rousseau in the seventeenth and eighteenth centuries. (See The Nature of the State)

The virtuous citizen will view events and make judgments with regard to the principles of justice as they affect individuals, groups, and the society as a whole. While the meaning ascribed to justice has varied historically in place and time, the concept itself is central to the moral basis of most societies, especially to liberal democracy. In *The Federalist* No. 51 (1788), James Madison argued that in a republic "Justice is the end of government. It is the end of civil society. It ever has been and ever will be pursued until it be obtained, or until liberty be lost in the pursuit."

A public sense of justice must govern the conduct of people in their relations to one another if society is to be well-ordered and secure. Citizens must accept the same principles of justice; and they must develop strong moral sentiments and effective desires to act as the principles of justice require.

The goals of justice continue to be pursued in modern societies wherever voices are raised in protest against perceived instances of injustice. It may be heard wherever children cry out "It isn't **fair**!" when their toys are snatched away by others. In 1989 it was heard in the cries of massed Rumanians who demanded immediate justice be dealt to their hated brutal dictator.

The idea of justice appears by name in some form in nearly all societies, and it ranges across a society's public affairs as well as the relations of individuals to one another. In a liberal democracy, it embraces the whole civil and criminal justice system erected by fairly elected legislators passing laws limited by constitutional restraints, administered by accountable officials, and held responsible by independent judges and juries. Justice in this sense refers to its procedural and corrective meanings. But justice also embraces the concept of distributive justice, i.e., the fair distribution of benefits and burdens to members of society, according to agreed criteria of desert. This form of justice has a long and rich pedigree, having been discussed in detail by Aristotle in the fourth century B.C.

The informed American citizen committed to civic virtue will be disposed to make decisions on public issues as well as in private dealings that will stand the tests of (1) fairness and (2) respect for the equal legal and civil rights of others. In a just democratic society, all persons are entitled to participate equally in the basic political liberties and to a fair share of the distribution of the social and economic benefits and burdens of the society, based on principles of just desert.

Justice should not be viewed simply as something one alone is entitled to, but as something to which all persons of equal or similar condition are entitled. There is a sense in which the claims of what is right or just are prior to the claims of what is good, since what is good is defined differently by different individuals and groups according to their particular ways of life and personal desires, whereas at least some of the claims of justice can more readily be agreed to. A just social system thus puts some limits on the actions stemming from what individuals may come to consider as "good;" and it can legitimately limit their efforts to impose those values upon unwilling others.

In a liberal democracy the principle of what is socially right or just puts limits and even imposes restrictions on what is good as perceived by some individuals or pluralist communities, if in practice that good deprives others of their "good." This is the principle of **reciprocal** rights. A just society thus defines the boundaries within which individuals and pluralist communities may realize their aspirations in practice. But a just democracy will widen those boundaries as far as is consistent with the public good and compatible with equal liberty for all.

The dynamic tension noted earlier between the values of the public good and of individual freedom affects the achievement of justice in a democratic polity. The concerned citizen will be alert to and informed about the persistent disparity between the ideas of those who favor a "minimalist" state and those who favor some version of a social welfare state.

Some who argue for a minimalist conception of justice argue that the state should be narrowly limited to protecting the individual's person and property against theft, force, violence, or fraud, and enforcing the validity of contracts. Justice requires that individuals be entitled to whatever they acquire under the processes guaranteed under the minimalist state. Certain inequalities are bound to result, because people are in fact unequal in ability, skills, and effort, but they are fully entitled to whatever they acquire justly, even if the results are unequal. They must not be subject to limitations or regulations by which the government attempts to redistribute property. Distributive justice, in this view, if it entails any attempt by government to meliorate the inequality of acquisition by redistribution, is unjust.

Some who argue for a more activist welfare state regard justice as including not only the principle that every citizen should have equal basic political liberties (the freedoms of suffrage, speech, religion, assembly, and the other civil liberties) but also a principle of distributive justice whereby the government has a reasonable role in regulating social and economic inequalities to protect and benefit the least advantaged persons in society. This idea of justice does not mean equality of economic condition, but it does entail the use of the processes of democratic government to provide a generous basic minimum of social and economic well-being for all (social security, health care, unemployment insurance, and aids for the poor, the disadvantaged, and the handicapped).

Many others hold neither of these views but rather lean toward one or the other without embracing complete minimalism on the one hand nor a generous and expansive, and therefore expensive, welfare state on the other.

Extreme libertarians view justice as being best served by maximizing liberty over equality; extreme egalitarians see justice as being best served by requiring greater equality of economic and social condition at the expense, if necessary, of some liberty for some. Others fall somewhere in between these views.

It is not our business to decide this issue but rather to point out that the civically virtuous democratic citizen, disposed and committed to justice, will support: (1) public arrangements that reinforce fair procedures for gathering and disclosing information and for free elections, passing legislation, enforcing the law, and adjudicating conflicts; (2) fair procedures for civil and criminal justice; and (3) fair treatment of all people—majorities and minorities alike—in the distribution of social and economic benefits and burdens. Thus equality of opportunity becomes a major goal of a just society, though not necessarily equality of result.

IV. Equality

Just as there is persistent tension between the values of the public good and individual rights, between justice and freedom, so there has been a continuing discord between the democratic values of liberty and equality. Along with justice and freedom, the idea of equality runs through the American creed of values deemed fundamental to democratic society. The proposition that "All men are created equal" is the first of the self-evident truths of the *Declaration of Independence*, even preceding the "unalienable" rights to "life, liberty and the pursuit of happiness."

One reason that Jefferson's proclamation became so spectacularly successful was that equality, which had been relatively neglected in the history of political affairs, was an idea whose time had come.

A limited sense of equality, it is true, had been expressed in the republican views of citizenship of the Greek city-states. Pericles had given classic form to the idea in his funeral oration in 431 B.C. as he defined Athenian democracy: "Wherein there is not only an equality amongst all men in point of law for their private controversies, but in election to public offices we consider neither class nor rank, but each man is preferred according to his virtue or the esteem in which he is held for some special excellence; nor is any one put back even through poverty, because of the obscurity of his person, so long as he can do good service to the commonwealth."

But scarcely a half century later in Athens, the idea of equality was being disparaged by no less a personage than Plato. He attributed a major flaw of democracy to demagogues who dispense "a peculiar kind of equality to equals and unequals impartially." Plato described democracy as "an agreeable, lawless, particolored commonwealth, dealing with all alike on a footing of equality, whether they be really equal or not."

In contrast, Plato's ideal commonwealth was made up of unequals dutifully doing the appointed tasks for which they were fitted by their natural talents and education. Plato did envision a certain limited equality among the members of the guardian ruling class, even including women, but the countless devotees of Plato over succeeding generations paid relatively little attention to this apparent aberration.

In his turn, Aristotle found a certain equality desirable in the Periclean view of the citizen class, but he clearly believed that the good life was only within reach of the citizen class, which did not include women, aliens, or those born by nature to be slaves. So, within a century following Pericles, the ideal of equality had been severely curtailed and confined within a rigidly hierarchical vision of society that proved to be especially congenial to conservative casts of mind in later centuries. Tyranny was often viewed as the result of democratic revolutions in which "inferiors revolt in order that they may be equal, and equals that they may be superior."

Equality was not a very attractive political concept in theory or practice for the next two thousand years. True, Christian spokesmen affirmed a spiritual equality among all persons in the sight of God by virtue of the existence of their immortal souls. But during ancient and medieval times this was seldom translated into a widespread command for social or political equality.

In fact, the decadence of the Roman Empire led St. Augustine in the fifth century A.D. to proclaim in *The City of God* that human nature was essentially evil as the result of the original sin of mankind. Thus, men could not achieve the good life in a political order of this world, but only through salvation bestowed by the grace of God in the supernatural world.

Furthermore, it was only the "elect" few who were predestined by God for eternal salvation in heaven, while most sinners were preordained for eternal punishment in hell. In this respect, all persons were by no means equal in the sight of God. Therefore, the spiritual power of God exercised by the church must take precedence over and give legitimacy to a subordinate secular government whose prime purpose was to keep order in an essentially evil world.

The term "election" now had a double meaning: (1) a political process whereby the citizens chose from among their equals those who would hold a public office in "this world" and (2) a spiritual process which viewed all human beings to be equally tainted with original sin but which held out the prospect that some would be chosen by God to be the object of divine mercy and salvation and others to be condemned to eternal punishment in the "next world."

During the Middle Ages the idea of a hierarchical society of unequals dominated the actual practices of feudalism and political statecraft. St. Thomas Aquinas viewed the state in Aristotelian terms as aiming at the common good under the tutelage of God through the church. In contrast, Dante's *De Monarchia* (c. 1313) idealized a universal secular monarch on the model of the ancient Roman emperor whose legitimate authority comes directly from God and not through the church. In neither case did the idea of civic equality play a part.

But social and religious unrest began to forecast a rising tide of protest against rigid class distinctions on behalf of greater equality. In the fourteenth century peasant revolts were fomented in nearly every country of Europe. Serfs were freed in England, France, and Germany by the end of the fifteenth century.

Religious and secular views of reformers often supported each other. In England, John Wycliffe and the Lollards proclaimed that each individual is a direct vassal of God and should render due service directly to Him as set forth in the Bible, rather than through an authoritative clergy. Similar views were expressed by John Huss in Bohemia, while Hans Bohm and the Bundschuh in Germany argued that all men were brothers and should share alike in the fruits of the earth.

In the sixteenth century the major actors in the Protestant Reformation, Martin Luther and John Calvin, began to win political and military victories against the rule of Roman Catholic hegemony in Northern Europe. Though neither preached the values of political democracy or equality, they loosened the claims of the Roman Church to a single ultimate authority in secular as well as religious affairs and paved the way for still more political reforms that did eventually embrace steps toward equality.

Although English Puritans generally followed Calvin's belief in the predestination of the elect, a radical sect arose in Oliver Cromwell's army, derisively called the Levellers because of their beliefs in extreme equality, who advocated abolition of the nobility and monarchy and universal manhood suffrage. Although wiped out by Cromwell in 1649, their views of complete religious and social equality did not die. Sporadic movements, such as the Agitators and the Diggers, returned again and again to claim greater religious and political equality.

Once the idea spread that the Bible alone set forth the rules whereby individuals could achieve salvation by faith and good works, the way was opening to claim the rights of freedom from civil as well as ecclesiastical authority in the exercise of religious and political conscience. In various ways, such views began to take form among those who were seeking freedom from the established Anglican Church in seventeenth-century England and who became known as separatists or independents.

Prominent among these religious reformers were the Quakers led by George Fox, who believed in the equality of all men and women and took the lead in the abolition of slavery. The Baptists adopted views of the Dutch theologian, Jacobus Arminius, that all persons, not just the elect, have the possibility to be saved by a combination of faith and good works. And Arminianism influenced the views of John and Charles Wesley and their Methodist followers.

In seventeenth-century America, these traditions of religious dissent fueled incipient beliefs in political equality, notably by the Pilgrims, Thomas Hooker, Roger Williams, Anne Hutchinson, and William Penn. In the early eighteenth century, vast numbers of American colonists were swept into the populist religious movements of Baptists, Methodists, Congregationalists, and Anglicans, known as the "Great Awakening." If all individuals could participate equally in their spiritual salvation, why could they not also participate in their political regeneration? The liberal Congregationalist minister, John Wise, made exactly that point: the goal was a democratic church in a democratic state, which would seek protection for natural rights, equality, and the general welfare.

Thus, from the sixteenth to the eighteenth centuries the idea of political equality began to emerge from both religious and secular sources and eventually to flourish as a goal of the first democratic revolutions of modern times. The secularization of politics played an important role in the development of the idea of political equality.

Thomas Hobbes wrote *Leviathan* in 1651. It may be said that his rejection of a natural hierarchy among men established the foundation for modern notions of democratic government. Dismissing those who, like "ignorant men and Aristotle, think one man's blood is better than another's," he insisted that the question of who is the better man can be established only as a matter of public policy. Having dismissed the idea of a natural hierarchy, he had also undercut the traditional justification for political authority. If political authority had traditionally been justified by a claim to some relevant superiority, Hobbes maintained that the only justification for the exercise of one person over others was the consent of those over whom the authority was exercised. This idea, so radical in 1651, had, of course become a "self-evident truth" by the time Jefferson pronounced the same doctrines of equality and political authority in "The Declaration of Independence."

Jean-Jacques Rousseau furthered the argument when he wrote **The Social Contract** in 1762. His passionate rhetoric that "Man is born free, but he is everywhere in chains" was heard around the world with ever increasing force as a justification for overthrowing the traditional privileged hierarchies of monarchy, nobility, established church, and landed property.

Redefining the older theories of social contract, Rousseau arrived at the concept of the "general will," which somehow represents the common good of all the people. Rousseau's radical egalitarianism became a source of inspiration and authority for later social democratic views as well as for totalitarian dictators of both fascist and communist leanings, who claimed that their ruling parties had exclusive authority to determine and express the people's general will on their behalf. But Rousseau also profoundly affected the rise of democratic constitutionalism in the political revolutions of Europe and America. "The people" became the ultimate source of political legitimacy, authority, and sovereignty.

Bernard Bailyn, eminent Harvard historian, makes it clear that the American founders were deeply influenced by the visions of equality being expressed by the religious dissidents of the European Reformation as well as by the political reformers of the Enlightenment. These attacks upon the oppressive privileges of aristocracy in church and state prepared the way for elevating the idea of political equality in the American and French revolutions.

In eighteenth century America the idea of equality was the counterpoise the colonists used in their struggle for democracy against the European-style tyrannies of inherited privilege and closed hierarchy. Equality was their remedy for the special privileges of the ruling elites, whose snobbishness, arrogance, pretense, and contempt for the common people infuriated not only the farmers and yeoman of the countryside, but also the middle classes of the towns. They rallied to the idea that there should be no impermeable boundaries separating social classes, that in public councils they should be considered of equal worth and equal merit as a matter of natural right, and that they deserved and were entitled to the same treatment and privileges enjoyed by their erstwhile rulers.

The American Founders did not define with exactitude what they meant by "all men are created equal." They did not include women, indentured servants, Native Americans, or slaves among those who were "equal." Furthermore, the Preamble to the Constitution did not refer to equality, while the Constitution itself embraced the superiority of white masters and the inferiority of black slaves. Still, the creed of equality achieved a kind of amorphous consensus that resonated two centuries ago throughout the first age of democratic revolution in much of Europe as well as America. But not only was this "equality" hard to define, practices that matched this ideal were also stubbornly difficult to establish.

Since the ideal of equality was elusive, it sometimes seemed to mean a social status in which all persons would have an equal opportunity to develop their inborn talents unhampered by inherited circumstances of family, property, class, or race. At other times, it seemed to imply that a rough economic equality or uniformity of condition would be desirable, even through enforced economic levelling. Most often, **political** equality was the prime goal.

Although the Founders assumed that even free individuals differ in their native physical and intellectual abilities, the important goal of equality was to keep the avenues of mobility open, so that inherited differences would not harden into political hierarchy and privileges such as those of the *ancien regimes* of Europe. Under the aegis of equality, rewards would ideally be made on the basis of individual achievement or merit in a society governed by equality of

opportunity. Furthermore, a republican government must be bulwarked by a democratic educational system whereby all children would have the opportunity to develop to the utmost their natural talents.

The American Founders did not expect that education would produce equality of condition or of result, but many did envision public education in which rich and poor would be instructed together. If they did not foresee an economically-levelled society, they rejected a society in which some have the right to rule and others only the obligation to obey. One might say that they accepted a differential society but opposed a deferential society.

The American Revolution did not confer equality upon the people but rather invited them to claim it through their own efforts at self-betterment. Since then, various egalitarian claims have often been muted or denied, but they have burst forth at critical times in our history, notably in the movements to abolish slavery, in the Civil War, and in the Reconstruction amendments to the Constitution which command the states to guarantee the equal protection of the law to all persons. But it was not until the civil rights movements of the 1950s and 1960s that positive government action was taken to wipe out long-standing legal restrictions on access to education, voting, housing, employment, and a wide range of other civil rights on behalf of historically disadvantaged and minority groups.

As the First Amendment was the charter for individual rights and freedom, so the Fourteenth Amendment became the charter for legal equality. It had become clear to the civil rights movement that stronger legal action by the federal government was required to overcome the historic discrimination and segregation embedded in state laws and practices. The legal turning point came in 1954 with the Supreme Court's unanimous decision in *Brown v. Board of Education* that the constitutional command of the national political community on behalf of equality must overrule the freedom of lesser political bodies to institute racial segregation practices.

Nearly four decades later, however, despite enormous gains, the legal, constitutional, and political struggles to desegregate schools and eliminate discrimination from other institutions continue almost unabated. Courts are still awash in cases claiming discrimination against women and ethnic, racial, and religious groups. Also in evidence are cases claiming reverse discrimination in practices said to form classes of second-class citizens denied the equal protection of the law. Civil disobedience and other forms of protest still occur over matters of school busing and the hiring or firing of school officials or employees on grounds of alleged racial or ethnic or gender discrimination.

The long, stubborn, complex search for equality is by no means confined to the United States or to recent history. From the Declaration of Independence and the French Declaration of the Rights of Man and of the Citizen, to the United Nations Universal Declaration of Human Rights, the Helsinki Final Act of 1975, and the Charter of Paris signed in 1990 by the thirty-five nations of the Conference on Security and Cooperation in Europe, the ideal of equality and equal rights has had a central role. We recall Abraham Lincoln's classic statement: "As I would not be a slave, so I would not be a master. This expresses my idea of democracy. Whatever differs from this, to the extent of the difference, is no democracy."

Enforced inequality, whether overt or covert, becomes an unendurable corruption of the ideal of democracy. The virtuous citizen strives to find a way to put the ideal of equality into practice—difficult, complex, and sometimes frustrating as that task may be. During the past forty years it has been almost as difficult for the concerned citizen to find a way through the labyrinth of public issues on equality as it has been for lawyers, politicians, judges, and bitterly contesting advocates. How do we go about the process of dismantling segregated public schools and other discriminatory institutions and practices in American society? What should be the role of government (whether by executive, legislative, or court action) in reducing unjustifiable disparities?

How do we equalize opportunity in education, employment, or other fields for the poor, deprived, disadvantaged, and handicapped without at the same time violating the fundamental right of all Americans to the equal protection of the law? How do we seek after our egalitarian ideals without discarding liberty for the sake of equality or, as critics argue, replacing the long-cherished American principle of equal individual rights for a new doctrine of group rights characteristic of universally-condemned regimes such as South African apartheid?

While generalizations about consensus on matters of equality are hazardous, it seems clear that the movement of public policies in the United States has been toward the view that opportunity for education, housing, jobs, and public entitlement should not be denied to any citizen solely on the grounds of their race, religion, ethnic background, economic or social status, sex, handicap, or way of life. The ideal of equality demands that none of these factors should count against any citizen.

Such questions involve some of the deepest tensions between the freedom of individuals to make personal choices on one hand and the obligations of a democratic community to act through law on behalf of certain forms of equality on the other. For example, these questions have become especially acute over affirmative action programs that seek to give some preference to applicants whose race has been discriminated against as a group for entry to jobs or education. Opponents of such programs have condemned them as "reverse discrimination" because, critics claim, they deny the equal protection of the law required by the Constitution.

The more government has been active by legislation or regulation in expanding compensatory or affirmative action programs for the benefit of the historically deprived, the more the resistance to such regulations has arisen from the Supreme Court to ordinary citizens, as shown in public opinion polls.

The continuing tension between the ideas of freedom and personal rights has escalated during the 1970s and 1980s. We do not attempt to settle these difficult issues here. Their contentious character is all the more reason why citizens concerned with the public good and the principles of justice must face the issues directly and honestly and with the best informed judgment available. Civically virtuous American citizens will seek some way to serve the cherished values of equality in a context that will also serve to the fullest extent possible the values of the public good, individual rights, freedom, and justice.

Americans cherishing civic virtue might well resolve to redouble their efforts to achieve an even more dynamic political equality by reaching for the goal of "one person, one vote" and reducing our economic inequality, **at least** to the extent that no American is without the economic necessities required for a safe and secure life of humane comfort, health, and education.

V. Diversity

Although not as boldly proclaimed in the historic American creed as are freedom and equality, diversity has marked American society ever since the first arrival of Europeans. At the beginning of colonization a small number of fairly homogeneous groups arrived, each marked by a common language, religion, national origin, and ethnic makeup. But the number of groups soon began to increase and proliferated enormously during the nineteenth and twentieth centuries. As millions of immigrants poured into the United States, the differences between established Americans and new arrivals tended to arouse suspicion and prejudice—even outright persecution and violence. But gradually the positive contributions of diversity and pluralism were recognized and took their places on the escutcheon of celebrated achievements of American democracy.

How to respect the rich cultural and intellectual rewards of pluralism despite often prickly racial, ethnic, linguistic, and religious diversity and at the same time serve the common American political values has again become a difficult and persistent obligation for the citizen. It requires striking a balance between unity and diversity—between the cultural enrichment that emerges from plural beliefs, ideas, and loyalties, and the necessity to strengthen commitment to the unifying values of political cohesion and the common identity of citizenship.

This effort is all the more important as large numbers of immigrants from Central America and South Asia continue to arrive legally or illegally. The recent influx, especially of illegal entrants, has prompted some to sound the alarm that certain alien groups are reluctant to learn English and that English should therefore be made the official language of government business. By the beginning of the 1990s, at least sixteen states had passed laws to this effect and a score of others were considering such action, usually accompanied by raucous debate between the advocates of multiculturalism and defenders of the majority's traditional values.

Among the alarms of the 1980s which have persisted into the 1990s were reports that a new generation of youth infected with the virus of racism was appearing at many universities. This same virus was also visible in violent inter-racial conflicts among inner city gangs. But on the positive side, thirteen of seventeen high school valedictorians in Boston in June 1989 were not born in the United States. There was no doubt that some minority youth were certainly "making the grade," though others were not.

As "minorities became the majority" in California's public school system and in large city schools around the country, the image that such diversity was linked with growing violence, drug abuse, and teenage pregnancies heightened the temperature of discussion and nervousness about the value of diversity itself. Some thought pluralism was becoming unmanageable and that traditional American values should be reinforced in schooling and social behavior. Others thought that Americans of African, Asian, Latino, and Native American descent have too long been victims of "intellectual and educational oppression" by traditional American culture. Thus the specter arose of the nation's growing fragmentation. Fears were expressed that America's much-vaunted ethnic and racial diversity was no longer a strength but rather a growing liability.

For a decade ethnic sensitivities have become increasingly visible—and audible—at all levels of American society, from local and state school board meetings to the Congress and the U.S. Department of Education. Factions of African, Asian, Hispanic, and Native Americans have accused textbook writers and curriculum guides from New York to California of neglecting or downgrading the positive role that their ancestors have played in U.S. and world history. Defenders of the central role historically played by Western culture and its political tradition have retorted that it is the Western values that have been neglected or played down by the rush to multiculturalism in the curriculum; and that dispassionate scholarship, not political partisanship or factional pride, should determine the content of the curriculum.

Nevertheless, in comparison with the racial, ethnic, and religious animosities in much of the world, the ideals of pluralism and, to a large extent, the practices of diversity in the United States are causes for hope that the tensions between political unity and cultural diversity, between public order and personal freedom, can be sufficiently balanced to maintain the welfare of American constitutional government. Understanding this argument requires an understanding of the contributions and values of pluralism as well as its problems and burdens.

First, it is important to recognize that in American history there have been ambivalent and sometimes bipolar attitudes toward the values of diversity. At times, all comers to American shores have been generally welcomed, while at other times voices were raised to exclude aliens or at least to subordinate them. Earlier in this century, public policy sometimes opted for rapid and thorough assimilation, seeking all to be mixed together in a melting pot "to form a breed new in the world." More recently it has been said that diverse groups should not only be welcomed but also encouraged to maintain their distinctive identities. So, "assimilation," "integration," "melting pot," and "cultural pluralism" have all had their powerful voices in defining an American solution to the problems of unity and diversity, order and liberty, the public and the private, *unum* and *pluribus*.

Civically virtuous democratic citizens will have in mind both the values of cultural plurality and of political cohesion. Professor Michael Kammen's analysis of plural societies in *People of Paradox* is a valuable tool in this context. He distinguishes between "stable pluralism" and "unstable pluralism." A "diverse" polity is one "containing distinct cleavages amongst diverse population groups." In a stable pluralist society there will be "a dispersion of power among groups bound together by crosscutting loyalties, common values, and a competitive equilibrium or balance of power."

In an unstable pluralist society "there will be a conflict between racial, tribal, religious, and regional groups, to such a degree that the whole must be maintained by regulation or force." At some point, the ruling regime may no longer be able to exert its authority even by military force, secret police, or intimidation. In such case, the cleavages in society threaten the very authority of the polity itself, each group forming its own political party or each group having its "own faction, each sect its own school, and each dogmatist his own ideology."

In contrast, a stable pluralist society has a "strong **underpinning** of legitimacy. A plural society is best insured by the rule of law—law made within the framework of an explicit constitution by elected representatives, executed by a partially autonomous administrative staff, and adjudicated by an independent judiciary. Insofar as all of these were created in 1787 and achieved in 1789, those dates do distinguish a genuine watershed in American history."

Kammen's further requirement of a "strong and lasting inventory of psychological legitimacy" is a useful way to define a goal of civic virtue: freedom for a variety of racial, ethnic, and religious groups is acknowledged and welcomed, while at the same time the values of the common good, justice, and equality in the democratic constitutional order are maintained and strengthened. It need hardly be added that common bonds rest upon a common language for citizens to communicate with each other. We should note the contrast between the United States, with all its pluralist problems, and countries where unstable pluralism either results in massive oppression of pluralist aspirations or results in seemingly endless guerilla warfare or anarchy.

Our democratic civic values should teach Americans to be citizens devoted to a stable pluralist democracy. These values enable the civically virtuous citizen to combat the main enemies characteristic of an unstable pluralism, described by Vaclav Havel in his first speech as president to his newly-free Czechoslovakian countrymen: "Our main enemy is our own bad traits: indifference to the common good...selfishness and rivalry. The main struggle will have to be fought on this field." So will it be in the United States and in any country that is trying to give maximum freedom for individuals as well as freedom for diverse groups, while pursuing the democratic values of justice, equality, and the common good. (For an extended discussion, see the section on Ethnic and Racial Diversity.)

VI. Truth

If we accept the principle that freedom of access to knowledge is a fundamental requirement for a democratic society, then the reliability and validity of public knowledge become of primary importance. The search for truth becomes a major goal of democracy. Democratic constitutional government is the only form of government in which every citizen has the obligation not only to tell the truth in personal matters but also to play a part in determining what the truth is in civic and political affairs. This has not necessarily been characteristic of other types of historical societies and certainly has not been the case in modern totalitarian societies.

In the past, the sources of truth have usually been limited to particular authoritative fountainheads of truth and purveyed only by certain specially qualified or anointed persons. For example, truth has commonly been assumed to arise from supernatural or divine sources as interpreted by rulers, prophets, scribes, or priests entrusted with unique powers to understand and interpret the truth that should be believed by their followers.

In literate societies, from the origins of the cuneiform tablets of Mesopotamia, the hieroglyphics of Egypt, and the alphabets of the major classical languages, the truth has been perpetuated over the centuries and carried around the world as embodied in various versions of the sacred books of Buddhism, Christianity, Confucianism, Islam, and Judaism. Believers acquired the truth from the books and from the teachers who taught the truth contained in their respective religious and moral codes.

Similarly, in the tradition of philosophical idealism of secular societies, truth was considered to be absolute, objective, and permanent, not a matter to be formulated or changed by human intervention. Plato's realm of ideas and immutable truth was thought to be beyond human manipulation and discoverable only by those few who had mastered a rigorous educational program in the liberal arts and philosophy. Only by contemplating the changeless forms of the true, the good, and the beautiful could the philosopher-kings rule wisely and justly for the benefit of the ruled.

For most of human history, the process of determining the truth-or the facts-involved in disputes and contracts in civil law and the relevant facts involved in criminal cases usually rested in the hands of rulers, kings, priests, magistrates, or judges who were recognized to have the right to determine the facts upon which civil law decisions were made or criminal law punishments inflicted.

In fact, in the early Middle Ages it was often assumed that only God knew who was telling the truth in a dispute or legal trial. Therefore, the one who could accurately recite an oath was the one who was considered to be making a true declaration or statement, namely "trial by oath." In other cases, "trial by ordeal" displayed in tests of physical strength or ability to resist torture would reveal which person was telling the truth. And for the nobility, victory in combat or "trial by battle" was a sign of truth telling.

Gradually, however, from the eleventh century onward in England, the practice arose whereby groups of one's peers or juries of freemen of property were called together to hear cases alongside the king's magistrates and to make a "declaration of truth" regarding the facts of a dispute. At first, it was believed that truth could best be ascertained by jurors who knew the disputants as neighbors and thus would have personal knowledge of the circumstances of the case. The practice of common law juries as agents of determining the truth came to be viewed as more just than trials by oath, ordeal, or combat. Gradually, this process of assembling twelve freeholders to determine the facts in suits at civil law was applied to criminal cases as well.

A still further refinement occurred when it was realized that the neighbors who knew a great deal about the disputants and the circumstances surrounding the case might be prejudiced for or against one of them and thus could not render a fair judgment. So jurors were chosen who did not already know the litigants or the case itself and thus would presumably be more impartial and decide the true facts of the case on the basis of clear and convincing evidence and the testimony of witnesses who in turn were sworn to tell the truth on pain of punishment. Elaborate rules of evidence as a means of arriving at the truth and the right to a trial by jury became staples of common law later embodied in the bills of rights of the American constitutional system.

A related aspect of the importance of truth-telling as a basic component of civic virtue in a constitutional order arose when printing made possible the widespread distribution of ideas in the form of books, broadsides, and eventually magazines and newspapers available to the citizenry at large. At that point, governments began to see that unauthorized printed speech, even more than oral speech, could become a threat to their authority. Thereupon, control of the press as a means of censorship of speech and ideas became a goal of royal governments, not only to prevent criticism but as a means to spread the official "truth" as they wanted it to be understood.

In England, licensing laws were passed by Parliament declaring published criticism of the king or officials of his government to be a crime, because it tended to degrade the government and cause discord among the people, especially if the common people were allowed to slander the "great men of the realm." Such criticism must not be allowed even if such criticism were true. Strict censorship by means of licensing approved publishers, prior restraint on what was written, confiscation of unauthorized materials, or destruction of printing presses as means of regulating the press fell into disrepute in England during the seventeenth century and especially following the passage of the Bill of Rights of 1689. But the laws of seditious libel were maintained as a means of controlling the press, on the grounds that published blame or criticism leveled at public officials would undermine the authority of the government and thus endanger national security.

The English laws of seditious libel were particularly galling to the American colonists of the eighteenth century. They objected to laws under which colonial publishers could be punished for publication of materials that tended to arouse ridicule, hatred, or contempt for the British officials even though charges of corruption or malfeasance proved to be true.

The most celebrated case of seditious libel in the American colonies arose when John Peter Zenger, publisher of *The New York Weekly Journal*, was imprisoned in 1735 for publishing a series of articles harshly critical of the New York royal governor. Zenger's defense attorney, Andrew Hamilton of Pennsylvania, surprised the court and the jury by arguing that since the criticisms of corruption and incompetence had not been proven false, their truth was a proper defense against the charges of seditious libel. Even though the judge instructed the jury to disregard the question of truth or falsity, a triumph for freedom of the press came when the jury agreed with the argument of truth and acquitted Zenger.

Though the Zenger trial did not set legal precedence, it accelerated the movement for protecting the freedom of the press to print the truth, which was later incorporated in the new state constitutions and in the U.S. Constitution in 1791. But the path to freedom of the press was not smooth or easy, then or now. As early as 1798, Congress passed the Sedition Act making it a crime to publish anything "with the intent to defame...or bring into contempt or disrepute" the president or other public officials. While the act was intended primarily to prevent criticism of the Federalist party then in power, it did permit the truth of statements to be recognized as a defense against charges of seditious libel. Yet, the long-established doctrine that criticism of government, even if true, is seditious, was hard to overcome in practice, especially when it took the tempting and milder form of argument that criticism of government, even if true, was at times unpatriotic.

The First Amendments's guarantee of the freedoms of religious belief, speech, the press, peaceable assembly, and petition is not only designed to protect those rights for the individual but also to insure freedom of public discussion as a fundamental protection for constitutional government itself. The freedom of public discussion requires freedom of access to knowledge and reliable information. The difficulty for citizens engaged in the public discussion of self-government is to determine what the truth is and who is speaking or writing the truth and who is not.

So long as freedom of speech and the press is untrammelled, there is the problem of winnowing and sifting the significant truth from the "plausible falsehood" and "beguiling half truth" so dear to the rough-and-tumble political process in an open society. From the founding of the American republic to the more recent perjury trials of former public officials, the search for truth has been a major goal of civic virtue in our democratic society. Politicians, Supreme Court justices, office holders, and ordinary citizens called to jury duty must all struggle to ascertain truth as the basis for decisions in law or policy as surely as scientists must doggedly seek scientific truth.

Justice Louis Brandeis once wrote that those "who won our independence believed...that freedom to think as you will and speak as you think are means indispensable to the discovery and spread of political truth; that without free speech and assembly discussion would be futile; that with them, discussion affords ordinarily adequate protection against the dissemination of noxious doctrines; that the greatest menace to freedom is an inert people; that public discussion is a political duty; and that this should be a fundamental principle of the American government."

In words that are eerily prescient of the European revolts against Communism in the 1990s and the revolts against apartheid in South Africa, Brandeis continued: "They [the Founders] recognized the risks to which all human institutions are subject. But they knew...that it is hazardous to discourage thought, hope and imagination; that fear breeds repression; that repression breeds hate; that hate menaces stable government; that the path to safety lies in the opportunity to discuss freely supposed grievances and proposed remedies; and that the fitting remedy for evil counsels is good ones."

How does the citizen distinguish between good counsels and evil ones? Surely one test is their truthfulness, the correspondence between what is said and factual reality. But testing the truth of theories is difficult at best even in the hard sciences. How is it to be done in politics? A classic reply was given in 1919 by Justice Oliver Wendell Holmes, Jr.: "...when men have realized that time has upset many fighting faiths, they may come to believe...that the ultimate good desired is better reached by free trade in ideas—that the best test of truth is the power of the thought to get itself accepted in the competition of the market, and that truth is the only ground upon which their wishes safely can be carried out. That at any rate is the theory of our Constitution."

Yet Justice Holmes was himself also the author of one of the most important doctrines for hedging about the freedom of speech and press with exceptions—and thus, one might argue, limiting the search for political truth. That exception is the right of government to prohibit and punish speech or press that poses "a clear and present danger" to the nation itself: "...we should be eternally vigilant against attempts to check the expression of opinions that we loathe and believe to be fraught with death, unless they so imminently threaten immediate interference with the lawful and pressing purposes of the law that an immediate check is required to save the country."

As with the other basic values of constitutional democracy, truth-telling sometimes conflicts with personal privacy, national security, the need for secrecy in war, presidential privilege in conducting foreign policy, and with the freedoms of speech and the press itself. But the overriding principle in a democracy is that truth-telling serves the common good while lying does not. Hence, effective civic education stresses the importance of distinguishing between the falsification that arises from ignorance, partial knowledge, or mistake from deliberate falsification intended to conceal misdeeds, to control others, or even harm them.

Thus, the laws against perjury and libel incorporate into the political system the moral sense that truth is better than lying and that deliberate untruths are punishable for the sake of the public good. Telling the truth is one of the compulsory obligations of citizenship. It is an integral part of testifying in court or in legislative hearings, in filing tax returns and fulfilling contracts, and in countless other ways. The principal purpose of the civic obligation to serve on juries in civil or criminal trials is to determine the facts of the case; in other words, to determine who is telling the truth and who is not.

In the complex arena of when, how, and why the truth should be told, or withheld or denied, several aspects deserve the citizen's careful attention. One concerns the rights and obligations of citizens to tell the truth about events or actions affecting others. The other, and in some respects even more important aspect, is the role of government officials in revealing, denying, withholding, shading, or hiding the truth from the citizens.

The attempt to balance these values has not been confined to courts of law and arcane legal disputes. In the 1980s many college campuses were wracked by disputes over the academic rules that should govern student freedom to defame, ridicule, disparage, or cast aspersion on the race, color, creed, or religion of minority individuals and minority groups by using belittling names or epithets. Minority student groups have claimed that such defamatory statements, posters, cartoons, or effigies should not be allowed by the college authorities; others have argued that such rules or regulations would stifle the robust freedom of expression guaranteed by the First Amendment and are especially inherent in the intellectual community's need for complete freedom to form and express the most widely varying and conflicting views, however unpalatable they may be.

During the past two decades, however, the most widely publicized controversies have concerned the role of government in revealing or hiding the truth from its citizens. Since World War II this fact has been repeatedly documented. Totalitarian states, both Communist and Fascist, as well as military dictatorships, have enforced controls over the flow of information and used falsification and lying to the public whenever it served their purposes. Deliberately deceiving the people is the essence of a closed society. Every *coup d'etat* is immediately accompanied by seizing radio and television stations, closing newspapers, reinforcing secret police to root out dissenters, cracking down on unauthorized assemblies or demonstrations, jailing political opponents, and possibly torturing prisoners.

We have learned to expect the strangling of truth by dictatorships of both the political Left and Right. Thus, it was all the more astonishing to see the democratic revolutions of the 1980s and 1990s begin the traumatic process of trying to face the facts of decades of deceit. Soviet educational authorities have begun to revise the history of Stalinism, revealing the brutal destruction of human rights under his regime. Germans have struggled to face up to the awful truths of the atrocities of the Holocaust. The newly constituted governments of Central and Eastern Europe have resolved to reveal the role of their Communist parties in falsifying their history of the past forty years. In Argentina families of victims of the deposed military junta insistently demanded that the truth about the fate of those who disappeared be publicly announced. Only the **public** affirmation of the truth would satisfy them. Similar demands for the public exposure of truth were heard in the former Communist countries of East Germany, Romania, and elsewhere—not least in the Soviet Union.

A crowning irony of the contemporary scene is that just as Communist countries begin to revise their histories in the interest of truth, the United States continues to struggle with the fundamental constitutional principles involved in the efforts to control information or cover up the truth of present, former, or would-be governmental officials. Major recent examples range from deceptions about the Vietnam War emanating from the government under Lyndon Johnson, the attempted cover-ups surrounding Watergate under Richard Nixon, and lying to Congress by administration officials in the Iran/Contra scandal under Ronald Reagan.

It may reveal the crucial importance of truth-telling in these cases to note that Vietnam led to Lyndon Johnson's withdrawal from reelection as president, that Richard Nixon resigned the presidency to avoid impeachment, and that charges of lying to Congress were involved in the trials and convictions of three national security aides of Ronald Reagan. When trust in the veracity of the presidency and of major government officials declines, the very foundations of a free society are at risk.

The basic principle was well stated by Walter Lippmann in 1954 as the country emerged from its tragic epic of innuendo, slander, and lying associated with McCarthy-era witch hunts for Communist party members and supporters: "...there are rules of evidence and parliamentary procedures, there are codes of fair dealing and fair comment, by which a loyal man will consider himself bound when he exercises the right to publish opinions. For the right to freedom of speech is no license to deceive, and willful misrepresentation is a violation of its principles. It is sophistry to pretend that in a free country a man has some sort of inalienable or constitutional right to deceive his fellow man. There is no more right to deceive than there is to swindle, cheat, or to pick pockets. It may be inexpedient to arraign every public liar, as we try to arraign other swindlers. It may be a poor policy to have too many laws which encourage litigation about matters of opinion. But, in principle, there can be no immunity for lying in any of its protean forms."

On the other side of the coin of truth is the query: Is there no limit to the right and freedom of investigative reporters to pry into the private affairs of public persons as well as into their affairs involving the public trust? As to national security reasons for government restraint on publication of "the truth," some absolutists believe that prior restraint is never justified, while others would take into account special circumstances of time and place surrounding the case. Similarly, it is sometimes argued that the private affairs of public personages is no business of the electorate. However, many instances of revelations about financial dealings, drug abuse, or wayward sexual affairs have led to difficulties for public officials from mayors to members of Congress to would-be presidential candidates and prospective Supreme Court justices. Public personalities found to be manipulating the stock market, financial institutions, real estate, sports, or even religious evangelism on television have had the same difficulties.

Citizens who do not insist upon the value of truth-telling of those who represent them and who do not try to distinguish the significant truth from plausible falsehoods, beguiling half-truths, or "plausible deniability" as set forth in news conferences, political campaigns, or other public statements put their freedom at risk. And a government that lies to its citizens as a matter of policy cannot expect to serve justice and equality, maintain its legitimate authority, or even command the unswerving loyalty of its citizens.

VII. Patriotism

Any defensible conception of citizenship and the civic virtue upon which the life of citizenship depends must take account of the extraordinary dynamic force that patriotic sentiments play in American life. At its best, patriotism binds the diverse segments of American society into an integrated whole, fostering mutual acceptance of citizens as members of a common political order. At its worst, patriotism can degenerate into nationalistic chauvinism. But in its best sense, patriotism is a positive force for national well-being. Patriotism and disreputable forms of nationalism are decidedly different and should not be equated or confused with each other. Simply put, patriotism is love of or devotion to one's country and to the fundamental values and principles upon which its security and welfare depend. Fifty years ago, the noted American historian, Merle Curti, in his pioneering work, *The Roots of Loyalty*, defined patriotism as "love of country, pride in it, and readiness to make sacrifices for what is considered its best interest." Too often, the voice of sacrifice, apart from military service, stands mute.

From colonial times our predecessors stressed the importance of the individual's obligation for the public good, including military service and loyalty to the republican values of the emerging nation. A sense of duty, discipline, and obligation was valued as the very essence of civic virtue, which must provide the social and political glue if democratic ideals were to survive, let alone thrive.

Even before the founding of the United States as a nation, the idea of the citizen-soldier, harking back to the Greek and Roman republics, was practiced in most of the American colonies. The early colonial militias typified the notion that it was the duty of individual citizens to engage in compulsory military preparedness without monetary pay as a form of personal obligation for the public good. (For details, see the section on Citizenship and Military Participation.)

The practice of periodic service in a local militia, aimed first against hostile Native American Indians, declined in the middle of the eighteenth century, only to be revived to oppose the British armies as the Revolutionary War approached. That war brought into being a professionally trained standing army in addition to the republican ideal of a part-time citizen soldiery. The two ideals have often been hotly debated in the history of American patriotism, especially whenever proposals for universal military service arose.

In the early nineteenth century, the militia idea retreated once again in the face of attractive pay and free land as incentives for men to volunteer for the armed forces on the frontier and in the Mexican War. Then, the Civil War brought the first national military draft and its attendant problems involving deferments and substitutions for those who could afford commutation fees. A mixture of patriotism and volunteerism continued to play essential roles in both North and South.

Each subsequent war evoked emotional controversies over the relative contributions to patriotism and to the public good of universal conscription versus voluntary service in the armed forces. These debates raised serious questions about the role of patriotism as a motive for military service as compared with the material benefits to be derived from it. It is generally agreed that the two World Wars elicited more public expressions of patriotic fervor both during and after the event, than was the case with the Korean and Vietnam Wars.

When the Persian Gulf War suddenly began, many of the well-trained members of the all-volunteer armed forces stated their views simply that they were ready and willing to "do our job and go home." But the war suddenly ended with massive outpourings of patriotism by the public scarcely exceeded by those at the end of the two world wars. And overt recriminations impugning the patriotism of those who were at first opposed to the war were far less bitter and hostile than in the preludes and aftermaths of the previous major wars.

As in the case of the earlier wars, there remained the long term questions concerning how best to prepare young people by education for the commitments of a "quiet patriotism" strong enough and sustained enough to enable them to face and solve the seemingly intractable problems of peace as effectively as the discipline, training, and motivation had apparently trained them for war. How can schooling and the other means of education help to form the patriotic character of citizens of a democratic republic in peacetime?

This question was dramatically posed in 1910 by William James as he pleaded for peaceful ways to achieve "the moral equivalent of war," by practicing the admirable elements of the "martial virtues," such as patriotism, discipline, "strenuous honor," cohesiveness, and obligation for the public good. His goal was action "to inflame the civic temper as past history has inflamed the military temper."

In modern, more prosaic phraseology, the questions might become: Can schools and other educational institutions learn how to transform the honorable values of a "combat culture" into the cohesive democratic values of a "civic culture"? Conversely, can the training given by the American armed forces be improved by requiring trainees to undertake a more substantive study of democratic "civic content" (like that in CIVITAS), which will enhance their political lives as citizens as effectively as the high quality technical training they receive enhances their economic lives as civilian income earners? And, can the enormous progress toward integration of races, minorities, and women into the armed forces be instrumental in improving the personnel practices of other American institutions in the direction of justice, equality, and diversity as means of promoting a patriotic sense of national community?

From the days of the early Republic, education has been called upon to serve as a prime means to help form the civic character of citizens. Today, of course, the schools alone cannot instill the necessary values of personal obligation and responsibility, especially when other major social institutions and their leaders are preaching and practicing self-aggrandizement and private interest. But the schools must play a major role along with kinship, ethnic, religious, community, and military agencies that are committed to the values of the democratic polity.

The goal is relatively easy to state: education has a major role to play in developing patriotic American citizens. How to reach that goal raises complex, often controversial, and always emotionally laden questions. These often involve little understood distinctions that need to be made between political dissent and disloyalty, between freedom of expression and obedience to civil authority, between criticism of government and traitorous actions.

The promotion of patriotism by schools has become especially complicated during the past fifty years. The once-powerful sanctions for patriotic civic education that came from moral, religious, political, and military institutions, have been weakened by world events as well as by domestic trends. The military defense of the nation as a reason for requiring patriotic civic education probably reached its peak in World War II, when a vast majority of the American people believed that Nazi and Fascist aggression must be opposed with military force and that the inhuman atrocities committed by the Axis powers justified war on moral grounds. But the Korean War seemed less immediately critical to the safety and security of the United States, and the protracted conflict in Vietnam increasingly convinced large numbers that it was an immoral war not justified as a reasonable cause for patriotic support or the risk to life and limb in military service.

On the home front, the Communist witch hunts of the 1950s, wrapped in the McCarthyite demands that loyalty oaths be extracted from teachers as an outward sign of patriotism, took its toll in the academic world. During the 1960s and 1970s, the unrest and disturbances on campuses almost obliterated overt expressions of patriotic symbolism in colleges and universities. Making a show of patriotism by singing patriotic songs, by waving and saluting the flag, and by pledges of allegiance became more than a little unfashion-

able. Outward showing of patriotic symbolism retreated to the academic closet. Merle Curti put it more gently by saying: "Perhaps the academic world felt that the whole matter of patriotism belonged to the twilight zone of the intellect." McCarthyism in the '50s and opposition to the war in Vietnam in the '60s and '70s combined to make patriotism disreputable in the eyes of many.

Gradually, however, the beginnings of detente and negotiations of arms agreement with the Soviet Union and the People's Republic of China began to reduce the rigors of the Cold War and thus to downgrade anti-communism as the prime reason for the encouragement of patriotism. With the virtual end of the Cold War by 1990 the political context of patriotism and schooling changed.

During the 1980s, President Ronald Reagan made his "new patriotism" a cornerstone of his policies in foreign and domestic affairs by emphasizing national pride in the American spirit. The intervention in Grenada in 1983, the Olympic Games in 1984, numerous campaign speeches in 1984, and his farewell speech in January 1989 all struck the patriotic theme. And President George Bush made it a keynote of his 1988 campaign when he repeatedly stated that he favored state laws requiring teachers to lead their students in the daily pledge of allegiance to the flag in the nation's schoolrooms, pointing out that his opponent had vetoed such a law in Massachusetts. The imputation was clear that such pledging was an act of patriotism that patriotic citizens would favor. The pledge of allegiance to the flag thus became an issue not only during the presidential campaign but long afterwards.

The point is not to try to resolve the issue here but to underline the fact that patriotism is a deeply felt emotion among the American citizenry and that it surges vibrantly across the spectrum of political partisanship. In 1988 the presidential candidates did not address the issue of the flag and patriotism in a substantive way. The public seemed ill prepared to make informed judgments about what the candidates did say. Most voters seemed ready to take sides on the pledge question, but the fundamental issues underlying the constitutional basis whereby public schools could properly play a role in promoting civic loyalty, patriotism, and commitment to the democratic values of citizenship were scarcely hinted at. The occasion for a constructive history and civics lesson was all but lost.

A few commentators and legal scholars of both conservative and liberal persuasion attempted to educate the public on the underlying issues, but the pace and character of the campaign gave little opportunity for the public to learn the relevant history and civics lessons, which they were not hearing from the candidates and which they apparently had not learned in their civics classes in school or college. What could be the rationale for and against using the authority of the state and of the public school system to require students and teachers to salute the flag and pledge allegiance to it? The answers could not be given in thirty-second campaign television advertisements during a rough and tumble campaign. This is one more reason why CIVITAS seeks to develop a reasoned historical perspective and a meaningful conception of the basic democratic values underlying civic virtue.

Even a brief look at the issue will reveal that, contrary to the implications of the campaign, a simplistic contrast that arrays conservatives against liberals on the values of the flag salute and pledge of allegiance in developing patriotism is not justified. Legal scholars and Supreme Court justices, as well as commentators and politicians, could be found supporting liberal as well as conservative points of view.

The conflicting principles were clearly set forth fifty years ago in two remarkable Supreme Court cases involving children of the Jehovah's Witnesses who refused to salute the flag on the grounds that the compulsory salute to the flag was in effect the worship of an image, which was forbidden to them by their interpretation of the religious teachings of the Bible. There is no better way to define the relevant principles than by quoting Supreme Court justices whose views do not fit a neat liberal/conservative classification.

In 1940 the issue was eloquently drawn in an eight to one decision by the Court. Writing for the majority in *Minersville v. Gobitis*, Justice Felix Frankfurter, appointed to the Court by Franklin D. Roosevelt but known at the end of his career as a conservative, wrote as follows: "A grave responsibility confronts this Court whenever in course of litigation it must reconcile claims of liberty and authority. But when the liberty invoked is the liberty of conscience, and the authority is authority to safeguard the nation's fellowship, judicial conscience is put to its severest test. Of such a nature is the present controversy."

After balancing these "two rights in order to prevent either from destroying the other," Justice Frankfurter came down on the side of national cohesion: "The ultimate foundation of a free society is the binding tie of cohesive sentiment. Such a sentiment is fostered by all those agencies of the mind and spirit which may serve to gather up the traditions of a people, transmit them from generation to generation, and thereby create that continuity of a treasured common life which constitutes a civilization.

"A society which is dedicated to the preservation of these ultimate values of a civilization may in self-protection utilize the educational process for inculcating those almost unconscious feelings which bind men together in a comprehending loyalty, whatever may be their lesser differences and difficulties. That is to say, the process may be utilized so long as men's right to believe, and their right to assemble in their chosen places of worship for the devotional ceremonies of their faith, are fully protected."

But it was precisely the effort of the state "to coerce these children to express a sentiment which violated their deepest convictions" that led Justice Harlan Fiske Stone to become the lone dissenter from the Court's decision. Stone was a Republican appointed to the Court by Calvin Coolidge. He came down on the side of the constitutional protections for religious liberty guaranteed by the First and Fourteenth Amendments: "The Constitution may well elicit expressions of loyalty to it and to the government which it created, but it does not command such expressions or otherwise give any indications that compulsory expressions of loyalty play any such part in our scheme of government as to override the constitutional protection of speech and religion."

Justice Stone even gave us the primary clue to an educational solution for the tension between religious conscience and national cohesion, a solution to which CIVITAS is deeply indebted. Justice Stone argued that the state and its public schools do not need to promote patriotism by coercing affirmation of belief; rather, they may require all students to study history and civics as the fitting road to developing a reasoned and committed patriotism: "...there are other ways to teach loyalty and patriotism, which are the sources of national unity, than by compelling the pupil to affirm that which he does not believe and by commanding an affirmance which violates his religious convictions. Without recourse to such compulsion the state is free to compel attendance at school and require teaching by instruction and study of...our history and...the structure and organization of our government, including the guaranties of civil liberty which tend to inspire patriotism and love of country."

Despite the Supreme Court's majority decision and the vigorous patriotic support for the flag salute at the onset of World War II, Jehovah's Witnesses' children persisted in refusing to participate in compulsory flag salutes and pledges of allegiance. They were excoriated, called traitors, rounded up and forcibly fed castor oil, and a mob burned a church in Kennebunk, Maine.

In 1942 Congress prescribed the wording of the pledge and changed the form of salute from the Nazi-like extended right arm to the right hand placed over the heart. Also in 1942, when the state of West Virginia made the salute and pledge compulsory on a state-wide basis, scores of students failing to comply were expelled for insubordination. Thus, another case reached the Supreme Court, which thereupon reversed itself in the landmark decision of *West Virginia v. Barnette.*

Justice Robert Jackson, former Attorney General under President Roosevelt, wrote the 6-3 decision for the Court, in effect adopting the *Gobitis* dissenting view of Stone who meanwhile had been raised to Chief Justice by Roosevelt: "The question here is whether this slow and easily neglected route to aroused loyalties [by study of history and civics] constitutionally may be short-cut by substituting a compulsory salute and slogan....National unity as an end which officials may foster by persuasion and example is not in question. The problem is whether under our Constitution compulsion as here employed is a permissible means for its achievement."

In his conclusion, Justice Jackson declared for the Court that compulsion was not permissible: "If there is any fixed star in our constitutional constellation, it is that no official, high or petty, can prescribe what shall be orthodox in politics, nationalism, religion, or other matter of opinion, or force citizens to confess by word or act their faith therein....We think the action of the local authorities in compelling the flag salute and pledge transcends constitutional limitations on their power and invades the sphere of intellect and spirit which it is the purpose of the First Amendment to our Constitution to reserve from all official control."

If in 1988 the presidential candidates had appealed to such arguments, the substance of the constitutional issue might have been confronted as a matter of serious public discourse and decision, namely, what is the proper role of public schooling in promoting patriotism? As it was, former Chief Justice Warren E. Burger, a Republican, attacked the discussion of the pledge as a "trivialization" of the campaign and described the argument as "a tempest in a saucer, not even a teapot."

Chief Justice Burger even went so far as to draft a voluntary citizens' oath that paralleled the citizenship oaths required of aliens and those entering the military and public service. The oath would give all citizens the same opportunity to exercise their patriotism by publicly supporting the Constitution, not the flag, as follows: "I do solemnly swear that I will support and defend the Constitution of the United States against all enemies, foreign and domestic, and that I will well and faithfully discharge my duties and responsibilities as a citizen of the United States."

In June 1989 a patriotic storm broke with increasing fury over the Supreme Court's 5-4 decision in *Texas v. Johnson* upholding the right to burn the American flag as a form of symbolic political expression protected by the freedom of speech clause of the First Amendment. This time the majority opinion was made up of three well-known liberals on the

Court joined by two conservatives, Justices Antonin Scalia and Anthony M. Kennedy; and the minority, led by conservative Chief Justice William H. Rehnquist, was joined by Harry Blackmun who usually voted with the liberals.

In his opinion for the Court, Justice William J. Brennan relied on the *Barnette* decision in saying "If there is a bedrock principle underlying the First Amendment, it is that Government may not prohibit the expression of an idea simply because society finds the idea offensive or disagreeable...Nor may the Government, we have held [in *Barnette*], compel conduct that would evince respect for the flag....The way to preserve the flag's special role is not to punish those who feel differently about these matters. It is to persuade them that they are wrong."

In a caustic dissent to this last point, Chief Justice Rehnquist commented: "The Court concluded its opinion with a regrettably patronizing civics lecture, presumably addressed to the members of both houses of Congress, the members of the forty-eight state legislatures that enacted prohibitions against flag burning....The Court's role as the final expositor of the Constitution is well established, but its role as a platonic guardian admonishing those responsible to public opinion as if they were truant school children has no similar place in our system of government."

Shortly after the decision, President Bush proposed an amendment to the Constitution prohibiting burning or desecrating the flag; and more than fifty resolutions were introduced in the Congress to that effect. Meanwhile, in the effort to forestall an amendment, Congress passed an act prohibiting harm to the flag, which President Bush allowed to become law without his signature. But the law was soon declared unconstitutional by federal district courts and, in June 1990, by the U.S. Supreme Court. Thereupon, President Bush again proposed a constitutional amendment to prohibit desecration of the flag as "good for the country." But after a bitter debate, the House of Representatives refused to pass the proposed amendment, failing to muster the required two-thirds vote. In effect, the desire to protect the integrity of the First Amendment won over the desire to protect the flag as a symbol of patriotism.

Whatever role the Supreme Court may play as schoolmaster to the republic on matters of history, civics, and patriotism, the schools must grapple with the task day in and day out. Our argument is that the schools' role in developing patriotism, loyalty, duty, and discipline is that of cultivating a civic virtue that grows out of acquiring the knowledge, skills, and values set forth in this framework.

Fortunately, there are signs in the academic world that patriotism is being brought out of the educational closet and into the daylight of scholarly analysis as well as of public discussion and advocacy. Liberal as well as conservative scholars are seeking to reformulate the role of education in developing **a sense of civic virtue as the essence of patriotism**. In the long run, however, the test will be whether American education can strengthen the sense of community and cohesion among successive generations through emphasis upon civic virtue and personal obligation for the public good, while at the same time strengthening the values of individual rights, justice, equality, diversity, and truth.

The closet door on patriotism may be opening a bit in the academic world and in public discussion, but the task of reconstructing the idea of patriotism in citizenship is a formidable one. Important as symbolic acts of patriotism are, and useful as scholarly analysis may be, the task of designing coherent, vibrant, and invigorating programs of civic education is even more challenging. The burden of carrying out long-term effective programs of civic education in the schools, in the colleges, and in the preparation of teachers rests with professionals in education collaborating with their academic colleagues and public counterparts. To this end the CIVITAS framework is dedicated.

PART TWO. CIVIC PARTICIPATION

PART TWO. CIVIC PARTICIPATION

INTRODUCTION

The ultimate goal of civic education is the widespread participation in the governance of the groups to which they belong by citizens who are knowledgeable, competent, and committed to the realization of the fundamental values and principles of our constitutional democracy. This governance includes localities, states, and the nation; it also includes governance of churches, labor unions, businesses, and other private associations as well as schools.[1]

The focus of civic education from the earliest grade levels should be to prepare students to take part in the governance of such groups beginning with their classes, schools, and social groups and then, at appropriate levels, dealing with formal political institutions and processes. By the end of secondary school this education should have culminated specifically in the development among students of the knowledge, skills, dispositions, and moral commitments required for competent and responsible participation in monitoring and influencing the formulation, implementation, adjudication, and enforcement of public policy.

Fostering participation

To be consistent with the values and principles of constitutional democracy, the student's decision to participate must be freely made. It is typical of some authoritarian systems to demand participation in order to "legitimize" their powers and to penalize those who do not vote or adhere in other ways to their notions of the proper role of the subject. A constitutional democracy, on the other hand, must rely upon education and example to inspire participation, a task which clearly indicates the importance of the civic mission of our schools.

Instructional programs based upon the CIVITAS curriculum framework should inspire among students a commitment to participate in governance by

- providing the knowledge and skills required to participate effectively;

- providing practical experience in participation designed to foster among students a sense of competence and efficacy; and

- developing of an understanding of the importance of citizen participation.

Providing a foundation for competent and responsible participation

Competent and responsible civic participation clearly requires a foundation of the knowledge and thinking skills linked with the dispositions and commitments described elsewhere in this framework. For example, suppose a citizen is concerned with a specific problem in the community. Competent and responsible participation requires a foundation of:

- **Knowledge and intellectual skills.** A knowledge of the fundamental concepts, history, contemporary events, issues, and facts related to the matter and the capacity to apply this knowledge to the situation.

- **Dispositions.** A disposition to act in accord with the traits of civic character noted in Part I in dealing with the matter, e.g., civility in discourse, open mindedness, disposition to compromise, and compassion.

- **Commitments.** A commitment to the realization of the fundamental values and principles described in Part I that are relevant to the matter, e.g., justice, the common good, and the rights of the individual.

The need for experience in participation

This foundation is essential for competent and responsible participation, but by itself it is insufficient. Civic participation requires certain additional skills needed to influence the governance of groups whether they be social clubs or the federal government. Civic education must provide students experience in participation designed to foster the development of these required participatory skills.

It is clear that learning experiences in political participation for students, especially young students, do not have to be confined to experiences associated with governmental institutions at local, state, and national levels. Much of what is required for competent and responsible citizen participation on the formal political level is identical with what is required for participation in the politics of the governance of families, schools, labor unions, churches, social clubs, and community groups.

---

1. This part of the framework draws heavily from the *Handbook of Basic Citizenship Competencies* by Richard Remy for the skills described under Topic I and from a variety of sources for those covered under Topics II and III.

This fact is of particular importance for civic education. The opportunities for students, particularly young students, to learn first hand about governance and to develop the skills required for effective participation are far greater in regard, for example, to the governance of schools and social clubs than the formal institutions of government. For this reason, this section of the CIVITAS framework begins with two central aspects of political participation. These are (1) the skills required for participation in the governance of any group to which one may belong, and (2) skills required for participation in the political process of governance of formal institutions of local, state, and national government and in global affairs. These are skills specifically related to the monitoring and influencing of public policy.

The section continues with historical perspectives on political participation and attention to civic and community action and participatory writing. It concludes with notes on methods of instruction for participation and a model scope and sequence statement for lower elementary grades.

CHARACTERISTICS OF COMPETENT AND RESPONSIBLE PARTICIPATION

Civic education's unique responsibility is not simply to increase participation rates, but to nurture competent and responsible participation. Such participation involves more than merely influencing or attempting to influence public policy. Competent and responsible participation must be based upon moral deliberation, knowledge, and reflective inquiry.

Moral deliberation

In contrast to many conventional approaches in civic education, the central point of this Framework is to foster the development of citizens who participate actively and knowledgeably in public affairs. Our emphasis on exerting influence, however, does not imply unconditional endorsement of all actions or policies that citizens may advocate. Since constitutional democracy itself is intended to advance such fundamental values as liberty, equality, justice, and the public good, citizens have an obligation to strive for governmental policies consistent with those values. Rather than providing a blank check for citizens to exercise their will in any direction, responsible self-government requires citizens to anticipate the consequences of their actions and to justify them in terms of fundamental democratic values. The process of assessing the extent to which proposed actions support or oppose fundamental values can be considered moral deliberation, and it must form a central strand in the curriculum.

The justification of all governmental actions should be based upon at least one of the fundamental values. The major problem for moral inquiry is to justify particular choices when two or more "good" values come into conflict. When, for example, should freedom of the press be limited in order to preserve national security, a fair trial, or, in the case of pornography, community values? When should the right of majority rule within towns or states be limited by Federal interests in the protection of health, the environment, or educational improvement? Under what circumstances is it legitimate for the state to deprive people of life itself, for example, in the case of capital punishment? While many of these issues cannot be resolved conclusively by even the most learned citizens, it is possible to develop thoughtful reasoned positions. If civic education is to build competent participation, it must assist students in devising defensible positions on value issues. To be consistent with democratic educational values, moral deliberation must be conducted in the spirit of free inquiry.

More elaborate discussion of fundamental values will be presented in the section on Civic Virtue, but here we call special attention to the role of the citizen in moral deliberation that is so often neglected. Aristotle, Jefferson, Dewey, and more recent analysts have argued that a principal responsibility of the democratic citizen is to deliberate with others about the nature of the public good, the means to achieve it, and ways to manage the inevitable tensions between the rights of the individual and the common good. Such deliberations need not be confined to the highest legislative halls or government agencies; they can occur in any situation where, in an attempt to govern, people must consider a common or collective good. Opportunities for collective deliberation can, therefore, be found in voluntary associations, businesses, unions, churches, political parties, neighborhoods, and schools.

Knowledge

Just as the health of constitutional democracy depends upon commitment to certain values, so, as Jefferson and others have warned, it also depends upon a well-educated, informed citizenry. The Framework helps to identify specific areas of knowledge that should inform civic participation. But in using this resource to develop a knowledge base aimed at civic participation, special effort will be needed to avoid two problems that have plagued formal education for decades.

First is the problem of **superficial coverage**. Curricula are usually organized around an extensive list of topics and skills.

In many subjects, especially social studies, the knowledge items are not connected to promote integrated, in-depth understanding. Instead, they are presented as sets of isolated knowledge bits with which we want students to be familiar. The lists are so long that teachers feel obligated to race through the material, which often promotes only the most superficial awareness. The press for broad coverage reinforces habits of mindlessness. Classrooms become places in which material must be learned even though students find it nonsensical because their teachers have no time to explain its value and relevance. Students are denied opportunities to explore related areas that arouse their curiosity for fear of straying too far from the official list to be covered. Teachers' talents for conveying subtle nuances and complexities are squelched.

Effective civic participation cannot function on superficial awareness; it requires in-depth understanding. The Framework presents a sizeable fund of knowledge from which to draw, but to guard against the addiction of coverage, it will be important for educators to be selective—willing to omit material that seems unimportant in order to develop a thorough understanding of topics that are more significant.

Second is the problem of **"knowledge first, application later."** This refers to the tendency to teach knowledge as static, abstract truth, to be deposited in the mind's bank for withdrawal at some future date. This pedagogical strategy assumes that students should not be involved in problem-solving or the use of knowledge until after they have first learned the basic knowledge. Research indicates, however, that when the knowledge taught is isolated from application to a concrete situation of contemporary interest, it is quickly forgotten. Even if it is temporarily committed to memory, it is unlikely to be called upon when an opportunity to use it arises in the future. Research also indicates that students generally do not simply deposit and retrieve pieces of knowledge as taught. Instead, they continually construct and shape knowledge, assimilating it with prior knowledge and experience.

This suggests that knowledge is often best assimilated in the process of solving a problem considered important by the student. For example, rather than studying provisions of the First Amendment abstractly as part of the Bill of Rights, one might present students with a case involving school censorship of a student newspaper. After discussing students' opposing viewpoints on the issue, one could then introduce the First Amendment and relevant court decisions that would presumably help students to further understand or resolve the problem of whether the school's action was justified. Civic participation is more likely to be well-informed if the knowledge base itself is learned in the process of addressing real issues of civic action.

Reflection

Beyond moral deliberation and the need for substantive knowledge related to specific problems, the thoughtful citizen is likely to confront persisting problems in dealing with the realities of everyday citizenship which call for reflection and decisive action. These problems are not usually studied as part of the formal subject matter of school, nor can they be dealt with solely by reference to a comprehensive fund of historical, political, and social knowledge. They are, nevertheless, likely to weigh heavily on the minds of citizens struggling to become active. To help citizens become more active, civic education programs ought to help students address these problems explicitly. These problems are discussed under the headings of uncertainty, strategy, and personal commitment.

Uncertainty. Thoughtful citizens wishing to participate must learn to deal productively with uncertainty, ambiguity, and conflicting interests and ideas. They must also realize the need to take positions and act responsibly under such conditions. Citizens are constantly faced with situations in which there is insufficient information or a lack of conclusive knowledge, conflicting interests, and persistent public issues or problems that, though they may be managed by the system, are not susceptible of resolution. At the same time, the politics of governing requires that choices be made and actions be taken. This work can be frustrating, and for understandable reasons students and adults alike may prefer to avoid the difficulties that attempting to deal with such situations entails. The challenge for the educator is to prevent the paralysis of participation which may result from critical inquiry and reflection on such complex and ambiguous situations.

Strategy. Citizens who wish to influence public policy are faced with the need to decide among strategies they may use. They must decide upon the scope and priorities of action. For example, suppose some students decide to act upon the goal of alleviating poverty. They wish to decide what ought to be done and what they themselves might do about some important public issue such as poverty.

Scope. How ambitious or comprehensive should their strategy be? Limited strategies might include volunteer tutoring in a low-income school or persuading neighbors to vote for a candidate who supports effective job training programs. More ambitious strategies might include programs to reduce taxation of the poor, or developing programs to create new jobs in low income areas. How much attention should be given to short term versus long term strategies (e.g. allocating temporary shelters for the homeless as opposed to providing permanent housing, income maintenance, or social service programs for them)? Students might also examine alternatives to government action to alleviate poverty.

Priorities. In choosing among the many ways to approach the poverty problem, a thoughtful citizen will try to establish priorities; that is, to decide which actions should come before others and which efforts might legitimately deserve a greater investment of resources than others. Asking about the relative costs and benefits of alternative actions, including the costs of **not** doing certain things (opportunity costs), can help to establish priorities. One might, for example, decide to work hard in the campaign of a candidate who is unlikely to win. One might do so on the ground that even an unsuccessful campaign could raise public awareness of the connection between poverty, education, and the local economy.

Reflection upon strategies helps first of all in deciding whether a proposed course is the best way to advance one's ultimate goals (e.g. "If we are successful in increasing the number of shelters for the homeless, to what extent will this reduce the burdens of poverty?"). Strategic reflection is also necessary in choosing steps to maximize achievement of intermediate goals (e.g. "If successful, will our proposed strategies actually produce an increase in the number of shelters?").

Commitment. If educators are to enhance civic participation, they will have to help students reflect upon their personal civic commitments. In doing so, they must generate excitement about the quest for the public good and try to replace pervasive cynicism about democratic participation with more hopeful moral inspiration. It may help to consider at least three factors that influence students' personal commitments: efficacy, integrity, and responsibility.

Efficacy. Civic education must foster among students both the feeling and reality of political efficacy rather than powerlessness. This involves setting goals that are not only attainable but which also carry enough challenge and significance that their fulfillment brings students a sense of efficacy, rather than merely the satisfaction of having finished an assigned task. Beyond successful action, efficacy depends also upon cognitive mastery—developing a better understanding of the problem. Students who have recognized the complexity of social issues need a sense of intellectual mastery at least over limited aspects of such issues, along with relief from the expectation that success consists only in exhaustive understanding.

Integrity. Effective participation often raises issues of the maintenance of one's integrity. The give and take of politics with the inevitable trade-offs, negotiations, and compromises may appear to the unsophisticated to require selling out, or otherwise abandoning basic principles. One may need to deal with people whose motives are suspect and whose interests may actually undermine the public good. In winning support, one may be tempted to become involved in one-sided advocacy, along with manipulation of opinions and votes, rather than in honest, open discussion of issues. And it may be necessary to take forceful stands with incomplete knowledge of the solutions to a problem. Such threats to integrity can reduce civic commitment, and ways to cope with them should be discussed. The main topic for reflection here is "How does one maintain one's integrity while participating in the real world of politics?"

Responsibility. The right of the citizen to participate in matters of public policy includes the corollary responsibility of being sure that public policy respects the rights and interests of the individual and the common good. That individual rights and the common good sometimes conflict is a truth that must be examined in detail using some practical example. The danger that appeals to the common good may be used to attack the basic rights of individuals is one example of the possible pitfalls that those concerned with responsibility in public deliberation should understand. They should also understand, moreover, that being responsible means realizing how uncertain the effects of public policy sometimes are.

Until this point, our discussion of effective civic participation has concentrated on underlying ideas not usually emphasized in the teaching of social studies, civics, history, or government but which are nevertheless critical to promoting competent and responsible civic participation. These ideas should guide the ways in which the goals and objectives of the **CIVITAS** Framework are organized into curriculum. That is, the specific topics selected for study from the broad Framework should be chosen and taught to enhance the student's capacity for monitoring and influencing public policy. The ways in which students monitor and attempt to influence public policies should, in turn, demonstrate moral deliberation, knowledge, and reflective inquiry of the sort we have described.

TOPIC 1. GOALS AND OBJECTIVES

I. **Governing and managing groups.** Citizens should be able to participate competently in the governance of the groups to which they belong, e.g., families, churches, schools and private associations, labor unions, business, and industry, as well as cities, states, and the nation. Competent participation is enhanced by the attainment of the objectives listed the other parts of the framework in hand with the following additional intellectual and participatory skills.

OBJECTIVES

The citizen, individually or collectively with others should be able to

1. acquire and process information about situations involving the governance of groups.

2. assess his or her involvement and stake in issues, decisions, and policies related to the governance of groups.

3. make thoughtful decisions regarding group governance and problems of membership.

4. develop and use standards helpful in evaluating positions, institutions, policies, and decisions, e.g., principles and values listed under Goals and Objectives and the UN Declaration of Human Rights.

5. communicate ideas to other members of one's groups, decision makers, leaders and officials.

6. cooperate and work with others in groups to achieve mutual goals related to the governance of groups.

II. **Monitoring public policy**

The condition upon which God hath given liberty to man is eternal vigilance; which condition if he break, servitude is at once the consequence of his crime and the punishment of his guilt.

John Philpot Curran (1790)

To be able to participate competently in the political process, the citizen must be able to actively and critically keep track of the formulation, implementation, adjudication, and enforcement of public policy. The citizen's ability to understand and evaluate public events requires the knowledge and intellectual skills described in Parts II and III. Monitoring public policy also requires the skills described below.

OBJECTIVES

The citizen, individually or cooperatively with others, should be able to

1. acquire, analyze, and evaluate information regarding public policy.

2. determine which parts of government are responsible for specific matters of public policy. This includes the ability to determine whether a matter is the responsibility of

   - local, state, and/or national levels of government.
   - the legislative, executive, or judicial branches of government, and certain agencies within these branches.

3. determine what, if anything, is occurring regarding matters of public policy that are of interest.

4. determine what matters, if any, are not being dealt with by public policy that should be.

III. **Influencing public policy.** The citizen must be skilled at influencing the formulation, implementation, adjudication, and enforcement of public policy by such activities as voting, corresponding with members of government, lobbying, campaigning, and taking part in the selection of judges. This skill is also enhanced by the attainment of the goals and objectives described in Parts I and III. Influencing public policy also requires the skills noted below.

OBJECTIVES

The citizen, individually or cooperatively with others, should be able to

1. determine whether a matter of public policy is of sufficient interest or importance to the individual or society to merit action.

2. develop an effective plan for influencing public policy.

3. carry out a plan to influence public policy.

FRAME OF REFERENCE
Conceptual perspective

The steps in the following strategy are rarely undertaken by the individual alone but are usually best accomplished in cooperation with whatever group or groups promote policies consistent with the individual's goals. The steps below are not necessarily listed in the order in which they will be taken since the sequence will vary with the situation, and some steps may be omitted.

I. **Deciding to act.** Deciding to act in a particular situation should be based upon an analysis of the impact of public policy upon one's individual or wider interests in light of the fundamental values and principles described in Part I. For example, a proposed policy may affect one's individual rights and the common good.

II. **Planning to affect public policy.** This task involves using one's knowledge and skills and the information gained by monitoring the political process to develop an effective plan of action. Steps to be taken include:

A. **Information gathering**—determining what is occurring regarding a public policy matter of interest.

B. **Identifying the actors**—determining what governmental agencies and non-governmental individuals or groups are involved in the decision-making process regarding the matter. This should include:

1. **Identifying sources of support**—determining which individuals and groups may be of assistance in attaining one's goals and the benefits and costs of associating with each.

2. **Identifying sources of opposition**—determining which individuals and groups may be opposed to the attainment of one's goals and the benefits and costs of seeking to overcome their opposition.

C. **Scheduling**—determining the schedule in which decisions regarding the matter will be made, e.g., determining when a board will hold a hearing or when a bill will be decided upon by a committee of the legislature.

D. **Selecting forms of participation**—determining what forms of participation are possible and desirable, taking into account the benefits and costs of each in order to determine the most effective and responsible ways to influence the process. Forms of participation may include voting, campaigning, writing letters to members of Congress, demonstrating, civil disobedience, etc.

E. **Estimating outcomes**—estimating what one can reasonably expect to achieve by participating in the decision-making process, e.g., can one expect one's entire proposal to be accepted, only partially accepted, or is success unlikely?

F. **Deciding to act**—deciding whether to attempt to influence or take part in the decision-making process in consideration of the results of taking the above steps and the benefits and costs of participation.

G. **Timing**—determining what steps to take in participating and when to take them, e.g., getting one's matter on an agenda, preparing a presentation, lobbying decision makers before the presentation, developing a supportive audience.

III. **Carrying out a plan of action.** Once a plan of action has been decided upon, the citizen individually, or with the cooperation of others, should possess the following abilities.

A. **Communicating.** The citizen must be able to clearly and persuasively present ideas and positions to others orally and in writing.

B. **Gaining support.** The citizen must be able to attain the support of key individuals or groups for positions on matters.

C. **Skill in carrying out planned steps.** The citizen must have the capacity, or work with others who have the capacity, to carry out whatever steps are planned to influence a particular policy, e.g., writing letters or articles, developing a position statement, drafting proposed policy statements or legislation, evaluating policies.

TOPIC 2. MODEL SCOPE AND SEQUENCE

The following illustrate ways the goals and objectives stated in "Topic 1. Goals and Objectives" can be translated into more specific goals and objectives and learning activities for students at lower elementary grades. Similar statements should be developed for the rest of the elementary and secondary curriculum.

A. Governing and managing groups

LOWER ELEMENTARY GRADES OBJECTIVES

Students should be able to

1. acquire and use information about the governance of the groups to which they belong

2. explain how the rules and persons in authority of the groups to which they belong affect their lives

3. take part in creating rules and selecting persons to serve in positions of authority in the groups to which they belong

4. evaluate rules and actions of those governing groups using criteria such as the need to protect individual rights and promote the common good

5. communicate their ideas about governance to others in their groups including persons in authority

6. cooperate with others in their groups to establish and achieve mutual goals regarding their governance

ILLUSTRATIVE ACTIVITIES

The following illustrate various educational activities appropriate for this level that may be used to foster the attainment of these objectives.

Acquiring and using information. Students may interview teachers, playground supervisors, crossing guards and other authorities of the groups to which they belong to determine the rules they are responsible for administering and their purposes.

Assessing involvement. Students may work cooperatively in small groups to review the rules which affect them and the responsibilities of those in authority over them to determine how they affect their lives.

Making decisions. Students may participate in the making of rules for their classrooms and schools and select persons to assist in their administration, enforcement, and in settling disputes over their meaning and application,

Making judgements. Students may evaluate the rules and actions of persons governing them in terms of their effects on their rights and the common good of their group.

Communicating and promoting interests. Students may work in small groups to develop proposed policies for their classrooms and schools. They may practice presenting these policies and the reasons for them within and among groups. They may then present their proposals to their teachers, school administrators, and PTAs.

Cooperating. Note: Learning to cooperate to establish and promote goals should be fostered throughout the curriculum by the use of cooperative group learning activities and specific projects devoted to this end. See specific suggestions in other sections of the framework.

B. Monitoring public policy

LOWER ELEMENTARY GRADES OBJECTIVES

Students should be able to

1. explain some of the basic functions of local, state, and national levels of government.

2. acquire information regarding public policy

3. identify current issues of public policy that are of interest to them

ILLUSTRATIVE ACTIVITIES

The following illustrates how various educational activities appropriate for this level may be used to foster the attainment of these objectives.

Exploring functions of local, state, and national government. Teachers may invite to class persons working in local, state, and national government to explain their responsibilities and the differences among the responsibilities of local, state, and national government.

Students may be assigned to draw pictures illustrating some of the functions of local, state, and national government and to explain their illustrations to the class.

Acquiring information. Students may be asked to inquire of their parents or other adults close to them about issues of public policy in their communities with which they are concerned, e.g, traffic safety, environmental problems, development, crime. In small groups they may discuss their findings and decide upon ways to report them to their class. Either in small groups or as a class they may develop murals depicting their community and some of the issues they have encountered.

Teachers may invite to class members of local government or groups concerned with local issues of public policy to present and discuss their views with the class.

Identifying issues of interest. By such means as speaking with adults or reviewing news media, students individually or in small groups should be assigned to identify a matter of public policy at the local level which is of particular interest to them. By means available to them, they should gather as much information on the issue as possible and then report what they have found to their class.

C. **Influencing public policy**

LOWER ELEMENTARY GRADES
OBJECTIVES

The student should be able to

1. decide whether a public policy is of sufficient interest or importance to him or her to wish to take some steps to influence the policy

2. develop an effective plan for influencing the public policy

3. carry out a plan to influence the public policy.

ILLUSTRATIVE ACTIVITIES

The following illustrates how various educational activities appropriate for this level may be used to foster the attainment of these objectives.

Deciding to act. Teachers may help their students decide how they wish to act on a local public policy issue by taking the following steps.

1. Have students identify a local public policy issue of particular interest to them by such means as speaking with adults or reviewing news media, e.g., an issue regarding littering, graffiti, or the recycling of waste.

2. Group students in accord with the positions they wish to take on the issue.

Planning to affect public policy. Teachers may help their students plan how to affect public policy by guiding them through the following steps.

1. **Information gathering**—Assign students the responsibility of gathering as much information as they can on the issue and then reporting their findings to the class.

2. **Identifying the actors**—Assign students the task of finding out what governmental and nongovernmental individuals or groups are involved in the making of public policy regarding the matter. This should include:

   a. **Identifying sources of support**—determining which individuals and groups may be of assistance in helping the students to make and carry out their plan

   b. **Identifying sources of opposition**—determining which individuals and groups may be opposed to the position the students are taking

3. **Scheduling**—Assign students the task of finding out when a decision may be made regarding the issue in which they are interested.

4. **Selecting forms of participation**—Assign students the task of deciding what forms of participation are possible and desirable, taking into account the benefits and costs of each in order to determine the most effective and responsible

ways to influence the process. Forms of participation may include developing a poster campaign for their schools and communities, developing and making presentations to other classes and to adult groups such as the PTA, sending letters to governmental officials, inviting government officials to class to discuss issues.

5. **Estimating outcomes**—Discussing with students what they can realistically expect to achieve by their efforts, e.g., making the public more aware of problems, developing support among students and adults for their positions, influencing the opinions and positions of members of government, getting a new policy made.

6. **Deciding to act**—Discussing with students whether they wish to influence public policy on the issue(s) they have selected in light of the results of taking the above steps.

7. **Timing**—Discuss with students what steps to take in participating and when to take them, e.g., developing posters on an issue and placing them just before an important meeting or election.

D. **Carrying out a plan of action**. Teachers may help their students carry out their plans by guiding them through the following steps.

1. **Communicating.** Arrange for students to communicate their positions to appropriate audiences orally, in writing, and graphically with the use of posters and drawings.

2. **Gaining support.** Arrange for students to meet to develop the support and cooperation of others with the same positions they hold.

3. **Cooperating in carrying out planned steps.** Arrange for students to cooperate with others to carry out whatever steps are planned to influence a particular policy, e.g., writing letters, creating posters and placing them in their school or stores in their communities.

TOPIC 3. HISTORICAL PERSPECTIVE ON POLITICAL PARTICIPATION

A. THE HISTORY OF NATIONAL PARTICIPATION

I. **Changing patterns of popular political participation.** Since the colonial period of American history, direct and indirect citizen involvement in politics has taken a variety of forms. Political participation includes official practices determined by law and unofficial practices arising out of changing customs and traditions, often regulated by law.

A. **Official or formal participation.** The most basic form of official participation is voting or suffrage. Based on several articles of the U.S. Constitution, voting rights are part of the definition of citizenship. The Constitution leaves it to the states to establish legal definitions and practices concerning the rights of suffrage, such as qualifications of voters, forms of ballots, and practical aspects of voting. During its entire existence as a nation, one of the burning themes of American politics has been the extension of the right to vote. Involving mass movements and social struggles for constitutional amendments, federal and state legislation, and court decisions at all levels.

1. **Voting rights.** At first the right to vote was generally limited to white male property owners. Then it expanded to include nearly all free white men, then males of all skin colors and origins, then women, and most recently all citizens over the age of eighteen.

2. **Government regulation.** Official control of participation also includes many regulations governing elections, running for office, financing campaigns, and other aspects of electoral politics. Over the years, the federal government has increased its involvement with elections and electioneering.

B. **Unofficial or informal participation.** Unofficial politics not sanctioned in the Constitution includes institutions such as political parties and clubs designed to influence elections and policy making, and interest groups usually formed to promote specific public concerns or private desires. Participation may take place through involvement of masses of people in political campaigning, demonstrations, and petition campaigns that apply pressure to influence the behavior of government policy makers and officials.

48 / CIVITAS: History of National Participation

Organized demonstrators and members of unruly mobs "vote with their feet" and their voices to bring changes in government policies.

II. **Development of formal and popular participation in the colonial and revolutionary periods.** Colonial politics included formal institutions based on limited popular representation and informal devices such as organized factions, interest groups, and electioneering. During the period of the American Revolution and the early republic, political leaders transformed and organized mobs into devices to exert informal pressure on official authorities.

A. **Participatory institutions in the colonies.** Many North American British colonies had representative legislative bodies elected by white male property owners.

1. **Elections with one candidate.** Customs of "deference" usually limited each contest for office to a single elite candidate. In New England, where town meetings served as governing bodies of incorporated towns, each male property owner could take part in discussions and have a single vote on decision making by the local government.

2. **Colonial electioneering.** Although organized promotion of candidates for office hardly existed in the American colonies, traditional practices in some areas encouraged local electoral festivities similar to political rallies. As a candidate for the Virginia House of Burgesses, for instance, **George Washington** (1732-1799) "treated" men who voted for him to food and drink in a kind of political barbecue or picnic.

B. **Revolutionary politics and mobs.** "Politics out-of-doors" as practiced by organized mobs was a respectable Anglo-American tradition. This type of resistance to alleged British tyranny and injustice arose in several American colonies. Often it was carefully organized by small groups of merchants, artisans, and professional men who formed networks of political agitators. Other forms of participatory resistance included planned riots and public demonstrations against colonial officials and policies. Occasionally, spontaneous mobs reacted against specific abuses. Popular rallies and demonstrations served as mass media of communication in politics.

1. **Organized resistance groups.** Secret committees of Sons of Liberty formed throughout the colonies in 1765 and often included men of wealth and high position. The Sons of Liberty clubs sought to rally public opinion against British policies by organizing orderly participatory public demonstrations. Members of these organizations also participated in Committees of Correspondence that aimed to coordinate resistance among the colonies.

a. **Planning the Stamp Act riots.** Stamp Act riots (1765-66) were planned by the Sons of Liberty to protest the stamp taxes. These organized demonstrations included attacks aimed strictly at stamp distributors in the colonies, intimidating and causing these officials to resign. Each riot enlisted several hundred respectable men and resulted in destruction of property owned by stamp distributors. Sometimes the leaders lost control of these events, bringing disorder and random destruction. In a number of instances obnoxious officials were treated to coats of tar and feathers.

b. **Organizing the Boston Tea Party.** Resistance to the British Tea Act in 1773-74 generally fell short of participatory demonstrations except at Boston when the famous Boston "Tea Party" (December 16, 1773) took place. At the Tea Party a disciplined group of respectable men disguised and dressed as "Mohawks" dumped chests of tea into Boston harbor.

2. **Disorderly mobs.** Sometimes in the pre-Revolutionary years political participation appeared in the form of mob violence developing spontaneously under immediate provocations. For example, the Boston Massacre (1770) was such an instance of unplanned violence that arose when a disorderly crowd of 50 to 60 persons harassed and attacked armed British troops. The troops responded by firing into the crowd, killing several colonists—hence the term "massacre." (The term was used by speech makers to stir the anger of crowds.) This mob was disavowed by Boston's revolutionary leaders.

3. **Citizen boycotts.** Another form of popular political participation consisted of agreements among colonial merchants and citizens to boycott certain kinds of imported British products. Women as well as men actively engaged in the boycotts against tea and textiles, reviving women's domestic crafts such as spinning and weaving and transforming their labors into political protests. Economics, craftsmanship, and

politics were thus combined into participatory resistance against consumption of British products.

C. **Popular politics of the early Republic.** Political participation ranged from mob violence to elaborate ceremonies honoring the Constitution and President George Washington. Later, with the formation of political parties, outdoor mass demonstrations became important methods of organizing and influencing public political opinion.

1. **Local disorders.** Many important local disorders took place during the 1780s. For instance, in June 1783, a mob of Revolutionary soldiers demonstrated at Philadelphia where Congress was in session, seeking financial settlements for their service. Unable to satisfy them, Congress fled to Princeton, New Jersey. One of the most serious episodes of public disorder, known as Shays' Rebellion, took place in Massachusetts in 1786-87, when debt-ridden farmers fought against the state government.

2. **Patriotic demonstrations.** Well organized orderly demonstrations quickly appeared to celebrate various patriotic anniversaries. The Fourth of July, Independence Day, was widely celebrated in the post-Revolutionary era with festive parades and participatory activities. Federalists organized elaborate parades and festivities in several cities and towns to celebrate ratification of the Constitution in 1788. During the largest of these, thousands of people paraded and feasted to honor the new government.

3. **Celebrations of Washington's inauguration.** Mass participation took place on a grand scale to honor George Washington when he was first inaugurated President in 1789. Crowds of well-wishers lined the route of his journey from Virginia to the national capital, then in New York City. Marching groups, bands, triumphal arches, and other participatory devices were assembled to honor the nation's leader. At the inaugural ceremony, immense crowds congregated to take part in processions and celebrations fit for a king and unprecedented in America.

4. **Small scale of early political parties.** The earliest political parties, evolving in the 1790s out of personal rivalries and disputes over the conduct of public affairs, did not encourage mass participation. Instead they consisted of small groups of leading men, mostly members of the elite. The Jeffersonian Republicans organized local clubs, called Democratic-Republican societies, that enrolled artisans and tradesmen and engaged in partisan agitation during the 1790s. Although there were some partisan gatherings, electioneering did not take place on a large scale. After the victory of **Thomas Jefferson** (1743-1826) over the Federalist party in 1801, members of the Republican party staged enthusiastic celebrations around the country in which thousands of rank-and-file supporters participated.

5. **Commemorations of Washington.** Following Washington's death in 1799, Federalist partisans organized many funeral and commemorative observances with quasi-political objectives. Thousands of Americans joined in or observed these ceremonies of mourning and partisan dedication. Cultivating the public in the early 1800s, Federalists also made Washington's birthday celebrations into occasions of general participation and promoted Washington Benevolent Societies, membership organizations that appealed to respectable men.

6. **The development of patriotic ceremonies.** Patriotic ceremonies served as models for later festivals of partisan politics. By the 1820s, Independence Day celebrations in cities and towns everywhere witnessed parades, "speechifying," and general hilarity similar to political party rallies. President James Monroe toured the nation in 1817, bringing out thousands of participants to commemorate his presence. When the French hero of the American Revolution, the **Marquis de LaFayette** (1757-1834) visited the United States in 1824-25, he stimulated outpourings of participatory enthusiasm wherever he appeared. These and other public festivities brought the people out in great numbers, serving as precursors of massive political gatherings of the 1840s.

III. **"Hurrah" style presidential campaigns.** Among the most spectacular occasions of American popular political participation were partisan campaigns for the presidency in the middle and late nineteenth century. The term "hurrah" campaign, as used by historian David M. Potter and other scholars, refers to a style of electioneering that features abundant drama and the direct involvement of masses of ordinary people in festive, often funny organized events such as parades, rallies, and outdoor gatherings. Enabling and encouraging participation from plain people, "hurrah" campaigns engaged masses of the public in electioneering, and stimulated huge turnouts during presidential elections.

A. **Andrew Jackson and early popular campaigning.** Andrew Jackson (1767-1845), a popular military hero for his victory over the British at the Battle of New Orleans in 1815, first ran for president in 1824. Defeated in that year, he tried for the presidency again in 1828 and won the election. His aggressive popular campaign changed the nature of electioneering.

1. **Building support for Jackson.** In the election of 1824, after a struggle of intense maneuvering among four candidates, Jackson, who had a popular majority, was defeated when the election was thrown into the House of Representatives. Enraged by the result that he believed had been achieved in a "corrupt bargain" between **John Quincy Adams** (1767-1848), the victor, and **Henry Clay** (1777-1852), who became Secretary of State, Jackson set out to ruin both Adams and Clay. He and his supporters developed a well-organized political group that later became the Democratic party. The Jackson faction aimed to build popular support for their hero among the millions of new voters permitted to vote under new, more liberal suffrage regulations in the states.

2. **The first popular political campaign.** During the presidential election of 1828, Jackson's party conducted the first enthusiastic truly popular campaign for the presidency. Although Jackson himself did not take the stump, hundreds of his supporters traveled through the country making speeches, organizing rallies and parades, and publishing campaign newspapers and advertising matter. Jackson the candidate was "sold" by means of image making. His partisans presented him as a grand old military man, the "Hero of New Orleans," a man of the people, nicknamed "Old Hickory" for his legendary bravery and strength. Opponents called him a tyrant, murderer, and adulterer, but Jackson propaganda carried the day and he was elected in a landslide.

3. **The evolution of partisan politics.** Partisan politics evolved during the 1830s. The Democratic party spread through the states with Jackson at its head, a small group of political professionals in command, and hosts of grass-roots enthusiasts in its ranks. A new opposition party, known as the Whigs, also formed, with particular strength in New England. By 1840 the Democrats and the

Whigs were ready to compete for the presidency on a national scale. The striking enthusiasm associated with presidential elections grew out of vigorous partisan competition.

B. **The Log Cabin Campaign.** "Hurrah" campaigning emerged fully in the election of 1840 when the Whig party organized an unprecedented popular contest of imagery and enthusiasm in behalf of their presidential candidate, an old general named **William Henry Harrison** (1773-1841).

1. **Harrison's campaign imagery.** At one level, the election of 1840 was a wonderful, outrageous image campaign. Candidate Harrison was presented, much as Jackson had been, as a noble military hero. Not only that, a spurious identity was invented for the old general: he was depicted through various campaign devices as a simple man of the people—a plain farmer and frontiersman who dwelled in a humble log cabin and drank the people's beverage, hard cider. In outbursts of spectacular political imagery, Harrison became the simple hero who left his plow to save his country. Despite the imagery's contrived exaggeration, the voters loved it and acquired a fond affection for their new hero. Campaign organizers staged numerous and varied participatory activities to advertise and popularize the imagery.

2. **Campaign festivities and the first speech by a candidate.** At another level, the 1840 contest was an outpouring of structured political enthusiasm dramatizing the log cabin and hard-cider themes. There were dozens of giant parades, rallies, and exciting party festivities throughout the nation where thousands of men, women, and children came together to celebrate the cabin and the man who occupied it. Paraders carried flags and banners, and pushed floats and other devices depicting log cabins. In a hundred or more towns, local men gathered for "cabin raisings" to construct with their own hands and materials Whig cabin campaign headquarters. They sang about Harrison, the cabin candidate, they shouted and drank hard cider, and listened to orators like **Daniel Webster** (1782-1852) and Henry Clay praise the old hero. Voters even heard, for the first time in any presidential election, the candidate Harrison speak in his own behalf.

3. **Growth of voter participation.** The results, like the enthusiastic electioneering, were unprecedented. Across the country 80 percent of eligible voters turned out at the polls on election day. Popular participation in dramatic rituals and activities of electioneering had translated into a mammoth increase in voter participation in balloting. Campaign festivities also resulted in Harrison's election to the presidency. The nation's lingering economic depression dating from 1837 may also have influenced the election's outcome. Nevertheless, the Whig party settled on the "hurrah" style of campaign as its chief means of seeking America's highest office. Although influenced by the new campaign style, the Democratic party did not emphasize election dramatics as did the Whigs.

4. **Continued participatory campaigning.** During the 1840s and '50s participatory campaigning continued as the norm, though it never achieved the extreme levels of imagery and festivity of the 1840 contest. Political rallies and parades were staged by both parties. Other devices such as personal ribbons and medalets spread the message and encouraged loyalties, while display pieces like banners and flags helped create a sense of celebration. Whig candidates Henry Clay and **Zachary Taylor** (1785-1850) tried to exploit popular campaign images. National turnouts at the polls fell to 79 percent of those eligible in 1844 and 73 percent in 1848.

5. **Republican party campaigns.** Partisan instability and turmoil in the 1850s began a national realignment of political parties, fueled by public issues such as economic change, sectional strife, and slavery. A new political organization, the Republican party, formed in 1854, grew rapidly, and replaced the old Whig party as the chief national rival of the Democrats. In 1856, with the heroic explorer, **John Charles Fremont** (1813-1890) as their standard bearer, the Republicans conducted a lively "hurrah" presidential campaign. Staging parades, rallies, picnics, music festivals, and other events, the Republicans produced a combined political festival and religious revival. The great issues of "free soil" and the future of the Union added to the outpouring of emotions across the nation. Voter turnout rose from 69 percent of those eligible in 1852 to 79 percent in 1856.

C. **Mob violence and civil demonstrations.** Informal mass behavior continued as an alternative form of participatory political action. Anglo-American patterns of crowd assemblies, demonstrations, and violence, so effective during the American Revolution, reappeared during the nineteenth century.

1. **Opposition to immigrants and abolitionists.** Violent mobs and demonstrations responded to a variety of social issues.

   a. **Nativists and anti-abolitionists.** Claiming that they aimed to reduce the growing influence of immigrant groups, especially Irish, numerous Nativist mobs destroyed property and injured people between 1830 and 1860. Mobs during the same period rioted against abolitionists—groups opposing slavery. Dozens of anti-abolition riots took place in northern cities and towns, attacking black people and aiming to prevent the slavery opponents from being heard.

   b. **Riots in New York and Philadelphia.** Examples of these disorders included a destructive anti-abolitionist and race riot in New York City in 1834 and a similar disorder in Philadelphia in 1838. The Philadelphia mob, with sympathy from local authorities, burned a meeting hall dedicated to freedom of speech, destroyed property owned by black people, and caused many injuries. Among the nation's most serious mob disorders ever were the New York City draft riots of 1863, in which thousands of participants, chiefly Irish-Americans, went on a rampage of looting, killing, and burning. The rioters protested against conscription during the Civil War and against the liberation of slaves.

2. **Labor demonstrations.** Organized demonstrations involving mass participation were also features of the struggles between labor and management during much of the nineteenth century. Labor disputes often resulted in strikes, and organized workers found that one of the few devices available to represent their views was the participatory demonstration. Management, viewing mass actions as "illegal," interfered and many confrontations became violent. Essentially, however, such activities belonged to the Anglo-American tradition of participatory politics.

IV. **The "hurrah" presidential campaign's evolution into army-style electioneering.** From 1860 until the 1890s, campaign styles continued in the "hurrah" tradition but added a strong element of militarism. Campaign organizations had earlier been compared to armies, but from the 1860s on, the military influence was especially pronounced. Paraders dressed in uniforms, marched in disciplined companies, executed drill maneuvers, and carried torchlights that resembled weapons.

A. **The "Wide-Awakes" in 1860.** According to many observers of the time, the most spectacular feature of the Republican presidential campaign of **Abraham Lincoln** (1809-1865) was a national marching group, some 400,000 strong, called the "Wide-Awakes." Organized in hundreds of local clubs throughout the northern states, "Wide-Awakes" consisted mostly of young men, although in a few places there were women's Republican marching clubs.

1. **Military trappings and torchlight parades.** Authorities believe that the "Wide-Awake" clubs originated in Hartford, Connecticut, early in 1860 when a local club of young Republicans began wearing uniforms and carrying torchlights in evening parades. It was not a new idea, for torches and night parades had been seen before, but the name "Wide-Awakes," the uniforms, and the military style caught on rapidly. By late summer and fall of the campaign, giant groups of as many as 20,000 marchers staged spectacular torchlight parades in cities like New York and Chicago. The impression made by thousands of marching men with their blazing torches was electrifying. In an election when the Union itself seemed threatened, the army-like discipline appeared truly ominous.

2. **"Honest Abe," the "rail-splitter:" campaign imagery renewed.** Besides the "Wide-Awake" clubs, the Lincoln campaign renewed a strong emphasis on candidate imagery much like that of the 1840 log cabin contest. Abraham Lincoln's managers presented their candidate as "honest Abe," a simple "rail-splitter" who had grown up in rural Illinois and possessed all the virtues and rustic savvy of the plain dirt farmer. To prove their man's authenticity, Lincoln's supporters displayed actual fence rails that the candidate had supposedly split. Shown at mass meetings and rallies, carried in parades, these rough souvenirs proved to be exciting crowd pleasers. As with the log cabin symbol, Lincoln rails caught the public imagination.

3. **Lincoln's campaign.** In 1860, as in the Tippecanoe campaign of 1840, political managers put together an effective organization. They saw to it that masses of Republican sympathizers participated in party festivities. Giant parades and rallies, musical and comic entertainments, and hundreds of local gatherings dramatized the candidate and his cause. Copies of prints and photographs of Lincoln were circulated by the thousands, displaying the rail splitter's homely but respectable features everywhere. But the candidate himself refused to appear in public or take any stand on the issues. Instead, following the old custom of remaining mute and appearing disinterested, Lincoln remained at home in Springfield, Illinois. Pictured as a kind of country bumpkin, he was in fact a skilled politician and, as we now realize, a remarkably thoughtful, articulate leader.

4. **Participation in the 1860 election.** The drama created by the "Wide-Awakes," the skilled organizing of the Republican party, and the brilliant achievements of Lincoln's image makers did the job. There were four candidates in the presidential election of 1860 and political parties were severely split between the North and the South. The election turnout surpassed all previous percentages. Eighty-two percent of the eligible voters went to the polls in 1860. Beneath all the extravagant electioneering, of course, was the crisis of a dissolving Union. In a strange way the threatening armies of Lincoln "Wide-Awakes" foretold the crisis of secession and the military struggle that followed Lincoln's election.

B. **Political participation in the post-Civil War years.** The war disrupted old habits and patterns of elections only temporarily. Lively campaigning took place even during the wartime election of 1864, and intense partisan rivalry resumed in the postwar era. Historians suggest that party politics was never more prominent, and political participation more widespread, than it was in the 1870s, '80s, and '90s. Electoral turnout stood at 81 percent of eligible voters in 1868, 83 percent in 1876, and 81 percent in 1880 and 1888. Dramatic campaigns in the army style attracted attention and invited participation from voters everywhere.

1. **Flourishing of party rallies and processions.** Both Republicans and Democrats sponsored massive popular involvement in presidential campaigns. As the party of the Union, the Republicans

recruited vast numbers of Civil War veterans who marched in partisan parades in uniform and became known as the "boys in blue." Party processions and rallies flourished everywhere, from small towns to great cities. Much like the "Wide-Awakes," these popular political armies conducted impressive torchlight parades at night, carrying brightly burning torches, lanterns, banners, and other partisan devices.

2. **Participation by African Americans and women.** Party celebrations influenced the electorate in several ways, encouraging participation, providing entertainment, and stimulating the emotional engagement and personal loyalty of the people who saw them. The Republicans even engaged newly freed African American slaves in the festivities. This short-lived appeal to blacks reinforced Republican efforts during Reconstruction to build their party in the South. In smaller communities, campaign celebrations brought out nearly all residents including women and children. Women often made banners for the marchers and participated in lively presentation ceremonies. Children also sometimes marched. These rituals and celebrations of politics helped to symbolize community cohesion and identity.

3. **Material culture as an element of participation.** A byproduct and integral element of political participation was a varied material culture. Consisting of banners, ribbons, buttons, posters, torches, uniforms, and novelties of every description, political material culture flourished during the era of mass partisan gatherings and parades. Campaign devices and political items added an enduring and colorful ingredient to American politics.

C. **Innovations in presidential electioneering of the late nineteenth century.** The changes of the post-Civil War era reduced the influence of army-style politics. Despite new techniques, established languages and imagery of campaigning persisted. Traditional since the first "hurrah" campaign of Andrew Jackson's time, these symbolic clusters included the language of festivity and celebration, images of humor and laughter, the language of partisan loyalty and personal commitment, candidate imagery, the language of attack, and the imagery of persuasion.

1. **"Front porch" electioneering.** One of the innovative techniques of the 1880s and '90s was a new kind of gathering, the front porch rally, that gave people a chance to see and hear presidential candidates. "Front porch" style electioneering first occurred on a significant scale in 1880 when supporters arrived at the home of Republican **James A. Garfield** (1831-1881) and called for the candidate to speak. Informal at first, these visits became more organized as the contest went on. Crowds assembled in the Garfield front yard at Mentor, Ohio; then the candidate appeared and greeted his supporters with a short message.

2. **The "front porch" style.** Participatory front porch campaigning became more orderly. The new technique served Republicans **Benjamin Harrison (1833-1901)** in 1888 and **William McKinley** (1843-1901) in 1896. These gentlemen found that front porch visits with partisans enabled them to celebrate and present their messages in a dignified way. Using the system of railroads that had developed after the Civil War, with special rates offered to them, thousands of enthusiasts traveled to hear the candidates speak. In 1896 an estimated 750,000 persons participated in visits to McKinley at Canton, Ohio. All the occasions were arranged beforehand. Party officials knew which groups would be present each day, so the leader could prepare appropriate remarks.

3. **Stumping by candidates and the "whistle stop" tour.** Another campaign innovation consisted of electioneering tours by the candidates themselves.

   a. **Traditional candidate behavior and its exceptions.** Traditionally, American presidential contenders had pretended to be disinterested, remaining silent and above the struggle for election. There had been exceptions to this rule, such as William Henry Harrison in 1840, **Stephen Douglas** (1813-1861) in 1860, and **James G. Blaine** (1830-1893) in 1884, but on the whole the rule was honored.

   b. **Bryan's departure from tradition.** In 1896, however, Democrat **William Jennings Bryan** (1860-1925) established a new precedent. Bryan ran hard and personally for president, conducting the first whistle-stop campaign trip by rail, traveling more than 18,000 miles and making more than 500 rear-platform speeches. For the next half-century, the whistle-stop tour was a typical presidential campaign technique. **Theodore Roosevelt**

(1858-1919), for instance, was an enthusiastic whistle-stopper.

4. **Continued prominence of imagery.** Candidate imagery remained a vigorous element in presidential contests. A series of Republicans presented themselves as Union generals and war heroes—**Ulysses Grant** (1822-1885), **Rutherford Hayes** (1822-1893), and others. The Republican party kept the imagery of war alive every four years until the century's end, a process caricatured as "waving the bloody shirt." Democrats responded by posing as the party of tolerance and reform in contrast to Republican corruption. Democrat William Jennings Bryan, a candidate in 1896, 1900, and 1908, ran as a reformer, the voice of the people, the "boy orator of the Platte," and the "great Commoner." The most effective image candidate of the early twentieth century, Theodore Roosevelt, invented many concepts of himself—the "Rough Rider;" "Teddy," the warmhearted, grinning friend of the common man; and the "Bull Moose" progressive.

5. **The paraphernalia of political imagery and voter interest.** Candidate images were translated into myriad campaign objects—buttons, pennants, flags, novelties of every description—designed to stimulate interest and loyalty among the people. Competitive partisanship, popular participation, and the wide distribution of souvenir artifacts helped keep voter interest high during this period. Seventy-nine percent of eligible voters turned out at the polls in 1896. In no presidential election since then has the level of voting been so high.

V. **Changes in political culture, political practices, interest groups, popular culture.** In the twentieth century popular participation in politics declined from the high levels achieved in the late nineteenth century. Numerous other developments accompanied these political changes. Historians and political scientists do not fully understand the reasons for these shifts, but they offer descriptions and speculations.

A. **Changes in the culture and practice of politics.** In the late nineteenth century new voting procedures and electoral institutions arose. After these new procedures took effect, there came a decline in the vitality and influence of political parties. Fewer dramatic campaign spectacles occurred, and candidates conducted more personal campaigns in their own behalf.

1. **Complications in the voting process.** New balloting procedures made voting less easy and reduced the potential electorate. Voters had to register and pass tests of residency and literacy to determine their qualifications to vote. Poll taxes in some states disqualified voters. Complicated "Australian" ballots (an official ballot, distributed at the polling place, marked in secret) replaced simple party ballots of earlier years. Instead of easily voting a straight party ticket, voters used a long ballot requiring a mark for each office. The result was a more secret and independent vote, and a system that intimidated many voters.

2. **Consequences of voting reforms.** Voting reforms changed the nominating process. The direct primary, introduced in many states in the early twentieth century, spread to the majority of states in the 1960s and '70s. Voters could participate in presidential nominations by voting in primary elections for candidates to be nominated at national party conventions. Candidates campaigned in primaries against other candidates of the same party. A byproduct of the new practice was an increase in "dirty" politics at the primary level. Other byproducts included a loss of control by party bosses over nominations and a reduction in the importance of national nominating conventions.

3. **Decline of political parties.** Fewer and fewer people thought of themselves as either Republicans or Democrats. Instead, the number of "independents" grew. These mavericks, who could not be relied upon as regular party voters, had to be courted by parties and candidates.

a. **The decline of party spectacles.** As their power waned, the parties were less able or inclined to stage the great "hurrah" festivities and parades of the army-style campaign era. General participation in political spectacles thus declined, replaced by spectator politics in various forms. Rather than joining in live partisan rallies, voters read about, listened to, or watched campaigning in the mass media of communications.

b. **The rise of the personal campaign.** Candidates themselves conducted personal campaigns, often through the media. Presidential candidates often seemed to come from outside the ranks of the regular party loyalists. In recent years, the "Jimmy Carters" and "Ronald Reagans" identified themselves not as devoted party men but as "outsiders," running "against Washington."

B. **Popular distrust of political institutions**. Trends in the politics of economic and social issues, and in the popular culture have intensified distrust of and disinterest in traditional political institutions.

1. **The expansion of special interest groups**. Since 1900 there has been a vast expansion in the number and influence of special interest groups that concern themselves with economic and social issues. Such interest groups often avoid acting through or identifying themselves with political parties. The range of these groups is astounding. They include huge labor and business organizations representing millions of individuals. In the early part of the century, groups such as the Ku Klux Klan, temperance, and woman suffrage organizations sponsored numerous parades, rallies, and other events attracting public participation.

2. **Post-war participation and social issues**. After World War II there was another surge of participatory groups representing positions on many social issues: civil rights organizations that carried out influential public demonstrations during the 1960s; women's rights groups that marched in the 1970s and '80s; anti-abortion organizations that paraded and carried out civil disobedience; peace groups, gay rights associations, and many others. These organizations rallied hundreds of thousands of Americans, persuading them to join in mass demonstrations. Thus, the initiative has shifted in mass political participation away from broadly based political parties toward rather narrow interest groups. The special interests, not the general social needs, seem to muster commitment and generate enthusiasm among thousands of ordinary people.

3. **Politics as mass entertainment**. Simultaneously with the development of interest groups, there have been massive changes in popular culture. The growth and influence of the communications media—film, radio, television, advertising, the print media—arouse public interest in alternatives to politics. Popular entertainment and professional sports, to mention only two areas of popular culture glorified in the mass media,

encourage a spectator culture throughout the nation. Politics itself has possibly become largely another form of mass entertainment.

VI. **Conclusions.** Direct participation in political activities has remained as a lively tradition in the United States since the colonial era. Although it has changed greatly in extent and significance, participatory involvement provides American political institutions with a characteristic vigor and intensity.

A. **Correlation between levels of political activity and voting**. In the nineteenth century when there was great popular involvement in political activities, there was also a high rate of electoral turnout. People gathered by the thousands at campaign rallies, formed marching clubs, paraded, and joined together. Later, when it was time to vote, they turned out at the polls. Eighty and more percent of eligible voters voted for the president in many nineteenth century elections.

B. **Decline in the twentieth century**. Electoral turnouts declined in the twentieth century. Fewer Americans vote in elections at the same time that fewer citizens become involved in partisan activities and electioneering participation. The public has not lost interest in public issues, however. Instead of taking part in party gatherings, great numbers of people seem to assemble into organized groups representing special interests. Giant rallies consisting of hundreds of thousands of participants can be organized around causes such as war and peace, civil rights, women's issues, and others.

C. **The decline of electoral participation**. The meanings of these phenomena and their relationships are not clear. It is likely, however, that an electorate not stimulated to participate tends toward apathy. Voters who are not motivated to become physically, personally involved in partisan demonstrations and parades may lose interest in electoral politics. The intensity of personal participation in demonstrations and parades of special interest groups suggests the persistence of public concern for significant issues. It also suggests that participatory action may serve important purposes in a democratic political system.

B. THE HISTORY OF LOCAL PARTICIPATION

INTRODUCTION

America has always prided itself on the strength of local communities and the vigor of local participation in public affairs. This unit traces the history of local participation from colonial times to the present. Even as the social system changed radically, the basic structures of local politics have been remarkably stable. (For example, people elected state legislators 300 years ago in almost exactly the same manner as today. Colonial communities had sheriffs, mayors, county clerks as well.) One reason for the stability is the deep and characteristically American distrust of central authority. Whether considering the prerogatives of Kings, Presidents, or Governors, Americans have worried about centralization of power and the danger that imposes. Various mechanisms to separate power into different hands have been one solution; another solution has been to keep citizens informed, interested and active. The ways in which Americans have participated in local affairs have depended in part on the rules of the game (such as what offices are to be voted for and who can vote), and even more on the "ideologies" of the people. That is, on their deeply-held values regarding what politics, government, and society ought to be like.

I. **Colonial and Revolutionary periods.** The colonial period was characterized by social hierarchy and the deference of lower social orders to their "betters." The revolutionary period embraced a different doctrine for a different orientation toward participation.

   A. **Suffrage extended to majority of male colonists.** Colonial political institutions were borrowed from England, with some important new features.

      1. **Colonial government structures.** The governments of the colonies were structured like business corporations; indeed, Virginia was originally a for-profit business enterprise. The governor was the chief executive officer; the board of directors (the legislature) was elected by the shareholders (voters).

      2. **Voter qualifications.** To qualify as a voter in England, or colonial America, a man had to own property. Very few Englishmen (under 1 percent) qualified as voters, because a small elite owned all the land and rented it out. But in America land was abundant and cheap, and a majority of adult men owned enough to qualify as voters.

Indentured white servants and black slaves were not allowed to vote, but Indians who gave up tribal life for farming were allowed to vote. Fewer than 10 percent of the population lived in cities; the unskilled workers there were usually too poor to qualify as voters.

   B. **Domination of deference, not democracy.** The widespread franchise and numerous elections help create a democratic environment. People could vote for officials who wielded genuine power, though they could not vote for the British Parliament in London that ultimately controlled each colony.

      1. **A hierarchical society.** It is important to stress that colonial America was a hierarchical society. Everyone agreed that there was a "natural" ordering of society, and that some men (usually rich ones, or scions of outstanding families) "deserved" to rule. This attitude is called "deference."

      2. **Election day gatherings, militias, and courts.** Throughout the colonies, communities gathered together on election day, or militia day, or on court day. There were no organized political parties before the late 1790s. Leading men would stand for office and rarely gave speeches, issued platforms, or debated opponents (they seldom had opponents). The militias were especially important because men were obliged to join, and because they elected some of their officers. Courts were important because the colonists were very litigious people, always suing and being sued. Service on a jury, or as a witness, gave men highly visible roles in their communities.

      3. **Ceremonial participation.** Ceremonies were especially important in a deferential society. The fact that a person showed up on court day meant that he recognized the authority of the court and paid deference to the judges. Community leaders never had the castles and retinues that characterized European aristocrats, but they did build bigger and bigger estates, and expected people to respect their "betters."

   C. **Republicanism.** Republicanism was the widely held political ideology of the Founders.

      1. **The tenets of republicanism.** Republicanism involved a rejection of anything tainted with aristocracy. It also included a powerful fear of

strong central government and warned citizens against luxury. On a positive note, it stressed the basic strength of the independent citizen (one who was not controlled by a local notable and not a slave). Citizens had a duty to be informed and participate in public affairs. Since a standing army was considered dangerous, citizens had the right to bear arms (through their locally controlled militias). The needs of the nation and the community ought to come before the special personal interests of the individual.

2. **The American rejection of formal caste.** At the time of the Revolution Americans opted for "republicanism" and systematically rejected the option of any sort of royalty or aristocracy. There would never be special political privileges that came about through inheritance or which were owned by a family. At the same time, many of the ceremonies were made deliberately plainer, and politicians began paying deference to the voter, instead of vice versa.

D. **Local governments.** The colonies (and states) had one of two types of local government.

1. **Township government.** In New England (and later, in New York and the upper Midwest), towns or townships had important responsibilities. Open town meetings that still exist debated and voted.

2. **County government.** Further south, the county was the most important organ of local government. In Virginia, local courthouse cliques took official control of county government, and when one of their members left, the reminder chose a successor. While people could vote for the state legislature, they were not allowed to vote for county or local officials. In the rural South to this day county affairs are largely controlled by courthouse cliques, though since the 1850s they have had to win elections.

E. **Participation to guarantee "rights."** Ever since the colonial era Americans had strongly stressed their "rights." The federal and each state constitution has a "bill of rights" that is the ultimate law. From the Supreme Court to the justice of the peace court Americans have demanded their rights. This is one reason the United States has far more lawyers per capita than any other nation. Since lawyers are so concerned with the technicalities of "rights" they are the group most trusted to become politicians.

1. **Contrast with emphasis on "privilege" in Europe.** It should be stressed that the emphasis on rights leads to a broadened perspective, an outreach, a universalism. It is easy for Americans to move from "we have rights" to "all Americans have rights" to "all people have rights." The logic of "rights" talk leads to the expansion of coverage, to blacks, women, children, aliens, prisoners—to everybody. This American emphasis can be contrasted to a European emphasis on "privileges," which led to narrowness and conflict among groups. In Europe, communities jealously guarded the special privileges that they had been specially awarded at some point in the past, such as control over certain territories. European constitutions do not have bills of rights. Canada, however, has adopted a bill of rights, though it does not always take precedence over parliamentary statues.

2. **Protestors demand their rights.** In American history, protest movements and violence typically have involved outsider groups that want to be included inside the protection of rights. Opponents of the protesters have often the "time is not yet ripe" for reforms. In Europe, protests and violence have been between hostile groups that want to guard their own privileges. But to the privileged, the time is never right to divest themselves of privilege.

3. **Distrust of government power.** "Rights language" heightens suspicions regarding power and the powerful. Americans fear that government may be dangerous because it may strip away rights.

   a. **Opposition to the limitation of American rights.** The major cause of the American Revolution was the intense fear that the British Crown was moving to limit or eliminate the rights of Americans.

   b. **Desire by minorities for protection against majorities.** Ethnic or religious minorities, however, have often welcomed state action as protection against the majority group that controlled the colony. Thus they tended to be Loyalist and pro-British during American Revolution.

4. **Tax revolts.** Revolts have been an important theme in American history since the colonial period. Taxes are a main point of contact—and abrasion—between government and governed.

When the people sense that they are not being properly consulted, or that the government is misspending the money, they protest vigorously. "No taxation without representation!" was the cry of the 1770s, while Proposition 13 (limiting tax rates in California) was the tocsin of the 1970s.

5. **Mob action to demand rights**. People who could not vote used other methods to assert their rights. Mob action was important during the eighteenth century. Sometimes, when it was a question of the British Crown usurping rights, leading citizens engaged in violent mob action (like the Boston Tea Party). In local affairs, poor, unemployed, or unskilled workers often formed mobs. With the dropping of property qualifications for the franchise, mob action dropped off. But lawless crowds could still be seen in action as late as the 1930s, when lynch mobs plied their grisly trade in the rural South.

II. **Modern politics since 1789**. With the adoption of the Constitution, the American nation moved to a new era of gradually widening political participation.

A. **The new nation and the party system.** In the nineteenth century the U.S. grew from a small country far away from the center of world affairs to a major economic power. In terms of political participation, the most important development was the creation of the party system. The Founders had expected that Americans would be devoted to the principles of Republicanism, and therefore not squabble amongst themselves or divide into parties. But by the late 1790s the nation's leaders were gravely divided over serious issues (especially over whether to support revolutionary France or conservative Britain in what became the Napoleonic wars). To gain power, each side began organize supporters at the local level. The Republicans (led by Jefferson and Madison) warned that the rights of the people were in danger; they stressed the power of the states to neutralize national power. In 1800 they won control of the national government.

B. **First party system (1796-1824)**. The First Party System is the name given to the era 1796 to 1824. The right to vote was expanded, political newspapers created, and the convention invented. The First Party System was, however, not fully or uniformly developed. Turnout in presidential elections averaged only 23 percent of the adult white men, though turnout in state elections was considerably higher, at 39 percent. The absence of long-established "first families" on the

frontier promoted a more egalitarian political culture, but the level of political participation varied drastically from place to place. In most places, local elites still controlled public affairs. However, the elites were in all cases committed to the spirit of republicanism, as hundreds of thousands of Loyalists with opposing views had fled the country.

C. **Second Party System (1828-1854)**. The "Second Party System," lasting between 1828 and 1854, saw the full development of American parties at the local level. The Democrats battled the Whigs in every state, every city, and every county in the land. Turnout soared, in both presidential and state elections, to 80 percent of more of the adult white men.

1. **Forms of political activity**. Besides voting, there were many other forms of participation. Men endlessly discussed the personalities of the day and the issues. Newspapers proliferated, each controlled by a political party to give detailed news, slanted editorials, and encouragement to the loyal party members. Absent baseball, football, television or paid vacations, politics was the spectator sport and the entertainment medium of the day. Vast crowds (counted by the acre) turned out for all-day barbecues and speech fests. Parades with floats and banners snaked through city streets.

2. **The army system**. A military metaphor is an apt description for the party organization of this era.

a. **Organization of the "armies."** The parties were organized like armies, with the top candidate as commander-in-chief, a series of ranks down to precinct captain, and the rank-and-file of loyal voters. Armies were the model because in the absence of large corporations, they were the only complex organizations that people understood. The strategy of victory was simple—get more of your soldiers to the ballot box than the other army.

b. **Party loyalty as a substitute for deference**. To be a loyal party member gave a man stature in the community; to be "independent" or "nonpartisan" was considered unmanly and rather dangerous. Local notables could no longer gain office simply through deference—indeed, little deference remained.

c. **Electoral practices.** There were a few "mercenaries" whose votes could be bought by either party. Somewhat more common was the practice, which was not illegal until late in the century, of paying loyal Democrats a few dollars to vote Democratic (or Whig or, later, Republican). The convention system was perfected, so that all candidates for all offices had to be approved by a cross-section of the party.

d. **Power and patronage.** Many self-made men like **Andrew Jackson**, **Stephen A. Douglas**, and **Abraham Lincoln** moved from poverty to power at the local level, and eventually the national level. Around 1850, many states made judgeships electives, so there were few lifetime public jobs left. Routine government jobs (post office, schools, police) were used as patronage by the winning party to reward its loyal workers with the spoils of office.

D. **Third Party System (1854-1896).** The Third Party System revolved around the issues of slavery, race, secession, and loyalty to the nation. The electorate expanded to include the freed slaves, but otherwise the rules of the game and the style of politics closely resembled the Second Party System. The intensity of popular participation reached a peak in 1896, when in many areas—including five entire states—over 95 percent of the eligibles voted.

1. **Women and populists protest.** Women were not allowed to vote, but they became especially interested in the question of prohibition (alcohol abuse was a major problem in most communities). They organized through the Woman's Christian Temperance Union, which in hundreds of towns, cities, and counties in every state crusaded—often successfully—for laws against saloons. In the early 1890s, a network of full-time organizers created the Populist Party, which captured about 12 percent of the vote in 1892-94, then fell apart. It was unable to compete with the much better organized major parties.

2. **Golden age of democracy?** Historians have debated whether the very high levels of participation seen in the Second and Third Party Systems indicated a "golden age" of democracy. Perhaps it was, but it was the parties that orchestrated most of the participation; while they did listen to their constituents, the parties were largely controlled by a small number of leaders (called "bosses" when they became especially powerful).

E. **Fourth Party System (1896-1932).** The old "army" style party system gave way to a more "consumer-oriented system."

1. **Advertising campaigns replace the army style.** As Americans became better educated, they saw themselves as "progressives," and were eager to abandon inefficient or corrupt old-fashioned ways. Uncomfortable with the rigid army-style political system, the progressives wanted to evaluate issues and choose candidates by themselves. Politicians responded by adopting a new campaign style, based on advertising. Voters were now seen as consumers, and candidates had to advertise their strengths to give the voters what they wanted. As politicians discovered they could package themselves better without the parties, they relied less and less upon the old organizations.

2. **Rules change.** The Fourth Party System saw dramatic changes in the rules of the game. Progressives complained that the tight party control of local affairs was unnecessary; fire departments, schools, highway departments, water systems, public health agencies, and similar services should be run by permanent well-trained professionals, not doled out periodically, after elections, as political patronage. Many smaller cities, especially in the west, adopted non-partisan forms of government. State by state civil service programs meant the only way to get a government job was to have qualifications and pass tests. The nation's newspapers began dropping their overt partisanship, and middle class Americans increasingly became more independent of older party loyalties.

3. **Political machines.** Large numbers of immigrants filled the major cities, but they had very low levels of participation. Strong party machines controlled politics in most cities, and the machine leaders did not want large turnouts that might be harder to control. Those who did vote were drilled like soldiers of the "army." In reaction against the machines, Progressives forced states to adopt the primary system, in which voters could have a direct voice in candidates selection.

F. **Fifth party system (1932-1968).** The Fifth Party System was dominated by the New Deal coalition and its Republican opposition.

1. **New types of participation.** The New Deal coalition was based on support from outsider groups (such as tenant farmers, Southerners, unskilled workers, Catholics, Jews, blacks, and the poor generally) that previously had low levels of participation.

   a. **New Deal politics and participation.** In order to rally support—and win elections—the New Dealers at the federal and state levels systematically promoted higher levels and new forms of participation. Turnout rose in the big cities, because President **Franklin D. Roosevelt** called upon the urban political machines to produce the largest possible pluralities. The only way he could win the electoral votes of the large states was for large urban majorities to offset Republican strength in the towns and rural areas.

   b. **Ethnic, rural, and blue collar groups courted.** During the 1930s, ethnic groups were given special patronage, and their rates of all forms of participation increased. The New Deal was especially eager to promote more civic participation on the part of ethnics, poor people, the working class, and farmers. It actively promoted labor unions and cooperatives, for example, and set up WPA educational programs to teach people how to hold meetings and organize themselves. Farmers (including blacks) voted on whether or not the government should adopt certain agricultural policies; these were the first (and only) national referenda in American history. In 1943-44, as a major war raged worldwide, the nation's 80,000,000 eligible voters had the opportunity to vote in 250,000 general elections held for local city, county, or school board offices.

2. **Restrictions dropped.** Old restrictions on voter registration—like the poll tax—were swept away. In the 1960s, extensive peaceful protests by blacks led to strong new voting rights laws. Ever since, Federal officials have monitored local elections and local election laws to guarantee that blacks and Hispanics have an equal opportunity to vote and to win elections. Blacks did begin to vote, and in response white Southerners began to register and participate in local politics as well.

G. **Sixth party system (1968-present).** After 1968, the old New Deal coalition no longer functioned as it had. A new party "system," presiding over the decline of parties as effective electoral instruments, might be said to have replaced it.

1. **Participation of the better educated.** The Sixth Party System saw strong local parties almost vanish. Election turnout continued its slow decline, until in 1990 only one-third of the adult population voted.

   a. **Americans and Europeans compared.** Fewer Americans voted than Europeans because Europe was still using army-style politics of the sort that characterized the Second and Third Party Systems across the Atlantic. Americans continued to have higher levels of knowledge about public affairs than Europeans and participated much more actively in local affairs.

   b. **Government complexity, education, and participation.** Government in America, with its multiple levels and very large number of offices, requires guidance to understand. The local party functionaries and precinct captains who once provided guidance were long gone. People relied increasingly on television, where the news coverage could be found, and paid political commercials increasingly negative and nasty. The better educated citizens were much more likely to discover what was going on, to talk about civic affairs, and to vote. In 1988, 14 percent of college graduates said the "never" discussed politics, compared to 56 percent of the people who had not finished high school. (The rates were 41 percent for people with 12 years of school; 24 percent for those with some college.)

2. **Distrust of government.** The level of distrust for government and for politicians rose sharply in the Sixth Party System.

   a. **State and local corruption.** Just as Watergate undercut trust in the White House, so too did a torrent of trials and convictions of state and local officials. The federal justice department was especially active in identifying and indicting corrupt local officials.

b. **Distrust and adversarial media.** The media became aggressively adversarial as well, feeding upon and encouraging the general distrust of government and politicians.

c. **Tax revolts.** The distrust of government carried over into tax revolts, and (in 1990) a movement to drastically limit the maximum number of terms of state legislators.

d. **Institutionalized protest and citizen activism.** During the era, the style of political protest became institutionalized. Civil rights, anti-war, environmentalist, feminist, anti-tax, anti-busing, and anti-abortion groups regularly scheduled rallies whenever they wanted to focus attention on a problem. The goal was usually to raise the level of awareness of the citizenry, and so protesters usually took care to remain peaceful, relying upon the guarantees of the Bill of Rights and the oldest American traditions of citizen activism.

C. THE HISTORY OF CITIZENSHIP AND MILITARY PARTICIPATION

INTRODUCTION

Throughout American history there has been a tension between individualism and community, and the tension has frequently focused on military service. During the seventeenth century, the colonies were small strips of settlements along the Atlantic coast, far removed from the mother country and exposed to dangers from foreign invaders and hostile Indians. Even the most individualistic settler saw the need for compulsory military service to protect the community. By 1765 the immediate dangers were gone, and American political thinking combined two contrasting themes, Lockean individualism and republican communitarianism. Lockean individualism stressed individual rights and benefits. The idea was that all men are naturally free and should be allowed to pursue happiness in their own ways. Regarding military service, the question individualists asked was "What's in it for me?"

Republicanism stressed the superior claims of the community. The republican idea was that all citizens have duties, foremost among them the duty (and right) to bear arms in defense of the community. (See also, "The role of the citizen"

in Civic Knowledge). John Kennedy's famous line was in the republican tradition: "Ask not what your country can do for you, ask what you can do for your country." Republicanism further held that regular standing armies were dangerous to the rights of the people; the best defense came through militias that were organized by local communities. American individualism, on the other hand, with its stress on the happiness—not the self-sacrifice—of each man and woman and its general aversion to coercive measures, has uneasily coexisted with republicanism on the question of the obligation and value of military service.

This tension is still very much with us today. To make sense of the issues it presents, and to evaluate the place of the military in the American constitutional order, citizens should be aware of the national experience of military service, its rationale in a free society, and the range of issues concerning military service that confront the nation.

OBJECTIVES

The citizen should be able to

1. explain the history of military service and the relationship between military and civilian authority in the United States.

2. explain the conflict between liberal democratic and classical republican views on military service.

3. explain the range of issues concerning military service that confront the nation.

4. take, defend, and evaluate positions on contemporary issues regarding military service.

FRAME OF REFERENCE
Conceptual Perspective

I. **Volunteer soldiers or draftees?** From the American Revolution to the Gulf War, the problem of military service has been much debated. On the one hand, there has been the need for a military force large enough to get the job done; on the other hand, the desire to avoid coercion and minimize American casualties.

II. **Pre-1940 policy.** Before 1940, the solution was to have a small volunteer army in peacetime, plus a militia or National Guard of part-time soldiers. When war came, most of the fighting was done by volunteers in new units, which were then disbanded as soon as the war ended.

Between 1940 and 1973—during World War II, the Korean War, the Vietnam War, and most of the Cold War —the country relied on a regular army fed by the draft (Selective Service). All men had to register, and 60% served in the military or National Guard. Volunteering was still possible (and desirable because it led to better service conditions). Since 1973 service has been entirely volunteer.

A. **Compulsory national service**. The "republican" (which refers to the traditional philosophy of republicanism, not to the political party) emphasis on the duty of the citizen to sacrifice for the benefit of the community as a whole never died out. Its call was always loud during wartime and was heard generally during the 1940-73 period. In the 1980s, some Democrats called for some form of compulsory national non-military community service. The purpose was to inculcate in the individual a sense of duty and accomplishment for the common good—what philosopher **William James** (1842-1910) called the moral equivalent of war. No such national service has ever been tried. The closest experiment was the Civilian Conservation Corps, which put some 2.5 million young men to work in outdoor projects during the New Deal. All were volunteers from families on relief.

III. **Rejection of Citizenship**. One corollary of republicanism is that rejection of military service is equivalent to rejection of citizenship. Generations of patriotic Americans recoiled in horror at the stunning story by **Edward Everett Hale** (1822-1909), "A Man Without a Country" (1863). A soldier was court-martialed and cried out he never wanted to hear his country's name again. He was sentenced to forever sail the seas and never again hear the name "America." Hundreds of thousands of Europeans immigrated to the U.S. in the nineteenth and early twentieth centuries in part to escape compulsory peacetime military service. In the Vietnam War era, 50,000 to 100,000 Americans fled to Canada or Sweden to avoid the draft. They were allowed to return without penalty in 1977, but many stayed abroad and changed their citizenship. One of the most striking indicators of the disunity within the USSR after 1990 was the refusal of large numbers of young men to serve in the Soviet army (even though they were willing to serve in the militias of their own republics, such as Lithuania or Armenia.)

IV. **Community benefits of military service**. The major benefit the community receives is protection. Perhaps that could be secured by paying someone else (as in the case of Japan since 1945), but national pride has supported a strong American military presence in world affairs since 1898.

A. **Traditional European promotion of national values through military service**. European countries have long used compulsory military service as a device to break down narrow localism; to teach a common language; to provide skills that the economy needs; and above all to instill a sense of nationalism.

B. **Immigrants in the U.S. military in World War I**. In 1917 the U.S. had large numbers of recent immigrants, many of whom planned to return to Europe. There was uncertainty about their loyalty and about their ultimate place in society. During the war, many were drafted; systematic "Americanization" programs allowed the immigrants to demonstrate their loyalty to the new country.

C. **Military service and self-worth**. An especially important benefit for cultural and political outsider groups in American history has been an enhanced sense of self-worth, of group pride, and of deserving equal treatment. The converse has been discrimination against soldiers in uniform—as when ten black veterans of World War I were lynched in 1919.

D. **Divisive wars considered failures**. So important has been the community component that wars which divided the country politically have been seen as failures (for example, Korea and Vietnam). The Civil War reunited a divided country, as the Confederates surrendered and returned to the Union; thus it is seen as a great success.

V. **Individual benefits of military service**. Military service has always had benefits for the individual.

A. **Benefits to individuals**. For some it provides better food and clothing; for others, training, self-discipline, and maturity; for the more privileged, a broadened perspective on the whole range of people who comprise society. Troublesome teenagers and juvenile delinquents have often been packed off to the service in order to provide them with a disciplined environment.

B. **Veterans' benefits**. The nation has always been very generous to war veterans, even if they served only a few months.

1. **Benefits from the Revolution to Vietnam**. Veterans received free land after the Revolution; the world's first old-age pensions after the Civil War;

large cash bonuses after World War I; and a package of benefits (the "GI Bill") after World War II, Korea and Vietnam. (The benefits included college tuition and stipends and lower interest rates for home mortgages.) Career members of the peacetime military get generous pensions. Candidates for civil service jobs get points added to their scores for military service. The Veteran's Administration has operated a network of free hospitals and provides disability payments and pensions for wounded veterans.

2. **Individualism and the minimization of casualties.** So important is the individualist component of military service that American soldiers have never been asked simply to die for their country. They are, of course, asked to **risk** their lives in combat, but special attempts are made to preserve life—individuals are not simply sacrificed for the sake of military expediency. Campaigns have been designed to minimize American casualties, for example, by emphasizing teamwork, extensive training, excellent defensive equipment, high technology, and a massive preponderance of firepower against the enemy.

VI. **The danger of standing armies.** The dangers of a standing army have always bothered Americans. (There has been much less fear of the navy.)

A. **The potential military threat.** Many countries have suffered grievously under military dictatorships. The fear is that the army will have its own interests contrary to the general good, and have the power over soldiers, and the community, to get its way.

1. **Jefferson's alarm over the military. Thomas Jefferson** was alarmed in 1798 when his arch-rival **Alexander Hamilton** started building a large army and filling it with Federalists. When Jefferson became president, he reduced the size of the army, and identified and removed most of the Federalists. At the same time he was reducing the army, Jefferson set up a military academy at West Point where cadets were appointed by members of Congress.

2. **A non-political military.** Having received their appointments to attend the national military academy from members of Congress, the officer corps therefore would exactly reflect the nation's political complexion. Since the Civil War, officers have been strikingly non-political; they have rarely even voted.

3. **Career armed forces members in politics. Dwight Eisenhower** (1890-1969) in 1952/56, **Zachary Taylor** (1785-1850) in 1848, and **Ulysses Grant** (1822-1885) in 1868/72 were the only career soldiers elected to the presidency, though others, such as **John C. Fremont** (1813-1890) were nominated for the office and ran, and others still, such as **Douglas MacArthur** (1880-1964), have sought nomination. In 1952 Eisenhower was an enormously popular figure; the most damaging attacks on him were to the effect that any soldier in the White House would be dangerous. A number of other generals have become president, but they came out of the state militia or were volunteers. Since 1900, a handful of career admirals have become senators, but no career generals.

4. **U.S. military's constitutional loyalty.** Fears of the military wielding too much power have been troubling since the 1930s, but there has never been a twentieth century instance of officers controlling the political behavior of their soldiers. In all of American history, the president has always controlled war and peace. The military has never asked to go to war.

Historical Perspective

I. **Colonial militias and volunteer units.** Colonial militias were necessary to ensure security against attacks by Indians.

A. **Membership in colonial militias.** The colonial settlements needed all possible military manpower to defend against Indian or foreign attacks. The old English "militia" was revived. Each white man was required to join, arm himself, and be trained a few days a year. Certain religious and student exemptions were made. Community leaders became the officers and non-commissioned officers (NCOs), and militia day was a popular holiday. However, the militia were only training units. When fighting units were needed, volunteers were called for. They were paid, and received pensions if disabled in combat.

B. **Indian alliances.** The colonial governments worked out military alliances with friendly Indian tribes; the governor of South Carolina led a mixed Indian-white army to destroy Spanish Florida in 1702. However, the tribes who participated did not receive citizenship rights, and were treated instead as foreign powers.

C. **Slaves excluded from militias**. No slaves were allowed to join the militias. Free blacks and runaways were excluded in Southern but allowed in Northern militia. In the South, the militia organized patrols to search for runaway slaves.

D. **The creation of militias in Quaker Pennsylvania**. In Pennsylvania the Quakers were in power and they abhorred military action, so there was no militia. The system of peace treaties with Indians broke down, and attacks by hostile Indians made Quaker pacifism intolerable. So in 1753 the Quakers voluntarily relinquished control over Pennsylvania. The new government raised a militia but provided for conscientious objector status for Quakers, Mennonites, Brethren and members of other pacifist churches. Since then, Conscientious Objection (CO) exemptions have always been available; the exemption was broadened in 1970 to include non-religious people who had a philosophical objection to all wars. (But objection to only one particular war does not confer CO status.)

E. **Citizenship promised to immigrants who served in military**. The colonies were eager for new settlers, and promised citizenship on easy terms. Pennsylvania advertised widely for British and German settlers, promising freedom of religion and freedom from compulsory militia duty. A 1761 Act of Parliament enabled foreigners who served two years in the British army in the colonies to become British citizens.

F. **American distaste for British army**. During the French and Indian War (1754-63), large numbers of young New England men volunteered for special units (paid by the British) for service against French Canada. They quickly learned to dislike intensely the highly authoritarian and brutal professional British army. This experience convinced Americans that regular armies were both unpleasant and dangerous.

1. **Need for voluntary army**. Virginia tried to draft unemployed men, but discovered that conscripts fought poorly and deserted quickly. An effective army had to be voluntary.

2. **Equality and individualism in the military**. The spirit of equality and individualism was rampant. "Our militia is under no kind of discipline," reported Cadwallader Colden, the lieutenant governor of New York. "The Inhabitants of the Northern Colonies are all so nearly on a level, and a licentiousness, under the notion of liberty, so generally prevails that they are impatient under all kind of superiority and authority."

II. **The American Revolution: citizenship and service**. **George Washington** (1732-1799) clearly expressed the republican theme: "Every Citizen who enjoys the protection of a free government, owes not only a portion of his property, but even of his personal services to the defense of it." **Albert Gallatin** (1761-1849) expressed the individual rights-oriented or liberal viewpoint: "Every man who took an active part in the American Revolution was a citizen according to the great laws of reason and of nature."

A. **Washington's army and the development of national identity**. The Continental Army was the voluntary national organization commanded by Washington. The officers came from the gentry and elite; the enlisted men were predominantly poor young men, Irish immigrants, and blacks. They received land grants after the war. The Continental Congress did a poor job supplying and paying the troops, and mutinies threatened in 1780. Washington, however, disbanded the army without incident when the war ended. The officers played a major role in developing a sense of national identity, and in supporting the Constitution proposed in 1787.

B. **Volunteers and paid soldiers**. Each state raised soldiers who fought in critical battles (and then went back to their farms.) At first they were a cross-section of the population, but states increasingly discovered that only the poorest were willing to fight for pay. The Philadelphia militia was a mediocre military force, but it became a power in city politics, demanding a more egalitarian political system.

C. **The role of national, racial, and other groups**. The role of a number of groups in the Revolution throws light on the relationship of citizenship and military service.

1. **Hessians**. The Hessians were German mercenaries who were rented to the British army by their Prince. (He kept their salaries and got a bonus for any who were killed.) Americans invited them to desert and become U.S. citizens, which many did.

2. **Blacks**. Some 5,000 blacks served in U.S. forces (out of 300,000 soldiers), mostly from the North. They served in both integrated and segregated companies.

a. **The enlistment of free blacks**. Free blacks enlisted in every state—mostly from the North. As available white manpower dwindled, states became eager to enlist blacks.

b. **Enlisted slaves gain freedom**. Northern states had some slaves; many were enlisted (the masters got the bounty) and given freedom. Some slaves in the South were treated likewise.

c. **British attempts to enlist slaves**. At first the British offered freedom for Virginia slaves who would desert rebel masters. The offer was generally unsuccessful, however. Blacks who did fight for the British were usually freed and made citizens of Canada.

d. **Abolition of slavery in the North**. After the war, the Northern states gradually abolished slavery, sometimes with a reference to "all men are created equal."

e. **Blacks excluded from the military in 1790s**. A conservative reaction came in the 1790s and 1800s, as Southern states tightened their slave laws. In 1792 a federal law prohibited any blacks from service in militia. No blacks were allowed to serve in the regular U.S. Army until 1862. Free blacks from Louisiana fought with Jackson at New Orleans, and blacks formed two New York regiments in the War of 1812. The U.S. Navy had a proportion of black sailors throughout the nineteenth century.

3. **Women**. Thousands of women accompanied the Revolutionary armies. They cooked, sewed and nursed (a very few were prostitutes). Some occasionally performed combat roles, such as helping artillery crews. A handful donned men's uniforms and fought in combat. Others still were spies and aided in intelligence gathering. After the war, women were honored for their contributions and obtained a special role as "Republican Mothers" with the responsibility of shaping the ideology of youth according to the themes of republicanism.

4. **Neutrals**. Many settlers tried to remain neutral during the war. They were seldom harassed and became full citizens.

5. **Loyalists**. The Loyalists were Americans who supported the Crown. Where the patriots were in control, they were forced to swear allegiance to the new government or flee. (In the latter case their property was seized.) None were executed. Many loyalists served in the British army. After the war, Loyalists were allowed to return on peaceful terms as full citizens. Most, however, resettled in Canada.

6. **Indians**. The Indians were generally pro-British. The U.S. warned they should stay neutral. British agents tried with some success to encourage them to fight. Severe fighting occurred in upstate New York and elsewhere on the frontier. Indians probably could have bargained for some citizenship rights in return for support for the U.S., but instead their opposition made them highly unpopular. After the war, the British army did not evacuate forts in the Great Lakes region and instead supported its Indian allies. The new U.S. government sent the regular army to Ohio and Indiana in 1790-91, but the soldiers (and the women camp followers) were massacred. President Washington then sent a volunteer army of 5,000 men under General **Anthony Wayne** (1745-1796), who crushed the Indians and restored the region to American control. The Indians were sent to reservations. Reservation Indians did not become citizens until 1924.

III. **War of 1812**. A violation of the rights of American citizens by the British was a principal U.S. complaint that led to the war.

A. **The impressment of American citizens**. A major cause of the War of 1812 was British violation of the rights of American citizens: they impressed (i.e. forced) American sailors into the Royal Navy.

B. **The republic imperiled**. A further factor in the War was the sense among leading Americans that the new American republic was in a fragile condition. They wished to go to war to protect the republic in peril.

C. **Opposition to the war by Federalists**. The Federalist party in New England not only vehemently opposed the war, it verged on treason. Connecticut and Massachusetts refused to furnish soldiers. The "Hartford Convention" made extremist demands that permanently ruined the Federalist party.

D. **Indian opposition**. The Indians again took the opportunity to fight against the United States. They were decisively defeated, and their lands thrown open to white settlement.

IV. **Regular army in peacetime**. The regular army and navy during peacetime in the nineteenth century were small, poorly paid organizations. Soldiers and sailors were held in contempt; most new enlistees deserted within a year or two. Compulsory militia service vanished, and republican ideals of military service as the responsibility of every citizen faded away. Some voluntary militias continued, chiefly as social clubs (similar to volunteer fire departments.)

V. **The Civil War**. Who served in the Civil War? The regular army was much too small and was comprised mostly of foreigners of dubious military ability. The national crisis represented by the war demanded an entirely new army. One-third of the officer corps (typified by **Robert E. Lee** [1807-1870]) switched allegiance to the Confederacy. (After the war they were allowed to swear a new oath of allegiance and become U.S. citizens again.) Very few enlisted men or navy personnel switched.

A. **The Union**. The military needs of the Union raised a host of problems that had substantial consequences for questions of citizenship.

1. **Politics and the new army**. The U.S. Volunteers was the name given to the new army raised to fight the war. It was comprised of regiments raised by political leaders in the states: the men elected junior officers (usually choosing the politicians who organized them); governors appointed colonels; and Washington appointed generals, with an eye to politics. In the first year (when most recruits joined), there was very little fighting or bloodshed, and a great deal of glory. The Democratic party supported the war. Hence many Democrats enlisted and many were made generals (like **Benjamin Butler** [1818-1893] of Massachusetts and Congressman **John Logan** [1826-1886] of Illinois).

2. **The vicissitudes of a partisan war**. In the year 1862, fighting started in earnest; abolition of slavery became a war goal; and the war became partisan, as about two-thirds of Democrats moved into opposition. Some Democratic troops deserted, but more often they switched parties (as did Butler's and Logan's men), seeing the Republican party as the soldier's friend. Soldiers used their influence on families and friends back home to support Lincoln's war.

3. **An unpopular draft**. Needing more men, Congress tried a draft. The rules were poorly thought out and quite unpopular. In July 1863, draft riots in

New York City were so serious that Lincoln was obliged to send troops to put them down. Draftees could hire a substitute (for about one year's average pay). One could volunteer and collect generous cash bonuses from states and local governments. It was possible to hide, or skip to Canada, or violently oppose draft agents. Very few men actually were drafted into service.

B. **The Confederacy**. The Confederacy raised its new army through the militia and through volunteers. Slaves were used extensively in building fortifications and as laborers, but not as soldiers. As the war dragged on, the Confederacy increasingly relied on conscription. Draft resistance was high, and desertions were so numerous that eventually the army ceased to function effectively. The episode demonstrated that nationalism depended on a strong army, which in turn required full community support. As more and more of the civilian Confederacy was overrun, the soldiers became more and more politically powerful.

C. **Indians**. Indians tended to favor the Confederacy; the Sioux launched a major war in Minnesota. Consequently the Indians did not gain from the war; they were not covered by the Fourteenth and Fifteenth Amendments (though slaves they owned were freed by the Thirteenth Amendment); and in 1871 Congress stopped the practice of making "treaties" with tribes. The War Department took control of the reservations, and after 1887 a systematic effort was made to break up the reservation system.

D. **Blacks in the army and citizenship rights**. In *Dred Scott v. Sanford* (1857), the Supreme Court said that blacks were not citizens. Intense racism threatened to weaken the Union cause if blacks enlisted in the army.

1. **Union recruitment of blacks**. The Union army began recruiting blacks in 1862. The official rolls of the army and navy include at least 180,000 blacks out of 2.5 million men. Some became officers, and some fought in combat. (The film "Glory" [1990] authentically recounts this service.)

   a. **Blacks treated equally under military law**. For the first time ever, blacks were treated as equals under the law—under military law. They were not necessarily treated as equals in practice, however.

b. **Black service as justification for abolishing slavery**. Black regiments justified adding the goal of abolishing slavery, and justified the Thirteenth, Fourteenth, and Fifteenth Amendments.

c. **Remarks by Lincoln**. President Lincoln recommended in 1864 that Louisiana give voting rights "especially to those who have fought valiantly in our ranks."

d. **Citizenship and blacks' motive to fight.** The citizenship motive of black soldiers was often noted. General Benjamin Butler said: "Poor fellows, they seem to have so little to fight for in this contest, with the weight of prejudice loaded upon them, their lives given to a country that has given them not yet justice, not to say fostering care. To us [whites], there is patriotism, fame, love of country, pride, ambition, all to spur us on. But there is one boon they love to fight for, freedom for themselves and their race forever."

e. **Frederick Douglass: black service to win right to citizenship. Frederick Douglass** (1817-1895) called upon his fellow blacks to enlist with this thought: "Once let the black man get upon his person the brass letters US; let him get an eagle on his button, and a musket on his shoulder, and bullets in his pockets, and there is no power on earth which can deny that he has won the right to citizenship in the United States."

f. **Permanent black regiments**. Black regiments were made permanent; after the war they provided an official position "better than that offered by any other large institution in American society." In 1866 there were four black regiments—two cavalry and two infantry, comprising some 2,000 men in an army of 200,000.

2. **Black regiments in the Confederate army**. In 1864 Lee demanded that blacks be called upon to aid in the war. It was understood that the Confederate black soldiers and their families would be emancipated. Finally the Confederate government agreed, and in 1865 black regiments were formed, though the war ended before any saw service. The episode demonstrated that Southern nationalism was stronger than support for slavery.

E. **Immigrants and the Civil War**. The Civil War was fought around the question of nationhood. Recent immigrants had a somewhat anomalous status.

1. **Aliens, citizenship, and military service**. Aliens were welcome to enlist; several German units became well-known. Immigrants who were still aliens but had started the process of naturalization by declaring their intention of becoming citizens were eligible for the draft. However, the North needed workers as well as soldiers and wanted to encourage immigration. Therefore, aliens who had not declared their intention to become citizens were exempt. Aliens honorably discharged could get citizenship in two years, instead of the five years normally required, with no declaration of intent required.

2. **Opposition to the war**. After 1862, some communities in the North vehemently opposed the war because it had become a war to abolish slavery. Irish and German Catholics, and some migrants from the South, were especially hostile. When the national draft threatened to conscript their young men, these communities resisted fiercely. In 1863 Lincoln had to pull regiments out of Gettysburg to send them to regain control of the streets of New York City, where tumultuous draft riots had broken out. Lincoln's own relatives in Illinois were involved in draft riots. Speaking the localistic language of republicanism, the draft opponents were welcomed by Democratic party leaders.

F. **The Civil War and black citizenship**. The main goal of the war was to reunite the Union. To do this, Lincoln felt the slave power had to be destroyed, and therefore the slaves had to be freed. But it was also necessary to win back psychologically the defeated Confederates. Amnesty and leniency became the policy in 1865. A handful of senior Confederates went into voluntary exile (there are still colonies of Southerners in Brazil), but most accepted the terms. The status of the freedmen (emancipated slaves), however, was a bitterly controversial matter. The ex-Confederates demanded that the blacks not be given full equality with whites. Civil rights laws to ensure equality were passed (and guaranteed by the Fourteenth and Fifteenth Amendments) but were not implemented until the time of the Vietnam war.

G. **The Civil War and woman suffrage**. Northern women vigorously supported the war effort (on the home front and in hospitals) and had some expectation of enhanced rights, including the right to vote. Once it was clear that blacks were seeking the vote, feminists made the same demand. However, the majority of women made clear that they were not seeking the right to vote.

VI. **Aftermath of Civil War**. After the Civil War, claims to patronage and citizenship were founded on service to the Union.

    A. **Grand Army of the Republic (GAR) and the "Bloody Shirt**." **Grover Cleveland** (1837-1908) had purchased a substitute when his name came up in the Civil War draft; as president he appointed more Confederate than Union veterans, earning the contempt of the organized Union veterans, the GAR. When he ran for president (1884, 1888, and 1892), political tensions over Civil War memories flared again. Some Republicans "waved the bloody shirt" (i.e., spoke of fallen comrades), and advised veterans to "vote the way you shot" (against Democrats). Government old age pensions (for Union veterans and their widows only) became a major item in the federal budget after 1888.

    B. **The Civil War and Catholic claims to citizenship**. **John Ireland** (1838-1918), briefly a chaplain during the war, and later, one of the most powerful Catholic bishops, worked closely with Republican leaders to validate the citizenship claims of Catholics. They had served in the Civil War armies and therefore deserved respect and equal rights. While most Catholics voted Democratic, Republicans were eager to get some of their support, and they endorsed Ireland's position. Thus, **William McKinley** (1843-1901), in his 1896 presidential campaign, made strong patriotic appeals to veterans and Catholics, and proclaimed the emerging ideal of a pluralist nation of equal citizens.

    C. **Army desertion frequent**. The regular army and navy after the war continued to have very poor conditions for enlisted men; over half of the new enlistees deserted. As one newspaper noted, "The average citizen regards desertion as but little worse than enlistment."

    D. **The National Guard issue**. In the late nineteenth century, the states began reorganizing their militias as "national guard" regiments. Service was voluntary and was closely tied to local community affairs. Guard officers were often more noted for their political acumen than for their military skills.

        1. **When the Guard was used**. By the late nineteenth century, Americans had come to accept the principle that only the government was allowed to use or threaten force in public matters. During labor disputes, strikers sometimes threatened to close down or destroy the factories or mines of the owners, or to beat up substitute workers. State governments frequently called out the Guard to intervene on the side of factory owners. In the aftermath of floods, hurricanes, riots, and other disasters, governors have sent in the guard to restore order. During the world wars, the National Guard was federalized, retrained, and sent to fight abroad.

        2. **Distrust of the National Guard by the regular army**. The regular army always distrusted the Guard as amateurish, but its special claims (enshrined in the Second Amendment of the Bill of Rights), its ties to local politics, and its stress on the community dimension of republicanism, have allowed it to continue as a major component of the nation's military force.

        3. **The National Guard and Vietnam**. In Vietnam, President Johnson did not call up the Guard because he wanted to avoid debate on his policies. Some were later criticized for service in the Guard because it was an "escape" from the regular army. After Vietnam, the Pentagon restructured the military so that in any major war the president would have to call up National Guard units. The Pentagon did this so that never again would it have to fight a war with unwilling conscripts. In the Gulf War, National Guard units were called up.

VII. **World War I and issues of military service**. World War I occasioned intense debate on the nature and purpose of military service. Both volunteering and the draft were used. The presence of large numbers of new immigrants raised the question of just what was the "community" that citizens ought to fight for. The spirit of republicanism was strong. For example, General **Leonard Wood** (1860-1927) said: "Real democracy rests upon one fundamental principle, and that is that equality of opportunity and privilege goes hand in hand with equality of obligation, in war as well as peace; that suffrage demands obligation for service, not necessarily in the ranks, but wherever it can best be rendered. The army of today is the army of the people."

    A. **The draft vs. a volunteer force**. Volunteering for service was found not necessarily always to be in the national interest.

1. **Loss of skilled employees and volunteering.** The problem with volunteering was that the wrong people signed up. Soldiers were necessary, but so too was a smoothly functioning industrial system that could not tolerate the loss of expert managers, engineers, and craftsmen. The discovery was made that the duty of some citizens was to not join the forces! Only the community could make the determination (not the individual).

2. **Promoting voluntary compliance with the draft.** The government carefully avoided the Civil War fiasco in which only a small number of men were actually drafted into service. The goal was to make conscription seem voluntary and honorable. Local draft boards, comprised of community leaders, handled the process.

3. **Draft resistance.** A small amount of draft resistance occurred, especially in the "Green Corn Rebellion" in Oklahoma, where antiwar Socialists tried to talk farm youth into evading the draft. The antiwar Socialists were sent to prison (but those Socialists who supported the war effort were honored.)

B. **Americanizing efforts: defining the community of loyalty.** During the war, ordinary Americans reacted with hostility toward immigrant cultures in general, and German culture in particular.

1. **Suppressing German culture.** A nationwide propaganda campaign lambasted every trace of German "Kultur" in the U.S., and millions of German-Americans were advised to appear patriotic and stop speaking German in schools, churches, or on the telephone. Sauerkraut became "liberty cabbage;" and dachshunds became "liberty pups." The German-Americans were in fact patriotic, and many served in the forces. However, the once-flourishing Germanic culture virtually disappeared except in a few remote rural areas.

2. **"Americanization."** Massive efforts were made to "Americanize" immigrants in the service and on the home front. The theme was that they could be, and should be, American citizens and should abandon their allegiance to foreign nations. (Americans have always been very uncomfortable about dual citizenship, even though it is both common and legal.) English language training was considered essential. The program worked well, for after the war, most of the immigrants who had originally planned to stay in the U.S. only long enough to make some money decided instead to stay permanently.

3. **Naturalization through military service.** Some 123,000 immigrants became naturalized through military service.

4. **Blacks in World War I.** Blacks were drafted, and served primarily in service units. A number of units went into combat, including one of the army's most decorated units, the 369th Harlem Hell Fighters, which was engaged with the enemy longer than any other army unit in the war. During the war, large numbers of blacks left the cotton belt and migrated to northern cities, where their legal rights were much more likely to be acknowledged.

5. **Women's roles.** In 1917-18, women were active in supporting the war effort as volunteers, housewives, and war workers. Thousands served in uniform as army and navy nurses, and as navy and marine clerical workers. After the war, the U.S. and most major nations recognized women's service by granting the right to vote.

6. **Suffrage and the obligation to military service.** Did having the vote imply the duty to fight? In an abstract way, the answer in law was "yes." The Supreme Court in 1929 upheld the federal law that denied citizenship to a woman who refused to promise to "bear arms" to defend the Constitution.

VIII. **Inter-war years.** In the aftermath of World War I, a system of reserve forces was given more emphasis.

A. **Federal reserve forces.** Beginning in 1916, the nation created a system of federal "reserve" forces. Totally distinct from the National Guard, they were civilians who trained on weekends and who could be called to active duty in a national emergency (most recently during the Gulf War).

1. **Compulsory ROTC in colleges.** Reserve Officer Training Corps (ROTC) courses were compulsory for most college men between the World Wars. A few thousand a year actually entered service for two-year terms, then reverted to the reserves.

2. **Upgrading requirements for service; excluding alien immigrants.** The postwar army tried to upgrade the calibre of its rank and file. Recruit-

ers promised "earn, learn, travel" and made no mention of warfare or patriotism. Immigrant non-citizens were no longer welcome. High unemployment during the Great Depression allowed standards to be raised; recruiters began requiring an 8th grade education and a suitable score on an aptitude test.

B. **The unique status of Filipinos.** Filipinos, who were U.S. subjects but not U.S. citizens, used service in the U.S. Navy as a route to full citizenship. They were eligible for 4000 billets, and could petition for citizenship after three years, beginning in 1919. In 1946 Filipino soldiers also became immediately eligible for citizenship because of their heroic wartime service. (Filipinos in the U.S. were not drafted in World War II, but could enlist.)

IX. **World War II.** After 1933, the liberal, working-class New Deal Democrats were increasingly identified with the republican/communitarian position, while conservative, middle-class Republicans favored Lockean individualism. (For further discussion of these positions, see The Nature of the State and The Role of the Citizen).

A. **A peacetime draft.** President Roosevelt, alarmed at the strength of the Nazi military juggernaut as it rolled over Europe, called for the first peacetime draft in 1940. All young men would register and a random selection would be chosen for one year's service. Republicans, who were more isolationist, opposed it without success. Despite the promises, terms of service were extended in 1941, and the men served until 1945.

B. **Wartime service.** During the war itself, the draft was no longer controversial. Support for the war effort was virtually unanimous.

1. **Military service, race, and social class.** The actual patterns of service cut across American society. Men from high status families were no more nor less likely to serve. However, about a third of the registrants were rejected for reasons of poor health; and rural politicians succeeded in having most farmers exempted. Blacks were about 4% less likely to serve than whites, and rural youth 11% less likely than city youth.

2. **Exempting fathers.** Local draft boards did everything they could to avoid drafting fathers. No one wanted war orphans. About 300,000 soldiers were killed, the vast majority of whom were single.

3. **Gaining citizenship through military service.** About 160,000 immigrants were naturalized through military service.

4. **Women's services.** Women were encouraged not only to take war jobs and do volunteer work, but to don a uniform and join the Army (WAC), Navy (WAVES), Marines (Women Marines) or Coast Guard (SPARS). A few hundred thousand enlisted, against the wishes of most male soldiers, who strongly indicated they did not want their sisters or friends to join. Soldiering was still a man's job. The Army and Navy nurse corps were acceptable, however, and enrolled 60,000 women. (No men were allowed.) President Roosevelt asked Congress to draft women nurses in 1945 because of expectations of high casualties; Congress refused.

5. **Black Americans and the "double-V" campaign.** Blacks called for a "double-V" campaign—victory against the Nazis abroad and victory against racism at home. Racial tensions were high both on the home front and inside the military.

6. **Interring the Japanese.** The most controversial domestic decision during World War II was the relocation of 120,000 West Coast Japanese to inland camps.

a. **Wartime hostility to Japanese Americans.** Fear and hatred of the Japanese was a characteristic of the war. The government's emphasis on community loyalty led it to fear that the Japanese communities would bear allegiance to Tokyo. (The younger Japanese, or "Nisei," were U.S. citizens by birth. However, they and their parents also held Japanese citizenship.)

b. **Japanese-American military service.** To prove their loyalty to the U.S., 33,000 Nisei served in the Army, mostly in Italy, where they distinguished themselves as fighters, because they still were not trusted in the Pacific Theater. Some units were highly decorated, and some war heroes (like Senator **Daniel Inouye**) became political leaders of the Japanese-American community in Hawaii. Release of detainees from the camps began in 1944. In 1988 the government formally apologized for the wartime internment and promised each survivor $20,000.

7. **Italians and Germans**. Italy declared war on the U.S. in December 1941. Italian immigrants were also enemy aliens if they had not taken out citizenship papers. In the 1930s, some had spoken favorably of Mussolini. Obviously there was no threat of an Italian invasion of the U.S., so their "enemy" status was dropped in 1942. Some 500,000 served in the military. The Army wanted German aliens interred as well, but there was very little pro-Nazi sentiment among them, and the government did not want to repeat the anti-alien crusading of World War I.

8. **The post-war draft law**. As soon as the war ended, liberal New Dealers moved toward a "Universal Military Training" (UMT), well before the "Cold War" began. The idea was that every young man owed his country service. Conservatives opposed UMT, and a compromise was reached involving a draft law with many exemptions. At the upper end of the scale college students were exempt; at the lower end, men of poor physical condition or low IQs were rejected; the result was that men in the middle served.

9. **The post-war status of women and the military**. After much debate, the WAC and other women's military services were made permanent. Conservative individualists wanted an Equal Rights Amendment, in part to reward women for their wartime performance. However, liberal New Dealers and labor unions successfully blocked it, arguing that ERA would destroy the elaborate labor laws that protected women from dangerous working conditions.

10. **Immigration law and war brides.** Immigration laws were changed to allow several hundred thousand war brides (or war husbands) and children of U.S. soldiers to immigrate and become citizens. Several hundred thousand war refugees were also allowed in.

11. **The position of blacks in the military**. Before 1945, blacks had a segregated, second-class status practically everywhere in America.

   a. **Legal equality in munitions employment**. A partial exception was in munitions plants, for President Roosevelt, after being threatened with a march on Washington by black union leader **A. Philip Randolph** (1889-1979), issued a famous executive order (#8802) that forbade discrimination in all war pro-

duction plants with federal contracts. In practice, however, the order was ignored in the South. Most munitions plants shut down when the war ended.

   b. **The abolition of segregation**. The military was segregated too, except for some combat units in Europe. Short of riflemen after the Battle of the Bulge in 1944, General Eisenhower invited blacks to volunteer for combat units, and they performed well—much better than blacks in segregated units. The services after the war realized that integrated units were much easier to train and command than segregated units. After prodding from the White House, all the services fully integrated themselves in the late 1940s and early 1950s.

Contemporary Perspective

A major shift in values took place during the Vietnam War. The appeal to community and to republicanism virtually collapsed, while Americans became intensely individualistic. Opposition to the war (and to the soldiers who were drafted to fight it) caused bitter splits at home. The idea of risking death for the government's policy was roundly rejected by the war's opponents. The "hawks," for example, complained about getting bogged down in a high-casualty land war in Asia. "Win and get out" was their prescription. The "doves" said that the war was unjust and that no national or community interest was worth the tens of thousands of deaths and the acrid divisiveness at home. The Democratic party, long champion of the "community" theme, broke apart on the Vietnam issue, allowing the more individualistic Republicans to become the nation's majority party.

I. **The creation of an all-volunteer army**. During the Vietnam War, the Army suffered severely from a variety of problems (much more than the Air Force and Navy, which did not have draftees). Many of the draftees did not want to serve, and morale and performance plummeted. The solution proved to be ending the draft and relying on an all-volunteer army, which was instituted in the early 1970s. The generals were dubious about the quality of soldiers they would receive. However, salaries were raised sharply, an attractive college tuition plan offered, pensions improved, and morale rebuilt. The Reagan Administration vastly increased spending on salaries, high-tech equipment, and training. By the 1990s an all-volunteer army of highly-trained specialists was touted as the best in the world.

II. **Issues concerning minorities in the military**. Some blacks, led by **Martin Luther King, Jr.** (1929-1968), opposed the Vietnam War and demanded reforms on the home front. Complaints about disproportionate casualties proved unfounded, however.

A. **Opportunity and risk for blacks in the military**. Blacks entered the draft army and the volunteer army at about the same rate as whites, but they were much more likely to reenlist. The reason was that they were given a much better opportunity for advancement than in practically any sector of civilian life except athletics. Combat troops, who suffered most casualties, were at first regulars (with a disproportionate number of blacks), but after 1968 they were mostly draftees. About 12% of the soldiers killed in Vietnam were blacks, about the same as their proportion in the population.

B. **Minority opposition to the Gulf War**. Blacks were much less likely to support military action in the Gulf War in 1991 than whites, and complaints were heard from the black and Hispanic communities about the risk of suffering disproportionate numbers of casualties in a ground war. The propriety of American wars with Third World countries was also questioned. When the war ended with remarkably few casualties, support for military service soared.

III. **Issues concerning women in the military**. The status of women in the military was increasingly controversial after 1978, when the WAC, WAVES, etc., were abolished and women integrated into regular units.

A. **Women not required to register for Selective Service**. Although the draft remained dead, young men were required to register for Selective Service beginning in 1980—but not young women. One of the main reasons for the defeat of the Equal Rights Amendment in the 1970s was the realization that it probably would require women to be drafted and possibly to serve in combat positions.

B. **The question of women in combat roles**. The proportion of women began to climb past 12%, but by law they were not allowed to enter combat jobs, even in peacetime, except in the Coast Guard, where women serve in all billets. It was not clear how many women actually wanted combat roles, but the fact they could never hold them was a serious brake on their career advancement. Most male soldiers held to a strong belief that combat should be exclusively a male activity. Tens of thousands of women served in the 1991 Gulf War in support roles near the front lines, including piloting helicopters ferrying troops to combat positions, but none was in combat itself. Several women were killed, however, and two were captured as POWs. (The two POWs were soon released). Immediately after the war, Congress began the process of dropping the rule against women in combat. The debate continues on whether the community as a whole has a special responsibility toward women, or whether they should be treated as individuals, exactly like men.

TOPIC 4. CIVIC AND COMMUNITY ACTION

Where everyman is...participator in the government of affairs, not merely at an election one day in the year but every day...he will let the heart be torn out of his body sooner than his power be wrested from him by a Caesar or a Bonaparte.

Thomas Jefferson (1816)

Americans of all ages, all stations in life, and all types of disposition are forever forming associations...at the head of any new undertaking, where in France you would find the government or in England some territorial magnate, in the United States you are sure to find an association.

Alexis de Tocqueville (1831)

Today we stand on the threshold of woman's era. In her hand are possibilities whose use or abuse must tell upon the political life of the nation, and send their influence for good or evil across the track of unborn ages.

Frances Harper (1893)

Democracy is a process, not a static condition. It is becoming, rather than being. It can be easily lost, but is never finally won.

William H. Hastie (1940)

The problems confronting us as a nation and as communities require immediate attention. The solutions will not come from government alone...Just as America's founders staked their reputations on representative democracy over 200 years ago, we must pledge our future to a prescription for a strong citizen democracy.

Henry G. Cisneros and John Parr (1990)

For centuries, Americans' voluntary and political involvements were closely intertwined and mutually reinforcing. Today, that link has been largely severed. Though participation in voluntary service and community-based groups is increasing, political involvement is decreasing. Democracy is in danger of becoming a spectator sport. The challenge facing civic education is to help overcome this divide.

Growing numbers of citizens feel disengaged from the political process and from public affairs. Voting levels have declined precipitously. Perceptions of the political process have soured. According to *New York Times* polling, 68% of the public thought the election in 1988 more negative than previous elections. Disengagement from politics, and from American institutions more generally, is especially acute among young people. In the 1988 election, only 36 percent of eligible Americans under the age of 25 voted for president. A Girl Scouts survey found that 65 percent of high school students would cheat on an important exam. The Times Mirror Center reported that for the first time since World War II, young Americans are less knowledgeable about major events than their elders. Only one in five follow major issues "very closely."

Citizens voice common complaints: the political process seems to reward posturing and hype; there is little serious discussion of the problems that the country faces; absent wide involvement, politics is dominated by extremes.

The problems with politics have not simply been inflicted **upon** the people, however. Americans have **allowed** politics to become the property of experts—professional politicians, consultants, media advisors.

Politics is like a spectator sport people try to avoid watching. Yet no matter how much complaint, or how many reforms are proposed, politics is unlikely to get much better until citizens reclaim their public roles.

Politics comes from the Greek word, *politicos*, meaning "of the citizen." Citizens need to include themselves again in politics for reasons of both practicality and reward.

In the first instance, issues have emerged that require for their resolution significant changes in behavior, values, and cultural assumptions—issues such as racial conflict, drugs, crime, homelessness, the education of a literate and sophisticated work force, entrepreneurial development, and protection of the environment. Recycling depends on citizen involvement. School reform requires parents as significant stakeholders and participants in the process. Reducing crime rests, in part, upon stronger neighborhoods and new cooperation between police and residents. Political problem solving is today too complex and many-sided a process to be satisfactorily left to political leaders, government, or any large systems alone. New ways to involve citizens as public problem solvers are essential.

Neither a simplistic and moralistic approach to politics nor a narrowly technocratic politics will work. The very complexity of the problems before us means that the nation needs the capacity for judgment that comes from learning how to listen to and draw from a variety of viewpoints. Today, Americans talk at each other and past each other because we have forgotten the arts of public argument.

In the second instance, public life is too rewarding to be left to professionals. For Thomas Jefferson and others among the nation's founders, freedom meant the ability to participate in the public realm. They believed that people have public needs—for recognition, voice, accomplishment, connection to larger purposes—just as they have private needs.

To meet the challenge of developing wider public leadership and creating a renewed practice of citizenship, civic education must show the connections between political society on the one hand, and citizens' daily lives and community interests on the other. Civic education must also demonstrate to young people the deep rewards of life-long involvement in the public arena.

OBJECTIVES

The citizen should be able to

1. explain how citizens' voluntary efforts have strengthened democratic institutions over the course of American history.

2. explain the scope and patterns of voluntary action today and what citizens gain and contribute through such efforts—how civic involvements are important to a successful and fulfilling life.

3. explain ways in which public life and citizens' public capacities have been weakened; the implicit connections between voluntary efforts and the formal political process; and concepts and approaches helpful in making explicit and cultivating those connections.

4. distinguish between voluntary efforts that involve monitoring and influencing public policy and those that do not.

5. evaluate voluntary efforts in terms of their effects upon the rights of individuals, the goals of the community, and the common welfare.

FRAME OF REFERENCE
Conceptual and Historical Framework

I. **The relations between civic and community action and politics.**

   A. **Government issues from the people.** Four states in the United States (Massachusetts, Pennsylvania, Virginia, and Kentucky) are officially "Commonwealths."

Through much of American history, however, **every** state was informally referred to as a commonwealth. The term conveyed something distinctive about the American political system: here government was understood to **issue** from the people. Thomas Paine captured this sense in his observation that "a constitution is not the act of a government, but a people constituting a government." This view is inscribed in the Constitution's Preamble: "We the People" created the legal framework for self-government.

In part, this meant that government leaders drew their authority from popular election. As James Wilson described it, "all authority of every kind is derived by representation from the people and the democratic principle is carried into every part of the government."

It also meant a particular relationship between the citizenry and government. Government was seen as the overall regulator of society, charged with tasks such as "promoting the general welfare" and providing for the nation's common defense and security interests. The public, however, fresh from the colonial experience, continued to view centralized governmental authority with suspicion.

As early as the 1790s, Democratic-Republican societies inspired by the French Revolution formed around the idea that the government could only be kept in check "by the display of power equal to itself, the collected sentiment of the people." Jefferson even urged a "revolution" every several decades, as antidote to concentrated authority.

Citizens also undertook many activities that in other nations were performed by governmental authorities. The work of settlers who created communities by clearing forests, forming militia, raising barns, and establishing religious congregations generated a distinctive view that government rests on an active citizenry who take it upon themselves to care for common projects, beyond the designated functions of government. As the historians Oscar and Mary Handlin put it, "for the farmers and seamen, for the fishermen, artisans and new merchants, commonwealth repeated the lessons they knew from the organization of churches and towns...the wisdom of common action."

   B. **Public action and the voluntary tradition.** In American history, "public" mainly referred to the citizenry or political society as a whole, not simply government. The voluntary tradition produced three distinct ways of seeing civil society and the role of "the public" in relationship to the political process: the public was a deliberative body; the public was a problem solver; and the public was a group of civic-minded reformers. These understandings are useful in mapping the ties between voluntary initiative and larger civic function.

1. **A deliberative body**. In 1776 in a letter to his wife, Abigail, John Adams expressed confidence that the citizenry of the emerging nation would be able to act wisely on the great challenges before them. "Time has been given for the whole People, maturely to consider the great Question of Independence and to ripen their Judgments, dissipate their Fears, and allure their Hopes, by discussing it in News Papers and Pamphletts, by debating it, in Assemblies, Conventions, Committees of Safety and Inspection, in Town and County Meetings, as well as in private Conversations."

Adams' view captured one basic meaning of public—the concept of the body of people **created** through a process of discussion and debate about current affairs. Such a sense of the public took shape through the press, libraries, clubs, education groups, coffee houses, electoral debates, and other associations that created awareness of a larger "thinking world" beyond family, friends, and daily interests.

American educational and media institutions have their roots in this understanding of the public as deliberator about political issues of the day. Thus, newspapers commonly described their mission as creating informed public discussion of current issues. In the nineteenth century, the expansion of public education came about often largely through the efforts of voluntary citizen organizations, and was seen as essential to a well-informed, deliberative citizenry. Similarly, public libraries were created through citizen efforts, and justified as "arsenals of democracy."

The view of the citizenry as a deliberative body produced large civic education movements. In the early 1830s, John Holbrook's Lyceum Movement created adult learning centers in order to provide forums for citizens to discuss public affairs. By 1837, the movement included an estimated 3,000 towns. After the Civil War, the Chatauqua Assembly movement continued this legacy,

eventually including 15,000 "home study circles" for discussion of public affairs and also artistic performances and public lectures. Similarly, university extension programs, adopted from England in the 1880s, were designed to promote better rural citizenship, as well as improved farming. In poor and immigrant communities, institutions like the Workmen's Circle and Settlement Houses sought to teach citizens how to understand and discuss public issues.

These traditions continue down to the present day through organizations like the League of Women Voters and, more recently, the National Issues Forums.

2. **An agent of problem solving**. The public was, secondly, a direct actor in problem-solving. This understanding of public was reflected in direct democracy, like the New England town meeting, which combined deliberation and action on public affairs. More informally, it appeared in our rich traditions of voluntary efforts that Alexis de Tocqueville observed when he travelled through the nation in the 1830s.

Immigrants from every corner of the world brought with them strong practices of community action. In English history, for instance, problem solving by villagers about the exercise of the rights and upkeep of common lands, footpaths, foodlands, and fishing areas, as well as maintenance of common buildings like the village church, gave to middle-level peasantry a constant, daily schooling in rough democracy. Villagers regularly promulgated laws, sometimes in joint consultation with lords, over "such things as gleaning after harvest, exercises of rights of common and the grazing of village paths and ways." Churches—the village site of feasts and celebrations, public deliberation, popular courts, refuge from raids, dances, marketplace, plays, and banquets—were public centers that entailed both rights to use and clear responsibilities. Parishioners "were called on to keep the nave in repair, the churchyard in good order, to provide many items of equipment including...bells for the steeple, a pyx, a Lenten veil, a font, a bier for the dea, a vessel for holy water and certain other items of equipment" as well as taxes and tithes of corn, garden produce, and livestock.

Such traditions flourished in a vast array of American voluntary activities—religious congregations that combined worship with community effort, barn raisings, quilting bees, immigrant mutual aid groups and voluntary fire departments. They also generated organizations like the National Council of Negro Women, 4-H, the Red Cross, the YMCA, the YWCA, and Rotary. Americans looked to their own initiative, rather than large governmental or business organizations, to undertake voluntary projects concerned with addressing public problems. Indeed, most functions later assumed by government were first designed and developed in community initiatives.

Practices of citizen problem solving have especially been revived in recent years in community and neighborhood organizations. Community groups take on a wide range of issues, from crime and drugs to commercial development, housing construction, landtrusts, and historic preservation.

3. **A civic-minded, reform-oriented citizenry**. Since the early nineteenth century, politics in America has included much more than electoral activity and government. Indeed, much of its most vital side took root in activist reform groups like missionary societies, educational groups, abolition crusades, and moral reform and temperance organizations. In the most dramatic instances, such groups were the seedbeds for large social movements which advocated expanding the "citizenry" itself by including within it those left out in original formal definitions. Thus, abolition, women's suffrage, the Farmers Alliances and Knights of Labor during the nineteenth century and the civil rights movement of the 1960s all sought to make political society more inclusive.

The key to their impact was that they combined struggles for power and reform with the assumption of **responsibility** for public affairs. The Women's Christian Temperance Union of the late nineteenth century, for instance, wedded decades of reform agitation against alcohol use with practical problem solving. Historian Ruth Bordin noted that by 1889, WCTU activities in Chicago included "two day nurseries, two Sunday schools, an industrial school, a mission that sheltered four thousand homeless or destitute women in a twelve month period, a lodging house that... provided temporary housing for over fifty thousand men, and a low cost restaurant." Similarly, the Citizen Education Program of the Southern Christian Leadership Conference in the civil rights movement of the 1960s helped disenfran-

chised blacks register to vote. It also trained thousands of local leaders as civic educators for teaching problem solving in their own communities.

The best examples of this public-spirited reform tradition in recent years are found in the public interest movement. Public interest organizations seek to make the large institutions of business and government more accountable, but they do more than voice criticisms. They also propose solutions which they believe are workable and realistic for problems facing the nation.

II. **Patterns of Contemporary Voluntary Involvement**.

A. **Overall pattern and historic continuities**. The extent of Americans' community and civic activities are extraordinary. Comparative research indicates that patterns of voluntary association and activity in the United States and Canada are notably higher than those of other industrialized nations with the exception of Scandinavia.

According to Peter Berger and John Neuhaus, in 1977 in the U.S. a great variety of privately supported institutions flourished: 1,900 colleges and universities, 4,600 secondary schools, 3,600 hospitals, 6,000 museums, 1,100 orchestras, at least 26,000 nongovernmental welfare agencies and nearly 500,000 local churches and synagogues. Alex Inkeles reported in 1983 that community involvements from Tocqueville's time to the present show strong continuities, though there were several significant differences. Notably, Americans today evidence increased tolerance of diversity. However, they also have less political confidence.

The level of voluntary efforts has recently grown. According to the Gallup-Independent Sector survey completed in 1989, an estimated 98.4 million Americans, 54.4 percent of adults 18 or older, volunteer an average of four hours a week for a total of 20.5 billion hours a year—an increase of 23 percent in numbers over three years.

Several new developments are noteworthy. Attendance at religious services has recently increased. Involvement in religious groups is the most widespread form of community and civic action. Nearly eight out of ten Americans report attending religious services in the last year, with 53 percent attending at least once or twice a month. Participation in religious groups is strongly connected to other forms of volunteerism.

Over the past two decades, several innovative forms of community and civic involvement have emerged. Adapting the model of Alcoholics Anonymous, more than 200 groups dedicated to various forms of self-help now exist, ranging from Mothers Against Drunk Driving, with 600,000 members, to peer support groups of students concerned with drug use, battered women's support networks, and groups of those with emotional problems. An estimated 15 million citizens are active in self-help groups.

Related to such self-help activity is a movement concerned with community stability and revitalization. By the late 1970s, a *Christian Science Monitor* poll found a dramatic growth of neighborhood activity. Twenty million citizens belonged to some sort of neighborhood organization. Several million had taken direct action in support of their communities. Neighborhood and community groups take a variety of forms, from community organizations aimed at gaining a voice in public decision making to community-based health clinics and day-care centers, urban garden clubs, and crime watch projects. According to the National Congress for Community Economic Development, the number of community development groups involved in low-income housing and commercial improvements increased throughout the 1980s, from 200 in the mid-1970s to the 1,500-2,000 range by 1989.

B. **Specific forms of community and civic involvement.** The Independent Sector study highlighted the range and extent of voluntary action:

1. **Religious organizations.** Beyond attendance at religious services, 51.7 million adults volunteer in religion-related organizations, including churches, synagogues, monasteries, convents, and seminaries, not including church-affiliated schools, nursing homes, or religious charity organizations.

2. **Informal voluntary effort.** 46.5 million citizens say they are active informally and on an ad-hoc basis in community activities such as helping neighbors, caring for the elderly, or babysitting for others without pay.

3. **Educational groups.** Some 29.5 million citizens volunteer time to educational and instructional organizations, including elementary, secondary, and higher education schools—public or nonprofit; libraries; and adult education.

4. **Youth development efforts.** 28.6 million adults volunteer in organizations considered "youth development" such as 4-H Clubs; youth groups with religious affiliations; Boy and Girl Scouts and Camp Fire Groups; and athletic groups like Little League.

5. **Human Services.** 25.3 million adults regularly contribute time to direct service efforts such as the YMCA, YWCA; foster care; emergency preparedness; Red Cross; United Way; Catholic Charities; and the United Jewish Appeal. According to the Independent Sector division, this category also includes such advocacy efforts as consumer protection and work with housing and shelter issues.

6. **Health efforts.** Slightly more than 21.5 million citizens volunteer in the health field, broadly defined to include programs around substance abuse; nursing homes; clinics; crisis counselling; organizations for mental health and developmentally disabled; and fund drives of health associations like the American Cancer Society and the American Heart Association.

7. **Work-related organizations.** More than 15.7 million Americans are active in work-related groups, including labor unions, credit unions, professional associations, and business groups like the Chamber of Commerce.

8. **Advocacy and public betterment groups.** Almost 14 million citizens volunteer time to groups defined broadly as "public benefit," which include in the Independent Sector terms a wide range—community improvement, advocacy groups like women's and minority rights organizations, anti-poverty groups and the nuclear freeze movement.

9. **Arts projects.** Slightly more than 13 million adults are active in arts, culture, and humanities activities, including a range from performing arts organizations to cultural and ethnic awareness groups, historical preservation, museums, theater, and public television and radio.

10. **Environmental efforts.** Some 11.4 million people contribute their time to an array of groups dedicated to environmental protection and welfare; wildlife sanctuaries; and also animal-related groups like zoos and humane societies.

11. **Political groups**. About 8.9 million Americans donate their time each year to groups which are explicitly "political," including political parties, the League of Women Voters, and other political causes.

B. **Personal goals and motivations for community involvement**. Americans give a number of reasons for their community, civic, and voluntary involvements. Most commonly, 53 percent express the conviction that people should help those less fortunate. Citizens also describe the strong personal satisfactions they gain from voluntary effort; see voluntary involvements as a central way to express their religious beliefs and values; appreciate the opportunity afforded by civic effort to give back to society some of the benefits they have received; and see voluntary efforts as a way to serve as examples and role models.

Civic and community activities serve many purposes. Volunteers' main goals include interest in increasing opportunities for others; protecting the environment; and improving the cultural life of communities. Large numbers of citizens also express concerns that reflect older civic, republican, and democratic traditions. Thus, 47 percent voice the desire to help improve the moral foundations of the society; 45 percent of respondents say that teaching people to become more self-sufficient is a major concern; and 41 percent say they have a strong interest in helping organizations "that work at the grass roots level."

Such patterns provide foundations for our civic culture. Yet the declining political confidence noted by Alex Inkeles requires attention, because it is the key to understanding the apparent paradox between widespread involvement and political disaffection. In particular, the loss of political confidence is rooted in the erosion of citizens' sense of their voice and authority in a public world of large institutions and expert decision-making.

III. **The erosion of public life**. Traditions of public life continue in the 1990s. Yet Americans' sense of public life has also greatly weakened. Television "soundbites" replace serious debate of issues; single issue groups crowd out reformers with a larger view of the public interest. A number of trends, from mobility to "consumer culture," have eroded public life by narrowing people's experiences to the world immediately at hand. Especially, the increase in institutional scale and the rise of expert authority have severed links between community life and public affairs.

A. **The problem of scale**. Throughout the nineteenth century, small towns and the rural landscape provided the matrix for most people's lives from birth to death. In this context, the explosive growth in voluntary organizations contributed to a broadening definition of "citizenship" and public affairs. Democracy suggested New England town meetings, or informally, decision making in business and voluntary groups.

But the developments of the late nineteenth and early twentieth centuries radically changed the texture of political and social experience. In enormous cities, many scarcely knew their neighbors, much less those on the other side of the tracks. Waves of immigrants brought new customs, traditions, and languages. Mass communication technologies weakened the ties between the press and the citizenry, and shattered the boundaries of local places.

As political scientist William Schambra of the American Enterprise Institute has observed, the **locus** of civic involvement shifted from community activity to government itself. In the view of many Progressive reformers, citizens could more than compensate for their loss of immediate involvement through various public agencies and electoral reforms—regulations, direct election of senators, referenda and initiative, and the like—that would allow them to shape the "great community" of the state.

Yet the reality proved different. Aside from a new rising professional class, most Americans continued to identify with their locales, traditions, and cultures. But their worlds seemed increasingly shaped by distant forces over which they had little control. Corner grocers gave way to chain stores; local decisions over education were removed to state or national bureaucracies; local businesses were bought out by national or global corporations. The weakening of citizens' power and authority in the midst of large-scale institutions was accelerated, moreover, by the growing authority of specialists and experts.

B. **The rise of expert decision-making**. As large government agencies and corporate structures came to predominate, a new generation of managers and technical specialists developed who drew their basic metaphors and language from science. A "culture of professionalism" detached knowledge from local communities in field after field, emphasizing rationality, methodical processes, and standards of "objectivity," in place of public deliberation. "Old functions of child welfare and training have passed over into the hands of sociologists, psychiatrists, physicians, home economists and other scientists dealing with problems of human welfare," wrote two child guidance experts in 1934. "Through parent education the sum of their experiments and knowledge is given back to parents in response to the demands for help."

Today, experts tend to **define** and **diagnose** the problem, **generate** the language and labels for talking about it, **propose the therapeutic or remedial techniques** for problem solving, and **evaluate** whether the problem has been solved. There are few opportunities for citizens to learn the skills of action, deliberation, and evaluation through which ordinary people move to the center of politics, and experts are "on tap, not on top."

Thus, voluntary groups have lost many of their public dimensions. Their goals shifted from public deliberation and problem solving to service provision for clients. The local union moved from the center of community life to a marketing operation around a series of specific benefits. Teenage programs deemphasized citizenship and developed programs around self-esteem and career skills. The civic group's problem-solving functions weakened as it came to compete with the local racquetball club.

IV. **Patterns of contemporary politics**. As strong experiences of public deliberation and public action eroded, a sense of active citizenship also weakened. As a result, we have today several dominant forms of politics, understood as distinctive patterns and cultures of decision making and action on public issues. All tend to conceal the link between citizens' everyday lives and the larger public world.

A. **Institutional politics**. When people refer to politics, they usually mean institutional politics—politics as represented by elected officials and government. Institutional politics encompasses voting, participation in political parties, discussions of important issues in the style of the League of Women Voters, petitioning, letters to the editor and other ways of letting citizen viewpoints be known. Instruments of direct democracy also exist, such as initiative and referenda, recall, and official citizen advisory mechanisms. According to the Independent Sector study, 8.9 million Americans are involved in "political" organizations today, understood as groups focused on the electoral process.

But most forms of institutional politics are in trouble, plagued by the growing role of money in campaigns, trivialized discussion of issues, personal and divisive attacks, antagonism between officials and the citizenry, and declining participation and knowledge on the part of the electorate. All these problems, in turn, feed the perception that electoral politics make little difference. Even mechanisms of citizen access are often overwhelmed by special interests and manipulative processes. As *The New York Times* observed about California initiatives, for instance, "This citizen tool of government has become just another tool of well-financed interests [and] the growing accumulation of such initiative-passed laws has also tied the hands of the Governor and the Legislature because ballot measures often award set budget allocations to programs that cannot be trimmed in the budget process."

Resolving problems of chronic antagonism among policymakers, the public, and the media will take education that can articulate a different view of politics and the benefits of effective public collaboration. Such education requires a retrieval of older concepts of **public** itself, in electoral politics and in various forms of citizen activism.

B. **Service politics**. Service involvements are often justified as an important way to restore commitment to citizenship. This rationale, for instance, framed the new National Service Act enacted by Congress in 1990. Yet volunteer service, while important, in fact generates little sense of a deliberative public, public policy, or the power relations of the modern service world. In fact, people often do "service" as an explicit **alternative** to what they conceive of as "politics."

Service efforts focus on one-to-one helping transactions in a variety of settings, from nursing homes to shelters, from literacy efforts to counselling programs. Service language stresses personal growth, self-esteem and charity. It tends to slight issues of larger public policy. In extreme form, therapeutic language personalizes every public experience.

Thus, for instance, in high schools, community service curricula emphasize personal growth and development as the main point. One leading publication of the new service movement made an illustrative list of "learner outcomes" (as the current educational language puts it) involved in youth service, including "self-esteem," "a sense of personal worth," "self-understanding," "independence," "consciousness about one's personal values," "openness to new experiences," "capacity to persevere in difficult tasks," and the "exploration of new identities and unfamiliar roles." "Politics" was completely absent.

From television talk shows to Congress, public terms and concepts like accountability, respect for public contribution, negotiation, and recognition of honest difference have been replaced by intimacies. But personalized language makes very difficult any honesty about racial, ethnic, economic, or religious differences, or attention to questions of power, politics, and accountability for serious problem solving.

A politics of intimacy colors formal mechanisms for citizen involvement in government and generates skepticism about "citizen participation," "citizen advisory committees," or "parent input" into education. Patterns of citizen input are often political therapy—"allowing citizens to be heard;" "helping people feel involved." They can create ways to obtain the appearance of citizen involvement without the substance. The politics of intimacy, in turn, feeds a moralistic politics of protest.

C. **Protest politics**. The protests of the 1960s were effective in dramatizing crucial, unaddressed problems in the nation. Martin Luther King, Jr., electrified a national audience with his description of the "forces of light" in their nonviolent confrontation with the "forces of darkness." But King also stood in the tradition of reform-minded public that combines demand for rights and recognition with acknowledgement of civic responsibilities. Through the decade, as every issue became "good versus evil" this combination disappeared. Anti-draft card protestors, for instance, commonly disclaimed **any** obligation to the nation.

Advocacy, issue, and protest organizations involve millions of citizens, drawing attention to a range of pressing issues. But issues are often framed in highly moralized fashion. From prayer in the schools to abortion, garbage incinerators to AIDS, partisans tend to claim their own righteousness and portray their opponents as depraved.

Today countless groups in politics position themselves as righteous and aggrieved. Yet seeing controversies as the clash between innocents and moral monsters constricts the possibilities of any constructive engagement with one's opponents, since no listening or exchange of views can occur. As a strong sense of public life has disappeared, **hierarchies** based on degrees of "innocence" or suffering are created, with a competition often occurring among groups for the mantle of being the most oppressed. When this occurs, demands for rights fail to acknowledge the legitimate self-interests of others with conflicting claims, or to voice complementary responsibilities. In sum, protest

politics puts citizens on the **outside** of political society. The politics of protest can also color community politics.

D. **Community politics**. Community organizations, neighborhood newspapers, community development corporations, and neighborhood festivals and crime watch programs have all become regular features of the urban landscape in the last two decades. One 1989 study of 834 large community-based organizations (less than half the community development groups operating) estimated that they produced about 125,000 housing units—90% for low and moderate income families. They had repaired an additional 275,000 units and developed over 16 million square feet of commercial property in economically depressed areas in recent years. Support for such initiatives is clearly expanding: a 1989 study of foundation support showed an increase in giving to community-based groups of 54% over five years, now 61% of the amount of support for the arts.

This community-based movement, championed by political leaders across the spectrum has made significant contributions to citizen capacity-building. Yet community politics does not directly translate into a larger politics of public problem solving or awareness of civic obligation. Leadership is often dependent upon charisma. Community action is difficult in a time when people often do not know their neighbors; and participation in institutions of church and synagogue, family, school, and local business has declined. Further, community politics is characterized by a "Small Is Beautiful" view that often leaves unaddressed larger problems which shape communities from the outside: economic development, toxic wastes, the power of television. External threats can breed a "Not in My Backyard" mentality. Community politics may effectively address local issues. But neighborhood interests can hinder public problem solving. Citizens need ways to link their communities to the larger world.

Contemporary Perspective

What gets lost in institutional politics, and politics focused on service, protest, or community is the sense of public as agent in serious, large-scale problem solving and deliberation. It is just this understanding of the public as agent that teaches the moral ambiguity and open-ended, provisional quality involved in the pragmatic tasks of the public world, where the search is not for "truth" or final vindication but rather appropriateness, fit, agreement, adjudication, and provisional but sound resolution of concerns. A critical challenge is how to revive and strengthen this tradition.

I. **The tradition of citizen education for public problem solving.** A number of attempts have been made in the past to provide for public problem solving.

   A. **The Citizenship School tradition.** A foundation for a politics of civic problem solving can be found in the Citizenship Schools of the Highlander Center and the Southern Christian Leadership Conference, organized by Ella Baker, Septima Clark, and others. During the civil rights movement, Citizenship Schools, while registering voters, also taught thousands of local leaders new approaches to addressing issues in their communities. "Teachers" and "students" were peers. Methods drew directly on the stories and experiences of participants. The formal political process was connected to people's daily lives.

   B. **Recent examples of education for public life.** Since the 1960s, certain community organizing networks have added to this tradition through developing a larger concept of the meaning of politics as **public life**, a diverse, challenging arena in which citizens reclaim responsibility and develop the power, skills, and knowledge seriously to address public issues.

   These community groups call themselves "universities for public life, where people learn the arts of public discourse and public action." Ed Chambers, director of Industrial Areas Foundation (IAF) network describes the shift toward political education as the major development in the network's fifty-year history. "We began to see every action as an opportunity for education and training," said Maribeth Larkin, an organizer with the IAF group, United Neighborhoods Organization, in Los Angeles.

   Such education results in a pragmatic rendering of the theme of "commonwealth." Classically, community organizing opposed any language of the common good. Yet IAF groups and others redefine "commonwealth" by changing the static idea of the common good into a dynamic, practical notion. In IAF terms, the commons, or basic public goods, cannot exist outside of politics. They are those larger public concerns affecting many communities and neighborhoods, like schools, roads, parks, the local economy and so forth, that politics identifies as occasions for pragmatic civic collaboration. Developing such collaboration means the shift from "protest to participation in governance," in the words of IAF staff member Gerald Taylor.

II. **Conceptual resources for connecting community and public.** Several concepts are helpful resources for strengthening the ties between community and political society:

   A. **Enlarged self-interest.** Effective education for citizen politics draws on participants' experiences, passions, and particular interests. It also reframes self-interest to highlight the **links** of individuals to the larger world and the **rationales for public relationships** with those whom one might well not "like" or agree with on many issues but who one recognizes have important contributions to make, nonetheless.

   B. **Free spaces.** Education in citizen politics depends upon people's sense of "ownership" of their action. This means the possibility of "free public spaces," independent associations and meeting grounds through which groups can develop their distinctive agendas, experiment with their own ideas, and develop their own sense of stake and initiative in public problem solving, reflecting their capacities.

   C. **Relational power.** Education in citizen politics entails teaching a different view of "power," not as a zero-sum resource (someone has it, someone does not) but rather as a dynamic and interactive set of relations. This understanding of power is especially important and useful in reestablishing citizen authority in the "information age," where all affected by public problems—not simply experts—have some legitimate contribution to the problem solving process. Understanding relational power means the ability to map the power relations (e.g., specialized knowledge and expertise, community know-how, political and economic power) as a precondition for effective action, not as static obstacles.

   D. **Relational politics.** Citizen politics is built on a "relational," interactive quality of public life that highlights the need for cultivation of ongoing public relationships among parties who have long-term overlapping interests or concerns in common. Relational politics generates respect for diversity, the ability to deal with conflict, and the skills of negotiation, compromise, bargaining, holding others and oneself accountable, and learning to understand their views.

   E. **Shared credit.** Citizen politics entails learning effective ways for diverse groups appropriately to share recognition and credit for their contributions to public projects.

F. **Public life as different from private life**. Finally, a conceptual framework that shows both the distinctions and the connections between public and private life proves a valuable resource for developing the skills of effective work with others beyond one's private life and community. In a fashion analogous to the legal distinction between substantive and procedural issues, this framework recognizes that personal concerns are relevant to public affairs, but how one acts upon them needs to vary with different settings. Public life is a realm of difference, public work, accountability, respect and recognition, negotiation and bargaining; private life is an arena of intimacy, spontaneity, similarity, and loyalty. There is nothing completely "either-or" about such distinctions—private life always has public dimensions; public life has personal elements; and there is an overlapping realm in between that can be seen as the "community" setting, where it takes thought to distinguish what is appropriate. This can be represented graphically by the following:

Private	Community	Public
family/friends	clubs/religious/ community groups, etc.	large institutions, public projects
loyalty	covenant relations	accountability
similarity	familarity	difference
intimacy/love	friendship	recognition/ respect
spontaneity	task orientation	strategic action
personal power	community power	public power

III. **Toward a problem-solving public**. In a problem-solving public, there are few saints or sinners but rather an interplay among a variety of interests, values, and perspectives. Knowledge is not simply divided between categories like "objective" and analytic or "subjective" and emotional. Different ways of knowing are valued because they are of practical **use**, in just the sense suggested by the fable of the six blind men surrounding an elephant who only know "the reality" by pooling their knowledge. In a public sphere of actors as well as helpers or protestors, no one is simply victim or innocent; all create public life. The development of some agreement about ethical standards for public life becomes essential. Everyone bears a measure of responsibility.

A. **Developing civic judgment**. Groups like the League of Women Voters or the Kettering Foundation's National Issues Forums have experimented with a variety of ways to develop citizen **judgment,** instead of simple **opinion**. Judgment is the larger perspective on issues that looks upon policy questions from a number of sides. It is longer range and more multi-dimensional than the views captured in opinion polls. There are now 1,500 forums, ranging from community college to business group, prisoner discussion to neighborhood.

B. **Measuring civic capacity**. The venerable National Civic League similarly focuses on ways to build "citizen democracy," a politics of citizen action and discussion in local communities. The League has a "civic index" that evaluates cities according to criteria like voluntary effort, the openness of government, and the vitality of citizen participation.

C. **Teaching politics to youth.** Several recent youth initiatives have moved from personal-service focus to concern for effective action around major public issues. On college campuses, the network of 600 service projects, Campus Outreach Opportunity League, has begun to make this a central theme, sponsoring an annual week of activities to highlight student contributions to resolution of social problems.

Similarly, Project Public Life at the University of Minnesota's Humphrey Institute of Public Affairs has shown how the concepts and skills of public life can be used to develop public leadership and reengage teens, young adults and others in politics, in settings as diverse as high schools, 4-H clubs, nursing homes and low income communities. The Project's Public Achievement, for instance, undertaken with the St. Paul city government and Minnesota 4-H, has found that teens today have great interest in problem-solving politics in which they design their own projects.

Such efforts suggest approaches for civic education that combine learning with substantial civic action to address major public issues. The key to such a process rests upon recognition that citizens are not simply objects of history but rather historical actors, whose everyday lives are imbued with larger public meanings and possibilities.

TOPIC 5. PARTICIPATORY WRITING

Writing conveys and records innovation, dissent, and criticism; above all, it can give access to political mechanisms and the political process generally where many of the possibilities for personal and social transformation lie.

Kenneth Levine (1983)

On several occasions, a single, thoughtful, factually persuasive letter did change my mind or cause me to initiate a review of a previous judgement.

Morris K. Udall (1967)

At first glance, civic literacy seems to refer only to a citizen's ability to read what is necessary for informed voting. But the ability to convey in writing one's ideas on matters relating to public life is equally critical for the proper functioning of democratic self-government. Participatory writing—the writing that citizens do as part of the process of democratic self-government—is, in fact, a necessary and inseparable component of democratic self-government.

There are a variety of forms of participatory writing. They include such formal writing for organizations as minutes of meetings, agendas, memos, and newsletters, as well as such formal writing as petitions, resolutions, and prepared speeches. Civic writing also includes a great deal of informal and personal writing, often in the form of letters—to friends, neighbors, public officials, and even to persons unknown. While some kinds of participatory writing can be identified by their forms, many others can be identified only by their purposes and the contexts of their use.

Participatory civic writing has a variety of purposes. One purpose of this writing is to persuade others of a particular point of view on a public matter, a familiar form of which is a "letter to the editor." However, there are a number of other purposes of civic writing that citizens need to be aware of to understand better the role their own writing can play in maintaining democratic institutions and in promoting the public good.

OBJECTIVES

The citizen should be able to

1. write lucid, engaging English on areas of concern to civic participation.

2. write critiques of political tracts, programs, and ideas for purposes of political participation.

3. explain why citizens in a republican form of self-government need to be able to write as well as to read.

4. explain the different purposes for which citizens may write or may need to write in a republican form of self-government.

5. recognize and discuss some of the most basic or most frequently used forms for participatory writing.

6. explain why freedom to write for these purposes and forms of writing used to further these purposes must be protected.

Conceptual Perspective

I. **Using writing to affirm relationships, obtain information or assistance, provide information or offer service.** A number of purposes for civic writing can be identified.

A. **Personalizing civic relationships and/or expressing civic identity.** Some kinds of civic writing affirm common civic identity with other citizens or officials.

1. **Writing that affirms civic identity with other citizens.** Citizens may write to personalize civic relationships in letters to private citizens whom they do not know. For example, in 1981 some citizens wrote welcome-home letters to former Iranian hostages. Others have written letters of sympathy to those affected after public tragedies, such as after the assassinations of President Kennedy and his brother Robert Kennedy. These expressions of welcome or sympathy are an affirmation of the bonds of citizenship, motivated by the perception of a civic identity or a sense of shared membership in a national civic community.

2. **Writing that affirms civic relations with public officials.** Citizens may write to public officials to put forward their ideas or analyses of public affairs or to express gratitude, sympathy, or other concerns. For example, they may thank a public official for assistance, congratulate a successful candidate for public office, or console a defeated candidate.

B. **Obtaining information or assistance**. Other purposes of writing are to acquire information or gain assistance from either private citizens or public officials.

1. **Writing to other citizens**. Citizens may need information or help from other citizens for a variety of reasons. For example, members of civic or political organizations often send out questionnaires to gather information for a voters' guide or to survey public opinion on an issue of concern to a particular community. Citizens, individually or as a group, often communicate to other citizens through the media seeking information or help, for example, to request information about a missing relative or to locate volunteers for an individual medical need, such as a particular type of blood.

2. **Writing to public officials**. Citizens may request a service for themselves or write on behalf of others. A pattern of requests for a particular service may alert legislators or other public officials to the need for new legislation or changes in administrative procedures.

C. **Providing public information or offering a public service**. Other purposes of civic writing are to provide information or to offer a service.

1. **Informing other citizens**. Citizens who are members of organized groups—ranging from legally-mandated citizen committees, such as school or library boards, to volunteer organizations, such as parent-teacher, neighborhood, taxpayer, or other civic associations—frequently provide information to other citizens or to serve their organizations.

   a. **Information about public issues**. Certain publications of the League of Women Voters provide examples of informative writing directed to other citizens. For example, the League regularly publishes guides to inform voters of issues in forthcoming elections. Also, PTAs often produce handbooks describing a community's schools.

   b. **Writings for civic organizations**. Members of a variety of civic organizations write memorandums, activity schedules, minutes, newsletters, agendas, and similar documents. Written records kept by members are vital for maintaining the continuity and democratic character of civic organizations.

2. **Volunteering service**. Citizens may write to public officials to volunteer their services as aides in libraries, schools, or hospitals—institutions that have long welcomed volunteers. People also write to volunteer talks in schools or other public institutes to advise others about problems they have overcome, such as alcoholism, drug addiction, or smoking.

II. **Using writing to evaluate and advocate**. Further kinds of civic writing include evaluative and advocacy writing.

A. **Evaluating public services, political structures, or the performance of officials**. Citizens are frequently called upon to write evaluations of public programs, services, or personnel. These evaluations may be formal or informal.

1. **Formal evaluation**. Members of school boards, library boards, health boards, and many other citizen boards are regularly required to assess the performance of professional administrators. Citizens are also often appointed or elected to evaluate a public service or political structure (e.g., public safety or crime control) to assist legislators or administrators in improving public services.

   a. **Committee evaluation reports**. Evaluations usually contain recommendations for general policies or specific actions as well as information. People appointed to gather information about the functioning of a service or individual—or to determine the need for a service—are expected to proceed impartially.

   b. **Purposes of evaluation reports**. Evaluations of public services, laws, professional persons, or officials are intended to ensure that the intention of voters is adhered to, that public funds are being spent efficiently, and that the common good is being promoted.

2. **Informal evaluation**. Citizens informally evaluate public services or officials in several ways. They may write, as individuals or as groups, to praise or blame services or individuals. Such writings may be sent directly to officials or public bodies, or they may be expressed indirectly through newspapers or other publications. Patterns of complaints can alert officials—or the public at large—to deficiencies.

B. **Advocating positions on public issues, organizations, or individuals.** Advocacy writing is indispensable for protecting political rights in a democracy and for promoting the common good. The purposes of such writing can be clustered around five distinct types of political activities:

1. **Soliciting support for a civic or political organization.** As de Tocqueville noted in the 1830s, Americans frequently form voluntary associations. These associations often serve as "mediating structures" between individual citizens and the wider society, and assist in knowledgeable participation in social, economic, and political life. Interests of many citizens are often advanced more effectively by an organized group than by solitary efforts. Much of the participatory writing in which the members of these associations engage focuses on recruiting new members or soliciting funds from their members or the public at large.

2. **Supporting or opposing public officials or candidates.** Writings may support or oppose individuals such as officials or candidates for office.

   a. **Supporting or opposing candidates for public office.** The bulk of the participatory writing citizens do for candidates for public office takes place at the local level. Large numbers of citizens write letters, postcards, and publicity releases; many design posters and advertisements that urge others to support candidates for the thousands of local public offices. At the national and state levels, most advocacy writing of this sort is now composed by paid professional staff.

   b. **Supporting or opposing public officials in a controversy.** Citizens may write to other citizens directly, to the media, or to other public officials to support or oppose a public official in a controversy.

   c. **Removing public officials from office.** Citizens may seek removal of a public official by bringing their complaints in writing to higher officials or by bringing their complaints directly to the voters through a recall petition. At least thirty-one states allow recall in some form.

3. **Supporting, opposing, or modifying existing or proposed laws or policies.** The ability of citizens to make or influence the making of law, directly or indirectly, lies at the heart of the democratic form of government. Their ability to do so indirectly is most often reflected in personal contacts, telephone calls, and written communications that try to influence others on matters of public policy.

   a. **Writing to fellow citizens.** Citizens may write to other citizens, urging them to support, modify, or oppose a proposed or existing law or administrative policy or to support or oppose policy positions of public officials. They may also write to other citizens to point out a problem they have identified and to recommend a particular solution.

   b. **Contacts with media.** Citizens may write to the media, such as letters to the editor, for these purposes.

   c. **Contacts with legislators or other public officials.** Citizens may write to legislators or other public officials for advocacy purposes. In several states, they can also compose public policy petitions and place them on the ballot in certain elections to register voter opinion.

4. **Creating or removing laws.** In some states citizens can directly or indirectly create laws. While professionals, usually attorneys, generally write the final form of proposed laws, civic writing by ordinary citizens can substantially contribute to the formulation and advocacy of such measures.

   a. **Directly creating laws—the initiative.** In this country, citizens may directly create law through the initiative process.

      (1) **At the state level.** Drawing upon traditions of democratic literacy, South Dakota in 1898 became the first state to allow private citizens to propose laws to be submitted for popular approval. As of 1984, citizens in twenty-one states are allowed to place proposed laws on a state ballot by means of an initiative petition. The number of successful citizen initiatives on the ballot increased from ten in 1968 to sixty in 1982.

(2) **At the local level.** Although provisions for local initiatives vary widely from state to state, citizens can also propose a law directly by means of an initiative petition at the local level in certain cities, counties, or other governmental units in all fifty states and the District of Columbia.

b. **Indirectly creating laws.** People can propose laws indirectly through their representatives at any level of government. In most cases, their representatives can decide whether or not to sponsor the proposed bill. In Massachusetts, state representatives are obligated to file a bill proposed by a constituent so long as it does not violate or replicate existing state law; this is known as the right of free petition.

c. **Directly removing laws—referendums.** Civic writing is also involved in initiating and advocating referendums. As of 1984, citizens in twenty-four states could directly seek recall of an existing state law through referendums.

d. **Proposing laws with symbolic value.** Citizens often propose laws about public issues that have a purely symbolic value but which can be powerful means of influencing public opinion and making public statements. Civic writing is directly involved in their formulation and advocacy.

(1) **Resolutions.** Resolutions at local and state levels can be proposed about a variety of concerns, including national and foreign policy issues.

(2) **Symbols.** Citizens may propose laws to create local, state, or national symbols or to establish special days for celebration. At the local government level, citizens may propose laws to honor or commemorate the name of a prominent citizen or national hero on a building or street sign.

5. **Advocating new political structures or procedural rules.** The most fundamental purpose for which citizens in a republican form of government may write is to devise the very structures and procedures that shape their participation in the governance of their society. The text they propose for their political community may be called a constitution or a charter.

a. **Civic or political organizations.** The opportunity to write or revise a constitution or charter arises frequently in civic or political organizations.

b. **Local government.** Constitution writing frequently takes place at the local or county level. In Massachusetts alone, as of 1982, forty-seven communities have elected charter commissions and adopted charters. Localities in other parts of the country offer other opportunities for proposing and adopting changes in government structures.

c. **State government.** Citizens in many states have the right to propose amendments to their state constitutions and to engage in a wide variety of civic writing in the proposal and advocacy of such changes. Since the turn of the twentieth century, twenty-three states have amended their state constitutions to permit citizens to propose state constitutional amendments.

d. **Altering the Constitution of the United States.** Although citizens cannot directly propose amendments to the Constitution of the United States, an enormous amount of civic writing underlies proposals for amendment. This writing occurs in pamphlets, articles, broadsides, petitions, books, and other forms.

Historical Perspective

I. **Significance of participatory writing in the development of democratic institutions.** Throughout history, people have often sought help from their rulers to deal with their grievances against local officials or others who they believed had dealt unfairly with them. In small countries, people often related their complaints orally directly to their rulers. Where distance prohibited a personal appearance, the grievance was frequently sent in the form of a written petition and presented at court by an intermediary.

A. **Parliamentary petitions in medieval England.** In medieval England, petitions to the Crown began to be presented at meetings of Parliament as well as at court. Although an origin of Parliament was to pass upon the Crown's request for taxes, the regular presentation of petitions in Parliament gradually led to members of Parliament themselves becoming the vehicle for their constituents' petitions to the Crown.

B. **The long-range effects of petitioning.** The petition, whether written by a paid scribe or other educated person, or by the citizen himself, soon came to serve the local poor as well as the gentry and townspeople. In this way, members of Parliament ultimately became the "collective voice for the needs of their local communities," as a British scholar, J.R. Maddicott, observed. Thus did the practice of presenting petitions to the Crown at meetings of Parliament influence the development of the House of Commons.

C. **Pamphlets and politics in civil-war England.** The first appearance of public opinion as a political force in the modern world occurred in seventeenth century England during the Civil War period. This took the form of pamphlets, thousands of which were published. Thus, in this form, wide-spread writing for civic concerns became a more common form of expression, instead of the exclusive province of a handful of the educated.

D. **Civic writing in America.** Civic writing became a developed form of communication in prerevolutionary America and continued its development in myriad forms long afterward. A few examples are the following:

1. **Writing on political issues before the revolution.** As pamphleteering was a force in the English Civil War, so also pamphlets and other forms of civic writing played a key role in the developing quarrel with the British colonial government and its slide into political rupture. Voluminous pamphlets, circular letters, and protests, such as those drafted by **Samuel Adams** (1722-1803), argued every shade of opinion and were at the core of the communication of political views that preceded the outbreak of revolutionary violence in 1775. *Common Sense*, written in 1776 by **Thomas Paine** (1737-1809), was perhaps the single most successful pamphlet of the time; and the Declaration of Independence might be thought of as the culmination of political writing during this period.

2. **Political writing and the ratification of the Constitution.** The framing of the Constitution in 1787 began an especially fruitful period of political writing. The controversy over ratification of the Constitution occasioned an enormous outpouring of political views in a steady stream of pamphlets and other writings, for and against. The publication of *The Federalist* as newspaper articles (1787-1788) and then as a volume of its own (1788), written by Hamilton, Madison, and Jay, became the most lasting contribution of this immense literature.

3. **Civic writing in the nineteenth century.** In the next century, civic writing in a vast range of forms became a staple of American democracy. Not limited to an educated elite but practiced by ordinary men and women, this writing delved into public issues such as slavery, the rights of women, the course of the Civil War, and innumerable other subjects. It appeared as pamphlets, letters, newspaper and magazine articles, petitions, and numerous other forms.

4. **Civic writing in the twentieth century.** One form of civic writing that developed substantially in the twentieth century was letters from citizens to elected officials. According to studies of political letter writing, constituent writing to political leaders has been increasing at an unprecedented rate since the turn of the century. As the level of literacy of the general population rose, so too did the number of communications sent by citizens to public officials. The presidency of Franklin D. Roosevelt (1933-1945) witnessed a dramatic increase in constituent writing to both the president and Congress. In 1984 the House of Representatives alone received 200 million pieces of constituent mail and the Senate another 41.5 million pieces, a five-fold increase in just twelve years. This phenomenal growth suggest that, despite the revolution in communications technology, Americans believe that participatory writing matters.

II. **Role of civic literacy in maintaining democratic institutions.** With few exceptions, literacy has been a necessary condition for the development and preservation of democratic institutions.

A. **Views of the importance of literacy in classical democratic theory.** Thinkers such as Thomas Jefferson and **John Stuart Mill** (1806-1873) believed that a democratic government could not survive without an educated people. That is why Jefferson supported free universal education at the elementary school level. To

Jefferson, the civic mission of the public schools was as important as their intellectual purposes.

B. **Education a necessary but not sufficient condition.** Twentieth century history teaches that a high degree of literacy does not guarantee a democratic society. The populace of Nazi Germany, for instance, was highly literate. However, literacy is associated with the existence and stability of democratic societies and appears to be a supporting condition for democratic self-government. According to recent international studies, democratic modes of participation seem to require an educated citizenry, regardless of cultural differences from country to country.

C. **Civic writing and constitutional documents.** Although written codes of law existed in many city-states in ancient Greece, the writing of complete constitutions by groups of citizens seems to be a fairly recent historical phenomenon. The state of Connecticut, to cite an American example, calls itself the Constitution State because the colony of Connecticut, under the leadership of **Thomas Hooker** (1586-1646), created and adopted in 1639 what is considered the first written constitution in the world. This constitution was superseded in later centuries by others, and today the Commonwealth of Massachusetts claims to have the oldest functioning state constitution in the country, written principally by **John Adams** (1735-1826) in 1780.

Contemporary Perspective

I. **The values participatory writing should reflect.** In order to promote genuine public discourse in a pluralist society, participatory writing should reflect both civic and liberal values. These values include independent thinking, honesty, fairness, willingness to seek out and consider all relevant information on controversial issues, tolerance of opposing views, responsibility for one's own thinking and behavior, respect for moral and civil law, concern for the common good, and respect for others as unique individuals rather than as representative members of groups.

II. **The role of writing in maintaining democratic institutions.** Both franchised and soon-to-be-franchised citizens need to be able to participate as writers in the civic process if they are to perform what R. Freeman Butts calls their "essential public, civic function." A contemporary incident in Brookline, Massachusetts illustrates the continuing importance of such forms of participatory writing as the petition and the minority report.

A. **A student petition.** In 1989, the Brookline School Committee voted to drop Advanced Placement European History from its course offerings at Brookline High School, even though the course was highly popular with students. Members of the administration and most members of the social studies faculty had argued that the course was no longer compatible with a "multicultural" curriculum. In the fall of 1990, a large group of students petitioned to have the course reinstated and were supported by a legal ruling of the State Department of Education. At a hearing in December, 1990, the School Committee listened to the petitioners' arguments and voted to reinstate the course.

B. **A minority report.** The teacher of the Advanced Placement European History course wrote a minority report to be included with a report written by the majority of the social studies faculty for a visiting high school reaccreditation team. The minority report presents a dissenting view of the strengths and weaknesses of the department's course offerings. The preservation of freedom of speech and the education of the general public often require that such minority reports be included with majority reports and receive wide publicity.

TOPIC 6. METHODS OF INSTRUCTION FOR PARTICIPATION

Conventional classroom activities such as reading, writing, and discussion, with the teacher as the major source of knowledge, can advance many of the goals of civic education. But if civic education is to place high priority on student competence in monitoring and influencing of public policy, it must also must depart in significant ways from conventional teaching. The main challenge is to provide experiences in which students not only learn about, but actually practice the monitoring and influencing of public policy. Without experience and practice in the classroom, the school, and in the world beyond the classroom, the study of participation is largely an academic exercise with no direct transfer to actual civic and political life.

To indicate ways of broadening the repertoire of learning experiences, we describe here a variety of activities needed to supplement more conventional classroom instruction. Many of the activities below place students in the active roles of finding and constructing knowledge, rather than memorizing what others have found and constructed for them, and of trying to exert influence in the world, rather than simply trying to understand how the world functions. Activities of this sort are essential to develop the capacities to monitor and influence public affairs.

Realizing that students of different ages and backgrounds have different interests and capabilities and that very few students can plunge successfully into the actual adult roles of lobbyist, legislator, or chief executive, it is important to regard participatory learning experiences in a developmental sense. In the initial stages, students may learn from activities that seem quite distant from typical forms of adult monitoring and influencing. As they develop greater interest and competence in comprehending complex policy issues, learning activities should change accordingly. Youngsters in elementary grades, for example, may attempt to set up fair rules for judicial proceedings dealing with discipline issues within the class. In contrast, high school seniors might actually attempt to bring about specific reforms in the juvenile justice system.

Many of the activities mentioned below, if considered in isolation from others, have only an indirect connection to students exerting actual influence on public policy in city halls, state houses, or the federal capitol. The mission of a complete civic education framework, however, is to organize activities of this sort so that they complement one another and, in concert with more formal instructional work, they constitute a developmental sequence which eventually enhances student competence to monitor and influence public policy in diverse arenas.

Study of exemplary citizens. Through biography and historical accounts of exemplary citizens, students can learn much about the process of trying to work for the public good. Beyond notable advocates and well-known political leaders, the study of "ordinary" citizens who have contributed to the public good is also important. While great and famous citizens can offer examples of coping with difficult major issues and can inspire students, their achievements can also be daunting to the "average" person, and so it is critical also to learn about the less heroic, behind the scenes, day-to-day efforts of those who labor outside the limelight but who nevertheless manage to "make a difference."

Participation in school governance. Student participation in the governance of the school can also offer a useful laboratory for the development of competence in monitoring and influencing policy. The governing role differs substantially from running for election or supporting candidates, and it can be exercised by participation in advisory committees, student courts, student legislative bodies, student town meetings, student representation on school boards. When students are given the opportunity to have a voice on such matters as school rules and disciplinary procedures, student participation can contribute to the development of civic efficacy.

Observations and interviews with active citizens. Major sources for community research are the adults who work in the processes of governing, maintaining the body politic, and attempting to influence public policy. Most of these people have not been written about, but they all have stories to tell which can help inform students of the accomplishments, frustrations, and the qualities needed for competent monitoring and influencing of policy. Student observation and interviews can be focused on the study of specific policy issues (e.g. child care), processes (e.g. how to obtain sponsors for a legislative bill), or general views on the opportunities for meaningful civic participation. Observations and interviews can be used as basic data for other activities such as developing positions on issues, completing community research projects, locating opportunities for community service, guiding one's electoral participation, and conducting action projects.

Community service. Student volunteer work in hospitals, nursing homes, day care centers, neighborhood organizations, other social service agencies and public offices provides concrete, real-life experience with the human side of some of the issues that policy must confront. Usually students gain a sense of personal satisfaction and increased competence working one-on-one to help others. If such experience is used as a basis for student reflection on policy issues dealing with quality of life, equity, and efficient service delivery, it can help to ignite student interest in monitoring and influencing policy, and in some cases this experience might provide a focus for further community research and public action.

Electoral participation. Students can run for office in organizations both in and outside of school, and they can work for the election of other students or adults. To be meaningful, electoral participation must go beyond completion of routine work such as addressing envelopes or conducting telephone polls. In addition, there must be occasions that challenge students to reflect carefully on issues of policy and strategy and to test their ideas in conversation with others.

Model government and simulation projects. Activities such as model United Nations, mock-trials, or simulations on diplomacy, passing legislation, or operating administrative agencies all place students in decision-making roles comparable to adult roles of public citizenship. If well-designed, these activities can realistically approximate the conditions and constraints that citizens and public officials face. Student preparation and participation in these activities can therefore contribute substantially to the knowledge, skills and dispositions needed for effective monitoring and influencing.

Public speaking, position papers, and debates on policy issues. Writing position papers and conducting debates on policy issues offer fertile opportunities for moral deliberation and for building in-depth knowledge on issues. Developing one's views on the issues is the basic step in monitoring policy. Trying to convey this persuasively to others is a critical step in exerting influence. Thus, public speaking is a key skill in myriad avenues of civic life. Students should be encouraged to cultivate this ability, including extemporaneously speaking to a variety of audiences.

Community research. Through original studies in their own communities and neighborhoods, students can acquire important information and skills relevant to monitoring and influencing policy. They can function as investigative journalists trying to get behind superficial news. They can gather information on citizens' attitudes and perceptions, on prices, accidents, taxes, living conditions, pollution, the quality of social services. They can collect oral histories and develop biographies of residents who have made interesting contributions. The results of such research can be made public through newspapers, talk shows, videos, special publications, and it can be used to influence policy through electoral politics or direct action.

Action projects. Electoral participation concentrates primarily on the selection of governmental leaders and representatives, but action projects attempt to influence policy more directly. Such projects might focus on new laws related to recycling or environmental protection, reducing government waste, welfare reform, or providing more efficient civic services—across a broad range of the political spectrum. Students can design their own group projects, and they can join forces as volunteers with existing advocacy organizations. Action projects provide a direct opportunities to monitor and influence public policy, and they can be the most challenging in terms of the amount of knowledge, skills, time, and perseverance required for success. In this sense, action projects can be considered powerful "dress rehearsals" for participation as an adult citizen.

PART THREE. CIVIC KNOWLEDGE AND SKILLS

THE NATURE OF POLITICS AND GOVERNMENT

POLITICS AND GOVERNMENT IN THE UNITED STATES

PART THREE: CIVIC KNOWLEDGE AND SKILLS

INTRODUCTORY NOTE

The Civic Knowledge section of the CIVITAS Framework that follows consists of summaries, by specialists in their respective fields, of what the specialists believe people should ideally know in order to be effective as citizens. These summaries outline what concepts citizens should be familiar with (the "conceptual perspective"); what historical knowledge they should have (the "historical perspective"); and how this knowledge may be brought to bear on the issues of society today (the "contemporary perspective").

Please note that CIVITAS has not attempted to include technical or scientific knowledge that might be relevant for the issues confronting citizens today. Such material would be both too voluminous in an already large document and much of it would be beyond the competence of the audience of the Framework to use profitably. Its accuracy would also be subject to swift alteration and therefore of limited usefulness.

Clearly the material of the Knowledge section extends far beyond what any student—or any adult—can be expected to comprehend. The material serves instead as a resource as well as a model to be emulated for those consulting the Framework.

The CIVITAS Framework is informed by the idea that rather than knowing the wealth of detail found in the large body of material that follows, citizens, to be civically literate in today's world should be familiar with the key elements in each of the topics selected for treatment.

THE NATURE OF POLITICS AND GOVERNMENT

TOPIC 1. POLITICAL AUTHORITY

It was from America that...ideas long locked in the breast of solitary thinkers, and hidden among Latin folios—burst forth like a conqueror upon the world...and the principle gained ground, that a nation can never abandon its fate to an authority it cannot control.

Lord Acton (1907)

As an essential basis for understanding the nature of politics and government the citizen should understand the nature of political authority, differing positions on the sources of its legitimacy, the difference between the legitimate use of authority and the use of power without authority, the history of the evolution of political authority, and contemporary events and issues related to authority.

OBJECTIVES

The citizen should be able to

1. discriminate between the exercise of political authority and the use of power without authority.

2. take and justify (or evaluate) positions on proper sources of authority and whether the exercise of authority is legitimate.

3. explain the significance of limitations on authority.

4. explain why consent is the basis of legitimate authority in a democratic political system.

5. distinguish between different forms of consent and explain the circumstances under which each form occurs.

6. explain the history of the idea that the self-determination of a people (freedom from external domination) is necessary to legitimize the authority of its government.

7. take, defend, and evaluate positions on the proper scope and limits of authority.

FRAME OF REFERENCE
Conceptual Perspective

I. **Political power and authority**. Power and authority are to be distinguished from each other.

   A. **Power.** Political power is the **capacity** to control, direct, or exert influence over something or someone, whether or not there is a right to do so.

   B. **Authority**. Political authority is the legitimized and institutionalized **right** to exercise power, whether or not adequate means are available to carry out what those in authority decide. Some of the basic characteristics of political authority with which citizens should be familiar are the following:

      1. **Legitimacy**. Legitimacy consists of the belief among the governed that the government has the right to claim and exercise its political powers.

      2. **Stability**. The idea of political authority usually implies that it continues over an extended period of time. Authority tends to disintegrate when it is changed with great frequency.

      3. **Limitations.** Constitutional governments are those in which the exercise of political authority is limited by law. These limits are enforced or strengthened by institutional arrangements such as checks and balances.

II. **Sources of political authority**. Historically the most frequently encountered positions taken on the sources from which political authority derives its legitimacy are as follows:

   A. **A supreme being**. Rulers have claimed that their authority is derived from a supreme being. Such rulers may include prophets and other religious figures as well as monarchs claiming a divine mandate for their authority, such as those in seventeenth century Europe who espoused the divine right of kings.

   B. **Birth**. Rulers have claimed their authority as a right of birth, usually rooted in an original divine mandate, passed on through generations by inheritance and sanctioned by tradition. Such rulers include hereditary monarchies and aristocracies.

   C. **Knowledge**. Rulers have claimed that their authority was based upon superior knowledge which was thought to legitimize their authority. Plato, in his conception of the ideal state, made this claim in his Republic, where a form of knowledge underlay the authority of the philosopher-king. According to traditional Marxist-Leninist theory, the Communist party ought to rule because only those with a correct understanding of the laws of history can properly guide society to the next stage of historical development.

D. **Consent of the governed.** Governments have claimed that their authority to exercise power is derived from the consent of the governed. Two forms of consent can be identified.

   1. **Express consent.** Express consent is explicitly stated consent; it consists of overt action that is either generally thought to be an act of consent, such as taking an oath of allegiance, or can be reasonably interpreted as an act of consent, such as voting in free elections. Express consent has often been given through elections such as in elective kingship, plebiscites, direct democracy, and constitutional democracy.

   2. **Tacit consent.** Tacit consent is implicit rather than explicit consent. It is reflected by an unarticulated acceptance of political arrangements or policies such as the compliance of non-voters with government regulations. This does not mean that all lack of opposition to government policies or actions implies tacit consent.

Historical Perspective

I. **Authority in pre-political societies.** Forms of authority have existed in the earliest known societies.

   A. **Hunting and gathering societies.** For thousands of years, authority in small-scale societies of hunters and gatherers flowed from those stronger, older, or wiser members of the kinship group who claimed the ability to guide the group and make rules for its protection and welfare. When means were devised to produce food by settling into more permanent agricultural communities or organizing roving pastoral communities for herding animals, arrangements for exerting authority became more complex.

   B. **Farming and pastoral societies.** Sometimes called neolithic or folk societies, these intimate groups of people were relatively isolated from contact with other groups.

   1. **Institutions not specialized.** These people lived under unspecialized social institutions based largely on the web of kinship relationships woven by family, clan, and tribal ties. Using oral communication and lacking systematic bodies of written knowledge, the functions of authority, social control, economic activity, religious ritual, and education were not often assigned to specialized institutions.

   2. **Few signs of political institutions.** There were few signs of formal political institutions like full-time rulers, legislators, judges, armies, police, or officials.

   3. **Custom rather than law controlled conduct.** A continuing deliberative or legislative body was seldom typical. A headman, chief, or council of elders performed the authoritative functions of making and applying rules as well as judging and punishing infractions. Controls were usually deeply ingrained customs and obligations learned informally in daily life with family and kinfolk.

   4. **Stability.** There was little deliberate effort to modify or change rules. Political functions in a folk society were diffuse, undifferentiated, and intermittent. Face-to-face primary relationships dominated these generally homogeneous societies. Status in the kinship hierarchy determined one's obligations and prerogatives. Rights and responsibilities were ascribed according to the status and role.

   5. **Authorities.** Nevertheless, in some folk societies, certain persons came to be recognized as having particular authority in the forming of customs and ideals. Elders, medicine men, seers, or storytellers were a kind of priestly or teaching class. Sometimes training in special skills or knowledge was required for preserving and passing on magical formulas, songs, rites, or ceremonies, all contributing to the legitimacy of the authority that was exerted.

II. **The origins of political authority in traditional civilizations.** The idea and practice of political authority appeared fairly late in history at around 3500 B.C. in the Mesopotamian region of Southwest Asia. It appeared somewhat later in Egypt, India, the Aegean, China, and pre-Columbian Central and South America. Typically, some of the neolithic village-farming communities began to organize themselves into larger towns, which became centers for a literate, urban way of life. These towns began to exert greater influence and authority over a number of other communities.

A. **The generative civilizations**. The primary or generative civilizations were characterized by social organization based on a territorial state; impersonal relationships rather than kinship; political structures somewhat differentiated according to function; and a ruling class differentiated from the ruled.

    1. **Institutionalization**. Some archaeologists and anthropologists emphasize the institutionalization of political authority based on territorial residence rather than on kinship, or at least overlaying the kinship webs of authority. Robert C. McAdams defines "state societies" as those "hierarchically organized on political and territorial lines rather than on kinship or other...relationships."

    2. **Stratification**. Morton H. Fried goes even further in stressing the coercive character of the state as a means of maintaining an established order of stratification, identifying formal education as one of the specialized institutions designed to indoctrinate the members of the state with the values of the stratified social order.

B. **Mesopotamian civilization as prototype**. Sumerian temple communities and city-states were early examples of organized authority.

    1. **Sumerian temple communities (3500-3000 B.C.)**. Something like a professional ruling class appeared in the form of temple communities or theocratic polities. The chief managers were priests who administered public affairs in the name of and on behalf of the gods.

        a. **How priestly authority was justified**. The rationale for legitimate authority was that all the land and the produce of a certain territory belonged to the gods. As stewards for the gods, the priests were at once political rulers and administrators, religious leaders, and economic planners and managers.

        b. **How priests were organized**. The priests organized themselves into colleges or corporations explicitly for the purpose of carrying out their political, religious, economic, and educational functions.

    2. **Sumerian city-states (3000-2500 B.C.)**. A more complex form of social organization took the form of city-states.

        a. **The purpose and social basis of the early city-states**. These city-states were groups who associated together for common political and military purposes, based upon territorial residence rather than upon kinship or religion. Inhabitants were in effect citizens of a city-type political organization embracing one or more of the temple communities.

        b. **Early kings**. The city-states often fell under the sway of an occasional strong man who rose to power on the strength of his military superiority. Such a semi-secular king, together with his aristocratic council of elders or nobles and his popular assembly of "men" or commoners, apparently constituted the earliest form of secular political structure that can be called a state.

        c. **Political loyalty through common identity**. As the kings came to exercise an increasing amount of political authority, they deliberately enlisted the loyalties of the people of the city-state to instill a consciousness of their common identity as members and to utilize the priestly class to strengthen their legitimacy as rulers.

C. **A succession of empires (2500-500 B.C.)**. For some two thousand years the elements of Mesopotamian civilization were absorbed, assimilated, adapted, and diffused by a succession of rulers. The Akkadian, Babylonian, and, above all, the Assyrian Empire covered most of Western Asia from the Mediterranean and Egypt to Iran. Of major importance in the development of political authority was the imperial bureaucratic system whereby the rulers of one people or society exerted direct rule over the lives and territory of another people or society.

    1. **Traditional imperium**. More people in the world have been ruled for longer periods of time by the political authority of empires than by any other kind of political authority. Even a partial list of the traditional empires that existed prior to 1500 A.D. is lengthy. Some lasted for several hundred years or more: Egyptian, Akkadian-Babylonian-Assyrian, Persian, Indian, Chinese, Japanese,

Arab Caliphates, Hellenistic, Roman, Byzantine, Holy Roman, Mongol, Aztec, and Inca.

2. **Legitimacy.** The political authority of empires has relied for legitimacy in various proportions upon divine sanction, hereditary privileges of birth, and special knowledge. Their power has usually been exerted through priestly or professional bureaucracies and always by military strength. In contrast, consent of the governed as the basis of political authority has been relatively recent, short-lived, and fragile.

III. **The rise of democratic/republican political authority.** The concept of democratic political authority received its first and clearest definition in the Aegean civilization of the Eastern Mediterranean region, when the Ionian Greeks developed a unique political organization in their compact and cohesive city-states.

A. **The democratic ideal of the Greek polis (c. 600-300 B.C.).** The significant fact about the rise of the Greek city-states from the seventh to the fifth centuries B.C. is that the authority for governing, for maintaining social order, and for administering justice was transferred from household patriarchs, tribal chiefs, military nobles, literate priests, or hereditary rulers to the political community consisting of the citizens of the polis.

1. **Loyalty to the state becomes primary.** Some of the terminology and outward forms of tribe and clan were maintained for the sake of ethnic identity or pride. But the Greek city-states downgraded the kinship ties typical of folk societies and established citizenship in the polity as the over-arching tie of unity binding the community together. The bonds of loyalty to the territorial state became the primary means of social cohesion, superior to family, class or caste, or any kind of voluntary association.

2. **Cleisthenes.** The key figure in this fundamental transfer of authority from kinship lineage to polity in Athens was **Cleisthenes** (fl. 510 B.C.), whose political reforms were apparently effected close to 500 B.C. Some adults—women, aliens, and slaves—even in Athens, were not regarded as citizens.

a. **Expansion of citizenship.** During the seventh century B.C., independent farmers were drawn into the rolls of citizens to fill the military ranks of infantrymen alongside the

mounted cavalry of noblemen. Under Cleisthenes, propertyless artisans and seamen in the mercantile and naval fleets also gained citizenship.

b. **Broadening the basis of authority.** These trends produced a broader base of political authority in Athens than in many other Greek city-states, leading to its boast of becoming a democracy.

2. **Pericles.** The classic statement of the high ideal of democratic citizenship as the wellspring for political authority came from the funeral oration of **Pericles** (495-429, B.C.) in the first year of the Peloponnesian War between Athens and Sparta in 431 B.C., as reported by the historian Thucydides. In the oration, Pericles evoked the glories of free, tolerant, democratic Athens and its glittering civilization. While the speech was an idealized patriotic rendition, it nevertheless bespoke a claim on the loyalties and commitments of Athenians similar to that which Lincoln's address on the battlefield of Gettysburg came to have for Americans.

3. **Plato.** Ironically, for most of the subsequent history of the West, the views of Cleisthenes and Pericles were eclipsed by those of **Plato** (427?-347 B.C.) and Aristotle, who wrote their treatises on political authority during the crises besetting the Greek city-states during the fourth century B.C.

a. **Plato's diagnosis of the ills of Athens.** Plato attributed the decline of Athens to a rampant individualism, a resurgence of traditional kinship and religious beliefs, a preoccupation with personal glory and private wealth, and the prejudices and ignorance of the common people whose passions as citizens led to successive coups and tyrannies.

b. **Plato's remedy.** Plato's remedy was a highly conservative, inward-looking state ruled by a wise, just, and well-educated aristocratic class who could keep the private passions arising from ethnicity, wealth, or religion under control and subordinate to the good of the state.

4. **Aristotle**. Aristotle (384-322 B.C.) made ethical judgments an integral part of his analysis of authority.

   a. **All incorrupt forms of authority have some value**. Aristotle was more flexible than Plato in finding some value in all three major forms of political authority, whether it resided in one person (a monarchy), few persons (an aristocracy), or many persons (a republic).

   b. **"Mixed" regimes most stable**. A state that combined elements of all three forms of rule, however, would be the most stable regime of all.

   c. **Primacy of public good over private interest the test of the state's legitimacy**. The test of the goodness of the state was whether the rulers were seeking the public good or their own private interests. Forms of political authority were legitimate if in practice the public good was foremost. But if private interest prevailed among rulers, then government degenerated into corrupted forms: monarchy into tyranny, aristocracy into oligarchy, and republic into democracy.

5. **Triumph of empire**. Between the deaths of Plato in 347 B.C. and of Aristotle in 322 B.C., the kings of Macedonia conquered and ruled the Greek city-states. The kingships of Philip and Alexander became imperial in scope, and the bright flame of democratic political authority flickered low in the Aegean. Nevertheless, it provided some fuel to Roman ideals during their republican years.

B. **The Roman Republic (fifth to first century B.C.)**. The early Roman experience somewhat paralleled the Greek shift from kinship to polis.

1. **Early Rome**. In early Rome, the authority and power of rural Latin tribal life was transformed by kings and aristocratic families into political institutions similar to those of the Greek city-states. The rural aristocracy, however, was deeply attached to the land and thus quite different from the warrior aristocrats of the Greek heroic age. The legendary founding of the Roman Republic is usually set at 509 B.C., but the aristocratic patricians continued to be the dominant political power in Rome during the fifth and fourth centuries B.C.

2. **Persistence of family authority**. In contrast to the Greek experience, the Roman republican state was overlaid on an extremely powerful network of family authority centered in the father (*pater familias*). He ruled an authoritarian structure that embraced his entire household of relatives, clients, servants, and slaves as well as wife and children. He was largely responsible for the safety, security, and welfare of the kinship group.

3. **Republican institutions**. The family rather than the individual was long the basis of Roman legal, religious, and social unity despite the outward republican forms of political authority. These republican forms resided in the Senate for the patrician families of large property and in the popular Assembly for the plebeian classes of small farmers, shopkeepers, tradesmen, and skilled workers.

IV. **The triumph and dissolution of traditional imperium**. The Roman Empire replaced the Republic and remained dominant for several centuries before dissolving in the onslaught of tribal invaders. Roman civilization, however, left a lasting legacy of ideas about authority.

A. **The Roman Empire**. During the second century B.C., the dynamism of the plebeian (lower) class declined rapidly because of the ravages of foreign wars and the long, debilitating civil wars between patricians and "plebs," from which the Senate seemed to emerge victorious. All classes were submerged when Octavian brought the Republic to an end and inaugurated the Roman Imperium, destined to last in some form for nearly a thousand years. Once again, the political authority of the few and the many was transferred into the rule of one, symbolized in the divine person of the Emperor Augustus.

1. **Legacy of Roman law**. Despite the presumption of absolutism, there was another legacy of imperial Rome, namely, the law that was later to be adapted and interpreted to give legitimacy to the rise of nation-states in modern times. The *Corpus Juris Civilis* compiled at the behest of Justinian in the sixth century A.D. consisted of all the constitutions promulgated by the emperors since Hadrian in the second century, the collected opinions of jurists, and a textbook on the law. Important principles included the following.

   a. **State has monopoly of legitimate force**. The political order has sovereignty over all other groups and interests in society, a monopoly of legitimate force, and a high degree of centralization.

b. **The state must approve all lesser associations**. No other form of association lawfully exists, unless it is granted that right by the political sovereign. Thus, Constantine proclaimed the right to make Christianity the established religion of the Empire, and Justinian projected the vision of a Universal Christian Roman Empire.

2. **The idea of citizenship**. The personal relations of citizens were considered to be legal only if based upon willing consent rather than ascribed social status. Thus hereditary, traditional customs had no standing in law unless they could be converted into contractual relations. And the only politically recognized units in society were individual citizens upon whom the rights and responsibilities of citizenship rested.

B. **Feudalism in the Middle Ages**. Authority during the Middle Ages took a number of forms.

1. **Plural relationships**. From the fourth to the eighth centuries A.D., a series of Germanic invasions revitalized the strength of tribal and kinship authorities and thereby weakened the centralized imperial authority.

a. **The eclipse of citizenship**. For the thousand years of the Middle Ages, citizenship in a political community was eclipsed by the pluralist relationships that characterized medieval society.

b. **The composition of medieval society**. Robert Nisbet summed up this point as follows: "Medieval society was a vast web of groups, communities, and associations, each claiming jurisdiction over the functions and activities of its members. The church was powerful, but, so, after the twelfth century, were guild, profession, monastery, and manor."

2. **Personal obligations**. Safety and political authority were to be found increasingly in the hands of a local strongman who possessed land, built a well-fortified castle, and could command the loyalty of subordinates who would fight for him.

a. **Political authority of feudal lords.** Political authority devolved into the hands of decentralized feudal lords who could provide some protection for the people of the surrounding territory against marauders.

b. **Absence of relationship between "citizen" and "state."** The essential political relationship in feudalism was no longer that between state and citizen or between ruler and subject, but one of personal relationships among a particular group of individuals.

c. **Primacy of personal agreements and authority**. The most important relationships were the personal agreements of allegiance between lord and vassal and the binding authority of the lord over the serf bound to his land. Political power was more personal than institutional.

d. **Europe inherits tradition of political contract**. Feudalism thus bequeathed to Europe a tradition of political contract and reciprocity of obligations.

C. **The idea of the Holy Roman Empire**. The theory of imperium was not dead during the Middle Ages.

1. **The reestablishment of the Empire. Charlemagne** (742?-814) was crowned successor of the Roman emperors by the Pope in 800 A.D. By 962 Otto I of Germany was strong enough to conquer Italy and establish himself in theory as the successor of Charlemagne and legitimate heir to the Roman Empire. The Empire was thenceforth to be ruled jointly with the Pope as a Latin Christendom or Holy Roman Empire.

2. **Claims to rule by the papacy**. By the thirteenth century Pope Innocent III, who exerted more secular power than any pope before or after, claimed that Christendom should be regarded as a great unified commonwealth with the pope as its head inspiring governments everywhere to righteousness. As successor to Peter, the pope should be regarded as superior to all secular and political authorities and feudal overlord to all kings. But Europe was on the verge of another major transformation in political authority, the rise of the modern nation-state.

V. **The rise of modern nation-states and their empires (1400-1700)**. One of the most transforming aspects of the onset of modern civilization was the decline of the medieval traditions of feudalism in the face of the growing centralized political power and authority of the European nation-states. The medieval conception of a universal Christendom with the pope and/or the emperor at its head was undermined. The Holy Roman Empire was beset by recurring challenges. The time was ripe for coalitions in various combinations in different countries of king, gentry, merchants, religious reformers, and "professional intellectuals" intent upon breaking the political, economic, and religious authority of the Roman Catholic imperium.

A. **Latinizing empires**. The states most successful in their early efforts to centralize royal power were Catholic Portugal, Catholic Spain, and Catholic France, soon to be challenged by Protestant England. They were first able to build superior royal power through centralized territorial authority. They did so by developing professional bureaucracies, strengthening loyal military forces and regional courts, harnessing or hobbling the upper aristocracy, and reducing the autonomy of cities or guilds.

   1. **Foreign conquests of Spain and Portugal**. Not content with consolidating power in their homelands, Portugal and Spain struck out to embrace literally the rest of the world. Their grasp was symbolized by a north-south line of demarcation in the Western Atlantic Ocean, proclaimed by Pope Alexander VI and confirmed by the Treaty of Tordillas in 1494.

   2. **Claims to the world** of Spain and Portugal. This line in effect authorized Portugal to possess and rule all non-Christian lands east of Brazil reaching across Africa and South Asia to China and Japan, while Spain was given authority to occupy all lands west of Brazil to include all of the Americas to the Philippines and the Spice Islands.

B. **The imperialist competitive edge**. Such an audacious division of the world was naturally disputed by the French, the English, and the Dutch, who were soon competing in the race to conquer, colonize, and Christianize the non-Europeans of the world. They sought to legitimize their power of political control by proclaiming a divine mission to bring Christianity to the heathen and a cultural mission to bring their respective versions of the language, moral norms, technology, and civility of European civilization.

   1. **The Anglo-Protestant empire**. The English won out over their Latin competitors and eventually had the largest impact on much of the world, especially on what became the United States. In an evocative phrase, historian Carl Bridenbaugh spoke of "the first swarming of the English" in the early sixteenth century. This "swarming" was the outpouring of thousands of people to places as near to the homeland as Ireland, the Netherlands, and France and as far away as India to the East and North America to the West.

   2. **New England Puritans' compact theory of government**. The Puritans established in New England a religious civil society, which was a combination of the theocratic conception of the state of **John Calvin** (1509-1564) and the constitutional liberties being won in Parliament. The result of the Puritan migration was a covenant or compact theory of political authority.

      a. **The state as a gift from God**. The state was viewed as a gift of God through which men obeyed His command to establish a civil government on earth.

      b. **The state to protect the church**. Thus, the state must be the protector and supporter of the ruling church, to do its bidding and enforce, with punishment if necessary, its moral laws and spiritual doctrines. While the Stuart kings were proclaiming their divine right to rule the Church of England, the Congregationalists were establishing their form of religion in New England.

   3. **The rise of constitutional thought**. Later in the seventeenth century, other American colonists were also embracing the rise of constitutional thought being expressed in the revolt of the Dutch Republic against Spanish rule as well as in the establishment of the English Commonwealth. In both, the civil rights of merchants, gentry, and free men were proclaimed as inviolable against autocratic usurpation by an absolute monarch. [See The Nature of the State and Individual Rights.]

VI. **The revival of republican political authority (1400-1800)**. From the fifteenth to the end of the eighteenth centuries there was a revival of republican political thought as well as the institution of republican political authority in various parts of Europe as well as in North America.

A. **Civic humanism**. Civic humanism had a marked influence in the Italian Renaissance and later in the Atlantic community, in England and France, and among the American colonists.

1. **Civic humanism in the Italian Renaissance**. Peter Riesenberg argues that the revival of learning in the Italian Renaissance, including the study of Roman law and the Greek philosophy of Aristotle as well as the experience of a vital urban life, led to a rise of civic consciousness in the Italian city-states well before 1400. In any case, the ideas of civic humanism were written out with persuasive force in the fifteenth and sixteenth centuries by **Leonardo Bruni** (1369-1444), **Francesco Guicciardini** (1483-1540), and, above all, by **Niccolo Machiavelli** (1469-1527).

2. **Civic humanism in the Atlantic community**. J. G. A. Pocock has portrayed how the Italian writers influenced the revival of republican political authority in the pre-revolutionary Atlantic community, especially in England, France, and British America. Pocock argues that civic humanism provides a vital link between the classical high ideal of republican citizenship and the modern ideas of republican and eventually democratic political authority. He even argues that the American Revolution and the U.S. Constitution in a sense form "the last act of the civic Renaissance."

B. **The age of democratic revolution (the eighteenth century)**. Robert R. Palmer argues that the democratic revolution that swept much of Europe and British America in the eighteenth century was a single movement that broke out in many parts of the heartland of Western civilization, especially in the decades from 1760 to 1800. The first manifestation was the American Revolution; the most extreme and violent was the French Revolution. Reform movements appeared in England and Ireland; short-lived republics were established in the Netherlands, Belgium, Switzerland, Italy, Hungary, and Poland in the 1780s and 1790s.

1. **Revolutionary ideas in Europe**. Each revolution had its own agitators, protests, and assaults on the established ruling orders, which had become ever more aristocratic, closed, self-recruiting, self-perpetuating, and increasingly more privileged.

   a. **Legitimacy of ruling powers denied**. Each band of revolutionaries denied the legitimacy of the ruling powers. They argued that political authority should not rest upon the asserted right of status, or of divine support, of custom or inheritance, or of the unalterable processes of history presumed to endow some special elite or revolutionary vanguard with the right to rule.

   b. **Objection to inherited privilege**. The revolutionaries especially objected to the growing emphasis on preferred status favoring the rights of particular families, kinship, wealth, property, or social class. The doctrines of natural rights, social contract, equality, and political liberty were in large part directed at doing away with the preferred status that had been forged into permanent legal relationships, fixing the rights and obligations of special groups into a hierarchical political order.

   c. **Demand for popular participation**. The revolutionaries demanded more participation in government by a greater share of the populace, more equality in such participation, and greater protection for the civil liberties and rights of an enlarged body of citizens.

2. **Revolutionary ideas in British America**. Bernard Bailyn has summarized the sources of the historical ideas that nourished the thought and actions of American revolutionaries and constitutionalists in the eighteenth century as follows:

   a. **Classical antiquity**. The most important were the Greek thought of Plato and Aristotle and the Roman thought of Cicero, **Sallust** (86 B.C.-c.34 B.C.), and **Tacitus** (55-117 A.D.), who wrote on the corruption and decline of civic virtue that undermined the Roman Republic.

   b. **The Enlightenment**. Another source was the Enlightenment literature on the social contract, ranging from works of **John Locke** (1632-1704) to those of **Voltaire** (1694-1778), **Montesquieu** (1689-1755), and **Rousseau** (1712-1778).

   c. **Common law**. A third source was the English tradition of common law, which stressed such key ideas as natural justice and civil rights.

d. **Puritan theology**. A further source was the Puritan covenant theology, which envisioned a special destiny in America for God's will.

e. **English republicanism**. Finally, American ideas were derived from the radical politics of the seventeenth-century revolutionaries in the English civil war and Commonwealth period. Influential republican writers of the period were **John Milton** (1698-1674), **James Harrington** (1611-1677), and **Algernon Sidney** (1622-1683).

3. **Popular consent as the source of authority**. The American solution was to reject the political authority of traditional constitutional bodies and to turn to "the people" as the sovereign constituent power for legitimate republican government. Such political authority must rest on the natural rights of liberty and equality, and function by popular consent through elected representatives.

VII. **The global embrace of imperialism (1700-1900)**. From the early eighteenth century to the turn of the twentieth century, European states spread their power throughout the globe.

A. **The modernization of the West**. The political, social, and cultural changes that gathered speed in the heartland of Western civilization during the eighteenth and nineteenth centuries were so portentous for the future of mankind that they can justly be compared with other major transformations in human history. In totality, the changes amounted to the transmutation of traditional society to modern civilization. Appearing first and most aggressively in Britain and France, (and later in the Netherlands, Denmark, Germany, and America), the modernizing leaders took several momentous strides.

1. **National power and industrialization**. Modernizing forces mobilized the centralizing political power of the nation-state. In the economic sphere, other forces energized massive industrialism and urbanization.

2. **Democracy and religious freedom**. Modernizing leaders fomented democratic revolution and stood in the forefront of secular enlightenment. In the newly freed American states, these leaders railed against religious establishment and rallied around religious freedom. Also in America, they championed the value of popular education as an essential ingredient of the new democratic order.

B. **The "civilizing mission" of the West**. The states of western Europe also launched their "civilizing mission" to embrace the world. This sense of "mission" was a compound of both noble and ignoble motives, but it served to legitimize, at least for itself, the extension of Western political power throughout much of the world. The sense of mission of these nations reflected a growing confidence in their cultural superiority over those they set out to "civilize."

1. **The ingredients of the sense of mission**. The compound factors that composed the sense of mission consisted of varying ingredients.

a. **Desire for power and profit**. Prominent ingredients were nationalist pride and military power as well as commercial aggressiveness and desire for profit.

b. **Religious and charitable motives**. Missionaries were generally moved by Christian evangelism and egalitarianism. Others were seized by humanitarian and philanthropic fervor to relieve the worst depredations of slavery, suffering, and poverty.

c. **Confidence in education**. Similarly, many who believed in the civilizing mission of the West had confidence in the power of knowledge and education to improve the conditions of the unenlightened or unfortunate.

d. **The drive for national stature**. A final factor was the desire to enhance self-esteem and stature in the eyes of the world.

2. **The West's sense of superiority**. Above all, the civilizing mission centered upon a growing feeling that Western society and culture were superior to those of Asia, Africa, the Americas, and the Pacific.

a. **Western imperialism justified by benefits to the conquered**. Through a sense of superiority, Western nations felt impelled to carry their civilization, including its political institutions, to the rest of the world and, if need be, impose it by force for the good of others as well as for profit and pride.

b. **The West's divine appointment or national destiny**. Many believed that their mission to the less fortunate was given to them by God, by national destiny, or both. And it so happened that they could profit not only from the international competitiveness with each other but from the dismantling of the Portuguese and Spanish empires.

C. **The spread of imperium around the world.** In the early modern period, the seafaring nations of Western Europe inaugurated explorations on a scale that later resulted in global empires.

1. **Seafaring empires of the West.** During the sixteenth century, imperialism, defined as the direct rule over the territory and lives of one people by the government of another, took on a worldwide character for the first time in history.

   a. **Limitations of pre-modern empires.** The pre-modern empires (except for the Greek city-states) were principally land-based empires with the rule of the farthest reaches of territory subject to the limited technology of overland travel and communication.

   b. **Unlimited scope of modern empires.** But with the onset of the early modern era, the seafaring governments of Western Europe formed the spearhead of waterborne empires that eventually encircled the globe.

   c. **The doctrine of imperium: the right to rule.** These Western nations proclaimed the doctrine of imperium, the right to assert lawful jurisdiction and to command obedience wherever they went, including the right to enforce their laws through coercion.

2. **Land-based empires of the East.** Meanwhile, the traditional land-based empires of the East also expanded their territorial powers to compete with the aggressive Westerners. Russia pushed eastward across the entire continent of Asia to the Pacific and southeastward into central Asia. The Ottoman Empire pushed across North Africa and deep into central Europe. The Chinese pushed north, west, and south from the Chinese heartland. And Japan moved onto the continent and the islands of east Asia.

3. **Conquest by the West.** By the middle of the nineteenth century, the age-old balance among the traditional land-based civilizations of East and West began to teeter uncertainly.

   a. **The acceleration of Western conquest.** From 1860 onward the aggressively modernizing empires of the West took the lead in the race for land and peoples to govern. After 1880, expansion accelerated so rapidly that the imperial powers of West and East alike carved up virtually the entire earth.

   b. **The decline of the East.** Within a decade or two after 1850 the major civilizations of the Middle East, India, China, and Japan, which had maintained a balance among themselves for nearly 2000 years and with the West for some 800 years, were beginning to be disrupted by the modernizing power of the Western nations.

4. **The dismemberment of Africa.** The most widely publicized symbol of Western imperium took place at the Berlin Conference in 1894-95 when thirteen states of Europe and the United States agreed upon the ground rules by which nearly all of Africa would be carved up. Within two decades the rulers of Africa were turned upside down. Whereas 90% of Africa was ruled by Africans in 1880, Europeans ruled 90% of Africa by 1900, the lion's share going to Britain and France.

5. **The fate of the traditional land empires.** While the Ottoman Empire and the Austro-Hungarian Empire were dismantled by World War I and the Japanese Empire and the Western empires collapsed after World War II, the Communist rule of the traditional empires of Russia and China over the peoples of vast territories of Asia was not seriously threatened until the fateful events of the late 1980s and the early 1990s.

Contemporary Perspective

The political revolutions in Eastern Europe and the Soviet Union in the 1980s and 1990s require a revision of what historians are likely to call "contemporary." In this case, what is meant by "contemporary" cannot be limited to the past decade or two. The recent rise of ethnic nationalism and calls for political democracy and self-determination have direct roots at least as far back as World War I. The noted exponent of world history William H. McNeill refers to 1917 as the "lever of history."

In the spring of 1917 the United States became a belligerent in World War I. In the fall of the same year, Bolsheviks overthrew the tsarist government in Russia and withdrew that country from the war. These events make the year 1917 a serviceable landmark from which to date a new phase in Western and world civilization, marked by the Communist transformation of Russia, the rise of the United States to world power, the eclipse of western Europe as undisputed center and arbiter of Western civilization, and by enormous advances in men's ability to manipulate human as well as inanimate energies.

It may be too soon to call 1989-91 another epochal date in human history, but the appeals that were heard for self-determination as the genuine source of political authority were undeniable. This "self-determination" had two parts: the first was **independence from foreign rule**; the second was the creation of **institutions of popular self-determination** as opposed to personal, military, or single-party rule. The former has been accomplished in most of the former colonial world, but not in places such as the Soviet Union. The latter form of self-determination—of some form of popular government—has not been accomplished in vast stretches of the earth and is among the most acute problems of political authority today.

I. **The warring of political authorities in the early twentieth century**. The Wilsonian doctrine of national self-determination announced at the end of World War I gained temporary recognition in some quarters, only to be eclipsed by the "era of tyrannies" of the 1930s.

A. **World War I and self-determination of peoples**. At the entrance of the U.S. to World War I in 1917, President Wilson defended democratic self-determination in words that have had continuing relevance.

   1. **Woodrow Wilson's war message**. After trying futilely for three years to keep the U.S. neutral in Europe's war between the Allied and Central Powers, Wilson's War Message to Congress of April 2, 1917, closed with these words:

      a. **Civilization in jeopardy**. "It is a fearful thing to lead this great peaceful people into war, into the most terrible and most disastrous of all wars, civilization itself seeming to be in the balance."

      b. **Struggle for democratic self-determination worth more than peace**. "But the right is more precious than peace, and we shall fight for the things which we have always carried nearest our hearts—for democracy, for the right of those who submit to authority to

have a voice in their own government, for the rights and liberties of small nations, for a universal dominion of right by such a concert of free peoples as shall bring peace and safety to all nations and make the world itself at last free."

      c. **The continuing invocation of Wilson's ideals**. Whatever other complex motivations may also have been involved, these ideals were being invoked again and again in the succeeding seventy years of world history.

   2. **Wilson's "Fourteen Points."** Even more effective as rallying points for the nearly exhausted Allied combatants at a particularly low point in the war were Wilson's famous "Fourteen Points," which he outlined in his State of the Union address to Congress in January 1918. They gave a rationale for the goals of the war that have been compared in effectiveness to the principles stated in the Declaration of Independence and in Lincoln's Gettysburg address.

      a. **"Disimperialism."** In the 1990s, some of the points have an uncanny contemporary sound: Point V states: "A free, open-minded, and absolutely impartial adjustment of all colonial claims, based upon a strict observance of the principle that in determining all such questions of sovereignty the interests of the population concerned must have equal weight with the equitable claims of the government whose title is to be determined."

      b. **Self-determination**. Points VI through XIII not only specify the return of territories overrun by the Central Powers in Belgium, France, and Italy but also proclaim freedom of self-determination specifically for the peoples of Imperial Russia, which Lenin had called "the prison house of nationalities," Austria-Hungary, Rumania, Serbia, Montenegro, Turkey, and Poland. "An evident principle runs through the whole programme I have outlined," Wilson said. "It is the principle of justice to all peoples and nationalities, and their rights to live on equal terms of liberty and safety with one another, whether they be strong or weak."

   3. **The Versailles Treaty**. Although Wilson's principles and political savvy could not prevail over

Clemenceau and Lloyd George at the Versailles Peace settlement, the political basis was laid for the independence of several Central and East European countries, now prominently in the news of the early 1990s: Lithuania, Latvia, Estonia, Czechoslovakia, Hungary, Rumania, and Yugoslavia. Wilson's principle of linguistic and ethnic nationalism gained some headway between the wars until snuffed out by new totalitarian imperialisms.

B. **Corruptions of political authority: the new imperialists**. The twentieth century spawned autocratic regimes that sought to impose new forms of empire on the world in the name of new ideologies. (For discussions of fascism and communism, see The Nature of the State.)

1. **Communism**. From the time that the Bolsheviks seized power in Russia in 1917, the "civilizing mission" of the Western empires began to pale in comparison to the worldwide "revolutionary mission" of communism.

    a. **Communism's reputed inevitability**. Marx had declared that communism was legitimized by the inevitable and scientific laws of history, which dictated that capitalism was doomed to pass into socialism and then finally to communism, when all peoples would be securely nourished by a just and egalitarian society.

    b. **Lenin's road to communist power: an elite party**. Lenin added the claims of the right of a highly disciplined, tightly knit Communist party to be the agent to overthrow the corrupt capitalist order and seize political power on behalf of the exploited workers. Only in this way could society be moved quickly and efficiently toward its preordained goals of social and economic equality.

    c. **Stalinism**. Stalin carried the doctrines of party infallibility and its right to rule to the extremes of ruthless brutal repression and the imprisonment and murder of millions. He declared that the monolithic power of the Soviet party extended to all Communist parties everywhere in the world. For the "capitalist hegemony" in liberal democracies, Lenin and Stalin sought to substitute a communist party which would engineer the overthrow of capitalism and lead to state socialism and finally to communism.

2. **Fascism and national socialism**. Another corruption of the meaning of political authority arising in the 1920s and 1930s was the doctrine that the "rule of one" was the only really viable basis of political authority. The "masses" must rally around and unquestioningly obey "the Leader" in order to achieve their common destiny as a people. The authority of the leader was claimed ultimately to rest upon the inherent superiority of his particular ethnic group or race. This leader must be strong enough to combat the egalitarianism of "evil communism" and "impotent, corrupt democracy."

    a. **Mussolini's fascism**. "Il Duce" turned Italy's humiliation at the Versailles Treaty into a nationalistic crusade, promising to lead the Italian people again to the heights of glory of the Roman Empire. Playing on the fear of communism and contempt for democracy, Mussolini built a highly centralized party, controlling all agencies of the state and emphasizing youth, discipline, strength, and ruthless suppression of dissent. Political authority resided solely in the leader.

    b. **Military dictatorships**. During the twentieth century, the fascist model was more or less followed around the world by military dictators too numerous to count: from Franco's Spain in the 1930s to Idi Amin's Uganda in the 1970s and Marcos's Philippines and Noriega's Panama in the 1980s.

    c. **Hitler's national socialism**. "Der Fuehrer" also played upon Germany's humiliation at Versailles, the fear of communism, the impotence of the Weimar Republic's failures in liberal democracy, and added the viciously potent virus of anti-Semitism. Combining the principles of strong leadership with racial inequality, Hitler vowed to restore the German people to their rightful place of superiority over all other ethnic groups and especially over such "inferior" races as Jews and Negroes.

    d. **Ultimate corruption of political authority**. Among all other twentieth-century dictatorships, only Stalin's regime rivaled the brutality of the Nazi onslaughts against humane values in their genocidal attacks on Jews, Poles, and countless others. The regimes of Hitler and Stalin represented the ultimate corruption of political authority.

II. **A second age of democratic revolution (1940-1990)**. War, decolonization, technology, and other factors have joined in the half-century since 1940 to foster a second age of democratic revolution.

A. **World War II and dissolution of the Western empires**. A long period of struggle by the West against expansionist dictatorships in World War II was followed by struggles for independence by the colonized peoples long ruled by Western European nations.

1. **War aims of the Allies**. The war aims expressed by the Allies returned to the Wilsonian democratic/republican ideals of self-determination of peoples and their rights to a voice in the political authority exerted over them. From the Atlantic Charter of 1941 to the United Nations Charter of 1945 and the Universal Declaration of Human Rights of 1948, the goals of self-government and consent of the governed were reasserted.

2. **"Disimperialism."** The Axis empires of Germany, Italy, and Japan were dissolved immediately upon the conclusion of the war in 1945. Taking the ideas of self-determination seriously, the peoples of the colonial Western empires agitated, fought for, and won "disimperialism" and independence. Beginning with the independence of the Philippines from American rule in 1946 and of India and Pakistan from British rule in 1947, the colonial peoples of Asia and Africa formed new nations and by 1990 were the majority of the one hundred-sixty member states that made up the United Nations.

3. **Nondemocratic rule in former colonies**. Independence, however, was only the first step in many countries toward the ideals of democratic political authority. Military dictatorships and one-party rule, whether of left or right, were often defended as necessary elements in the transition from colonialism to self-government. Their ideology often promised the eventual authority of democracy, but in reality simply rested on the exercise of unlimited power.

B. **Threats of dissolution of the Eastern empires**. The last great empires to respond to the democratic revolution

following World War II were those of China and the Soviet Union.

1. **Democracy's challenge to Chinese autocracy**. Falling to the Communist rule of Mao Tsetung in 1949, China gradually began to open cultural and economic contacts with the West in the 1970s. But in 1989, when Chinese students challenged the Communist party's claims to complete control, the Tiananmen Square massacre and nationwide crackdown strangled the open movement toward democracy and freedom. Afterwards, the Chinese rulers continued to stifle the calls for democracy both in China and in Chinese-controlled Tibet. Western analysts wondered how long Chinese autocracy could last in the new age of democracy.

2. **Democracy sweeps Eastern Europe**. By 1990, popular regimes had taken power nearly everywhere in Eastern Europe. One exception was Romania, where a harsh government, no longer labeled communist, survived. Even in Albania, the last holdout of communist oppression in Europe, signs of freedom of travel and of religion began to appear.

3. **The rise of democratic authority in the USSR**. Led by the declarations of independence by the Baltic republics, struggles for autonomy and popular government arose in many Soviet republics, especially in the Russian republic, which freely elected **Boris N. Yeltsin** president.

a. **New meaning for the word "republic."** The term "republic" was taking on a new meaning in the USSR as the leaders of the Soviet republics appealed to the ideals of constitutional democracy for the legitimacy of their claims to political authority, whether increased sovereignty or greater autonomy within the Soviet Union, or complete independence.

b. **End of former basis of authority**. The old basis of authority for the whole USSR—a Communist party appointed to power by history—seemed to have collapsed, especially after the abortive coup of August 1991. What kind of unifying authority would take its place was unclear.

C. **The reassertion of ethnic and religious nationalisms**. An important factor complicating the basis for authority was the powerful dynamics of ethnic and religious nationalism unleashed not only in Eastern Europe and the USSR but also in nearly all parts of the world. Group after group bound by ties of ethnic kinship and religious heritage was demanding fundamental alterations of political authority and territorial borders imposed by wars or revolutions decades or centuries ago. These groups included Europeans such as Basques in Spain, and Serbs, Croats, and Slovenes in Yugoslavia; Middle Easterners such as Muslims, Christians, and Jews in Lebanon, and Kurds, Sunnis, and Shiites in Iraq; Asians such as Muslims, Sikhs and Hindus in India; Palestinians battling Israeli authority in the occupied territories; and blacks achieving a greater share of political authority in South Africa.

III. **Twilight or high noon for political authority in the United States?** The democratic revolts around the world not only raised serious questions for American foreign policy, but also political authority within the nation was undergoing severe tests of its historic viability.

   A. **Privatism and privatization.** Since the mid-1960s the public mood of the United States has soured, and the sense of legitimacy of government at all levels has been increasingly eroded. "Privatism" in this context may be called the **affirmation** of transferring attention and concern from the public sphere to the private, especially personal, sphere. "Privatization" is the **process** of this transfer. Moreover, private interest has increasingly been praised by conservatives as a necessary brake on the expanded role of government, which had been powered by Roosevelt's New Deal, Truman's Fair Deal, Kennedy's New Frontier, and Johnson's Great Society.

      1. **America's "traumatic years."** In 1978 Sidney Ahlstrom, Yale historian, called the preceding period of a decade and a half "the traumatic years," in which "the nation's sense of purpose fell to its lowest ebb," and our national consensus was shattered by years that were "tumultuous, troubled, and traumatic." Five issues around which protest and reform movements were mobilized constituted "a full-scale critique of the American way of life: both the social injustices of the system itself and the ideological, philosophical, and theological assumptions that have justified and legitimated the existing social order."

         a. **Race and racism.** The civil rights movement pervaded public consciousness, while racism continued to preoccupy minority races and their allies, especially students.

         b. **War and imperialism.** The war in Vietnam met widespread opposition, particularly among youth. For periods of the 1960s and '70s the country was torn apart by controversy. Opponents labeled the war an "imperialist" adventure.

         c. **Sex and sexism.** A revolt against the puritanical streak in American culture led to a pervasive attention to issues of sex and the appearance of newly cohesive sexual minorities demanding toleration. At the same time, women organized to wage war against all aspects of the inferior status assigned to their sex.

         d. **Ecological exploitation and environmentalism.** In the 1970s environmental questions began to concern large numbers of Americans. It was argued that environmental damage was being inflicted by uncontrolled and uncaring private (or public) enterprises that poisoned air, land, and water to the detriment of all forms of life.

         e. **The misuse of government power.** Charges of government lying to the public followed by the Watergate scandal led to intense public awareness of corruption in government. Further episodes of lying or corruption such as "Abscam," "Iran-Gate," and the savings and loan scandals reinforced such perceptions.

      2. **Political alienation.** It can be argued that all five of the above issues are still alive and troublesome in the 1990s. Poll after poll since the 1970s and repeated scholarly judgments have underlined the public's growing cynicism and skepticism about government and its alienation from politicians, public institutions, and insensitive bureaucracies; venality and corruption in government; and voter apathy. All of these were matched if not surpassed by the greed, corruption, and self-seeking in the private sector as exhibited in the parade of super-rich convicts on their way to prison and in the savings and loan scandals.

      3. **Youth and privatism.** Of special concern to observers was the succession of studies showing

that privatism had become the dominant mood of youth as well as of adults. From the Yankelovich surveys of youth values in *The New Morality* of the early 1970s to the Hart study of *Democracy's Next Generation* in 1989, the prominence of "deauthorization" among youth has been noted; that is, a marked rise since 1969 in the values assigned to privatism and a corresponding decline in values assigned to constituted authority, obligation to others, and patriotism.

4. **A disconnected citizenry**. A whole generation seems to have acquired little commitment to the civic values which American society traditionally regarded highly and which the schools presumably teach. The Markle Commission on the Media and the Electorate in 1990 documented a widening gap between the citizens and their government. Citizens wanted public services, but they did not want to pay taxes for them: their attitude was, "Let the government pay for them."

B. **The ideologies of social pluralism**. Another contemporary movement that often seemed at odds with attachment and support for political authority was a growing stress upon the values of "social pluralism" in American life.

1. **The historical roots of the new ideologies of "social pluralism."** Germinating in the 1960s and blossoming in the 1970s and 1980s, the attraction of various groups to "social pluralism" resulted in part from the loss of credibility of government authority. The growth of "social pluralism" also stemmed from the glorification of the '60s notion of "doing one's own thing" in the search for self-fulfillment.

2. **The larger significance of "social pluralism" ideologies**. As critics have noted, withdrawal from general political involvement to personal or group concerns was much more than what met the eye. It was nothing less than a search for nonpolitical authorities upon which to base one's life goals and values. The argument of the new ideologies of social pluralism can be read as claiming that authority arises from and therefore should rest upon the diverse ("pluralist") communities in American society rather than upon the political or civic community common to all such groups.

3. **Diversity as ideal community**. The new social pluralists seek primary moral authority and legitimacy for their lives in the many different communities that serve to bind individuals and groups together on the basis of religion, race, ethnicity, language, or common culture. They see such positive values in the diversity and variety of pluralist associations that they consider them to be the essence and foundation of a sense of community. They appear to see little or no connection to a common American community as a whole.

4. **Cultural pluralism**. The popular rebirth of "cultural pluralism," prefigured by Horace M. Kallen in the early 1920s, has come from several sources. On one hand, there has been a growing demand of political liberals that American institutions should recognize the values inherent in different racial and ethnic identities. On the other hand, there has been a resurgence of a conservative economic and social philosophy that prefers voluntary and private group action to government activism.

5. **The "new ethnicity."** The civil rights movement of the 1960s and 1970s focused national attention on the historical discriminations against black Americans. It achieved notable successes in desegregation and equality of opportunity for African Americans.

   a. **Heightened ethnic consciousness**. It was soon evident that other forms of discrimination continued to frustrate the descendants of white immigrants to America from southern and eastern Europe and, especially in more recent times, the immigrants from Latin America and Asia.

   b. **New ethnic pride**. As a result of heightened ethnic consciousness, a new and sometimes fierce pride in ethnic traditions stoked demands for renewed self-knowledge and self-consciousness among all ethnic groups.

6. **The "multiculturalism" controversy**. One of the demands for the recognition of minority ethnic and racial groups took the form of ethnic heritage studies, "multicultural" studies, and bilingual education in schools and colleges.

   a. **Controversy over school and college curriculums.** In the 1980s, the movement for "multicultural" studies exploded into national controversies over the values of requiring a core or canon of studies emphasizing Western civilization as against a "curriculum of inclusion" that would pay special attention to the wide diversity of backgrounds and cultures that critics charged were not given their due in American education and culture.

b. **Arguments for "multicultural" curriculums.** "Multicultural" studies, it was argued, would promote the self-esteem of minority groups historically discriminated against as inferior in American life. Ethnicity as well as race became powerful and often explosive ingredients confronting America's historic political authority. Adding to these demands was the fact that, added together, minority groups were nearing a majority in many major cities such as New York and Los Angeles and in certain large states such as California, Texas, Florida, and New York. Non-European minorities are expected to comprise about 25 percent of the nation's population by the year 2000.

7. **A new conservative pluralism.** While the new ethnicity was often supported by politically liberal, even radical, advocates of greater civil rights for minorities, a new conservative pluralism also appeared to call in question the whole range of institutions that make up liberal democratic government in the United States.

a. **Conservative responses to social reformism.** Notable academic voices like those of Robert Nisbet of Columbia University, Robert Nozick of Harvard, and Milton Friedman of the Hoover Institution at Stanford reflected a growing ideological reaction against the social reform movements of the 1960s, much as Ronald Reagan symbolized the conservative political movements of the 1970s and 1980s.

b. **The conservative program.** In various idioms, theirs was a call for a reassertion of the values of private freedoms, individual rights, free market mechanisms, the minimal state, and the free play of voluntary groups and mutual aid associations. The converse was their attack upon an overweening welfare state, the inquisitional and repressive measures of governmental regulation and bureaucracy, the mentality of the "leviathan state," and a general neoconservative disen-chantment with the liberal welfare state and its policies.

c. **The twilight of authority?** In his book with the evocative title, *Twilight of Authority*, Robert Nisbet put it this way: "I believe that the most remarkable fact at the present time in the West is neither technological nor economic, but **political**: The waning of the historic political community...the whole fabric of rights, liberties, participations, and protections that has been, even above industrialism, I think, the dominant element of modernity in the West...."

d. **A restoration of authority?** Nisbet's prescriptions for the restoration of authority were to recover the central pluralist values of ethnicity, decentralized localism and regionalism, religion, and kinship rather than national political authority. At root, he would revive the prestige of the private as contrasted with the public and rely as much as possible on informal custom, folkways, spontaneous tradition-sanctioned habits of mind—rather than formal law, ordinance, or administrative regulation in the "name of a vain and vapid equality."

At the opening of the last decade of the twentieth century, a renewed, revised, and revitalized conception of the role of political authority in American life is clearly called for. A major purpose of the following sections of CIVITAS is to provide a comprehensive and scholarly basis of knowledge upon which to conduct this examination. Such an examination may also be of use to the reinvigorated nations of Eastern Europe, the Soviet Union, and the Third World.

TOPIC 2. THE NATURE OF THE STATE

What is the state without justice but highway robbery on a grand scale?

St. Augustine (c. 400)

I am the state. I alone am here the representative of the people....France has more need of me than I of France.

Napoleon Bonaparte (c. 1800)

The republican is the only form of government which is not eternally at open or secret war with the rights of mankind.

Thomas Jefferson (c. 1785?)

A knowledge of the nature of the state provides citizens with a basis useful in analyzing and evaluating the goals and operations of their own and other governments. The perspective gained by this knowledge facilitates citizens' understanding of the purposes of government in general, as well as their ability to identify the strengths and weaknesses of particular governments and to propose and implement effective remedies for those weaknesses. Thus, a historical grounding in the experience which gave rise to the American political order is essential for citizens to be able to judge its achievements, the social forces and policies that could undermine it, and its future prospects. Knowledge of other forms of government and of competing political ideas and ideologies makes it possible for citizens to identify the distinctness of liberal democracy in America; free choice to adhere to its ideals and institutions is possible only in light of alternative forms of government and of the ideas that underlie them.

OBJECTIVES

The citizen should be able to

1. identify the purposes served by various kinds of states. This should include the ability to identify the purposes served by a government's acts, laws, and policies.

2. evaluate the degree to which states are successful in meeting their purposes.

3. evaluate the purposes and priorities of various states using explicitly stated criteria such as the listing of fundamental values and principles of American constitutional democracy.

4. describe historical and contemporary examples of states exemplifying the various views of the proper role and organization of the state, i.e., aristocratic traditionalism, liberal-democracy, Marxism, twentieth-century communism, and fascism.

5. explain the underlying rationale held by the advocates of varying views of the state and know something of the historical record of varying kinds of states.

FRAME OF REFERENCE
Conceptual Perspective

I. **Government and the state.** The state is the means through which political authority is exercised; it is also the vehicle through which authority is made stable by becoming institutionalized. A state is an independent political community claiming sovereignty over a defined territory. The organization that exercises the state's authority is the government.

II. **Purposes of government.** Depending on the character of the society of which they are an expression, different governments may serve some or all the purposes set forth below. Governments typically have varying priorities among these purposes.

   A. **Order, predictability, internal security, external defense.** Nearly all governments at least claim to have as their purpose the establishment of an order that permits predictability, which in turn promotes a sense of security among the governed. This may be true whether a government is authoritarian or democratic. Sovereign states also take as a primary purpose the defense of their territory against external attack.

   B. **Distribution of resources.** All governments play a role in controlling the distribution of resources in their societies. These may include capital, labor, and natural resources. Governments determine which resources will be publicly controlled and which will be in private hands.

   C. **Conflict management.** All governments develop institutions and procedures for the management of conflict. These may include legislative, executive, and judicial institutions with established procedures for managing disputes that arise in society. Governments may also provide other institutional and informal means of conflict management such as voting rights, majority rule, protection of minorities, and the freedom to express and discuss conflicting ideas, beliefs, and proposals.

D. **Fulfillment of societal or group aspirations.** All governments strive to fulfill the goals of society as a whole and of various groups within a society. Aspirations may include the promotion of human rights, the common good, and international peace. Goals of some governments might include the conquest and acquisition of territory and the subjugation of other peoples or of some groups within society.

E. **Fulfillment of individual aspirations.** Some governments preserve and promote opportunities for individuals to pursue their own fulfillment in their own way. The Declaration of Independence, for example, speaks of "the pursuit of happiness." Such governments preserve social diversity and enhance the liberty of individuals and groups.

F. **Protection of individual rights.** Some governments, those of constitutional democracies, are established for the protection of each citizen's basic rights against encroachments by government itself or by other groups or individuals. Constitutional democracies are created to serve individuals, not to dominate them.

G. **Improvement of moral condition.** Some governments attempt the moral improvement of citizens. Laws and institutions are designed to mold citizens' character in accordance with some standard of goodness. Ancient Sparta cultivated discipline and austerity among its citizens, and the early Roman Republic fostered civic virtue or devotion to the well-being of the state. Certain modern states promote religious or secular moral ideals.

H. **Protection of property.** States provide means such as police and legal systems that protect private and public property. States also provide legal facilities for the use of their members in defense of their property through a system of rules and law.

III. **Views of the state.** The most prominent philosophical positions on the nature of the state, its organization, and its purposes are in varying degrees reflected in historical and contemporary political debate in the U.S. and abroad. Prominent among these views are the following:

A. **Aristocratic traditionalism.** Several key ideas inform the view of society held by aristocratic traditionalism.

1. **Society is naturally hierarchical and unitary.** This position holds that society is a naturally hierarchical, unitary (corporate) body whose leaders form a natural aristocracy.

2. **Hereditary government and political inequality.** The form of government is usually thought to be hereditary aristocracy. Social classes should participate unequally in political decision making, according to their place in society.

3. **Denial of social contract theory.** Society is not governed by a legalistic "contract" as in commercial relations; rather society should be considered bound together by a moral partnership between present, past, and future generations.

4. **Diminished role for reason.** The role of reason in social and political affairs should be limited; instead, custom and tradition, inherited ideas, benign prejudices, and ingrained habits should be depended upon to guide society.

B. **Liberal-democracy.** "Liberal" in this term means a society that is not bound by authoritarianism or rigid orthodoxy; it does not refer to the contemporary division between "liberals" and "conservatives."

1. **Citizens as creators of the state.** Liberal-democracy views the state as the creation of its citizens, who contract together, agreeing to obey the authority they set up, in order to protect certain individual rights they believe to be their birthright.

2. **Citizens are sovereign.** The citizenry, which collectively is sovereign, has the right to abolish or change governments that fail to protect these rights. No customs or prejudices, however benign, ever take precedence over legally guaranteed rights. Citizenship is *membership* in the sovereign body politic.

3. **Citizens have equal rights.** All citizens have an equal right to participate in making laws or choosing legislators; in political decision making, this equality is to take precedence over all social hierarchies.

C. **Classical Marxism.** Classical Marxism tended to a uniformly negative view of the state.

1. **State as instrument of class domination.** In the view of Marx and his followers, the state is the

politically organized power of the dominant class in society. The state is created to maintain and further the interests of this class.

2. **Modern state as means of bourgeois domination of working class**. The modern capitalist state is dominated by the bourgeoisie, the owners of the means of production. The state oppresses the interests of the working class, who are non-owners of the means of production and must sell themselves on the labor market in order to survive. The capitalist state is thus the political instrument of bourgeois rule, its claims to allegiance are unfounded, and its version of justice favors the ruling class.

3. **The working class should struggle to achieve power**. It is the historical task of the working class to achieve power, if necessary through violent means, and establish a revolutionary socialist state, which will eventually wither away as communism is achieved. The working class accomplishes this task through its own political party, which acts as its vanguard,

D. **Social democracy**. In its original nineteenth-century form, social democracy was another term for democratic socialism.

1. **Social democracy called for peaceful change**. Although many of its ideological underpinnings were Marxist, social democracy called for a peaceful and democratic transition from capitalism to socialism. This strategy therefore opposed the violent revolution usually deemed necessary by orthodox Marxism.

2. **Change from hostile to positive view of the state**. Prior to the turn of the century its concept of the state was, being Marxist, hostile and negative. In the new century, however, this hostility diminished. Before World War II, social democrats generally advocated wholesale public ownership of industry, with a central role given to the state.

3. **Post-war changes**. Since World War II, European social democratic parties have changed in several principle respects.

   a. **State control of industry rather than ownership**. Social democracy has tended since the war to advocate regulation and control of industry by the state rather than outright ownership.

   b. **Advocacy of welfare state**. Social democracy has come to stand for large-scale welfare programs designed to promote social equality and alleviate poverty.

   c. **Positive role for the state**. Social democracy thus places considerable emphasis on a positive, active role for the state. In America, the New Deal is sometimes thought to be a form of social democracy.

E. **Twentieth-century communism**. Prior to the change occurring in the late twentieth century, communism, when it achieved power, viewed the state as its possession.

1. **State as means to develop socialism**. Under Lenin, Stalin and their successors, the state was seen as an instrument of total social control in order to establish socialism.

2. **State controlled solely by Communist party**. The state was strictly subordinated to the Communist party, which held a monopoly on political power, allowing no organized opposition. The party was controlled by a small number of top leaders or by a single individual.

3. **State controlled every facet of society—the idea of totalitarianism**. The state was responsible for the economic life of society and owned nearly all means of production. The state also controlled all facets of social and cultural life, outlawing independent expression. An official Marxist ideology pervaded all areas of public life. On account of the attempt to direct and control the total life and personal expression of the individual, twentieth century Communist states have been termed "totalitarian."

4. **Use of secret police and terror**. State regulations were enforced by an extensive system of secret police, armed militia, informers, and prisons. In the Stalinist model, the use of terror was the means of controlling the population, through widespread executions or imprisonment.

F. **Fascism**. Fascist regimes in the twentieth century have differed considerably amongst themselves. Certain characteristics, however, have generally been prevalent.

1. **State as an autocratic corporate unity**. Fascism, a form of autocracy, views the state as an

organic unity, a corporate whole, which embodies in itself the noble spirit of the people. This view contrasts with liberal democracy, which considers the state an institution set up to protect the individual's rights.

2. **Subordination of the individual.** In the fascist view, the individual must always be subordinate to the state, which is the embodiment of the national will.

3. **Dominant role of the Leader.** The national will is personified by the Leader and his party, which stand above everyone. Resistance and dissent cannot be tolerated.

4. **Purpose of the state is power and glory.** The purpose of the state is not a search for justice or liberty but for power; military prowess is venerated over discussion, as is action, especially violent action, over rational thought. The purpose of the state is the maintenance and increase of national glory.

G. **Chinese traditionalism.** Traditionally, China viewed itself as a "universal state," founded on a "universal kingship."

1. **All of humanity should be ruled by China.** China assumed that all of humanity should be governed by a single ruler bound to act on universal principles. This one ruler, the Chinese emperor, called the "Son of Heaven" was the only person in the world who could communicate between the cosmos and the human world.

   a. **Emperor's rule to be righteous.** The emperor's rule had to be moral and righteous. He maintained order through an emphasis on family and social ritual and a complex and well-educated administrative bureaucracy.

   b. **The heavens punish unjust rule.** If the heavens were displeased with his rule, it would show up in such phenomena as poor harvests, women giving birth to cows, and natural disasters.

   c. **The people could resist unjust rule.** If the emperor failed to rule in a moral way, the people were entitled to rebel against him, to terminate his "mandate of heaven." One ruling house would replace another, however,

and the people were "represented" only temporarily, while rebelling.

   d. **Excluded peoples seen as "barbarians".** China viewed itself as an empire, not as one state among equals. Those not part of its empire were considered "barbarians". They were ranked as more or less barbarian according to the degree to which they accepted rule by the "Son of Heaven" and other Chinese cultural principles.

   e. **Chinese cultural principles.** Chinese cultural principles that all were expected to obey included the Confucian concept of a patriarchal order, and a political order based on strict adherence to the rites, rituals, and obligations forming the essence of relationships of inequality.

   e. **The regime as an ethical-cultural entity.** China saw itself as an ethical-cultural entity, not a political structure. Legitimate rule of the political domain was based on ethical and cultural values. If invading barbarians accepted these ideas, they could even rule China with Chinese support.

2. **China's view of the state in the nineteenth century.** China's confrontation with the superior fire power of the industrializing West in the nineteenth century led to a major transformation of its views about the state.

1. **Competing "empires" not accepted as cultural equals.** Chinese learned of other "empires" that considered themselves superior to China. But China conceded only their military, not cultural, superiority.

2. **The idea of equal "states."** In the nineteenth century, China was introduced to the idea of equal and sovereign "states" based on concepts of political structure, an idea at odds with the Chinese notion of China as a cultural entity. But by 1900 many leaders began to accept the Western notion of the equality and sovereignty of states under international law.

3. **The survival of tradition.** China continued to be governed by a "foreign" emperor, a Manchu, who based his right to rule on traditional values. He was assisted by an administrative bureaucracy well-versed in the moral precepts embodied in the Confucian classics, but not in "modern"

knowledge of science and technology. China continued to be ruled as if it were a moral polity until the collapse of its last empire (the Ch'ing Dynasty) in 1911.

Historical Perspective

I. **Ancient Israel**. The ancient Israelites had an extraordinary influence on Western civilization, including the West's political ideas and practice. While it is impossible to present all of the effects of the Israelites' history and ideas here, several basic lines of influence can be outlined. Those that will be considered are monotheism; the Exodus story as a model of liberation from bondage; and Messianism. In addition, the influence of the Exodus story on the West's view of history as leading to a definite end or purpose (the "unilineal" view of history) and the act of "covenanting," which forms part of the Exodus story, will be considered.

The story of the Exodus of the ancient Israelites from Egypt, their wanderings in the desert and eventual arrival in Canaan, the "promised land," as told in the first books of the Hebrew Bible (Old Testament) deeply influenced Western political thought and action and remains with us today as a cultural prototype of liberation from oppression. The story also incorporates a view of history quite at odds with the view of Greece and Rome. The Exodus story and its view of history enter the mainstream of Western culture through the influence of Christianity, which incorporated the Hebrew Bible into its own expanded version. A principal feature of the story that has had enormous influence is the idea of the covenant—the mutual promising of the Israelites with Yahweh (God). The model of the Exodus story is peculiar to Western culture.

A. **Monotheism: the deity as lawgiver**. The ancient Israelites adopted the monotheistic god that they called Yahweh. This single God was conceived as both creator of the universe and as ruler and lawgiver. The whole of humanity is subject to one God and one moral law; humanity is *under* God. This fundamental idea was transmitted by Christianity throughout Western culture and its political ideas. After much development and mixture with Greek thought, in its secularized form, God's rule became the ideal of the rule of law—law to which even monarchs and princes are subject. The notion of a "higher" law—which is also present in Greek culture—in the modern era is found in the idea of *constitutionalism*: the constitution is conceived as a higher law to which all, including rulers, are subject. This significant invention

of Western political thought and practice was deeply influenced by the ancient Israelites' view of God and God's law, as described in the Hebrew Bible, transmitted and developed by Christianity, and further developed by secular forces.

B. **The Exodus story**. The basic structure of the Israelites' Exodus story is as follows: slavery in Egypt; deliverance from slavery; wandering in the wilderness; and, finally, entrance to a "promised land." During the bondage in Egypt phase, a leader (Moses) emerges who eventually guides the Israelites out of Egypt. According to biblical accounts, God promises the Israelites their own territory, a land of plenty after being delivered from Egypt. The deliverance of the Israelites occurs with divine assistance. After the Exodus from Egypt, the next stage of the biblical story is the Israelites' wandering for forty years in the wilderness. Here there is trouble, for there are "murmurings" against Moses by the recalcitrant, building an idol in Moses' absence, and purging the unfaithful. There is also the key event of the Covenant, a promise by God to his people to favor them if they keep His moral law. Reaching the Promised Land, the "land of milk and honey," is the last stage of the Israelites' liberation.

1. **Bondage in Egypt**. Bondage in Egypt involves both oppression and corruption. The Israelites' enslavement accounts for their oppression. But Egypt, an advanced civilization, also has its attractions. These attractions are its "fleshpots," not only the luxury of eating meat, but all manner of luxuries. The rejection of these luxuries by the Israelites is often regarded as the rejection of urban civilization by a nomadic tribe.

2. **The Exodus: "let my people go."** According to the biblical version, the Israelites escape the bondage of Egypt through the leadership of **Moses** (c. 1200 B.C.) and by direct divine intervention. God punishes Egypt and its tyrannical Pharaoh for failing to release the Israelites by sending a series of plagues to haunt and ravage the land. When the first-born males of the Egyptians are killed (the angel of death passes over the homes of the Israelites), pharaoh at last consents to the Exodus. When Pharaoh's forces nevertheless pursue the Israelites, threatening calamity, God intervenes again to save them, silencing the doubting Israelites by parting the Red Sea and allowing them to escape.

3. **The Wilderness.** The "exodus" proper—the "deliverance" (from the Hebrew word "to go out")—from Egypt is only the first step in preparation for coming into the promised land. Under the leadership of Moses, the Israelites wander in the desert for forty years. Moses becomes their lawgiver and educator, for slaves cannot go directly from bondage to freedom; they must be educated for freedom. This means that they must internalize the law—God's law—before they can become a free people.

a. **The covenant.** God's promise to provide a land "flowing with milk and honey," was made while the Israelites were still in Egypt. It was one-sided: God demanded no return promise by the Israelites. In the wilderness, however, a key moment arrives when God tells the Israelites that if they will promise to obey him and keep this covenant, He will favor them above all other peoples and make them a "kingdom of priests, and an holy nation" (Exod. 19:5-6). The terms of the covenant on God's side are the moral law that He announces through Moses, beginning with the Ten Commandments.

b. **The covenant as an act of political foundation.** The covenant between God and the Israelites is a founding act, such as the creation of a constitution by agreement of a people. Through the covenant, Israel is created as a people in a way they had not been before. The law they agree to obey has a defining, shaping, disciplining force to it that molds the Israelites as a single people as they had not been before. The process of making the covenant is an act of **mutual consent** by God and people: "And all of the people answered together, and said, 'All that the Lord hath spoken we will do.' And Moses returned the words of the people unto the Lord" (Exod. 19:8). Through the act of covenanting, the Israelites take moral obligations upon themselves, obligations that, to their cost, they do not always obey. Thus they take upon themselves moral responsibility; they show themselves to be **moral agents**. (Michael Walzer, *Exodus and Revolution*, 1985).

c. **Backsliding and "murmuring."** The desert is a hard place after the settled life of Egypt. Some of the Israelites long for the "fleshpots of Egypt." While Moses is on Mt. Sinai, some of the people, backsliding into their old ways, unsure of Moses' whereabouts, disobeying the commandment to have no other gods before them and to make no graven images, ask Moses' brother Aaron to make them a god. Aaron fashions a Golden Calf, which many of the people worship. Seeing this, God is so infuriated that Moses must dissuade Him from destroying the people (Exod. 32: 11-14).

d. **The purges of the unfaithful.** Descending from Mt. Sinai to confront the unfaithful, Moses destroys the idol worshipped by the morally weak and asks, "Who is on the Lord's side?" In reply, "all the sons of Levy gathered themselves together unto him." Thus was born a priest caste in a people not yet ready to become a "kingdom of priests," as promised in the covenant. On Moses' instructions from God, this caste of the morally pure, the Levite priests, then kill the men among the faithless, "and there fell of the people that day about three thousand men" (Exod. 32: 28-26). This slaughter has been termed history's first revolutionary purge, a model for later purges such as the Terror of revolutionary France and the long and bloody line of purges after the Russian Revolution.

e. **Education.** One moral of the story of the Israelites in the desert is that newly-released slaves cannot become free men and women in an instant. They are "freed" but not "free," their irresponsible mentality still exhibiting the inward marks of the outward bondage they have cast off. The rigors of the desert serve the purpose of recreating the Israelites into a people fit for freedom. They need to be reeducated for a life without masters and bondage, and the inhospitable desert is an ideal site for enforcing moral discipline after the lax regime of Egypt. They can only be a free people if they obey the moral law and behave responsibly; irresponsibility fits them only for destruction or for the acceptance of a new master and a new bondage.

4. **The "Promised Land."** According to the Exodus story, God promised the land of Canaan to the Israelites while they were still in Egypt without

demanding a reciprocal promise by the people. It was to be "a land flowing with milk and honey." Scholars have interpreted this promise as an inducement for the Israelites to leave an advanced urban civilization for the severity of a nomadic life in the desert. While the promise seems straightforward enough, there are a number of complexities.

a. **The promised land and the covenant.** God not only promised a land of their own to the Israelites. According to the Sinai covenant he also promised to make them a favored people and "a kingdom of priests and a holy nation"—**if** they kept the moral law. Eventually they do enter Canaan, but it does not live up to expectations. By way of explanation, the prophets argue that God has not (yet) fulfilled the promise because the people have not lived up to the law.

b. **The two-fold material and moral aspect of the promised land.** After the Sinai covenant, there were two aspects to the idea of the promised land—the satisfaction of needs and desires on the one hand; and the keeping of moral law on the other. The failure to keep the law first occurred in the desert in the Golden Calf incident. The immediate result was that the promise to make them a "kingdom of priests" was compromised with the creation of the Levite priest caste.

c. **Delay of the promised land until the future.** The result of the prophets' explanation of Israel's failure to realize God's promise was to push attainment of the land of milk and honey into the future. Thus, while the future might be an egalitarian state where all are priests, the law is kept ("a holy nation"), and while the needs of all are satisfied in a land of plenty, the present is otherwise.

C. **Messianism.** Messianic ideas began with Judaism and were adopted by Christianity.

1. **Messianism in Judaism.** Later in the history of the ancient Hebrews, the character of the promised land underwent a change with the coming of Messianism. The original idea of the promised land did not include the idea of its utter perfection. It was not a return to the Garden of Eden. But in the Messianic tradition, the promised land is perfected; there is a final

triumph of good over evil. "...[A]fter the final overthrow of evil powers, the righteous nation [of Israel] would live in harmony and prosperity in a 'renovated' earth, which would center in the New Jerusalem" (Ernest Lee Tuveson, *Millennium and Utopia*, 1964). Thus, the triumph is this worldly and political as well as moral. It is also conceived as benefitting all of humanity, not only the Jewish people, though at various times in biblical history God's redemption of the Israelites as a nation was emphasized over its wider significance. Further, at some periods, it was suggested that the Messianic age would come without an individual Messiah (or "anointed" one, as kings and other superiors were once anointed).

2. **Messianism in Christianity.** Christianity adopted Messianism from Judaism. Jesus of Nazareth, whom Christians call "Christ," from the Greek for Messiah, disappointed Jewish Messianic expectations by declaring his kingdom "not of this world." According to the New Testament Book of Revelations, the Messiah will return and the New Jerusalem will descend from Heaven after cataclysmic natural and political events (the "Last Days") to rule for a thousand years.

3. **The influence of Messianism.** Messianism is not only a Western idea—it is found in ancient texts of Buddhism, Islam, and in other religions. But it has had a deep and lasting influence on Western thought and, at various times, action.

a. **Utopia and utopianism.** Although the sources of utopianism in Western thinking have Greek as well as Judeo-Christian roots (Plato's *Republic* is a sort of Utopia), the Messianic tradition is an important one because it envisages an age of human perfection. The ideal of a perfect society has been explored in Western culture by a long series of "Utopias." (**Sir Thomas More** (1478-1535) coined the word in his *Utopia* (1516), meaning "nowhere.") Messianism, with its prophecy of a final battle between good and evil, injects an element of emotional frenzy into utopianism.

b. **The tragedy of messianic politics.** Many of the nineteenth century's political ideas and movements have been described by scholars as embracing political Messianism, the "expectation of universal regeneration" and "a coherent, complete, and final solution to the problem of social evil" (J.L. Talmon, *Political Messianism*, 1960). Those embracing Messianic politics, believing that their cause advances the purpose of history, embodies the idea of "unilineal" history. Secularized Messianic politics is represented most familiarly in traditional Marxism, in which the Communist party is considered the deliverer of the enslaved working class. The party is to lead the suffering workers to Socialism, a secular equivalent of the promised land. The faith and fervor historically vested in various communist parties—especially in the Soviet Union—have been considered by a number of scholars as a secular form of religious Messianism. In its Bolshevik version, the inner core of the Party plays a role like the Levite priest caste at Mt. Sinai. They are pure and fervent instruments furthering History's "divine" mission. No limits bind the morally pure from committing violence on behalf of the sacred cause. The necessarily disappointed expectations of perfection, together with the possibility and historical realization of limitless violence, constitute the tragedy of political Messianism, which must always fail.

G. **The Exodus story and Western culture.** The Exodus story and various of its special features, such as the covenant and the idea of a "promised land," have had a remarkable effect on both thought and action in the West. The basic idea of the Exodus story is unique to Western culture; it "isn't a story told everywhere; it isn't a universal pattern; it belongs to the West...." (Michael Walzer, *op. cit.*)

1. **Unilineal vs. circular view of history.** The view of history encompassed by the Exodus story is the opposite of the cyclical view held by the ancient Greeks and Romans.

   a. **The cyclical view of history.** In the Greco-Roman view, time moves through political forms, which, like the seasons of the year, inevitably return to their point of origin only to begin the cycle again.

   b. **The unilineal view of history.** In the Exodus story, on the contrary, time moves forward toward a stated end or purpose. There may be regress—the backsliding of a stubborn people—but history then moves onward toward entrance into the promised land. In the Christian version, history moves toward the return of the Messiah and the termination of human history with the apocalypse (the destruction of evil and the triumph of good) and the rule of Christ.

   c. **Secular versions of the Judeo-Christian view of history.** Secular versions of the unilineal view of history have been monumentally important for more than the last two centuries. The idea of Progress is a direct descendent of unilineal history, infecting much of the Western world since the eighteenth century. Thus, the view of history adopted by Marxism is a secular version of the Judeo-Christian view. In the traditional Marxist view, human history moves inexorably toward the end point of Socialism, the perfection of human society.

2. **The reappearance of Exodus ideas.** The reappearance of the central ideas of the Exodus in Western political theory and practice is virtually endless. Among many other instances, it was cited by religious reformers such as **Savanarola** (1452-1498) in Florence; the protestant **John Calvin** in Geneva; the Presbyterian **John Knox**, (1514?-1572) in Scotland, and the Puritan leader in the English Civil War **Oliver Cromwell** (1599-1658). It was likewise cited by contemporary South African blacks. The Exodus tradition was a deep impetus in the foundation of Israel in 1948. In addition, cultural figures as remote as the eighteenth century English reformer **Jeremy Bentham** (1748-1832) and the founder of psychoanalysis **Sigmund Freud** (1856-1939) compared themselves to Moses in their struggle to lead humanity to a better existence. (See below for a discussion of the influence of the Exodus story in America.)

3. **The influence of the idea of a "covenant."** The influence of the covenant idea upon Western culture, both in its ideas and many of its political practices, is immense. The Latin word for covenant is *foedus*, from which the English word federal is derived. To covenant is to federate; and the freedom to make political covenants was traditionally called "federal" liberty. (See the section below in this fFamework on Federalism). The Exodus story was not the only Western source of the idea of society created by a mutual agreement or contract—in

Plato's account the idea was discussed by **Socrates** (469-399 B.C.) in his refusal to escape from his death sentence. But political writers of sixteenth and seventeenth century Europe, although they knew of the idea of contract from Roman and medieval law, often drew upon the example of the Sinai covenant in defending a contractual view of society. In 1537 Calvin literally reenacted the Sinai covenant in Geneva, having his followers swear to the Ten Commandments in a civic ceremony. Such covenanting was repeated "in the Mayflower Compact, in the Scottish National Covenant,...in the [English] Puritan army's Agreement of the People, in the American constitutions of the 1780s....The study of the Bible leads to a view of political action as a kind of communal performance; what happened at Sinai provides a precedent for early modern (and **present day**) efforts to mobilize men and women for a politics without precedent in their own experience" (Walzer *op. cit.*).

4. **Influence of the Exodus story in America**. Biblical accounts of the ancient Israelites and the Exodus story had an enormous influence in America in the first centuries after colonization and continue to exert inspirational power among wide sections of the American people. Below are examples of this influence.

   a. **The colonial era**. Early colonists such as the Pilgrim fathers actively identified themselves with the ancient Israelites and believed that they to be on an "errand into the wilderness," having been "singled out by God to be an example for the nations (especially England)" (Conrad Cherry, *God's New Israel*, 1971). An example of this outlook is found in **John Winthrop** (1588-1649). Writing in 1630 while at sea aboard the *Arrabella*, Winthrop, member of the founding Massachusetts Bay Company and later the colony's governor, citing Moses and the Israelites, wrote that "wee shall be as a Citty upon a Hill, the eies of all people are uppon us"—a model community to be emulated. Early colonists saw themselves as God's new "chosen people," as the Israelites had been in the past; America was the new promised land. The covenant of the Israelites was now reenacted in the wilderness of the New World. In the work of building a new holy community, Winthrop wrote that "Wee are entered into covenant with [God] for this worke..."

(Cherry, *op. cit.*; and see Perry Miller, *Errand into the Wilderness*, [1956]).

   b. **The revolutionary and founding era**. The Great Awakening, the religious revivals that swept the American colonies for decades beginning in 1720, saw a renewal of the view of the New World as the new "promised land." But the American Revolution was a powerful stimulus to the view of the new policy as "God's new Israel," with Great Britain playing the part of Pharaoh. Asked by Congress in 1776 to design a seal for the new American polity, Benjamin Franklin and Thomas Jefferson both chose Exodus themes that compared Americans to the ancient Israelites. Franklin proposed "Moses lifting his hand and the Red Sea dividing, with Pharaoh in his chariot being overwhelmed by the waters, and with a motto in great popular favor at the time, 'Rebellion to tyrants is obedience to God'." Jefferson favored "a representation of the children of Israel in the wilderness, led by a cloud by day and a pillar of fire by night." Jefferson also alluded to the Exodus story on his first inaugural address. In 1783, **Ezra Stiles**, president of Yale, was much in the mainstream when he preached a sermon in Connecticut citing the Exodus story and designating the newly emancipated United States as "God's American Israel" (Cherry, *op. cit.*).

   c. **The era of Westward expansion**. The era of westward expansion in the nineteenth century saw a renewed consciousness of the idea of the American nation as a chosen people reenacting the story of the Israelites. American paintings were a powerful medium in the representation of this view. Thus, *Daniel Boone Escorting Settlers through the Cumberland Gap* (1851-52) by **George Caleb Bingham** (1811-1879) depicted a latter-day reenactment of Moses leading his people through the wilderness. Also representative was the theme of **William S. Jewett's** *The Promised Land—the Grayson Family* (1850), which showed a pioneer family gazing out upon a vast distant landscape (see *The West as America: Reinterpreting Images of the Frontier*, Washington, D.C., 1991). The idea of the divine appointment of the American nation was an influential force among those who supported the "Manifest Destiny" of American expansion to the Pacific Ocean.

    d. **The Civil War era.** Exodus and the biblical imagery and belief in a divinely appointed mission were invoked by both sides during the Civil War. Each side assumed that its military "was the advance guard of the New Israel crossing the Red Sea of war" (Cherry, *op. cit.*). For example, in a sermon in April 1861 the New England Congregationalist preacher **Henry Ward Beecher** (1813-1878) compared Americans to Israelites in the struggle that was upon them: "Right before us lies the Red Sea of war. It is red indeed. There is blood in it." For the Confederacy, in June of the same year, a Presbyterian minister in New Orleans, **Benjamin Palmer**, compared the South to the oppressed Israelites in Egypt and the North's government to Pharaoh and invoked the Israelites covenant with God as a model for the confederacy: "Eleven tribes sought to go forth in peace from the house of political bondage: but the heart of our modern Pharaoh is hardened, that he will not let Israel go." The day when the ancient Hebrew tribes had accepted divine law was, Palmer said, "a memorable day." "Not less grand and awful is this scene to-day, when an infant nation strikes its covenant with God of Heaven" (Cherry, *op. cit.*).

    e. **Black American history.** The ideas and imagery of the biblical Exodus have had a special force and influence in black American history. In the nineteenth century, the biblical story was frequently invoked by blacks and their supporters to explain the position of slaves and to provide religious weight to demands for their freedom and to give divine sanction to their ultimate vindication and succor in a promised land. "Without doubt, the Exodus story was the most significant myth for American black identity whether slave or free." As one former slave related, preachers exhorted slaves to believe that they were the children of Israel in the wilderness sent by the Lord to take them to the land of milk and honey. "Emancipation proved that God was faithful to his people...." (Albert J. Roboteau, "The Black Experience in American Evangelism:

The Meaning of Slavery," in Leonard Sweet, ed., *The Evangelical Tradition in America*, 1984). At a meeting of blacks in 1865, the "Celebration by the Colored People's Educational Monument Association," held in Washington on the fourth of July, the celebrated white poet **John Pierpont** read a poem that compared Moses and Lincoln, "Led thy people through a redder sea/Than Israel passed, to light and liberty." Exodus imagery did not die out with emancipation but continued to be frequently cited by black Americans in the nineteenth and twentieth centuries, especially in the post-World War II Civil Rights movement (see also, for example, Nell Painter, *The Exodusters*).

II. **Nature and purpose of the state in the ancient world.** Philosophical reflection about the state in the ancient world was articulated by philosophers and expressed in the practice of government.

  A. **Ancient Greece—the influence of geography.** The nature of the Greek city-state or *polis* was heavily influenced by geography.

    1. *Polis* **is small and homogeneous.** As opposed to Rome in its later centuries, the *polis* was usually composed of a small, homogenous population, making consensus easier.

    2. **Mountainous terrain impedes expansion.** City-states were usually located in the many valleys of Greece's mountainous terrain that restricted expansion and maintained separation.

    3. **Athens an exception.** With its easy access to the sea, Athens was an exception. It developed an urban policy open to diverse ideas and peoples but also favored direct democratic rule by its citizens. Athenian democracy was notably portrayed by its leader **Pericles** (c. 495-429 B.C.) in his funeral oration as reported in the *History of the Peloponnesian War* by **Thucydides** (c. 471-400 B.C.).

  B. **Purposes of the *polis* as justice and the good life.** In Greek political culture, morality and politics were thought to be inseparable. Thus the creation of a just political order was a paramount purpose of the *polis*. Its political order was often viewed as an educating force that molded citizens in accordance with a shared ideal of what a good life is. In this way the collective and individual aspirations of the members of the state could be fulfilled.

1. **Plato.** As outlined in the *Republic*, **Plato** (427-347 B.C.) placed an aristocratic concept of justice at the heart of his ideal state.

    a. **Plato's view of justice as harmonious order.** In Plato's view the attainment of justice is a central purpose of any proper political order. Justice consists of individuals performing the assigned task they were most fitted by nature and education to do, thereby promoting harmony between the parts of the state and the whole.

    b. **Justice and the division of labor within a social hierarchy.** Wise guardians were to rule, courageous warriors were to fight, and industrious workers were to work. The practice of justice promoted the stability of the state.

    c. **Public education at the heart of the republic.** The just social system of the republic had at its center the state's education of its members, harmoniously molding their character for the good of the whole.

    d. **Advancement by merit alone.** Entrance into the highest class of society was to be according to merit only, without distinction between the sexes.

2. **Aristotle.** Aristotle (384-322 B.C.) discussed the purpose of the state in his *Politics* and *Ethics*.

    a. **The *polis* as creator of human beings by a system of justice.** Aristotle saw the purpose of the *polis* as raising humanity above the level of beasts by subjecting its members to the rules of justice. Although ideas of justice may diverge to some extent under varying constitutions, justice is not the arbitrary creation of humanity but is founded on nature. Thus, what is right is right by nature—a universal standard. The idea of natural right or, as it was later called, "natural law," was passed to the modern world from Greek thought through Christianity. The idea of the law of nature was a key ingredient in the English political thought that influenced the ideas of the American Revolution.

    b. **Pursuit of public good at the heart of a just order.** In non-perverted forms of the *polis*, the rulers (whether one, few, or many) rule on behalf of the public good. In corrupted forms, the rulers rule for their own benefit. Citizens are obligated to promote the public good.

    c. **The state as an arena for self-development.** The *polis* provides the means for safety and security. But it also provides the means that allow the self development of citizens, fostering the moral and intellectual qualities that are uniquely human.

    d. **Distributive justice and the Good Life.** The overall purpose of political power is the achievement of a morally good life. The *polis* or state also maintains a system of distributive justice in which goods are distributed in accordance with the merits of those who receive them.

    e. **Citizens share common understanding of the Good Life.** The purpose of the state can be agreed upon by citizens because they share a common understanding of justice and the good life. The small size and homogeneity of the *polis* is reflected in this view.

3. **The *polis* and immortality.** Classical Greek culture regarded the political realm as an arena in which the virtuous citizen could gain immortality through heroic words and deeds that would be remembered by the *polis* virtually forever.

4. **The *polis* in historical experience.** The political and legal arrangements of the city-states were not uniform.

    a. **Well-developed legal systems.** A number of Greek city-states had highly developed judicial systems, with written laws, courts, and juries. **Socrates** (370?-399 B.C.) was tried under a provision of the Athenian system.

    b. **Slavery.** Many of the ancient Greek city-states were based on slavery. Slaves suffered the severest legal disabilities under legal systems that might serve full citizens well. Slavery existed both in liberal Periclean Athens and in authoritarian Sparta, with its system of "helots" or serfs.

c. **Political participation for males only**. Participation was exclusively male, though occasionally a woman might have political influence, as was thought to be true of Pericles' brilliant and cultivated companion **Aspasia** (c. 440 B.C.). Participation varied by city-state. Some were aristocracies; others were democracies; still others were ruled by kings or by strong men known as tyrants.

5. **The *polis* as educator**. The central place that the Greek states assigned to education is reflected in the writings of leading Greek writers.

   a. **Education in Plato's *Republic***. Plato's elaborate proposals for the education of the guardian class in his *Republic* mirror the idea of *polis* as educator. Education was aimed at developing the whole person, including intellect, spirit, and body.

   b. **The state as educator in Aristotle**. In the *Politics* and *Ethics*, Aristotle states that "All would agree that the legislator should make the education of the young his chief and foremost concern" since "the constitution of a state will suffer if education is neglected." "The citizens of a state should always be educated to suit the constitution of the state (*Politics* 1337 a). Education was thus to be the same for all citizens and was to be public, not private.

   c. **The state as educator: Sparta**. Education in the two chief rivals of classical Greece, Athens and Sparta, reveal much about the character of the state in each case.

      (1) **Harsh and puritanical education**. For centuries Sparta's education system was rigorously puritanical, harsh, and authoritarian. An early system educated both boys and girls. But by c. 550 B.C. it had given way to an exclusively military education for young men that emphasized discipline, austerity, and brutality. Education of young women was reduced to training for their future role as mothers.

      (2) **Education as military boarding school**. Completely in the hands of the state, the boy's education began when he left his family for a military-type boarding school at the age of 7 to 20. He was imbued with total subservience to the state, to the exclusion of all other forms of fulfillment. The security of the state was the supreme good.

   d. **The state as educator: Athens**. Athenian education was based upon principles completely different from those practiced at Sparta.

      (1) **Balanced education**. By the sixth century B.C. Athens had rejected military prowess as the primary purpose of education. Instead, it aimed at a balance between physical, cultural, and moral elements.

      (2) **Variety of schools**. Education took place in a variety of schools, which all male youth of the citizen class (10-20% of population) were expected to attend. Separate schools were devoted to gymnastics, music (including dance and drama), and reading and grammar.

      (3) **Special schools**. In the fourth century, schools of philosophy (Plato's Academy and Aristotle's Lyceum), rhetoric, and, eventually, a college for military training were added.

      (4) **Purpose of education**. Education played a central role in the state, expressing its ideals and other aspects of its identity. Education had a moral purpose: the creation of a good and wise individual. While the citizen was obligated to fight for Athens, he was also free to pursue his own self-development.

      (5) **Classic balance and its undoing**. In its classic age, Athens came close to achieving an equilibrium between individual freedom and political obligation. The political and spiritual upheavals accompanying the Peloponnesian War (431-404 B.C.) were the undoing of this balance. The conviction of Socrates in 399 B.C. for unorthodox teachings perhaps illustrates the erosion of freedom; his refusal to escape capital punishment shows that, at least among

the older generation, a sense of civic obligation remained.

C. **Ancient Rome**. As opposed to the diminutive size of the Greek city-states, Rome in its republican period grew steadily.

1. **Geography and adaptation to ethnic diversity**. Geography played a central role, since Rome lay on a plain without natural defenses. Allying itself with alien peoples who had their own laws and customs, the Roman state and legal system, as opposed to its Greek counterparts, adapted itself to ethnic diversity.

2. **Cicero and the state as moral community**. In his *Republic, Laws, De Oratore,* and elsewhere, **Marcus Tullius Cicero** (106-43 B.C.) argued that the state is a community that exists for ethical purposes. These aims are the improvement of life by the thought and effort of its members. The state is a moral community possessed in common by its members, united by common agreement about law and rights and by the desire to participate in its advantages. These include just government and mutual aid.

3. **Cicero and the state as the common wealth of its members**. For Cicero the state is a "**res populi**" or "**res publica**"—a "thing of the people," a "public thing," a "commonwealth". The state is thus a single corporate body whose power is derived from the collective power of the people.

4. **Cicero's view of the state as subject to higher law**. Not only is it governed by law; the laws of the state are subject to a higher divine or natural law. States that do not adhere to these principles lose their character as states.

5. **Ideal citizen devoted to public good**. Drawing on the views of **Isocrates** (436 B.C.-338 B.C.), Cicero believed the ideal citizen has these qualities:

   a. **Citizen as orator**. The ideal citizen is an **rhetor** or orator, devoted to the public good, accepting the responsibilities of citizenship.

   b. **Citizen educated in the humanities**. The citizen is informed by a broad liberal education in the "humanities" (studies proper to humanity).

6. **Transmission of the ideal of educated citizen**. The tradition of educated citizen from Isocrates and Cicero was reinforced by **Marcus Fabius Quintilian** (A.D. c.35-c.95) whose *Institutio oratoria* (the schooling of the Orator) became virtually the educational bible of civic humanists in the Italian Renaissance.

7. **Roman law**. Roman law has been called "undoubtedly one of the great achievements of the human mind and spirit."

   a. **Compilations of Roman law**. Roman law was compiled in 533 in the *Digest* and the *Institutes* written under the emperor **Justinian** (reigned 527-565).

   b. **Law as civilizing force**. An important Roman idea was law as the principal ordering and civilizing force of the state. Law protects individual rights, secures expectations, and improves people's moral condition by subjecting them to its requirements.

   c. **Varieties and sources of law**. In the Roman tradition, there are several kinds and sources of law. Not all law comes from the acts of will of a legislature or ruler. Reason is a source of law, and all proper law is compatible with reason. At its full development, Roman law made women the equals of men in controlling property and children, though not in inheritance. It also sought to protect slaves by outlawing cruelty and making it easier for them to be freed.

8. **The purposes of the Roman state in practice**. No brief summary of Rome's thousand-year political history can be adequate; but certain generalizations may be offered.

   a. **Rome pursued both ideals and self-interest**. Both as republic and as empire, Rome's purposes combined the pursuit of ideals with naked self-interest, promoting the polity's aspirations. Rome pursued both the protection of its citizens and the conquest of neighbors. In early times conquest was to be morally justified as defensive war, though this rule was not always followed. Civic devotion seems to have been widespread.

   b. **Highly developed legal institutions embodied inequalities**. Law and legal institutions were always prized and became highly developed by the early empire. The inequality of women and, at various times, of aliens combined with extensive slavery meant that the protection of rights was not uniform. At the height of the empire, the subjection of barbarian tribes to the civil law was justified as a means to improve their moral condition.

c. **Public works**. The Roman state also had a highly developed system of public works that distributed various resources.

d. **The decline of security**. By the end of the fourth century A.D., the western empire no longer fulfilled its purpose of creating security; less than a century later it had collapsed, leaving barbarian rule and anarchy in its wake.

D. **Christianity**. The triumph of Christianity in the Roman world brought with it a fundamental alteration in the relationship of the individual to the political order.

1. **The moral relationship of the classical citizen and the state**. In the classical world of Greece and republican Rome, the individual was regarded as owing the state complete moral and spiritual allegiance as well as military service and general obedience. The classical citizen was not split between two competing realms that Christians were to call "this world" and "the next" world. Although Socrates claimed a religious obligation to pursue philosophy that he refused to abandon, in the end he believed in an ultimate obligation to Athens—not to philosophy—and drank the hemlock. Demanding the allegiance of the whole person, the ancient republic was thus "morally greedy." In Sophocles' *Antigone*, Antigone disobeys the state in the name of a higher law—and is destroyed for her trouble.

2. **Christianity and divided loyalties**. Espousing a doctrine of divided loyalty, Christianity claimed the moral and spiritual portion of the human person for itself, leaving the physical portion to the command of the state.

a. **Breaking the state's moral monopoly**. In Jesus' injunction to "render unto Caesar the things that are Caesar's and unto God the things that are God's," Christianity broke the monopoly of the ancient state on the whole person.

b. **Obedience to a higher power**. Moreover, deriving its monotheistic ideas from Judaism, Christianity placed a power higher than the state—the power of God and God's laws—to sit in judgment over it. For many centuries, Christian teaching led believers to obey constituted authority. But eventually the revolutionary potential of Christian ideas was realized. Acting in the name of this higher power, Christians found themselves obliged to *dis*obey a state that demanded obedience outside its limited sphere. By the nineteenth and twentieth centuries, secularized versions of Christian ideas called for "civil disobedience," based on the state's lack of a moral monopoly over the citizen on the one hand, and knowledge of higher moral principles by the individual, on the other.

c. **From individual salvation to the "pursuit of happiness."** In later centuries it became apparent that Christianity introduced a radical individualism with its revolutionary doctrines, for each Christian was deeply concerned with his own salvation. Christians demanded a state that accommodated their search for salvation. Ultimately, in the eighteenth century, the search for "salvation" was transformed into the secular terminology of the "pursuit of happiness." By separating spiritual and physical realms, Christianity introduced **freedom** from the state's total grasp of its subjects.

d. **Freedom, equality, and the individual**. Two of Western Civilization's great ideas—freedom and individualism—are in great measure the outgrowth of Christian ideas. In championing the idea of the **equality** of each person, of man and woman alike (for Christianity "there is neither male nor female for all are one in Christ"), Christianity introduced a third great idea of the West. Without these ideas, the course not only of Western history but also of world history, would have been fundamentally altered.

III. **Absence of the state in the Middle Ages; its development in the early modern period.** Examples of reflection on the state and significant incidents in the historical experience concerning its development follow.

A. **The Middle Ages**. The state as we now understand it did not exist in Medieval Europe. The purpose of the fragmented political power that did exist tended to be considered as an adjunct to the Christian Church.

1. **Medieval theory**. There was no separate idea of the "state" in the Middle Ages.

   a. **Divine justification for political power**. The existence of political power was justified through the Christian belief in man's sinful nature. The most influential biblical source for the justification of political power and the obligation of obedience was a passage in the New Testament *(Romans* 13: 1-7), which stated that everyone is to be "subject to higher powers."

   b. **Theory of the "two swords."** Thought to be naturally hierarchial, Christian society was composed of two "swords," one secular, the other ecclesiastical. The main purpose of the secular sword was to protect the Church, its officers, and believers, and to maintain a just social order which allowed the faithful to lead a Christian life.

   c. **Lack of religious toleration**. There was no toleration for non-Christians or the unorthodox, who were persecuted; there was thus no freedom of belief or conscience.

2. **Political ideals of Aquinas. Thomas Aquinas** (1225-1274), combining Aristotelian with Christian philosophy, argued that the purpose of secular power is primarily ethical. This ethical purpose rests ultimately on divine will, which underlies law. To be legitimate, human law must conform itself to Natural Law, which is the part of God's law that can be known through human reason unassisted by revelation and is therefore common to all mankind, not only to Christians. Rulers are to maintain peace and preserve life. Law is to promote "felicity and beatitude" which are the purposes of human life; law is not to contradict natural law. Legitimate political power is founded on the community as a whole; rulers are obliged to promote the **common good**, an idea borrowed from Aristotle.

3. **Medieval historical experience**. Although a main purpose of the political order was to maintain social peace, in practice the period between the fall of the Roman Empire and the Renaissance was one of almost continuous violence.

   a. **Lack of control of means of violence**. While the modern state claims a monopoly on the legitimate means of violence, conditions in the Middle Ages were different. With no centralized control on the means of violence, medieval society was incapable of remedying its insecurity. Private armies directed by powerful nobles, feuds among family clans, marauders such as the Vikings, and general political instability made the management of conflict always precarious and often impossible.

   b. **Conflict between secular and sacred authorities**. The superiority of the Christian church to decide various matters was frequently challenged by rulers anxious to increase their own prestige. Confrontations between kings and the papacy reached a peak in the twelfth and fourteenth centuries.

   c. **Few purposes of political power fulfilled**. In general, few of the ordinary functions of what is now called the state were fulfilled by the warriors who populated the castles of medieval Europe. Even the unifying agency of the papacy broke down at various times, as rival "popes" challenged each other, and unsuitable individuals occupied the Holy See in Rome.

B. **Early modern era: political ideas**. The modern state developed in England and on the continent of Europe from the sixteenth century onward.

1. **The purpose of the modern state: renaissance Italy**. The separation of political thought from theology and the secularization of the political realm marked the thought of Renaissance writers on politics and history.

   a. **Guicciardini. Francesco Guicciardini** (1483-1540), a master historian of the Renaissance, illustrated the separation of political thought from theology, discussing political matters on their own. One of his concerns was the political instability of his native Florence.

   b. **Machiavelli**. For **Niccolo Machiavelli** (1469-1527) the purpose of the state was its own perpetuation and aggrandizement as well as the fulfillment of group aspirations of independence and glory. These ideas became part of the background for the **nationalism** that became so powerful a factor in Europe in the nineteenth century and throughout the world in the twentieth century.

2. **The purpose of the modern state: seventeenth-century England**. Both the political theory and historical experience of seventeenth-century England are an important example of European influence on the later evolution of the modern state in America and elsewhere.

a. **Hobbes and the modern state**. Certain assumptions of **Thomas Hobbes'** (1588-1678) otherwise authoritarian *Leviathan* (1651) formed part of the basis of later liberal theory. The authoritarian character of Hobbes' theory is mainly due to its creation during the English Civil War (see below). Hobbes was anxious to derive a view of political obligation that would preclude the breakdown of civil order that so convulsed his own time.

(1) **State as a contract among equals**. The state should be considered as arising from a contract among the governed, who agree to obey one person or group. The governed are considered as equals, since potentially each can kill any other.

(2) **Protection of the subject as the state's sole purpose**. The state's sole purpose is to protect the lives of its subjects. Subjects' obligations end if this protection ceases.

(3) **Denial of a sole "good life"**. There is no one "good life" for the state to promote. The absence of a single "valid" moral ideal limits the proper scope of the state's authority.

(4) **State to monopolize means of violence**. Hobbes' idea of a single sovereign power advanced the key idea that the modern state claims for itself a monopoly on the legitimate means of violence, making order and conflict management possible.

(5) **Will of the sovereign as sole source of law**. In another departure, contrary to Roman Law which recognized a number of sources of law, Hobbes said that all law comes from the will of the sovereign.

(6) **State as a "mortal god"**. Hobbes also described the state as a "mortal god," a description fulfilled only later with the worship of the state in the extreme nationalism of the twentieth century.

b. **Locke**. In his *Second Treatise* (published in 1690 but written in the early 1680s) **John Locke** (1632-1704) set forth ideas essential for the development of liberal democracy. The historical setting of his theory differed from that of Hobbes, in that, writing two decades after the restoration of the English monarchy, Locke set out to justify overthrowing authority that he believed had overstepped its bounds, not to defend the prerogatives of authority, as Hobbes had done during the Civil War. Not long after Locke wrote his *Two Treatises*, the "Glorious Revolution" overthrew Charles II and placed the Dutch **William III** (1650-1702) and his wife **Mary** (1662-1694) on the English throne.

(1) **State as a "compact" among its members**. Locke followed Hobbes in viewing the moral basis of the state as a "compact" among its members set up to protect life, liberty, and property.

(2) **Purposes of the state limit its authority**. Political power is a kind of legal "trust". In the theory of liberal democracy, Locke's ideas helped to establish the character of the state as the creature and servant of the people.

(3) **The "right to revolution"**. If political authority habitually fails to meet the terms of its trust, citizens have a right to change or abolish it. This later became known as the "right to revolution" (Locke's own term was an "appeal to heaven") and formed an important philosophical basis for pre-revolutionary American thought.

C. **Early modern era: historical experience**. The modern state was born in Europe. While much of the continent remained politically fragmented, it was nevertheless in Europe that the development of the modern state took place. Such development occurred, for example, in the unified countries of France and England, where monarchs were able to establish powerful centralized states by the early seventeenth century. The English example is outlined below.

1. **Struggle between king and Parliament in England.** Under the Tudors, especially **Henry VII** (d. 1509), **Henry VIII** (d. 1547), and **Elizabeth I** (d. 1603), the English state was increasingly centralized and dominated by the executive. Under Henry VIII, England broke with the Catholic church and formed the Church of England in its place.

    a. **Parliament's power challenged by "divine right of kings" doctrine**. To maintain their power, however, English monarchs were dependent on Parliament to provide taxation venue. When **James I** (1567-1625) proclaimed the divine right of kings and the subservience of Parliament to his prerogative, a struggle between legislative and executive powers ensued.

    b. **Monarch attempts to dominate judiciary**. The king also claimed a prerogative over the judiciary. For example, a dispute arose in 1610 when the distinguished jurist **Edward Coke** (1552-1634) told the king that he had no more prerogative than the law allowed. in reply, James dismissed him. Although the rule of law, a principal norm of constitutional modern states, was already an ideal, it had yet to be achieved in practice.

2. **The English Civil War** (1642-1649). The failure of king and Parliament to resolve their dispute led to civil war. During this struggle the opposition of the religious ideas of Anglican and Puritan played an important role.

    a. **Popular debate vents influential new ideas**. At the same time, debate about the organization, character, and purpose of political rule gave rise to popular movements and ideas that were widely influential. In the two following centuries many of these ideas reappeared in radical democratic and social-

ist movements that altered the character of the state.

    b. **First appearance of "public opinion"**. In the creative outburst that accompanied the Civil War period and the Commonwealth period that followed (roughly 1640-1660), some 20,000 pamphlets were published. For the first time public opinion made its appearance as a factor in politics. The state was in the process of becoming a "public thing". Two groups whose ideas were important for future development are the Levellers and the Diggers.

    c. **The Levellers and liberal ideas**. Led by **John ("Freeborn John") Lilburne** (1614?-1657) and others, the Levellers advocated ideas that later became influential in America and elsewhere.

        (1) **Individual natural rights and political equality**. The Levellers believed in individual, inalienable natural rights that the state is obliged to defend. They stood for equality before the law and male political equality.

        (2) **Opposition to monopoly and religious intolerance**. The Levellers also opposed economic monopolies, aristocratic privilege, and religious intolerance.

        (3) **State exists to serve individuals**. The purpose of the state is to aid individuals; its legitimacy rests on individual consent expressed in the selection of representatives.

        (4) **Written list of guaranteed rights and written constitution**. Rights should be guaranteed by a written list. In 1653 the Levellers urged the adoption of a written constitution, the Instrument of Government, that would limit Parliament's power. It was the only such attempt in English history.

    d. **The Diggers and communist ideas**. Led by **Gerrard Winstanley** (1609-1676?), the Diggers were a tiny but influential agrarian communist movement.

(1) **An experiment to feed the poor**. In 1649 a small group of Diggers attempted to take over a plot of common land and planted crops to feed the poor. After a year the attempt failed, but the Diggers' ideas were transmitted in Winstanley's books *New Law of Righteousness* (1649) and *Law of Freedom* (1652).

(2) **Collective ownership the cure for human corruption**. The Diggers appealed to the law of nature that gave all land to the community to own in common. Individuals have rights only to a common share of the labor and its produce; no one should rule or be landlord over others. The principal cause of human corruption is the ownership of property. Lawyers and clergy are forces for oppression.

(3) **Economic equality necessary for political freedom**. Only material equality can yield freedom; economic exploitation, such as the wage system, is incompatible with democracy. There is thus an intimate connection between the economic order and the political order.

3. **The "Glorious" or "Bloodless" Revolution**. The restoration of the English monarchy in 1660 did not settle all important constitutional questions.

   a. **Executive power**. A paramount constitutional question concerned the power of the executive. This question was critical to the development of the modern constitutional democracy.

   b. **The exile of James II in 1689**. After James II ascended to the throne in 1685, it was feared that he would reestablish the Roman Catholic religion, forcing it upon the country. Parliament was determined to thwart this challenge to its power and in 1689, without bloodshed, forced James into exile.

   c. **Parliament's restrictions on the new monarchs: the Bill of Rights**. William and Mary of the Dutch House of Orange were invited to take James's place if they accepted Parliament's conditions. These conditions, set forth in the Bill of Rights of 1689 and in successive legislation, guaranteed the power and independence of Parliament from the monarchy.

   d. **English Bill of Rights unlike American Bill of Rights**. The English Bill of Rights differed in fundamental respects from the American one of a century later.

      (1) **English Bill does not restrict Parliament**. The English Bill was a declaration by Parliament, not by a sovereign people, of restrictions on the powers of the executive. Unlike the American version, the English Bill put no restrictions on Parliament, which claimed a free hand to enact any laws it pleased without legal restriction.

      (2) **Influence of English Bill on American Bill of Rights**. Nevertheless, in some places, the American Bill of Rights contains language found in the English Bill. For example, the English Bill states that "excessive bail ought not to be required, nor excessive fines imposed, nor cruel and unusual punishments inflicted."

   e. **Judicial independence and effective limits on executive**. By 1701 judges were made independent of the crown. By this settlement, effective limitation on executive power was achieved.

IV. **Modern views of the state**. From the eighteenth to the twentieth centuries a number of theories of the state were discussed by different writers and expressed in the practice of government.

   A. **Aristocratic traditionalism**. By "aristocratic traditionalism" is meant the form of European conservatism in vogue among some segments of European society after the outbreak of the French Revolution. This set of ideas advocated a leading role in society for the traditional aristocracy and similarly influential groups.

   1. **Aristocratic traditionalism in the eighteenth century**. While the French Revolution was the stimulus for the creation of a self-conscious school of thought, a doctrine of aristocratic traditionalism was already visible before 1789.

      a. **The importance of non-rational factors for social order**. Before the French Revolution, various writers point out the importance in society of non-rational factors (factors that do not stem from reason or are not necessarily justified by reason) such as customs and habits.

b. **The idea of an organic society.** In its classic eighteenth century form as well as afterwards, those who espoused aristocratic traditionalism were not primarily concerned with the nature of the state. They were concerned instead with the nature of society, of which the political realm was seen as an important aspect.

    (1) **Society is a single body.** In this account, society is organic—it is like a single physical body. This idea was as old as Plato's *Republic* and had been preserved in Christianity through the idea of believers belonging to a single body, the "Corpus Mysticum," the mystical body of Christ.

    (2) **Society naturally hierarchical.** Because it is organic, society is also naturally hierarchical. That is, just as the limbs of the body follow the directions of the head, so the lesser parts of society are directed by natural leaders, whose political influence should be paramount.

    (3) **Influence of the "organic analogy".** The organic view, which was inherited in a modified form from the Middle Ages, can be seen in the writings of the poet **Alexander Pope** (1688-1744) and the critic **Dr. Samuel Johnson** (1709-1784). Tampering with this natural order of things imperils society; overthrowing the natural order leads to society's destruction, as illustrated in the French Revolution.

2. **The ideas of Burke. Edmund Burke** (1729-1797), the Anglo-Irish parliamentarian and political writer, may be taken as the chief eighteenth century representative of aristocratic traditionalism. Many of his most important ideas are summed up in his *Reflections on the Revolution in France* (1790).

a. **Natural leaders and "prescription".** For Burke, the well-ordered society is ruled by its natural leaders. It is also ruled in accordance with inherited institutions and usages ("prescription"), since they have been found by long experience to suit the peculiar character of the nation. Thus no society should be ruled by the principles of another.

b. **Leadership not a class monopoly.** Burke thought that the natural leaders of his own society were not only the powerful members of its aristocracy. Also included were "the leading landed gentlemen, the opulent merchants and manufacturers," and "the substantial yeomanry," prosperous independent farmers. Society is best directed by these, who are its great "shady oaks," called by a later age "the pillars of society".

c. **Society an interdependent community.** These natural leaders are not to attempt to stop all change. Still less are they to ignore the interests of the lower orders. Rather, the stability of society is assured by a sense of obligation at the top of the social hierarchy and a sense of deference to them by lower orders, who are never to be denigrated. Thus the idea of an interdependent community plays a major role in this view.

d. **Abstract reason no guide to action.** In leading and directing society, the natural aristocracy should not be guided by ideas of abstract reason to the exclusion of the traditional practices. If such practices are to be reformed, they are not to be changed in haste or in violence, lest man's animal nature break out of the restraints so carefully constructed by society and chaos result. This is precisely what Burke and his allies saw occurring in the Terror of the French Revolution.

e. **Higher law limits legitimate action.** In preserving and safeguarding the institutions and customs passed on from time immemorial, those exercising political power should recognize and act within the confines of a higher law, sanctioned by a divine creator.

3. **The influence of aristocratic traditionalism in the nineteenth and twentieth centuries.** Similar voices were heard in the nineteenth and twentieth centuries. Aristocratic traditionalism retained its most influential following in England, which

avoided the social revolutions that by the end of World War I had swept aristocratic influence from much of the continent.

a. **Thomas Carlyle**. In nineteenth century Britain, figures such as the Scottish historian **Thomas Carlyle** (1795-1881), in his *On Heroes, Hero-Worship, and the Heroic in History* (1841), discussed at length the influence of history's great figures, to the exclusion of lesser men and all women. Carlyle had little respect for ordinary people; he held out no hope of a stable society under democratic rule.

b. **Benjamin Disraeli**. Another adherent to a version of aristocratic traditionalism was the British Conservative politician and prime minister **Benjamin Disraeli** (1804-1881). Disraeli held a more sanguine view of the possibilities of the democracy state. He believed that "the wider the popular suffrage, the more powerful would be the natural aristocracy". In works such as *Sybil* (1881), he declared his faith in "a new generation of the aristocracy." They were "the natural leaders of the people."

c. **T. S. Eliot**. In the twentieth century, Britain continued to be the main source of traditionalist thought and sentiment. The Anglo-American poet **Thomas Stearns Eliot** (1888-1965) expressed a variant of this philosophy in his *The Idea of a Christian Society* (1939). He argued that both liberalism and democracy were insufficient for a decent and stable social order; the **weight of tradition** was a necessary ingredient. Alienation from tradition and religion makes people "susceptible to mass suggestion: in other words, a mob."

d. **American figures**. In the United States this form of conservatism never took root because it grew out of a class system created by feudalism which was not part of American experience.

(1) **The Old South in the nineteenth century**. One American region that did approximate a caste system was the Old South with its agricultural economic base. Certain southerners adhered to ideas akin to aristocratic traditionalism.

In the nineteenth century, **John C. Calhoun** (1782-1850) sought to preserve the South's traditional social order.

(2) **The Old South in the twentieth century**. In the twentieth century, the "Fugitive" poets and critics at Vanderbilt University such as **John Crowe Ransom** (1888-1974) and **Allen Tate** (1899-1979) sought in their work to preserve the history and customs of the Old South. Deeply imbued with their southern heritage, they opposed industrialization of the South in the name of the old agricultural order.

B. **Liberal democracy**. The word "liberal" in liberal democracy refers to the generosity—the liberality—of the allowance the political order makes for political, personal, and economic liberty. Many historians argue that the liberal idea of the state has found its fullest expression in the United States. **"Liberal" in this section does *not* refer to the opposition in American politics between "liberals" and "conservatives."**

1. **Conditions for liberal democracy**. The ease with which liberal democracy grew in America is due partly to the absence of a feudal background.

a. **Absence of feudalism in America**. European political ideologies such as Marxism and continental conservatism had their roots in the social class system inherited from the feudal system. But America had no feudal system—it had no peasantry or nobility. It had only middle classes of varying degrees of wealth and poverty. This was one reason that in eighteenth-century America the liberal-democratic state found ready soil in which to take root.

b. **Liberal democracy and capitalism**. Liberal democracy is also associated with the development of capitalism.

(1) **Barriers to free markets in Europe.** In Europe, the legal privileges and rights of the social classes inherited from the Middle Ages combined with traditions of state control of economic affairs formed barriers to capitalist development, especially the formation of free markets.

(2) **Absence of barriers to free markets in America.** The absence of a European class system in America facilitated the creation of a capitalist economy. The emergence of a strong middle class, a key ingredient in the social basis of liberal democracy, followed from the development of a capitalist economy.

c. **The role of geography in America.** In the American case, geography played a significant role in the development of the liberal-democratic ethos.

(1) **Availability of land.** Until the late nineteenth century, the availability of land meant that personal freedom could be exercised by all who were not slaves and able to move west. Both the fact and the mythology of "wide open spaces" with its frontier mentality nurtured the spirit of freedom and individualism.

(2) **Role of ocean barriers.** Secondly, the ocean barriers at the ends of the continent meant that social organization requiring the regimentation of individuals to resist invasion was unnecessary.

d. **Central ideas and institutions of American liberal democracy.** Not all liberal democracies practice the same ideas in the same way. Not all profess the idea of popular sovereignty, preferring instead the form of constitutional monarchy, as in the case of Britain and the Netherlands. But most of the following ideas generally characterize the practice of liberal democracy.

(1) **Freedom of the individual.** Perhaps most central to liberal democracy is the freedom of the individual both as an idea and as a reality. In this context, liberty of conscience may be said to be a "**first freedom**," since other essential freedoms, such as speech and worship, suppose it.

(2) **Popular sovereignty.** The idea of popular sovereignty is that the polity is the joint creation and common property of the body of citizens as a whole. This idea is not accepted in constitutional monarchies such as Britain. But in the United States "We the People" established the Constitution.

(3) **Toleration.** A further central idea is toleration of varying religious, political, and other beliefs, and of social mores. Early ideas of toleration, often restricted to varieties of religious belief, have expanded as liberal democracies have become increasingly diverse.

(4) **Market economy.** Another central idea of liberal democracy is the existence of a market economy, which makes possible a dispersal of the economic power which, if centralized, could curtail individual liberty.

(5) **Distrust of the state.** Especially in America, liberal democracy has tended toward a distrust of the state. Political power is viewed with suspicion on account of its potential to subvert liberty in all of its forms.

(6) **Welfare state.** The "welfare state" is a further set of ideas and institutions that became a central feature of liberal democracy only in the twentieth century. The idea of the welfare state is that government rather than private charity alone is responsible for relieving extremes of poverty and privation among its citizens. A certain minimum is to be guaranteed to all citizens as a matter of right.

e. **A "balance of forces" in society.** Liberal democracy is not attainable or is not readily attainable in all social conditions. If a single social element—the army, a religious group, an organized aristocracy, the poor—dominates the social fabric, it is unlikely or impossible that liberal democracy can develop or prosper.

f. **Strong "civil society".** "Civil society" is a key idea in understanding liberal democracy. "The words 'civil society' name the space of uncoerced human association and also the set of relational networks—formed for the sake of family, faith, interest, and ideology—that fill this space" (Michael Walzer, "The Civil Society Argument," Gunnar

Myrdal Lecture, 1990). Thus, the term refers to all those voluntary associations, economic groups, religious organizations, and other social relationships that in a free society are not under government control. Stable liberal democracy requires a strong civil society. Authoritarian societies attempt to control independent social activities, while totalitarian societies suppress civil society altogether. The associations of civil society often achieve public purposes independent of government itself.

g. **A strong middle class.** A strong and stable middle class is nearly always a condition essential for the development and continuance of liberal democracy.

    (1) **Middle class not dominated by rich or poor.** "Strong" in this context means in part that the middle class must be numerous enough not to be politically dominated by either the rich or the poor.

    (2) **Necessity for economically stable middle class.** The middle class must also be economically stable, for events such as catastrophic inflation or depression that wipes out middle-class wealth undermines democratic institutions by undermining its middle class basis.

h. **Education a prerequisite to liberal democracy.** The United States may be taken as an example of a liberal democracy in which education has been seen as a prerequisite for full, successful participation in self-government.

    (1) **Common education.** Common education for all was recognized early as a necessary underpinning of liberal democracy. Many Founders believed that a diverse people had to be bound together to remain unified. Common education must stress the virtues and responsibilities as well as the rights of citizenship. Thus many supporters of public education drew upon classical republicanism. In that tradition, common education is the political glue binding citizens together.

    (2) **Leading early figures.** Spokesmen as varied in their political philosophies as **George Washington** (1732-1799), **John Adams** (1735-1826), **Thomas Jefferson** (1743-1826), **Benjamin Rush** (1745?-1814), and **Noah Webster** (1758-1843) all argued for public institutions of education that would instill in all children and youth the responsibilities and rights of American citizenship.

    (3) **Supporters of the common school movement.** Similarly, in the nineteenth century, the common school movement was promoted by such diverse figures as, among others, educational statesman **Horace Mann (1796-1859)**, lawyer-statesman **Daniel Webster** (1782-1852), and progressive social reformers **Florence Kelly** (1859-1932), **Lillian Wald** (1867-1940), and **Jane Addams** (1860-1935).

    (4) **The common school movement and Catholic education.** One effect of the Common School movement was that it stimulated Catholics to form schools of their own because the Common Schools were Protestant in orientation.

    (5) **Education and the Americanization of immigrants.** The massive immigration of the late nineteenth and early twentieth century underlined the demands for a common political education in the public schools. Most Americans supported civic assimilation in the schools called "Americanization". Progressives such as **John Dewey** (1859-1952) and Jane Addams were strong supporters of these efforts.

2. **Constitutional popular government.** The historical roots of constitutional government and popular sovereignty, twin principles of liberal democracy, are found in the ancient worlds of Greece and Rome, in the medieval opposition to the unlimited power of popes and princes, and in the constitutional struggles in England in the seventeenth century. Eighteenth century political struggles in America and in Europe established the first regimes that recognized legal limitations on all branches of government as well as popular sovereignty. Those included in the "sovereign

people" were initially relatively few; but by the early twentieth century, most liberal democracies had universal adult suffrage.

a. **Principles of the American Revolution.** Basic principles of the American Revolution, begun in 1775 and declared in 1776, were outlined by Thomas Jefferson in the Declaration of Independence as "self-evident truths." All of them, save the idea of the "pursuit of happiness," can be found in Locke's *Second Treatise.*

   (1) **Natural equality.** "All men are created equal." This meant that no person or class of persons is the natural ruler of other adults. That no one is the natural ruler of another is found in Locke, based on the Law of Nature.

   (2) **Inalienable rights.** A second key idea was also based on the Lockean concept of the Law of Nature: every person is endowed with certain "unalienable rights" such as "Life, Liberty, and the pursuit of Happiness." Because they are not rights created by man-made law, they are the natural rights of individuals.

   (3) **Securing rights the purpose of government.** Government, and thus the state itself, is the creation of the governed, who set it up to secure their natural rights.

   (4) **Government's authority derived only from consent.** Legitimate government powers (as opposed to illegitimate **claims** of government) originate solely in the consent of the governed.

   (5) **Limits to legitimate government power.** As a consequence of the necessity for the consent of the governed, the legitimate powers of government are limited by what the governed consent to. Thus there should be "no taxation without representation."

   (6) **Right to revolution.** If government fails to fulfill the purposes for which it is set up, if it attacks the very rights it was designed to protect by those who creat-

ed it, then it is the right of the people to alter or abolish it. Prudence, however, dictates that this not be done for light or transient causes.

b. **The U.S. Constitution and the Bill of Rights.** The Constitution, written in 1787 and ratified in 1788, institutionalized limited government and recognized popular sovereignty by stating in the Preamble that the Constitution is established by "We the People." These limitations and guarantees of civil rights were further spelled out in the first ten amendments (known as the "Bill of Rights") ratified in 1791.

c. **The stability of liberal-democratic views in America.** The fundamental American liberal-democratic views announced during the Revolution have been uncontested outside of the slave-holding states of the South in any serious way in the subsequent two hundred years of American history. Some views may have been modified and extended to meet changing needs and expectations, but none of the basic assumptions has been rejected.

d. **The French Revolution.** The French Revolution begun in Paris in 1789 had a number of root causes. Some were proximate, such as the social conditions in Paris at the time of the outbreak; others were in the realm of ideas, such as the influence of Rousseau's *The Social Contract.* The Revolution was also inspired in part by American events. It demanded constitutional limits on government, embodied in a written document. Thus a "Declaration of the Rights of Man and of the Citizen" was issued in 1789. In the 1790s successive constitutions were written. The idea of popular sovereignty also became entrenched after the abolition of the monarchy in 1792.

e. **The spread of liberal democracy.** The French Revolution was followed by the rule of Napoleon Bonaparte.

   (1) **Spread of democratic ideas in Europe.** The democratic ideas of the French revolution were spread by Napoleon's armies throughout much of Europe.

(2) **Spread of democratic ideas to Central and South America**. Liberal ideas also spread in the early decades of the nineteenth century to Central and South America, where Spain's colonies rebelled. After a period of reaction during which monarchies were returned to power, democratic and constitutional ideas reappeared.

(3) **Liberal democracy in the twentieth century**. Liberal-democratic ideas of limited government and popular consent are institutionalized today in western or western-style democracies in North America, Australasia, Europe, Japan, India, Israel, South America, and elsewhere.

f. **The expansion of suffrage**. At the outset of liberal democracy in America and Europe, not everyone was accorded the rights of full adult membership.

(1) **White suffrage in America and Europe**. Only white, male, property owners were allowed the vote in the **United States** until after 1800. In the U.S., universal white male suffrage was not achieved until 1860. In **Britain** property or income requirements restricted the electorate. Only a handful of men voted when the first Reform Bill was passed in 1832, enlarging the male electorate but excluding the majority. A second Reform Bill in 1867 still left many men as well as all women disenfranchised.

(2) **Black suffrage in the United States.** Black males were formally guaranteed suffrage by the Fifteenth Amendment, but in some states they were excluded in large numbers from voting. Literacy tests were used for this purpose, as was the "Grandfather Clause," which excluded blacks whose grandfathers did not vote. Blacks in the South gained the vote in the 1960s, when the Civil Rights movement successfully launched voting rights drives. In 1965 Congress passed the Voting Rights Act that aided in securing the vote for blacks.

(3) **Woman suffrage in the U.S.** After the American Revolution women voted in an election in New Jersey because of a legal loophole. The loophole was soon closed and women were denied the right to vote in all states. The Seneca Falls Declaration of 1848 demanded woman suffrage. In 1859 Wyoming was the first state to grant suffrage to women.

(4) **International woman suffrage**. In most countries, women did not gain the right to vote until after World War I. But in some places suffrage was gained earlier. Sometimes it was initially restricted to municipal or provincial elections. Woman suffrage was instituted, for example, in New Zealand, 1893; Australia, 1894 and 1902; Canada, 1918; Great Britain, 1918 and 1928; and United States, 1920. After 1921 many others followed.

(5) **Suffrage of indigenous populations**. The peoples indigenous to areas colonized by Europeans did not vote until the twentieth century. American Indians gained the vote in 1924; in Australia, the suffrage was extended to Aboriginals in 1967.

3. **Toleration**. Another central idea of liberal democracy is toleration of varying religious, political, and other beliefs, and of social mores. Early ideas of toleration, often restricted to religious belief, have expanded as liberal democracies have become increasingly diverse. But, generally speaking, the idea of toleration was only a transitional step toward the ideal of genuine religious freedom. Even though their religious worship was tolerated, dissident religious minorities were often at a political and cultural disadvantage in comparison with the legally recognized and orthodox established religions.

a. **Religious toleration in Europe.** A degree of religious toleration in Europe was inaugurated in the wake of the "Wars of Religion" of the sixteenth century. Catholic France tolerated Protestantism by the Edict of Nantes (1598), though it was revoked in 1685. Toleration was practiced later in the seventeenth century in the Netherlands. In Great Britain the Toleration Act of 1689 extended religious liberty to all Protestant sects.

b. **Religious toleration in America.** It is a truism that many colonists came to America seeking freedom of religious conscience and worship from the discrimination and oppression of established Catholic and Protestant churches in Europe. But it is also true that nine of the thirteen colonies established their own churches in seventeenth century America. Toleration of religious diversity did not come easily in three Congregational colonies of New England, five Anglican colonies of the South, or in New York. The eighteenth century was the great watershed in American religious history, when the many diverse religious and ethnic groups flowing into the colonies gradually claimed toleration for themselves and then forced the practice of toleration toward the ideal of genuine religious freedom, eventually enshrined in state and federal constitutions.

c. **Toleration of diversity.** Toleration of a wider variety of differences in political belief, social mores and ways of life, and other aspects of social diversity has gradually spread in the western democracies in the twentieth century. This has been partly as a result of increased immigration, communication, and travel as well as other cultural changes. There is no general agreement, however, about what limits should be set either in law or social attitudes to such toleration.

4. **Market economy.** A third factor is the existence of a market economy. A market economy helps to ensure that no element in society, such as government or powerful individuals and groups, can curtail or eliminate individuals' freedom by controlling and directing either their livelihood or what they buy and consume.

5. **Welfare state.** The idea of a welfare state is that the **state**, as opposed to some less-inclusive group, private charity, or individuals themselves, assumes ultimate responsibility for the general well-being of its members.

a. **Origins of the welfare state.** The welfare state originated in the paternalist legislation of Elizabethan England, the Poor Laws first codified in 1597-1598 and 1601. These laws provided public assistance for the old, the sick, and the unemployed.

b. **Early defenders of the welfare state.** The welfare state was defended by **Thomas Hobbes**, many of whose ideas form the basis of liberalism. Since the purpose of the state is to preserve its subjects' lives, he argued, it must provide the means to life when the subject cannot. Early liberal writers such as **Jeremy Bentham** (1748-1832) likewise defended the existence of some version of the welfare state against those who wished to abolish it (see, C.F. Bahmueller, *The National Charity Company*, [1981]).

c. **The welfare state under social democracy and liberalism.** Welfare state policies have been adopted in the twentieth century by social democrats as well as by some adherents of liberalism. What distinguishes the two approaches is the greater latitude and degree of benefits provided by social democracy, such as socialized medicine, universal unemployment insurance, and more generous payments for social programs.

d. **The welfare state in the United States.** Modern welfare state policies began in the United States as a response to the Great Depression of the 1930s.

(1) **The New Deal.** National welfare state programs were inaugurated after 1933 during the New Deal administration of President **Franklin Roosevelt** (1882-1945). For example, the Social Security Act of 1935 provides for old age and survivors insurance for most of the population.

(2) **Post-war developments.** The Fair Deal of President **Harry Truman** (1884-1972) and the Great Society programs of President **Lyndon Johnson** (1908-1973) continued Welfare State programs.

e. **The welfare state in post-war Europe.** The fullest development of welfare state programs is found in post-World War II Europe as part of the policies of social democracy.

6. **Classical American political thought: central ideas of *The Federalist.*** *The Federalist Papers* or *The Federalist* represents the most sophisticated political thinking of America's Founders. Eminent American scholar Clinton Rossiter wrote, "*The Federalist* is the most important work in political science that has ever been written, or is likely ever to be written, in the United States. It is, indeed, the one product of the American mind that is rightly counted among the classics of political theory." The contents of *The Federalist* were originally a series of eighty-five essays published in New York newspapers between 1788 and 1789. They argued the case for ratification of the new Constitution for the United States. Written by **Alexander Hamilton** (1755-1804), **James Madison** (1751-1836), and **John Jay** (1745-1829) under the pseudonym, "Publius," *The Federalist* presents the most authoritative understanding of the conceptual underpinnings of the American constitutional system from the Founders' perspective.

a. **Concept of human nature.** The Founders' concept of human nature is crucial to understanding the philosophical basis of the American system of government.

   (1) **Government a reflection of human nature.** In one of the most famous passages of *The Federalist,* James Madison in No. 51 stated, "But what is government itself but the greatest of all reflections on human nature? If men were angels, no government would be necessary. If angels were to govern men, neither external nor internal controls on government would be necessary."

   (2) **Positive aspects of human nature.** Madison wrote further in *The Federalist* No. 55, "As there is a degree of depravity in mankind which requires a certain degree of circumspection and distrust, so there are other qualities in human nature which justify a certain portion of esteem and confidence. Republican government presupposes the existence of these qualities in a higher degree than any other form. Were the pictures which have been drawn by the political

jealousy of some among us faithful likenesses of the human character, the inference would be that there is not sufficient virtue among men for self-government; and that nothing less than the chains of despotism can restrain them from destroying and devouring one another." That is to say, human beings possess many faults (they are not "angels"), but they are capable of self-government if a popular regime is constituted to complement instead of clash with human nature.

   (3) **U.S. Constitution to constrain but not alter human nature.** Thus, the framers of the U. S. Constitution proposed a system that would constrain (and when possible, properly motivate) rather than attempt to "change" human nature. In a sense, the entire American constitutional edifice of a democratic republic is based on the Founders' concept of human nature derived in part from their reading of history and their experience. Without this particular understanding of human nature (that is, if men were, or could become, angels) the checks and balances of the American constitutional structure would not be necessary.

b. **The problem of popular governments.** According to the Founders, most popular (republican) governments in the past had failed to secure either good government or liberty.

   (1) **The disorder of weak governments.** *The Federalist* noted that in many cases weak popular governments unable to maintain order had been replaced by tyrannies that extinguished liberty and ignored justice. Hence, the danger was that republican regimes could become too weak (and thus inept, unable to secure liberty or establish effective government) or too strong (and thus tyrannical and unjust).

   (2) **Securing liberty in the face of faction.** The problem for the framers of the Constitution was stated succinctly by James Madison in *The Federalist* No.

10, "To secure the public good and private rights against the danger of such a faction [an overbearing majority], and at the same time to preserve the spirit and the form of popular government, is then the great object to which our inquiries are directed."

(3) **Channeling and restraining human passions.** In other words, the Founders hoped to create a constitutional framework that provided for popular sovereignty (representative democracy), liberty (individual rights), and good government (justice). However, the Founders knew this would be difficult to achieve. They would have to create a political system that would guard against the "mortal diseases" of popular government, i.e., that would restrain and channel the exigencies of human nature, and at the same time establish self-government and secure political freedom.

(4) **What faction is.** Specifically, overcoming the danger of "faction" was critical to the well-being of republican government. A "faction" was defined by Publius as a group of citizens united around some common impulse, passion, or interest adverse to the rights of other citizens, or to the interests of the community as a whole.

(5) **The problem of majority faction.** Since republican government was to be based on majority rule, the greatest danger to liberty and justice occurred when a "faction" became the majority. Hence, how to avoid (or lessen) the formation of "factious majority" was a major problem for the framers of the Constitution. The Framers were not, however, opposed to the formation of majorities per se, because that would have been against the spirit of self-government.

(6) **Faction not to be eliminated.** Moreover, Publius noted that it was neither desirable nor even possible to eliminate the cause of faction. It was not desirable because it would require "destroying liberty" and thus the remedy "was worse

than the disease." It was not possible because, "the latent causes of faction are...sown in the nature of man."

c. **The solution to the problem of popular government.** The solution offered by *The Federalist* to the "mortal diseases" of popular governments was the creation of a regime founded on the principles of republicanism (i.e. representative democracy), separation of powers, federalism, and constitutionalism (limited government). Crucial to this framework was the theory of an **extended republic** that encouraged a "multiplicity of interests."

(1) **The extended republic.** *The Federalist* authors pointed out that the United States, unlike the failed popular government of the past, consisted of a relatively large population and territory. Because it was an "extended republic," they insisted it possessed crucial advantages over smaller republics for the maintenance of ordered liberty and the alleviation of the problems of "faction."

(2) **Madison's view of the extended republic.** Madison wrote in *The Federalist*, No. 51, "In the extended republic of the United States, and among the great variety of interests, parties, and sects which it embraces, a coalition of a majority of the whole society could seldom take place on any other principles than those of justice and the general good....In other words, the new government was a popular regime, majorities could be formed, and they would prevail. However, since the United States was an "extended republic," a "multiplicity of interests" existed. This multiplicity made it unlikely (but not impossible) that a "factious" majority coalition could be formed around unjust, foolish, or tyrannical policies.

(3) **Commercial republic.** The United States, according to Publius, was fortunate to be not only an extended republic, but a commercial republic as well. In a large commercial republic with a diversified economy, political conflict occurred over "degrees" and "kinds" of

property (landed interests, manufacturing interests, mercantile interests, monied interests). This kind of conflict was preferable to the "factious" disputes over "amounts" of property (rich v. poor) that had destroyed the republics of antiquity.

(4) **Securing the republic's well-being.** *The Federalist* argued that in order to secure its well being, the American republic must: 1) protect the interests of small (as well as large) property holders and individual citizens, allowing them to be free to seek economic gain; 2) insure that commercial life "be made honorable and universally practiced"; and 3) attain a reasonable degree of prosperity. Publius believed that the large commercial republic of the United States possessed a number of institutional features critical to its success and survival.

(5) **Representation.** Unlike the turbulent direct democracies of the past, the new government was a republic (representative democracy). This permitted the enlargement and refinement of public views through the process of deliberation.

(6) **Separation of powers.** Powers at the national level were separated into three branches of government: the legislative (Congress), executive (president), and judicial (courts). This separation operated as a barrier to tyranny and "faction" because it motivated officials in the three different branches to defend their respective prerogatives against possible encroachments from the other two. Publius suggested that the psychology of "human nature" be put to use so that ambition would "be made to counteract ambition."

(7) **Federalism.** Federalism divided governmental power between the national and state governments. *The Federalist* described the new government as a "compound republic," a combination of a national regime (with a central authority) and a confederation (where power rested chiefly in regional and local entities). Considerable power was to reside in state governments under the new Constitution.

(8) **Limited government.** *The Federalist* argued that the Constitution contained limits on the authority of the national and state governments. The judiciary, Publius stated, can limit the actions of the executive and legislative branches of the national government and the state governments as well.

(9) **Judicial review.** *The Federalist* No. 78 developed the justification for giving the courts the power to declare acts of Congress unconstitutional. In accepting the concept of limited government the American framers (unlike ancient political theorists), distinguished between the legal role of government and the public, but nongovernmental, activities of civil society (churches, voluntary associations, professional organizations, etc.). Eighteenth-century America was a thriving civil society; the deeper questions of morality and virtue were, for the most part, presumed to fall within this realm.

d. **Comparison with French revolutionary thought.** It is significant that the views of the American framers about human nature and, therefore, on the philosophical basis of constitutional government, differed considerably from those of the theorists and leaders of the French revolution. Unlike **Rousseau** (1712-1778), **Condorcet** (1743-1794), **Robespierre** (1758-1794), and **St. Just** (1767-1794), the American revolutionaries believed that popular government must be erected in accordance with a human nature that included both positive and negative characteristics. The French revolutionaries, on the other hand, believed that the negative aspects of human nature were the result of oppressive government, and that the end of tyranny would free human beings and lead to the perfection of mankind; hence these negative characteristics were "unnatural" and would disappear with the elimination of tyrannies.

e. **The Founders' perspective of *The Federalist*.** From the perspective of America's Founders, *The Federalist* essays represented not only the best explanation of the proposed American political order, but a major contribution to universal political thought. For example, Thomas Jefferson wrote James Madison that *The Federalist* was "the best commentary on the principles of government ever written." Similarly, George Washington wrote to Alexander Hamilton, "that work [*The Federalist*] will merit the notice of posterity because in it are candidly and ably discussed the principles of freedom and the topics of government—which will always be interesting to mankind so long as they shall be connected in civil society."

f. **Contemporary significance of *The Federalist*.** The central ideas of *The Federalist* retain significance today.

(1) **Creating stable democracy.** The issues facing the authors of *The Federalist*—how to create a stable, prosperous, representative democracy that provided for ordered liberty and justice—are essentially the same issues that face the fledgling new democracies in Eastern Europe, Asia, Africa, and Latin America in the 1990s. It is significant that *The Federalist* is the single most requested book by Polish and Czech educators who are struggling to develop a new democratically-based citizenship education in their countries.

(2) **The realism of the central ideas of *The Federalist*.** In a sense, *The Federalist* offers a realistic, non-utopian yet democratic framework for analyzing the serious issues that have always confronted nation builders: the interplay of self-government, power, representation, reason, emotions, rights, responsibilities, and the common good. Starting with the sobering premises that human beings are neither perfect nor perfectible, *The Federalist* delineates a tough-minded perspective based on history, experience, observation, and reason that contrasts sharply with political philosophies premised on effecting changes in human behavior.

C. **Classical Marxism.** Classical Marxism is the theory and practice of **Karl Marx** (1818-1883). Most scholars distinguish his ideas from those of his collaborator, **Friedrich Engels** (1820-1895).

1. **The state and Marxist theory.** Marxism is a theory of the basic character of society and how it changes. It purports to show the relationship between economics, which it regards as most fundamental, and social change. It also tries to show the influence of economic systems on the whole of culture.

a. **Historical law and the fate of capitalism.** Marx believed that he understood the character of certain basic historical processes. He also believed that he had discovered the fundamental laws of capitalist economics showing why capitalism creates increasingly severe crises. In the end these crises would drive the people suffering most—proletarians and bankrupt members of the bourgeoisie—to overthrow it and install a system that solved its problems.

b. **"Historical materialism."** Marx called his view of history "historical materialism." In his *Contribution to the Critique of Political Economy* (1859) he said: "The mode of production in material life determines the general character of the social, political, and spiritual processes of life." In order to live, men enter into economic relations with each other. "The sum total of these relations of productions constitutes the economic structure of society—the real basis on which rises a legal and political superstructure."

c. **The division of labor and ownership of the means of production.** To Marx, one key feature of the economic base of society is the division of labor. Another is the ownership of the means of production. These two factors combined account for the creation of social classes. Throughout history, those who own or control the means of production exploit those who do not. Marx adopted the French words for the dominant social classes in capitalist society. The "proletariat," or working class, own no productive instruments and are obliged to sell their labor to the "bourgeoisie," the middle class owners of productive means such as factories.

d. **The oppressive function of capitalist culture**. As outlined in *The Communist Manifesto* (1848) Marx wrote with Engels, all history consists of the struggle for domination among economic classes; contemporary history consists in the struggle of the bourgeoisie and the proletariat. In this struggle, important parts of the cultural "superstructure" are controlled by the dominant class, the bourgeoisie. The superstructure as a whole functions as the instrument of class oppression. For example, religion acts as a narcotic, soothing workers' suffering, preaching acquiescence to the political status quo.

e. **The character and fate of the modern state**. The state and its legal apparatus is the most direct instrument of class domination. While politicians might deal directly with an electorate of greater or lesser size, behind them stood the real power, the power of monied interests—of capitalists. Thus for Marx, the state is no more than "the ruling committee of the bourgeoisie." And since its sole function consists in class oppression, in a new system devoid of this oppression the state would become unnecessary.

f. **After the revolution: "withering away of the state."** Marx thought that after a proletarian revolution won "the battle of democracy," the state, a superfluous appendage of a deposed class, would simply "wither away."

(1) **Socialism as the first stage of development**. The first stage of the post-revolutionary process would be **socialism**, whose economic essence was the collective ownership of the means of production.

(2) **Communism as the final stage of development**. At the end of the post-revolutionary process would be **communism**, in which economic scarcity would vanish along with private property.

g. **The "inevitability" of revolution**. The proletarian revolution was bound to occur—it was **inevitable**—because, try as it might, capitalism was caught in internal contradictions it

was powerless to solve. Sooner or later, suffering humanity would be led by sheer misery to overthrow capitalism and with it the capitalist state.

h. **The relationship between the party and the proletariat**. It was the task of those who understood this process to form a political party that would act as a "vanguard" to hasten the revolution—to "ease the birth pangs" of the new social order.

(1) **The possibility of non-violent revolution**. Marx thought that in some places, such as Britain, the process might be peaceful; in others it would be violent.

(2) **The superiority of the party over the proletariat**. Whether or not the revolution was violent, Marxist philosophy was the "head" of the movement; the proletariat was the "heart." This formula describes a hierarchial division of labor in which a philosophically-informed party directs a proletariat that necessarily assumes a subordinate-position. Carried out in practice in twentieth century communism, this relationship between party and people had far-reaching consequences. It meant the tyranny of parties once in power over all of society.

2. **The sources of Marxist theory**. Marx's doctrine was a unique synthesis derived from three main sources. These were German philosophy, especially of **G.F.W. Hegel** (1770-1831) and **Ludwig Feuerbach** (1804-1872); French utopian socialism, especially of **Henri Saint-Simon** (1760-1825); and British economics, especially **Adam Smith** (1723-90) and **David Ricardo** (1772-1823).

a. **Hegel and Feuerbach**. From Hegel, Marx adopted the view of history as a rational process. Hegel viewed this process as the unfolding of an idea, leading in the end to human freedom. In place of this idealism Marx substituted a materialist basis for history, grounded in economic processes. Marx found such a materialist philosophy in Feuerbach's *Essence of Christianity* (1841).

b. **Smith and Ricardo**. From Smith and Ricardo, Marx took important categories of his economics such as ideas concerning the rate of wages, rents, and profits. He derived from them, for example, the theory that wages tend to be no higher than workers' subsistence level and that labor is the chief source of the economic value of products (the "labor theory of value").

    c. **Saint-Simon**. From Saint-Simon, Marx took elements of his vision of post-revolutionary communism. Contrary to Saint-Simon, Marx insisted, however, that this new society could **not** be planned. It would grow of its own accord. Attempting to plan a future socialist society would be merely "utopianism"—irrelevant dreaming. Marxian socialist doctrine, based on objective evidence and knowledge of historical laws, was said to be "scientific."

3. **Socialism in practice**. The historical development of socialism took place in nineteenth-century Europe during a period of rapid industrialization.

    a. **Socialism and the hardships of industrialization.** Working conditions for the industrial workers in nineteenth century Europe were usually grim. Long hours were combined with low pay, unsafe practices, monotonous or grueling labor, and laws forbidding the formation of trade unions. Child labor, often in dreadful conditions, was commonplace. With few exceptions, employers made no provision for the health care of employees. Workers had few legal protections. They could be fired at will and had no unemployment compensation. Socialist movements, whether or not of Marxian persuasion, were a protest against these circumstances.

    b. **The formation of socialist parties**. Marx and Engels wrote the *Communist Manifesto* during the series of revolutions that broke out in Europe in 1848. But their ideas had little immediate impact on workers' movements.

        (1) **Formation of the First International.** In 1864, an International Workingmen's Association, known as the First International, was formed in London. It consisted of workers' representatives from various countries on the Continent as well as from Britain.

        (2) **Spread of Marxism on the Continent**. Although Marx's ideas still made little headway in England, they spread rapidly on the Continent, especially in Germany. Socialist movements of a Marxist bent sprang up in a number of countries. By 1876 it was clear, however, that they could not be directed by a central authority, and the International disbanded.

    c. **The problem of socialist strategy**. In 1889, six years after Marx's death, a Second International was founded. By then, powerful socialist parties were active throughout most of Western Europe.

        (1) **Second International incapable of action.** The International acted as an umbrella organization of these separate parties. But like its predecessor, the Second International was incapable of achieving common action among participants.

        (2) **Disputes about doctrine and strategy**. The Second International was split by numerous doctrinal and strategic disagreements. Among the most serious and chronic of the latter disputes were two in particular.

            (a) **How to achieve power**. One key question was whether socialist parties should participate in parliamentary politics, or whether they should aim at achieving power solely through revolutionary means.

            (b) **Reform or revolution**. A different form of this question was whether socialist parties should aim at reform or revolution. Twentieth-century social democracy grew out of the socialist movements that favored reform over revolution.

    d. **The failure of socialist internationalism**. The socialist internationalism of the nineteenth century broke down, however, at the outbreak of World War I in 1914. At that time, initial socialist efforts were to abort the war by urging their adherents to refuse participation. But when this tactic failed, member organizations generally supported their respective countries. Thus nationalist adherence to the state won out over Marxism's internationalist hostility to both nation and state.

D. **Twentieth-century communism**. The legacy of classical Marxism was an anti-state bias. The state was seen as little more than the agent of class oppression. After a proletarian revolution it would eventually dissolve of its own accord; it would "wither away." Communism in practice, however, was quite different; the state became all powerful. It owned nearly all means of production, including (with national variations) agriculture and industry. The USSR will be used as the principal example and China as a secondary example of communism in practice.

1. **Leninism and the state.** At the outbreak of World War I, the Russian empire, ruled by hereditary czars, was a mainly peasant society. Industrialization had only recently begun. Accordingly, only a small percentage of the population consisted of industrial workers or proletarians. Compared to Western Europe, it was undeveloped. In 1905, once-mighty Russia was shocked by its military defeat at the hands of Japan. The end of czarist rule was in sight.

   a. **The revolutionary theory of orthodox Marxism**. It was in this context that **Vladimir Ilyich Lenin** (1870-1924) developed his new directions in Marxist theory and practice. Orthodox Marxism assumed that socialist regimes would come to power in the most industrially advanced nations. Over an extended period these nations cast off feudalism and developed a capitalist form of production and a state dominated by the middle class and its ideas. Only then would a large, increasingly well-organized and politically-conscious working class develop that could challenge the middle class state with a new socialist program. To Marxism, this was the standard course of development.

   b. **Lenin's impatience for revolution**. Lenin, on the other hand, did not wish to wait for backward Russia to catch up with the West. He wanted Marxist revolutionaries to take power as soon as possible. Still, even shortly before the outbreak of World War I, Lenin thought that he would not live to see a communist revolution in Russia. But in 1917 Lenin's party succeeded in taking power.

   c. **Lenin's innovations: revolution in an underdeveloped country**. By making revolution in czarist Russia, Lenin and his doctrine departed from previous theory and practice in four principal ways.

      (1) **Revolution in a developing country**. First, Leninism was a formula for making revolution in an underdeveloped country.

      (2) **Changing party organization**. Second, to accomplish this novel task, it was necessary to change the character of the communist party capable of making revolution, since it would operate in quite different conditions than those of Western European.

      (3) **Voluntarism and revolution**. Third, Leninism rejected the inevitability of revolution in favor of an emphasis on a necessity for the will to revolt.

      (4) **Popular mandate unnecessary**. Fourth, Lenin separated the right of the party to rule from an actual popular mandate.

   d. **The role of geography**. One of the problems that Lenin confronted was geographical, for the Russian empire was immense. It was nearly as large as the present-day Soviet Union, the largest country in the world. Pockets of workers who might be receptive to Marxist ideas were scattered across the cities of European Russia.

   e. **Lenin's idea of the party.** Lenin's second innovation was formulated to cope with these conditions. He abandoned the idea of a large, openly visible party. In its place he built a small, elite, secretive party that was highly disciplined from top to bottom. It was ruled by his new doctrine of democratic centralism. As outlined in Lenin's *What is to be Done?* (1901), decision-making was to be democratic, from the bottom up, but once a decision was made, it would be rigorously enforced from top to bottom, from the central leadership to those beneath.

f. **The absence of party democracy**. From the beginning, however, the emphasis in Lenin's party was on centralism, not democracy. In a meeting of Soviet revolutionaries in 1901, Lenin found himself in the minority. But once most of the delegates left the meeting hall, his followers composed a majority—the "bolsheviks," in Russian. Lenin's claim of "majority" status for his party, was a propaganda tool rather than a reality.

g. **The rejection of historical inevitability**. Lenin's third innovation was a rejection of the revolution's inevitability. Left to themselves, he argued, workers would travel no farther on the road to revolution than trade unionism. They could be bought off with concessions and benefits and would make no revolution. But even in the largely agricultural Russian empire, revolution was possible. Thus Lenin substituted the idea of voluntarism for inevitability. The united **will** of an elite, conspiratorial party could make a revolution where it would otherwise not occur.

h. **The basis of the Bolsheviks' right to rule**. The fourth innovative part of Leninism was its refusal to base its right to rule on popular approval, as evidenced in elections. As opposed to his fellow socialists, the Mensheviks, Lenin refused to wait for economic development to create a working class majority. Instead, Lenin based the party's right to rule on the correctness of its cause, regardless of popular support in elections. The Marxist idea of the "dictatorship of the proletariat" became the dictatorship of the party over the whole of society, proletariat included.

2. **Leninism in practice**. After the 1917 revolution, Leninism departed from earlier views of the state.

a. **The fate of doctrine in practice**. The new version of Marxist theory exhibited the old hostility to the state as the creature of an oppressive ruling class. But after taking power, new realities took precedence over theory. This is illustrated by Lenin's views before the Bolshevik *coup d'état* of November 1917 and his actions afterwards. In *The State and Revolution*, written shortly before taking power, Lenin argued that after the revolution the state's bureaucracy must be "smashed." But upon assuming power, he found it necessary to rely upon the old czarist bureaucracy.

b. **Civil war**. The fate of the new Soviet state was uncertain. Having taken power during World War I, the Bolshevik government withdrew from the fighting and signed a separate treaty with the Central Powers (March, 1918). Civil war broke out in May, accompanied by Allied intervention against the Bolsheviks (known as "Reds" for their red flag). In 1920, the Red Army, formed and led by the brilliant revolutionary **Leon Trotsky** (1879-1940), was victorious.

c. **"War Communism."** Wholesale nationalization of industry and similar measures had accompanied civil war. With peace, this "war communism" was abandoned. To bring stability to a badly tottering economy, a New Economic Policy was declared in 1921, allowing private economic activity and private ownership of property. A degree of cultural freedom also prevailed.

3. **Stalinism and the state**. When Lenin fell ill in 1922, the Bolsheviks rejected the leadership of Trotsky, in favor of a troika of leaders, including **Josef Stalin** (1879-1953).

a. **Stalin's rise and the fate of Trotsky**. Stalin (Russian for "steel") was the name adopted by the future dictator while a member of the prerevolutionary Bolshevik underground. While he was ill, Lenin opposed Stalin's power. His "political testament" called for Stalin's removal from office.

(1) **Power struggle between Trotsky and Stalin**. Upon Lenin's death in 1924, a power struggle ensued. The charismatic Leon Trotsky, who preached "permanent," international revolution, was politically inept and was suspected of Napoleonic ambitions. The seemingly moderate and conciliatory Stalin, with his doctrine of "Socialism in one country," won out over Trotsky, whom Stalin exiled and eventually had murdered.

(2) **Foreign policies similar**. The foreign policies of the two men, however,

differed little. Stalin's victory was mainly due to his position as General Secretary of the party. From this vantage, he could pack party posts and committees with his followers, who duly supported him.

b. **Stalin's triumph**. Having dealt with the left by exiling Trotsky, Stalin proceeded to defeat competitors from the right. By 1927-28, he had achieved a large measure of personal mastery. He engineered the removal from the Politboro of the "Right Opposition" leaders **Nikolai Bukharin** (1888-1938), **Lev Kamanev** (1883-1936), and **Grigory Zinovyev** (1883-1936), all of whom he later had executed. But his power was not yet absolute. Stalin now began the first stage of what was to become a policy of achieving total personal dominion over party, state, and society by means of organized terror.

c. **Agricultural collectivization**. First came the "collectivization" of agricultural land. "Collectivization" meant that private land and farm animals were forcibly taken from owners without compensation, and peasant farmers were compelled to live and work on "collective farms." In 1929-30 the more prosperous peasants, the Kulaks, were systematically starved and killed when they resisted. About 6.5 million died. In all some 11 million peasants died from 1930-1937; about 3.5 million more later died in labor camps. By 1936 all of the country's farms had been collectivized. (See Robert Conquest, *The Harvest of Sorrow*, 1986.)

d. **The "Five Year Plan."** At the same time, the first of a series of five-year economic plans was inaugurated, geared to force an unwilling population to rapid industrialization. Collectivized agriculture was to help pay for this industrial investment. The tightly controlled, centralized economy under an all-powerful state that marked the Soviet Union for more than half a century was taking shape.

e. **Purges and the GULAG**. Next, in 1934, Stalin used the murder of a popular party boss, **Sergi Kirov** (1886-1934), to begin a policy of purging the party and society of potential opposition. Stalin is reliably thought to have ordered the murder himself.

(1) **Executions and camp system**. During the following five to six years, millions were executed or sent to a huge system of prison camps where many others died. GULAG is an acronym for the camp administration. The camp system was compared by **Alexandr Solzhenitsyn** (b. 1918) to a chain of islands, a world of its own.

(2) **The GULAG as death camps**. In *The GULAG Archipelago* (3 vols., 1973-75) Solzhenitsyn argued that many of the "islands" were death camps; that is, prisoners were treated in ways calculated to kill them. Some camps, for example, required hard labor at sub-zero temperatures of prisoners who were ill-clad and kept on a starvation diet.

f. **The "show trial."** In 1936 and 1938 new purges were inaugurated which included a novel tool of autocratic rule—the "**show trial**." Show trials featured prominent opponents of Stalin confessing to fantastic charges of subversion and sabotage. The novel *A Darkness at Noon* (1941) by **Arthur Koestler** (1905-1983) explored the psychology of those who "confessed." They did so perhaps in the belief that their confessions, however false, might aid the Party and help to fulfill their life's work.

g. **Origins of the Soviet secret police**. As a means of terror and suppression, Stalin used an elaborate secret police force. Such police had been part of the Soviet system from its inception. Within weeks of the Bolshevik *coup* in 1917, a secret police force, the "Cheka," was formed. It soon had extra-legal powers to arrest, imprison, and execute "enemies of the people." Disbanded in 1922, the Cheka was immediately replaced by a similar organization, the GPU. Under various names, the secret police under Stalin came to hold enormous power, including hundreds of thousands of operatives and its own armed troops.

h. **Stalin's use of secret police**. The secret police were responsible for carrying out

Stalin's purges, conducting show trials, and running the GULAG. The slave labor of the millions of inmates was exploited for public works and other purposes. (Solzhenitsyn's *The First Circle* [1968] deals with the most favored of such prisoners, who did scientific work.) Successive heads of the organization during the height of Stalin's purges, **Genrikh Yagoda** (1891-1938) and **Nikolay "the dwarf" Yezhov** (1895-1939), were themselves arrested and executed. **Lavrenti Beria** (1899-1953), who headed the secret police at Stalin's death was similarly executed.

i. **Stalin's culpability.** In all, Stalin was responsible for the death through murder, starvation, and other means of between 20 and 60 million Soviet people.

4. **Post-war Soviet expansionism and the Cold War.** Soviet expansionism after World War II precipitated the Cold War (1947-1990). Soviet surrogates in Eastern Europe set up a series of communist states in areas occupied by the Red Army, which had entered them in pursuit of the retreating German Wehrmacht. These included communist regimes in Bulgaria, East Germany, Hungary, Poland, and Romania. In 1948 Soviet-backed communists took over the government of Czechoslovakia, which then entered the Soviet orbit. Events such as Soviet sponsorship of communist insurgents in Greece (1946-49), the Berlin Blockade (1948-49), and the Korean War, begun in 1950 by Soviet-satellite North Korea, deepened the Cold War and convinced western democracies of the reality of the communist threat.

5. **Eastern Europe under Stalin.** In the Soviet satellites under Stalin the most powerful individual was the Soviet ambassador, who was instructed from Moscow. Later, power was held by a Soviet-backed strong man such as Polish party head **Wladyslaw Gomulka** (1905-82) or **Janos Kadar** (b. 1912) in Hungary. In East Germany, communist oppression was symbolized by the **Berlin Wall**, erected in August 1961.

6. **Post-Stalinist developments.** Upon the dictator's death in March 1953 the character of the Soviet state was altered. While the use of secret police and surveillance went on unabated, wholesale mass terror and execution was abandoned. The GULAG prison camp system continued, but many of Stalin's victims were released. The period

became known as the "Thaw," after a 1954 novella by Soviet writer **Elya Ehrenberg** (1891-1967), in which Soviet society, frozen in the locked embrace of Stalinism, was partially released. There was, however, little or no independent civil society.

a. **Khrushchev and the seeds of a new revolution.** The state's grip on society was periodically loosened under **Nikita Khrushchev** (1894-1971); but subsequently it was reapplied. Khrushchev, however, sowed the seeds of orthodox communism's undoing with his "Secret Speech" ("On the Cult of Personality and its Consequences") at the 1956 Communist Party Congress. In this speech, since published, he denounced Stalin's murderous lawlessness. Young party members such as Gorbachev were deeply impressed by the revelations.

b. **Gorbachev's revolution.** Under the leadership of **Mikhail S. Gorbachev** (b. 1931), who came to power in 1985, fundamental reforms were launched.

(1) **Attempts to dismantle the post-Stalinist state.** Gorbachev and his supporters, and the Soviet peoples themselves, attempted to dismantle the post-Stalinist state. Limited but important political and cultural expression undirected by authority was increasingly allowed after Gorbachev took power. This led to further demands for free expression and other freedoms by ordinary people, who began to behave more as active citizens than the passive subjects of autocracy.

(2) **The reemergence of "civil society."** The partial dismantling of the repressive Soviet state in the late 1980s meant that groups and organizations with their own views independent of state control could emerge spontaneously from society. This independent activity as a whole, "civil society," had been suppressed under the Stalinist and post-Stalinist states.

(3) **The emergence of Eastern European democracies.** In the Eastern Europe of the early 1990s, deep and far-reaching

changes were under way. Democracies were founded in Poland, Hungary, and Czechoslovakia and Communist party domination discarded. No longer Soviet satellites, these countries began asserting their independence in foreign as well as domestic affairs. The Warsaw Pact, the Soviet-dominated equivalent of NATO, had collapsed in all but name and was later disbanded.

7. **The party that became the state**. Paradoxically, the institutions called the state had little power in themselves. They were facades behind which stood the party. In essence, the party **became** the state. Before the late 1980s, the power of the party was directed by a single man. In the Soviet Union this was Stalin, Khrushchev, and **Leonid Brezhnev** (1906-82). In each case, by dominating the party, the leader dominated the state. After Stalin's death, however, the Politburo, the Communist party's highest governing body, acquired greater influence. But in 1990 in a far-reaching decision, the party formally relinquished its claim to be the sole guiding force in Soviet society. Thus a central pillar of Leninism was abandoned.

8. **China**. The modern Chinese state began with the 1911 Revolution that overthrew the Manchu (Ch'ing) Dynasty (1644-1911) and in 1912 established the "Republic of China." But Western institutions ill-suited a politically inexperienced and generally illiterate people. After 1916, the shell of political democracy was undermined completely by corruption, rising warlordism, and Japan's invasion of Manchuria in 1931 and full-scale attack in 1937. Attempts at political reform failed.

   a. **The founding of the Chinese Communist Party**. During the "May Fourth Movement," which began in 1919, Chinese intellectuals searched for ideas to make the Chinese state strong, wealthy, and democratic. The Chinese Communist Party (CCP) was founded in 1921, in the context of a search for a new political, social, and economic framework.

   b. **CCP strategy for Chinese development**. Western political forms having failed in China, the CCP focused on social and economic democratization as the key to a powerful Chinese state.

   c. **Moscow's advice and the Kuomintang**. Moscow advised the CCP to ally with the more promising and militarily powerful Kuomintang (KMT or Nationalist party) instead of making revolution on its own. The KMT was led first by **Sun Yat-sen** (1866-1925), founder of the Republic of China, and after his death by **Chiang Kai-skek** (1887-1975).

   d. **CCP-KMT alliance and its aftermath**. Lacking conditions for a Marxist revolution, the CCP, agreed to a "united front" with the KMT. The front's purpose was to unify China under one government, but it was short-lived, ending in 1927. The history of China from then until the CCP's victory in 1949 is one of betrayal, internal CCP factionalism, Japanese invasion, and civil war.

   e. **The establishment of the People's Republic of China**. After fighting the Japanese from 1937 to 1945, the Chinese Communists, led by **Mao Tse-tung** (1893-1976), and the Nationalists turned on each other in a bitter civil war ending in 1949. The Nationalists then fled to Taiwan, where they carried on the name of the Republic of China, and the CCP proclaimed the People's Republic of China. The issue of which government properly represents the Chinese state is still not entirely resolved.

   f. **Soviet support and Chinese allegiance**. Despite Stalin's erratic support of the CCP and collusion with the KMT throughout the 1930s and 1940s, the new Chinese regime turned to the Soviet Union for support. For ten years China followed the Soviet model of development.

   g. **Breakup of the Sino-Soviet alliance**. When China's leaders refused to heed Soviet political and economic advice, the Soviets withdrew all their assistance. It was a bitter lesson for China and soured any prospect for renewal of close relations. Ultimately it led to the rupture of relations between the two states.

   h. **The Cultural Revolution**. In 1966, to regain control over party policy, attack a repressive bureaucracy, and prevent the abandonment of socialism, Mao launched the "Cultural Revolution" (1966-1976) or "CR."

(1) **Revolution of the young brings chaos.** Mao called on China's youth to "challenge authority" and "make revolution." This invited abuse and led to torture, murder, suicide, ruined careers, and broken families. Chaos resulted as people tried to protect themselves by attacking others, even friends and relatives.

(2) **Counting the CR's costs.** By the CR's end in 1976, production had virtually halted. An estimated 100 million people had become the CR's targets. Hundreds of thousands died. After Mao died, several of his accomplices, the "Gang of Four," were sentenced to jail. Until the early 1980s they served as scapegoats for all China's problems.

i. **Reform policies.** After a brief transitional period, control over CCP and the government fell to vice-premier **Deng Ziaoping** (b. 1904). An arch-pragmatist, Deng once said he did not care if the cat was black or white, as long as it caught mice.

(1) **Economic decentralization.** Pragmatism underlaid Deng's willingness to put aside centralized state economic controls. In agriculture, market forces were allowed to govern, giving greater control over production to the peasantry, who still composed 80% of the population. The result was a rapid increase in agricultural production and the release of millions from the land.

(2) **Continued controls.** In the urban, industrialized sector, however, state control remained strong, though individuals could begin their own businesses or "collectives." The result was a part-socialist, part-capitalist economy.

j. **Liberalizing reforms blamed for China's problems.** By 1988, despite a decade of rapid modernization, many problems existed. Most seemed to stem from mixing market and socialist economies.

(1) **Corruption.** Corruption was rife, for the state controlled access to resources. The simplest decision in the industrialized economy still required official approval.

(2) **Party economic intervention.** Worse, party officials continued to intervene in these decisions. The Communist party and the state were coterminous, with the CCP making policies for the state to carry out, and then interfering in their execution. Deng's repeated efforts to remove the party from governance failed.

(3) **Inflation, unemployment, and crime.** A third problem was rapid inflation, estimated in 1988 to be nearly 50% in some sectors. Although this had little affect on those in the free market economy, it hurt those on state salaries. Finally, increasing unemployment gave rise to criminality.

(4) **Reversal of reforms.** By the fall of 1988, the CCP reversed many reforms in an effort to regain control over the economy and society.

k. **Intellectuals challenge the authority of the Communist Party.** During the reform period, educated Chinese began to question the CCP's authority. China experienced the greatest degree of press freedom and cultural ferment in the year preceding the military crackdown in 1989. Students were no longer forced to study rigid Marxist-Leninist ideology. Tens of thousands could go abroad for study. This "open door" policy benefitted both the economy and intellectual life.

l. **The Tiananmen Square massacre.** The period of liberalization dramatically ended with the June 1989 military attack on the Tiananmen Square pro-democracy student-led movement. Hundreds if not thousands of lives were lost. Thereafter, repression by the state silenced students, intellectuals, and ordinary citizens.

E. **Social democracy.** Social democracy began in the nineteenth century as a variant of socialism advocating that socialist programs be enacted only by peaceful and democratic means.

1. **German origins of social democracy.** Politically organized social democracy originated in Germany.

    a. **Early parties and leaders.** Social democratic parties began with the formation in Leipzig of the German Social Democratic Workers' Party in 1869. In 1875 the party merged with the German General Workers' Union to form the German Social Democratic Party. Until the end of the century, the party was led by **August Bebel** (1840-1913), a self-taught craftsman, and his friend **Wilhelm Liebknecht** (1826-1900), a university-educated close associate of Karl Marx.

    b. **The rise and influence of German social democracy.** In the hands of the two leaders, the tenets of social democracy remained Marxist in essential respects. But despite severe repression at the hands of Chancellor **Otto von Bismark** (1815-1896), German social democracy never embraced violence as a means to power. In spite of Bismark's restrictions, the party continued to grow under the influence of its two leaders. By 1912 it held more legislative seats than any other party. Because of its success in Germany, social democracy radiated its influence to other parts of Europe.

2. **The revision of Marxism.** By 1900 the orthodox Marxism previously espoused by German social democracy was undergoing revision.

    a. **Capitalism's appearance of solving its problems.** Marx thought capitalism would meet increasingly severe crises it would be powerless to remedy. But a number of social democrats came to believe that capitalism was solving many of its problems. Instead of becoming more concentrated, as Marx predicted, industrial ownership was becoming more widespread. Marx had also portrayed the middle class as parasites once its historical function was fulfilled. But social democrats came to see the middle class as playing a more positive economic role.

    b. **Bernstein and the rejection of revolution.** All of this and more was argued by **Eduard Bernstein** (1850-1932) in his ground breaking *Evolutionary Socialism* (1899), the most important early work of Marxist revisionism. To Bernstein, the interests of the working class and of society generally would be advanced by steady, evolutionary progress, not by revolutionary upheaval.

    c. **The new view of the state.** Evolutionary socialism entailed a radically different view of the state and its possibilities than was implied by its Marxist description as the "ruling committee of the bourgeoisie." Instead, social democracy now saw the state as an instrument capable of promoting a more just and equable society.

3. **Social democracy in Britain.** A similar, non-revolutionary view of social progress had been evolving in Britain since the late nineteenth century among members of the **Fabian Society**. Early members of the Society, founded in London in 1883-84, included the playwright **George Bernard Shaw** (1856-1950) and the influential writers and social reformers **Sidney Webb** (1859-1947) and his wife **Beatrice Webb** (1858-1943).

    a. **Fabianism and the Webbs.** Sidney Webb wrote "Facts for Socialists" for the *Fabian Essays* (1889). This important essay launched an effort to create a socialist Britain by educating the public. Only through an informed public could socialism evolve democratically.

        (1) **Founding of the London School of Economics.** To this end the Webbs founded the London School of Economics and Political Science and were instrumental in reforming the University of London.

        (2) **Educational opportunity and popular participation.** As a member of the London County Council, Sidney Webb sponsored measures for extending primary and secondary education among previously excluded classes. The Fabian Society sponsored lectures, conferences, summer institutes, and discussions. Popular participation was considered a key factor in the success of social democratic aims.

b. **Fabianism in the twentieth century.** The Fabian view of peacefully evolving democratic socialism deeply influenced the British Labour Party from its inception in 1906.

    (1) **Advocacy of social insurance.** Beatrice Webb championed the idea of social insurance in her famous *Minority Report* (1909) following service on a commission on poverty. In 1942 the *Beveridge Report*, which set the agenda for the post-war Labour government which came to power in 1945, advocated a similar plan.

    (2) **Positive role of the state.** Thus democratic socialism in Britain, like its counterpart on the continent, put great emphasis on the state's potentially positive role in the amelioration of lower-class suffering and in fostering the aims of socialist democracy.

4. **Post-war social democracy.** Social democratic parties came to power in continental Europe after World War II, for example, in Denmark, Germany, Norway, and Sweden.

a. **Abandonment of Marxist orthodoxy.** The post-war social democratic parties abandoned ties to Marxist orthodoxy as well as emphasis on public ownership of the means of production.

b. **Concentration on developing the welfare state.** Instead of Marxist orthodoxy these parties advocated a pragmatic approach, including government regulation and control of industry. They concentrated on developing the welfare state, with its system of state-guaranteed benefits. But significant state ownership might still be practiced, as in Britain and Sweden.

c. **Fundamental difference with traditional Marxism and communism.** Post-war social democracy rejected ideological dogmatism and wholesale socialization of industry and commerce. Social democratic parties insisted on achieving power democratically and advocated a positive role for the state to promote its aims. They supported democratic liberties. Thus modern social democracy differs fundamentally from both traditional Marxism and latter-day communism.

F. **Fascism.** Fascist movements originated and first came to power in Europe in the 1920s and '30s. The most important examples were Italy under **Benito Mussolini** (1883-1945) and Germany under **Adolf Hitler** (1889-1945). The history of fascism may be divided into intellectual roots, social and political context, and examples of fascism in practice.

1. **Intellectual roots.** Important nineteenth-century roots of fascism lie in the extreme reaction of some parts of European society to the French Revolution. While some enemies of the Enlightenment were traditional conservatives, others were forerunners of fascism.

a. **Reaction to the French Revolution—rejection of the Enlightenment.** Some who reacted with horror to the overturning of French society, especially to the execution of the king and the Terror, sought refuge in the belief in a rigid social hierarchy headed by monarch or aristocracy. They rejected the Enlightenment, with its values of freedom, social equality, individualism, rationality, and the application of reason to social problems, and chose traditional social and political structures emphasizing tradition and religious faith.

b. **Irrationalism and glorification of the state.** Glorification of the state and the view that power is its essence can be traced to Machiavelli during the Renaissance.

    (1) **Hegel.** After the French Revolution, Romantic philosophers such as Hegel, himself no proto-fascist, glorified the state, depicting it as the pinnacle of historical development and the instrument of divine will.

    (2) **De Maistre. Joseph de Maistre** (1754-1821) saw dogmatic faith, inflexible social hierarchy, and unbending authority as foundations of social order. Throne and alter—monarchy and church—were the twin pillars of his social edifice. Although an extreme reactionary, de Maistre's ideas look forward to fascist doctrine. A supreme elitist, he rejected reason for mystery

and the irrational, demanded total submission and subservience of the individual to the state and its rulers, glorified violence and the divinity of war, with its "five or six kinds of intoxication," and repudiated the idea of the free expression of ideas. (See Isaiah Berlin, *The Crooked Timber of Humanity*, 1991.)

c. **Racial doctrines and anti-semitism.** Later writers such as **Joseph Gobineau** (1816-1882) and **Houston Chamberlain** (1855-1927) popularized doctrines of Teutonic racial superiority combined with anti-semitism and demands for racial purity. These ideas were adapted to form the basis of Nazi anti-semitic and racial doctrines.

d. **The discovery of the irrational.** A number of brilliant nineteenth century writers such as **Fydor Dostoyevsky** (1821-1881) and **Friedrich Nietzsche** (1844-1900)—neither of whom was a proto-fascist—explored human irrationality.

(1) **Dostoyevsky and the psychology of submission.** Dostoyevsky exposed aspects of man's dark side such as the need to renounce freedom and responsibility by submitting to an authority figure. By conviction a religious conservative, Dostoyevsky explored this theme in the "Parable of the Grand Inquisitor" in *The Brothers Karamozov* (1879-80). Fascism often successfully appealed to these impulses. (The psychology of submission in fascism was later examined by psychoanalyst Erich Fromm in *Escape from Freedom* [1941].)

(2) **Nietzsche's diagnosis of European decadence.** Human irrationality and the ills of modern Europe were explored by Nietzsche. Contemptuous of democracy and social equality, Nietzsche mercilessly unmasked the non-rational bases of the Judeo-Christian European culture he believed to be crumbling. He looked to new cultural heroes to establish a new set of values. Nietzsche's ideas were misused by twentieth-century fascists to bolster their racial, elitist, and authoritarian doctrines.

e. **Elitism and vitalism.** In the early twentieth century theories of "vitalism" and "elitism" helped shape an intellectual climate favorable to the acceptance of the irrationalist politics that characterized fascism.

(1) **Vitalism.** Vitalism saw some version of a "life force" as a central philosophical category. The "life force" or some other form of the irrational took precedence over reason and intellect. In his *Reflections on Violence* (1908), **George Sorel** (1847-1922), for example, denounced liberal democracy and championed the idea that irrational myths were needed by the working class to fulfill its historical role.

(2) **Elitism.** Elitist theories held the rule of political and cultural elites to be inevitable aspects of the social order. Influential Italian social scientists **Gaetano Mosca** (1858-1941) and **Vilfredo Pareto** (1848-1923), for example, emphasized the universal role of elites in human history. For Mosca, in his *The Ruling Class* (1896), societies are always divided into elite and mass and are dominated by their ruling class. For Pareto, irrational and non-rational factors are permanent features of human society. Irrational myths (or ideologies) are manipulated by elites to control and inspire the masses.

2. **Political and social context.** Forces opposed to individual freedom, social equality, and democracy had varying influence in nineteenth-century Europe.

a. **The Dreyfus Affair.** An important example of these forces in action took place in France. After that nation discarded its monarchy to become a republic in 1870, traditionalists remained unreconciled to the new state. These forces were apparent in the **Dreyfus Affair** (1894-1906) in which **Alfred Dreyfus** (1859-1935), an innocent Jewish French officer, was found guilty of treason and imprisoned on Devils Island, off French Guiana in South America. Dreyfus was eventually pardoned and finally exonerated, but those arrayed against his cause were revealed as strongly anti-republican and anti-semitic. The Dreyfus Affair split French society for a generation.

b. **War and the rise of fascism**. World War I (1914-1919) was the catalyst that led to the initial formation of fascist movements. The war, which killed the flower of an entire generation of men, had a profoundly destabilizing effect on Europe. The threat of communist revolutions, such as the successful Bolshevik *coup d'état* in Russia in 1917 and the unsuccessful "Spartacus Revolt" in Germany in 1919, had a similar effect.

c. **Modernization, depression, and fascism.** Rapid modernization in countries like Germany and Italy, together with the dislocations of war, left whole societies in a state of uprootedness. Part of the appeal of fascism was to those who were uprooted by the rapid social change of industrialization, urbanization, economic depression, and the decline of traditional beliefs. The extreme nationalism and anti-modernism of fascist ideology appealed to those who had lost faith in both church and political institutions.

3. **Fascism in Italy**. Because Italy was united only in 1870, its political institutions lacked the weight of tradition. The north had rapid economic development before World War I, but the south remained economically and socially traditional, overpopulated, and poor. Italy's failure after the war to secure territorial gains secretly promised by the Allies in 1915 provoked nationalist complaints.

a. **Mussolini takes power.** Previously a Marxist, Benito Mussolini became an ardent nationalist during World War I. After the war he organized former soldiers and others into a movement that pressed nationalist claims. Looking back to ancient Rome, Mussolini promised restored greatness to Italy but otherwise had few ideas. His movement rejected thought in favor of violent action. In 1922 he organized a march on Rome to demand an end to social disorder. Italy's king invited Mussolini, a member of parliament, to form a government.

b. **The corporate state**. Once in power, "Il Duce" ("the leader"), as he was known, transformed the country into a dictatorship, violently suppressing opposition and forcing education, the press, and other social institutions into compliance.

(1) **State control of the economy**. By 1930 a "corporative state" was in place that left the means of production in private hands but gave the government complete control over economic life. The economy was divided into a series of associations that were represented in a "council of corporations."

(2) **Suppression of free activity**. Labor unions were absorbed into the Council of Corporations. Free political activity and independent unions were suppressed. Civilian consumption was reduced to enhance militarization. This model was also adapted in Germany by Hitler and to a lesser extent in Spain by military dictator **Francisco Franco** (1892-1975), whom Mussolini aided in 1936 during the Spanish Civil War.

(3) **Primacy of the state**. The *Doctrine of Fascism*, published under Mussolini's name but written by the Italian philosopher **Giovanni Gentile** (1875-1944), declares that "[t]he State is not only authority that governs and molds individual wills...but it is also power that makes its will prevail abroad....For the Fascist, everything is within the state and...neither individuals or groups are outside the State....For Fascism the State is an absolute, before which individuals and groups are only relative."

c. **Mussolini's military adventures**. Mussolini's militaristic nationalism led to an attack on Ethiopia in 1935-36 followed with an alliance with Hitler. In 1939 he occupied Albania. In 1943 military reverses during World War II led to his being deposed; with the occupation of Italy by the Allies, the country's fascist period came to a close.

4. **Fascism in Germany**. Nazism in Germany represented the most extreme form of fascism.

a. **The role of geography**. Germany's geographic position, between east and west without barriers to invasion, made it especially insecure. Like Italy, Germany lacked rooted political institutions since it was not united until 1870. Rapid industrialization and urbanization in much of the country had also led to social dislocation. But Prussia, Germany's eastern region which politically dominated the country, retained an archaic, authoritarian social structure.

b. **Military defeat and desperation**. Germany's defeat in World War I and the harsh terms of the Versailles Treaty (1919) were important causes of the rise of extreme nationalism.

(1) **Weak foundations of Weimar Republic**. Demoralized by defeat, Germany also suffered acute starvation after the war. Without historical roots, the new Weimar Republic that replaced the German Emperor's regime rested on flimsy foundations. These were seriously undermined by the catastrophic hyperinflation of 1923, which wiped out the savings of much of the middle class.

(2) **Rise of authoritarianism**. Political chaos and social disorder were furthered in 1930 by the onset of the Great Depression. Desperate and unemployed, great numbers were ready to put their faith in an authoritarian movement whose leader promised to restore national greatness and prosperity.

c. **Hitler and Nazi ideology**. Adolf Hitler, known as the "Fuhrer" (leader), perfectly embodied the fascist leadership principle.

(1) **Hitler's rise**. Though born in Austria, Hitler emerged from fighting in World War I as an extreme German nationalist. He blamed the German defeat on betrayal by Marxists and Jews. By 1921 he was head of the National German Workers' or "Nazi" party. In 1923 he gained national attention by attempting a *coup d'état*, the Munich "beer-hall putsch."

(2) *Mein Kampf*. In the same year, while in jail for his crime, Hitler began writing *Mein Kampf ("My Struggle")*, the Nazi bible that outlined the theory of an Aryan "master race," an especially vicious form of anti-semitism, and a plan for world domination.

d. **Nazi techniques of rule**. To gain political power and to wield it once in office, Hitler and his chief lieutenants adopted a number of techniques that typified Nazism.

(1) **Propaganda and mass meetings**. Hitler used oratory, huge rallies, and torchlight parades to whip up mass nationalist frenzy. Propaganda vilified the opposition. It used the technique of the "Big Lie," according to which colossal untruths were said to be more readily believed than trivial ones.

(2) **Use of private armies for political repression**. Private armies of Nazi adherents were used to intimidate and assault opponents. Unpopular groups such as Jews and political enemies such as communists were made scapegoats. Murder and terrorism were resorted to without hesitation. No moral limits to action were respected; political expediency alone was consulted.

e. **Nazi totalitarianism in practice**. In 1932 Hitler ran for president against **Paul von Hindenburg** (1847-1934) and lost. The Nazi state took shape after Hitler legally became chancellor in 1933, appointed to the post by President Hindenburg.

(1) **Terror and concentration camps**. Opponents of the Nazis were murdered or imprisoned. Secret police, the Gestapo, arrested and tortured whomever they pleased. The first concentration camp was established at Dachau, near Munich, just five weeks after Hitler became Chancellor.

(2) **Jewish persecution**. "Racial" laws (the "Nuremburg laws") that persecuted Jews were enacted in 1935, and organized massacres were mounted against them. The worst of these was **"Kristallnacht"** ("Crystal Night") in 1938, when Jews and Jewish property throughout the country were attacked.

(3) **Militarization**. Militarization proceeded at breakneck speed. The Versailles Treaty was violated with impunity. Preparation for war was placed at the center of state policy.

(4) **Totalitarian controls**. All of German culture, including law, religion, education, the press, music, films, and theater, was ruthlessly controlled by the Nazi state. A cult of the leader was fostered.

f. **The outbreak of World War II**. After forcing a merger with Austria in 1938 and seizing neighboring lands, Hitler precipitated the outbreak of World War II in 1939 by invading Poland. By the end of the war, the Nazi regime was responsible for the deaths of more than 40,000,000 people.

g. **Genocide of the Jews**. Several years after the outbreak of war, Hitler began the so-called "Final Solution" to the "Jewish question." This "solution" was genocide, the mass-extermination, of the Jews, of whom some 6,000,000 perished. This event is now known as **the Holocaust**. Also killed were perhaps 2,000,000 others, including gypsies, homosexuals and Slavs. To kill on such a massive scale, the Nazis used scientifically designed and organized death camps, such as those in Poland at Auschwitz and Treblinka.

h. **The legacy of Nazism**. Fascism under Hitler abolished much of traditional morality and glorified irrationalism, violence, and persecution. The individual was ruthlessly subordinated to the state's aim of total power. Nearly the whole of the population that did not take part voluntarily was forced through terror and intimidation into some form of political participation, always as the manipulated subjects of state power.

i. **The god-like powers of the Nazi state.** Nazism claimed for the state the divine powers of defining who is human and who is not and of killing or enslaving all those judged inferior.

5. **Fascism outside Europe**. A variety of stridently nationalist dictatorial regimes outside Europe that exhibited other fascist characteristics qualify as full-fledged fascism. Two important examples of non-European fascism were Japan and Argentina.

a. **A fascist phase of development?** In the 1930s and afterwards some liberal democratic or monarchial regimes were too weak to withstand problems of economic depression, social dislocation, and disorientation arising from industrialization and other aspects of modernization. Some scholars have argued that rapidly developing societies risk undergoing a "fascist phase." In this phase, irrationalist movements espousing traditionalist values seek the support of the uprooted and dispossessed in order to gain power.

b. **Fascism in Japan**. In Japan, the militarist factions of society gained ascendancy from the 1920s. Although there was no fascist political party as in Europe, Japanese militarism has generally been included among fascist regimes.

(1) **Militarism and "tribal mysticism."** In 1936 the Japanese army took over the government in the name of a kind of "tribal mysticism" that venerated the nation and traditionalist values such as those of the warrior.

(2) **Role of the emperor**. In place of the fascist leader, the state was personified by the emperor, who stood above the law and was virtually worshiped.

(3) **Suppression of western liberal ideas**. The army massacred or suppressed those it believed promoted such western ideas as liberalism, individualism, and internationalism.

(4) **Territorial conquest and World War II**. In possession of Manchuria since 1931, the army launched a full-scale attack on China in 1937. Its attempt to create an East Asian empire precipitated American opposition and led to the Japanese attack on Pearl Harbor in 1941.

c. **Peron and Argentine fascism**. In Argentina, a group of army officers seized power in 1943. In 1946 one them, **Juan Peron (1895-**

1975), emerged as strong man. Peron was elected president, mainly with the support of workers, among whom he had built a political empire. Peron ruled by increasingly authoritarian means, using his nationalist movement to whip up frenzied support from crowds. His wife **Eva Peron** (1919-1952) was made the object of cult worship. In 1955, amidst economic chaos, Peron was overthrown by the army.

Contemporary Perspective

In much of the world, the state is undergoing a series of dynamic changes as the result of technological innovation, international economic factors, demographic forces, changes wrought by the spread of ideas, and other factors. The following are examples of these changes that are of special concern to the citizen.

I. **Spread of democracy.** Late in the century a number of seemingly well-entrenched autocracies were overthrown or are presently in a state of flux. In many places, the power of the state to dictate to docile populations seems to be waning. But, however positive these developments may be, there is no guarantee that democratization will be long-lasting, especially where poverty and illiteracy continue.

The spread of democracy has been uneven in less developed countries. Movements for democracy have been most successful in Latin America and least successful in Africa, though this could change as the democracy movement continues its sweep. In the early 1990s, Asia has seen mixed results from attempts at democratization. Whether constitutional governments that respect basic human rights are brought to power, and whether once in power they can endure are momentous questions that looms large in the political future of each region.

A. **The Soviet Union and Central and Eastern Europe.** Since 1985 democratic forces have been unleashed by new leadership. The theory and practice of a centralized state, especially centralized state economic planning, has been in full retreat. By the early 1990s, the totalitarian state, which attempted to control every facet of its people's life, had been largely dismantled in the USSR. In most of Central and Eastern Europe, it had been entirely dismantled.

1. **The Soviet Union.** The future character of the democratization process is uncertain in the Soviet Union. Whether the USSR—or a rump successor

—can transform itself into a western-style market economy without a prolonged period of acute economic and social dislocation and civil disorder is unknown. The future course of democratization may depend upon the degree of disorder. Demands for democratization throughout the USSR became irresistible with popular fury after the coup attempt of August 1991.

a. **The problem of national fragmentation.** The future character of the Soviet Union as a multi-national state is also uncertain. As many of the peoples who comprise the USSR demand sovereignty and most republics have declared independence, the future shape of the Soviet state cannot be predicted. The state's capacity to influence (still less to control) events is likely to wane as economic problems and ethnic rivalries and aspirations threaten to become overwhelming.

b. **The party apparatus and the KGB.** Although much progress toward democratization had been made by the early 1990s, much power was left with the state security agency, the KGB, and Communist party officials. These groups and the armed forces threatened to form the kernel of a new authoritarian regime. But the end of Communist rule and the deepening of the popular basis of power that followed the abortive August 1991 coup eliminated the possibility of party-led autocracy. Whether democracy can survive the severe economic difficulties that lay ahead, however, was a question that only the future could answer.

2. **Eastern and Central Europe.** In the revolution of 1989, most of the previously communist states of eastern Europe—Czechoslovakia, East Germany (part of Germany since 1990), Hungary, and Poland—cast off their Soviet-backed regimes and moved decisively toward democracy. These countries, however, face severe economic problems, and in some cases, ethnic and national rivalries. These grave difficulties may imperil the future of democracy. Any prolonged period of social dislocation and disorder could give rise to the entrenchment of autocratic governments.

B. **Sub-Saharan Africa.** The spread of democratization in Africa is perhaps more problematic than in any other part of the Third World. Nevertheless, calls for democratization have been heard in a number of countries whose governments embody some form of autocratic or authoritarian rule.

1. **Few democratic regimes.** Of the dozens of regimes that rule African states in the early 1990s, no more than a small handful could be called democratic. Among them were Botswana, Senegal, and Namibia. Most embody some form of autocratic rule, though some—perhaps many—may be in the process of democratizing, as calls for multi-party systems are heard across the continent.

2. **Human rights violations.** Human rights violations have been endemic to much of the continent since decolonization in the 1950s and '60s. Such violations have occurred at various times and places on a colossal scale, for example in the Central African Republic, Nigeria, South Africa, and Uganda.

3. **Uncertainty of future democratization.** The future of democratization in sub-Saharan Africa is uncertain. The establishment in 1991 of a new democracy in Namibia was a positive development.

    a. **Spread of demands for democracy.** Demands for democracy appear to be spreading. They have been heard in Cameroon, Ivory Coast, Kenya, Nigeria, South Africa, Togo, Zambia, Zimbabwe, and elsewhere.

    b. **Factors tending to undermine democracy.** Endemic poverty, illiteracy, population explosion, disease, economic mismanagement, internal violence, tribalism, and corruption put the future of democratization at grave risk.

4. **Possible democratization in South Africa.** In South Africa, the African majority has struggled for decades against a system of "apartheid" (racial "separateness") that systematically deprived them of political and human rights.

    a. **Peaceful dismantling of apartheid uncertain.** Whether the African, Asian, mixed-race, and white people of South Africa can find a stable, long-term, peaceful solution for a mutually acceptable constitutional order in South Africa is difficult to judge.

    b. **Possibility of constitutional democracy uncertain.** If the African majority is successful in achieving power, it is also uncertain whether constitutional democracy will result or if the experience elsewhere on the continent of dictatorship or civil war will be repeated in South Africa.

C. **China.** After the repression of the pro-democracy movement in 1989, the future of Chinese democracy was uncertain.

    1. **Suppression of the democratic movement.** After the military suppression of the student-led pro-democracy movement in June 1989, the Chinese Communist Party (CCP) suppressed all free political activity through a series of totalitarian controls.

        a. **Surveillance of the population.** The Chinese people are under close scrutiny at all times. The regime has used such devices as the "Big Lie," secret surveillance cameras, a large-scale system of informers, arbitrary imprisonment, and public executions.

        b. **Use of propaganda.** Students must attend regular propaganda classes, the military is under tight control to prevent a possible *coup d'état*, and the media are subjected to the tight discipline of the CCP Propaganda Department.

    2. **Influence of Eastern European events on the regime.** Events in Eastern Europe in 1989 alarmed China's leaders. Events in East Germany and Czechoslovakia indicated how quickly pro-democracy demonstrations can escalate. Events in Poland, where the trade union Solidarity successfully challenged the government, suggest the power of workers to challenge CCP rule.

    3. **Influence of Eastern European events on Chinese democrats.** For Chinese democrats, Eastern European events provide hope. Communism has proven its inability to bring about modernization and ruling communist parties everywhere have been shown to be corrupt to the core. From a Chinese perspective, the CCP's immorality in massacring the innocent means that it, too, has lost its right to rule, and therefore rebellion is justified. Most Chinese appear to be waiting patiently for the right moment again to demand

greater democracy and the end of communist rule.

4. **Implications of Chinese fear of chaos.** For the ordinary Chinese, however, there is a darker side to the events in Eastern Europe. Now, as for centuries, the Chinese fear chaos more than they hate autocracy. If Eastern Europe and the Soviet Union disintegrate into civil war, the Chinese may well decide that one-party communist rule is preferable to chaos.

D. **Southeast Asia, the Indian subcontinent, and the Middle East.** Movements for democracy have been active in various parts of Asia and to a lesser extent in the Middle East. But the stability of already-established popular regimes is uncertain. Several examples are the following:

1. **Southeast Asia.** Since the late 1980s Myanmar (formerly Burma) has been the scene of agitation for democratic elections and popular government. But democratization has been opposed, often violently, by the ruling military regime. The democratic government of the Philippines, established after the overthrow of **Ferdinand Marcos** (1917-1989), is not firmly established, having endured multiple attempts to overthrow it by military coup. It also faces a formidable communist insurgency movement as well as severe economic problems.

2. **The Indian Subcontinent and central Asia.** Democracy in India has in recent years become increasingly violent, as illustrated by the assassination of two members of the dynastic Gandhi family in 1984 and 1991. The fragmentation of the Indian people among myriad ethnic groups speaking some 1,500 languages and dialects places increasing pressures on democratic norms and processes. Violence over religious issues has increased. Democracy in Pakistan is also problematic, since popularly elected governments face intervention and replacement by military forces. Efforts toward democratization and constitutionalism have been made in Nepal, where calls have been heard for such staples of the rule of law as institution of the writ of habeas corpus. In 1990 Mongolia moved squarely into the ranks of democratic nations.

3. **The Middle East.** Movements for popular government have manifested themselves from time to time in certain Middle Eastern countries such as Algeria. But in many others, tight restrictions backed up in some cases by extensive secret police networks and draconian punishment for dissent makes the free expression of the popular will impossible. Moreover, popular government is not necessarily constitutional democratic government in the western sense, making it difficult to hazard generalizations about popular demands in the Middle East. The growing strength of Muslim fundamentalism makes the stability of democratic regimes that might be established problematic. Demands for popular government in Kuwait followed in the wake of its liberation by American-led forces in 1991.

E. **Latin America: the move towards democracy.** The decade of the 1980s saw the vast majority of Latin American nations turn towards democracy. During the previous twenty years every nation on the mainland of Latin America suffered some period of authoritarian rule, except Colombia, Venezuela, Costa Rica and Belize. In fact, authoritarianism has been the norm in Latin America since the region was liberated from Spanish colonial domination in the early 1800s. Today, however, only three governments in all of Latin America have no claim to democratic legitimacy: Cuba, Surinam and Guyana.

1. **Obstacles to democracy.** But the Latin American road to democracy will not be easy or without obstacles. While elections are an important step, they alone do not constitute full democracy. In societies steeped in authoritarian traditions, developing and consolidating democratic habits and institutions will likely require decades. In addition, the continent's horrendous economic crisis stands in the way of democratic progress. During the 1980s, known there as the "lost decade," the regional GDP **fell** by 9 percent. Latin America has witnessed increasing poverty, a large disparity of wealth between rich and poor, and a decline in the countries' already small middle classes, developments contrary to what is normally expected of democratic societies. In 1989 the region's average inflation rate was 1000 percent, and by 1990 Latin America had amassed a combined foreign debt of $420 billion.

2. **Economic policies.** To combat their economic difficulties, Latin America's young democracies have turned to orthodox, free-market policies, which show signs of being effective but entail large social costs. Economic austerity and

increased hardship in turn cause increased social instability that threatens to weaken the fragile foundations on which Latin American democracies are built. Alone, either these tasks—democratization or economic recovery—would be a complex and precarious process. Undertaking both at once will be much more so. This will be the great challenge to Latin America and the world in the coming decades.

3. **U.S. policy.** United States policy towards its southern neighbors has taken a turn from the past. Formerly, direct military and economic aid were funneled into the region to combat the threat of Communism. But in the last few years both the United States' ability to give direct aid and the fear of Communism have declined. In December of 1990, President George Bush traveled through the region to promote his new "Enterprise for the America's Initiative." The Initiative is intended to bolster the economic and political changes that have taken place in Latin America by encouraging free trade, free markets, debt reduction, privatization and private foreign investment in Latin America. The following is a country by country breakdown of the democratic outlook for mainland Latin America.

4. **Mexico.** Since the end of the 1910 revolution Mexico has been ruled by the Institutional Revolutionary Party (PRI), a heterogeneous coalition of various interest groups. Although PRI has not allowed open, organized political opposition, traditionally there has been reasonable competition for power among inter-party factions, and civilian presidents have passed on power every six years. Seeking a clear political mandate in order to tackle his country's severe economic problems, President **Carlos Salinas de Gotari**—elected in 1988—pledged to open the electoral process. Consequently, non-PRI parties have increased their representation in Mexico's Congress and for the first time in the twentieth century an opposition candidate was elected governor of one of Mexico's states.

5. **Central America.** In Central America, the 1980s was a period of revolution and insurrection when political battles were fought with guns. But at the dawn of a new decade peace and civilian democracy have started to take seed. With the election of **Violeta Barrios de Chamorro** in 1990, Nicaragua's "Contras" laid down their arms after nine years of war and abandoned their Honduran

bases to return home. In spite of political strife in Honduras, El Salvador and Guatemala, in 1989 and 1990 relatively free elections were held in all three countries. In 1991 prospects were better than ever for negotiated settlements that would end the guerrilla wars that have plagued El Salvador and Guatemala for over a decade. The United States' removal from power of military strongman **Manuel Noriega** gives hope that Panama will also become more democratic. Another budding democracy is English-speaking Belize, a former British colony that gained independence in 1981. Much of the trend towards democracy in this area of the world has come about thanks to the example and vigorous diplomatic efforts of another Central American country, Costa Rica. A self-styled "Switzerland of Latin America," Costa Rica is one of the region's strongest democracies.

6. **South America.** As in Central America, South America has had its share of military dictators and military-controlled governments. Only Surinam and Guyana have not seen the disappearance of military dictatorship and the emergence of freely elected civilian regimes. But throughout the region these developments are precarious.

   a. **Nations where democracy has taken root.** Of the South American nations, Colombia and Venezuela have had the longest uninterrupted democratic rule. Although in the early 1990s Columbia negotiated an end to its decade-long guerrilla wars, the increasing power of drug traffickers threatens the country's civilian democratic institutions. In the 1980s three hundred-fifty Colombian judicial employees and fifty judges were murdered. Venezuela does not face such extreme problems, due in part to its oil reserves, which ensure a source of economic wealth that other South American countries do not have. But even there economic problems have spawned civil violence. When Venezuela's newly-elected President **Carlos Andres Perez** raised prices and devalued currency to reduce the country's budget deficit, the 31-year old Venezuelan democracy was rocked by riots that reportedly left hundreds dead and thousands wounded.

   b. **Other nations turning to democracy.** All of the remaining nations have turned towards democracy and held elections, with differing degrees of legitimacy, during the 1980s. In Ecuador (1979), Bolivia (1982), and Paraguay (1989) well-established military dictatorships fell from power and civilian governments elected. But in each country the government retains close ties to the military. In some cases the fairness of the elections has been openly questioned. Nonetheless, progress toward democracy has been made. In Ecuador, Bolivia and Paraguay the difficult transition away from authoritarian regimes has been made and democracy has steadily been consolidated.

c. **Consolidation of democracy difficult.** In other countries where authoritarian military governments have fallen—Peru (1980), Argentina (1983), Uruguay (1984), and Brazil (1985)—the move away from the military has been more rapid, but the consolidation of democracy equally difficult. Rampant inflation, drug trafficking, and the "Shining Path" guerrillas have greatly destabilized Peru's eleven year-old democracy. Brazil's $112 billion debt is the biggest in the world. Immediately after his inauguration as the country's first popularly elected president in 29 years, President **Fernando Collor de Mello** announced the most radical economic package yet in Latin America, but one year later hyperinflation was still a looming threat, and the Brazilian economy was not improving. Debt and hyperinflation are problems in Argentina as well, where the young democracy has also been confronted with several small but open revolts by a faction of the Argentine military known as the "carapintadas," or painted faces.

d. **Chile.** Chile, on the other hand, is a sign of hope for Latin America. Between 1973 and 1989 the country was ruled by General Augusto Pinochet, one of the most repressive of the Latin American dictators. But tough austerity and free-market changes undertaken by the regime were reaping benefits by the early 1990s. In recent years the country has cut its foreign debt, built up currency reserves and stimulated economic growth. In a 1989 plebescite the country voted against allowing Pinochet to extend his rule eight more years. Since his 1990 inauguration, democratically elected President **Patricio**

Aylwin has led perhaps the most healthy economy and the most rapidly developing democracy in Latin America.

7. **Conclusion.** In Latin America, building mature, stable democracies on the democratic gains of the 1980s will not be easy. Young democratic governments will be hard pressed to consolidate civilian democratic rule and, at the same time, combat inflation, pay off debt, and improve their citizens' standards of living. But, as never before, there is consensus in Latin America that the key to the region's problems lies in democracy and free-market economies.

II. **Opposition to traditional liberal-democracy.** Notwithstanding the spread of democracy in the world, assaults on liberal-democratic notions of the state flow from various sources. Anti-liberal views either of a corporatist or collectivist nature have had considerable influence in the modern world, usually (though not always) through the medium of fascist or Marxist movements.

A. **Secular states opposed to liberal democracy.** In the early 1990s a number of Marxist and non-Marxist states opposed to liberal democracy remained in existence.

1. **Marxist states.** Marxist states governed by communist autocracy include examples such as China, Cuba, North Korea, and Vietnam. Traditionally, the Marxist state's purpose is to preserve "progressive" forces in power for the collective benefit of the whole, including the creation of a socialist form of production and distribution. The state, possessed by the Communist party, is the agent of this end. Some Marxist states have liberalized economic institutions, allowing elements of the free market. But they have refused meaningful political liberalization or democratization.

2. **Non-Marxist states.** A variety of non-Marxist states such as Iraq and Syria in the Middle East, Malawi and Zaire in Africa, and Indonesia in Asia reject liberal democracy in the name of personal rule, political necessity, and other reasons. Some are simply autocracies based on a single faction or ruler's desire for power. In other cases, ethnic rivalry or tribalism is cited as the reason for not attempting to institute multiparty democracy.

B. **Non-secular states opposed to liberal democracy.** Finally, some states see the goal of the state as enforcement and preservation of the laws and institutions they consider divinely mandated and therefore solely legitimate. As a result they reject liberal democracy and its policy of toleration for those of all faiths or no faith. Such states can be divided into fundamentalist and traditionalist examples.

   1. **Fundamentalist theocratic states.** The "Islamic Republic of Iran" is an example of a "fundamentalist" theocracy. It is a theocracy because it is ruled by religious leaders. It is fundamentalist because it believes in the literal interpretation of religious dogma, which it enforces as law with the whole power of the state.

   2. **Traditionalist religious states.** Saudi Arabia is an example of a state that rejects liberal democracy in the name of traditional institutions and religious beliefs. Because it is ruled by a hereditary monarchy, it is not a theocracy. But it does enforce strict Islamic law in accordance with traditional Muslim practice, including grossly unequal treatment of women, and does not allow freedom of religion. There are few such states, and it must be assumed that most of their days are numbered. But it cannot also be assumed that liberal regimes will take their place.

III. **Debate over the democratic state.** Within western democracies, debate rages over the size and scope of government activity and over what should be permissible in a free society.

A. **The scope of the state's welfare activities.** Questions frequently debated in western democracies include whether the state should increase its kind and level of benefits to society's poor and disadvantaged, whether it has gone far enough, or whether it has gone too far. What welfare benefits the state should provide for middle-class citizens and whether the state should redistribute wealth at all are further objects of disagreement.

B. **Government regulation and degree of activity.** The degree to which the state should regulate economic life and whether it should own and operate any basic industries are also matters of debate in western democracies. Examples of questions asked include: Are the governments of western democracies, in particular that of the United States, so large and overbearing that the individual is overwhelmed? Is the character of the contemporary state largely to blame for political withdrawal?

C. **Individual liberty and moral questions.** Debate in America, and to a lesser extent Britain, often centers upon a cluster of controversial questions over the legal enforcement of certain traditional moral norms, including abortion, publication of pornography, and alleged "victimless crimes" such as homosexuality and prostitution. Should these be considered strictly moral questions unregulated by law in a free society? Or should the moral issues embodied in them be decided by society and enforced legally?

IV. **Decline of territorial sovereignty.** Economic and demographic forces have combined in many cases to lessen the state's control over its territory.

A. **Third World immigration.** Large numbers of Third World people fleeing poverty or oppression have emigrated to industrialized states, especially Europe and North America. Some have done so legally; many others have done so illegally. The ability or will of some democratic states, especially the United States, to control their borders appears to have declined. Large numbers of illegal Third World immigrants can potentially change the political, social, and economic character of affected countries.

B. **International economic forces.** At the same time, the free movement of capital across state boundaries, large-scale international ownership and investment, the power of multi-national corporations, the relative ease of illicit import and export, and similar considerations, have lessened the state's ability to control its own territory.

C. **International communication.** Other forces, such as the export and import of popular culture, the ease of international travel and communication, the awareness that some environmental and economic problems can only be dealt with on an international or global scale, and similar factors have in some cases fostered a decline in attachment to a single state. The modern state, both democratic and authoritarian, appears to be in flux, and its future character is uncertain. In particular, whether it can command the depth and breadth of loyalty of previous generations is open to question in an age of geographic mobility in the "global village." (See also the discussion in "America and the international system.")

V. **Political and economic disintegration and integration.** Two contradictory trends, one toward the political disintegration of multi-national or multi-ethnic states, the other toward the creation of trans-national political and economic entities can be identified as the twentieth century draws to a close.

A. **Political and economic integration.** In several parts of the world "common markets"—groups of states that lower tariffs among themselves while maintaining them for others—have been formed. These countries may also allow free movement of capital and populations across their borders. The extent to which economic integration leads to political integration is of great importance. This is so because larger states can be expected to exercise more influence in the world. They may also become stronger economic competitors in world markets.

1. **The European Community (EC).** The most important example of the process of economic and political integration is the EC, which has already established a "European Parliament." By 1992 it eliminated all tariffs and restrictions on the movement of people within its borders. A super-national United States of Europe may be developing, though resistance, especially in Britain, is apparent.

2. **Other economic integration.** Some degree of economic integration is taking place or is proposed in a number of other parts of the world. For example, a Central American common market is in partial operation. The United States and Canada have agreed to a gradual elimination of tariffs and may do so with Mexico. International institutions such as the General Agreement on Tariffs and Trade (GATT) have gradually lowered trade barriers among its members. A common market has been proposed among South American countries.

B. **Nationalism and political disintegration.** Paradoxically, at the same time that trans-national political organizations such as the European Community are taking shape and vying for the loyalties of the citizens of member states, a contrary trend is appearing.

1. **Former Communist countries.** Foremost of the examples of this contrary trend is the disintegration of the Warsaw Pact and the fragmentation of the USSR itself, with declarations of sovereignty at one time or another by virtually all of its constituent republics.

2. **Canada and Yugoslavia.** Other examples of movements toward political disintegration include Canada, where French-speaking Quebec has demanded cultural autonomy and may seek full independence; and Yugoslavia, where national antagonisms among its constituent peoples threaten its complete disintegration.

3. **The USSR.** The abortive coup of August 1991 underlined the current instability of the Soviet Union in its present form. Whether the USSR will permanently break up or will be reconstituted in some form of confederation only the future will determine.

VI. **Conclusion.** While the modern nation-state is in a condition of flux, there is little reason to believe that it will either disappear or become overshadowed by supernational entities such as multi-national corporations or the United Nations. On the contrary, while certain states (Yugoslavia, the USSR, India, Canada) may break up and others may give up some of their sovereignty to a federation (members of the European Community), the modern state—flux or no flux—seems destined to remain the principal means of international political organization for the foreseeable future. For much of the world—certainly the whole of the developed world—the modern state performs the literally vital function of protecting the lives of those within its borders from internal and external attack. Beyond this primordial task, constitutional democracies such as the United States have been and will continue to be the focal point of the loyalty of their members. Where national identity and the state coincide—in nation-states as opposed to multi-national states—loyalty to the polity appears to be an enduring facet of the modern world; national cohesion has proved to be a tenacious force, in the communist world, for example, outlasting decades of suppression. Moreover, at least in the developed world, constitutional democracies have the capacity as never before to establish the conditions in which the individual may freely develop his or her talents and faculties as a conscious, autonomous adult, the fulfillment of an age-old dream.

SCOPE AND SEQUENCE
Grades K-12

CIVIC KNOWLEDGE AND SKILLS
THE NATURE OF POLITICS AND GOVERNMENT

Scope and Sequence
Lower Elementary
Grades Kindergarten - 3

OBJECTIVES[1]

Students should be able to

1. explain some the most important purposes served by government in the United States.

2. describe the essential characteristics of American constitutional democracy, i.e.:

   a. the people are the ultimate source of the government's authority.

   b. all citizens have the right to vote and influence government in other ways.

   c. the government is run by the people either directly or through representatives selected by them.

   d. the powers of the government are limited by law.

   e. all people have certain basic rights guaranteed to them by the Constitution.

3. explain the fundamental values and principles of American constitutional democracy, i.e.:

   a. freedom of belief, expression, and religion.

   b. equality of opportunity.

   c. the use of fair procedures in gathering information and making decisions.

   d. the importance of diversity.

4. plan and implement a community service program designed to serve one of the purposes of government, e.g., an anti-litter campaign.

FRAME OF REFERENCE
Conceptual Understanding

To attain the objectives noted above, students should be able to provide simple definitions and explanations of the following concepts:

I. government.

II. important purposes served by the government of the United States, i.e., the laws and actions of the government: (See Frame of Reference in the Goals and Objectives statement for details.)

   A. promoting order, predictability, and feelings of security.

   B. controlling the distribution of the benefits and burdens of the society, e.g., opportunities for education and jobs, taxes.

   C. providing a means for the peaceful management of conflict among individuals and groups.

   D. protecting the rights of individuals.

   E. promoting the common welfare.

Historical Perspective

To attain the above objectives students should become familiar with key figures and events in American history which illustrate the above concepts. (See Illustrative Activities below for specifics.)

Contemporary Awareness

To attain the above objectives students should develop an awareness, based on experiences in their homes, schools, and communities, of how their government protects their rights and promotes the common welfare. For example, they may

---

[1] Upon first review it may appear that the attainment of the objectives suggested for grades K-3 and 4-6 are beyond the capacities of students at these levels. The reader is invited to look at the illustrative activities designed to foster the attainment of these objectives to see how, by providing learning activities closely related to student experiences at these levels, it is possible to lay the groundwork for the development of the suggested learnings and skills. The reader will also note that the same objectives are treated with increasing sophistication throughout the K-12 curriculum.

learn how government provides for public education, lunch programs, school nurses, after school day care, sanitation, transportation, pure food and beverage controls, environmental controls, and public safety.

ILLUSTRATIVE ACTIVITIES

Activities which foster these objectives include:

Identifying purposes served by government in the United States. Students may participate in experiential learning activities designed to help them understand how rules in their school provide a means of

1. promoting order and feelings of security, e.g,. playground safety rules, traffic rules.

2. providing for the fair distribution of resources and opportunities, e.g., rules giving all students their turns using playground equipment, rules followed by teachers in giving all students a chance to participate in classroom activities, rules providing for the fair distribution of books and other educational materials to students.

3. providing fair means of managing conflict, e.g., rules enabling each person in a conflict to give their side and to be judged impartially, promoting peaceful rather than violent means of resolving conflicts.

4. protecting the rights of all students to private property, to freedom of thought and religion, etc.

Students may role play and discuss how members of government agencies in their communities serve various purposes of government, e.g., teachers educating students, crossing guards protecting lives, sanitation workers controlling waste, police officers maintaining order and protecting citizens.

Students may interview visiting representatives of governmental agencies to learn about their jobs and the purposes they serve, e.g., people serving in fire and police departments, public parks and recreational facilities, health and safety inspectors, and civil rights compliance workers.

Describing essential characteristics of American constitutional democracy. Students may create a student government in their classrooms or schools which embodies essential characteristics of constitutional democracy, e.g., the right of each student to have a voice in the creation of their government and its rules and to select representatives to serve in their government, and limitations on the powers and privileges of representatives they have selected to serve them.

Explaining fundamental values and principles. Students may research and report to the class their findings on the lives of persons who exemplify important principles and values of the American constitutional democracy, e.g., Thomas Jefferson, Rosa Parks, Elizabeth Cady Stanton, Theodore Roosevelt, Ceasar Chavez.

Students may create a series of displays for their school and community illustrating the principles and values embodied in the Declaration of Independence, the Preamble to the Constitution, and the Bill of Rights.

Planning and implementing community service programs. Students may plan and implement a community service project such as an anti-litter campaign or a community beautification project.

Scope and Sequence
Upper Elementary
Grades 4-6

OBJECTIVES

Students should be able to

1. define the terms monarchy, liberal democracy, and totalitarianism.

2. explain the major purposes/priorities served by each of these types of governments.

3. explain the relevance of key figures/events important in the history of the growth of liberal democracy in the United States.

4. evaluate how actions and laws of the government of the United States affect individual rights and the promotion of the common welfare.

5. propose effective means of changing laws/policies in the United States which do not properly serve the legitimate purposes of government.

6. plan and implement a community service program designed to serve one of the purposes of government.

FRAME OF REFERENCE
Conceptual Understanding

To attain the objectives noted above, students should be able to provide simple definitions and explanations of the following concepts:

I. government.

II. important purposes served by the government of the United States, i.e., by the laws and actions of the government. (See Frame of Reference in the Goals and Objectives statement for details.)

    A. promoting order, predictability, and feelings of security.

    B. controlling the distribution of the benefits and burdens of the society, e.g., opportunities for education and jobs, taxes.

    C. providing a means for the peaceful management of conflict among individuals and groups.

    D. fulfilling societal or group aspirations.

    E. protecting individual rights.

III. types of government:

    A. monarchy.
    B. liberal-democracy.
    C. totalitarianism.

Historical Perspective

To attain the above objectives students should develop an historical perspective which includes a familiarity with

I. modern views of government focusing upon:

    A. monarchy and aristocracy in Great Britain and France in the eighteenth century.

    B. liberal-democracy in the United States focusing upon the founding period and highlighting key individuals and events to the present day which have contributed to the evolution of constitutional popular government, e.g., the extension of suffrage.

    C. totalitarianism in countries such as China, Germany, Argentina, Chile, Rumania.

II. legislation and other acts of the federal and state governments which did and did not further the legitimate purposes of the American government, e.g., Bill of Rights; Amendments 14, 16, 18, and 21; Dred Scott Decision, Jim Crow laws, Native American relocation acts, Japanese internment.

III. landmark decisions of the Supreme Court and civil rights legislation which have extended the government's protection of individual rights.

IV. major events in U.S. history in which individuals and groups have sought to influence public policy in order to further the realization of the fundamental values and principles of American democracy, e.g., abolitionist movement, labor movement, child labor movement, suffrage, and civil rights movement.

Contemporary Awareness

To attain the above objectives, students should become familiar with the following:

I. current debates over the degree to which the state is responsible to care for the disadvantaged, guarantee a minimum standard of living, guarantee basic child and health care services, to protect the environment.

II. the efforts to attain democracy in the Soviet Union and Eastern Europe, China, Asia, Africa, and South America.

ILLUSTRATIVE ACTIVITIES

Activities which foster these objectives include:

Identifying purposes served by governments. Students may

1. research and report to class on key figures and events important in the history of the evolution of constitutional democracy in Great Britain and in the United States with special attention to the establishment and growth of suffrage and the extension of individual rights under the Fourteenth Amendment, judicial decisions, and Civil Rights legislation.

2. read and discuss excerpts and adaptations from the writings of such leaders as Jefferson, Madison, Lincoln, and Martin Luther King which set forth their ideas regarding the proper purposes of government.

3. interpret graphs and charts illustrating major categories of the budget of local, state, or federal

government to determine the purposes the budget is intended to serve and the priorities among these purposes it represents.

4. select an issue of interest regarding the purposes and responsibilities of government and invite to class advocates of varying positions on the issue after which the students prepare and hold a debate on the topic, e.g., provision of day care or medical care benefits, care for the homeless, control of off-shore drilling.

Evaluating policies and laws. Students may

1. obtain newspaper clippings regarding the activities of various agencies of our local, state, and federal government, analyze them to determine what purposes they serve, and write editorials which evaluate how well the agencies are protecting individual rights and promoting the common welfare.

2. obtain newspaper and magazine clippings concerning issues of governmental activities related to the protection of human rights and create a human rights bulletin board for their school or public library.

Proposing means of influencing policies and laws. Students may

1. examine ways various public interest groups and other organizations attempt to influence public policy by interviewing representatives of those groups

2. gather information from news media and other sources on current laws or policies which they think do not adequately protect the rights of individuals and/or promote the common good. Then they may develop alternative proposals and outline ways to get their ideas to influence public policy. For example, students may review local policies regarding waste management, the use of illegal drugs, truancy laws, welfare regulations, or graduation requirements. They may then propose alternatives and develop campaigns to promote them, e.g., letter writing campaigns, petitions, and meetings with influentials to present their positions.

Planning and implementing community service programs

Students plan and implement a community service project such as participating in a petition drive on an issue of local concern.

Scope and Sequence
Grades 7-9

OBJECTIVES

Students should be able to

1. identify the purposes served by several types of governments and the priorities they set among them by analyzing the governments actions, policies, laws, and the allocation of resources in their budgets.

2. describe historical and contemporary examples of monarchies/aristocracies, liberal-democracies, communism, and fascism.

   a. explain the major purposes served by each of these types of governments.

   b. explain the rationales of advocates of these types of governments.

   c. evaluate how the governments affect individual rights and the promotion of the common welfare.

3. propose effective means of changing laws and policies which they believe do not properly serve the legitimate purposes of government.

4. plan and implement a community service program designed to serve one of the purposes of government.

FRAME OF REFERENCE
Conceptual Understanding

To attain the objectives noted above, students should be able to provide simple definitions and explanations of the following concepts. (See Frame of Reference in the Goals and Objectives statement for such definitions and explanations.)

I.   Government and state

II. Purposes of government

   A. Order, predictability, security
   B. Distribution of resources
   C. Conflict management
   D. Fulfillment of societal or group aspirations
   E. Protection of individual rights
   F. Improvement of moral condition
   G. Protection of property

III. Types of government

  A. Monarchy/aristocracy
  B. Liberal-democracy
  C. Twentieth-century communism
  D. Fascism

Historical Perspective

To attain the above objectives students should develop an historical perspective which includes a familiarity with

I. ancient Greece focusing upon key individuals and events in the political history of Athens and Sparta.

II. ancient Rome focusing upon key individuals and events in the political history of the Roman Republic and Roman law.

III. government in the Middle Ages and early modern period focusing upon highlights of the political history of Europe between the fall of the Roman Empire and the "Glorious Revolution."

IV. non-Western perspectives on the state or political rule such as those of China, Africa, and the indigenous populations of North and South America.

V. modern views of the state focusing upon:

  A. liberal-democracy to the present day with special attention to the evolution of the concept of constitutional popular government, the importance of an educated citizenry, the extension of suffrage, toleration of diversity, the market economy, and the welfare state.

  B. twentieth-century communism in such countries as the Soviet Union, China, and Latin America.

  C. fascism in Italy, Germany, Japan, and Chile.

VI. key events and figures important in the historical struggle for human rights and the promotion of the common good, e.g., Susan B. Anthony, Louis Brandeis, Ghandi, Martin Luther King, Jr., Desmond Tutu, Mother Teresa.

VII. the positions, strategies, and experiences of individuals and groups attempting to influence public policy on matters affecting human rights and the common welfare, e.g., religious groups, abolitionist groups, consumer groups, and environmental groups.

Contemporary Awareness

To attain the above objectives students should become familiar with

I. opposition to traditional liberal democracy, e.g., from governments dominated by the clergy such as Iran.

II. current debate over the responsibility of the state to care for the disadvantaged, the extent to which it should regulate the economy.

III. efforts to achieve democracy in the Soviet Union, Eastern Europe, China, Asia, Africa, and South America.

ILLUSTRATIVE ACTIVITIES

Activities which foster these objectives include:

Identifying purposes served by governments. Students may

1. research and report on key individuals and events in the history of the governments of Athens, Sparta, and Rome which illustrate differing ideas on the proper purposes of government, e.g., Plato, Aristotle, Cicero and the founding of the Roman Republic.

2. develop a time line of key persons and events in the history of the evolution of constitutional democracy in Western civilization focusing upon the establishment and extension of individual rights as a basic purpose of government.

3. compare and contrast their state constitutions and the federal constitutions in terms of protection of the rights of individuals and promotion of the common welfare.

4. identify an issue regarding the proper purposes of government and invite advocates of varying positions on the issue to participate in a school forum conducted by the class. Afterwards, students should determine what position they would support on the issue.

Evaluating policies and laws. Students may

1. obtain information from newspapers and other sources on the activities of agencies of our local, state, and federal government; analyze them to determine what purposes they serve and their effects on individual rights and the common good; and

present their findings and opinions on the activities in the school or local newspaper.

2. visit and observe hearings of local administrative, legislative, or judicial agencies; analyze them to determine what purposes they serve; and write a report on how well the agencies appear to be protecting individual rights and promoting the common welfare which may be sent to the agency they have observed.

3. use excerpts from the UN Declaration of Human Rights as a set of criteria to identify and collect news clippings on situations in several nations to determine to what degree they are meeting the criteria of the Declaration. Then students may stage a "meet the press" television show to examine the situations related to such topics as freedom of religion, the right to political dissent, and due process of law.

Proposing means of influencing policies and laws.

Students may identify and explain examples of current laws or policies which they think do not serve the legitimate purposes of our government, e.g., campaign financing practices. Students may then outline the steps in a strategy which they think should be used to improve or eliminate the laws or policies.

Planning and implementing community service programs.

Students may plan and implement a community service project such as writing and producing informative public service announcements about adult literacy campaigns, meals-on-wheels programs, etc.

Scope and Sequence
Grades 10 - 12

OBJECTIVES

Students should be able to

1. identify the purposes served by various governments and the priorities they set among them by analyzing the government's actions, policies, laws, and the allocation of resources in their budgets

2. describe historical and contemporary examples of monarchies/aristocracies, liberal-democracies, social democracies, communism, and fascism, and:

    a. identify the major purposes served by each of these types of governments.

    b. explain the rationales of advocates of these types of governments.

    c. evaluate how the governments affect individual rights and the promotion of the common welfare.

3. propose effective means of changing laws/policies which they believe do not properly serve the legitimate purposes of government.

4. plan and implement a community service program designed to serve one of the purposes of government.

FRAME OF REFERENCE
Conceptual Understanding

To attain the objectives noted above, students should be able to provide simple definitions and explanations of the following concepts. (See Frame of Reference in the Goals and Objectives statement for such definitions and explanations.)

I. Government and state

II. Purposes of government

   A. Order, predictability, security
   B. Distribution of resources
   C. Conflict management
   D. Fulfillment of societal or group aspirations
   E. Fulfillment of individual aspirations
   F. Protection of individual rights
   G. Improvement of moral condition
   H. Protection of property

III. Views of the state

   A. Aristocratic traditionalism
   B. Liberal-democracy
   C. Classical Marxism
   D. Twentieth-century communism
   E. Social democracy
   F Fascism

Historical Perspective

To attain the above objectives students should develop an historical perspective based upon a study of

I. Ancient Greece focusing upon:

A. the political ideas of Plato and Aristotle.

B. the political history of Athens and Sparta.

II. Ancient Rome focusing upon:

A. the political ideas of Cicero.

B. the political history of the Roman Republic and Roman law.

III. the state in the Middle Ages and early modern period focusing upon:

A. the political ideas of Thomas Aquinas, Machiavelli, Hobbes, Locke, Montesquieu, Beatrice Webb, etc.

B. political history of Europe between the fall of the Roman Empire and the seventeenth century.

C. non-Western views of the state or political rule such as those of traditional China and India, selected African cultures, and the indigenous peoples of North and South America.

IV. modern views of the state focusing upon:

A. aristocratic traditionalism in the eighteenth century, through selected writings by Edmund Burke, Benjamin Disraeli, and John C. Calhoun.

B. liberal-democracy to the present day with special attention to the evolution of the concept of constitutional popular government, the importance of an educated citizenry, the extension of suffrage, toleration of diversity, the market economy, and the welfare state.

C. classical Marxism, as expressed by Karl Marx and Frederick Engels, and the historical development of socialism in Europe up to the time of the Russian Revolution.

D. twentieth-century communism, Leninism, Stalinism, Maoism, the dissident movements leading to changes in Eastern Europe, the pro-democracy student move-

ment in China, the free election movement in Central and South America, etc.

E. social democracy, its German origins, its development in Great Britain and Scandinavia.

F. fascism's intellectual roots, development in Italy and Germany, Japan, Argentina, Chile.

V. key events and figures important in the historical struggle for human rights and the promotion of the common good, e.g., apartheid.

VI. the positions, strategies, and experiences of individuals and groups attempting to influence public policy on matters affecting human rights and the common welfare, e.g., religious groups, abolitionist groups, consumer groups, environmental groups

Contemporary Awareness

To attain the above objectives students should develop a contemporary awareness of the

I. efforts to establish democracy and market economies in the Soviet Union, Eastern Europe, Asia, Africa, and South America.

II. opposition to traditional liberal democracy, e.g., from such sources as theocratic states like Iran.

III. contemporary controversy over whether or not the extent of freedom in modern democratic states undermines moral norms which should be enforced by the state.

IV. current debate over the responsibility of the state to care for the disadvantaged, the extent to which it should regulate the economy and individual rights such as privacy, speech, etc.

V. rise of a global economy, creation of common markets, the political integration of formerly sovereign states, and, and the implications of these developments on governmental institutions and public policy.

ILLUSTRATIVE ACTIVITIES

Activities which foster these objectives include:

Identifying purposes served by governments

Students may

1. read, analyze, and discuss excerpts from the writings of political thinkers such as Plato, Aristotle, Cicero, Aquinas, Machiavelli, Beatrice Webb, V.I. Lenin, Vaclav Havel, and Jeanne Kirkpatrick which set forth their ideas regarding the proper purposes of government.

2. read and discuss excerpts from the history of the governments of Athens, Sparta, and Rome which illustrate the purposes served by their governments.

3. read and discuss the history of the evolution of constitutional democracy with special attention to the purposes such governments are intended to serve.

4. compare constitutions of various nations throughout history in terms of their protection of individual rights and promotion of the common welfare. Students may then write critical essays regarding the degree to which these nations have in fact achieved these purposes.

5. invite to class advocates of varying views of the state and its purposes to present their positions and discuss them with the class. Then write a pamphlet advocating their position on the issue.

6. invite to class advocates of varying policies or laws which they believe serve to promote fundamental purposes of our government to present their positions and discuss them with the class. e.g., persons representing various positions on the environment, abortion, civil rights, the homeless, medical care.

Evaluating policies and laws

Students may

1. obtain policy statements and regulations of various agencies of our local, state, and federal government, analyze them to determine their purposes, and write critical evaluations of how they might affect individual rights and the common welfare.

2. review a simplified version of the budget of the federal government to determine the purposes it is intended to serve and the priorities among these purposes it represents. Then, students may participate in a simulated budget hearing to negotiate the allocations of funds according to priorities they decide upon.

3. observe congressional hearings on television on such issues as human rights, international affairs, military spending, law enforcement and drug abuse, and environmental matters. After debating their observations, they produce majority and minority reports on the issues which they may present to their congressional representatives.

Proposing means of influencing policies and laws

Students may

1. identify and explain examples of current laws or policies which they think do not serve the legitimate purposes of our government, then outline the steps in a strategy designed to improve or eliminate the laws or policies.

2. visit and observe hearings of local administrative, legislative, or judicial agencies, determine what purposes these agencies are serving, how well they are serving them, and whether the purposes are legitimate in terms of the fundamental purposes of our government. They may then create editorials or letters to editors expressing their opinions on the matters observed.

Planning and implementing community service programs

Students may plan and implement a community service project such as a ballot petition campaign, voter's registration drive, or an adult literacy campaign.

TOPIC 3. TYPES OF GOVERNMENTS

Power tends to corrupt and absolute power corrupts absolutely.

Lord Acton (1887)

No legislative act...contrary to the Constitution can be valid. To deny this would be to affirm that the deputy is greater than his principal; that the representatives of the people are superior to the people themselves; that men acting by virtue of powers may do not only what their powers do not authorize, but what they forbid.

Alexander Hamilton (1788)

The basic difference between constitutional governments and non-constitutional governments is among the most indispensable ideas required of democratic citizens. Only by a clear understanding of this vital difference will citizens be able to know how serious—how potentially calamitous—is the overstepping of proper bounds by their own government and raise their voices to oppose such dangerous behavior. This knowledge should include comprehension of the essential characteristics of each type of government and common differences among them, especially limitations upon power and treatment of individual rights.

OBJECTIVES

The citizen should be able to

1. explain the essential differences between constitutional and non-constitutional governments.

2. examine historical and contemporary governments and determine if they are constitutional or non-constitutional.

3. identify actions of their own and other governments that fail to adhere to principles of constitutionalism.

4. take, defend, and evaluate positions on issues of constitutionalism.

FRAME OF REFERENCE
Conceptual Perspective

I. **Constitutional governments.** A constitution is a set of fundamental customs, traditions, rules, and laws that sets forth the basic way a government is organized and operated. Most constitutions are in writing, some are partly written and partly unwritten, and some are not written at all. Having a constitution does not mean that a nation has a **constitutional government**. The following are the essential characteristics of constitutional government.

A. **Limited government.** Constitutional governments are those governments whose actions are **in practice limited** by law and institutions and not just by the rulers' calculations of how to protect and increase their power. If a constitution provides for the unlimited exercise of political power—by one, few, or even many   it is not the basis for a constitutional government. If a constitution says that the power of a government is to be limited, but it does not include ways to enforce the limitations, it also is not the basis for a constitutional government.

B. **Higher law.** In a constitutional government, the constitution is considered a higher law which those in government must and do obey. The constitution or higher law has the following characteristics:

1. **Individual rights.** It provides for the protection of the rights of the individual against unfair and unreasonable infringement by the government and other individuals. This typically includes the establishment of **a private domain** which the government may not intrude upon. The individual also typically enjoys the stringent protections of **due process of law** intended to protect the rights of both innocent and guilty alike from the full and arbitrary power of the state.

2. **Methods of limiting power.** Methods of limiting power typically include **formal means** such as the separation of powers, checks and balances, and other constitutional restrictions. Power is also limited by **informal means** such as publicity given to government actions and group pressure such as lobbying and demonstrations. In addition, consciousness among citizens and public officials of traditional limits on power may serve as an effective restraint.

3. **Stability.** The constitution cannot be changed without the widespread consent of citizens and in accord with established and well-known procedures.

C. **Forms of constitutional governments.** Constitutional governments were traditionally categorized as monarchies, aristocracies, and democracies. In the modern world, nearly all constitutional governments are representative democracies.

1. **Constitutional monarchies vs. republics.** Constitutional governments are either constitutional monarchies or republics.

   a. **Constitutional monarchies.** Some governments have a monarch as head of state and are called constitutional monarchies. Great Britain, the Netherlands, and Sweden are examples of constitutional monarchies. Some members of the British Commonwealth who accept the British monarch as their own monarch, such as Australia, Botswana, and Canada, are also constitutional monarchies.

   b. **Republics.** Other constitutional states have no monarchs and are called republics. Examples include Germany, the United States, and Venezuela.

   c. **Role of representative democracy in each form.** Nevertheless, in all of these cases, in practice the process of government is through the mechanism of representative democracy.

2. **Presidential vs. parliamentary government.** Governments may be either parliamentary or presidential.

   a. **Parliamentary systems.** The difference between parliamentary and presidential systems is that in the former case, the chief executive is chosen from among members of the legislature and is directly responsible to them. Britain, India, and Japan are examples of parliamentary systems.

   b. **Presidential systems.** In presidential systems, the chief executive is not a member of the legislature, is independently chosen, is not directly responsible to the legislature, and is removable by the legislature only in extraordinary circumstances, if at all. The United States is an example of a presidential system. France is a modified presidential system, combining a strong presidency with elements of a parliamentary system.

3. **Unitary vs. federal systems.** Constitutional governments may be unitary, in which case power is

centralized as in France and Japan; or they may be federal, in which power is divided between a central government and territorial subdivisions, as in Australia, Canada, and the United States.

II. **Non-constitutional governments.** Non-constitutional governments may also have constitutions that set forth the basic way they are or are said to be organized and operated. However, they may be distinguished from constitutional governments by the following characteristics:

A. **Ineffective limitations on powers.** In non-constitutional governments there are no effective means available to the general public of limiting the powers of the rulers. Rulers typically are not effectively restrained by law in the exercise of their powers. Governmental rulings, actions, and decisions may be made arbitrarily, at the discretion of the rulers, instead of within prescribed limits and according to established procedures. In the Soviet Union under Stalin, for example, the fate of whole peoples were decided by the decision of the dictator. Thus, the Crimean Tartars were moved en masse from their homeland and transported hundreds of miles to strange territory.

B. **Uncertainty or absence of individual rights.** Any rights of the individual that may be claimed to exist are subject to the arbitrary violation of the ruler or rulers. Typically, there is no private domain into which rulers may not intrude. Whatever rights the individual may be considered to possess, rather than being protected by stringent standards of due process of law, are typically subject to arbitrary and summary decree and deprivation. Uganda under Idi Amin, for example, was terrorized by Amin's Bureau of State Research, which arrested and tortured people at will.

C. **Forms of non-constitutional governments.** Autocracies and totalitarian states are forms of non-constitutional governments.

   1. **Autocratic regimes.** Autocracies or dictatorships now generally call themselves republics. Autocracy may take various forms, in which unlimited power is exercised by one person or a small group, either civilian or military. Examples of autocratic regimes are Haiti under "Papa Doc" Duvalier; Spain under Franco; Nicaragua under Samosa; and the Philippines under Marcos.

   2. **Totalitarian regimes.** Some dictatorships do not attempt to control every aspect of society; those

that do attempt to exercise absolute control over all spheres of human life are called totalitarian dictatorships. Non-constitutional governments may be organized as presidential or parliamentary governments; they may also call themselves federal rather than unitary systems, but these names are only used to obscure the true nature of autocratic government. The classic examples of totalitarianism are China under Mao; Germany under Hitler; and the Soviet Union under Stalin.

For the Historical and Contemporary Perspectives, see The Nature of the State.

TOPIC 4. POLITICS AND GOVERNMENT

A. MORALITY AND POLITICS

If politics were to say: "Be ye therefore wise as serpents," morality might add, by way of qualification: "and harmless as doves."

Immanuel Kant (1795)

Politics ain't beanbag.

Mister Dooley (Finley Peter Dunne 1898)

I am not a crook.

Richard M. Nixon (1973)

The terms "morality" and "politics" are slippery and hard to pin to one or two fixed ideas. **Morality**, roughly speaking, is the point of view from which we contend about the ways of living and acting that are worthy of human beings. When we ask ourselves what is decent and good, what is evil and vile, we are asking ourselves moral questions. The vocabulary of morality speaks of rights and duties, virtue and vice, responsibility and blame, purity and defilement, justice and desert.

Politics, roughly speaking, defines a certain approach to government and power. A democratic political regime settles matters of governance and control through public debate, openly contested elections, and representation of interests. Political rule stands in contrast to rule by tyrants, experts, or priests. Democratic political systems govern by appeal to public opinion rather than by reference to special knowledge, divine ordinances, or unbreakable tradition. Morality-and-politics, consequently, refers to the standards of decency, honor, and justice that guide assessment of political activity, political actors, political institutions, and political goals.

Morality-and-politics may be divided into five lines of questions. First, political choices often have moral content. They sometimes directly **express**, **embody**, or **implicate** ideas of justice, propriety, decency, or goodness. Consequently, citizens need to be able to understand the moral issues involved and give voice to their own views about them. Moreover, citizens need to settle among themselves what kinds of moral beliefs may properly affect policy choices and what limits there should be to public implementation of moral ideals, goals, and requirements. They need to have some understanding of how moral differences can be discussed and, if possible, resolved.

The second line of questions focuses on the ethics of public office. What moral duties specifically apply to political representatives and public servants? How are they to understand their roles and carry out their duties both effectively and honorably? Public office can be corrupted by personal greed, treachery, and deceit. It can also be subverted by occupants who, on the one hand, over-reach or exceed their authority to promote particular goals or, on the other, obstruct through neglect and delay the implementation of policies they dislike.

The third set of questions concerns "politics" in its popular sense, the partisan competitions for office. Political campaigning is often a rough-and-tumble affair and frequently leaves a foul taste in electors' mouths. Is it reasonable to hold campaigns (and campaigners) to high standards of honesty, fairness, decency, and accuracy? Does partisan political competition poison the very political process it is supposed to serve?

The fourth set of questions concerns the personal value of politics and political activity. According to Aristotle, political activity is an important constituent of a good life. A person who abdicated from political engagement and took no part in political affairs would lead a deficient life, in some sense. A contrasting conception views political activity as necessary evil. Partisan politics is unpleasant, even sordid, but necessary to sustaining a system of government that isn't tyrannical or inhumane. A third conception, intermediate between the two extremes, views politics as worth pursuing for its own sake, but not essential to a good life.

The issues at stake here go beyond merely assessing the personal fulfillment political activity can bring. They point to the moral hazards intrinsic to politics. An office holder, for example, not only represents constituents in a political district, he or she also represents a political party and various partisan causes. To be true to party or cause, one may have to neglect or betray the interests of some constituents. Political leaders, whether in office or not, are expected by their followers to be successful in the struggle for power and have an obligation to be as effective as they can. Personal scruples against "playing hardball" may have to be put aside. The vocation of politics, then, may require practitioners to overcome or suppress some of their moral sensitivities. It may require habits and attitudes that are incompatible with particular virtues—such as gentleness, kindness, humility, inoffensiveness, fairness—virtues that people are usually loathe to stunt or stifle in themselves.

Finally, the fifth set of questions touches on the duties and responsibilities of citizens toward political campaigns and political office. Are citizens required to moderate the demands they make upon their representatives? From what point of view should they cast their votes? How should they assess candidates?

Objectives

The citizen should be able to

1. explain moral arguments about the content or implications of public policy.

2. explain the special duties and rights of various political roles (party leaders, elected representatives, administrative officials, etc.).

3. explain both the value and the limitations of politics.

4. take, defend, and evaluate positions on morality and public policy.

FRAME OF REFERENCE
Conceptual Perspective

I. **The structure of moral reflection and argument.** Morality is a social practice of judgment and criticism, whose vocabulary supplies concepts, standards, and pictures of what is worth doing and being in life—worth doing not because it gives us advantage in any particular aim we might have but because it is good in itself, or leads to things that are good in themselves. Moral appraisal is distinct from legal, prudential, and technical appraisals. The latter, which supply standards for criticism and decision where certain ends are taken for granted, can themselves be the subject of moral appraisal.

A. **Right and wrong.** One part of morality contains concepts and principles that constrain or require conduct in various ways. This part is the domain of duty, obligation, justice, and rights. Arguments from this domain are about what we ought or ought not do, what we do or do not have a right to do, and what it would be just or unjust for us to do.

1. **General prohibitions and duties.** "Thou shalt not kill," one of the Ten Commandments, is representative of the general prohibitions and duties that people typically understand as applying to them and all people living in society. These prohibitions and duties come in the form of simple precepts—e.g., don't steal or cheat, help others in need, take your turn, to each according to his desert—which, in fact, contain exceptions and qualifications, some well-established and widely understood (e.g., the permissibility of killing an aggressor in self-defense) and others more contentious and uncertain (e.g., the permissibility of

the state executing a duly convicted kidnapper, spy, or murderer).

2. **Specific prohibitions and duties.** Through valid promises and acts of consent, or through special relationships, people acquire special moral duties and rights. For example, in taking an oath of office, a judge acquires a special moral duty to uphold the law and a soldier a special moral duty to defend his or her country. Through marriage vows, spouses acquire the obligation to remain faithful to one another. In having a child, parents assume a duty to care for it, and the child, in turn, has rights not to be neglected by them.

3. **Rights.** A special kind of idea is captured in the concept of "having a right." To have a right is to be able to claim as your due some forbearance or performance on the part of others. It is common in American political debate to appeal to legal and constitutional rights; and, sometimes, to moral "natural" or "human" rights that are thought to underlie the legal and constitutional ones.

4. **Justice and fairness.** One way we can act wrongly is to fail to treat people justly or fairly. Justice is giving people their due. What is considered to be due to people depends on the rules of the systems and institutions they live under. The rules establish property rights, set penalties for crime, lay the basis for entitlements to benefit from productive labor, and support claims to restitution for wrongful injury. There may also be "natural" justice (e.g., "an eye for an eye") and injustice (e.g., failure of social systems and institutions to protect people's "natural" rights or distribute social burdens fairly). "Desert" and "merit" are often thought to be appropriate grounds for apportioning some things, "need" for other things. Any apportionment or division of benefits and burdens, including responsibility and blame, can be assessed as just or unjust.

B. **Moral goodness.** A distinct part of morality contains concepts and ideals for evaluating goodness or badness. There is no unique direct relationship between moral goodness (which concerns the worthiness of ideals) and moral rightness (which concerns following moral rules). Sometimes goodness supplies the standard of rightness; sometimes rightness supplies the standard for goodness. Whereas rightness is generally a characteristic of conduct or rules, goodness can be a property of a variety of things.

1. **States of affairs.** When we say that it would be good if people could live together in peace, we describe an ideal (or at least better) state of the world. Sometimes there may be good states of affairs that no one has a duty directly to bring about. For example, a world of peace might be good, but individuals do not have the duty to forego justified defense of their rights or lives, even if this disturbs the peace.

2. **Character.** We judge people as good or bad, virtuous or vicious. Among other things, what makes the character of people good is that they do their duty or act justly and responsibly. Negative character-evaluating concepts include "trimmer," "hypocrite," "two-timer," "coward," "sneak," "unreliable," "irresponsible," "hard-hearted," "selfish," and "vain." Positive concepts include "honest," "trustworthy," "charitable," "decent," "upright," and "sensitive." A central evaluating concept applying to persons is "integrity." Integrity, in one of its important uses, means not honesty or reliability but wholeness and unity. In a life that has integrity, its various parts—its commitments, projects, avowals, and deeds—fit together, rather than conflict or war with one another.

3. **Conditions.** Some ideals have to do with being in, or getting into, a certain condition, e.g., being holy, pure, or innocent.

C. **Sources of morality.** Two very different things can be meant by "the sources" of morality.

1. **The origin or cause of moral beliefs.** We learn our moral beliefs from family and community. More broadly, a community's moral beliefs may arise from a particular religious or other tradition, document, or founding moment.

   a. **The "historical" origin of moral beliefs.** Our moral beliefs have historical origins; we are not born with them. Sometimes we explain a particular person's beliefs as induced or caused by peer pressure, psycho-sexual processes, wish-fulfillment, or indoctrination. Moreover, we may show that the prevailing moral beliefs in a society have the effect of preserving or masking hierarchy, privilege, or power.

   b. **Attempting to "explain away" moral ideas.** People often think that by thus explaining the generating cause or psychological/sociological function of a moral belief, they have "explained it away." They think, that is, that they have debunked it, showing it in error or without foundation. But this is to confuse the first sense of source (genesis or cause) with the second (authority).

2. **Authority of moral beliefs.** When we are asked about the "source" of our moral beliefs in this second sense, we are not being asked why they are believed by us (their causes), but why they are worthy of being believed (their authority). There are **proximate** and **ultimate** authorities.

   a. **Justifying moral ideas with common authorities.** If our questioner shares with us a commitment to a specific dogma (say, a religious doctrine or text), then we can justify a belief to the questioner by showing that it is explicitly or implicitly included in the dogma. We would be appealing to a "proximate" authority.

   b. **Justifying moral ideas with rational argument.** If our questioner does not share with us a specific dogma, then we try to offer reasons for a belief that would lead any reasonable person to accept or endorse it. Although we may look for proximate shared commonalities, our appeal here ultimately is to the authority of reason itself. Where we share very little with our questioner, it may be impossible to make "reason itself" overcome our differences.

D. **Moral disagreement.** The life of citizenship often involves disputes about whether proposed policies or states of affairs are morally justified or not. Moral disagreements stem from many sources. Disagreements may be merely **verbal** (where disputants use different words to mean the same thing) or **substantial** (where a real difference of belief is at stake). Substantial disagreement about particular cases or policies may reflect different **predictions of outcomes**, different **assignments of fault**, different **weightings of options**, different **personal commitments or loyalties**, different **interpretations of motive or aim**, different **understandings about which principles apply**, and different **restrictions on the scope** of applicable principles. Moreover, beneath the surface of disagreement, that is, beneath the various verbal representations and arguments that disputants make, may lie causes that have nothing to do with the merits of those representations and arguments. A person may disagree with another out of spite, or unwillingness to be seen as giving in, or need to maintain good relations with third parties, and so on.

1. **Moral reasoning.** Moral reasoning, like practical reasoning in general, seeks conviction by bringing the considerations that bear on a case or policy into a satisfying balance. To achieve this balance, a reasoner invokes general rules or principles that are thought to bear on the case or policy in question, considers comparable situations in which these rules or principles have been applied, and looks at reasons for classifying the present case or policy with (or distinguishing it from) the comparable situations. A "reasoned agreement" is reached when persons converge, through a process of mutual reasoning, on a common interpretation of principles or a common judgment about a case or policy.

2. **The intellectual virtues.** Moral disagreement has the best chance of being resolved through reasoned agreement in a context of mutual respect and good-faith argument. In good-faith argument, each side puts forward claims and reasons it genuinely believes provide the strongest rational support for its views. Mutual respect is most in evidence when each side to a disagreement practices the virtues of **charity** and **humility** in argument.

   a. **The principle of charity.** This principle recommends that we view our opponent's arguments and beliefs in their best light. According to this principle, one should always look for the interpretation or construction of our opponent's arguments or beliefs that give them the best chance of being true.

   b. **The principle of humility.** This principle tells us to assume that, regardless of their strength, our own arguments and beliefs are likely to be one-sided, partial, and incomplete in important ways and can benefit from being tested against opposing arguments and beliefs.

   c. **The principle of tolerance.** This principle acknowledges that reasonable people can remain in disagreement about many important moral issues and urges us to respect differences and support policies for getting along with others where agreement cannot be reached.

II. **Politics and the content of public policy.** The need for citizens to understand and argue moral views arises in part because the content of political choices and public policies can have moral import. Public policies can **express, enforce,** or **implicate** particular moral views.

A. **Politics expressing moral views.** Sometimes a law, administrative rule, or legislative policy **expresses,** or stands for, a particular moral view. For example, restrictions imposed by Congress on the National Endowment for the Arts, forbidding it to underwrite art projects that are "pornographic" or "blasphemous," would have this expressive character, signifying that Congress does not (collectively) "stand for" these kinds of "offensive" art.

B. **Policy enforcing moral views.** A related matter is that laws, regulations, and rules have sometimes been passed that prohibit certain kinds of activity as immoral. For example, laws against adultery, prostitution, gambling, and doing business on Sunday are often meant to enforce certain moral views about proper and improper kinds of activity. The same is true of laws or rules that require school sex education classes to instruct students that chastity is the right policy for them. Some critics argue that laws that enforce controversial moral stances often needlessly infringe on the liberty of those who disagree, trampling on the rights of minorities. Other critics argue that the enforcement of morality is a proper purpose of law.

1. **Civil rights and affirmative action.** Civil rights laws which prohibit discrimination on the basis of race, gender, or religion are grounded, in part, on a public moral sense that such discrimination affronts the dignity of its victims as persons and denies them basic respect. Civil rights laws not only give expression to this moral sense but aim to enforce widespread compliance with non-discriminatory standards. The efforts at achieving compliance, especially through various "affirmative action" policies, spark controversy, and reveal public division about the proper way to understand the moral principles that underlie disapproval of discrimination.

2. **The abortion controversy.** The political struggle over abortion reflects deeply held moral views about the rights of women to exercise control over their bodies and the rights to life of fetuses. The debate turns on views about the humanity of the fetus, the woman's right to choose, the protection of helpless life, and the proper role of the state when moral disagreement is intractable. It also turns on broader issues about the proper way to conceive of women's roles and rights in society, and about the place of gender categories in shaping social expectations and roles. The struggle is political because the contending sides want law to enforce moral views.

C. **Policy implicating moral views.** Legislation and policy on any number of matters may raise moral issues. Policies about strip-mining, tax rates, diplomatic relations, gun control, genetic screening, highway construction, and the preservation of endangered species, as examples, not only involve questions of budget costs, economic incentives, risks of harm and injury, and enforcement effectiveness. They also raise questions either directly or indirectly about justly distributing social benefits and burdens, invading privacy, infringing liberty, associating with evil regimes, and acknowledging the dignity of non-human life forms. Seldom will wide-ranging and central social policies be debated only on their technical, economic, or scientific merits and not also on their moral merits.

1. **Welfare policies.** Various schemes of public assistance and aid generate moral controversy. A government that failed to help the destitute and homeless would be charged with lacking compassion. Yet, it is argued that policies of support seem to make recipients even more dependent and to undermine their self-respect. Is welfare assistance grounded in the moral duty of people to help others in need or in the moral right of recipients to be compensated for being left out of an economic system that benefits the rest of society? Does welfare express an idea of social solidarity or does it betray class divisions and condescension of the well-off toward the poor? Welfare policies, in short, invite debate about the public's very sense of itself as a community and about the principles of justice it subscribes to.

2. **Environmental policies.** Although policies toward pollution control, work place safety, wilderness protection, and preservation of endangered species have economic and prudential justifications, they also draw upon moral and religious ideas about the meaning of nature and the place of humanity in it, the integrity and dignity of non-human life forms, and the place of wilderness in the nation's cultural self-understanding. Endemic to these policies are trade-offs between economic development and environmental protection, which raise questions about justice: is it right to preserve wetlands, green spaces, or endangered

species at the cost of jobs for workers who need them?

D. **Foreign affairs and war.** Few areas of policy are as morally troubling and perplexing as those that have to do with war and peace, and the relations among nations generally. Great disparities of power and wealth exist among nations; in many parts of the world whole populations live impoverished and precarious lives while in other nations citizens enjoy enormous abundance and opportunity. Moreover, the relationships among nations rest, ultimately, on power and violence, and as a consequence, the personal security of people both in poor and rich countries is continually at risk.

1. **Realism in foreign policy.** Because nations exist in a condition of mutual distrust, and because there are no international institutions to enforce a common law, each nation lacks **assurance** that other nations will follow norms of peaceable conduct or make sacrifices to benefit others; and in the absence of such assurance a nation has no choice but to act to protect its own security and enhance its own power. Whatever a nation's moral values and however just its own domestic institutions, its foreign policy must be amoral and self-protective.

2. **Moralism in foreign policy.** Where a nation is powerful, it may peacefully or coercively try to influence the internal affairs of other nations to reflect its own views of the morally best way to live. The United States may, for example, seek to "export" democracy or to deter human rights violations by other governments. The United States also provides "humanitarian" relief to nations suffering from disasters or calamities like starvation, and, through institutions like the Peace Corps, seeks to aid self-development in poorer countries: these it does as an expression of its own moral values rather than to change the values of others. (Additionally, the United States provides aid to other countries for reasons of realism: to protect its power and advantage vis-a-vis other nations.)

3. **Overcoming the assurance problem.** Through its policies, a nation can encourage and support the existence of world institutions (like the United Nations) which may lay the ground for a trust and mutuality that would allow nations to approach a rule of law rather than a rule of power. For example, the United States might oppose human rights violations explicitly within the context of widely accepted United Nations declarations concerning

human rights, while simultaneously supporting a framework of international pluralism, that is, a framework that acknowledges and respects a diversity of political regimes and ways of life. When states have assurance that other nations do not threaten their basic security, they can forego the use of war as an instrument of policy.

4. **War and morality.** Traditional just-war standards, elements of which are reflected in international conventions, the Nuremburg Tribunal, the United Nations Charter, and domestic law, permit the moral use of force under certain conditions and by certain means.

   a. *Jus ad bellum*. The idea of *jus ad bellum* (the right to go to war) comprises the grounds that warrant a state legitimately to resort to war. To be just, a war must be fought for a **just cause** (e.g., to resist aggression), as a **last resort** (after alternative solutions are no longer feasible), with **reasonable hope of success**, and for **proper ends** (e.g., to restore a just peace, not to exact revenge or eliminate a nation). Moreover, the destruction in the war must be **proportionate** to the good aimed for.

   b. *Jus in bello*. The idea of *jus in bello* (law regarding the **conduct** of war) refers to the constraints on how a nation carries out a war. It must **discriminate** between combatants and noncombatants in its application of force. The latter may not be directly targeted. Unintended damage to noncombatants is permitted as a side-effect of attacking legitimate military targets where the amount of damage is **not out of proportion** to the value of the targets.

III. **Morality and public office.** Officeholders, whether in the administrative, judicial, or legislative branches of government, have special obligations and rights defined by their roles and offices. One dimension of morality-in-office involves abuse of authority and corruption, that is, officeholders using their position and authority for their own financial or personal advantage. Abuse of power need not be for personal or financial advantage, but for political advantage, as when the authority of office is used to cover up criminal wrongdoing or political dirty tricks (e.g., Watergate). Even apart from corruption and abuse of power, however, moral problems arise for officeholders because of uncertainty about the duties their roles impose or because of conflicts among those duties or with other duties, both personal and professional.

A. **Corruption and conflict of interest.** Many officeholders are granted considerable power and authority. They oversee large sums of money, dispense lucrative contracts, purchase and control expensive equipment, and regulate the economic and professional activity of various powerful groups. The justification for these grants of power and authority is that the public good may be served. But the same power and authority can be turned to personal gain by officeholders. Consequently, "ethics in government" laws and regulations often narrowly circumscribe an officeholder's latitude regarding sources and amounts of outside income, non-governmental use of equipment, letting of bids and contracts, and similar matters.

1. **Money.** Money is often a lure and temptation to those in position to acquire it. Rules of the U.S. House of Representatives, for example, limit the amount of income members of Congress can derive from giving speeches but not the amount they can derive from book royalties. In one case, a former Speaker of the House sought to evade the rule by accepting artificially large royalties, and was disciplined accordingly.

2. **Conflict of interest, "the revolving door," and corrupt use.** Because officeholders are not supposed to have personal interests in the matters they regulate or decide upon, ethics laws and rules limit their receiving gifts and other favors from individuals or organizations affected by their activities. Likewise, laws restrict "revolving door" employment, where an officeholder leaves government to go directly to work for an or institution he or she formerly regulated, often in the capacity of lobbyist before the very agency previously worked for. Many government officials now by law must wait a year or more after leaving office before they may lobby their former agencies on behalf of private firms. Finally, rules strictly limit non-governmental use of government property (even to the point of prohibiting an official from letting his Boy Scout troop use office computers on weekends to gain merit badges in computer proficiency).

3. **Political corruption.** The powers of office are easily turned to partisan and political ends. Officeholders at the highest levels of government are appointed directly by the chief executive and serve at that person's pleasure—which pleasure generally includes re-election or at least maintaining the party in power in office.

   a. **Justifiable use of the powers of office.** Consequently, the powers of office are often turned to securing these ends. Typically, the political exercise of these powers falls within a zone of legitimate if not particularly salutary activity, e.g., the dispense of patronage and favors to party faithful, the use of government organs to promote favorable publicity, etc.

   b. **Unjustifiable use of the powers of office.** However, the powers of office are sometimes used criminally to promote political victory—for example, to extort campaign contributions or to cover up political dirty tricks. Sometimes there is only a fine line between "politics as usual" in office and corruption of office; this is a troubling arena for officeholders who want to be responsible both to their political party and their office itself.

B. **Role-related moral issues.** Roles specify particular tasks and activities that role-holders are to carry out, and define their areas of authority and responsibility. A particular office may cast its holder into multiple roles or define the role in multiple ways, making it hard to reconcile all his duties.

1. **Representation.** Elected officials "represent" their constituents. A centuries-old debate concerns how to understand the scope and meaning of this representation. Do officials represent the **expressed wishes** of their constituents or constituents' **real interests**? Do officials represent the interests only of **those who voted for them** or **all the members** of their districts? Is their duty to promote **the good of their respective districts only**, even at the cost of the common good, or is it to promote the **common good as well**? It should be apparent that there are no easy resolutions to these questions and that elected officials can find themselves in moral quandaries about what to do.

2. **Administrative authority.** Administrators of programs and policies are charged with carrying out the aims of laws while being limited by the laws' terms and by their own place in the larger scheme of legitimate authority.

a. **Stretching the law.** Administrators may use their powers to give greater scope to the law than intended by its authors, to limit its effect, or to implement its provisions more or less systematically and adequately. Their exercise of discretion may represent good faith efforts to carry out a law as written, or it may reflect their hostility to the very aims of the law.

b. **Restricting the law.** Their actions may represent their view that the law's terms unreasonably hobble accomplishment of its larger aims, or that as written, the law is incapable of being fully put into operation. Similarly, lower-level administrators may feel hindered by higher-level administrators or feel that they have been given incoherent or ill-advised directives.

c. **The inevitability of interpretation.** In all these cases, administrators have to judge how far to substitute their own interpretation of the law or directive for the interpretations of superiors, or whether they should defer to superiors. Because it is not desirable that they be blindly obedient, administrators have considerable discretion in which to act responsibly. This means acting on commitments not only to the particular programs they administer but also to the long-term effectiveness of their agency and to the various constituencies it serves, commitments that in particular circumstances may point in different directions: thus moral quandaries.

3. **The problem of "dirty hands."** Sometimes an office may seem to permit or even require its holder to violate ordinary morality. Presidents of the United States, for example, may feel themselves compelled to deceive the public, to sanction covert violence, or to inflict cruelty on undeserving parties—all for the good of the country. According to Machiavelli, effective political leaders must "learn how not to be good." They must be prepared to get their hands dirty or else risk, not only personal defeat, but also the ruin of the state and its citizens.

a. **The paradox of dirty hands.** "Dirty hands" should be distinguished from merely unpleasant duties of office.

(1) **Situations in which common morality is not necessarily violated.** Leaders must often do unpleasant things—such as firing close associates or signing execution warrants—but these actions are not to be confused with "dirty hands" behavior. Moreover, a leader may sometimes properly use counter-deception or counter-force against opponents who have wrongfully initiated the use of deception or force. Such a response need not cause "dirty hands" because common morality itself allows for deception or force in self-defense.

(2) **"Dirty hands" as the violation of common morality.** True "dirty hands" situations involve doing genuinely morally wrong actions, although actions that are justified, all things considered. At first glance this seems a paradox. However, true "dirty hands" situations are possible because a leader may have to do something that wrongs other people (that truly violates their rights, for example) as part of a larger policy or action necessary, all things considered, to preserve the peace or safety of the nation. Thus, even though the leader's act can be plausibly viewed as morally right, it includes wronging others as a component that does not disappear in the overall justification.

(3) **Dirty hands and guilt.** Consequently, the leader may appropriately feel guilty about the act and may even owe redress, penance, or expiation for it.

b. **Democracy and "dirty hands."** In a democracy, leaders are authorized to act by public consent. In "dirty hands" situations, several questions can be asked. Have citizens by their consent joined in their leaders' wrongful acts? Are they guilty of complicity? Does this remove a certain responsibility from leaders who perform such wrongful acts? As with other aspects of democratic theory, much depends on the idea of consent and what, specifically, citizens have consented to, and what such consent legitimates.

IV. **Morality and political competition.** It is in regard to political competition that we encounter "politics" in the vernacular. "Politics" means the vying for votes, the deal-making, the campaigning, and the partisan wrangling endemic to a democratic electoral system. It is seldom an attractive process and has been the subject of complaint and comment from Mark Twain to H.L. Mencken to this week's newspaper editorials. One newspaper, for example, once published a four-part editorial series on the subject "Why Politics Stinks."

A. **The perpetual campaign.** Once in office, elected officials measure their actions by their effects on the next election. Presidents, for example, carry on elaborate, continuous polling operations throughout their period of office to keep their fingers on the public pulse. Every choice of policy is made with at least one eye toward its political popularity.

1. **Political effect and conflict or convergence of interest.** Because of the demands of the "perpetual campaign," officeholders are always tempted to support policies that are popular rather than best. They may put their interest in re-election ahead of the public good. According to the theory of government made famous by the Scottish writer **James Mill** (1773-1836) in the early nineteenth century, the need of officeholders to seek re-election produces a **convergence** of interest between representatives and their constituents: officeholders' interests are most effectively advanced by satisfying constituents' interests. But this convergence thesis presupposes that constituents always know their own interests and are always effectively organized to express them. Moreover, the interests of a district or constituency may **conflict** with the interests of a larger whole, so that the representative may be prompted to serve the narrow interest of his constituents (and his own re-election) over the common good.

2. **Corruption by money.** The perpetual campaign, especially at the national level, is driven by the voracious need for money. A U.S. senator, for example, though elected only every six years, needs to raise approximately $12,000 a week throughout the term to finance the last stages of the forthcoming re-election contest. To raise that kind of money, senators need to be doing many favors for many people, and their autonomy of action and judgment—on some issues at least—are invariably compromised. The conflict between the public good and personal interest discussed above is intensified.

B. **Campaigns and the "stink" of politics.** Electoral campaigns, where the stakes are very high, tend toward name-calling, extravagant charges, and unrealistic promises. These tendencies are not rooted in the correctable misfortune of having "bad" people in politics; they are rooted in the very nature of politics.

1. **Manipulating voters in ancient Rome.** Twenty-two hundred years ago the Roman **Quintus Cicero** was advising his now renowned brother **Marcus** (106 B.C.-43 B.C.), in his canvassing for the Roman consulship, to play on the affections of followers, feign an interest in voters' problems, seem sincere, make promises he cannot keep, adopt a flattering manner, cater to the feelings and tastes of everyone he meets, and "start a scandal" against his opponents.

2. **Manipulating voters.** Such tactics are bound to recommend themselves to any competitor for power who must win by popular acclaim. In theory, campaigns are opportunities to "inform" the voters about candidates' stands on the issues and to provoke public debate about the merits of policy alternatives. In practice, candidates find they do better flattering voters' opinions or stirring up their fears and hatreds. Modern techniques of polling can tell candidates within hours how a particular position is being received by voters, allowing them to adjust and fine-tune their messages for maximum effect.

3. **Strategic versus "good-faith" argument.** Campaigns are not ideal occasions for public debate because most candidates adopt a strategic attitude toward argument. They frame arguments with an eye toward effect, not toward accuracy and completeness. Arguments are most effective in the political arena when they are simple, frame issues in black-and-white terms, and do not seriously upset or challenge the views of voters.

4. **Negative advertisements.** Political campaigns have always used the tactic Quintus Cicero recommended, i.e., starting a scandal against one's opponent. Campaigners attack their opponents as inept, incompetent, unpatriotic, dishonest, and as potential or actual disasters in office. They try to associate their opponents with despised groups, outcasts, enemies of the country, political untouchables. They leak personal information about their opponents' health, sanity, sexual habits, and drug use. Contemporary campaigns rely heavily on television "spots," many of which are

"negative," attacking or criticizing a candidate or his record rather than making positive proposals for reform or change. Citizens complain about this aspect of campaigns, but the negative advertisements are common because campaigners find them effective.

5. **Dirty tricks and other shenanigans.** Campaigns not uncommonly plant spies in an opponent's camp, employ hecklers to disrupt his or her speeches, sabotage campaign arrangements, and hire private eyes to "dig for dirt." Sometimes such tactics blur into outright crime, such as the break-in at the Democratic Campaign Headquarters in Washington that began the "Watergate" affair.

6. **The "stink" of politics and the collective action problem.** Politics is a competition for power and the stakes can be enormous. Those who put themselves forward as candidates take on an obligation to their party and supporters to compete as effectively as they can.

    a. **Political necessity and moral limits**. Candidates face moral quandaries about how far to go. What falls within the range of legitimate rough-and-tumble? When does an opponent's resort to low blows justify one's own retaliatory blows? Most candidates would rather not resort to simplistic slogans, negative advertisements, and the constant groveling for money, but no candidate can unilaterally refuse to play the game as it is without self-destruction.

    b. **Difficulty of enforcing common rules**. If candidates could all agree to play by better rules, and not break ranks, both they and the public would benefit. But it is hard, in politics, to enforce any agreement. For politics to be politics, it has to be a free appeal to opinion. And, in the absence of enforcement, some candidates will do better to break ranks. If some do, all the rest will have to follow or contend at a disadvantage.

    c. **Political innocence as a moral failing**. Politics, within the bounds set by the criminal law, is a relatively unregulated competition for great stakes, and as long as it is unregulated, it will be an indelicate competition at best. Innocence in politics may be as much a moral failing as overweening ambition and self-delusion. Effective political leaders may

not have to be morally bad, as Machiavelli thought, but they may have to be hard and calculating and willing to press close to the line between good and bad.

V. **The duties of citizens.** The quality of political activity and public service reflects, in good measure, what citizens expect from politicians and demand from them. Although citizens lament the negativity in campaigns and think all politicians untrustworthy, they are at the same time moved by the same negative advertisements, appeals to fear and prejudice, and rumors of scandal they deplore. And although citizens condemn politicians for giving in to special interests and not acting for the common good, they are at the same time the very "special interests" that incessantly pressure their representatives to fix their problems with government, reward them with patronage jobs, and ease the way for their obtaining contracts, awards, pensions, and other benefits from government.

A. **The citizens' point of view.** In assessing candidates, policies, and actions of government, may citizens use their own self-interest as the measure, or are they duty-bound to consider the common good? The idea of self-government suggests that "citizenship" is an office requiring its holders to support policies that are for the common good, not just their own good. Otherwise, policies would never reflect the united will of the people but only the power of some to impose their desires on others. However, as a realistic concession to the tendency of people to favor their own interests, the institutions of self-government may be arranged to pit self-interest against self-interest so that they cancel out and the institutions lead to genuinely public policies. This last idea unites two of the main strands in political theory, the "republican" tradition, typified by **Jean-Jacques Rousseau** (1712-1778) and **Immanuel Kant** (1724-1804), and the "liberal" tradition, typified by James Madison and James Mill.

B. **Citizens and the intellectual virtues**. Citizens, ideally, should be able to distinguish "good-faith" from strategic arguments, and should be disposed to penalize candidates and causes that flagrantly transgress against the principles of tolerance and humility. Candidates would abandon simplistic slogans, "straw man" arguments, and playing on emotions if these were not effective among voters. Citizens ought to be well-enough informed to follow the main arguments in important public debates, and to make political choices with some understanding of the issues. Ideally, citizens will be able to contribute to some debates, especially on matters that involve their own communities. Finally, because public issues are often quite complex and technical, citizens need to know when to defer to expert opinion and when to substitute their own judgments.

C. **Citizens and political obligation.** Citizens generally are obligated to obey just laws. "Democratic closure" requires that once policies are decided upon after due debate and deliberation, citizens should do their best to comply with them, even if they opposed the policies in the first place and think them unwise. Citizens who resist or try to sabotage policies they believe to be wrong face a dilemma, since they do not want to give up democratic closure in general, and closure does not happen without widespread willingness to live with final political decisions.

Historical Perspective

I. **Moral and philosophical traditions.** The literature of the Jewish and Christian religions abounds in moral instruction and commentary. On the one hand, there are theological speculations about the unifying principle of virtue (as an aspect of God's goodness and perfection) that underlies all right action; and on the other, there are detailed codifications and classifications of cases and rules (in Jewish writings, rabbinical law expressed in the Talmud; canon law and casuistry in Christian writings). Parallel to this literature is a body of secular philosophical writings, from Plato to the present, that also divides into two. One part is speculative and theoretical, the other part advisory about the best way to live, the best ends to pursue. Similarly, there are religious and secular literatures that grow out of Muslim, Hindu, and Buddhist traditions, but that are less well known in the United States and that have had little effect on American institutions and culture.

II. **Morality in office—the misuse of office.** The history of government service and political office in the United States does not discourage the conclusion that we are a better society today than formerly. Politicians have historically used office to enrich themselves, reward their followers, and punish their enemies.

A. **Patronage.** Political patronage was common at the very beginning of our nation.

1. **Rewarding supporters.** Thomas Jefferson was the first president faced with a bureaucracy staffed by people of an opposing political party. He began the process of replacing some with members of his own party, and speculated whether there should be a rule giving each party half the appointments in government.

2. **The "spoils system."** The "spoils system" in government derives from the era of **Andrew Jackson** (1767-1845), who began to apply at the federal level practices already well established in state and local governments. Jackson insisted that holding government office was "not a matter of right" and that it served the democratic cause to have periodic "rotation" among the people's public servants just as among the people's representatives.

3. **Reform of the "spoils system."** After the Civil War, the use of government jobs as "spoils" was so pervasive and corrupt that political pressure arose to reform government employment. The result was the Pendelton Act (1882), which created the beginnings of a professional civil service.

B. **Conflicts of interest.** These conflicts have been a common problem in our history. In the early years of the nation, representatives and officeholders were less fastidious about mixing together private and public business. In fact, much of their behavior would today be criminal.

1. **Webster's retainer. Daniel Webster** (1782-1852), for example, applied to the directors of the Second National Bank for renewal of his "retainer" if they wanted his further political support in the Senate.

2. **The "revolving door."** In World War I, naval officers openly moved back and forth between jobs at ship-building companies and in War Department procurement offices responsible for ship-building contracts, enriching themselves and the companies in the process.

3. **Regulating conflicts of interest.** It is only in recent decades that the Senate and House of Representatives have actually adopted rules regulating the behavior of their members to avoid conflict of interest.

C. **Plain corruption.** Ordinary corruption is also well represented in American history. Bribery, fraud, and misconduct of all kinds have always existed at every level of government.

1. **The Yazoo land scandal (1795).** The nation's first decade witnessed the great Yazoo land scandal, in which the entire Georgia legislature was bribed to sell at a penny and a half an acre 35,000,000 acres of Georgia's western territory

(virtually the entirety of Alabama and Mississippi) to a land company that included senators, representatives, state officials, federal judges, and a Supreme Court justice. Controversy and legal action continued into the early nineteenth century.

2. **Police corruption.** Corrupt activities by local authorities is a continuous theme running through American history. A recent example involved the uncovering in 1970 by the Knapp Commission of extensive and widespread police bribery in the New York City Police Department. The majority of the department was "on the take." New York has hardly been the only city where such corruption has occurred.

3. **Corruption in high office.** In 1973, Vice President Spiro Agnew resigned from office and pleaded no contest to one count of income tax evasion in a plea bargain that disposed of bribery charges against him. "On the take" while Governor of Maryland, Agnew was still getting payments after going to the White House.

4. **The "Abscam" case.** In 1980, an FBI undercover operation called "Abscam," in which agents posed as wealthy businessmen and Arab sheiks, implicated seven congressmen and a senator in bribery, recording all the corrupt transactions on video tape for posterity.

D. **Abuse of office.** Abuse of office for partisan gain is as old as offices to abuse.

1. **The 1960 election in Cook County, Illinois.** The Daley Machine in Chicago is widely believed to have stolen the 1960 presidential for John Kennedy by using its control of city election machinery to stuff the ballot boxes. Kennedy won in Illinois, a pivotal state in the election, by 8,000 votes.

2. **The Watergate scandal.** The Watergate affair is the most notorious instance of abuse of office because it brought about the only resignation of a president in our history.

a. **Scope of those involved.** Watergate involved members of the Office of the President obstructing the investigation of the break-in at the Democratic Campaign Headquarters—a break-in that was authorized by the President's campaign chairman. Members of President Nixon's staff suborned and committed perjury, destroyed documents, and engaged in other acts to prevent FBI and Justice Department investigators from following up leads that would have uncovered the authorization of the break-in.

b. **Watergate-era wrongdoing.** The subsequent Watergate investigation and impeachment hearings by the Congress shed light, as a by-product, on the range of dubious campaign practices that were standard operating procedure in the White House (and, presumably, under other Administrations as well). These activities included mounting a false write-in candidacy to confuse the electorate and draw votes away from an opponent; planting stories in newspapers through the use of friendly columnists; organizing bogus telegrams and letters to congressmen; using a spy in another candidate's campaign to steal documents; instructing the FCC, IRS, and Justice Department to threaten or start investigations of unfriendly media; and staging "black advances," i.e., sabotage and harassment of opposition campaigns.

Contemporary Perspective

I. **Moral education.** If citizens are to be able to understand the moral content of many public debates, they have to be adequately educated in the community's moral traditions. A contemporary challenge is to sustain, or create, institutions that support moral education.

A. **Moral vocabulary and moral argument.** A good moral education introduces citizens into the various vocabularies of criticism available in the community, and supplies them with a common stock of models and examples as starting points in arguments.

B. **Learning other perspectives.** A good moral education encourages in citizens the ability to detach themselves from their own points of view and to imagine how matters look from other perspectives. This ability makes possible the practice of intellectual generosity and humility.

II. **Campaign reform.** Among the most pressing contemporary problems in morality-and-politics is reform of campaigns to remove the need for candidates to raise so much money and to create incentives for candidates to avoid name-calling and character assassination.

A. **Alternative means of campaign finance.** Various schemes of public financing have been broached as a way to diminish the domination of politics by money. Alternatively, the costs of campaigns could be reduced by developing sources of free media exposure for candidates. Changes in rules that limit the amount of individual donations and that make PACs independent receivers of unlimited donations may affect campaigns for the better as well.

B. **Monitoring campaign tactics.** Some newspapers have begun to monitor political advertisements for distortion and falsification, as a counterweight to the tendencies of campaigns to become increasingly shallow and negative. Voluntary monitoring organizations and voluntary pledges by candidates might also create incentives or opportunities for better campaigning.

III. **Citizen sophistication.** Citizens need not only moral sophistication but political sophistication, as well.

A. **Necessity for political sophistication.** Institutions of adult political education can help adults understand political issues and political procedures, and help them give voice to their political views. The contemporary challenge is to create a richer supply of such institutions than we presently have.

B. **Learning while in office.** Occupying elective or appointed office can give citizens an appreciation of role-duties and of the sources of conflict within the role of representative.

IV. **Politics as a vocation.** Citizens need to reflect on the moral attractions and perils of political life. Active participation by citizens is a textbook ideal of democratic politics, but many citizens are alienated from or hostile to politics. Citizens may benefit by a sharper appreciation of the personal fulfillment that comes from collective effort on behalf of a cause, as well as by a clearer sense of the temptations that make politics morally hazardous.

A. **The rewards of political life.** Political activity enlists an individual's powers in the collective formulation of goals and values, and in the joint activity of like-minded persons in pursuit of those goals and values. Whether successful or not, there is usually something gratifying and ennobling in having "fought the good fight."

B. **The political actor as an empty vessel.** One central personal danger in political activity is loss of integrity. By using contemporary political technology, candidates can "test-market" various positions to identify the most effective positions and most effective ways to get them across. Political actors can find themselves driven more and more by purely strategic considerations, creating a wider and wider gulf between what they sincerely believe to be reasonable and true and what they present as their views to various audiences. At the limit, political actors can become entirely empty persons, with no real beliefs of their own and guided only by strategic concerns.

C. **Politicians' attitudes toward electorate.** There is also a danger that political actors and managers will come to view the electorate with contempt. In using modern techniques of persuasion, political actors see how little these techniques have to do with "good-faith" arguments and the rationality of the audiences upon which they work their effects. As they increasingly view the electorate as just a field for application of scientific manipulation, it is hard for political actors to continue to respect electorate opinions.

B. THE AMERICAN ECONOMIC SYSTEM

It is not from the benevolence of the butcher, the brewer, or the baker, that we expect our dinner, but from their regard to their own interest....Every individual...intends only his own gain, and he is in this, as in many other cases led by an invisible hand to promote an end which was no part of his intention.

Adam Smith (1776)

The ideas of economists and political philosophers, both when they are right and when they are wrong, are more powerful than is commonly understood. Indeed the world is ruled by little else. Practical men, who believe themselves to be quite exempt from any intellectual influences, are usually the slaves of some defunct economist. Madmen in authority, who hear voices in the air, are distilling their frenzy from some academic scribbler of a few years back.

John Maynard Keynes (1936)

Economics is all about how people make choices; sociology is all about how people have no choices to make.

James Duesenberry (1960)

Economics can trace its lineage to Aristotle, who coined the term when referring to managing household resources—almost the modern definition of home economics. The modern founding of economics as a discipline is generally considered to center on the publication of Adam Smith's book *An Inquiry into the Nature and Causes of the Wealth of Nations* in 1776. In a little over two centuries since that renowned treatise appeared, economists have defined their area of study and forged the tools of analysis that help to provide important insights into the contemporary world.

Economists generally agree that economics is the discipline that focuses on how people use scarce resources to satisfy their wants. In the words of James Duesenberry, "Economics is all about how people make choices." These choices can be divided into micro- and macroeconomics. Microeconomics focuses on the allocation of resources by individual units within the economy. These scarcity-based decisions help determine prices, production, and the distribution of income; whereas macroeconomics studies the functioning of the economy as a whole. Macroeconomics studies the levels and trends in measures of national output, employment, and prices, with an eye toward such long term issues as full employment and economic growth.

Political choices that confront citizens are replete with the ideas—and choices—of economics. Citizens can scarcely make sense of policies advocated in print and on the airwaves by those within and outside of political institutions unless they have a basic grounding in economic ideas and issues. Economics may have been dubbed "the dismal science;" but ignorance of economics on the part of citizens called upon to judge the ideas, criticisms, warnings, policies, and proposals that swirl about them in public debate is more dismal by far. Like ignorance in general, ignorance of economics in today's world forms a prison from which citizens—if they are to be adequate judges of public discussion—must be given the tools to escape.

OBJECTIVES

The citizen should be able to

1. explain the characteristics of the American economic system.

2. explain the basis of reasoned judgements regarding fundamental economic principles.

3. explain the nature of scarcity and the limits it imposes.

4. explain the idea that personal and societal choices have costs as well as benefits.

5. describe the relationship between productivity and our standard of living.

6. explain the idea that there are tradeoffs everywhere, even among broad social goals.

7. take, defend, and evaluate postures on public policy regarding contemporary economic issues.

FRAME OF REFERENCE
Conceptual Perspective

I. **Economic consensus.** Economists are often accused of disagreeing with one another on major issues. On closer inspection, however, this disagreement can often be understood as a lack of consensus on a normative rather than a positive economic issue.

A. **Normative economics.** A normative statement is a value judgment—an "ought statement"—rather than a testable statement. "Everyone should have enough to eat," or "The price of gasoline should not be so high," or "The minimum wage should be increased," are all examples of normative statements. No one can refute or prove these statements because they are based on opinion, with no means of making a scientific test of their accuracy.

B. **Positive economics.** A positive statement is a testable statement that can be proved or disproved. For example, "Ten percent of U.S. children are undernourished by USDA standards," or "If gasoline prices reach $1.50 per gallon, profit margins of taxi companies will fall," or "Full-time minimum wage workers who support three or more dependents fall below the federal poverty line" are all statements that can be tested.

C. **Economic consensus.** Recent research has shown that most economists agree on those questions that fall into the positive economics domain. In other words, there is a well accepted body of economic theory that all practitioners agree upon. Nevertheless, there is room for disagreement on the normative issues because, while two economists may see similar outcomes from a given action, one may see the outcomes as favorable, while the other may find them undesirable. Economists may also disagree about economic ideas that lie outside the accepted body of theory.

D. **Rational choice.** Despite the normative controversies among economists, all would agree that an understanding of fundamental economic principles helps citizens make reasonable estimates of the consequences of different policies. Such knowledge forms the basis for an informed choice.

II. **Economic goals.** Economic decisions generally involve broad social goals. Citizens' perception of the desirability of social policy will be formed by the perceived outcomes of that policy with respect to these goals. The following are among those most often relevant to economic policy decisions:

A. **Economic freedom.** Freedom of action and thought form the core of democratic values. Economic freedom generally refers to the freedom of action in the marketplace as it relates to production and consumption of goods and services. Nevertheless, this freedom is not unfettered. Certain goods like alcohol, tobacco, and heroin may be deemed unhealthful, and restricted or banned outright. Government regulation of economic activity is clearly a limitation on economic freedom. Differences in viewpoint and discussion are an integral part of the democratic process.

B. **Economic efficiency.** This goal concerns producing the most highly desired goods at the lowest possible cost. This goal does not mean producing with the fewest inputs, but rather with the least costly bundle of inputs. All other conditions being equal, economists favor societal policies that encourage the most efficient use of resources to achieve society's other goals.

C. **Full employment.** Benjamin Franklin once wrote, "An idle mind is the devil's workshop." Economists view idle resources with equal disdain. Their view is that resources (other than those preserved for various reasons, such as national parks and wilderness areas) are meant to produce goods and services. If resources are unemployed for no good reason, society is sacrificing the output that would have been available—fewer homes, health services, and other outputs are available. The nation is poorer as a result.

D. **Economic growth.** An increase in the economy's output of goods and services is defined as economic growth. In the popular analogy between society's output and a pie, annual economic growth can be characterized as baking a larger pie each year. When a larger pie is baked, we can each get a larger slice without diminishing the share of others, so long as we don't add too many more people sharing the pie.

E. **Economic equity.** Economic equity refers to the fairness of the system. Does everyone have an equal opportunity to demonstrate their abilities? Does everyone have an equal opportunity to improve their abilities? Economists point out that policies in pursuit of **equity** as an attribute of an economic system do not imply equality of "outcome," but rather equality of "opportunity." Some commentators confuse these concepts. (Whether it is desirable or equitable for society to redistribute resources—to the needy, for example—is a separate question not addressed here.)

III. **Fundamental economic concepts.** Fundamental economic concepts include scarcity and choice; and the factors of productivity, opportunity costs, and similar notions.

A. **Scarcity and choice.** Scarcity is considered the core concept of economics. Scarcity exists when our wants exceed our resources. This is sometimes called "The Economic Problem." A basic premise of economic theory is that "people want more." "More" may refer to many kinds of things—clean air or safety or space to live in as well as homes and autos and vacations, since people's choices differ.

1. **Economic wants defined.** Economic wants are desires that can be satisfied by consuming a good or a service. Thirst, hunger, shelter, and transportation are all examples of economic wants. They could be satisfied by getting a drink, a meal, an apartment, or a bus ride. Eternal salvation or love are not economic wants because there are no economic goods or services produced that can satisfy them.

2. **The consequences of scarcity in society.** Scarcity exists for society as well as individuals. National defense, education, public transportation, medical care, and police services are all examples of societal wants that exceed our society's resource base. If wants exceed resources, then scarcity exists, and choices must be about how to use our resources to satisfy our wants.

3. **The factors of production.** Society's resources can be divided into three categories: natural resources; capital resources; and human resources.

   a. **Natural resources.** Gifts of nature like deposits of iron ore, coal, and petroleum are examples of natural resources. Their presence is not related to human intervention.

   b. **Capital resources.** While natural resources are important, they are no guarantee of a nation's prosperity. Capital goods are more important. They are manufactured goods that are used to produce other goods and services. Tools, machines, and factories are all examples of such resources. Capital resources enhance a worker's ability to produce goods and services thus increasing labor productivity.

   c. **Labor resources.** Human resources, sometimes called labor, represent the quantity and quality of human effort directed toward producing goods and services. The quality of human resources is composed of the skills and knowledge of members of the labor force. A worker's skills and knowledge are often referred to as "human capital" because they enhance a worker's ability to produce goods and services. An increase in the skills (human capital) of members of the labor force will increase their productivity and ultimately their income. Skilled workers earn generally more than semi-skilled workers who, in turn, earn more than unskilled workers— depend-

ing on the market forces of supply and demand. One of the major thrusts of economics is to emphasize the importance of students investing in themselves—investing in their own "human capital." Economists also stress the correlation between improving skills, productivity, worker income, and economic growth.

   d. **Entrepreneurship.** Economic risk taking is another type of human resource. It entails the ability of some people (called entrepreneurs) to organize economic activity by taking the risks of starting a new business or introducing a new product in the hope of making a profit. The entrepreneur must judge the merits of different ways of producing goods or services and decide how to apply new production methods or how to produce new goods. The great entrepreneur is often an innovator, but only rarely an inventor.

B. **Productivity as the basis for a high standard of living.** Productivity refers to the amount of goods and services produced per unit of productive resources used—the ratio of output per unit of input. From a macroeconomic viewpoint, productivity is the basis of our relatively high standard of living. No society can continue to consume at high levels without having a highly productive labor force. Moreover, it is probable that no modern democracy can maintain itself without experiencing economic success, at least in the long term. The roots of productivity advance can be achieved through the organization of production, especially through specialization and division of labor, through new technology, and through additional investment in capital equipment and/or the labor force.

1. **Specialization and the division of labor.** Specialization occurs when people produce a narrower range of goods than they consume. The Scottish professor **Adam Smith** (1723-1790) was the first to describe the advantages of workers concentrating their energies on a narrow range of production activities and thus increasing their output. He referred to his observations of ten workers in a pin factory who were able to produce 48,000 pins per day as a result of their specialized labors. Our modern automobile assembly lines are similar examples of such specialization of labor.

2. **Technology as society's pool of useful knowledge.** Technology is a way of making our limited resources produce more output. New technology is incorporated into the world of work through a process called technological change. Technological change can be as simple as a new way of organizing the production process—assembly lines, for example, or "quality circles." Or technological change may involve the introduction of new goods or services like the jet airplane or word processing. In any case, technology plays a key role in improving productivity and ultimately improving the standard of living.

3. **Increasing productivity with capital investment.** Productivity can also be increased by providing labor with additional capital resources like tools and machines. Simply providing workers with greater capital resources is not sufficient to increase labor productivity. Workers must learn how to use these capital resources in order to enhance their productivity. They must study, practice, and generally invest time and energy in the learning process.

C. **Opportunity cost.** One of the most repeated lines in economics is: "There is no such thing as a free lunch." At one time this referred to the nineteenth century American saloons that provided patrons with sandwiches as long as they bought a beer—the equivalent of "free" hors d'oeuvres in today's saloons. But the cost of the "free" food is always included in the price of the drinks.

1. **The "free lunch" analogy and the multiple uses of resources.** The free lunch analogy can be applied to any situation where scarce resources are used. Public schools, for example, are not truly cost-free because they use scarce resources that have alternative productive uses. Those resources could have been used for medical care, highways, police protection, or many other uses. The point is that resources have a variety of uses. Once a choice has been made to use resources for a particular end, for example, building a new school, the highest valued alternative use for that resource, such as building a new police station, is called its "opportunity cost."

2. **All choices involve "opportunity costs."** Students, and adults for that matter, will often try to rationalize their choices by arguing that they aren't giving anything up by so choosing—that there is no opportunity cost. They may maintain that they

can create more wildlife preserves, eliminate air pollution, rebuild the armed forces, build homes for the homeless, and feed the hungry without raising taxes or incurring debt. Economists hold that these are unrealistic arguments.

3. **"Guns" versus "butter:" the idea of "trade-offs."** Citizens need to be aware of the reality of opportunity costs so their decisions are made with full information about what they are giving up. They must understand that a "tradeoff" exists between creating more wildlife preserves (or anything else) and improving educational programs for disadvantaged youth, or between health care and national defense expenditures (or any other desired choice). Because of scarcity, this is a necessary truth: one can have some of one and some of others and all of one and none of others; but one cannot expend all resources on all goals at once. Economists often call defense programs and the like "guns," and domestic programs "butter." Thus there is always a trade-off between guns and butter. Much political debate revolves around this issue.

D. **Weighing costs and benefits.** Good decision making always involves considerations of opportunity costs. But benefits must be identified as well. Weighing the costs and benefits associated with choices constitutes effective decision making.

a. **Wildlife preservation vs. education.** The trade-off between wildlife preservation (or other goals) and education (or other goals) may illustrate the process of weighing costs and benefits. The opportunity cost of wildlife preserves might be fewer educational programs (or some other equally desirable purpose). To some this may seem to be a small price to pay for the enjoyment of seeing animals in their natural habitat. Of course, in principle one could have both education and wildlife preserves, but then some **other** program people desire would have to be cut. The point is that the economic facts of life make difficult choices a necessity.

b. **The complexities of weighing cost and benefits.** Other observers may view the benefit of these two activities differently. They may argue that educational programs provide significant long term benefit in terms of improving the academic ability and productivity of children. Education amounts to an investment in human capital and stimulates economic growth, whereas the enjoyment of a leisure activity like a wildlife park does not have such long term benefits for those seeking leisure. On the other hand, wildlife preserves can be enjoyed repeatedly by oneself and future generations in the long term. Also the long term preservation of wild life for other reasons would have to be taken into account, complicating the matter further.

E. **Economic systems.** An economy is society's answer to the three basic economic questions: What to produce? How to produce it? For whom to produce it? There are three model economies: traditional, command, and market.

1. **Traditional economies.** Tradition based economies are the oldest form of economy. Production and distribution decisions are largely based on custom—the way things were done in the past. The economic actors in this system do as their ancestors did and do not introduce new techniques.

2. **Command economies.** In a command economy a central authority, usually the government, makes the major production and allocation decisions. Unlike the tradition based economy, the command system is able to change its technological base and grow economically. However, the system is ultimately based on authoritarian rewards and punishments and sharply restricts the liberty of those who live under it.

3. **Market systems.** In a market system the major economic decisions are made by households and firms which follow their self-interest. While no modern economy could be classified as an example of one of these ideal types, the U.S. economy resembles the market economy more closely than it resembles either the tradition or command model. In the U.S., individual liberty is also far greater than in societies whose economies resemble command or traditional economies. It is important to understand that political and economic systems are closely interlinked.

4. **Basic components of market systems.** All market economies have three basic components: a director, a motivator, and a regulator.

   a. **"Consumer sovereignty."** Consumers are the ultimate directors of what gets produced in a market economy. If businesses produce something consumers do not want, consumers may refuse to buy it. In this case the firm either

produces something else, or goes out of business entirely. Slide rules, Edsel automobiles, Old Gold Cigarettes, IBM PC Jr. computers, and New Coke are all examples of products consumers chose not to support with their dollars.

   b. **Role of profits.** Profit, which can be defined as the difference between a firm's total revenues and total costs, is a firm's motivator (incentive) for successfully anticipating the market demand.

   c. **Role of competition.** Competition is the regulator in this process. In a market economy, strong consumer demand and large profits act as signals for other firms to enter the marketplace, thus increasing supply and competition.

IV. **Microeconomic concepts.** Microeconomics is the study of the behavior of households, firms, and markets, of how prices and outputs are determined in those markets, and of how prices allocate resources and distribute income. Microeconomics is sometimes referred to as the economist's "tool box," because it contains the tools of analysis most often used.

A. **Markets and prices.** Markets are arrangements that enable buyers and sellers to exchange goods and services. Markets provide a way to organize the production and distribution of goods and services. Prices of goods and services are defined in markets, and these prices signal the relative scarcity of the good or service being exchanged. Relatively high prices ration commodities to those who are most willing and able to buy, and encourage firms to produce more of the relatively scarce good. But how are prices established? And why do they change?

B. **Supply and demand.** It is the interaction of supply and demand that determines prices in the marketplace. A market economy is dependent on freely operating forces of supply and demand to function effectively.

1. **Definition of supply.** Supply can be defined as the quantity that producers are willing to sell at different prices in a given time period. As the price of a good or service rises, the quantity supplied tends to increase.

2. **Definition of demand.** Demand can be defined as the quantity that consumers are willing to buy at different prices in a given time period. As most

people intuitively understand, higher prices cause the quantity demanded to decrease.

3. **The "market price."** In competitive markets these laws of supply and demand lead to a market clearing price where the quantities that demanders wish to purchase is exactly equal to the quantities that suppliers are willing to produce. This market clearing price is often called the "equilibrium price."

4. **The function of price fluctuation.** If the producers charge prices that are above equilibrium, there will be a "surplus" because firms want to produce more than consumers wish to buy. If prices are below equilibrium, buyers will want more than firms are willing to produce, and there will be a "shortage." In the final analysis, the value of a good or service in a market economy is determined by supply and demand—by the costs of production (supply) and by the ability and willingness of consumers to buy (demand).

5. **Supply factors that change prices.** Changes in the costs of production (supply) will cause a new equilibrium to be established. For example, technological change that leads to higher productivity will tend to increase supply and depress the equilibrium price. The markets for personal computers and agricultural commodities have seen dramatic technological changes that lowered their equilibrium prices.

6. **Demand factors that change prices.** On the demand side, a change in consumer income, tastes, or the prices of related goods can affect the demand for a product. Teenage consumers, for example, are especially susceptible to peer group pressures when it comes to defining their tastes and preferences for goods. Last year's popular clothes become this week's discards. Nevertheless, changes in a teenager's income can have a dramatic effect on the quantity and quality of items these consumers demand. Firms must be mindful of the essentially fickle nature of much of teenage demand if they hope to benefit from it. But why would firms cater to teenage consumers?

C. **Economic incentives.** The incentive for most human action is the belief that after engaging in some economic activity, whether it is buying, selling, working, or saving, one will be better off. In other words, there must usually be some tangible reward, or economic incentive, for people to engage in an economic activity (as opposed to other kinds of activities). Savers expect to receive a premium for allowing others to borrow their buying power. Interest is the term we use when referring to this incentive. Workers expect to receive an incentive in the form of wages and/or fringe benefits if they are to provide services. Entrepreneurs expect to earn a profit in return for their contribution to the production process. Economic incentives can be powerful motivating forces that propel the economic actors to do what is in the best interest of society.

D. **Voluntary exchange.** The system where consumers and producers follow their individual interests leads to a mutually beneficial exchange. Voluntary exchange is at the heart of a market economy. For example, when consumers buy flower seeds and plant them in the front yard, their buying behavior shows that they want to have some lovely flowers. By the same token, the merchant is clearly happier with the money than with the flower seeds. Both are better off after the exchange. Society has also benefitted from the exchange, which is rooted in consumer and producer self-interest.

1. **Zero-sum game.** The idea that both the buyer **and** the seller benefit from voluntary exchange is important. Many consumers fail to grasp the mutually beneficial nature of voluntary exchange. They may see the economy as a "zero-sum game" where the amount that one group wins is exactly equal to the amount that another group loses.

2. **Positive-sum game.** In reality the economy is a "positive-sum game" where buyers and sellers can **both** gain through specialization and exchange. Like the flower example above, there need not be a winner and a loser in a positive-sum game.

E. **Externalities.** There are occasions, however, when the actions of one person or group have a significant impact on a third party—someone not directly considered in the action. If some of the costs or benefits of a consumption or production activity spill over onto innocent bystanders, then an externality exists. Externalities can be either positive or negative.

1. **"Positive externalities."** Positive externalities involve benefits to third parties. Goods and services that have significant positive externalities tend to be underproduced because not all the benefits are reflected in the consumer's demand for the product.

2. **Examples of positive externalities.** Examples of goods with positive externalities include public health, mass transit, and education. A patient who gets a flu shot benefits privately by avoiding a bout with the flu, but others also benefit because they will not contract flu from the patient. By the same token, a student clearly benefits from a good education, but other members of society benefit, too, because that student will ultimately be a more productive, tax-paying citizen. A further significant point is that the private marketplace tends to underproduce goods with significant positive externalities.

3. **"Negative externalities."** Goods and services with significant negative externalities tend to be underpriced and overproduced in a market society because the full cost of production is not reflected in the price. Some of the costs of production or consumption are pushed onto third parties.

4. **Examples of negative externalities.** Pollution is an example of a negative externality. If a steel mill uses a nearby river as a sewer for its waste, then part of the cost of producing steel falls on those who use the river for other uses, like fishing, drinking water, and recreation.

5. **Negative externalities and government intervention.** Cases of significant externalities often justify some form of government intervention which may take the form of subsidy, regulation, taxation, or outright prohibition.

F. **Public goods.** Most goods and services in a market economy are privately produced and consumed, but some goods have the characteristics of a public good: non-exclusion and shared consumption.

1. **Non-exclusive consumption.** Non-exclusion means that producers cannot prevent consumers from enjoying a good once it is produced. Street lighting, mosquito abatement, and national defense are examples of services that cannot exclude consumers.

2. **Shared consumption.** Shared consumption means that once a service is produced, any number of consumers can enjoy it without disturbing others. The previous examples all qualify along with public television broadcasts and lighthouses.

3. **Production of public goods.** Public goods tend to be underproduced by the private sector and are generally produced by the government and paid for through taxation.

V. **Macroeconomic concepts.** The relationship between national income, output, employment, inflation, and the money supply is all part of macroeconomics, which focuses on the functioning of the economy as a whole.

A. **GNP defined.** Gross national product (GNP) is an estimate of the value of an economy's output of all final goods and services for a specific year. It is the most comprehensive measure of the value of an economy's output.

1. **Per capita GNP.** The U.S. has the world's largest economy with a GNP of more than $5 trillion, but comparing the absolute size of GNPs can be misleading. India has a GNP that is twice the size of Sweden's, but on a per capita basis Sweden's GNP is 44 times larger.

2. **The idea of "constant dollars" in comparing GNP at different times.** Price fluctuations make intertemporal comparisons of GNP hazardous. Economists compute an inflation adjustment index called the GNP Deflator to assist in making such comparisons by putting current (nominal) GNP in constant (real) dollars.

a. **"Real GNP."** Real dollars have the same purchasing power, regardless of the time period considered. By comparing Real GNP in different time periods we can get an overall idea of the health of an economy.

b. **"Nominal GNP."** Nominal GNP increased every year between 1960 and 1990 with a cumulative increase of more than tenfold, but much of that increase was the result of inflation. Real GNP rose less than threefold over this period, and actually fell in the recession years of 1975 and 1982.

3. **Economic growth.** Economic growth is defined as an increase in real GNP over time. The sources of economic growth include technological change as well as the growth in the quantity and quality of the factors of production: land, labor, and capital.

B. **The "business cycle."** Fluctuations in economic activity over time are called business cycles. They have four phases: peak, recession, trough, expansion. A complete cycle involves all four parts and is usually measured from trough to trough or peak to peak.

1. **Studying the business cycle.** The trough and peak are officially designated by the National Bureau of Economic Research, an independent non-governmental organization that commissions studies of the economy. It has data on thirty business cycles in the U.S. from 1854 to the present.

2. **Recessions.** By definition, recession involves a decline in real GNP. As a rule of thumb, an economic downturn must last two quarters (six months) to be classified as a recession. It is accompanied by an increase in unemployment and by business and personal bankruptcies as well as by a decline in output and tax revenues. In the post-World War II period, the average length of a U.S. recession has been eleven months.

3. **Causes of recessions.** The causes of recessions vary, but they generally involve a shift in aggregate demand or aggregate supply.

    a. **Declining demand.** Recessions often begin with a decline in aggregate demand, usually investment demand. Such a decrease in investment may be precipitated by a rise in interest rates that stifles new construction and mortgage lending. If a decline in demand is the cause of the recession, then "someone in the economy begins to spend less."

    b. **Declining supply.** Recessions may also begin with a supply-side shock that drives prices up and lessens the economy's ability to produce the same level of output without raising prices. Supply-side shocks produce upward wage-price spirals that ultimately lead to higher prices and higher unemployment.

4. **Federal attempts to regulate the business cycle.** The federal government can take an active counter-cyclical role by manipulating its budget (taxes and expenditures) to counteract periods of recessions or inflation. This role is called exercising discretionary fiscal policy.

    a. **Keynesian measures by government. John Maynard Keynes** (1883-1946), a British economist whose followers are known as "Keynesians," argued that it was fluctuations in aggregate demand that caused most business cycles. From this insight his followers developed a demand-based theory of managing the economy. To avoid a recession, government should intervene to stimulate demand by raising government expenditures and/or lowering taxes. To avoid inflation, government should lower its expenditures and/or raise taxes.

    b. **Problems with fiscal (spending) policy.** Discretionary fiscal policy has proved to be especially difficult to practice when inflation is the macroeconomic illness. Tax hikes are difficult to enact, and spending programs are politically difficult to cut. Only in recessionary times have Keynesian policies been successfully implemented, and even in these times they need the cooperation of the nation's central bank, the Federal Reserve System.

    c. **Rejection of Keynesian fiscal tools.** Many economists are wary of dependence upon the ability to fine-tune the economy by using Keynesian tools of fiscal policy. They prefer a return to the laissez-faire approach of lower government expenditures, regulation, and taxation. Some of these economists may be labeled as supporting the "supply-side" view that lower tax rates and decreased governmental regulations provide increased incentives for additional work effort, investment, and entrepreneurship.

    d. **Limits to government fiscal measures.** Other economists who hold "rational expectation" views argue that discretionary fiscal policy may be destabilizing at worst and ineffective at best because of unforeseen time lags and offsetting behavior by groups within the economy. They see government as much more constrained in its ability to correct business cycles and manage the economy.

C. **The role of money.** Money is something generally accepted as payment for goods and services. It is thus a medium of exchange. Without money every economic transaction would involve barter (exchanging one set of goods for another)—a very inefficient mechanism of exchange. Money allows people to separate their consumption activity from their production activity.

    1. **The functions of money.** Money has three basic functions.

a. **Money as a medium of exchange.** If something is not generally acceptable as payment for goods and services, then it is not money. In the U.S. the most restrictive definition of money (M-1) amounts to more than $800 billion and includes currency (27%), check deposits (72%), and travelers' checks (1%).

(1) **Cash.** The dollar is fiat money. It is not backed by gold or any other precious metal. It is acceptable because people have faith in it.

(2) **Credit cards.** Credit cards are not money since they represent debt rather than payment. A credit card allows you to borrow money at the instant the purchase is made. But the debt must eventually be paid with money.

b. **Money as storing value.** Money must be able to retain its ability to command goods and services over time. It must represent stored buying power. Price inflation hampers the ability of money to serve this purpose. Because of inflation, one dollar today buys about what 30 cents would purchase 20 years ago. At the end of World War II, one could buy a good steak dinner for 50 cents.

(1) **International inflation rates in the developed world.** U.S. inflation is considerably less than most other nations. While U.S. inflation rates have averaged about 5 percent a year over the last two decades, other industrial nations have experienced even higher annual rates: Canada, 7; Sweden, 8; France, 8; Italy, 11; Spain, 12; Israel, 67.

(2) **Inflation in less developed countries.** Less developed nations have considerably higher inflation rates that lead many of their citizens to prefer American money as a store of value. The average annual rate of inflation from 1980-85 for all middle income countries as defined by the World Bank was 57.4 percent—more than ten times the annual inflation rate in the United States.

c. **Money as a unit of account.** Money is the counting system we use to translate the value of all transactions into a single monetary unit. But if the money of one nation is not easily convertible into another nation's money, then the exchange rate may be distorted. Once free exchange is established, this could result in the rapid decline in the value of one nation's currency. This "devaluation" occurred in the early 1990s with the Soviet ruble vis-à-vis western currencies.

2. **Relationship between money and inflation.** There is an important relationship between the quantity of money and the level of prices. While money is not the only determinant of inflation, no long-run inflation can be sustained without a subsequent increase in the money supply. By the same token, the supply of money and credit in an economy has a major influence on the level of interest and output. But simply increasing the money supply is not a panacea for a healthy economy. Economists believe that too great an increase in the money supply creates inflation, as too many dollars chase too few goods—with more money to spend on scarce goods, people bid up prices.

D. **The role of savings institutions.** Financial intermediaries are business firms that act as middlemen by taking deposits from savers and making them available to borrowers. They earn profits based on the differential between the interest they pay depositors and the interest they charge to borrowers. They keep very little of their depositors' money in reserve.

1. **Deregulation of savings institutions.** Until the passage of the Depository Institutions Deregulation and Monetary Control Act (1980), there were sharp distinctions between commercial banks and other financial intermediaries. Since 1980 all intermediaries that accept deposits can create transaction accounts that allow easy transfer of funds.

2. **Non-banks competing with banks.** Financial deregulation has allowed non-bank financial intermediaries to compete with banks in a variety of lending activities, and to offer market rates of interest to depositors with no official government-imposed ceiling—the abolition of regulation Q. The nefarious activities of some of the newcomers to this industry and their subsequent bankruptcies have led many experts to call for re-regulation of the entire industry.

3. **Insurance of bank deposits.** Since financial intermediaries keep a very small proportion of their

deposits on hand, they will fail if a large number of depositors request their money immediately.

a. **The FDIC.** The invention of the Federal Deposit Insurance Corporation (FDIC) assures depositors that they will receive their money back up to $100,000 if a bank should fail. The FDIC was created to prevent bank panics, but it also absolved depositors from risk of loss.

b. **A "moral hazard" created by the FDIC system.** This system creates a moral hazard since it can lead to depositors seeking the highest interest rate regardless of the financial solvency of the bank offering these rates, because they are assured of their money.

c. **How "good" banks are punished and "bad" banks rewarded.** This insurance arrangement also creates a perverse system of incentives in which the banks that act in the most profligate manner get more deposits, whereas economically responsible banks lose deposits.

E. **Role of the Federal Reserve System.** The Federal Reserve System, commonly called "the Fed," is the central bank of the United States. It has a greater quantifiable influence on the quantity of money, the structure of interest rates, and the health of the economy than any other entity in the United States.

1. **The history of the Federal Reserve System.** The Fed was established by Congress in 1913 to regulate the supply of money and credit in the economy. Twelve federal reserve districts were established in different regions of the country to provide services and regulate the financial institutions in their respective districts, and a board of governors with seven members was located in Washington, D.C., to serve as the headquarters of the system.

2. **The structure of the Federal Reserve.** There are three major parts to the Fed: the board of governors; the district banks; and the federal open market committee.

a. **Insulation from politics of the board of governors.** The board of governors consists of seven members, called governors, who are appointed by the President (with the advice and consent of the Senate), and who serve fourteen-year terms that are staggered so that a new term for some members begins every two years. Governors may be reappointed and can serve the remainder of another member's term. One of the governors of the board is named to a four-year term as chairman and may be reappointed to that post. Once appointed, the members' positions are secure for the length of the appointment.

b. **District banks.** Each of the Federal Reserve district banks is governed by nine directors with one-third appointed by the board of governors and the remaining two-thirds elected by member banks in the district. These directors appoint the district bank's president with the approval of the board of governors. The twelve Federal Reserve bank cities are: Boston; New York; Philadelphia; Cleveland; Richmond; Atlanta; Chicago; St. Louis; Minneapolis; Kansas City; Dallas; and San Francisco.

c. **Policy-making bodies.** The federal open committee is the main policy-making body of the Federal Reserve System. It consists of the board of governors, the president of the New York District Bank, and the presidents of four other Federal Reserve district banks elected on a rotating basis. It meets monthly to establish U.S. monetary policy.

3. **The tools of the Federal Reserve.** There are three major policy tools available to the Fed. It can alter the discount rate, the reserve requirement, and open market operations.

a. **The Fed's "discount rate."** The "discount rate" is the interest rate the Fed charges banks that wish to borrow reserves. If the Fed raises the discount rate, it is a signal that it is pursuing a tighter monetary policy; that is, loans will be more expensive and difficult to obtain. If the Fed lowers the discount rate it is a sign that it wants to encourage borrowing and is willing to augment bank reserves.

b. **The Fed's "reserve requirement."** The "reserve requirement" is the legal minimum level of reserves that banks must keep on hand either as vault cash or on deposit with the Fed. Required reserves are specified as a minimum percentage of different kinds of deposits. Checking accounts, for example, have higher reserve requirements than savings accounts. If the Fed raises reserve requirements, it is a signal that it is pursuing a tighter monetary policy, and loans will be more difficult and expensive to obtain. A lowering of the reserve requirements frees additional bank reserves to be loaned, expanding the supply of money, easing credit and increasing loan activity.

c. **The Fed's "open market operations."** Open market operations involve the direct purchase or sale of government securities like U.S. Treasury bonds or notes in the open market. These operations are ordered by the federal open market committee, and they lead to a direct change in bank reserves. If the Fed wants to pursue a tighter monetary policy, it moves into the financial markets and sells government securities from its portfolio. This contracts bank reserves and ultimately decreases the economy's money supply. On the other hand, if the Fed wishes to expand money and credit within the economy, it buys government securities in the open market and thus puts new reserves in the banking system.

VI. **International economic concepts.** With the coming of global markets and international convertibility of currencies, national economies are more open to international influences than ever before. The American economy is becoming part of a global economy.

A. **International trade defined.** International trade is the exchange of goods and services between people and institutions in different nations. It occurs for the same reasons that trade and specialization take place among different regions of a nation.

1. **Economic consequences of world trade.** Trade promotes specialization and thus increases world output. It also increases the interdependence of nations.

2. **Why nations trade.** International differences in factor endowments and relative prices are the basis for international trade. Economists once believed that nations traded based on their absolute advantage in output. But the relevant concept for trade is not absolute advantage, but rather comparative advantage.

a. **Absolute advantage.** A nation has an absolute advantage if it can produce more of a good with the same level of resources than another nation can. France can produce better wine than England using the same amount of capital, land, and labor. Therefore, it has an absolute advantage in wine.

b. **Comparative advantage.** Comparative advantage is the economic principle that says nations should export those goods and services in which they have a lower opportunity cost. To use the earlier example, suppose France could also produce more sheep than England using the same amount of capital, land, and labor that was involved in the wine example. Once again it has an absolute advantage, but does it have a comparative advantage? Look at the table below:

France	100 sheep	1000 wine casks
England	80 sheep	400 wine casks

The opportunity cost of 100 sheep produced in France is 1000 wine casks, or 1 sheep costs 10 wine casks. In England 80 sheep cost 400 wine casks, or 1 sheep costs 5 wine casks. Sheep are cheaper in England than they are in France. Since sheep cost half as much in England, England has a comparative advantage in sheep and should export them to France.

3. **Protectionist devices.** Despite the benefits of free trade, many nations restrict the flow of imports through a variety of protectionist devices such as tariffs, quotas, voluntary export restraints, and governmental regulations.

a. **The GATT.** The U.S. has been a leader in the free trade movement, helping to establish the General Agreement on Tariffs and Trade (GATT) in 1947. GATT provides an organization for promoting free trade through simultaneous negotiations among all members.

(1) **Trade among GATT members.** Today more than 80 percent of world trade is carried on by nations associated with GATT.

(2) **GATT and the reduction of tariffs**. The World Bank credits GATT with helping to reduce tariffs on manufactured goods from a world average of 40 percent in 1947 to 5 percent today.

b. **U.S. protectionism**. Despite the U.S. official position on free trade, it has put significant non-tariff barriers on imports. Some restrictions are very old, like U.S. book manufacturing protection (1891); while others, like domestic automobile protection, are more recent (1980s); but all cost the consumer significant amounts of money—$500 million for book manufacturing and $5.8 billion for autos.

c. **The high cost of protectionism**. Saving domestic jobs has been a powerful argument in favor of protectionism, but according to recent research, the cost per job saved has been very high. Estimates of the cost of saving a worker's job varies from a low of $30,000 in the rubber footwear industry to a high of $750,000 in the steel industry.

B. **International exchange rates**. International currency exchange rates are regulated by some governments and not by others. As the value of a currency rises and falls, economic consequences follow.

1. **Government policies regarding exchange rates**. The value of a nation's money can be expressed as a price in terms of another nation's money. This price is called the exchange rate. Exchange rates may be allowed to float in a free market based on the supply and demand of the currency, or the government may allow them to fluctuate within a price range (managed float), or they may be set (pegged) by the government.

2. **Consequences of exchange rate fluctuations**. If one nation's currency, the dollar for example, begins to buy more of another nation's currency, we say the dollar is becoming "stronger." A stronger dollar is good news for U.S. consumers who can buy imported goods more cheaply, and who can depend on lower priced imports to help fight inflation. A stronger dollar is bad news to U.S. firms and workers who find their products becoming more expensive overseas, and therefore less competitive in world and domestic markets. A weaker dollar favors U.S. production at the expense of consumption. In the case of travel, a strong dollar makes it cheaper for Americans to travel abroad; a weak dollar attracts tourists to the United States. Foreign tourism in the U.S. is a U.S. export; U.S. tourism abroad is a U.S. import.

C. **The balance of payments**. All nations that participate in foreign trade maintain a balance sheet that measures the value of exports and imports as well as the flow of financial resources with the rest of the world.

1. **Balance of payments accounts**. The three major sections of a nation's balance of payments are the "current," "capital," and "official reserve" accounts.

a. **The current account**. The current account records the international exchange of all goods and services, as well as all income transfers across the nation's borders. The difference between the export of goods and the import of goods is called the balance of trade. The balance of trade excludes services and transfers. A deficit or surplus in the current account must be offset by a surplus or deficit in the capital account plus changes in the official reserve account.

b. **The capital account**. The capital account records international investments. On the credit side, these investments include foreign direct investment in the U.S. such as Toyota building a new production facility for autos, as well as foreigners purchasing American stocks and bonds. The debit side of the U.S. capital account would include American firms or private individuals investing abroad in a similar manner.

c. **The reserve account**. The official reserve account shows the net change in the U.S. government's holdings of gold, special drawing rights, and foreign currencies.

2. **Deficits made up from other accounts**. Countries often run a surplus or deficit in their current or capital account, but the overall balance of payments adds up to zero. A deficit in one account is necessarily offset by a surplus in another account.

3. **The U.S. as a "debtor nation."** A deficit in the current account means that a nation must borrow from other nations via the capital account. If this

borrowing persists, it must eventually result in "debtor status" which means that the claims of foreign nationals on the resources of the debtor nation exceed the claims of the debtor nation on the rest of the world. In 1988 the U.S. economy became a debtor nation for the first time since 1913.

4. **Foreign acquisition of U.S. companies.** U.S. debtor status can be clearly seen in the series of American firms that have been acquired by foreign firms. MCA, Inc., owners of Universal Studios and Theme Parks as well as, at the time of purchase, the Yosemite Park & Curry Co., was purchased by a Japanese firm, Matsushita in 1990. Other American firms that have become subsidiaries of foreign multi-nationals are: General Tire by Continental Tire (German); Baskin-Robbins by Grand Metropolitan (U.K.); Citgo by Petroleos de Venezuela (Venezuela); Chesebrough-Ponds by Unilever (Netherlands); White-Westinghouse Appliances by Electrolux (Sweden), and Mack Trucks by Renault (France).

5. **Competing successfully in international markets.** International economic isolation would not solve the U.S. balance of payments problems. Many U.S. firms compete successfully at the international level. The following U.S. multi-nationals earn more than 30 percent of their profits from foreign sales: IBM, Exxon, Dow Chemical, Eastman Kodak, Dupont, Coca-Cola, Johnson & Johnson, Goodyear, H.J. Heinz, Gillette, and Xerox. The answer to international competition, most economists believe, is to become more productive, not more restrictive.

Historical Perspective

I. **The Medieval economy.** Medieval society illustrates economics in a tradition-based society.

A. **A limited agricultural economy.** Production was largely subsistence agriculture. Markets were very limited in Europe, and the emphasis was on continuity, protection, and stability. The feudal system can be seen as a contract between the lord of the manor and his peasants where the noble provided protection and adjudication of disputes in exchange for labor and tax revenue.

B. **Lack of significant economic growth.** The economy was viewed as a zero sum game where the winnings of some equalled the amount lost by others.

1. **Vilification of the rich.** Since it was a zero sum game, the rich were vilified. Religious writings dictated the economic philosophy of the time. The biblical passage saying that "It is easier for a camel to go through the Eye of the Needle than for a rich man to enter the Kingdom of Heaven" was cited to bolster the case against the wealthy.

2. **Wealth as theft.** Wealth was considered to be stolen from other less fortunate souls. The attitude of organized Christianity toward trade was summed in the statement *"Homo mercator vix aut numquam Deo placere potest"*—"the merchant can scarcely or never be pleasing to God."

3. **Attempts to eliminate lending at interest.** Usury, originally the process of lending money at interest, was declared a mortal sin, and charging more, or paying less, than the "just price" for an item was considered sinful.

C. **The modern influence of "normative economics."** The judgmental or "normative" economic philosophies of the medieval period influence the modern economy in such legislation as rent controls, excess profits taxes, and minimum wage laws.

II. **The emergence of a mercantilist economy.** The economy of early modern Europe was influenced by the doctrines of mercantilism.

A. **The ideas of mercantilism.** Mercantilism was the first set of economic doctrines created to guide rulers and set state policy. Its tenets were developed in the sixteenth and seventeenth centuries in Western Europe. Mercantilist tenets preserved some of the medieval notions such as those that implicitly viewed the economy as a zero sum game, but they added new ideas on the importance of trade and the nation. Mercantilists favored a command style economy run by a strong monarch.

1. **"Bullionism."** Bullionism was a major concept in mercantilism. Mercantilists believed that the nation with the greatest accumulation of gold and silver would be the strongest and therefore most prosperous nation in the world. To achieve these riches, a nation had to pursue policies that limited imports of goods, and stressed exports. Goods that could not be produced domestically should be produced by subjugated colonies.

2. **Strong national government.** Mercantilists favored a strong national government that would protect their merchants, grant monopolies to favored merchants, regulate production and consumption, and wage war on other nations to disrupt their trade.

3. **Low wages desirable.** Mercantilists also favored policies that would depress domestic wages, believing that such low wages would provide the nation with a cost advantage in foreign trade. They did not recognize the importance of workers as buyers of the goods they produced. As the Englishman **Bernard de Mandeville** (1670-1733) wrote in his *Fable of the Bees* (1714), "In a free Nation where Slaves are not allow'd of, the surest Wealth consists in a Multitude of laborious Poor."

B. **Modern influence of mercantilism.** Mercantilistic theories continue to influence modern nations that see a surplus in their balance of trade as crucial to their prosperity, or who insist upon regulating economic activity because they fear unfettered competition may be harmful to the economy.

III. **The modern economy and analysis.** Modern economic analysis began with the "laissez-faire" (literally, "allow them to do" or "let them alone") school and proceeded to other schools of thought. Some modern economists have returned to the "free market" doctrines of Adam Smith and his followers.

A. **Classical economics.** Adam Smith is considered the founder of economics. His *Inquiry into the Nature and Causes of the Wealth of Nations* (1776) laid the foundation for modern economic analysis.

1. **Criticism of mercantilism.** Much of *The Wealth of Nations* criticizes the basic premises of mercantilism. Classical economists see the economy as a positive sum game based on specialization and the division of labor. Smith's classic example of specialization involved a pin factory where, by dividing the tasks, workers were able to produce an average of 4800 pins a day, whereas working independently they could not have produced twenty. The moral was that by participating in an organized system of production, everyone could benefit.

2. **Criticisms of government regulation and the "invisible hand" principle.** Smith was also highly critical of the wisdom of government regulation. He believed the economy worked best under the laissez faire principle, when citizens followed the "invisible hand of self-interest." Economic freedom was a highly prized element in his philosophy. It is more than coincidence that the date of the publication of his important book is also the date of the Declaration of Independence. Great minds around the world were rebelling at the imposition of mercantilistic regulations.

B. **The industrial revolution and beyond.** The industrial revolution created conditions for unparalleled prosperity.

1. **Effects of the industrial revolution.** The modern standard of living in today's developed nations is unequaled in the history of the world. Average life expectancy, health, income, and education levels are all unprecedented. Much of this advance is a direct or indirect consequence of the industrial revolution which began in England in the late eighteenth century and spread throughout the world over the next two hundred years.

2. **Standard of living and economic growth.** In the U.S. today, "the great majority of American families live on a scale that compares well with the way wealthy families lived 200 years ago." The source of this gain in living standards for the average American family can be traced directly to the growth of the American economy. Between 1840 and 1960, U.S. per capita national product increased at a 1.5 percent annual rate. Thus, in 1960 U.S. per capita GNP was approximately six times greater than it had been in 1840.

3. **The Great Depression.** The improvement in U.S. economic output was accompanied by periods of negative growth. Panics, recessions, and depressions were interspersed throughout U.S. economic history. The nineteenth century produced several significant business cycles, but none was more important than the period of stagnation that occurred in the 1930s following the Great Stock Market Crash of October 1929.

   a. **Gross unemployment.** Between 1929 and 1933, the U.S. unemployment rate rose from 3 percent to 25 percent, and real national output fell by 36 percent. But even in 1939, the U.S. economy was still operating well below full employment with an unemployment rate of over 17 percent.

b. **The advent of Keynes.** The Great Depression gave added importance to a new economic theory on national income determination developed by an English economist, John Maynard Keynes. His book *The General Theory of Employment, Interest, and Money* (1936) led to what became known as the Keynesian Revolution.

c. **Keynes' ideas.** Keynes argued that market economies would not normally reach full employment. Thus, he offered the prospect of long and continued depressions unless there was government intervention to manipulate aggregate demand. Even today, these demand-side prescriptions exert a strong influence on policy makers. In fact, it was the large deficit spending brought on by World War II (not the New Deal) that pulled the U.S. out of the Great Depression.

Contemporary Perspective

I. **Applied microeconomic theory.** Economists have proposed solutions to a variety of modern economic problems based on what they know about microeconomics.

A. **Environmental economics.** The public's perception of pollution problems has grown to crisis proportions, but until recently economists were not given much credence by environmentalists. However, because of their understanding of cost-benefit analysis, economists are uniquely positioned to offer some solutions.

1. **Marginalism vs. absolutism.** Economists think in marginal terms—a little more of this, or a little less of that. This is distinct from those who have an "absolute" point of view—all or nothing.

2. **Counting costs an economic necessity.** Economists view cleaner air or water as a good that can be purchased, but only when one understands that it has an opportunity cost. Economists would never agree with the statement that "protecting the environment must be done regardless of cost."

3. **Some degree of pollution inevitable.** A pollution-free society is unattainable based on the laws of nature—the "law of conservation of matter and energy" holds that nothing simply vanishes. If we wish to have production, we must learn to live with some pollution.

4. **Using resources efficiently.** Pollution standards that require a 100 percent reduction are the most costly. One study that focused on such a standard for benzene concluded that the OSHA benzene standard would result in one less death every three years, a noble accomplishment, but at a cost of $100 million each year. Economists view such regulations as a very inefficient use of resources. Many more lives could be saved at a lower cost by using resources in more efficient ways.

5. **The efficiency of market-driven policies.** Market-based approaches like emissions taxes and permits are much more efficient ways of limiting pollution and encouraging households and firms to preserve the environment. A law that forbids consumers to throw away their soft drink cans is not as easily enforced as one that establishes a deposit on the cans. Deposits encourage consumers to recycle. A refundable deposit puts the powerful self-interest motive to work for a less polluted environment, while minimizing the enforcement bureaucracy.

B. **Free trade.** Most economists argue that free trade is in the best interests of the vast majority of U.S. citizens. As Adam Smith wrote in the *Wealth of Nations*: "If a foreign country can supply us with a commodity cheaper than we ourselves can make it, better buy it of them with some part of the produce of our own industry, employed in a way in which we have some advantage."

1. **Protectionism not extinct.** Despite the clear advantages of free trade in terms of specialization, productivity, and output, many politicians still vote for protectionism—usually because their constituents may lose jobs which politicians find in their interest to protect. Most economists argue that such policies, consistently followed, in the end would hurt everyone.

2. **Protectionism and special interests.** The arguments for protecting U.S. industry are usually made by special interest groups trying to benefit at the expense of the public interest. But since the amount of the gain is concentrated on a small group, and the loss is dispersed over the general public, it is difficult to stop protectionist legislation.

II. **Modern macroeconomic problems.** Macroeconomic policy making is the area of least consensus within the economics profession. There are several distinct schools of thought regarding the proper role of government in the macroeconomy. A literate citizen should be aware of their basic positions.

A. **Demand-side economics: the Keynesian view.** Economists trained as Keynesians believe that the modern economy is intrinsically unstable, but largely driven by demand. Too little demand in the economy leads to recession; too much demand leads to inflation. They view the federal government as the only entity within the economy that can smooth out the business cycles caused by fluctuations in demand.

1. **Government expenditures.** By raising expenditures in a recession, government can create additional demand when it is needed. Conversely, inflation can be slowed by a decrease in expenditures, although Keynesians will readily admit the difficulty of reducing expenditures.

2. **Taxation.** Tax decreases are the appropriate remedy for recessions and tax increases would help fight inflation—as long as the taxes did not fuel additional federal spending. However, Congress has shown little willingness to use Keynesian prescriptions when confronting inflation. Part of the reason clearly lies in voters' dissatisfaction with politicians who raise taxes.

3. **Monetary policy.** Partly as a result of their inability to convince Congress to adopt anti-inflationary fiscal policies, Keynesians have looked to the Federal Reserve Board to raise interest rates when the economy needs to slow down. High interest rates will slow spending, but they also result in increased unemployment.

B. **Supply-side economics.** Some economists are skeptical of government's ability to manage the economy. A subset of this group emphasizes the importance of government establishing the ground rules and then allowing the markets to work. They return to the laissez-faire ideas of Adam Smith and emphasize the deregulation of economic activity.

1. **The "Laffer Curve."** Some supply-side economists have gone so far as to argue that a cut in income tax rates will actually raise government revenues because people would work more and be less likely to defraud the Internal Revenue Service. The well-known Laffer Curve (after California economist **Arthur Laffer**) described this phenomenon.

2. **"Voodoo economics."** The income tax cuts enacted during the Reagan Administration were based on such supply-side theories. These were the same theories that George Bush once labeled "voodoo economics."

3. **Skeptical views of supply-side economics.** Economists do not doubt the importance of incentives in promoting economic growth, but they are generally skeptical of the grandiose claims made by supply-siders. Empirical evidence has not confirmed the claims that government revenues would rise once the income tax rates were cut. In fact, the federal budget deficit grew dramatically and the national debt doubled from one to two trillion dollars during the Reagan presidency.

C. **Monetarism.** Some macroeconomists doubt the efficacy of demand side economics without embracing the tenets of the supply-siders. Monetarists, for example, believe that it is the growth of the money supply that predicts the well being of the economy. Led by Nobel Laureate **Milton Friedman**, monetarists urge the Federal Reserve Board to adopt a monetary rule that ensures a slow but steady growth in the money supply. Monetarists deny government's ability to manage the economy.

D. **The national debt and the federal deficit.** Do we have anything to fear? The short answer is yes, we do have something to fear, if we allow gargantuan federal deficits to accumulate year after year.

1. **The deficit rise of the 1980s.** Tight monetary policy in the early 1980s was one factor that led to a dramatic recession in 1981-82. The federal deficit rose because expenditures for social welfare programs like unemployment compensation rose automatically while tax revenues declined. But even after the recession ended, the deficit continued to rise.

2. **Interest payments a growing percentage of the national budget.** In order to finance the deficit, the U.S. Treasury had to sell large amounts of government securities, and the interest payments on this debt became a larger share of the federal budget. Interest payments comprise more than 10 percent of federal expenditures, and 20 percent of these payments go abroad. But taxpayers get no benefits from interest payments other than the maintenance of the credit of the U.S. Treasury and the ability, therefore, to borrow more in the future. Later generations, which have not

benefited from monies borrowed in previous decades or centuries, will still be required to continue interest payments, from tax dollars or tax cuts that would otherwise be available to benefit them.

3. **Dangers of long-term federal deficits**. A federal deficit is understandable in times of recession, but not during times of high employment. The inability of Congress to control its budget led it to pass legislation (the Gramm-Rudman-Hollings deficit reduction legislation) that mandates a balanced budget, but which may or may not work or which might work only after trillions of dollars of further debt is accumulated. Such legislation would not be necessary if the electorate did not punish their representatives in Congress for dealing directly with the fiscal dilemma by either raising taxes or cutting expenditures.

C. PUBLIC CHOICE THEORY

INTRODUCTION

In all political systems there exists a potential conflict between a politician's duty (to promote the welfare of the nation) and his personal interest (to gain and retain power). Traditionally, democratic theory has argued that this potential conflict can be overcome by subjecting politicians to the periodic judgment of the voters, so that only by winning the approval of the voting public are they able to gain and retain power. It was argued that this powerful check would ensure that politicians promote their own interests only by promoting the good of the whole community. This is the political equivalent of Adam Smith's theory of the free market, according to which individuals pursuing their own interests are led by an "invisible hand" to promote the prosperity of the entire community.

In the twentieth century, political scientists have modified this simple model of democratic government by recognizing the important role that interest groups play in politics. Politicians today deal mostly with lobbies and try to retain power by cobbling together legislative programs that favor not so much a simple majority of citizens but rather a winning coalition of minorities. In the 1950s, **Professor Robert A. Dahl** coined the term "polyarchy" (rule by minorities) to describe this system. Dahl argued that polyarchy had many advantages: above all, it avoided the "tyranny of the majority" that some of the Founders feared would be the outcome of democratic government. Instead, polyarchy allowed all social groups a voice in determining political outcomes. This open political system, it was theorized, would automatically register the existence of fresh minority groups once their preferences crossed a publicly visible threshold of intensity. In this view, the "public interest" had no ultimate reality beyond the agreements that the democratic political system allowed the interest groups to make.

In recent decades this belief that interest group activity was essentially benign and consistent with liberal-democratic values has come under increasing criticism from "Public Choice," a school of political economy based principally at the Center for Study of Public Choice at George Mason University, under the direction of **Professor James Buchanan**, winner of the 1986 Nobel Prize in Economics. "Public Choice" theory predicts that where the Constitution fails to impose appropriate limits of government, interest groups in collusion with politicians and bureaucrats will exploit the powers of government to redistribute resources towards themselves at the expense of the general public and future generations of citizens. Democratic checks are regarded as no longer operating; the duties of politicians are regarded as conflicting with their personal interest. Public Choice further argues that government intervention in the economy, while often justified as a cure for "market failure," is questionable since it is not assured that government can produce superior outcomes and typically produces worse ones.

According to Public Choice theory, the most obvious and serious indication of a breakdown in the democratic process is the federal budget deficit. Politicians acknowledge that the deficit should be eliminated, but many are driven by self-interested deals with pressure groups to oppose the policies—like tax increases and spending cuts—that would decrease the deficit. The "invisible hand" mechanism in politics that promotes the good of the community has broken down, in this view, and will not be repaired until the Constitution is amended to prohibit budget deficits and upper limits on taxation are imposed.

OBJECTIVES

The citizen should be able to

1. explain the incentives that confront politicians and voters at different stages of the political process.

2. explain the underlying constitutional make-up of the political system; that is, not just the written rules of the Constitution but also its unwritten conventions.

3. explain the relationship of political outcomes to political processes and interpret outcomes in light of the interests of the actors, the incentives that confront them, and the constitution that shapes those incentives.

4. identify and explain areas of constitutional weakness, that is, areas where reform is needed to ensure that political actors have incentives to behave in ways that do not harm and may promote the public interest.

5. take, defend, and evaluate proposals to reform our constitutional system, e.g., one term Presidency, limitations on terms of legislators, line item veto.

FRAME OF REFERENCE
Conceptual Perspective

I. **Political actors**. Public Choice theory is often characterized as "the application of the methods of microeconomics to the study of politics." This means that participants in politics are assumed to have the same motives as

participants in economic life: predominantly self-interest, but also a degree of altruism. (This assumption is in deliberate contrast to that of traditional political philosophy and of much modern political thought as well. This contrast is explained below in the Historical Perspective.) The term "Public Choice" is meant to convey the application of the techniques of studying "private" choice to the public realm. Sometimes this method is called "**methodological individualism**." The following are considered by Public Choice theorists to be the primary actors involved in the democratic political process.

A. **Politicians**. Politicians are conceived of as entrepreneurs, seeking to maximize political "profit," that is, power and influence. They do not necessarily adopt those policies and programs they believe are "right," but those they believe will maximize the support they receive from voters and other politicians. **Political parties** are conceived of as "corporations"—groups of entrepreneurs seeking to maximize their gains through cooperative effort.

B. **Voters**. Voters are conceived as "buying" policies with their votes, as consumers buy goods with money. Again, voters are assumed to support those policies that give them the greatest satisfaction as individual voters, which may or may not coincide with the general good of the nation.

C. **Interest groups**. Interest groups form the third principal group of political actors in Public Choice theory. Interest groups share the characteristics of both politicians and voters. They act as entrepreneurs to bring together groups of citizens around certain shared interests. They also offer their support to politicians in exchange for favorable treatment.

D. **Bureaucrats**. Bureaucrats are a fourth important group of actors for some Public Choice theorists. They are assumed to be in the business of "empire-building" like corporate managers, constantly exploiting opportunities to increase the amount of resources they control.

II. **The political process in Public Choice theory**. Constitutionally, **elections** are the crucial process in a democratic system, since it is here that the citizens choose their representatives. But Public Choice theorists tend to regard elections as little more than the rubber-stamping of decisions made elsewhere in the system through the informal processes of **interest-group formation** and **logrolling**. In this they are not unlike more conventional political scientists such as Robert Dahl, but their interpretation of these processes is very different.

A. **Methodological individualism**. The concept of **methodological individualism** is most important in understanding Public Choice theory.

1. **Groups as basic units of analysis**. Conventional political scientists such as Dahl and others adopt a sociological perspective that sees groups as the main elements in society; and like society as a whole, these groups are held together by shared norms and values.

2. **Individuals as basic units of analysis**. Public Choice, in contrast, considers individuals as the fundamental elements in society. Individuals, of course, act collectively to secure shared goals, but group behavior cannot ultimately be explained except by reference to the incentives that prompt individual members to cooperate. In short, individuals will cooperate in groups to achieve shared goals only when the benefits of such cooperation outweigh the costs to them **as individuals**.

B. **Interest-group formation**. The main Public Choice critic of the standard interpretation of interest-group activity as a benign aspect of democratic politics is Mancur Olson. In *The Logic of Collective Action* (1965) Olson attempts to refute the "polyarchic" analysis of interest-group formation. He argues that in the real world only certain kinds of groups are able to organize, and these groups secure benefits for themselves mainly at the expense of the general public.

1. **Why all groups cannot organize: the role of size**. Why can only certain groups organize? The crucial factor is not the **intensity** of the preferences of the group members but the **size** of the group. According to Public Choice, what counts is not the balance of benefits over costs for the group as a whole, but the balance for the **individual member**.

   a. **Ease for small groups to organize**. Small groups can organize easily, since the resulting benefits for the members who take the initiative exceed their shares of the costs of organizing.

   b. **Difficulty for large groups to organize**. Organizing large groups is more difficult, since the members who take the initiative often find that their shares of the potential benefits are not only relatively small, but are also exceeded by their shares of the organization costs.

2. **Latent groups**. Olson calls groups incapable of organizing for these reasons "latent" groups. Since they are not organized, "latent" groups are systematically excluded from the bargaining process. The most important latent groups are taxpayers and consumers. So, for Public Choice, Dahl's "polyarchy" turns out to be an unrepresentative form of minority tyranny after all.

C. **Logrolling**. The other main process identified by Public Choice theorists is called "logrolling" and likewise involves costs as well as benefits. In the process of logrolling, legislators exchange support for the lobby groups they represent among themselves. In this way the lobbies get the benefits they seek. However, the costs are passed on to the general public via taxation or borrowing. Whether logrolling is a benign process, as Dahl and others claim, depends on whether the benefits outweigh the costs.

1. **Interest-group influence as contrary to the public good.** Olson's doubts about the desirability of the results of interest-group bargaining are summarized concisely in the following passage from *The Logic of Collective Action* (1965): "Even if such a pressure-group system worked with perfect **fairness** to every group, it would still tend to work **inefficiently**. If every industry enjoys, to a fair or equal degree, favorable government policies obtained through lobbying, the economy as a whole will tend to function less efficiently, and every group will be worse off than if none, or only some, of the special-interest demands had been granted. Coherent, rational policies cannot be expected from a series of separate *ad hoc* concessions to diverse interest groups."

2. **Public Choice and the costs of group bargaining**. As noted above, conventional political science concentrates on the **benefits** of group bargaining. Public Choice also looks at the **costs** and finds that existing political processes may be systematically biased against taking costs into account. Thus, the free play of interest groups may not in fact produce the best outcomes.

3. **Why the political system ignores costs**. Why does the political system tend to ignore costs in this

way? Such costs might not be ignored if elections really did register the wishes of the majority—the "latent" groups of taxpayers and voters. But the legislative process has been largely influenced by lobbies representing special interests. Where there are no budgetary constraints on legislation favorable to these interests, logrolling by legislators is likely to get out of control.

4. **Costs as accruing to everyone; benefits to only some**. Political deals differ crucially from economic transactions between individuals in that in politics **everyone** can be required, via legislation, to carry some of the **cost** of the deals, while the **benefits** may be concentrated only on a few, that is, on effectively organized interest groups. Thus, political actors have little incentive to conclude deals that are efficient from the standpoint of the whole community.

5. **Legislative majority rule as producing inefficiencies**. In *The Limits of Liberty* (1975), James Buchanan has shown how easy it is for the simple majority rule to have the effect of over-all inefficiency. A sequence of legislative measures that pass through Congress may leave everyone worse off than if none had got through. This happens when the costs to each voter of those (few) proposals that the voter opposes exceed the benefits of the (many) proposals that the voter supports. One example is the construction of too many highways with federal funds. Logrolling delivers federally-financed highways to each state; but the overall result may be more highways than can be justified on strict cost benefit criteria, and the nation as a whole is the poorer for it.

III. **Some criticisms of Public Choice theory**. Commentators have levelled two significant criticisms against Public Choice theory, one theoretical and the other practical.

A. **Emphasis upon interest over ideas**. The theoretical criticism is that Public Choice unduly emphasizes the role of interests at the expense of ideas. Political outcomes are explained by reference to the special interests that benefit from them. But is this sound? How, for example, would Public Choice theorists explain the success of free-market policies in the 1980s, given that many such policies **conflicted** with the interests of some influential lobbies? Thus, Public Choice theorists would have had to predict in the 1970s that the privatization of state-owned enterprises would be vetoed by the many special interests in the public sector. Yet, during the 1980s, the privatization

movement swept the world, reflecting the widespread belief that the private sector was more efficient than the public sector.

B. **Ignoring public opinion**. Public Choice thus seems to ignore any role for **public opinion** in determining political outcomes. But if we accept that public opinion has a role, then we must accept that the ideas that influence public opinion are important. Public Choice has not really specified the conditions under which public opinion may be able to defeat the special interests that oppose it.

C. **Devaluing democratic rights**. Some commentators have claimed that the Public Choice assumption that political outcomes are determined by special interests and not by rational public debate devalues democratic rights like free speech. The Virginia School theorists would reply that rational debate can play a role in determining **constitutional** change. But if public opinion really is influential on ordinary political outcomes, then the budget deficit problem may possibly be soluble not by constitutional reforms but by political leaders persuading the public that budget deficits really are harmful. Already there is some evidence of voters accepting that certain problems can be solved only by higher taxes.

D. **The problem of special interest lobbying**. The practical criticism of Public Choice is that the constitutional road to reform is unlikely to solve the problem of special-interest lobbying. History suggests that constitutional limits can be eroded by ordinary politics. American Courts have failed to uphold the economic liberties enshrined in the Constitution. The Congress has already found many ways of getting around the Gramm-Rudman-Hollings law; why shouldn't they do the same with a balanced-budget requirement enshrined in the Constitution? This practical criticism supports the theoretical criticism in that it suggests that governments will balance their budgets if and only if public opinion demands it: constitutional limitations appear to work only when they reflect the broad consensus of society.

Historical Perspective

The Public Choice assumption that political outcomes are determined by processes in which actors promote their individual interests is not at all new. But it has always had to compete with a different view of politics according to which outcomes are determined by governments acting directly to promote the good of the whole community.

I. **Plato's "Philosopher-Kings."** The latter view of politics was given its most famous exposition by the ancient Greek philosopher **Plato** (427?-347 B.C.) in his work *The Republic*. Here Plato stated his view that the ideal state is one ruled by philosophers. He argued that rule by philosophers was desirable not merely because they were the wisest individuals, but because—thanks to their proper selection and their education—they were **incorruptible**. Their devotion to truth was so great that they had no self-interest to advance and so would use their political power solely to promote justice and the common good.

II. **Machiavelli and Hobbes.** Modern political philosophy has been strongly influenced by two thinkers of the early modern period: **Niccolo Machiavelli** (1469-1527) and **Thomas Hobbes** (1588-1679).

A. **Machiavelli's denial of moral politics.** Machiavelli saw politics as the pursuit of power and influence, an endless game from which some won and others lost (and most winners eventually became losers). It was governed by its own standards that were quite distinct from traditional Christian morality and largely in conflict with it. For Machiavelli, the attempt to unite politics and morality inevitably fails: the moral life is possible only as a **private** pursuit.

B. **Hobbes' affirmation of "moral" politics.** Like Machiavelli, Hobbes interpreted political life in individualist and power-seeking terms. But, unlike Machiavelli, he thought politics could be reconciled with morality: the laws of God (or "laws of nature") were also "precepts of reason" that guided humanity towards its own preservation. To Hobbes, morality is rational, collective self-interest: in circumstances of law and order, self-interested behavior promotes the common good. Hobbes' identification of morality with self-interested behavior, however, was quite idiosyncratic.

III. **The Keynesian Revolution.** The Hobbesian view of human nature prevailed for several centuries.

A. **Influence of the idea of human nature as self-interested.** The view of human nature as self-interested was espoused, with some modifications, by the classical political economists of the eighteenth and early nineteenth centuries, who wanted government to restrict itself to a few essential tasks, with little interference in the lives of individuals.

1. **Framers of the U.S. Constitution.** The American Constitution was drawn up by thinkers who thought it best to **assume** that people were in-

clined to wickedness and corruption (even if in practice most of them were not). A version of this view is found in the famous No. 51 of *The Federalist*, where Madison writes, "But what is government itself but the greatest of all reflections on human nature? If men were angels, no government would be necessary."

2. **British Utilitarians.** British Utilitarians such as **Jeremy Bentham** (1748-1832) and **James Mill** (1773-1836) espoused radical democratic reforms in which politicians would be motivated by fear of electoral dismissal to govern in the public interest.

B. **Twentieth-century view that unrestrained politicians can promote public good.** But during the twentieth century a more traditional view of government gained currency in some quarters, according to which politicians and their advisers could best promote the common good if they were **unrestrained** by constitutional checks and limits.

1. **Role of the Great Depression.** The event that gave this viewpoint a decisive impetus was the Depression of the 1930s. At the time, the Depression was blamed on the strict "economic constitution" that politicians observed, consisting of rules that forbade budget deficits and arbitrary government intervention and fixed the currency to the gold standard.

2. **Ideas of Keynes. John Maynard Keynes (1883-1946),** the brilliant British economist and civil servant, argued that the "economic constitution" could be safely ignored and budgets allowed to go into deficit **for short periods** so as to counteract the economy's boom-slump cycle and sustain employment levels.

IV. **The Public Choice critique of Keynes.** Public Choice theorists argue that the "Keynesian Revolution" has turned out to be a disaster in the United States, for two main reasons.

A. **The persistence of inflation.** First, unlimited economic intervention by government has led to persistent **inflation** with no guarantee that employment levels can be sustained. In fact, a permanent threat to modern economies is **stagflation**, a combination of high inflation, low economic growth, and relatively high unemployment.

B. **The permanence of budget deficits.** Second, budget deficits have become **permanent** as special-interest lobby groups trap politicians in high levels of public spending and low levels of taxation. In this view, instead of wise politicians intervening to improve things, politicians appear no different from anyone else intervening in ways that make things worse. Thus, for Public Choice, the long-term problem is not "market failure" but "government failure".

Contemporary Perspective

Public Choice offers a perspective on modern government dysfunction. It purports to explain the intractability of the federal budget deficit. Public Choice sees itself as deliberately restoring the constitutional wisdom of the Founders, who put their trust not in individuals but in laws. Hence the emphasis in Public Choice theory on a new constitutional settlement that restores and entrenches the "economic constitution" worked out by the classical political economists.

I. **The malaise of democracy.** Public Choice explains the widespread sense of the futility and irrelevance of democratic politics in terms of a failure to balance the costs and the benefits of political outcomes.

A. **Government's failure to control costs.** Existing institutions are highly attuned to delivering visible benefits but not to controlling the corresponding costs.

1. **Benefits short-lived.** As a result of not controlling costs, the benefits of politics are short-lived and illusory, gradually overwhelmed by the slowly rising tide of costs. The system both raises people's expectations and fails to fulfill them.

2. **The public's assumption of unlimited government funds.** Citizens often seem to assume that governments have unlimited funds to dispense, when in fact its funds are limited by the productivity of the economy and by the willingness of citizens to pay taxes. The actual remark of a citizen opposed to increased taxes, "Let the government pay," illustrates the assumption of limitless government resources.

3. **Federal budget deficit as sign of democracy's malaise.** The federal budget deficit is the clearest manifestation of the democratic malaise. The benefits of logrolling have been continuously dispensed to the general public over the years. But the costs of the process have gradually accumulated and have begun visibly to outweigh the benefits. Critics argue that the budget deficit causes high interest rates, dampens the economy, unjustly burdens future generations, and gives government a permanent incentive to inflate the currency in a fraudulent attempt to reduce its debt burden.

II. **A constitutional reform agenda.** James Buchanan calls for a revival of what he calls the "constitutional attitude," that is, approaching reform by concentrating on political **processes** (on which a high level of agreement can be reached) rather than political **outcomes** (which often divide society between winners and losers). The following constitutional reforms have been promoted by Public Choice theorists.

A. **Balanced federal budget.** A balanced federal budget is the central Public Choice reform proposal. It would require all public spending to be covered by tax revenue rather than by the present combination of tax revenue and public borrowing.

1. **Control of logrolling.** Public Choice advocates believe that the immediate effect of the adoption of this reform proposal would be to control logrolling by bringing its costs quickly to the fore. Since a balanced budget requirement would control logrolling, lobby groups would have a much harder job securing their demands. Lobby group activity would diminish, enabling legislators to concentrate on issues of genuinely common concern.

2. **Gramm-Rudman-Hollings and balanced budget reform.** The balanced budget rule has been implemented at the legislative level in the form of the Gramm-Rudman Hollings act, whose framers were influenced by Public Choice. This law seeks to take the decision to cut public spending out of the hands of legislators, devolving it to an automatic process. However, law makers are strongly tempted to tamper with the law itself, allowing the budget deficit to continue to grow or to continue at high levels. Critics argue that only if the law is entrenched in the Constitution itself can it be made immune from political meddling.

B. **A two-thirds decision rule for Congress.** Another device for controlling lobby group activity that has been suggested is a rule requiring that measures pass by a two-thirds majority, rather than by the current simple majority.

1. **Simple majorities and ease of logrolling.** At present, the simple majority rule makes it relatively easy for logrolling deals to pass through Congress, even if their social costs exceed the benefits to the groups involved.

2. **"Weighted" majority and difficulty of logrolling.** A "weighted" (two-thirds) majority rule would make logrolling more difficult, simply because the more individuals involved in a decision, the less likely it is that some can benefit at the expense of others.

3. **Drawbacks of a unanimity rule.** A unanimity rule is theoretically ideal since it would make logrolling virtually impossible. But since it gives each member of Congress a veto, the costs of negotiating any agreement would be astronomical. Even deals that benefitted everyone might be impossible to achieve.

4. **Presidential enforcement of a two-thirds rule possible today.** The two-thirds rule is already used for some purposes, such as Senate ratification of international treaties and congressional overriding of Presidential vetoes. The President could easily implement this particular reform simply by announcing that all bills passed by Congress with a less than two-thirds majority would be vetoed. A two-thirds vote in Congress would be necessary to override such vetoes.

C. **Constitutional limits on the tax-transfer system.** This third reform would place agreed limits on the amount of tax revenue the government could collect and the amount of welfare it could dispense.

1. **Growth of the tax-transfer system.** The reasoning behind this proposal is that under the simple majority rule and the logrolling that it permits, taxes and transfers have grown beyond the level acceptable to the great majority of citizens.

2. **Guarantee of basic income in place of welfare system.** Public Choice thinkers believe that a constitutional referendum on this issue would decrease the share of the national product taken in taxes and also guarantee to each citizen a basic income which the present welfare system fails to provide, primarily because it is subject to logrolling.

D. **A greater role for citizens' initiative and referendum.** Public Choice theory tends to favor citizen initiative and referendum.

1. **Opening decisions to larger numbers.** As already indicated, Public Choice thinkers favor bringing as many individuals as possible into a decision in order to promote genuinely shared interests and to prevent some groups from benefiting at the expense of the general public.

2. **Decisions to be on rules, not on outcomes.** However, such decisions should ideally be taken on the rules of the game rather than on particular outcomes. Public Choice theorists argue that in thinking of what fair rules are, people subordinate their particular interests to those of representative citizens or citizens in general. Rules conceived in this way are likely to benefit everyone.

III. **Civic education.** Public Choice attempts to offer a significant lesson in civic education by highlighting the redistributive effects of most government interventions and stressing the costs that accompany political gains.

A. **Government intervention always at others' expense.** Public Choice argues that normally individual citizens cannot benefit from government intervention except at the expense of other citizens.

1. **Irrelevance of "good intentions."** According to Public Choice theorists, the "good intentions" of government in its interventions are not relevant in judging the outcomes of such interventions. The costs of government intervention cannot be eliminated by good intentions or by getting the "good guys" into office.

2. **Guarding against unrealistic expectations of government.** The assumption that political actors operate from normal private motives can guard citizens against the distractions of political rhetoric. This assumption may also prevent unrealism in people's interpretation of politics and in the expectations they have of the political process.

B. **Public Choice and political processes.** The constitutional attitude advocated by Public Choice directs attention toward the processes of politics and toward reforms from which everyone can genuinely benefit.

1. **Benefits promised from elimination of logrolling.** Public Choice theorists consider constitutional agreement to resemble market exchanges from which all parties benefit. Such agreement generates moral behavior from ordinary motives. It moves away from the narrow egoism of the present logrolling system, under which those who refrain from selfishness lose out and are made to subsidize those who are effectively organized to promote their own selfishness.

2. **Human nature and civic idealism.** Public Choice thus assumes that basic human motives which involve self-interest cannot be changed. But by reviving the constitutional tradition, Public Choice also attempts to provide for civic idealism.

D. GEOGRAPHY AND CITIZENSHIP[1]

Geographic ignorance results in voters entering polling booths unequipped to make important decisions [about] the problems facing our nation.

National Geographic Society (1988)

An understanding of human distribution over the earth, the fragile interrelationship with the environment, the different uses to which people have put different parts of it, the cultures and economies they have created, and the spatial interrelations which exist between and have influenced these patterns—or in a word, geography—has a fundamental place in the equipment of an educated person.

Rhoads Murphey (1982)

As you read this, take a look outside your window. What elements of the natural environment—hills, forest, lakes or rivers, clouds or rain—can you identify? What elements in the environment, such as buildings, roads, gardens, have been added by people? Geography is concerned with all of these elements and, perhaps more importantly, with explaining how these elements are related and how they affect our lives.

Geography provides a basis for understanding the world we live in: its physical environment, its various peoples and the way they live, and the way people interact with their environments. If fact, everything in the world that has a spatial element—everything that you can describe in terms of where it is located or where it occurs—is part of geography.

Salter and Kovacik (1989)

Geography, in its most basic expression, is the study of four fundamental elements that interrelate. The quartet is Place, People, Pattern and Process. The primary concern with Place comes from the fact that geography is a spatial science, and knowing where events occur tells us something about what has influenced their development. People are basic to all geography because it is through our perception of environments, resources, and potentials that we set in motion the transformation of the landscape. Patterns are critical to

---

[1]Adapted for CIVITAS from Joseph P. Stoltman, *Geography Education for Citizenship.* Bloomington, Indiana: The Social Studies Development Center, ERIC Clearinghouse for Social Studies/Social Science Education (1990). Edited for CIVITAS by Christopher L. Salter. Material on the history of geography and geopolitics added by the Center for Civic Education.

geography because it is through the observation and determination of the patterns on the surface of the earth that we begin to understand the impact of human activity, and the nature of the changes that we have wrought. Process, finally, provides the systematic means for analyzing the way in which these four components come together in the creation of the cultural—that is, the humanized—landscape. It is by understanding the landscape and its implications that we can begin to make intelligent decisions about the direction of land use and landscape change.

In a thematic sense, geography is the location of the place where we reside and the relation of that location to all other places. It is the physical and human characteristics of the places where we live, the places we visit, and other places in the world that we can only imagine. It is the relationship established between individuals or groups and the environment of those places. Geography includes the regions—both micro and macro—where we play out our individual roles as citizens.

Geography in its widest interpretation includes certain interactions between people and their environments on or near the earth's surface. All people depend upon and share common environmental elements of land, water, and air. Literacy and competency in geography are essential if citizens are to be equipped to determine the necessary tasks related to the natural environment and human concerns and efforts to modify the environments of the earth.

Geographic education complements citizenship. When geography and citizenship are joined, citizenship gains a potent and practical context which may be local, national, international, or global in its concern and practice.

OBJECTIVES

The citizen should be able to

1. identify the location of political, economic, or natural events.

2. explain how geography has shaped the past and continues to be a dominant force influencing events.

3. explain the interrelationship between geographic factors (e.g., physical, historical, cultural, and economic) and national and international politics.

4. explain how knowledge about geography and about geographic influence on politics developed from the fifteenth to the twentieth centuries.

5. explain the various geographic factors that should be taken into account in making decisions regarding land use and landscape change

6. take, defend, and evaluate positions regarding issues of public policy affecting land use and landscape change.

FRAME OF REFERENCE
Conceptual Perspective

The information and perspectives included in the attainment of geographic literacy are important to citizenship. Geography, as a discipline from the social and physical sciences that contributes to a more informed citizenry, has several unique characteristics.

I. **Fundamental themes.** The fundamental themes represent those aspects of geography that are most appropriate for school geography, whether taught as a separate subject or as part of the social studies. As such, they embody a major contribution of geography education to citizenship. These themes are the five fundamental themes derived from the 1984 *Guidelines for Geographic Education.*

   A. **Location: position on the earth's surface.** Absolute and relative location are two ways of describing position on the earth's surface. In many situations, identifying location, whether absolute or relative, is important. On a global scale, locations of major physical features (e.g., oceans, seas, rivers, mountains, plains, forests, or deserts) and important human features (e.g., countries, boundaries, population concentrations, or cultural regions) set the context in which social, political, and economic connections and relationships occur. For example, the location of an industrial complex may affect a town's fresh water supply.

   B. **Place: physical and human characteristics.** All places on earth have distinct physical and human characteristics that give them meaning and distinguish them from other places. This theme presents the physical landscape as that scene that has not been modified by human activity, while the other aspect of place is that composed of the cultural landscape, sometimes called the human or built environment. Taken together, characteristics of place provide keys to identifying and interpreting both basic and complex interrelations between people and their environments.

   C. **Human-environment interaction.** People modify and adapt to natural settings in ways that reveal their cultural values, economic and political circumstances, and technological abilities. The development and consequences of such human-environment interactions—these relationships between people and place—have an immediate bearing on common civic issues, both locally and in larger areas.

D. **Movement: humans interacting on the earth.** The most visible evidences of geographic interdependence and the interaction of places are the transportation and communication lines that link every part of the world. These linkages demonstrate the daily interaction between people and place through travel, communications, and commerce, during which they come into contact with tangible things, people, information, and ideas from beyond their immediate environment. The geographic and social changes that result from such movement have a profound effect on individuals and the community, and the country as a whole.

E. **Regions: how they form and change.** The basic unit of geographic study is the region. A region is a human construct. It is defined as any area that displays unity in terms of selected criteria. There are almost countless ways to define meaningful regions, depending on the issues and problems being considered. Regions define convenient and manageable units upon which to build our knowledge of the world. They provide a context for studying contemporary issues and current events. They frequently help to establish identity and, as such, have powerful influence over the ways people decide to participate in significant decision-making processes.

II. **Essential skills.** The skills recommended for use in geography education are applications of the content, concepts, and processes of the discipline. Geography education assists citizens in developing and presenting effective rationales, an important aspect of participating in group decision making and influencing public policy.

A. **Looking at the world through geographer's eyes.** Fundamental to being able to utilize geographic knowledge is understanding the way in which a geographer views the world. A simple quartet of skills sets the stage for more effective evaluation of geographic facts.

1. **Observation.** No matter what question is considered, the geographer looks to see what visual elements are in the scene being studied. "What can be seen there? What is the nature of this landscape in question?" Whether in the field, looking at a photograph, or reading about an issue, the first step in any geographic equation must be an answer to "What is in this scene in front of me?" This leads to the next essential skill, speculation.

2. **Speculation.** Intelligent education requires that a person be able to make sense, oftentimes, out of incomplete data. "Why is there this pattern here? What has caused people to create such a landscape?" This act of speculation leads to a consideration of all that is observed, set in the context of a person's knowledge and beliefs. Questions come from this process which lead to the third skill, analysis.

3. **Analysis.** From the base of observation and speculation, a geographer decides what specific questions have to be answered in order to clarify the speculations that this exercise has engendered. This leads the observer to the library, to residents of the scene, to experts who have a greater knowledge of this setting. In that process, a fuller understanding is gained of the landscape in question, and the stage is set for the final skill, evaluation.

4. **Evaluation.** It is the step of evaluation that makes geography a vital cog in the education of a citizen. It is not enough to see and learn what makes up the heart of the scene in question, it is often essential to be able to make an assessment of its appropriateness as a humanized landscape. Decisions about land fills, airport expansion, tract developments, forest depletion, and countless other real world landscape modifications all evolve from the presence or absence of citizen interest and consequent participation in the decision-making process. If the role of the geographer is played out fully through the use of these skills, then each scene in question is taken through this four-lens filter and final evaluation is given the benefit of much more comprehensive understanding before decisions regarding change and development are made. These skills, therefore, are vital to intelligent and productive citizenship.

III. **Developing geographic skills.** Development of these skills derives from utilization of the following processes.

A. **Asking geographic questions.** Geography is distinguished by the kinds of questions it asks—the "where?" and "why there?" aspects of an issue or problem. Useful citizenship education encourages skills in asking such questions and searching for answers.

B. **Acquiring geographic information.** Skills requisite for acquiring geographic information include being able to identify location using grid systems, making observations and acquiring information during field study, and obtaining and organizing geographic information from different graphic modes, including maps, tables, photographs, and graphs. These data are increasingly computer-generated and continually grow in complexity and detail. A "geographic eye" learns how to read and see these data, just as an educated person learns to read the landscape of the real world in an effort to make more intelligent land use and landscape change decisions.

C. **Interpreting geographic information.** Interpreting involves the ability to discover what a particular map, table, or graph says or implies about the landscape question or issue being investigated. Interpreting information requires the development of a critical approach, examining information for its accuracy and the extent to which it represents major patterns or single occurrences. Pattern and process, people and place all have significance in these considerations.

D. **Developing and testing geographic generalizations.** Skills in developing and testing geographic generalizations include the ability to make inferences based on information presented in maps, tables, graphs, and in oral and written narrative form. These skills also include the development and testing of hypotheses regarding both observable and non-observable geographic characteristics of the earth, its environment, and human inhabitants. They involve the ability to distinguish those generalizations that apply at the local level from those that apply at a larger level. The geographer sees the system of landscape modification as part of a system of human intent to make the earth more productive, more satisfying, and more accommodating with every move. The fact that many of these moves—at both local and larger levels—do not achieve these goals, or achieve them at too great an environmental or social cost—is part of the geography that must be understood by all citizens.

IV. **Geography and spatial organization.** Geography is the only discipline primarily concerned with the spatial arrangement of and relationships between and among phenomena on or near the earth's surface. This is referred to as spatial organization. Spatial organization is important in making decisions about issues related to environmental perception, location, landscape change, and movement—issues that commonly affect citizens.

V. **Geography and a perspective on the world.** Geography and citizenship interact and complement one another in building a perspective on the world. In geographically informed citizens, this "world" includes local, regional, and national dimensions, as well as distant countries and peoples, linked together in complex ways to form a perspective on the whole earth. Without accurate geographic knowledge, such perspectives will be fundamentally skewed. Too narrow a view of the power of landscape change and design will make it difficult for the citizen to see the significance of geographic change and what it engenders.

A. **The idea of "geographic perspective."** In general terms perspective may be thought of simply as the way one perceives the world. Perspective is learned through formal education and as well as through the informal education provided by ordinary experience. Consideration of the geographic processes of observation, speculation, analysis, and evaluation will help to better develop a geographic perspective.

B. **Levels of perspective.** One of the most complex problems in citizenship is the determination of the realm in which one should invest energy and importance. Local perspectives on change need continual attention, and geography's attention to land use and landscape change prepare the citizen for productive involvement in that domain. However, the skills that lead to such involvement also prepare a person for intelligent and useful concern in larger areas of concern. The lessons of geography may be used at both spatial levels. The decision for involvement is to be made by the citizen.

VI. **Geography and global connections.** Complex and rapidly changing world conditions are characterized by webs of interactions between natural and human/cultural environments. Understanding the relationship between environmental and socio-cultural systems is important to understanding a range of civic issues and responsibilities.

A. **Environmental systems.** Among the social science disciplines, only geography provides a link between the natural and physical sciences (National Commission on Social Studies, *Charting a Course* 1989).

1. **The relationship of natural systems.** Understanding the connections of natural systems develops knowledge of the natural environment as a holistic, interconnected global system as well as of regional or local subsystems. Thus understanding one's community's dependence upon a limited supply of natural products (such as clean air, potable water, fertile soil, open space) supplied

by natural systems helps foster awareness of the universal dependence of all life upon complex interactions with their environments.

2. **Fostering a sense of responsibility**. Developing a perspective incorporating the natural systems all people on earth share fosters responsible citizenship through becoming aware of the consequences to the natural environment of such elements as economic production, consumption and waste disposal patterns, and public policy.

B. **Socio-cultural systems.** Socio-cultural systems link the world's people through a vast spatial network that includes political, economic, and social interaction. The spatial aspects of socio-cultural systems—the locations and distributions of activities by people and how they are linked across the earth's surface—are important to the geographic perspective and have significant applications to the more complete understanding of civic issues.

1. **Geographically varying political systems**. The world's division into political divisions includes units of widely varying size. Often geographic features have an important bearing on the delineation, development and character of political systems, political policies, and national character.

a. **Ancient Greek city-states**. One example of the influence of geography on political systems is the city-states of ancient Greece. These polities were divided and distinct largely in response to the country's mountainous barriers that separated these city-states and impeded effective communications between them.

b. **The United States**. Geography has played an immense role in American historical development, national character, and political life. Several examples among many are the following:

(1) **Optimism**. The large, open frontier, the availability of cheap land, and the seemingly limitless resources of the early centuries of national development are often credited with having a direct bearing on American character. For example, optimism amidst hardships and hazards was encouraged by the seemingly boundless prospects for land ownership and economic self-improvement.

(2) **Individualism**. It has also frequently been argued that frontier life and the continual renewal through migration fostered such traditional American characteristics as self-reliance and individualism.

(3) **Political isolationism**. Geography in the form of two vast oceans at the margins of the North American continent also played a direct role in traditional American political isolationism. Fortified between two ocean barriers for the first century and a half of their existence, Americans largely wished to remain aloof from the world, especially from European affairs. Such isolationist sentiment was responsible in great measure for the defeat of the Versailles Treaty in the Senate in 1919. Later in the century, faster transportation and improved communications considerably diminished the political isolation of America. But these developments have not eliminated the influence of geographic separation imposed by the Atlantic and Pacific oceans.

2. **Geographic interdependence**. People rely upon the environment for such essentials as food, clothing, and shelter. Knowledge of what products they depend upon, where those products come from, and how far they must be transported for production and distribution helps citizens understand the complex economic interrelationships that occur within and among countries. Our historic sense of relative isolation is being replaced by an increasingly broad linkage to global economic and political systems. Understanding these linkages with other parts of the world is essential knowledge of for a well-educated citizen.

3. **Geographic distribution of wealth and poverty**. The economic well-being of people varies internationally, regionally, nationally and even locally. Awareness of such differences fosters empathy for others and is a factor in shaping the citizen's perspective on the world.

a. **North-South relations**. The geographic factor in the distribution of wealth in the world economy is referred to increasingly in the familiar idea of "North-South relations." "North" and "South" refer to the nations of the northern and southern hemispheres, respectively. Most of the industrialized world lies in the north and much (though not all) of the developing world lies in the southern hemisphere or not far north of the Equator.

b. **The future of North-South relations**. A number of analysts believe that a key factor in the future of world affairs is the relationship between the developed nations of the northern hemisphere and their poorer neighbors to the south, often in the southern hemisphere.

c. **Geographic features of U.S. distribution of wealth**. Geographic features also shed light on the distribution of wealth within the United States. Examples include the variations between regions; between certain rural and urban areas; and between suburban and inner-city districts. Understanding of these patterns and their causes is further benefit of the learning of a geographic perspective on the local world.

4. **Geography and demographic shifts.** Americans have always been a mobile people. Changing environmental perception, more sophisticated telecommunications links with distant places, the increasing willingness to uproot and relocate, and the spatial shifts in American industry have all combined to cause major shifts in our population map. New political—as well as economic and social—influence is being manifest by the Southwest, the West Coast, Florida, and the Northwest as our national center of population moves further west and south. Geography is critical to understanding what these changes in centers of influence and power mean to the country.

VII. **Geography and civic participation.** Effective citizenship involves more than just participating in the electoral process. It also involves participation in policy decision making. A geographic perspective and knowledge can often contribute to more effective participation through the light they shed on political, economic, environmental, and social questions. In addition, knowledgeable civic participation is enhanced by the development of geographic skills in acquiring and using information, assessing involvement, making decisions, and making judgments.

A. **Acquiring and using geographic information**. Acquiring information entails obtaining data from sources that are known to be reliable. Using information entails making judgments about its appropriateness and organizing the information in a coherent manner. The

particular skills and discipline required for geographic studies encourage careful inquiry and provide a framework for organizing and thinking about facts concerning the interaction of people with the earth's environments and with one another at all levels of society and within the world at all scales. The human population shares a history of ever increasing landscape change. Change in one place sets in motion transformation at other places as well. Geographic knowledge helps us comprehend and anticipate such spatial relationships.

B. **Promoting involvement.** Involvement is an essential part of citizenship that varies greatly among individuals and groups. Geography helps the citizen to understand how decisions regarding land use and landscape change can stimulate such involvement.

C. **Making decisions.** Decision making of one kind or another forms a notable portion of the role of citizenship practiced individually and in groups. Geographic knowledge and skills provide valuable insight into decision making. Geographic knowledge and skills are involved, for example, in such issues as foreign trade, immigration and in an increasing variety of environmental questions.

D. **Making judgments.** Making judgments is one of the most frequently exercised elements of citizenship. The study of geography contributes to the making of judgments by helping to establish criteria related to how people move about in, respond to, and change the environment. On the local level, for example, an individual's criteria for what constitutes a safe and appropriate location for placing potentially dangerous or noxious industries, prisons, landfills, or similar facilities are affected by knowledge of geographic factors—both physical and cultural—involved.

VIII. **Political geography: Geopolitics**. Martin Glassner and Harm de Blij, noted political geographers, state that "Unfortunately, many people, including some geographers, confuse political geography with geopolitics. Geopolitics, however, is only one of the subjects studied by political geographers" (Martin Glassner and Harm de Blij, *Systematic Political Geography*, 1989). Political geography is a branch of human geography that is concerned with boundaries, the extent of territory, divisions, resources, internal and external political relations, and the effects of political actions on social and economic conditions. It has continued to develop as a sub-field of geography in the latter half of the twentieth century with a relatively more scientific methodology than that which characterized its earlier development.

Within political geography at the end of the nineteenth century there emerged two major strands of thought that were geopolitical in their makeup: geopolitics and geostrategy. Geopolitics came into being as a scholarly field of study during the period when a broader view of the world emerged among academics and policy makers, especially with regard to imperialist spheres of interest. Geostrategy, on the other hand, was based mainly upon geographic facts and how they could or should influence governmental policies. There has always been a certain inexorable geographic set of influences that worked upon political realities, and geostrategy is concerned with understanding, accommodating, or attempting to modify those influences. Geopolitics in this context refers generally to the role of geographic factors in political life. Such factors are often of considerable significance in international politics. Today the terms "geopolitics" and "geostrategy" are used interchangeably.

A. **The emergence of Social Darwinist and Imperialist geopolitical theory.** While ancient Greeks and Romans addressed political structure and geography in their writings, it was not until 1896 and the publication of *Politische Geographie* by **Friedrich Ratzel** (1844-1904) that Geopolitics within the context of Social Darwinism appeared. (Social Darwinism entertained the notion that those who reached the top of the social ladder translated, in this case, to the pinnacle of international power—deserved to, since they were the "fittest.") Ratzel's theory of the state was land occupied by people, people linked together through the ideas of the state. The state was equated with a biological organism that conformed to natural laws and physical boundaries, and with its development tied directly to the natural environment.

B. **The development of geopolitics and geostrategy as a theory.** Geostrategy introduced a global view of geopolitical affairs that developed with geopolitical theory among another group of scholars and writers. An early geostrategist was **Alfred T. Mahan** (1840-1914). A career naval officer, Mahan's major interest as a geostrategist was sea power. His interests in geography and politics were closely associated with the location of countries relative to oceans, coastlines, and their defenses; the development of naval and merchant marine influences; and the willingness of states to promote sea power. Mahan believed, for example, that the U.S. should occupy the Hawaiian Islands, control the Caribbean, and build a canal to link the Caribbean Sea to the Pacific Ocean—all policies eventually adopted by the United States. **Theodore Roosevelt** (1858-1919) was an ardent admirer of Mahan's Theory of Geostrategy and, as Assistant Secretary of the Navy and as president, influenced both U.S. domestic and foreign policy with his commitment to a strong navy and the construction of the Panama Canal.

C. **Modern geostrategy.** Theories of geostrategy influential earlier in the twentieth century were developed by Mackinder and Spykman.

1. **Mackinder's geostrategy.** Scottish geographer **Sir Halford John Mackinder** (1861-1947) advanced the thesis, now discredited, that world politics can be characterized as a continuing conflict between the powerful continental nations of inner Eurasia and surrounding maritime nations characterized by sea power. Mackinder proposed the theory that the Euro-Asian "Heartland" was the pivotal region in this struggle, and that the nation which controlled this "Heartland" would ultimately control the world.

2. **Weaknesses in Mackinder's theory.** Three major weaknesses plagued Mackinder's "Heartland" hypothesis. First, he underestimated the growing importance of North America. Second, he failed to consider the political and economic weaknesses of Russia/USSR until World War II. Third, he did not take into consideration the growing importance of air power and other new technologies. For example, Mackinder's hypotheses were based upon the Mercator map of the world, for that is the only way that North America could be considered distant from Eurasia. The relative location of North America and Eurasia changed greatly with the advent of air power and great circle aerial navigation.

3. **Spykman's geostrategic theory.** Nicholas John Spykman (1893-1943) took issue with Mackinder's theory and pointed out two basic weaknesses. First, he believed that Mackinder overemphasized the power of the Heartland. Spykman felt it would never reach its political potential due to major difficulties in developing internal transportation. Second, Spykman believed the real power potential of Eurasia rested with the area Mackinder had called the "Marginal Crescent." Spykman called this area the "Rimland." The "Rimland" area of northern, western, and southern Europe was vulnerable by both land and sea, and consequently had to develop land and sea oriented economies and governmental policies. Such a geography also stimulated the establishment of far reaching alliances. On a map of Eu-

rope, NATO is the practical application of geostrategic thinking.

D. **Contemporary geopolitical theory**. The term **geopolitics** (or geostrategy) is used today to characterize analyses of the geographic influences on the political problems and concerns of particular nations. The word is used by scholars, journalists, politicians, and others.

1. **The diversification of contemporary geopolitical theory**. Researchers interested in the role and influence of geographic factors in political affairs study the features of national and international politics which are influenced by natural boundaries, specific geographical characteristics, and the desire for control of strategically or economically important regions (for example, access to sea routes or control of oil fields). Contemporary geopolitics has become more diversified and interdisciplinary in its field of inquiry. It may now also include the influences of such elements as land and sea area, population, military deployment, production, transportation, and industry on national and international policies and power relationships.

2. **Hans Morgenthau and the role of geography in international politics**. An influential post-World War II theorist of international politics, **Hans J. Morgenthau** joined other scholars in attacking the geopolitical theories of Mackinder. But Morgenthau staunchly supported the idea of geopolitics as used today.

   a. **Importance of the geographic element**. Morgenthau warned against underestimating the geographic element in international politics, calling it "The most stable factor upon which the power of a nation depends ...." (*Politics Among Nations*, 1961). America's oceans might not isolate it as they did a century ago, but they are still a dominant feature of the nation's geopolitical position.

   b. **Examples of the geographic factor in European politics**. Other examples of the influence of geography cited by Morgenthau include the vast reaches of Russia, which have themselves conquered a number of would-be conquerors; the lack of natural barriers between Germany, Poland, and Russia, which is another vital geographic fact of that area of Eastern and Central Europe; and the English Channel, which has been a key geographic feature for Britain's security and political perspective. In addition, the Alps have separated Italy from the North and posed formidable barriers to invaders; and the Pyrenees mountains have separated Spain from the continent of Europe and have been instrumental in keeping that nation from European wars and in partially isolating Spain's development.

Historical Perspective

The study of geography reflects a basic human desire to investigate and understand the world. For millennia the human mind has been fascinated with the interaction of physical, biological, and human elements, the differences between various environments, and the cultural, social, economic, and political patterns which occur in these environments. Early geographers, whether assuming the role of explorers, travellers, philosophers, or scientists, made observations about the earth's landforms, climates, bodies of water, natural vegetation, and animal life. They also provided the groundwork for later descriptions and analyses of human populations and their interactions with the environment, such as the development of agriculture and technology and the influence of geographic factors on social and cultural institutions.

The composite of all these various geographic influences came together in a nation's—or locale's—politics. In trying to understand the personality of these places, the citizen is greatly benefitted by geographic understanding. The development of such a geographic perspective and knowledge has spanned a long time and knowledge from the past still has an influence on what occurs today.

I. **Ancient geographers and philosophers**. Since the beginning of recorded history—and certainly for eons preceding writing, human beings have attempted to chart, explore, and understand the physical features of the earth. The accounts of travelers and philosophers provide the earliest record of the attempt to comprehend the earth as a physical body and to understand other lands and peoples.

A. **Early explorers**. Egyptian, Phoenician, and possibly Chinese explorers journeyed great distances by sea prior to 1500 B.C. Archeological evidence suggests that Phoenician ships sailed to England prior to 800 B.C. and made voyages around Africa by 600 B.C. Early explorations such as these contributed to the development of geographic knowledge.

B. **The geographic observations of Herodotus**. In the fifth-century B.C., the Greek writer and traveler **Herodotus** (c. 482-420 B.C.) provided detailed geographic observations of his many travels to other lands. These documents are among the earliest of such accounts and inspired later geographic descriptions and explorations. Herodotus, along with **Hecataeus** (c. 500 B.C.), who also wrote a treatise on geography, are often described as the "fathers" of the study of geography.

C. **Early Greek concepts of the earth**. The ancient Greeks not only attempted to describe various geographic regions of the world but also speculated about the shape of the earth and its relationship to other heavenly bodies in the cosmos. For instance, the philosophers **Pythagoras** (d. 497 B.C.) and **Aristotle** (384-322 B.C.) postulated that the earth is a sphere, a theory so advanced that it only became accepted by the scientific community centuries later.

D. **Eratosthenes' calculations of the earth's circumference**. In the third century B.C., **Eratosthenes of Cyrene** (c. 276-194 B.C.) corroborated earlier theories of the earth as a sphere by producing an extremely accurate calculation of the earth's circumference. Eratosthenes' deductions were expressed in his *Geographica* (meaning "earth description"), the first treatise to use the word geography as a title of a major work.

E. **Strabo's treatise on geography**. Around the time of Jesus of Nazareth, the Greek geographer and historian **Strabo** (c. 64 B.C.-A.D. 23) wrote a monumental seventeen-volume treatise on the geographic knowledge of the time. Strabo reviewed earlier Greek and Roman works on geography, characterized the methods and goals of geographic inquiry, and provided lengthy descriptions of various geographic regions.

F. **Ptolemy's tabulations of latitude and longitude**. In the second century A.D., the Greco-Egyptian geographer and astronomer **Claudius Ptolemy** (c. 110-150 A.D.) developed the theory that locations could be accurately tabulated through latitude and longitude. However, this and other theories by Ptolemy (for example, that the earth is at the center of our planetary system) were not necessarily reliable and led geographers astray until the fifteenth and sixteenth centuries, even though the world maps he created were really the first steps in our cartographic understanding of the globe.

G. **Advances by Arab geographers**. During the eleventh and twelfth centuries, Arab geographers perpetuated and advanced the study of geography, preserving much of the geographic knowledge of the Greeks which had been lost during the decline of the Roman Empire. European contacts with Arab learning during the First, Second, and Third Crusades (c. 1095-1192) stimulated a renewed interest in the study of geography.

H. **Early explorations**. In the Medieval era geographic knowledge and exploration did not make great advances in Europe. The discoveries of the Vikings, however, form an exception. The Vikings explored and raided the European coast in 900 A.D., **Eric the Red** (fl. tenth century) sailed to Greenland in 985 A.D., and Viking ships are believed to have reached North America by the year 1000 A.D. The adventures of the Italian traveller **Marco Polo** (c. 1254-1325) near the end of the thirteenth century helped revive interest in geographic exploration and discovery, particularly in the designing of accurate navigational maps.

II. **Cartography, topography, and the exploration of earth**. In the fifteenth and sixteenth centuries, the study of geography became an increasingly systematic discipline as the result of the developments in cartography and topography. From the fifteenth to eighteenth centuries, numerous explorations and voyages also furthered the knowledge of the world.

A. **The age of geographic discovery**. The fifteenth and sixteenth centuries are often considered to be the "Golden Age of Exploration," an era in which the knowledge of the world increased enormously. Improvement in the design and use of the magnetic compass, map projections, and ship building initiated an exploratory fervor throughout Europe and beyond.

1. **Fifteenth-century explorers**. Early explorers included the Italian navigator **Christopher Columbus** (1451-1506), credited with discovering America, and the Portuguese voyager **Vasco da Gama** (?1469-1524), who sailed around Africa to India. **Amerigo Vespucci** (1454-1512), from whom the name of the American continents is derived, was an Italian navigator who made several journeys to the New World between 1499-1502.

2. **Sixteenth-century explorers**. In the sixteenth century, explorers included **Vasco de Balboa** (1475-1519), who sighted the Pacific; **Hernando De Soto** (1496?-1542), who explored what is now Mexico and the Southwest; **Ferdinand Magellan** (1480?-1521), who proved the earth to be spherical by circumnavigating it; **Giovanni da Verrazzano** (c. 1485-1528), who explored the coast of North America for France; **Sir Francis Drake**

(1540?-1596), who was the first Englishman to circumnavigate the globe; and **Henry Hudson** (d. 1611), who, sailing for the Dutch, explored the Hudson River region of New York and parts of Canada. These figures, among others, added greatly to the geographic knowledge of the period.

B. **The first world atlas.** In 1570, the Flemish cartographer **Abraham Ortelius** (1527-1598) created the world's first atlas (*Epitome of the Theatre of the World*) by binding together numerous maps of regions of the world in book form. His contemporary and traveling companion, **Gerardus Mercator** (1512-1594), also from Flanders, was the most prominent cartographer of the sixteenth century and coined the term *atlas* (derived from the depiction on the frontispiece of many early atlases of the Greek god Atlas holding up the heavens).

C. **Varenius'** *General Geography*. In 1650, the German geographer **Bernhardus Varenius's** (1622-1651) *General Geography* was published. This volume, which was based on detailed observations and measurements, set the precedent for later geographic works and remained a prime reference work for over a century.

D. **Topographic surveys by the Cassini family.** From the end of the seventeenth century to the late eighteenth century, generations of the **Cassini** family (**Gian Domenico** [1625-1712], **Jacques** [1677-1756], and **Cesar-Francois** [1714-1784]) of astronomers and surveyors in France developed accurate methods for surveying land surfaces. The Cassinis conducted a topographic survey of France (the first survey of a large nation) which became the basis for the national atlas of France published in 1791.

E. **The scientific voyages of Captain Cook.** English navigator and explorer **Captain James Cook** (1728-1779) established new levels of expertise and precision at sea through his three scientific voyages to the Pacific (1769-71, 1772-75, 1776-79). Cook circumnavigated the globe, conducting geographic exploration and research in the North and South Pacific, the Antarctic, and along the coasts of New Zealand and eastern Australia.

III. **The beginnings of modern geography.** Many of the highly formulated methodological and theoretical approaches used by geographers today have their origins—at least in part—in the eighteenth and nineteenth centuries.

A. **Humboldt's methodology.** At the end of the eighteenth century, **Alexander von Humboldt** (1769-1859) began his explorations of the earth, which were based on direct field observation, precise measurements of geographic phenomena, systematic and detailed descriptions, and a sophisticated analysis of the relationships of altitude, temperature, flora and fauna, agriculture, human populations, trade, and the differential uses of resources. The monographs he produced as a result of his surveys of South and Central America (1799-1804) provided the foundation for modern geography, which stresses the importance of direct observation and accurate measurements from which theoretical generalizations are then made.

B. **Kant's promotion of geography.** The eighteenth-century German philosopher **Immanuel Kant** (1724-1804), in his seminal *Critique of Pure Reason*, argued for the importance of geography as a scientific discipline. Kant maintained that geographic study of phenomena located in space (i.e. the external world) was a necessary complement to the historical analysis of phenomena located in time.

C. **University support for the study of geography.** The flourishing of European universities in the early nineteenth century produced geography specialists who not only taught but conducted original geographic research. Von Humboldt, for instance, lectured on physical geography at the University of Berlin, which later established the first chair of geography at a modern university. By the late nineteenth century, universities in many European countries had established chairs in geography.

D. **The founding of geographic societies.** As a result of the increasing numbers of university teachers and specialists, geographic societies were soon formed, for example, in France (1821), Germany (1828), England (1830), Russia (1845), and the United States, where the **American Geographical Society,** founded in 1851, promoted geographic knowledge through lectures and publications. Also in U.S. the **National Geographic Society** was established in 1888 with the goal of promoting geographic knowledge. The Society, which has now over 10,000,000 members, supports various research expeditions and publishes the *National Geographic Magazine*, which features topics of geographic interest from around the world. In 1904 the **Association of American Geographers** was formed by the renowned geographer and geologist **William Morris Davis** (1850-1934) to promote the academic and scholarly study of scientific geography; and the **National Council for Geographic Education** was begun in 1915 to enhance the teaching of geography at all levels of the curriculum.

E. **The rise of government surveys.** In the United States and Russia, government surveys were employed to chart resources, natural features, and specific regions for future settlement.

1. **American surveys.** In the United States, **Thomas Jefferson**, who had an intense interest in geography, appointed **Meriwether Lewis** (1774-1809) and **William Clark** (1770-1838) to lead an expedition (the **Lewis and Clark Expedition** of 1804-06) in an exploration of the lands obtained as the result of the 1803 Louisiana Purchase. Later expeditions surveyed the western territory of the United States for potential railroad routes, settlement areas, and mineral resources. In addition, the first survey of modern oceanography (*The Physical Geography of the Sea*) was published in 1855 by the American hydrographer **Matthew Fontaine Maury** (1806-1873). In this same era, **George Perkins Marsh** published *Man and Nature* (1864) in which strong data were advanced for the major impact human effort was having on the natural flora and fauna—and landscapes—of the world.

2. **Russian surveys.** In Russia, the czar **Peter I "the Great"** (1682-1725) supported numerous geographic expeditions and publications in order to expand the knowledge of his country. The first geographic and economic survey of Russia was completed in 1727, and the first atlas of the Russian Empire was produced in 1734.

F. **The growth of geographic awareness.** While there was no true coherence between all of these various geographers, cartographers, explorers, and literate travellers, the knowledge and data that they brought to print, and to public awareness through lectures, began to change the geographic understanding of the world. As people took advantage of this new knowledge, they began to see the networks that humanity had established—and would continue to establish—through economic, social, and political interaction. By the end of the nineteenth century, geography had developed a strong position in American education.

IV. **Areas of contemporary geographic inquiry.** Geographic study in the twentieth century may be divided into three general areas of inquiry: physical geography, regional geography, and human geography. Geographic knowledge in human geography, particularly in the areas of **historical** and **political geography**, is of particular relevance for an informed citizenry.

A. **Historical geography.** Historical geography studies the changes in natural landscape over time and the relationship between geographic and cultural forces throughout history. The evolution and development of present social, cultural, and political patterns and landscapes are also dominant themes in historical geography. The most well-known example of the historical geographic approach involves analysis of the famous Domesday Book, which was a survey of culture and land use in England conducted in the year 1086. This early geographic document was created at the request of **William I the Conqueror** (1027-1087) as an inventory of the resources and lands of his country. It has provided a wealth of data for geographers interested in analyzing England's history through geographic records and reconstructing everyday life late in the eleventh century. Although the mid-eleventh century was the focus of the Domesday Book, the compilation and analysis of its data were developed within this century by H. C. Darby (*Domesday England,* 1977).

B. **Political geography.** The analysis of the relationship of geography to political organizations is called political geography. This field of research studies a wide range of subject areas, such as the relationship of geography to the organization of the world into states, the political alliances within nations, their divisions into political and administrative units, and the international relations between and among nations. Other areas of study concentrate on the history of "metropolitan" powers and their colonies, the bases of political power, issues of regionalism, separatist movements, and the ways voting patterns reflect the interests of people from specific geographic regions.

C. **Social geography.** The traditional interest in understanding the human forces that played a major role in the shaping of landscapes was part of cultural geography. However, in the recent decades new interest in the power of ethnic identity, urban residential patterns, and class differentiation in American society—particularly in the cities—has led to the emergence of **social geography.** In trying to comprehend the nature of life and spatial organization as well as economic interaction in city space, social geography has become very important. Traditional cultural geography is seen to be more frequently associated with non-urban settings, or popular culture while social geography attempts to deal with city realities as they exist today. For the citizen who is trying to make intelligent decisions about city resources, city land use, and landscape design, the themes of social geography bring many aspects of real moment to the fore. Ethnic and racial tensions, the problem of the underclass and the increasing gap between the wealthy and the unemployed or underemployed in American cities all receive attention in social geography. In this material the citizen can find important relevant urban themes.

V. **Geography in the American school curriculum.** Geography as part of the school curriculum has a long pedigree in the history of American education.

   A. **Founding a new nation.** Geography has been a part of American education since the seventeenth century, when it was introduced as map and globe study at Harvard College (founded in 1636).

      1. **Geography in elementary schools.** Elementary schools of the time found the subject, which most certainly included stand-and-recite memory exercises, ideally suited to the intellectual activities and abilities of children. A premium was placed upon geographic knowledge as one trait of a liberally educated citizen (Warntz, *Geography Now and Then*, 1964).

      2. **Geography and citizenship.** Early textbooks also presented geography as an important part of education for citizenship. *Geography Made Easy*, by **Jedidiah Morse** (1784), required students to memorize standard answers to standard sets of questions. The text was strongly biased in favor of New England, reflected religious orthodoxy, and was extremely conservative regarding morals—all essential characteristics of the idealized eighteenth-century New England citizen.

   B. **Geography and early public policy.** Geography education was often required by law in public schools in the early nineteenth century.

      1. **Legal provision for geography education.** After about 1830, several states enacted laws requiring the teaching of geography—often that of the home state—in the elementary schools (Rumble, "Early Geography Instruction in America," 1946). This legislation was an early example of public policy that mandated geography education, with citizenship development as a principal motive.

      2. **Study of local geography.** The study of local geography to enhance more effective citizenship in one's immediate area flourished during the period from 1820 to 1870. Map drawing, the study of the home region through direct observation, and experimentation using globes became the recognized

ways to teach geography (S. Rosen, "A Short History of High School Geography," 1957).

   C. **Shifting currents.** Later on, other trends in geographic studies appeared, especially physical geography.

      1. **Trend to physical geography education.** Toward the end of the nineteenth century, shifting emphasis within the discipline of geography resulted in greater attention to more scientific studies in physical geography and less attention being given to local studies. This trend perhaps weakened the early link between geography and citizenship.

      2. **Reenforcement of study of physical geography.** The trend toward physical geography was further reenforced by a report of the National Education Association's Committee of Ten in the late nineteenth century. The report, published in 1894, recommended that physical geography be the most important geography offering in secondary school. Worthy of note, however, was the minority report from the committee predicting that physical geography courses would not meet the cultural or intellectual demands of a changing citizenry.

   D. **Undercurrents of change.** Early in the twentieth century, the Committee of Seven of the Science Section of the National Education Association recommended greater emphasis on the response of human populations to physical geography; the interrelationship between peoples and the environment; examination of regional differences; and geography for all students. Strong support was given to geography's role in liberal education, which was in turn believed to be important to the development of an enlightened citizen. As a result, geography began to show its more humanistic traits through the people-and-places approach of regional geography (Chamberlain, "Report of the Committee on Secondary School Geography," 1909).

   E. **Emergence of social studies.** In 1916 the National Education Association's secondary school curriculum review included an assessment of the social studies movement and its role in the curriculum. As the writers of the report conceived of the subject, social studies was to represent a single field of study encompassing all the social sciences, without disciplinary boundaries. A major goal of the social studies, in which the social aspects of geography were included, was citizenship education (U.S. Bureau of Education, *The Social Studies in Secondary Education* 1916).

VI. **Geography's four traditions.** Geography as a school subject experienced a steady decline during the 1940s and 1950s due, in part, to a confusion among social studies educators about the nature of geography as a division of the subject (Winston, "Teaching and Learning in Geography," 1986). Because of the breadth of geographic concern, teachers and laymen alike had difficulty in seeing exactly what it was that geographers gave most attention to. W.D. Pattison helped to clarify the nature of the subject for educational purposes through his synthesis of the discipline into four dominant traditions.

A. **Geography as a physical science.** The physical science tradition of geography is concerned almost exclusively with natural elements and natural occurrences. Knowledge of physical geography makes one a more comprehending and observant citizen with regard to physical processes in the natural environment.

B. **Geography as human-environment relationships.** The second tradition of geography is concerned with the pervasive activities of people on earth. The human-environment tradition provides knowledge about how humans affected and were affected by the environment. This tradition provides an understanding of the range of choices a particular environment offers and includes the activities people have undertaken to change, control, harness, and use the earth and its resources.

C. **Geography as a spatial science.** The third tradition involves the organization and distribution of phenomena across the earth's surface, or earth space, and provides skill in analyzing patterns. The potential for geography to serve as a basis for decision making and critical thinking in citizenship rests in this tradition. The spatial tradition is concerned primarily with three aspects of the earth's surface: the location of something; the effect of location on people; and the effect of one location on another. Why are things located where they are?

   1. **Spatial patterns.** Many things have spatial patterns and relationships with other elements, including people and their patterns of behavior as shoppers, commuters, voters, and workers, to name only a few roles. All physical phenomena, as well, can be expressed in spatial patterns, so this theme serves as a foundation for geographic learning. Again, the blend of observation, speculation, analysis and evaluation comes to

   2. **Application of spatial relations.** Analysis of voter participation is one example of the application of spatial relations to the study of citizenship. Spatial analysis is also important in shaping civic responsibility in decision making involving, for example, selection of locations of schools or highways. The spatial tradition has much to contribute when citizens begin examining issues of land use, community change and development, resource depletion and utilization, and environmental modification.

D. **Geography as a regional science.** The fourth tradition in geography is the study of the region. The physical, social, economic, and emotional attachment of individuals to regions gives this tradition a powerful claim to developing citizenship. People who believe they have a vested interest in a region, whether it be a small hamlet, a farmstead, or the nation, are more likely to manifest involved citizenship. The study of regions provides a prominent descriptive element and a powerful analytic technique by which the complexity of physical and social conditions may be studied, thus enhancing the individual's competence as a citizen.

VII. **High School Geography Project.** In the 1960s, the High School Geography Project attempted to outline the basis for the return of the study of geography as an academic subject and to promote the image of the discipline as a subject critical to the management of the contemporary patterns of social and economic development.

A. **A national curriculum project.** The High School Geography Project (HSGP) was a national curriculum development project intended to demonstrate the academic foundations of geography as a discipline, present current ideas and thinking in the discipline, and involve students in doing real geographic problem-solving. In discussing the newly emerging project, Gilbert White ("Geography in Liberal Education," 1965) alerted fellow geographers to the importance of geography to active and effective citizenship by encouraging an "intellectual experience which we might wish for every citizen who seeks coherent methods of comprehending the world's diversity." The design of the HSGP from the very beginning reflected the belief that citizenship was an important education outcome.

B. **Practicing citizenship.** HSGP was a major attempt to reintroduce geography to the high school curriculum through the preparation of materials designed specifically for the secondary school. A major benefit of the project's inquiry approach to learning was that it involved students in practicing citizenship. For example, one activity entailed role playing in which students portrayed the citizens and elected officials in a hypothetical state. The activity was designed to enable students to address a major problem while balancing the special needs and concerns of five different regions within the state.

VIII. **Guidelines for geographic education**. The 1980s saw further attempts to include geography in the social science curriculum in the schools in light of widespread geographic illiteracy among youth. Surveys found that not only were school children geographically ignorant, but college students were plagued by the same unawareness of the world beyond the most local scene.

A. **Educational reform.** The late 1970s saw the beginning of several educational reform movements in the United States, including the back-to-basics movement in reading and mathematics. Geography was not greatly affected by the reforms until early in the 1980s, when the news media began carrying articles describing the geographic illiteracy of American students. Commentators repeatedly asked how effective U.S. citizens could be in the world economic and political arena when they were alarmingly ignorant of the geography of their own country as well as the rest of the world. The most significant product of this media attention was the decision of the National Geographic Society to take up the banner and begin—through teacher training, materials development, and heavy media attention—to prod American educators and curriculum specialists to give attention and curricular space to better geography education. In 1986 the Society began a steady expansion of a grassroots collaboration of classroom teachers, university geographers, and educational administrators built around the concept of the state Geographic Alliance. Many citizens became aware of the role and the importance of geographic learning because of the media attention given to the new Alliances.

B. **The guidelines.** The leading academic societies of geographers responded to this call for educational reform by publishing the *Guidelines for Geographic Education: Elementary and Secondary Schools* (Joint Committee on Geographic Education 1984). This publication offered a focus for K-12 geography and posited forty-six learning outcomes that could help guide the discipline's efforts to return as a significant subject in the American schoolroom. The *Guidelines* also suggested how the discipline could address the problems associated with the nation's low level of geographic literacy. As a part of the rationale for the *Guidelines*, it was noted that "training in geography gives us unique perspectives about places and their relationships to each other over time. It is an essential ingredient in the total process of educating informed citi-

zens" (*Guidelines* 1984). In the current climate of continuing media attention to the high costs of geographic ignorance, these concepts in the *Guidelines* and the strategies promoted have helped to greatly increase the geographic education made available to the American citizenry.

Contemporary Perspective

Every citizen possesses a personal geography. In each individual's perception of location or place where he or she lives, of landscapes that are favored or feared, and of the environment, the individual acts out a personal geography. This body of knowledge and preference has a number of discrete elements.

I. **Mental maps.** An accurate mental map of the earth's major physical and political features equips the citizen with a knowledge of where places are located as a means to understanding how the shape and location of land and water create critical relationships. Mental maps of geographic proximity of nations and the location of resources also inform the citizen's sense of nations' economic and security interests. These maps also give shape and meaning to places that have been heard of but not visited. One's mental map of a particular place is often a mixture of objective information and subjective imagination. As such, these mental maps are susceptible to the influences of popular culture as well as formal education.

A. **Citizen uses of geographic knowledge.** Citizens use geographic knowledge to shape their perceptions of the world in myriad ways. For example, a knowledge of the location of the earth's major mountains or deserts is a necessary antecedent to a perception of their role as barriers to cultural diffusion or protection from invasion. Awareness that Japan is an island country is key to understanding its history of isolation and cultural uniqueness. Likewise, a knowledge of the distribution of scarce resources leads to an appreciation of differences in opportunities and limitations among the world's countries and regions.

B. **Conflict, cooperation, and geographic relationship.** A knowledge of the political, economic, demographic, and historical relationships among places furthers an understanding of the potential of states or peoples for cooperation or conflict. Further, a knowledge of the relationship of one's own location relative to theaters of conflict or potential conflict contributes to one's sense of place in an interdependent world.

II. **A way of looking at the earth.** While an awareness of place is a starting point, geography's greater concern is with the spatial aspects and consequences of the human presence on the earth. Every geographic equation must begin with careful observation, thoughtful speculation, diligent analysis, and intelligent evaluation if the citizen is to be an informed judge of and participant in events.

A. **Physical diversity.** The geographically literate citizen cultivates an understanding and appreciation of the physical diversity of the earth—the variations in land and water features, in climates and ecosystems, in resources—for it is on these natural systems that we all depend. Ultimately, our survival and that of future generations rests with our ability to develop and maintain sustainable uses of the environment.

B. **Human diversity.** The human presence on earth alters—and in many cases dramatically remakes—the natural environment. Therefore, the geographically literate citizen develops an understanding of the human diversity on the earth—the variations in peoples, in cultures, in economies, and in political systems—and the ways in which different peoples respond to the opportunities and limitations of the natural environment. A major component in this learning process relates to an understanding of the power and cost of ever-changing technology. Our human capacity to modify our setting, the "climate" of our homes, factories, shopping malls, and the resources available to us from place to place is a facet of human development that must be ever more present in our decision making about land use and landscape change. The scale of our capacity to bring change to the world is changing and growing so rapidly that this is now an area of extraordinary citizen responsibility and decision making.

III. **Changing realities.** Pivotal to developing a geographic sensitivity is the recognition of the principal sources and locales of ongoing environmental change which act as critical forces at work in today's world. If the citizen can begin to see the edges and centers of cities, the forest and wilderness areas not too distant from urban space, family farms, the lines of transportation that link together populations within cities and bond city to city then they are becoming more attentive to the landscapes that are most threatened by change today. In this understanding comes the ability—as geographically literate citizens—to make relatively better-informed decisions about the positive and negative aspects of the transformation of such places.

A. **Environmental stress.** Environmental change has been a constant throughout the earth's natural history. However, rapidly increasing rates of change over the past century, and particularly since the end of World War II, resulting from increases in population and technology use, have yielded evidence of unparalleled stress in the environment. In much of historic time, environmental change has been assumed to be the right of the owner of the locale being transformed. As we have learned, however, that landscape change in one place has a powerful capacity to visit change upon other locales, there has been increasing citizen involvement in the nature of such transformation.

1. **The distribution of water resources.** One example of environmental stress is on fresh water supplies that are being strained by the competing demands of agriculture, industry, and urban areas. At the same time, fresh water supplies are at risk due to contamination from these same sources. The environmental tension caused by water or its absence will shape major political battles in this and the next decade. Awareness of the geographic distribution of such water supplies and of their increasing environmental and fiscal cost adds to the citizen's knowledge and understanding of the world's political economy.

2. **The distribution of oxygen producing plant life.** Another example of environmental stress on which geography can throw light concerns the world's rain forests, many of which lie in the southern hemisphere. Destruction of significant portions of these sources of oxygen—which also consume carbon dioxide—may add significantly to world climate change.

3. **The relative imbalance in the distribution of resources such as petroleum.** As the citizen geographer looks at the map of world petroleum reserves distribution, it can been seen that there is a major political tension that can derive from that pattern. The Gulf War of 1990 is a bold example of what happens when a single resource becomes profoundly important to all of the world's populations but is found in only a limited number of regions or nations. Understanding the geography of resources and their disequilibrium in distribution helps the citizen to understand regional conflicts.

B. **Demographic realities.** The citizen requires an awareness of the implications of changing populations both at home and abroad.

1. **National population change**. For example, in the case of the U.S., whether population change is manifested in a maturing age-structure or redistribution of settlement patterns toward the south and west, the impact will have political repercussions in new voting patterns and Congressional reapportionment.

2. **International population change**. The geographic distribution of world population growth is also a key factor in assessing significant trends in international politics and economics. Features of physical, economic, and demographic geography of the Americas likewise cast light on the political and economic consequences of population growth for both the U.S. and the hemisphere. The human potential for migration is powerfully stimulated by population growth and associated patterns of poverty and perceived opportunity elsewhere that make distant locales take on an attractiveness that leads to migration. The U.S. has a long history as a magnet for international migration. The current regional disparity in international population growth rates between rich and poor countries will have an influence on American responses to demographic shifts beyond its borders. Millions of people from poor countries have already crossed American borders, and millions more can be expected to wish to follow.

C. **Economic realities.** Changes in the world economy have forced nations to reckon with the realities of limited and unevenly distributed resources. The classic example of Japan being so destitute of natural resources—especially iron ore and petroleum—that it could not be expected to play any significant role in world economic competition has been replaced by a very different assessment. However, while science and technology have given people greater command over natural systems, they have at the same time increased human dependence on the resources and those systems. Because of this dependence, countries cannot afford to ignore international economic trends in the availability and cost of these resources.

D. **Political realities.** Changes in transportation and communication systems have redefined boundaries and frontiers. The collapse of the post-World War II Cold War alliance in Eastern and Central Europe (the Warsaw Pact) that shaped the political geography of Europe and the Soviet Union has uncapped major points of ethnic stress within and among countries once thought to be fully stable under Soviet rule. Examples include the nations of Yugoslavia and of the USSR

itself. In addition, new technologies such as FAX that instantaneously diffuse information have forced people to review the political geography of international and internal regional boundaries.

1. **Political geography and foreign policy**. After World War II, Americans found it necessary to reevaluate their own political geography. Atlantic and Pacific ocean barriers no longer seemed impenetrable obstacles to external threats. That reality, coupled with expanding global economic interdependence has led to a reevaluation of the role of geographic factors and their contemporary importance. Just as the traditional geography of mountains and oceans seemed to be losing significance, the new geography of diffusion and human migration was gaining ascendence. For the citizen attempting to maintain an understanding of the forces that were shaping the world, geographic literacy became ever more important.

2. **The politics of local landscape change.** Citizen participation in decisions about transportation systems, industrial facilities, sanitary landfills, and other essential components of the city has increased enormously. Advisory committees, referenda, and bond issues are increasingly the norm in such decision-making. A citizen who is geographically aware of what such change means will be better able to help make intelligent judgments about what ought to be, or ought not to be, done.

IV. **Legal issues.** Geographic knowledge provides opportunities to address legal issues, especially as they relate to the environment. For example, cities, townships, and counties use geographic information in developing zoning ordinances; these ordinances are enacted by citizens who serve on legally appointed boards or vote in community-wide referendums. In addition, the new technology of geographic information systems (GIS)—a computer based manipulation of spatial data—has made redistricting ever more complex and sophisticated. Such changes have made an understanding of the origins and significance of political boundaries even more important.

V. **Social Issues.** Certain geographic themes are germane to understanding a variety of social issues. For example, the geographic distribution of wealth may shed light on aspects of poverty; patterns of home ownership and tenancy may assist in understanding racial and ethnic problems and realities; and the comparative distribution of crime and unemployment may allow deeper understanding of social pathologies and their spatial patterns. These contemporary social issues all derive from geographic patterns and processes that become clearer as the citizen has a better understanding of geography.

VI. **International knowledge.** Since World War II, international knowledge among Americans has been immensely expanded through powerful new technologies, foreign travel to and from American shores, new immigration, economic ties abroad, cultural imports, cold and hot wars, high-profile diplomacy, and more. Geography education fosters awareness among citizens of the complex ways in which the world beyond their borders impinges upon their nation and themselves. Geography in its very infancy was concerned with bringing news of outsiders to home folk. Today geography can not only help play this role but may also allow the citizen to organize what might otherwise be a flood of bewildering data into usable information.

A. **Informed citizens.** Citizens who are informed about geography are better able to develop a sense of how their nation and they themselves are connected with the larger world, not isolated in a universe strictly of their own making. American citizens need to be reminded that, even as they strive to preserve their nation and their identity as Americans, they cannot live as if they were unaffected by foreign influences or maintain an erroneous sense of self-sufficiency. This reality calls for a familiarity with the world map and with the location of political and economic power as well as problem areas.

B. **An interrelated world.** In an interrelated world, it is desirable and increasingly necessary for civic judgment to reflect upon international as well as local and national issues. Citizens who buy sneakers from Taiwan, cameras from Brazil, headsets from South Korea, or beer from Canada must begin to comprehend this international network of cooperation and competition that characterizes the world they are part of. Through an exploration of geography's basic themes in an international setting, geography education yields essential preparation for citizenship in an age of a mutually involved and interconnected world.

VII. **Geography education for citizenship.** In summary, the study of geography is relevant for civic education for the following reasons:

A. **Knowledge.** Geography education provides knowledge and a unique perspective on the world, its nations, and their peoples. Geographic knowledge forms part of the basis on which citizens can make wide-ranging decisions and judgments. Such knowledge encompasses traditional placename geography that gives the citizen the capacity to know the setting of stories and reports

from Lima, Peru; Kuwait City, Kuwait; Bonn, Germany; and Beijing, China. While such geography does not tap the discipline's full range of concerns, it does establish an essential base for any citizen's intelligent discussion of issues.

B. **Awareness.** Geographically literate citizens know what is occurring and where it is occurring. They comprehend how actions in one part of the world—whether political, economic, or natural—can affect people in other parts of the world directly and indirectly. Geographic literacy leads citizens to ask where things are happening, why they are happening, and why they are happening **there**.

C. **Involvement.** Geography provides information individuals and groups need to make critical judgments and rational decisions about issues ranging from the environment to international trade. In this involvement, the well-informed citizen makes an effort to observe just what the scene is that is being called into question; to speculate on why reported or observed patterns have the shape they seem to have; and to analyze what additional questions have to be answered in order to bring this observation and speculation to a reasonable conclusion. This process is not only part of essential education for the geographically literate citizen, these three learning steps support all education.

D. **Perspective.** Geography education provides the perspectives and the essential information to understand ourselves and our relationships to the earth and to other people in other places. This development of perspective leads to the fourth step in our quartet of skills—evaluation. To develop the capacity to evaluate the good and the bad in a specific decision about land use, about resource extraction, about landscape modification is the goal that should be central to the geographic education of any citizen. It is in decisions about land use and landscape change that geography ought to be most critical in the minds of citizens. Knowledge of this discipline will help shape the world in which they live—and which their children will inherit.

Conclusion

By taking note of the geographic themes of place, people, patterns, and processes a citizen can see the world through geographic eyes; and by developing the capacity to look at the world with the four skills of observation, speculation, analysis, and evaluation, the geographically literate citizen learns to create the geographic equation. This is an essential step in understanding how geography plays a major role in influencing human development. Finally, by giving special attention to the components of location, the nature of place, human-environment interaction, movement, and regions, the citizen can bring order to the role of geographic influence in the shaping of human events.

To make informed analysis and judgment of the world, American citizens require the capacity to see how geography has shaped the past and how these same geographic factors will continue to be a dominant force in molding the future. Knowledge of geographic themes, skills, and perspectives will assure this vision.

E. RELIGION AND PUBLIC LIFE

The Religion then of every man must be left to the conviction and conscience of every man; and it is the right of every man to exercise it as these may dictate. This right is in its nature an unalienable right.

James Madison (1785)

The Religious Liberty clauses of the First Amendment to the Constitution are a momentous decision, the most important political decision for religious liberty and public justice in history. Two hundred years after their enactment they stand out boldly in a century made dark by state repression and sectarian conflict. Yet the ignorance and contention now surrounding the clauses are a reminder that their advocacy and defense is a task for each succeeding generation.

The Williamsburg Charter (1988)

From the colonial era to the present, religions and religious beliefs have played a significant role in the political life of the United States. Religion has been at the heart of some of the best and some of the worst movements in American history. The guiding principles that the Framers intended to govern the relationship between religion and politics are set forth in Article VI of the Constitution and in the opening sixteen words of the First Amendment of the Bill of Rights. Now that America has expanded from the largely Protestant pluralism of the seventeenth century to a nation of some three thousand religious groups, it is more vital than ever that every citizen understand the appropriate role of religion in public life and affirm the constitutional guarantees of religious liberty, or freedom of conscience, for people of all faiths or none.

The philosophical ideas and religious convictions of Roger Williams, William Penn, John Leland, Thomas Jefferson, James Madison, and other leaders were decisive in the struggle for freedom of conscience. The United States is a nation built on ideas and convictions that have become democratic first principles. These principles must be understood and affirmed by every generation if the American experiment in liberty is to endure.

OBJECTIVES

The citizen should be able to

1. explain the position that religious liberty is a universal human right, the preservation of which depends

upon a reciprocal responsibility to respect that right for everyone.

2. explain how the constitutional principles of religious liberty are the ground rules that enable people of all faiths and none to live together as citizens of one nation.

3. explain the principles of religious liberty, freedom of conscience, and separation of church and state, found in the First Amendment of the U.S. Constitution.

4. explain various interpretations of the constitutional relationship of religion and government in American political life.

5. explain the role religion and religious beliefs have played in American history and politics.

6. explain the relationship of religious liberty to the strength and diversity of religious life in the United States.

7. take, defend, and evaluate positions on constitutional issues regarding religious beliefs and practices.

FRAME OF REFERENCE
Conceptual Perspective

I. **The central place of faith in the idea of religion.** The radical pluralism of faiths in the United States today makes it difficult to define religion without excluding religions that may not fit a chosen definition. If, however, citizens are to understand the role of religion in American public life and support religious liberty for all, they need to appreciate that faith is of central importance to so many Americans.

A. **The centrality of religion in the lives of many Americans.** Without defining what religion **is**, we can, for purposes of civic understanding, focus on what religion **does** in the lives of believers. Ultimate beliefs and world views shape the lives of many people because they are regarded as the deepest source of meaning and belonging. In the United States, arguably the most religious of all the industrialized nations, religious beliefs are at the center of life for millions of Americans. These beliefs are not confined to worship and family life; they also shape the political and social views of vast numbers of citizens.

B. **The expansion of religious pluralism.** The United States has moved beyond the largely Protestant pluralism of its early history to a pluralism that includes almost every religious expression in the world. This expanding diversity presents new challenges for American public life.

C. **Religious liberty as freedom of conscience for all, including non-believers.** A growing number of people in the United States express no religious preference at all. Any discussion of pluralism and the role of religion in public life, therefore, must include secularists, non-believers, and others who do not profess any religious beliefs.

1. **The protection of religion in its broadest sense.** The Supreme Court has accepted the necessity of a broad recognition of world views (and the dangers of too narrow a definition of religion) by giving conscientious objector status to those who have "a sincere and meaningful belief which occupies in the life of its possessor a place parallel to that filled by the God of those admittedly qualifying for the exemption..." (*U.S. v. Seeger*, 1965).

2. **No one excluded from protection.** The important point for citizens to keep in mind is that religious liberty, or freedom of conscience, was intended by the Framers to protect the beliefs of everyone, not just those of recognized faith communities.

II. **The American experiment in religious liberty.** Religious liberty in America is a key part of the boldest and most successful experiment in freedom the world has known. The strength and diversity of religion in the United States is due almost entirely to the full protection of religious liberty, or freedom of conscience, guaranteed by the Constitution.

A. **Religious liberty as the "first liberty."** Religious liberty has been called America's "first liberty" because freedom of the mind is logically and philosophically prior to all other freedoms protected by the Constitution.

B. **Definition of religious liberty.** In the American experiment, religious liberty is defined according to the following elements.

1. **Freedom of conscience.** There shall be full freedom of conscience for people of all faiths or none.

2. **Religious liberty an inalienable right.** Religious liberty is considered to be a natural or inalienable right that must always be beyond the power of the state to confer or remove.

3. **Right to practice any or no religion.** Religious liberty includes the right to freely practice any religion or no religion without governmental coercion or control.

C. **Guarantees of religious liberty in the Constitution.** The guiding principles supporting the definition of religious liberty are set forth in Article VI of the Constitution and in the opening words of the First Amendment to the Constitution. These principles have become the ground rules by which people of all religions or none can live together as citizens of one nation.

1. **Article VI of the Constitution.** Article VI concludes with these words: "no religious test shall ever be required as a qualification to any office or public trust under the United States." With this bold stroke, the Framers broke with European tradition and opened public office in the federal government to people of all faiths or none.

2. **Religious liberty clauses.** The First Amendment's religious liberty clauses state that "Congress shall make no law respecting an establishment of religion, or prohibiting the free exercise thereof...." Taken together, these two clauses safeguard religious liberty by protecting religions and religious convictions from government interference or control. They ensure that religious belief or non-belief remains voluntary, free from government coercion.

   a. **State and local government included.** The clauses apply equally to state and local government actions because the Supreme Court has ruled that the Fourteenth Amendment's command that states are not to deprive any person of liberty makes the First Amendment applicable to the states.

   b. **Meaning of "no establishment."** No establishment means that neither a state nor the federal government can establish a particular religion or religion in general. Further, government is prohibited from advancing or supporting religion. This does not mean that the government can be hostile to religion.

The government must maintain what the Supreme Court has called "benevolent neutrality" which permits religious exercise to exist but denies it government endorsement. The "no establishment" clause serves to prevent both religious control over government and political control over religion.

c. **Meaning of "free exercise." "Free exercise"** is the freedom of every citizen to reach, hold, practice, and change beliefs according to the dictates of conscience. The free exercise clause prohibits government interference with religious belief and, within limits, religious practice.

   (1) **The difference between belief and practice.** The Supreme Court has interpreted free exercise to mean that an individual may believe anything he or she wants, but there may be times when the state can limit or interfere with practices that flow from these beliefs.

   (2) **The traditional "compelling interest" test.** Traditionally, the Court has required a government to demonstrate a compelling interest of the "highest order" before it can burden or otherwise interfere with religious conduct. Even then, the government has to demonstrate that it has no alternative means of achieving its interest that would be less restrictive of religious conduct.

   (3) **Weakening of the "compelling interest" test.** A 1990 Supreme Court decision, however, appears to have reduced significantly protection of free exercise of religion. The decision, *Employment Division v. Smith* (1990), indicates that government will no longer have to demonstrate a compelling government interest unless a law is specifically targeted at a religious practice or infringes upon an additional constitutional right such as free speech.

III. **Religion, public life, and politics.** The First Amendment separated church and state but not religion and public life.

A. **The involvement of religious groups in public life.** Many religious groups consider it an article of faith to speak out on issues of moral concern in the public sphere. The Constitution protects the right of religious individuals and organizations to attempt to shape public policy and to exercise their influence. There are presently hundreds of nonprofit groups concerned with religious issues and public life in the United States.

B. **Tax-exempt status dependent on non-partisanship.** However, religious organizations that are charitable institutions with tax-exempt status may not engage in partisan politics by endorsing a political candidate or party or by directly lobbying Congress.

C. **Religious liberty and political responsibility.** In certain cases, the injection of religious views into political debate, though constitutionally protected, may be irresponsible.

  1. **Religious views in political debate are protected.** In the American experiment in self-government, disestablishment of religion, or separation of church and state, prevents religious institutions from establishing their faith as the law of the land and from receiving financial support from the state. At the same time, "free exercise" protects the right of religious views to be part of the political debate.

  2. **Religious attacks in political debate may be irresponsible.** It is important to remember, however, that some actions taken by religious organizations or individuals in the political arena (for example, attacks against the fitness of people to hold public office because of their religion) may not be unconstitutional but may be politically irresponsible violations of the spirit of religious liberty.

Historical Perspective

The relationship of politics and religion has been a central issue in American life since the colonial era. For most of the European settlers who came to North American shores in the seventeenth century from England, France, and Spain—all nations with established churches—a society without an established faith was unimaginable. The unity and morality of the community, it was believed, depended upon divine sanction of political authority and conformity of the populace in matters of faith. Eventually, however, by separating religion and government and by granting freedom to all religious groups, America launched a new political experiment unprecedented in the world's history.

I. **The religious liberty sought by the Puritans.** Like many who arrived on these shores in the seventeenth century, the Puritans of Massachusetts Bay came to America seeking religious freedom.

A. **Religious freedom not sought for others.** The freedom they sought, however, was for themselves and not for others. The Puritans felt called by God to establish "new Israel," a Holy Commonwealth based on a covenant between God and themselves as the people of God.

B. **All laws to be grounded in God's law.** Though there were separate areas of authority for church and state in Puritan Massachusetts, all laws of the community were to be grounded in God's law and all citizens were expected to uphold the divine covenant. Massachusetts was to be an example to the world of God's kingdom on earth, "a city upon a hill."

II. **Roger Williams and the origins of freedom of conscience in Puritan America.** Very early in the Massachusetts' experiment, dissenters arose to challenge the Puritan vision of a holy society. The first dissenter, **Roger Williams** (c.1603-1683), was himself a Puritan minister but with a very different vision of God's plan for human society. Williams argued that God had not given divine sanction to the Puritan colony. In his view, the civil authorities of Massachusetts had no authority to involve themselves in matters of faith. The true church, according to Williams, was a voluntary association of God's elect. Any state involvement in the worship of God, therefore, was contrary to the divine will and inevitably led to the defilement of the church.

A. **"Soul liberty" means freedom of conscience for all.** Williams' arguments for religious liberty had two principal parts.

  1. **Freedom of conscience as God's will.** Central to Roger Williams' arguments for separating church and state was his conviction that it was divine will that every individual's conscience remain free to accept or reject the word of God. Williams defined freedom of conscience, which he called, "soul liberty," as the freedom of each person to follow his or her own heart in matters of faith without interference or coercion by the state.

2. **Religious intolerance and war.** Citing Europe's long history of wars and divisions, Williams pointed out that coercion in matters of faith inevitably leads to persecution and bloodshed.

B. **Rhode Island's experiment in religious liberty.** Williams found it necessary to seek religious liberty outside of Massachusetts Bay.

1. **The founding of Rhode Island.** Banished from Massachusetts in 1635, Roger Williams founded Rhode Island, the first colony with no established church and the first society in America to grant liberty of conscience to everyone. Jews, Quakers, and others not welcome elsewhere made their home there.

2. **The wider significance of the Rhode Island's religious liberty.** Eventually, Williams' conception of soul liberty had an impact far beyond the Rhode Island experiment. In the eighteenth century, dissenting religious groups, particularly the Baptists, were inspired by Williams' ideas to advocate separation of church and state and freedom of conscience. Some historians also argue that Williams' writings influenced the Enlightenment philosopher **John Locke** (1632-1704), a key source for Thomas Jefferson's views concerning religious liberty.

C. **Freedom of conscience as an American conviction.** The Puritans' demand for religious liberty for themselves became, in the vision of Roger Williams, a requirement of religious liberty for all.

1. **Early religious liberty outside Rhode Island.** This revolutionary idea was echoed to a lesser degree (and for only a brief period) in seventeenth century Maryland and later more fully in the eighteenth century "holy experiment" of Quaker William Penn's colony of Pennsylvania.

2. **Gradual extension of religious liberty.** Gradually, the extension of liberty to include not only one's own group but also others, even those with whom "we" disagree, became a central American conviction. It is this principle of full freedom for people of all faiths and of none that was embodied one hundred and fifty years later in the First Amendment to the Constitution.

III. **The movement toward full religious liberty in the United States.** The momentous decision by the framers of the Constitution and the Bill of Rights to prohibit religious establishment on the federal level and to guarantee free exercise of religion was related to a number of religious, political, and economic factors in eighteenth century America. Underlying all of these factors, of course, was the practical difficulty of establishing any one faith in an emerging nation composed of a multiplicity of faiths (mostly Protestant sects), none of which was strong enough to dominate the others.

A. **From toleration to free exercise.** The period between 1776 and the passage of the First Amendment in 1791 saw critical changes in fundamental ideas about religious freedom.

1. **The Virginia Declaration of Rights.** In May 1776, just prior to the Declaration of Independence, the leaders of Virginia adopted the Virginia Declaration of Rights, drafted by George Mason. The first draft of the Declaration argued for the "fullest toleration in the exercise of religion according to the dictates of conscience." This language echoed the writings of John Locke and the movement in England toward toleration.

2. **Madison's objection: "toleration" versus "free exercise."** Although toleration was a great step forward, a twenty-five-year-old delegate named **James Madison** (1751-1836) did not think it went far enough. Madison, also deeply influenced by the ideas of the Enlightenment, successfully argued that "toleration" should be changed to "free exercise" of religion. This seemingly small change in language signaled a revolutionary change in ideas. For Madison, religious liberty was not a concession by the state or the established church, but an inalienable or natural right of every citizen.

3. **"Free exercise and the First Amendment."** In 1791, the free exercise of religion proclaimed in the Virginia Declaration became a part of the First Amendment, guaranteeing all Americans freedom of conscience.

B. **From establishment to separation.** The decisive battle for disestablishment came in the large and influential colony of Virginia where the Anglican Church was the established faith. Once again, James Madison played a pivotal role by leading the fight that persuaded the Virginia legislature to adopt in 1786 Thomas Jefferson's "Bill for the Establishment of Religious Freedom."

1. **Madison, Jefferson, and the struggle for disestablishment.** Madison and Jefferson argued that state support for a particular religion or for all religions is wrong because compelling citizens to support through taxes a faith they do not follow violates their natural right to religious liberty. "Almighty God had created the mind free," declared Jefferson's bill. Thus, "to compel a man to furnish contributions of money for the propagation of opinions which he disbelieves and abhors, is sinful and tyrannical."

2. **The "Great Awakening" and the struggle for disestablishment.** Madison and Jefferson were greatly aided in the struggle for disestablishment by the Baptists, Presbyterians, Quakers, and other "dissenting" faiths of Anglican Virginia. The religious revivals of the eighteenth century, often called The Great Awakening (1728-1790), produced new forms of religious expression and belief that influenced the development of religious liberty throughout the colonies. The revivalists' message of salvation through Christ alone evoked a deeply personal and emotional response in thousands of Americans.

3. **Evangelical fervor and religious self-government.** The evangelical fervor of the Awakening cut across denominational lines and undercut support for the privileges of the established church.

   a. **Support of religious choice by evangelicals.** Religion was seen by many as a matter of free choice and churches as places of self-government. The alliance of church and state was now seen by many as harmful to the cause of religion.

   b. **Leadership in Virginia of John Leland.** In Virginia this climate of dissent and the leadership of such religious leaders as **John Leland**, a Baptist, provided the crucial support Madison needed to win the battle for religious liberty in Virginia.

4. **The final demise of religious establishment.** The successful battle for disestablishment in Virginia is a vital chapter in the story of religious liberty in America. By the time of the ratification of the First Amendment in 1791, all of the other Anglican establishments (expect in Maryland) were ended. The Congregational establishments of New England lasted longer. Not until 1818 in Connecticut and 1833 in Massachusetts were the state constitutions amended to complete the separation of church and state.

IV. **The Constitutional prohibition of religious tests for office in Article VI.** The only mention of religion in the Constitution of the United States prior to the adoption of the First Amendment was the "no religious test" provision of Article VI. The significance of this often forgotten provision cannot be exaggerated. At the time of the Constitutional Convention in 1787, most of the colonies still had religious establishments or religious tests for office. It was unimaginable to many Americans that non-Protestants—Catholics, Jews, atheists and others—could be trusted with public office.

A. **"No religious test" proposed at the Constitutional Convention.** One aspect of religious liberty was inserted into the Constitution during its framing in Philadelphia.

   1. **The role of Charles Pinckney.** At the Constitutional Convention, **Charles Pinckney** (1757-1824), a delegate from South Carolina, proposed that "no religious test shall ever be required as a qualification to any office or public trust under the United States." Though he came from a state that had established the Protestant faith as the state religion, Pinckney represented the new spirit of religious liberty exemplified in the Enlightenment thinking of Jefferson.

   2. **A tool for oppression outlawed.** Remarkably, the "no religious test" provision passed with little dissent. For the first time in history, a nation had formally abolished one of the most powerful tools of the state for oppressing religious minorities.

B. **Religious tests imposed in some states.** Most states followed the federal example and abolished tests for state office. But it was not until 1868 in North Carolina, 1946 in New Hampshire, and 1961 in Maryland that religious tests were abolished entirely. Maryland had required since 1867 "a declaration of belief in God" for all officeholders. When the U.S. Supreme Court struck down this requirement in 1961, freedom of conscience was fully extended to include non-believers as well as believers. No religious test can be imposed for any office at any level of government.

C. **Informal religious tests a factor in elections.** Though the Constitution barred religious tests as a formal qualification for office, many American voters continued to apply informal religious tests in the political arena, particularly in presidential elections.

1. **Exclusion of Catholics.** With two exceptions (Al Smith in 1928 and John Kennedy in 1960) all presidential candidates nominated by the two major parties have been Protestants. The election of Kennedy, a Roman Catholic, broke the informal political barrier that had long excluded non-Protestants from the presidency.

2. **Religious dissension among Protestants.** Even with Protestant candidates, religion has frequently been an issue. Beginning with attacks on the Deist religious convictions of Thomas Jefferson (Deism is a faith based on reason rather than revelation) and continuing to the recent discussions about which candidate is "born again," questions about the "correctness" of a politician's religion have played an important role in many national elections.

V. **The First Amendment principles of religious liberty.** In the mind of James Madison and some of the others at the Constitutional Convention, the Constitution established a limited federal government with no authority to act in religious matters. That others were unsure had momentous consequences.

A. **Reassurance of those fearful of religious intolerance.** Many Americans, including leaders of the Baptists and other religious groups, feared that the Constitution offered an insufficient guarantee of the civil and religious rights of citizens.

1. **Madison's promise of a bill of rights.** Many of those who suspected the proposed new constitution demanded a bill of rights as their price of moderating their heated opposition to its adoption. To win ratification, Madison promised to propose a bill of rights in the First Congress.

2. **The enshrinement of religious liberty in the Bill of Rights.** Madison kept his promise, and the religious liberty clauses adopted by the first Congress in 1789 became, when ratified by the required number of states in 1791, the opening words of the Bill of Rights.

B. **Religious liberty and the first principles of American liberty.** Full religious liberty was first applied to acts of the federal government alone. Later it was applied to the states as well.

1. **The First Amendment and the federal government.** With the passage of the First Amendment, the principles of nonestablishment and free exercise became the first principles of American freedom. The federal government was constitutionally prohibited from establishing or sponsoring religion, and prohibited from interfering with the natural right of every citizen to reach, hold, exercise, or change beliefs freely.

2. **The First Amendment and state governments.** These prohibitions were extended to the states in the twentieth century following Supreme Court rulings that the Fourteenth Amendment made the First Amendment applicable to the states.

VI. **Religious influences in American political life.** Disestablishment was never meant to keep religious beliefs or institutions from influencing public life. From the beginning of American history, religions and religious beliefs have played a central role in shaping public policy and political debate.

A. **De facto Protestant establishment.** For many Protestants in the nineteenth century, disestablishment meant an end to the coercive power of the state in matters of faith and barred any faith from becoming the legally established religion. But disestablishment did not extinguish the Protestant vision of creating and maintaining a "Christian America." By numbers and influence, Protestantism became the de facto established religion of the nation. Many no doubt agreed with Daniel Webster when he argued in 1844 that "general tolerant Christianity is the law of the land."

B. **Protestant contributions to social reform.** The close ties between Protestant churches and American culture led to many social and political reforms. This can most clearly be seen in the "Second Great Awakening" of the early nineteenth century when some Protestant leaders mounted a crusade to reform and revitalize America. Urban social work, schooling for poor children, the abolitionist movement, supported by Quakers, Methodists, and others were only a few of the many reform movements inspired in large measure by the religious awakenings.

C. **Nativist reaction to expanding pluralism.** A dark side to the Protestant vision of America became evident in the nineteenth century.

1. **The effects of immigration.** The waves of immigrants coming to these shores in the nineteenth century challenged the Protestant domination of the culture. By 1850 Catholicism was the largest single American denomination, and by the end of the century large numbers of Jews had arrived to become citizens.

2. **The rise of anti-Catholicism and anti-Semitism.** There were only a few Catholics and Jews in America from the earliest days of colonization. This dramatic influx of non-Protestants created fear and anxiety among some Protestants.

   a. **Intolerance and the "Know Nothings" at mid-century.** An anti-Catholic and antiforeign nativist movement emerged in the first half of the nineteenth century, culminating in the 1840s and 1850s in the Know-Nothing Party. Catholics were the victims of violence and discrimination in many parts of the nation.

   b. **Intolerance at the turn of the century.** A resurgence of similar sentiments in the late nineteenth and early twentieth centuries contributed to widespread anti-Semitism, opposition to immigration, and the rise of the Ku Klux Klan.

D. **The positive role of religion in helping shape public policy.** The ugly expressions of religious bigotry in the nativist movement represent some of the worst examples of religious involvement in politics and public policy. But religion has also been at the heart of some of the best movements in American social and political life.

   1. **The contribution of African American churches.** The black churches have played a central role in the political and social history of African Americans from the colonial period to the present. Indeed, black churches have shaped the lives of all Americans by providing much of the moral and political leadership of the Civil Rights Movement.

   2. **The contribution of Judaism and other minority religions.** In the late nineteenth and early twentieth centuries, churches, synagogues, and temples provided vital support for Catholic, Eastern Orthodox, Jewish, and Asian Buddhist immigrants as they adjusted to life in the United States. Religious communities were also at the forefront of many reform movements during the Progressive Era early in this century. Various religious groups, notably Unitarians, Quakers, and Reform Jews, have been particularly visible in the peace movements and in the advocacy of social justice.

3. **Constitutional separation and the role of religion in public life.** In these and in many other ways, religious institutions and beliefs have significantly influenced public policy in the United States throughout our nation's history.

   a. **Benefits of religious moral leadership.** Again, the constitutional separation of church and state was not meant to separate religion from public life. Politics and government in America have clearly benefitted from the moral leadership and values of many religious traditions and convictions.

   b. **Costs of religious zealotry.** At the same time, the nation has suffered from violations of the spirit of religious liberty by religious groups who have at various times in our history used the public square to attack the religion of others or to deny others the full rights of citizenship.

Contemporary Perspective

More people have died because of their religious convictions in the twentieth century than in any previous century. And there appears to be no end to the tragedy. Of the more than thirty wars that raged in the world in 1990, more than two-thirds have religious or ethnic differences as a root cause. From Northern Ireland to Lebanon to Sri Lanka, religious differences contribute daily to death and destruction around the globe.

Even the explosion of freedom in Eastern Europe and the Soviet Union, by any measure a tremendous advance for democratic principles, has been accompanied by a serious outbreak of religious and ethnic bigotry and division. One of the most frightening developments has been the dramatic rise of anti-Semitism throughout the region, particularly in the Soviet Union. Tensions between Muslims and Christians have resulted in violence in Soviet Azerbaijan and Armenia as well as in Bulgaria where thousands recently demonstrated against religious freedom for the Muslim citizens of that country.

How has the United States, the most religiously diverse nation in the world, managed to avoid the "holy wars" so prevalent today and throughout history? This remarkable achievement may be traced directly to the religious liberty clauses of the First Amendment. In spite of occasional setbacks and outbreaks of religious bigotry, the American experiment in religious liberty has held.

I. **Religions remain active in American political life.** Religious liberty has allowed religions in the United States to grow and prosper as in few other places in the world. Not only are a large number of Americans deeply religious, but their religious communities continue to be actively involved in political life. This is evident, for example, in the civil rights and peace movements. Also, since the late 1970s, Fundamentalist Christian communities together with other evangelical Christians have become a significant force in American politics speaking out on a variety of social and moral issues.

II. **Confusion about the role of religion in public life threatens religious liberty.** There are disturbing signs that the American experiment in liberty may be in danger from two extremes.

   A. **Two extremes on the issue of religion and public life.** On one end of the political spectrum there are those who seek to establish in law a "Christian America." On the other end are some who seek to exclude religion from public life entirely. Both proposals violate the spirit of religious liberty.

   B. **Teaching religion versus teaching about religion.** The controversy surrounding the role of religion in public life has left many citizens confused about the principles of religious liberty. This confusion is made worse by the absence of teaching **about** religion and religious liberty in many public schools. Teaching **about** religion in the schools is often confused with the teaching **of** religion, or religious advocacy and indoctrination.

      1. **Change in some public schools.** In the last few years a number of states, most notably California, have mandated more teaching about religion in the schools.

      2. **Change in textbook treatment of the role of religion.** As a result, textbooks have begun to include more about the story of religious liberty and the role of religion in American history and society.

III. **The Supreme Court's interpretation the religious liberty clauses.** Another factor that contributes to the confusion about the principles of religious liberty is the bewildering number of church/state cases decided by the U.S. Supreme Court in recent years. Prior to 1940, only a half-

dozen cases involving the Religious Liberty clauses had come before the Court. Since that date, the Court has reviewed hundreds of such cases. Many of these cases have seriously divided the Court and the nation. In the face of the complexity and confusion surrounding the church/state battles, the Supreme Court has attempted to articulate some guidelines for interpreting the religious liberty clauses.

   A. **The Free Exercise test.** In a 1963 unemployment compensation case, *Sherbert v. Verner*, the Supreme Court adopted a test for evaluating free exercise claims.

      1. **The "Sherbert test."** The "Sherbert test" has two parts.

         a. **"Compelling state interest."** Under the Sherbert test, government would not prevail against a person claiming violation of his or her religious freedom unless it could show a "compelling governmental interest."

         b. **No alternative means.** The government also had to demonstrate that it had no alternative means of achieving its interest that would be less restrictive of religious freedom. Despite this high level of protection, the Court in the 1980s rejected many claims by individuals seeking a free exercise exemption from generally applicable laws.

      2. **Weakening of the Sherbert test.** In 1990, in *Employment Division v. Smith*, the Supreme Court issued an important ruling in a case that concerned the firing of drug rehabilitation workers who used peyote as part of a religious ceremony. The Court found that they were not entitled to use peyote because the state's aim under the applicable law was to outlaw drug use. It was only coincidental that some religious activities would be barred under the law. The Court indicated that the Sherbert test will not apply to laws outside the unemployment compensation area unless one of two conditions is met.

         a. **Targeting a religious practice.** One condition is if the law specifically targets a particular religious practice, such as the use of sacramental wine. In that case, the Sherbert test will be applied to the practice.

         b. **Linking free-exercise claims to other constitutional rights.** The Sherbert test will not be applied unless the free exercise claim is linked with another constitutional right such as free speech.

   c. **Narrowing the scope of the Sherbert test.** Since few, if any, laws single out religious practices for discriminatory treatment, the Sherbert test is likely to be of little practical use outside the unemployment compensation area.

B. **The No Establishment test.** The Court fashioned a three-part test in *Lemon v. Kurtzman* (1971) to evaluate cases arising under the "no establishment" clause. The present Court is sharply divided about the value of the Lemon test, raising questions about its use in future decisions.

   1. **Legitimate secular purpose.** According to one part of the Lemon test, in order not to violate the "no establishment" clause, a government action must have a legitimate secular purpose.

   2. **Neutral toward religion.** Another part of the test is that the government act must have a primary effect that neither advances nor inhibits religion.

   3. **No excessive involvement with religion.** The third part of the test is that a government action must not foster excessive entanglement between government and religion.

IV. **The new challenges of exploding pluralism.** The confusion and ignorance surrounding the religious liberty clauses of the Constitution leave Americans in a weak position to meet the challenges of exploding religious pluralism in the United States. The violent religious divisions throughout the world serve as a dramatic reminder of how vital it is for Americans to understand and affirm the principles of religious liberty in a nation of some three thousand religious groups.

A. **Pluralism as meaning all faiths or none.** Religious pluralism in the United States has expanded beyond the Protestant, Catholic, and Jewish pluralism of the 1950s.

   1. **Expanding pluralism.** Pluralism now includes a growing number of people from all the world's religions, especially Islam and Buddhism. Pluralism must also take into account the nearly 12% of Americans who express no religious preference at all. This expansion will only continue. Califor-

nia alone now receives one third of the world's immigration.

   2. **The burdens of exploding pluralism.** The challenges of this diversity can be seen throughout American society. This pluralism is particularly evident in public schools. For example, dozens of different native languages are often found among the students of large urban schools. Similarly, many different religions are represented.

B. **The First Amendment as providing ground rules for living together.** As the United States begins its third century of constitutional government, the nation faces certain important questions.

   1. **Living together without religious consensus.** Two urgent questions are how Americans of so many faiths will continue to live together as citizens of one nation and, since there is not (and cannot be) a religious consensus, what the civic values are that Americans of all faiths or none hold in common.

   2. **Adherence to the principles of religious liberty.** To answer these questions, American citizens must return to the democratic first principles articulated in the religious liberty clauses of the First Amendment. Religious liberty, or freedom of conscience, is at the heart of what it means to be an American citizen. Only in these principles can Americans find the ground rules that allow all citizens to live together with deep religious differences.

C. **The Williamsburg Charter.** One effort to return to first principles is the Williamsburg Charter. Drafted by members of America's leading faiths and revised over the course of two years in close consultation with political, academic, educational, and religious leaders, the Charter was signed in 1988 by former Presidents Gerald Ford and Jimmy Carter, the two living chief justices of the United States, and by nearly two-hundred leaders of national life. With their signatures these individuals strongly reaffirmed the principles of religious liberty as essential for developing a common vision for the common good. The Williamsburg Charter states in part:

We affirm that a right for one is a right for another and a responsibility for all. A right for a Protestant is a right for an [Eastern] Orthodox is a right for a Catholic is a right for a Jew is a right for a Humanist is a right for a Mormon is a right for a Muslim is a right for a Buddhist—and for the followers of any other faith within the wide bounds of the republic.

That rights are universal and responsibilities mutual is both the premise and the promise of democratic pluralism. The First Amendment, in this sense, is the epitome of public justice and serves as the golden rule for civic life. Rights are best guarded and responsibilities best exercised when each person and group guards for all others those rights they wish guarded for themselves.

F. ETHNIC AND RACIAL DIVERSITY

Give me your tired, your poor,
Your huddled masses yearning to breathe free.
The wretched refuse of your teeming shores,
Bring these, the homeless, tempest-tossed to me:
I lift my lamp beside the golden door.

Emma Lazarus (1886)

What then is...this new man? He is an American, who leaving behind him all his ancient prejudices and manners, receives new ones from the new mode of life he has embraced, the new government he obeys, and the new rank he holds. The American is a new man, who acts upon new principles....Here individuals of all nations are melted together into a new race of men.

J. Hector St. John de Crevecoeur (1782)

There she lies, the great Melting-Pot—listen! Can't you hear the roaring and the bubbling? Ah, what a stirring and a seething! Celt and Latin, Slav and Teuton, Greek and Syrian,—black and yellow—Jew and Gentile...East and West, and North and South, the palm and the pine, the pole and the equator, the crescent and the cross....Here shall they all unite to build the Republic of Man....[W]hat is the glory of Rome and Jerusalem where all nations and races come to worship and look back, compared with the glory of America, where all races and nations come to labour and look forward?

Israel Zangwill (1908)

The principle on which this country was founded and by which it has always been governed is that Americanism is a matter of the mind and heart; Americanism is not, and never was, a matter of race and ancestry. A good American is one who is loyal to this country and to our creed of liberty and democracy.

Franklin Delano Roosevelt (1943)

The one absolutely certain way of bringing this nation to ruin, of preventing all possibility of its continuing to be a nation at all would be to permit it to become a tangle of squabbling nationalities...each preserving its separate nationality.

Theodore Roosevelt (c. 1912)

America is woven of many strands; I would recognize them and let it so remain....Our fate is to become one and yet many.

Ralph Ellison (1952)

[T]here never was a melting pot; there is no melting pot; there is not now a melting pot; there never will be a melting pot; and if there were, it would be such a tasteless soup that we would have to go back and start all over!

Bayard Rustin (1972)

We embrace the American dream as culturally pluralistic—a nation having a unity of spirit and ideal, but a diversity of origin and expression.

The Orchard Lake Center for Polish Studies and Culture (c. 1971)

We must all hang together, or assuredly we shall all hang separately.

Benjamin Franklin (July 4, 1776)

INTRODUCTION

Ethnicity, race, and immigration have been central factors in American history. The diversity of the United States as a society was influenced in highly significant degrees by a number of cultures and groups. Knowledge of the history of ethnic and racial diversity and the conditions that shaped and reshaped it throws light on a fundamental problem of all modern societies, which the United States has faced in acute form because of its origins in international migrations: what conditions enable people of dissimilar backgrounds not simply to coexist but also to act in concert under new conditions?

Important legal and ethical developments in American history have resulted from efforts to govern the contact between different ethnic groups. This contact challenged the nation's commitment to its stated beliefs and sometimes exposed the contradictions between its democratic ideals and social realities. Knowledge of these developments forms an essential part of the perspective necessary in building a just and pluralist nation.

OBJECTIVES

The citizen should be able to

1. describe the ethnic and racial diversity of the United States with a perspective based on historical knowledge of the origins of groups and the American social order they have shaped.

2. describe the history of governance related to racial and ethnic groups.

3. describe the evolutionary changes of ethnic groups and their relationship to the wider society; and describe the evolution of the nation as ethnic groups were integrated.

4. describe the principle patterns of acculturation, social mobility, changes in status, and national integration of ethnic groups.

5. take, defend, and evaluate positions on constitutional and public policy issues regarding ethnic and racial diversity.

FRAME OF REFERENCE
Conceptual Perspective

Ethnic and racial groups should be envisioned as key building blocks of the American nation. Their role developed through the historical process of international migration and absorption through conquest. Ethnic and racial groups introduced new dynamics of cultural, economic, and social change. The interaction between these groups and the social order has been shaped by a variety of government policies and private priorities. These have both provided and limited opportunity for individual members of groups. Over time, a trend developed toward equalization of opportunity and inclusion.

I. **Ethnic group experience in America**. Since the nineteenth century, public officials, cultural representatives, and scholars have described the historical changes experienced by ethnic groups in American society. These changes defined the distinctive forms of group relations and ethnic diversity in the United States.

   A. **Assimilation and pluralism**. These changes can be divided into two basic categories: assimilation and pluralism. The former increases homogeneity in society while the latter increases heterogeneity.

   B. **Relationship between assimilation and pluralism**. Assimilation and pluralism can be viewed as twin aspects of historical change. One cannot occur without affecting the other: they are dynamic categories that cannot exist without the other. They can change on account of the development of new factors defining group identity, as well as from reaction to tradition.

II. **Types of assimilation**. Three directions toward assimilation have existed historically, marking three different types of assimilation. Different groups have taken these paths in different eras of American history.

A. **Assimilation into the dominant culture**. The first direction is conformity toward the dominant culture. It has produced the absorption of groups within the dominant Anglo-Saxon ethnic group. These groups lost their original identity and adopted Anglo-Saxon identity. It has been said that Dutch Calvinists and German Lutherans have often taken this route.

B. **Assimilation into non-dominant groups**. Another direction of assimilation has been absorption into another group that is socially non-dominant. The result has been the formation of broader ethnic collectivities based on pre-existing or traditional traits. Some scholars argue that Catholic groups were merging into an all-encompassing Catholic group, while different Jewish groups were merging into a Jewish group. Other examples of this type of assimilation are the absorption of West Indian blacks in the native black population; the mixing of Caribbean, Central, and South American Hispanics and Mexicans; and the merging of Chinese, Japanese, and Koreans.

　　1. **Relative ethnic similarity**. These processes of assimilation hinged on relative similarity of ethnic background.

　　2. **Retention of ethnic distinctiveness**. Moreover, these processes of assimilation did not result in the radical loss of ethnic distinctiveness.

C. **The melting pot metaphor**. The "melting pot" is a metaphor for assimilation toward a radically mixed new ethnic identity and culture. The social result was one in which no ethnicity or tradition was dominant and in which a cultural and social synthesis produced a wholly new and transformed group. A radical loss of ethnic distinctiveness is an inevitable byproduct. An example of this process is the so-called "part-Hawaiian" group of mixed European, Asian, and Polynesian ancestry.

III. **Stages of assimilation**. Within the three pathways or directions of assimilation, three stages in assimilation can be distinguished.

A. **Cultural assimilation**. The first and most superficial to be established was cultural assimilation in which cultural patterns from one group were borrowed by another.

B. **Institutional assimilation**. The next stage was structural assimilation in which an ethnic group infiltrated into institutions and social structures to replicate the pattern of representation of other groups.

C. **Primary group assimilation**. The final and ultimate stage was primary-group assimilation in which an outsider group was absorbed into the most intimate "primary" networks of another group defined by kinship and other intimate bonds. Intermarriage was the ultimate process for assimilation into primary groups.

IV. **Pluralism as counteracting assimilation**. Pluralism, defined as the maintenance or increase of ethnic differences, counteracted assimilation.

A. **Heightening ethnic differences**. Pluralism preserved and heightened ethnic differences. It assumed the necessity for intergroup toleration and cooperation in the larger framework of society.

B. **Ethnic persistence and the decline of the urge to assimilate**. The societal product of pluralism was the persistence of ethnic components and the dissipation of the urge to assimilate. Pluralism tended toward a mosaic system of different cultures which maintained their distinctiveness, with little intergroup homogenization.

C. **"Pure" ethnicity rare**. Groups have historically found it hard to achieve pluralism in a pure sense because of the extreme difficulty of resisting intergroup exchanges and mixing in a dynamic modern society, and the limited resources for ethnic maintenance in a polity where government has not historically given support to ethnicity.

V. **Government and the historical maintenance of ethnic groups to the mid-twentieth century**. In the United States, ethnic institutions were the result of voluntary effort rather than government support.

A. **Lack of government support for separate political status**. In the United States, government declined to give political status to ethnic groups.

B. **Lack of government support for ethnic maintenance**. In addition to giving no political status to ethnic groups, government declined to support ethnic maintenance.

C. **Government ethnic policy as parallel to laissez-faire economics**. State officials did not support the establishment of religious institutions, ethnic newspapers, language schools, and ethnic mutual aid societies. Eschewing support for ethnic maintenance was a parallel to the principle of laissez-faire in economic policy.

D. **The prevalence of voluntarism.** As a result, the voluntary principle shaped ethnic institutions and communities far more than government. Ethnic groups had to take the initiative to establish their own language schools, churches, hospitals, cemeteries, and social welfare agencies.

E. **Voluntarism as undercutting ethnic traditionalism.** The ability of the group to maintain adherence to tradition was undercut by voluntarism.

1. **No legal requirement to honor ethnic traditions.** No ethnic group could get government to pass laws ordering that ethnic traditions be honored.

2. **Necessity to compete for loyalty of young.** Thus, ethnic groups had to compete for the loyalty of the youngest generations and new members who entered the groups through intermarriage and religious conversion.

F. **Difficulty of keeping ethnic allegiance of young.** Holding on to the new generations was very difficult. Ethnic groups had to change in order to maintain their appeal to their membership. For example, the Jews and Italians of New York in 1900 tried to reduce the cultural differences that set them apart from the host society. They diluted their ethnic features through symbolic forms of patriotic activity and adopted a public identity conforming to the dominant culture.

G. **Difficulty of ethnic groups in isolating their members.** Ethnic groups in America lacked the size and power to completely isolate their members.

1. **Links with other groups.** Their members forged and dissolved linkages with people from other groups as made necessary by self-interest.

2. **Increase of opportunity by variety of social links.** An individual's opportunities increased according to the ability to diversify social contacts. To maximize economic opportunity, it was necessary to overlook ethnic loyalties. The enterprising immigrant worked for the best-paying boss, hired the most efficient worker, shipped on the cheapest carrier, and sold to the best-paying customer.

3. **Toleration for ethnic differences of others.** Ethnic-group members were willing to ignore the religion or ancestry of the person with whom they developed instrumental and mutually beneficial relations.

H. **Necessity for ethnic alliances to gain political power.** Immigrants could only gain political power and office by forming alliances with outsiders. No ethnic group constituted a secure majority except at the most localized level. In order to become a force, groups had to form coalitions that transcended ethnic divisions.

I. **Necessity to broaden ethnic/religious constituencies.** Groups that founded institutions to serve their own members soon discovered that they had to broaden their constituency to survive. For example, Catholic parochial schools and colleges had to recruit non-Catholics to survive and to expand.

J. **The endurance of ethnic identity.** Despite governmental aversion toward ethnic maintenance, ethnic identity endured.

K. **Being American a matter of mind and heart, not ethnic background.** The American idea of unity within diversity is symbolized by the oath sworn by aliens during the naturalization ceremony marking their passage to American citizenship: "I hereby declare on oath, that I absolutely and entirely renounce and abjure all allegiance and fidelity to any foreign prince, potentate, state, or sovereignty of whom or which I have heretofore been a subject or citizen; that I will support and defend the Constitution and laws of the United States against all enemies foreign and domestic; that I will bear true faith and allegiance to the same; that I will bear arms on behalf of the United States when required by the law; that I will perform non-combatant service in the Armed Forces of the United States when required by the law; that I will perform work of national importance under civilian direction when required by the law; and that I take this obligation freely without any mental reservation or purpose of evasion: so help me God."

VI. **Ethnicity and religious diversity.** In the American experience, the disestablishment of religion—the refusal of the state to support the church—was similar to the refusal of the state to support particular ethnic identities.

A. **Relationship of religious and ethnic groups to government.** Historically, a close parallel existed between the relation of ethnic groups to government and the relation of religious bodies to government. The historical policy of government toward religion basically followed the principle of non-support and non-recognition of political status practiced toward ethnic groups.

B. **Government policy and development of religion-based ethnic diversity**. As a consequence of the separation of church and state, the polity has fostered conditions hospitable toward the toleration and development of multifarious ethnic subcultures and institutions based on religion.

VII. **Ethnicity and political diversity**. Ethnicity in the United States has had a marked effect on the responsiveness of its political system.

A. **Immigration and political responsiveness**. The history of continuous migration from foreign regions to the United States produced a political system that was highly responsive to the interests of ethnic groups.

1. **Ethnicity and voting**. The effects of ethnic affiliation on voting behavior were particularly strong in the era of unrestricted immigration that corresponded to the industrial expansion of the United States.

2. **Effects of immigration restriction**. From the 1920s, restrictive laws prevented mass immigration from constantly reinvigorating ethnic attachments and identities that could shape politics.

3. **Ethnic loyalties undercut by the Great Depression**. The connection of ethno-cultural attitudes to political loyalties changed in the Great Depression of the 1930s. After the Depression, economic interests became a force undercutting ethnic interests as a factor in popular voting. The New Deal's focus on economic democracy weakened ethnicity as the basis for party support.

B. **Pursuit of public measures by least advantaged racial minorities**. Racial minorities which experienced the sharpest legal and social inequalities developed political traditions of pursuing public measures designed to limit discrimination and to expand opportunities.

C. **Ethnic divisions over government activism**. Two broad divisions of ethnic-group behavior toward government can be discerned from the nineteenth century to the early twentieth century.

1. **Preferences for moral activism by government**. Ethnic groups favoring moral activism in government, that is, a government seeking to regulate moral and civic behavior, gave support to the Whig or the Republican Party. Examples of these groups included evangelical Yankees who espoused sabbatarianism and prohibition, and blacks who supported moral crusades to reform race relations.

2. **Adherence to Democratic party by ethnic groups preferring government moral neutrality**. Ethnic groups preferring a government with a policy of staying out of cultural, civic, and moral issues supported the Democratic party. Examples of these groups include French and Irish Catholics, and white Southern fundamentalists wishing to maintain religious traditions or customary inter-racial relationships.

D. **Democratic politics and ethnic representation**. Because of democratic suffrage and mass party voter organization, the political system has been able to represent ethnic diversity. It has allowed policies and agendas to be shaped by the dissimilar expectations of government held by different ethnic groups.

Historical Perspective

I. **The colonial origins of the American ethnic pattern**. The Indian population of North America inhabited the areas of early British colonization.

A. **English colonists and Native Americans**. The English colonists' encounter with the indigenous population of North America known as American Indians became the first confrontation with the issues of ethnic difference and diversity.

1. **The indigenous population**. Although the features of the American Indian population of the seventeenth century are difficult to ascertain, experts believe there were over 200 tribes or nations in North America, comprising between 850,000 and a million inhabitants.

2. **Population density**. The eastern region of North America was more heavily populated than the land west of the Mississippi. The areas of greatest density included southern New England and tidewater Virginia.

B. **Lack of common front among Native Americans**. Although living in highly organized societies with settled patterns of subsistence, Native Americans did not present a unified front that could thwart European colonization.

1. **Loss of Atlantic Coast lands.** The Indian tribes of the Atlantic Coast were unable to retain control of their lands when English settlers began to occupy it.

2. **Decimation of Indians by war and disease.** Intermittent war and armed conflicts, along with the spread of communicable diseases brought by the colonists, destroyed over 90 percent of the eastern coastal Indian population by the eighteenth century. The surviving remnants formed small pockets of assimilated or proselytized Indians living on the margins of colonial civil society.

II. **European immigration in the colonial era.** In the seventeenth century, most immigrants were English; by the next century, other parts of the British Isles were heavily represented, as well as the continent of Europe.

A. **Emigration and the English drive for empire.** In the seventeenth century, the English drive for overseas empire brought the first settlers to America.

1. **America populated by English farmers.** The commercialization of the English rural economy displaced many farmers from their land holdings. These farmers were recruited to the New World colonies so they could supply raw materials to the mother country and consume its manufactured goods.

2. **Colonies' efforts to increase immigration.** The colonies employed advertising, land grants, labor incentives, arranged transportation, and easy legal requirements to attract immigrants.

3. **England as suppliers of most early immigrants.** In the seventeenth century, a very large majority of settlers came from England.

4. **Differences between immigrants to New England and the South.** In New England, the migrants came in families and were independent farmers. In the southern colonies, many were single laborers who came as indentured servants.

B. **Immigrants from British Isles and Germany.** In the eighteenth century, newcomers arrived from Scotland, Ireland, and the European continent. The largest new waves of immigration came from Germany and Ireland.

1. **Prerevolutionary German immigration.** Before 1776, 100,000 Germans migrated to the colonies. Most came from the Rhineland of Germany, driven away by religious persecution and war.

2. **Prerevolutionary Scotch-Irish immigration.** By 1776, 250,000 Scotch-Irish emigrants arrived from Northern Ireland, impelled abroad by religious persecution and economic setbacks.

3. **Receptivity to non-English settlement.** Non-English newcomers received generous rights and easy naturalization.

C. **Eighteenth century immigrants from British Isles not fleeing persecution.** Immigration crested in the decade before the American Revolution. Most newcomers came from the British Isles. A wave of middling farmers from central and northern England took immigration to America as an opportunity rather than as economic or religious exile.

III. **The origins of the African American population.** African slaves were brought to the colonies in small numbers early in the seventeenth century. After the 1670s, however, their numbers grew substantially.

A. **Slavery not envisaged by colonies' founders.** Neither a sizable black population nor institution of slavery had been envisioned or expected by the founders of the colonies.

1. **Few African arrivals by mid-seventeenth century.** The first handful of Africans to arrive in the British North American colonies were brought to Virginia in 1619. The African population grew slowly. In 1650 only a few hundred Africans lived in Virginia.

2. **African's position akin to indentured servants.** Their position in society roughly overlapped with that of indentured servants from England. They were enslaved but the terms of their condition would not evolve into the legal and institutional form of chattel slavery until the end of the seventeenth century.

B. **African share in labor force increases.** In the second half of the seventeenth century, African Americans occupied a growing share of the labor force. The key changeover to the commitment to recruiting African slaves as the central part of the agricultural labor force in the southern colonies began in the 1670s.

C. **By the 1690s, blacks outnumber white laborers in some areas of Virginia and Maryland.** This drive was an effort to compensate for a fall in the supply of English indentured servants. By the 1690s, blacks outnumbered whites in the key areas of labor-intensive agriculture, such as the coastal regions of Virginia and Maryland.

D. **Creation of chattel slavery.** By the 1690s, a wholly new institution for slavery was created: chattel slavery. Henceforth, the black laborer was a chattel slave.

   1. **Chattel slave a form of property.** He or she was a person in bonded servitude for life—a form of property, not a person.

   2. **Status of slave inheritable.** As property, a slave was subject to the unlimited will of the owner. This status was restricted to the African race only. Finally, this status was inheritable.

E. **Growth of slave population by natural increase in North American colonies.** Despite the exploitative treatment given to blacks under chattel slavery, the slave population was able to grow by family formation and natural increase. Elsewhere in the Western Hemisphere, in the slave societies of the Caribbean and Latin America, the slave population was only able to grow through continuous immigration.

F. **African American population in 1776.** By the American Revolution, African American slaves numbered over half a million. They comprised over 20 percent of the entire population of the colonies. In the colony of South Carolina, they had grown to become the demographic majority.

G. **Distribution of African American population.** Eleven percent of African Americans resided in the northern colonies from Maine to Pennsylvania. Fifty-four percent lived in Virginia and Maryland. Thirty-four percent of the black population inhabited the Carolinas and Georgia in 1770.

H. **Black settlement as reflecting cultural patterns.** The three major regions of black settlement reflected different patterns of social and cultural integration.

I. **Economic assimilation of blacks in North.** The black population was most economically assimilated in the northern colonies from Maine to Pennsylvania. At no time did slaves represent a numerical threat to white dominance in this area. The diversified northern economy led to a limited integration of blacks within mainstream economic activities in which the white population engaged.

J. **Economic compartmentalization of blacks in South.** By comparison, in the South, slaves were compartmentalized into a separate sector of labor-intensive agriculture. In the early formative era of the Southern colonies, most worked alongside white servants, as cattlemen and farm workers, but eventually they became a segregated labor force.

K. **Position of blacks in the lower South.** The position of the black population in the southernmost colonies—the Carolinas and Georgia—was the extreme antithesis of the status of the northern black population.

   1. **Early relationship of blacks and white servants.** In the late seventeenth century, whites and blacks intermingled despite slavery. A rough functional equivalence existed between white servants and black slaves much as in the early seventeenth century Chesapeake area. There is evidence that blacks brought certain skills from Africa such as fishing, rice farming, and animal husbandry that made them very valuable in the early frontier.

   2. **The coming of rigid racial segregation.** In the eighteenth century, however, the loose accommodation of white and black was replaced by a rigidly segregated social order. A separate sphere for blacks was created. It was centered on rice and indigo plantation districts. Gang labor under the terrible conditions of mud-field agriculture produced a high death rate and curtailed family formation. In these areas, the rate of acculturation was slow. The master class were usually absentee landlords who took few programmatic efforts to acculturate their slaves.

   3. **Blacks in some southern towns lived in intimate contact with whites.** A small segment of the black population in the lower South were employed in towns such as Savannah, Charleston, and Beaufort. They worked as artisans, porters, and house servants. They often lived intimately with whites. Some laborers were given semi-autonomous privileges, whereby they could hire themselves out for temporary periods to other employers.

L. **Unique status of blacks in the Chesapeake and coastal areas of Virginia and Maryland**. The status of the black population in the Chesapeake was different from that of the North or the lower South, and had the greatest significance for the future development of African American society in the United States. The Chesapeake was profoundly reshaped by the growing flow of slaves. The social structure was a combination of the northern pattern of the assimilated black population and the lower South pattern of mass black segregation.

1. **Key role of large plantations**. The key unit of African American society in the Chesapeake was the large plantation under resident landlords. These landlords gave a high priority to the acculturation of African slaves.

2. **Plantation encouragement of families among slaves**. Plantations also encouraged the formation of families. As a consequence, an Americanized community and a large native-born generation was already in existence in the early eighteenth century. By the time of the American Revolution, the plantations of Virginia and Maryland were peopled by blacks who had native parents and grandparents.

3. **Plantation encouragement of sophisticated skills**. These blacks were not restricted to field labor as were the slaves in the lower South. Like their counterparts in the north, they learned sophisticated artisan and domestic skills. Unlike their northern counterparts, however, they were not as dispersed throughout the society and economy; they lived and worked within a self-sufficient plantation.

4. **Paternalism of plantation owners**. In this setting, the master class practiced a form of paternalism in the management of their slaves. The great planters tended to view slaves as similar to children, as part of an elaborate kinship network. They proselytized Christianity to their African slaves, which served as a means of social control.

5. **The development of African American culture**. The slaves actively reshaped the elements of Anglo-American culture to which they were exposed to establish the first forms of a distinctive African American creole culture. Blacks created their own syncretic and dialectical culture as a response to the tutorialism and domination of the master class. They developed a unique extended family culture overseen by matriarchs. They created an African version of gospel Christianity. African American forms of musical and folk expression developed.

M. **Enduring Chesapeake African American culture**. The forms of Chesapeake African American society and culture would be far more durable and influential than the regional patterns developed in the North and in the lower South. They would expand to the west and south as plantations spread into that region. The Chesapeake forms became a model for race relations between white and black in the half-century before the Civil War.

IV. **The evolution of slave society**. The evolution of slave society along different lines in the North, the Chesapeake, and the lower South was critical in determining the impact of the American Revolution upon the future of slavery.

A. **The contradiction between slavery and the principles of the American Revolution**. The whole thrust of the Revolution ran counter to slavery; the republican theory of citizenship was based firmly upon the notion that persons were equal before the law and any differences among them were the product of momentary circumstance, "accident."

B. **Variation in regional effects**. The Revolution's promotion of civil equality affected the new states according to the kind of social evolution slavery had undergone. The Revolution thus produced different regional effects upon the black population.

1. **Where slavery destroyed**. In the areas where slavery was most tenuous and where slaves were most integrated into the social fabric, slavery was destroyed. The new states north of Maryland and Delaware drafted constitutions that abolished slavery.

2. **Where slavery protected**. In the lower South, where slavery was deeply woven into the economic fabric, where the proportion of the slave population was the greatest, and where slaves were reduced to a barbarized cultural state, the new state constitutions protected the legitimacy of slavery.

3. **Significance of the Chesapeake region**. The Chesapeake displayed a curious mixture of the trends in the North and the lower South in its response to the American Revolution. In Virginia,

slavery was challenged strenuously by an abolitionist movement in the 1780s, which almost succeeded in legislating slavery out of existence. A popular voluntary manumission movement produced the freeing of ten thousand slaves. The Chesapeake's response embodied the contradictory impulses released by the ideology of the Revolution. The states were left free to determine their constitutional principles but the Revolution had clearly challenged slavery by institutionalizing the idea of equality before government.

4. **Slavery made a moral problem.** The Revolution turned slavery into a problem, both governmental and moral. There was never to be a time after the Revolution when slavery ceased to be regarded as a problem by lawmakers and those concerned with simple justice.

5. **The appearance of racial theories.** In response to the American Revolution's thrust toward equal citizenship that made slavery a political anomaly, certain defenders of the institution began to turn to racial theories to allege that the natural inferiority of blacks made slavery legitimate.

THE AMERICAN ETHNIC PATTERN IN THE INDUSTRIAL ERA, 1800 TO 1940

I. **European immigration in the industrial era.** European immigration to America increased dramatically after the turn of the nineteenth century.

A. **Rate of immigration increase.** The yearly volume of migration multiplied by over twenty-fold in the nineteenth century. An average of ten thousand immigrants had arrived each year in the eighteenth century; but in the nineteenth century an average of 200,000 immigrants came annually. Annual totals rose steadily toward several hundred thousand arrivals.

B. **Immigration from Germany and Ireland.** Most newcomers came from Germany and Ireland. Two million Irish Catholic immigrants and 1.5 million German immigrants arrived from 1830 to 1860, comprising two of every three immigrants.

C. **Cultural disparity of immigrants and natives.** The cultural distance between immigrants and natives widened. By 1860, 10 percent of the U.S. population was Catholic. The cities included an even higher proportion of Catholics.

D. **Congregation in urban areas.** The nineteenth-century immigrants helped build cities and industries. In contrast to colonial era immigrants who settled in the countryside to take agricultural occupations, nineteenth-century immigrants concentrated in the cities. They helped fill the demand for labor in the early industrial economy.

II. **Immigration from Southern and Eastern Europe.** After 1880, streams originating from southern and eastern Europe swelled the flow of immigration.

A. **The "new immigrants."** The arrivals from southern and eastern Europe were called the "new immigrants" to distinguish them from the "old immigrants" from northern and western Europe. The largest groups, in the order of size, were the Italians, the Slavs, and the Jews. They came respectively from three areas: Italy, Austria-Hungary, and Russia.

B. **Italian immigration.** From 1899 to 1924, 3.8 million Italians immigrated to the United States. Italy's southern provinces produced 80 percent of these immigrants.

C. **Slavic immigration.** The Slavs constituted the second largest group in the new immigration: 3.4 million Slavs arrived from 1899 to 1924. The Russians, the Ruthenians, and Ukrainians were most numerous among the eastern Slavs. Among the western Slavs, the Poles, Czechs, and Slovakians predominated. Among the southern Slavs, the Slovenians and Croatians were the largest groups.

D. **Jewish immigration.** Jews from eastern Europe were the third major factor in the new immigration; 1.8 million arrived from 1899 to 1924. Three out of four Jewish immigrants in the United States came from Russian territory. One out of four emigrated from Austria-Hungary (Galicia, Bukovina, and Hungary) and the independent state of Romania.

E. **Other European immigrants.** Although Italians, Slavs, and Jews were by far the largest groups in the early twentieth century, other groups such as the Greeks, the Hungarians, and the Finns were an important part of immigration. Five hundred thousand Greeks, 500,000 Hungarians, and 300,000 Finns entered the United States from 1899 to 1924.

III. **Early immigration from Asia, Latin America, and the Caribbean.** Immigration from areas of the world other than Europe was small but not insignificant.

A. **Immigration from Asia and Latin America.** Immigration from Asia and Latin America composed a small fraction of total immigration from 1850 to 1930—less than five percent.

B. **Sources of Asian immigration.** Asian immigration was the first mass migration from outside Europe to the United States. Over a million Asians came to the U. S. and Hawaii from 1850 to 1930. The Chinese, Japanese, Koreans, Asian Indians, and Filipinos arrived roughly in sequence. Asian immigration shifted from one sending country to another. American lawmakers placed restrictions on the admission of male laborers at different times for different countries in Asia, thus generating a periodic series of migrations.

C. **Sources of Latin American immigration.** Immigration from Mexico, Puerto Rico, and the West Indies became significant in the early twentieth century. Unlike immigration from East Asia and southern and eastern Europe, the influx from the New World was not limited. Puerto Ricans faced no restrictions for they were American citizens and Congress decided not to impose quotas or annual ceilings on Western Hemisphere nations until 1965. From 1901 to 1940, 750,000 immigrants came from Mexico; over 320,000 immigrants arrived from the West Indies; and 90,000 came from Puerto Rico. They filled labor shortages caused by the restriction of European and Asian immigration.

IV. **The social mobility of immigrants.** Immigrants of working class backgrounds were, over time, able to achieve upward economic mobility.

A. **Gradual upward mobility.** From the beginnings of the Industrial Revolution, immigrants in the working class had been able to achieve gradual upward social mobility. Regional studies have shown that a quarter to a third of unskilled and semiskilled workers moved up to a higher occupation in their lifetime. More impressive still was the process of cumulative or intergenerational mobility. In one major industrial city, forty percent of the sons of unskilled and semi-skilled workers rose to white-collar jobs, and 15 to 20 percent moved up to become skilled craftsmen. Nevertheless, many low manual-labor workers did not gain superior employment. Others became part of a migratory force of industrial laborers.

B. **Differences in upward mobility.** Ethnicity remained an important factor in producing differences in rates of social mobility. Native-born people of native parentage had notable advantages over immigrants or their children in moving upward. Particular groups such as the British, Germans, Jews, Japanese, and West Indians made rapid advances up the social scale. Other immigrant groups—such as the Irish and Italians—found white-collar occupations difficult to penetrate.

C. **Barriers to upward mobility.** Immigrants encountered a variety of customary and legal barriers to opportunity. Labor unions refused to accept aliens and foreigners from areas outside of northern Europe. Asians and Mexicans in the West faced local laws and practices that segregated them according to education and residency.

D. **Political exclusion of Asians.** Classified by U.S. law as permanent aliens without the right to become naturalized citizens, Asian immigrants were excluded from democratic politics. Local and state governments enacted anti-alien laws that limited their rights to enter certain occupations. California and other states passed anti-alien land laws restricting the right of Asian aliens to purchase and transfer farm land.

E. **Limits to effectiveness of discriminatory practices.** These discriminatory practices that denied opportunity were harmful to the social position and mobility of immigrant groups. However, in historical perspective, it appears that they hindered or impeded social mobility but could not prevent progress. Immigrant groups were adaptive and resourceful enough to circumvent and overcome barriers. Some of the groups facing the fiercest discrimination, such as the Jews and Japanese, achieved economic and educational mobility of an exceptional magnitude.

V. **Immigration policy and its evolution.** Immigration policy gradually evolved over the course of more than a century.

A. **Immigration policy in flux.** Legal policies enacted by Congress both shaped and reflected the changing demographic patterns of American immigration. Like the influx of newcomers, immigration policy was in a constant process of evolution. It regulated immigration not only according to the shifting characteristics of immigrants, but also according to a changing vision of the agenda for national development.

B. **Decentralized immigration.** In the first century of the new nation, immigration policy produced a decentralized form of government administration of immigration. Lawmakers refused to enact policies that would select immigrants according to notions of social desirability.

VI. **The era of free and unlimited immigration: American Revolution to the era of Reconstruction**. The policy of unrestricted citizenship of the early days of the Republic largely remained until the Civil War.

   A. **The American Revolution and universal citizenship**. In the century after the American Revolution, immigration policy was guided by the assumptions of universal citizenship and decentralized government. A cosmopolitan attitude shaped the federal government's view that immigrants from all lands could have a place in the forming of the new nation. Main jurisdiction over immigration resided in state governments and local authorities until the decades after the Civil War.

   B. **The era of unrestricted citizenship**. In the ante-bellum era, the federal government did little to restrict or to promote immigration. Congress established immigration policy as a corollary to the axiomatic concept of universal individual citizenship. Rights to admission and to settlement could not be apportioned according to national identity or origin.

VII. **The era of regulation and restriction**. The increase in immigration after the Civil War led to expanded federal government activity to deal with it as well as to a rise in nativism.

   A. **Growth of federal government regulation**. Gradually but steadily the federal government assumed a more active stance toward immigration. By the 1870s, over 280,000 immigrants a year were disembarking in American ports. In the 1880s, immigrants from southern and eastern Europe began to arrive in large numbers. In the 1890s, the volume of immigrants arriving from eastern and southern Europe began to eclipse the total from northern and western Europe. The federal government could no longer rely on informal processes to manage this powerful social force. The emergent national administration of immigration became the tool for an effort to regulate immigration.

   B. **The rise of nativism**. Popular movements to oppose immigration and the presence of immigrants began to grow with the reaction to Catholic immigration, especially from Ireland and Germany. They intensified with the response to immigrants from Asia and southern and eastern Europe in the late nineteenth century. Nativists who came from patrician elites and organized labor criticized the immigrants for a variety

of ills: the lowering of employment conditions, the spread of slums and crime, and the growth of poverty. Some nativists believed that immigrants from Asia and southern and eastern Europe could not be assimilated.

   C. **Anti-immigration appeals by labor**. Labor organizations appealed to Congress to proscribe further immigration of Chinese workers. In 1882 Congress enacted the first Chinese Exclusion Act banning all Chinese laborers and preventing Chinese immigrants from acquiring American citizenship through naturalization.

   D. **Government regulation of immigration part of a wider trend to regulation**. Although the shift in the national origins of immigration stirred restrictionist sentiments, the increased number of all immigrants was probably the main stimulus for more stringent federal regulation. The movement to establish progressive government, improved schools, and social services in the midwest and the northeast popularized the idea of increased government activism. The federal entry into the field of immigration was part of a general trend toward strengthening public controls over social processes.

   E. **Restriction of immigration by law**. From 1891 to 1929, Congress built a complex body of law which steadily restricted the kinds of immigrants qualified for admission. Its goal was to admit only those who theoretically could be assimilated into the host society. This movement coincided with the rise of laws limiting opportunities for aliens.

   F. **Opposition to restrictive regulation**. The growth of restriction was far from a smooth and unimpeded process. The Democratic Party was indifferent or opposed to restriction well into the first decade of the twentieth century. The urban electorate of the northeast and midwest applied pressure to keep open the door to immigration. Industrialists and businessmen who required a steady supply of labor lobbied for a liberal admissions policy. Several presidents were unwilling to sanction a literacy test as a qualification for entry. In 1896, a bill to impose a literacy test as a prerequisite for entry was passed by Congress but vetoed by President Grover Cleveland. Senator Henry Cabot Lodge of Massachusetts had formulated the bill to exclude any immigrant unable to read forty words in any language. Cleveland vetoed the measure because he felt that it violated the traditional principle of free immigration. Renewed attempts to enact a literacy bill failed to pass Congress in 1898,

1902, and 1906. Congressional literacy bills were vetoed by President William H. Taft in 1913 and Woodrow Wilson in 1915. Not until 1917 was the literacy law enacted when Congress finally passed it over another veto by Wilson.

G. **Growth of legally restricted immigrant categories.** Still Congress enacted, piece by piece, measures which set more stringent requirements for immigrants and which enlarged the category of exclusions. In 1892, the Chinese Exclusion Act was renewed on a trial basis for ten more years. Further refinements and additions were made to the categories of those excluded from entry. Partly as a reaction to the assassination of President William McKinley in 1901, but largely in response to growing radicalism, Congress barred anarchists from entry.

H. **Asian restriction most extensive.** The most far-reaching restrictions, however, developed in the laws controlling Asian immigration. Since the 1880s, congressmen from the far western states made the permanent exclusion of Chinese laborers one of their paramount legislative goals. In 1902, they succeeded in passing a law that indefinitely prohibited the immigration of Chinese workers. About this time, however, new immigrants from Asia, the Japanese, began to arrive in numbers equaling the peak annual totals of previous Chinese immigration. Congressmen proposed to extend the ban on Chinese immigrants to the Japanese as well. They also sought to exclude Korean immigrants, whose homeland had been annexed by Japan in 1905. Anti-Asian restrictionism received an unexpected breakthrough in 1907 and 1908 when the so-called "Gentleman's Agreement" was arranged between Washington and Tokyo. The Japanese government pledged to restrict emigration of Japanese laborers to the United States in exchange for the admission of Japanese American pupils to San Francisco's public school system.

I. **The Immigration Act of 1917.** This act was a major step toward creating an omnibus policy of discriminatory restriction based on national origins. It introduced the long-sought literacy test whose supporters believed it would have the practical effect of excluding immigrants from southern and eastern Europe. It established an Asiatic Barred Zone from which no laborers could come, covering all of India, Afghanistan, and Arabia as well as East Asia and the Pacific. This act represented an expansion of the principle of exclusion based on national origins begun by Congress in the Chinese Exclusion Act of 1882. This controversial law was passed over the veto of Woodrow Wilson.

J. **Resurgence of immigration after World War I.** After a slowdown in arrivals, partially due to the initiation of the new exclusionary provisions but mainly because of the international disruption of World War I, annual immigration rebounded. From slightly over 110,000 in 1918, the influx climbed to 141,000 in 1919; 430,000 in 1920, and 805,000 in 1921. Alarmed by the resurgence of immigration fueled by a renewed tide of southern and eastern European immigrants who passed the literacy test, restrictionists groped for more drastic devices to stem the flood.

K. **Immigration quotas.** In 1921 Congress introduced into law a system of discriminatory quotas for immigrant admissions.

1. **Constructing a system of national preference.** Using the U.S. Immigration Commission 42-volume report (1911) as evidence, congressmen began to devise a ranking system in which groups of particular national origins were preferred over others. This innovation constituted a turning point in the history of American immigration policy. Henceforth, the number of aliens of any admissible nationality would equal three percent of the foreign-born population of that nationality enumerated in the United States census of 1910.

2. **Where the quotas applied.** These quotas were limited to Europe, the Near East, Africa, Australia, New Zealand, and Siberia. They did not apply to nationalities excluded previously by the Asiatic Barred Zone, Chinese exclusion laws, and the Gentleman's Agreement. The quotas also did not apply to countries in the Western Hemisphere.

3. **Ceilings on total immigration.** Finally, the 1921 act installed for the first time an annual ceiling on admissions of 355,000; 200,000 of which were available to immigrants from northern and western Europe; and 155,000 going chiefly to those from southern and eastern Europe. This act was passed over yet another veto by Woodrow Wilson.

L. **Regulating immigration quotas.** Led by congressmen from western and southern states, Congress passed the Johnson Act of 1924, imposing even smaller quotas on southern and eastern European immigrants. The annual ceiling on total immigration was slashed to 165,000, by recalibrating the quotas to two percent of the foreign-born population in the United

States in 1890. The 1890 baseline for quotas favored immigrants from northern and western Europe even more since they were more heavily represented in 1890 than 1920. Resetting the quotas reduced the southern and eastern European share of annual admissions to only 20 percent.

M. **The high water mark for Asian exclusion.** The Johnson Act also marked the high point of restrictionist policies against Asian immigrants. It dictated that "no alien ineligible to citizenship shall be admitted to the United States." The Chinese Exclusion Act of 1882 had rendered Chinese immigrants ineligible to citizenship in 1882 and court decisions put the Japanese in the same position. The development of the status of aliens ineligible for citizenship in naturalization law became the key in immigration law to the complete exclusion of Asian immigrants.

N. **New ceiling on immigration.** Restrictionists used the Johnson Act as a temporary measure until an even more severe law was finally installed in 1929. The annual ceiling for immigration shrank once more, this time to 150,000. A formal "National Origins" plan was invoked in which quotas were allocated to immigrants of an eligible nationality in proportion to their representation in the population in 1920. According to this formula, northern and western Europeans received 82 percent of the total annual quota, southern and eastern Europe 16 percent, and the rest of the world two percent.

O. **Ability to assimilate a criterion for entry.** The national origins system produced the desired goal of distributing quotas according to a hierarchy of nationalities ranked in grades of assimilability. American lawmakers had redefined the place of immigration in American life.

VIII. **The role of immigration in the industrial era.** Immigration was a key factor in the development of a dynamic economy.

A. **Immigration as varying with economic cycles.** The American economy had a cyclical capacity to absorb mass immigration. Annual immigration rose in long upswings during phases of economic expansion, and declined in long downswings during recession.

B. **Immigration and economic growth.** Immigration stimulated the growth of the gross national product. It multiplied the labor force, savers, and consumers that made national commercial markets and industrial economies of scale possible. Immigrants provided the cheap labor that made mass manufacturing industries cost effective. The foreign-born and their children held most of the manual-labor jobs in the industrial economy.

IX. **African American slavery: the new republic to the Civil War.** Slavery before the Civil War was concentrated in the South, where it was economically entrenched.

A. **Extent of slavery.** By 1820, nine out of ten American blacks were held in slavery. (Free blacks were about equally divided between the northern states and the southern states. Delaware, Virginia, and Maryland had especially large concentrations. All faced racial discrimination and social, political, and economic restrictions.)

B. **Slavery and Southern agriculture.** By 1820, slavery supported a dynamic agricultural economy based on the commercial production of cotton. The highly productive labor of black slaves made economic expansion in the South possible. As cotton agriculture became immensely profitable, Southerners gave increasing political support to the maintenance and spread of slavery.

C. **Slave resistance.** Slaves continually resisted slavery from its inception, frequently through passive resistance and sabotage. Sometimes resistance was overt as in the revolt of **Nat Turner** (1800-1831) who led an uprising in Virginia in 1831.

D. **Anti-Slavery movements.** Anti-slavery movements were spawned in the early nineteenth century.

1. **American Colonization Society.** In 1816 the American Colonization Society was formed by prominent ministers and politicians (some of whom were slave holders) to phase out slavery and to resettle free blacks in West Africa. In 1820 the society, with some federal support, settled 88 blacks in West Africa, establishing the colony of Liberia. The society was against the presence of the free black as much as it was against slavery.

2. **Incitement to slave resistance. David Walker,** a free man from North Carolina who migrated to Boston, wrote an *Appeal* (1828) in which he assailed slavery as a barbaric institution and urged slaves to rise up in open rebellion.

3. **Garrison's *Liberator*. William Lloyd Garrison,** (1805-1879) militant abolitionist from Boston,

published an antislavery newspaper, *The Liberator*, the first such publication to demand immediate abolition of slavery.

4. **American Antislavery Society**. The American Antislavery Society was formed in 1833 to coordinate antislavery action throughout the North. The organization sponsored the publication of hundreds of abolitionist books and pamphlets, antislavery rallies, and lecture tours by **Frederick Douglass** (1817-1895), **Sojourner Truth** (1795?-1883) and many other black and white antislavery speakers.

X. **The abolition of slavery in the Civil War and the changing position of freedmen**. The aftermath of the Civil War led to changes in the legal position of African Americans.

A. **The abolition of slavery**. The Civil War abolished the institution of slavery. Enacted at the close of the War, the Thirteenth Amendment to the U.S. Constitution outlawed slavery within the United States, thus freeing over four million slaves.

B. **Equal citizenship in law**. During the Reconstruction Era, Congress passed amendments to the federal Constitution to give blacks equal citizenship. Blacks were to have the same civil rights as white citizens.

C. **Blacks made citizens**. The Fourteenth Amendment, ratified in 1868, established the rights of black men as citizens. It enabled black Americans to vote.

D. **Suffrage and the Fifteenth Amendment**. Ratified in 1870, the Fifteenth Amendment guaranteed suffrage to black men in all states of the Union.

E. **Segregation outlawed**. The Civil Rights Acts of 1875 barred segregation in public facilities and provided restitution to former slaves who had suffered damages by segregation.

F. **Creation of the Freedman's Bureaus**. Congress founded the Freedman's Bureau to assist newly freed blacks and poor whites who were displaced by the War to establish themselves.

G. **White resistance**. Southern whites who did not accept the outcome of the Civil War adopted a number of devices to ensure their continued dominance over blacks.

1. **Black Codes**. Southern states established discriminatory laws called "black codes." They included vagrancy laws and restrictions on renting and property ownership, and made unemployment and absences from work illegal. Many African Americans were convicted, fined, or imprisoned under these codes.

2. **White vigilantes**. Vigilante groups were organized by whites to spread terror and intimidate newly freed blacks. The white supremacist organization known as the Ku Klux Klan was the most prominent and enduring.

H. **Legal discrimination against blacks**. From 1880 to the turn of the century, limitations on the status of blacks became legally entrenched.

1. **Denial of legal redress**. The United States Supreme Court declared in 1883 that the Civil Rights Act of 1875 was unconstitutional. Thus, African Americans who were refused equal accommodations or service by privately-owned facilities were denied legal redress.

2. **The "separate but equal" doctrine**. The Supreme Court ruled in *Plessy v. Ferguson* (1896) that, in places of public accommodation, such as railroads, restaurants, and schools, segregation was legal so long as "separate but equal" facilities were provided. The "equal facilities" provision of the ruling was never enforced adequately.

3. **"Jim Crow" laws**. "Jim Crow" laws began appearing on state and local dockets at the turn of the century. These laws established legal forms of racial segregation. They allowed for disenfranchisement, residential segregation, separate public accommodations, and curfews. Thousands of such ordinances were established over the next five decades.

XI. **New patterns of black mobility from 1900 to World War II**. After the turn of the twentieth century, black geographical mobility increased in response to urban economic opportunity and rural oppression.

A. **Source of cheap labor**. After the destruction of slavery, blacks became the major source of cheap non-white labor.

B. **Concentration of blacks in the South**. The vast majority of blacks remained in the South after the Civil War.

C. **Few blacks in industry.** A very small number of blacks had penetrated the industrial labor force by 1900. In that year, 86 percent of all black workers were still employed in agriculture or in personal-domestic service.

D. **Role of World War I in black industrial employment.** Nevertheless, blacks were beginning to move out of these employments, a process that speeded up during World War I with its high demand for labor in manufacturing. By 1920, agriculture and domestic service accounted for only two-thirds of the black labor force while one-third of blacks worked in the industrial sector.

E. **Migration from rural South.** As the structure of the black labor force changed, its geographic distribution shifted. The first important migrations to the North from the "cotton South" occurred during World War I. The majority of migrants located in large cities. Over 80 percent of all blacks in northern and western states lived in urban areas.

F. **Migration and economic opportunity.** Like the immigrant movement to the cities, black migration was a response to real changes in the structure of economic opportunity—changes such as the price of labor.

   1. **Attraction to Northern cities.** The rise in northern demand for industrial labor caused by war and an economic boom in the 1920s, and the decline of cotton agriculture in the South attracted black labor to industrial cities in the North.

   2. **Escape from oppression in the South.** The black migration from the South was an effort to escape from persistent discrimination and inequality in the South. As limited as the opportunities in Northern cities were for the black migrant, they were still broader than found in the South. In the South after World War I, the position of blacks was worsened by the consolidation of "Jim Crow" policies, the rise of lynchings, and the re-emergence of the Ku Klux Klan.

XII. **The subjugation of American Indian tribal society.** In the course of the nineteenth century, Native Americans were subjugated by whites.

A. **Native Americans east of the Mississippi.** By the late 1820s, more than 125,000 American Indians still lived east of the Mississippi River. Some 60,000 Cherokee, Choctaw, Chickasaw, and Creek Native Americans owned land in Georgia, Alabama, and Mississippi.

B. **Eviction of Indians by settlers.** Land-hungry settlers began to push Indian communities off their land, with the assistance of state and local governments which ignored the federal Supreme Court's orders to cease eviction.

C. **Large-scale eviction of Indian communities.** Wholesale expulsions of Indian communities were inaugurated. In the winter of 1831, in the first of a series of forced marches known as the "Trail of Tears," Indians departed from their eastern homelands for Oklahoma and Arkansas. One hundred thousand were ultimately removed by eviction operations which lasted until the 1840s. By 1844, whites in the South claimed 25 million acres of land formerly held by Indians.

D. **Displacement by frontiersmen.** The future plight of Indian populations was determined by the westward migration of white frontiersmen and adventurers. Mountaineers, cattlemen, miners, and trailblazers flocked to the West. They displaced Native American Indians from their western lands and killed off the buffalo, their principal economic resource.

E. **Defeat by the U.S. Army.** The U.S. Army's defeat of the Indians in the Great Plains and the Southwest paved the way toward the programmatic subjugation of surviving tribes.

F. **Divide-and-rule policies.** A new policy of concentration, according to which tribes were to live separately from each other, was implemented. This policy was designed to reduce intertribal contact and enable the federal government to negotiate separately with each tribe.

G. **The "reservation."** Furthermore, it established an institutional environment, the reservation, in which the Indians were to be "de-tribalized" and assimilated into the official culture of the external society.

H. **Abortive attempts at improving the lot of Native Americans.** The Dawes Act of 1887, to create independent farms and individual landholdings for Indians who left reservation communities, failed to improve their circumstances.

I. **New Deal legislation.** New Deal legislation attained some limited improvements. The Wheeler-Howard Act or "the Indian Reorganization Act" passed by Congress in 1934, provided for tribal self-governance, loans for Indian business ventures, and funds to educate Indian youth. It made the Indian population legal successors to the aboriginal tribes. They were authorized to control the reservations in cooperation with Bureau of Indian Affairs officials.

POST-INDUSTRIALIZATION PATTERNS OF ETHNIC DIVERSIFICATION AND INCLUSION: THE POST WORLD WAR II ERA

I. **Post war immigration mobility and assimilation**. The decades after World War II brought immigrant populations to a higher stage of social mobility and cultural assimilation.

A. **The upward mobility of immigrants**. By the post-war years, nearly all immigrant groups who arrived in the industrializing era displayed rates of upward movement that increased with their length of residence. On the whole, immigrants to the United States achieved an improved life for themselves because they helped to build a dynamic economy that raised overall material welfare. Immigrant groups displayed consistent rates of upward social movement that increased with length of residence and intergenerational succession.

B. **Rise of European assimilation**. By the 1960s and 1970s, descendants of European immigrants began to lose strong identification with a dominant traditional ethnicity. Secularization, acculturation, social mobility, and intermarriage combined to weaken both objective involvement in ethnic group life and subjective identification with ethnic culture.

II. **Asian mobility**. Asian Americans made rapid progress toward middle class status after World War II. Their mobility marked the opening of new opportunities to groups which suffered historic ethnic discrimination.

A. **Japanese internment**. In one of the great miscarriages of constitutional justice in history, Japanese Americans were interned in prison camps during World War II, on false suspicions of disloyalty. But after the war, the climate of persecution dissipated and they entered business and professional fields from which they had been formerly excluded.

B. **Growth of Chinese middle class**. For Chinese Americans, World War II had stimulated the growth of a middle class. Many were hired for jobs in defense industries, the sciences, and the professions.

C. **Increased educational opportunity**. Both the Chinese and Japanese found that educational opportunities had also improved markedly in the post-war years; they became among the most highly educated groups in the population.

III. **Immigration policy: from restriction to liberalization**. From the 1930s to the mid 1960s immigration tended to decline but then rose when the quota system was abolished.

A. **Decline of immigration**. In the 1930s immigration slumped due to restrictionism and the Great Depression. At the end of the war the admission of refugees and war brides started a new rise in the influx.

B. **The resumption of mass immigration**. A new era of mass immigration began with the passage of the Hart-Cellar Act of 1965. This was a landmark act because it abolished the discriminatory national quotas and exclusions that had been established from 1882 to 1929. It raised the annual ceiling on quota admissions from 150,000 to 290,000. It provided for equal but limited admissions from all countries.

IV. **The return of mass immigration and the rise of the Third World**. Immigration rose in the 1960s, much of it from Third World countries.

A. **Increase in immigration**. The annual volume of immigration surged after 1965 toward levels reached in the peak intervals of the late nineteenth and early twentieth centuries.

1. **Rise of illegal immigration**. Official yearly totals were underestimated and therefore misleading. The flow of undocumented immigrants (who illegally entered the country or overstayed their visas) mounted in the 1960s.

2. **Sources of illegal immigration**. The western hemisphere was a principal source of undocumented migrants. They came from Mexico, the Caribbean islands, and parts of Central and South America. Illegal immigration from Europe also increased.

3. **Third World arrivals outpace European immigration**. At the turn of the century, European immigration comprised 97 percent of annual admissions; in 1975, however, Asia and the other Americas sent 77 percent while Europe accounted for 19 percent.

B. **Post-war policies on Hispanic immigration.** Hispanic immigration in the post-war period grew through new policies and produced new social controversies.

1. **The "bracero" program.** The "bracero" guest-worker program had been instituted by the U.S. and Mexican governments during World War II to supply labor for American agriculture. A shortage of workers during the Korean War, as well as the American desire to control the flow of Mexican labor, caused the program to be extended annually until 1964.

2. **The position of illegal immigrants.** "Undocumented" (illegal) Mexican workers continued to move to the United States in ever-increasing numbers. Since they were not legal residents of the United States they lacked protection from exploitative practices and were reluctant to draw attention to themselves.

3. **Repatriation.** By 1954 a stable and regulated labor pool had been established for agriculture, leading the Immigration and Naturalization Service to initiate "Operation Wetback" to remove the unwanted illegal residents. Some 3.8 million Mexicans were expelled within the next five years, most by only the threat of deportation, without formal proceedings.

V. **Immigration of refugees.** Refugee immigration became a major factor from the middle of the twentieth century.

A. **Admittance of the oppressed.** Inspired by the historic position of America as an asylum for the oppressed of the world, Congress granted special permission to those fleeing from Nazi persecution, persons displaced by war, and war brides.

B. **Increase in Third World refugees.** After 1960, the largest waves of refugees came from Asia, Africa, and Latin America. By the 1980s, an average of 100,000 refugees from these regions were admitted annually.

VI. **The changing position of African Americans.** From the end of World War II to the 1970s, blacks achieved unprecedented advances. In charting these improvements in position, it must be kept in mind how disadvantaged they were at the start of this period.

A. **Voting and holding public office.** The Civil Rights Acts of the 1960s produced large gains in voting power. Black voters in the South increased from 1.5 million to 3.3 million from 1962 to 1970. Black registration rose from 30 percent of those eligible to nearly 60 percent. In 1965, there were 70 elected black officials in the South; in 1970, 700 blacks were sitting in elected positions; in 1975, 1600 blacks held office.

B. **Education levels.** Blacks achieved new levels of education. The median number of school years for blacks jumped from 10.7 in 1960 to 12.7 in 1970. College attendance among blacks increased by 500 percent from 1963 to 1977.

C. **Economic advancement.** Economic progress was not as impressive as political and educational gains, but it was nevertheless substantial. The economic expansion of the post-war years combined with government efforts to improve the occupational status of blacks. Income for black families increased by 109 percent in the 1960s, while income for white families grew by 69 percent. This accelerated change lifted black family income from 48 percent of white earnings to 61 percent in 1970. Moreover, black families headed by gainfully employed husbands and wives earned 88 percent of the annual income of two-income white households.

VII. **Post-war organization against discrimination.** The post-war years saw both new opportunities and increasingly sophisticated organizational efforts among disadvantaged groups to secure rights under law and to protect their interests.

A. **Actions to combat discrimination against African Americans.** After World War II, attempts to improve the status and condition of blacks were renewed. In 1948 the Democratic Party's platform included a plank for the improvement of civil rights for blacks. The National Association for the Advancement of Colored People (NAACP), founded in 1909, launched new legal challenges to *de jure* racial segregation.

B. ***Brown v. Board of Education.*** In the landmark 1954 case, *Brown v. Board of Education*, the Supreme Court, under the leadership of Chief Justice **Earl Warren** (1891-1974), ruled that segregated public schools violated the Fourteenth Amendment—that separate facilities are inherently unequal. This case overturned the *Plessy v. Ferguson* decision of 1896.

C. **The leadership of Martin Luther King Jr. Martin Luther King Jr.** (1929-1968) began his historic leadership of the civil rights movement when he was elected president of the Montgomery boycott organization in 1955. He organized protest and petition campaigns for civil rights, based on a philosophy of non-violent resistance.

D. **Expansion of LULAC and allied Hispanic organizations**. Mexican-American leadership groups began to press for more equality and opportunity. The League of United Latin American Citizens (LULAC), founded in 1928, expanded into a national organization to obtain protection against discrimination. The Mexican American Legal Defense and Educational Fund (MALDEF) searched for new legal remedies against discrimination. **Caesar Chavez** became a symbol of the increased activism among Mexican Americans when he led the organizing of the United Farm Workers Union.

E. **Japanese Americans organize**. The Japanese American Citizens League (JACL), founded in 1930, expanded its efforts to oppose prejudice and discrimination toward Japanese Americans, along the advocacy lines taken among black and Hispanic civil rights groups. It began to explore ways to seek redress for the setbacks caused by World War II internment.

F. **Federal legislation to bar racial discrimination**. The federal government passed new laws and established new agencies to end legal discrimination based on race. The 1957 Civil Rights Act created a Civil Rights Commission and authorized the attorney general to protect voting rights. The 1960 Civil Rights Act strengthened enforcement of voting rights. The 1964 Civil Rights Act empowered federal agencies to eliminate discrimination in public accommodations and federal programs, and generally to protect equal opportunity.

G. **Termination of legally sanctioned racial discrimination**. As a consequence of changes in judicial holdings, the gains of the civil rights movement, and new federal initiatives, *de jure* racial discrimination was set on the road to termination.

Contemporary Perspective

The diversity of the American people is proverbial. Americans differ from each other in innumerable respects. They live in distinct regions, each of which retains, even in an age of geographical mobility and cultural homogenization, its own defining characteristics—its own speech and intonation, mores, and customs—even its own cuisine. Again, Americans differ in age, in education and occupation, in religious belief, in wealth and lifestyle, in skills, capacities, and interests—and in other ways too numerous to mention.

These and other sources of American diversity are not, however, those that concern us here. We are concerned instead with the ethnic and racial diversity of the American people, since that aspect of diversity has become an increasingly common source of public discussion and controversy.

That America's ethnic and racial diversity is truly remarkable is a matter of frequent self-congratulation. But a number of often contentious issues regarding this diversity have arisen in American public life from the very dawn of the nation's history. Beyond social fragmentation and political controversy, however, the American public has a stake in fostering among its citizens a conscious commitment to the values capable of transcending differences. Effective civic education can foster a consciousness of national identity within the differences that diversity implies. Key elements in this education are knowledge of the democratic values and principles that animate American political institutions; and a solid grounding in the nation's history—warts and all. Americans need to know that their past is at once the story of a favored and successful people as well as a history that is troubled and tragic, colorful and variegated, endlessly fascinating, and instructive. Americans of all races and groups have inherited these institutions and this past from those who have come before. Uninstructed, or falsely instructed, they are disinherited. But wisely instructed, they can hardly escape the realization that they share both a common identity and a common destiny.

I. **Demographics**. America's racial and ethnic diversity is represented in the nation's demographic breakdown.

A. **America's demographic diversity**. Observers have sometimes pointed out the ways in which American society has become homogenous on account of increasing geographic mobility and the development of a common popular culture. Nevertheless, in recent decades, many of America's ethnic and racial groups have put forward claims to uniqueness that have brought a new consciousness of difference.

1. **The division of citizens by race and ethnicity**. breakdown of American citizens by race and ethnicity cannot be precise for several reasons. For one, the published 1990 census figures represent an undercount estimated to be up to 5.4 million or about 2.1 percent of the population, most of these racial or ethnic minorities. For another, the census does not distinguish between citizens and aliens, known to number some millions, though just how many can only be estimated. Taking these factors into account, the following breakdown of American citizens is

likely to err by no more than 1 percent: white—76.5 percent; black—13 percent; Hispanic—7 percent; Asian—2.75 percent; Native American 0.75 percent.

2. **The diversity of groups**. It may be argued that these categories are unsatisfactory tools in discussing American demographic diversity. They lump all American Indians, Asians, blacks, Hispanics, and whites into single categories, thereby obscuring the great diversity *within* each group. A more accurate and interesting view of the demographic diversity of American citizens would look to variety within both racial and ethnic categories. For example, the category "Hispanics" include Argentines and Mexicans; Puerto Ricans and Cubans; Spanish and Guatemalans—groups often as different from each other as they are from other ethnic groups. Similarly the category "Asians" include Koreans and Indians, Chinese and Vietnamese, Japanese and Malaysians who also differ markedly from each other and who have in some instances expressed ethnic hostilities toward each other. The category "whites" harbors similar differences.

B. **The political determination of group identity**. One problematic aspect of diversity is that the question of which groups are identified as worthy of government attention is a political matter, not an ethical or scientific one. Only those groups that have achieved a sufficient degree of self-consciousness and organization combined with an effectively articulated set of demands are in a position to protect and advance their interests. In society at large and within the political system, fairness in the abstract is thus not the test of whose concerns are noticed or which interests are serviced. The bromide that "the squeaky wheel gets the oil" expresses the truth that in politics organized interests tend to receive most attention. The interests of unorganized groups—especially very large groups, which are notoriously difficult to organize—German-Americans, for example—are often not represented in legislative chambers.

II. **Public policy issues**. Examples of public policies involving racial and ethnic diversity issues range from those regarding education to those regarding immigration and preferential treatment.

A. **Issues in education**. A series of issues such as curriculum content and racial integration divides the nation with regard to education policy.

1. **Curriculum**. The content of the curriculum in the schools and in higher education has been a special source of controversy.

a. **Advocates of expanded multi-cultural education**. Some critics argue for radical revision of curriculums in the schools.

(1) **Under-represented groups to be included**. Especially with regard to the social sciences, calls are heard to include in the curriculum under-represented groups to reflect the contributions of a wider range of cultural groups than have been recognized in the past.

(2) **Minority history as source of self-esteem**. Critics further argue that racial and ethnic minority children need to study the history of their own people to achieve self-esteem. Self-esteem is necessary in order to overcome social disadvantages. Moreover, the preservation of ethnic culture and identity is itself good and desirable for its own sake.

(3) **Europe to be deemphasized**. Since various racial and ethnic minorities do not originate from Europe, European history and culture as well as the achievements of white Americans, especially men, should be deemphasized in the curriculum, and the history and achievements of African, Asian, Latin American, and Native American peoples, histories, and cultures emphasized in their stead. Thus, a "curriculum of inclusion" should replace a "curriculum of exclusion."

(4) **Growth of minority populations**. The change in curriculum is especially warranted because of the large number of non-European immigrants who have arrived in recent years. In a number of urban school systems such as in Los Angeles and parts of Texas, most students are racial and ethnic minorities, and their needs must be properly met. Indeed, California will soon become the first state with a majority of minorities in its schools.

b. **Critics of expanded multi-cultural education.** Critics of proposals for radical revision in school curriculums site a number of objections.

(1) **Historical accuracy not to be sacrificed.** Critics argue that changes must not do violence to historical truth. The politicization of the curriculum threatens to transform questions of historical accuracy into political struggles, where truth matters less than power.

(2) **Dangers of a "Balkanized curriculum."** A "Balkanized" curriculum will fail to create a common sense of civic identity among a diverse population. Such a curriculum would constitute another symptom of the disintegration of American society, a society in danger of finding itself progressively less a "nation" than a geographical expression where ethnic clashes rule the day.

(3) **"Europe" not a monolithic culture.** Europe should not be considered a unitary, undifferentiated culture, any more than China and Japan, for example, are culturally unified components of a unitary Asian culture. It should also not be overlooked that more than 75 percent of American citizens are of European heritage.

(4) **Self-esteem argument fallacious.** The argument that the study of the history of one's own ethnic group is necessary for self-esteem is incorrect. Self-esteem is the product of many experiences and results from a child's pride in his or her own achievements. Empirical research shows that lack of self-esteem is a symptom, not a cause, of social pathologies. And if children are taught falsehoods to shore up self-image, they will be rudely awakened later when they discover the truth.

(5) **Objections to hostility to whites.** It is also argued that any revisions made to the curriculum should not be hostile to whites or to Western civilization, contrary to some revisionist plans. Such hostility is simply racism and ethnocentrism in a barely disguised form.

2. **Diversity in the schools and in higher education.** A series of diversity issues concern education in the schools and in the nation's colleges and universities.

a. **Racial integration in the schools.** Racial integration is still far from complete in the nation's schools.

(1) **Need for busing and federal court supervision.** Advocates of the use of busing, if necessary under federal court supervision, point to the distance between realities in the classroom and the ideal of racially integrated schools. Pointing to the language of the landmark *Brown v. Board of Education* decision, they argue that "separate is inherently unequal." Four decades after *Brown*, the national disgrace of racial segregation in education continues, and the will to alter its ancient patterns appears to be flagging.

(2) **Opposition to busing and federal court supervision.** Opponents of school busing say that busing has been unsuccessful in many areas. They maintain that because some parents place their children in private schools to avoid the consequences of busing, public education is undermined. The best criteria of judging a policy are results—not just ideals and intentions. Judged by these standards, the policy is clearly a failure and should be abandoned. In 1991 a Supreme Court ruling made it easier for school districts to stop busing in order to achieve racial balance, even though one-race schools might result (*Board of Education v. Dowell*).

b. **Racial and ethnic diversity in higher education.** Another set of diversity issues is found in higher education settings.

(1) **Arguments for increasing faculty and student racial and ethnic diversity.** Critics of traditional colleges and universities argue that special efforts, including preferential policies (see III.

C. below), should be made to increase the numbers of racial and ethnic minorities among students to reflect the demographic composition of the community, thereby ensuring a fair distribution of scarce goods and the enhancement of academic programs resulting from the perspectives of those from different racial and ethnic backgrounds. In addition, disadvantaged groups should have the opportunity to better themselves, thereby ameliorating the enormous disparity between rich and poor in the United States. Minority faculty should be increased to promote diversity and to ensure that minority students have teachers with whom they can identify and work with effectively.

(2) **Arguments for deemphasizing race and ethnicity of faculty and students**. Critics of preferential policies argue that placing less qualified students and faculty in colleges is unfair to those not favored, denying them the fundamental right to the equal protection of the law. The policy also injures the quality of education and is a principal cause of racial and ethnic incidents on college campuses. Students admitted under "special" admissions programs fail to complete their degrees in large numbers, thus keeping the places from those who could benefit from them. There is also the "mismatch" problem: students who would fare best at a second-rank university are recruited to first-rank institutions, where they may do poorly and unnecessarily feel defeated. The same occurs for students recruited for second-rank universities, and so on through the academic hierarchy of higher education. Also, those who know they are given preference can never gain full satisfaction for their accomplishments, which are also devalued by others. They argue that the diversity that is critical to quality education is diversity of academic opinion, not race and ethnicity.

3. **Racist and anti-ethnic incidents in educational settings**. Incidents of a racist or anti-ethnic character have blighted a number of the nation's institutions of higher learning, among them some of the most prestigious institutions. Such shameful episodes have led to calls for censorship of campus student publications and broadcasts and penalties for students who make overtly racist statements or acts, or remarks deemed "insensitive."

a. **Arguments for campus censorship**. Proponents of campus censorship and penalties for proscribed student speech argue that such measures are required so that the university, which should be a citadel of toleration and learning, takes a stand against intolerance and ignorance. In addition, such incidents directly attack the well-being of those groups targeted.

b. **Arguments against campus censorship.** Opponents of such measures argue that press censorship is blatantly unconstitutional and that rules against "insensitivity" are excessively vague and attack freedom of expression, preservation of which lies at the heart of the university's mission. Censorship also breeds an atmosphere of ideological purity and conformism, promotes the very resentments it is designed to stamp out, and is often enforced with a double standard.

B. **Immigration policy**. Controversial issues have arisen over immigration policy, especially over how many immigrants should be allowed into the country annually. Illegal immigration is a further issue raising controversy.

1. **Levels of immigration**. One issue is the level of immigration is in the national interest. A second issue is whether the sources of such immigration should be controlled. Proponents of large immigration quotas argue that the nation is economically and socially benefitted by immigration. Critics argue that the benefits of large-scale immigration are exaggerated and that the nation's social fabric is in danger of disintegration from such policies.

2. **Problem of illegal immigration**. Hundreds of thousands (during some years a million or more) of illegal immigrants, nearly all of them impoverished and often illiterate people from developing countries in search of a better life, pour across the nation's southern border. Although a large majority of American citizens oppose allowing

such illegal immigration, measures to deal with the problem have been ineffective.

    a. **Arguments in favor of stopping illegal immigration.** Some critics argue that the federal government should allocate the resources to stop this immigration, which is a drain on economic resources in fields such as health, education, and welfare. They also argue that such immigrants place a heavy strain on the nation's social fabric, especially when they do not learn English, even after a number of years residence. Although the economy needs workers, its principal needs are for skilled labor, while those who arrive illegally are generally unskilled. Moreover, because the country's capacity to absorb immigrants is limited and because so many millions from around the world would arrive if they could, the time is past when America can simply open its doors to all comers.

    b. **Arguments against stopping illegal immigration.** Other critics argue that the nation benefits economically from such immigrant labor, which more than outweighs its costs. "Undocumented" (illegal) workers perform important agricultural labor without which crops would rot in the fields. In the case of agriculture, as with other jobs, these workers accept work that Americans refuse. Moreover, it would be cruel to stop poor people from seeking a better life; America has traditionally been a refuge for just such people from around the world, as inscribed on the Statue of Liberty.

C. **Preferential policies.** Certain kinds of affirmative action policies are especially controversial because they involve preferring one set of groups over others on account of its race, gender, or ethnicity. These policies are applied in such areas as hiring and promotion decisions and college admissions. In some cases, for example, the scores of favored groups on competitive examinations for jobs are raised so that the scores are equivalent to those of groups whose scores are higher but are not favored. This practice is known as "race norming."

1. **Arguments in favor of preferential policies.** Proponents of preferential policies argue that such policies are temporary measures designed to compensate for past unfair discrimination against groups such as African Americans, Asians, Latinos, Native Americans, and women. When these wrongs have been remedied, preferential policies will end. They also argue that these policies are designed to promote equality among the poor members of disadvantaged groups and that social equality is an essential characteristic of democracy. It is idle to expect social cohesion in a society where millions of minority people live in squalor and danger, while majority people live in secure comfort. The idea of equality of opportunity is inapplicable where some groups are extremely disadvantaged and others are born with advantages through which they cannot help but win the race. Without the intervention of preferential policies, most minority groups do not compete on a level playing field. Rather than "equal" opportunity that is inherently *un*equal, justice demands that equality of result be achieved. Preferential policies are the indispensable means to that end.

2. **Arguments against preferential policies.** Opponents of preferential policies argue that such policies are unjust ("reverse") discrimination against unfavored groups and deny those groups the equal protection of the laws and equality before the law. Instituted in many countries, such policies have never been temporary. These policies constitute the same racial and ethnic discrimination that their proponents decry. They also sanction punishment of the innocent in order to favor others. It is also unfair to create "instant minorities" of groups which do extremely well in society without preferences given them, but who, being identified as members of some minority group are nevertheless given needless benefits. Those in the past who were unjustly benefited and injured are all dead; guilt for past wrongs cannot be inherited. Preferential policies breed resentment against favored groups and are responsible for much of the racial and ethnic tension on college campuses. In other countries, over time these policies have fostered civil turmoil, including civil wars, with more than a million lives lost. Further, these policies mainly help middle class minorities, not the poor in whose name they are created. Preferential policies are opposed by a large majority of Americans. Justice does not mandate equality of result; nor in a world without discrimination would one expect groups to be economic equals; all empirical research contradicts such assumptions. Finally, according to a 1991 opinion poll, 71 percent of Americans oppose preferential

hiring policies (ABC News-Washington Post poll, May 30-June 2, 1991). Other polls have shown majorities of more than 80 percent.

III. **Finding unity within diversity**. With the range of divisive issues concerning racial and ethnic diversity, Americans have a considerable stake in finding common ground on which to base the democratic enterprise of self-government.

A. **The costs and benefits of diversity**. Social diversity in American society is commonly celebrated as a strength. Although this celebration is sometimes justified, diversity is not always or necessarily a positive attribute of society.

1. **Diversity as a positive force in society**. Diversity may be—and in American society has been—a positive force by providing a wide range of cultural enrichment and by enlarging personal freedom by presenting a wider range of choice than in homogeneous circumstances.

a. **The enrichment of American life**. Skills and abilities of immigrants from around the world have made a myriad of remarkable contributions to the intellectual, artistic, economic, scientific, and other aspects of America's national life.

b. **The enhancement of personal freedom**. An example of the positive effects of diversity is that in some areas of social life diversity can have the effect of promoting freedom. Thus, religious diversity promotes freedom by legitimizing a range of choices of religious beliefs. The individual is freed from irresistible demands for conformity to a single religious orthodoxy. The same is true of other kinds of choices.

2. **Diversity as a negative force in society**. However positive its contributions, diversity may also be— and in American society at times has been—a negative factor.

a. **"Balkanization."** Ethnic and racial diversity can "Balkanize" society. That is, members of racial and ethnic groups may adopt exclusive loyalty to their own groups rather than to the public good and the principles of fairness and equality of all citizens regardless of race, religion, and ethnicity. They could refuse to practice the spirit of toleration for others of different groups. In that case, society would look like a collection of mini-nations, each suspicious of and hostile to the others and prepared to strip them of equal access to society's desired goods. This is the condition of "Balkanization."

b. **The necessity for a common language**. A further problem of social diversity can result from linguistic diversity. This occurs when there is no common language among citizens. Above all, democratic citizens must be able to communicate with each other to carry on a common discussion of public issues. Without a common language, society tends to split apart into linguistic groups with a strong tendency to fight each other. The historical and contemporary experience of multi-lingual countries confirms this tendency.

c. **Social cohesiveness as a problem**. At the same time that Americans celebrate diversity, they must look as well to the problem of social cohesion in a diverse society. Society is weakened insofar as group rivalry is deepened. The ultimate consequence of intense and prolonged struggle among groups is violence, even civil war, and the possible breakup of the polity. The threat or fulfillment of this process is found throughout the world—as close to home as Canada, in the Indian subcontinent, among the pieces of Yugoslavia, in the Soviet Union, in parts of Africa, in Sri Lanka, and elsewhere.

4. **Search for the public good, group loyalty, and personal responsibility**. A transcendent principle of American democracy is that citizens must not think and act exclusively for the benefit of their own group, whether by group one means any of the myriad secondary associations of civil society or an ethnic or racial group. To the extent that such exclusivity is practiced society moves toward disintegration. Those imbued with the values and trained in the arts of citizenship accept that the public good forms a limit to the demands of lesser groups, however legitimate those demands may be. The legitimacy of the claims of one group is predicated upon reciprocal recognition of the claims of other groups; the unlimited selfishness of any group has no rightful place in the conversation of democracy. Of equal

importance is the key idea that in a liberal democracy citizens are born to individual responsibilities and rights; they are not forced by some inheritance of blood or clan to an adherence to race or ethnicity. As they have rights as individuals—not as groups—so also they have responsibilities as individual citizens to preserve the constitutional order which they join.

B. **Conclusion: what Americans hold in common**. Increasing controversy over issues of diversity points to the necessity of finding sufficient common ground among citizens to prevent American society from disastrous internecine conflict and social breakdown. The nation's motto "*e pluribus unum*" reflects the idea of unity in diversity. But any semblance of unity is under siege when the social fabric is rent by various racial and ethnic groups angered and defensive on account of the claims and accusations of others. (See Arthur M. Schlesinger, Jr., *The Disuniting of America*, Knoxville, Tenn., [1991]). One critic has charged that we are in danger of reducing our renowned national motto to "*e pluribus plures*." Americans should not underestimate the danger of today's social divisions. All Americans have an interest in finding a common understanding and a common identity—common ground upon which inevitable controversies can be thrashed out.

1. **Common political values and institutions**. Whatever ethnic, racial, and cultural differences divide the unique tapestry of their society, civically educated Americans hold a set of political values and institutions in common. These are the values of liberal democracy as practiced under the U.S. Constitution and its institutions, discussed in detail elsewhere in this framework.

2. **Common history**. Americans also hold in common a rich history. Shared historical memory constitutes the most tenacious bonding agent available to a diverse nation; knowledge and appreciation of a common history creates the core of a collective historical memory that can bind citizens together in a public enterprise belonging equally to everyone. Thus, American history can be seen as the history of a society of immigrants who came to a New World to escape religious persecution, political tyranny, and poverty; or who, having escaped from the shackles of servitude, struggled to overcome past injustices. It is the story of a people who "brought forth a new nation," an experiment in the self-government of a free people. This unique population trace their origins to every inhabited continent on the globe. All share the search for personal fulfillment—the "pursuit of happiness"—within a constitutional structure of ordered liberty. The American nation—"one people," in the words of the Declaration of Independence—was founded in rebellion from colonial rule, preserved by a bloody civil war, and enriched by vast waves of immigration to become one of the world's great nations. Fully conscious Americans see themselves in the **whole** of this history, not solely in the history of their own particular group. Paradoxically, diversity can be made secure only within the context of a common identity.

3. **Common destiny**. Whatever their differences and divisions, as citizens of one nation, Americans share their nation's destiny. America may prosper from its diverse population, or it may decay because the forces of group hostility or self-aggrandizement overcome those that seek mutual acceptance and equality under law. Whatever that destiny might be, it cannot be divided but will form the common fate of all.

G. GENDER ISSUES

[I]n the new code of laws which I suppose it will be necessary for you to make, I desire you would remember the ladies and be more generous and favorable to them than your ancestors. Do not put such unlimited power into the hands of the husbands. Remember, all men would be tyrants if they could. If particular care and attention is not paid to the ladies, we are determined to foment a rebellion, and will not hold ourselves bound by any laws in which we have no voice or representation.

Abigail Adams (1776)

We hold these truths to be self-evident: that all men and women are created equal; that they are endowed by their Creator with certain inalienable rights....The history of mankind is a history of repeated injuries and usurpations on the part of man toward woman, having in direct object the establishment of an absolute tyranny over her.

Seneca Falls Declaration (1848)

...[S]ince sex, like race or national origin, is an immutable characteristic determined solely by the accident of birth, the imposition of special disabilities upon the members of a particular sex because of their sex would seem to violate the basic concept of our legal system that "legal burdens should bear some relationship to individual responsibility."

Weber v. Aetna Casualty & Surety Co. (1972)

Although the study of gender issues in politics is relatively new, there are a number of reasons for exploring the subject. First, the history of gender politics in America is a key part of American political life, especially for the slightly more than half of citizens who are women. During periods of American history, women have been excluded from voting, holding public office, serving on juries, and serving in the armed forces. A complex set of ideas existed to justify these exclusions, and these ideas continue in part to shape the way some people view women's roles in politics.

Since women have traditionally been associated with domestic life, and politics has traditionally been seen as arising outside of domestic life, looking more closely at gender also helps us to think about what the proper boundaries of politics are.

Third, most changes in the status of women can be traced to social and economic changes not directly attributable to political action specifically aimed at the betterment of women's conditions. For example, the legal status of women has been radically affected by the influx of women into the work force (especially after World War II), by the rise in the power of labor unions in the 1940s and 1950s, and by changes in public attitudes toward discrimination embodied in or sanctioned by unfair statutes. Nevertheless, women have been able, individually and as a group, to act to help bring about social and political change and their activities serve to illustrate some of the ways such changes can be attained.

OBJECTIVES

The citizen should be able to

1. explain the similarities and differences between men's and women's political participation throughout American history.

2. explain how the changing roles that have been deemed appropriate for men and women have affected their participation in American politics.

3. explain how the effects of public policies vary by gender, affecting men and women differently.

4. take, defend, and evaluate positions on constitutional and public policy issues regarding gender and political participation.

FRAME OF REFERENCE
Conceptual Perspective

I. **The basis for past exclusion of women from politics.** The historical exclusion of women from politics rests upon views about the differences between men and women and the appropriate spheres of life for men and women.

   A. **Differences between men and women.** Men and women may be distinguished in several ways, depending on the reason for making the distinction.

      1. **Gender and sex distinguished.** Scholars generally distinguish between sex and gender. Sex refers to the biological distinctions between males and females; gender refers to the social and cultural distinctions made between men and women.

         a. **Gender a consequence of nature.** Some critics say there is not much difference between gender and sex. They argue that the social division of labor is due to the natural reproductive differences between women and men.

b. **Gender a social construct.** Other critics argue that gender is almost entirely a social construction. They claim that while men and women do have different reproductive roles, except for child bearing and breast feeding, few differences between women and men are biologically determined. Most people's views lie between these two notions of gender as a natural or as a social construct.

2. **The political importance of the difference between men and women.** Various arguments have been used to justify the exclusion of women from politics.

   a. **Biological arguments.** In the nineteenth century biological arguments about women's alleged smaller brains and supposed frailty were used to exclude them from politics.

   b. **Social division of labor.** In the twentieth century, however, arguments for excluding women from politics are not premised on a natural inability to engage in politics. Instead, they have appealed to the social division of labor that arises from men's and women's different reproductive roles.

B. **Social role differences between men and women.** Some views about the role of women place them in a sphere separate from the worlds of business and politics.

   1. **Separate spheres.** According to one argument, different social roles for men and women and different spheres of life where each sex should concentrate its efforts arise from biological differences between them. Women's role of bearing children has given rise to their primary identification as wives and mothers. Women have been associated with the domestic sphere since Aristotle distinguished between the household and the polity in *The Politics*. Traditionally, men have been associated with the world of politics and affairs outside the household. However, in recent decades with so many women working outside the home, this view has become less popular.

   2. **Arguments against separate spheres.** Others argue that marking some spheres as appropriate only to women or to men diminishes the prospects for both sexes.

      a. **Male/female spheres as social constructions.** These critics argue that gender roles are

created by the social order, and the roles can be therefore reshaped to match the aspirations of women and men.

      b. **Reconstructed roles as superior.** They further argue that reconstructed roles will be better because they will allow all men and women to pursue their own desires and capitalize on their talents for the benefit of society as a whole. Men could choose to play a larger part in domestic life, allowing women to play a larger part in public life.

   3. **Boundaries between public and domestic life.** Another aspect of the past exclusion of women from politics is the question of how rigid the line distinguishing domestic life and public life is. In general, in a liberal democracy the state may not, unless criminal statutes are violated, intervene in people's private lives. As a result, the state has often played only a small role in women's lives, except in regulating marriage, divorce, and similar matters.

II. **The role of feminism.** Feminists have been among those who have led the challenge to inherited gender roles; but changes in women's roles also reflect other social processes.

A. **Feminism defined.** Although there are many definitions of feminism, the term generally refers to advocacy of equality between men and women in all spheres of life.

B. **Factors influencing women's changing roles.** Historically, women were legally excluded from some spheres of life outside the home. For example, they were banned from certain occupations.

   1. **Political activity.** Feminists argue that their political activity has been a significant factor in removing restrictions on women. For example, feminists have pressured legislators to provide legal protection for women's rights to equality in employment.

   2. **Increased education.** In addition to legal changes, the changes in the status of women in society have been the result of other changes elsewhere in the wider culture. Women have become more involved outside of the domestic sphere in a number of ways. An important factor in this century has been that women have received more

formal education, including more college and post-graduate education.

3. **Economic change**. Perhaps the main reason for the new attitudes to women in nondomestic roles is that many more women now work in paid occupations outside the home.

C. **Changing spheres**. The separate spheres of domestic life and work life have changed in Western societies over time. During the eighteenth century, for example, most economic work was done in the household. Starting in the latter half of the nineteenth century, men went out to work, and women stayed at home. Since World War II, women have constituted a far larger percentage of the work force than previously. How women carried out their responsibilities of child rearing and housekeeping changed with these altered circumstances. Whether women in households become politically active depends partly on their decisions or assumptions about how exclusively they should devote their energies to homemaking.

III. **Arguments for and against changing women's roles**. Some critics believe that arguments for changing women's roles in society are more influential when put in terms of women's rights, that is, claims on the basis of role equity rather than directly on a demand for role change. For example, changing institutions such as the family is far more difficult than arguing about equal gender rights. Using arguments about **role equity** are more effective than those about **role change**, which men are more likely to resist. Role equity refers to an issue of fairness, that people in the same circumstance should be treated the same way. For example, women should be paid the same amount as men for the same job. On the other hand, role change refers to transformation of existing roles. Thus, the idea that wives should not assume more responsibility for certain household chores than husbands challenges the idea of the separation of spheres. Other critics, however, argue that men have traditionally had their own set of household chores and that attempts to politicize internal family relationships are liable to harm the family as an essential unit of the social order. The decline of the family over the past half century has already substantially injured society; the family today is in need of renewed support. Future changes that have the effect of undermining the family will further injure society.

IV. **Change in women's place in politics**. The place of women in American politics has changed dramatically over time as the result of social movements for political change.

A. **Two waves of feminism**. There has been more than one wave of feminist political activism in American history. The term "feminist" first gained wide usage in the U.S. in the 1910s but is more closely identified with the continuing "second wave" of women's activism that began in the 1960s. The first wave was primarily concerned with legal matters pertaining to equity. The second wave has remained more controversial since many of its leading theorists see women as living under an oppressive patriarchal system, a perspective that most American women do not accept.

B. **Feminism and other social movements**. Women's movements for political change often grow out of other movements for social change, in part because women do not always see their interests as the interests of a single group. It is when other social movements have begun to call widespread social practices (such as slavery and segregation) into question that women's movements have historically arisen.

C. **Women and political change**. The success of women's political movements shows that relatively powerless groups in American society can have a profound impact on politics if they are well organized.

V. **Women's role in formal political power much smaller than men's**. Despite the growth of women's political involvement, women hold very few formal roles in American politics.

A. **Women as elected officials**. Women constitute only about 5 percent of members of Congress and only about 16 percent of local elected officials on a national level. Were women office holders in proportion to their membership in the population, they would hold slightly more than 50 percent of offices.

B. **Differences in women's socialization for leadership.** Women do not necessarily think of their political involvement in the same terms as men: surveys of female office-holders and party volunteers suggest that they are less likely to label their interests in politics as professional rather than as altruistic. They are less likely to be involved in professions that facilitate their entrance into politics. They are likely to enter politics at a much later age than men, after raising a family. Thus a significant reason why there are fewer women office holders than male office holders is that women have made different choices regarding their professions and their role in child rearing.

C. **Difficulties of pioneering**. Women who do enter politics face special difficulties which may be one reason that women politicians remain rare in the United States. The images, models, and ideals for successful politicians have been shaped mostly by male politicians. Further, images of successful women have for many people been shaped by women's traditional roles in the household. These customs put women politicians in "a double bind." If they appear to be too much like traditional women, they are not taken seriously as politicians. If they appear to be too much like men, they are criticized for not being feminine.

D. **Possible consequences of more women in politics.** The image of the successful politician and of the successful woman have seldom coincided in the past. This circumstance makes it more difficult for women to enter politics. One present sign of change is that the percentage of voters who say they would not vote for a woman for President has declined precipitously since the 1960's—from 39 percent in 1969 to 12 percent in 1987. In 1937, 65 percent said they would not vote for a woman for president.

Historical Perspective

I. **Women in politics at the founding of the U.S.** At the time of the American founding, women were almost totally excluded from politics.

A. **Political thought.** The first modern stirring of debate in political thought over the place of women in politics occurred about the time of the American founding.

1. **Prevailing views.** Most eighteenth century Anglo-American thinkers believed that women's place was in the home, under the rule of a male head of the household. In the writings of Hobbes, Locke, Hume, and Rousseau this model of the household meant that women had no real involvement in political life.

2. **Arguments to improve women's household roles.** At the end of the eighteenth century, some thinkers began to argue that men had too much power over their wives.

a. **Abigail Adams.** It was for this reason that **Abigail Smith Adams** (1744-1818) wrote to her husband **John Adams** (1735-1826) as he worked with the Continental Congress fashioning American independence. Thinking of the role of women in the new political order, she said to her husband, "remember the ladies."

b. **Thomas Paine.** In 1775, **Thomas Paine** (1737-1809) wrote *An Occasional Letter on the Female Sex* that declared, "Who does not feel for the tender sex?...Man, with regard to them, in all climates, and in all ages, has been either an insensible husband or an oppressor...."

3. **A bold argument for women's equality: Mary Wollstonecraft.** The strongest eighteenth century argument for the equality of women was made in the *Vindication of the Rights of Woman* (1792) by **Mary Wollstonecraft** (1759-1797). Wollstonecraft argued for the equal education of women. "To render mankind more virtuous, and happier of course, both sexes must act from the same principle; but how can that be expected when only one is allowed to see the reasonableness of it?" She stopped short of calling for allowing women to vote, however, saying that her readers would think such a provision ridiculous.

B. **Colonial political practices.** Traditional political practices in the colonies, with few exceptions, excluded women from political life.

1. **The franchise.** Prior to independence women were not entirely removed from politics, however, since a few were permitted to vote during the colonial era. Women who had been widowed but who owned property were enfranchised as property holders in colonial New Jersey. But the post-independence reforms of voting laws disfranchised those few women voters.

2. **Women and the War of Independence.** Women played a variety of roles in the War of Independence. These roles consisted of encouraging and in many ways supporting and assisting the revolutionary soldiers. Various women travelled with the Continental Army, though Washington repeatedly objected to their riding in wagons, on the grounds that the army was slowed. Within the army, women's main duties were nursing sick or injured soldiers, sewing, and cooking. **Martha Washington** (1731-1802) spent every winter during the war with her husband at the battle front, including the severe winter at Valley Forge, where she organized local women and women in the camps to roll bandages, knit socks, and mend shirts. (See Margaret Branson, *America's Heritage*, Lexington, Mass., 1986.) Some loyalist women acted as spies or couriers. Women in Philadelphia, including **Sarah Backe Franklin**, wife of

Benjamin Franklin, and **Esther De Berdt Reed**, wife of the president of Pennsylvania, raised monies for Washington's armies. After announcing their cause in a broadside that proclaimed they were "born for liberty," they went door-to-door to solicit donations. Many other women assisted by caring for family farms in the absence of their husbands. (See Linda K. Kerber, *Women of the Republic*, 1980.)

C. **Restrictions on women in the family**. Women's activities were largely confined to the household in the eighteenth century. Women labored under various legal disabilities.

1. **Laws of coverture.** Family law in the eighteenth century generally excluded women from owning property or from having a separate legal identity. Fathers were the guardians of their daughters until they married, at which point they became the legal extension of their husbands. Divorce was next to impossible, so there were few options in the face of abusive husbands. If a woman fled her husband, she lost her children since fathers were presumed to be their guardians.

2. **Protection from domestic violence.** Although the first law ever enacted against wife abuse was passed in Massachusetts in 1641, few prosecutions for domestic violence occurred in the eighteenth century. However, many criminal acts against women continued to be dealt with under the general laws against violence.

3. **Women's importance in household production.** Despite restrictions, women had a relatively large hand in the country's economy. Most production occurred in the household. While women spent a great deal of their time in the household, so also did men. Women were essential to the economic life in the colonies, even if they were rarely involved politically; for example, they were active in businesses outside the home.

II. **The beginning of women's political activism.** The first stirring of women's political activism grew up in the anti-slavery movement.

A. **Slavery as woman's cause.** The abolitionist **Frederick Douglass** (1817-1895) wrote in his autobiography, "When the true history of the antislavery cause shall be written, women will occupy a large space in its pages, for the cause of the slave has been peculiarly woman's cause."

1. **Female anti-slavery societies.** Women were involved in the abolitionist movement from its earliest years. In 1832 the Boston Female Antislavery Society and the Philadelphia Female Antislavery Society were organized by black and white women and men in those cities. By 1837 over one hundred local antislavery societies existed and they formed a national organization.

2. **Women's rights and abolitionism.** Many women's rights advocates saw their condition connected with the institution of slavery. **Sarah** (1792-1873) and **Angelina Grimke** (1805-1879) were Southern white sisters who argued that putting slaves to work in the fields so that slave-holding women could be pampered reflected two sides of the same coin.

3. **Controversies over women's roles in the abolitionist cause.** Nevertheless, what part women should play in the abolitionist movement remained controversial.

   a. **Women as public actors.** On the one hand, women such as **Lucretia Mott** (1793-1880), **Elizabeth Cady Stanton** (1815-1902), and **Lucy Stone** (1818-1893), argued that they could not be very effective unless allowed to take a public role. In 1870 Stone founded the *Women's Journal*, for nearly fifty years a major voice for woman suffrage.

   b. **Feminists who were abolitionists first.** On the other hand, abolitionists such as **Theodore Weld** and his wife and sister-in-law Sarah and Angelina Grimke argued that the cause of abolition was too important to have it sidetracked by the attention paid to whether or not women were speaking. The Grimke sisters withdrew from public speaking.

   c. **Maria Stewart's argument.** Women had traditionally been proscribed from public speaking, following the dictates of St. Paul's biblical injunction to obey. In 1832 when **Maria Stewart**, a black woman, was the first woman to speak in public in Boston, she assured her audience, "Did Saint Paul but know of our wrongs and deprivations, I presume he would make no objections to our pleading in public for our rights."

4. **The transition from the abolitionist cause to women's rights.** During the World Anti-Slavery Convention in London in 1840, Elizabeth Cady Stanton and Lucretia Mott were denied membership at the meeting because they were women. Afterward, Stanton and Mott resolved to fight as forcefully for women's rights as for the anti-slavery campaign.

B. **The rights movement.** The women's rights movement began before the Civil War.

1. **Convention at Seneca Fall, 1848.** Mott and Stanton convened a meeting of three hundred men and women in Seneca Falls, New York, on July 19, 1848, to consider the question of women's rights.

2. **"Declaration of Sentiments."** At the end of the meeting they issued a "Declaration of Sentiments" that paralleled Jefferson's "Declaration of Independence."

   a. **Demand for equality.** It began, "When, in the course of human events, it becomes necessary for one portion of the family of man to assume among the people of the earth a position different from that which they have hitherto occupied, but one to which the laws of nature and of nature's God entitle them, a decent respect to the opinions of mankind requires that they should declare the causes that impel them to such a course."

   b. **List of grievances.** Among the grievances they included were: "He has never permitted her to exercise her inalienable right to the elective franchise....He has compelled her to submit to laws, in the formation of which she had no voice....He has made her, if married, in the eye of the law, civilly dead....He has made her, morally, an irresponsible being, as she can commit many crimes with impunity, provided they be done in the presence of her husband. In the covenant of marriage, she is compelled to promise obedience to her husband, he becoming, to all intents and purposes, her master—the law giving him power to deprive her of her liberty, and to administer chastisement."

C. **Early opposition to women's rights.** The unprecedented demands for women's rights created many opponents.

1. **Religious opposition.** Opponents of women's rights frequently objected to women's expanded role on religious grounds. They cited Christian practice that women should submit to their husband's control.

2. **Women on a pedestal.** Opponents argued that women's proper roles made them too dainty to serve in professions or to become involved in public life.

D. **Response of Sojourner Truth to critics.** In 1843 a freed slave, abolitionist, and women's rights activist from New York named Isabella felt a calling to speak against slavery and the oppressed condition of women. Taking up the name **Sojourner Truth** (1795?-1883), she left domestic employment to travel throughout the North with her message. In 1851 she answered these criticisms in her famous speech "Ain't I a Woman?"

1. **Women as workers.** "That man over there says that women need to be helped into carriages, and lifted over ditches, and to have the best place everywhere. Nobody ever helps me into carriages, or over mud-puddles, or gives me any best place! And ain't I a woman? Look at me! Look at my arm! I have ploughed and planted, and gathered into barns, and no man could head me! And ain't I a woman? I could work as much and eat as much as a man—when I could get it—and bear the lash as well! And ain't I a woman?

2. **Women's religious role.** "I have borne thirteen children, and seen them most sold off to slavery, and when I cried out with my mother's grief, none but Jesus heard me! And ain't I a woman?....That little man in black there, he says women can't have as much rights as men, 'cause Christ wasn't a woman! Where did your Christ come from? From God and a woman! Man had nothing to do with Him. If the first woman God ever made was strong enough to turn the world upside down all alone, these women together ought to be able to turn it back, and get it right side up again! And now they is asking to do it, the men better let them."

E. **Women's rights at the conclusion of the Civil War.** At the conclusion of the Civil War, a rift developed among the women's rights advocates who had worked actively for women's rights.

1. **"The Negro's Hour."** Some, including Frederick Douglass, **William Lloyd Garrison** (1805-1879),

and Lucy Stone saw the enfranchisement of former slaves as their first priority.

2. **Woman suffrage first.** Others, such as **Susan B. Anthony** (1820-1906) and Elizabeth Cady Stanton wished to push at the same time for women's vote. Stanton angered her former allies when she opposed adoption of the Fifteenth Amendment to the Constitution because it did not give the franchise to women as well as to blacks.

3. **Dissolution of the abolitionist-women's rights coalition.** The women's rights advocates formed two different woman suffrage organizations, the American Woman Suffrage Association led by Lucy Stone and the National Woman Suffrage Association led by Susan B. Anthony and Elizabeth Cady Stanton. At Stone's death in 1893, the Lucy Stone League was founded to continue her fight for women's rights.

III. **The campaign for women's suffrage.** The campaign for women's suffrage was a long and complex political struggle.

A. **The post-Civil War period.** The former abolitionist women's suffrage activists worked from the 1860s until the turn of the century. The American Woman Suffrage Association and the National Woman Suffrage Association differed philosophically about the best way to pursue women's suffrage.

1. **The American Woman Suffrage Association (AWSA).** The AWSA, led by Mott and Stone, was the more moderate organization. It favored lobbying activities and improving the condition of women so that they would be worthy of the vote.

2. **The National Woman Suffrage Association (NWSA).** The NWSA, led by Anthony and Stanton, was the more radical organization. It believed in making more forceful demands for women's rights. An example of the Association's more radical tactics occurred in 1873 in Rochester, New York, when Anthony attempted to vote. She was arrested, tried, found guilty of voting illegally, and fined $100, though she never paid the fine.

B. **Cultural context for the demand for women's rights in the late nineteenth century.** Suffragists faced an uphill struggle during this period since the prevailing image of women as the weaker sex remained a strong cultural norm.

1. **Women's education rare.** Although some colleges devoted to women's education had appeared in the first half of the nineteenth century, the notion still prevailed that education taxed women physically and mentally and ruined their ability to bear and to raise children.

2. **Changing family responsibilities.** With urbanization and the emergence of work for men outside the household, the model for women's lives reflected in women's magazines and elsewhere was for women to absorb themselves in their duties as housewives, duties now much less demanding than the colonial wives' tasks.

3. **Exclusion from professions and other work.** Few professions were open to women in the nineteenth century. Although a few exceptional women became doctors and lawyers, most clerks and secretaries remained men. Women were employed mainly as school teachers for the lower grades, as factory workers, as farm workers, and as domestic help.

4. **Abortion laws and control of reproduction.** During the second half of the nineteenth century statutory abortion laws were adopted in the United States. They were a response to the fear that women were increasingly resorting to abortion. They were also intended to impose medical standards upon practitioners.

5. **The "cult of true womanhood."** The "cult of true womanhood" prescribed a role for women as providing moral and spiritual sustenance for the household while keeping the home a place for families to enjoy. There was little in this image of women that corresponded to women as active citizens.

C. **The renewed push for suffrage.** Women's suffrage attracted only a small following in the remainder of the nineteenth century. The two suffrage organizations continued to exist but lost membership over time.

1. **The Creation of the National American Woman Suffrage Association (NAWSA).** In 1890, the AWSA and the NWSA merged to form a new organization, called the NAWSA. This organization was more solidly middle class in social composition and less radical than the earlier National Association. It was more interested in constitutional reform than the earlier American Association.

2. **Single-minded focus of NAWSA.** After Susan B. Anthony resigned from its presidency in 1900, **Carrie Chapman Catt** (1859-1947) assumed the organization's leadership.

   a. **Exclusion of divisive issues.** Under her direction, all issues except women's suffrage were kept off the Association's political agenda. Catt tried to avoid issues that would divide women.

   b. **The question of black membership.** One such potentially divisive issue was whether blacks should be admitted to the Association. The arguments made by NAWSA frequently stressed that there were more educated white women than black or immigrant men, so that extension of the franchise to women would appeal to the interests of white, middle class men.

D. **The adoption of the Nineteenth Amendment.** Women finally won the right of suffrage in 1920.

   1. **Catt's false start.** The woman suffrage movement's strategy of relying on state legislatures to pass women's suffrage had virtually no impact in the first decade of the twentieth century.

   2. **More radical tactics.** During the 1910s, some suffragists adopted more militant tactics. **Alice Paul** (1885-1978) led a march of five thousand women the day before Woodrow Wilson's inauguration in 1913 and collected two hundred thousand signatures for a federal constitutional suffrage amendment. In 1917, Alice Paul and her group, the Congressional Union, began to picket Woodrow Wilson in the White House. After the American entry into a war billed as "the war to make the world safe for democracy," they carried signs that said, "democracy begins at home." Two hundred women were arrested and detained when violence broke out after one of their marches on the White House.

   3. **Combining strategies: state and federal pressure.** By 1916, a state by state strategy was in place. Members of Congress from states where woman suffrage had been passed began to support a federal constitutional amendment. Strongly supported by President Wilson, the amendment was passed by the House of Representatives in January 1918, and the Senate followed in late 1919. By August 1920, the required thirty-six states had ratified the amendment.

E. **Opposition to woman suffrage.** A number of groups opposed suffrage for women.

   1. **Southern opposition.** Southern males, whose Jim Crow regulations effectively denied blacks the right to vote, were reluctant to allow women the vote. None of the states in the deep South ratified the Nineteenth Amendment.

   2. **Urban machines.** Big city machine politicians opposed women's suffrage out of the fear that women would try to clean up politics.

   3. **The liquor industry.** The liquor industry, afraid that women voters would add impetus to the temperance movement, helped to establish and fund anti-suffrage organizations.

   4. **Religious opposition.** Tradition-minded churches such as the Roman Catholic Church opposed woman suffrage because they believed that it would change relations between men and women.

   5. **Additional opposition.** The National Association Opposed to Woman Suffrage was headed by the wife of New York Senator James Wadsworth.

      a. **Woman's suffrage as socialism.** Wadsworth believed that woman suffrage was attached to socialism. She called them "branches of the same tree of social revolution."

      b. **Other criticisms.** In a speech given in 1918, Ruth B. Sacks, the Secretary of the Missouri Anti-Suffrage League, said: "Feminism advocates non-motherhood, free love, easy divorce, economic independence for all women and other demoralizing and destructive theories."

F. **Other political activities at the time of the suffrage movement.** Since the late nineteenth century politically active women did not devote all of their attention to the suffrage issue. Among other activities were the following:

   1. **Labor unions and working conditions for women.** Both middle class and working class women and men were involved in helping women workers.

a. **Trade unions.** The International Ladies' Garment Workers Union was founded in 1900. Although the leadership was primarily composed of white men, women were the majority of members. In 1909, some twenty to thirty thousand women went out on strike.

b. **Protective labor legislation.** Activists had pushed for labor reforms to shorten hours and improve working conditions throughout the last quarter of the nineteenth century. These efforts were most successful in protecting women and children workers. In 1908, in *Muller v. Oregon*, the U.S. Supreme Court upheld labor legislation that provided special protection for women workers. The Court said that women's physical well-being "becomes an object of public interest and care in order to preserve the strength and vigor of the race."

2. **Settlement houses and the National Consumers League.** Although the experience of **Jane Addams** (1860-1935) at Hull House in Chicago is best known, a large number of urban settlement houses were set up by middle-class, college-educated women to help the poor and immigrant groups. As part of the progressive movement, women were active in other groups to improve living conditions for the less well off. Women were active in the establishment of Children's Aid Societies and the National Consumers League.

3. **Women's clubs.** Organizations such as the General Federation of Women's Clubs and the National Association of Negro Women were involved in more activities than their names identify. At the beginning of the twentieth century, hundreds of women's clubs existed throughout the United States. They were involved in popular women's concerns such as gardening, sewing, and cooking. But they were also involved in the suffrage movement, in book discussions, and in self-help movements.

4. **Temperance movement.** Many politically active women in the early twentieth century were involved in the temperance struggle. Led by **Frances Willard** (1839-1898), the Women's Christian Temperance Union (WCTU) was the largest organization pushing for the passage of local, state, and federal temperance regulations.

5. **Birth control.** Early in the twentieth century, women activists were also involved in making birth control information more widely available, especially for poor and working-class women. **Margaret Sanger** (1883-1966) was an early and central advocate of wider dissemination of birth control information. When the birth control pill became available in 1960, advocates of contraception pointed out the effect it could have of freeing women from an endless cycle of child bearing and rearing, creating opportunities for economic activity outside the home as well as for political action.

6. **Black issues.** **Ida Wells Barnett** (1862-1931) was a black journalist and co-owner of a Memphis newspaper who wrote on a variety of issues, such as the education of black children. During the last decade of the century she led an influential campaign against lynching, including a British lecture tour, persevering against violent opposition. She also advocated women's rights and founded one of the first black women's suffrage groups.

IV. **The end of the first wave of feminism.** Although political leaders were at first deferential towards new women voters, by the end of the 1920s, issues of special concern to women were not at the forefront of the public agenda.

A. **Initial successes of women's new political standing.** Immediately after the passage of the Nineteenth Amendment, women seemed to have much political power.

1. **The League of Women Voters.** At its greatest strength, two million members belonged to the NAWSA. Immediately after suffrage was granted, NAWSA changed its name to the League of Women Voters. It expected, by representing such a large bloc of voters, to exert considerable political pressure in the United States.

2. **Initial results of woman suffrage.** A number of gains for women followed the passage of the Nineteenth Amendment.

a. **Jury eligibility.** By 1922, for example, twenty states allowed women to be eligible for jury selection.

b. **Political parties.** The Democratic National Committee in 1920 adopted a short-lived rule that their composition should be 50 percent women.

    c. **The Sheppard-Towner Act.** Congress passed the Sheppard-Towner Act in 1922, the first direct social welfare program in the United States. Sheppard-Towner was designed to provide training, information, and milk to disadvantaged mothers. Forty-one states joined the program.

B. **The end of women's collective political power.** It was clear soon after passage of the Nineteenth Amendment, however, that women did not vote as a bloc; at that point, women's political power diminished.

    1. **Internal divisions about strategy.** Women were divided about how to pursue their further political goals. One of the most divisive issues was the question of a second federal constitutional amendment, one that would provide for women's equal rights. The Equal Rights Amendment was first introduced into Congress in 1923 at the behest of Alice Paul. Other women, **Florence Kelley** for example, thought that an Equal Rights Amendment would undo all of the accomplishments of working women in gaining special protective legislation for women workers. Accordingly, these women opposed an Equal Rights Amendment.

    2. **The failure of the child labor amendment.** Perhaps another signal of the lack of strength of women voters was the failure of women's groups to pass their "Child Labor Amendment," an amendment to the Constitution outlawing child labor. The issue was not, however, exclusively a women's issue.

    3. **The effects of weakness.** With the waning threat of a women's voting bloc, political leaders paid less attention to women's issues. From 1922-35 only one state made women eligible for jury service. In 1928, the Sheppard Towner Act lapsed. By the end of the 1920s, women's organized political power had clearly not materialized.

V. **Women's activities in the doldrums: the 1930s to the 1960s.** Women's political activities continued from the 1930s to the 1960s, but they were neither widely supported nor widely effective.

A. **The 1930s: the Depression.** During the Great Depression, although women's organizations continued to exist and women continued to remain active in the labor movement, there was not much activity for the advancement of women's rights.

    1. **Negative effects of the Depression.** Women who had become professionals in the 1920s were often forced out of their jobs by nepotism laws adopted in the 1930s. Alice Paul's post-suffrage organization, the National Women's Party, had only eight thousand members in 1923. By the 1930s it dwindled to a few hundred members.

    2. **Hopeful developments.** But women began to appear in high government positions during this period. In 1933 **Frances Perkins** (1882-1965) became the first woman to serve in the cabinet when President Roosevelt appointed her Secretary of Labor, a position she held until 1945. Perkins played significant roles in supporting two path-breaking labor laws, the Wagner Act (1935) and the Fair Labor Standards Act (1938). The Wagner Act allowed workers to join unions without penalty and compelled collective bargaining; the 1938 Act limited the standard work week to 40 hours and set a minimum wage of 25 cents an hour, rising over eight years to 40 cents an hour.

B. **The 1940s: wartime opportunities.** With the demand for men to serve in the armed forces, World War II brought a dramatic influx of women into the work force. Moreover, thousands of women served in various capacities in the armed forces.

    1. **Numerical changes in the work force.** In 1930, 24 percent of all women worked, and women constituted 22 percent of the work force. In 1940, 29 percent of all women worked, and women constituted 24 percent of the work force. By 1945, 38 percent of all women worked, and 36 percent of the work force were women. Not only did the number of women working increase dramatically, but women took jobs that were traditionally reserved for men. Women joined unions in increased numbers; the Congress of Industrial Organization (CIO) had eight hundred thousand women worker members in 1939 and over three million women members in 1945. At the outset of the war, 95 percent of women workers said that would like to quit when their men returned; but by 1945, 80 percent said they wanted to continue working. Nevertheless, beginning in 1946 corporations such as IBM said they would no longer hire women.

2. **Cultural changes in the work force.** Although middle class white women in the work force had previously been young and unmarried, during World War II half of working women were married, thereby changing both women's self-image and the public perception that married women did not work. Child care centers were set up at some job sites, though the extent of organized child care was small. "Rosie the Riveter" became a symbol of the changing possibilities for women workers. A poll conducted during the Depression in 1935 had shown that 80 percent of Americans thought it was wrong for women to work, particularly if they were married. By 1942, 71 percent thought more married women could and should be employed. This shift in public opinion was not due to feminist "consciousness raising" but to the exigencies of the war. Nevertheless, much of the change persisted well after the war was over. Not only did the war open blue collar jobs to women; more women were also accepted in the professions, in journalism, and even as members of orchestras.

3. **Women in the military and government.** World War II also expanded women's opportunities in the military and government. It marked the beginning of an organized women's presence in the armed forces. For the first time nurses could become regular commissioned officers. And women served in all branches of the armed forces in significant numbers. In addition, more women moved into supervisory positions in the federal government. **Eleanor Roosevelt** (1884-1962), the First Lady, was an important representative of the Administration both within the United States and around the world.

4. **Professional women's political efforts.** Professional women, who had organized in the 1920s, were able to exert some political influence. In a drive largely spearheaded by the organization called Business and Professional Women, the Republican Party added a plank supporting the adoption of a federal Equal Rights Amendment to their 1940 Platform. The Democrats followed suit in 1944. Large scale concern about this issue was still several decades away, however.

5. **Post-war gains.** Several categories of women gained most from employment practices brought on by the necessities of the war. Black women, who were overwhelmingly employed before the war in domestic and farm positions, after the war found other positions more readily available. Women over 35 years old, who before the war found it difficult to find employment, were hired in greater numbers after the war. And married women similarly found their prospects for employment significantly better after the war than before.

C. **The 1950s: reduced opportunities.** At the end of the war, many women found themselves constrained to leave their more public roles in the work force to return to the household.

1. **Changes in the work force.** With the soldiers returning from World War II, government manpower officials actively encouraged women workers to leave their jobs and return home. By 1950, the percentage of women who worked dropped to 32 percent, and women were only 28 percent of the work force. During the 1950s, women were more likely to work in sex-segregated occupations and to be supervised by male workers.

2. **Cultural changes.** During the 1950s, American culture extolled women's roles as wives and mothers and warned of the dangers of becoming unsatisfied career women. Women's magazines, full in the '40s of quick supper recipes and stories of successful career women, in the '50s focused on housewives as the best model for American women.

3. **Educational changes.** Middle-class women continued to enter colleges in ever larger numbers. But some were now being encouraged to think of themselves as educated for motherhood and the duties of homemakers.

4. **Limited political advances.** Despite the continued existence of women's rights organizations, they remained small and relatively ineffectual in the 1950s. More women were appointed to ambassadorial and other important government posts, though, and several prominent women served in Congress, among them: **Senator Margaret Chase Smith**, and Representatives **Martha Griffiths** and **Edith Green**. In addition, when the Department of Health, Education, and Welfare was created in 1953, President Eisenhower appointed **Oveta Culp Hobby** to his cabinet as its first Secretary.

VI. **The rebirth of the feminist movement in the 1960s.** In the 1960s, a second wave of feminist activity emerged in the United States.

A. **Dissatisfaction among women.** In the 1950s women had become increasingly disaffected with their roles. In 1962, a Gallup poll indicated that 92 percent of housewives did not want their daughters to pursue the same path. They wished their daughters to receive more education and marry later. In 1963, **Betty Friedan** captured this mood in her book *The Feminine Mystique* (1963). Friedan captured this sense of frustration and presaged the beginning of a new wave of feminist activism.

B. **Two feminist movements.** The women's movement that reappeared in the 1960s and 1970s had two different origins and two different styles.

1. **The mainstream women's movement.** The mainstream women's movement arose out of the political organizations that had existed for decades and that were well connected to the new Kennedy administration.

   a. **The Commission on the Status of Women.** Women who had been active in Kennedy's campaign pressured the new President to establish a Commission on the Status of Women. Kennedy appointed such a commission and asked Eleanor Roosevelt to chair it. The president hoped to create a moderate commission, one that would oppose the Equal Rights Amendment, since organized labor, a more important constituency, continued to oppose an ERA. The commission was a popular idea; in a short time many governors also created commissions on the status of women.

   b. **Founding of the National Organization for Women.** In October 1966, delegates from these commissions met in Washington, D.C. Frustrated with their slow progress, they created the National Organization for Women (NOW). The purpose of NOW, as its Statement of Purpose explained, was "To take action to bring women into full participation in the mainstream of American society **now**, exercising all the privileges and responsibilities thereof in truly equal partnership with men." Within five years, NOW had over ten thousand members. By 1980, NOW had over two hundred thousand members; by 1991 its membership was about the same, at 215,000.

2. **The emergence of a radical women's movement.** Another group of women also came to feminist awareness in the second half of the 1960s.

   a. **Origins in the civil rights and anti-war movements.** Women actively involved in the Civil Rights Movement and the Anti-War Movement argued that these supposedly "progressive" organizations were dominated by men. By the late 1960s, loosely organized women's liberation groups, often initially organized as consciousness-raising groups, had emerged throughout the United States from groups of these radical women.

   b. **Loosely organized groups of radical women.** The feminism of the new groups was more radical as well; often their concern for improving women's status was mixed with proposals for transforming American society economically and socially. They engaged in more radical actions, such as demonstrating against the Miss America pageant in 1968. They also concerned themselves with questions of sexuality and violence against women.

3. **Common traits.** Women in both of these movements tended to be white, upper middle class or middle class, and college educated. They tended to live in urban areas, hold professional positions, and were less likely to be involved in organized religious activities.

C. **"The personal is political."** The feminist slogan "the personal is the political" captures several important features of this second wave of feminism. First, feminists insisted on raising as questions of public concern issues that had previously seemed either too private or too trivial for public attention. Second, feminists insisted that the exercise of power, whether between individuals in a household, in patterns of social convention, or in government activity, all deserve to be treated as "political," that is, public concerns. Third, feminists in broadening this understanding of politics were not calling for broader government intervention but for a public reassessment of values. Critics, however, take issue with an endorsement of "the personal is political." The editors of the respected weekly *The New Republic*, for example, write: "On the left, the chief axiom is that the personal is political and that the continuum of authenticity must know no boundary....The genius of liberalism consists partly in the attempt to separate the passions of private life from the reason of the public arena. Conflating the two realms, by contrast, has been a hallmark of theocratic and totalitarian regimes. A liberal society eschews such invasive identifications." (*The New Republic*, August 19 & 26, 1991.)

VII. **Women's movements in the 1970s and 1980s.** During the 1970s and 1980s the concerns of these two disparate groups of women merged, and the appeal of feminism was somewhat broadened.

  A. **The changing place of women in America.** During the 1970s and 1980s, women continued to move out of the household into other spheres of life.

   1. **Social and economic changes.** More women entered the labor force during this period. By the end of the 1980s, over half the nation's women were employed outside the home. An additional social development was that the average age for marriage increased and divorce rates increased dramatically. During the late 1970s, almost one of every two marriages ended in divorce. As a result, more women were placed in a vulnerable economic status during some part of their adult lives. An increasing number and proportion of female-headed households were below the poverty level. Over half the households headed by women of color were below the poverty line.

   2. **Expanding professional opportunities.** More women entered the professions, the armed forces, and government than ever before. By the early 1990s women constituted about a third of new doctors and lawyers. Although only a small proportion of the highest ranks in colleges and universities are women, they receive an increasing proportion of doctoral degrees.

  B. **The political goals of feminist organizations.** Feminist organizations have been active in trying to effect changes in women's place in society through political means.

   1. **Changing laws.** NOW and other organizations advocated broadening legal protections for women starting in the 1960s. The Equal Pay Act of 1963 provided for equal pay for men and women doing the same job. "Sex" was added as an outlawed ground for employment discrimination in Title VII of the Civil Rights Act of 1964. Title IX of the Education Act of 1972 outlawed discrimination in education based on sex. A national child care act reached President Nixon's desk in 1972, but he vetoed it.

   2. **The Equal Rights Amendment (ERA).** First introduced in Congress in 1923, the ERA became the most widely recognized single issue of the second wave of feminism.

    a. **The legal rationale for ERA.** The amendment provided that "Equality of rights under the law shall not be denied or abridged by the United States or by any State on account of sex." By the early 1970s, many laws already had been passed by Congress and by the states to provide equality for women. The main task of the ERA narrowed from its initial purpose to protect women from inequalities generally. Now its task was to guide the courts to interpret sex as a suspect classification in gender-bias cases. While the courts had begun to interpret laws that discriminated on the basis of gender as unfair, the Supreme Court had also advised that it would not apply exactly the same standards to issues of gender equality as to other suspect classifications such as race.

    b. **Defeat of ERA.** The Equal Rights Amendment was finally passed by Congress in 1972. Its initial prognosis for ratification seemed favorable, as states rushed to be first to ratify it. Within a few months, over thirty states had ratified the Amendment. When sufficient states failed to ratify it during the seven years allotted for its adoption, the deadline was extended. Nevertheless, on June 30, 1982, when the time allotted for ratification passed without the agreement of three-fourths of the states, ERA died.

    c. **Why ERA failed.** Public opinion polls showed that most Americans favored the ERA. While equality of the sexes was generally agreed to, an implied weakening of conventional gender roles was a matter of public concern. It appears that many citizens who support legislation that removes discriminatory constraints believe that it should be done without a constitutional amendment that might have unintended consequences. Certainly many were disturbed by national trends negatively affecting the family; there was also concern about combat military roles for women under ERA. It was also feared that women might lose rights to economic support from their husbands. Insofar as the ERA was simply an abstract question of fairness, citizens supported it. But in the end it came to represent more fundamental change in the relations between men and women and did not gain the support of legislators. Some argue that ERA was unnecessary: "Perhaps it is ironic that the great progress made by the advocates of women's rights under the Fourteenth Amendment was a substantial cause" of ERA's defeat. "Apart from symbolism, there was little need for ERA. Few, if any, remnants of the once-pervasive discrimination against women could any longer survive attack under the Equal Protection Clause" (Archibald Cox, *The Court and the Constitution*).

3. **The politics of abortion**. Another area in which the feminist movements of the 1970s and 1980s was active is the area of legalized abortion.

   a. **Legislative activity.** The National Association to Repeal Abortion Laws, NARAL, had begun to pursue a state-by-state lobbying effort in the late 1960s to have laws against abortion removed. While abortion laws were liberalized in some states, the remaining state laws forbidding abortion were overturned in 1973 when the Supreme Court decided *Roe v. Wade*. NARAL then changed its name to National Abortion Rights Action League to lobby against an alteration of the law under *Roe*.

   b. **Judicial action.** In *Roe*, the U.S. Supreme Court extended considerations of the right to privacy to include a woman's decision about whether to have an abortion. *Roe* said that the question of abortion required a balance to be struck between women's compelling right to privacy in deciding whether to seek an abortion and the state's compelling interest in preserving life. Deciding not to reach the question of when human life begins, the majority opinion by Justice **Harry Blackmun** in *Roe* established that the state's interest is inviolable during the last trimester of pregnancy. But the Court also ruled that a woman's interest is inviolable during the first trimester of the pregnancy. During the middle trimester, the Court said, states could regulate abortions, provided that they recognize the fundamental rights involved.

   c. **Controversy after *Roe*.** The controversy surrounding *Roe* did not abate in the 1980s.

Some legal scholars saw the decision as a blatant form of judicial legislation, with the Court replacing the decisions of legislatures with its own judgment. Others saw the decision as a positive step in the judicial protection of individual rights. Still others viewed with dismay the Court's unwillingness to consider the question of when human life begins.

4. **Violence against women and other issues**. Another issue that has gained attention since the 1960s is violence against women, especially rape and domestic violence. A further issue is pornography.

   a. **Rape**. Concerns that have been raised about rape in recent years include the following:

      (1) **Changing treatment of rape.** A long-standing tradition in Anglo-American law made it difficult to sustain the charge of rape without corroboration for the woman's testimony that she had been raped. As a result of activity by women's groups, rape laws have been reformed to make rape a crime of violence, not of passion. Charges of police insensitivity in dealing with rape victims led women to set up rape crisis centers to help victims cope with the crime. Rape is now treated more like any other form of forcible attack.

      (2) **Extending the meanings of "rape."** In recent years some women have argued that acquaintance rape ("date rape") and marital rape should also be treated as severe crimes. Others have argued that these extensions, when given legal status, go too far in interfering with intimate relationships; they argue that excessive broadening of the definition of rape is an attempt to give women total control in sexual relations with men, especially if no corroboration of rape is required for conviction.

   b. **Domestic violence**. Domestic violence laws were adopted first in the seventeenth century in Massachusetts, but domestic violence has not always been taken seriously by police. Attitudes have changed over time, however. By the end of the 1980s, after widespread publicity, the public had come to perceive domestic violence as a serious problem. Estimates of physically abused wives and partners range as high as 25 percent to 50 percent. No reliable statistics are available however. A small number of men were also victims of their wives or partners. Actions designed to address this problem include setting up shelters for abused wives and their children, allowing *ex parte* court orders to prevent abusive spouses from approaching potential victims, and training police to deal more effectively with domestic violence.

c. **Pornography**. Another issue given public attention is pornography.

   (1) **Arguments against pornography**. Anti-pornography advocates argue that pornography degrades women. Moreover, it is argued that sadistic pornography contributes to some men's willingness to engage in violence against women. Pornography should therefore be outlawed.

   (2) **Opposing views**. Critics argue that outlawing pornography among adults is a paternalist attempt to interfere with the actions of free men and women which is not the legitimate interest of the state. The case that some forms of pornography lead to violence against women rests on weak research and has not been proved. Beauty pageants might also degrade women in the sight of some, but in a free society mere disapproval of behavior in the absence of harm more substantial than alleged degradation is insufficient grounds for its being outlawed.

   (3) **Attempted legislative action**. Several municipalities passed ordinances outlawing pornography that critics argue is harmful to women. However, the laws were struck down by the Supreme Court as violating First Amendment protections of freedom of speech and the press.

5. **Lesbian and gay rights**. Early in its history, women's groups were reluctant to recognize the presence of lesbians in their membership, fearing that such recognition would make it less attractive to mainstream America. This argument soon gave way to the view that since lesbians are

women, the absence of protection for their rights casts a shadow on the rights of all women. In this way, the movement for lesbian and gay rights was linked with gender issues.

C. **Anti-feminist women's movements**. In response to feminist activism, many women have become politically active in opposition to feminist demands.

1. **STOP ERA**. One movement that emerged in the 1970s was STOP ERA, organized in 1973 to defeat the Equal Rights Amendment. The organization argued that the amendment would undermine the American family.

2. **"Right to life" movement**. Many women have also been active in the anti-abortion movement, though men are also among its leaders.

   a. **Opposition to judicial activism.** The anti-abortion movement has been critical of the Supreme Court's decision on *Roe v. Wade*, proposing constitutional amendments to overturn the decision.

   b. **Legislative activity.** The movement has also attempted to pass greater restrictions on abortions within states and localities.

   c. **Use of civil disobedience.** One branch of the Right to Life Movement, Operation Rescue, uses civil disobedience to keep women from entering abortion clinics.

3. **Opposition to changing the family**. During the early 1980s, conservatives united to support the Family Protection Act, a bill aimed at undoing the kinds of transformations brought about by feminists. It included provisions to restore the father as the head of the household and to prevent homosexuals from obtaining federal benefits.

4. **Neo-conservative opponents**. These critics claim that American women have already been given the freedom and equality they should legally have. They now have more choices than any women before them in history. They are free to choose marriage and careers, to get an education, and even to engage in sample mating. Of course, a woman may be dissatisfied with her life and look for external reasons. According to author and editor Midge Decter, "the primary appeal of the women's movement lies in the message that

everything troubling her is somebody else's fault."

D. **From social movements to conventional politics.** Over two decades a number of changes have occurred within the women's movement. Some groups have disappeared, others continue to flourish. Politically the most significant change has been from the protest politics of the late 1960s and early 1970s to more conventional political tactics. More women's groups now lobby in Washington and in state capitals than hold street demonstrations. This shift marks both a change in national climate and in the power of the concerned groups. It also marks a change toward greater involvement in electoral politics. In the 1980s the issue of gender entered electoral politics in concerns about a "gender gap." Polls showed that men and women seemed to hold somewhat different opinions on certain issues. Women were somewhat more likely than men to support Democrats; men somewhat more likely to support Republicans. Ironically, the gender gap does not affect questions of women's rights. There is no difference between men and women in support for women's rights.

E. **Advances for women in the 1980s.** The advancement of women in the 1980s is illustrated by the fact that fewer women chose many of the more poorly paid occupations that typified their work in the past. More opted for business, science, and the professions, such as law and medicine. The first woman astronaut, **Sally Ride**, was chosen; **Geraldine Ferraro** was a vice-presidential candidate in 1984; and **Sandra Day O'Connor** was appointed to the U.S. Supreme Court.

Contemporary Perspective

I. **Thinking about gender issues.** What issues should be regarded as "gender" issues and how they should be considered are open political questions in the United States.

A. **What a "gender issue" is.** It could be argued that questions such as whether the federal government should increase defense or social welfare spending have a gender impact: more men are employed in defense related industries; more women are employed in social welfare agencies. So thought of, almost every policy question becomes a gender issue.

B. **Gender issues as issues of special concern to women.** Opponents of this wide view believe that it dilutes the understanding of gender issues. They assert that gender issues consist of issues of special concern to women. These include issues of women's rights, including

equality in the work place and similar issues of gender discrimination, the family, and children. Gender issues in this view are conceived as issues that directly concern the lives of women as women.

II. **Controversies for the 1990s.** A number of controversial issues raised during the last several decades of activity over gender issues remain unresolved. These issues remain controversial in large part because they reflect underlying disagreements about deeply held values, especially views about the proper roles for women and men in society.

A. **Women and work: Wage inequality and job segregation.** Nearly half the nation's women now work. In 1990, according to the U.S. Department of Labor, women constituted 45.3 percent of the work force, yet the pay for the average woman remains at about 60 percent of the pay for the average man. How much if any of this disparity is due to unfair practices and how much is due to other factors is a matter of controversy.

1. **Existence of job segregation.** One argument is that the discrepancy between the pay of women and men is explained by the types of jobs that each group occupies. The job market remains gender segregated, with women largely concentrated in such traditional female fields as clerical, non-commissioned sales, cashiering, nursing and other health care professions, and waitressing and other service jobs. Despite decades of affirmative action, most women remain in a small assortment of jobs near the bottom in terms of salary and prestige in the work force.

2. **Explaining job segregation.** A number of explanations are offered to explain this persisting pattern. One explanation is that women are still victims of employment discrimination. Another is that women prefer these jobs, because they allow the flexibility necessary to work and assume household responsibilities simultaneously. A third argument is that for a variety of reasons many women simply prefer these types of jobs to those favored by men.

3. **The "comparable worth" proposal.** Some critics advocate a controversial "comparable worth" policy as a solution to the disparity in pay between the sexes.

   a. **Arguments supporting "comparable worth."** The basic premise of the comparable worth argument is that traditional women's jobs have a depressed value on the labor market because they are women's jobs. Hence, nurses are paid less than truck drivers because nurses are women, even though the difficulty of their job, arguably, rivals that of truck drivers. Several states have implemented comparable worth compensation schemes within the ranks of their state employees.

b. **Arguments against "comparable worth."** Opponents of comparable worth point out that it represents a fundamental assault on the free market system. Jobs traditionally filled by men may not be higher paid because of discrimination, but because the tasks are less desirable. Truck drivers, for example, often need to be away from home for extended periods of time and have a difficult and uncomfortable job, making it less attractive than nursing. Many truck drivers are members of a strong union, which may also be a factor. As a result of these and other factors, it is argued, the pay is better. In other cases, women's pay may be lower for other reasons, such as market forces. For example, their jobs may be easier to perform and therefore lower paid because market forces (the ease of filling these jobs) keeps pay at a low level.

c. **How the issue is perceived.** Comparable worth illustrates well the point that how an issue is perceived affects one's judgment of it. To its proponents, comparable worth is a simple question of fairness, of ensuring that people are paid the same for similar work. To its opponents, comparable worth is an attempt by women to overthrow free market forces in an attempt to gain advantages for themselves.

4. **Affirmative action.** A further issue involves the use of preferential policies to promote gender equality in the work place. For arguments about this issue, see the section in this framework on Racial and ethnic diversity, Contemporary Perspective.

B. **Women and work: child care.** Another problem for women who work is the problem of child care. Since work schedules rarely match school schedules, women have difficulty working and taking care of their children. As more women with small children work, pressure mounts for government to make provisions for child care. Child care is not, however, exclusively a women's issue or women's responsibility since men are also concerned about the care of their children and bear responsibility for it. Thus, child care may be called a family issue.

1. **Arguments for government-provided child care.** Among the arguments for child care paid through tax dollars are the following:

a. **Allowing women to work profitably.** Advocates of government-sponsored child care argue that such child care advances the public good by freeing mothers who wish to work, contributing to more prosperous families and, in particular, aiding disadvantaged women for whom most of their wages would otherwise be expended in child care costs, driving them from the work force.

b. **Promoting equity in the work place.** For those who advocate government provision of child care, the assumption that women take care of children is an illustration of how women are disadvantaged in the work force by the assumption that they are the primary caretakers of the household. Women point out that the assumption that they are expected to make child care arrangements, to stay at home and care for sick children, etc., puts them at a competitive disadvantage in relation to male colleagues who do not bear these responsibilities.

2. **Arguments against public child care.** Opponents of more government intervention in child care provision view the issue differently.

a. **Abdication of responsibility.** For these critics, questions of child care are not questions of job equity between men and women, but an attempt on the part of women workers to abdicate their more important responsibilities as mothers.

b. **Increasing the role of government.** Opponents also argue that increasing government's role in child care reduces the family's ability to raise children as family members see fit. Most parents appear to want child care that most approximates the family setting—a difficult undertaking for a government program. Moreover, there is the basic question of whether government can afford to provide such a potentially costly program in an era of huge budget deficits and competing alternatives for available resources.

3. **Other child care questions**. Additional difficult questions face those who would expand the public provision of child care. Should child care be simply custodial, or should it be enriching? If so, how will child care workers be trained? How much should child care workers be paid? Other alternatives are possible, such as provision of day-care by employers, though this model requires employers to absorb the expense, which may be considerable. Research has shown, however, that companies may also gain from such programs through reduced absenteeism and increased productivity. On the other hand, under this model, women with children might be constrained to work for companies with child care arrangements, whether or not these jobs provided them with the best opportunities. To solve this and similar problems would require a completely funded, universally available child care system which some have estimated could cost as much as ninety billion dollars a year.

4. **The issue of child care in the 1990s**. More American women are working today than ever before. Given the structured requirements of the work day, however, many women and their families confront difficult child care decisions. Whether these are private matters for each family to resolve for itself or whether there is a broader public mandate to help families resolve these problems will remain a difficult political problem in the 1990s.

C. **Women and reproduction: abortion and other issues**. Another area of controversy raised by the women's movements of the last decades are questions about the control of reproduction. Questions about reproduction reflect issues of deeply held values as well as the need to respond to rapidly changing medical technology.

1. **Views on the abortion issue**. Public opinion on abortion remains deeply polarized. On one hand, abortion is viewed by some as tantamount to murder by those who view human life as created at the moment of conception. On the other hand, abortion is seen by others as involving a right of privacy. They argue that women should have the right to control their own bodies and that there should be few if any restrictions on abortion. Some consider the idea that human life is created at conception to be a matter of moral or religious faith, not a matter of fact. Most people—men and women alike—hold some qualified version of these positions. The majority appear to favor a right to abortion in certain special circumstances, for example, when pregnancy is the result of incest or rape, when the mother's health is endangered, or when the mother will not be able to take care of the child. The more compelling the reason appears to people, the larger the majority favoring a right to abortion in that case.

2. **Recent developments in the abortion issue**. Legal developments over the abortion question in recent years include the U.S. Supreme Court decision in *Webster v. Reproductive Health Services*(1989), in which the Court raised doubts about the continuing validity of the analysis *Roe v. Wade* had developed but did not overrule *Roe*. The Court implied that stricter state regulations of abortion might now pass constitutional muster. As a result, state legislatures have begun to consider more restrictive abortion regulations.

3. **Complexity of the abortion question.** The abortion question is complicated because it involves many dimensions of moral and political judgment. It is not only a question about when life begins, about the interests of the state in fetuses's lives and about the rights of women to control their own bodies. The question of abortion is also a question about values, about sexual conduct, and about the role of government in protecting the rights of women, on the one hand, and of the unborn on the other.

4. **Other issues of reproductive control**. There are a number of other issues regarding reproduction. One, for example, concerns sterilization of poor and disadvantaged women. Another concerns surrogate parenthood, either through artificial insemination or the use of third-party "birth mothers" paid to bear children. At present these practices are not widespread and are not highly regulated by law. With practices such as surrogate parenthood, the issue of abortion is more complex, since it involves aborting someone else's fetus. In general, as options for using new medical technologies appear, questions of legal intervention in reproductive conduct become more difficult.

D. **Women, the family, and divorce**. As family structures change in the United States, they also pose difficult questions about gender and politics. While people may disagree about the cause of the high divorce rate, it is clear that divorce is increasing and that women are usually left less well off financially after divorce than are men. The causes of the current divorce rate and the means to reduce it are disputed. Although reformers at first supported easier "no-fault" divorce laws, the consequences of such laws now seem unfavorable to women. In California a study of no-fault divorce showed that men's incomes went slightly up and women's incomes dramatically down after divorce. Whether government has a positive role to play in changing divorce law is an open question.

E. **Women and government.** Women still comprise only a small number of high-ranking government officials and public office holders and about 12 percent of American military personnel.

   1. **Military service.** Some forms of military service for women have become increasingly controversial. Some argue that admitting women into the services in certain capacities, especially combat roles, creates problems such as divisions among troops and battlefield difficulties in which male soldiers may be overly solicitous toward the welfare of female soldiers. Similar problems could inhibit efficient military functioning. Others argue that real equality among the sexes requires equality of opportunity in the armed services as elsewhere in society. If women are physically able to perform a job, including combat positions, they should be allowed to do it. Women performed successfully in the Gulf War of 1991.

   2. **Women in government.** Far fewer women serve in elective and appointive office than might be expected given a random distribution of the population. Affirmative action plans have increased the hiring of women in the upper echelons of government service. While additional action can be contemplated, critics argue that solutions must not violate the same principle of fairness to which women's rights advocates appeal.

III. **Effect of women in politics a question.** There is a final question about the significance of all of these issues. What difference does it make if women and men are treated in the same way? What difference does it make if women do not represent half of the elected officials in society? A variety of answers can be given to this question.

   A. **Women's special contributions?** Some critics argue that women bring with them to public life a unique set of sensibilities; increasing the number of women in political life would change political outcomes and make the political world more homelike, more peaceful, and kinder. Variations on this argument have been made since the nineteenth century. But, it is argued, these contributions cannot be made while men continue to dominate public life.

   B. **A division of labor between men and women?** Others argue that the dangers of trying to enforce similar opportunities and roles for men and women greatly outweigh any abstract benefits of fairness or benefits from restructuring society. Societies only work well if there is a division of labor between men and women. Attempting to alter that division of labor invites confusion and pain. It is also argued that there is no compelling reason to believe that women should be 50 percent of office holders, anymore than they should be 50 percent of wine makers, automobile mechanics, restaurant managers, etc. It is also argued that the proportion of women in office should depend upon their own and the electorate's choices, not on a preconceived percentage. There might be fewer women in office than their proportion of the population without any of the disabilities under which women have labored in the past. Thus, many women may dislike the cut and thrust of competitive political action for reasons quite independent of social pressures or unfairness.

   C. **Kinder, gentler government?** It is further argued that the claim that the political world would be gentler and more peaceful is contradicted by the toughness of leaders such as **Margaret Thatcher**, **Indira Gandhi** (1917-1984), and **Golda Meir** (1898-1978), some of whom were quite ready to fight wars they felt to be justified. Opponents of this view see these leaders as having inherited a male-dominated world which forced them into tough postures they might otherwise have been unwilling to take.

IV. **Conclusion.** There is at present no consensus about the direction the nation should take regarding a number of gender issues. Many Americans are wary of the fundamental changes in institutions that are demanded by advocates who wish to provide men and women with complete equality in every sphere of life. On the other hand, most Americans recognize questions of fairness in the treatment of both women and men as an important part of their values.

It is important to be aware of the long history of inequity in the status of women when evaluating the gains made by women in this century. Compared with other centuries, the twentieth century has witnessed spectacular progress in breaking down legal barriers and discriminations under which women have long suffered. Equality of opportunity has expanded. The percentage of women in college now exceeds that of men. And while women are less than half the work force much of this disparity is, arguably, due to their own preferences and not to any widespread discrimination against women as such. It is now unthinkable to assume that women who divorce should legally lose custody of the children. It is unthinkable to condemn women to the second class citizenship they had in previous centuries in respect to elementary property rights. It is now unthinkable to discriminate against women in education or in their legal right to hold office. On the whole, it is fair to say that most legal discrimination against women has been eliminated. What remains is under assault and much of it is not likely to persist.

The doors to women in the work place, to higher education, and to political life have, arguably, been effectively opened. Some historians believe that much of what has been accomplished since World War I is probably due more to vast social and economic changes than it has been to agitation for specific reforms.

It is, of course, hard to compare the relative effects of focused political activity for reform on behalf of women to the effects brought about by many social changes that were not the result of reform activity but which nevertheless have clearly affected the social and economic status of women. These changes include the rise of labor unions like the International Ladies Garment Workers Union, the progress made by the Civil Rights Movement, the new democratization of higher education caused by the influx of veterans into colleges after World War II, the phenomenal growth of the American economy, vast technological innovation, and similar forces. Indeed, war itself is a great democratizing force, during which egalitarian forces are set loose that remain in existence long after fighting stops. America's participation in wars in this century is well known to have aided the cause of race and gender equality.

Changes like these have been responsible for enhancing equality of opportunity throughout American society. Women's movements did their share, especially in achieving the suffrage. But the slow erosion of women's political power that ensued when politicians realized that women were not voting as a bloc suggests that women are not convinced that they constitute a political class. The defeat of the ERA again suggests that many women at the grass roots reject the idea of class solidarity or "Sisterhood" that was being promulgated by the more radical elements of the women's movement. In some respects the gains made by women were made in spite of their political fragmentation and not because American women were solidly behind some formal programs like those of NOW (not to speak of some of the programs promoted by the more radical feminists).

Citizens will continue to think deeply about women's issues in the coming years. Underlying familiar questions of gender and politics are fundamental questions about what Americans, as a nation, value most highly, such as liberty and equality, the peace and stability of the social order, and fairness and efficiency in political and economic arrangements.

H. AMERICA AND THE INTERNATIONAL SYSTEM

...they shall beat their swords into plowshares, and their spears into pruning hooks: nation shall not lift up a sword against nation, neither shall they learn war any more.

Micah 4:3 (8th Century B.C.)

...you know as well as we do that right, as the world goes, is only in question between equals in power, while the strong do what they can and the weak suffer what they must.

Thucydides (*Melian Dialogue*) (5th Century B.C.)

For what can be done against force without force?

Cicero (1st century B.C.)

If we do not want to die together in war, we must learn to live together in peace.

Harry S. Truman (1945)

The management of a balance of power is a permanent undertaking, not an exertion that has a foreseeable end.

Henry A. Kissinger (1979)

[The problem is] deciding correctly when, where, how, and to what ends we shall exert the enormous power and influence which we are able to generate.

Walter Lippmann (1948)

INTRODUCTION

It has been a hundred years since Americans have felt that events in the world beyond their shores were breaking so favorably as they have been in recent years and that the future held so much promise. But it is evident that the promise of tomorrow will require more knowledge than ever about the basic character and process of international life, about specific issue areas, and about international institutions. To discover what we need to know, we must have the prior ability to organize our thinking. We need to be able to apprehend international relations—how states "classically" deal with each other and how new forms of activity among states are now complicated by novel institutions and issue areas.

To be capable and enlightened citizens, Americans must have some idea of the course of the American experience in foreign affairs and of the international system in which their country plays so important a role. We must be conscious of international and global issues and concerns; and we must realize how the world is growing increasingly interconnected. We need to know something about the course of the Cold War, why it was waged, and how it was concluded. We need to have an appreciation of the mechanisms for ameliorating conflict between groups—especially the uses for a resuscitation of diplomacy. These are the requisites of informed citizenship.

America's isolationist heritage. Democracy functions well if citizens know both their own interests and have a responsible idea of the interests of others. For over one hundred years we Americans did not need an elaborate knowledge of people and places beyond our own frontiers. For much of our history, the American destiny was hammered out in substantial isolation from Great Power politics. As Washington enjoined in his famous farewell address, "The great rule of conduct for us in regard to foreign relations is, in extending commercial relations, to have with them as little political connections as possible."

The American experiment was best achieved, most Americans believed, as a result of a felicitous detachment from Old World struggles. Our forbears maintained that our independence and our institutions would prosper only if we were detached from the "corruptions of Europe," for the old order was characterized by dynastic war, a scramble for colonies, and the willful vanities of monarchs.

Well into the twentieth century, most Americans were isolationists. World War II and its aftermath, however, transported us an enormous psychological distance. The rest of the world was brought home by the millions who served overseas and later via television. The world was coming closer to a land many had once felt could be an impregnable fortress cut off from unhappy foreign conflicts. Even well into the late 1940s opinion polls found most Americans hoping to detach themselves from the rest of the world once again. This illusion is no longer imaginable.

From isolationism to Cold War Consensus. The post-World War II transformation of American foreign policy from "entangling alliances" to a permanent peacetime involvement in the fortunes of the world had **three immediate circumstances**:

First, **the collapse of former great powers in Europe**—Britain, France and Germany—leaving the Soviet Union as the only intact and viable military power poised, it seemed, to reap the benefits of the vast dislocation of war.

Second, the **economic analysis** U.S. policy makers gave to events: the belief **that in the long run, war was caused by exclusive markets and restrictive trade**. And, in the short run, a European economic collapse would fit the interest of communism, an ideological servant of a totalitarian state with many of the same limitless appetites of dictators just defeated in the most devastating war in history.

Third, the **changed character of war**. Previously war was finite. There had always been a shortage of munitions and a surplus of targets. But the **atomic bomb** foretold a world in which war might not serve policy or defense. Rather, the only purpose of armed force, if nuclear war was to result from the initial spark, might be to avoid war altogether. The option to fight an all-out war in the nuclear age defied rationality altogether. War became, in the words of the renowned Prussian military strategist **Karl von Clausewitz** (1780-1831), "a thing unto itself."

Given the high perception of danger after World War II, it is not surprising that much of the public agenda was shaped in terms of defense. The greatest public works program in the last forty years, the interstate highway program, was described and defended as a "National Defense Highway" system. Monies given to education were debated in terms of racing the Soviets and voted under the rubric of "National Defense Education." Even the civil rights agenda of the 1960s was framed in terms of the effectiveness of the United States overseas and our call to democracy elsewhere.

Among the studies that prospered in the Cold War period was the formal study of international relations. By divorcing the study of international affairs from law and history, it was hoped that Americans could derive an independent knowledge of the mechanics of world affairs. To be sure, as with any field, international relations involved a separate idiom as it emerged as a full blown academic field of inquiry. The following objectives state a core of principal concepts that emerged from that inquiry that are helpful in allowing citizens to evaluate world affairs.

OBJECTIVES

The citizen should be able to

1. explain the basic character of international relations including the concepts of state, sovereignty, nationalism, balance of power, and international order.

2. explain the relationship between force and order in international relations.

3. explain the role of diplomacy in international relations including how states relate, negotiate, and manage conflict.

4. explain key events and issues in the history of the United States in world affairs.

5. explain the ways in which individuals can participate in a world of "sovereign states."

6. take, defend, and evaluate positions on issues of public policy regarding international relations.

FRAME OF REFERENCE
Conceptual Perspective

I. **International Relations: distinctions and definitions**. International Relations are the relations between states. States are legal entities.

A. **Definition of a "state" and "international relations."** The strict definition of a state is a government that has effective domain over a territory. International relations are the relations between sovereign units.

B. **Definition of "sovereignty."** Sovereignty is the ability to effectively make law within a territory and uphold agreements with other states.

C. **States and nations not the same**. Nations are historically developed communities of people who share a common language and culture and a common identity. Some nations have no state; and states are not necessarily single "nations."

   1. **Nations without states**. There are nations without states. For example, the Basques of northern Spain and southern France are an ancient people who speak a language very different from that of France or Spain. The Kurds of Iraq, Turkey, and the Soviet Union are another example of a nation without a state.

   2. **States with many nations**. There are also states composed of many nations. The Soviet Union has over a hundred different linguistic groups and dozens of major ethnic groupings. States frequently contain a dominant linguistic and ethnic group.

   3. **Most states are "multi-national."** Most states are not, strictly speaking, "multi-cultural" or "nation-states" but rather "multi-national" states. The

United States with its racial and ethnic diversity is said to be an example of the former and the Soviet Union an example of the latter.

4. **States do not require a single culture or language.** States do not need the same culture or language to function in international society, or to be peaceful, or to have a sense of a common identity. For many years Canada, with some difficulty, showed that it could have separate nationalisms within the same boundaries, remaining an effective member of international society.

D. **Woodrow Wilson and the idea of a system of "nation-states."** The idea (as opposed to the reality) of the nation-state is a thread that joins the mid-eighteenth century to our own time. **Woodrow Wilson** (1856-1924) believed that if nations were free to choose their own government, they would likely choose democracy.

1. **A system of free peoples.** After World War I, Wilson envisaged an international system of democratic free peoples joined together in a "**League of Nations.**" This system, he believed, would be stable and peaceful. It would have no cause for war.

2. **Wilson's failure and the perpetuation of the "nation-state" idea.** Wilson failed in his attempt to create an international system of democracies when the U.S. Senate refused to ratify the League of Nations treaty. But nationalism and the idea of the nation-state remain powerful ideas, as the continuing revolts of the peoples within the Soviet Union and elsewhere attest.

E. **"International society" and the "international system."** Some one hundred-sixty states, from tiny city-states such as Monaco to giant multi-national states like the Soviet Union, now comprise the "international system."

1. **Contacts as comprising the "international system."** States that have some contact with one another are said to form **international society**. The **sum of these contacts** is usually called the **international system**.

2. **"Great powers" as historically comprising "international society."** The history of international society—the society of states who regularly "relate" to one another—has been dominated by a handful of major "powers." Those powers that share a number of common values and interests are said to form an "international society."

II. **The problem of international order.** The problem of international order is the classic problem of international relations. Order may be defined as regular and predictable behavior.

A. **Need for methods to reduce violence.** To maintain order there must be methods by which states deal with each other to smooth relations and reduce the potential for violence.

B. **Means of keeping order in domestic society absent in international society.** International society is unable to keep order through the same means as domestic society. In well-governed states, the legitimate means of violence are under the disciplined control of one or more levels of government.

1. **Domestic society and order through monopoly of legitimate means of violence.** States try to organize and control violence domestically by **centralizing the use of violence**, if possible, claiming a **monopoly** on the use of violence.

2. **Domestic society and the professional use of arms.** In domestic society, arms are used by a **constabulary** (an organized body)—by **professional police** at home and a professional military abroad.

3. **International society as lacking a monopoly on legitimate means of violence.** In domestic society, the police and the national militia have the wherewithal to compel compliance. But in international society, the members have arms distributed among themselves.

   a. **States as separate actors.** Each state must, as best it can, decide for itself when its interests are challenged in a way that requires force.

   b. **No international police or mandatory judge.** There is no international police and no single magistrate to whom an appeal can be directed. **The analogue of domestic police in international society is self-help.**

   c. **Disorder and expansion of number of states.** Much international disorder can be traced to the **abrupt expansion in the number of states** in the international system.

C. **Existence of order in international society**. States do not live in a true condition of international anarchy. There is order.

1. **Abundant examples of international order**. Letters mailed from almost anywhere will, with reasonable certainty, arrive at their destination. Telephone services function world-wide. Radio signals are received over clear bands. Planes operate in separate air paths. These procedures and institutions are signs that states generally live in peace and have regular, predictable means of dealing with each other.

2. **States as guarantors of international order**. If states did not guarantee order, then a livable society would not be possible. States in a position to implement law can and do pattern human activity, from insisting that everybody drive on the same side of the road, to enforcing rules of world-wide commerce, to guaranteeing property.

3. **The relationship between force and order**. The state's monopoly on force is largely seen as the precondition for orderly conduct within the state. But in international society, each member retains substantial access to force. No higher power enforces "order," that is, predictable and reasonably peaceful relations between the members of this "international society."

D. **Alliances and order**. Order in the international system, classically, has been achieved by negotiation and through alliances.

1. **Alliances and "balance of power."** A general description of international behavior is that states align themselves in juxtaposition to one another so that no power can dominate the "system" and thus dictate to the others. This system is commonly called the "balance of power."

2. **Central place of military alliances**. Power, classically, has largely been measured in terms of force. Thus, these alignments or alliances within the balance of power system were (and still are) historically defined in terms of military alliances.

3. **"Balance of power" as a check on states' ambitions**. The system of states poised in equilibrium has been seen by some as the best way for international society to contain excessive ambition and guarantee the independence of its members. An **equilibrium of power** is thought to help

minimize the violence attendant to war and to help keep the peace.

4. **America's historic ambivalence toward "balance of power" politics**. Most of the Founders believed that the European system of shifting alliances and wars to restore or maintain the balance of power was an enterprise typical of corrupt European potentates. From its inception as a nation, the United States attempted to remain aloof from the European balance.

   a. **Nineteenth century cooperation with Britain**. After the War of 1812, the United States and Great Britain worked—with some exceptions such as during the Civil War and the dispute over Venezuela—in tacit cooperation. With British help in patrolling the seas, the United States prevented any other European power from extending its control to the Western Hemisphere and allowed the hemisphere to throw off Spanish domination.

   b. **Acceptance of "balance of power" politics after 1945**. *De facto* Anglo-American cooperation in maintaining the Monroe Doctrine was not an alliance. Not until the late 1940s, after much debate, did Americans accept the idea of an alliance with Europeans to make a permanent commitment to a balance of power.

   c. **The new balance of power**. This new balance of power excluded the Soviets from expansion beyond their World War II gains. It was formalized when the North Atlantic Treaty Organization (NATO) was begun in 1949 by fourteen states, joined in 1954 by West Germany. NATO stands as the preeminent post-war American alliance.

E. **Diplomacy and order**. Diplomacy is an essential mechanism for organizing peace and waging war.

1. **Diplomacy defined**. Diplomacy is the **practice of negotiating with friends** to keep their friendship and **negotiating with adversaries** or potential adversaries to reduce their enmity.

2. **The purpose and use of diplomacy**. Diplomacy is a professional undertaking that evolved, along with the state system, as **an instrument for managing relations between states**. All states use

diplomats to formalize, routinize, and regularize communication with each other. Diplomacy is a primary tool of interstate relations. Diplomats work to solidify alliances, make treaties, and gain information to assist national decision making.

3. **Diplomats as commissioned public servants.** Diplomats are professionals in the arts of persuasion and representation as much as soldiers are versed in the use of arms and coercion. Private individuals and corporations may try to influence governments, but they are not diplomats. **Diplomats are commissioned officials.** They are **public servants representing each state's own interest** by a highly developed mechanism of communication with other governments. In the United States, some important diplomats, i.e. ambassadors, are nominated by the president and confirmed by the Senate.

4. **Diplomats organize the state's purposeful international behavior.** Diplomats and soldiers have an intimate relationship with one another. These professions developed in the same context and over the same period as methods for organizing the state toward purposeful behavior, securing interests, and making the environment for state activity as congenial as possible.

5. **Origins of modern diplomacy.** Beginning with heralds, who were ambassadors acting as official messengers among leaders, diplomats have been seen as unmolestable messengers. By the eighteenth century, diplomats were viewed as a discreet corps or profession whose task was to bring reason, persuasion, and tact to overseas courts and conferences. Diplomats' assignments were to help build up confidence in their own states and minimize friction with the states that hosted them.

6. **Legal documents called treaties as the products of diplomacy.** The brief of the diplomat has always been persuasion. In a sense, diplomats are lawyers, in that the result of diplomacy is agreements. Agreements that are signed conventions between states are called **treaties**, and they have the status of international law.

7. **The resurgence of diplomacy in the twentieth century.** Diplomacy in the twentieth century retains its importance and is re-emerging after a long hibernation. One main reason for its temporary eclipse was that diplomacy was never very popular in either the Soviet Union or the United States.

a. **Distaste for diplomacy in early Soviet Russia.** Leon Trotsky (1879-1940) and **V.I. Lenin** (1870-1924) believed that diplomats were capitalist or monarchist affectations.

(1) **Relations with capitalists unnecessary.** Lenin and Trotsky thought the Bolsheviks would deal with workers and peasants and their representatives but not with the illegitimate and doomed institutions of capitalism.

(2) **Embassies packed with spies.** Stalin became ever more fearful that those who had contact with the West could not be trusted. He therefore laced his overseas diplomatic missions with more spies than diplomats.

b. **America's early distrust of diplomats.** The United States did not think kindly of diplomats for much of its history.

(1) **High-level diplomats viewed as undemocratic.** In the nineteenth century, the U.S. did not send envoys above the rank of minister, lest its democracy be thought to share the pretenses of European courts.

(2) **Wilson's view of diplomatic "deals" as immoral.** Woodrow Wilson typified American attitudes in believing that the practice of secret "deal-making"—away from the inspection of the people—was immoral. Wilson's call "for open covenants openly arrived at" contributed to practices that were not efficient in securing the national interest.

(3) **Professional diplomatic corps founded in 1920s.** Illustrative of the American attitude is that it did not have a professional diplomatic service until 1926.

8. **Modern specialization of diplomatic missions.** By the latter twentieth century, the character of diplomats and others in diplomatic missions had changed considerably.

a. **The onset of specialization.** Diplomatic missions have come to include intelligence representatives, treasury officials, military officers, commercial specialists, and a host of other technicians.

b. **Costs of specialization.** The advent of specialization within and beyond the normal diplomatic enterprise has been a source of concern to some diplomatists. For example, American ambassadors have sometimes found their authority and effectiveness undermined by the presence of intelligence officers on their staff.

c. **Benefits of specialization.** To the extent that problems can be reduced to sub-specializations within diplomacy, they appear to be more manageable and therefore more likely to end in the harmony that diplomats have always sought. With the diminution of Great Power enmity in international affairs in recent times, the extent to which problems are reduced to "technical" and "managerial" issues is to be welcomed. This is not to say, however, that conflicts of interest do not remain.

F. **International law and international order.** As with law in domestic society, international law is an instrument to create or preserve order.

1. **International law regulates states, organizations, and individuals.** International law consists of those rules that regulate how states and their agents and citizens behave toward one another. More recently, international law has begun to cover individuals and international organizations as proper subjects of international law.

2. **International law traditionally created through treaties.** There is an intimate connection between international law and the balance of power. International law has traditionally been the product of treaties.

3. **International law enforced only by states themselves.** The mechanism of enforcement of international law is "self-help." That is, states must enforce the law themselves if it is to be enforced at all. States and individuals often agree to argue their positions in terms of existing international law. But there is no international equivalent of a court bailiff to serve writs and make arrests.

Thus, enforcement is up to the members of international society individually or collectively.

4. **International society as anarchical.** Municipal law (law within a state) is maintained by central authority. But international society is an anarchical society with no real central authority.

5. **International legal procedure similar to its domestic counterpart.** Despite the absence of central authority, the language and procedure of international law are remarkably close to domestic law. There are lawyers and courts who by the agreement of the participants render decisions that are generally obeyed. If they are not obeyed, however, the only choice is default of remedy or war.

6. **International law usually followed.** Virtually every state has specialists devoted to understanding international law. Since it provides basic rules for safe air travel, mail delivery, protection of diplomats, and declaring war and waging war, few states have had an interest in wholesale defiance of international law. Like people in domestic society, most states, most of the time, heed the law.

7. **Politically radical states' disregard of international law.** Only those radically revisionist states such as those guided by Lenin in its early years, Mao Tse-tung, Hitler, Saddam Hussein, or the Ayatollah Khomeini, have an interest in dramatically redefining the structure of international law.

8. **States' formal allegiance to international law.** When the United States was found to be flying a reconnaissance plane called the U2 over the Soviet Union in 1960, President Eisenhower defended the action by saying there was an overriding necessity of self-defense. But he did not deny the general principle that states control their own airspace.

9. **States' attempt at legal justification for illegal acts.** Even when "vital interests" compel an illegal action, a legal justification is expected and inevitably offered by the offending state.

10. **International law as covering the conduct of war.** The habit of consulting international law makes international relations more predictable and orderly. There are laws of war and laws of peace.

Therefore, when the balance of power fails to maintain peace, international legal principles attempt to mitigate the excesses of war. Law helps to structure and limit war's violence. Along with diplomacy, it also provides a way of formalizing an end to war by the signing of peace treaties.

G. **The decline of diplomacy during the Cold War.** Force is the last resort of politics, whether domestic or international politics. But power does not always mean force. States use economic power and the power of persuasion or "soft power" more routinely than military power. (For "soft power," see Contemporary Perspective below). But coercive diplomacy became commonplace during the Cold War.

1. **Compromise identified with appeasement.** In part, this decline was due to the depreciation of traditional diplomacy after the experience between World War I and World War II. At that time, compromise, the classic diplomatic routine, became identified with appeasement.

2. **Appeasement as not satisfying the dictators.** Appeasement in the inter-war period (1919-1939) did not sate the appetite of aggressors. On the contrary, the hunger of Japan and Germany grew with the feeding. Similarly, the wartime negotiations of the Powers were stigmatized by the poor reputation of the 1945 Yalta accords, which were attacked for agreeing to Stalin's swallowing up of Eastern Europe.

3. **Lack of diplomatic tradition in both the U.S. and the USSR.** Neither major power in the Cold War had any real diplomatic tradition. Publicly, in the United States, diplomacy fell on harder times. Diplomats were besmirched by McCarthy and politicized by various presidencies. With diplomacy in decline and the politics of confrontation ascendent, force achieved public esteem as an instrument to contain adversaries and sustain international order.

III. **The decline of force because of nuclear weapons.** The destructive force of nuclear weapons has made their use unthinkable.

A. **Nuclear weapons as changing the character of war.** Traditionally, weapons had been acquired by states to secure one of four political objectives: wealth, land, prestige, or defense. Karl von Clausewitz said "War is the extension of politics by other means." This under-

standing of the usefulness of war was changed by nuclear weapons.

B. **Nuclear weapons as altering the traditional scarcity of munitions.** There had previously always been a deficit of munitions among warring states. There had never been "enough" bullets or guns when compared to the targets available. But with nuclear weapons, there was a deficit of targets. The nuclear age was an age of overkill, in which it has been argued that von Clausewitz' understanding of war was rendered almost meaningless.

C. **Decline of threat of nuclear war among superpowers after the Cold War.** Clausewitz also observed that wars tend to produce violence in excess of their objective. Wars tend to become "things unto themselves"—violence out of control. Nuclear war between states has been more a threat than an option. As the Cold War loses its meaning, nuclear weapons are receding as an eminent danger in the developed world. With the decline of the Soviet threat, force has faded from its position of primacy in the relations between industrialized states. The use of force in relations among less developed countries and between industrialized and the developing countries is, however, another matter.

D. **The spread of nuclear weapons among developing countries as increasing the danger of their use.** The decline of the nuclear threat could change significantly if such weapons proliferated among developing nations. In these countries, lingering ethnic hatreds and national rivalries tend to be exploited by leadership for short-term gains.

1. **Indian-Pakistan rivalry.** Before the advent of nuclear weapons in the Third World, communal rivalry in the Indian subcontinent led, at the time of the partition into India and Pakistan in 1947-48, to the loss of millions of lives in communal warfare. The recent acquisition of nuclear weapons in the subcontinent and the persistence of these rivalries augur poorly for the future.

2. **The Middle East.** The persistence of the hostility between Israel and her neighbors makes the area another possible site of nuclear war, should Islamic states obtain such weapons. Irresponsible leaders in such countries as Iraq, Iran, Libya, and Syria have not scrupled to use excessive force, terror, or forbidden weapons to achieve

their aims. The use of nuclear weapons by such states cannot be discounted.

E. **The continuing relevance of military power**. In an ideal world, force would assume a place more like its position in domestic politics. Domestically, force is an understated but real possibility, having its effect more by its potential than by its actual use. Whether this effect is possible in an international arena lacking a central authority is highly uncertain. The Persian Gulf crisis and war of 1990-91 illustrates stark limits to the notion that military force has lost its relevance in a post-Cold War world.

IV. **The persistence of force and the decline of war**. To understand what war is, we must distinguish between its legal and its "material" senses.

A. **War as a legal idea, not just military fighting**. The organization of violence by states against other states is called war. War should not be understood only in the "material" sense of military fighting; war is also very much a legal concept. War (as opposed to other forms of fighting) takes place only among states, which are legal structures.

1. **In the legal but not "material" sense, Israel is at war with some neighbors**. Examples of war in the legal as opposed to "material" sense may clarify the matter. In a legal sense, Israel is still in a state of war with all of its neighbors except Egypt, with whom it has signed a peace treaty. In a material sense, it is at peace with some of them, notably Jordan and Saudi Arabia.

2. **In the legal sense, U.S. not at war with Nicaragua in the 1980s**. In the 1980s, the United States was not at war with Nicaragua in a legal sense. There continued to be an exchange of Embassies between the two countries. But in its actions, the U.S. embargoed trade, armed rebels, and generally tried to undermine the Nicaraguan economy and government.

3. **Panama intervention and Korean War were not wars in legal sense**. The U.S. did not declare war on Panama when it landed two divisions for a fifty-four-day operation to overthrow the infamous dictator, **Manuel Noriega**. Even the Korean War of 1950-53 was not officially or legally a war, but a "police action" of the United Nations led by American forces.

B. **Gradations of war and peace**. Classically, states have been at war or they have been at peace. But for the United Sates of the twentieth century, gradations of war and peace have developed. Strictly speaking, the U.S. has not been at war with Cuba. In the 1960s, however, both the Eisenhower and Kennedy administrations tried to topple the regime of **Fidel Castro** by a combination of sabotage, economic pressure, and, on more than a few occasions, by assassination attempts.

C. **Why no full-scale wars among industrialized countries**. There are two main reasons why war-like acts on the part of states of the developed world no longer lead to full-blown war. One is legal; the other is rooted in war's dynamic to become absolute.

1. **The legal reason for the decline of war**. Various conventions (the League of Nations Covenant [1919], the Kellogg-Briand Treaty [1928], and the United Nations Charter [1945]), have all but outlawed war except in the face of an armed attack.

2. **Deterrence**. A second reason is deterrence. Deterrence is restraint among armed powers that arises from fear of retaliation in kind. The conduct of war has always risked outrunning its purposes. With the rise of industrial democracy, more people have become available both to fight war and to become war's target. This expansion of violence has culminated in nuclear weapons. But states possessing them have shown some restraint in war.

   a. **Nuclear weapons not used in Sino-Soviet conflict**. The Soviets and Chinese, both nuclear powers, fought in the late 1960s but did not use nuclear weapons.

   b. **Deterrence in Soviet-American relations**. During the Cold War, the Soviets and the United States had confrontations that at other times would have led to war. For example, nuclear war came perilously close during the Cuban Missile Crisis of 1962. But nuclear weapons have disciplined the two sides in their behavior toward each other.

   c. **The stability of nuclear deterrence**. Nuclear deterrence has seemed reasonably stable in that there have been really few direct attempts to exploit atomic power diplomatically and virtually no test on the battlefield since World War II. The future of deterrence among developed states seems likely to be reasonably benign.

V. **The usefulness of nuclear force and its decline.** There is clearly a discrepancy between most policy goals and the means associated with nuclear weapons. Nuclear weapons have brought about revolutionary changes by stabilizing international political relationships and by limiting arenas in which the "superpowers" can clash.

A. **Nuclear weapons' lack of usefulness in waging war.** In both Soviet and American cases, nuclear weapons have had little usefulness in extending the wealth, power, and esteem that large states have traditionally sought or in furthering other aims of national policy. The reason for this is that nuclear weapons are unusable by either side and are known to be unusable.

B. **Nuclear weapons' limited usefulness.** Nuclear weapons and massive armaments have had some utility. They served to conserve a system of alliances and associations for over forty years. It is unclear, however, whether nuclear weapons have had the kind of utility that, for example, British sea power yielded at the end of the nineteenth century.

1. **Arguments that nuclear weapons have not been useful.** One argument is that nuclear weapons have not been of much demonstrable benefit in obtaining the goals of policy makers of powerful nations such as the United States. For example, during the Vietnam war a hint was dropped about the possible use of such weapons, but North Vietnam ignored it with impunity.

2. **Arguments that nuclear weapons have been useful.** A contrary argument is that nuclear weapons were useful in preventing the Soviet Union from neutralization if not outright occupation, of some portion of Western Europe. It is also argued that President Eisenhower's threat to use nuclear weapons was instrumental in securing a cease-fire in Korea in 1953.

C. **Divorce between means of force and achievement of foreign policy goals.** In some cases, the divorce between the possession of the means of force and the fulfillment of policy and maintenance of order seems to have accelerated since the early 1970s.

1. **The Arab oil embargo of 1973-74.** The Arab oil embargo of 1973 could not be countered by the threat of using massive force. In such an event, the Arabs threatened to blow up the oil fields, making the use of force counterproductive.

2. **Policy objectives of superpowers in the Third World.** In the Third World, the arbiter of events has been less a deterrent effect of the coercive resources of the superpowers than it has been the political and military conditions "on the ground" and the fearful costs and the toll associated with "conventional" weapons. Two notable examples in which superpowers failed to achieve their aims are the U.S. in Vietnam and the USSR in Afghanistan.

VI. **Why deterrence was stable.** In the forty years of the Cold War until its demise in 1989-90, there has been no nuclear explosion set off in anger. To that extent, at its core, deterrence was stable. It is important to consider why this was so.

A. **Lack of "first strike" capability.** First, there was little chance of a first strike against nuclear-armed states that would completely disarm the state attacked. In every declared nuclear state, there has been a second strike capability, i.e., the ability to retaliate after being attacked, on the part of states that could be attacked, that would visit terrible punishment against a nuclear aggressor.

B. **Acceptability of the status quo.** Second, among the NATO and Warsaw pact forces in Europe, there was a realization that the status quo was livable for both sides. Neither side required anything of the other. On the contrary, each side wanted to keep what it had.

C. **Abhorrence of nuclear war.** Third, both sides carried a common abhorrence for war and for nuclear weapons. The Soviets lost 26 million lives in World War II. The Germans lost over 11 million lives. World-wide, the war cost the lives of nearly 100 million people. No Soviet leader—not a Stalin, a Khrushchev, or a Brezhnev—has been motivated to embrace the apocalyptic numbers of deaths implied by nuclear war.

D. **Common American-European culture.** Fourth, among Americans and Europeans a common culture and fraternity of experience suffused relationships. Prosperity and cooperation disciplined many ancient animosities to the point that they are hardly more than footnotes to the text of memory.

VII. **Change and continuity in international life in the late twentieth century.** New circumstances in international life in the last half century have given rise to a more complex international arena. When non-governmental actors such as the IBM or the Roman Catholic Church both have larger budgets and more practical influence in world affairs than many nation-states, some rethinking of how to accurately describe the present world political system is needed, without claiming, however, that the state system has in any essential respect been superseded.

A. **"Transnational" actors.** In the late twentieth century, states acting through traditional diplomacy as well as through other means remain the principal players on the international stage. Nevertheless, the international arena is replete with various entities—some of them quite old, others newly established—that sometimes alter the flow of international events. When they do, it is argued that they become international actors in their own right, perhaps competing with states for power and influence. Various of these "transnational" actors are not under direct government control; others are. (See *Transnational Relations and World Politics*, ed. Robert O. Keohane and Joseph S. Nye, Jr., Cambridge, 1972.)

1. **Economic organizations.** Internationally based financial institutions and myriad other multinational corporations exert important influences in international economic affairs and are sometimes able to alter international events.

2. **International nongovernmental organizations (INGOs).** INGOs such as the International Red Cross and Amnesty International are examples of a second category of transnational actors. Today there are many thousands of such organizations.

3. **Intergovernmental organizations.** A third category of transnational actors are intergovernmental agencies which are not directly controlled by individual governments such as international air transport and climate control agencies.

4. **Religious and political organizations.** A fourth category are religious and political transnational organizations, eg. the Roman Catholic Church, the World Council of Churches; and national organizations, eg. the AFL-CIO, the National Democratic Institute for International Affairs, the National Republican Institute for International Affairs, the Overseas Development Council, and the English Aldermaston March Committee.

5. **Prominent individuals.** Also among transnational actors are prominent individuals who are sometimes able to help shape international events. Examples include former president **Jimmy Carter**, who undertakes to promote international peace and is active in other international projects; the late businessman **Armand Hammer**, who often intervened in US-USSR relations from the 1920s, when he knew Lenin, until his death in 1990; and former Secretary of State **Henry Kissinger**, head of Kissinger Associates, a prominent international consulting firm. Other such individuals include former German Chancellor **Helmut Schmidt** and former British Prime Minister **Margaret Thatcher**. Others include dissidents such as the human rights activist and physicist **Andrei Sakharov** (1921-1989), **Willy Brandt**, head of the Socialist International, Pope **John-Paul II**, and **Mother Theresa**, a moral and cultural figure.

B. **Technological innovation.** Changes in technology have introduced innovations that have radically altered international transportation, communication, trade, and other aspects of international life. For example, jet passenger travel, satellite television, FAX machines, fiber-optic telephone lines, and the like have revolutionized vital areas of international interaction.

C. **Changed public attitudes toward armed conflicts and its ethical ground.** A third factor is that since World War II there are changed attitudes in many industrialized countries toward the use of armed force in international affairs.

1. **More difficult for democratic states to wage war.** It is now more difficult than in previous eras for governments to wage wars. The U.S., for example, went through a period after the Vietnam War in which the thought of committing U.S. troops to armed conflict abroad was widely viewed with alarm and skepticism. While interventions in Grenada (1983) and Panama (1989-90) followed by triumph in the Gulf War have altered this climate, public attitudes at home and abroad weigh heavily against any impulsive or ill-considered use of military power. In general, domestic opinion, especially of elites, in most Western countries is far more sensitive to ethical questions regarding the use of military power than ever before. One reason for this change is that since 1945 there has been a significant growth both of agencies that shape ethical concepts of how states should behave and

of agencies through which moral judgments are pressed upon states, such as the papal encyclicals (*Pacem in terris* [1963]) or the world-wide human rights movement.

2. **When peace is unethical**. Ethical sensitivities have more than one direction, however; in certain cases, some citizens and moralists find it unethical **not** to fight—for example, in coming to the aid of victims of aggression, especially when one's treaty obligations require such aid. The British sellout of Czechoslovakia in 1938 is a classic example. The British expulsion from the Falkland/Malvinas Islands of the forces of an unsavory Argentine junta in 1982 and the U.S.-led coalition's expulsion of Iraq from Kuwait in 1991 are two further examples in which powerful ethical arguments for resorting to military force were made. Thus, ethical arguments on some occasions call for war; those who believe in "peace at any price" are few and far between.

3. **The continuation of war**. Analysts point out that "the fighting never stops;" that whatever the calls for world peace have been, wars continue to be fought without cease in the late twentieth century. Thus, in 1988, some 80 wars were being fought, with little prospect of general world peace in sight. (See, Patrick Brogan, *The Fighting Never Stops*, New York, [1990]).

D. **Ferment in ideas of national identity and community**. In some areas of the world, especially in parts of Europe and Asia, changing concepts of personal and group identity and community have undermined loyalty to the established political order. This tendency is most dramatically illustrated in the Soviet Union, where personal attachment to the Union itself is virtually nonexistent among large numbers—perhaps a majority—of the population. Instead, they long for autonomy of their individual nations. The same longing is apparent in Yugoslavia. Peoples such as the Basques in Spain likewise claim political independence. Czechoslovakia (the "Czech and Slovak Federal Republic") may split in two. In much of the rest of Europe, although the idea of European Community has considerable support, the nation-state still appears to be the central organizing concept of political identity, though moving toward some form of confederation. In Asia, separatist movements are active in the Indian subcontinent, including Sri Lanka, where preferential policies at the expense of the Tamil minority have fomented a violent separatist movement. In India itself, Sikhs seek independence in the name

of religion. Among the majority Hindu population there is a resurgence in religious fervor. Even in North America, Canadian unity is challenged by Quebec nationalism. In the United States, segments of various racial and ethnic groups appear to be withdrawing from primary national identification as Americans in favor of group loyalty. In addition, certain American elites espouse notions of world community at odds with the central tenets of American political loyalty, citizenship, and popular sentiment.

E. **What has not changed: American citizenship and the U.S. role in world politics**. Changes in the international scene have led to varying interpretations of the meaning of change.

1. **For and against a "state-centric" view**. Some critics argue that states are no longer the central actors in international politics, that a "state-centric" view is no longer a tenable picture of international relations in an age of global concerns. Other critics point out, however, that this view ignores the fact that final decisions on war and peace, on economic and military aid, on key areas of economic policy, and much else of vital concern are made by states, not by subunits or superunits.

2. **Transnationalism and American leadership**. Moreover, leading students of transnationalism such as Harvard University's Joseph S. Nye, Jr. argue that, whatever the positions of some small and medium countries, the United States, the world's only superpower, is both in a position to promote and defend its interests and should be guided by prudence to lead the world to new international order (see Joseph S. Nye, Jr., *Bound to Lead*, [New York, 1990]).

3. **The primacy of American citizenship**. Critics take special issue with those seeking to undermine the attachment of Americans to membership—citizenship—in their country in the name of government entities that do not exist and which have no real prospect of being created in the foreseeable future. If America is indeed "bound to lead," it is essential that civic attachment, including substantive civic education, be renewed and revitalized so that the ill-prepared or irresponsible do not gain credence in directing the course of national policy. (See commentary by Robert Pickus in *Approaches to Peace*, ed. W. Scott Thompson et al., United States Institute of Peace, [Washington, 1991]).

Historical Perspective

From the earliest days of the Republic, the United States has been involved with the world beyond its shores—often more than deemed desirable by those of an isolationist bent. The foreign policy of the new nation was determined by an epochal event that began unfolding just as the United States was organizing its government under the newly adopted federal Constitution. That event was the French Revolution, which commenced in 1789 and did not finally run its course until 1815. By 1792 the revolutionaries had toppled the monarchy and made France a republic. Wars lasting a generation then broke out between the radical new French republic and a coalition of conservative European powers. These wars provided the setting for the initial development of American foreign policy.

I. **The Federalist and Jeffersonian Periods—1789-1815**. Issues concerning relations with Britain and France dominated American policy during this period.

A. **Consequences of Washington's neutrality policy**. At the outset of the European War between the conservative coalition led by Great Britain and the French Republic, President Washington seized the constitutional initiative by announcing the policy of the United States in his Neutrality Proclamation of 1792. In it, he stated that the United States was to remain "friendly and impartial" toward the belligerent powers. This policy had several consequences.

1. **Divided opinion**. Since these wars were ideological, opinion in the United States itself was divided. For Washington and three successors, this internal division made their stated policy difficult to maintain. Disagreement over policy with regard to France exacerbated developing domestic political divisions and the opposing views of emerging political parties.

2. **Difficulty of maintaining policy**. The United States, profiting commercially from the European wars, insisted as a concomitant of its neutrality policy that non-contraband trade with the belligerents be allowed. From the beginning this policy was difficult to maintain.

a. **Great Britain a threat**. Great Britain, with its sea power, was the principal threat to American interests. Its harassment of U.S. shipping and its stated policy of impressment (the forcible drafting of American sailors on the high seas into the Royal Navy) put it on a collision course with an Administration determined to avoid a ruinous war.

b. **Unpopularity of the Jay Treaty**. The outcome was the Jay Treaty, signed in 1794, which was so unpopular that, although it was ratified by the Senate the following year, it received a number of negative votes, passing by a margin of 20 to 10. Silent on the issue of impressment, the British promised, once again, to evacuate western forts. Above all, the treaty said nothing about British respect for the neutral rights of American trade which had been claimed since 1778 and placed humiliating restrictions on U.S. trade with the British West Indies. In addition, British ships were to be admitted to American ports on "most favored nation" terms.

c. **The Jay Treaty and Anglo-American peace**. The Treaty did keep the peace between the U.S. and Britain. To Washington and his Anglophile treasury secretary, Alexander Hamilton, that sufficed.

3. **The "X, Y, Z Affair."** The consequence of the Jay Treaty was a quasi-war with France. French depredations on U.S. shipping intensified.

a. **French demand for a bribe**. President John Adams sought to maintain the peace with France and in 1797 sent a negotiating team to France to end the undeclared naval war. Three French agents, known as "X, Y, and Z," demanded a bribe in exchange for facilitating negotiations with the French foreign minister, **Talleyrand** (1754-1838).

b. **War fever in America**. News of this attempted extortion led to war fever in America when Adams informed Congress of it. "Millions for defense," Americans proclaimed, "but not one cent for tribute." Adams was able to resume negotiations which were successful in evading war and eventually ending the treaty the U.S. had established with France during the American revolution.

4. **The Louisiana Purchase**. In 1803 the purchase from France of the Louisiana Territory doubled the size of the United States. Its $15 million price also purchased a measure of national security for the new nation, making isolationism a workable policy.

5. **Problems with Britain and France**. President Jefferson's second administration foundered on the European problems of this era. Great Britain again seemed the greater threat.

   a. **The *Chesapeake* affair and the Embargo Act**. Early in Jefferson's second term (1807), an American ship, *Chesapeake*, was attacked by the British *Leopard*. Again there was war fever. In the belief that France and Britain badly needed U.S. trade, the Administration sought to maintain American neutrality and rights by economic coercion. At the urging of the president, Congress passed an Embargo Act, forbidding American ships to leave for foreign destinations. At great political and economic risk, Jefferson hoped that the British and the French would cease and desist their depredations.

   b. **Depredations continue**. Neither country ceased its attacks on American shipping, and the economic and political costs of the embargo were too high. At the end of Jefferson's term, the Embargo was repealed.

6. **The War of 1812**. Under President James Madison's leadership, efforts to solve problems peacefully were attempted but failed.

   a. **Continued tensions with France and Britain**. In 1809 Congress replaced the Embargo Act with a less stringent measure, the Non-Intercourse Act, opening non-European ports to U.S. shipping. It was not enough to accomplish its purpose of protecting American ships and was replaced by another measure allowing trade with both Great Britain and France. But the new law tried to entice each to cease its seizure of American shipping.

   b. **Peace with France; war with Britain**. In 1810 France moved to remove its restrictions on American shipping, though Napoleon continued to seize U.S. ships. At the same time, new members of Congress called the **"War Hawks,"** began to demand war with Britain. They came from the West and saw that British support of the Indians strengthened Indian resistance to new settlements. Madison adopted a tougher attitude toward British interference with American shipping. But, since the British were unwilling to compromise, in 1812 Madison's policy led to a war which lasted until 1815.

B. **Main ideas of early American foreign policy**. By the end of the Federalist and Jeffersonian periods, the United States had acquired a stance toward the outer world.

   1. **"Isolationism."** Washington's Farewell Address of 1796 stated the policy and its rationale. The United States should and could remain aloof from European political camps, maintaining friendship and trade relationships only. Jefferson seconded this in his First Inaugural, warning of "entangling alliances."

   2. **"Freedom of the seas."** As a corollary to the policy of isolation, the U.S. argued its right, as a neutral, to trade freely with warring nations. The second war with Great Britain was fought in the name of this policy of a neutral's rights on the seas.

   3. **Trade and whaling in the Pacific**. Isolationism did not interfere with the commercial spirit of the "Yankee trader" abroad.

      a. **The China trade**. Trade with China was inaugurated in 1784 when the *Empress of China* left for Canton and returned the following year, having turned a profit. In 1785 the first U.S. consul arrived in Canton.

      b. **Trade in Australasia**. Trade with the colony of New South Wales, Australia, began with the arrival in 1792 of the ship *Philadelphia* in Port Jackson (Sydney harbor). Interrupted only by the War of 1812, trade between the U.S. and ports in Australia and, from the 1840s, New Zealand flourished. By the 1840s, U.S. consuls could be found in ports throughout the region.

      c. **Whaling**. From early in the nineteenth century, American boats could be found in various parts of the Pacific, acquainting the young republic with an enormous region of the world in which it was destined to play a significant role after 1890. Herman Melville learned much that he put to use in *Moby Dick* while engaged in South Pacific whaling in the 1840s.

II. **The Middle Period—the War of 1812 to the Civil War.** The War of 1812 led to a surge of American nationalism. In foreign policy this was manifest in a "spread eagle" policy—the projection of American power abroad—toward the newly independent Latin American republics, and in an aggressive stance toward whatever power stood between the U.S. and its "manifest destiny," the control of the North American continent from sea to sea.

A. **Latin American independence.** During the first quarter of the nineteenth century, Latin American dependencies of Spain seized opportunities to form independent republics. In 1817, however, a mission to Washington from Buenos Aires found a "lack of American sympathy," for the U.S. was prepared neither to aid the rebellious governments financially nor to recognize them diplomatically. But in 1822, the year after a number of Latin American republics declared their independence, President Monroe recommended they be recognized.

B. **The context of the Monroe Doctrine.** The Congress of Vienna, which worked out a post-Napoleonic European settlement, was committed to the reactionary principle of "legitimacy." This principle implied that the major powers might assist Spain in an attempt to restore the independent American republics to Spanish rule. The Monroe Doctrine was the American response to the possibility of the reestablishment of Spanish rule in Latin America.

1. **Opposition to European assistance of Spain.** Secretary of State **John Quincy Adams** (1767-1848) argued in the Cabinet that the U.S. should oppose any attempt by the European powers to assist Spain. He also urged that the U.S. should announce this policy unilaterally, although for commercial reasons Great Britain also favored independence for Latin American republics.

2. **Russian expansion on the Pacific Coast.** Also of concern to the Monroe Administration was possible Russian expansion on the west coast of North America, as well as a rising sentiment in the U.S. for intervention in the Greek war of independence against the Turkish Empire, which broke out in 1821.

C. **Content of the Monroe Doctrine.** On December 2, 1823, President Monroe proclaimed in his annual message to Congress what became known as his Doctrine:

1. **Non-colonization.** The continents of North and South America were said to be no longer available for European colonization.

2. **Hostility to European expansion.** The U.S. would look upon any attempt of the European powers to extend their system of monarchy to the newly independent republics as an unfriendly act. In effect, the Doctrine said "the Americas for the Americans."

3. **U.S. non-interference in European Latin American possessions.** The U.S. would not interfere in the existing European colonies in the Americas.

4. **U.S. non-interference in Europe.** The U.S. would not interfere in purely European affairs; it would not, for example, intervene in the Greek war for independence (1821-1830). In effect, this was another statement of the policy of "isolationism" with regard to Europe. In a famous Fourth of July lecture in 1821, Secretary of State Adams replied to those who demanded that the U.S. pursue a policy of liberating oppressed nations: "Wherever the standard of freedom and independence has been or shall be unfurled, there will [America's] heart, her benedictions, and her prayers be. But she goes not abroad in search of monsters to destroy. She is the well-wisher to the freedom and independence of all. She is the champion and vindicator only of her own."

D. **U.S. power in the Western Hemisphere.** The announcement of the Monroe Doctrine implied a U.S. sphere of influence in the Western Hemisphere, but the European powers probably paid it little heed. The doctrine was resurrected in the late nineteenth century, however, by a more powerful and outward-looking United States.

E. **Internal preoccupations.** Much of U.S. foreign policy in the middle period relates to the expansion of the nation to the West Coast, to issues involving the U.S. border with Canada, and to acquiring land from Mexico.

1. **Disarming the Great Lakes.** To forestall a costly arms buildup, in 1817 the Rush-Bagot agreement with Great Britain banned naval armaments on the Great Lakes.

2. **Oregon treaty with Britain.** The U.S. also negotiated a treaty in 1846 dividing "Oregon country"

with Great Britain. The U.S. gained the area south of latitude 49.

3. **Acquisition of Texas**. Americans first entered the Mexican state of "Texco-Coahila" when Stephen Austin and two hundred settlers arrived in 1821.

    a. **Americans populate Texas**. In 1825 Mexico opened Texas to American immigration but repealed the law in 1830. The new law could not be enforced, however, since Americans far outnumbered Mexicans.

    b. **The Texas Revolution**. In 1835, after the Americans petitioned but failed to receive separate statehood from Mexico, the Texas Revolution broke out and independence was declared. The following year Mexican forces were defeated at San Jacinto, and the independence of the Lone Star Republic became a fact.

    c. **Texas joins the Union**. For a decade Texas was denied statehood because of the opposition of abolitionists, who opposed Texas's entry to the Union as a slave state. Mexico still claimed Texas as a province when an annexation treaty between Texas and the U.S. was signed in 1844. Although the treaty was rejected by the Senate the same year, in 1845 Texas accepted annexation, which was confirmed by Congress that year.

4. **The Mexican War (1846-48)**. War with Mexico broke out in April 1846 over the disputed Texas territory. The Treaty of Guadalupe Hidalgo in 1848, which ended the war, granted to the United States a large tract of territory, nearly 1.2 million square miles, including Texas, stretching to the Pacific Ocean.

F. **America and the Pacific**. Although still isolationist in outlook during this period, American interest in the Pacific and its trade manifested itself in a number of ways.

1. **Commerce in Siam and China**. In 1833 and again in 1856 the U.S. signed commercial treaties with Siam (Thailand). In 1839 American merchants in Canton, China, petitioned for an American agent to protect their interests when the Anglo-Chinese war, from which they were profiting, was concluded. The American naval squadron in the China seas was too small, however, to influence events.

In 1844 a commercial treaty with China announced the "open door" principle, by which China was to trade with all nations equally, thus protecting American trade interests.

2. **Commodore Perry and the opening of Japan (1854)**. In 1852 Commodore Matthew Perry was instructed to obtain a commercial treaty with Japan. The Japanese had previously allowed only one Dutch ship per year to trade with their deliberately isolated country. Beyond trade, for strategic reasons, Perry also wanted to occupy several of their islands if the Japanese refused to allow their use.

    a. **Initial treaties with Japan**. In 1853 Perry sailed into Tokyo harbor and successfully demanded that a message be taken to the emperor. The following year, a treaty was signed granting the U.S. trading privileges in several ports as well as humane treatment for shipwrecked American sailors. A further commercial treaty was signed in 1857.

    b. **Diplomatic relations established**. In 1858 a more far-reaching treaty was signed, this time establishing formal relations. Six Japanese ports were opened for American trade, tariffs were fixed, and Japanese were invited to study U.S. naval construction and to buy American warships. In 1860, seventy-seven Japanese officials arrived in San Francisco to a gala welcome, after which they toured Eastern cities and displayed Japanese culture and products.

III. **The Civil War Era**. A number of foreign policy issues intruded themselves during the "War Between the States."

A. **Prevention of Confederate recognition**. After the Southern secession of 1860-61, the principal goal of U.S. foreign policy was to prevent European recognition of the Confederacy.

1. **Capture of Confederate diplomats**. The U.S. seizure of two Confederate diplomats on *H.M.S. Trent* threatened this goal as it led to righteous indignation in both Britain and the Confederacy.

2. **The *Alabama* claims**. British shipyards built Confederate blockade runners and other ships which endangered U.S. commerce. In particular,

the C.S.S. *Alabama* wrought havoc with U.S. shipping and led to a post-war suit for damages.

B. **French threat to the Monroe Doctrine**. French intervention in Mexico in the guise of the installation of the Austrian archduke **Ferdinand Maximilian** (1832-1867) as the emperor of Mexico (1864-1867) threatened the nascent Monroe Doctrine. The U.S. moved troops near the border; and French forces withdrew. Maximilian's forces were defeated by his opponents in 1867, and he was executed.

C. **The U.S. and the Pacific**. In 1864 and 1866 the U.S. participated with several European powers in naval action against Japan to protect trading privileges that Japanese isolationists wished to terminate. In 1867 U.S. warships attacked Taiwan in reprisal for the murder of a shipwrecked American crew. In 1868 the Burlingame Treaty was signed between the U.S. and China, after Chinese representatives arrived in San Francisco and travelled, amid popular acclaim and hospitality, to Washington. Among other provisions, the treaty provided for Chinese consuls in America, for unlimited Chinese emigration to the U.S., and for tolerance for Chinese religious practices.

IV. **Post-Civil War policy**. For decades after the Civil War, foreign policy took a back seat as the nation undertook to subdue American Indians and promote industrial expansion. By the 1890s the U.S. was an economic giant. The consequences of these momentous changes had important effects on foreign policy. The U.S. underwent a metamorphosis from youthful self-preoccupation to flexing its economic and military muscle outside its borders, demanding that the world recognize its maturing power and thus its status as a major player on the world stage.

A. **American influence in the Western Hemisphere**. The revival of the Monroe Doctrine and American influence in the Western Hemisphere resulted from threats from Great Britain and Germany in the two Venezuelan border crises. Secretary of State **Richard Olney** (1835-1917) and, later, President **Theodore Roosevelt** (1858-1919), asserted United States' primacy in the Americas.

1. **The first Venezuela crisis**. In 1895 the first Venezuelan crisis occurred over a long-standing border dispute with the colony of British Guiana. Olney invoked the Monroe Doctrine, arguing that Britain must agree to arbitrate the dispute. After much tension and some war talk, an arbitration commission was appointed. Privately, Olney asserted that "the U.S. is practically sovereign on this continent."

2. **The Roosevelt Corollary to the Monroe Doctrine**. A second Venezuela crisis occurred several years later. In 1902-03 a blockade of Venezuela by Germany and Britain sought to force it to pay its debts. In 1904 the crisis came to a head, when President Roosevelt asserted that preservation of the Monroe Doctrine—keeping European powers from intervening to collect debts or for similar reasons—meant that the U.S. might have to intervene in Latin American countries guilty of "chronic wrongdoing."

3. **The Roosevelt Corollary and U.S. intervention**. Roosevelt's "corollary" became U.S. policy until the 1930s. The U.S. intervened on numerous occasions in Central America and the Caribbean to assume what Theodore Roosevelt called "the exercise of an international police power." Thus, marines occupied Haiti from 1915, when the U.S. effectively took over the political and economic affairs of the country, until 1934. Other examples included interventions in Cuba (1917); Honduras (1912); Mexico (1914); and Nicaragua (1912). In the latter case, troops remained from 1912 until 1925, and returned in 1927.

B. **The Spanish-American War and its aftermath**. Insurrection in Cuba in the 1890s led to the Spanish-American War and a mini-empire for the United States.

1. **The background to war**. American sympathies with Cuban rebels who had sought independence for decades were one factor that led to war with the colonial power Spain. The influence of those seeking U.S. expansion was another factor. A third factor was the appearance of "yellow journalism," which inflamed American opinion during a series of provocative events early in 1898, including publication of a stolen Spanish letter insulting President McKinley, and the sinking of the battleship *Maine* in Havana harbor in February. In April Congress declared war on Spain.

2. **Annexations and the treaty with Spain**. The war ended in August 1898 after fighting in Cuba and the Philippines. Americans debated whether or not to annex the remnants of the Spanish Empire, especially the Philippines. President **William McKinley** (1843-1901) included the

annexations of the Philippines, Puerto Rico, and Guam in the Treaty of Paris signed at the end of the year. The Senate ratified the treaty in early 1899.

3. **Occupation of Cuba and the Platt Amendment.** Cuba was occupied by American forces until 1902. Under the Platt Amendment (1901) giving the U.S. the right to intervene in the island to ensure its independence from other foreign powers or to preserve order, Cuba effectively became an American protectorate.

C. **America and the Pacific.** Prior to the Spanish-American War and its portentous consequences for the U.S. position in the Pacific, American policy often focused on ensuring that American interests were not excluded by European powers from trade with Pacific nations.

1. **Purchase of Alaska.** First proposed in the 1850s, the purchase of Alaska from Russia was undertaken in 1867. Secretary of State **William Seward** (1801-1871) saw the territory useful as a way station for Pacific trade, though at the time he was ridiculed—Alaska was "Seward's icebox," or "Seward's folly."

2. **Trade with Korea.** Just as it had "opened" Japan and sought to protect trading privileges in China and elsewhere in the Pacific region, the U.S. sought trade with Korea. In 1882 this effort succeeded, when a commercial treaty was agreed to by Korea.

3. **The "Open Door policy" with China.** In 1899 Secretary of State **John Hay** (1838-1905) issued a diplomatic note to the European powers who had "spheres of influence" in China. The note reaffirmed the "open door" policy originally supported by Britain in the 1840s, according to which the U.S. and a number of European states were to have equal commercial access in the various European spheres of influence in China. Hay was thus attempting to protect U.S. trading interests. The Open Door policy continued to be pursued by Secretary of State **Elihu Root** (1845-1937).

4. **Putting down the Boxer Rebellion.** The U.S. contributed to the international force that successfully fought the Chinese anti-foreigner society known as the Boxers, which wished to expel the foreigners who had forced themselves upon China for decades. In 1900 the Boxers besieged the diplomatic compound in Beijing for fifty-five days. In 1901 a settlement required the weak Chinese state to execute ten Boxers and to pay a $333 million indemnity. Resentment of the occupation by European powers and of China's humiliation set the stage for prolonged Chinese hostility to the West, including the U.S., after the Chinese communists took power in 1949.

5. **The annexation of Hawaii.** As a prelude to statehood in the twentieth century, the annexation of Hawaii was preceded by stages in which ties between the U.S. and Hawaii were gradually strengthened.

a. **Early relations with Hawaii.** Although the Senate rejected a commercial treaty with Hawaii in 1867, by 1875 the U.S., recognizing the significance of Hawaii for its interests, signed a treaty giving the U.S. a virtual protectorship over the islands. A further treaty followed in 1884.

b. **Annexation.** A revolution in 1893 overthrew the Hawaiian monarchy, though doubts were raised that it represented the popular will. A treaty of annexation in 1894 was rejected by the Senate at President-elect Cleveland's request, and Hawaii remained a republic. A second annexation treaty was signed in 1897 and, over Japanese objections, Hawaii was annexed the following year. The islands were to serve as a way-station to America's Asian possessions.

6. **Acquisition of other Pacific islands.** Prior to about 1890, the U.S. was often reluctant to pursue the acquisition of Pacific naval bases or territory, though there were exceptions. After 1890, more territory was added besides Hawaii and the Philippines.

a. **Midway and Wake Islands.** Midway Island was occupied in 1867 as a coaling station for U.S. shipping. Wake Island, first taken in 1897, was occupied by the navy in 1899.

b. **Samoa.** In Samoa, in the western Pacific, an attempt in 1872 to further American naval and commercial interests proved abortive when the Senate refused to ratify a treaty. A second attempt in 1878 was successful, however, and the U.S. gained Pago Pago as a naval station. Conflicts in Samoa with rivals Britain and Germany followed later in the century. In 1889 armed conflict with Germany over its interference in the island's self-government was narrowly averted. In 1899, the two nations divided Samoa between them, and American Samoa was born.

D. **America as a world power: the Great White Fleet circumnavigates the globe**. In 1908, in a bid to impress Japan with American naval prowess and shore up support in Congress for the navy, President Roosevelt decided to showcase the strength of the nation's newly enhanced navy by sending a "Great White Fleet" of sixteen battleships around South America from Virginia to California. On the way, however, Roosevelt decided to send it on a world-wide tour. In Australia, where it was greeted ecstatically by crowds who saw it as a counterweight to growing Japanese ambitions, and in Japan itself, where it was greeted with gracious friendliness, to ports in the Mediterranean, the fleet was a resounding success. The growth of the American navy owed much to the ideas of American naval officer and historian **Alfred T. Mahan** (1840-1914), whose seminal *The Influence of Sea Power upon History, 1660-1873* (1890) persuaded many that naval power is essential to success in international affairs.

V. **World War I and its aftermath**. At the outbreak of World War I, American opinion was strongly on the side of non-involvement. Indeed, in 1914, it was unknown, if the U.S. did enter the war, whether it would enter on the side of Britain and France or of Germany and its allies. One factor in swaying public opinion was the effectiveness of British anti-German propaganda and the ham-handed character of German propaganda.

A. **U.S. neutrality**. At the outbreak of general European War in August 1914, President Woodrow Wilson announced an American policy of "neutrality in thought as well as deed."

1. **Protection of American rights of neutrality**. President Wilson insisted on America's neutrality rights and, unlike Jefferson with his Embargo, was unprepared to abandon them and U.S. prosperity by pulling U.S. ships off the high seas to keep America out of the war.

2. **Sinking of the Lusitania and German submarine warfare**. Horror at underwater warfare was one potent factor in enlisting American sympathy for Britain. Germany's use of the U-boat made it seem the greater threat to American principles.

Public opinion was greatly inflamed in 1915 when the British liner *Lusitania* was torpedoed off the coast of Ireland on its way to the U.S., with the loss of 1,195 lives, of which 195 were U.S. citizens. By 1916 the Wilson Administration was on a collision course with German policy.

3. **Declaration of war**. Germany's resumption of unrestricted submarine warfare in early 1917 led to a U.S. declaration of war in April 1917.

B. **U.S. war aims**. President Wilson drew up a set of war aims which were eventually considered to be overly idealistic.

1. **Magnanimous treatment of the defeated enemy**. Even before U.S. entrance, Wilson called for a "peace without victory," one without indemnities and annexations.

2. **The purpose of U.S. entrance**. In his War Message of April 2, 1917, Wilson called for a crusade to "make the world safe for democracy," for the rights of all peoples to live under governments of their choice.

3. **Wilson's Fourteen Points**. In 1918 Wilson proclaimed his Fourteen Points, which he thought would create a just and lasting peace. World War I would indeed be "the war to end all wars." These war aims included: "open covenants of peace [treaties] openly arrived at;" reduction of trade barriers; reduction of armaments to defensive levels; freedom of the seas; self-determination for all peoples; and, most importantly, a League of Nations to replace alliance systems with the principle of collective security.

4. **Wilson at Versailles**. Wilson led a peace delegation to France to ensure that the Peace Treaty would reflect American war aims.

5. **Rejection of the Versailles Treaty**. In 1919 the Senate rejected the Versailles Treaty with Germany. Many provisions of the Treaty created opposition within the U.S., but the principal reason for its rejection was its incorporation of the Covenant of the League of Nations.

   a. **The League threatens isolationism**. Membership in the League of Nations would have ended the hallowed policy of U.S. isolationism toward European political alignments—a step which the U.S. Senate and a disillusioned American public was not prepared to take in 1919. Another wing of opposition was led by Senator **Henry Cabot Lodge** (1850-1924), who opposed the treaty on the ground that it compromised U.S. sovereignty.

b. **The abdication of great power responsibility**. In effect, the Senate's action represented a refusal to accept the role of a great power.

VI. **From "normalcy" to the New Deal—(1919-1933)**. In the 1920s Americans recoiled from foreign commitments, so deep was their disillusionment with the Great War's aborted crusade. U.S. foreign policy vigorously pursued the nation's interests in the Western Hemisphere.

A. **Intervention in the Soviet Union**. The Russian Revolution of 1917 culminated in the demise of the liberal government and the victory of the Bolsheviks, who seized power by coup d'etat in October.

1. **Intervention in north Russia**. In 1918, the year following the Bolshevik coup, Britain and France urged the U.S. to join them in intervening to topple the Bolshevik regime, which had announced a policy of world revolution.

   a. **Wilson's hesitation and agreement**. President Wilson at first refused to intervene, but after a plea from the democratic Czech leader **Thomas Masaryk** (1850-1937) for American protection of Czech forces in Russia who were under attack, Wilson agreed.

   b. **The purpose of intervention**. Accordingly, in July Wilson dispatched U.S. troops to northern Russia and Siberia, though he denied doing so to intervene in Russia's political affairs. The aim, he said, was only to protect the Czechs.

   c. **The termination of intervention**. The force was withdrawn from North Russia the following summer and from Siberia in 1920. It was almost wholly passive, engaging in only one skirmish with the Bolsheviks. The Americans opposed Japanese occupation in Siberia, and the one American accomplishment of the intervention came when the U.S. successfully demanded Japan's withdrawal.

2. **The Red Scare**. In the U.S., in the wake of domestic violent incidents undertaken by radicals, some of them inspired by events in Russia, fear of communist revolution underlay the "Red Scare" hysteria of 1919-20 during which suspected radicals—most of them aliens—were hunted down in a series of raids. Civil liberties and due process of law were flagrantly violated, and few radicals found. Most deportation orders were canceled when a courageous government official realized that the accusations were groundless; and the scare ended as abruptly as it began. Opposition to the revolutionary new communist state continued, however, and the U.S. refused to recognize the Soviet regime until 1933.

B. **The Washington Naval Conference**. The U.S. hosted the 1921-22 Washington Naval Conference. Agreements on naval armaments were reached by the major powers. The diplomatic codes of Japan, a major participant, were broken by the Americans, making it possible to negotiate an agreement with the minimum armaments acceptable to Japan.

C. **Restrictive tariff and immigration policies**. Tariff and immigration policies of the 1920s exemplified the "America First" spirit of the day, which rejected European goods and its peoples.

D. **Outlawing war**. The Kellogg-Briand Pact of 1929, ratified by sixty-three nations, renounced the use of war as a means of national policy. The U.S. signed, as the pact provided for no enforcement machinery.

E. **Relations with Mexico**. U.S. relations with Mexico reached a low point between 1925 and 1928, when Mexico's land redistribution laws reminded some U.S. officials of communism, and U.S. oil investments appeared to be in jeopardy from a law that placed all mineral rights in the hands of the government. President Coolidge's appointment of an outspoken anti-Mexican ambassador who spoke no Spanish did little to improve matters. However, the ambassador's replacement by the tactful and pro-Mexican Dwight Morrow soon warmed relations, and Morrow's adept diplomacy solved the oil nationalization question for some years.

F. **Allied debt repayment**. The U.S. pursued a policy that required its World War allies to repay their debts. This policy was, as a practical matter, null and void after the world-wide economic collapse of 1929.

G. **The "Stimson Doctrine."** In 1931 Japanese forces invaded the north Chinese province of Manchuria. Secretary of State **Henry L. Stimson** (1867-1950) proposed forceful opposition but was limited to the statement of the "Stimson Doctrine" or non-recognition of military gains by the Japanese in China.

VII. **The New Deal years to Pearl Harbor**. The mandate of President **Franklin D. Roosevelt** (1882-1945) was to deal with the economic catastrophe he inherited. Foreign policy in the early New Deal years was secondary. But Roosevelt, a Wilsonian internationalist by training and inclination, kept a watchful eye on foreign developments.

A. **The "Good Neighbor" policy toward Latin America**. The Roosevelt Administration sought cooperation and improved relations with Latin America by renouncing U.S. interventionism and proclaiming a desire to be a "Good Neighbor." The Platt Amendment, which declared the U.S. right to intervene throughout the Hemisphere, was abandoned.

B. **Isolationism and neutrality**. As fascist aggressions in Europe were launched in the mid-1930s, Congress responded to the isolationist mood, passing a series of Neutrality Acts (1935-1937). These laws had a number of major provisions:

1. **Arms sales to belligerents forbidden**. U.S. citizens were barred from selling armaments to countries at war, with no discrimination between aggressors and victims.

2. **Travel on ships of belligerents forbidden**. American citizens were forbidden to travel on the ships of belligerents (except at their own risk), a reaction to the *Lusitania* episode of 1915 in which Americans were killed in a torpedoed British vessel (see V.A.2, above).

3. **Loans to belligerents outlawed**. Americans were forbidden to make any loans to belligerents, a belated response to the "merchants of death" explanation for U.S. intervention in World War I.

4. **Credit for trade with belligerents prohibited**. Other trade with belligerents was put on a "cash and carry" basis.

5. **Neutrality in the Spanish Civil War**. With the outbreak in 1936 of civil war in Spain, the Acts were amended to apply to civil wars.

C. **Fascist aggression and American public opinion**. German and Italian advances in Europe and the Japanese invasion of China in 1937 effected a change in American public opinion. Aid to victims of fascist aggression became permissible.

1. **Repeal of the arms embargo**. Shortly after the German invasion of Poland in September 1939, triggering World War II, Congress repealed the arms embargo, instituting a policy of "cash-and-carry."

2. **Destroyers for Britain**. In 1940, Roosevelt authorized the "destroyer deal" by which the U.S., in return for 99-year-leases on British bases in the Western Hemisphere, gave Great Britain fifty World-War-I-vintage ships.

3. **Peacetime conscription**. Congress passed a measure drafting men for one year of military service, the U.S.'s first peace-time conscription.

4. **The Lend-Lease Act**. After Roosevelt's re-election to a third term in 1940, he asked for, and Congress passed, a Lend-Lease Act. At the president's discretion, goods of all types would be made available to countries whose defense he deemed to be in the American interest. The U.S. had, in his words, become "the arsenal of democracy."

5. **Aid for Soviet Union approved**. Lend-Lease aid was extended to the Soviet Union after it was attacked by Germany in June 1941.

6. **Agreement for an "Atlantic Charter."** In August 1941, Roosevelt and British Prime Minister **Winston Churchill** (1874-1965) met in Argentia Bay off Newfoundland and agreed to the Atlantic Charter. Its eight points stated common principles to guide the two nations in their hopes for a better post-war world. They included such items as self-determination for all peoples; equal access to trade and raw materials; and improved labor standards and social security.

7. **Policy towards Japan**. In 1931 Japan attacked Manchuria and set up a puppet state. In 1937 it invaded China proper, slaughtering Chinese in great numbers. In response, the Roosevelt Administration decided to withhold from Japan the raw materials it needed to wage war. This action risked Japan's seizure of the resources of Southeast Asia. As a further warning to Japan to cease and desist its depredations, Roosevelt ordered most of the Pacific fleet to Pearl Harbor in Hawaii.

8. **"Europe first" policy**. Staff talks between U.S. and British officers resulted in a "Europe first" policy in the event of U.S. entrance in the war in more than one theater. This decision meant that the Pacific theater of World War II received a lower priority in receiving men and material until after the war in Europe had been decided.

D. **The Japanese attack on Pearl Harbor**. On December 7, 1941, dubbed by Roosevelt "a day that will live in infamy," the Japanese attacked the U.S. fleet in Pearl Harbor, Hawaii, inflicting heavy damage. The following day, the president asked Congress for a declaration of war with Japan, and Congress assented. Shortly afterward, the U.S. also declared war on Germany and Italy.

VIII. **World War II (1941-1945)**. President Roosevelt as "Dr. Win-the-War" replaced his role as "Dr. New-Deal." Allied victory in the war against the Axis became the fundamental purpose of U.S. foreign policy. Foreign and military policy were intertwined.

A. **The "Europe first" policy in action**. America pursued a policy of committing the main body of its resources toward the defeat of Nazi Germany.

1. **The Manhattan Project**. After a plea in 1939 by **Albert Einstein** (1879-1955), who with other scientists feared Nazi progress on atomic research, President Roosevelt inaugurated the top-secret Manhattan Project to develop a weapon based on release of energy from splitting the atom.

2. **Aid to the Soviet Union**. Aid to the Soviet Union continued during the war, and cooperation with the Soviets became a principal strand of American policy, as essential to the defeat of Nazi Germany.

3. **Soviet calls for a "second front."** Differences with the Soviets and the British emerged over the timing and site of the Allied invasion of Western Europe—the Second Front. The British urged the U.S. to invade the "soft-underbelly" of Europe in Italy. The British based their policy on their suspicions of Soviet intentions in Eastern Europe should they "liberate" it from the Nazis.

4. **Policy of "unconditional surrender."** The Western Allies announced a policy of "unconditional surrender" at the Casablanca Conference of January 1943. Stalin acceded to it; no terms or negotiations would be considered with existing Axis governments, or any which might replace them.

5. **Plans for occupation of Germany**. At several wartime conferences, general plans for the division of Germany into temporary occupation zones left to the post-war era the precise conditions under which a united Germany would be created.

B. **Hopes for democracy in Eastern Europe**. U.S. policy toward Eastern European countries such as Czechoslovakia, Hungary, and Poland was based on American principles of government by consent, most recently expressed in the Atlantic Charter.

1. **The Yalta Conference**. At the Yalta Conference of February 1945, the Soviets agreed in the Declaration on Liberated Europe that free, democratic elections would be conducted in the nations their army had liberated from the Nazis. Soviet domination of the Eastern European countries occupied by the Red Army received de facto assent and drew continuing fire from critics in the 1950s and 1960s.

2. **Hopes for democracy dashed**. The goal of postwar democracy was threatened by the Red Army arriving in Eastern Europe ahead of the western allies. Despite his promises at Yalta, Stalin had no intention of allowing free elections in the lands the conquering Red Army occupied on its way to Berlin.

C. **Plans for a United Nations Charter**. The U.S. sought to create a new world organization, the United Nations, to replace the League of Nations. ("United Nations" was a term coined in 1941 by Franklin Roosevelt in describing the nations allied to fight the Axis.) After officially announcing a need for such an organization in 1943, the Big Four allied powers (Britain, France, the U.S., and the USSR) met at the Dumbarton Oaks Conference in Washington, D.C., in 1944 to draw up basic proposals for a post-war world organization to replace the League. Further discussions at the Yalta Conference concluded that the Big Four would have a veto over important decisions of the United Nations.

D. **American plans for post-war Asia**. China became the keystone of Roosevelt's plans for post-war Asia. During the war, the U.S. supported the Nationalist government of **Chiang Kai-shek** (1887-1975) and urged, through General **Joseph Stilwell** (1883-1946),

Roosevelt's emissary, that it assume a greater fighting role against the Japanese invaders.

E. **The Nuremberg Trials.** In 1945-46 the U.S. and other allied nations sponsored war crimes trials of former Nazi leaders held in Nuremberg, Germany. The Allied High Military Tribunal was headed by **Robert Jackson** (1892-1954), Associate Justice of the U.S. Supreme Court. In October 1946 ten of those found guilty were hanged; others received lesser sentences. The Nuremberg verdicts established a new kind of crime, "crimes against humanity," and provided a precedent for holding those who direct military operations responsible to the international community.

F. **Truman becomes president.** After Roosevelt's death in April 1945, the vice-president, **Harry S. Truman** (1884-1972), "the man from Missouri," became president.

1. **United Nations.** In 1945 plans for a United Nations charter continued. In June, the Charter was signed in San Francisco; and in October, the new organization formally met in London, moving afterward to New York.

2. **The Potsdam Conference.** In July and August Truman met with Churchill and Stalin in Potsdam, Germany.

   a. **Truman told of atomic bomb success.** Told of the successful explosion on July 16 of an atomic bomb at a secret site code-named "Trinity," near Alamogordo, New Mexico, Truman decided to use the weapon against Japan in order to avoid the massive U.S. casualties calculated to result from an invasion. A demonstration drop, to show the bombs' destructive potential should Japan not surrender, was not carried out, since only two bombs were available, and it was unknown if they would go off successfully.

   b. **Inability to agree on German reunification.** The Western Allies and the Soviets were unable to agree on how to reunify Germany, setting the stage for a German nation that remained divided for fifty-five years.

3. **The atomic bomb and the end of World War II.** On July 26, the U.S. and Britain issued an ultimatum to Japan demanding unconditional surrender and warning that non-compliance would lead to the use of vast, destructive force against Japan. Two days later, U.S. planes dropped 27 million leaflets over Japanese cities, giving a list of eleven cities, four of which would be destroyed if Japan did not surrender. On August 6, an atomic bomb was dropped on Hiroshima causing 160,000 casualties; three days later, a second bomb fell on Nagasaki, with 100,000 killed or wounded. On August 15, Japan surrendered unconditionally, but with the understanding that it could choose to keep the emperor.

IX. **The outbreak of the "Cold War" and the abandonment of isolationism.** The uneasy cooperation between the U.S. and the Soviet Union during the war broke into an open and active distrust in its aftermath, with disputes over the reconstruction of Germany, Soviet domination of Eastern Europe, and U.S. economic control of Western Europe. At the end of the war, the U.S. had rapidly demobilized in the expectation of the democratization of Europe and peaceful relations with the Soviets. But the progressive communization of Eastern Europe alarmed the Truman administration, which then decided to resist further Soviet expansion. By 1946, the expression the "Cold War" had been coined to describe relations between the Soviet Union and its former western Allies. In the same year, Winston Churchill gave a memorable speech in Fulton, Missouri, warning that an "iron curtain" was descending across Eastern Europe.

A. **Abandonment of isolationism.** While the American public was weary of foreign entanglements by the end of World War II, President Truman and such key former isolationists as Senator **Arthur Vandenberg** (1884-1951), believed that the world political balance was in jeopardy and that the U.S. must take an active role in safeguarding Western societies. Vandenberg, for example, was a firm advocate of bipartisan support for Truman's foreign policy and played a principal role in Senate approval of the NATO Treaty.

B. **Containing communism.** Soviet incursions into Eastern Europe and plans to communize Turkey and control Iran reinforced the belief within the Truman Administration that the Soviets were intent on global expansion.

1. **The "containment" doctrine.** The policy of "containing" Soviet expansionist tendencies originated in 1946 in a long telegram to the State Department from a U.S. diplomat stationed in Moscow, **George F. Kennan**. The telegram is said to be "probably the most important, and most influential, message ever sent to Washington by an American diplomat." In his message,

afterwards published as "The Sources of Soviet Conduct" by "X," Kennan advocated the patient but firm resistance to attempts by the Soviets to expand its power in Europe and elsewhere in the world.

2. **The Truman Doctrine.** With the British withdrawal from Greece and Turkey in March 1947, President Truman asked Congress to appropriate money to aid these countries against Communist subversion. The Truman Doctrine declared it American policy to aid free peoples everywhere who resist threats to their independence. Truman thus declared an American vision of world order that also marked the transfer of global leadership from Britain to the United States.

3. **The Marshall Plan.** The Truman Administration's concern that economic crisis in Europe in the years after the war would provide fertile soil for communist influence led Secretary of State **George C. Marshall** (1880-1959) to propose a policy of massive economic aid to the region. Marshall proposed a "European Recovery Program," soon known as the Marshall Plan, in his commencement address at Harvard University in June 1947. The Plan was an economic application of the Truman Doctrine. An immense sum was allocated for its success—some 16 percent of the federal budget.

4. **The Berlin blockade and allied airlift.** In 1948 the Soviet Union took action which it hoped would scuttle plans for an autonomous west German state that would join an alliance with the Western powers. Thus, from July 1948 to May of the following year, the Soviets blocked all ground transportation to West Berlin, in an attempt to starve the city into submission to Soviet plans for its absorption into the eastern bloc. The "Berlin blockade" was met with an American-led airlift, which successfully flew essential supplies twenty-four hours a day to the beleaguered city. As a result of the "Berlin airlift," the blockade was defeated and finally lifted.

5. **The formation of NATO.** In early 1949, U.S. entrance into the North Atlantic Treaty Organization, (NATO) marked its first "entangling alliance," aside from the United Nations Treaty, since 1778. The collective security provisions of NATO commit the U.S. to come to the defense of member nations (currently sixteen) if they are attacked.

C. **Support for a Jewish state.** President Truman was a firm supporter of a homeland in Palestine for the Jews, who had suffered so much at the hands of the Nazis. A movement for such a state ("Zionism") had begun in the nineteenth century, but matters came to a head in May 1948, when Britain, which had exercised a mandate over Palestine, was to withdraw. An alternative to recognizing a Jewish state (its name was not announced ahead of time, and some members of the American government believed it would be called "Judaea") was a UN mandate for Palestine, forestalling the birth of the new state. Immediate U.S. recognition for the Jewish state was a hotly contested issue in the Truman Administration. The refusal of American recognition would damage the new state's reputation and perhaps aid in its still-birth. Truman, however, maneuvered around intense opposition from within the State Department, including Secretary Marshall, **Dean Acheson** (1893-1971) (later Truman's Secretary of State), **George Kennan**, **Dean Rusk**, and others. On May 14, 1948, when the state of Israel was proclaimed, the U.S. government immediately extended recognition.

D. **The Korean Conflict.** In January of 1950 Secretary of State Acheson gave a speech at the National Press Club in Washington during which he placed South Korea outside the U.S. defense perimeter in the Pacific. Many analysts later believed that Stalin saw this as a denial that the Americans would resist a communist takeover and was therefore willing to approve a North Korean invasion. The invasion was launched in June 1950. Putting aside its previous doubts of the importance of the Korean peninsula to American security, the Truman Administration believed the invasion to mark a shift in Soviet tactics toward overt aggression through client states and that Japan was their ultimate target. The U.S. believed that resisting communist aggression was vital to Western security.

1. **United Nations involvement.** Military response to the invasion was a collective action sanctioned by the UN Security Council. Some fifteen Western nations, including Australia, Britain, Canada, and France, contributed men and materiel to the UN forces. The U.S. furnished most of the troops, however, and did most of the fighting, losing more than 50,000 dead and 100,000 wounded. All UN forces operated under U.S. military command, headed first by General **Douglas MacArthur** (1889-1964).

2. **The conflict ends.** The Korean conflict ended when an armistice was signed in July 1953 under the Eisenhower Administration. The U.S. had successfully contained communism, but some considered the result a stalemate since North Korea remained communist.

3. **Long-term significance.** U.S. involvement in this conflict marked the assertion of the willingness to use military force to support the "containment" policy. Concerns of future communist aggression led to the reestablishment of U.S. forces in Europe within the framework of the NATO alliance.

X. **Waging "Cold War."** The policies of President **Dwight D. Eisenhower** (1890-1969) and Secretary of State **John Foster Dulles** (1888-1959) incorporated the global pursuit of "containing" the Soviet Union. However, President Eisenhower was determined to engage in containment at a lower financial and human cost to the United States than did Truman with the Korean conflict. Military and economic aid and covert operations along with diplomatic support were the principal tools used to counter Soviet subversion.

A. **Post-war decolonization.** After World War II, a succession of colonial nations fought successful struggles against continued European rule. India, which gained its independence in 1947, was at the forefront of the emancipated nations.

1. **Loyalty to Europe vs. self determination.** From the 1950s onward, scores of other countries followed suit, sometimes after bitter fighting. American policy in a succession of administrations found itself situated among contradictory historical currents. The U.S. was frequently caught between the tides of loyalty to its European allies, partners in the struggle against Soviet communism, on the one hand, and historic and philosophical allegiance to the idea of national self-determination and independence, on the other. In the case of some developing nations, it was often considered that communism could only be countered by a strong American presence. In more than one instance, this policy led to support of anti-communist strongmen, whose autocratic regimes were an embarrassment to democratic values.

2. **Relations with emerging nations.** Secretary of State Dulles, in many ways the embodiment of the American moralistic approach to foreign policy, believed neutrality in the struggle between Soviet communism and the Western democracies to be immoral and urged nations neutral in the Cold War to join the Western cause.

a. **The nonaligned movement.** Unpersuaded by Dulles's appeals to join the opposition to the Soviet Union were members of the movement of nonaligned nations. The movement had its birth in 1955, when twenty-nine African and Asian countries met at the Bandung Conference in Indonesia. During the Eisenhower years and afterwards, relations with the U.S. were sometimes strained between newly independent nations in Asia and Africa, who resented the legacy of European empire, and as a result were sensitive to perceived meddling in their affairs or to attempts to enlist them in Western alliances.

b. **Marxist rhetoric and decolonization.** The "nonaligned" states employed the rhetoric of Marxian socialism in their struggles for national independence. Once they achieved independence, newly emancipated states often tried to play off the U.S. and the Soviets against each other. Both powers eagerly competed to develop influence among the former colonies, which accepted military and economic aid from both East and West.

B. **A global system of alliances.** In pursuit of the containment policy, American diplomacy set about constructing a worldwide system of alliances directed against communist expansion anywhere in the world, all of which was believed to be the result of Soviet activity rather than from solely indigenous causes. Besides NATO, these alliances included the Rio Treaty with most of South and Central America; the ANZUS Treaty with Australia and New Zealand; and a number of bilateral treaties, such as those with Japan and the Philippines. In addition, the Southeast Asia Treaty Organization (SEATO), was established in 1954. A protocol to SEATO put several non-signatories, including Laos and Vietnam, under the treaty's protection and provided the formal basis for American involvement in those countries. The U.S. also supported the Baghdad Treaty. (See E. the Middle East, below). Critics called the American penchant for alliances "pactomania."

C. **Relations with the Soviet bloc**. With the death of **Joseph Stalin** (1879-1953), new leadership took the helm in the Soviet Union. The new Soviet leader to emerge after several years of Kremlin power struggle, **Nikita S. Khrushchev** (1894-1971), secretly denounced the policies and tactics of Stalin (in the "secret speech" of 1956) and publicly seemed more willing to negotiate on arms control and other Cold War issues than the previous leadership under Stalin. But a deep sense of distrust remained and few concrete changes occurred in U.S./Soviet relations in the 1950s.

1. **The arms race**. In 1957, the USSR tested a long-range intercontinental ballistic missile (ICBM) and launched its first satellite, leading U.S. analysts to assume that the Soviets possessed weapons technology equal to that of the United States. Although that assumption was mistaken, it lead to a reexamination of U.S. defense capabilities. Also, in 1957, the U.S. successfully tested an intermediate-range ballistic missile (IRBM) and secured agreement for its deployment in Europe until U.S.-based ICBMs were developed. In 1958 the first American ICBM was successfully tested.

2. **"Massive retaliation."** In 1955 the Eisenhower Administration announced its doctrine of "massive retaliation" against the Soviets. Since the Soviets and their satellites had far larger armies than NATO, armies whose numerical strength it would be financially ruinous and politically impossible to duplicate, the U.S. declared that a Sino-Soviet Bloc invasion of Europe or Asia would trigger a massive nuclear response. This doctrine remained in place until the "flexible response" posture of the Kennedy years and after.

2. **Summit meetings**. In July 1955 a "Big Four" (U.S., U.K., France, and the USSR) summit conference opened in Geneva, attended by President Eisenhower and Soviet Premier **Nikolai Bulganin** (1895-1975). Although the meetings were cordial, agreement with the Soviets over German membership in NATO was not achieved. Eisenhower's proposal for mutual aerial inspection to prevent surprise attack was well received by the Western public but was later rejected by the Soviets. In 1960 a second summit between Eisenhower and Khrushchev was angrily canceled by the Soviets after a U.S. U2 spy plane was shot down over the USSR, and its pilot was put on public display. Summit meetings continued to be a feature of U.S.-USSR relations throughout the Cold War period.

3. **The China question**. When the Chinese communists under **Mao-Tse-Tung** (1893-1976) launched their People's Republic in 1949, the question of who was responsible for its "loss" bedeviled American politics. At the height of the McCarthy era, it was claimed that disloyal U.S. foreign service officers were at least partly to blame. Although no evidence for the charge was ever uncovered and the accused were repeatedly exonerated after investigations, the careers of a number of "China hands" were ruined. The U.S. refused to recognize the Beijing regime, and instead supported nationalist Chinese leader **Chiang Kai-shek** (1887-1975), who had fled with the remnants of his army to Taiwan. Chiang continued to claim to represent the legitimate government of China and sat in China's seat on the UN Security Council. Chiang's government received substantial economic and military aid from the United States. Washington repeatedly warned Beijing against invading Taiwan.

D. **Southeast Asia**. President Eisenhower believed that the struggle for containment in Southeast Asia would be lost if pivotal countries were lost to communism. These countries were like dominoes which would all topple if the lead domino fell. American policy was accordingly directed toward combatting communist insurgency in Laos, Vietnam, and elsewhere.

1. **Laos**. Laos was politically divided during much of the 1950s between royalist forces and communist insurgents known as the Pathet Lao. Although a coalition government was formed in 1957, by 1959 it had broken down. In 1960 a number of coups resulted in a three-way struggle for power between right, left, and neutralist forces. The Eisenhower Administration viewed Laos as a critical Southeast Asian domino and sought to preserve the country's independence from communist domination. In 1961 it recognized a rightist government and sent it six fighter bombers, but the policy was not backed by some parts of the Administration. Eisenhower himself believed that if Laos fell to the insurgents, the whole of Indo-China would fall with it. At the end of his term, he impressed upon the incoming Kennedy Administration the importance of maintaining a non-communist Laos, using U.S. troops if necessary to do so.

2. **Early involvement in Vietnam**. Vietnam had been colonized by France since the nineteenth century. After World War II, nationalists, led by

the communist **Ho Chi Minh** (1890-1969) struggled with the French for independence. In January 1950 President Truman gave some aid to the French effort in Vietnam; and after the outbreak of the Korean War in June, he authorized huge amounts of aid for the same purpose. Eisenhower and Dulles thought the French cause vital to the containment of communism everywhere, and contributed to its funding. But by 1954, the French could no longer sustain the battle, then in its eighth year. At a Geneva Conference in the same year, France negotiated a provisional demarcation of Vietnam and scheduled national elections for 1956 to determine the fate of the whole country. A communist government under Ho ruled in the north, while a U.S.-backed government under **Ngo Dinh Diem** (1901-1963) ruled in the south. The split between north and south Vietnam became formalized when Diem refused to conduct elections as agreed, claiming the pre-conditions for democracy did not exist in the north. No one seemed to doubt that Ho Chi Minh was the most popular leader in the country and would easily win any election.

E. **The Middle East.** As the U.S. sought to fill the power vacuum left by the withdrawal of the British from this region, the U.S. was concerned both with the communist threat to world order and the strategic importance of oil. To address these concerns, an air base in Saudi Arabia was leased, and the Navy's Sixth Fleet patrolled the Mediterranean.

1. **Iran.** In 1951 the nationalist government of **Mohammed Mossadegh**, who was supported by the Iranian communist party, seized the Iranian oil industry, which Britain protested. A running dispute over the issue lasted until 1953, when Royalist forces, aided by the U.S. Central Intelligence Agency (CIA), reinstalled the Shah, **Reza Palahvi,** who had fled the country. Thereafter, until the Shah was deposed in 1979 and replaced by Muslim fundamentalists, Iran was an important regional American ally.

2. **Containing Soviet influence.** Carrying out the containment policy in the Middle East became a major American preoccupation, so much so that the U.S. tended to see politics in the area solely in Cold War terms.

   a. **The Baghdad Pact.** To counter Soviet attempts to gain influence, the U.S. supported the Baghdad Pact, a collective security treaty signed in 1955 by Turkey and Iraq, followed soon by Britain, Iran, and Pakistan. Though the U.S. established economic ties with the Pact and joined its military committee, it did not formally enter the pact, in deference to the Israelis.

   b. **The Eisenhower Doctrine, the Syrian crisis, and the landing in Lebanon.** In 1957 the "Eisenhower Doctrine" was approved by Congress, committing the U.S. to use force if necessary to counter communist aggression in the Middle East. Later the same year, the president announced an arms lift to Jordan and aid to Lebanon, Turkey, and Iraq to counter plans for communist subversion from Syria, where it was said that communist elements were planning a takeover with Moscow's backing. In 1958, marines landed near Beirut, Lebanon, at the Lebanese government's request, to prevent civil war alleged to have been fomented by the United Arab Republic (UAR), the short-lived union of Egypt and Syria.

   c. **The Suez crisis.** The most serious breach between the U.S. and important NATO allies Britain and France arose over the Suez crisis.

      (1) **The immediate cause of the crisis.** In July 1956, after Secretary of State Dulles canceled a loan promised to the Egyptian nationalist government of **Gamal Abal Nassar** (1918-1970) to finance an important dam at Aswan, Nassar nationalized the Suez canal, owned by an Anglo-French company. Nassar said he would use the canal's toll income, of which Egypt had been receiving only a fraction, to build the dam.

      (2) **Onset of the crisis.** Britain and France considered the canal vital to their interests. A crisis ensued as they maneuvered for its return. Britain, France, and Israel agreed in a secret plot unknown to the U.S., that Israel would attack Egypt and an Anglo-French "peace keeping force" would intervene, seizing the canal. When the attack occurred at the end of October, Eisen-

hower bluntly demanded the withdrawal of the Anglo-French troops.

(3) **Resolution and consequences of the crisis.** The U.S. used "strongarm" tactics, including weakening the pound sterling, to enforce its demand. The American view was that Western actions so reminiscent of the days of colonialism could no longer be tolerated. Britain and France backed down, but Anglo-American relations had been badly shaken. British feelings were permanently bruised, with wounded or angry references to the affair made in Parliament for decades. Britain had been publicly humiliated, her slip to the status of a second-class power held up for the world to see, by her NATO ally and former colony.

d. **The Hungarian Revolution.** While events in Suez were unfolding, another drama was taking place in Hungary. There an anti-communist uprising, begun on October 23, 1956, and led by Hungarian premier **Imre Nagy** (1895?-1958), deposed the Soviet puppet regime, declared neutrality, and appealed to the United Nations for aid. Although for years the U.S. had called for the liberation of Eastern Europe, no action was taken by the Eisenhower Administration to aid the Hungarian revolutionaries. As the Suez crisis came to a climax, the Soviet Union invaded Hungary and in brutal fighting crushed the revolution. Nagy was abducted and later executed. The episode embarrassed an administration and its allies who lent their support to calls for the overthrow of communism in Eastern Europe or "rollback" and forced a change in the public presentation of policy.

F. **Latin American policy.** For most of the 1950s, Latin America was a neglected area of American policy, preoccupied as it was with Europe, Korea, the Soviet Union and global communism, armaments, China, and several crises. Cold War concerns dominated foreign policy, with most U.S. aid reserved for the fight against communist subversion. Thus the three small Benelux countries (Belgium, the Netherlands, and Luxembourg) received three times the aid allocated to all of Latin America, with its many tens of millions of impoverished inhabitants. Later in the decade, this neglect became apparent in episodes of explosive anti-American resentment in South America.

1. **Guatemala and the Cold War.** An episode in Guatemala illustrated the tendency of the Cold War to dominate American foreign policy perceptions. Elected president of Guatemala in 1951, **Jocobo Arbenz Guzman** sought to assuage rural unrest with land reform. Accomplishing little, in 1954 Arbenz decided to confiscate 75 percent of the land of the American-owned United Fruit Company, a dominant force in the country. A U.S. demand that the company be compensated was refused. Secretary Dulles was concerned about communist influence in the Arbenz government, as evidenced by Guatemala's acknowledgement of receiving 900 tons of arms from communist Czechoslovakia. Dulles secured the agreement of the Inter-American Conference at Caracas to denounce communism and to approve action to prevent and eradicate it in Latin America. The CIA aided the training of opposition soldiers for a coup, which took place in June, 1954. The rebels' leader, **Castillo Armas,** came to power. He disenfranchised 70 percent of the population, suspended Guatemala's Congress, and halted agrarian reform.

2. **Anti-Americanism.** Late in the decade American neglect of the area was brought forcibly to Washington's attention.

a. **Anti-American mobs.** When Vice President **Richard Nixon** toured South American cities in 1958, he was greeted by anti-American mobs throwing stones and eggs. In Caracas, the vice president found himself in personal danger when his limousine was set upon and nearly overturned before he was rescued. The following year, more than a dozen anti-American riots took place in South American cities. The most serious, however, occurred in La Paz, Bolivia, where for three days rioters attacked American-owned property, burned flags, and denounced the Yankees.

b. **The U.S. response to anti-Americanism.** In December 1959, in an attempt to improve Latin American relations, the Eisenhower Administration established the Inter-American Development Bank, funded with $1 billion. The purpose of the bank was to funnel low-interest loans to South America.

The following September, a meeting held in Bogota, Columbia, announced long-range plans for U.S. aid to stimulate economic growth in the continent. The Americans agreed to establish a special fund to assist in Latin America's social development. The meeting marked a new American awareness of the acute needs of the nation's southern neighbors.

3. **Cuba and Castro**. The alliance between Cuba and the Soviet Union made **Fidel Castro** a thorn in the U.S. side for decades after his rise in the late 1950s to become the undisputed dictator of Cuba.

   a. **Castro comes to power**. After years of guerilla warfare in the Cuban mountains, Castro overthrew the corrupt regime of strongman **Fulgencio Batista** (1901-1973) and early in 1959 took power. The U.S. recognized his government and sent an ambassador.

   b. **American doubts about Cuba's new regime**. Castro's hundreds of executions in the early months in power alarmed the Eisenhower Administration. Castro's declaration during a visit to Washington in April that his regime was "humanistic" rather than communist, allayed fears in some quarters, but not in the Administration, which began plans for the new regime's overthrow. After he was well established in power, Castro announced that he was and had always been a Marxist revolutionary, confounding observers who originally described him as an "agrarian reformer."

   c. **Cuba's nationalization program**. In June, however, a far-reaching nationalization of sugar plantations brought U.S. protests of confiscation that went unheeded. Castro denounced opponents to his policies as "traitors," and by August, moderates were fleeing to the U.S.

   d. **Cuban-Soviet friendship and the U.S. trade embargo**. The following February saw formal Cuban-Soviet economic ties and friendship. In March, Eisenhower, with congressional approval, cut the quota of Cuban sugar imported to the U.S. by 95 percent. Castro retaliated by confiscating all U.S. property, which had dominated the Cuban economy. In October, 1960, the U.S. placed an embargo on all trade with Cuba.

   e. **Preparations for an invasion**. In March 1960 Eisenhower approved CIA training of Cuban exiles for an invasion to topple Castro's regime. By the end of the year, some 1,200 men were training for the invasion that came a year later under President Kennedy.

   f. **Diplomatic relations broken**. When in January 1961 Castro demanded the U.S. embassy reduce its staff to eleven persons within 48 hours, the U.S. broke relations. The stage was set for the serious confrontations of the Kennedy years.

XI. **Flexible response: the Kennedy years**. In 1961, as **John F. Kennedy** (1917-1963) assumed the presidency, the Soviets and the Chinese had become more supportive of insurgencies in Asia, the Middle East, and Africa; a communist government under Fidel Castro had come to power in Cuba; and the USSR was becoming a greater nuclear threat. President Kennedy sought to effect containment by exploiting a wide-range of responses, from Third World economic development to low-level conventional warfare to nuclear threats. In his inaugural address, he invoked the traditions of civic republicanism in declaring that the nation must "pay any price, bear any burden" in the defense of freedom.

   A. **The Peace Corps**. Soon after the advent of the Kennedy Administration in 1961, a bill was signed establishing the Peace Corps. The purpose of the Corps was to send American emissaries to poor nations around the world to help alleviate social and economic problems. Idealistic volunteers, many of them young, could spread good will for America and democracy around the world, helping to assuage the conditions that led to communism. Headed by the president's brother-in-law, the program achieved great popularity at home and a good measure of success abroad.

   B. **The Alliance for Progress**. Announced by President Kennedy in March 1961, the Alliance for Progress was a ten-year, $20 billion program to infuse economic aid into struggling Latin American countries. The goal was to provide a credible alternative to communism through economic modernization and to ensure stability by strengthening military institutions. Launched with great fanfare, the program in the end accomplished few of its aims.

C. **The Bay of Pigs.** The Kennedy Administration inherited from its predecessor a plan to aid foes of Fidel Castro by invading their island to foment a counter-revolution. The invasion by 1,600 U.S.-trained Cuban exiles, which took place at Cuba's Bay of Pigs on April 17, 1961, less than three months after Kennedy's inauguration, was a complete failure. The Kennedy Administration then began a series of efforts to harass and assassinate Castro, none of which succeeded in ousting the dictator and his increasingly repressive regime. Much further ill-will in Latin America toward U.S. interventionism was sown by the Bay of Pigs episode.

D. **A limited response in Indo-China.** Like Eisenhower, Kennedy considered Vietnam along with Laos as central dominos in the effort to contain communism in South East Asia.

1. **Threat of war in Laos.** So impressed was the new administration with the importance of the situation in Laos, that it seriously considered going to war when the U.S.-backed rightist government lost popular support and a communist military victory seemed near. In March the president ordered U.S. forces to move closer to Laos. An aircraft carrier moved into the Gulf of Siam; marines were dispatched to Thailand, and troops on Okinawa were put on alert. The new secretary of state, **Dean Rusk**, asked a meeting of SEATO for support for U.S. military action. But once the Joint Chiefs told the president that massive troops and nuclear weapons would be necessary for success, American policy rejected the military option. Moreover, neither France and Britain, who were members of SEATO, nor the Soviets, wanted war in Laos. Thus, in May a cease-fire was announced, followed by a Geneva conference, which reached agreement the following year. A coalition government was formed; Laos became a neutral country.

2. **Increased U.S. forces in Vietnam.** With the Geneva Conference on Laos dealing with the Laos problem, attention shifted to South Vietnam, where communist insurgents were attacking with increasing intensity and success. While Kennedy rejected recommendations for a massive American troop buildup, the prestige of the U.S. government was at stake in matching results on the ground to official rhetoric. Kennedy was fully determined to keep Vietnam from communist hands. Thus, by October 1961, U.S. advisors increased from 700 to 3,000 and to 12,000 by the end of 1962. By the end of 1963, 3,000 more "advisors" were in place, and Americans were engaged in combat missions under the guise of assisting the Vietnamese. According to historian Stanley Karnow, "[t]he growing U.S. military investment was kept secret, partly because it violated the [1954] Geneva Agreement, and partly to deceive the American public." (*Vietnam: A History*, 1983).

E. **Crises in U.S./Soviet relations.** A pair of crises, each of which brought the nuclear powers to the brink of direct confrontation, occurred in the Kennedy years, and ensured a rapid increase of U.S. and Soviet armaments.

1. **The Berlin Crisis.** In 1961 the U.S. and the Soviets found themselves in a showdown over the status of U.S. military forces in West Berlin. This, coupled with the Soviet desire to conclude a separate peace treaty with East Germany, threatened to finalize Germany's division into two states. Moreover, East Germany had for some time been hemorrhaging at this border, its dramatic loss of manpower auguring ill for its economic future. Nor was the flow of refugees a positive advertisement to the world for communism.

a. **Face off on the border.** Throughout the summer of 1961, as tension rose, each side began a massive buildup of military forces on the border between East and West Berlin.

b. **The Berlin Wall.** On August 13th, the Soviets suddenly began to erect a wall along the entire border between the two parts of the city. The wall would stop the flow of refugees from the east and demonstrate their control of the city. When the wall was completed, orders were given to border guards to shoot to kill anyone attempting to scale it. In the ensuing years, many died attempting to cross it. Until its dismantlement nearly thirty years later, the wall stood as a bleak symbol of communist tyranny.

c. **Stalemate.** The crisis dissipated as the Soviets backed down and removed their tanks from the border, and the U.S. decided against launching an attack to stop the building of the Berlin Wall.

2. **The Cuban Missile Crisis.** The thirteen-day Cuban Missile Crisis marked the climax of the cold war. In October 1962, the U.S. discovered that the USSR had built forty-two sites for medium-range missiles in Cuba.

   a. **A blockade.** President Kennedy responded by erecting a naval blockade around Cuba and demanding the removal of all missile facilities by the Soviets. The world waited anxiously as twenty-five Soviet ships approached Cuba, and the superpowers came close to a direct military confrontation. Khrushchev diverted the ships, however, and they returned to the USSR.

   b. **A deal made.** Khrushchev proposed to remove the Cuban missile sites in exchange for U.S. missiles based in Turkey. In the end, Khrushchev agreed to remove the missiles if the U.S. would not invade Cuba; assurances were also given that Cuba would not promote revolutionary activity abroad, an undertaking that was not fulfilled. The U.S. told the Soviets it would remove the missiles from Turkey later.

3. **A clear victory.** As a result of these crises, U.S. military superiority was evident to both sides. On account of U.S. strategic supremacy, the Soviets had already begun a massive armaments buildup before the crisis in an effort to achieve strategic parity. Khrushchev's plans to moderate the pace of this buildup were scrapped as a result of the crisis, while the U.S. attempted to maintain its lead. Between 1960 and 1964 American ICBMs jumped from 18 to 834 and the Soviets' ICBMs increased from 35 to 200.

4. **The Test Ban Treaty.** In the summer of 1963 the U.S., Britain, and the USSR reached agreement to ban all testing of nuclear weapons in the atmosphere, under water, or in space, and a treaty was signed in Moscow. One effect of the ban was that radioactive material that endangered health would no longer be released into the atmosphere. By the time the treaty went into effect in October, it had been signed by more than 100 nations. It was not signed by France, however, which has continued to conduct atmospheric nuclear testing, to the dismay of nations such as New Zealand, which find themselves uncomfortably close to French test sites in the Pacific.

XII. **The Johnson Administration and the Vietnam War.** During the administration of **Lyndon B. Johnson** (1908-1973), the U.S. became embroiled in a protracted war that brought an end to his political career, radically divided the American public, and for years dampened U.S. tolerance for direct foreign intervention.

A. **Growing U.S. involvement.** By the time of Kennedy's assassination in November 1963, the situation in South Vietnam had deteriorated to the point that without a significant increase in U.S. involvement, Johnson feared South Vietnam's collapse.

   1. **Gulf of Tonkin Resolution.** In August 1964, Congress passed a resolution authorizing the president to take any action necessary to repel an attack by North Vietnam. The resolution was a reaction to alleged naval attacks by North Vietnam on U.S. ships in the Gulf of Tonkin. Evidence revealed later provided some grounds for the view that the U.S. had actually provoked one attack and fabricated another to provide the casus belli, but the evidence was ambiguous, and historians are not agreed on the actual course of events.

   2. **Bombing of North Vietnam.** Despite his campaign pledges of peace, Johnson had begun planning for extensive bombing of North Vietnam well before the 1964 elections. Bombing began in February 1965 and, with occasional pauses, lasted for three years.

   3. **Escalation.** The bombing did little to soften the position of the North Vietnamese on unifying the country. At the same time the South Vietnamese army was demonstrating its inability and unwillingness to fight the war.

      a. **Americanization of the war.** By April 1965, Johnson ordered an escalation of U.S. troops and made the decision to begin a ground offensive, with the U.S. taking command of the war. By April 1969, there were 543,000 U.S. troops in Vietnam.

      b. **Intense bombing of North Vietnam.** By late 1974, more bombs had been dropped on North Vietnam than in all of Europe during World War II.

   4. **The Tet offensive.** The massive "Tet offensive" (so-named after a Vietnamese holiday) launched by the North in January 1968 marked the turning

point for U.S. involvement in the war. While the Vietcong sustained heavy casualties and were militarily defeated, the attack stunned the American public. Many believed they had been misled about the war's progress and the strength of the Vietcong enemy. At the same time, the administration recognized that the U.S. could not successfully execute the war at a level acceptable to the public. As a result of this battle, both the U.S. and North Vietnam began to reconsider negotiation.

5. **Public dissent.** Opposition to the war began to build in late 1967. By the spring of 1968, American public opinion was solidly against the war. Americans were uneasy about defending a series of corrupt and inept governments in South Vietnam which the Vietnamese people did not support. American public opinion was referred to as the most important "domino," and it was falling.

XIII. **Nixon/Kissinger and the balance of power.** President **Richard M. Nixon**, with the aid and support of his national security advisor and later secretary of state, **Henry A. Kissinger**, began to shift U.S. foreign policy away from ideological politics and toward geopolitical power politics. In this view, true stability required an equilibrium of the principal actors on the world stage to achieve a "balance of power." A new policy of "detente" (relaxation of tensions) toward the USSR and China would require a level of public support that could only be achieved with a successful conclusion to the Vietnam War.

A. **Vietnam.** For Nixon, Vietnam was not a vital U.S. interest. He began to de-escalate U.S. ground forces and to turn the war over to the Vietnamese. At the same time, however, Nixon intensified the bombing raids and expanded into Cambodia with secret bombing missions.

1. **Secret negotiations.** In addition to continuing public negotiations, in August 1969, Kissinger began a series of secret meetings with the North Vietnamese, unknown to U.S. allies and even the State Department. These talks occurred intermittently until January 1973, and ultimately resulted in a truce.

2. **Truce.** Agreement was reached between the United States and North Vietnam in January, 1973. The last U.S. military forces left Vietnam

two months later. South Vietnam surrendered to the North in April, 1975.

3. **The aftermath of the American withdrawal from Southeast Asia.** After the U.S. withdrawal and South Vietnamese capitulation, the North established a repressive dictatorial regime. Former supporters of South Vietnam were placed in concentration camps for extended periods for "reeducation." Poverty and repression became so onerous that thousands of Vietnamese fled the country in boats (becoming known as "boat people"), risking death at sea through starvation, thirst, or piracy. Attempted escapes in this manner continued into the 1990s. In Cambodia, the regime of **Pol Pot** carried out genocidal policies that led to the death of more than a million Cambodians. (Events in Cambodia were described in the American film *The Killing Fields*, 1984).

B. **Detente.** In his 1969 inaugural address, Nixon claimed the end of the post war world and the beginning of a new era of "detente" (a French word meaning a lessening of tension or hostility), with the Soviets. Although U.S./Soviet relations remained competitive, Nixon rejected the Cold War notion of the USSR as a pariah nation with which the U.S. could not establish a relationship.

C. **The SALT talks.** As the USSR achieved rough strategic parity with the U.S. in the late 1960s, it became clear to Nixon and Kissinger that an endless arms race was not beneficial to either side or to international stability. While the share of U.S. GNP devoted to defense spending began to decline, the Soviet Union under Brezhnev annually increased its defense allocations in an effort to reach parity with the U.S. Nixon revived the stalled Strategic Arms Limitation Talks (SALT) with the Soviets in 1969 in an attempt to slow the rapid increase of Soviet nuclear forces.

1. **An arms limitation treaty.** The first SALT treaty was completed in 1972, freezing forces at current levels. In 1972 the USSR had surpassed the U.S. in both strategic land-based and submarine-launched strategic missiles. The U.S. retained a substantial lead in bombers and in the quality of weapon technology.

2. **Significance of SALT.** The SALT treaty, which expired in 1977, made a short-term contribution to slowing the arms race, but it also brought a

measure of order to U.S./Soviet relations that had previously been absent.

D. **The opening of China.** Nixon sought to exploit the rivalry between China and the Soviet Union to obtain a three-way global balance and to give each communist power a stake in improved relations with the West. Nixon actively sought to open discussions with the communist Chinese government, not recognized by the U.S. since its birth in 1949.

1. **Secret diplomacy.** The process of normalization of relations with China began in July 1971, when Kissinger secretly flew to China to conduct exploratory talks with the Chinese. One obstacle to overcome was that the American desire to conduct a "two Chinas" policy—recognizing both the Beijing and the Taiwan governments—was unacceptable to the communist regime. At the same time the Americans insisted they would not countenance a Chinese takeover of Taiwan. China, for its part, insisted that Taiwan was an integral part of China.

2. **The outcome.** In a radical shift from previous U.S. policy, Nixon agreed that there was one China, represented by the communist government, not by the nationalist government of Taiwan. It was also agreed that the U.S. would accept China as a member of the United Nations. In February 1972, President Nixon travelled to China, meeting with Mao Tse Tung. China was warned, however, that the U.S. would oppose any attempt to overthrow the nationalist government in Taiwan.

E. **Limits of the balance of power—the power of oil.** International powers and dynamics began to emerge that fell outside of the trilateral relationships being established by Nixon and Kissinger. One of them was the power of oil. In reaction to U.S. support for Israel in the Yom Kippur War in 1973, Arab members of the Organization of Petroleum Exporting Countries (OPEC) imposed an oil embargo in October 1973, against the U.S., Europe, and Japan. The embargo was lifted in March 1974, but prices were again increased.

1. **Economic consequences of the oil embargo.** While the embargo was difficult for the U.S., causing long lines of autos at service stations, it led to an economic crisis in nations more dependent on imported oil, such as Japan and much of western Europe.

2. **Political consequences.** The oil embargo demonstrated the extent of international economic interdependence and the political, as well as economic, power emerging in oil-rich countries.

XIV. **America in decline: the Carter Administration.** When President **Jimmy Carter** took office in 1977, the American psyche was suffering from the trauma of the Vietnam War, the disgrace of President Nixon's forced resignation in 1974 over his role in the Watergate affair, a loss of influence around the globe, and the elimination of strategic superiority over the Soviets. Despite Carter's best intentions to bring a humane spirit to foreign policy, the national mood was reinforced with a series of disappointments and failures.

A. **Human rights.** In his inaugural address Carter stated that "our commitment to human rights must be absolute." However, as a principle of foreign policy this stand was problematic. The cultural variance over what constitutes human rights, the question of what role the U.S. should play in championing human rights abroad, and the poor human rights records of some U.S. allies, such as those in Central America, precluded application of a coherent policy.

B. **U.S./Soviet relations.** The Carter Administration was split into two camps—those who sought to place U.S./Soviet relations on the periphery of U.S. foreign policy, and those who sought to place them at the center. By the end of his term in office, Carter had clearly moved into the latter camp.

1. **Arms control.** Completion of a SALT II treaty was a major goal of the Carter Administration. A treaty placing limits on modernization and expansion of strategic forces was agreed to in June 1979. However, the treaty faced strong opposition in the Senate by those still uncomfortable with the Soviet lead in ICBMs. The Soviet lead, however, was only in raw numbers of weapons and nuclear megatonnage; it was not in deliverable war heads, where U.S. warheads were always more accurate.

2. **The end of Detente.** U.S./Soviet relations became strained in the late 1970s due to a range of issues. The Soviets felt that Carter's human rights policy interfered in Soviet domestic affairs and were uneasy about the increasingly close U.S./China relations. The U.S. continued to have reason for concern about the Soviets' adventures in the Third World, particularly in Ethiopia, Mozambique, and elsewhere, as well as through

their Cuban allies, in Angola, Somalia, and Yemen. After 1979 Nicaragua and Grenada were added to the list.

3. **Soviet invasion of Afghanistan.** In December 1979, the Soviet Union invaded Afghanistan to support a threatened pro-Soviet regime. This marked the first overt Soviet invasion outside of Eastern Europe in the post-war era. In response, Carter withdrew the SALT II treaty from consideration by the Senate, placed an embargo on sales of high technology and grain, increased defense spending, announced a boycott of the Moscow Olympics, and launched a nuclear modernization program.

C. **Success and failure in the Third World.** While attempting to fashion a more equitable American role in the Third World, Carter achieved mixed success.

1. **Camp David accords.** Under Carter, the U.S. served as mediator to the chronic conflict in the Middle East over the lack of a Palestinian homeland and the status of territory seized by Israel in the 1967 and 1973 wars.

   a. **Achievements.** Meeting at Camp David, Maryland, in September 1978, the leaders of Israel and Egypt entered into agreements that normalized relations between the two largest military powers of the region and settled some territorial questions.

   b. **Impasse over the Palestinian issue.** The accords, however, made no progress in settling the most difficult problem, the Palestinian issue, and merely established a framework for future discussions on that issue.

   c. **Soviet and Arab hostility to the Camp David accords.** The Soviets, who had been excluded from the meeting, were antagonized by the Camp David process, as were many Arab states.

2. **Nicaragua.** In 1979 the revolutionary Marxist Sandinista government came to power in Nicaragua. Carter quickly recognized the new government and provided economic assistance. However, the president received considerable domestic criticism for withdrawing effective support from the U.S. client government overthrown by the

Sandinistas, thereby allowing the fall of Nicaragua to communism.

3. **Iran.** Also in 1979, another client government faced popular revolution. Again the Carter Administration was criticized for failing to act decisively to prevent the replacement of the Shah with the Islamic fundamentalist government of the Ayatollah **Ruhollah Khomeini** (1900-1988).

   a. **The hostage crisis.** Carter misread the level of anti-U.S. feeling in Iran, which intensified when the Shah arrived in the U.S. for medical treatment. On November 4, 1979, militant students in Tehran took over the U.S. Embassy, taking sixty Americans hostage and demanding the return of the Shah and his wealth. After a failed American rescue attempt and despite protracted negotiations, the Americans remained in captivity for over a year. Not until Carter left office were the hostages released.

   b. **Significance of the hostage crisis.** The inability of the U.S. to secure the release of the hostages was seen as the nadir of U.S. power in the post-World War II era. To some the affair demonstrated a lack of respect for the U.S., and to others it showed a lack of willingness to use force to support American influence and prestige.

XV. **The Reagan years and the revival of American confidence. Ronald Reagan** came into the presidency in 1981 promising to restore America's power in the world and pride in itself. During his first term, he stood as a staunch anti-communist, emphasizing containment. His second term ended with a pragmatic foreign policy and unprecedented cooperation between the two superpowers.

A. **The "evil empire."** In a 1983 speech President Reagan proclaimed that the Soviet Union was "the focus of evil in the modern world" and that it was America's duty to undermine and contain the USSR. He would negotiate with the Soviets from a position of strength, and he launched the largest peace-time military build-up in U.S. history.

1. **Defense spending.** Beginning in 1981, defense budgets rose an average of 6.8 percent a year, levelling off in 1986. Between 1980 and 1988, the U.S. spent over $2 trillion on defense, much of it

for the procurement of high-cost, high-technology strategic weapons.

2. **Strategic Defense Initiative (SDI).** In January, 1983, the Reagan Administration unveiled its plan for a ballistic missile defense that would render nuclear weapons "impotent and obsolete." This Strategic Defense Initiative, dubbed "Star Wars" by the press, generated a debate over whether the space defense system could actually succeed and over the shift in nuclear policy, as symbolized by SDI, away from sole reliance on offensive weapons and deterrence as opposed to a defensive shield against a surprise attack.

3. **Arms Control.** Reagan considered most arms control negotiations inherently flawed since in his view the U.S. and the Soviets did not have corresponding interests.

   a. **SALT limits.** Reagan made it clear that his administration would not abide by the arms limits established by the unratified SALT II treaty that both sides had agreed to honor.

   b. **Missiles in Europe: the "Zero option."** In 1981 Reagan proposed that the U.S. would deploy no intermediate range missiles in Europe, if (and only if) the Soviets removed their existing missiles. This was the "zero option." In 1983, while negotiations over the issue continued, the U.S. deployed Pershing II and cruise missiles in Europe. As threatened, the Soviets walked out of the negotiations, but later they returned. Key European governments, Germany, Britain, Italy, and the Netherlands, in particular, agreed to the U.S. deployment in the face of vociferous opposition of the left, who marched in the streets of European capitals in large numbers. The American deployment was directly responsible for the subsequent Soviet agreement to remove their missiles in exchange for the removal of the U.S. missiles. (See below, C.2.a)

B. **The Reagan Doctrine.** In an effort to contain communism in the Third World, President Reagan proclaimed that the U.S. had a moral responsibility to aid insurgencies against communist regimes. By relying on indigenous rebels to challenge Soviet-backed governments, the U.S. could exert military pressure without becoming mired in what the public often saw as irrelevant foreign conflicts. Through this principle, the U.S. financed rebels in Nicaragua, Afghanistan, and Angola.

1. **The Nicaraguan Contras.** The primary focus of the Reagan Doctrine was Afghanistan; but also receiving attention was the Sandinista government in Nicaragua, which was being aided by advisors from the Soviet bloc. Through the "Contras," U.S.-financed and trained rebels, the U.S. engaged in a highly controversial five-year war against the Sandinistas.

   a. **Iran/Contra.** In 1986, it was revealed that the Reagan Administration had covertly sold arms to Iran in exchange for the release of American hostages held by terrorists, in contradiction to Reagan's stated policy of never negotiating with terrorists. Since Congress had made it illegal to supply the Contras, the funds raised through the arms sale to supply the Contras were in violation of U.S. law. Public and congressional support for the Contra war, already weak, was further eroded, eliminating future aid to the Contra forces.

   b. **Elections.** Convinced by opinion polls that they would be returned to power, the Sandinistas held free elections in 1990. However, they were voted out of office by a hostile public. Fearing government reprisals, Nicaraguans had not told their true intentions to pollsters. Nevertheless, the Sandinistas retained a significant organized following and influence in the government.

2. **The Grenada intervention.** The Reagan Administration also made use of limited but direct U.S. military force.

   a. **Birth of a new Soviet ally.** In 1979 a coup removed the constitutional government of the tiny Caribbean island of Grenada (population 100,000) and installed a government of the Grenada Communist Party. The close relations of the new government with Cuba and Nicaragua alarmed the United States. Construction by hundreds of Cubans of a new airport capable of servicing Soviet or Cuban military jets further heightened tensions with Washington. The Grenada government sought close relations with Moscow, sending an ambassador. Documents captured in 1983 showed that revolutionaries from neighboring islands left via Grenada for terrorist training in Libya, justifying fears of the export of revolution by nearby governments.

b. **The crisis of 1983**. In October, 1983, fighting among factions of the government left the prime minister dead and an army general of unknown intentions in charge. His intentions toward the scores of American students who studied medicine on the island were especially sensitive to the Reagan Administration, in light of the recent hostage situation in Iran that had ruined the presidency of Jimmy Carter. To restore constitutional government, eliminate the latest communist stronghold in the hemisphere, and safeguard the Americans on the island, U.S. troops, supported by neighboring governments, landed on the island and defeated Cuban defenders in heavy fighting. The American troops were greeted as rescuers by the Grenadan people, 91 percent of whom, according to a poll taken soon afterward, approved the U.S. action.

C. **The Cold War begins to subside**. In 1985, a new leader emerged in the Soviet Union who would begin steps to end the Cold War. **Mikhail Gorbachev** recognized that the Soviet Union was rapidly becoming a second-rate economic power. In an effort to modernize the Soviet economy, Gorbachev expressed a commitment to ending the arms race and bringing the Soviet Union into the international community.

1. **The pragmatic Reagan.** A new relationship emerged between the U.S. and the USSR that began to change the face of international politics. In addition to real changes occurring in the USSR, Reagan faced pressure for improved relations from Congress and the increasingly popular peace movement that had mushroomed during Reagan's first term.

2. **Progress on arms control.** Arms control agreements that had seemed impossible just two years before, were suddenly acceptable.

   a. **Intermediate-range Nuclear Forces (INF) Treaty.** In December 1987, the presidents of the U.S. and the USSR signed a historic agreement, the INF Treaty, to eliminate an entire class of nuclear weapons. It was the first actual arms **reduction** treaty, in contrast to previous arms **control** treaties that limited

future deployment. The INF treaty grew out of the "zero option" and the deployment of Pershing II and cruise missiles over Soviet objections.

   b. **START talks.** Negotiations to make significant reductions of longer-range strategic weapons, the START talks, began in earnest in 1985 and continued through the Reagan years.

3. **Cooperative efforts.** The superpowers began to work together successfully to resolve a range of regional conflicts in southern Africa, Central America, and Asia. The Soviets withdrew from Afghanistan, though fighting continued there; progress on peace in Angola took place, reaching fruition in 1991; and a reduced Soviet commitment to Nicaragua helped lead, in time, to a peaceful succession to the Sandinista regime via the ballot box.

4. **Defense and deficits.** The upward spiral of the defense budget ended in 1986 when public support for military spending fell dramatically. The Reagan fiscal and defense spending policies had created an unprecedented federal budget deficit of $220 billion. To finance these deficits, the nation required a massive foreign influx of cash. As a result of deficit spending and a huge trade deficit, the nation catapulted from its position as the world's largest creditor nation to being the largest debtor nation.

D. **The U.S. as provider of aid in the post-World War II era.** A principal feature of American foreign policy in the post-war period has been foreign aid, in various forms. These forms have included economic grants and loans; military grants and loans; and humanitarian assistance. The following is a summary of these programs. The dollar amounts in each category would have to be increased by the rate of inflation from the year the aid was given until the present in order to arrive at constant dollars, or, in other words, today's money. For example, Marshall Plan aid to Europe between 1949 to 1952 amounted to $26.1 billion in grants. In 1990 dollars, this would amount to about $130 billion.

1. **Decline in economic assistance in the 1980s.** From 1946 to 1988, the U.S. gave about $212 billion, of which about $55 billion was loans and the remainder was grants. In the 1980s, annual economic aid declined. In 1985, for example, the

U.S. gave $10.75 billion in grants and $1.58 billion in loans; but in 1988 $7.9 billion was given in grants and $.85 billion in loans. The decline was actually greater than the dollar figures since inflation was not taken into account.

2. **Decline in military assistance in the 1980s.** During the same period (1946-1988), the U.S. gave $130.9 billion in military assistance. Of this amount, $91.1 billion was grants and the remainder loans. Like economic assistance, total annual military aid also declined in the 1980s, although grants as opposed to loans rose slightly. In 1985 military grants amounted to $3.44 billion and loans were $2.37 billion, while in 1988 grants were $4.83 billion and loans $.763 billion.

3. **Humanitarian assistance.** This assistance was given for an array of disasters, natural and man-made. From the formal inception of the program in 1964 until 1989, the Agency for International Development (A.I.D.), through its disaster assistance program, gave $4.51 billion in aid. Of this, $2.6 billion was in the form of food under the Food for Peace program. By contrast, the rest of the world during the same period gave some $6.6 billion for the same disasters and voluntary American organizations gave $480 million. An average of thirty-two countries a year received disaster assistance.

XVI. **The superpowers at the end of the Cold War.** The decline of the Cold War witnessed a great reversion to a "normal" international society in Europe, mixed with novel elements of friction.

A. **The basis of the Cold War.** The Cold War rested on twin pillars.

1. **The dominance of ideology.** The first pillar was ideological. Soviet Marxism was pitted against western liberal democracy.

2. **The status of Central Europe.** The second pillar was the question of the freedom of Central European states, forcibly occupied since 1945 by the Soviets, to choose their own destiny.

B. **The end of the Cold War when the Soviets changed.** The principal reason for the change in the European map was a radical shift in thinking in the Soviet Union. On both of the principal issues of the Cold War, the Soviets conceded. Examples of Soviet change in their policy in Central Europe are the following:

1. **Soviets' encouragement of change in Poland.** The late 1980s saw a remarkable example in the case of Poland. Poland was a Russian security interest since the eighteenth century. But in the Poland of 1989, a non-communist Premier could argue for the transformation from socialism to capitalism. Indeed, when the Communist Party of Poland objected to this process, Soviet premier Gorbachev telephoned instructions to be more cooperative.

2. **Change in Hungary and the "Sinatra Doctrine."** Similarly Hungary, crushed in 1956 by Soviet tanks for opting out of the Warsaw pact, rapidly moved out of the Soviet orbit. Senior Soviet spokesmen, alluding to a popular song, explained that this was all part of a new "Sinatra Doctrine," according to which Socialist states can proceed "their way," to non-socialist destinations.

3. **Destruction of the Berlin Wall.** The twenty-nine-mile-long Berlin wall, constructed with Soviet approval in August 1961 by East Germany, was one of the lasting and hated symbols of the Cold War. Its demolition beginning in December 1989, with Soviet acquiescence if not active encouragement, allowed free movement of Berliners and marked a fundamental change in Soviet policy.

C. **Fulfillment of the "containment" doctrine.** By the early 1990s, the hopes of America's post-war policy of containing Soviet power were being realized.

1. **Withering of Soviet power.** Soviet power, constrained from real expansion, is withering. As George Kennan predicted in 1947, the Soviet system faced radical transformation or a shattering implosion at the end of the Cold War.

2. **Withering of Soviet ideology.** Like some ancient bog-bound Cro-Magnon ancestor, the Soviets began shedding their previously indispensable ideology as well as their hitherto vital European buffer states, as they struggled for release from impending disaster.

D. **The role of the United States in the post-war era.** Important lessons can be drawn from American experience from 1945 to the end of the Cold War.

1. **The necessity of sacrifice for the preservation of freedom.** The domination of the industrialized states of western Europe by the Soviet Union after World War II would have made the enor-

mous industrial resources of the region, once it had recovered from the ravages of war, a potential military threat to the United States. The U.S. would have been virtually isolated in a world whose balance of power had tilted, perhaps decisively, toward communist autocracy. Thus the American role in preserving the freedom of Western Europe was the means to preserve its own freedom. This role included considerable sacrifice of human effort, economic resources, military investment, and American lives.

2. **Recognition of the American role: the testimony of Vaclav Havel.** The American role in the preservation of freedom in Western Europe and in the recovery of freedom in Eastern Europe was the subject of remarks by Czechoslovakia's president Vaclav Havel in his 1990 address to the U.S. Congress. Havel said:

   a. **American sacrifices in the World Wars.** "Twice in this century, the world has been threatened by a catastrophe; twice this catastrophe was born in Europe, and twice you Americans, along with others, were called upon to save Europe, the whole world, and yourselves....[Between the wars] the United States was making great strides. It became the most powerful nation on earth, and it understood the responsibility that flowed from this. Proof of this are the hundreds of thousands of your young citizens who gave their lives for the liberation of Europe, and the graves of American airmen and soldiers on Czechoslovak soil.

   b. **Growth of Soviet power after World War II.** "But something else was happening as well: the Soviet Union appeared, grew, and transformed the enormous sacrifices of its people suffering under totalitarian rule into a strength that, after World War Two, made it the second most powerful nation in the world. It was a country that rightly gave people nightmares, because no one knew what would occur to its rulers next and what country they would decide to conquer and drag into their sphere of influence, as it is called in political language.

   c. **Division of Europe into arsenals.** All of this taught us to see the world in bipolar terms, as two enormous forces, one a defender of freedom, the other a source of nightmares.

Europe became the point of friction between these two powers and thus it turned into a single enormous arsenal divided into two parts.

   d. **America's contribution to western survival.** "In this process, one half of the arsenal became part of that nightmarish power, while the other—the free part—bordering on the ocean and having no wish to be driven into it, was compelled, together with you, to build a complicated security system, to which we probably owe the fact that we still exist. So you may have contributed to the salvation of us Europeans, of the world and thus of yourselves for a third time: you have helped us to survive until to-day—without a hot war this time—but merely a cold one."

Contemporary Perspective

INTRODUCTION

Americans often view international events and U.S. relations with other countries through the prism of the post-World War II era when American military, political, and economic power was at its height. While the United States remains a predominant international actor of enormous wealth and power, the global context has changed. The preeminent place of the geopolitical structures that defined the post-war era—structures such as NATO—is complicated by an increasingly interconnected world where power and influence are not limited to superpowers. These changes have an impact on American foreign policy, military and economic security, and citizens' perception of the American role in the world. Outlined below are some of the most important international challenges—strategic, political, economic, and cooperative—faced by Americans preparing to enter the twenty-first century.

I. **Strategic challenges.** Since the end of World War II, the rivalry between the U.S. and the Soviet Union has defined the strategic balance in Europe and often pulled conflicts in other regions into a superpower tug-of-war. The Soviet-American competition gave birth to a costly nuclear and conventional arms race that simultaneously maintained an uneasy peace and threatened the survival of humanity. But as the 1980s progressed, it was argued that economic strength, rather than military might, was the future path to world power. The Iraq crisis and war of 1990-1991, however, showed the limits to this argument, since American military might was the key to deterring further Iraqi aggression after its initial invasion of Kuwait, denying to the Iraqi dictator immense economic power through control of the world price of oil; and in 1991 American military power was the predominant factor that defeated Iraq. Thus, the notion that economic strength has superseded military power is at best an overstatement.

A. **Decline of Cold War rivalry.** Faced with a faltering domestic economy, the Soviet leadership began to search for ways to lighten the burden of military expenditures and change its adversary relationship with the West. Likewise, growing budget deficits in the U.S. have created pressures to reexamine U.S. security needs and the international U.S. military role. As a result, the prevailing defense issue of the 1990s will likely focus on the changing nature of the threats to U.S. national security and how to manage the necessary changes in our defense posture. However, wary observers warned that it was not impossible for East/West tensions to flare up as forces of reaction in the USSR asserted themselves. These forces—the Communist party apparatus, security agencies, and the military—tended to hold traditional Cold War views and to advocate assertion of Soviet interests at the expense of the Western allies.

B. **U.S. interests abroad.** The role of the U.S. military abroad is to protect American and allied security and interests. The continuing debate over the nature of those interests becomes more crucial as resources to be directed to the military become more scarce. As the future U.S.-Soviet relationship becomes uncertain, questions arise as to what are the primary threats to U.S. security.

1. **Continuing Soviet military threat.** One argument is that although the Cold War has abated, the Soviet Union's nuclear capabilities continue to pose a threat to the U.S. and its European allies. Moreover, a new Cold War might arise.

2. **Third World military threats.** It is also argued that threats to U.S. interests arise from Third World governments with strong ideological differences or from aggressive dictatorships. The threat to American interests by Iraq in 1990-91 illustrates the latter threat. Developing countries are expected to have increasing access to technologies that could threaten the U.S. and its allies. These threats could arise from chemical, biological, and atomic weapons delivered either through such means as planes, missiles, and battle field weapons, or through terrorists. Even

relatively poor countries, critics have warned, could develop chemical and biological weapons capabilities.

3. **Economic and environmental threats.** Another view argues that notwithstanding military threats, economic and environmental problems pose the greatest threats to American security.

   a. **Economic problems.** Examples of economic problems include the chronic trade deficit, loss of employment to foreign countries, dependence on foreign oil supplies, and the control of American industries by foreign owners.

   b. **Environmental problems.** Examples of environmental problems include the rise of greenhouse gases from burning fossil fuels and the effect on health from pollution.

4. **Importance of this debate.** The response to these questions determines the strategic posture that the U.S. adopts and the size and character of the military capabilities it maintains. Equally, the response to these questions also informs American policy in its relationships with other nations.

C. **Arms control.** The 1970s and 1980s saw a costly and spiralling race of the superpowers to arm with nuclear and conventional forces.

1. **Arms ceilings v. arms reductions.** During the 1970s and 1980s, arms control efforts sought to place ceilings on future production of weapons. With economic pressures and improved East/West relations, arms control negotiators began to seek actual reduction in existing weapons stockpiles and military forces. The 1987 U.S./Soviet treaty to eliminate all intermediate range nuclear weapons in Europe was the first step in this direction.

2. **Reversing the arms race.** Debate over arms control now centers on the pace of reductions and the size of military forces necessary to provide an adequate defense and deterrent. For the first time, there exists the possibility of reversing the arms race and the nuclear threat between the U.S. and the USSR.

3. **Arms reductions and Third World threats.** Although the dangers between the U.S. and the USSR appear to have receded, the extent to

which it will be prudent for the U.S. to limit conventional arms reductions is limited by the possibility of previously unexpected threats from developing countries. Development or threatened development of nuclear, chemical, and biological weapons, and ballistic missiles, as discussed above, along with the formation of large conventional forces by such countries, may to some degree restrict U.S. reductions in weapons procurement.

D. **Strategic modernization**. At the same time that the U.S. is negotiating strategic and conventional force reductions, defense planners continue to pursue development of new, more advanced weapons. Some defense policy analysts believe that the U.S. should delay further production of increasingly expensive strategic systems until a full examination can be made of U.S. defense needs and the usefulness of each new weapon to a reduced defense force. Other analysts, unsure of Soviet intentions and the future of U.S.-Soviet relations, and keeping the experience of the 1991 war with Iraq firmly in view as an example of new sources of threats to American security, contend that such weapons are vitally necessary to ensure continued U.S. security and to provide negotiating leverage.

II. **Political challenges**. Due to its enormous economic and military power, the U.S. has been able to wield a great deal of political influence in much of the world through bilateral relationships, formal and informal alliances, and through a variety of international organizations such as the United Nations, the World Bank, and the International Monetary Fund. But as other countries, often with U.S. aid, have become economically strong and politically mature, they have demanded a greater share of international decision making and have demonstrated independence from U.S. political objectives. Thus, the U.S. may be unable to exercise effective influence over many of the political changes occurring in the 1990s. The American ability to exert world leadership, however, should not be discounted. In this regard, analysts have distinguished "soft power"—leadership ability to set the international agenda and gain support for one's positions—from the traditional "hard power" of armies, navies, and weapons. Listed below are some of the significant international political circumstances that concern Americans.

A. **Burden sharing**. Western European nations have fully regained status as significant international powers. As East/West military tensions ease, many questions arise about the relationships between Eastern and Western

Europe, and between Western Europe and the United States.

1. **Reducing U.S. presence in Europe**. Many Americans perceive the increasing political and economic contact between Western European nations and the USSR as justification to reduce U.S. military defense of the region.

2. **Maintaining U.S. presence in Europe and burden sharing**. Other analysts are concerned that a reduction of U.S. forces will further erode U.S. political influence in Europe. It is often argued that Europe should equally share the financial burden of any American contribution to its security.

B. **Shifting power in Eastern Europe**. In the late 1980s and early 1990s the shift in the Soviet government's attitude toward its former Eastern European satellites precipitated remarkable and unanticipated changes in the political make-up of that region. Although the political shape of Eastern Europe will be unclear for quite some time, one thing is certain—the legacy of Stalinism has ended, definitively changing life in the Soviet Union and the nations of Eastern Europe.

1. **The Revolution of 1989**. In the last months of 1989, the communist governments of Eastern Europe fell in rapid succession. The once communist countries of Europe have begun experimenting with free market mechanisms, democratic elections, new constitutions, and less repressive social controls.

2. **Difficult years ahead**. Despite the international euphoria over such changes, these countries face difficult years ahead. The region confronts enormous challenges in providing a standard of living comparable to their western neighbors, in preventing ethnic or ideological power struggles, and in resolving ambiguous military relationships within what was once the Warsaw Pact.

C. **The new Europe**. As Europe approaches the next century, its internal structure is changing due to several factors.

1. **Political realignment and integration**. The end of Soviet domination of Eastern Europe has created a fluidity in the relations of former communist countries and Western Europe. Some may wish to join an expanded European Community (EC). The place of the Soviet Union, especially when

its future is so uncertain, is an imponderable that promises to be an important subject in the future. How united a role in world affairs the new Europe will play is likewise an imponderable.

2. **Economic integration**. The end of tariff barriers in 1992 for members of the EC signals the beginning of a new era of economic cooperation and integration in Europe. With the largest single market in the industrialized world, the economic strength of the EC will potentially be a force to be reckoned with.

3. **The role of a united Germany**. In October 1990 East Germany peacefully united with West Germany. The Soviet Union agreed to a gradual withdrawal of its troops from former East German territory. Germany, economic powerhouse of Europe, appears destined to become more politically influential as a result of both its unification and the retreat of Soviet power.

D. **Third World debt**. Foreign debt has become an economic and political crisis for many developing nations and for much of Eastern Europe, as well. In South America, for example, the issue of foreign debt relief is, and will continue to be, of paramount importance. After years of austerity measures, it is becoming clear that this debt, totalling $426 billion at the end of 1988, will never be repaid in full.

1. **Dealing with Third World debt**. The task at hand for the U.S. and other western nations and the governments of developing countries is to find a politically viable means of relieving the debt burden and rebuilding the potentially dynamic economies of the region.

2. **Threat posed to western banks by debt default**. Some American and other Western banks face severe losses or even closure if developing countries default on loans. Thus the stakes in finding means to manage the problem of Third World debt may be high.

E. **Prolonged regional conflicts**. While many Americans point to the absence of armed conflict between the United States and the Soviet Union and in Europe as evidence of an era of peace and stability, in other parts of the world armed struggle has become a way of life. Prolonged wars have raged in such places as southern Africa, Afghanistan, Ethiopia, Central America, and the Middle East. Two of the cases in

which the United States has important interests at stake are outlined below.

1. **Central America**. Long-term economic distress, exacerbated by recurring human rights problems, has generated prolonged and widespread political unrest throughout Central America. The region's most unyielding conflict is the civil war in El Salvador—a tiny nation that, since the mid-1970s when the war began, has lost much of its population to war, death squads, or emigration. Although in 1989 the United States supported El Salvador at $386 million per year, the war effort has not come to a conclusion militarily and politically. The country remains one of the hemisphere's poorest.

2. **The Middle East**. The Middle East is a region of long-simmering political rivalries and enmities. It is also of vital importance to American and Western interests generally because of the importance of Middle Eastern oil in the world economy. It is also important to the U.S. because of America's historic commitment to maintaining the existence of Israel. The political fallout from the Persian Gulf War of 1990-91 means that the future configuration of alliances of Arab states is in flux, making generalizations hazardous.

a. **The Arab-Israeli conflict**. The *intifada*, or uprising, of Palestinians in Israeli-occupied territories of the West Bank and Gaza focused world attention and created political pressures for a negotiated settlement of this forty-year conflict. Such negotiations would attempt agreement on Israeli security and Palestinian self-determination and would most probably require mediation by the U.S. But radical Palestinian and other Arab hostility to the existence of Israel, as well as forces in Israel hostile to allowing an independent Palestinian state, make a final settlement of the Arab-Israeli conflict problematic at best.

b. **Other chronic conflicts**. Enmities and rivalries among Arab and other states in the region such as Iran (which is Muslim but not Arab) have numerous, sometimes ancient, origins. Two salient roots of some of these rivalries center upon the possession of oil wealth and the degree of modernization of each country. Rich Arab countries are often opposed by poor ones, who demand they share their vast wealth. Traditionalist Islamic countries may be opposed to their modernizing neighbors who have cast off strict adherence to Muslim tradition. A third root of conflict lies in the claims of Islamic fundamentalists—hostile to Muslim secularism, to the West and to oil-rich Arab governments allied with the West—who are a growing force in much of the region. Conflicting ambitions of the region's dictatorial strongmen have led to tensions and hostilities. Such instability makes the protection of American and Western interests both difficult and dangerous.

F. **The rise of Asia.** As a region, Asia has experienced remarkable economic growth in recent years. As a result, Japan's political influence has also increased. Led by Japan, new political and economic forces are arising in the region. In addition to Japan, the new Asian economic forces include the "Four Tigers"—South Korea, Taiwan, Hong Kong, and Singapore. The average annual growth rate for South Korea in the 1980s was ten percent. One of the "tigers," Hong Kong, is scheduled to revert to Chinese rule in 1997. Its future economic health is difficult to predict.

1. **Japan.** Japanese economic leadership has brought it both political power, which it is often reluctant to accept, and an evolving relationship with the United States. Neither the United States nor Japan has adequately addressed the tensions produced by Japan's economic rise, such as the growing bilateral trade deficit and a growing cultural antagonism. During the next decade both nations will struggle to adjust their former political relationship of patron-client to meet the economic realities of two, relatively equal, world economic powers. But there is no indication that Japan's military power will approach that of the United States.

2. **China.** Through much of the 1980s, China also experienced rapid economic growth. But unlike Eastern Europe and the Soviet Union, China attempted to combine free market reforms with political repression. China's economic developments and its growing international respect were sharply reversed when the government violently suppressed the Chinese democratization movement led by students. The future of China's role in the area may hinge upon whether it can evolve into a stable democratic state.

III. **The debate on the "decline" of American power.** On the other side, America's power relative to Europe and Japan has also declined compared with its position in 1945 when the ruin of war had decimated Europe and Japan alike. But whether the country was "in decline" at the end of the Cold War was vigorously debated.

A. **Evidence of decline.** For a time in 1989, Japan, in terms of its market capitalization, was wealthier than the United States. American crime rates in the 1980s had increased 47 percent, while infant mortality hovered around rates more familiar to the developing world. Drug use was rampant. Education was faltering. American national debt grew, while capital formation and savings declined. A large national budget deficit continued. Fragmentation of society into racial, ethnic, and linguistic rivalries, and the existence of a chronic "underclass" could be read as signals of social decay. In some quarters, there was a sense that the United States had reached the Cold War's finish line "exhausted."

B. **The case against decline.** Other critics argued against this analysis, arguing that the American position in 1945, when Europe and Japan were exhausted by war, was an anomaly. A truer comparison is with the pre-World War II American position, which shows the U.S. as far more powerful at the close of the Cold War. The U.S. is destined to retain its power through its immense wealth, technological prowess, military strength, political stability, and the political will to exercise power in pursuit of perceived national interests. The American-led military victory in the Gulf War illustrated American political will, diplomatic skill, and military prowess, adding weight to the anti-declinist case. In this view, the strength of American liberal democracy far outweighs the liabilities of its social problems.

IV. **Economic challenges.** International economic changes are perhaps felt more acutely by Americans than are changes in the strategic and political spheres. Since the 1970s, competitors to a once dominant U.S. economy have emerged. While the U.S. continues to be the world's largest economy, it is also the world's largest debtor and suffers from grave budget and trade deficits. Today's global economy is characterized by predominance of transnational economic forces and the interrelationship of the world's domestic economic policies. Such policies as fiscal, monetary, tax, and employment legislation enacted by one major international actor affect the global economy. These developments demand greater degrees of economic coordination between major economic players. Although attempted with limited success to date by the western industrial nations, efforts to coordinate domestic economic policies are likely to increase in the future.

A. **Trade**. The growth of international trade since the 1970s has made a significant contribution toward the creation of an interconnected world with multiple centers of economic power. American businesses and citizens often feel threatened by this new economic environment. At the end of the 1980s, the U.S. recorded an annual trade deficit nearing $200 billion. This deficit induced some U.S. policy makers to favor "protectionism" (trade barriers against foreign competition) as opposed to the traditional American "free trade" policies. This debate is likely to continue for some time to come.

1. **Trading blocs**. Some analysts suggest that international relations are moving from the bipolar U.S.-Soviet world to a tripolar world of trading blocs—North American, the EC, and East Asia. The 1988 U.S.-Canada Free Trade Agreement, reducing restrictions on the flow of goods, services, and capital across their border was a large step in this direction. The U.S. and Canada are each other's largest trading partners. Furthermore, members of the EC are integrating their economies into a single market in 1992. The economies of the Association of South East Asian Nations (ASEAN) have been moving toward their own common market, as well.

2. **The pros and cons of trading blocs**. There is no consensus among economists as to whether the consequences of trade blocs will be positive or negative.

    a. **Trading bloc rivalries as leading to protectionism**. Some analysts predict fierce economic rivalries will arise from such a trading bloc system. These rivalries, they argue, will increase protectionist sentiment globally, thereby reducing international trade.

    b. **Trading blocs as a boon to small states**. Others see trading blocs as the only means for smaller, more vulnerable economies to meaningfully participate in a world of economic superpowers.

B. **Poverty**. The 1980s was a high growth period for a handful of newly industrialized countries such as Asia's Four Tigers. But many other developing nations during the same period saw earlier economic gains reversed.

1. **Grim statistics**. Currently, 25 percent of the world's people live in dire poverty. The lives of these impoverished people are marked with severe malnutrition, illiteracy, and rampant disease. For sixteen African and Latin American nations, per capita income was lower in 1985 than in 1965, and in twenty African countries, calorie supply of the average diet was lower in 1985 than in 1965.

2. **The example of Africa**. At a time when great hope for economic progress has been rising in much of the world, many African nations are sinking deeper into poverty and debt.

    a. **Poverty**. Twenty of the world's thirty-four poorest nations are in Africa. While child mortality rates are declining in every other region of the world, they continue to rise in Africa.

    b. **Population increase**. The African population is expected to more than double from 1990 to 2025, rising from 647 million to 1.58 billion. In one dramatic example, Nigeria is projected to more than double its population by 2025, rising to more than 300 million, or about equal to the U.S. Such increases in the continent will further strain the fragile environment and declining food resources.

    c. **Absence of Western interests in Africa**. Because the West does not perceive much of sub-Saharan Africa to have the strategic and economic importance of other regions, it is often passed over for substantial foreign aid and economic investment—two factors that may be increasingly necessary to reverse Africa's slide into widespread human tragedy.

3. **The debate over foreign aid**. While much of the world's sustained poverty arises from such factors as environmental deterioration, political instability, high population growth, and low commodity prices, the policies of wealthy nations can have significant impact on world poverty. Whether large increases in Western economic assistance are desirable, however, is a subject of debate.

a. **Arguments for increasing foreign economic aid**. As of the late 1980s, 66 percent of U.S. foreign aid was allotted for military assistance, with 24 percent of total aid going to the world's poorest nations. Critics argue that economic aid is far too low. Shifting U.S. foreign aid priorities, along with easing these nations' foreign debt burdens, would help renew economic growth in poor regions. While Japan and much of Western Europe already outspend the U.S. on development aid, in the future they may be expected to take stronger political leadership on the issue of poverty.

b. **Arguments against increasing foreign economic aid**. Other critics argue that foreign aid has been shown to be often wasted in poor countries. While emergency assistance should be granted to victims of famine and other natural calamities, in the long term, large-scale foreign aid is not the panacea that its supporters imagine. Poor countries must practice the virtue of self-help and take effective measures to reduce excessive population growth where it is a hindrance to reducing poverty.

C. **Technological revolution**. During the 1980s, the world witnessed a new economic revolution—that of information and communication technologies—that has had an impact on the shape of the international economy and the future of individual countries. Through this revolution, trade and other economic transactions know no national borders. Products often have the components of many nations, making the country of origin difficult to pinpoint. While this revolution has created truly international, intertwining Western economies and caused the Soviet bloc to strive for access to it, it is leaving others behind. Those nations whose industrial base is undeveloped may find the new world economy even further out of their reach.

V. **Challenges of international cooperation**. Problems of the twenty-first century, such as environmental issues, poverty, economic development, regional conflicts, and international arms sales are sometimes truly global in nature and often require the cooperation of nations from every corner of the world. While many governments conceptually acknowledge the need to coordinate efforts to resolve world problems, such coordination often contradicts national agendas. Many of these issues cannot, however, be tackled by a handful of countries, while others continue to contribute to the problem. Broad-based international efforts are often essential.

A. **International organizations**. Since the end of World War II, attempts have been made for regional organizations such as the Organization of American States and the Organization of African Unity, and international organizations such as the United Nations (UN) to serve as agencies to deal peacefully with disputes between nations. In some cases they have been successful to a degree, while in others they have failed. For example, the UN was originally designed as a forum for the peaceful resolution of conflict and as an advocate for social and economic justice and human rights. Support for the UN's record in preventing and mediating conflict varies among critics.

1. **Evolution of the United Nations**. In its early years the United Nations was dominated by the wealthy and powerful nations of the West, which were the leading lights behind its creation. With decolonization in the 1950s and '60s, the newly-formed nations of the Third World embraced the UN as an international forum to voice their concerns. Because these nations were often hostile to the West in general and to the U.S. in particular, many Americans began to see the UN as anti-American and ineffective, and withdrew their support for the organization.

2. **The return of multilateralism**. In the late 1980s, the UN began enjoying a period of renewed confidence. In recent years, several successes in peacekeeping and conflict resolution helped to restore international faith in the organization. These included the UN's positive role in negotiated settlements in Southern Africa and the Persian Gulf and in the negotiated withdrawal of Soviet troops from Afghanistan, combined with the award of the Nobel Peace Price to the UN peacekeeping forces. The UN as a forum for organizing resistance to the Iraqi invasion of Kuwait in 1990-91 likewise aided the UN's reputation.

3. **The limits to multilateralism**. Some of the weighty issues facing the U.S. and other states are global in nature and require an international forum. Other crucial issues facing the U.S. are not "global" but require attention at bilateral, regional, or other levels. Critics argue that it remains true that the UN or similar international organizations can only be effective when member

states find their interests to be sufficiently compatible to justify their cooperation. Decisions by multilateral organizations are not autonomous but are at bottom the decisions of sovereign states, the ultimate players on the international stage. Thus, in the final analysis, unless it decides to take the momentous step of giving up sovereignty, the U.S. itself, rather than multilateral organizations, is responsible for the decisions it makes regarding international affairs.

4. **The debate over American policy.** The character and extent of American international cooperation is a matter of debate among citizens.

   a. **Argument that American policy should be more internationalist.** One side holds that the U.S. should adopt a consistently internationalist approach, cooperating with majorities in international organizations in tackling global problems. Some who hold this position argue that the U.S. should subordinate itself to international organizations for the sake of ensuring international peace, the redistribution of wealth to the poorest nations, and the solution of pressing global problems. In any case, these problems demand that national sentiment be put aside, if for no other reason than the welfare, even the survival, of humanity, Americans included.

   b. **Argument that American internationalism should remain limited.** Another approach holds that the goal of American foreign policy should be the pursuit of enlightened, national self-interest and believes the American tendency to embark on moralistic crusades to be fundamentally mistaken. Some international bodies, such as the UN General Assembly and UNESCO, are hostile to American interests and sometimes behave irresponsibly. Far from ensuring humanity's survival, subordination to them would be foolhardy, perhaps suicidal to American democracy. International cooperation is generally desirable, but not on terms that undermine legitimate American interests. In any case, the question whether the U.S. should relinquish some degree of sovereignty to international bodies is a political question for the American people to debate and decide openly. A policy of abandoning sovereignty should not be inculcated into

unsuspecting youth under the guise of "education."

B. **The environment.** The deterioration of the global environment is a problem of truly international dimensions. It can only be dealt with through the cooperative efforts of many nations. Decades of industrial development without regard to its environmental impact, coupled with the additional strain on resources from world population growth of 90 million people each year, will have a lasting impact on all of humanity. For example, water and air pollution know no national boundaries; and global warming and a thinning ozone layer affect everyone.

   1. **Global warming.** Global warming is caused by an increase in carbon dioxide and other chemicals in the earth's atmosphere, brought on by heavy use of fossil fuels. It is exacerbated by the loss of the world's forests, which are receding by some 28 million acres a year. Scientists are divided over the severity of the warming trend or what the effects will be over the next several decades. Few doubt, however, that international efforts are required to deal with whatever problems global warming may bring.

   2. **Implications of environmental degradation.** Environmental degradation may have dramatic economic, social, and political implications as well as adversely affecting people's health. For example, changes in the environment can cause agricultural belts to shift geographically, thereby changing the relative economic strength of nations. The displacement of large numbers of persons by environmental deterioration causes social disorder and political instability. Domestic and international peace may become precarious as a result. In many cases, means of managing or resolving problems arising from environmental degradation, such as the effects of burning fossil fuels, deforestation, and large increases in population, can only be accomplished through the cooperation of many nations.

C. **International terrorism.** Terrorism is a threat or act of illegitimate violence meant to achieve a particular political objective. Terrorism relies on creating fear and insecurity and gaining public attention for the terrorist's grievances and differs fundamentally from ordinary acts of war.

   1. **Illegitimacy of terrorism.** The notion that one person's terrorist is another person's freedom

fighter is false. A just cause—freedom from oppression or self-defense, for example—does **not** make it legitimate to use outlawed means of attaining these ends. Legitimate ends do not justify illegitimate means.

2. **Examples of terrorist acts.** Means outlawed by international law and by the conventions of civilized humanity include indiscriminate attacks on innocents, such as hijacking or bombing civilian modes of transport, bombing or shooting in public places, kidnapping civilians, assassination of politicians, and taking hostages.

3. **Where terrorism occurs.** Most terrorism occurs in the Middle East, Latin America, and Europe. Relatively few incidents of international terrorism occur in the United States.

4. **Need for international cooperation to combat terrorism.** While there is no one proven method for effectively dealing with terrorism, most experts agree that international cooperation is needed for applying sanctions against states that support terrorists, for extradition of suspected terrorists and for exchanging information. The possibility of terrorist access to nuclear, chemical or biological weapons technology makes this cooperation essential for international stability.

5. **New terrorism versus old.** The use of force by terrorists is not a new phenomenon. But there are a number of differences between the new terrorists and the anarchists and terrorists of the nineteenth century.

   a. **Civilians excluded under old terrorism.** The targets of terrorists have expanded. Until the mid-twentieth century, virtually all terrorist acts were directed against agents of the state such as police, military officers, rulers, and politicians. The practice of terrorism has become so commonplace that its origins hardly matter, but the taboo against targeting civilians seems to have been broken in the Middle East in the 1920s and '30s as well as during the 1948 Israeli War of Independence.

   b. **State terrorism.** Those who perpetrated the old terrorism were members of revolutionary groups of one kind or another. Although certainly not all of the new terrorism is state-sponsored, many terrorist acts today and in the recent past have been directly or indirectly directed, carried out, or fostered by states. During their communist phases, East European states such as Hungary, Bulgaria, and Czechoslovakia carried out or sponsored terrorist acts. In the Middle East, states such as Iran, Iraq, Libya, and Syria have been implicated in such acts.

   c. **Limits of the old terrorism.** The logic of terrorism appears to have changed. In the nineteenth century, terrorists hoped to drive fear into the hearts of the ruling houses of Europe. In the twentieth century, the aim of terrorists has been to spread apprehension as far as possible—to everyone.

   d. **Television as propagator of terrorist aims.** Third, this enlarged arena of terrorism accomplishes its purposes less by the propaganda of the deed and more by the medium by which the deed is conveyed. Terrorism has become a new, sordid political theater, which works best on television.

D. **Nuclear proliferation.** Although U.S.-Soviet efforts to reduce their nuclear arsenals met with some success, the proliferation of nuclear weapons is increasing.

1. **Recognized nuclear powers.** The five recognized nuclear powers are the U.S., the Soviet Union, Britain, France, and China.

2. **States believed to possess nuclear weapons.** It is reasonably certain that several other countries possess small nuclear stockpiles. These are Israel, India, and South Africa.

3. **States working toward possession of nuclear weapons.** States that are reliably thought to be approaching nuclear weapons capability are Argentina, Brazil, and Pakistan, although in 1990 Argentina and Brazil declared publicly that they would not build nuclear weapons. Before the Persian Gulf crisis of 1990, it was widely believed that Iraq was five years or less from producing such weapons. It is also believed that North Korea, one of the last hard-line communist dictatorships, is actively developing nuclear weapons.

4. **Problems with the Nuclear Proliferation Treaty.** While the U.S., the USSR, and Britain are

signatories to the international Nuclear Non-Proliferation Treaty (NPT), none has strictly adhered to its precepts, thus enabling the spread of nuclear weapon know-how. The NPT is scheduled to be reconsidered in the 1990s, providing an opportunity for the world's nuclear powers to renew their commitment to plugging the hazardous leak of nuclear technology.

VI. **America's neighbors: Canada**. The United States and Canada share a continent. They also share the world's longest unfortified border. The two nations simultaneously have much in common and much that distinguishes them from each other. Each is extremely important to the other for cultural, economic, political, and security reasons. Americans tend to know far less about Canada—its geography, people, and government—than Canadians know about the United States. This is at least partly so because Canada's southern neighbor, with enormous wealth and more than nine times its population, perpetually threatens to overwhelm it culturally and economically. Thus, to Canada, the U.S. is a colossus that in some ways poses significant problems. The two nations have for long maintained warm relations, although the British repelled several American invasions during the War of 1812, and Irish nationalists ("Fenians") raided Canada from the U.S. after the Civil War. For more than a century, however, friction between the two countries has not included military tension or political rivalry. Still, former Canadian Prime Minister **Pierre Elliott Trudeau**, once said that living with the U.S. was "comparable to a mouse sleeping with an elephant." The elephant might be very friendly, but when it turns over in bed, it is liable to cause considerable commotion.

A. **Canada's geographical and demographic context**. Canada is the world's second largest country, after the Soviet Union, comprising some 3,851,000 square miles, more than 6 percent larger than the U.S. Its population in 1991 was approximately 27 million, compared with 250 million in the U.S. The vast majority of Canadians live within 100 miles of the U.S. border. While those of English, Scottish, and French backgrounds comprise the majority of the population, a number of other groups have emigrated to Canada in the nineteenth and twentieth centuries, many of them after World War II. Thus, Chinese form one of the largest recent immigrant populations in British Columbia; many Canadians of Eastern European origin can be found in such plains cities as Winnipeg, capital of Manitoba; and cosmopolitan Toronto is a mosaic of ethnic groups, among them Asians, Caribbeans, Eastern Europeans, Germans, Italians, and others.

B. **Canada's origins**. The origins of today's Canada lie in the competition between French and British claims to the country in the early seventeenth century.

1. **Early history**. A series of armed clashes and wars culminated in France's defeat and the Treaty of Paris in 1763, which ceded nearly all French North American territories to Britain. By then, a considerable number of French settlers inhabited today's Quebec. During and after the American Revolution large numbers of British loyalists fled north and settled in the Maritime Provinces and Quebec. Conflict between English and French inhabitants led the British to separate "Upper Canada" (Ontario) from "Lower Canada" (Quebec). In 1840 an Act of Union brought the two parts under one government.

2. **Canada's first constitution**. Canada remained a colony until 1867, when the British Parliament passed the British North America Act (BNA Act) creating the Canadian federation. The federation also included the predominantly English-speaking former colonies of Nova Scotia and New Brunswick. Beginning in 1870 with Manitoba, new provinces joined the Federation; in 1949 Newfoundland became the last to join. The BNA Act served as the country's constitution until 1982, when it was "patriated," i.e., its status changed from British law to Canadian law. Until then, Canada could not amend its own constitution directly but had to make appeals for changes to the British Parliament.

3. **National character**. The country's origins provide some explanation for its national character as well as its political predilections. Anglophone Canada is known for its "touch of Toryism," whose roots can be traced to its Loyalist origins. This "touch" of Toryism is found in Canadian communalism as opposed to American individualism. Thus, Canadian voters have supported social democratic political parties to an extent unknown in their neighbor to the south. There have been social democratic governments in Saskatchewan, Manitoba, British Columbia, and, beginning in 1990, in the most populous province of Ontario.

C. **English and French Canada: a linguistic and cultural bifurcation**. One of the distinctive ways in which Canada and the U.S. differ is that the native language of about 25 percent of Canadians is French. Most Francophones reside in Quebec, marking the province off from the rest of the country. Quebec, with an 83 percent French speaking majority, has for long feared and resisted cultural domination by the English-speaking majority in the rest of the country. The fact that historically Quebec was a conquered colony forced to accept British rule, while Anglophones settled by consent has colored Canada's history down to the present day. Religion historically magnified the cultural divide, Quebec being overwhelming Roman Catholic and the majority population predominantly Protestant. This primary cultural/linguistic division is a fundamental factor in Canada's constitutional politics and may lead to the country's ultimate breakup. To cope with it, English and French have been both declared official languages. Linguistic parity in law and bilingualism at the federal level and in certain sectors of the bureaucracy, however, have not satisfied much of Quebec. In 1976 Quebeckers elected to office the Parti Quebecois, which advocated Quebec's secession from the federation. Nevertheless, in 1980 the same electorate defeated a provincial referendum providing for Quebec's separation from Canada. (See G. below, Canada's Constitutional Crisis.)

D. **Fears of American domination**. The overwhelming presence of American popular culture, especially in English-speaking Canada, is a source of great concern to some Canadians. Fears of American cultural domination are not allayed by U.S. economic strength, as some 75 percent of Canada's international trade is with the United States. Television airwaves do not stop at the border, and millions of Canadians nightly watch American networks along with the Canadian Broadcasting Corporation (CBC) and other Canadian channels. The result in recent decades has been a resurgence of Canadian nationalism, especially in powerful Ontario. To deal with the American influence on Canadian television, the federal government has specified that Canadian television stations must provide a minimum percentage of "Canadian content," that is, programs produced in Canada. Moreover, majority ownership of newspapers and broadcasting stations by law must be under Canadian control.

E. **Regionalism**. The distinctiveness of Francophone Quebec is only one aspect of the deep regional rivalry that has increasingly been reflected in Canadian politics and stands as a major factor threatening to undermine the country's political stability.

1. **Lack of economic integration**. Many of the regional tensions and fissures in Canadian politics arise from the lack of economic integration of the

country. As opposed to the U.S., with its integrated national economy, Canada's economic regionalism has been accentuated, not reduced, by modernization. Thus, the economy of the Atlantic Provinces is largely dependent on fisheries; the Prairie Provinces on wheat and potash; Alberta on oil and gas; British Columbia on fisheries and timber; Ontario and Quebec on manufacturing. Ontario is considerably richer than most of the other provinces and usually has significantly lower unemployment, creating long-standing resentment in other parts of Canada.

2. **Resurgence of regionalism in the 1970s**. A particularly bitter resurgence of regionalism arose during the early 1970s when world oil prices rose dramatically but Canadian oil prices were regulated by the federal government at much lower levels for Canadian consumers. The oil-producing regions, especially Alberta, were outraged that the manufacturing regions of Ontario and Quebec were to become more economically competitive at their expense. They noted that hydroelectric power and other national resources were not sold to the West at cut-rate prices. This confrontation brought about widespread animosity against the East, best captured by the popular bumper sticker slogan, "Let the Eastern bastards freeze in the dark."

F. **Parliamentary Federation: Canada's political system**. Modern Canada was born after the American Revolution, when loyalists fled north from the revolted colonies, settling alongside French-speaking "habitants" already there. Canada's political system in large measure reflects its British origins. In 1867 when it became self governing, the parliamentary system was adopted. Canadian government incorporates no U.S.-style "separation of powers;" the executive, as in Britain, is dependent on the legislature. That is, the government will usually fall if it loses a vote of "no confidence" in the House of Commons. Also, members of the cabinet, known as ministers, must be members of the House of Commons or the appointed upper house, the Senate. A further constitutional arrangement of great significance is that Canada is a federal state, with ten powerful provinces and two territories in the North.

1. **Canada's federalism vs. American federalism**. Because Canada and the U.S. are both federal systems, it must not be thought that these systems are more or less the same, for in key ways they are quite dissimilar. For example, the

British monarch is formally Canada's head of state, although the Canadian government-appointed Governor General performs all the associated functions of this position. More important is the relative weakness of the Canadian central government compared to the federal government in Washington. It is ironic that while the central government under the U.S. Constitution began life in 1789 as relatively weak in comparison to the states but in time became much stronger, just the opposite occurred in Canada. In 1867 the central government appeared to have formidable powers under the BNA Act, but in time those powers diminished considerably. The most important reason for this weakening is that many judicial interpretations of the Constitution made by the British-based Judicial Committee of the Privy Council prior to 1949 were skewed in favor of the provinces. (After 1949, however, the Canadian Supreme Court became the highest court of appeal and its decisions have tilted back in favor of the federal government, as originally intended in the Constitution.) An additional factor is that the Province of Quebec has played a major role in resisting centralizing tendencies of the federal government, thus blazing a trail for other provinces to follow. It has also been argued that the differing patterns in the division of powers in Canada and the U.S. have led to differences in centralization. In Canada, the federal and provincial governments were given **exclusive** jurisdiction over areas of governance, rather than **concurrent** jurisdiction, as in America, where dual federal-state responsibility often operates, and where in many areas, for a variety of reasons, Washington has gained the upper hand over the states.

2. **The Constitution of 1982**. In 1982 a new Canadian Constitution brought significant changes. One such change was the inclusion of a "Canadian Charter of Rights and Freedoms," akin to the U.S. Bill of Rights, which sets forth basic political and legal rights and, in the process, sets limits on the formerly almost unlimited powers of Parliaments at both the provincial and federal levels. At variance with American practice was the provision in the document allowing for either federal or provincial legislatures to exempt certain laws from a limited number of provisions of the Charter of Rights. That is, by explicitly stating they wish to do so, they may violate certain parts of the Charter's terms. (This provision is known as the "notwithstanding clause.") Though this arrangement may be surprising to Americans, it is no more than an accommodation to Parliamentary supremacy. It is a denial of the right of the judiciary to overrule legislatures in the instances in which the legislatures claim an exception to constitutional provisions. The Charter also includes an affirmative action provision that allows any "law, program, or activity" that attempts to reduce the disadvantages of specified individuals or groups, such as races or ethnic groups. The provision for a constitutionally sanctioned departure from equality before the law and the inclusion of group rights sharply separate the Canadian Charter from its U.S. counterpart.

3. **Judicial Review**. Before the enactment of the 1982 Constitution, the power of the Canadian Supreme Court to declare law unconstitutional was limited to decisions concerning whether federal or provincial law breached its powers by legislating in an area reserved for the other. But after 1982, the Court could practice judicial review for all laws not explicitly excepted by federal or provincial legislatures. In the ensuing years the Court has made stunning use of its powers. In 1988, for example, it struck down Canada's abortion law. In another instance, however, the decision of the Supreme Court abrogating a section of Quebec's language laws was circumvented with the passage of another law which, by using the "notwithstanding" or exceptions clause in the Charter of Rights, allowed Quebec to forbid any but French language outdoor signs in the province.

G. **The free trade agreement with the U.S.** In 1990 Canada and the U.S. signed a far-reaching trade agreement that will eventually sweep away all tariffs from trade between the two countries. The agreement elicited considerable and heated opposition in Canada, especially in Ontario, where critics said it represented a giant step toward the eventual absorption of Canada into the United States. Americans, on the other hand, saw no such ultimate result, which was in any case not advocated by any significant sector of American opinion. In 1991 trilateral talks began between the two countries and Mexico for a North American Common Market that would eventually include some 400,000,000 people in the world's largest free trade zone.

H. **Canada's constitutional crisis and the United States.** The Province of Quebec refused to sign the 1982

Constitution, which nevertheless became law. Quebec demanded a veto on all federal legislation, a provision other provinces found objectionable. In the absence of such a veto, Quebec's secession from Canada might be more attractive to the same Quebec electorate that had previously rejected it.

1. **The Meech Lake Accord.** To deal with the simmering constitutional crisis over Quebec's demands for a special position in the constitution, the federal Prime Minister and the ten provincial premiers met in 1987 at a First Ministers Conference at Meech Lake, Quebec. The conference agreed upon a constitutional amendment that would satisfy Quebec's aspirations by declaring it a "distinct society" within Canada and affirming Quebec's right to "preserve and promote" its distinct identity.

2. **The failure of the Meech Lake Accord.** Although most provincial legislatures agreed to the constitutional amendment that incorporated the Meech Lake accord, the agreement was scuttled when in June 1990 Manitoba refused to ratify it.

3. **Canada's continuing constitutional crisis, the U.S., and the future.** The status of Quebec and its future in Canada remain in question. The province's continued membership in the Canadian federation is by no means certain. Much hostility among Anglophones was generated by Quebec's demands for special status and policies restricting the use of the English language and limiting access to English language schools. From time to time, the possibility of Canada's breakup and the disposition of secessionist movements has been discussed in the American press. Talk is occasionally heard on both sides of the border of the possibility of one or more provinces joining the United States. Little enthusiasm for such an eventuality, however, is heard on the American side. Political, historical, and financial considerations make inclusion of most if not all provinces undesirable to many Americans. Nevertheless, in 1990 the Premier of Nova Scotia stated that if Quebec seceded from Canada, the Maritime Provinces would have "no choice" but to apply for admission to the United States (*The Wall Street Journal*, May 17, 1990). Thus, the future of Canada and its relationship to the U.S.—a topic of great significance for Americans—remain in flux.

VII. **Mexico.** The U.S. and Mexico (officially named the United States of Mexico) share a 2,000 mile border, one of the longest bilateral borders in the world. U.S.-Mexico relations have always been marked by both antagonism and cooperation. Much of the southwestern United States was originally Mexican territory and many Mexicans are still sensitive about the loss. But more immediate concerns exist as well. Throughout this century Mexicans have often fretted about being dominated by their powerful neighbor, while the exponential jump in illegal Mexican immigration northward is causing increasing concern among Americans. But in spite of such tensions, cultural affinities and the two countries' significant economic ties have encouraged continuing better relations. The most obvious sign of this trend has been the movement toward a free trade agreement to link both countries with Canada in the largest free trade zone in the world.

A. **Mexico's geographic and demographic context.** Mexico occupies some 761,000 square miles, an area nearly as large as California, Arizona, New Mexico, Colorado, and Texas combined. In mid-1991 Mexico's population was approximately 90,000,000, or 36 percent of the U.S.; by 2025 Mexico's population is projected to become 150,000,000, or 50 percent of the projected U.S. population. If the 2025 estimate is reached, Mexico will have trebled its population in fifty-five years. Most Mexicans are of mixed Spanish and Indian descent, with several million of only Indian descent.

B. **Government.** Following in the wake of the Mexican Revolution, the Institutional Revolutionary Party (PRI) was founded in 1928 and has ruled Mexico ever since. Although general elections are officially free, traditionally only token opposition has been allowed and the party has maintained a virtual monopoly on political power to this day. Some observers have argued that Mexico, if not a full democracy, has at least been a one-party democracy. Political competition for power among PRI's heterogeneous factions is common within the party and civilian president's have passed on power every six years. But serious outside challenges to PRI have not been permitted: until 1988 PRI had never lost a presidential, gubernatorial or senatorial election.

There are signs that Mexico is on its way to becoming more democratic. In the 1980s the Party of Democratic Revolution (PRD) and the National Action Party (PAN) seriously challenged PRI. President **Carlos Salinas de Gotari** (PRI), elected by a very slim margin in June 1988, pledged to open the electoral process. In 1989 a PAN candidate was elected governor of the state of Baja California Norte and became the first opposition governor in 60 years.

C. **Trade.** Trade between Mexico and the U.S. increased steadily during the 1980s and shows no signs of slowing down.

    1. **Significant trading partners.** Mexico is the third largest U.S. trading partner and the nation's third largest export market, behind Canada and Japan. In 1989, bilateral trade reached $52 billion, an increase from $44 billion in 1988. The U.S. is by far Mexico's largest trading partner, accounting for nearly 60 percent of its trade. Investment between the U.S. and Mexico is also significant. Total U.S. direct investment in its southern neighbor totals more than $5.5 billion; estimated Mexican investment in the U.S. is about $1 billion.

    2. **Proposed free trade agreement.** In September 1990, President George Bush notified Congress that the U.S. and Mexico would initiate negotiations for a free trade agreement under which the countries' border would disappear for purposes of trade and industry. Tariffs would be lowered and eventually eliminated. Restrictions on U.S. investment in Mexico would be reduced and the Mexican market would be opened up, especially to U.S. agriculture. Proponents of the agreement argue that it would stimulate mutual economic prosperity and foster regional harmony. In combination with the 1988 U.S.-Canada free trade agreement, the three countries would form the world's largest free trade zone, including 360 million consumers from the "Yukon to the Yucatan." But American opposition to such a pact is strong. Organized labor warns that under the agreement U.S. manufacturers would move south of the border, where labor costs are 10 percent of those in the United States. Perhaps thousands of U.S. jobs would be lost. Environmental groups have also joined the vocal opposition, arguing that industrial development would have dire environmental consequences in Mexico, where environmental regulations are minimal or nonexistent.

D. **Debt.** Mexico's $110 billion external debt is the second largest in the world (after Brazil) and is another issue of importance between the two nations. In the past, Mexico has had difficulty in meeting its loan obligations, and in the summer of 1982 had to temporarily suspend its payments. But Mexico has distinguished itself from the non-payment policies of other Latin American countries and is widely considered a model debtor. In February 1990, in what was the first application of the "Brady plan" to encourage voluntary debt-reduction schemes, Mexico reached an accord with 450 commercial creditor banks to restructure its debts. The plan includes a combination of loan extensions and reductions, as well as new loans in order to reduce the country's annual debt repayment burden enough to stimulate economic growth.

E. **The political economy of immigration.** Mexican citizens have been crossing the U.S. border in search of work for nearly as long as the two nations have been settled.

    1. **Mexican immigration to the U.S.** Mexicans have emigrated to the U.S. throughout the twentieth century, usually in flight from economic and political hardship in their own country. Because emigration eased the plight of the Mexican population and lightened the burden of solving pressing social problems, the Mexican government has never actively discouraged the emigration of its citizens to the U.S. Some critics have maintained that the government even encouraged emigration in the hopes that this would serve as a safety valve against any nascent political and social unrest.

    2. **Immigration a problem to the U.S.** In the 1980s Mexican immigration to the U.S. surged dramatically. Mexico's drastic economic slump and its rapidly increasing population (between 1990 and 2000 population is projected to increase from 88.3 million to almost 110 million) have sent millions northward in search of jobs and a decent standard of living. Since 1980 the Mexican population of the U.S. has risen from 8.7 million to 12.6 million, a 45 percent increase. Most of these newcomers reside in the U.S. illegally. Some observers believe that nearly a million Mexicans entered the U.S. illegally in 1985 alone. This large population influx has caused problems in the United States. American labor claims they are the victims of abusive employers, and take jobs and undercut the wages of American residents. Also, because the newcomers are poor and uneducated, they constitute an enormous burden on state and local governments, especially in the southwest, where the preponderate majority resides.

3. **Immigration reform**. The Immigration Reform and Control Act of 1986 attempted to solve some of these problems by offering resident alien status to illegal aliens, providing they could prove prolonged residence in the U.S., and by penalizing the U.S. employers who hire illegal aliens. While the legalization program has met with considerable success, sanctions against American employers have been considerably less successful. In recent years, thousands of Mexicans each day have continued the risky border crossing in search of work.

F. **Oil**. Mexico has one of the largest oil deposits in the world; indeed, some geologists consider them to approach Saudi Arabia's vast reserves.

1. **Mexico as a source of stable oil supplies**. Mexico's proximity makes it an important source of oil imports for the U.S., which receives about 55 percent of Mexico's oil exports. Oil exports now account for one-third of Mexico's annual foreign exchange earnings, down from two-thirds in 1985.

2. **Exclusion of foreign oil investment**. The two nations have not always been this friendly over the oil question. Oil was first discovered in Mexico in the early 1900's, and U.S. and British companies owned most of the oil industry in Mexico. After a labor dispute between the foreign companies and the oil workers union in 1937-38, President **Lazaro Cardenas** (1895-1970) expropriated all of the companies' holdings. There has been no foreign investment allowed in the oil industry since this took place. This is one of the items that can be expected to be discussed during negotiations for a free trade agreement.

G. **Conclusion**. The 1990s should see a strengthening of the relationship between the United States and Mexico, with the possibility of a North American Common Market that would unite them in a single trading area with Canada. This free trade zone would be the world's largest and would encompass a population greater than 400 million by the turn of the century.

VIII. **Citizens and the making of foreign policy**. Many Americans feel that issues of international relations have no relevance to their lives. They have little knowledge of the world outside of the United States and pay scant attention to how the U.S. government interacts with that world. But in fact the lives of Americans are closely tied with key international events. By the same token,

American actions may have a significant impact on the lives of others.

A. **The role of elected officials in making foreign policy**. According to the U.S. Constitution, power to make foreign policy is divided between the executive branch and Congress.

1. **Executive powers**. The president is the Commander-in-Chief of the armed forces. The president has the power to appoint ambassadors and negotiate international treaties, with the advice and consent of the Senate. The president also appoints the principal cabinet officials and other members of the executive establishment who carry out foreign policy such as the Secretaries of State and Defense and the Director of the Central Intelligence Agency. Many such appointments require Senate approval.

2. **Congressional powers**. The Congress has the power to declare war, to regulate commerce, and to appropriate funds for the military and other foreign policy functions. The Senate has the power to reject certain presidential appointments, such as ambassadors and cabinet officers with foreign policy duties.

3. **Dispute over the War Powers Act**. Especially since the Vietnam War, Congress and the executive branch have contested and attempted to limit the foreign policy powers of each other. In 1973 Congress passed the War Powers Act, which requires congressional approval within sixty days after the president commits American forces abroad. Presidents have disputed the constitutionality of this act.

B. **The role of American values**. Though this vision has sometimes been clouded by war or other events, Americans have generally enjoyed a clear and positive image of themselves and their nation's place in the world. They see their nation as wealthy, generous, and humanitarian as well as militarily strong but peace loving. They have faith in their basic political and economic values—freedom, democracy, the free market. The actions of their government abroad affect this image, which may be undermined when government policy strays from the values they hold dear. Two sets of sometimes competing values can be identified.

1. **National defense**. In the international sphere a primary imperative for Americans is founded on

their expectation that their government protect them from external threats of all kinds. They wish their government to do what is necessary for the defense of the nation and to punish aggressors. The concern with defense is not necessarily incompatible with altruism, but at times the two sets of values have appeared to some to be in conflict.

2. **Generosity and humanitarianism.** Americans often wish their government to work toward ending arms races with other nations; search for peaceful solutions in regional conflicts such as in Africa, Central America, and the Middle East; prevent starvation; help the poor in Africa and Asia; and join cooperative efforts on bilateral, regional, and global problems. But when these objectives conflict or appear to conflict with other goals, some citizens have in recent decades involved themselves in influencing foreign policy. To this end they have joined appropriate organizations, voted for candidates supporting their foreign policy views, and behaved in other ways to further their goals.

C. **The role of citizens.** Avenues for participation open to citizens to influence foreign policy are varied.

1. **Voting.** Because the U.S. government represents its citizens abroad in its military, political, and economic relationships with other governments, it is the role of American citizens to hold the government of the day accountable and ensure that U.S. foreign policy meets the will and the needs of the people. Where foreign policy issues form substantial campaign issues, voters can exhibit their will to elected officials, policy makers, and analysts.

2. **Organized lobbying.** Citizens may join membership organizations that reflect a particular interest, such as Amnesty International for those concerned about human rights. Others join multi-issue organizations whose goal is to provide educational resources and opportunities for community discussion on issues, such as the League of Women Voters.

3. **Local discussion and debate.** In many local communities, people gather at public forums, debates, and group discussions to discuss international relations issues and how they affect themselves and their communities. Communities with immigrant populations, with import and export businesses, with sister-city relationships, and with military installations all have an interest in international relations and U.S. foreign policy.

4. **The role of citizens' economic life.** Political and economic change in the world often affects citizens most tangibly in their economic lives as producers and consumers.

   a. **Citizens as producers.** Americans' ability to sell their products overseas, to compete with foreign products sold at home, or to keep a manufacturing job despite lower foreign wages are issues that affect the lives of millions of Americans as producers.

   b. **The choice of consumer action.** As consumers, citizens have demonstrated important power, once a significant number have been aroused to action. Some examples of how citizens as consumers have used their power include "buy American" campaigns to promote U.S. domestic industries; actions to oppose unsavory regimes by boycotting their products or opposing investment in their economies; and movements to avoid products that harm the environment.

IX. **Conclusion: a shrinking planet.** Through modern communications, international trade, and the mobility of individuals as visitors or migrants, the peoples of the world have more direct and indirect contact with each other than ever before.

A. **Global interconnection.** Moreover, global interconnection is evident in the emergence of a world economy and in the prevalence of common world problems, such as the threat of large-scale war and the consequences of environmental degradation.

B. **The need to understand.** Through travel and study, Americans can encounter other cultures and inform themselves as never before of the wider international world beyond their shores. Americans need to understand this emerging world to develop rational and enlightened policies to cope with its dangers and opportunities. Americans have the opportunity to influence the course their government takes in domestic and foreign policies that affect countries and their peoples the world over and in great measure determine the destiny of the American democratic order. (For further discussion of interna-

world beyond their shores. Americans need to understand this emerging world to develop rational and enlightened policies to cope with its dangers and opportunities. Americans have the opportunity to influence the course their government takes in domestic and foreign policies that affect countries and their peoples the world over and in great measure determine the destiny of the American democratic order. (For further discussion of international issues, see The Nature of the State, Contemporary Perspective).

C. **The persistence of danger**. From time to time Americans come to the conclusion that the world has fundamentally changed, that military aggression by the enemies of liberal democracy is a thing of the past, and that the world can be safely ignored. Such was the dominant American view at the end of World War I and throughout the 1920s. The uncertainties generated by the abortive Soviet coup of August 1991 **further underline the vicissitudes of the international system and their potential threat to the United States. Bitter experience thereafter gave the lie to this faith.** As the twentieth century comes to a close and a new millennium approaches, weapons of awesome destructive power, the ambitions of existing lawless or unstable regimes, and the likelihood of the proliferation of the means of destruction, including mass destruction, to new rulers adverse to the security of liberal democracies remind Americans that they dare not forget the ancient saying that "eternal vigilance is the price of liberty."

TOPIC 5. LAW AND GOVERNMENT

A. THE CONCEPT AND PURPOSES OF LAW

No freeman shall be taken, or imprisoned, or outlawed, or exiled, or in any way harmed, nor will we go upon him nor will we send upon him, except by the legal judgment of his peers or by the law of the land.

Magna Carta (1215)

Wherever Law ends, Tyranny begins.

John Locke (1690)

The people made the Constitution, and the people can unmake it. It is the creature of their own will, and lives only by their will.

John Marshall (1821)

In view of the Constitution, in the eye of the law, there is in this country no superior, dominant, ruling class of citizens. There is no caste here. Our Constitution is color-blind, and neither knows nor tolerates classes among citizens. In respect of civil rights, all citizens are equal before the law. The humblest is the peer of the most powerful.

John Marshall Harlan (1896)

Two important ideas about law lie at the foundation of American government. The first is the idea that "We the People" have the power to make and change the law—a concept commonly known as popular sovereignty. In a government based on popular sovereignty the people use law as an instrument for reforming society and setting its future direction. The second idea is that government by the people must itself be subject to the rule of law. This is the idea of constitutionalism, which states that government's power should itself be limited by a fundamental law, the constitution. In a government based on the rule of law, decisions by officials that negatively affect individuals must be made on the basis of legal principle rather than arbitrary preference, political influence, or public opinion. Under the rule of law, individuals who are adversely affected by government action have the right to have the basis of that action reviewed by neutral and impartial decision makers (judges) who apply the requirements of fair legal process that would apply in disputes between two individuals.

Much of American political culture is a continuing effort to define the relationship between varying ideas about the role of law in our society. In the abstract, popular sovereignty seems to apply to questions usually addressed by legislatures—decisions for the future that affect society as a whole. In contrast, enforcing the rule of law seems to apply questions addressed by courts—decisions about people's actions in the past that affect others' rights or the relative balance of power and advantage between individuals. Are these really separate domains, or do they in many instances overlap? Americans engaged in politics, both national and local, often claim that certain decisions about the interpretation of law that affect the future of social policy should sometimes be addressed directly by the courts and not left exclusively to legislatures. Just as typically, other Americans tend to argue that efforts to resolve conflicts between individuals and groups on the basis of legal principles also have implications for the future of society and should therefore be addressed through exercising popular sovereignty in legislation. Both arguments involve claims about the role of law in American society, focusing not only on the proper functions of legislatures and courts in our system of government, but also on which of these two forums it is most appropriate that matters of public concern be decided.

OBJECTIVES

The citizen should be able to

1. explain what a legal system is and the various types of law that make up a legal system.

2. explain the special role that the U.S. legal system plays in American politics.

3. explain the role of legal ideas in the civic order and how legal notions of appropriate procedure have been adapted for use in organizations and relationships that are not part of the legal system.

4. explain the conflicts arising from different concepts of legality.

5. take, defend, and evaluate positions on prominent approaches to law.

FRAME OF REFERENCE
Conceptual and Contemporary Perspectives

I. **The legal system as a body of rules**. Philosophers have never agreed upon a single definition of law, but there is some measure of agreement on what constitutes a legal system. Essentially, a legal system is a body of rules

enforced by the authority of a political order in which the key officials profess to act according to those rules and to accept the rules as binding. A legal system is made up of four distinct kinds of rules: rules that directly govern the conduct of officials and private individuals; rules for determining what constitutes an authoritative rule in the legal system; rules for changing the rules; and rules for interpreting the rules and settling controversies about them.

A. **Rules governing conduct**. These rules, created for a variety of purposes, generally proscribe behavior (forbidding, for example, acts of force or fraud); prescribe behavior (commanding, for example, performance of public service); or establish institutions or practices (telling us, for example, the procedures for voting in elections or how to establish a business.) Laws of this type are almost always enforceable by courts that are backed by the coercive power of the state.

B. **Rules for identifying valid rules**. These rules allow officials to distinguish between those norms that are authoritative within the legal system, and other norms that may be widely accepted, but that are not backed by the coercive authority of the state. In modern states these rules often define the basis of sovereign authority in the society. In a constitutional democracy the people are sovereign, but the rules of the constitution define the conditions under which the people are conceived to have exercised their sovereignty.

C. **Rules for changing rules**. These rules specify how and by whom existing rules may be validly changed, or new rules may be added to the legal system. In modern states these rules are often called rules of legislation. In democracies, most legislation is enacted by representatives duly elected by the people, or by administrators whose power has been delegated by elected officials.

D. **Rules for interpreting rules**. These rules specify how and by whom controversies arising under the rules, or about their interpretation, may be authoritatively resolved. In modern states these rules are often called rules of adjudication. The rules of adjudication in most modern states set up a process that is independent of the legislative process.

II. **The U.S. legal system**. The legal system plays an especially important role in the system of government in the United States.

A. **General functions of law**. As in most societies, law in the United States performs a variety of important roles.

1. **Defining relationships**. Law defines and regulates personal, economic, and other relationships among members of a society. It spells out what activities are permitted or prohibited, what rights will be protected, and what duties will be enforced by the government.

2. **Maintaining order**. Law is part of the system through which order is maintained in a society. Authority and the right to use physical sanctions—such as force, arrest, and detention—in the exercise of authority are allocated by law.

3. **Managing conflict**. Law provides a method of managing conflicts over things of value by defining those conflicts as matters involving judicially enforceable rights. The legal method of resolving conflicts can apply to conflicts between individuals over particular entitlements, and to larger conflicts among racial, ethnic, economic, or other groups within society.

4. **Implementing social change**. In addition to its role in maintaining the social order, law may be used as an instrument to bring about social change initiated by political leaders, or, in some societies, by the people themselves.

5. **Defining and limiting power of officials**. Law defines what authority shall be exercised by respective public officials, thereby circumscribing the scope of their legitimate power. In societies governed by the rule of law these legal limitations on the power of public officials may be enforceable by the courts.

6. **Respecting liberty and securing expectations**. Law defines the boundary between the willingness of the state to respect the interest of citizens in liberty on the one hand, and security on the other. Expanding the scope of legally protected liberty may require the contraction of legally protected security; expanding the scope of legally protected security requires the contraction of legally protected liberty.

B. **Categories of American law**. Courts in the United States recognize several distinct categories of law. There are established rules of primacy among these categories.

1. **Constitutional law**. The modern idea of constitutional law is an American invention. Because the U.S. Constitution is conceived to be a legally interpretable document, the courts and legal system play a special role in American political life.

   a. **Constitutions and regimes**. A constitution describes the structure of legitimate power in a political regime. In most countries constitutional history is a story of changes in fundamental political relations brought about by legislation, revolution, civil war, and coups. Although the U.S. has not been immune from political upheaval (a bloody civil war killed half-a-million men and fundamentally altered the Constitution), a large part of its constitutional history is a history of judicial opinions on questions of fundamental law.

   b. **Judicial review**. The U.S. Constitution has been treated as a legal document subject to interpretation by the courts using techniques similar to those that courts use to interpret other legal documents such as contracts or statutes. Because the Constitution is the highest law in the American legal system—superior to statute—a judicial interpretation of the Constitution may not be reversed by statute. The only way the Supreme Court's interpretation of the U.S. Constitution can be changed is by the Supreme Court itself or by an amendment to the Constitution (seen as a direct expression of popular sovereignty.)

   c. **Law and politics**. Because Americans tend to believe that their Constitution is effective only because it is judicially enforceable, they tend to see many political issues as also having a legal dimension. For this reason, many political issues are debated in the language of constitutional rights, and many of the major developments in U.S. political history are the direct or indirect result of judicial reinterpretations of the U.S. Constitution.

2. **Statutory law**. Statutory law is written law created by legislative bodies. (The Constitution does not establish procedures making for state or local statutory law.)

a. **Statutory interpretation.** The courts have the task of interpreting statutes as they apply to individuals. If the legislature disagrees with the way that the courts interpret a statute, the legislature has the power to change the statute, or to remove the court's jurisdiction to so interpret it in the future.

b. **Statutory delegation.** In addition to the implicit enforcement power that most statutes confer on the courts, many statutes confer enforcement power on specific administrative bodies such as regulatory agencies and the police.

3. **Common law.** Even in the absence of statutory law to guide them courts often have a responsibility to decide cases involving controversies between individuals who make conflicting claims to legal rights. Common law is the body of legal ideas based on the record of judicial decisions in such cases.

a. **Precedent.** In deciding a particular case, judges are obliged to take account of the past body of judicial decisions in relevant cases, and to explain how the case at hand is different from or similar to the previous cases. The common law that develops from the continuing interpretation of these past decisions ("precedent") is also known as "case law" or "judge-made law."

b. **Legislative supremacy.** Where legislation conflicts with common law, judges are generally obliged to follow legislation. The main exception is in the area of constitutional law: legislation that conflicts with the judicial interpretation of state constitutions or the U.S. Constitution is invalid, and hence not binding on the courts.

4. **Administrative law.** In twentieth-century America many functions once performed by legislatures and courts have been taken over by administrative agencies operating under authority that has been delegated by the legislature and that may often be reviewed by the courts. Administrative law is the body of statutes and judicial decisions that governs the regulatory power of administrative agencies. In addition, administrative law refers to the body of rules and regulations made by administrative agencies insofar as these are recognized by the courts to have the force of law.

a. **Judicial review.** Individuals who are adversely affected by administrative decisions are often entitled to have those decisions reviewed by the courts in order to determine whether the administrative agency acted properly. In reviewing the conduct of administrative agencies, courts are typically concerned with whether the agency acted according to its own rules, whether its rules serve the purposes envisioned by the legislature, and whether the process through which the administrative agency reached its decision took adequate account of the likely impact of that decision on affected individuals.

b. **Administrative due process.** Legislatures and courts have often required that administrative agencies adopt certain procedures of "fair hearing" that incorporate some of the procedures that courts would use in reaching decisions that affect individual rights. The degree to which the requirements of administrative due process approximate those of judicial due process varies widely from agency to agency, and according to the interests at stake in particular decisions. Provided that administrative agencies adhere to the requirements of due process, courts typically allow the results of administrative hearings to stand in lieu of proceedings under the common law.

5. **International law.** International law may be defined as the body of rules of conduct accepted as legally binding by states in their relations with each other. Whether international law can legitimately be called law in the conventional sense is controversial, since there is no world state with the power to enforce international law against states that are parties to international disputes. Nevertheless, some aspects of international law (such as treaties) may be interpreted and applied by domestic courts insofar as this is necessary for the resolution of domestic disputes falling within the jurisdiction of those courts. (For further discussion, see the section on international law below.)

III. **Legal ideas in American civic life.** Because of the special importance of the legal system in the U.S. system of government, legal ideas have come to play an important role in areas of American civic life that lie outside the legal system.

A. **The role of lawyers in American public life**. Throughout American history lawyers have played a prominent role in politics, bureaucracy, and business. Whether as a cause or an effect of the role of lawyers in American public life, legal ideas of appropriate process and rule-based decision making have entered many areas that have only marginal connections with the courts and the legal system.

B. **Law and private organizations**. Many complex bureaucratic organizations, both public and private, have internal procedures and rules that resemble those of the larger legal system. (Among such organizations are schools, hospitals, and business corporations). Often the internal rules and practices of these organizations embody internal notions of due process that are potentially enforceable in the courts. There has been considerable debate in recent years about the extent to which courts and regulatory agencies should recognize some of these internally-generated standards and practices as having a status equivalent to that of governmentally-imposed law.

IV. **Two concepts of legality**. Debates about public issues in America often reflect a tension between two concepts of official legality, one grounded on the power of legislative bodies to create and change law; the other grounded on the power of courts to decide cases in which there is controversy about what the law requires.

A. **The legislative model**. The legislative model of legality focuses on the power of a legislative body to create the substantive rules that regulate society and to empower government officials to implement those rules, when necessary by coercion. According to this model, existing law governs a particular matter when a valid rule clearly applies to it. Laws are valid when they are made according to some accepted criterion of legitimacy, such as enactment by a duly elected legislature. Problems arise under the legislative model when one or more of these conditions is not met. If, for example, relevant laws are unclear or incomplete, the officials charged with enforcing them may find it difficult to distinguish between interpreting the law as it already exists and engaging in a fresh instance of law-making. When confronted with such cases, judges or administrators operating under the legislative model may base their decisions on their own view of what the law ought to be. To do so openly, however, might undermine the notion of legality under which public officials are bound to uphold the law as it is. Judges and administrators therefore tend to argue that good law has certain general characteristics to which public officials are permitted to refer, but only

when the existing laws enacted by the popularly elected legislature are incomplete or unclear. These characteristics include the following:

1. **Public benefit**. Inasmuch as law is costly to implement and tends to interfere with the ability of some people to pursue their private benefit, a good law should produce public benefits at least sufficient to outweigh these effects.

2. **Fairness**. The distribution of benefits and burdens of the law should be relatively broad and should fall within society's generally accepted standards of fairness. No groups should be burdened by a law because of inappropriate criteria (such as race, religion, or gender), and no individual should be unduly burdened with the cost of providing a general social benefit.

3. **Effectiveness**. Laws should be clearly and intelligibly written, adequate to meet their stated purpose, and designed so that voluntary compliance is possible. Laws that do not meet these standards of effectiveness are likely to raise issues that require extensive judicial and administrative interpretation, that therefore point to the limitations of the legislative model.

B. **The judicial model**. The judicial model of legality focuses on the power of the courts to decide cases in which the requirements of the law are unclear or controversial. According to the judicial model a disputed matter may be governed by law, even when the relevant laws are ambiguous or incomplete—or when the principles that would justify enforcing those laws are in conflict. In such circumstances the courts have a responsibility to justify their decisions by interpreting the relevant rules and principles in a manner consistent with the underlying rights of the parties to the dispute. Under the judicial model there is a tendency to interpret the law in a way that leads to justifiable outcomes in particular cases. Judicial legitimacy, according to this model, has the following characteristics:

1. **Principled decision making**. Good judges must articulate the rationale for their decision according to the principles of justice and legality that underlie the claims of the various parties to legal rights. The judicial model is based on the premise that basing official decisions on these principles is intrinsically different from basing such decisions on personal preference, political influence, or public opinion.

2. **Impartiality**. Good judges must be personally disinterested in the matter at hand, and must not exercise a personal bias on behalf of either side in the dispute.

3. **The right to be heard**. Before being made to permanently suffer a harm at the hands of government or a private actor the individual has a right to some kind of hearing.

4. **Answerability**. Those who impose harms on others, whether they are government officials or private individuals, can be made to answer for their conduct before an impartial body that is empowered to bring about some sort of rectification.

5. **Due process and equal protection**. Individuals who are singled out by a legal regime to suffer especially severe burdens have rights to greater than usual procedural safeguards before those burdens are finally imposed.

C. **Compatibility of the models**. The two models described above focus, respectively, on what makes for good legislative or judicial decisions. There are essentially three distinct positions on whether the two models are compatible.

1. **One as dominating the other**. Some would argue that one of the two models dominates and encompasses the other. The legislative model, for example, might be said to seen as the dominant picture of the role of law in American society, even while allowing the judicial model to address the issue of what makes for legitimate decisions in cases where the laws are incomplete or unclear. On the other hand, the judicial model might be seen as the dominant picture of a society governed by legal principle, with legislation seen as one way in which laws can be changed, subject to judicial review.

2. **One or the other**. Some would argue that as a general matter there is only one model of legality and that it is focused on either the substance of law or on the process of legal reasoning. From this perspective, legality is in essence either a striving for clear general rules under the legislative model or for the principled differentiation of individual circumstances under the judicial model.

3. **Models in tension**. The coexistence of the two models of legality reflects an underlying tension between the twin ideals of popular sovereignty and the rule of law. According to this view, much of American political debate is an attempt to move back and forth between these partially conflicting impulses. Law is both a means to reform society and a means to articulate and enforce the underlying principles that justify existing social relations. When we express our political differences in legal terms, we attempt to see our institutions simultaneously from the outside and from the inside—as critics on the one hand and as participants on the other.

D. **Controversies about law**. For the reasons sketched above, almost all social and political issues in the U.S. take the form of controversies about law and about the role of law in society. Some of these controversies are of enduring significance, such as the ongoing debates about the use of law to enforce sexual and other forms of moral virtue, or about the use of law to promote social equality.

V. **Schools of jurisprudence**. Modern debates about legal philosophy focus on two major problem areas—the relation of law and morality, and the autonomy of law.

A. **Law and morality**. Philosophers have traditionally debated the relation between legal and moral obligation. Does identifying what the law requires have any necessary bearing on what one really ought to do? Can there be a conflict between one's legal and moral obligations? There are many views on this question. At two extremes are the following:

1. **Natural law**. Although natural law for some philosophers is merely the law of reason that would prevail in the absence of man-made law, most believers in natural law also argue that it contains universally obligatory standards of justice. This strong theory of natural law implies that man-made laws that are in conflict with universal principles of justice are not really laws, and hence are not obligatory: "an unjust law is no law."

2. **Legal positivism**. In traditional legal positivism, all law is the product of the state; moral principles, however universal, have no legal force unless they are incorporated in man-made law. Although the legal positivist accepts the likelihood of a substantial overlap between legal and moral obligation, what a law is and whether it is

morally obligatory must remain for the positivist two separate questions. In legal positivism law and morality are necessarily distinct, and neither diminishes the effect of the other. Thus, an unjust law does not cease to be law on account of its injustice, but no one has a moral duty to obey the law simply because it is law.

B. **The autonomy of law**. Theorists of law frequently debate about whether law is a closed or an open system. Are judges who are charged with interpreting law confined to considering rules and principles that are direct products of the legal system, or are they required (or at least allowed) to take into account a range of other considerations?

1. **Formalism**. Legal formalism is the view that legal decisions can in many, if not all cases, be justified by reference only to the rules and principles that constitute the legal system, much as the decisions of an umpire in baseball can be justified without going outside the rules of baseball.

2. **Realism**. Legal realism is the view that legal rules and principles do not determine a judge's decision: legal rules constrain what a judge can say—he is obliged to describe his decision in terms of rules—but they could not require him to decide an issue one way or the other. Instead, in reality, law is nothing else than the actions of judges. Many legal realists view judges as political actors in exactly the sense that legislators are political actors. Legal realism has several off-shoots that attempt to apply the techniques of mid-century American social science to the study of legal decision making.

   a. **Sociological jurisprudence**. The version of legal realism that says that judicial opinions (like legislative choices) should be assessed by their practical social effects is called sociological jurisprudence.

   b. **Judicial behavior**. The study of judicial behavior is a form of legal realism that seeks to explain patterns in judicial decision making on the basis of subjective factors that are abstracted from the judge's stated reasons for deciding a case one way or the other.

   c. **Political jurisprudence**. Another variant of legal realism, political jurisprudence, studies the courts as a political institution like Congress or the presidency. Proponents of political jurisprudence typically focus on the ability of the courts to mobilize political constituencies and to respond to changing configurations of interest groups in society.

3. **Legal reasoning**. Since mid-century a large number of American legal scholars have directed their attention to the reasons judges give to justify their decisions. The modern study of legal reasoning attempts to encompass some of the insights of both formalism and realism by exploring the connection between what judges say and what they are obliged to do when they decide a case. To what extent must judges go outside the scope of established legal doctrine in order to give the sort of reasons that would justify their decisions?

   a. **Neo-positivism**. Modern versions of positivism focus on why a judge must say what he says in order for his decision to count as law. According to this theory, judges must act according to rules that govern the sort of reasons that would count in favor of their decisions. These rules may not determine which party wins a case (any more than the rules of baseball determine the winner of a game); but in order for a judicial decision to be legally valid the rules must be followed.

   b. **Law and ethics**. In recent years some leading academic legal scholars have argued that the American legal system can best be understood as embodying the implications of a small subset of moral principles that have particular legal relevance. These scholars typically sidestep the issue of whether these principles have legal force in the U.S. because they embody a minimal content of natural law, or because they are directly incorporated in American positive law via the Constitution. In the literature on law and ethics there are two contending moral principles that are said to have a special weight in American legal reasoning: the principle of equality and the principle of liberty. Some recent literature in jurisprudence has been devoted to reinterpreting egalitarianism and libertarianism as alternative conceptions of the basis of American legal reasoning.

c. **Law and economics**. A growing number of academic legal scholars have argued in recent years that the substantive basis of legal rules is economic efficiency (or the maximization of social wealth). This thesis is generally taken to explain both what the law is and what it ought to be. Some recent literature on law is devoted to reinterpreting legal rules on the basis of rational actors would have chosen in perfect or imperfect markets. The study of law and economics has had growing influence in American law schools, and has been adopted increasingly as a technique of rule-making by administrative agencies that are faced with the charge (common in the 1980s) that government over-regulates the economy.

d. **Law and history**. Historical research is now increasingly invoked by scholars and judges as a source of legal authority. Proponents of "original intent" argue that authentic discoveries about the lives and opinions of the Framers of the Constitution or the authors of legislation can justify setting aside past judicial opinions as "mistakes." Other legal historians in the realist tradition argue that the more one discovers about legal history, the more one sees arbitrariness and contradiction, rather than a clear basis of legal authority that can be distinguished from subsequent judicial invention.

For the Historical and Contemporary Perspectives, see under B. below and The American judicial system.

B. MAJOR TYPES OF LEGAL SYSTEMS

The knowledge and understanding of the major and influential contemporary legal systems of the world provide citizens with a frame of reference useful in critically evaluating their own legal system, identifying its possible shortcomings, and appreciating its strengths and achievements in the protection of both individual rights and the welfare of society.

Laws, both substantive and procedural, are particularly strong indicators of the values of a society, especially of the importance the society attaches to the protection of individual rights and what the society perceives as the group welfare. Although no two countries' legal systems are exactly alike, they can be grouped into types that share important traits. These commonalities can be traced to the same earlier traditions from which they were derived.

OBJECTIVES

The citizen should be able to

1. describe some of the major legal systems of the world today, their basic characteristics, their historical backgrounds, and their contemporary character.

2. explain how this understanding can be applied to the critical evaluation of the American legal system, in both its substantive and procedural aspects.

3. explain the implications of this comparison in the consideration of long-standing questions concerning the universality of values regarding individual rights and human dignity.

FRAME OF REFERENCE
Conceptual Perspective

I. **The common law tradition.** The common law tradition originated in England and was carried to other parts of the world through the colonization process.

A. **The place of case law in the common law tradition**. Historically, common law systems are based mainly on English case law. They include the body of concepts, rules, and principles developed over many centuries in the English courts. Common law is derived primarily from judicial decisions rather than from systematic legal codes enacted by legislatures.

B. **The principle of *stare decisis* in common law systems.** The law develops by applying and reinterpreting judicial precedents under the general doctrine of *stare decisis* (literally, "to stand by decided matters"), the idea that precedents should generally be followed.

C. **The place of the adversary procedure in common law systems.** Common law systems use the adversary system of court procedure. Lawyers for each side present the best arguments for their side under strict rules of evidence, and the outcome is decided by a judge or jury.

II. **The civil law tradition.** Civil law systems are spoken of as "codified systems."

A. **Statute law in civil law systems.** The basic law is set out in codes or general statutes which arrange the various areas of the law in orderly, logical, and comprehensive ways. Although there are national differences, the categories of legal duty, the methods of transferring interests in property, and the rules of inheritance are similar.

B. **Judges not bound by precedent.** Judges are not bound by judicial precedent; more reliance is placed on the writings of academic lawyers in interpreting the codes.

C. **The place of inquisitorial procedure in civil law systems.** In civil law systems, the so-called "inquisitorial system" (as distinguished from the adversary system of common law systems) of court procedure is used in criminal proceedings. The typical criminal proceeding in the civil law tradition is divided into three basic parts: the investigative phase, the examining phase, and the trial.

1. **The investigative phase.** The investigative phase comes under the direction of the public prosecutor, who also participates actively in the examining phase which is supervised by the examining judge.

2. **The examining phase as the heart of the trial procedure.** The examining phase is primarily written and not public. The judge controls its nature and scope and is expected to investigate the matter and prepare a written record, so that by the time this stage is complete, all relevant evidence is in the record. If the examining judge concludes that a crime was committed and that the accused is the perpetrator, the case goes to trial. If the judge decides otherwise, the matter does not go to trial. In the great majority of civil law countries, the examining phase is the heart of the criminal procedure system. Trial by jury is not generally employed in non-criminal cases.

3. **Procedural safeguards.** A number of procedural safeguards have been developed to help the accused during the examining phase, including the right to counsel. The dossier compiled by the examining judge is open to inspection by the defense.

4. **Variances with common law trials.** Because of the nature of the examining phase, the trial itself is different in character from the common law trial. The evidence has already been taken and a record made and is available to both the accused and the prosecution. The purpose of the trial is to present the case to the trial judge and jury and to allow the prosecutor and defendant's counsel to argue their cases—in public.

5. **The jury in civil law trials.** The jury is an established tradition in civil law systems, although its form may differ from that of common law systems. It may not consist of twelve persons, it may frequently take the form of lay advisers who sit on the bench with the judge, and it may not have to render a unanimous verdict of guilty for the accused to be convicted.

III. **Religious legal traditions.** In some societies, legal systems are based, in varying degrees, on the religious laws embodied in the dominant religion of the society. Examples of such religious legal systems include those of Christian Europe from the Middle Ages and the Holy Roman Empire through the Reformation, classical India, Israel, and the Islamic societies. Traditional Islamic law, or Shari'a, in particular, is an influential force in the Muslim world today. In some Arab countries and in Iran, it has official status. In other countries, it coexists with a secular legal system, governing or influencing certain areas of the law, such as family or personal law. The distinctive characteristics of Christian and Islamic law are described below.

A. **Christian law.** Christian law, known as **canon law**, consists of the system of laws which form the basis for the organization and government of the Christian Church. From the time of its formation, the Christian Church developed its own laws and rules which often addressed different issues or interpreted subjects differently than secular law did. Canon law is not an unchanging body of rules but reflects changing cultural, social, political, and ecclesiastical contexts and has been constantly adapted to new conditions. Although various doctrines of canon law were adopted into church practice in the United States, canon law has never been a part of the law of the United States.

1. **The role of canon law**. Canon law, defined as the principles of divine Christian law, plays a fundamental role in the organization of what is today's Roman Catholic Church, its liturgy, and teachings. Canon law outlines the rules or codes concerning the beliefs and behavior of individuals and institutions, addressing issues concerning values, morals, and church law. In Roman Catholic countries today, canon law continues to be a primary form of law for believers, directly influencing their personal lives and faith.

2. **The basis of canon law**. Canon law is based on Roman law, the New Testament, and legislation by popes and Church councils, as well as upon tradition and precedent. Canon law has characteristically borrowed and adapted concepts and practices from a multiplicity of sources.

3. **The influence of canon law on other legal systems**. During the Middle Ages, canon law formulated by the Roman Catholic Church exerted a strong influence on civil law systems, ranging from the subject of property rights, marriage, and the prosecution and punishment of criminals, to the formulation of the principles of international law and the development of the modern idea of the state. The inquisitional methods of canon law were also adopted in civil courts along with the practice of public prosecution.

4. **Relations between church and state**. The relation of *sacerdotum* to *imperium* (church authority to state authority) is addressed throughout canon law writings and became the basis for the development of the legal principles concerning church-state relations. It should be understood, however, that according to classical Christian theory, there are no such separate entities as "church" and "state," but rather two "swords," the sacred and the secular, both part of a single, unified "Respublic Christiana."

5. **The humanizing influence of canon law**. Canon law had various humanizing effects on the procedures of criminal law, punishment, and reform. For instance, Christian doctrine maintained that human nature allowed for criminals to be reformed and that reform rather than death should be part of punishment. As a result, canon law advocated prison sentences and reform instead of the death penalty.

6. **Canon law influence on the concept of natural law**. Christian doctrines promoted the concept of "natural law" as the supreme law of the universe. Natural law, according to the canon law interpretation, is a reflection of the laws of God or divine law. This concept of divinely created "natural law" was later modified and applied to secular interpretations of the law, which looked to fundamental law—constitutional law—as a kind of "higher law" which rules over rulers, just as kings and princes were subject to divine law in the canon law conception. The influence and importance of the "higher law" idea can hardly be exaggerated.

7. **The role of canon law in the social and secular sphere**. Canon law also had a profound effect on secular aspects of Christian civilization, influencing such areas as the legal proceedings regarding marriage, divorce, wills, and inheritance; proof or evidence; property rights and property acquisition; and possession and obligations.

    a. **Consensual Contracts**. Unlike civil law which claimed that consensual contracts must be those of a specific class or be qualified by particular conditions, canon law claimed that the simple act of consent was sufficient to establish a contract.

    b. **Possession and the law**. The canon law principle of *actio spolii*, (an action for stolen goods) which protected peaceful possession, became the model for similar actions in secular interpretations of the law.

B. **Islamic law and Islam.** To understand the character of traditional Islamic law, it is necessary to know certain basic tenets of the religion of Islam. It must be understood, however, that the idea of Islamic law as presented here is far from actual practice in most Islamic societies today, where (as noted below) civil courts and political administration have often supplanted traditional ideas, especially in matters of commercial and criminal law. In conservative Saudi Arabia, on the other hand, tradition still reigns; and in revolutionary Iran, fundamentalist Muslims have reinstated their version of Islamic law.

1. **Fusion of religion and life in Islam.** Islam, which means submission or surrender to the will of God, is a religion that encompasses the whole of life. "Islam makes no distinction between religion and life, nothing being excluded from religion, or outside it and 'secular'" (*Encyclopedia of Islam*). Islam thus rejects any distinction between sacred and secular. As a result, in principle there can be no "separation of church and state" in Islamic society, no area of life that sacred law should not govern. Islamic law is thus an integral part of Islamic religious doctrine, claiming authority to direct every aspect of the believer's life. Moreover, God is considered the only lawgiver. What purports to be law must therefore find a religiously sanctioned root or be rejected.

2. **The Koran as primary source of Shari'a (Islamic law).** Islamic law, or Shari'a, is based first of all upon the Koran (or Quran), the Muslim equivalent of the Bible, the writings accepted by Muslims as divine revelation to the prophet **Muhammad** (570?-632). In Islam, Muhammad is believed to be "God's messenger;" that is, Allah (Arabic for God) Himself is said to have spoken through Muhammad. Thus, the writings of the Koran are believed to be God's words, not those of Muhammad, who only transmitted them. As source of law and as word of God, the Koran illustrates the fundamental Muslim message regarding law: Law is the command of God. Indeed, in classical Islam, God is not only a lawgiver; God is the *only* lawgiver.

3. **Further sources of Shari'a.** In addition to the Koran, there are other sources of Shari'a. In some instances, the treatment of these sources varies among different Islamic sects.

   a. **The *Hadith* (acts of the Prophet) and Sunnah (traditions).** Islamic law, Shari'a, all of which is believed to be divinely inspired, is also founded upon the *Hadith*, reports or compilations of the acts and words attributed to Muhammad, and the *sunnah* or traditions that are based upon the *Hadith*. It should be understood that tradition had considerable authority in Arab societies even before Muhammad. Accordingly, the form of tradition embodied in the *Hadith* is of great authority.

   b. ***Kiyas* (reasoning by analogy).** Another source of law are opinions established by *kiyas*, or reasoning by analogy. This is the oldest form of reasoning in Islamic law, having been established by the second century after the death of the Prophet. *Kiyas* refers to the application of reasoning to a present case which is like a case in which a rule accepted as valid has already been applied. For example, four witnesses are prescribed in the Koran to convict someone of unchastity (sura [chapter] xxiv 4). An early case of reasoning by analogy that has survived to modern times demands four confessions—by analogy to the four witnesses—from the defendant before he is given the prescribed punishment (Joseph Schacht, *An Introduction to Islamic Law*, 1964).

   c. ***Ijma* (consensus of religious scholars).** The fourth source of Islamic law is the consensus (*ijma*) of the community (ummah), meaning the community of legal scholars. This consensus, however, is not a consensus newly formed in the present day, but the consensus that grew during the formative years of the growth of Islamic jurisprudence in the centuries after the death of the Prophet. Variations in the idea of consensus are found among the various schools of Islamic jurisprudence. Respect for tradition, noted above, and the idea of *ijma* mean that the precedent (or *sunna*) of the formative periods of Islamic law is given great weight and authority.

   d. **The principle of *ijtihad* ("effort").** A special feature of the process of the creation of the body of Islamic law is the principle of *ijtihad*, "effort" or exercise—the use of individual reasoning—the intellectual effort required to extrapolate law from the above sources. For Sunni Muslims, the period of "effort" is, at least officially, deemed to be over, having ended in the ninth century; that is, Islamic law is considered by orthodox religious traditionalists to be a fixed and static body of doctrine. The only form of reasoning officially permitted is reasoning by analogy, *kiyas*. Nevertheless, means have been found to accommodate various aspects of Islamic societies to the modern world, so that *ijtihad* continues in some form. Such accommodation, however, is denounced by fundamentalists, who demand a return to strict adherence to Shari'a in every avenue of life.

4. **Law and the division of Islam into Sunni and Shi'ite branches.** This picture of Islam and the sacred law that forms such an integral part of it is complicated by differences among the sects into which the religion is divided. The main division in Islam is between Sunni (or orthodox) and Shi'ite Muslims. A primary difference between them is that while for the Sunnis divine revelation ceased with the death of the Prophet, this is not so with the Shi'ites, most of whom believe certain "leaders," *Imams*, are divinely guided and therefore infallible, and who accordingly add to the *sunna*, or obligatory tradition. (Shi'ites are themselves divided into various branches, one of which, the Ithna-asharites, or "Twelvers," recognize only twelve Imams, the last of whom died in 874 A.D. and will, in time, reappear. Most Iranians are members of this sect.) Thus, the law for the two principal branches of Islam is often at variance; for Shi'ites law can be changed by Imams in a way unrecognized by Sunnis, who maintain the unalterable authority of tradition.

5. **Schools of jurisprudence.** The sacred law of Islam, though universally based upon the Koran and other sources listed above, is not given identical interpretations throughout the Muslim world. This lack of agreement was given sanction within Islam in the eighth century, when a maxim had it that such disagreement was a sign of divine indulgence. Four principal schools of jurisprudence, each of equal validity, have been established over the centuries among Sunnis, and others grew up with the Shi'ites and a further sect, the Ibadis. A single school of jurisprudence tends to be recognized in a particular geographical area; for example, the Hanafi school predominates in India and the Middle East; the Maliki in Central, North, and West Africa; and the Shafi'i school in East Africa, the south of the Arabian peninsula, Indonesia, and Malaysia. Other schools predominate elsewhere.

6. **Modernization vs. traditionalism.** The doctrine already mentioned that Shari'a is unalterably established has created problems for its adaptation to the modern world. In practice, means have been found for Muslim societies to deal with later-day realities. For one thing, because of the limits of its subject matter, Shari'a can only be a part of an Islamic legal system. For another, "Islamic government has never meant, in theory or in practice, the exclusive jurisdiction of Shari'a tribunals" (N.J. Coulson, *A History of Islamic Law*, 1964). In some countries, practicality has meant relegating Shari'a to family law and similar settings less subject to the exigencies of modern conditions. Modernizing movements have in some countries swept Shari'a away entirely or lessened its influence through statutory law; generally, however, Shari'a has at least to some extent been adapted to modern conditions. (For further discussion, see the Historical Perspective, below.)

7. **Basic characteristics of Shari'a.** Some of the basic character of Islamic law can be appreciated from the following considerations.

a. **The scope of Islamic law.** While Islamic law is essentially religious, it is intended to regulate all aspects of Islamic society: "Islamic law takes...the whole of human action as its field" (Salah El-din Abdel-Wahab, *An Introduction to Islamic Jurisprudence*, 1963). It is concerned with economic matters such as property and contract rights, taxes, and laws related to usury; family matters such as marriage, divorce, and inheritance; and the definition and punishment of crimes. It is meant to embody correct Muslim practice in all matters, from religious to everyday practical concerns, and from the level of families to matters of the state and its relations with the outside world, both Muslim and non-Muslim.

b. **Compulsory acts in Islamic law.** In Islamic law, distinctions are made between acts that are required, "neutral" acts, and acts that are forbidden. Within the category of neutral acts, subdivisions are found between acts that are recommended and those that are discouraged. In the "required" category, there are varying degrees of compulsory behavior. Things that are commanded include prayer; fasting during daylight hours, as well as other observances, during Ramadan, the ninth month of the Muslim year; and the paying of religious taxes. Slightly less compulsory is the obligation of every adult Muslim to perform the "hajj" or pilgrimage to Mecca. (One who has made the trip is known as a "hajji.")

c. **Centrality of the idea of duty.** The concept of duty rather than right is central. Shari'a seeks to enforce the whole range of religious duties set down in the Koran and other sources. Thus, detailed rules exist for such subjects as acceptance of the faith, obligatory bathing, prayer, fasting, tithing and other taxes, fighting and defense, business dealings, and a host of social relationships and family ties. Vows and oaths, marriage and divorce, the slaughter of animals and hunting, and the general rules of virtue and vice are all covered (Imam Khomein, "The Practical (Social) Laws of Islam," in H.S. Bhatia *Studies in Islamic Law, Religion and Society*, New Delhi, [1989]).

d. **Forbidden acts and punishments in Islamic law**. Forbidden acts include murder, theft, adultery, eating pork, drinking wine, cursing the religion of Islam, and marriage to more than four wives. (In some Islamic countries, a man cannot marry a second or subsequent time unless he can show that he has the means to support his wives adequately). Punishment for six specified crimes (highway robbery, adultery, fornication, false accusation of the two latter crimes, apostasy, and drinking alcohol) is fixed or *hadd*. *Hadd* punishments range from fines to flogging, imprisonment, the cutting off of hands for theft and similar punishments in some jurisdictions, and capital punishment by various means, including decapitation and stoning. (Stoning to death is an ancient practice alluded to in the New Testament admonition against "casting the first stone.") Cutting off of hands or feet is relatively rare but does occur in such countries as Saudi Arabia and the Sudan.

e. **Trial and criminal procedure**. The rules of procedure of Shari'a court trials are not nearly so extensive or complex as in the West, especially as compared with the adversarial system as practiced in the United States. Traditionally courts were presided over by a single judge or *qadi* and procedure was informal. Today, in most countries uniform codes of procedure and evidence govern the courts applying Shari'a law. In criminal cases, the idea of the intention of the accused is of great importance, and the accused enjoys a presumption of innocence. Circumstantial evidence is excluded in favor of eye witness testimony, though modern legal systems have often modified such rules. A special feature of punishment for criminal acts such as murder and certain other crimes is that the victim or the victim's family can choose monetary compensation from the wrongdoer in place of the prescribed punishment. Again, Muslim countries today have often altered or abolished such practices.

f. **The position of women in Islamic law.** Under the traditional Shari'ia, women do not as a rule occupy a position of equality with men. Although the Shari'a gave women certain rights at a time they had virtually none at all; nevertheless, especially in marriage, it placed women in a position decidedly inferior to men. Thus, for example, under traditional law men can divorce women by disavowing marriage three times in successive menstrual cycles. Many other inequalities also obtain.

Historical Perspective

I. **Origins and extent of common law systems.** Common law systems had their origin in England and were spread through British colonization. They include the body of concepts, rules, and principles developed over many centuries in the English courts which emphasize precedents as a basis for law. The common law prevails wherever English is the major language, including the United States (except Louisiana), Australia, Canada (except Quebec), Jamaica, New Zealand, Trinidad, most of the Indian subcontinent, and most former English colonies in Africa.

A. **The beginnings of common law**. Prior to the year 1100 A.D., "law" in England consisted of traditional or customary law, as well as the canon law which governed the clergy. The conquest of England by the Normans in 1066 introduced new legal practices, such as the restriction of the legal authority of the church and consideration of serious crimes to be matters of public concern, rather than simply the concern of the injured party. **William I**, "the Conqueror" (1027-1087) provided the initial impetus for the development of common law by attempting to separate ecclesiastical and secular authority and by strengthening the feudal courts. **Henry I** (1068-1135) further attempted to codify the common law tradition. Although Roman law (civil law) was being reestablished throughout Europe, the Normans opposed the establishment of Roman law in England. With their emphasis on customary law and the establishment of a central judiciary that carried out laws based on the system of writs, the Normans helped create the common law system.

B. **Early administration of common law.** Common law emerged from the *curia regis* (royal law), the administrative part of the Norman and Plantagenet rule, in which the king's **curia** or clerics, administered the king's justice throughout England. The first English royal court of law, the Exchequer, was established to facilitate the accounting by royal officials to the king, as "lord" of all feudal estates and manors. The king's laws also extended to vassals and others in his domain, protecting people on the king's highway and in the coastal areas, for example.

C. **The establishment of a system of writs.** Under Henry I, a "system of writs" was established, which involved a sheriff issuing a summons to a litigant to appear before the *curia*, consisting of the king's justices, to answer the questions concerning the supposed offense. These hearings were not organized under the auspices of customary law as was typical during that time but were guided by the principle of *secundum aequitatem* ("following principles of equity"), and by considerations of overall fairness and justice.

D. **The rise of the royal court.** The jurisdiction of the king greatly expanded with the increase of royal manors during the reign of **Henry I** (1100-1135) and **Henry II** (1154-1189), with the royal court interceding in place of the feudal courts. The extensive use of the royal court by private citizens for personal matters quickly led to the creation of a separate Court of Common Pleas (c. 1190). By 1297 the law of the royal courts had become known as "common law."

E. **Bracton and the development of common law.** During the rule of **Henry III** (1207-72), the itinerant judge **Henry de Bracton** (d. 1268), wrote *On the Laws and Customs of England*, a monumental and systematic treatise on common law. The document, known simply as "Bracton," discussed and elaborated upon previous court rulings, limitations on royal power, and specific judicial actions, procedures, and methods of pleading. Bracton's treatise was based on a discussion of several thousand common law cases, and incorporated ideas

associated with the Roman law of Justinian and aspects of canon law. Bracton's work had a substantial and lasting influence on the development of the common law system.

F. **Promotion of common law by the Inns of Court in London.** In England the teaching of the common law was developed by the Inns of Court in London, the only organization that formally offered lectures and apprentice training in the subject. Under the reign of **Edward I** (1239-1307), the status of judges and lawyers changed from that of a clerical, informal position to a full-time profession. As the right to practice law became a professional occupation, formalized education in the theoretical and practical skills became necessary for individuals to practice law in the royal courts. Members of the Inns of the Court were required to eat their meals ("eat their commons") at the Inns, facilitating interaction with learned members. Their more formal education consisted in attending the courts themselves, becoming familiar with the courts' practical working.

G. **Littleton's treatise on common law.** Jurist **Sir Thomas Littleton** (1422-1481) wrote the *Littleton Treatise on Tenures*, the first major English legal text not written in Latin or heavily influenced by Roman law, as well as the first printed book on common law. Written in a specialized Anglo-Norman language called "law French," Littleton's work distinguishes between various types of medieval land tenure.

H. **Sir Edward Coke and the preservation of common law.** During the Stuart-Tudor period, lawyer and judge **Sir Edward Coke** (1552-1634), developed numerous treatises that reformulated and preserved common law in the seventeenth century. Coke was made chief justice of the Court of Common Pleas in 1606. In 1607-08, in a ruling concerning the limits of the king's power, he asserted that common law was the supreme law of the land and that the king had no authority in common law matters. In a later case in 1610, Coke again challenged the king's authority in a case before the royal council, when he insisted that the king did not have the authority to change any part of existing common law or create an offense by pronouncement that was not previously an offense. Coke helped develop the *Petition of Right* (1628), in response to the conflict between **Charles I** (1600-1649) and Parliament. His eleven-volume *Reports* (1600-1615) was the only formal collection of court cases and became the basis for ensuing judicial decisions. Throughout his life, Coke defended the supremacy of common law against the royal claims to powers outside the jurisdiction of the law, and his moral standards and unwillingness to compromise before the law later earned him the title of "the personification of common law."

I. **Blackstone and the modernization of common law.** Jurist **Sir William Blackstone** (1723-1780) played a fundamental role in the development of common law and in its spread to other parts of the world. Blackstone's *Commentaries on the Laws of England* (1765-69) was used throughout the world during the eighteenth and nineteenth centuries and came to be regarded as the definitive statement on common law. Consisting of four books, the treatise provided an extensive discussion of real-property law, family and public law, civil liability, courts and procedure, and criminal law. The work was extremely influential in the United States, being regarded as the second most important source of information on common law next to the Declaration of Independence.

J. **Criticism of common law.** English philosopher and reformer **Jeremy Bentham** (1748-1832) violently disagreed with Blackstone's adulation of common law and advocated a radical reformulation through systematic codification (a word Bentham invented). In his *An Introduction to the Principles of Morals and Legislation* (1789), Bentham insisted that legislators, not the courts, should determine the law and that the objectives of the law must necessarily be revised over time. Bentham argued that common law grew in a haphazard fashion and, being unsystematic, was virtually unknowable. This aspect of common law, combined with certain obscurities of English legal procedure, made pleading before the courts like taking a chance in a lottery. Bentham emphasized making law more accessible to people and less the domain of specialists, whom he found to be little more than predators and parasites. His call for legal codification, as well as other of his ideas for social reform, had an influence in much of Europe and the United States.

K. **The beginning of common law in the United States.** The law of the English settlers in America was based on common law, although there were at first relatively few lawyers, judges, and lawbooks in the colonies. Governors and legislative bodies operated as courts, lay juries had extensive powers, and each colony passed its own statutes. Knowledge of new English laws and court decisions did not immediately reach the colonies, and these new laws were not considered binding or even necessarily adopted in the colonies.

L. **The development of common law system in the United States.** By the end of the seventeenth century, the number of lawyers had increased in the colonies, and common law was the basis for the settlement of legal disputes. After 1776, many lawyers recommended changing the common law system as an expression of anti-British sentiment, but the principles of the European legal system were not easily accessible or familiar. Blackstone's *Commentaries on the Laws of England*, printed in America in 1771, became the most important document on common law. The U.S. Constitution is worded in legal terms reflecting English common law. The common law tradition was further developed in the United States by the influential judges **James Kent** (1763-1847) and **U.S. Supreme Court Justice Joseph Story** (1779-1845), who wrote extensive commentaries on the law. The practice of common law continues today in the United States, except in Louisiana, where legal procedures based on French civil law persist.

II. **Origins and extent of civil law tradition.** Civil law systems are derived from Roman law, particularly from the Roman civil law codified by the Byzantine emperor **Justinian I** (483-565 A.D.) in 534 A.D., which was termed the *corpus juris civilis* ("The Body of the Civil Law"). This manuscript was divided into a "Code" which consisted of "constitutions," a "Digest" which was comprised of the writings of Roman jurists, and the "Institutes," a handbook for students of law, which was added in 553. Roman law began as the law of the city of Rome and eventually encompassed the entire Roman Empire. Roman law was not inspired, like so much of Roman culture, from Greek culture. In fact, some scholars have even asserted that it is "the most original product of the Roman mind." In Roman hands, law "became for the first time a thoroughly scientific subject...." (Barry Nicholas, *An Introduction to Roman Law*, 1962).

A. **The survival of Roman law.** Although the Roman Empire was overthrown, the ideas inherent in Roman law were perpetuated by the Roman Catholic Church in the form of canon law. Roman law was revived in the Middle Ages, and today civil law systems, which stem from Roman law, represent the most widely distributed legal tradition in the world.

1. **Resurgence of interest in Roman law.** In northern Italy in the eleventh century, the teaching of law was given impetus by the rediscovery of Justinian's "Digest," as well as by changes within the Papacy which resulted in the "Christian Renaissance." Re-evaluations of canon law

inspired interest in civil law, as did the increasing power struggles between the Holy Roman Empire and the Church. In addition, the Roman law found favor with various rulers of the Holy Roman Empire, who claimed to be successors of the Caesars and therefore emphasized the importance of Roman law as a continuation of Roman practices.

2. **The appeal and acceptance of Roman legal principles**. Roman law, with its apparent emphasis on secular as opposed to clerical authority, appealed to feudal lords and those desiring independence from Church influence. Although the study of Roman legal principles was initially forbidden in the medieval period by the Church, students of civil law eventually were recognized, and many early Roman tenets were adopted as an improvement over a confusion of existing local laws, as a means of systematizing legal practices. Jurists trained in Roman law soon developed a systematic and superior knowledge of legal principles and practices.

3. **The Renaissance enthusiasm for Roman culture**. Long before the period of the high Renaissance, the study and application of Roman law had reappeared. From the latter eleventh century onward, universities in the south of France and in the Italian cities of Bologna and Ravenna had become learned centers for the study of Roman law and jurisprudence. The Renaissance resurgence of interest in Roman and Greek culture helped to establish the legitimacy of the study of Roman civil law. Roman civil law, *corpus juris civilis*, soon supplanted local custom and city statutes.

B. **The influence of the Code Napoleon**. The most influential of the modern civil law codes was the French Code of 1804, known also as the Code Napoleon of 1804 or the "Code Civil," which is still in existence in modified form in France. Created after the French Revolution as an attempt to codify the law in continental Europe, this code was a culmination of the characteristics of civil law stemming from the eleventh century. The underlying propositions of the code include the general equality of citizens; respect for freedom of contract and the freedom of persons; respect for private property; and the separation of civil law from ecclesiastical authority. As a prototype of civil law, this document inspired other codes throughout the world.

C. **The diffusion of the civil law system**. The civil law system has been diffused to many parts of the world and continues to be a dominant form of law in many countries today.

1. **Civil law countries in Western Europe**. The civil law system is dominant in much of Western Europe—France, Germany, Italy, Spain, Portugal, the Netherlands, and Belgium have civil law systems.

2. **Spread of civil law to European colonies**. Through Spain and Portugal, the civil law tradition was extended to Latin America. The French established it in their colonies in Africa, and it is the prevailing system in the French-speaking province of Canada, Quebec.

3. **Civil law in Louisiana**. Louisiana adopted the civil law system when it enacted its Civil Code (adapted from the Code Napoleon) of 1825.

4. **Recent adoption of systems based on civil law**. Japan and Turkey have developed legal systems in recent times based on the civil law tradition. The legal systems of the Soviet Union and the other Eastern European socialist countries had their origins in the civil law tradition but departed in many ways from the legal systems of western Europe as a result of differences in their political and economic structures. Ongoing political and economic changes in these areas will undoubtedly be reflected in their legal systems.

III. **Origins of Christian law**. Throughout most of the history of Western Civilization, Christianity was not only the primary spiritual institution, but the dominant legal institution as well, with Christian laws regarded as superior to all other laws. The history of medieval Europe cannot be understood without an understanding of the pervasive influence of canon law, which played a crucial role in the transmission and dissemination of Roman law in the Middle Ages throughout Europe.

A. **Early development of canon law**. The early Christian Church quickly developed into an organization with its own system of laws and rules. By the third century, early forms of canon law were being formulated by **Tertullian** (c. 160 A.D.-230 A.D.) and **Cyprian** (d. 258 A.D.). These early canons, most of which were initially in Greek and later translated to Latin, Coptic, Arabic and other languages, were based on the New Testament and the writings of the apostles.

B. **The influence of emperors on the development of canon law**. Once religious tolerance of Christianity was granted by **Constantine** (280?-337), numerous synods created rules of discipline, or *canons*. These written laws soon began to replace customary law. Later emperors, such as **Justinian** (483-565), influenced canon law through various mandates and religious constitutions which were then incorporated into the existing canonical collections.

C. **Early canonical collections**. During the sixth century, attempts were made to order and consolidate the various councils and canon laws in order to produce a standardized corpus of Christian law that would be universally applicable. Numerous countries produced their own collections, such as the Italian *Collectio-versio* (c. 500-23) and *Thessaloni* (c. 531) and *Avelana* (c. 555); the Spanish *Collectio Hispana Chronologica* (c. 601); and the *Statuta Ecclesiae Antiqua* (c. 485) from Gaul.

D. **The changing role of canon law**. In the tenth century, the weakening of papal authority and the social and political turmoil in Europe lead to a decrease in the authority of canon law. By the early eleventh century, the Gregorian reform of the Church emphasized the pope as the principal source of canon law, which was made manifest through councils and decretals. Collections of canonical literature emerged during this period, such as the *Collectio* by Ivo of Chartres, a major work which attempted to synthesize traditional canons with newer interpretations. Conflicting canons of law had existed since the time of the early church and it was not until the Middle Ages that the many canonical collections were organized into a central body of law.

E. **Gratian and the classical period of canon law**. The classical period in the formation of canon law occurred between 1140-1350. It was during this time that the first systematic and scientific studies of canon law were undertaken by **Gratian** (flourished c. 1140), who attempted to organize and unify the numerous canonical collections, many of which offered differing interpretations of the law. Basing his method of organizing disparate texts on that of the French theologian and philosopher **Peter Abelard** (1079-1142), Gratian identified and extracted certain universal principles from earlier canonical writings and decisions. The product of his efforts was the *Concordia discordantium canonum*, the "Harmony of Contradictory Laws," (c. 1140), which became the definitive collection of classical canon law. In this monumental work Gratian applied a rigorous scholas-

tic method to material gathered from conciliar, patristic, and papal teaching which dealt with everything from the structure of the Church, the nature of the Sacraments, liturgy, and worship, to procedural law, heretics, schismatics, marriage, penance, and church ordinations and elections. The *Concordia* provided the basis for the assembling and discussion of legal materials and was accepted universally as the foundation of church government and justice.

F. **The study of canon law**. Gratian's work stimulated further inquiry into canonical thought and served as the basis for the teaching of canon law at Bologna, which was the center of such studies, as well as Padua, Oxford, Canterbury, Paris, Orleans, and elsewhere. By the early thirteenth century faculties of canon law existed in the majority of universities in Europe, and the study of canon law was emphasized along with the subjects of civil law (Roman law) and theology.

G. **The effect of the Reformation on canon law**. In the transformation of Christian Europe brought about by the Reformation, many nations were no longer under the jurisdiction of papal authority and canon law. However, even the countries that did separate from the Church continued to use in modified form the principles and terminology of pre-Reformation canon law. The Reformation inspired a body of canonical literature which addressed the concerns of the Church at that time, such as schism, church and state relations, etc.

H. **Canon law and the Council of Trent**. The Council of Trent (1545-63) attempted to revise and augment existing canon law in an effort to update and modernize older concepts and practices. The decisions of the council became the basis for later changes in canonical thought and practice. During the appointment of pope **Gregory XIII** (1572-85) canon law was further codified in the work *Corpus Juris Canonici*, which was issued as an official Roman edition in 1580-82 after it was approved by a commission of cardinals and experts.

I. **The establishment of a new codex and commission on canon law**. In 1904, Pope Pius X introduced a plan for the complete codification of canon law. Unlike secular law, which had been codified since the end of the eighteenth century, canon law was dispersed in numerous collections, such as the *Corpus Juris Canonici* and various private collections. The new code, *Codex Juris Canonici*, was completed in 1917 and became effective in 1918. The clarification and interpretation of this new code was assigned to a special council called the Commission for the Interpretation of the Code of Canon Law. The Commission administers and re-evaluates the canon law system, clarifying controversial interpretations and determining the precise meaning of the law.

J. **The impact of Vatican II and the revision of canon law**. The changes instituted as a result of the second Vatican Council (Oct. 11, 1962-Dec. 8, 1965) had a profound effect on canon law. The second, revised *Codex* was promulgated and went into effect in 1983. This new canon of law reflects the theological transformations of Vatican II, emphasizing, for instance, the democratization of the organization of the church and its decentralization, the importance of the involvement of the laity, and ecumenical respect for the religious beliefs of every human being. During the 1980s, changes similar to those which now characterize the new Roman Catholic canon law were also being incorporated into the canon law of the Eastern Catholic Churches.

IV. **Origin and extent of Islamic law systems.** Islamic law has a long and rich history, only a small portion of which can be discussed here. The origins of traditional Islamic law must be sought in the history of Islamic society after the death of the Prophet. The history of that law has three periods. The first occupies the first two centuries of Islam, the seventh to the ninth centuries A.D., culminating in an attempt to unify the body of Islamic law; the second extends from the Middle Ages to the eighteenth and nineteenth centuries, when the Islamic world came under increasing Western influence; and the third, modern times, is characterized, on the one hand, by attempts to adapt Islamic law to the modern world; and on the other, by fierce opposition to modernization and demands for a return to a pure Muslim law unsullied by the "corrupting" influence of the West.

A. **The empire of the Umayyads.** At the time of his death in 632, the Prophet Muhammad ruled an expanding empire centered in Medina, in the Arabian peninsula. A series of rulers or caliphs succeeded him. In 661, **Ali** (c. 600-661), the Prophet's cousin and husband of his last surviving daughter, governed as the fourth caliph but was opposed by the Umayyad clan. When Ali was murdered, his son, who succeeded him, abdicated in favor of the Umayyads. This succession brought about the schism between Sunni and Shi'ite Muslims, who refused to recognize the legitimacy of the Umayyad caliphate.

B. **The diversity of early legal practice**. The rapid expansion of the Umayyad empire carried Islam into new regions, each with its own local customs, resulting in a marked disparity in law among parts of the empire. The Umayyad administration appointed local judges *(qadis)*, who administered the law, functioning as the delegate of the local governor and sometimes doubling as chief of police or Master of the Treasury. These officials, though not unmindful of their religious duties under the Koran, interpreted local law that necessarily varied widely in a polity that stretched from the Pyrenees nearly to the Indian subcontinent and which had come in contact with legal systems foreign to Islam. Thus Roman and Persian legal traditions crept into early Islamic practice in conquered territory previously under their influence. To this geographic cause of legal diversity a second must be added, for each *qadi* had the power to decide the cases before him according to his personal opinion or *ra'y*. Without some unifying influence, disparity in legal interpretation and practice was inevitable.

C. **The appearance of schools of judicial thought in the eighth century**. By the early eighth century, from about 720 onward, a critical spirit embraced the legally educated, who bemoaned how far the Umayyad's lust for power and territory had led the law from the unblemished principles of the Prophet's days.

1. **Growing reliance on Islamic tradition**. As a de facto check on the centrifugal forces of *ra'y*, the individual opinion of judges which might lead to multiple legal interpretations, there arose a greater consensus regarding correct legal interpretation; and similarly, there was a growing reliance on the idea of *sunna* (literally "beaten path" or tradition). While *sunna* was at first only the tradition of the tribe or locality in question, it came to embody a wider region and to express the ideal doctrine of a legal school. Such legal consensus stood quite at odds with the parochialism of the Umayyad courts.

2. **The problem of false "traditions."** The increasing reliance on *sunna* had the side effect of a growth in the false ascription of tradition to Muhammad, as the doctrines of various schools sought legitimacy by cloaking themselves in the Prophet's authority. By 770, however, opposition to such loose practice had made its appearance, characterized by a doctrinaire adherence to the Koran, and therefore to the prophet Himself, as

ultimate authority. Nevertheless, fallacious material crept into the growing body of the *Hadith* (traditions). By the latter third of the eighth century, three sources of Islamic law, apart from the Koran itself, coexisted uneasily: the reasoning of individual scholars; the consensus of varying schools of legal scholars; and the growing traditions of the Prophet. Despite a move away from disintegration, the period was marked by the diversity of competing views (Coulson, *op. cit.*).

D. **Muhammad Ash-Shafi'i and the attempt to unify Islamic law.** The diversity of competing legal schools set the stage for the entrance of a unifying force attempting to reconcile them. This force arrived in the person of **Muhammad Ibn-Idris Ash-Shafi'i** (767-820), the "colossus" of Islamic legal history, the father of its jurisprudence.

1. Developing a unified, authoritative law. Shafi'i was able to encompass the contending schools through his periods of study in the most important centers of jurisprudence in the Islamic world—in Mecca and Medina, in Iraq and Syria. Standing apart from the schools, Shafi'i developed doctrines that gave authoritative status to sources of the law which previously could be ignored, interpreted in endless variations that led to a multiplicity of views rather than to the unified opinion, or packed with localisms that splintered the law into parochial fragments.

2. **The sources of Islamic law.** As previously stated, these sources are the Koran; the *sunna* (traditions) drawn from the *Hadith* (acts and sayings of the Prophet); the *ijima* (consensus) of the Muslim (legal) community; and the use of analogical reasoning (*kiyas*). None of these was original with Shafi'i; rather, he gave them a novel twist. Thus, Shafi'i argued that the Koran could not contradict itself: if one provision was in conflict with another, then the earlier one was repealed by the later. In a doctrine scholars consider among his greatest contributions, he argued that the *sunna* of the Prophet possess divine authority, and he devised principles to provide its uniform interpretation. The consensus he approved as a source of law was not a series of local consensuses of jurists, but the consensus of the entire community of Muslim jurists, thus pointing to a uniform law. Finally, he admitted that the reasoning process might on rare occasions provide conflicting views, but it was entirely

subordinate to the divine sources of law (where it would have to find a source if it was to operate at all).

3. **Tradition as the key to a unified legal system.** In untangling the conflicting claims of reason and tradition, he leaned toward the latter but left space for the former. Shafi'i's message to the Muslim world was that the divine will had expressed itself far more precisely than previously believed. If this was so, then a unified Shari'a or holy law was indeed within Islam's grasp. That later events found this to be impossible detracts little from Shafi'i's achievement.

E. **"Closing the gate of independent reasoning:" Islam's period of stagnation.** At the end of the ninth century the creative force of Islamic jurisprudence had been spent. Although there were still schools of law, a far greater unity of the system had been achieved. But variance with received doctrine was formally forbidden; creative effort was suppressed with the doctrine that the "gate is shut," and henceforth Muslim legal scholars could only be imitators of previously established forms of legal reasoning and method. Since the *sunna* was now accepted as divinely inspired, efforts were made to distinguish authenticity from apocrypha. But after this period, Islamic legal thought remained in stagnation for centuries. Further schools of jurisprudence were born, but inventive imagination was largely stifled until the birth of the modern age.

F. **The modern age: reform and reaction.** From the nineteenth century on, Islamic societies came into increasing contact with the West and its legal systems, especially in the process of colonization in Africa, Asia, and the Middle East.

1. **The role of European colonial rule.** Where continental powers ruled, civil law tended to be implemented; and where Britain ruled, common law or other features of English legal practice were introduced. Thus, for example, in Islamic Northern Nigeria, stoning to death of murderers by the aggrieved family was outlawed by British colonial authorities (Norman Anderson, *Law Reform in the Muslim World*, London, 1976).

2. **Indigenous reform.** Reforms were also introduced by non-colonial governments seeking to adapt to the modern world. For example, Islamic law was abolished in Turkey in 1926 and replaced by Swiss family law, but this was the only Muslim country to do so. Modernist legislation was

introduced in Iran in the 1920s and 1930s (repealed in 1979 after the fundamentalist revolution), Egypt in 1948, Jordan in 1951, Syria in 1949 and 1953, and Tunisia in 1957; similar reforms were enacted elsewhere.

3. **Contradictory currents: Islamic law in the late twentieth century.** In a few cases, such as Saudi Arabia, traditional Shari'a is still the dominant legal system and is applied in its entirety, including public beheadings and amputation of limbs. Still, the influence of European legal systems after the end of colonial rule has continued in many Muslim countries or countries with significant Muslim populations, where civil authorities enact law as in the West. But movements to restore Shari'a to its previous position of dominance are often active and energetic, sometimes to the point of fanaticism. As a result, civil authority has sometimes found it necessary, as in Egypt, to make concessions to Islamic tradition to quell popular demands for reform. Such moves generally reflect a deep division between educated elites who favor modernization, such as improving the unequal status of women under Shari'a, and uneducated masses of a conservative persuasion, led by religious traditionalists. The force and complexity of the pressures driving Islamic societies in contrary directions—some toward modernization, in the emancipation of women, for example; some against modernity, favoring a return to rigid Koranic principles—cannot be exaggerated. Ruling elites cannot entirely discount the possibility of fundamentalist uprisings such as the Iranian Revolution that destroyed the regime of the Shah of Iran in 1979. Indeed, observers in the 1980s and 1990s remark upon the fundamentalist "revivalism" sweeping much of the Muslim world (H.S. Bhatia, *op. cit.*).

Contemporary Perspective

I. **The convergence of common law and civil law systems.** Although the traditional differences between common law and civil law systems outlined above still generally exist, a number of scholars have commented on the ways in which both the procedures and substance of civil and common law systems have tended to converge.

A. **Convergence in legal procedure.** In certain areas of legal procedure, common law and civil law systems appear to be converging to some extent.

1. **The decline of jury trials in non-criminal matters in many common law systems.** The general absence of trial by jury in non-criminal cases in civil law systems increasingly appears to characterize common law systems, though not in the United States. For example, jury trials in civil cases, while still a constitutional right in most jurisdictions in the United States, are rarely used in England, and in certain other common law systems have been abolished. The right to a jury trial in criminal cases is still prevalent in both systems.

2. **The spread of codification in United States.** The dependence of civil law systems on codified law rather than on precedents embodied in case law has made substantial inroads in the U.S. federal law and in the individual states; much of the common law has been codified, and new law has been created by legislatures. These statutes have themselves been subject to interpretation by the courts, forming a new body of case law.

3. **The development of case law in civil law systems.** While precedents are not binding in civil law systems as they are in common law systems, convergence of the two systems is nevertheless evident. For in civil law jurisdictions, a considerable body of case law has developed as a result of judicial interpretation of codified law.

B. **Convergence in substantive law.** Convergences in substantive law have also been noticeable.

1. **Convergence in non-criminal law.** Convergence between the two systems in non-criminal matters has come about through the operation of similar economic and social processes in all developed countries. For example, the development of technology in modern Western societies has created similar problems and led to similar laws to handle them. Thus the invention of the railroad—and later the automobile—resulted in the creation of whole bodies of law that are basically the same in France and England.

2. **Convergence in criminal law.** Substantive criminal law in Western civil law countries does not differ greatly from that of common law countries. The same kinds of actions are considered criminal, and the same general approaches to corrective justice are discussed and debated throughout these societies.

II. **Contemporary canon law**. The changes instituted as a result of the second Vatican Council (1962-65) had a profound effect on canon law, reflecting contemporary cultural, social, political, and ecclesiastical changes. In Roman Catholic countries today, canon law continues to be a central form of law, directly influencing the personal lives of the faithful. Changes similar to those which now characterize Roman Catholic canon law were also underway in the Eastern Churches in the 1980s.

   A. **Vatican II and the new Codex**. The second, revised *Codex*, which reflected the theological transformations of Vatican II, was promulgated and went into effect in 1983. The new body of law contained in the *Codex Juris Canonici*, consisting of 1,752 canons comprising seven books, emphasizes the democratization and decentralization of the organization of the church, and the importance of the involvement of the laity. The seven books address the following general subjects: "General Norms," which includes the operating principles of canon law, definitions of juridical persons and ecclesiastical offices; "The People of God," which describes the rights and duties of the clergy and laity and the organizational structure of the church; "The Teaching Office of the Church," which details catechismic and missionary activities and the use of print and electronic media; "The Sanctifying Office of the Church" which discusses the nature of the sacraments and worship; "The Temporal Goods of the Church," which addresses issues concerning property, contracts, etc.; "Sanctions in the Church," which delineates various crimes, offenses, and penalties; and "Procedures" which clarifies the administration of justice by ecclesiastical courts.

   B. **The new approach**. As a result of the new formulations resulting from Vatican II, the Roman church is no longer conceptualized solely as the "perfect society," the members of which are subordinate to the church hierarchy. Instead the Roman church is redefined as "the people of God," a community through which all members participate in proclaiming the Gospel. In this new conception of the church, canon law is considered a means of guidance, rather than a form of religious regulation of people's behavior, taking into consideration pastoral concerns and emphasizing cooperation and communal participation. While the application of the principles of canon law to one's own personal life is advocated, conflicts between personal conscience and public law are discouraged, particularly in the areas of marriage and penal law. Vatican II canon laws are said to be offered in a "spirit of love, fairness, and humanity"

with an ecumenical respect for the religious beliefs of every human being.

III. **Islamic law today**. Islamic law applies in modern nations where there is an Islamic ruler to enforce it, not by virtue of citizenship but by virtue of religious affiliation. It is applied primarily to Muslims although it contains provision for non-Muslims within the jurisdiction.

   A. **Islamic law incorporated in some countries' constitutions**. In some countries, Islamic law is made explicitly part of the law of the land as part of its basic law. In the Islamic Republic of Iran, for example, it is expressly stated in the constitution that all laws must be based on Islamic law, and the legislature has no right to formulate laws repugnant to Islamic injunctions. The constitution of the Islamic Republic of Pakistan is also devised expressly to be compatible with the Koran and Sunna. Traditional Islamic law also predominates in Saudi Arabia, where religious police stand guard over morals, applying Islamic standards to Muslims and non-Muslims alike.

   B. **Islamic law combined with common or civil law**. In other Muslim countries, Islamic law is combined with elements of common law or civil law, as a result of their colonial histories. For example, Bangladesh and Malaysia, in common with other former British colonies, inherited and have adopted the common-law system, although much of family and personal law is governed by Islamic law. The influence of Western law and legal systems is found throughout much of the Muslim world, with notable exceptions such as Iran.

   C. **Islam at the crossroads: reform or reaction?** In the Islamic world today pressures to continue the process of adapting to the modern world vie with social movements for a return to Muslim purity as expressed in the classic works and doctrines of the Shari'a.

      1. **Secularism vs. fundamentalism**. This clash was dramatically illustrated in the 1980s in the war between fundamentalist Iran and secular Iraq, led by the modernist Baathist party. The hopes in some quarters for a convergence of Islamic states and western-style democracy seem unjustified in light of the incompatibility of traditionalist Islam, and its many fervent supporters, on the one hand, and a secularism that attempts to separate religion from social policies, such as the role of women or the liberty of the individual, on the other. Fundamentalism and

secularism seem destined to predominate in different places and different times, and no general victory for one or the other seems likely to occur in the foreseeable future.

2. **The status of women**. To critics, the status of women in traditionalist societies is especially vexing. For example, in accordance with Shari'a, women remain the decided inferiors of their husbands in marriage and can, to cite one instance, be unilaterally divorced. Multiple wives are allowed in various places. In Saudi Arabia women suffer many inequalities, such as being barred from driving automobiles. Women who are not covered in accordance with traditional practice are liable to be accosted by religious police, who frequent public places in search of offenders. In addition, within some countries the practice of clitorectomy continues. Also, in various countries restrictions are placed on the employment of women, and other disabilities obtain.

C. INTERNATIONAL LAW

Roper: So now you'd give the Devil benefit of law!

More: [Lord chancellor of England] Yes. What would you do? Cut a great road through the law to get after the Devil?

Roper: I'd cut down every law in England to do that!

More: Oh? And when the last law was down, and the Devil turned round on you—where would you hide, Roper, the laws all being flat?...yes, I'd give the Devil benefit of law, for my own safety's sake.

Robert Bolt (1961)

International law, like all the laws that regulate our daily lives, is a liberator as well as regulator of conduct. Individuals as well as nations share in the benefits of the freedom of activity created by international order, the rules of which are governed by international law. The mail we receive from Hong Kong, Nigeria, and France, the produce from Mexico and New Zealand, the radio programs from London, are all a product not only of the airlines, farmers, artists and writers, but also of the international lawyers, politicians, and diplomats who helped to create the social, legal, and economic milieu in which international life proceeds and prospers. The citizen

should appreciate these roles in assessing how the rules of international order are constructed and recognized. They should also realize what benefits arise from the operation of international law and what consequences flow from its partial or complete breakdown.

To judge the controversies that sometimes surround international legal issues and the claims and counterclaims of wrongdoing by the states that make up the international system, citizens must also know that international law differs significantly from domestic law. Those differences—the absence of an international legislature, courts with compulsory jurisdiction to interpret law authoritatively, and, especially, the lack of a generally available agency to enforce it by applying sanctions—put international law in a special status. On the one hand, advocates argue that it must be followed on all occasions, for to do otherwise is to invite the law of the jungle to hold sway, with disastrous consequences. On the other, critics claim that rigorously followed legalism will in time lead to the demise of the democratic order and the dominion of ruthless international predators who care little for law and much for the aggrandizement of their own power at the expense of the liberty and safety of others. To debate issues of foreign policy and international order, citizens must be knowledgeable of these arguments and attempt to apply them intelligently to the issues of the day.

OBJECTIVES

The citizen should be able to

1. explain the history and development of international law.

2. explain how international law is formed, applied, enforced, and adjudicated.

3. evaluate the activities of national, state, and local officials in the context of the law of nations.

4. take, defend, and evaluate positions on the obligations of the United States to adhere to various international laws, including agreements with other states.

FRAME OF REFERENCE
Conceptual Perspective

I. **The character of international law**. International law must be distinguished from domestic law.

A. **Domestic law**. The domestic law of the United States is a product of a political process regulated by the U.S. Constitution and those of the various states. It regulates the relationships among persons within the country, between federal, state, and local governments and members of society, between states, and between states and the federal government.

B. **International law**. International law is a product of national state consent. It regulates primarily the relationship between states. Recently, it has also begun to encompass the obligations and rights of individuals with regard to states, including their own states.

C. **Incorporation of international law into domestic law**. International law is frequently a part of domestic law.

1. **The incorporation of treaties and other agreements**. Treaties (international agreements—also known as "conventions") are incorporated into U.S. law in accordance with the Constitution, which (in Article VI) states "This Constitution, and the laws of the United States which shall be made in Pursuance thereof; and all Treaties made, or which shall be made, under the Authority of the United States, shall be the supreme Law of the Land; and the Judges in every State shall be bound thereby, any Thing in the Constitution or Laws of any State to the Contrary notwithstanding."

   a. **Treaties**. International treaties, which are negotiated by the executive (president), normally must be ratified by the president after procuring the consent of the Senate—by a 2/3 vote of those present—in order to be binding on the U.S. vis-a-vis other countries and to be "supreme law" within the U.S.

   b. **Executive agreements**. So-called "executive agreements" need not be endorsed by the Senate, since they deal with areas of activity entrusted exclusively to the executive branch by the Constitution.

2. **Incorporation of customary international law**. The Supreme Court of the United States has held that customary international law is part of the law of the United States (The Paquete Habana, [1900]). Since it is part of the law governing an area over which the federal government has primary

constitutional authority—international relations—it too takes precedence over all state law.

3. **Conflicts among laws**. Conflicts between federal law and international law include the following:

   a. **Federal statutes and treaties**. One set of conflicts is between a federal statute and a treaty—the one more recent in time takes precedence.

   b. **Federal statutes and customary law**. A second set of conflicts is between a federal statute and a rule of customary international law—the statute takes precedence.

   c. **International customary law as part of federal common law**. There can be no conflict between a rule of customary international law and the federal common law, since customary law is part of federal common law.

4. **Domestic effects of international law**. Each country decides for itself how international law will be given effect domestically, the international obligation being satisfied if it is given effect pursuant to its stated purpose.

II. **International organizations**. International organizations are products of multi-lateral treaties (usually referred to as "conventions").

A. **Worldwide organizations**. The United Nations (UN) is the most important worldwide organization. Some of its constituent institutions have limited rule-making powers, the resultant law being binding on member states.

1. **The UN Security Council**. The Security Council is a fifteen-member body. Its resolutions are binding on all states. No resolution may be passed if any permanent member (the U.S., the United Kingdom, France, the USSR, and China) votes against it.

2. **The International Court of Justice**. Upon the agreement of two or more states which submit their dispute for decision, the International Court of Justice (ICJ) may decide the case. Its written decisions indicate rules which are part of customary international law. Only states and international organizations—not individuals—may be parties to actions in the ICJ; and

only those states that, with regard to a specific dispute, have consented to the court's jurisdiction, or generally, are subject to its authority.

3. **The General Assembly**. Each member of the United Nations is a member of the General Assembly and has one vote. Its resolutions are not binding on member states. However, the resolutions, along with other official state acts, help to create customary international law.

B. **Regional international organizations**. An example of such regional associations is the Organization of American States. Another is the European Community. These organizations have their own charters, operating regionally in a manner somewhat similarly to the United Nations. They may not operate inconsistently with the obligations of their members under the United Nations Charter.

III. **International human rights law**. International human rights law is a product of both treaties and customary law. It is rooted in the United Nations Charter and is further amplified by a growing number of implementing legal documents. (For a discussion of human rights law, see the section on Human Rights in this Framework and see below under the Historical Perspective of this section under "Twentieth century developments").

IV. **Importance of international law**. Prior to World War II, opinion in the United States widely deprecated international law. It was thought of as rules of good manners among governments; power was the only significant factor in international relations. Since 1945, this point of view has waned gradually; and this body of law has played an increasingly important role. Treaty law has grown dramatically, governing such topics as the following:

A. **The environment**. One set of treaties attempts to deal with environmental degradation. An example is the border waters agreement between the U.S. and Canada that regulates water pollution of the Great Lakes and connecting and tributary waters.

B. **Labor law**. Other treaties deal with the rights of labor. The International Labor Organization (ILO), based in Geneva, has drafted and brought into effect many such treaties, governing the right to organize in unions, freedom from arbitrary discrimination, etc.

C. **International borders**. Treaties regulate international borders. For instance, the U.S. and Canada have delineated their common border by treaty.

D. **International commerce**. Treaties also regulate international commerce. For example, the General Agreement on Tariffs and Trade (GATT) binds many of the major trading countries of the world to reduce customs duties on imports to levels mutually agreed to by treaty, and otherwise restricts their freedom to act in ways considered destructive of the world community's interest in expanding international trade.

V. **Controversy over international law**. Several controversies over international law that have continued to engage the interest of governments and scholars are of concern to citizens.

A. **International law as publicly invisible**. International law nearly always comes to our attention in the context of conflict between countries involving its content or application. In these cases, the focus in media attention is usually upon facts which have created high emotion and extreme rhetoric. Seldom does the public witness the unfolding of the process of legal decompression and settlement, which may be years in the making. Consequently, there is a certain skepticism about the very existence of an international legal order, or at least as to its effectiveness as a tool to affect state conduct. This view ignores the enormous amount of orderly intercourse among the nations of the world in such spheres as trade, tourism, military security, communications, and other areas. All of these areas are regulated by international rules that are, in the main, effective.

B. **Limits to the effectiveness of international law**. International law cannot be expected to be effective in all situations in the absence of courts with mandatory jurisdiction and the equivalent of an international police force to enforce commonly agreed-upon rules. Any state may be faced with a legal prescription that is, or which it views as, running counter to a vital interest—one that threatens or appears to threaten its existence. No government can be expected to obey a law that requires what is, or may be considered to be, national suicide. Whether such non-observance is justified is a matter of continued controversy.

VI. **Effects of international law upon individuals and organizations within the U.S.** International law has wide and sometimes unsuspected authority. Even such activity as the hunting of certain bird stocks in the Mid-West (migratory) is controlled by treaty.

VII. **Enforcement of international law in U.S. courts**. Courts in the U.S. enforce international law as a matter of course, as do a growing number of administrative agencies.

Historical Perspective

I. **Need for order in the international arena.** From the earliest times, the transnational flow of goods, people and ideas created a need for laws which would regulate international relations. Early international law, like all law, was rooted in a need for order, predictability, and stability, conditions which are essential for the proper functioning of societies.

    A. **Ancient origins of international law.** The rules and customs which regulated and governed the relations of various political groups in ancient China, India, Egypt, Assyria, and the Hittite Empire were early forms of international law.

    B. **International law in classical Greece and Egypt.** The city-state politics of ancient Greece resulted in the creation of rules dictating interstate relations. The presence of foreign inhabitants required city-states to address the question of whether specific groups should be allowed to have their own specific laws.

        1. **The appointment of *prostates* and *proxeni*.** Local officials, called *prostates* and *proxeni*, were appointed to perform certain judicial functions and for the specific purpose of deciding disputes involving foreigners. These local officials applied a special body of law applicable only to foreign inhabitants. This early example of the development of a body of law dictated by the problems of international relations was a forerunner of international law as we know it today.

        2. **The development of personal law.** During the sixth century, B.C., Greek representatives succeeded in convincing the Egyptian government to permit local Greek inhabitants to select *prostates* from among their own number to apply a special "Greek" law to disputes involving them. At about the same time, Jews living in Egypt had their own courts which applied "Jewish law" to disputes within their own community.

    C. **Early Roman international law.** The Romans adopted various Greek institutions and procedures, among which was the application of a special body of law to foreigners in their midst. Like the Greeks, the Romans appointed an official whose duty it was to administer justice to foreigners.

        1. ***Praetor peregrinus*.** While the term *praetor* was applied to an official who performed general judicial functions, *peregrinus* defined one type of *praetor* whose duties included those legal issues involving the *peregrini*, or foreigners.

        2. **The creation of special laws for foreigners.** Specific laws were created by Roman officials for the benefit of foreigners. Known as *jus gentium* (law of peoples), these laws consisted of a body of principles considered universally appropriate, which were dictated by the social nature of humanity. This special body of familiar law was used as a means of encouraging foreigners to come to Rome, particularly for purposes of commerce.

    D. **Dissolution of the Roman Empire and the need for international order.** The gradual decline of the Roman Empire, the conquests by Islamic and Turkish armies, the development of city-states, and the emergence of various political regimes from the sixth to tenth centuries, created a need for laws which regulated interactions between diverse political groups.

        1. **Islamic and Turkish conquests.** From 634 to 712 A.D., Arabic forces overran most of the Middle East, as well as all of the African provinces of Rome. Turkish armies captured the city of Constantinople (now Istanbul) and much of southeastern Europe. These conquests created problems of ordering the relationship between the newly created polities and the remnants of the old regime.

        2. **Italian city-state evolution.** City-states, such as Venice, Genoa, and Amalfi, arose in Italy from the sixth to the tenth century, A.D. The life-blood of these emerging city-states was trade, and it soon became necessary for them to develop a legal regime to regulate their relations among themselves, as well as with other independent communities rising from the ashes of the Roman Empire.

        3. **Development of Hanseatic League.** In Northwestern Europe, during the thirteenth and fourteenth centuries, the Hanseatic League, composed of commercial city-states similar to the Italian city-states, developed, further increasing the need for a new, international legal order.

II. **The development of international law by scholars and publicists.** European international law developed amid the disintegration of the medieval system, the ensuing growth of a limited number of powerful political bodies in Europe, and the widespread recognition of the concept of territorial sovereignty in the fifteenth century. The efforts of legal scholars and "publicists" (still defined as "experts in international law") contributed greatly to the advancement of methods and theories about international law. While legal decisions and documents have not been widely published in the past, during this period scholars began to compile information about the law and made legal materials and interpretations more readily accessible. For the sake of understanding their differences, these scholars may be divided into three general schools: the Naturalists, the Positivists, and the Eclectics.

A. **Early scholars of international law.** From the fourteenth to eighteenth centuries, international legal development was dramatically influenced by the writings of European theologians, lawyers, philosophers, and other scholars. For instance, the treatises of political theorists such as the Frenchman **Jean Bodin** (1530-1596) had implications for policies of international law, while in the fifteenth century, Italian lawyers attempted to develop a doctrine of international law. These and other scholars organized existing legal materials, suggested principles, and provided interpretations of various legal sources, all of which greatly advanced the study of international law. Thus, international law should be seen as the result of a long evolution which gradually expanded its province over a course of centuries.

B. **Natural law models for interpreting international law.** The approach of the "Naturalists" for interpreting international law stressed the moral and rational principles of "natural law." The Naturalists claimed that international law should be founded on ethical principles deduced from basic norms of the natural order.

1. **The Spanish natural law school.** In Spain, **Francisco de Vitoria** (c. 1485-1546) and **Francisco Suarez** (1548-1617) developed the Spanish Naturalist school. Vitoria's writings, inspired by Spain's then recent conquest of Mexico, questioned the right of Spain to conquer indigenous rulers of the New World. The result was his system of rules based on natural law theory that he argued should be the basis for regulating the interactions of culturally and religiously diverse sovereign states.

2. **The natural law approach in Germany. Samuel von Pufendorf** (1632-1694), was a German public-

ist and lawyer who advocated the precedence of natural law over positive (that is, "actual" or written) law. Pufendorf, who was influenced by the English political philosopher **Thomas Hobbes** (1588-1679), founded a naturalist school which considered natural law to be the source of international law and the basis of human rights. Pufendorf believed that principles of logic inherent in natural law would sufficiently regulate international legal decisions and disputes.

C. **The positivist approach to international law.** Rivals of the naturalist school were members of the positivist school, who emphasized the historical precedence of actual legal practices and agreements and the logic behind such practices. The Positivists based their interpretation of international law on legal analysis, rather than stressing what they considered the somewhat abstract and metaphysical principles of "natural law."

1. **Gentili and Bynkershoek.** Positivists included the Italian jurist **Alberico Gentili** (1552-1608), who served as an advisor to Queen Elizabeth I, and the Dutch judge **Cornelis van Bynkershoek** (1673-1743), who developed the concept of a three-mile limit for national territorial waters.

2. **The Positivist approach in England.** The English judge **Richard Zouche** (1590-1661) initiated positivist interpretations of international law in England. Zouche analyzed the distinctive characteristics of the premises of natural law and international law, examining these as they were manifested in state practice.

D. **Grotius and the "eclectic" interpretation of international law. Hugo Grotius** (1583-1645) and his followers, referred to as members of the Grotian school or the Eclectics, adopted aspects of both the naturalist and positivist approaches. Much of contemporary international law has its basis in Grotius's integration of the moral principles of natural law, legal principles, and actual practices. The Statute of the International Court of Justice at The Hague, The Netherlands, for instance, exemplifies this approach.

1. **Grotius and modern international law.** The Dutch jurist, theologian, and philosopher **Hugo Grotius** is often credited with being the founder of modern international law.

a. **Grotius's masterwork.** Grotius's prominence was based on his masterful *The Law of War* *and Peace* (1625), considered by many scholars as the classic statement of international law. Written in response to the brutality of the Thirty Years' War (1618-1648), this work embodies a synthesis of concepts which quickly gained wide appeal among his colleagues as well as among future scholars of international law.

b. **Grotius' methods and ideas**. Grotius' work systematically combined aspects of Roman law, natural law, moral principles, historical precedents, and state practices, and claimed that sovereign states were the basic unit of international law. His treatise emphasized the destructive and unproductive character of warfare, while also providing certain sanctions for governments to do what they considered advantageous in certain circumstances, without legal restrictions. Grotius maintained that international law was based on natural law, independent of God, and founded on human nature.

2. **Other Eclectic approaches to international law**. Other scholars considered to embrace the "eclectic" approach were the philosopher **Baron Christian von Wolff** (1679-1754), and the jurist **Emmerich von Vattel** (1714-1767). Wolff emphasized the concept of the "great society," or "*civitas maxima*," as the basis of authority for international law, while Vattel stressed the idea that the balance of power between nations forms the basis for international law. Vattel's work in particular, because it was written in French rather than Latin, received widespread acclaim among the constitutional founders of the United States. While Vattel and Wolff are generally considered Eclectics, their treatises were heavily influenced by naturalist principles.

E. **The decreased importance of publicists in influencing international law**. Today, information regarding national and international activity is widespread and readily accessible. The dissemination of decisions by courts, agencies, and other tribunals has reduced the importance of treatises on international law. While the Statute of the International Court of Justice does list such works as a subsidiary means of determining the existence of international legal rules, the accessibility of original legal materials and the development of international institutions has substantially decreased their significance.

III. **Twentieth century developments**. International law undoubtedly has developed faster during the twentieth century than in all of its previous existence. The most important feature of that growth has been the development of international institutions.

A. **Permanent Court of Arbitration**. Established by treaties signed at conferences in The Hague in 1899 and 1907, this court was the first permanent institution created for the resolution of disputes among nations.

B. **Permanent Court of International Justice**. The establishment of this court was a post-World War I development in conjunction with the League of Nations. The U.S. was never a member of the court, though an American justice always sat on it. The court was dissolved in 1945 and replaced by the UN International Court of Justice.

C. **The United Nations**. One of the principal purposes of the United Nations is to attempt to promote and maintain respect for international law. The UN includes in its membership nearly every country in the world.

D. **International Court of Justice**. This is a court created by the United Nations Charter (the treaty that gave birth to the United Nations). All United Nation member states are also parties to the statute of the International Court of Justice. Only states or international organizations (not individuals) may be parties to actions in this court.

E. **International protection of human rights**. Prior to World War II, international law conferred no rights directly on individuals; only states were recognized actors under it. More particularly, no state or person had the authority under international law to protest the treatment, however vicious, by a state of one or more of its own nationals. Since World War II there has been a rapid evolution of a body of rules seeking to protect individuals against certain kinds of state conduct, regardless of the relationship of the victim and the offending state. Among the many treaties and institutions are the following:

1. **The United Nations Charter.** The UN Charter, signed in San Francisco in 1945, is the basis for a number of succeeding treaties and other documents that attempt to promote the idea of human rights and adherence to its norms.

2. **The Universal Declaration of Human Rights.** This resolution of the General Assembly of the United Nations was passed in 1948 with the universal assent of its membership. Originally a statement of aspirations, it has been so broadly adhered to by members of the world community, and so often cited by states as proof of legal obligation, that it has found its way into customary international law.

3. **The International Covenant on Civil and Political Rights.** This treaty came into effect in 1976. It comprehensively protects individual rights against transgression by any state. The United States was a major actor in negotiating and drafting this convention and was an original signer of it. By 1991, however, the U.S. Senate had not ratified the treaty.

4. **The International Covenant on Economic, Social and Cultural Rights.** This treaty, due to the nature of its subject matter, imposes few absolute duties. Unlike the Covenant on Civil and Political Rights, in which the obligations imposed on the states party to it are mostly negative (i.e., **not** to interfere with certain protected interests, such as life and liberty) it imposes positive duties, requiring state action to improve the economic, social, and cultural climate in order to promote individual progress. The United States is not a party to this convention.

5. **The Convention on the Prevention and Punishment of the Crime of Genocide.** This treaty came into effect in 1951 and was ratified by the United States in 1988. It requires states party to it to make criminal any actions intended to destroy defined minority groups, in whole or in part.

6. **Convention Against Torture and other Cruel, Inhuman or Degrading Treatment or Punishment.** This Convention came into effect in 1987. The United States has ratified it with reservations seeking to make it conform with U.S. law.

7. **Regional pacts.** A number of regional pacts have been created in the twentieth century.

    a. **The American Convention on Human Rights.** This treaty is the product of a 1969 conference of Western Hemisphere nations held in San Jose, Costa Rica. It came into effect in 1978. Twenty states have become party to it, not including the United States.

        (1) **The Inter-American Commission on Human Rights as an institution created by the Convention.** This commission receives and investigates complaints of violations of human rights as defined in the Convention. It may bring an action against a transgressor state in the Inter-American Court of Human Rights.

        (2) **The Inter-American Court of Human Rights.** This court was created by the Convention. Only states or the Commission may bring actions in it. Although it is relatively new, it has begun to have an effect. For example, in 1988, at the instance of the Commission, it heard and decided a case against Honduras on behalf of the dependents of two Honduran citizens who "disappeared" while in the custody of the government. Honduras was held liable for violation of the rights of those citizens. The government has made no claim that the decision is in any respect invalid and must pay an indemnity to the dependents.

    b. **The European Convention for the Protection of Human Rights and Fundamental Freedoms.** The Council of Europe, as the states party to this treaty are known, now consists of twenty-two countries. The treaty, which entered into force in 1950, also created a Commission and a Court with powers similar to their counterparts in the Americas. Both have been increasingly active over the years. They have made so many decisions that their reports fill many volumes in the libraries of the world.

Contemporary Perspective

I. **Effectiveness of international law.** A key question in considering the present status of international law is its effectiveness.

    A. **Reciprocity.** Reciprocity is one of the most important concepts in the arena of international law. Reciprocity involves a state's adherence to the same rules or norms it expects other states to follow.

        1. **Reciprocity v. self-contradiction.** A government that is convinced that its people are better off in

a rule-governed world is likely to conform its conduct to that rule. Similarly, a government that wishes another state, with which it has a treaty, to act consistently with obligations defined by the agreement will feel itself obliged to do so. It will realize that disregarding the same treaty obligations it demands that others follow, places it in a state of self-contradiction.

2. **Reciprocity and the growth of world order**. To the extent that reciprocity in adherence to international law becomes generalized to the entire international community, states tend to be induced to be law-abiding even if no immediately discernible reciprocal benefit is apparent. The motivating hope is for the long-term stability of international relations and the security of expectations that can result when the web of reciprocal legal conduct is truly seamless.

3. **The need of law-breaking states to justify themselves**. States have not willingly complied with laws that run counter to their vital interests as they have perceived them to be. It is interesting, however, that in the very act of breaching a clearly defined rule, states invariably insist upon placing a construction on the factual context that attempts to prove that they are not law breakers. It is further worth noting that the number of cases in which perceived national interests prevent compliance with law are few indeed, compared with the totality of state actions.

B. **Compliance with international law**. The level of state compliance with international law is very considerable. Governments operate meticulously within the rules governing the international mails, whereas, for example, motorists in many nations violate automobile traffic control rules, tax laws, and other legal norms on a grand scale. Strict compliance to international law can also be seen when a British plane takes off from Los Angeles airport, picks up passengers in Germany, and transports them to Moscow, where fuel is purchased for the return trip to London, all pursuant to a system of laws governing provision of that service.

C. **Violations of international law**. Like all law, international law is violated from time to time, sometimes with impunity.

1. **The Iran-Iraq war as legal violation**. In the early 1980s, Iraq invaded Iran for the purpose of seizing the waterway lying at their border. This was clearly a violation of international law, both customary and conventional. The United Nations Charter explicitly outlaws the use of force against another state except in self-defense.

2. **Lack of world response to Iraqi aggression**. No attempt was made by the international community to punish the aggression; indeed, many states, including the United States, Western Europe, the Soviet Union, and Japan, went on with business as usual. During the course of the ensuing war, Iraq was believed to have used poison gas extensively against the Iranians, a further serious breach of international law. Even after Iraq used lethal gas on its own nationals, nothing was done to apply sanctions for its transgression against international law.

3. **Reasons for the lack of world response**. The world response to Iraqi aggression illustrates the complexities of international behavior. When it was attacked by Iraq, Iran had recently (1979) undergone a revolution led by fanatical Muslim fundamentalists who were perceived as a threat to their more conservative neighbors, and indeed to the regimes of much of the Muslim world. The vital interests of many states in keeping the world's dominant source of energy (oil) out of the hands of religious zealots (who had recently held dozens of American diplomats hostage) known to hate the West, convinced those states that the defeat of Iran was in their interest.

II. **Enforcement of international law**. One of the essential characteristics of international law is the absence of the equivalent of a domestic police force either to stop legal infractions as they occur or to enforce the decisions of international courts or other bodies such as the UN. This does not mean, however, that no enforcement at all is available to aggrieved parties.

A. **Self-defense**. A state may use whatever force is necessary to protect against the possibility of injury from an illegal act. A foreign military plane that fails to turn back at the border may be forcibly dealt with, if necessary, by shooting it down. A civilian craft may be forced to land, and its pilot punished. The force must be proportionate to the perceived threat.

1. **Aiding other states**. An extension of selfdefense is the right of a state to seek the help of other states in repelling aggression. For example, the U.S. in part justified its 1990 blockade of Iraq upon the Kuwaiti government's request for assis-

tance. The U.S. also relied upon U.N. Security Council resolutions.

2. **Humanitarian intervention.** A related doctrine is humanitarian intervention, the use of force by one state against another to prevent widespread abuse of human rights there. In the early 1970s the Pol Pot regime in Cambodia systematically maltreated millions of its nationals and was responsible for extensive suffering and loss of life. Ultimately, Vietnam invaded Cambodia, with the claimed purpose of preventing further human rights violations. There is disagreement among international legal scholars as to whether humanitarian intervention is ever permissible, particularly in view of the explicit prohibition of armed force in international relations included in the UN Charter.

B. **Retaliation.** A state whose rights are violated by another state may legally make a proportionate response, even one that would be itself illegal if the first illegality had not occurred. If France breaches its extradition treaty obligation to return an escaped convict to the United States, a permissible reaction would be to refuse a similar extradition request from France.

1. **Retaliation not necessarily identical.** Retaliation need not, however, be identical to the violation. The United States might, for example, choose to refuse to permit the landing of French aircraft at U.S. airports pursuant to a treaty under which they otherwise would be entitled to land.

2. **Retaliation against innocents outlawed.** Retaliation may not include acts against innocent civilians in the other state. The United States would not have been entitled to take Iranian citizens hostage in response to the holding of the U.S. diplomats in Tehran. Nor, in the case of the 1991 war with Iraq, could it have tortured and executed Iraqis in response to similar Iraqi actions. Similarly, there is no right to respond to terrorist attacks by deliberately bombing innocent civilians of a state believed to have supported it in some manner. The reason is that innocent civilians have rights (to life, and against torture) independent of, and even **against**, their own state. Those rights are protected by international law against the acts of any state. These considerations do not, of course, prohibit retaliation against those guilty of terrorist or similar acts.

C. **Institutional responses: United Nations procedures.** Enforcement of international law may also occur within the institutions of the UN.

1. **Security Council.** If a breach of international law is thought to constitute a threat to peace, application can be made to the Security Council for United Nations action against the wrongdoer.

2. **Human rights violations.** Human rights violations may be investigated by bodies created by the General Assembly; and efforts may be made to intercede with the offending state. Although this is an advance over the previous total lack of institutionalized response, it is still far from adequate.

D. **Institutional responses: regional pacts.** Such organizations as NATO and the Warsaw Pact are essentially community defense organizations. Each purports to be primarily for the purpose of resisting aggression against one of its members from without.

E. **Institutional responses: specialized organizations.** Examples of responses by specialized institutions include:

1. **General Agreement on Tariffs and Trade (GATT).** The primary purpose of GATT is to regulate trade among its members. It includes special provisions for punishing a member which violates its obligations. For example, if a state was to establish a subsidy for exports from its territory, the organization could permit another state or states to impose countervailing customs duties on goods from that state, which would not have been permissible absent the violation.

2. **International Monetary Fund.** A borrowing state may be foreclosed from further borrowing if it violates its obligations under the lending agreement. For example, in the 1980s Mexico had its right to further borrowing interrupted when it suspended payments on its debts to the Fund.

3. **International court action.** The decisions of the ICJ may be enforced by the UN Security Council, by use of sanctions or any other action that can command the necessary votes. Of course, as in all Security Council activity, no resolution may be passed over the negative vote of a permanent member. Thus, a judgment against the United States could not be the subject of a Security Council resolution if the U.S. chose to veto it.

Enforcement procedures in regional courts, such as the European Court of Justice, depend on the treaties by which they are constituted.

4. **Domestic court action.** The enforcement of international law in the local courts of the various countries of the world is becoming increasingly significant. To the extent that a judgment is a product of international law, that law is enforced as effectively as is the domestic law of the state where the court sits. As an example, the father and sister of a young man who was tortured to death by a torturer paid by the Paraguayan government, sued him for damages in a U.S. court on the grounds that torture is a violation of international human rights law. The U.S. courts held for the plaintiffs. (*Filartiga v. Pena-Irala*, [1980].) As a result, there is one fewer safe haven country for the property of torturers. Further, once such decisions become more common in local courts, international law appears likely to be increasingly effective to control conduct by states and their agents.

CONCLUSION

As the world shrinks, people in one corner of the globe increasingly have important interests in others. Governments naturally feel pressure to create a dependable legal system to protect these interests. Neither domestic law nor raw military and economic power will suffice. Only in cooperation with other states, themselves having a similar stake in establishing a dependable order, joining together in a world community of law and order, will it be possible to satisfy these demands.

The international legal process has begun to meet the need for world order, though the deficiencies of the international legal system (the absence of courts with mandatory jurisdiction and the equivalent of an international police force to enforce their decisions) make it impossible under current conditions for endemic violence around the world to be prevented or terminated. But to participate intelligently in public affairs, citizens need to be aware of the character, limitations, province, and myriad functions of international law. Only then are they able to judge international law itself and the relevant issues, actions, and policies of their own and other societies.

POLITICS AND GOVERNMENT IN THE UNITED STATES

TOPIC 1. FUNDAMENTAL VALUES AND PRINCIPLES

Civic values embody expressions of political ideals considered worthy of achievement by citizens. They identify moral objectives and provide a general standard for judging action and for choosing among alternatives. Civic principles are fundamental doctrines or assumptions of our constitutional system.

The fostering of a reasoned commitment to the values and principles of American constitutional democracy among each generation of citizens lies at the heart of civic education. This commitment requires citizens' (1) understanding of the history of these values and principles and their importance to the preservation and improvement of American democracy, and (2) capacity to intelligently discuss their application to contemporary issues.

A knowledge of the fundamental values and principles of the American system of government provides citizens with a frame of reference useful in analyzing and evaluating the goals and operations of their government. The perspective gained by this knowledge should facilitate citizens' understanding of the importance of these values and principles to the preservation and improvement of a free society. It should also shed light on progress and shortcomings in the implementation of these values and principles and enhance citizens' capacity to propose and promote the implementation of effective remedies for apparent weaknesses.

A. FUNDAMENTAL VALUES

These values are set forth either explicitly or implicitly in the nation's basic documents such as the Declaration of Independence, the Constitution, and the Bill of Rights. These values are described below.

1) THE PUBLIC GOOD

The public interest may be presumed to be what men would choose if they saw clearly, thought rationally, acted disinterestedly, and benevolently.

Walter Lippman (1955)

The concept of the public good assumes that the democratic political community as a whole has a discernible set of values and interests that define a public good affecting all its members in common. These values and interests are usually assumed to be superior to the special interests of particular groups within the political community and are considered essential for the security and general welfare of all individuals and groups within the community. In the United States, the values of the public good have been spelled out in the basic charters of the Declaration of Independence, the U.S. Constitution, the Bill of Rights, and in the succeeding two hundred years of public discussion and debate, legislation, and judicial decision.

In a democratic society, there are major differences of view concerning how the public good should be defined, who the definers should be, and how the values of the public good are to be achieved. This does not mean, however, that there is no core public good upon which reasonable citizens can agree. The security of the nation from destruction and economic collapse; public health; and well-functioning political institutions are examples of the public good to which reasonable citizens give their assent.

In this topic, we define two major visions of the public good which have contested with each other since the beginning of the Republic. They provide the context within which debate has proceeded concerning how the public good may best be achieved.

OBJECTIVES

The citizen should be able to

1. explain the idea of the public good, its importance, and how it might be identified.

2. identify issues in which the public good is involved.

3. analyze situations in which the public good may conflict with other important values and interests, e.g., individual rights.

4. take, defend, and evaluate positions on the proper scope and limits of basic rights when they appear to conflict with the public good.

FRAME OF REFERENCE
Conceptual Perspective

I. **The republican ideal of the public good.** The founders of the American republic drew heavily upon the republican ideal of the public good. Stemming from classical Greco-Roman times, this view is summed up in the term **respublica**: a form of governing whose primary goal was to achieve that which benefited the society as a whole rather than particular groups or individuals.

A. **The "common good."** Sometimes the public good is referred to as the totality of common goods of the political community, which all the members of the community share in common. They transcend the private goods which many people may share in their respective particular groups. The good of the whole community is viewed as greater than the sum of its parts. The public good is common in the sense that it is indivisible and available to all, as in the defense of the nation in time of war.

B. **The "general welfare."** Sometimes the public good is referred to as the general welfare of the people as a whole, including all those goods necessary for their safety, security, health, and basic necessities of well-being.

C. **The "public interest."** The "public interest" is referred to, in Madison's words, as the "permanent and aggregate interests of the community," which elevate the good of the country as a whole above private, self-seeking interests of class, dynasty, race, religion, or ethnicity.

D. **"Public happiness."** Public happiness is a term often used by the Founders to include those benefits to be provided by government through adequate public facilities as well as the sentiments of civic trust and fraternity to be enjoyed by membership in the commonwealth or **civitas**.

E. **Civic virtue.** In the civic republican tradition, civic virtue is the duty of the members of the political community to seek to promote the public or common good as one of the major obligations of citizenship.

F. **Welfare government.** The New Deal and its successors elevated physical and material well-being for all citizens as a prime goal of activist welfare government, nicely summarized by sociologist Robert Bellah and his associates as follows:

1. **National harmony and economic growth.** "This emphasis on governmental intervention in the market leads to Welfare Liberalism's conception of politics. The public good is defined as national harmony achieved through sharing the benefits of economic growth. It is the purpose of activist government to promote economic growth and to guarantee individuals a fair chance to benefit from it."

2. **The moral dimension to economic intervention.** "The intervention in economy and society has moral purposes to provide all citizens with an 'equal opportunity' to engage in economic competition, to prevent economic exploitation, and, since the early 1970s, to conserve environmental resources."

II. **The individual interest model of the public good.** The Founders of the American republic also drew heavily upon a tradition of individualism, stemming from a seventeenth and eighteenth century philosophy that looked upon the public good as the total sum of private interests and benefits.

A. **Individual dignity.** In one sense, the individual interest model is based upon a view of human nature that elevates the inherent dignity and sanctity, even sacredness, of each human person. Each person has a potential of individuality and a uniqueness that deserves to be expressed and developed. Thus, personal fulfillment and happiness are the ultimate goals of the political order and of the public good.

B. **Self-interest.** Another strand of individualist thought stressed the baser characteristics of human nature, arising from innate and inherently selfish passions and fears (see, for example, Machiavelli and Hobbes). These desires for self-preservation and power lead individuals to enter into social contracts, including government, in order to preserve each one's well-being and property (see Locke) and to promote each one's self-interest.

C. **Interest conflicts.** Inevitably, the interests of some individuals will be different from and often in conflict with the interests of other individuals. The function of government is to set the rules whereby the conflict of interests can be resolved in an orderly and fair fashion. The public good emerges from vigorous advocacy by the multiplicity and variety of interest groups.

D. **Limited government and minimal state**. Since all individuals and groups have full entitlement to whatever property they have acquired justly according to the rules, they can dispose of it as they please without interference by the government. Certain inequalities are bound to result, because individuals are inherently unequal in talent, skills, and effort, but the individual, and not someone else, is entitled to what those talents, skills, and efforts produce.

E. **Interest advocacy**. In this view, the public good arises out of the clash of self-interested individuals and groups operating in the political arena, so long as there is open access for vigorous self-advocacy. The role of government in achieving the public good is limited to the enforcement of contracts and protection against any theft, fraud, or force that may interfere with the process of interest advocacy among those individuals and groups who are seeking to fulfill their differing wants and preferences.

F. **Voluntarism**. In general, the public good arises from the assertion of private freedoms, individual rights, the free market mechanism, the minimal state, the free play of voluntary groups, mutual aid associations, and the reinforcement of pluralist groupings of all kinds: "a politics of privacy." The sense of community revolves around the image of a voluntary association of like-minded neighbors who know and respect one another.

G. **Business enterprise**. The demands of a highly industrialized and commercialized society underlined the view that prospering business enterprise, creating jobs through its efficient productivity, was the best guarantor of achieving the public good for all. Often allied with the frank admission that business activism, even greed, was the basis of the public good, was a glorification of the traditional values of family, hard work, and religious belief as the primary sources of individual and civic virtue.

Historical Perspective

I. **Conceptions of the public good that influenced the Founders**. Several traditions and concepts of the public good influenced the American Founders.

A. **Hebraic-Christian tradition**. One tradition may be termed "Hebraic-Christian." It may be broken down into two strands.

1. **The Hebraic tradition**. In the Hebraic tradition, the rules for the common good of the society emanate from God and are handed down to the people through divinely appointed lawgivers such as Moses and his successor kings and prophets.

2. **The Christian tradition**. In the Christian tradition, human rules for proper moral conduct that will serve the good of the whole society are also based on God's word as taught by Jesus of Nazareth and eventually revealed by the Holy Bible and its authoritative interpretation by a divinely-sanctioned clergy. The idea of the common good constantly reappears in Christian political thought of the Middle Ages. Thus, images of the good ruler were drawn from biblical metaphors such as the good shepherd who ensures the welfare of his flock by acting for its common good.

3. **The Reformation**. In the Reformation, Protestant leaders like **Martin Luther** (1483-1546) and **John Calvin** (1509-1564) rejected the claims of the Pope to be the authoritative interpreter of divine will for the good of the people, as well as the papal views of the political roles of church and state in enforcing rules for the public good. They looked to the Bible itself and the individual's faith in it to be the moral guides to the public good, enforceable by the state.

B. **Greco-Roman traditions**. Other traditions of the public good emerge from the ancient world of Greece and Rome.

1. **Greece**. In ancient Greece, the idea of the common good was one of the most basic and pervasive concepts defining the purpose of the state.

   a. **Plato**. The idea that the proper form of political rule is rule for the good of the whole is found throughout the *Republic* and other dialogues of **Plato** (427?-347 B.C.). Through rigorous selection and education, the elite guardian rulers are enabled to contemplate the ultimate and ideal Good and then make wise and just laws for the rest of the people.

   b. **Aristotle**. In his *Politics,* **Aristotle** (384-322 B.C.) defines the legitimacy of all major forms of government according to whether the one, the few, or the many rule for the common good, or whether they degenerate into corrupted forms in which they rule in their own interests.

2. **Rome**. In Rome, **Cicero** (106-43 B.C.) and **Quintilian** (c.35-c.95 A.D.) revived the civic ideals of the "statesman" propounded in Greece by **Isocrates** (436-338 B.C.) some centuries earlier. The highest human good is not only to be realized through the political community, but only when the people are led by wise leaders steeped in an education and experience that prepares them to make judicious practical judgments through reasoned public discussion and discourse.

C. **Early modern views**. A variety of views of the public good can be found among writers of the early modern period in Europe and America.

1. **In Europe**. European views of the public good were divided between traditionalists and the new doctrines of liberalism and, later on, democracy.

   a. **Traditional views**. Prior to the seventeenth century, there was seldom any doubt that the whole society or state should be the primary focus in thinking about the common good. Writers on the subject directed their attention to the perspective and the obligation of rulers. The ruled, with some exceptions, such as those who attained the status of free citizens in certain city-states, had little to do with public affairs. In Britain, traditional Tories and Whigs believed that the duty of society's natural leadership—its governing class—was to act for the common good, exercising paternalistic care over the weak and unfortunate.

   b. **Liberal and democratic views**. With the growth of liberal and later overtly democratic views, the idea of the common good underwent fundamental change.

      (1) **Locke**. John Locke (1632-1704) made much of the "public good" in his *Second Treatise* (1690). In that work, he was concerned both with mapping out its contents—protection of life, liberty, and property—and with the individual's connection to the public good by way of membership in the political community.

      (2) **Rousseau**. Jean-Jacques Rousseau (1712-1778) developed the fullest and most original treatment of the idea of the public good. He wished to show how a political community could best assure that public deliberations would result in the common good. In *The Social Contract* (1762) he urged that the public good is only reached by the "General Will," the will that seeks the benefit of society as a whole rather than that of some lesser part.

   c. **Utilitarianism**. Other intellectual currents treated the idea differently. One of the most influential was the English utilitarian tradition influenced principally by **Thomas Hobbes** (1588-1679) and later **Jeremy Bentham** (1748-1832) and his followers. The focus shifted from the common good as an abstract idea to the common good as the sum of the interests of individuals as components of the whole. These writers deny the existence of a "common good" other than a sum of the good or interests of the individual members of the political order.

2. **American revolutionary period**. The founders of the American republic drew upon this variety of Western views to shape the unique formulations of the public good that have been in dynamic tension ever since. Concern for the public good was apparent in the American Revolution's fundamental charter, the Declaration of Independence.

   a. **The Declaration's main themes**. The Declaration is justly famed for its generalized affirmations of the principles of equality; "unalienable" rights to life, liberty, the pursuit of happiness; and the consent of the governed as the sole legitimate basis for political obligation.

   b. **The Declaration and the "public good"**. It is seldom noticed, however, that the long list of grievances charging the British monarch with tyranny repeatedly recites the king's alleged violations of the colonists' public good as set forth in the laws passed by their legislatures. The very first grievance declares, "He has refused his assent to laws the most wholesome and necessary for the public good."

3. **American constitutional period**. During the period of the writing and ratification of the Constitution, the idea of the public good was never far from view.

   a. **The Preamble to the Constitution**. One of the ultimate purposes of the new federal government framed by the Constitution was to "promote the general welfare." Whether or not this phrase had a purely economic meaning to the Framers, as Mortimer Adler has argued, it has come to signify to successor generations a much broader meaning of the public good.

   b. **The Federalists**. The writers of *The Federalist* (1787-88) never doubted the existence of a common good that was not simply the sum of individual interests.

      (1) **The language of the public good in *The Federalist***. In discussing the aims of government in general and of the new Constitution in particular, the *Federalist* papers are peppered throughout with references to the public good and several variations in terminology on that theme: the common good, the public weal, public voice, public spirit, public service, and the general welfare. These terms are often linked with the public happiness, public safety and security, and justice.

      (2) **The public good as the purpose of the new government**. The whole purpose of forming a truly federal government was to serve a larger public good than the several states could achieve by themselves. The prime evils to be overcome were self-serving factions and special interests.

   c. **Madison in *The Federalist***. **James Madison** (1751-1836) discussed the public good in various numbers of *The Federalist*. Two important instances are the following:

      (1) ***The Federalist* No. 10**. In this famous essay, Madison carefully distinguished between what even a majority in society conceived as their interest and the actual common or public good. Madison does not argue that the common good is the sum of all the small interests in society. Rather, the benefit of a large republic is that the people's elected representatives can "refine and enlarge the public views" and "discern the true interest of their country."

      (2) ***The Federalist* No. 45**. In this essay, referring to the purpose of government, Madison says that "the public Good, the real welfare of the great body of the people, is the supreme object to be pursued;...no form of government whatever has any other value than as it may be fitted for the attainment of this object."

   d. **Hamilton's views**. No less than Madison, **Alexander Hamilton** (1755-1804) stressed that the public good could best be achieved by an enlarged active role for the federal government in regulating and guiding the economy on the basis of deliberate, reasoned, and disinterested discourse among the elected legislators.

II. **The nineteenth century**. With important exceptions, the role of voluntarism in the search for the public good was paramount in the nineteenth century. But by the end of the century, voices for government intervention in various areas of social and economic life were being heard.

   A. **Voluntarism**. In the nineteenth century, voluntarism—individual action or spontaneous association for the accomplishment of some purpose—may be considered at both small- and large-scale levels.

      1. **Small-scale voluntarism**. By the middle of the nineteenth century, it was apparent to key observers like **Alexis de Tocqueville** (1805-1859) that Americans were forming a great variety of voluntary associations to achieve purposes through private efforts rather than through government. The assumption was that the public good could best be achieved by enlightened self-interest, whereby individuals get what they want through their own efforts. Community service was a fully voluntary matter rather than a civic duty, especially as realized most fully in small-scale local communities.

2. **Large-scale voluntarism.** By the end of the nineteenth century, business, financial, and industrial leaders were arguing that the public good was best achieved through private means, especially through corporate enterprise, rather than through government.

B. **The expanding role of government and the national public good.** Especially toward the close of the nineteenth century, demands were heard that the pursuit of the national public good required an expanded role for the federal government. But that role had already been called for in a different context by those seeking the abolition of slavery.

1. **Slavery, states' rights, and the public good.** In the course of the nineteenth century, great national issues surrounding slavery and states' rights elevated issues of the public good to the federal level with the onset and aftermath of the Civil War. As Republican candidate and as president, **Abraham Lincoln** (1809-1865) appealed for strengthening the role of the federal government in order to achieve the overriding purposes of the national public good. He became the foremost spokesman for the civic ideals of "government of the people, by the people, and for the people."

2. **The reaction to laissez-faire capitalism.** After Reconstruction, the voluntary ideals of laissez-faire capitalism and free enterprise gained enormous headway, so much so that counter-demands for a greater role for government regulation arose from two sources: Populists argued for more active grass roots government to promote the welfare "of the people" in local and state communities; and Progressives demanded more active welfare legislation by a strengthened federal government.

3. **Populism and the public good.** Harking back to the Democratic-Republicanism of Jefferson's faith in the independent yeoman, Populism of the late nineteenth century not only expressed faith in the "common man," but viewed government as a prime means to improve the economic welfare as a common good for all. Appeals to moral and religious values often served as powerful bulwarks for this civic faith.

4. **Progressivism and the public good.** Progressives followed the Populists but with a growing realization of the need for the federal government to tackle national and international problems, as illustrated by **Theodore Roosevelt** (1858-1919) for the Republicans and **Woodrow Wilson** (1856-1924) for the Democrats. These problems included demands for better public services for health and education, as well as government regulation of business and industry in the interests of the public good.

5. **Activist or limited government and the public good.** Following the Great Depression and the New Deal of **Franklin D. Roosevelt** (1882-1945), the role reversal of the two major parties in their attitudes toward the role of the federal government in achieving the national public good had been substantially completed. By and large, the Republican party came to stand for conservative, limited government and the Democratic party for liberal, activist government as the preferred roads to achieving and protecting the national public good.

Contemporary Perspective

In the last decade of the twentieth century, American democracy faces a series of fundamental issues regarding the meaning of the public good. How is it to be achieved? Who is to be regarded as its ultimate keeper? How do we take due account of the legitimate role of government and the legitimate interests of particular individuals and groups in a pluralist society? The persistent encompassing question facing the American citizenry: Where does the greater public good lie?

Listed here are some of the glaring issues that cause controversy regarding the meaning of the public good and how it is to be achieved without serious damage to the legitimate interests of particular individuals and groups.

I. **Reordering the U.S. military posture at home versus protecting the national interest abroad.** With the easing of the Cold War between the Western allies, including the United States, and the Soviet Union and the rise of democratic movements throughout much of the Communist world, it was assumed by many that the United States was faced with a reduction, or at least a reexamination of its military posture in the world. Such assumptions were given a rude jolt with the invasion of Kuwait by Iraq in August 1990.

A. **Reordering the U.S. military posture.** During the long negotiations over budget deficits in the 1990s, Congress and the Administration had to decide how large the military budget should be in comparison with the domestic budget. No one denied the importance of a military establishment strong enough to protect U.S. interests at home and abroad (the public good). But the question was how much military power was enough and what kind was necessary? The added expense of deploying huge forces to the Persian Gulf region further complicated the problem of reducing the federal budget deficit.

B. **American military presence overseas.** Negotiations had scarcely begun with the Soviet Union and with America's allies concerning the amount and timing of the withdrawal of American forces from Europe when the Iraqi invasion of Kuwait suddenly added a new dimension to the problem. As hundreds of thousands of American troops were rapidly sent to the Persian Gulf by President Bush, a rising public debate began to focus on what paramount public good was being served—and threatened—by massive American military involvement in the Middle East.

C. **Kinds of weapons needed for the future.** In view of less likely war in Europe and more likely regional conflicts, extremely complicated estimates had to be drawn up regarding such major items as the new B2 bombers and the Strategic Defense Initiative, popularly known as "Star Wars," as compared with more varied and rapid military forces.

D. **Reducing military presence at home.** Debates arose in many parts of the country concerning which military industries and installations should be closed down or reduced, with attendant loss of jobs and of business in the surrounding regions.

   1. **Job retraining for military personnel.** If the armed forces were reduced, the problem of finding appropriate jobs and job training for large numbers of men and women had to be faced, especially for the 96% of enlisted personnel (including a large proportion of minorities) who had no more than a high school education.

   2. **Volunteer military or draft?** The Persian Gulf crisis drew new attention to the high proportion of low income and minority personnel who made up the all-voluntary military force. Questions were raised once again about reinstituting a universal draft to spread the obligation of military service more equitably among the various segments of the American population.

II. **Need for efficient sources of energy versus protection of the environment.** A growing and prosperous modern economy requires abundant sources of energy, but some sources have had serious negative effects on the environment. Wherein lies the greater public good?

A. **Energy Shortages.** In a modern technological world the search for efficient and affordable supplies of energy has led to persistent debates over the relative advantages of the use of irreplaceable fossil fuels (like coal, oil, and natural gas) as compared with nuclear, water, solar, and wind power. The reliance of the industrialized nations of the world on the oil of the Middle East was once again driven home to the people of the world by the Iraq/Kuwait crisis. As the threat of war increased, debates arose concerning the importance of Persian Gulf oil to the U.S. national interest (the public good) as compared with the possibility of thousands of casualties inflicted upon the U.S. military and the Arab civilian populations of Kuwait and Iraq.

B. **Threats to the environment from nuclear power.** For the more than forty years of the Cold War the threat of nuclear war had been clear; but by the 1980s the threats to the environment and thus to the well being of humanity itself from nuclear power came into focus.

   1. **An efficient source of power.** Nuclear power is argued by its proponents to be an efficient and inexhaustible source of power to meet the needs of an industrialized and modern world.

   2. **Threat of nuclear war.** During the Cold War the most threatening problem in the public's mind was the danger of nuclear holocaust in a war between the U.S. and the Soviet Union. The possibility that third world countries like Iraq might develop nuclear weapons and threaten the peace of the world came to the fore in the Persian Gulf crisis of 1990-1991.

   3. **Threat of nuclear accident.** Critics of nuclear energy argue that unsafe nuclear power plants themselves pose a threat to the environment and to the civilian population from the radiation released in nuclear plant accidents, such as those at Three Mile Island in Pennsylvania and at Chernobyl in the Soviet Union. Proponents of nuclear power respond that new generations of nuclear power technologies are safe.

   4. **Waste disposal.** A further factor complicating the nuclear power question is the difficulty of the safe disposal of nuclear waste, since such waste

remains toxic for prolonged periods and its secure storage is problematical.

C. **Threats to the environment from fossil fuels and chemicals.** With the easing of fears of nuclear war, the public became more directly aware that threats to the environment arise from the burning of coal, oil, and gas and from the industrial and agricultural use of chemicals and pesticides.

    1. **Air pollution.** Release of pollutants by millions of automobile exhausts and thousands of factories threaten an alarming rise of cancer and other diseases in industrial and urban areas. An historic clean air bill was enacted by Congress and signed by President Bush on November 15, 1990.

    2. **Water pollution.** Massive chemical wastes threaten the water supplies for human consumption as well as the ocean and river habitats of marine and bird life. Underground water supplies are threatened by billions of tons of waste material in non-toxic garbage dumps and by the hard-to-detect leakage of gasoline and oil from six million underground petroleum storage tanks scattered throughout the U.S.

    3. **Acid rain.** Industrial effluents released in the atmosphere threaten the forests, lakes, and urban areas of territories far beyond their source, often crossing international boundaries.

    4. **Oil spills.** Accidents to oil tankers and oil rigs threaten the ecology of sea and coastal areas in many parts of the world.

    5. **Global warming.** It is widely believed that the burning of fossil fuels already has increased and will continue to raise the earth's temperature and thus threatens potentially destructive changes in the earth's environment. Such predictions raise fundamental questions of how to achieve the public good of humanity as well as of individual nations.

III. **Governmental versus private approaches to domestic social problems.** Some of the most controversial questions about the public good concern whether government action or private agency is the better approach to domestic social issues. These debates reflect a concern that the very fabric of American society is coming unravelled in fundamental ways.

A. **Drugs and crime.** High on the list of worries is the rapid spread of drug use and attendant crime, especially among youth.

    1. **Drugs.** A huge consumption of illegal drugs, and crime surrounding the manufacture, sale, and import of drugs have led to chronic social problems. Statistics in many large cities about the number of premeditated murders, random shootings, and gang killings are appalling.

    2. **Remedies.** Remedies in the name of the public good range from better interdiction of drug traffic, and more convictions and prisons for drug dealers and users, to more preventive education and rehabilitation. Some critics argue for the legalization of drugs, a policy, they say, would relieve pressure on public resources. Opponents say that such policies would effectively abandon the victims of drug addiction and alienate citizens who find such legalization morally wrong.

B. **Abortion and teenage pregnancy.** In the early 1990s one of the most inflammatory and divisive social issues has to do with public policies concerning abortion.

    1. **Arguments against abortion.** Opponents of legal abortion argue that human life begins at conception and that the fetus is a human being entitled to full legal protection to the right to life guaranteed by the Fifth and Fourteenth Amendments. Thus, government should neither finance nor permit abortion for unwanted pregnancies except for strictly limited reasons.

    2. **Arguments for the right to choose abortion.** Supporters of the right to abortion argue that the Fifth and Fourteenth Amendments' guarantees to the right to **liberty** includes a basic constitutional right of privacy. The right to privacy protects what a woman chooses to do with her body and that a fetus, at least in the early stages, cannot be considered a full human being, because it lacks the development inhering in such status.

    3. **Teenage pregnancy.** Especially critical is the legal debate over whether pregnant teenagers have a right to an abortion without the consent of their parents or a court. As the rate of teenage pregnancy mounts, advocates of abortion counselling argue that the public good is not

served by the birth of unwanted children, destined to substandard lives. Opponents argue that public funds should not be used for such counselling without parental consent and that adoption is preferable to abortion.

C. **Child abuse**. Increasing public awareness of widespread child abuse by parents who physically or sexually abuse their own children as well as by other adults who sexually molest children has raised questions about how far the fundamental interest of the state may go to protect the young against their own parents as well as other adults charged with their care.

D. **Health care**. As the cost of medical and hospital care has risen enormously in the 1980s and 1990s, the debate over the role of government in health care has also heightened.

1. **Arguments for more public aid for health care.** Demands for improved health care financed by state and federal sources escalated during the 1980s as the public became aware of the millions of poor as well as middle-class families who were not being cared for adequately in what was viewed as a grossly inequitable system. The increasing political influence of the elderly has helped to increase the demand for some kind of universal health insurance on a national level.

2. **Arguments for limiting public support of health care.** Many began to argue that health care programs like Medicare had become so burdensome on public budgets that the limit had been reached. For example, the Family and Medical Leave Act requiring employers to grant twelve weeks of unpaid leave to employees who needed time off to care for newborn or adopted babies or elderly parents was passed by both houses of Congress in July 1990. But it was vetoed by President Bush as being not flexible enough to meet various needs of employees and as involving excessive government intrusion in employers' affairs.

E. **Education**. Few doubt that an effective education available for all is an essential foundation for achieving the public good in a democracy. But policies for attaining this goal differ markedly.

1. **Constitutional commands to equalize public education.** Federal and state courts have interpreted the Fourteenth Amendment's guarantee of "equal protection of the laws" for all persons to mean that states cannot segregate public schools by race or otherwise discriminate on the basis of sex, color, religion, or national origin. The courts have also ruled that within states, financial resources must be reasonably equalized among all school districts, even if taxes must be increased.

2. **National goals for educational achievement.** The educational reform movements of the 1980s emphasized the need for high quality education as a necessity for the public good. Most visible was the "education summit" held in 1989 by President Bush and all fifty state governors to try to agree on a set of national goals that should frame the guidelines for all American public education during the 1990s, principally to enable the United States to compete in world markets. Public debate has been complicated by controversies over how such goals should be achieved, monitored, and paid for in a time of huge deficits and economic recession.

3. **Promotion of parental choice.** One particularly controversial proposal is to make public funds available for use by parents to send their children to private or religious schools as they wished. In some places, experiments were begun to allow parents to choose among schools through the use of vouchers or tax credits, on the theory that competition for students would require schools to become more effective. Critics contend that such a system would undercut the ideal of public education and institutionalize unequal education for rich and poor.

IV. **Governmental versus private approaches to domestic economic problems.** Among the most important debates before the nation in the search for the public good are choices between government and private action in dealing with the economy.

A. **Poverty and human deprivation**. Despite widespread feelings of well-being among many Americans in the 1980s, the evidence grew that the economic deprivation of millions of poverty-stricken people would not resolve itself and was even getting worse. The plight of the urban poor, especially of minority blacks and Hispanics, the growing visibility of chronic homelessness, and the labeling of a "permanent underclass" finally etched themselves on the consciousness of government and philanthropy alike. Especially poignant was the recognition that the majority of the poor were children and that the gap between the rich and the poor was growing larger.

B. **The federal deficit.** A major threat to the national weal is the continued existence of large federal budget deficits.

1. **Cutting spending.** Advocates of private economic priorities urge cutting taxes, especially capital gains taxes, reducing government expenditures, and lowering interest rates to encourage investment and economic growth.

2. **Raising taxes equitably.** Advocates of governmental priorities in the economy argue that the decay of the social infrastructure like education, health care, and transportation facilities require greater support from government, including fair tax reforms.

3. **Budget compromise.** During 1990 the congressional leadership and the president began to grapple seriously with the huge and growing federal government deficit. In a budget which consisted of about one-half entitlements (like social security, medicare, pensions), one-fourth military, and one-fourth discretionary (almost everything else), there was little inclination on the part of politicians to cut entitlements or raise taxes. When they did arrive at budget compromises, firestorms of protest arose within both political parties during the elections of 1990.

4. **Further drains on the federal budget.** All was made more harrowing by the unfolding of the dimensions of the savings and loan bailouts and the cost of the Persian Gulf crisis.

C. **Trade gaps and balance of payments.** Another threat to the public good is the existence of chronic and large trade deficits that transfer wealth abroad. Among other undesirable consequences is that these deficits mortgage the nation's economic independence by placing many billions of dollars in the hands of foreigners.

D. **International competitiveness.** In addition to persistent worries about the unfavorable trade position of the United States and its growing debtor status, the easing of the cold war raised disturbing questions about how the United States should deal economically with rival nations. Was the public good to be served by increasing exports of agricultural products to the Soviet Union and thus help its movement toward a market economy? Should the rulers of China be rewarded with most-favored-nation status before they reformed China's human rights policies? Should economic sanctions against the white South African government be removed before political rights are achieved by the African majority? Should vast military expenditures be continued for the defense of nations who now compete successfully with the United States (Japan, Germany, and South Korea)?

V. **Racial and ethnic nationalisms versus political cohesion.** The choice that individuals must make is whether their primary loyalty is to the political community as a whole or to a lesser part, such as racial, ethnic, or religious groups. This choice is a continuing one, both in the world at large and in the United States.

A. **Release of nationalisms outside the United States.** With the loosening of authoritarian controls in recent decades, ethnic and religious nationalisms have reappeared with stunning force in Eastern and Central Europe, the Soviet Union, the Indian subcontinent, the Middle East, and in many parts of Africa. Often exploding with sudden violence and savage assaults, the search for political identity along historic linguistic, religious, and cultural lines reasserted itself in new movements for independence.

B. **Growth of European Community idea.** A force opposed to national or ethnic particularism is the increasing strength in Europe of a trans-national economic and political unity linking states and peoples that had in many instances been historically opposed to one other. It is paradoxical that the growing success of the European Community (EC) has taken place at the very moment when elsewhere in Europe and the world, political entities are being fragmented. The reason may be that the EC is evolving voluntarily, while peoples striving for independence have been kept from autonomy by force—without their consent.

C. **Rise of racist and religious assaults inside the United States.** "Hate crimes," including anti-Semitic, anti-black, anti-white, and anti-Hispanic incidents, have been widely noted. Of special concern has been the rise of such assaults on the nation's college campuses, sometimes at the most prestigious institutions of higher learning. Lesser versions of outright assault are racist and ethnic slurs and personal "fighting words" and disparagement. When the rights of free expression confront the rights of individual dignity and group equality, the very idea of a university as a guardian of civility as well as learning is severely tested.

VI. **Freedom of expression.** Freedom of expression is another vital concern of the public good in a democratic society. Problems have arisen involving freedom of artistic, political, and religious expression.

A. **Federal support for the arts: freedom of artistic expression versus community moral standards.** A further question of the public good is whether the federal government's support of the arts should be limited by a particular community's standards regarding what is immoral or obscene.

1. **The decay of community standards.** In some quarters there is a sense that public standards of art and morality have been eroded, as the limits on what can be said or portrayed in the public media have steadily eroded. Of special concern were the debates over federal funding by the National Endowment for the Arts of paintings and photography deemed by outspoken political and religious leaders to be obscene or pornographic and thus not worthy of federal support. Some went so far as to say that the public good would best be served if the federal government should cease supporting the arts altogether.

2. **The rights of free expression.** Others decry what seem to them to be attempts to institutionalize philistinism and the establishment by law of the tastes of the culturally insensitive and ignorant. They maintain that America's public life is enriched by the free exercise of artistic expression, encouraged and supported by the federal government without official control such as that which had stifled the public cultural life of Communist and other authoritarian countries.

B. **Freedom of political expression: flag burning and patriotism.** Symptomatic of contemporary disputes over the constitutional principles of freedom of speech were the heated controversies involving the appropriate treatment of the American flag. A key question of the public good was at stake when outrage over flag burning in 1989 led to calls for a constitutional amendment to outlaw desecration of the flag. These calls were heard after the Supreme Court struck down state laws that punished flag burning as a crime. The Court ruled that flag-burning intended as a form of symbolic political expression is protected by the First Amendment. The upshot in June 1990 was that a two-thirds majority of the Congress consisting of conservatives and liberals alike agreed that protecting the integrity of the First Amendment and the Bill of Rights was a greater public good than protecting individual flags against destruction.

C. **Freedom of religious expression.** Controversies over the extent to which freedom for unlimited religious expression and actions motivated by religious belief were consonant with the public good continued to fuel debate on political and educational policies. (See the sections on Religion and Public Life; and on the Separation of Church and State.)

VII. **Securing Civil Rights and Liberties in a Pluralist Society.** The 1950s and 1960s saw great strides in removing the legal barriers to equal civil rights for racial minorities, especially African Americans. In the 1990s, arguments over justice, freedom, and equality as ingredients of the public good lie at the heart of controversial issues of civil rights.

A. **Affirmative action versus reverse discrimination in employment, promotion, and tenure.** A host of controversies surrounds the advocacy of affirmative action to secure racial and gender equality throughout American society.

1. **Affirmative action as justice.** Advocates justify preferential policies on the grounds that they compensate for past injustices and promote socially desirable equality of opportunity and condition. Civil rights advocates argue that the public good and the principles of justice are best served by laws and regulations that prohibit employment practices that discriminate against persons on the basis of race, gender, ethnic origin, or religion.

2. **Affirmative action as quotas.** Critics of affirmative action policies argue that employment practices that discriminate on the basis of race, gender, ethnic origin, or religion are contrary to justice and the public good. They argue that such preferential policies amount to "reverse discrimination" punishing the innocent in favor of those groups historically discriminated against. The result, they claim, is to classify whites and males as legally sanctioned second-class citizens who are in turn denied the equal protection of the laws. (See also, Diversity, Contemporary Perspective.)

B. **Voluntary school desegregation versus court-ordered desegregation.** A further question of justice and the public good concerns desegregation of public schools. Voluntary desegregation has not produced racially balanced schools in some states and districts after decades of effort. On the other hand, opposition among whites to court-ordered busing as a solution seems unrelenting and has led to a massive white exodus from public schools, placing the very institution of public education in jeopardy.

VIII. **Threats to U.S. political health.** As the struggles for democracy broke out in many countries of the world in the late twentieth century, an increasing number of observers began to worry about the growing signs of ailment in the American polity itself, so often looked to as a model by embryonic democracies abroad.

A. **Voter apathy and frustration.** Numerous studies of electoral behavior underlined the fact that fewer and fewer eligible Americans took the trouble to register and still fewer took the trouble actually to vote at election time.

   1. **Low turnout.** American voter turnout is generally the lowest in the Western world. In the 1990 national elections only 36% of eligible voters voted; and presidential elections do not draw much more than 50%. Widespread frustration and anger among the electorate about the perceived inadequate performance of members of Congress and state legislators over deficits and taxes was a counterpoint to the apathy that kept citizens from the polls in 1990.

   2. **Ignorance of issues.** Similar studies reported how little many voters understood about the basic issues confronting them. Blame was levelled at the press, television, and education as well as the electorate's preoccupation with making a living and being entertained instead of seeking hard information about public issues.

   3. **Excessive complexity.** In some states, the trend to making major political decisions by referring them directly to the electorate through complex initiatives and referendums rather than through legislative deliberation may lead some citizens to recoil from voting altogether.

      a. **Arguments in favor of the initiative.** Proponents of the initiative argue that this is a democratic procedure desirable in itself or made necessary by bumbling and self-serving legislators.

      b. **Arguments against the initiative.** Critics argue that the voters are being asked to

decide measures whose complexity is beyond their competence to understand and are being hoodwinked by special interest groups seeking to bypass the representative legislative process.

B. **The special case of youth indifference to politics and government.** Of special concern are the repeated studies that have revealed the lack of interest in politics and government among young people of school and college age. Gross political indifference among youth bodes ill for the future of the public good of liberal democracy.

   1. **Disconnection from politics.** One study reported that the predominant mood of youth aged 15 to 25 was one of disconnectedness between politics, government, and their own personal lives and interests. Their major goals in life dealt with getting a job, being part of a close-knit family, having a good time, and making money. Such goals far outdistanced being involved in community affairs or voting as a responsibility of citizenship.

   2. **Lowest voting rate.** Of all age groups, young people are the least likely to vote; and they firmly reject the idea of compulsory national service by a three-to-one margin. One study by the Times Mirror Center for the People and the Press summed up the attitudes of 18 to 29-year-olds as a generation that "knows less, cares less, votes less and is less critical of its leaders and institutions than young people in the past."

   3. **The good news: community service activism.** In contrast, many organizations reported an increasing activism among school and college youth in community service and civic participation; but there was general agreement that civic education must become much more effective if a sense of the public good is to be generated to combat the general prevalence of apathy and alienation. Critics cautioned against counting civic participation required by schools as evidence of community voluntarism.

C. **Degradation of campaign tactics.** Some observers point to campaign tactics as another element in the deterioration of political attitudes in the 1980s and 1990s.

   1. **Negative advertising.** The use of sleazy and *ad hominem* attacks on political rivals and smear

techniques in newspapers and, especially, in thirty-second television advertisements have alienated the thinking voter and appealed to the lowest motivations of the unthinking voter.

2. **Financing by special interests**. A special problem is the growing dependence of candidates, especially of incumbents, on money raised through political action committees (PACS) funded by special interests.

D. **Decline of ethics in public life**. The evident power of large campaign funds and lobbying of special interest groups and PACs has left many citizens with feelings of helplessness, cynicism, and a growing lack of trust in the word and actions of their political leaders.

1. **Infractions by appointed government officials.** In the 1980s, the Iran-contra scandal led to the trial and conviction of several appointed officials in the Reagan administrations. Subsequently, scandals involving kick-backs and pay-offs by officials in the Department of Defense and the Department of Housing and Urban Development were uncovered.

2. **Infractions by elected government officials.** Charges of the violations of Congressional ethics among senators and representatives of both political parties widened the circle of blame and outrage directed at elected officials during both the Reagan and Bush administrations. These changes ranged from revelation of moral and sexual offenses to involvement in the financial dealings of the savings and loan scandals.

E. **Failure of ethics in the private sector**. Far outdoing the financial peccadillos of the politicians were the misdeeds of some giants of the business world.

1. **Financial manipulators**. Illegal stock transactions and corrupt practices in manipulating markets and corporate finance were two areas in which well-known business leaders were tried, found guilty, and jailed in an intense public spotlight.

2. **Linkage of politicians and private scandals.** When unethical business practices came at the expense of the public treasury to the possible extent of $500 billion, and when political leaders were linked with business leaders in the savings and loan bailouts, the public finally began to realize that "the full faith and credit of the U.S. Government" really means that **they** as individual

taxpaying citizens **are** the government. The connection between the public good and the individual's good, at least in this instance, became plain for all who would see.

2.) INDIVIDUAL RIGHTS

We hold these Truths to be self-evident, that all Men are...endowed by their creator with certain unalienable Rights....To deal intelligently with issues regarding individual rights and to protect these rights from encroachment, the citizen should be aware of the basic individual rights of Americans, their evolution, their functions, and how they are embodied in basic documents and court decisions.

OBJECTIVES

The citizen should be able to

1. explain the history of individual rights.

2. explain the importance of individual rights in a free society, e.g., political freedom.

3. analyze and evaluate situations in which individual rights conflict with each other or with other important values and interests, e.g., fair trial v. free press.

4. take, defend, and evaluate positions on the proper scope and limits of these rights in specific situation, e.g., freedom of the press and the libel of an individual.

FRAME OF REFERENCE
Conceptual Perspective

Fundamental to American constitutional democracy is the belief that individuals have certain basic rights that are not created by government but which government should protect. These are the rights of life, liberty, property, and the "pursuit of happiness." It is the purpose of government to protect these rights, and it may not place unfair or unreasonable restraints on their exercise. These rights are explained below.

I. **Life.** With few narrowly defined exceptions, the individual's right to life is considered inviolable. The state may not act as if it owned and disposed of the lives of its members, nor may private persons, except in certain cases of self defense, jeopardize another's life. Only in extreme circumstances, such as when certain criminal acts are being committed or in capital punishment may the state be justified in using deadly force. Citizens may be obligated to risk their lives in military service, but this is not an obligation to die.

II. **Liberty.** In the American political tradition, the right to liberty is considered an unalterable aspect of the human condition. Central to this idea of liberty is the understanding that the political or personal obligations of parents or ancestors cannot be legitimately forced on people; the obligation by adults to live under a political system or to obey the authority of private persons, such as in the course of employment, is derived from individual consent, not from force or inheritance. Such obligations remain in force only so long as that consent continues.

    A. **Personal freedom.** "The right of the people to be secure in their persons, homes, papers, and effects against unreasonable searches and seizures, shall not be violated...." Central to the notion of personal freedom is the idea of privacy, i.e., that there is a private realm in which the individual is free to act, to think, and to believe and which government cannot legitimately invade. This realm includes, for example, the individual's rights to freedom of religious conscience and belief, to freedom of association and expression, and the right to be let alone.

    B. **Political freedom.** "Congress shall make no law...abridging the freedom of speech, or of the press; or the right of the people peaceably to assemble, and to petition the Government for a redress of grievances." Central to the notion of political freedom is the idea that the people of a nation have the right to participate freely in the political process. This process requires the free flow of information and ideas, open debate, and the right of assembly. Elections occur at stated, agreed-upon intervals; political candidates and their supporters may not be subject to arbitrary arrest, harassment, or intimidation; and electoral corruption—such as buying votes, intimidation, and obstruction of voters—and fraud, plays no significant role.

    C. **Economic freedom.** "No person shall be...deprived...of property, without due process of law; nor shall private property to be taken for public use, without due compensation." Central to the notion of economic freedom is the right to acquire, use, transfer, and dispose of private property without unreasonable governmental interference. In addition, economic freedom includes the right, for example, to seek employment wherever one pleases; to change employment at will; and to

engage in any lawful economic activity either by oneself or in combination with others in units such as labor unions or business corporations.

III. **The pursuit of happiness.** The "pursuit of happiness"is derived from the idea of freedom in a liberal democracy. It includes the idea that while no government can guarantee the happiness of citizens, it is the right of citizens in American democracy to attempt to attain—to "pursue"—happiness in their own way, so long as they do not infringe upon rights of others. The idea of "the pursuit of happiness" supposes a fundamental human longing to seek fulfillment and establishes the right of individuals to conduct that search without unwarranted political interference.

For the Historical and Contemporary Perspectives see under Individual Rights in the Role of the Citizen.

3) JUSTICE

We the people of the United States, in order to...establish justice,...do ordain and establish this Constitution for the United States of America.

           United States Constitution (1787)

The responsibility of citizens and the government to promote justice requires of the citizen an understanding of the concept, its history, the ability to identify issues in which justice is at stake, and the ability to take informed positions on issues of justice when it conflicts with other important values and interests.

OBJECTIVES

The citizen should be able to

1. explain the concept of justice and the differences between distributive, corrective, and procedural justice.

2. explain the utility of the idea of justice in evaluating public policy.

3. identify issues in which justice is involved, e.g., the distribution of the tax burden.

4. analyze and evaluate situations in which justice may conflict with other important values and interests, e.g., procedural justice and public safety.

5. take, defend, and evaluate positions when different forms of justice conflict among themselves or with other important values and interests, e.g., failure to compensate victims.

6. evaluate positions and proposed policies to determine the degree to which they promote justice as opposed to other interests.

FRAME OF REFERENCE
Conceptual Perspective

Justice, another basic value of the American system, is embodied in the Declaration of Independence and the Constitution. Justice, as used here, is essentially synonymous with the idea of fairness. Three types of justice are generally recognized.

I. **Distributive justice.** Central to the concept of distributive justice is the idea that the distribution of benefits and burdens in society should be fair. These distributions should be determined by agreed-upon standards such as the application of the principle of equality or similarity according to need, capacity, and desert. This principle requires that in a particular situation, people who are the same, or similar, in certain important ways (such as need, capacity, or desert) should be treated the same or equally.

II. **Corrective justice.** Central to the concept of corrective justice is the idea that fair and proper responses should be used to correct wrongs and injuries. Fair and proper responses may, under certain circumstances, (1) correct a wrong or injury but not deter or prevent others, (2) fail to correct a wrong or injury but deter or prevent others, or (3) promote a number of values and interests such as corrective justice, deterrence, prevention, rectification, forgiveness, charity, etc.

III. **Procedural justice.** Central to the concept of procedural justice is the idea that procedures used for gathering information and making decisions should be fair. Procedures of due process in the legal system as well as in other governmental institutions should be guided by such principles as impartiality and openness of proceedings. Standards of procedural justice may also be applied in the private sector.

For the Historical and Contemporary Perspectives see Justice under Civic Virtue.

4) EQUALITY

We hold these truths to be self-evident, that all men are created equal....

Declaration of Independence (1776)

...nor shall any State...deny to any person...the equal protection of the laws.

Fourteenth Amendment (1868)

OBJECTIVES

The citizens should be able to

1. explain the concept of equality and its various forms such as political, legal, and social equality.

2. explain the utility of the idea of equality in evaluating public policy.

3. explain issues in which equality is involved, e.g., inequalities in political power and influence and effects on the political system of American democracy.

4. analyze and evaluate situations in which equality may conflict with other important values and interests, e.g., equality of opportunity in employment and freedom to hire at will.

5. take, defend, and evaluate positions on conflicts between equality and other important values and interests, e.g., equality of condition and distributive justice.

6. evaluate positions and proposed policies to determine the degree to which they promote equality as opposed to other interests.

FRAME OF REFERENCE
Conceptual Perspective

Both the Declaration of Independence and the Constitution contain prominent statements of the value placed upon equality in the American system of government. Directly related to the concept of distributive justice, three notions of equality are of particular interest.

I. **Political equality.** Central to this concept is the idea that all people who attain the status of adulthood have equal political rights. For example, each adult citizen is to have an equal right to vote and to run for and hold political office. No one is to be denied this right except under certain narrowly-defined circumstances, such as when one is convicted of a felony.

II. **Legal equality.** Central to this concept is the idea that government should treat all people as equals, without favoritism toward any individual or group. This ideal is contained in various provisions of the Constitution, such as the clause of the Fourteenth Amendment which guarantees equal protection of the laws.

III. **Social equality.** Central to this concept is the idea that there should be no classes sanctioned by law, e.g., no nobility in which individuals, by virtue of their membership, have certain privileges and duties that others do not have.

IV. **Economic equality.** Some have argued that economic equality is foundation for and *sine qua non* of political and legal equality, and that without it they will be unrealized ideals.

For the sections on Historical and Contemporary Perspectives see Equality under Civic Virtue.

5) DIVERSITY

Congress shall make no law respecting an establishment of religion, or prohibiting the free exercise thereof....

First Amendment (1791)

One of the marked characteristics of American society is its diversity. America is a nation of great differences, e.g., social, ethnic, religious, racial, economic, and political. Americans have celebrated this diversity and placed a high value upon it. However, diversity is not without its costs. There is the question, for example, of how much diversity a nation can tolerate without losing its cohesion and identity. This is an issue that concerns every citizen. American citizens should understand the value of diversity as well as be able to deal responsibly with the issues it raises.

OBJECTIVES

The citizen should be able to

1. explain the concept of diversity, its value, and the different forms it takes in American society.

2. identify issues in which diversity is involved, e.g., bilingual education.

3. analyze and evaluate situations in which diversity may conflict with other important values and interests, e.g., the need for a common language.

4. take and defend positions when diversity conflicts with other important values and interests, e.g., reaching consensus on the common welfare.

5. evaluate positions and proposed policies to determine the degree to which they promote diversity as opposed to other interests.

6. explain the utility of the idea of diversity in evaluating public policy.

FRAME OF REFERENCE
Conceptual Perspective

The initial phrase from the First Amendment to the Bill of Rights stated above is one of the most prominent manifestations of the value placed on the right of the individual to differ in beliefs and lifestyles. Central to this concept of diversity is the idea that variance in cultural and ethnic background, race, lifestyle, and belief is not only permissible but desirable and beneficial in a pluralistic society. Although there may be problems caused by diversity, benefits include social and individual enrichment through the interaction of varying ideas, perceptions, and practices; enhanced personal freedom and enlarged perspective through acquaintance with a range of choice of beliefs and practices; and the prevention of the domination of the interests of a single group.

For the Historical and Contemporary Perspectives see Diversity under Civic Virtue.

6) TRUTH

"I swear (or affirm) to tell the truth, the whole truth, and nothing but the truth."

Court oath

Questions of truth are a fundamental and enduring aspect of political life; truth has long been held as a fundamental value of American democracy. And yet issues of truthfulness and the conflict between truth and other important values are perennial in the political world. The evaluation of competing resolutions of these issues requires of the citizen an informed judgment.

OBJECTIVES

The citizen should be able to

1. explain the concept of truth and the value placed upon it in American democracy.

2. explain issues in which truth is involved, e.g., disclosure of official malfeasance or incompetence, of sources of financial support, or of public policy or action.

3. analyze situations in which truth may conflict with other important values and interests, e.g., national security or public order.

4. take, defend, and evaluate positions when truth conflicts with other important values and interests, e.g., the effective conduct of foreign policy.

5. evaluate the consequences of the widespread and chronic public disregard for truth.

6. explain the utility of the idea of truth in evaluating public policy.

FRAME OF REFERENCE
Conceptual Perspective

Two general issues may be thought to concern truth as a value in American democracy; truth as opposed to falsehood, and truth as opposed to secrecy. Truth as a value in the first sense declares lying by public officials to be an offense against the body politic; in the second sense truth demands disclosure and affirmation of matters that governments often wish held in secret in the name of some necessity of state, usually national security.

In neither of these cases, however, can citizens expect complete truth-telling by government, since legitimate interests of state may be fatally compromised by admission and disclosure. Yet citizens can just as legitimately demand that truth-telling as refraining from lying not be disregarded cavalierly, since trust in the veracity of government constitutes an essential element of the bond between governors and governed. Citizens have also found the public disclosure of unpalatable truths to be an important political

value in its own right as public atonement for crimes committed in their name or as a palliative for an atmosphere of deceit.

For the Historical and Contemporary Perspective see Truth under Civic Virtue.

7) PATRIOTISM

Breathes there the man, with soul so dead,
Who never to himself hath said,
This is my own, my native land!

Sir Walter Scott (1805)

Patriotism is a value of the American political system which is often confused with certain forms of nationalism, e.g., jingoism. A clear understanding of the meaning of patriotism provides citizens with a basis for understanding the nature and limits of loyalty to the nation and the difference between dissent and disloyalty.

OBJECTIVES

The citizen should be able to

1. explain the concept of patriotism and the value placed upon it in American democracy.

2. distinguish between patriotism and destructive nationalism.

3. analyze situations in which patriotism may involve a conflict between competing values and interests, e.g., conflict between religious and moral ideas and the national interest.

4. take, defend, and evaluate positions when patriotism conflicts with other important values and interests, e.g., loyalty to friends and family.

FRAME OF REFERENCE
Conceptual Perspective

Patriotism is the devotion to one's country, including the fundamental values and principles upon which is depends. In this sense, patriotism serves as an essential unifying force within the considerable diversity of American society and facilitates the perpetuation of its democratic institutions. Patriotic citizens willingly undertake actions intended to enhance the common good. They act, within the bounds of conscience, to protect the country in time of national danger.

Patriotism is entirely compatible with criticism of and opposition to the policies of any government of the day, including during time of war. This is the idea of a "loyal opposition." There is a need in democracy for responsible critics.

for the Historical and Contemporary Perspectives see Patriotism under Civic Virtue.

B. FUNDAMENTAL PRINCIPLES

The citizen should understand the most basic principles of American constitutional democracy and be familiar with the conceptual tools useful in dealing with issues regarding their application to specific situations.

1) POPULAR SOVEREIGNTY

We hold these truths to be self-evident, that...Governments are instituted among Men, deriving their just powers from the consent of the governed, that whenever any form of government becomes destructive of these ends, it is the Right of the People to alter or abolish it....

Declaration of Independence (1776)

We the People of the United States...do ordain and establish this Constitution for the United States of America.

United States Constitution (1787)

OBJECTIVES

The citizen should be able to

1. explain the concept of popular sovereignty and alternative concepts of sovereignty.

2. explain the ways in which popular sovereignty operates in the American political system.

3. identify political systems in which popular sovereignty does not operate and explain what difference this makes in their operation.

4. take, defend, and evaluate positions on issues in American politics that involve the principles of popular sovereignty, e.g., initiatives, referendums, judicial review.

FRAME OF REFERENCE
Conceptual Perspective

Both the Declaration of Independence and the Preamble to the Constitution clearly establish the principle of popular sovereignty as fundamental to American constitutional democracy—the idea that the only legitimate source of government authority is the consent of the governed. The citizenry as a whole is the sovereign of the state and holds the ultimate authority over public officials and their policies. Consent is given by the people through their regularly-elected representatives and through approval of all constitutional changes. Popular sovereignty also means that the people have the right to withdraw their consent when the government fails to fulfill its obligations to them under the Constitution. Popular sovereignty in American democracy assumes the principle of majority rule, which means that within constitutional limits majorities should have the right to make political decisions. Such decisions are made within the framework of regular elections and include the choice of who should be elected to public office and what laws should be passed by legislative bodies.

For the Historical and Contemporary Perspectives see Liberal Democracy under The Nature of the State.

2) CONSTITUTIONAL GOVERNMENT

The government of the United States is "a government limited...by the authority of a paramount Constitution."

James Madison 1788

The Constitution of the United States is law
for rulers and people, equally in war and in peace, and covers with the shield of its protection all classes of men, at all times, and under all circumstances. No doctrine, involving more pernicious consequences, was ever invented by the wit of man than that any of its provisions can be suspended during any of the great exigencies of government.

Ex Parte Milligan (1866)

OBJECTIVES

The citizen should be able to

1. explain the essential characteristics of American constitutional government, their history, and evolution: the principles of the rule of law, separation of

powers, checks and balances, minority rights, judicial review, civilian control of the military, the separation of church and state, and the power of the purse in the hands of the legislative representatives of the people.

2. explain the ways in which the above principles operate in the American political system.

3. identify, take, and defend positions on issues related to governmental adherence to each of these principles.

FRAME OF REFERENCE
Conceptual Perspective

Central to the American principle of constitutional government is the idea that in order to protect the basic rights of the people, government should be limited both in its scope and in its methods. By consenting to the Constitution, the sovereign people agrees not only to limit the powers of their government but their own powers as well. The principle of constitutional government typically includes the following related principles.

I. **The rule of law.** The principle of the rule of law means that both government and the governed are subject to the law. Government decisions and actions shall be made according to established laws rather than by arbitrary action or decree.

II. **Separation of powers.** An essential part of the American constitutional tradition is the idea that legislative, executive, and judicial powers should be exercised by different institutions and that government should be federal, with power distributed between the central government, the states, and the people.

III. **Checks and balances.** The powers given to the different branches of government are balanced so that no branch can completely dominate the others. Many of the powers of one branch are shared and checked by those of the other branches.

IV. **Minority rights.** The idea of minority rights means that decisions made by in accordance with the principle of majority rule should not unreasonably and unfairly infringe upon the rights of minorities. Constitutionally-guaranteed rights should be placed out of the reach of legislative majorities.

V. **Civilian control of the military.** The principle of civilian control of the military is implied in the constitutional provisions that the president is the commander-in-chief of the armed forces and that Congress has the power to declare war.

VI. **Separation of church and state.** The principle of the separation of church and state is embodied in the First Amendment of the Constitution, "Congress shall make no law respecting an establishment of religion, or prohibiting the free exercise thereof," and in subsequent court decisions.

VII. **Power of the purse.** This principle states that all federal laws for raising revenue must originate in the legislative house closest to the people (the House of Representatives) and be approved by the Congress as a whole.

VIII. **Federalism.** According to this principle, the sovereign people establish political unity while preserving diversity by delegating certain enumerated powers to a general ("federal") government and certain powers to constituent governments (the states), reserving other powers to themselves. Federalism is therefore an aspect of limited government.

For the Historical and Contemporary Perspectives of items not discussed below see Liberal Democracy under the Nature of the State.

2) a. SEPARATION OF POWERS AND CHECKS AND BALANCES

[T]he great security against a gradual concentration of the several powers in the same department consists in giving to those who administer each department the necessary constitutional means and the personal motives to resist encroachments of the others....Ambition must be made to counteract ambition. The interest of the man must be connected to the constitutional right of the place.

James Madison 1787

The separation of powers is perhaps the salient characteristic of American national government. The Framers of the Constitution saw the chief threat to liberty to be the concentration of powers in the hands of one person or body and therefore set out to parcel out the powers of government among its three branches. But they did not separate this power completely. On the contrary, ensuring that ambition "be made to counteract ambition" meant **sharing** certain powers. Thus the executive was given certain sanctions in dealing with the legislature and vice versa. Not even the judicial branch, whose independence, the Framers believed, must be ensured, was completely separated: courts were to be established by Congress; and Supreme Court justices were to be appointed by the president and approved by the upper house of the legislature.

Yet, effective as the separation of powers has been in the preservation of American liberty, the doctrine has turned out to be a double edged sword. For if no branch has all the power in its hands, government as a whole may find itself incapable of action if its parts are warring together. In the frequent deadlock of Congress and the president, the wheels of government may work only by fits and starts or may come to a halt altogether.

OBJECTIVES

The citizen should be able to

1. explain why the Framers thought the separation of powers and checks and balances were essential components of constitutional government.

2. describe the three branches of government, what they do, and the relationships among them.

3. describe key historical changes in the relationships among the three branches of government.

4. take, defend, and evaluate positions on issues regarding the separation of powers and checks and balances, e.g., the role of Congress in making foreign policy, the proposal for a line item veto, and congressional oversight of administrative agencies.

FRAME OF REFERENCE
Conceptual Perspective

Separation of powers and checks and balances are organizational means of limiting the powers of a constitutional government and preventing their abuse or misuse.

I. **Separation of powers.** The principle of the separation of powers divides the powers of government into several functions and places principal responsibility for carrying out each function in a separate part or "branch" of government.

   A. **Legislative function.** One of the principal functions of all governments is to make laws. Article I of the Constitution places this authority in a Congress, consisting of a Senate and a House of Representatives.

   B. **Executive function.** A second principal function of government is the carrying out and enforcement of laws. Article II of the Constitution places this authority in the executive branch of the federal government.

   C. **Judicial function.** The third principal function of government is the management of conflicts over the interpretation and application of the laws in specific situations. Article III of the Constitution places this authority in the judicial system.

II. **Checks and balances.** The principle of checks and balances limits the separation of powers by giving partial responsibility for certain functions to more than one branch. Thus, checks and balances eliminate or at least compromise the complete autonomy of any branch.

   A. **Legislative branch.** The Constitution gives the legislative branch certain powers which make it possible to check the exercise of power by the executive and judicial branches. Examples are ratification of treaties; the confirmation of executive and judicial appointments; impeachment; and control of the budget.

   B. **Executive branch.** The Constitution gives the executive branch certain powers which make it possible to check the exercise of power by the legislative and judicial branches. Examples are the presidential veto power; the president's power to make judicial appointments; and the president's power as military commander-in-chief.

   C. **Judicial branch.** The Constitution gives the judicial branch certain powers which make it possible to check the exercise of power by the legislative and executive branches. Thus, federal courts review the constitutionality of laws passed by Congress and acts of the executive.

Historical Perspective

The principle of separation of powers is firmly embodied in the Constitution through Articles I, II, and III that establish and set forth the structure, responsibilities, and powers of three coordinate and independent branches of government: the legislative, executive, and judicial. So highly regarded was this constitutional principle at the time of founding that it is extremely doubtful that the Constitution would have been ratified without its incorporation. Indeed, many Anti-Federalist (or opponents of ratification) argued that the

Constitution did not go far enough in providing for separation between the branches.

I. **Ancient Origins.** The origins of the doctrine of separation of powers can be traced back as far as Aristotle in ancient Greece and Polybius in ancient Rome.

    A. **Aristotle and the idea of "mixed government."** Aristotle can be said to have introduced in a rudimentary fashion the notion of a **mixed** government; one wherein a dominant middle class would mediate the extreme demands of the rich and poor. In his view, only in states where the middle class was large enough to hold a balance of power between the rich and the poor was stable, orderly, and decent popular government possible.

    B. **Polybius and the idea of "checks and balances."** Polybius (203? B.C.-120 B.C.), for his part, sought to explain the success of the Roman Republic in terms of the institutional checks and balances available to the dominant social orders. These checks and balances, he maintained, produced accommodation, compromise, and harmony among interests and orders that would otherwise have caused disorder and fragmentation.

II. **English background.** The developments most relevant to the American system of separation of powers arise from the struggles between parliament and monarchy in seventeenth-century England. During this period, the character of the English constitution changed from a mixed regime to a system of Parliamentary supremacy; the system changed, that is, from a one in which the principal institutions (the monarch, the House of Commons and the House of Lords) representing the three dominant orders (monarchy, aristocracy, and commons) each had to consent to measures before they could become law, to one clearly dominated by Parliament. This transformation and the historical circumstances surrounding it are reflected in the writings of **John Locke** and **Baron de Montesquieu** that form the basis for the modern version of separation of powers.

    A. **Locke and separation of powers.** Locke looked upon separation of powers as a means to prevent the arbitrary and capricious rule characteristic of so many of the British monarchs through the exercise of the powers of prerogative.

        1. **The problem of executive and judicial power in the same hands.** In his *Second Treatise of Civil Government*, Locke wrote that the dangers and inconveniences of the "state of nature," where each man was judge of his own cause, were scarcely avoided in a regime "where one Man commanding a multitude, has the Liberty to be Judge in his own Case, and may do to all his Subjects whatever he pleases, without the least liberty to any one to question or control those who Execute his Pleasure...."

        2. **Connection between oppression and the lack of separation of powers.** Locke believed that if "the Same Persons who have the Power of making Laws,...have also in the hands the power of executing them, whereby they may exempt themselves from Obedience to the Laws they make, and suit the Law, both in its making and execution, to the private advantage,...[they] thereby come to have a distinct interest from the rest of the community, contrary to the end of Society and Government."

        3. **Separation of powers and the prevention of oppression.** Although Locke advocated parliamentary supremacy based upon majority rule, he believed that the separation of legislative and executive functions would serve to prevent oppressive rule: "in all well order'd Commonwealths...the **Legislative** Power is put into the hands of divers Persons who duly Assembled, have by themselves, or jointly with others, a Power to make Laws, which when they have done, being separated again, they are themselves subject to the Laws, they have made; which is a new and near tie upon them, to take care, that they make them for the public good."

    B. **Baron de Montesquieu, the American Founders, and the separation of powers.** The French aristocrat Baron de Montesquieu is generally regarded as the father of the modern version of the separation of powers.

        1. **The English basis of Montesquieu's views.** Montesquieu formulated the doctrine of the separation of powers primarily from his observations of the English system of government. Montesquieu shared Locke's view that separation of the legislative and executive powers was essential to prevent arbitrary and capricious rule. This separation also insured the rule of law, that is, the uniform, equal, and predictable application of known, standing laws.

        2. **Montesquieu and Madison.** That the Founders looked primarily to Montesquieu for their under-

standing of the purposes and requirements of separation of powers is well known.

  a. **Accumulation of powers as tyranny**. In *The Federalist* No. 47, Madison quotes extensively from Montesquieu in support of the proposition that the "accumulation of all powers, legislative, executive and judiciary, in the same hands, whether of one, a few, or many, and whether hereditary, self appointed, or elective, may justly be pronounced the very definition of tyranny."

  b. **Blending of powers a necessary addition to the separation of powers**. Montesquieu is also used to defend the blending of powers found in the Constitution such as presidential participation in the legislative process. According to Madison, by separation of powers Montesquieu "did not mean that [the three departments] ought to have no **partial agency** in, or no **control** over the acts of each other. His meaning, as his own words import, and still more conclusively as illustrated by the example in his eye [the English system], can amount to no more than this, that where the **whole** power of one department is exercised by the same hands which possess the **whole** power of another department, the fundamental principles of a free constitution are subverted."

III. **The Framers and the separation of powers**. The Framers also shared the views of Montesquieu and Locke regarding the ends or objectives of the separation of powers.

  A. **Separation of powers, the rule of law, and liberty**. Separation of powers, the Framers believed, was necessary for the rule of law—the impartial administration and adjudication of known laws as opposed to edicts or decrees made up on the whim of those in power. The observance of the rule of law would also secure liberty. The Framers, following Montesquieu, took liberty to mean "a right of doing whatever the laws permit" and a "tranquillity of mind arising from the opinion each person has of his safety."

  B. **Separation of powers and prevention of the abuse of power**. Moreover, use of the doctrine of the separation of powers enabled the Framers to solve the perplexing problems of how to prevent the rulers from abusing the ruled. As Madison put this matter in *The Federalist* No. 51, "what is government itself but the greatest of all reflections on human nature? If men were angels, no government would be necessary. If angels were to govern men, neither external nor internal controls on government would be necessary. In framing a government which is to be administered by men over men, the great difficulty lies in this: You must first enable the government to control the governed; and in the next place, oblige it to control itself."

  C. **Problems of implementing the separation doctrine in the Constitution**. The critical question facing the Founders was how to devise a system of separation of powers to achieve these objectives, a question not easily answered given the peculiarities of the American political landscape.

    1. **Social differences with Britain**. Separation of powers could not be based upon the British model because, as **Charles Pinckney** (1757-1824), among others, pointed out in the Philadelphia Convention, the United States "contain but one order than can be assimilated to the British Nation, this is the order of Commons." Thus, the Framers could not emulate the British system where the three dominant social orders—monarchy, aristocracy, and commoners—found institutional representation.

    2. **Lack of social basis for a "mixed regime."** Lack of distinct royal and aristocratic classes also meant that the Framers could not very well establish the "mixed regime," which, in its classic formula, required elements of monarchical and aristocratic rule as well as the democratic element.

    3. **The necessity for republican government**. As a consequence of the structure of American society, the Framers had to construct a system of separation of powers upon republican principles; i.e., provision for direct or indirect control over the rulers by "the great body of society, not from an inconsiderable proportion, or a favored class of it."

    4. **Providing for the independence of each branch**. To establish a system of separated powers on such foundations was unprecedented. The task was made extremely difficult by the realization that for the separation of powers to serve its avowed purposes required "that each department should have a will of its own." This, in turn, the Framers realized, meant that the members of

"each department should have as little agency as possible in the appointment of the members of the others." A major portion of the debates and deliberations at the Philadelphia Convention were devoted to how best to secure independent channels for the composition of the three branches.

5. **Legislature, not executive, the source of danger in republics.** In *The Federalist* No. 48 Madison took pains to emphasize still another complication with which the delegates of the Constitutional Convention had to deal. During the period of British rule, and particularly in the years leading up to the Declaration of Independence, Americans had been concerned with curbing the powers of the king. But, he continued, "In representative republics," such as that called for by the proposed Constitution, the people now had to focus their concern, "indulge all their jealousy and exhaust all their precautions," on controlling the representative assembly.

   a. **Executive power effectively limited in republics.** He remarks that, on the one hand, "the executive magistracy is carefully limited, both in the extent and the duration of its power," so that it is scarcely in a position to pose much of a threat to liberty.

   b. **Potential danger in legislature.** On the other hand, the "legislative power is exercised by an assembly, which is inspired by a supposed influence over the people with an intrepid confidence in its own strength; which is sufficiently numerous to feel all the passions which actuate a multitude, yet not so numerous as to be incapable of pursuing the objects of its passions, by means which reason prescribes."

   c. **Jefferson on dangers of despotic legislatures.** One of Jefferson's charges against the Virginia government, for example, was that "All the powers of government, legislative, executive, and judiciary, result to the legislative body." Such a concentration, he declared, in keeping with the universal sentiment of the times, constituted "despotic government." "It will be no alleviation," he maintained, "that these powers will be exercised by a plurality of hands, and not by a single one. One hundred and seventy-three

despots would surely be as oppressive as one."

   d. **Necessity for legislative predominance.** "In republican government," Publius writes in *The Federalist* No. 51, "the legislative authority necessarily predominates." This had certainly been the case at the state level, where the legislatures had even assumed executive and judicial powers when it suited their fancy. Thus the problem for the Framers was that the same legislatures that must predominate in republics were at the same time sources of potential threats to liberty.

D. **The Framers' solution to the problems of the separation of powers.** For the Framers, perhaps the most critical problem was how to prevent the Congress from gradually usurping the executive and judicial powers. They knew from the experiences in the states that parchment barriers—i.e., constitutional declarations that the legislature ought not to invade the executive or judicial provinces—were entirely unreliable.

1. **Devising means of keeping each branch in its place.** The Framers' eventual answer, outlined by Madison in *The Federalist* No. 51, was "contriving the interior structures of the government, as that its several constituent parts may, by their mutual relations, be the means of keeping each other in the proper places."

2. **Making "ambition counter ambition."** The chief and essential ingredient of this solution, in turn, was "giving to those who administer each department, the necessary constitutional means, and personal motives, to resist the encroachments of the others." In this fashion, "Ambition" could be used "to counteract ambition."

3. **Making defense commensurate with danger: the role of checks and balances.** This solution also recognized that "The provision for defense must...be made commensurate to the danger of attack." Here the Framers introduced what is today called "checks and balances" to maintain the necessary separation.

   a. **Strengthening the judiciary.** The judiciary, possessing neither the power of the purse nor the sword, was considered by far the weakest of the branches. This necessitated that it be strengthened by giving its members life tenure during good behavior and providing that judicial salaries could not be diminished.

b. **Arming the executive**. The president was constitutionally vested with a qualified veto—a veto which could only be overridden by a two-thirds vote in both houses of Congress. The primary purpose of this veto, as Hamilton points out in *The Federalist* No.73, was to protect the president against being "stripped of his authorities by successive resolutions, or annihilated by a single vote;" an objective which Madison suggests in *The Federalist* No. 51 might be more appropriately fulfilled by equipping the president with an "absolute veto." But Madison implicitly holds out the prospect that the Senate, because it shares appointment and treaty-making powers with the president, might unite with him to the extent of upholding justified vetoes.

c. **Dividing the legislature**. The Framers were not content simply to strengthen the weaker departments; they also weakened the strong. Accordingly, the legislature was divided into two branches with the end, as Madison put it, of rendering them "by different modes of election, and different principles of action, as little connect with each other, as the nature of their common functions, and their common dependence on the society, will admit."

d. **The weak strengthened; the strong weakened**. In sum, in order to insure that the separation between the departments as laid down in the Constitution would be maintained, the Founders adopted the strategy of weakening the strong (the Congress) and strengthening the weak (the president and the courts). They also counted upon the interest of the office holders being "connected with the constitutional rights of the place" so that "ambition" might counteract "ambition" to preserve the constitutional separation.

Contemporary Perspective

Contemporary issues in historical perspective. From the outset of the operations of government under the new Constitution, friction arose between the branches over their respective powers. Over the course of American history, conflict between the Congress and president has dominated; though in recent years the role and function of the courts, particularly the Supreme Court, has become a subject of intense controversy. The source of the disputes between the branches are both constitutional and extra-constitutional.

I. **Executive privilege.** From Washington's administration forward, presidents have asserted wide powers in the field of foreign relations and policy.

   A. **Precedent established by Washington**. Washington's refusal (1796) to comply with the request of the House of Representatives to provide it with documents related to the negotiation of the controversial Jay Treaty with Great Britain constitutes the first of the innumerable assertions of executive privilege by presidents.

   B. **The practice of presidents**. That is, when the occasions have arisen, presidents have insisted that certain of the communications with subordinates, as well as executive department documents, must be treated with confidentiality and that a president is well within his constitutional authority in refusing to disclose the communications to Congress or its investigating committees.

   C. **The status of executive privilege today**. The constitutional status of executive privilege was never fully established in the courts until *United States v. Nixon* (1974), a case that arose out of the Watergate scandal. In this case, the Court rejected the claim that executive privilege is an "absolute privilege" which rests upon the doctrine of separation of powers. It held that the privilege does not automatically extend to materials which are relevant to "ongoing criminal prosecution[s]." It did give wide scope to this privilege, however, in matters relating to military, diplomatic, and national security matters.

II. **The Congress, president, and foreign policy**. Another, and far more significant, dispute during Washington's administration provided the backdrop against which Congress and the president have struggled ever since.

   A. **Controversy over Washington's Declaration of Neutrality**. At the outbreak of war between England and France, Washington issued a Proclamation of

Neutrality which declared that the United States would "pursue a course friendly and impartial to both belligerent powers."

1. **Hamilton's defense of Washington.** The issuance of this Proclamation was assailed by many as being beyond the constitutional authority of the president. Alexander Hamilton, writing under the pseudonym "Pacificus," set out to answer critics of the Proclamation. In this endeavor he asserted and defended the proposition that setting the direction of foreign policy was the constitutional responsibility of the president, not Congress.

2. **Madison's reply to Hamilton.** Madison, at the urging of Jefferson and using the pseudonym "Helvidius," responded to Hamilton's position. He reasoned that Congress, possessing the power to declare war, clearly bore the responsibility for setting down foreign policy which was a lesser responsibility, though clearly related to matters of war and peace.

B. **Periodic conflicts and unresolved questions today.** Conflicts between the president and Congress over the direction of foreign policy have occurred throughout history. Prior to our entry into World War II, for instance, the Congress sought to maintain a stance of neutrality, whereas President Roosevelt pursued policies decidedly favorable to Great Britain and the allied forces. That this tension remains unresolved to this day is evidenced by the Iran/Contra affair, particularly the struggle between the Reagan administration and the Congress over aid to the Contras in Nicaragua.

III. **The Congress, the president, and the power to make war.** A related and even more persistent tension surrounds the nature and extent of the president's powers as "Commander-in-Chief" of the armed forces.

A. **Early debates.** An early debate (1797) in the House of Representatives over giving the president complete discretion in the deployment of three newly commissioned frigates indicates the intricacies involved with regard to this presidential power.

1. **President's actions to be restricted by Congress.** Representative Smith, echoing the concern of some members, points out that "If the power of employing the frigates was wholly left with the President, though he had not the power of declaring war, yet he might so employ them as to lead to war." For this reason, Representative

Gallatin argued that Congress ought to stipulate "upon what business they [the frigates] ought to be employed."

2. **Lack of congressional authority to restrict president.** Those opposed to Gallatin's position argued either that the Congress lacked the constitutional authority to limit the president's discretion or that such a restriction would prove to be imprudent and possibly disastrous since it would tie the president's hands in cases of unforeseen contingencies.

B. **Making war without congressional declarations.** The early concerns of those who sought to limit the president's discretion have proved to be well founded. On well over a hundred occasions presidents have ordered American forces into hostile situations without authorization.

1. **Polk and war with Mexico.** Perhaps the most blatant example of this was President Polk's (1846) ordering troops into disputed territories with full knowledge that this would precipitate hostilities with Mexico, thereby leaving the Congress with no alternative but to declare war.

2. **Vietnam and the War Powers Resolution (1973).** The undeclared war in Vietnam, which gradually came to involve massive national commitment of men and matériel largely through the exercise of the president's power as commander-in-chief of the armed forces, prompted Congress to pass the War Powers Resolution (1973). Through this resolution Congress sought to control the president's powers to commit forces to situations in which hostilities appear "imminent."

IV. **The Congress and president: political deadlock.** Conflicts between the president and the Congress have arisen for extra-constitutional reasons.

A. **Which branch most representative of the people?** While the Framers regarded Congress as the institution most representative of the American people, with the emergence of political parties and the election of Andrew Jackson in 1828, presidents could and have claimed that they represent all of the American people. Likewise, presidents are regarded as the leaders of their political parties.

B. **Increasing conflicts between Congress and presidents.** These developments have led to increasing conflict between the president and Congress over matters of public policy and who best represents the popular will.

1. **Increasing use of veto**. One measure of this conflict is seen in the use of the president's veto power. Prior to the Civil War, presidents exercised their veto power only fifty-two times; since then it has been used well over two thousand times.

2. **The rise of stalemate between president and Congress**. When a president is able to command majorities in both houses of Congress—such as Franklin Roosevelt was able to do in the 1930s—he clearly assumes the role of "chief legislator," setting a coherent legislative agenda before Congress. When the president is of one party and Congress another—as has often been the case in recent decades—stalemate often arises over key issues of public policy.

3. **Congressional use of "riders."** In this situation, Congress will often attach "riders" or amendments to measures, such as appropriations, which the president for political reasons cannot afford to veto.

4. **Stalemate and proposals for constitutional reform**. The political infighting between the president and Congress, as well as the frequent stalemates between them on matters of policy, have led many observers to advocate a change in the constitutional system to provide for a cabinet system with responsible and disciplined political parties along the lines found in Great Britain. Short of this, there have been several reforms suggested to provide for greater cooperation between the Congress and president such as allowing cabinet members to speak on the floor of the House and Senate.

V. **Judicial Activism**. To the conflicts and tensions between the executive and legislative branches must be added those involving the courts.

A. **Conflicts between the Supreme Court and the president**. At various times, particularly in the twentieth century, the Supreme Court has crossed swords with the executive and legislative branches. In the mid-1930's, the Court invalidated much of Roosevelt's New Deal program which prompted him to propose his famous Court "packing" plan—the addition of one justice for each member over seventy years of age up to a total of fifteen. This plan was rejected by the Senate, principally on grounds that it would intrude upon the independence of the judicial branch.

Shortly thereafter the Court reversed its position relative to the New Deal programs.

B. **Controversies over the role of the Court**. In recent decades, however, Court decisions concerning, among others, abortion, busing to achieve racial integration, voluntary prayer, affirmative action and, criminal procedures have spurred charges that the Court is moving beyond its legitimate constitutional authority. Critics contend that the Court has ignored original intent in interpreting the Constitution; that it has read its own values into the Constitution, not those of the Founders.

2) b. SEPARATION OF CHURCH AND STATE

Congress shall make no law respecting an establishment of religion, or prohibiting the free exercise thereof....

First Amendment (1791)

The constitutional principle of the separation of church and state is embodied in the First Amendment of the Bill of Rights, cited above. This guarantee of religious freedom imposed on Congress was subsequently applied by the Supreme Court to the states by incorporating it into the Fourteenth Amendment's limitation on the power of states to deprive any person of **liberty** without due process of law. This section deals primarily with the "establishment clause" and focusses on its relationship to schools and education. The section in this framework on "Religion and public life," as its title indicates, presents a fuller and more general discussion, with special reference to the "free exercise clause."

OBJECTIVES

The citizen should be able to

1. explain the historical background and contemporary relevance of the establishment clause of the First Amendment.

2. take, defend, and evaluate positions on contemporary issues involving the establishment clause.

FRAME OF REFERENCE
Conceptual and Historical Perspectives

I. **Original meanings of "an establishment of religion."** Today, "an establishment of religion" is an unfamiliar term to most Americans, but it was very familiar to the peoples of Europe and America in the sixteenth, seventeenth, and eighteenth centuries.

A. **A single established church.** This policy originally meant that a close legal alliance of mutual support and preference existed between a particular state and a single church.

 1. **Roman Catholic establishments.** The very name of the Holy Roman Empire, which lasted for 800 years in Europe until 1806, symbolized the linkage of the spiritual authority of the Roman Catholic Church with the secular power of the ancient Roman Empire. Roman Catholic establishments flourished in many states of Europe and eventually in Central and South America.

 2. **Protestant establishments in Europe.** During the bloody wars of the Reformation the leaders of dissident Protestant sects joined powerful secular rulers to throw off this intermixture of governmental and Catholic spiritual power. Lutheranism became the established religion in the several states of Northern Germany and Scandinavia; Anglicanism was established in England; and Calvinism was established in the Reformed Church of the Netherlands, in the Presbyterian Church of Scotland, and in the Puritan Commonwealth of England.

 3. **Protestant establishments in America.** Establishments of religion were brought to British North America in the seventeenth century by Calvinist Puritans and Congregationalists to New England and by Anglicans to the Southern colonies. Although there were differences among the British colonies, "an establishment of religion" in seventeenth century North America meant that the legal power and authority of the state were used to support a single established church in two major ways:

 a. **Enforced religious belief and worship.** The particular religious doctrines, beliefs, and public worship of the established church were enforced by law on all inhabitants and all clergy. Physical torture, imprisonment, or fines were meted out to those found guilty of blasphemy, heresy, or idolatry as well as for failing to attend faithfully the authorized and compulsory public worship, or of conducting unauthorized worship services in private. There was little toleration or freedom for dissenters. Anyone who held unorthodox religious beliefs could not be regarded as a moral person or good citizen.

 b. **Public financial support for the established church.** The state levied taxes or tithes upon all inhabitants and used the public funds to support the established clergy and to build churches and maintain church property, with penalties of jail or fine for those who failed to pay the religious taxes, no matter what their religious beliefs might be.

 c. **Most American colonies had establishments of religion.** During the seventeenth century, nine of the original thirteen colonies installed various forms of established religion, where-as religion was not established in Rhode Island, Pennsylvania, New Jersey, or Delaware.

B. **A new meaning in America: multiple establishment of religion.** During the eighteenth century, however, the establishments of single churches were weakened politically by the increasing number and variety of religious and ethnic groups who poured into the colonies.

 1. **Separatists grew in number and power.** Especially important was the increase in political power of such "separatist" groups as Quakers, Baptists, Moravians, Methodists, and others whose religious beliefs opposed state control over religious doctrine or worship. They rejected the obligation to pay taxes for a religion in which they did not believe. They campaigned to separate the state from all churches.

 2. **Multiple establishments became the rule.** Six of the colonies with single established churches gradually permitted an increasing number of Protestant sects to conduct public worship and even to share in public funds for their support on a non-preferential basis. Customarily, a taxpayer could designate the church to which his taxes would go. If he did not designate a settled minister or church, his taxes would be divided among the established Protestant churches.

3. **South Carolina a prime example of Protestant establishment.** A clear case of the meaning of a multiple form of establishment is found in the South Carolina Constitution of 1778; "The Christian Protestant religion shall be deemed, and is hereby constituted and declared to be, the established religion of this State....All denominations of Christian Protestants in this State...shall enjoy equal religious and civil privileges."

4. **Maryland included all Christian churches.** With its large Catholic population, Maryland's Constitution of 1776 permitted its legislature to "lay a general and equal tax for the support of the Christian religion," leaving each individual to decide to which minister his tax money should go.

C. **The movement to disestablishment.** Between 1776 and 1789 three states disestablished religion (New York, Virginia, and North Carolina). All six states that still had an establishment of religion at the time of the framing of the Constitution and the establishment clause of the First Amendment had a multiple form in which several churches could share in tax funds for the support of their own clergy and worship (Massachusetts, Connecticut, New Hampshire, Maryland, South Carolina, and Georgia). This was the only kind of establishment left in the American states, and this is what the Framers meant by an establishment of religion. These six states eventually changed their constitutions and laws to disestablish religion along the lines of the First Amendment.

II. **The rise of separation of church and state.** Thus, at the beginning of the new Republic the growing consensus was that the legal and financial connections of the state and one or more churches had to be broken, if the equal rights of conscience and the free exercise of religion were genuinely to be achieved.

A. **The role of Thomas Jefferson.** Under the preeminent leadership of such Founders as **Thomas Jefferson** and **James Madison**, the legal separation of church and state was embedded in the laws and constitutions of the several states and in the First Amendment of the U.S. Constitution. Jefferson's use of the phrase "separation of church and state" is well known. His 1779 Bill for Establishing Religious Freedom in Virginia eventually became the Statute of Religious Freedom, passed in 1786 with the indispensable aid of Madison. This was a landmark event, prohibiting general assessments by the state for supporting religious teachers and guaranteeing the free exercise of religion.

It specifically defeated a 1779 competing bill modelled on the provisions of the South Carolina Constitution.

B. **The role of James Madison.** Less well known are Madison's efforts in the First Congress to use the power of the federal government to require the states to protect what he called the "choicest liberties of the people."

1. **Madison's proposal to limit the states.** In his proposals for adding a Bill of Rights to the Constitution made in his speech to Congress on June 8, 1789, Madison would have put limits on the states as well as on Congress. He proposed that "No state shall violate the equal rights of conscience, or the freedom of the press, or the trial by jury in criminal cases." He argued that "...it is proper that every Government should be disarmed of powers which trench upon those particular rights....[I]t must be admitted, on all hands, that the State Governments are as liable to attack those invaluable privileges as the General Government is, and therefore ought to be as cautiously guarded against."

2. **Defeat of Madison's proposal.** The Congress was not ready at that time to authorize the federal government to prohibit the states from violating the full equal rights of conscience for all persons. The nation had to await the Fourteenth Amendment and subsequent interpretations by the Supreme Court to achieve Madison's original intention that the First Amendment should protect the religious freedoms of all individuals (not just Christians) against encroachment by the states as well as protecting minorities against majority actions in state and local communities.

Contemporary Perspective

I. **Religious conflicts abound in the twentieth century.** The ideals and practices of the separation of church and state have enabled the United States to embrace into equal citizenship millions of people from all races, nationalities, and religions of the world and to avoid the worst outbreaks of religious violence and wars that have characterized so much of modern history in the twentieth century.

A. **Conflicts around the world.** There has been nothing in the United States to compare with the violent and intractable conflicts among Jews, Muslims, and Christians in the Middle East; among Hindus,

Muslims, Sikhs, and Buddhists in Southern Asia; between Sunni Muslims and Shiite Muslims in Iraq and the Persian Gulf; between Catholic and Protestant Christians in Northern Ireland; between Christians and Muslims in Soviet Armenia and Ajerbaijan; and between Roman Catholics and Greek Orthodox Catholics in Yugoslavia.

B. **Conflicts in the U.S.** This is not to say that there has been no religious violence, intolerance, or discrimination in the U.S. in the twentieth century. Successive groups of religious minorities have been subjected to open ridicule, prejudice, and personal abuse, as well as quiet quotas in admissions to educational, civic, and business and industrial work places. But the civil rights movement of the 1960s increased efforts to reduce or eliminate discriminatory practices based on religion as well as on race, ethnicity, and sex.

II. **Continuing controversies over education in the U.S.** For most of the twentieth century the constitutional principle of separation of church and state has been constantly debated in communities, legislatures, and courts of law throughout the country. Of special interest to CIVITAS is the fact that much of the legislation and litigation has had to do with educational policies and practices in schools and colleges. Two major questions about education have been persistently and contentiously debated:

A. **Public financial support for religious schooling.** Does the constitutional principle of separation of church and state permit the use of public funds to aid religious schools?

1. **Direct aid.** In general, direct aid from the state for teachers' salaries, buildings, and maintenance of religious schools has been prohibited under the establishment clause of the First Amendment.

2. **Indirect aid.** In contrast, debate has been intense over indirect aid, as represented by such practices as the following: reimbursing parents for bus fares to send their children to religious schools; providing public tax funds to supply free textbooks, tests, and other services to children who attend religious schools; paying salaries of public school teachers who teach non-religious subjects in religious schools; and, most recently, the proposals for parental choice, whereby public funds would be granted to parents who choose to send their children to private or religious schools rather than to the public schools.

a. **Narrow or accommodationist views.** Proponents of such practices as those listed above argue that the establishment clause should be interpreted narrowly; that is, it simply prohibits the Congress and the states from supporting or favoring a single church or religion. So, the Congress and the states may aid religion in general by accommodating their policies and practices to the religious views of the populace. Such policies and practices are constitutional so long as the Congress and the states do not give preference to one church or one religion over another.

b. **Broad or separationist views.** Opponents of such practices argue that the establishment clause broadly prohibits engagement of the state with religion and that even non-preferential or impartial aid from public funds for religious activities, practices, or institutions is effectively and historically an establishment of religion and thus unconstitutional.

B. **Religious instruction and observances in public schools.** Does the principle of separation of church and state permit the states to require, endorse, or promote religious instruction or observances in public schools?

1. **Controversial practices.** The most conspicuous cases at issue in recent years regard the following practices in public schools: organized daily prayer, Bible reading, or recitation of the Ten Commandments; prayers at graduation ceremonies; required teaching of creationism along with evolution; censorship of secular humanist textbooks as inimical to common religious values; Christmas ceremonies and observances; required pledge of allegiance and salute to the flag in spite of students' religious scruples to the contrary; and exemption of private religious schools from meeting state requirements concerning the certification of their teachers, courses required for high school graduation, required textbooks, or compulsory attendance laws.

2. **Narrow or accommodationist views.** Proponents in favor of such practices as listed above argue that the First Amendment permits the states to accommodate themselves to the religious consensus of the majority of the people in a state or local community as determined by the political process rather than by the federal courts.

3. **Broad or separationist views.** Opponents argue that the principle of separation in the establishment clause prohibits government from promoting or endorsing religious beliefs or practices in general, just as it prohibits the state from promoting specific religious doctrines of a particular church.

C. **Religion and public issues.** The principles of religious freedom and the equal rights of conscience are also involved in a whole range of controversial public policy issues beyond schooling, e.g., conscientious objection on religious grounds to draft registration and military service; punishment of parents who refuse, on religious grounds, to permit medical treatment for their critically ill children; controversies over tax exemption for the business activities of churches; nativity scenes on public property at Christmas time; official U.S. representation to the Vatican; Sunday closing laws; and paid vacations for employees whose religious observances do not fall on the Christian Sunday. (See the section in this Framework, Religion and Public Life.")

III. **Landmark decisions on the establishment clause.** For more than 50 years the meaning of the establishment clause has been a matter of contentious debate.

A. *Everson v. Board of Education*: **a broad or separatist view.** In 1947 a broad, separationist interpretation was defined by Justice Hugo Black for a unanimous Supreme Court in the *Everson* case, which arose over the use of public funds to pay for bus fares of children attending Roman Catholic parochial schools: "The establishment of religion clause of the First Amendment means at least this: Neither a state nor the Federal Government can set up a church. Neither can pass laws which aid one religion, aid all religions, or prefer one religion over another....No tax in any amount, large or small, can be levied to support any religious activities or institutions, whatever they may be called, or whatever form they may adopt to teach or practice religion....In the words of Jefferson, the clause against establishment of religion by law was intended to "erect a wall of separation between Church and State."

B. *Lemon v. Kurtzman*: **the consensus view.** After 1947 hundreds of local and state laws were passed involving the establishment clause and education. Scores of cases reached the federal courts, many reaching the Supreme Court under Chief Justices Earl Warren and Warren Burger.

1. **The Burger decision.** In 1971 the Supreme Court summarized and consolidated twenty-five years of decisions on the principle of separation of church and state in an 8-1 decision written by Chief Justice Warren Burger in *Lemon v. Kurtzman*. The case dealt with use of tax funds to pay for teachers salaries and instructional materials related to secular subjects taught in religious schools, which the Court prohibited (Justice Byron White dissenting).

2. **The principles of the three-fold test.** Constitutional government action must meet a three-fold test: (1) The state action must have primarily a secular purpose rather than religious. (2) The principal effect of the action must be neither to advance or inhibit religion. (3) The action must not result in excessive entanglement of government with religion.

C. *Wallace v. Jaffree*: **rising dissent.** During the 1980s, attacks upon the broad and separationist views of the establishment clause sharply increased in state courts and legislatures, in Congress, in the Reagan and Bush administrations, and in the federal courts on the way to the Supreme Court.

1. **The broad or separationist views.** In 1985 an Alabama law endorsing organized prayer as a part of authorized moments of silence in the public schools was struck down by a majority of 6-3 in an opinion by Justice John Paul Stevens reaffirming the broad principle of separation of church and state stemming from *Everson*. The opinion was agreed to by Justices Lewis Powell, William Brennan, Thurgood Marshall, and Harry Blackmun. While Justice Sandra Day O'Connor voted with the majority, she made it plain that being new to the court she was not ready to abandon all aspects of *Lemon* but that she **was** ready to have it "reexamined and refined."

2. **The narrow or accommodationist views.** Premonition of the future was forecast, however, by the long dissent by Justice William Rehnquist who explicitly called for reversing the *Everson* principle: "The Establishment Clause did not require government neutrality between religion and irreligion nor did it prohibit the federal government from providing non-discriminatory aid to religion. There is simply no historical foundation for the proposition that the Framers intended to build the 'wall of separation' that was constitutionalized in *Everson*....The 'wall of

separation between church and state' is a metaphor based on bad history, a metaphor which has proved useless as a guide to judging. It should be frankly and explicitly abandoned." Chief Justice Burger and Justice Byron R. White also dissented, White supporting "a basic reconsideration of our precedents."

D. **An uncertain future.** Controversies over the meaning of the establishment clause and the future of the principle of separation of church and state itself are still in the offing.

1. **A fundamental sea-change in the Court.** The Supreme Court has agreed to hear arguments on its docket for 1991-92 concerning the constitutionality of prayers at public high school graduations (*Lee v. Weisman*). The decision will be made by a Court on which Chief Justice Rehnquist and Justices White and O'Connor still sit, but a Court without Justices Powell, Brennan, and Marshall, all of whom voted with the majority in *Jaffree* and who were strong supporters of a broad and separatist meaning of the establishment clause. Justices Stevens, Blackmun, and O'Connor are the only members of the *Jaffree* majority of six who will hear the new case involving the establishment clause.

2. **The establishment clause at stake.** In future decisions, much will depend on whether the establishment clause will be viewed broadly or narrowly in defining federal restrictions on state action in the realm of religion and education. And much will depend on the way the history of the original intentions of Jefferson and Madison are read by the new members of the Supreme Court, all appointed by Republican Presidents since *Jaffree*. It remains to be seen whether the Rehnquist Court seeks to overturn its precedents on the establishment clause as it began to do in 1990-91 on defendants' rights in criminal cases.

2) c. FEDERALISM

There is a twofold liberty, natural...and civil or federal. The first is common to man with beasts and other creatures....The other kind of liberty I call civil or federal, it may also be termed moral, in reference to the covenant between God and man, in the moral law, and the politic covenants and constitutions, amongst men themselves. This liberty is the proper end and object of authority, and cannot subsist without it.

John Winthrop (1645)

In considering...the system before us, it is necessary to mention another kind of liberty,...**federal liberty**. When a single government is instituted, the individuals of which it is composed, surrender to it a part of their natural independence....When a confederate republic is instituted, the communities, of which it is composed, surrender to it a part of their political independence....The states should resign to the national government, that part, and that part, only, of their political liberty, which, placed in that government, will produce more good to the whole, than if it had remained in the several states. While they resign this part of their political liberty, they retain the free and generous exercise of all their other faculties, as states, so far as it is compatible with the welfare of the general and superintending confederacy.

James Wilson (1787)

...the proposed government cannot be deemed a **national one**; since its jurisdiction extends to certain enumerated objects only, and leaves to the several States a residuary and inviolable sovereignty over all other objects.

James Madison (1788)

The question of the relation of the states to the federal government is the cardinal question of our constitutional system....It cannot, indeed, be settled by the opinion of any one generation.

Woodrow Wilson (1908)

...you can clear a room almost any place by talking about federalism.

Charles S. Robb (1986)

Federalism and the intergovernmental relations that arise from it are central features of the American system of democratic governance. The federal principle, which emphasizes covenantal relationships of cooperation and partnership, also shapes American society as a whole, as reflected in federated church governance, federated nonprofit associations, quasi-federated corporate structures, and covenantal/contractual relations among persons.

OBJECTIVES

The citizen should be able to

1. explain the purposes of federalism as a form of democracy that seeks to promote liberty, justice, equality, and human diversity.

2. explain the importance of federalism and intergovernmental relations as central features of American democratic governance that shape virtually all politics and public policy.

3. explain the types of powers in the U.S. Constitution, the constitutional division and sharing of powers between the states and the U.S. government, the constitutional prohibitions on and obligations of the states and the U.S. government, the role of rights in shaping the federal system, and changing views of the Tenth Amendment.

4. explain the forms of cooperative sharing and intergovernmental regulation in the federal system, the politics of federal-state-local relations, and the disputes that arise over the extent of state powers and U.S. government powers.

5. explain the ways in which Congress, presidents, and the Supreme Court shape the federal system; and the expansion of U.S. government powers in the twentieth century.

6. take, defend, and evaluate positions on issues regarding contemporary federalism.

FRAME OF REFERENCE
Conceptual Perspective

I. **The concept of federalism.** Modern federalism is an original contribution of the American people to democratic government.

  A. **The covenantal root of federalism.** The word "federal" comes from the Latin *foedus*, meaning "covenant." Covenant signifies a marriage or partnership in which persons or groups consent to unite for common purposes without giving up their fundamental rights or identity.

  B. **A definition of federalism.** Federalism establishes unity while preserving diversity by constitutionally uniting separate political communities into a limited, but encompassing, political community. Power is divided and shared between a general government having certain nationwide responsibilities and constituent governments having broad local responsibilities.

    1. **Mutual integrity.** The distribution of power is intended to protect the integral authority of both the general and constituent governments as well as the existence of their respective political communities.

    2. **Partnership.** A democratic federation is a republic of republics, which emphasizes partnership and cooperation for the common good, while also allowing diversity and competition to foster liberty and efficiency.

  C. **Varieties of federalism.** Different federal arrangements can be found around the world (e.g., Australia, Belgium, Canada, Germany, Nigeria, and Switzerland) and even with respect to the United States (e.g., the relationship of Puerto Rico and the U.S.).

  D. **Confederation.** Confederation is a particular form of federalism. In practice, the distinction between a federation and a confederation is sometimes blurred (e.g., Canada and the European Community). Examples of confederation are the United Nations and the U.S. under the Articles of Confederation. The following generally distinguish confederation from federalism.

    1. **Confederations as composed of constituent political communities.** In confederations, plenary power resides in the constituent political communities, which expressly delegate certain responsibilities to the general government.

    2. **Power of constituents to withdraw wholly or in part from the union.** Usually, the constituent governments can withdraw delegations of power unilaterally, and often they can secede from the union.

    3. **Confederal government's laws not enforceable against individuals.** The general government cannot usually enforce law against individuals.

4. **Sovereignty in constituent communities.** A confederation ordinarily has a written covenant or charter, but sovereignty resides either in the separate peoples or in the governments of the constituent communities.

E. **Factors distinguishing federalism.** Federalism can be distinguished from unitary government. It is characterized by non-centralization and the necessity for the different units of government to interact.

1. **Unitary government.** In a unitary polity, plenary power resides in a central government. A unitary government may or may not have a written constitution.

2. **Non-centralized government.** Federalism is "non-centralized" government as opposed to "decentralized" government.

   a. **Non-centralized government.** In non-centralized government, neither the constituent governments nor the general government can unilaterally alter the constitutional distribution of power. The U.S. Constitution, for example, can be amended only by the concurrent consent of three-fourths of the states and two-thirds of the Congress or a constitutional convention.

   b. **Decentralized government.** In a decentralized polity, the central government devolves selected powers to regional or local units of government or administration. Those powers can be re-centralized unilaterally. This is not the case in the American federal system.

3. **Intergovernmental relations.** Governance in every federal polity is intergovernmental (e.g., federal-state-local relations), but intergovernmental relations also occur politically in non-federal systems where regional or local governments exercise some self-governance.

II. **Federalism and sovereignty.** Sovereignty was defined by the French philosopher **Jean Bodin** (1530?-1596) in 1576 as "a power over citizens and subjects that is supreme and above the law." Sovereignty implies self-sufficiency, completeness, legal independence, and the ability to make, amend, repeal, and execute law. Because the concept of sovereignty helped legitimize the unitary nation-state by providing a rationale for justifying the growth of centralized power, it has been viewed as inalienable and indivisible and, thus, basically alien to federalism. Modern federalists, who see sovereignty as residing in the people, have had to view sovereignty as divided, shared, and dualistic.

A. **Dual sovereignty.** The U.S. Supreme Court held in 1792 that "the United States are sovereign as to all the powers of government actually surrendered. Each State in the Union is sovereign as to all the powers not conferred" (*Chisholm v. Georgia*). In 1819, the Court declared that "the powers of sovereignty are divided between the government of the Union and those of the States. They are each sovereign with respect to the objects committed to it." (*McCulloch v. Maryland*)

B. **Dual citizenship.** The people of the United States are held in American thought to be sovereign, and thus have the right to delegate and limit government powers, but in two capacities: (1) their citizenship in the United States and (2) their citizenship in a state. The Fourteenth Amendment (1868) to the U.S. Constitution states: "All persons born or naturalized in the United States...are citizens of the United States and of the State wherein they reside."

C. **Dual constitutionalism.** Dual citizenship is reinforced by dual constitutionalism. Thus, the Massachusetts Constitution of 1780, the oldest written constitution still in effect, was ordained by "We...the people of Massachusetts." The U.S. Constitution was ordained by "We the People of the United States...."

1. **The "complete constitution" of the United States.** The "complete constitution" consists of the U.S. Constitution and the fifty state constitutions.

2. **U.S. Constitution incomplete.** The U.S. Constitution may be thought of as "incomplete" in that it is a document of limited, delegated powers, which relies greatly on the states for its operation. Thus, **Alexis de Tocqueville** (1805-1859) referred to the U.S. government as an "incomplete national government."

D. **Dual governments.** The union and each state have a full complement of legislative, executive, and judicial institutions.

E. **Limited union supremacy.** The U.S. government is supreme within its spheres of delegated powers. But it is not supreme in all matters because the Constitution limits these powers. State law is supreme within its realm. State legislative authority is limited only by the U.S. Constitution and by the people of each state.

Thus, state law cannot contradict the U.S. Constitution.

F. **Sovereignty as a diffused property of the federal union.** Given that the U.S. Constitution was ratified by popular conventions in the states rather than by a direct national referendum, and that the Constitution was not in force until nine states signed on, there is ambiguity about whether "We the People of the United States" refers to a single body of sovereign people or to a partnership of sovereign peoples. This is why Madison referred to the U.S. Constitution as being neither wholly federal nor wholly national.

1. **Limits on state sovereignty.** The people of a state possess limited sovereignty because they have delegated certain powers to the federal union. Thus, they can be overruled by the people of the U.S. on certain matters.

2. **Limits on union sovereignty.** The people of the union as a single entity possess limited sovereignty as well. The union's powers are delegated powers; the U.S. Constitution limits union powers; and the people of the union possess no way to express their majoritarian will as a single body. Neither the U.S. Constitution nor any law or any public servant is subject to a direct national majority vote.

3. **Non-centralized sovereignty.** The American people are "sovereign" in that all government power in the states and the federal government derives from them. But another meaning of "sovereignty" is "having the final say" in all matters. In this latter sense, there is no center of sovereignty under the U.S. Constitution; that is, the general government does not have a final say in all matters. Instead "sovereignty" is a diffused property of the federal union, not a possession of any one part of it.

III. **Federalism and democracy.** Not all constitutionally federal polities are democratic (e.g., the USSR), but those that fairly conform to their federal constitutions are democratic (e.g., Austria, Australia, Canada, Germany, Switzerland, and the U.S.). The term "democracy" is used here to include electorally representative government or what most of the Founders called "republican government."

A. **Concurrent consent.** A federal union is fundamentally democratic insofar as it is founded on the concurrent consent of the constituent peoples or governments representing them. In the U.S., new states are admitted to the Union by consent of the people of each new state and of the people of the union, as represented in the Congress.

B. **Republican government.** The U.S. Constitution establishes a "republican" general government and requires the United States to guarantee every state "a republican form of government." Republican government means representative government, which belongs to the people and in which the people are sovereign. This guarantee is intended to protect states from an internal dissolution of republican government and from a usurpation of republican government by other states, the federal government, or foreign powers.

C. **Federal democracy versus unitary democracy.** In a federal democracy, power is sufficiently diffused to make it difficult or impossible for a simple national majority to rule the general community. Instead, the general community is governed by a majority or super-majority of territorially based constituent majorities. In a unitary democracy, power is sufficiently concentrated to make it easy for a simple majority or plurality to rule the nation. The French Revolution produced the modern idea of unitary (or Jacobin) democracy; the American Revolution produced federal democracy.

D. **The question of federalism as anti-democratic or super-democratic.** Arguments have been made that federalism is anti-democratic or "super-democratic."

1. **Antidemocratic.** Because the will of the general majority can be frustrated by minority constituent communities, some people say that federalism is anti-democratic. A federal polity empowers too many veto points. If democracy is defined simply as national majority rule, then federalism is anti-democratic, although simple majority rule may prevail in the constituent communities.

2. **Super-democratic.** A federal polity, however, is super-democratic in the sense that it compels the general majority to court constituent minorities, thus broadening the base of public consent. Fundamental matters, such as U.S. constitutional amendments, require super-majority consent (i.e., two-thirds of the Congress and three-fourths of the states). Hence, politics in a federal democracy does not operate by command but by bargaining, negotiation, and compromise among multiple centers of power.

E. **Democratic multiplicity**. In addition to creating a union of multiple power centers, federalism, especially when combined with separations of powers within governments, creates a multiplicity of small-to-large democratic arenas and of democratic arrangements— from the U.S. Supreme Court with its unelected justices to the direct democracy of statewide referendums and of town meetings.

IV. **Values of federalism**. The values of federalism, most of which are listed in the Preamble to the U.S. Constitution, include the following:

A. **Large-scale democracy**. The U.S. was the first new nation created in the modern era. It was also the first continental-size polity in history to be governed democratically.

1. **Size and democracy.** All territorially large democracies are federal (i.e., Australia, Brazil, Canada, India, and the U.S.). The two other territorial giants, China and the USSR, are essentially empires, as was true of large-scale political systems before the American union.

2. **Viable democracy.** Modern federalism has made democracy widely viable for the first time in history, on both a large scale and a small scale. As de Tocqueville observed, a federal republic that preserves itself also preserves its smaller constituent republics against both one another and foreign enemies (e.g., the U.S. Constitution's republican guarantee clause).

B. **Pluralist democracy**. Federalism also has made democracy more viable by providing a way for ethnic, religious, racial, and linguistic communities to benefit from union without surrendering total sovereignty or fundamental rights of self-government and communal identity to another group (e.g., Belgium, Canada, Czechoslovakia, India, Malaysia, Nigeria, Switzerland, and Yugoslavia). This type of federalism, however, is often fragile because these federations experience pressures for dissolution or dictatorial centralization. But the emergence of the European Community may provide a more stable model for this type of federalism.

C. **Peace and security**. As **Alexander Hamilton**, **James Madison**, and **John Jay** argued in *The Federalist*, the more that small republics can federate, the more likely they are to enjoy mutual peace and security.

D. **Common-market prosperity**. Peace and security are two preconditions of prosperity. In turn, creating a common market through federation greatly expands opportunities for economic development and entrepreneurial freedom.

E. **Liberty**. Federalism endeavors to protect and enhance liberty by providing for (1) **mutual consent** in the formation and alteration of the union, (2) a **written constitution** specifying and protecting the terms of union, (3) a **defense** against internal and external aggression, (4) a **diffusion of power** to prevent the formation of an imperial or tyrannical central government, (5) **participation by the constituent governments** in the make-up and operation of the general government, (6) constitutional guarantees of **local self-government** and autonomy, (7) **guarantees of the territorial integrity** of the constituent communities (e.g., no alteration of U.S. state boundaries without state consent), (8) general and constituent government **protection of individual rights**, and (9) the protection of both **individual and communal diversity**.

1. **"Communitarian liberty"**. Historically, federalism aimed first at protecting communitarian liberty, namely, the right of the constituent communities to govern themselves in all matters of local relevance and to maintain their identities and ways of life. In the American context, "communitarian liberty" refers to the limited sovereignty of the states. Protecting communitarian liberty indirectly protects individual liberty by preventing one group from unilaterally imposing burdens on individuals of another group or of depriving those persons of their lives, rights, property, or historic identity. Every government that suppresses individual liberty must also destroy communitarian liberty.

2. **Individual liberty**. Federalism is not necessarily aimed directly at protecting individual liberty in the way we understand rights protection today. But such protections may be incorporated into federal systems, as they have been in the American system.

   a. **Protections from general and constituent governments**. Provisions may be made to protect communities and individuals against powers exercised by the general government (e.g., the U.S. Bill of Rights), and against anti-Union and anti-rights powers that might be exercised by the constituent governments (e.g., the U.S. Constitution's privileges and immunities clause).

b. **Communitarian liberty**. Limited local sovereignty within a federal system allows the constituent communities to define and protect certain rights according to their preferences, within the limits set forth in the federal charter. Thus, each U.S. state constitution has its own declaration of rights. States may grant **more** rights than the federal Constitution but not less.

3. **"Communitarian" versus individual liberty**. There is a tension between "communitarian" and individual liberty. "Communitarian liberty" refers to freedoms of the constituent governments from control of the general government.

a. **Federalism and slavery in the U.S.** Among the most abhorrent examples in American history were U.S. guarantees of the liberty of southern states to maintain slavery and then racial segregation. Federalism neither caused nor perpetuated slavery; it was the price of union, and was later abolished by the perseverance of the Union through the Civil War.

b. **The legacy of slavery for liberty and federalism**. However, because of the legacy of slavery, and also because the U.S. has no state comparable to Quebec in Canada where the liberty of a constituent government to pursue policies of cultural autonomy is a major issue, many Americans developed a distrust of "communitarian liberty" (e.g., old-style states' rights) and consented to (1) the Fourteenth Amendment, (2) federal statutory limits on the states, and (3) a transfer of fundamental rights protection from the states to the union through the judicial "incorporation" of the Bill of Rights into the Fourteenth Amendment.

F. **Citizen participation and self-governance**. By providing not only for a democratic general government but also for numerous smaller arenas of democratic governance (e.g., fifty U.S. states and 83,166 local governments), federalism offers citizens many opportunities to hold elected office (497,692 positions) and otherwise participate in public affairs, influence public officials, monitor government, hold public officials accountable, and gain a greater sense of purpose and control over their lives and communities.

G. **Multiple access and checks and balances**. Federalism offers citizens multiple points of access to public power and, thus, an ability to appeal to other governments when one is unresponsive. Multiple governments also check and balance each other, thereby limiting the potential for tyranny. In addition, multiple governments provide citizens with competing sources of information.

H. **Human diversity**. By promoting unity without homogeneity, federalism seeks to protect and moderate human diversity, which serves not only to enhance liberty and the richness of life but also to produce innovation and adaptation to change. Of course, the permissible limits of both diversity and unity are debated perennially in federal polities.

I. **Creative experimentation**. As Justice Louis D. Brandeis said in 1932, a federal polity benefits from a system in which "a single courageous state may, if its citizens choose, serve as a laboratory, and try social and economic experiments without risk to the rest of the country" (*New State Ice Co. v. Liebmann*).

J. **Citizen choice**. By providing for regional and local self-government and for freedom of interstate travel, a federal union gives citizens many choices of government jurisdictions offering different "packages" of taxes, public services, and civic values. In extreme cases, citizens can flee oppressive jurisdictions, as did many black Americans who migrated north and west, first to escape slavery and then to flee legalized discrimination.

K. **Public service efficiency**. Federal systems are often said to be inefficient because there can be duplications of services. It can sometimes take longer to make decisions than may be true under benign centralization. However, history seems to show that centralized governments are less efficient and more wasteful.

1. **Service scales**. A federal system allows for an efficient delivery of public goods by enabling governments to provide public services that are economically appropriate to their territorial jurisdiction (e.g., defense by the general government, highways by state government, and trash collection by local government) and responsive to citizen needs and preferences.

2. **Freedom to seek a more benign state or local government**. This system also permits citizens to "vote with their feet" by leaving a jurisdiction so

as to put pressure at least on constituent governments to match public services with public preferences. Short of leaving a jurisdiction, citizens can vote and otherwise seek to influence government.

L. **Justice**. The above values contribute to one of government's highest objectives, namely, justice. Federalism also makes unique contributions to justice.

1. **Matching burdens and benefits.** Where most domestic services are provided by constituent governments, benefits are more likely to be matched to burdens. That is, citizens get what they pay for, rather than paying for what they don't want, need, or get.

2. **Mutual aid.** Federalism allows for mutual aid and a distribution of resources (e.g., federal grants-in-aid) to jurisdictions that lack the capacity to provide fully for their needs.

3. **Justice in diversity.** In the absence of a universally accepted definition of justice applicable to every case, federalism permits a degree of diversity of conceptions of justice. For example, capital punishment is lawful in thirty-seven states, and its use varies among those states. To majorities of citizens in many of the other states, the death penalty is abhorrent.

V. **The tension between federalism and equality**. Alexis de Tocqueville argued that the modern drive for individual equality would spell the death of federalism (and liberty) because only centralized government would be able to enact thoroughgoing equality. If there is more than one government, then citizens and businesses will be treated differently across the nation. However, no unitary government has ever achieved thorough equality, and those claiming to do so have produced, since the French Revolution, both inequality and tyranny.

A. **Representation**. The basic tension is between community equality and individual equality. The constituent communities (i.e., states) are represented equally in the U.S. Senate; hence, individuals are represented very unequally. This is counteracted to some extent by the House, where representation is by population.

1. **Presidential elections**. Similarly, because the U.S. system of electing presidents apportions electoral votes among the states according to their representation in Congress, citizen votes do not count equally nationwide. There have been many calls to abolish the electoral college, but citizens have not been sufficiently disturbed by it to do so. Also, some minority groups with sizable populations in large states benefit from the electoral college because it magnifies their presidential vote.

2. **Equal representation in state and local legislative bodies**. Representation in state and local legislative bodies has, since the U.S. Supreme Court's "one person, one vote" ruling in *Reynolds v. Sims* (1964), been based on individual voter equality.

3. **Territorial neutrality**. The territorial basis of representation moderates the effects of unequal representation in four ways.

a. **Freedom to choose jurisdiction**. Voters are not compelled to live in a particular jurisdiction. Persons can choose to live in jurisdictions that give their vote more or less weight.

b. **Local self-government of minorities**. Territorial representation allows minority groups to exercise some measure of self-government in states and localities where they are the majority or near-majority. In such local jurisdictions, for example, black Americans are often able to win mayoral and other elections.

c. **Minority representation in large governments**. Territorial representation allows minorities to gain representation in larger governments in ways often otherwise impossible, because they can elect members of their own group to office from any district where they are the majority or near-majority. Thus, for example, there have been more black congressmen than senators, but only one black governor, and no black president. One of the egalitarian ends of federalism is to compensate for what Madison called majority tyranny by providing ways for minorities to gain at least a toehold in government and to have some measure of local self-government.

d. **Establishing new forms of equality**. Territorial representation allows jurisdictions to pioneer new forms of equality, such as in the many states that extended voting rights to women prior to the Nineteenth Amendment to the U.S. Constitution in 1920.

B. **Unequal burdens and benefits democratically chosen.** Ordinarily in a federal democracy, the burdens (e.g., taxes, rules, conscription) and benefits (e.g., public services, financial aid) produced by the general government are to be distributed as equally or equitably as possible among communities and individuals.

1. **Unequal burdens.** The existence of independent state and local governments, however, makes the distribution of other burdens and benefits unequal across the nation (e.g., some states and localities have higher taxes and/or better services than others). Within each jurisdiction, though, burdens and benefits are to be distributed as equally or equitably as possible among localities and/or persons.

2. **Unequal burdens not necessarily objectionable.** Such inequalities are not necessarily objectionable if some jurisdictions democratically choose to have higher taxes or to have better services or different kinds of services than others. In effect, jurisdictions have equal opportunities to make themselves more or less equal, or simply different, from others.

C. **Compensating for unchosen inequality.** Some inequalities, however, are due to wealth or natural-resource endowments. Less well off jurisdictions lack the financial ability to provide better or even minimally adequate services. Some jurisdictions also face higher per capita costs than others because of such things as harsh weather, long stretches of rural highway, or many school children. Hence, just as democracies use tax and spending policies to redistribute some income from high-income to low-income persons, so too do most federal democracies empower their general government to redistribute some income from high-income to low-income places.

D. **Equality on fundamental rights and benefits; local variation on those not fundamental.** In all federal democracies, citizens must make hard choices between rights, benefits, and burdens that are to be regarded as fundamental and, therefore, distributed equally across the nation, and those that are to be allowed to vary according to the preferences of state and local voters. In effect, federalism seeks to balance people's desires to be equal and different.

E. **Discrimination and externalities.** A further feature of federalism is that federal democracies are able to prohibit certain forms of discrimination and to deal with positive and negative externalities.

1. **Discrimination.** Generally, federal democracies prohibit state and local policies that significantly discriminate against or disadvantage other jurisdictions and their citizens.

2. **Externalities.** Similarly, federal democracies endeavor to deal with externalities (or spillovers), both positive and negative. An example of a positive externality is a public park built by a community with its own funds that also is used by people from other communities. A community can charge for this spillover, however, by levying a user fee. A negative externality is air pollution produced in one state that blows over other states.

3. **Federal floors and state ceilings.** An emerging trend is for the federal government to require all states to comply with minimum national standards, but to allow states to impose higher standards if they wish to do so. Externalities are not peculiar to federalism; they are present in all government systems and in international relations. Lessons learned in federal systems can be applied to these other arenas.

F. **No consistent winners or losers.** Given the complexity of equality and the difficulty, perhaps impossibility, of achieving absolute equality, federal democracies seek to compensate in many ways. In the end, in a federal democracy no citizen or group is necessarily a consistent winner or loser in electoral contests. Thus, for example, in a single year, a citizen may vote for a winning presidential candidate, losing senatorial candidate, winning congressional candidate, losing gubernatorial candidate, winning mayoral candidate, losing school-board candidate, and so on.

VI. **The framework of the American federal union.** The overall constitutional-legal framework of the American federal union includes the Declaration of Independence, Articles of Confederation, Northwest Ordinance, Constitution of the United States of America (including the Bill of Rights), state constitutions (including their Declarations of Rights), Indian treaties, federacy covenants, and, some would argue, municipal charters.

A. **The Declaration of Independence (1776).** The Declaration does not have the force of law, but it is the fundamental document that established the American people and thereby, in time, their union. The Declaration sets forth common values that underlie the American identity and the chief principles of American government.

B. **The Articles of Confederation (1781).** The Articles were replaced by the U.S. Constitution. However, debts incurred and treaties concluded by the U.S. under the Articles remained in force after 1789. Furthermore, the Articles established the Union for perpetuity, which is why the Preamble to the U.S. Constitution speaks only of forming "a more perfect Union."

C. **The Northwest Ordinance (1785 and 1787).** The Northwest Ordinance provided for governance in the old Northwest Territory. Certain provisions of the ordinance still have the force of law in states formed from the territory (i.e., Ohio, Indiana, Illinois, Michigan, Wisconsin, and northeastern Minnesota).

D. **State constitutions.** State constitutions preceded the Articles of Confederation and the U.S. Constitution and provided the framers of both documents with many models of what to do and not do. Most state constitutions are longer than the U.S. Constitution, in part because they must provide for more functions (e.g., education and local government). In addition, because of residual state plenary powers, citizens must limit power in state constitutions.

E. **Indian treaties.** Indian treaties are part of the Union's constitutional-legal framework because Native American communities were initially treated as sovereign nations, and many Indian treaties remain in force, in whole or in part.

1. **Supremacy of U.S. law.** Although the U.S. Constitution and U.S. laws now have de facto supremacy because Native Americans were unilaterally made citizens by the Congress, prior treaty law is applicable to certain tribes and limits the exercise of federal and state power over them.

2. **Indian nations not federal constituent governments.** Self-governing Native American reservations are not states, nor are they creatures of the states like other local governments. Hence, self-governing Native American communities cannot fundamentally be regarded as constituent governments of the federal Union because most of them did not truly consent to join the union, and because some tribes live on lands to which their ancestors were removed forcibly.

F. **Federacy covenants.** "Federacy covenants" include the various quasi-constitutional agreements that exist by mutual consent between the U.S. and American Samoa, the Federated States of Micronesia, Guam, the Marshall Islands, the Northern Mariana Islands, the Panama Canal Zone, Puerto Rico, the Republic of Palau, and the Virgin Islands.

G. **Municipal charters.** Some observers argue that municipal charters, especially in home-rule states, should be viewed as part of the nation's basic constitutional framework. Even in states where cities can only exercise powers expressly granted to them, municipalities sometimes enjoy substantial self-government. Although states are not formally federal, the tendency has been to disperse power in a federal-like manner. Also, several states (e.g., Rhode Island) were formed in fact or in essence as federations of local communities. The degree of centralization within states varies greatly.

VII. **The Constitution of the United States.** The U.S. Constitution is the authoritative basis of the American federal union and the supreme law of the land within its sphere of authority. Through the U.S. Constitution, the American citizens delegate limited powers to a general, nationwide government (i.e., the U.S. government), which is usually called the federal government. This government is not a traditional national government; instead, as Madison noted, it is partly national and partly confederal. We designate this "compound republic" as simply "federal."

A. **Policy-making powers delegated to federal government.** The policy powers delegated to the U.S. government fall into two general categories:

1. **Foreign affairs and defense powers.** These powers allow the U.S. government, for example, to regulate immigration, declare war, and conclude treaties.

2. **Land and commerce powers.** These powers allow the U.S. government to, among other things, regulate foreign and interstate commerce and commerce with the Indian tribes; coin money; establish post offices and post roads; grant patents and copyrights; and admit new states to the Union.

B. **Integrity powers.** The remaining powers delegated to the U.S. government serve to protect the integrity and operational independence of that government in the federal union (e.g., the powers to tax, spend, and borrow money; make all laws necessary and proper for executing the powers listed in the U.S. Constitution; and initiate amendments to the U.S. Constitution by a two-thirds vote of both houses of Congress).

C. **Post-1789 U.S. powers.** By amendments to the U.S. Constitution, the U.S. government was empowered to enforce the constitutional ban on slavery and involuntary servitude (Amendment 13, 1865); enforce the Fourteenth Amendment (1868); enforce voting rights for racial minorities (Amendment 15, 1870), women (Amendment 19, 1920), and then all citizens age 18 and over (Amendment 26, 1971); levy an income tax (Amendment 16, 1913); and enforce a ban on poll taxes (Amendment 14, 1964). No new powers have been constitutionally delegated to the U.S. government since 1971.

D. **Powers prohibited to the U.S. government.** The powers prohibited to the U.S. government by the U.S. Constitution fall mainly into five categories:

1. **Power to compromise states' integrity.** Powers are denied that would destroy the existence or concurrent independence (or co-sovereignty) of the states (e.g., no state can be formed from existing states without the consent of said states; also constitutional amendments must be ratified by three-fourths of the states).

2. **Power to deny equal treatment to states.** Powers are denied that would deny states equitable treatment by the U.S. government (e.g., no preference can be given by any regulation of commerce or revenue to the ports of one state over those of another).

3. **Power to deny state representation in Congress.** Powers are denied that would alter states' representation in Congress and presidential elections (e.g., each state is guaranteed two senators and at least one representative).

4. **Power to deny citizens' rights.** Powers are denied that would deprive citizens of rights (e.g., the prohibition of bills of attainder, ex post facto laws, and religious tests for U.S. office; and the entire U.S. Bill of Rights).

5. **Power to establish an aristocracy.** Powers are denied that would destroy fundamental political equality by establishing an aristocracy; that is, neither the U.S. nor any state can grant any title of nobility.

E. **Roles and powers of the states.** The states are mentioned fifty times in forty-two separate sections of the U.S. Constitution. The roles and powers of the states as affected by the U.S. Constitution fall into six categories.

1. **States as basis of representation and of the electoral college.** States are the basis of representation in the Senate, and they are the electoral basis of voting for the president and vice president.

2. **States and procedures of government: the "political safeguards" of federalism.** States directly affect the operations and powers of the U.S. government through their people's representation in Congress, their power to call for a constitutional convention (by petition of two-thirds of the states), and their exclusive authority to ratify or reject proposed amendments to the U.S. Constitution. Ratification requires the approval of the legislatures or conventions of three-fourths of the states. The compositional and procedural roles of the states are often called the "political safeguards" of federalism.

3. **State obligations.** The U.S. Constitution requires each state to (1) give full faith and credit to the public acts, records, and judicial proceedings of every other state; (2) extend all privileges and immunities of its own citizens to the citizens of other states; (3) extradite indicted persons to the state of indictment on demand of the indicting state's governor; and (4) uphold the U.S. Constitution.

4. **Unconditional prohibitions.** The U.S. Constitution prohibits states from, for example, (1) entering into any treaty, alliance, or confederation; (2) coining money; (3) enacting any bill of attainder or ex post facto law; (4) impairing the obligation of contracts; (5) making any law that abridges the privileges or immunities of citizens of the states; (6) depriving any person of life, liberty, or property without due process of law; and (7) denying any person the equal protection of the laws.

5. **Conditional prohibitions.** Without the consent of the Congress, states may not, for example, keep troops or ships of war in time of peace; enter into any agreement or compact with another state or foreign power; or engage in war unless invaded or in imminent danger.

6. **State integrity**. In addition to the prohibitions on U.S. powers and the political safeguards of federalism, three other provisions protect state integrity: (1) state maintenance of militias; (2) the clause guaranteeing each state a republican form of government and protection against invasion; and (3) the Tenth Amendment.

F. **Categories of governments' powers**. Generally, the powers of governments (federal and state) in the American federal union fall into eight interpretative categories.

1. **Delegated powers**. Delegated powers are those given to a government by the people. These are the powers spelled out in the U.S. Constitution. Strictly speaking, the people do not delegate powers to state governments.

2. **Enumerated powers**. Enumerated powers are those explicitly listed in the U.S. Constitution, such as the power to regulate interstate commerce.

3. **Implied powers**. Implied powers are those not expressly listed in the U.S. Constitution but judged "necessary and proper" (the "elastic clause") to execute enumerated powers.

4. **Inherent powers**. Inherent powers are those deemed necessary and essential to the U.S. as a nation-state, even though they are not enumerated or implied in the U.S. Constitution. There is no clear evidence that the framers of the U.S. Constitution contemplated inherent U.S. government powers, but the U.S. Supreme Court recognized such powers in *U.S. v. Curtiss-Wright Export Corp* (1936).

5. **Exclusive powers**. Exclusive powers are those exercised only by one type of government, such as the power to declare war exercised by the U.S. government, and the power to choose presidential electors exercised by the state governments.

6. **Concurrent powers**. Concurrent powers are those exercised by both the U.S. government and the state governments. There is no list of concurrent powers in the U.S. Constitution, as there is in some federal constitutions, because states can exercise powers not denied them by the U.S. Constitution. The powers to tax, spend, and borrow money are examples of vital concurrent powers.

7. **Plenary powers**. Plenary powers are, in principle, the complete powers of government, which originally (before the Constitution was ratified) belonged to the states. These powers are limited by the sovereign people through the U.S. Constitution and state constitutions. A state can exercise any powers not prohibited to it by the U.S. Constitution or the state constitution. Strictly speaking, the U.S. government has no plenary powers, although it is often said that its enumerated powers are plenary within their spheres (e.g., Congress has plenary power to regulate interstate and foreign commerce).

8. **Reserved powers**. Reserved powers are those retained by the states or the people after their delegations of powers to the U.S. government. There is no list of reserved powers; instead, there is the summary statement found in the Tenth Amendment: "The powers not delegated to the States by the Constitution, nor prohibited by it to the States, are reserved to the States respectively, or to the people."

G. **Supreme Court as federal umpire**. The U. S. Supreme Court has traditionally been viewed as the umpire of the federal system because of its power to interpret law and to declare acts of Congress (e.g., *Marbury v. Madison*, 1803), acts of states (e.g., *U.S. v. Peters*, 1809), and local ordinances (e.g., *Weston v. City Council of Charleston*, 1829) to be in violation of the U.S. Constitution and, therefore, null and void. Likewise, conflicts between U.S. statutory or treaty law and state or local law are often adjudicated by the Court. Lower federal courts and state courts also adjudicate such conflicts.

H. **Congressional discretion in interpreting federal powers**. The Congress, however, is usually the driving force in determining the powers exercised by the U.S. and/or the states. This is so because only Congress can make federal law and ratify treaties, and because, since 1937 (e.g., *NLRB v. Jones and Laughlin Steel Corp.*), the U.S. Supreme Court has given the Congress broad discretion to interpret the scope and nature of U.S. powers.

VIII. **Historical change in operation of federalism**. Key operational aspects of American federalism have, of course, changed during the past two centuries because of political and socio-economic developments and constitutional change and interpretation.

A. **Dual and cooperative federalism**. Dual and cooperative federalism have been the two general conceptions of federalism dominant in American history.

 1. **Dual federalism**. Dual federalism was developed mainly by the U.S. Supreme Court in the early nineteenth century to settle federal-state jurisdiction issues. The U.S. Constitution was said to create a division of labor in which the U.S. government and the state governments operate in two separate spheres of independent authority. The doctrine of dual federalism was replaced by cooperative federalism during the New Deal.

 2. **Cooperative federalism**. The idea of "cooperative federalism" was developed by such early leaders as **Albert Gallatin** (1761-1849) and then by political reformers, such as the Progressives, in the late nineteenth century.

   a. **Problem of fragmentation of power**. Dual federalism was said to fragment public power, making it difficult for government to cope with the rise of a national economy and big business and with the social problems created by economic cycles, urbanization, and immigration.

   b. **Obligation to work cooperatively**. Cooperative federalism holds that the U.S. government and the state governments are constitutionally obligated to work cooperatively, with few sharp boundaries between them, and with the U.S. government having broad authority to exercise power on behalf of the states.

B. **Intergovernmental cooperation**. Practically, dual federalism never really existed.

 1. **Impracticality of "dual federalism."** From the beginning, the U.S. government relied greatly on the states for many tasks, and the states relied on the U.S. government for post offices, post roads, public works projects, land grants, military assistance, and other aid. In essence, the U.S. government and the states must cooperate to make federalism work.

 2. **Increase in scope of government action**. Under cooperative federalism, the scope of action of all governments has increased; virtually every public policy field involves the federal, state, and local governments; and the U.S. government is the dominant partner in many fields.

C. **Forms of federal-state cooperation and sharing**. There are many forms of cooperation and sharing in the federal system. These occur informally and through explicit compactual agreements, contracts, and statutory arrangements. For example, grants-in-aid to state and local governments are a major form of fiscal sharing today, totaling $123.6 billion in 1990, or 10.7 percent of U.S. government outlays.

D. **Prohibition and coercion in the federal system**. There also are forms of prohibition and coercion in the federal system.

 1. **Constitutional prohibitions**. Since 1789, the U.S. Supreme Court has struck down more than 1150 state and local laws as being unconstitutional. State supreme courts also exercise this authority with respect to state and local laws that contravene the U.S. Constitution and the state constitution.

 2. **Judicial mandates**. Court orders involve U.S. court commands that a state or local government do something (e.g., provide prisoners more cell space) or not do something (e.g., cease racial segregation). State courts also exercise this authority with respect to the state and local governments.

 3. **Other government mandates**. Mandates are requirements of action (e.g., to provide disabled persons access to public transit) imposed by the U.S. government on state or local governments or by a state on its local governments. Mandates are sometimes funded, or partly funded, by the mandating government, but often they are not, thus requiring the mandated government to pay the compliance costs.

 4. **Federal preemption**. Preemption allows U.S. law, under the supremacy clause, to supersede state or local law. Since 1789, the U.S. government has enacted at least 351 preemption statutes, 187 of which (53 percent) have been enacted since 1969.

E. **Dualistic cooperation**. Dualistic cooperation remains a characteristic of the American federal system in most policy fields (e.g., antitrust law, banking, environmental protection, narcotics, and telecommunications). Both the U.S. government and the state governments exercise lawful regulatory authority. Sometimes this involves parallel or competing institutions, such as

U.S. regulation of U.S.-chartered banks and state regulation of state-chartered banks.

F. **Burden of state and local government**. Most domestic laws and public policies are enacted or administered by state and local governments. For example, more than 99 percent of the nation's judicial business is handled by state courts. State and local governments, with 14.2 million employees, also carry out most of the domestic policies of the U.S. government, which has only 3.1 million civilian employees. State and local governments also provide the public services that affect the daily lives of citizens, such as police and fire protection, public education, roads, streets, water, and sewer services.

IX. **Influence of federalism on policy-making**. Federalism and intergovernmental relations shape all policy-making in the United States. If, as former U.S. House Speaker Tip O'Neil once said, "All politics is local," then this is all the more true in a federal system. A perennial issue in federalism, however, is the appropriate balance of power to be maintained between the general government and the constituent governments.

Historical Perspective

The American federal union is arguably the most successful experiment in democracy in history. Before 1789, there was no historical precedent for an entity like the United States of America. In 1789, no sane person would have wagered on the union lasting for more than two hundred years and also growing to encompass fifty states and citizens representing virtually every racial, ethnic, nationality, religious, and linguistic group in the world.

I. **Origins of American federalism** The origins of American federalism lie in political theory, cultural practice, and political necessity.

A. **Federal theology**. The first political ideas systematically articulated in North America were derived from the Puritans' federal or covenant theology, which drew heavily from the Hebrew Bible (i.e., the Old Testament).

1. **Federalism in Puritan thought**. The Puritans regarded all relationships as federal, beginning with the relationship between God and humans. In turn, men and women covenanted to form families, families to form congregations, congregations to form towns, towns to form larger civil associations, and so on.

2. **The influence of covenant theology**. Covenant theology was deeply embedded in Reformed Protestantism, which came to include such denominations as the Baptists, Congregationalists, and Presbyterians.

   a. **The Mayflower Compact**. The first American expression of Reformed Protestantism's civil federalism was the Mayflower Compact (actually a covenant) of 1620.

   b. **The Constitution as a "Presbyterian" document**. By the 1780s, at least half of the union's religious congregations were based on covenant principles. In the republic's early days, some people referred to the U.S. Constitution as a "Presbyterian" document because of its similarity to federated church governance in Reformed Protestantism.

B. **Practical federalism**. In America, making covenants as a basis of government predated the classic English contract theorists.

1. **Civil covenanting in colonial America**. Often overlooked is the fact that, before **Thomas Hobbes** and **John Locke** formulated their secular theories of civil covenant and social compact, settlers in North America were already engaged in civil covenanting. After the Mayflower covenant of 1620, hundreds of communities, especially in the northern colonies, were founded by covenants among settlers.

2. **Movement toward larger societies**. Over time, steps were taken toward larger civil societies, including the Colonies of New England in 1643, the Albany Congress in 1745, the Stamp Act Congress in 1765, the first Continental Congress in 1774, the Declaration of Independence in 1776, eighteen state constitutions prior to 1789, the Articles of Confederation and Perpetual Union in 1781, and, finally, the U.S. Constitution.

C. **Shareholder rights**. Economic bases of federalism can be traced to the sea laws that governed settlers on the Atlantic voyage and to the trading companies that sponsored British and Dutch settlement.

1. **Voyagers' agreements**. Generally, voyagers signed articles of agreement on governance for the ocean crossing. (This system reappeared in the organization of wagon trains, whose members

compacted to provide for governance during their journey.)

2. **Shareholders' agreements.** On shore, relationships between the shareholders and non-shareholders in North America and the shareholders in Europe developed a quasi-federal character in which the North American settlers sought greater rights and autonomy.

3. **The British Empire as a federal system.** The agreements with shareholders in Europe is one reason why many Americans by the 1770s saw the British Empire as a kind of federal system and, therefore, demanded both local autonomy and actual representation in decisions affecting them.

D. **The Iroquois Confederacy.** Some observers hold that the origins of American federalism lie partly in the model of the League of the Iroquois. There were favorable references to such a confederacy by Benjamin Franklin (e.g., his Albany Plan) and other colonists. But there is little evidence that the political organization of the Iroquois had a significant, independent impact on American federalism.

E. **Minimal influence of secular European political thought.** Although Americans were greatly influenced by European ideas, secular European political thought offered little on federalism. Outside of Switzerland and the Dutch provinces, the federal ideas of covenanters were overshadowed by monarchies, theories of the unitary state, and the emerging idea of the General Will. Attention was given to biblical Israel's federalism and to other historical confederations and leagues, but it was left to the Founders to pioneer a modern, workable federalism, along with written constitutions and bills of rights. The idea of a written constitution was not prevalent in Europe, and few of the rights found in state declarations of rights and the U.S. Bill of Rights existed in European documents.

F. **Practical necessity.** Finally, the origins of American federalism lie in the practical fact that the confederation consisted of thirteen independent-minded states spread across a large territory. Citizens of the states were unwilling to accept a unitary national government, and no monarch or military force existed to unify the states under one central regime.

II. **From confederation to federation.** On July 12, 1776, the Articles of Confederation were submitted to the Second Continental Congress by a committee set up to compose them. After revision, they were adopted by the Congress

in November 1777. Ratified by all states but one by 1779, they were finally adopted in March 1781. The Articles established a "perpetual union," but many nationalist leaders believed the confederal government was too weak to protect the union against domestic and foreign dangers.

A. **Weaknesses of the Articles of Confederation.** The weaknesses of the Articles of Confederation were held to be primarily the Congress's lack of authority to perform a number of functions.

1. **Enforcing government law.** The confederal government could not enforce confederation law against states and persons.

2. **Levying taxes.** The confederal government could not levy taxes; instead, it was dependent on the states to make contributions, which the states were often loathe to make.

3. **Regulating commerce.** The confederal government lacked the power to regulate interstate and foreign commerce.

4. **Raising armies.** The confederal government could not directly raise military forces.

5. **Protecting individuals rights.** The confederal government lacked the power to protect individual rights.

B. **Strengths of the Articles of Confederation.** The strengths of the confederation should not be overlooked, however.

1. **Policy accomplishments.** During and after ratification of the Articles, the States won the War of Independence, concluded a treaty of peace, obtained the cession to the union of state claims on western territories, provided for settlement and governance of the Northwest Territory, established diplomatic and trade relations, created a perpetual union, and provided a vehicle for moving toward a stronger union.

2. **Holding tyranny and anarchy at bay.** Perhaps most important, under the Articles, the Americans became one of the few peoples in history to fight a revolution, or war of national liberation, without plunging into despotism or civil war afterwards.

C. **The Constitutional Convention.** The convention, which met in Philadelphia in 1787, formulated remedies for the weaknesses of the Articles of Confederation.

1. **New government authority.** Granting the new general government authority to enforce law against individuals was the most singular innovation, according to Hamilton. This enables the U.S. government to levy taxes, raise an army and navy directly, regulate interstate and foreign commerce, and protect some rights, such as certain property rights under the Constitution's contracts clause.

2. **Federal government no longer the mere creature of the states.** As a result, another key innovation of the new federal Constitution was that it was established directly by the people of the states, rather than by state governments per se. Thus the Preamble speaks of the Constitution's establishment by "We the People of the United States."

3. **Supremacy of federal Constitution.** Making the U.S. Constitution and laws conforming to it supreme over state and local law was another innovation.

4. **Implied federal powers.** Granting the new general government implied powers was another important innovation.

5. **Concurrent and exclusive powers.** Providing for concurrent and exclusive powers to be exercised by the general government and the constituent governments was a further innovation.

6. **Equality for new states.** Providing for the admission of new states to the union on an equal footing with the original states was another extremely important and almost unheard of (outside of North America) innovation.

7. **The Connecticut Compromise.** The Connecticut Compromise solved a knotty procedural problem in creating a stronger general government. It was another innovation, providing for equal representation of the states in the U.S. Senate (although senators vote as individuals) and variable representation in the U.S. House, according to population as determined by a constitutionally mandated decennial census.

8. **"Compound republic."** Finally, the idea of the "compound republic" articulated by Madison stands as a general innovation in federalism.

Madison (see *The Federalist* No. 39, especially), noted how various features of the U.S. Constitution make the general government partly confederal and partly national (e.g., the Senate leans in a confederal direction; the House leans in a national direction).

D. **Ratification campaign.** The campaign to ratify the proposed constitution produced two general camps commonly called Federalists and Anti-Federalists.

1. **The Federalists and Anti-Federalists.** Federalists, who supported the draft constitution, included such prominent leaders as **George Washington**, **James Madison**, **Alexander Hamilton**, **John Jay**, and **Benjamin Franklin**. The Anti-Federalists, who opposed the draft constitution because (among other reasons) they believed it would create a consolidated national government, included such prominent leaders as **George Clinton**, **George Mason**, and **Patrick Henry**.

   a. *The Federalist Papers.* *The Federalist Papers* written by Hamilton, Madison, and Jay, were not popular in 1787-1788, but have since become the single most authoritative source for interpreting the Founders' intentions, and the greatest single expression of American political thought.

   b. **Bill of Rights as Anti-Federalist contribution.** The U.S. Bill of Rights remains the most important Anti-Federalist contribution to the U.S. Constitution. (The Bill of Rights originally limited only the U.S. government, not the states.)

2. **Small republic v. large republic debate.** The Anti-Federalists advanced a number of arguments against a large republic.

   a. **Fear of tyranny.** Given that, historically, attempts to create large political societies had produced empires, Anti-Federalists feared that the proposed general government would become tyrannical. Federalists argued that the draft constitution contained sufficient safeguards against tyranny, while also having enough power to protect the states against a major weakness of small republics, namely, their inability to defend themselves against aggression.

b. **Weakening of democracy.** Anti-Federalists also held that democracy can only work in a small republic where citizens can deliberate rationally on public issues, elected officials can be held accountable, and government can approximate direct democracy. Federalists argued that the bane of small republics is majority tyranny in which one political faction dominates others. A large republic would have too many factions to allow one faction to bring about tyranny.

c. **Weakening of civic virtue.** Anti-Federalists argued that a large republic would produce an anarchic politics of selfish interest-group bargaining and conflict that would undermine civic virtue and the common good. Federalists argued that good government cannot rely on virtue because self-interest is the natural basis of human behavior, and, in fact, operates more perniciously in small republics. Instead, interests must be constantly checked, balanced, and prevented from coalescing behind tyranny.

III. **Pre-Civil War federalism.** Federalism before the Civil War was characterized by a combination of competition between the U.S. government and the states, fairly regular intergovernmental cooperation, and rising conflict over slavery.

A. **Competition among governments.** Competition occurred as the U.S. government sought to establish itself as a viable government while states sought to retain power.

1. **Proposal for a bill of rights.** Congress quickly established the new government by proposing a bill of rights as promised by the Federalists during the ratification campaign, creating institutions of government (e.g., the courts), and asserting powers (e.g., establishing the Bank of the U.S.).

2. **Early executive leadership.** President George Washington provided legitimacy for the new government and ended the Whiskey Rebellion amicably, and President Thomas Jefferson expanded U.S. powers by making the Louisiana Purchase.

3. **U.S. Supreme Court's assertion of national authority.** The Supreme Court, under Chief Justice John Marshall, a Federalist, asserted U.S. powers.

a. **Federal government independent of states.** In *McCulloch v. Maryland* (1819), the Court as-serted national supremacy in an implied sphere of constitutional authority by upholding the Bank of the U.S. and holding that states could not tax the bank without U.S. consent because the bank was an instrument of the U.S. government. (Congress later allowed state taxation of U.S.-chartered banks.)

b. **Federal law enforceable against state officials.** In *Osborn v. Bank of the U.S.* (1824), the Court held that the U.S. government may enforce U.S. law against state officials.

c. **Broad federal power to regulate commerce.** In *Gibbons v. Ogden* (1824), the Court asserted a broad interpretation of "commerce" subject to U.S. regulation.

4. **State-related resistance.** State-related resistance to the new government took several forms.

a. **The Virginia and Kentucky resolutions.** The Kentucky resolutions (1798 and 1799) drafted by Thomas Jefferson, and the Virginia resolutions (1798) drafted by James Madison, asserted state authority to nullify U.S. law deemed unconstitutional by a state legislature. They were responses to fears of U.S. tyranny arising from the Alien and Sedition Acts of 1798. Among other provisions, the Acts proscribed written or spoken criticism of the government.

b. **The Hartford Convention (1815).** The Hartford Convention reflected New England's resistance to the War of 1812. The convention made many proposals to limit U.S. power, but concern ended with the close of the war.

c. **States' rights and nullification of U.S. law.** John C. Calhoun (1782-1850), in his "South Carolina Exposition and Protest" (1828), mounted a defense of states' rights and state nullification of U.S. law. Later, he propounded his compact theory of the U.S. Constitution.

d. **The Ordinance of Nullification (1832).** The Ordinance of Nullification was enacted by a convention in South Carolina to nullify the U.S. tariff acts of 1828 and 1832. In response, **President Andrew Jackson** (1767-

1845) alerted U.S. forces in Charleston and proposed both a compromise tariff bill and a bill (the Force Bill) to allow him to use troops to enforce the tariffs. Both bills passed the Congress. In 1833, South Carolina rescinded its tariff nullification but passed an ordinance nullifying the Force Act.

B. **Intergovernmental cooperation.** Despite competition and conflict, the predominant modes of daily intergovernmental relations were cooperation and mutual forbearance. States administered and enforced federal law, and members of Congress provided "pork-barrel" benefits. The U.S. government participated in "internal improvements" (e.g., roads and canals), and formal and informal cooperation developed between the federal government and the states in such fields as agriculture, banking, education, and economic development. On several occasions (e.g., 1833 and 1836), the U.S. distributed surplus revenue to the states, usually as loans that were never recalled.

C. **Conflict over slavery.** After the War of 1812, slavery became the centerpiece of federal-state conflict because it was a fundamental moral issue drawn along regional lines.

1. **Growing economic disparities.** The conflict was heightened by the growing industrial character of the North and continuing agricultural character of the South. Also, tariff disputes intensified the regional conflict embedded in slavery.

2. **Enforcement of the "fugitive slave clause" of Article IV of the Constitution.** Southern states urged U.S. enforcement of the fugitive slave clause, while Northern states asserted states' rights to harbor fugitive slaves.

3. **Admission of new states.** The conflict was also expressed in the admission of new states to the Union, as various compromises (e.g., the Missouri Compromise, 1820) were forged between pro- and anti-slavery forces.

4. **The Dred Scott case.** A major factor in precipitating the Civil War was the U.S. Supreme Court's decision in *Dred Scott v. Sanford* (1857)which, among other things, voided the Missouri Compromise.

5. **South Carolina's secession from the Union.** On December 20, 1860, South Carolina seceded and was followed the next year by ten other states, thus opening the Civil War.

IV. **From the Civil War to the New Deal.** Although conflict lingered between southern states and the U.S. government during Reconstruction, and new conflicts developed between East and West, this period was marked by remarkable continuity in the federal system, even though the nation experienced tremendous expansion and dramatic social and economic changes. Post-Civil War federalism was affected mainly by growing class and ethnic conflict in which reformers advocated expansions of U.S. powers to counteract the power of big business and urban political machines.

A. **Constitutional amendments.** Four constitutional amendments adopted during this period laid foundations for greatly expanded U.S. power: the Fourteenth Amendment (due process and equal protection applied to the states), the Fifteenth Amendment (right to vote), the Sixteenth Amendment (federal income tax), and the Seventeenth Amendment (direct election of U.S. senators).

B. **Supreme Court policies.** Near the end of this period, the U.S. Supreme Court pursued policies viewed by many scholars as hostile to government regulation of the economy and overly supportive of dual federalism. However, other scholars believe that the true picture was more mixed. Among significant Court decisions related to federalism were:

1. *Texas v. White* (1869). In this crucial case, the Court held that: "The Constitution...looks to an indestructible Union, composed of indestructible States."

2. The *Slaughterhouse Cases* (1873). These cases upheld a Louisiana act, which in effect granted a monopoly, and refused to construe the Fourteenth Amendment's due process clause as a substantive limit on state regulatory powers, thus upholding states' rights.

3. *Plessy v. Ferguson* (1896). Here, the Court upheld a Louisiana law requiring "separate but equal" racially segregated railroad facilities.

4. *Lochner v. New York* (1905). In *Lochner*, the Court struck down a New York law setting maximum work hours for bakers.

5. *Missouri v. Holland* (1920). In *Missouri v. Holland*, the Court upheld U.S. authority to

override state powers under treaty law (a treaty involving migratory birds), an authority that was earlier held to be invalid in the absence of a treaty.

6. *Gitlow v. New York* (1925). *Gitlow* upheld New York's criminal anarchy law but opened the door to nationalization of the U.S. Bill of Rights as protection against state actions.

C. **Congressional-presidential expansions of U.S. powers.** Expansion of federal powers occurred mainly in economic regulation, as reflected in enactment of the Interstate Commerce Act (1887), Sherman Antitrust Act (1890), Federal Bankruptcy Act (1898), Pure Food and Drug Act (1906), Meat Inspection Act (1906), and Clayton Antitrust Act (1914).

D. **Intergovernmental cooperation.** Cooperation between the federal and state governments continued and became more formal as the U.S. government made land grants to states, land grants to railroads to facilitate economic development, and, later, cash grants-in-aid. This period also marked the height of U.S. military assistance in settlement and development of the West. Several examples are the following:

1. **The Morrill Act (1862).** The Morrill Act made land grants to states to endow agricultural colleges, which resulted in 69 land-grant colleges.

2. **The Selective Service Act (1917).** The Selective Service Act created an intergovernmental cooperative system for military conscription (e.g., local draft boards).

3. **The Sheppard-Towner Act (1921).** The Sheppard-Towner Act provided federal grants for the health and welfare of pregnant women and infants.

4. **The Air Commerce Act (1926).** The Air Commerce Act provided federal aid to promote civil air transport and build airports.

E. **State reforms.** Although the turn of the century saw the rise of powerful urban political machines and corporate dominance of a number of states, this was also a period of state reform activity. Some "firsts" were **woman suffrage** (Wyoming, 1869), the **income tax** (Hawaii, 1901 and Wisconsin, 1911), **direct primary** (Mississippi, 1902 and Wisconsin, 1903), **workers' compensation** (Maryland, 1902), **public assistance for women with dependent children** (Illinois, 1911), and

minimum-wage law (Massachusetts, 1912), which was struck down by the U.S. Supreme Court in 1923.

V. **From Roosevelt's New Deal to Reagan's New Federalism.** This period was marked by (1) a tremendous expansion of U.S. government power in response to the Great Depression, World War II, the civil rights revolution, the war on poverty, and the environmental protection movement; (2) the nationalization of the U.S. Bill of Rights by the U.S. Supreme Court and the rise of a more active federal judiciary that viewed the Tenth Amendment as "but a truism" (*U.S. v. Darby*, 1941); (3) a proliferation of federal grants-in-aid, funding for which peaked in 1978 as a percentage of federal outlays and state and local revenues; (4) a resurgence of the states as reformed polities by the 1970s; and (5) the rise of the Reagan new federalist reaction to U.S. government activism.

A. **Increase of federal power by executive-legislative action.** Congressional-presidential expansions of U.S. government activity brought the U.S. government into virtually every policy field relevant to state and local governments.

1. **Public finance.** The power shift can be seen in the relative amounts spent by the federal, state, and local governments. The U.S. government accounted for only 26 percent of all government expenditures in 1929 (when states accounted for 20 percent and local governments for 54 percent). By 1939, the U.S. government's share had increased to 51 percent, which then increased to 70 percent in 1949—about where it has remained since then. The U.S. government also collects the largest share of taxes.

2. **New Deal precursors of contemporary federalism.** New Deal legislation that laid the groundwork for the intensive cooperative federalism and rising federal regulations of the 1960s and 1970s includes the following:

   a. **The Glass-Steagall Act (1933).** The Glass-Steagall Act created the Federal Deposit Insurance Corporation (partly modeled after state deposit insurance systems). It maintained the dual federal-state banking system but opened the way for greater federal regulation of financial institutions and use of that regulation for purposes of domestic social policy.

b. **The Civilian Conservation Corps Reforestation Relief Act (1933) and Soil Conservation Act (1935)**. These acts expanded the U.S. government's role in conservation, which had begun with the establishment of Yellowstone National Park in 1872. They were followed by numerous environmental laws, including the Water Pollution Control Act (1948); the Clean Air Act (1963); National Environmental Policy Act (1970); and Low-Level Radioactive Waste Policy Act (1980), which makes each state responsible for its own waste and encourages interstate compacts for waste disposal.

c. **The National Guard Act (1934)**. The National Guard Act substantially integrated state National Guard units into the U.S. Armed Forces, a process that continued through the Montgomery Amendment (1986), which denied governors a veto over presidential orders to send Guard units on peacetime training missions abroad (upheld by the U.S. Supreme Court in *Perpich v. Department of Defense*, 1990).

d. **The Motor Carrier Act (1935)**. The Motor Carrier Act brought buses and trucks engaged in interstate commerce under the Interstate Commerce Commission, opening the way for more federal highway-related regulation, including billboard rules in 1965, imposition of the 55-mph speed limit in 1973, and the 21-year-old drinking-age requirement of 1984 (upheld by the U.S. Supreme Court in *South Dakota v. Dole*, 1987).

e. **The Social Security Act (1935)**. The Social Security Act, in addition to its retirement program, became the springboard for the U.S. government's massive role in social welfare, including Aid to Families with Dependent Children (1950), Food Stamps (1961), Medicare and Medicaid (1965), the Family Support Act (1988), and nearly one hundred other welfare-related programs—most of which are federal-state programs.

f. **The National Housing Act (1937)**. The National Housing Act became the basis for the U.S. government's involvement in public and low-income housing, urban renewal, and expansion of home ownership.

3. **The Truman Administration**. The Truman Administration, largely preoccupied with international affairs, produced one significant federalism initiative: the Housing Act of 1949, which created a major role for the U.S. government in urban renewal and community development, a role expanded by later legislation, including creation of the U.S. Department of Housing and Urban Development (1965).

4. **The Eisenhower Administration**. The period of the Eisenhower Administration saw reactions to the U.S. government's expanded powers as well as further extensions of that power.

a. **The Bricker amendment (1953)**. The proposed Bricker amendment to the U.S. Constitution, which failed by one vote in the Senate, would have limited the treaty power, in part to protect state powers.

b. **Commission on intergovernmental relations**. A National Commission on Intergovernmental Relations was formed in 1953 "to study the proper role of the Federal government in relation to the States and their political subdivisions." This led to creation of the permanent Advisory Commission on Intergovernmental Relations (1959).

c. **Civil Rights Acts**. The Civil Rights Acts of 1957 and 1960 opened the way for the U.S. government's massive role in rights protection.

d. **The Highway Act (1956)**. This act provided for new motor fuel taxes and creation of the federal Highway Trust Fund to finance 90 percent of the cost of a state-administered program of constructing the interstate system and 50 percent of the cost of other federally aided roads.

e. **The National Defense Education Act (NDEA) (1958)**. NDEA initiated the U.S. government's now wide-ranging role in K-12 and higher education.

5. **The Kennedy Administration**. The Kennedy Administration produced no major new legislation affecting federalism, but it was greatly involved in countering sometimes violent resistance to desegregation in southern states, at times requiring the use of U.S. marshals and troops.

6. **The Twenty-Third Amendment (1961)**. The Twenty-Third Amendment to the U.S. Constitution conferred quasi-state status on the District of Columbia by giving its residents three or more electoral votes in presidential elections.

7. **The Johnson Administration**. The Johnson Administration's Great Society program produced a flood of legislation affecting federalism, some of it already listed above (e.g., Medicare and Medicaid).

   a. **The Economic Opportunity Act (1964)**. The Economic Opportunity Act initiated the "War on Poverty" and inaugurated Johnson's "Creative Federalism" involving (a) intensi-fied federal-local relations so as to bypass uncooperative state legislatures and gover-nors, and (b) federal funding for nongovern-mental organizations, such as community action groups and nonprofit organizations, so as to bypass uncooperative mayors and city councils.

   b. **The Civil Rights Act (1964)**. This act was aimed mainly at desegregating public accom-modations, ending discrimination in employ-ment, and enhancing voting rights.

   c. **The Voting Rights Act (1965)**. This act suspended literacy and other voter tests and authorized federal supervision of voter registration in states and districts having pervasive discrimination. Later amendments expanded the U.S. role.

   d. **The Uniform Time Act (1966)**. This act preempted state powers in order to standard-ize the dates for daylight savings time.

   e. **The Omnibus Crime Control and Safe Streets Act (1968)**. This Crime Control Act was one of the first large block grants enacted by Congress. Block grants are sums given to the states for a generally stated purpose, but the details of how to spend the funds are left largely to the states, with relatively few federal restrictions.

8. **The Nixon Administration**. Nixon's "New Federal-ism" program was aimed mainly at "rationalizing" the federal system and channeling more aid to state and local governments with fewer federal

rules. Major new environmental legislation was also enacted during Nixon's terms.

   a. **The Occupational Safety and Health Act (1970)**. This act partially preempted state powers, allowing states to choose to enforce federal standards and receive federal aid for enforcement, or to let the U.S. government enforce the standards in the state.

   b. **The Twenty-Sixth Amendment (1971)**. The Twenty-Sixth Amendment lowered the voting age to eighteen after the U.S. Supreme Court held in *Oregon v. Mitchell* (1970) that Congress does not have authority to alter the voting age for state and local elections.

   c. **General Revenue Sharing (1972)**. General revenue sharing, Nixon's major New Federal-ism program, distributed largely unrestricted federal revenues to state and local govern-ments by formula. This act brought federal aid directly to some 36,000 small local governments for the first time. Funding for states was terminated in 1980 and for local governments in 1986.

9. **The Ford Administration**. President Ford contin-ued prior trends but also became known for refusing federal aid to help bail New York City out of its financial difficulties.

   a. **The Education for All Handicapped Children Act (1975)**. This act requires states to provide a free "appropriate" education to all handicapped children, with modest funding assistance from the U.S. government.

   b. **The Anti-Recession Fiscal Assistance Act (1976)**. This act, passed over Ford's veto, directed more federal public works aid to distressed states and localities. The act was reauthorized and funding increased with President Carter's support in 1977.

10. **The Carter Administration**. Attempting to cope with deepening "stagflation," the Carter Adminis-tration produced the first slow-down of federal aid, which peaked at 26.5 percent of state-local spending in 1978, even though the number of grant programs peaked at 538 by 1981. Carter, former governor of Georgia, also sought to forge a "New Partnership," mainly to assist distressed communities.

11. **The Reagan Administration.** Reagan's "New Federalism" sought to reduce the size of the U.S. government and increase state powers. The results, however, were mixed.

   a. **Levels of federal aid.** A real reduction in federal aid occurred in 1981 (from $94.8 billion to $88.2 billion), but aid increased again in absolute terms ($123.6 billion in 1990) while still falling as a percent of federal spending.

   b. **Shift from places to persons.** Federal aid shifted from places to persons as the percentage of grants for payments to individuals (i.e., the social safety net) rose from 35 percent of all federal grants in 1980 to 53 percent in 1989.

   c. **Curtailment of direct federal-local relations.** Direct federal-local relations were curtailed, and federal aid to local governments declined more steeply than aid to state governments.

   d. **Decentralization of responsibility.** Devolution of domestic responsibilities to states and localities was also promoted by the Reagan Administration.

   e. **The Tax Reform Act (1986).** The Tax Reform Act reduced "tax expenditure" subsidies for state and local governments by placing limits on tax-exempt state and local bonds and by eliminating the deductibility of state and local sales taxes from personal federal income-tax liabilities.

   f. **Increase in federal preemption of state and local authority.** Federal preemption of state and local authority, however, increased dramatically, with 88 preemption laws enacted during Reagan's years, the largest number ever under one president. This rise was due mainly to political pressure for popular programs (e.g., environmental protection), business pressure for uniform national regulation, and Reagan's desire to preempt state and local authority to regulate economic activities (e.g., buses, airlines, and cable television) deregulated by the federal government.

   h. **Federalism Executive Order 12612 (1987).** The last Reagan federalism initiative requires executive agencies to review all regulatory and legislative proposals for conformity to a set of federalism principles.

   g. **Federal mandates.** Federal mandates, which require state and local governments to follow certain procedures and perform certain services, also increased significantly. Federal funding does not necessarily accompany mandates.

12. **The Bush Administration.** The Bush Administration entered office with a general commitment to the New Federalism of its predecessor but to no major new federalism initiatives. Bush revived presidential relations with local officials and generally improved "dialogue" with state and local officials. His "education summit" with 49 governors in 1989 reflected the administration's initial approach to intergovernmental policy-making.

B. **Increase of federal power by judicial action.** The U.S. Supreme Court has expanded U.S. government power considerably since 1937 by upholding expansive congressional-presidential initiatives, enlarging preemption, striking down state and local policies under the Fourteenth Amendment, and continuing the "nationalization" of the U.S. Bill of Rights begun in *Gitlow v. State of New York* (1925).

   1. **Expanding federal regulation of commerce.** In *NLRB v. Jones & Laughlin Steel Corp.* (1937), the Court upheld the National Labor Relations Act and endorsed a broad view of the "stream of commerce." In *Steward Machine Co. v. Davis* (1937), which upheld the Social Security Act, the Court affirmed comprehensive congressional taxing and spending powers, authority to loan money to municipalities to build electric power plants, and authority to subsidize state social welfare programs through conditional grants-in-aid.

   2. **Applying the U.S. Bill of Rights to state law.** In *Palko v. Connecticut* (1937), Justice Benjamin Cardozo wrote that "the due process clause of the Fourteenth Amendment may make it unlawful for a state to abridge by its statutes the freedom of speech which the First Amendment safeguards against encroachment by Congress...[or] the right of one accused of crime to the benefit of counsel....In these and other situations, immunities that are valid as against the federal govern-

ment...through the Fourteenth Amendment, become valid as against the states."

a. **Nationalization of rights.** Cardozo's view became the basis for the Court's "selective incorporation" doctrine, that is, application of most of the U.S. Bill of Rights to the states via the Fourteenth Amendment. This view underlay the Court's many modern holdings applying the Bill of Rights to state law in decisions on freedom of speech, press, and religion; establishment of religion; criminal procedures (e.g., Miranda warnings); capital punishment; privacy; abortion; and so on.

b. **Court orders.** The application of the Bill of Rights to state law is also one basis of the many orders issued by federal courts in recent decades requiring state and local governments to provide certain public services, and to reform certain institutions, such as jails, prisons, schools, and mental health facilities, held to violate rights protected by the U.S. Constitution.

3. **Expansion of congressional power over regulation of commerce.** The Court's opinion in *U.S. v. Darby* (1941), which upheld the Fair Labor Standards Act, reasserted that Congress's power over interstate commerce "is complete in itself," repudiated dual federalism, and remarked that the Tenth Amendment is "but a truism...."

4. **Outlawing racial segregation.** *Brown v. Board of Education of Topeka* (1954, 1955), one of the Court's most historic decisions, overturned *Plessy*, ruled that racial segregation violates the Fourteenth Amendment's equal protection clause, and ordered school desegregation to proceed "with all deliberate speed." This decision helped to spark the Civil Rights Movement and the U.S. government's assault on racial and, later, other forms of discrimination.

5. **Expansion of abortion rights.** *Roe v. Wade* (1973) vacated state anti-abortion laws as violations of a woman's right of privacy. Although the Fourth Amendment provides some protection for privacy, no privacy right is specifically listed in the U.S. Constitution. The Court had found this right in "penumbras, formed by emanations" from the rights listed in the Constitution (*Griswold v. Connecticut*, 1965, which voided state laws banning the use of contraceptives).

6. **Appeal to the Tenth Amendment denied.** *Garcia v. San Antonio Metropolitan Transit Authority* (1985) said that states cannot expect the Court to protect them by invoking the Tenth Amendment; instead states must rely on "the workings of the National Government itself" to protect their interests.

7. **Judicially ordered taxation.** *Missouri v. Jenkins* (1990) held that a federal judge cannot directly levy a local tax but can order a local government to do so in order to pay for a court order to remedy a condition (i.e., school segregation) said to exist and judged unconstitutional by the court.

8. **The new judicial federalism.** The new judicial federalism is a state court response to the U.S. Supreme Court's perceived retreat from rights protection. Since the mid-1970s, state high courts have issued more than 600 decisions granting broader individual rights protection under state declarations of rights than the U.S. Supreme Court has granted under the U.S. Bill of Rights. States cannot grant less protection than the U.S. Supreme Court, but they can grant more protection under state constitutions.

C. **State resurgence.** This new judicial federalism exemplifies the resurgence of the states by the 1970s as innovative and reformed polities. In the 1930s, many observers thought states were bound for extinction and that federalism was obsolete. Many states were dominated by a monopolistic or oligopolistic business interest, an urban political machine, white supremacy, or some combination of these.

1. **The reform surge.** After World War II, however, reform spread throughout the states.

a. **Reform fostered by federal government.** The U.S. government fostered reform through its grants-in-aid, statutory regulations, and judicial decisions.

b. **Reform fostered by economic diversity.** Growth and change in the U.S. economy diversified the economic bases of states, making it more difficult for any one corporate interest to dominate government.

c. **Reform fostered by social change.** Rising levels of education along with suburbanization and ethnic assimilation undercut the political bases of virtually all courthouse gangs and political machines.

d. **Emergence of strong local interests.** Labor unions, public school teachers, and then other non-business groups—including movements for civil rights, environmental protection, and consumer rights—emerged as strong interests in state and local governments, thus increasing pressure for reform.

e. **Role of increasing state tax revenues and rising federal deficits.** By the mid-1970s, facing stagflation in the national economy and then retrenchment by the U.S. government during the 1980s, state and local governments were more or less compelled to strengthen their capacities and become more innovative.

2. **Constitutional reform.** Constitutional reform occurred in nearly every state after World War II, with twelve states adopting new constitutions.

3. **More active state legislatures.** State legislatures, which range in size from 424 members in New Hampshire to 49 in Nebraska's unicameral legislature, now meet in annual sessions in 43 states. By contrast, four legislatures met in annual sessions in 1941.

4. **Stronger governors.** Governors now serve four-year terms in forty-seven states. Most states allow a governor to serve two or more consecutive terms.

5. **Reforms of state courts.** State court reform has included the adoption of some form of merit selection of judges, especially the Missouri Plan, which combines merit appointment with retention elections; better methods for disciplining judges; and unifying the court system under the state's chief justice.

6. **Improvement of state administration.** The administration of state law has been improved by emphasizing merit hiring and civil service reform.

7. **Improvement of state revenue systems.** State financing has been improved by diversifying revenue sources (e.g., forty-one states now have a broad-base personal income tax), making state taxes less regressive.

8. **Strengthening of local governments.** Many local governments have undergone similar reforms.

Contemporary Perspective

The seeming paradox of contemporary federalism is the expanded power of the U.S. government coupled with state resurgence. This paradox exists because state resurgence was necessary, in part, to take advantage of the U.S. government's fiscal incentives and to comply with U.S. mandates. Also, one government's gain in power is not always another government's loss. As the role of the U.S. government in American life has increased, so too have the roles of state and local governments. The paradox may also reflect a transition in American history, one requiring a better balance between the states and the Union in an era of global interdependence and competition. Key issues facing American federalism include the following:

I. **Fiscal problems of the U.S. government.** Fiscal problems of the U.S. government, such as large budget deficits and the savings-and-loan bailout, have dominated intergovernmental relations since 1978, producing a decline in federal aid and a shifting of costs to state and local governments. Deeper effects of these problems appear to be a decline in innovative U.S. government policy-making and a reduced ability of the U.S. economy to compete effectively in the global economy.

II. **Decline of federal aid.** The decline in federal aid has sparked debate over the purposes of grants. A few observers argue that aid should be abandoned because it distorts state and local priorities and expands federal government powers. Others argue that aid should be extended only to persons, not to state and local governments. Two issues lie at the center of the debate.

A. **Which government's objectives to be financed.** One question is whether aid should advance the U.S. government's objectives, or help state and local governments achieve their own objectives. There is also the question of what kinds of objectives should be emphasized: capital improvements aid for infrastructure (e.g., ports, highways, power plants), which has declined greatly since the 1950s; or aid for social welfare, which has increased greatly.

B. **Criteria for distributing aid.** A further question is whether aid should be dispersed widely or given only to persons "truly in need" and/or to states and localities that lack the fiscal capacity to provide a certain level of services.

III. **Questions raised by federal mandates**. Federal mandates on state and local governments that require state and local expenditures for compliance have raised questions of autonomy, accountability, and capacity.

A. **Question of self-government**. It is contended that the self-governing autonomy of state and local governments is compromised by mandates because they limit state and local discretion and extend U.S. control over state and local budgets.

B. **Questions of accountability**. Questions of accountability arise when the public officials who gain from making policy do not experience the pain of presenting the tax bills to voters.

1. **Federal mandates weaken accountability**. Some critics argue that mandating allows presidents and members of Congress to enact popular programs, such as expanded Medicaid eligibility, while requiring state and local elected officials to pay for all or a portion of these programs.

2. **Federal mandates defended**. Other critics argue that because federal programs are national and benefit all citizens, state and local governments should bear all or a portion of the costs. It is also argued that some mandates (e.g., voting rights and handicapped access) are responses to derelictions of duty on the part of state and local governments and, therefore, should be paid for by those governments.

C. **Questions of government capacity**. Questions of federal capacity have been raised because mandating partly reflects an inability of the U.S. government to finance all of its policy preferences without incurring larger deficits or increasing taxes. Shifting costs to state and local governments does not solve the problem, however, and may, to some extent, exacerbate the problem.

IV. **Federal preemption of state and local authority**. Federal preemption of state and local authority has risen dramatically since the 1960s and may continue increasing because Congress and the Supreme Court have construed the U.S. government's constitutional powers broadly.

A. **Floor or ceiling federalism?** A new "states' rights" doctrine may be emerging in preemption, however. As the U.S. government encountered fiscal problems and became more conservative, and as states became more progressive and fiscally healthy, debate arose as to whether federal preemption should set floors or ceilings.

1. **Federal government to set minimum standards**. One option is that the U.S. government establish minimum standards ("floors") in policy fields (e.g., environmental protection) and allow states to set higher standards if they wish.

2. **Federal government to set sole permissible standards**. A second option is that the U.S. government set the only permissible standards ("ceilings") and prohibit states from exceeding those standards (e.g., air pollution standards).

3. **Support and opposition to federal preemption**. Many interests that once supported total federal preemption, now oppose preemption in many areas or support only partial preemption in which the U.S. government establishes a floor but not a ceiling for state and local action.

V. **Issues of federal and state responsibility**. Questions of sorting out which responsibilities should be federal ones and which should be reserved for the states remain on the intergovernmental agenda. Two important issues are involved.

A. **Federal overload**. One question is whether the U.S. government has assumed so much responsibility that Congress operates as if it were a super city council and as a result is less able to give adequate attention to matters of truly national importance.

B. **Shared responsibilities**. A second question, given that virtually all policy fields are intergovernmental, is what decision-making, administrative, and funding responsibilities are appropriate for each type of government and how these responsibilities should vary among policy fields.

VI. **Global economic competition**. Global economic competition has sparked fundamental debate about federalism.

A. **Arguments for increased federal power**. Opponents to strengthening state and local powers argue that global competition makes federalism obsolete because diverse state and local regulation hinders efficient movements of domestic and foreign capital and blocks global product marketing. For example, can there be fifty state rules for food-product labeling? If the U.S. is to compete against such giants as the European Community, these critics argue, it must have a strong national government able to preempt state and local authority and to impose uniform rules and taxes so as to create a uniform national marketplace.

B. **Arguments against increasing federal powers.** Critics opposed to increasing powers of the federal government argue that because national boundaries are increasingly irrelevant to economic activity, federalism is an asset because it allows states and localities to fend for themselves and to experiment and compete with each other to promote prosperity. Federalism also allows failures to be confined to particular states rather than affecting the nation.

   1. **Failures of federal regulation.** Opponents of increasing federal government power point to its regulatory failures during the 1970s and 1980s. They also point to state and local export-promotion, investment-attraction, and tourism programs that did much to counteract weak U.S. policies and to slow the erosion of the nation's global economic position.

   2. **Preference for decentralized power.** Opponents of federal-government powers argue that the U.S. government should set basic rules and assist fiscally weak states and localities, creating "a level playing field." Otherwise, however, substantial state and local self-government should be maintained to promote traditional ends of federal democracy.

C. **"Globalization."** The globalization of American life poses many challenges for federalism. For example, treaties increasingly cover previously domestic matters, such as individual rights and environmental protection. To what extent should the U.S. government use its treaty powers to override state and local powers? How far can state and local governments go in international affairs? With their pension funds and other financial resources, state and local governments wield increasing power in financial markets and can use that power to reward or punish other nations (e.g., divestment from South Africa) independently of U.S. foreign policies.

VII. **The power of television and attention to local issues.** The rise of the national media, especially television, has also posed challenges for federalism because the media focuses heavily on national and international affairs. Attention to state and local questions may decline should the public become increasingly distracted with issues farther afield.

VIII. **Questions of constitutional reform.** Questions of constitutional reform to restore balance in the federal system have recently arisen as a result of the decline in federal aid, the rise of federal preemption and mandates, and the U.S. Supreme Court's treatment of the Tenth Amendment.

   A. **Reform of constitutional amendment procedures.** There have been proposals to amend Article V to permit single-issue constitutional conventions or to allow states to initiate amendments with a congressional veto.

   B. **Reform of U.S. Supreme Court.** Another proposal is to require the U.S. Supreme Court to adjudicate cases under the Tenth Amendment, to limit the jurisdiction of the Court, or to require at least a 7-2 vote of the Court to overturn state law.

   C. **Opposition to proposed reforms.** Opponents argue that the nation should not tamper with the Constitution, that state and local governments should use the political process more adroitly to protect their powers, that new appointments may make the Supreme Court more friendly to states in the 1990s, and that limiting the Court will hamper the federal government's ability to make policy and protect rights.

IX. **Impending worldwide federal revolution.** Finally, there are signs of an impending federalist revolution worldwide, arising from three sources.

   A. **A general reaction against centralization.** In many parts of the world, notably in eastern and central Europe and throughout the Soviet Union, there is opposition to overbearing centralized political power. The Soviet Union may find that its sole hope of becoming a democratic and prosperous political entity is through a new federal system that decentralizes power, giving far greater autonomy to its constituent republics and to other national and ethnic groups demanding self-determination.

   B. **Federalism as promoting democracy and economic development.** Secondly, there is a belief among some observers that federalism can help to promote both democracy and economic development. It does this primarily by preventing the over-centralization of political power or reforming such centralization where it has occurred under non-federal systems. Decentralized political power fosters democratic participation. It also tends to prevent heavy-handed policies of central authorities that stifle economic development.

C. **The success of federal systems**. Thirdly, there is a recognition that the kind of federal democracy practiced in the U.S., Canada, Australia, Switzerland, and Germany, for example, has been highly successful—politically, economically, and culturally.

X. **Promise and turmoil**. The promise of federalism—as laid out in the U.S. Constitution, state constitutions, *The Federalist* (which has been translated into many languages), and other documents in both the U.S. and other federal democracies—continues to have popular appeal as well as a solid record of performance. Yet, as Americans adapt their federal covenant to the circumstances of its third century, there will be considerable debate and controversy. In many other places, there will be turmoil and bloodshed as peoples whose aspirations were suppressed by colonialism and centralized regimes seek to sort themselves out into territorially acceptable federal arrangements in their efforts to promote liberty, democracy, security, peace, and prosperity.

2) d. CONFLICTS AMONG FUNDAMENTAL PRINCIPLES

American citizens should understand that there can be discrepancies between practices justified by one principle believed to be fundamental and practices justified by another principle believed to be equally fundamental. The freedom of the press to publish certain facts, for example, can sometimes make it difficult to assure a fair trial. These conflicts do not arise because of a flaw in the conduct of politics. Rather, they arise because of the necessary interplay of the principles that, taken as a whole, constitute the basis of the American way of life.

OBJECTIVE

The citizen should be able to

take, defend, and evaluate positions on conflicts among fundamental values and principles of American constitutional democracy.

FRAME OF REFERENCE
Conceptual Perspective

There are several important conflicts that can arise among American principles. Among these are

I. **Liberty v. equality.** American government is founded on the principle of equality of rights. The truth of this principle, announced in the *Declaration of Independence*, is argued in John Locke's *Two Treatises of Government* (1690). The basic rights declared by Locke are the rights to self-preservation, liberty and property. The fundamental rights declared by Jefferson are life, liberty, and the pursuit of happiness.

A. **Equal rights; unequal results**. A right is the authority to choose the means necessary to life and to happiness; liberty and property are the most important of those means. When we exercise the liberty that we hold equally as a right (or attempt to amass property), inequalities in wealth, knowledge, status, and political office often result. These inequalities may seem to violate the basic equality in rights. But, when they stem from the proper use of liberty, they are a outgrowth of our equal freedom to pursue happiness. Different talents lead to different results when all are equally free to use their talents.

B. **How equality may conflict with liberty**. The political conflict between equality and liberty, i.e., between equal rights and the unequal results that arise from freely exercising these rights, comes about because our respect and love for equality in rights often tends to make us believe that our national goal is to secure as much equality as is possible in all things. To secure such equality, however, would be to deny people the freedom to pursue their rights whenever that freedom resulted in inequality.

C. **Equal rights not subordinate to equal results**. This would be to understand equal rights to be subordinate to equal results. Such an understanding is opposed to our country's founding principles, as we see them in the *Declaration*, Locke's Treatises, the Constitution and the *Federalist Papers*. Not only are equal rights considered to be naturally just, they also are believed to be the key to creating prosperity that will benefit all. When each is free to pursue his or her abilities to the fullest, under a representative democracy, the intended, and in our country, largely actual, result is an explosion of skill and ingenuity that by any historical standard vastly increases common wealth and plenty and helps to alleviate poverty.

D. **How inequality can limit liberty**. Nonetheless, inequalities can arise that make it more difficult for some than it is for others to pursue their liberties effectively. The ideal of equal rights can be weakened if the opportunities that allow them to be pursued to maximum advantage are unjustly limited. A life lived in squalid, even lawless conditions, for example, makes it extraordinarily difficult to obtain the discipline and education that are necessary to pursue rights vigorously and thoughtfully. Unequal conditions may so restrict opportunity that there is no genuine equality in rights. Unequal restrictions on ability to advance in careers, to be educated to the level of one's natural abilities, or to hold and dispose of property also lead to diminished equality in rights. (Indeed, slavery is the outright denial of equal rights.)

E. **Government to redress unjust inequality.** The purpose of much of what government is designed to achieve is to prevent the emergence, and redress the effects, of such inequalities when they arise unjustly. This is a purpose of criminal justice and public education, for example. The difficulty, however, is that not all such restrictions on opportunity are unfair and unjust. Some arise because of the results of the free, proper and energetic exercise of rights. Those with greater wealth, for example, will often be best able to secure the day-to-day freedom from crime and misery that most easily allows moral training and the growth of character. They will often have the leisure that permits significant education and cultivation. Those with natural intelligence or deep faith will, in the privacy of their homes, pass on traditions of moral discipline and intellectual curiosity that will often give their children a head start.

F. **Dealing with the conflicts between liberty and equality.** It is not possible for each to have perfectly equal opportunities at the same time that each has simply untrammeled liberty. The question then becomes the degree to which unequal opportunities result in genuine restrictions on rights, or, rather, are easily enough overcome; the degree to which measures to ensure equal opportunities significantly restrict liberty and the public benefit that comes from it, or, rather, are acceptable inconveniences; and the degree to which legal control, as opposed to public persuasion or the action of private groups is the best way to restrict individual liberty when such restriction appears to be necessary.

II. **Rights v. duties.** A second important conflict that can arise among our principles arises from the tension between our rights and our duties.

A. **The results of rights without limits.** When each of us exercises the rights that are his or hers by nature, but does so in a context where there are no commonly agreed upon limits, the result is a situation that none of us would rationally accept. This situation is described in detail in Locke's *Second Treatise* and Thomas Hobbes' *Leviathan*, where it is argued that the "state of nature," a condition in which there is no government, soon becomes a "state of war" of each against the others.

B. **Government as setting limits to rights for their effective exercise.** Individuals agree or consent to enter civil society, and then choose a government to make common decisions that will replace the unintended public consequences (war and poverty) of complete individual license. Legitimate government rests upon the transfer to a common, political body of some of our natural individual authority to choose the means to our happiness. Legitimate government, as Jefferson said, must be based on the consent of the governed. The laws passed by the legitimate government become authoritative and replace some of our freedom to make individual choices. But the justification for law and government is merely that it is sometimes necessary to make authoritative public decisions in order for individual rights to be exercised effectively.

C. **Preference for voluntary action.** Because a purpose of government is to protect the fruits of individual effort, and because political authority rests on individuals as members of the sovereign people, there is always a great preference for individual as opposed to government action in American life. Individual judgment reigns supreme when no law exists. Moreover, our Constitution proscribes whole areas from government intrusion, and severely limits it in other areas. The civil or political rights of free speech, freedom of press, and defined rules for criminal prosecution speak to this restriction on government. For government action to be justified, it must both respect these civil rights and demonstrate reasons, through legislative and executive deliberation, why natural individual authority must be replaced by common action.

D. **Indifference to obligations.** If the government is to act effectively, it sometimes must call upon citizens to lay aside their individual preferences, or, indeed, to work actively on public matters. The country requires that taxes be paid, that soldiers serve during wars, and that citizens vote, run for office, and make government forcefully aware of their opinions.

1. **Difficulty in developing public spirit.** The conflict or conundrum is this: the protection of the rights of individuals that the country fosters sometimes makes it difficult to develop the necessary degree of public interest and public spirit. The duties of

citizens can become submerged under a sea of individual activities; and public obligations can appear to be intrusions, rather than privileges.

2. **Ineffectiveness of law in developing public-spiritedness.** Although law prevails where it exists, law cannot guarantee active participation in political life. Nor is its threat of punishment sufficient to guarantee the habitual compliance that is necessary in any healthy country.

3. **Emphasis on individual rights and blunting the sense of public obligation.** The United States is superior to many other countries in this regard because a country that serves individual liberty can call forth its own intense loyalty. Nonetheless, the American emphasis on individual rights makes it a permanent challenge to bring forth in citizens a firm sense of public obligation.

III. **Rights v. rights.** A third basic conflict concerns the possible contradictions that arise from attempting to protect equally important rights. The Constitution creates certain civil rights as a way of protecting our natural rights once we have entered society. These include the rights guaranteed by the first ten amendments to the Constitution. Beyond these guarantees, the Constitution seeks to secure the individual's natural right to hold property, move freely from job to job and place to place, and otherwise choose how to "pursue happiness."

A. **Conflicts among rights.** When these rights are exercised, they may come into conflict. Toleration of religious belief, for example, may conflict with the basic protection of life if religious practices put others, e.g., children, in danger. Completely uncontrolled freedom of speech may create danger in life-threatening emergencies. Unrestricted access by the press to all government activities, including, for example, jury deliberations while they are occurring, may make fair trials impossible. One person's property holdings in newspapers and television may create monopolies that reduce the effective right of others to publish.

B. **The necessity for limits.** To a large degree, the daily activity of all three branches of government involves sorting out these difficulties. It is precisely the uncomfortable result of full individual license that forces the social order to be created in the first place, and much of government involves limiting individual actions in order to secure the common good. These limits prove necessary even when we acknowledge constitutionally guaranteed civil rights, because no perfect system can be devised in which the exercise of

rights automatically adjusts itself so that everyone is completely unrestricted and fully satisfied. Good government must attempt thoughtful deliberation that adjusts competing claims and enforces the results of these deliberations in laws that limit individual action. These laws are open to challenge and change because there is no general set of rules that can cover all cases or consider in advance changing circumstances.

IV. **Democratic control v. effective government.** A fourth fundamental conflict is the one that occurs between our wish that government be as effective and energetic as necessities demand, and our wish that our leaders be subject to popular control.

A. **Openness v. secrecy.** Effective government sometimes demands secrecy; action with a minimum of consultation; and quick, authoritative decisions. These demands are most obvious in connection with foreign affairs. A system of government such as the American system, with separated powers, open access to the press, and, of course, the need to stand for election, does not always permit these restraints on shared power and full disclosure. Indeed, a representative democracy is composed of many institutions that work against such restraints. These institutions foster opinions that make any limit on access or consultation appear to be illegitimate. Still, we generally recognize that a government with no ability to deliberate or act with at least some distance from the immediacy of popular wishes and oversight will often fail to be as successful as we desire.

B. **Governmental responsiveness v. long-term policy.** Democratic control in the form of frequent elections, different centers of power (i.e., the three branches of government) and constant attention to the fluctuations of public opinion also makes it more difficult than we would wish for government to plan for the long term, to set a steady course and stick to it. The ready access of lobbyists to legislators and the massive attention of the media to often fleeting issues make it difficult to construct sweeping measures and to keep them in place. The vagaries of contemporary tax and budget legislation are good examples. Yet, we would hardly desire a government that disregards public opinion or is immune from defeat in elections. Nor, in a federal system with separation of powers, have we chosen a government with only one center of political power. The requirement for democratic control cannot be perfectly meshed with every need for effective and farsighted government.

C. **Majority control v. minority rights.** Another instance of this dilemma can be found in the potential discrepancy between democratic control in the form of majority rule and the protection of individual liberty. Effective government is not only government that meets imminent and long term dangers successfully. In a regime whose purpose is to protect rights, effective government also is the protector of individual liberties. Sometimes these liberties can be protected only by ignoring, or, indeed, contravening, the wishes of the vast majority of citizens.

1. **Ending racial segregation.** The most significant general example in our time is the provision of full civil rights to blacks in the South against the wishes of the majority of white Southerners. Segregation in the 1950s and 1960s was not unpopular; it was what the majority of Southerners wanted their democratically elected officials to enforce.

2. **Protecting individual liberties.** Our representative democracy seeks to balance democratic control with the effective protection of individual liberties. The need for balance makes clear that majority control, however important we know it to be, does not automatically secure, and may conflict with, the effective defense of individuals.

V. **Central government v. local control.** A fifth area of basic conflict is that between central government and local control. This conflict takes the form of unitary control as opposed to federalism, i.e., of the authority of the central government as opposed to control by the states. This conflict also takes the form of the split between any government activity at all, and the autonomous private actions of neighborhoods and communities.

A. **National unity v. local diversity.** The United States is a large and diverse country, with a variety of regions, interests, and modes of life; its politics is based upon the consent of the governed. This combination of pluralism and citizen responsibility leads to a preference for government that can properly reflect diversity while also enforcing the principles and regulations that bind the whole country. State law often goes beyond federal law, or covers areas, such as education, on which the national government does not legislate extensively. The result is that different conditions and customs may arise that can threaten the reality of equality of opportunity.

B. **Complete national control undesirable.** Simple national control, however, often seems to be too remote from the day to day influence of citizens genuinely to call forth their public efforts in the way that, for example, the politics of the local school district often will. And simple national control may exacerbate the tendency to uniformity and intrusiveness that weakens the diversity and privacy that nourish liberty and self-government. Again, there is no magical formula that resolves all tensions. Rather, the tension is a necessary concomitant of the duality of the governing principles—nationalism and localism—that we believe to be important.

Historical Perspective

I. **Liberty v. Equality.** Several events and concerns in our history clarify and illustrate this conflict.

A. **The ratification period.** The essays of *The Federalist*, written during the ratification debate of 1787-1788, make clear that, on the basis of political equality, a conceivable "tyranny of the majority" might arise that can trample individual liberties. Hence, the Constitution was designed to frustrate such a possibility by forming a complicated system of separated powers and checks and balances designed to limit government. Moreover, the adoption of the Bill of Rights was motivated by the wish to be certain that the federal government would properly respect important individual liberties.

B. **The "Lochner era" and the New Deal.** A second significant historical example is the series of Supreme Court decisions regarding property rights in the first third of the twentieth century (sometimes called the "Lochner era," after a famous 1905 Supreme Court case), and the New Deal reaction to those decisions. An interpretation that supported the individual's right to dispose of property more or less completely as he saw fit eventually gave way to an interpretation that more readily allowed the formation of labor unions and government intervention in other contractual arrangements. The new understanding seemed necessary to deal fairly with economic opportunity in modern economies, in general, and the depression of the 1930s, in particular.

II. **Rights v. duties.** Elements of this controversy have been present throughout our history. One area of special significance has been the series of questions surrounding the obligation of citizens to risk their lives in war. Such questions, with attendant protests and violence, characterized, among other events, both the Civil War and the war in Vietnam. A related series of questions involved civil disobedience whose purpose it was to extend genuine civil rights to blacks. When, if ever, is it just to seek to advance the public good by violating public laws? Writings on civil disobedience by **Henry David Thoreau** (1817-1862), the works of **Harriet Beecher Stowe** (1811-1896) and other abolitionists, Lincoln's speeches and debates, and the books and sermons of **Frederick Douglass** (1817-1895) and **Martin Luther King, Jr.** (1929-1968) are milestones in both the discussion and the concrete working through of these questions.

III. **Rights v. rights.** The potential conflict among equally important rights has made itself visible in a variety of historical situations. Since the Second World War, for example, legislation and court decisions have adjusted the boundaries between freedom of association and civil rights. Similar adjustments have been made between property rights and civil rights. Freedom of speech and press have come into conflict with individual privacy from the beginning of the Republic and have been dealt with in ever-shifting interpretations of what constitutes libelous speech. Publicly guaranteed religious freedom has often been at odds with legal private behavior in employment and association: discrimination against Catholic immigrants from the "Know Nothing" period in the mid-nineteenth century at least through the 1920s is a case in point.

IV. **Effective government v. democratic control.** This debate has raged in the United States since the founding period. The constitutional convention itself was devoted to replacing the ineffective Articles of Confederation with a document that formed a more energetic government; the Anti-Federalists who opposed the new regime did so in part because they feared that the new government would become a tyranny that would overwhelm democratic rule. Andrew Jackson's presidency was a battleground on this very issue, with the debate over a national bank being the central question. The progressive period at the beginning of the twentieth century was an attempt to institute reforms, such as a neutral civil service, that would allow effective and "scientific" management. Finally, during roughly this same period, a populist sentiment arose that sought to control large and alien government and business.

V. **Central government v. local control.** This split also has been significant since the founding period. The constitutional convention attempted to allow both energetic central government and powerful states. During the tenure of **John Marshall** (1755-1835), the U.S. Supreme Court attempted to assert the necessary powers of the central government in several cases, notably *McCulloch v. Maryland* (1819). The Civil War, of course, turned this

question around, as did many of the most renowned congressional debates and personalities, such as **Daniel Webster** (1782-1852) and **John C. Calhoun** (1782-1850).

Contemporary Perspective

I. **Liberty v. equality.** Over and above the continuation today of several historical areas of controversy, one subject of current debate is especially worth pointing out: should we consider each person primarily as the individual possessor of a variety of rights, or should each of us be considered primarily in terms of our membership in this or that religion, race, or other group, and having the rights to which that group is entitled? Although thinking in terms of group as opposed to individual rights has never been a valid part of the principled natural rights tradition that gave birth to our country, today's confusion about whether we are first of all individuals or members is a contemporary version of the distinction between individual liberty and equality of condition.

II. **Rights v. duties.** Two contemporary examples of this problem are worth noting. One is the concern over falling voter turnout. Without responsible citizens, government threatens to become passive and inattentive in some matters, and capricious or even tyrannical in others. How can a country based on rights properly justify, teach, and enforce civic duty? A second example involves recent controversies about the arts. Are they primarily or exclusively matters of individual expression, or should public funding of artists, and their patrons and viewers be restrained by the standards of public taste and decency that some argue are a necessary part of moral education in a free country?

III. **Rights v. rights.** Two controversies today are especially useful in helping us to frame this issue. One is the split between the freedom of the press to publish and the right to a fair trial. The Iran-Contra prosecution and the legal situation of Panamanian strongman Manuel Noriega, along with the briefs and editorials on these cases, are interesting examples. The second controversy is the debate about abortion, which often is conducted in terms of the split between the "right" of the fetus versus the "right" of the mother, and is also often conducted in terms of an enforceable right of privacy versus the right to allow religious belief to find its place in the making of law and the determination of acceptable behavior.

IV. **Effective government v. democratic control.** Several of today's issues shed light on, and are often discussed in terms of, this controversy. One is the growing tendency in states such as California to use the referendum, which is example of direct or popular control, to limit the amount of discretion available to elected officials and civil servants. A second is the continuing controversy about the degree of secrecy that the executive branch must be permitted if it is to conduct foreign affairs effectively. If there is too much secrecy, will Congress and public opinion have the time and leisure to choose the nation's course? If there is too little secrecy, can any military or diplomatic policy be successful?

V. **Central government v. local control.** The wish to have appropriate central guidance at the same time that one has local control, and the inevitable political confusion, are evident in discussions of several important areas of policy, ranging from control of crime to the protection of the environment. The problem is perhaps most visible in agriculture, education, and immigration. Farming communities pride themselves on local independence, yet fight fiercely for price supports mandated by the federal government. Education is considered to be a national problem requiring a national solution, but funding for and control of public schools remain, by clear popular demand, in local hands. And, the wish of many to encourage immigration (or public transportation, or safe sites for toxic wastes) when they take the national or broad point of view runs counter to their desire to have strong means of local control so they can be certain that the costs in public assistance or a disrupted neighborhood do not cut too close to home.

Each of these five areas of conflict is intertwined with the others. None admits of a perfect solution; each requires thoughtful deliberation and practical judgment. The citizen of a democracy should be aware of their existence and complexity, and, especially, of the documents of our political life that give life to the principles that underlie these conflicts.

TOPIC 2. POLITICAL INSTITUTIONS AND PROCESSES

The citizen's capacity to participate effectively in the political process requires an understanding of the relationship of American political institutions to the basic principles of the American political system. This understanding should be accompanied by a knowledge of (1) the origins and development of the formal institutions and process of the American political system, and (2) the informal components of the political system of which political parties, interest groups, and a variety of methods of exerting influence play important roles.

A. FORMAL INSTITUTIONS AND PROCESSES

The constitution establishes the following formal institutions and processes of the American system.

1. CONGRESS AND THE PRESIDENCY

The tyranny of the legislature is the most formidable dread at present, and will be for long years. That of the executive will come in its turn, but it will be at a remote period.

Thomas Jefferson (1789)

Oh if I could be President and Congress too, for just ten minutes.

Theodore Roosevelt (1908)

The Congress looks more powerful sitting here than it did when I was there in the Congress. But that is because when you are in Congress you are one of 100 in the Senate or one of 435 in the House. So that the power is divided. But from here I look at the collective power of the Congress, particularly the bloc action, and it is a substantial power.

John F. Kennedy (1962)

The Constitution makes cooperation between the president and Congress both necessary and difficult. One scholar has described the separation of powers and checks and balances as "an invitation to struggle." To protect citizens from the tyranny of both the legislature and the executive, James Madison said, "Ambition must be made to counteract ambition. The interest of the man must be connected with the constitutional rights of the place." (*The Federalist* No. 51). The principles of separation of powers and checks and balances are reflected in the president's veto power, the congressional powers of the purse and impeachment, the

Senate's treaty powers and the requirement that the Senate approve presidential nominations of cabinet officers, judges, and ambassadors.

The Constitution establishes the rules of the game, but not the outcome of the contest between president and Congress. At the hundredth anniversary of Congress in 1989, Senate Majority Leader George Mitchell observed that those two hundred years had produced "forty-one presidents and no kings" and that "no institution has contributed more to that success than Congress." But the battle is never over. The inauguration of a president simply marks the beginning of a new time period in this ongoing contest. It is a contest that is fueled by what former Chief Justice Warren Burger called the "hydraulic pressure inherent within each of the separate branches to exceed the outer limits of its power."

What happens between the president and Congress is a reflection of what is happening within the executive and legislative branches. What are Congress and the presidency like in the 1990s? Is the modern president "the Wizard of Oz," as one presidential scholar has written? Was it accurate for a senator to compare the actions of Congress to "a hippopotamus rolling a pea?" Citizens have the opportunity to judge presidential candidates every four years and members of Congress every two years. There are additional opportunities for citizens to influence what Congress and the president do in between elections. An understanding of fundamental concepts, historical developments, and contemporary behavior helps to make citizens' judgments and participation both informed and effective.

OBJECTIVES

The citizen should be able to

1. explain the key functions of Congress in the American political system and the inherent conflict between representation and lawmaking.

2. explain the importance of the president as the "responsible" officer of government and the gap between the real and imagined powers of the president.

3. explain how congressional elections and different styles of representation affect Congress as the primary representative institution in the federal government.

4. explain how the committee system, political parties, staff, rules and norms, and patterns of floor voting contribute to congressional lawmaking.

5. explain the distinction between the power of executive prerogative that a president can use in a crisis and the power of persuasion that is needed in the normal governing process.

6. explain how the presidential selection process contributes to the view of the president as the responsible officer of government and how the institutional presidency supports the president's actual role in the governing process.

7. explain the possibilities and limits of citizen influence on congressional and presidential policy making.

8. take, defend, and evaluate positions on constitutional issues regarding the relationship between Congress and the presidency.

FRAME OF REFERENCE
Conceptual Perspective

I. **The functions of Congress.** The Framers put the powers of Congress in Article I, before the articles on the president and the courts. They intended Congress to have the primary responsibility for making laws and to be the central branch of government except during wars or emergencies. There is general agreement on the primary functions of Congress, but less agreement on which functions are most important and of the conflicts between some of those functions.

A. **Legislation.** Lawmaking is the chief responsibility the Constitution assigns to the national legislature ("All legislative powers herein granted shall be vested in a Congress of the United States.") Congress governs by considering and passing legislation. The First Congress (1790-91) considered 167 bills and passed 117 laws; the 100th Congress (1987-88) considered more than 11,000 bills and passed 713 laws.

B. **Representation.** Representation is the process by which members of the House of Representatives and the Senate speak for those who live in their district and state. The republican form of government established under the Constitution is one in which citizens elect others to represent their interests. Elections provide the mechanism for holding senators and representatives accountable to their constituents.

1. **Delegate model.** Members of Congress sometimes see their role as that of delegates who should vote as a majority of constituents want them to

vote. Thus in this model, members simply carry out the instructions of their constituents.

2. **Trustee model.** Members of Congress sometimes consider themselves as trustees, who vote in the long-term interests of constituents regardless of current opinion. Thus in this model, instead of merely carrying out constituents' instructions, members decide for themselves how they should vote.

C. **Oversight of administration.** Administrative oversight is the process of assuring that the laws passed by Congress are carried out as intended.

1. **Investigative hearings.** Investigative hearings are the most common form of administrative oversight. Hearings are held by committees or subcommittees that hear testimony of relevant officials. Members, many of whom are experienced lawyers, have the opportunity to cross-examine witnesses.

2. **Legislative vetoes.** Congress continues to use the legislative veto, a resolution that prohibits or overrules an executive branch decision, for administrative oversight. In 1983, however, a Supreme Court decision declared some types of legislative vetoes unconstitutional.

3. **Control of funding.** Congressional control of agencies' funding is another means Congress can use to oversee administration. In addition, informal agreements between members and administrators are used as a means of oversight.

D. **Education.** Education is another important function of Congress. When members of Congress go home to explain their actions in Washington to constituents, they are also teaching the "folks at home" about issues and the congressional process. Woodrow Wilson considered this "instruction and guidance in political affairs" to be the most important function of Congress. Open committee hearings on Watergate in the 1970s and the Iran-Contra affair in the 1980s served to educate the public, as does the now routine practice of televising floor proceedings in both chambers.

E. **Service to constituents.** Constituent service is the term for legislators and their staffs intervening to help constituents who are having problems with a government agency, such as Social Security or Veterans Affairs. Constituent service, or casework, is a form of representation that usually does not require the passage of any legislation. The annual workload of cases now exceeds 4 million, or an average of three hundred per week for Senate offices and one hundred per week for House offices.

F. **Tension among functions.** Members of Congress engage in all of these functions, but not all at the same time or to the same degree.

1. **Representation v. legislation.** Representatives and senators who emphasize lawmaking concentrate their activity on committee work in Washington. Those who stress representation direct more of their time and effort to their home district or state. Recognizing this tension between representation and lawmaking is key to understanding the behavior of Congress and its individual members.

2. **Decentralization v. centralization of power in Congress.** There is a similar tension at the institutional level between decentralizing reforms in Congress, such as those giving subcommittees more policy-making responsibility, which facilitate representation; and centralizing reforms, such as those strengthening the Speaker's control over floor proceedings, which facilitate lawmaking.

II. **Presidential powers.** The president shares the task of governing with Congress, the courts, the bureaucracy, and state and local political leaders. But the American public regards the president as the responsible officer of government and chief symbol of the nation's well-being. As former President Jimmy Carter pointed out: "When things go bad, you get entirely too much blame," and "when things go good, you get entirely too much credit."

A. **Constitutional grants of power.** The Constitution grants five major powers to the chief executive. Because many of these powers are shared with Congress, however, they have contributed over the years to many conflicts between the executive and legislature.

1. **The "executive power."** The executive power is not limited to specific laws passed by Congress or other powers of the Constitution. Article II states: "The executive power shall be vested in a President of the United States" and "He shall take care that the laws be faithfully executed." Over the years, the Supreme Court has ruled that presidential acts have the force of federal law. But the Court also overturned President

Truman's seizure of the steel mills in 1952 and President Nixon's attempt to prevent publication of the Pentagon Papers in 1971. The Court did so on the grounds that those actions exceeded the limits of the president's executive powers.

2. **Appointment power.** The president's power to appoint, with the Senate's advice and consent, important executive branch officials, judges, and ambassadors is another key presidential power. The president is responsible for appointing approximately 4,000 officials throughout the federal government.

   a. **Senate rejection of cabinet nominees rare.** Presidents generally have little trouble winning Senate approval of cabinet nominees. The Senate's 1989 rejection of Defense Secretary nominee John Tower was only the ninth cabinet rejection in U.S. history.

   b. **Senate rejection of Supreme Court nominees not unusual.** In contrast, the Senate's 1987 rejection of Supreme Court nominee Robert Bork was more typical. One of every five presidential nominees to the Supreme Court has been rejected by the Senate.

3. **War power.** Article I of the Constitution gives Congress the power "to declare war," but Article II makes the president the commander in chief of the armed services. The concept of "defensive war," first advanced by President Jefferson in 1801, expanded the president's war powers by saying hostile actions by another country initiated a state of war and permitted the president to respond as commander in chief even if Congress had not formally declared war. Congress sought to make this more of a shared power by passing the War Powers Resolution of 1973.

4. **Legislative power.** The president has the legislative power to call special sessions of Congress, recommend legislation, and veto legislation. Custom and subsequent statutes have augmented these constitutional powers to such a degree that it is now the president's legislative program that determines most of the congressional agenda.

   a. **Use of veto power.** On average, presidents veto less than one percent of the bills passed by Congress, and Congress musters the required two-thirds vote to override only about seven percent of those vetoes.

   b. **Threat of veto power.** It is the threat of a veto more than its actual use that helps a president bargain with Congress. Presidents must sign or reject entire bills; they do not have the selective line-item veto that most state governors have.

5. **The treaty power.** Article II of the Constitution says the president "shall have power, by and with the advice and consent of the Senate, to make treaties, provided two thirds of the senators present concur."

   a. **Senate's role restricted.** President George Washington established, early on, that the constitutional provision meant that presidents would seek Senate approval after a treaty was negotiated rather than having the Senate participate in or approve of ongoing negotiations.

   b. **Executive agreements.** Presidents have increasingly turned to executive agreements between the leaders of two or more nations as an alternative to treaties because such agreements do not require Senate approval. About ninety-five percent of all agreements between the United States and other countries since the end of World War II have been executive agreements.

B. **Executive prerogative.** The constitutional powers of the presidency establish the basis of presidential power in the twentieth century but by no means account for the totality of that power. The right that executives have to perform certain functions without the requirement of public or legislative approval is known as executive prerogative.

   1. **Locke's definition.** In 1690, English philosopher John Locke, a strong proponent of legislative power, defined executive prerogative in *The Second Treatise of Government* as "the power to act according to discretion for the public good, without the prescription of law and sometimes even against it."

   2. **President's "inherent powers."** The theory of executive prerogative states that there are inherent powers that belong to the executive even if the Constitution does not grant those powers. The language of the Constitution supports this idea of implied executive powers. Contrast Article I: "All legislative powers **herein granted** shall be

vested in a Congress of the United States" with Article II: "The executive power shall be vested in a President of the United States of America." The grant of executive power has no limiting phrase of "herein granted".

3. **Use of prerogative to expand presidential power.** Presidents have used the concept of executive prerogative to expand presidential power most effectively during international or domestic crises. President Lincoln, for example, claimed executive power to establish blockades, raise troops, and spend money without congressional action, suspend basic civil liberties, and substitute military for civilian courts in some areas during the Civil War. Subsequent presidents have claimed executive prerogative to respond to domestic crises such as strikes and economic depression and to international crises and threats to national security.

4. **Relationship of past and present prerogative power.** Executive prerogative rests on a general acceptance that in times of crises certain functions must be carried on by someone in government and that the executive is better suited than the legislature to respond quickly and effectively to crises. It is the actions of past presidents more than the words of the Constitution that establishes the executive prerogative powers of contemporary presidents.

5. **Public support of prerogative power.** Polls show the American public supports the concept of executive prerogative by identifying the president as the responsible officer of government, ranking as "great presidents" those who expanded the powers of office (Washington, Lincoln, Franklin Roosevelt), and identifying strong leadership as the trait they most want in a president.

6. **Limits to prerogative.** After a war or a crisis is over, the Supreme Court and Congress have established outside limits on the powers a president can claim under executive prerogative. Watergate, the Vietnam War, and the Iran-Contra scandal have triggered similar limits. But Congress and the Court also recognize and accept executive prerogative and the inherent powers of the presidency.

C. **The power to persuade.** In 1960, Richard Neustadt said that a central fact of the presidency is that "powers are no guarantee of power." The theme of Neustadt's seminal book, *Presidential Power*, is that the essence of presidential power is the power to persuade others to do what he wants or to support his actions. The formal powers of office provide a foundation of power for all presidents, but some are more powerful than others because they succeed at persuading the public, the press, and other political leaders to support their programs.

1. **Power to command limited.** Neustadt provided case studies of presidential leadership under Franklin Roosevelt, Truman, and Eisenhower (and in later editions, Kennedy to Carter) to demonstrate the limits of presidential commands or orders and the ingredients of successful persuasion.

2. **Persuasion v. management.** Presidential scholars Marcia Lynn Whicker and Raymond Moore have expanded on Neustadt's theme in their analysis of presidential effectiveness. Presidents today, they say, need persuasion skills to generate support from others and managerial skills to direct the executive branch of government.

3. **Rating recent presidents.** In their book, *When Presidents Are Great*, Whicker and Moore concluded that some presidents since FDR have been ineffective both as salesmen and managers (Ford and Carter), one has been a poor salesman but good manager (Nixon), two have been good at selling but ineffective managers (Johnson and Reagan), and four have been effective at both persuading and managing (FDR, Truman, Eisenhower, and Kennedy).

4. **Basis of persuasive power.** A president's power to persuade members of Congress to support his programs greatly depends on his ability to use three key resources: the political party, the president's approval rating in public opinion polls, and legislative skills such as personal involvement and the ability to provide tangible rewards to supporters.

Historical Perspective

American political development has seen successive periods of congressional government (for example, the decades following the Civil War), presidential government (the mid-1960s to mid-1970s), and deadlock or stalemate between the president and Congress (the late 1950s and the 1970s).

The balance of power between the president and Congress has swung back and forth in response to partisan changes in the electorate and government, leaders and leadership styles in both branches, social and economic developments, and international events. Although at any particular time it might seem like the president or Congress has gained the upper hand, the one true constant in the history of executive-legislative relations in the United States has been that of change.

One result of that change is that both institutions are quite different today than they were at the time of their creation, not only because of the dynamics between and inter-development of the two branches, but also because of the greatly expanded role of the federal government in the twentieth century.

I. **Congress**. Delegates to the Constitutional Convention drew on their experience with the English Parliament, colonial legislatures, the Continental Congress of the Revolutionary War, state legislatures, and the Congress of the Articles of Confederation in creating the Congress in 1787. The national legislature established by the Framers was a compromise institution reflecting the interests of large and small-population states, agricultural and mercantile economies, slave-holding and free states, other regional differences, those who favored a strong national government, and those who wanted to maintain states' rights in a federal system. The central compromise was the decision to have a bicameral legislature, with a popularly-elected House of Representatives and a Senate elected by state legislatures to represent state interests.

A. **The size of Congress**. When the first Congress met in New York City in 1789, it consisted of sixty-five representatives and twenty-six senators (two from each of the original thirteen states). The size of the House is established by law and has remained at 435 since 1913.

1. **Constitutional provisions for the House**. A member of the House today has more than 520,000 constituents, in contrast to the 30,000 or fewer constituents in 1789. The Constitution provides that each state will have at least one representative constituents and will have no more than one representative for each 30,000 constituents.

2. **Constitutional provisions for the Senate**. The Constitution provides that each state will have two senators, regardless of population, and the number of senators has been 100 since the admission of Alaska and Hawaii as states in 1959. The Seventeenth Amendment, adopted in 1913, provided for the direct election of senators.

B. **Length of sessions**. Congress was essentially a part-time institution up to the twentieth century; it was in session for less than twelve months of its two-year term until about 1911 (with the exceptions of the seventeen-month First Congress and even longer sessions of the Civil War and Reconstruction Congresses in the nineteenth century). Since then Congress has been in session for more than half of every two-year term, and in recent decades has become a year-round institution. Since the 1950s, the number of hours in session, committee meetings, and floor votes has doubled, and senators and representatives devote most of their time when Congress is not in session to constituency work back in their state or district.

C. **Institutionalization**. Congress has become a structured institution of established traditions and predictable routines. This institutionalization is reflected in the development of:

1. **Congressional careers**. The current practice of "professional legislators" making a career of service in Congress did not emerge until the latter part of the nineteenth century. Prior to that time, the typical senator and representative was a "citizen legislator." To illustrate, before 1880 the average length of service for a representative was two years and a senator four years. In 1989, however, it was about eleven years in the House and ten in the Senate.

2. **Party leadership**. Although there were important partisan divisions in early Congresses, it was not until after the Civil War that party committees and party leaders such as the House Speaker took on the important role they have today of managing conflict and organizing the business of the House and Senate.

3. **Committee system**. The division of labor reflected in the highly structured committee systems of the House and Senate is one of the hallmarks of the institutionalized Congress. Regular criteria and procedures for selecting committee members and chairs and stability in committee membership and jurisdictions are characteristics of the modern Congress, which emerged in the late nineteenth century.

II. **The presidency**. The expansion of presidential power is like a ratchet wheel: after executive power has been moved up a notch or two to meet a crisis, it almost never falls back to its earlier level. The exercise of a presidential power that was once regarded as exceptional becomes routine. Strong presidents have drawn on the grants of power in Article II and on the concept of executive prerogative to establish precedents that successive chief executives can use to justify their own claims to particular powers. The emergence of the modern presidency after World War II has consolidated and institutionalized those powers.

A. **Contributors to presidential power**. Presidential scholar Edward Corwin has suggested that not more than one in three presidents has contributed to the development of presidential power but that the precedents established by those strong presidents have greatly determined the evolution of the American presidency.

1. **Washington** (1789-1797). As the first to hold that office, George Washington's many contributions included creating the president's cabinet, asserting presidential dominance in foreign policy by proclaiming neutrality in the French-British war in 1793, establishing a doctrine of executive privilege, and serving an important symbolic role as chief of state to encourage stability and national unity.

2. **Jefferson** (1801-1809). Thomas Jefferson downplayed the symbolic, chief of state aspects of the presidency and relied more on personal persuasion, especially in his dealings with Congress. He also chose to be an active party leader rather than remaining "above politics." In 1801 Jefferson established a precedent of broad presidential powers as commander-in-chief when he sent ships and troops into the Mediterranean even though Congress had not declared war. The President advanced a concept of "defensive war" to justify his actions, saying that a state of war existed even without a congressional declaration because Tripoli had attacked American ships.

3. **Jackson** (1829-1837). Andrew Jackson's tenure in office coincided with the transformation of political parties from legislative caucuses to grass-roots organizations of the electorate. The party convention replaced the caucus in presidential nominations and a state's popular vote rather than its legislature's vote determined its electoral votes. Jackson's independent electoral base allowed him to claim that only the president spoke for the entire nation. Acting as the people's "tribune,"

Jackson vetoed twelve acts of Congress—more than the combined total of his six predecessors.

4. **Lincoln** (1861-1865). Abraham Lincoln's presidency is often described as a constitutional dictatorship (and some even question its constitutionality).

   a. **Powers used by Lincoln**. The crisis of the Civil War permitted Lincoln to invoke executive prerogative in claiming extraordinary war powers. When war broke out in 1861, the President spent $2 million that had not been appropriated by Congress, closed the post office to "treasonable correspondence," imposed a blockade on southern ports, suspended the constitutional guarantee that a person could not be held in jail indefinitely, and ordered the arrest and detention of anyone suspected of "treasonable practices."

   b. **Congressional approval after the fact**. Three months after the fact, Congress approved Lincoln's actions, and after his presidency, Congress once again gained the upper hand in governing.

   c. **Lincoln's legacy of presidential power**. The extraordinary powers that presidents can claim in times of war are a legacy of the Lincoln presidency.

5. **Wilson** (1913-1921). In Woodrow Wilson's first term he effectively combined the roles of party leader and people's tribune to win approval of progressive legislation. In his second term, he exercised extraordinary wartime powers that Congress had delegated to him. After Wilson's tenure, these wartime powers, the personal direction of foreign policy, presidential initiative in congressional policy making, and broadened economic responsibilities all became accepted prerogatives of the executive.

6. **Franklin Roosevelt** (1933-45). The Great Depression, World War II, and the precedent-shattering twelve-year tenure of Franklin Roosevelt revolutionized the presidency. Roosevelt's personal leadership skills provided the model for Neustadt's discussion of the power to persuade. Presidents since Roosevelt have differed in their ability to maximize presidential power through persuasion. The most enduring legacy of Franklin

Roosevelt's tenure of office, however, is the institution of the modern presidency.

B. **The modern presidency and the roles of office.** Since 1933, the public, press, members of Congress and other political leaders expect presidents to propose legislation and budgets and seek congressional approval of them, be the central political figure in the nation, advance and defend this country's interests internationally, and control the resources needed to meet those goals. Under the traditional presidency, some presidents were active leaders of Congress and the nation while others were not. Under the modern presidency, all presidents are expected to be the central figure of American politics and government.

C. **The post-modern presidency and the limitations of power.** Do the expectations and responsibilities of the president now exceed the resources of the office? Some scholars have suggested that the Vietnam war marked the arrival of the post-modern presidency. The country's military, economic, and political commitments to other nations mean that a president must be able to influence foreign political leaders and shape international events in order to be successful. Post-modern presidents are expected to meet these international expectations, but the opportunities and resources for doing so are limited.

Contemporary Perspective

I. **Congress and representation.** Although lawmaking is the chief responsibility of Congress, the authority of the national legislature to pass laws rests on its being a representative body. It is the selection of legislators and their behavior once in office (both in Washington and at home) that determines congressional representation.

A. **Selection.** Most members of Congress first win election by winning a seat left open by a retiring or deceased incumbent rather than by defeating an incumbent. Two-thirds of the members of the 101st Congress (1989-90) first came to office that way. But the distinguishing characteristic of congressional elections is that almost all the incumbents seeking reelection are returned to office.

1. **Nominations.** Incumbent senators and representatives have little to fear from challengers within their own party. In recent years, less than two percent of the House incumbents running for reelection have been defeated in a primary, and no senator has been defeated that way since 1980.

   a. **Lack of opposition.** The power of incumbency makes it difficult for the party out of power to recruit strong candidates, especially for the House. In 1988, for example, one of every five incumbents seeking reelection faced no major party opponent at all.

   b. **Male majority.** The incumbency effect at the nomination stage helps to account for the fact that there are few women in Congress. Most incumbents are male, and fights for the party nomination in open-seat races generally attract many male candidates with experience in elected office. Men held 88 percent of the elective political offices in the United States in 1989.

2. **The general election.** Since 1946, voters have returned nine of ten House incumbents seeking reelection and three of four incumbent senators seeking reelection. In some elections the incumbent reelection rate has been even higher. In 1988, for example, it was 98.5 percent for representatives and 85 percent for senators. The following are some reasons for incumbent reelection.

   a. **Support services.** The perquisites of office, such as staff and other support services, are often cited as one of the reasons for incumbents' electoral success. In recent elections, these "perks" have been valued at $1 million for representatives and even more for senators.

   b. **Fund raising.** Incumbents also have an edge in fund raising. For instance, in 1988, political action committees (PACs) contributed four times as much to incumbent senators than to challengers and eight times as much to incumbent representatives than to challengers.

   c. **Name recognition.** Incumbent representatives have a two to one advantage over challengers in name recognition among voters. But in Senate races, where the challengers tend to be highly visible figures, this advantage all but disappears.

d. **Decline of party affiliation.** The declining importance of party affiliation in congressional elections has benefited incumbents. About twenty percent of the electorate votes against their normal party affiliation in congressional elections, and ninety percent of those defectors are switching to support an incumbent.

e. **Voter perception of issues.** Somewhere between twenty and thirty percent of the electorate know enough about the issue position of each candidate to be considered issue voters, but even with this group, incumbents gain an advantage from voters' perceptions of issues and candidates' positions.

B. **Representatives focus.** Legislators serve as representatives by acting on behalf of others. But who are those "others?" To what extent do members of Congress represent constituents, important special interests, or the general public and a national interest?

1. **Constituencies.** Contrary to the common notion that legislators must follow constituency opinion or risk electoral defeat, members of Congress know that most constituents lack information on and interest in most of their congressional votes. It would be difficult for representatives to follow majority constituency opinion because in most cases there is none. Instead, representatives view their constituents as a series of concentric circles, and respond to them in different ways.

   a. **Geographic constituency.** Representatives respond to important economic interests, demographic groups, and prevailing ideology within the physical boundaries of their district, but the geographic constituency is not an important referent on most issues.

   b. **Reelection constituency.** This is the smaller group within the geographic constituency made up of those who members of Congress felt supported them the last election. Representatives' behavior in Washington is influenced to some extent by the anticipated reaction of the reelection constituency.

   c. **Primary constituency.** This group has demonstrated a more intense and durable support over a number of elections and has often helped to recruit the representative for his or her first campaign. These are the people

members say they "owe" and whose opinions will be sought on issues of importance to them.

   d. **Personal constituency.** This innermost circle is made up of political or personal friends whom the members trusts completely. Legislators may discuss political strategy with this group and draw on it for emotional support, but they seldom look to it for cues on how to vote.

2. **Special interests.** Congress has always regarded the representation of economic interests as one of its functions. The First Congress, for instance, considered requests from domestic manufacturers for protective tariffs on paint, rope, cotton cloth, and imported mustard.

   a. **PACs.** Political action committees (PACs) have changed the nature of interest representation in Congress because of the extent of their involvement in financing congressional campaigns.

   b. **Growth and variety of PACs.** The number of PACs has gone from about 600 in 1974 to over 4000 today. There are corporate, labor, ideological, trade, and health PACs representing almost every private interest in the country.

   c. **PAC funds to incumbents.** In 1988, House candidates spent a total of nearly $250 million and Senate candidates spent about $200 million. PACs contributed about one-third of all funds raised by candidates that year but almost one-half of incumbents' campaign funds.

   d. **PAC funds to congressional leaders.** PAC contributions are also directed toward congressional leaders, members of important money committees (such as House Ways and Means and Senate Finance), and members of committees with jurisdiction in a particular area of importance (such as transportation, communications, and agriculture).

   e. **PAC funds and ethics codes.** Both chambers have ethics codes, most recently revised in 1989, which seek to prevent the representation of special interests from becoming bribery, extortion, or any other type of illegal behavior. The House Committee on Standards of Official Conduct and the Senate Select Ethics Committee investigate alleged ethics violations and enforce the ethics codes.

3. **The national interest.** If representatives and senators are servicing their constituencies and special interests, who is looking out for the national interest? Presidents often present themselves as the one true representative of the national interest. Members of Congress use the president's position on national issues as well as national public opinion polls as reference points on national issues, but they also maintain that their actions in areas such as environmental protection and foreign policy collectively represent the national interest.

II. **Congress and lawmaking.** Many of the activities that make up representation take place in the home district and state, whereas lawmaking is mostly confined to Capitol Hill. Individual legislators can be effective representatives, but lawmaking is a collective effort that requires the building of coalitions. A decentralized Congress supports representation; a centralized one is most effective at lawmaking.

Individual members of Congress can satisfy public expectations about issues by talking about them and explaining their votes on those issues. But citizens expect more from Congress as a whole when it comes to lawmaking. They expect Congress to resolve pressing national issues such as the deficit and drug abuse, which is much more difficult than representing interests. Citizens hold the institution of Congress accountable for lawmaking just as they hold individual legislators accountable for representation.

A. **Committees.** These are the workshops of congressional lawmaking. There are twenty-two standing committees in the House, sixteen in the Senate, and a total of more than two hundred subcommittees between the two chambers. Their control over the legislative process is suggested by the fact that five of every six bills introduced in Congress dies in committee.

1. **Committee jurisdiction.** House and Senate rules specify committee jurisdictions, and their parliamentarians routinely refer bills to committee after they are introduced. Overlapping jurisdictions sometimes require that more than one committee consider proposed legislation.

2. **Role of sub-committees.** Committee chairs will usually refer bills to a subcommittee, following the subcommittee jurisdictions created by the full committee. Subcommittees then hold hearings, "mark-ups" or make changes in the bill, and report it to the full committee.

3. **Reforming "subcommittee government."** A number of decentralizing reforms that increased the number and importance of subcommittees led to "subcommittee government" in the 1970s. Subsequent reforms in the House moved that institution away from subcommittee government by strengthening the speaker, party leaders, and full chamber consideration of the budget, while the Senate continues to be a decentralized body.

4. **Members' committee assignments.** Party committees in both chambers assign members to committees on the basis of members' preferences, seniority, constituency or region, and sometimes additional factors such as ideology, party loyalty, professional background, race, sex, and religion.

5. **Factors in members' committee preferences.** Legislators seek out committees that will help them serve their own goals of reelection, influence within the chamber, and policy making. The relative importance of those goals helps to determine on which committees legislators seek membership.

6. **Committee membership and receipt of PAC funds.** Political action committees consider senators' and representatives' committee assignments to be one of the most important factors in deciding how to distribute campaign contributions. In 1989, for instance, 154 PACs identified by *Congressional Quarterly* as having a significant stake in the outcome of clean-air legislation gave more than $600,000 to members of the House Energy and Commerce Committee, the committee with primary jurisdiction in that area.

B. **Parties.** Political parties and their leaders are responsible for organizing Congress by determining the size and makeup of committees and setting the rules for floor action. In addition, party leaders try to get policies favored by their party passed by Congress and to block policies favored by the opposition.

1. **Party leaders' resources.** Resources available to party leaders include House and Senate rules, tangible rewards (such as office space and cam-

paign support), status within Congress, and information.

2. **Party affiliation and voting.** Even though congressional parties often appear to be toothless organizations, political party affiliation is the single most important influence on congressional voting. Seven of every ten members of Congress regularly vote with a majority of their party on votes that divide a majority of one party against a majority of the other.

3. **Effects of single-party domination.** Political parties historically have been vehicles for translating changes in the American electorate into changes in national policy. Today, however, Congress appears to be insulated from national trends that in the past have produced new party majorities in Congress. This is particularly true in the House of Representatives where Democrats have held a majority for more than 35 consecutive years. Republicans ended a similar 26-year Democratic reign in the Senate in 1980, but gave way again to a Democratic majority in 1986. This longstanding Democratic control has led some observers to charge that Congress is unresponsive to political change.

C. **Staff.** The congressional bureaucracy of more than thirty thousand employees makes it larger than some executive bureaucracies such as the Department of Labor and Housing and Urban Development. The number of congressional staff members has increased dramatically over the last four decades and is now about six times what it was in 1947.

1. **House and Senate members' personal office staff.** Representatives receive about $400,000 annually to hire as many as twenty-two personal staff members. The amount senators receive for staff depends on their state population but ranges from $470,000 to $1.4 million and permits senators to have an average of forty people on their office staffs.

2. **Committee and subcommittee staff.** Committee chairs and ranking minority members hire committee and subcommittee staff in both chambers, and each senator also hires three committee staff members to cover his or her own assignments.

3. **Responsibilities of staff.** Congressional staffs carry out most of the constituency casework of Congress, conduct most of the preliminary research on legislation, draft bills, arrange for and organize committee and subcommittee hearings, perform administrative oversight through program evaluations and investigations, and participate in bargaining sessions with legislators and representatives of the executive branch, constituents, and special interests.

4. **Effects of staff increase.** The increase in congressional staff has reduced legislators' dependence on the executive branch and interest groups for information, increased their ability to put new issues on the legislative agenda, and heightened Congress's impact on national issues. But staff growth has not permitted members to gain control over a constantly increasing work load. Indeed, many people suggest that the increase in staff has actually added to that workload.

5. **Power of congressional staff.** The great increase in the size and influence of congressional staffs over the last four decades has troubled many members of Congress and outside observers. This is particularly true when staff members become what one scholar has termed "unelected representatives" and staff-to-staff negotiations take the place of member-to-member deliberations.

D. **House-Senate differences in rules and norms.** The rules and norms of the House of Representatives serve primarily to establish limits on representation and reinforce lawmaking, while those of the Senate maximize representation.

1. **Formal and informal rules.** The formal rules and informal norms of the House of Representatives make that chamber more formal, hierarchical, and impersonal than the Senate. Committee and subcommittee work is generally more important to representatives than it is to senators.

2. **Hierarchial system of the House.** There are fewer opportunities for individual participation in the House and more of a hierarchy in which a member's influence depends to a great extent on his or her formal position. Leaders strictly control the business of the House floor.

3. **Greater participation in the Senate.** While representatives tend to be policy specialists, senators are policy generalists. Senate rules and norms support a wide range of individual participation.

4. **The "new breed" legislator.** In recent years, both chambers have seen an increase in members characterized as independent policy entrepreneurs. "The New American Politician," as one congressional scholar has called this type of legislator, often has little patience with rules and norms that limit full participation in all arenas of congressional politics. As a result, the House has become more like the Senate in its individualism. Many members and congressional experts also think that the ability to engage in productive deliberations on pressing national issues has declined in both chambers.

E. **Congressional voting.** Congress averages between eight hundred and nine hundred recorded floor votes every year, in addition to hundreds of voice votes on the floor, committee and subcommittee votes, and votes in party caucuses and conferences. What factors determine how members vote on the floor?

1. **Factors influencing voting.** Analyses of roll-call voting in Congress show that party affiliation, region, ideology, the president, and certain constituency traits such as urbanism and the number of blue-collar workers are the most important influences on members' voting.

2. **Relative influence of factors.** The relative influence of these factors depends on the issue under consideration. Party affiliation is the most durable influence and for most members a party vote is also a constituency vote. Those senators and representatives who most often defect from their party (southern Democrats and northeastern Republicans) also tend to represent constituencies that are different from the typical constituency of their party.

3. **The conservative coalition.** The conservative coalition, made up of a majority of voting southern Democrats and a majority of voting Republicans, has been the primary regional influence on congressional voting. The coalition emerged in the 1930s in opposition to many New Deal programs but has been less important since the 1980s. It now appears as a voting bloc in fewer than ten percent of the recorded votes in Congress.

4. **"Cue networks."** Members of Congress develop a cue network of colleagues whose opinions are sought on particular issues. Two of the most important cue sources for most legislators are party leaders and members of the state party delega-

tion. Members follow what one scholar calls a "consensus mode" of decision making in using their cue networks. If there is an agreement among the primary cue givers about how to vote, the legislator can cast his or her vote that way without having to worry much about any repercussions.

5. **Relative weight of "cue networks."** The internal nature of these cue networks, in which Capitol Hill cue sources are consistently regarded as more important on most votes than constituency cue sources, again raises questions about the insulation of Congress and whether it is unresponsive to pressing national issues.

III. **Presidential selection.** Richard Neustadt points out that the White House "is not a place for amateurs." The presidential selection process has generally been successful at keeping amateurs out of the White House. Eight of the nine presidents since Franklin Roosevelt held an elective office in national or state government before becoming president (The ninth, Eisenhower, was a career military officer with extensive Washington experience.). The extent of that experience ranged from eight years (Carter and Reagan) to twenty-eight years (Johnson), but the average for all eight was seventeen years of experience in elective office before becoming president.

A. **Nominations.** The Democratic and Republican nominees for president are formally chosen by the national conventions. In effect, however, they have been chosen in presidential primaries since 1972.

1. **Increase in states holding primaries.** The number of states holding presidential primaries went from seventeen in 1968 to thirty-seven in 1988. Less than half the convention delegates in both parties were chosen in primaries in 1968, compared to more than three-fourths in 1988.

2. **Importance of early primaries.** Not only is winning primaries the only way to win the nominations, but winning early primaries has also become key. In 1968 New Hampshire was the only primary before the middle of March, but in 1988 twenty states had held their primaries by then. The importance of early wins has created the "invisible primary"—a series of low visibility and usually informal state party contests and fund raising competition that takes place a year or more before the first primary.

3. **Importance of early fund raising.** Candidates capable of raising funds early have an advantage in the long primary season. In 1988, the sixteen major party candidates for president spent almost $200 million trying to win the nomination, with the two eventual nominees—Bush and Dukakis—accounting for more than a quarter of that total ($55 million).

4. **Absence of coalition building and difficulty in governing.** Presidential candidates are able to win primaries and the nomination without having to build coalitions, as they were required to do under the old convention system. The ability to build coalitions, however, is considered essential to governing once in office. Many scholars feel that a candidate's being able to win the nomination without having to build coalitions is a basic flaw of the presidential primary system.

5. **Problems raised by decentralized nominations.** The presidential nominating process also raises a number of other issues about politics and governing. Some critics suggest that the emphasis primary voters in both major parties place on the ideological acceptability of candidates produces nominees with limited appeal in the general election. Despite efforts to provide for the representation of party elites as "super-delegates" at the convention, national party elites still have little influence over the selection of their party's nominee. And the primary system leaves little or no room for either party to draft a reluctant but qualified candidate for president.

B. **Elections.** The president is indirectly chosen by the people through the electoral college, in which states have as many electoral votes as they do senators and representatives in Congress. The candidate with the most popular votes in a state wins all of that state's electoral votes. To be elected president, a candidate needs a majority (270) of the total (538) electoral votes. The electoral college is sometimes said to favor one party or the other. In 1988, for instance, there was talk of a "Republican lock" on the electoral college and of a Democratic strategy late in the campaign to try to win an electoral majority without winning a popular majority. But most studies show that neither party has a standing advantage in the electoral college. The following are factors that help determine how people vote in presidential elections.

1. **Demographic factors.** Demographic factors such as race, religion, and occupation sometimes determine how people vote in presidential elections. The New Deal coalition that dominated presidential elections from 1932 to 1968 was often described in demographic terms. There have been so many changes in the voting habits of demographic groups over the past twenty years, however, that some political scientists have concluded that a realignment has taken place in the American electorate.

2. **Party affiliation.** Party identification is closely connected to how people vote. About two out of three Americans identify with a party, but the number describing themselves as independents has been steadily growing since the 1960s. Recent surveys show that about forty percent of Americans think of themselves as Democrats, thirty percent Republicans, and thirty percent independents.

3. **Opinion of issues.** Issues also influence how Americans vote in presidential elections. Between forty and fifty percent of the electorate can be classified as issue voters. These are voters who correctly identify both candidates' positions on important issues and vote on the basis of the proximity of candidates' issue positions to their own.

4. **Retrospective judgments.** Voters also make retrospective judgments in presidential elections. Prospective issue voting requires speculating about what candidates will do in the future, and that can be a very difficult task. Retrospective voting is based on voters' judgments on the nation's economic performance for the past year or so. Poor economic performance tends to hurt incumbent presidents and their parties.

5. **Candidate image.** Candidate image—voters' perceptions of candidates' personal and political qualities—has an immediate impact on voting in presidential elections. Many commentators express concern about "image" voting displacing issues in presidential elections, but voters' perceptions of candidate image are often sophisticated judgments about candidates' competence and leadership ability.

6. **Factors affecting decrease in voting.** Only half the eligible voters turned out to vote in the 1988 presidential election—the lowest turnout since 1924. Compared to other democracies and compared to earlier periods in American history, the

"turnout problem" is one of the most serious issues and greatest challenges facing U.S. citizens today. Whatever the causes, the low turnout in presidential elections is a serious flaw in how we select presidents and should be an issue of great concern to all citizens. Political scientists have found that there are a number of reasons for low voter turnout. The most important are the following.

    a.   **Youth**. Age is a factor, with fewer voters among those under thirty-years old.

    b.   **Registration requirements**. Registration requirements prevent others from voting.

    c.   **Alienation**. Attitudes of political alienation and feelings of ineffectiveness also depress voter turnout.

IV. **The institutional presidency**. The modern presidency includes more than 1500 officials and staff members who assist the president in information gathering, decision making and the implementation of decisions.

  A. **Cabinet**. The Constitution says nothing about a president's cabinet. It does say a president "may require the opinion, in writing, of the principle officer" in the executive departments. George Washington effectively created the cabinet by calling his department heads together for joint discussions of important issues.

    1.   **Factors in cabinet selection**. In appointing a cabinet, presidents select a mix of policy specialists, representatives of broad interests such as business or agriculture, Washington careerists, and long-standing political allies.

    2.   **The "inner" and "outer" cabinets**. The attorney general and secretaries of state, treasury, and defense make up the "inner cabinet" and the heads of such departments as agriculture, labor and commerce make up the "outer cabinet." This is not a formal distinction, but in most administrations members of the inner cabinet see the president more often and are more involved in presidential policy making than are members of the outer cabinet.

    3.   **Relations between presidents and cabinets**. Presidents usually begin their terms with a commitment to cabinet government but come to depend less and less on cabinet meetings and collective decision making as time goes on. Conflicts also develop in most administrations between White House aides and cabinet officials and between cabinet officials' dual roles of advising the president and representing the interests of their departments.

  B. **White House Office**. The president's personal staff in the White House Office numbered about 50 members under Franklin Roosevelt, 350 under President Bush and was as large as 560 under President Nixon.

    1.   **Campaign staff and presidential appointments**. Presidents find it necessary to have more than one pool of candidates for presidential appointments.

      a.   **Campaign staff**. Presidents naturally turn to their campaign staff in filling positions in the White House Office. These individuals have devoted themselves to the president's election. It is prudent to reward the faithful, and promises are sometimes made to outstanding members of the campaign team or are made for other political reasons.

      b.   **Need for appointees beyond the campaign team**. Presidents also benefit by filling some of these positions with people experienced in governing as well as campaigning. The increasing professionalization of presidential campaigns, the growing emphasis on negative campaigning, and the expanding gap between running a campaign and governing that have become evident in recent elections make it particularly important for presidents to cast their nets wider than the campaign staff in selecting White House aides. Candidate George Bush made that point during the 1988 campaign when he was said to tell one election aide: "You know, if I were elected president, I wouldn't want people like you in government."

    2.   **Purpose and organization of White House staff**. The purpose of the White House staff is to provide the president with complete and reliable information for decision making. Franklin Roosevelt employed a competitive approach to staffing, in which aides had overlapping responsibilities and reported directly to the president. In contrast, Presidents Truman, Eisenhower, and Nixon organized the White House Office as a formal

hierarchy with only a few aides having regular direct access to the president.

3. **Detail oriented v. "minimalist" presidential styles.** President Carter's personal attention to the details of governing (such as closely reading and making a critique of the Air Force budget) and President Reagan's detached "minimalist" style (reflected in his often not knowing key elements of his administration's own policy proposals) represent two extremes in how presidents use White House staff in decision making.

   a. **Disadvantages of minimalist style.** On the one hand, a minimalist management style raises issues about unelected staff members making policy as well as concerns similar to those about congressional staff discussed earlier.

   b. **Disadvantages of detail orientation.** On the other hand, a president bogged down in the details of governing is not likely to be able to carry out the policy of selling and personal persuasion needed for effective presidential leadership.

C. **Executive Office of the President.** The Executive Office of the President (EOP) was created in 1939 to support presidential planning and fiscal policy making. The EOP was intended to be a staff agency to gather information and coordinate the actions of other agencies, not a line agency to implement policies. The Bureau of the Budget was the original central agency of the EOP but more than forty agencies have been a part of the office for different periods of time.

1. **Agencies of the EOP.** Currently, the Executive Office consists of thirteen separate agencies, including the National Security Council, Council of Economic Advisors, and the central budgeting unit of the executive branch, the Office of Management and Budget (OMB), which replaced the Bureau of the Budget in 1970. As the congressional agenda has become increasingly dominated by budget issues, the Budget Director, who heads the OMB, has come to play a key role in executive-legislative relations.

2. **EOP as a "counter-bureaucracy."** Many of the key agencies of the EOP have changed from being strictly information-gathering and coordinating agencies into operational units. This is a result of presidents since Kennedy using the EOP as a "counter-bureaucracy." The National Security Council, for example, has provided a counter to the sprawling bureaucracy of the Pentagon and State Department. Reagan administration reforms after the Iran-Contra scandal were designed to reduce the dangers of the National Security Council carrying on its own operations.

3. **White House Office not same as EOP.** A distinction is sometimes made between the White House Office, which is the personal staff of the president that is also a part of the Executive Office of the President, and the broader Executive Office, which is designed to serve the institution of the presidency rather than the current occupant of that office.

4. **Dangers of over use of EOP.** There is a tendency for all presidents to use the EOP as an extension of their personal staff, as their own government within the government. But the Bay of Pigs fiasco in the Kennedy administration, the presidential isolation that bred Watergate in the Nixon administration, and the Iran-Contra affair in the Reagan administration all suggest the dangers involved when presidents use agencies in the Executive Office for implementing policies rather than for advice and coordination.

D. **The vice presidency.** Fourteen of the forty individuals to serve as president have previously been vice president and nine of those fourteen took over when the incumbent president died. One of those nine, Lyndon Johnson, likened a vice president to "a raven hovering around the head of the president, reminding him of his mortality."

1. **Selection of vice presidential nominees.** Presidential candidates select their own running mates. The last time the choice for the number two slot on the ticket was left up to the convention was in 1956. That means that vice presidents have a constituency of one: the president.

2. **Desire to "balance the ticket."** The electoral strength of vice-presidential candidates is a key ingredient in their selection. Presidential candidates and parties want to "balance the ticket" by selecting vice-presidential candidates who represent a geographic region, ideological faction, or age group different from the presidential candidate.

3. **Change in vice-presidential responsibilities.** Vice presidents have traditionally had political responsibilities and often played a strong partisan role that permitted the president to stay "above politics." Since the Carter administration, however, presidents have assigned vice presidents policy responsibilities in areas such as drug interdiction and space programs.

4. **Dependency of vice president's role on the president.** Because there is no room in the American system for a co-president or assistant president, the role of the vice president will always depend on what the president wants it to be. And while a vice president today does have some policy responsibilities, he or she is likely to continue to function more as an administrative spokesperson and representative than as a policy maker.

V. **Citizen participation.** In 1787, Robert Yates and John Lansing, delegates to the Constitutional Convention from New York, walked out of the convention and later worked with other Anti-Federalists to oppose the ratification of the Constitution. Yates and Lansing said that the national officials' "remoteness from their constituents and necessary permanency of office" would make it difficult for them to work for the people's welfare and happiness. More recently, public opinion polls have found that the number of people who feel "people like me don't have any say about what the government does" and "I don't think public officials care much what people like me think" has more than doubled between 1960 and 1988 and that more than one third of the public now agrees with both statements. Were the fears of Yates and Lansing and other Anti-Federalists about the national government becoming remote and isolated from its citizens justified? Have the routine reelection of incumbents to Congress and the high cost of congressional campaigns compromised the democracy of Congress? Has presidential power expanded to the point where presidents are indeed constitutional monarchs isolated from the realities of American life and its citizens?

A. **Congress and democracy.** Congress is widely regarded as the most democratic of the national government's three branches. Frequent elections are the primary instruments for achieving democracy in Congress, and the accessibility of the institution and its members provides many opportunities for citizen participation.

1. **Means of citizens gaining influence with members.** The regularity with which incumbents are reelected and the high costs of campaigns would appear to make it difficult for fresh faces to be

elected to Congress or for average citizens to have any influence on congressional elections. But the number of resignations, retirements, and electoral defeats combine to make the average tenure of members of Congress less than eleven years. Citizens can maximize their influence and establish close ties between members and constituents by helping to recruit candidates for Congress and working in their campaigns. A strong campaign, even if it results in defeat by an incumbent, can lay the groundwork for a future campaign when the seat becomes vacant.

2. **Congressional accessibility.** Since the 1970s, congressional reforms and the emergence of a new breed of representatives and senators extremely attentive to their districts and states have made Congress a more accessible institution than it was before.

   a. **Attendance and testimony at committee meetings.** Any citizen can attend committee and subcommittee hearings and provide testimony or other information to their own representative or senator for submission.

   b. **Contact with district and state offices.** More and more congressional staffers are being assigned to district and state offices to respond to constituent requests.

   c. **Personal contact with members.** Representatives now spend about one of every three days in their districts and senators one of every four days in their states—more than double what it was in the mid-1970s. In addition to regular appointments and speeches, many legislators hold open office hours and open meetings to hear citizens on any issues of concern to them.

3. **Congress and the citizen.** Congress acts as a democratic institution not only by listening to constituents and representing the interests of their district and state, but also by deliberating and passing laws in the national interest. Citizens cannot personally engage in the debate on the floor of the House or Senate, but they can now watch those deliberations on cable television and participate in the broader national debate reflected in the deliberations of Congress. By taking advantage of the educational function of Congress in this way and by conveying ideas to their representatives, citizens help to bring

Congress closer to Madison's vision of the House of Representatives "as a substitute for a meeting of citizens in person." *(The Federalist* No. 52).

B. **The Presidency and democracy**. A former White House aide in the Kennedy administration once told presidential scholar Thomas Cronin that "everybody believes in democracy until he gets to the White House." Others who have served in the White House have made similar comments about the aura of power and the trappings of monarchy that make life in the White House seem like that in a royal court. But presidents are not like the French "Sun Kings" of the *ancien régime*. On account of the provisions of the Constitution, they cannot say "I am the state," as Louis XIV of France once did. As political leaders in a democracy, they depend on public support, not just on election day, but throughout their term of office.

1. **Public opinion**. Studies of presidential influence in Congress have found a direct relationship between the president's standing in public opinion polls and his support in Congress. Even those citizens who play no active role in Washington politics help to influence the dialogue between a president and Congress. But that does not mean that citizens should hang around the house waiting for a pollster to show up. Instead, it means participating in the broad national deliberations discussed above.

2. **Agenda setting**. Just as presidents set much of the congressional agenda, so too does the public influence the relative attention that presidents give certain issues. The high priority that recent presidents have given to anti-drug programs and family issues and the relatively low priority given to actually reducing the budget deficit, reflects the relative importance the general public assigns those different issues. Grass roots lobbying by senior citizens, public demonstrations by farmers, and massive rallies by advocates on both sides of the abortion issue are all ways of gaining the public's attention and moving issues higher on the agenda of the president and Congress.

3. **Recognizing the limits on presidential power**. Because presidents are chiefs of state as well as chief executives and the responsible officers of government, they are the central symbols of American government. That results in the general public having an exaggerated view of presidential power and expecting more from presidents than they can possibly deliver. Citizen participation at any level of government makes one aware of the limits on any particular office and of government in general. Knowing where to direct one's energy in order to get results is an important element of citizen participation in America. Active participants are less likely to credit the president for everything that goes right during his term of office and to blame the president for everything that goes wrong.

2. THE CITIZEN AND THE BUREAUCRACY

In our day it is a constant fact that the most outstanding Americans are seldom summoned to public office, and it must be recognized that this tendency has increased as democracy has gone beyond its previous limits. It is clear that during the last fifty years the race of American statesmen has strangely shrunk....In democratic eyes government is not a blessing but a necessary evil.

Alexis de Tocqueville (1835)

INTRODUCTION

For most Americans, "bureaucracy" is a word with unpleasant connotations. It represents what we like least about government, and "bureaucrats" epitomize what we like least about bureaucracy. Ironically, however, we expect a great deal from government and expect that its programs be run effectively and efficiently. That necessarily requires a strong and energetic bureaucracy. There is a fundamental paradox here.

This paradox has deep roots in American history and political thought. Americans have always distrusted governmental power yet have increasingly demanded more governmental services. If there is to be a government, there must be a bureaucracy to do its work. Since the American revolution, however, we have been profoundly ambivalent about what role the bureaucracy ought to play. We resent having bureaucrats meddle in our lives to collect taxes, but we insist on the programs the taxes fund. We want government to protect us, but we are annoyed at the restrictions on our freedom that accompany government's protection.

Some of our antipathy toward bureaucracy is thus clearly American, rooted deep in our national culture. Some of our suspicion also comes from the inevitable dilemma of bureaucratic power. If it is to be effective and efficient, bureaucracy must have expertise and power. However, if bureaucracy is powerful, it can threaten democratic rule. Much of the activity in American government is, and always has been, devoted to making bureaucracy strong enough to be effective but not so strong as to be threatening. This is one of the central problems of American democracy.

Bureaucracy has power because its bureaucrats develop specialization in particular tasks. Bureaucracies and their bureaucrats are also powerful because their job is administering the law. That puts bureaucracy in an awkward, often conflictive, position between the legislature as law maker and the chief executive as law administrator.

It is little wonder, therefore, that we have such ambiguous and contradictory feelings about bureaucracy. Bureaucracy stands at the center of historical conflicts about the role of government in society and at the center of the continuing struggle over the balance of power in American government. It is the source of much unpleasantness, from tax collection to "red tape;" but it is also the foundation of the government's valued programs. The debate over the role of government bureaucracy is thus a reflection of the broader arguments over American politics.

The problems that de Tocqueville pointed out are ageless. New challenges face us as well, challenges requiring that elected officials and citizens alike support an effective bureaucracy if the nation's government is to meet the demands of future problems.

OBJECTIVES

The citizen should be able to

1. explain the reasons why bureaucracy exists, and why it is a generic phenomenon which is important in both the public and private sectors.

2. explain the role that bureaucracy plays in democracy and the dilemma that bureaucratic power creates.

3. explain the historical evolution of the modern American administrative state.

4. explain why public confidence in bureaucracy has declined.

5. explain the problems facing bureaucracy today.

6. take, explain, and defend positions regarding the central problem of bureaucracy: the dilemma of accountability—entrusting it with enough power to be effective, yet controlling the exercise of that power to keep it accountable to elected officials.

FRAME OF REFERENCE
Conceptual Perspective

I. **What bureaucracy is.** Although we often use the word "bureaucracy," we aren't necessarily clear about what it means.

A. **Bureaucracy as a "dirty" word?** "Bureaucratic" is often used as a pejorative description of the way citizens are treated by government. In fact, bureaucracy is a universal phenomenon of all large and complex organizations, public and private.

B. **Bureaucracy as inevitable.** Bureaucracy, in government or in the private sector, exists for two reasons:

1. **Division of labor.** Large, complex tasks must be broken down into smaller pieces to be accomplished. These individual pieces must be coordinated from the top if they are to add up to a whole. This coordination occurs through the organization's **authority** structure.

2. **Specialization.** The tasks of modern society are also usually too complex for any one person to master completely. The breaking down of tasks in a bureaucracy allows workers to **specialize** and become expert.

C. **Sources of bureaucratic power in a democracy.** Like the meaning of the word "bureaucracy," the sources of its power are sometimes elusive.

1. **Delegation of power by legislatures.** Legislatures, such as Congress, cannot possibly define every detail of a governmental program. If they tried, they surely would get nothing else done. Hence, they delegate to the bureaucracy the job of implementing the law. That means, in turn, that the bureaucracy can only what the legislature allows it to do.

2. **Exercise of discretion.** Implementing the law, however, inevitably means that administrators must exercise discretion. Because the legislature has neither the expertise nor the time to decide every detail, administrators must fill in the gaps with their own knowledge, experience, and decision-making capabilities.

D. **Dilemma of bureaucracy.** The workings of delegation and discretion produce a dilemma. In a democracy, a strong bureaucracy is inevitable to produce effective government. On the other hand, government must work hard to shape and control bureaucratic power to prevent it from overwhelming democracy.

II. **Who the bureaucrats are.** Citizens are often unaware of who government bureaucrats are, where they work, and other basic facts about them.

A. **Location.** Most federal government bureaucrats work outside Washington. Only 10 percent of all federal civilian employees work in the Washington area, while 85 percent work in the government's 22,000 field offices around the country, and another 5 percent work abroad.

B. **Growth.** The number of federal civilian employees has actually stayed about the same over the last twenty years, at about 3 million. State and local government employment, however, has grown by 62 percent over the last twenty years, to about 15 million. This puts the size of America's public bureaucracy at about the same level as that of France and Germany, and lower than the United Kingdom's. Sweden has almost twice as large a share of its population working for the government as the United States.

C. **Where bureaucrats work.** Most federal bureaucrats—about 70 percent of the total—work for one of the fourteen cabinet departments. The rest work in the legislative and judicial branches (as staff members or clerks) and in the independent agencies and government corporations (such as the U.S. Postal Service and AMTRAK).

D. **How bureaucrats get their jobs.** Most government workers are covered by the *civil service system.* This system has three key elements:

1. **Position classification.** All positions are classified according to the kind of knowledge and education required and the responsibility of the task. The salary is determined by the position, not by the person filling it. In general, the positions in the federal government are classified according to the "General Schedule," the GS-system, ranging from GS-1 for the lowest clerical employees to GS-18 for top-level executives.

2. **Hiring by merit.** Individuals are supposed to be hired for positions on the basis of merit. At lower levels, merit hiring usually means that citizens interested in working for the government must take a test. Agencies that want to hire new workers must hire from those who have received top scores on the test. At upper levels, individuals

submit a statement of their experience and qualifications. Again, agencies are required to hire the most qualified individuals.

3. **Promotions.** Government employees can advance within the bureaucracy if they have at least the minimum requirements for higher positions. It is the position, not the employee's qualifications, that determines the salary and the job's requirements.

III. **The difference between *public* bureaucracy and *private* bureaucracy.** Reformers are continually promising that they will "shape up" the government bureaucracy by making it run more like the private sector. They quickly find out that public and private bureaucracies are very different.

A. **Nature of the job.** In the private sector, organizations can do anything not prohibited by law. In the public sector, organizations can do **only** those things allowed by law.

B. **Goals.** The pursuit of individual interest, especially profit, is the keystone of the private sector. Public administrators are supposed to pursue the public interest, as defined by the law.

C. **Openness.** In the private sector, organizations can operate cloaked with as much secrecy in their internal operations as they desire, subject to accounting and other legal standards. In the public sector, we expect almost all governmental decisions to be reached in the open.

D. **Equity.** It is acceptable and common in the private sector to favor some customers over others. In the public sector, we expect that everyone will be treated equally.

E. **Time horizon.** In the private sector, organizations set their own deadlines. In the public sector, expectations for quick and immediate results are very high.

F. **Criteria of success and failure.** In the private sector, there is a clear bottom line that determines success or failure. The public sector has no such bottom line. "Success" and "failure" are subjective terms defined by public support for an agency's programs.

IV. **The problem of "red tape."** Bureaucracies are frequently criticized for being "bureaucratic" and imposing massive amounts of "red tape" on innocent citizens.

A. **What red tape is.** The term "red tape" actually comes from the red ribbons used once to tie up the official papers presented to kings. Now we use it to describe the rules and regulations that bureaucracies issue.

B. **Why these rules are written.** Government regulations serve three interests:

1. **Govern the behavior of government.** To ensure that everyone is treated fairly, no matter who he or she might be or where he or she might live, many rules define how government employees must treat citizens.

2. **Govern the behavior of citizens.** Whether through the tax code, environmental, or other such rules, the bureaucracy tries to define clearly what members of the public must do to comply with laws passed by Congress.

3. **Establish standards for accountability.** The government's rules, finally, set principles by which both the executive and the legislature can hold the bureaucracy accountable for its actions.

C. **Cost and benefits.** The government's regulations are often criticized for being too complicated, too cumbersome, and too costly.

1. **Costs.** Government regulations, in fact, often are costly. Compliance with the federal government's environmental standards alone has cost billions of dollars.

2. **Benefits.** The costs are imposed because elected officials believe that the benefits are worth it. Both the air and the water are far cleaner now than before the environmental laws were passed. The comparison of costs and benefits is usually a political, not an economic, judgment. Regulations are created and endure because elected officials believe that the benefits exceed the costs. Bureaucrats cannot write regulations without the explicit authority of these elected officials.

D. **Deregulation.** It is tempting to think that we could do away with the existing regulations that we find costly or troublesome. To be sure, judicious pruning of red tape is always useful. The lesson of the 1980s, however, is that too little regulation can be as dangerous as too much. Left underregulated and undersupervised, the nation's savings and loans associations created a debacle that might cost $500 billion. Airline prices for many travelers from smaller cities have actually risen since deregulation. Deregulation can sometimes be effective, but it is not a universal remedy.

V. **Bureaucracy in the political world.** While federal agencies are part of the executive branch, the laws governing them, as well as their annual budgets, must be passed by the legislative branch.

A. **Bureaucracy as the servant of two masters.** We want bureaucracy to be accountable to elected officials, but it is simultaneously accountable to both the legislative and executive branches of government.

1. **Legislative branch.** The legislature writes the laws that bureaucracies implement. It also appropriates the money and creates the very structure that government bureaucracies use to administer the law. The bureaucracy and its programs thus are truly creatures of the legislature.

2. **Executive branch.** At the same time, the chief executive—whether president, governor, or mayor—is charged with seeing that the laws are faithfully executed. The chief executive appoints the heads of the key agencies and directs their behavior.

3. **The dilemma.** The bureaucracy is thus subject to both branches at the same time. Both branches expect obedience, but following the directives of both simultaneously is often impossible. Administrators thus must often make hard choices about which values to emphasize.

B. **Judicial influence.** The courts also have important influence over the bureaucracy. The decisions of administrators are subject to judicial review. Especially with regard to government regulations, litigation often shapes the nature of the bureaucracy's behavior. Furthermore, the courts recently have seized control of the direction of important administrative activities in some states, such as school busing and the administration of the prison system.

C. **Interest groups.** Because of the bureaucracy's considerable and inevitable power, interest groups seek to influence bureaucratic decisions. They are allowed by law to submit reactions to proposed regulations. They also often attempt to influence administrative actions by filing suit in the courts to block or change those actions.

D. **"Iron triangles."** Sometimes, critics warn, a triangle of interests shapes government policy. This triangle is composed of members of key interest groups, members of Congress (especially congressional committees), and the bureaucracy. Such triangles increase the responsiveness of the system, but they also risk steering government decisions to benefit small minorities instead of the broader public interest.

E. **Accountability.** The importance and power of "iron triangles" only underline the underlying theme. Bureaucratic power is inevitable in a democracy. It is the task of democratic institutions—especially the legislature and the courts—to control that power and to steer it in the public interest.

Historical Perspective

I. **Bureaucracy at the beginning of the American republic.** Government bureaucracy at the dawn of the American republic existed almost entirely at the state level.

A. **Early days.** The American revolution was also a war of ideas. Those who fought it knew what they did not want—a new nation that repeated the abusive power of a strong monarch—but they had not given much thought about what they did want. What they most clearly did not want was a powerful governmental apparatus, full of bureaucrats, which could undermine their liberty. Despite these strong feelings, however, the nation's important early documents are strangely silent on the issue of bureaucracy and bureaucratic power.

1. **Articles of Confederation.** The nation's executive power was almost nonexistent in the era of the Articles of Confederation. Policy making required the unanimous agreement of the states. The states, not the national government, were responsible for carrying out the decisions they reached. The federal government essentially had no bureaucracy, since state governments were responsible for administering what governmental policies there were.

2. **Absence of mention in the Constitution.** There is no mention of bureaucracy in the Constitution, but the Founders anticipated that there would be a bureaucracy. They gave the president, for example, the power to appoint "Officers of the United States," but they did not say who the officers would be or what they would do. That was left to the new Congress and president to decide. Only

the evolution of the new nation's structure was to shape the kind of bureaucracy that would conduct the nation's business.

B. **The Hamilton-Jefferson debate.** In the early days of the government created by the Constitution, there was much debate over just how strong the national government should be and, within the national government, how strong the president should be compared with the Congress. The debate revolved around positions taken by **Thomas Jefferson**, the nation's third president, and **Alexander Hamilton**, the first secretary of the Department of the Treasury.

1. **The Jeffersonians.** Led by Thomas Jefferson, an important group of political leaders, known as "Republicans," feared that a strong government would repeat the dangers of British rule. (These Republicans built the foundation for today's Democratic party.)

   a. **Leave power to the states.** They argued that the national government should be given only enough power to keep the peace and to deal with foreign nations. Otherwise, important questions ought to be left to the states to decide.

   b. **Supremacy of Congress.** A strong executive, they feared, was the root of repression. Better, they believed, to base national power in the people's representatives in Congress than in a single person who could accumulate control.

2. **The Hamiltonians.** Led by Alexander Hamilton, a competing faction argued that the nation required a strong national government, led by a powerful executive, to achieve its potential. This faction was known as the "Federalists."

   a. **Promoting commerce.** Hamilton had a vision of the nation's potential economic strength and the riches that stretched out into the unsettled land. To realize that potential, he argued, a strong national government was needed to overcome the petty disagreements of the states and to promote development.

   b. **A strong executive.** Such an assertive role demanded an effective government. Hamilton believed that was most likely to happen if the president was empowered with the authority to guide and shape the nation's potential.

3. **The conflict**. This conflict was resolved in three different ways.

   a. **The short run**. In the short run, the Jeffersonians triumphed. After Jefferson's election as president in 1802, the Federalist party crumbled and the Republicans (soon renamed the Democrats) ruled for a generation.

   b. **The medium run**. The Jeffersonians soon drifted from their original principles. Jefferson himself put aside his ideas about restrictions on presidential power to negotiate the Louisiana Purchase (1803). The idea of a strong national government vested with powers to promote development took hold.

   c. **The long run**. The debate between the Hamiltonians and the Jeffersonians has never been fully resolved, however. Americans continue the Hamiltonian tradition by expecting a great deal from their government. They also continue the Jeffersonian tradition by seeking at every opportunity to restrict government's power. This fundamental tension remains.

      (1) **The role of bureaucracy**. American bureaucracy sits squarely in the middle of this tension. To pursue Hamiltonian ideals, a strong and effective bureaucracy is essential. On the other hand, to pursue Jefferson's vision of a limited government, the bureaucracy must be kept small and checked at every opportunity. We thus often expect great things but demand a weak bureaucracy. A weak bureaucracy often cannot achieve what we ask, but a strong bureaucracy raises our deep worries about the abuse of government power.

      (2) **Bureaucracy's place in government**. This ageless dilemma shapes bureaucracy's place in government. We cannot do without a strong bureaucracy, yet we tend to distrust its power. We thus often face individual bureaucrats with a love-hate relationship.

II. **Development of the modern administrative state**. American bureaucracy has developed to today's position through six periods. (These categories are drawn largely from Frederick C. Mosher's classic, *Democracy and the Public Service*.)

A. **"Government by gentlemen" (1789-1829)**. Early public service was governed by an ethos of guardianship for the new nation.

   1. **Public servants drawn from elite**. George Washington believed strongly that only "fitness of character" should determine who was hired for federal service. In general, however, society's elite populated key government positions.

   2. **Few public services**. Government was small, with basic functions, especially raising revenue, dominating government activities. The federal government provided very few services, so there was little need for bureaucracy except for collecting taxes.

   3. **Small size of federal bureaucracy**. This early period was a period of guardianship: of the new nation's freedom, of the balance of power between the national government and the states and between the government and the people. It was a time of rapid growth in the size of the nation but not significantly in the bureaucracy's power.

B. **"Government by the common man" (1829-1883)**. Jacksonian democracy altered the character of public service.

   1. **Rise of the spoils system**. **Andrew Jackson** is credited with "reform" of bureaucracy: movement away from the government of the elite and toward the rise of the "spoils system."

      a. **Jobs for the common people**. Instead of allowing government to be dominated by the elite, he argued that government jobs ought to be held by common citizens. That, he argued, would improve the people's voice in shaping government policy.

      b. **Jobs as rewards for political support**. These citizen-bureaucrats would be chosen from among the supporters of victorious politicians. The motto: "To the victor belongs the spoils."

c. **Public office as not beyond common capacity.** Jackson argued: "The duties of all public offices are, or at least admit of being made, so plain and simple that men of intelligence may readily qualify themselves for their performance; and I cannot but believe that more is lost by the long continuance of men in office than is generally to be gained by their experience."

2. **Jacksonianism in practice.** With regard to the distribution of offices, the Jacksonian period only partially lived up to its principles.

   a. **Contradiction between promise and reality.** In fact, Jackson himself was devoted to securing government workers of top ability and did not open the doors of government service to just anyone. Government was thus not completely turned over to rank amateurs.

   b. **Spoils and the rise of politicians.** The spoils system changed government power from one small group—the gentry—to another—politicians and their loyal band of supporters. This was a far more important implication of Jackson's reform and marked the end of the Federalists' power in American government.

   c. **Problems of the new system.** The spoils system produced important problems.

      (1) **Problems of transition between administrations.** One problem was that there was chaos with every change in presidential administration. With many positions changing hands with each election, government lost continuity and institutional memory.

      (2) **Bureaucracy associated with crass politics.** There was a tendency among the people to associate bureaucracy with crass politics and administrative incompetence. When political loyalty, more than just competence, was the prerequisite for holding office, it was inevitable that the public's image of the bureaucracy's professionalism would decline.

      (3) **Competition between branches of government over appointments.** A growth in conflict developed between the presidency and Congress, especially over appointments. The more that positions were filled on the basis of partisan loyalty, the more inevitable were conflicts among politicians over who should fill them.

      (4) **Post-election job stampedes.** There were overwhelming demands by office-seekers on elected officials after every election. Supporters of the victors swarmed to Washington seeking jobs. The old saying that politics creates thousands of disappointed friends and one ingrate stems from this feature of the spoils system.

      (5) **Turnover and lack of institutional experience.** There was a problem in running the government effectively with frequent turnover and little accumulation of wisdom or experience. With little institutional memory, there was no continuing source of expertise regarding how past problems had been resolved. Each new administration had to begin from scratch, so much time was wasted inventing new solutions to old problems.

C. **"Government by the good" (1883-1906).** The problems created by the old spoils system led to efforts to reform it.

   1. **An egalitarian public service.** A new movement arose: to make the public service truly egalitarian and open it to all citizens.

      a. **Merit as the basis for employment.** This open public service was based on the idea of merit: the best person ought to be hired for the job, regardless of personal background or political affiliation.

      b. **Principles of the Pendleton reform act.** The Pendleton Civil Service Act of 1883 established key principles:

         (1) **Competitive examinations.** Competitive examinations for public office were established. The new civil service system sought to select bureaucrats on the basis of what they knew, not whom they knew.

(2) **Political neutrality**. The act aimed to restore public confidence in the civil service by convincing Americans that they would be treated fairly by politically impartial bureaucrats.

(3) **Job security for public servants**. Stable and continuous public service would provide continuity in government across political changes. A steady cohort of skilled administrators would help new administrations manage government. Civil servants were expected to devote their knowledge to the goals of elected officials, regardless of party.

2. **Similarities and differences with the British system**. Principles were borrowed from the British system, but with a distinctive American stamp.

   a. **Political appointments in top American positions**. Unlike the British system, with its administrative class filling top positions, the American civil service has been dominated at the top by presidential political appointments.

   b. **Political neutrality a problem**. The idea of a politically neutral yet popularly responsive bureaucracy also posed problems. How can a bureaucracy resist the political pressures of politicians yet be responsive to the wishes of the people who, after all, elect the officials? The dilemma was unresolved and continues today.

   c. **The rise of public morality**. The rise of the merit system associated public personnel with public morality, an important theme for nineteenth-century reformers.

D. **"Government by the efficient" (1906-1937)**. The Progressive era had a marked effect on public service. A new movement grew at the end of the nineteenth century—first from the cities, then to the states, and on to the national government—to promote efficiency in government.

1. **Principles of scientific management**. The movement was based on the principles of the scientific management movement, such as the following:

   a. **Rationality**. There was the expectation that reason could guide management, and that managers could apply logic to management problems.

   b. **Planning**. The scientific management movement believed that government could improve its ability to deal with future problems by looking forward and anticipating solutions to those problems.

   c. **Specialization**. As managerial tasks became more complicated, the scientific management movement sought to develop highly skilled employees and unique tools that could produce better results.

   d. **Quantitative measurement**. Scientific managers developed numerical measures for all parts of the system. By using these measures, even for assessing the qualifications of employees, government administration could improve.

   e. **"One best way."** Scientific management argued that there is a single best technique for doing any job—and "one best worker" to do it. The scientific management approach could help government managers discover that approach.

   f. **Standards and standardization**. Once the "best way" was discovered, efficiency demanded that the way be repeated through standard operating procedures that everyone had to follow.

2. **Results for bureaucracy**. The theory of scientific management had a number of implications for bureaucratic practice.

   a. **Personnel examinations**. If one could determine the best qualifications for particular positions, then special examinations could be designed to select the best employees. Standard examinations were developed.

   b. **Training**. If one could determine the "one best way" for completing the bureaucracy's tasks, workers could be trained in the knowledge and skills needed.

   c. **Efficiency ratings**. If there is "one best way," workers could be rated on how well their performance matched the objectives.

d. **Specialization**. A bureaucracy staffed with individuals seeking the "one best way" would become populated with specialized experts.

3. **Role of government promoted**. This period promoted, as well, the belief in government's positive role. The New Deal marked the high point of the high expectations about government's potential.

E. **"Government by managers" (1937-1968)**. From the New Deal to the Great Society years of the 1960s, bureaucratic reform was influenced by the idea that a stronger executive was required to improve government efficiency.

1. **Need for strong executive**. Government officials argued that efficiency measures alone were not sufficient. Effective government required a stronger president.

2. **Guidelines for assisting the executive**. The Brownlow Committee reported in 1937 that "the president needs help" to govern effectively. These guidelines suggested ways to improve the president's ability to govern.

   a. **Clear lines of authority**. There should be clear and uninterrupted lines of authority from the top of government to the bottom.

   b. **Span of control**. No executive can control too many agencies at the same time. The president's span of control should be a manageable number of agencies that he can supervise adequately.

   c. **Controlling independent agencies**. Such agencies, which had proliferated in the regulatory movement of the early twentieth century, should be brought under the president's direction.

   d. **Need for staff**. To help the president direct government more effectively, he should be supplied with a small White House staff. This staff should have a "passion for anonymity," in the words of the report. The president should also have control over the key staff functions of budgeting, personnel, and planning.

3. **Results**. Many of the Brownlow Committee's recommendations were implemented. Some were not.

a. **Successful implementation**. Among the recommendations successfully implemented were the following:

   (1) **Authority**. The president's authority was improved, but his ability to control all parts of the bureaucracy remained limited. Bureaucracy remained in its fundamental constitutional position between two masters, the president and Congress; and Congress was unwilling to cede its power.

   (2) **Staff**. The president did gain significant leverage over the bureaucracy through the creation of the Executive Office of the President. The budget and personnel functions were moved to this office. The president also gained a personal staff that has grown significantly in both size and power. This staff, while scarcely full of persons with a "passion for anonymity," have enormously increased the president's leverage over governmental affairs.

b. **Unsuccessful implementation**. Recommendations unsuccessfully implemented include the following:

   (1) **Span of control**. The number of bureaucracies over which the president had control was scarcely diminished. In fact, the number of cabinet departments and other agencies continued to increase.

   (2) **Independent agencies**. Nearly all of the independent agencies remained independent, and new ones were created. Presidents sometimes did not want control over some activities. Congress, at other times, did not want the president to control them. The notion of independent agencies, such as the Environmental Protection Agency, violated the norms of bureaucratic efficiency but fit the political needs of those who proposed it.

4. **Promotion of a strong bureaucracy**. These themes guided presidential power for a generation. They promoted a strong bureaucracy under the control of the chief executive. The ideas, furthermore,

spilled over into state and local government as well.

F. **"Government through partners" (1968-present)**. From the late 1960s until the present, there has been a growing reliance on partnership between federal agencies and both the private sector and state and local governments.

1. **The growth of public-private partnership**. After World War II, the federal government began subtly relying more and more on administration of government programs through a broad variety of relationships with partners in the private sector. With the programs of President **Lyndon Johnson's** Great Society, especially with the creation of new intergovernmental grant programs and Medicare, these partnerships began growing in number and importance.

2. **Kinds of partners**. The federal government has several kinds of partners:

   a. **Contractors**. Contractors are private organizations hired through a negotiated contract to perform jobs, such as building weapons or cleaning waste dumps, according to goals defined by the government.

   b. **Intergovernmental grantees**. These grantees are state and local governments administering federal programs with their own bureaucracies. The federal government sometimes has given state and local governments substantial discretion in implementing these programs. The goal: to pursue national goals but to permit the programs to be responsive to the views of local citizens.

   c. **Private grantees**. These grantees are universities and other research centers pursuing basic and applied research in areas defined by the federal government. Major breakthroughs in health and other advanced technologies have frequently come as a result of these grants.

3. **Reasons for increasing partnerships**. Several considerations have promoted the trend toward partnerships.

   a. **Resistance to expanding public bureaucracy**. For many new and ambitious programs, the choice was either expanding the national bureaucracy significantly or hiring these partners to do the job instead. Especially as time has gone by, the public has been evermore resistant to expanding the size of the bureaucracy. The use of partners provided a pragmatic solution to the problem.

   b. **Insufficient federal expertise**. The federal government often does not have sufficient expertise to conduct many of these sophisticated programs itself. Using partners allows the government to obtain the expertise needed.

   c. **Efficiency of using private partners**. In some cases, the use of these partners is cheaper than using government workers to perform the same task. Even when it is hard to prove that using partners is cheaper, many people believe that contracting out is cheaper, and that belief has driven the expansion of this system.

4. **Implications of the partnership**. The trend toward partnership has in practice implied the following:

   a. **Importance of non-federal performance**. The more the federal government has relied on private and state and local government organizations to administer its programs, the more their performance has determined the effectiveness of government programs. Furthermore, these private and state and local partners have also been drawn far more deeply into the federal government's sphere and in some measure have lost their independence.

   b. **Difficulty in managing partnerships**. These partnerships often are extremely complex and hard to manage. The government has often relied on them often because its own expertise is lacking. Thus, the federal government creates the partnerships but often has a difficult time in controlling them.

   c. **Boundaries between public and private blurred.** The rise of such partnerships thus is a clever accommodation to the complexity of new programs and to citizens' demands that bureaucracy not get bigger. The result is a blurring of the boundaries between public and private, and among the federal, state, and local governments. The result is also a system that defies most of the principles of scientific management and that is hard to control effectively. Some of the major headlines of the 1980s, such as defense procurement scandals, are a result of these problems. As the chain between those who make policy and those who implement it becomes longer and the links sometimes become indirect, it becomes harder to ensure accountability.

III. **Changing public policy and changing public administration**. What results have these trends produced?

    A. **The growth of the regulatory state**. The sweep of the federal government's programs is remarkable. Along with each program comes a set of rules, both to guide the behavior of bureaucrats and to govern those affected by the program. As a result, bureaucracy's regulation of society has increased.

    B. **Policy implementation through partners**. Few governmental activities of any kind are the sole province of any one level of government, or even of government itself. Nearly everything the government does is part of a partnership: among the federal, state, and local governments; and between government and the private sector.

    C. **Growing reliance on *public* policy**. Society as a whole, meanwhile, relies increasingly on government to solve its problems. While we struggle to maintain the Jeffersonian tradition—to keep government's power limited—at the same time we demand the Hamiltonian promise of a strong government to solve our problems. As the problems and their solutions become more complex, the bigger the issue government bureaucracy and its power becomes.

Contemporary Perspective

I. **Expansion of government programs**. Government programs have expanded markedly since World War II. As the programs have grown, however, public confidence in government—and especially in bureaucracy—has decreased.

    A. **Reasons for decline in confidence in bureaucracy**. A number of reasons can be cited for the decline in public confidence in the public bureaucracies.

    1. **Anti-tax sentiment**. The anti-tax movement, which bubbled up from the property tax revolts at the state and local level, has hit all of government hard. Demands for services continue to grow, but many Americans struggle to pay for these services. When demands for lower taxes and lower government spending surface, government administrators have been the first to feel the bite: No one wants to pay taxes to support bureaucrats, even if the bureaucrats are responsible for providing the services that citizens demand.

    2. **Waste-fraud-abuse**. Widespread allegations of waste, fraud, and abuse in government programs have led to demands for reducing government and, with it, reducing the role of bureaucrats.

        a. **Defense horror stories**. Famous tales of overpriced hammers and toilet seats in Department of Defense contracts galvanized political attacks on the bureaucracy. In some cases, they were legitimate prices for specialized products. In other cases, they were rare departures from ordinary practice. Sometimes, they really were instances of waste and fraud. The real cases of waste and fraud, however, were far less than the publicity suggested.

        b. **Different expectations**. Some allegations of waste, fraud, and abuse were simply reflections of the different expectations that different participants in the policy process—especially in Congress—have about government programs. Some instances of apparent bureaucratic waste, in fact, are cases in which Congress demands that programs be administered in prescribed ways.

        c. **Comparison with the private sector**. Critics claimed that the private sector is far more efficient and, therefore, that government should be shrunk and more responsibility given to the private sector.

            (1) **Waste and efficiency**. A comparative study by University of Arizona political scientist John Schwarz shows that the public sector is neither more wasteful nor less efficient than the private sector. (John E. Schwarz, *America's Hidden Success*, 1988.)

(2) **Value differences**. Many of the criticisms of public sector performance represent a preference for different **political** outcomes. The hope of critics is that private administration of public programs will produce a different set of winners and losers.

(3) **Privatization**. Privatization—different forms of transferring public sector responsibilities to the private sector—can indeed produce beneficial changes.

    (a) **Smaller size of government**. It reduces the size of government (and the bureaucracy) compared with what would otherwise be the case.

    (b) **Market-based incentives**. It replaces political demands for programs with market-based incentives.

    (c) **Remaining management problems**. However, it does not always eliminate management problems. It replaces one set of administrative tasks with another: ensuring adequate management of the private sector organizations performing public tasks. Contracting scandals, along with the savings-and-loan debacle, illustrate that the private sector's behavior does not always promote the public interest. Continuing government supervision is often necessary.

3. **Potential problems of privatization**. Confidence in government and its bureaucracy may have declined, but the reasons are complex. Simply transferring public responsibilities to the private sector will not automatically solve the problems. It may, moreover, create serious new problems.

B. **Continued reliance on government**. No matter what our preferences in government programs—liberal, conservative, or somewhere in between—there is an irreducible core of government required.

1. **Protecting citizens from harm**. One of government's key roles is to protect us from threats to our health and safety.

    a. **National defense**. Government's foremost responsibility is to ensure peace and create a shield from foreign perils. That creates the necessity for the armed forces. We can quarrel over how the military should be equipped and how it should be deployed, but protecting citizens through the armed forces is a central responsibility of government.

    b. **Police powers**. Closely associated with protection from foreign threats is protection of life and property at home. That creates the need for police, especially at the state and local levels, as well as for the judicial and prison systems.

    c. **Regulatory programs**. Related to international and domestic security is protection of citizens from a broad range of other dangers. Whether preserving the security of the banking system or inspecting the quality of the food stocked in stores, government provides a broad array of services that protect us from the unscrupulous.

2. **Promoting the general welfare**. Government engages in many programs designed to improve our lives. Education, of course, ranks high on the list. Other programs, from air-traffic control to highway construction, are also significant.

3. **Helping the disadvantaged**. From Medicaid to food stamps, from public housing to job training, a sense of social obligation drives the argument for these government programs.

4. **Guaranteeing equal treatment**. Government seeks to ensure that all citizens are treated equally, regardless of race, gender, or creed: in the voting booth, on the job, and in housing.

5. **Providing for entitlements**. Increasingly, many citizens have come to believe that they are entitled to some government services. Social Security and Medicare are at the top of this list. Underlying the political demands for these programs is a sense of social contract: having paid into the programs during their working lives, retirees believe that government owes them basic support.

6. **Collecting revenue**. Like it or not, performing government's functions requires money. No one likes the tax collector, whether the Internal Rev-

enue Service or those in biblical lore. A tax collection role is essential and inevitable.

C. **The inevitability of bureaucratic power**. We can argue over just what government ought to do. We must admit, however, that there is a group of functions that government must do. Performing those functions requires a strong and effective government—and that means a strong and effective government bureaucracy.

II. **The challenge of bureaucratic accountability**. The inescapable need in modern society for a strong and effective government bureaucracy raises the old problems of bureaucratic accountability anew.

A. **Tension between bureaucracy and democracy**. The ageless dilemma of bureaucracy—an effective government requires a strong bureaucracy, but a strong bureaucracy poses a threat to democracy—continues.

B. **Increasing problems of accountability**. The old problems of accountability—controlling and directing bureaucratic discretion—are becoming greater. As government programs have become more complex, from launching space shuttles to overseeing the financial industry, the technical problems that government must solve have become more difficult.

C. **New problems of accountability**. The new methods government is using to implement its programs—especially through federalism and through privatization—create new problems. The task now is not only ensuring that government administrators themselves remain accountable but also guaranteeing that the partners with whom government works also perform according to the government's standards.

III. **Strengthening the public service**. The old and new problems combined create new problems for the public service.

A. **Need for a strong public bureaucracy**. There is no alternative to a lean, strong, and effective bureaucracy. The challenges facing government are growing, and without a strong bureaucracy, America will lag behind the rest of the world.

B. **Difficulty recruiting skilled public servants**. There is disturbing evidence, however, that it is getting harder to recruit the skilled public servants needed.

1. **Public service not recommended to the young**. Only 13 percent of senior government executives in one survey would recommend that young people start their careers in government.

2. **Recruitment of talent becoming more difficult**. Half of the federal personnel managers surveyed said recruiting top-quality new staff members has become more difficult in the 1980s.

C. **Volcker Commission's recommendations**. The Volcker Commission, headed by former Federal Reserve Board Chairman **Paul Volcker**, made an impassioned argument in 1989 for a strong public service: "Faced with these challenges, the simple idea that Americans must draw upon talented and dedicated individuals to serve us in government is uncontestable. America must have a public service that can both value the lessons of experience and appreciate the requirements for change; a public service that both responds to political leadership and respects the law; a public service with the professional skills and the ethical sensitivity America deserves."

D. **Implications**. The following are implied by the need for an effective bureaucracy:

1. **The public interest in competent public servants**. Creating a strong public service is everyone's business. If we criticize bureaucrats unfairly because we do not like the way government is run, we will only suffer more. If government cannot recruit able workers, it will not be able to effectively oversee defense contractors, regulate the banks adequately, promote research on AIDS, or keep the skies safe.

2. **Value of a public service career**. The public service is a stimulating career. Government faces society's cutting-edge problems. Working in government gives individuals the chance to wrestle with them. Educating individuals for the public service is an important activity. Making a career in the public service is an exciting challenge.

3. **Recruiting and keeping public servants**. Recruiting, training, and rewarding good public servants are essential if government is to work well. We will surely get what we pay for if we do not do our best to find and keep the best public servants.

   a. **Uncompetitive pay**. We often lose top officials in whom we as a nation have invested years of experience because the private sector often pays much more than government jobs.

b. **Need for public support.** The "bash-the-bureaucrat" syndrome, in which candidates for electoral office appeal to voters' dislike for some government programs by blaming those who administer them, has weakened government. It is demoralizing to work hard for the public interest only to have that work castigated in political campaigns. The work of government officials must be respected if the best of government officials are to stay.

E. **The broader obligations of citizenship.** As government programs have grown more complex, as we have asked more of government, and as the administration of government programs has involved more private-sector partners, it has become much harder to draw the line between government and the rest of us. Indeed, in ways we might not realize, all of us, in one way or another, are partners with the government in its programs. As citizens we have a responsibility to ensure that those programs work well.

3. THE AMERICAN JUDICIAL SYSTEM

The power vested in the American courts of justice of pronouncing a statute to be unconstitutional forms one of the most powerful barriers that have ever been devised against the tyranny of political assemblies.

Alexis de Tocqueville (1835)

The judiciary on the contrary has no influence over the sword or the purse, no direction either of the strength or of the wealth of society, and can take no active resolution whatever. It may truly be said to have neither Force nor Will, but merely judgment; and must ultimately depend upon the aid of the executive arm even for the efficacy of its judgments.

Alexander Hamilton (1788)

Let us now set a salutary precedent that will never be violated. Let us, the Seventy-fifth Congress, declare that we would rather have an independent judiciary, a fearless Court, that will dare to announce its honest opinions in what it believes to be defense of liberties of the people, than a Court that, out of fear or sense of obligation to the appointing power or factional passion, approves any measure we may enact.

U.S. Senate Judiciary Committee Report (1937)

From the traffic courts to the Supreme Court, from the smallest claims to the most dramatic constitutional rulings, the American judicial system is relied upon to resolve disputes, interpret the law, and protect our most cherished rights. Courts provide a peaceful forum to settle disputes; when individuals suffer injuries and injustices they turn to the judiciary for redress. Courts interpret and apply the law to protect the innocent and punish the guilty, to implement the will of legislatures, and to regulate human affairs.

Perhaps most importantly, the judiciary is entrusted with enforcing the Constitution and possesses the power to invalidate government actions that transgress our basic freedoms. Judges are expected to render decisions based on reason and mercy, not passion or prejudice. But inevitably the law is ambiguous, and judges often possess considerable discretion in deciding cases. The quality of justice thus depends very much on who sits on the bench.

The complex structure of the courts reflects the existence of both state and federal court systems, with trial and appellate courts in both. A detailed set of rules determines where cases belong and how they are handled in every court. Although at times it seems that procedural rules are given more weight than substantive concerns, court procedures are designed to provide fairness to the litigants, accurate decisions, and the efficient handling of disputes.

The record of the courts, like that of any institution, is somewhat mixed. There are examples of biased and incompetent judges committing gross injustices. But far more often, courts have withstood public pressure and corrupting influences and have been models of integrity and even courage.

OBJECTIVES

The citizen should be able to

1. explain the structure of the American judicial system.

2. explain varying views on how judges should be selected and held accountable.

3. explain what matters come before the judiciary.

4. explain the different bodies of law applied by courts—the Constitution, treaties, statutes, common law, administrative regulations.

5. explain the different types of remedies courts can provide.

6. explain the nature of judicial discretion in deciding cases.

7. explain the importance of judicial review in enforcing the Constitution and the alternative approaches courts can use in interpreting the Constitution.

8. take, defend, and evaluate positions on contemporary issues regarding the judicial system.

FRAME OF REFERENCE
Conceptual Perspective

I. **The structure of the American judicial system.** The judicial system includes both federal and state courts and trial and appellate courts of each type.

A. **State and federal courts: types of cases.** The jurisdiction of each court is determined by provisions in the United States Constitution and federal and state statutes.

1. **Criminal cases.** Government at all levels—federal, state, and local—enacts laws making

certain behavior illegal and punishable by fines, imprisonment, or community service. Violations of federal laws are heard in federal courts, while state laws are enforced in state courts and violations of city ordinances are generally tried in municipal or state courts.

2. **Civil cases.** If individuals or entities seek money damages, or a court command (such as an injunction halting behavior), or a declaration of rights (such as a divorce decree), a civil case is filed. Whereas only the government can initiate a criminal prosecution, the government, individuals, or entities (like corporations) can bring civil suits.

   a. **Jurisdiction of state courts.** State courts are courts of "general jurisdiction." Any civil case—including an issue of federal law—can be brought in state court unless there is a federal law creating exclusive federal court jurisdiction. Only in limited areas, such as patent and copyright law, do federal courts possess exclusive jurisdiction. In all other areas where federal courts have jurisdiction, the lawyers may choose whether to proceed in federal or state courts.

   b. **Jurisdiction of federal courts.** Federal courts are courts of "limited jurisdiction." Federal courts may not hear civil cases unless there is both a provision in the United States Constitution and a federal statute authorizing jurisdiction. Federal courts generally exercise jurisdiction in only three situations.

     (1) **U.S. Government a party.** According to Article III of the U.S. Constitution, federal courts hear suits where the United States government is a party to the lawsuit. At the time the Constitution was written, state courts were not trusted to adequately protect the interests of the federal government.

     (2) **Citizens of different states as parties.** Federal courts also hear suits where there is diversity of citizenship between the parties to the lawsuit—that is, the plaintiff and the defendant are from different states—and there is more than $50,000 at stake. The fear that state courts might be biased in favor of their own citizens caused the creation

of diversity jurisdiction. There have been repeated attempts to eliminate diversity jurisdiction on the grounds that such parochialism no longer exists. About 25 percent of the cases in federal court are brought under diversity jurisdiction.

(3) **Cases involving constitutional claims.** Federal courts may hear cases that arise under federal law where the plaintiff's claim rests on the United States Constitution, a treaty, or a federal statute. This is referred to as "federal question jurisdiction." Law professors debate whether federal courts are more likely than state courts to adequately enforce federal law, especially the Constitution.

(a) **Limiting federal jurisdiction.** Those who believe there is parity between federal and state courts generally support restrictions on federal court jurisdiction and more deference to state courts.

(b) **Expanding federal court jurisdiction.** Those who believe there is not such parity favor more expansive federal court jurisdiction, particularly in constitutional cases.

(c) **Practice from the 1950s to the 1990s.** In general, the Warren Court during the 1950s and 1960s enlarged the ability of the federal courts to review state court decisions and minimized federal court deference to state courts. In contrast, the Burger and Rehnquist Courts during the 1970s and 1980s proclaimed parity between state and federal courts, restricting federal court review of state courts and expanding federal court deference to the state courts.

B. **State and federal courts: trial and appellate courts.** In both the federal and the state systems, cases initially are filed in a trial court and courts of appeals can review the trial courts' decisions.

1. **State courts.** Every state judicial system has as its "lowest level" trial courts.

a. **Cases found in state courts.** Trial courts may have general jurisdiction and the ability to hear all types of cases or they may be specialized. For example, in some states there are separate civil and criminal trial courts; in other states the same trial courts hear both types of cases. In many states there are separate trial courts for matters such as domestic relations cases (such as divorce courts) and for juvenile cases. Small claims courts are one type of specialized civil court with authority to hear cases involving less than a certain amount of money.

b. **Names of trial courts.** The title of the trial courts varies from state to state. In many states, such as California, some trial courts are called "superior courts." In other states, such as Illinois, the courts are termed "circuit courts." In New York, the **trial** court is labeled the "supreme court."

c. **Review of lower court decisions.** In most states, decisions of the trial court are reviewable in an intermediate court of appeals; that is, a court that is in-between the trial court and the state's highest court.

(1) **Right of appeal.** Generally, the losing party has a right to appeal to the intermediate court of appeals. That court is obligated to hear and decide the appeal.

(2) **Review of law vs. review of facts.** A court of appeals usually will not review the lower court's finding of facts, but instead will decide only questions of law. The trial court, which saw the witnesses and heard the evidence, usually has the final say in deciding what occurred. But the court of appeals will decide "de novo"—without deference to the lower court—issues of what the law means.

d. **State supreme courts.** The title or name for the highest court varies from state to state. Often it is simply called the state supreme court. Sometimes it is called the "court of appeals," as in New York. Especially in states where there is an intermediate court of appeals, review in the state's highest court is generally discretionary—that is, the court decides whether or not to hear a particular case. In California, for instance, the Supreme Court has complete discretion to decide what cases to review, except that it must hear all cases where capital punishment was imposed by the trial court.

2. **Federal courts**. Like state courts, federal courts have several levels.

   a. **Federal district courts**. The lowest level of the federal court system is the federal district court. There is at least one federal district court in each state and some states are divided into more than one district. They are courts of general jurisdiction, hearing both criminal and civil cases.

   b. **Specialized courts**. Some specialized federal courts, such as federal bankruptcy courts, which decide matters involving federal bankruptcy laws, are adjuncts of federal district courts. There are also specialized courts such as the Court of Claims (to hear some types of monetary claims against the U.S. government) and the Tax Court (to hear some types of tax cases).

   c. **Federal appeals courts.** The United States Courts of Appeals review the decisions of the federal trial courts. There are thirteen courts of appeals.

      (1) **Varieties of appeal courts**. Eleven are numbered, for example, the U.S. Court of Appeals for the First Circuit. The U.S. Court of Appeals for the District of Columbia Circuit reviews the federal trial court decisions in the District of Columbia. It also reviews rulings by some federal administrative agencies. Finally, there is the United States Court of Appeals for the Federal Circuit which hears appeals from tribunals such as the Court of Claims.

      (2) **Jurisdiction of appeal courts**. The courts of appeals have mandatory jurisdiction; that is, the court is obligated to hear and decide appeals properly brought to it. Each court of appeals has jurisdiction to review trial courts located in more than one state.

   d. **The U.S. Supreme Court**. The United States Supreme Court generally reviews only final judgments by a United States court of appeals or by a state's highest court.

      (1) **What questions the Supreme Court decides**. The Supreme Court almost always decides only questions involving federal law—whether a federal or state law is consistent with the United States Constitution; whether a state law is inconsistent with and therefore preempted by federal statutes or treaties; or how a federal statute or treaty should be interpreted. The state's highest court has the final say as to matters of state law. The Supreme Court is the ultimate arbiter of the meaning of federal laws and of the United States Constitution.

      (2) **Deciding which cases to hear**. Review in the Supreme Court is now almost entirely discretionary, that is, the Supreme Court is almost never obligated to grant review in a case.

         (a) **Discretion is recent**. The Court's discretion is a very recent change in the law. Early in American history, federal statutes required the Supreme Court to decide every case properly brought to it. In 1925, Congress specified that in some situations the Court would be required to decide the case, but in other instances the Court would have discretion as to which cases to hear. In 1988, Congress eliminated virtually all instances in which the Court has mandatory jurisdiction.

         (b) **The writ of certiorari**. In almost all situations, Supreme Court review is sought by filing a legal document called a "writ of certiorari." The Court grants certiorari if four justices vote to hear the case; otherwise, review is declined. A denial of certiorari does not mean that it necessarily agrees with the lower court ruling but that fewer than four justices wanted to hear the case. The Supreme Court decides only about 170 cases a year and is unable to hear more than a small fraction of the matters it is asked to review.

C. **State and federal courts: their interrelationship.** Although the federal and state court systems have a good deal of autonomy, the relationship between them is obviously very important.

1. **Federal cases which stay in the federal court system.** If a matter is properly brought in a federal court, it generally remains in the federal court system for all stages of the litigation.

2. **State cases which may be brought to federal court.** If a civil case that could have been brought in federal court is brought in state court, the defendant usually can remove the case from the state trial court to the federal trial court at the very beginning of the litigation.

3. **When federal courts review state court cases.** Once litigation has begun in state court, the case is almost always litigated all the way through the state court system. Federal court review of a state court decision is available only in two ways.

   a. **U.S. Supreme Court review.** One means of gaining federal court review is to seek U.S. Supreme Court review of federal law questions decided by a state court.

   b. **Use of writ of habeas corpus.** Also, those convicted of a crime in state court who have exhausted all state court appeals may seek federal district court review by filing a writ of habeas corpus if they claim that the conviction violates the Constitution or U.S. laws.

4. **Recent limitations on federal court review.** In the past two decades the U.S. Supreme Court has greatly limited the availability of federal habeas corpus for those convicted in state courts. This is a major example of the Burger and Rehnquist Courts' restriction on federal court jurisdiction and their deference to state courts.

D. **Decision-making.** A central question is which matters should be decided by juries and which by judges.

1. **Juries.** The concept of a trial decided by one's peers is deeply imbedded in the American legal system.

   a. **The right to a jury trial.** The right to a trial by jury in federal courts is guaranteed by the Constitution in both criminal cases and in some civil cases.

      (1) **Criminal cases.** The Sixth Amendment to the U.S. Constitution guarantees a right to a jury trial in criminal cases in both state and federal courts. Defendants, however, can waive their right to a jury trial and elect to have the matter decided by a judge.

      (2) **Civil cases.** The Seventh Amendment guarantees a right to a jury trial in civil cases in federal court if the plaintiff is seeking money damages. But if the plaintiff is seeking only a court command, such as an injunction, a jury is not available in civil cases in federal court. The Seventh Amendment has not been applied to the states, thus allowing each state to decide for itself whether to use juries in civil cases. Most states, following provisions in state constitutions, allow juries in some civil cases.

   b. **Decisions by juries.** When juries are used, they decide questions of fact, that is, what happened. Judges rule on questions of what the law is and instruct juries on the law to be applied. Furthermore, a judge will not allow a case to be decided by a jury unless the judge believes a reasonable jury could decide the matter either way.

   c. **Controversy over continued use of juries.** The jury remains a controversial institution, particularly in civil cases. On the one hand, it is thought to provide trial by one's peers and is thus a check on government power. But jury trials take much longer than judges (more than twice as long on average) and many question the ability of juries to decide competently in complex areas of the law.

2. **Judges.** The method of choosing judges and holding them accountable varies greatly between the federal and state courts, and among the states.

a. **Independence of federal judges**. Federal judges are nominated by the President and require Senate confirmation. Once confirmed, judges remain in office until they die, resign, or are impeached. The Constitution also guarantees that federal judges shall not have their salaries decreased during their term of office.

b. **Election of state judges**. Most states have some form of electoral accountability of judges. In some states, especially in the south, judges run for election in partisan elections and must stand for reelection at prescribed intervals. In other states, judges are appointed (usually subject to some confirmation process) and must stand for retention elections at regular intervals. A few states have systems like that used at the federal level, with executive appointment and life tenure.

c. **Should judges be elected**? An important question is whether electoral selection or review of judges is desirable. Some argue that in a democracy all office holders, including judges, should be chosen and held accountable by the voters. But others maintain that judicial independence and electoral accountability are inherently incompatible. Because judges should decide cases according to their view of the law, and not to please the voters, judges should not be reviewed at the polls.

d. **Should a judge's ideology be a criterion in appointment**? A related issue is what criteria should be used to select and review judges. For example, should the process examine only the individual's professional qualifications and experience, or should the process also examine the candidate's ideology and views on controversial issues? For example, ideology was an issue in the 1986 retention election of California Supreme Court Justice Rose Bird and the defeat of conservative Supreme Court nominee Robert Bork. The debate remains whether ideology should be a major factor in selecting and reviewing judicial candidates.

II. **Matters which can come before the courts**. Unlike legislatures which can consider virtually any matter introduced by a member, courts are limited to deciding those cases **properly** brought before them, that is, according to the law.

A. **When actions can be brought**. A criminal prosecution can be brought by the government only if there is a statute prohibiting specific conduct. A civil suit can be initiated if the law creates a cause of action—that is, if there is a legal entitlement to a court-imposed remedy. Not every injury a person suffers can be redressed by the court. Causes of action come from three major sources:

1. **Common law**. A large body of American law is the result of published judicial decisions.

    a. **Extent of common law**. Many causes of action—legal entitlements to court relief—come from court decisions.

        (1) **Civil wrongs (tort law)**. The body of tort law which determines when individuals can recover for injuries to their person or property is almost entirely judicially created. Court decisions authorize the right to sue and have articulated the requirements which must be met for the plaintiff to succeed.

        (2) **Contract and property law**. Contract law and property law, among other areas, are largely based on court decisions and not statutes. The slogan, "judges should apply the law and not make it," fails to reflect the American (and English) legal system where much of the law is judicially created.

    b. **Limitations on common law**. The legislature by statute can override or modify the common law. The U.S. Constitution, can, of course, also be used as a defense to a common law cause of action. For example, the Supreme Court has made it clear that the First Amendment's protection of freedom of speech limits plaintiffs' ability to recover for the common law torts of defamation and libel.

    c. **No general federal common law**. Common law causes of action—such as tort, contract and property law—are almost exclusively state law. There is no body of general federal common law. People bringing actions continually ask state courts to recognize new common law causes of action. For example, during the 1960s and 1970s many state courts created a cause of action for "wrongful birth." A typical case would involve a suit to recover costs of childbirth and even raising a child from a doctor for negligently performing a sterilization operation.

2. **Statutes**. Statutes adopted by all levels of government can authorize law suits and judicially imposed remedies. For example, many environmental protection statutes specifically provide for suits by citizens to halt pollution and recover damages for harms suffered.

3. **Constitutions**. Actions under constitutional law are brought under federal or state constitutions.

   a. **The U.S. Constitution**. The United States Constitution protects individual rights and assures equal protection of the law. Plaintiffs may sue to invalidate and halt unconstitutional government conduct and recover damages for injuries they have suffered. A federal statute authorizes suits against state or local governments and their officers for violations of the Constitution or laws of the United States. Also, the Supreme Court has inferred directly from the Constitution a cause of action against federal officers for violations of the Constitution.

   b. **State constitutions**. State constitutions can create rights greater than those provided in the United States Constitution. State courts are responsible for interpreting and applying state constitutions.

4. **Varieties of legal remedies**. Lawsuits are initiated only if the plaintiff believes that the court can provide a desired remedy. There are three major types of remedies available:

   a. **Money damages**. Generally, money damages are awarded to compensate individuals for the injuries and losses they have suffered. Damages serve both a compensatory and a deterrence function. For example, malpractice liability damages both compensate an injured patient and discourage negligent medical practice. Also, if the defendants' conduct is particularly egregious and wanton,

courts can impose punitive damages—damages designed to punish.

   b. **Court commands**. Often the plaintiff seeks not compensation but to halt an offending practice. For example, a plaintiff might want to stop a factory from emitting noxious pollutants. A court can issue such an injunction only in a situation where money damages would not suffice to remedy the harm and where, on balance, it is desirable to grant such relief. Courts also can issue temporary commands (such as temporary restraining orders and preliminary injunctions) to preserve the situation so that it can decide if a command is appropriate.

   c. **Declarations of rights**. Sometimes a court is asked to issue a declaration such as one changing a person's name, granting a divorce, or determining ownership of a patent. Federal law and the law in most states specifically authorize plaintiffs to seek declaratory judgments—court declarations of rights —in certain instances. For example, if a government adopts an unconstitutional statute, a person might bring an action for a declaratory judgment to have the law invalidated.

B. **Factors which discourage or limit law suits**. Even when there is a cause of action and remedy, a court suit still might not be filed. Among the factors that might account for this are the following:

1. **Access barriers**. Many people cannot afford the costs of initiating lawsuits. Attorneys' fees are high and there are also court filing fees and other litigation costs. Much of the poor and middle class lack meaningful access to the civil justice system, except where attorneys accept "contingency fee" cases—cases where there is no cost to the client unless damages are recovered. The most common example of these cases is personal injury suits.

2. **Expected costs outweigh expected benefits**. Sometimes individuals make an on-balance judgment that the benefits to be gained from a lawsuit do not justify the time, cost, and effort required.

3. **Ignorance of legal rights**. Many people are unaware of their legal rights and thus do not

know they have an opportunity to use the legal system for compensation or prevention of harms.

4. **Lack of confidence in the judicial system to provide a fair resolution.** Individuals will turn to the courts only if they trust judges to provide a fair resolution of the matter. If courts lack legitimacy, cases will not be brought to them.

5. **Alternative methods of dispute resolution.** Increasingly, society is exploring alternatives to the judicial system as a way of resolving disputes. Some contracts now prescribe that disputes arising under them will be handled by private arbitration, not court adjudication. Even some statutes now provide that certain matters should be resolved through arbitration. (See Contemporary Perspective, below)

III. **How courts interpret and apply the law.** Some cases are resolved without judicial decision, that is, they are settled out of court. When the parties to a suit disagree about questions of facts and/or the meaning of the law and/or how the law should be applied to the facts, courts are asked to resolve them.

A. **Judicial discretion.** Judges usually have a range of permissible alternatives to choose from in deciding cases.

1. **What judicial discretion is.** Courts have to decide what the law means and how it should be applied. Inevitably judges have discretion in interpreting and applying the law. There are several reasons why this discretion is inevitable.

    a. **Necessity to decide what the facts are.** The fact-finding process is inherently discretionary. The trier of fact, whether judge or jury, must decide whose story is more believable, which often involves deciding which witnesses are most credible.

    b. **Ambiguity of statutes.** Statutes and constitutional provisions often use vague or ambiguous language. Courts must therefore make choices in application and interpretation.

    c. **Example of an ambiguous statute.** An example of an ambiguous statute is 42 U.S. Code section 1983, which states: "Every person, who under color of any statute, ordinance, regulation, custom or usage, of any State or Territory or the District of Columbia, sub-

jects, or causes to be subjected, any citizen of the United States or other person within the jurisdiction thereof to the deprivation of any rights, privileges, or immunities secured by the Constitution and laws, shall be liable to the party injured in an action at law, suit in equity, or other proper proceeding for redress."

(1) **The importance of this statute.** As statutes go, this is a very short provision. But it is especially important because it authorizes federal courts to remedy state or local government violations of the Constitution and federal laws.

(2) **Ways in which the statute is ambiguous.** This statute presents numerous interpretive questions for courts.

    (a) **Meaning of "person."** Does the word "person" at the beginning of the statute only apply to individual government officers, or is the government itself a "person"? (The Supreme Court has held that local governments are persons, but state governments are not.)

    (b) **Meaning of "under color of."** What does "under color of" law mean? If a government officer acts in violation of the law, can it still be under color of law? (The Supreme Court has answered affirmatively, that acts by government officers are under color of law even if they violate the law.)

    (c) **Is the government's good faith a defense?** Is it a defense that the government officer acted in good faith? (The Supreme Court has allowed good faith as a defense and even has held that some officers, such as judges and legislators, are absolutely immune from suits). These are only a few of the questions that courts have had to answer in interpreting this one brief statute.

d. **Discretion applying law to facts**. Courts also have discretion in applying the law to the specific facts. The common law method is inductive in that judges are supposed to follow precedents. Judges compare previously decided cases to the current one and determine whether the precedent is controlling. Inevitably, prior decisions can be characterized broadly or narrowly and courts have discretion to apply or distinguish them.

2. **When judicial discretion can be overruled**. Exercises of judicial discretion in interpreting the law can be overruled by the legislature in the common law and statutory areas, but not in constitutional law.

a. **Statutory override of judicially created common law**. If, for example, a court develops a common law cause of action for "wrongful termination"—allowing suits against employers for unfairly firing employees—the legislature could adopt a statute eliminating that cause of action in future cases.

b. **Revision of statutes to override judicial interpretations**. When a court narrowly interprets a statute, the legislature can respond by amending the statute to accomplish its desired result. For instance, in 1989, several Supreme Court rulings narrowly interpreted federal civil rights laws and made it more difficult for plaintiffs in civil rights cases to seek remedies for discrimination. Members of Congress responded by proposing a bill, called the Civil Rights Protection Act of 1990, to overturn these restrictive Court interpretations.

c. **When Supreme Court rulings can be overturned**. However, when the Supreme Court is interpreting the United States Constitution, its rulings cannot be overturned except by a constitutional amendment or a later Supreme Court decision. For example, the Supreme Court's recent decisions holding that flag burning is a constitutionally protected form of expression can be overturned only by amending the Constitution (or by a later Supreme Court decision).

B. **The special problem of constitutional law**. The power of the judiciary to invalidate statutes or government actions when they violate the Constitution is controversial, both as to the authority for the power and the proper manner of its exercise.

1. **Creation of the authority for judicial review: *Marbury v. Madison***. The Constitution does not expressly authorize federal courts to invalidate government actions that violate the Constitution. This power of constitutional judicial review was created by the Supreme Court in *Marbury v. Madison* (1803).

a. ***Facts of Marbury v. Madison***. At the end of John Adams' presidency, Congress created a number of judgeships. William Marbury was appointed to one of these positions and was confirmed by the Senate on the day before Adams left office. However, Marbury's commission—the piece of paper officially bestowing his judgeship—was not delivered before Thomas Jefferson became president. Jefferson ordered his Secretary of State, James Madison, not to deliver the commission to Marbury.

b. **Marbury's suit**. Marbury filed suit against Madison directly in the United States Supreme Court. Marbury argued that a provision in the Judiciary Act of 1789 authorized the suit to be filed originally in that Court rather than beginning in a lower court.

c. **The Court's ruling in *Marbury v. Madison***. Chief Justice Marshall's decision had several steps. Although the Court found that Marbury had a right to the commission and that it had the authority to review the constitutionality of the executive branch's conduct, it held that it could not provide relief to Marbury.

(1) **Declaring a federal law unconstitutional**. The Court concluded that the Judiciary Act of 1789 was unconstitutional in authorizing the matter to be filed originally in the Supreme Court.

(2) **The Court's rationale**. The Court stated that Article III of the Constitution prescribed a few instances in which the Supreme Court possesses original jurisdiction; Marbury's claim was not among them. Therefore, the statute authorizing jurisdiction was, according to the Court,

inconsistent with the Constitution and invalid.

d. **Importance of *Marbury v. Madison*.** *Marbury v. Madison* is the single most important judicial decision in American history. The case established the authority of the Supreme Court to review the constitutionality of both presidential and congressional actions. The Court explained that the Constitution imposes limits on government powers and that those limits are meaningless unless subject to judicial enforcement. The Court concluded that: "It is emphatically the province and duty of the judicial department to say what the law is."

e. **Chief Justice Marshall's brilliance.** The brilliance of Chief Justice John Marshall's opinion cannot be overstated.

   (1) **Marshall finds way to avoid confrontation with the executive branch.** Politically, Marshall had little choice but to deny Marbury relief. The Jefferson administration surely would have refused to obey an order to deliver the judicial commission to Marbury.

   (2) **Marshall strengthens the judiciary's power by establishing judicial review.** Marshall did more than simply rule in favor of the Jefferson administration. He used the occasion of *Marbury v. Madison* to establish the power of the judiciary and to articulate a role for the federal courts that survives to this day. Because the Supreme Court ruled in favor of the then ruling political party, its decision was not seriously questioned. Thus, the power of constitutional judicial review was established and remains essentially unchallenged.

2. **Competing theories of constitutional interpretation.** After almost two hundred years of judicial review, the question of how the Supreme Court should interpret the Constitution remains unanswered. For example, how should the Court decide whether the Constitution protects a right of women to obtain abortions, or whether the Constitution prohibits school prayer, or whether the Constitution protects a right of individuals to choose to die by refusing needed medical treat-ment? There are two major competing theories as to how the courts should interpret the Constitution.

a. **Intent of the Framers.** One method of interpretation, termed "originalism," provides that the Constitution's meaning is limited to what is clearly stated in the text or clearly intended by its Framers. The U.S. Supreme Court should protect only rights that are stated in the Constitution or intended by the Framers.

   (1) **The case for "originalism."** Originalists argue that constitutional judicial review is inherently at odds with the basic premises of a democratic society. Unelected judges, beyond the requirements of limited ("constitutional") government, substitute their views for the choices of popularly elected legislatures and executives. Thus, originalists contend that the Supreme Court should invalidate a government action only when it is clear that the Constitution, in its text or intent, prohibits the action.

   (2) **An example of originalist reasoning.** Originalists would argue, for example, that the Constitution does not protect a right to abortion because the document does not mention abortion and the Framers surely did not intend to create such a right. Chief Justice William Rehnquist, and former judge and Supreme Court nominee, Robert Bork, are prominent originalists.

   (3) **The positive/negative argument.** According to this argument, the proper role of federal courts, including the Supreme Court, with regard to judicial review is essentially negative—to void unconstitutional law. But under "judicial activism," the courts appoint for themselves a positive role—setting forth what public policy shall be. Thus the courts have commanded jails to be built or prisoners to be released; they have also ordered taxes to be levied, thereby flatly contradicting the fundamental idea that taxes shall be raised only by the people's representatives.

b. **An alternative view: non-originalism.** In contrast, non-originalists maintain that the Court is not limited to the text or the Framers' intent in protecting constitutional rights. Non-originalists contend that the Constitution was intentionally written in broad, open-textured language, using phrases like "due process of law" and "equal protection." The Constitution, by this view, is a living document that justices apply to society's changing circumstances. Supreme Court Justices William Brennan and Thurgood Marshall are prominent examples of non-originalists. Non-originalists make several arguments.

(1) **The Framers did not want their intentions to govern.** One argument is that originalism as a theory "self-destructs." Originalism commands adherence to the Framers' views, but the Framers did not want their intent to control those who came after them. James Madison took the notes at the Constitutional Convention, but he prohibited looking at them until after his death so that the Constitution would be interpreted on its own.

(2) **Originalist results unacceptable.** Opponents maintain that originalism leads to unacceptable results, for society cannot be governed by the views of 200 years ago.

(a) **Presidents would have to be male.** For example, Article II of the Constitution refers to the President as "he." The Framers certainly intended that only men would occupy the office. Fidelity to originalism would make the election of a woman as president unconstitutional.

(b) **Schools could not be desegregated.** The Supreme Court's decisions finding segregation unconstitutional—perhaps the most socially significant rulings in American history—cannot be reconciled with originalism. The same Congress that passed the Fourteenth Amendment (which contains the equal protection clause) also voted to segregate the District of Columbia's public schools.

(c) **Importance of the debate.** Whether the debate is phrased in terms of originalism and non-originalism, or in the more familiar language of judicial activism and restraint, there is continuing heated debate over which method of Supreme Court decision-making is correct. The debate has strong political overtones.

(1) **Illegitimacy of "judicial legislation."** "Conservatives" object to judicial protection of rights, such as abortion and rights for criminal defendants, and decry "judicial legislation."

(2) **Protection of fundamental values.** "Liberals" argue that the Constitution was meant to protect fundamental values from majoritarian interference, and that it is the role of the judiciary to identify and protect basic rights from infringement. Ultimately, this debate is about the proper place of the Constitution and the judiciary in the American system of government.

Historical Perspective

I. **Historical changes in court structure and procedure.** Since adoption of the Constitution there have been a number of alterations in court structure and procedure.

A. **Court structure.** Although the overall structure of the judicial system is remarkably the same after 200 years, many particular aspects have been altered.

1. **Debate at the Constitutional Convention over how to structure the federal judicial system.** At the Constitutional Convention there was a major disagreement as to whether or not there should be federal trial courts. One faction distrusted state courts and wanted a system of lower federal courts. Another group felt that state courts could be trusted and that Supreme Court review of state court decisions would be sufficient. A compromise was reached: Article III of the Constitution created the United States Supreme Court and left it to Congress to decide whether to create lower federal courts.

2. **Provisions of the Judiciary Act of 1789.** In the Judiciary Act of 1789, Congress created lower federal courts and they have existed ever since. The major change since 1789 is in the creation of permanent court of appeals judgeships. Under the Judiciary Act of 1789, the courts of appeals were staffed by district court judges and Supreme Court justices who travel and also sat as appeals court judges. This practice was termed "riding circuit" and led to the courts of appeals gaining the title "circuit courts." Not until 1891 was the practice of riding circuit eliminated and permanent court of appeals judgeships created.

3. **Number of Justices on the Supreme Court.** The number of justices on the Supreme Court fluctuated for the first seventy years of American history but has remained constant at nine ever since 1869.

   (a) **Fluctuation prior to 1869.** Initially, there were six justices on the Supreme Court. This number was increased every time a new circuit court was added until there were ten justices on the Court in 1864. In 1866, in an effort to prevent President Andrew Johnson from making appointments to the Court, the number of justices was reduced to seven. In 1869, after President Johnson left office, the number was increased to nine, where it has remained ever since.

   (b) **Roosevelt's "court-packing" scheme.** The only serious proposal for a change in size came during the mid-1930s, when President Franklin Roosevelt advocated his famous "court-packing plan."

      (1) **Why FDR wanted more justices.** Angry over the Supreme Court's invalidation of New Deal legislation in the midst of the depression, Roosevelt proposed adding one new justice to the Court for each justice over the age of seventy, to a maximum of fifteen justices.

      (2) **The effect of adopting FDR's plan.** The effect would have been to allow Roosevelt immediately to appoint a majority of the Court, thus securing approval of his legislative programs.

      (3) **Opposition to FDR's plan.** Despite Roosevelt's immense popularity at the time, the court-packing plan was severely criticized and even renounced by a Senate Judiciary Committee controlled by the Democratic Party.

      (4) **FDR's plan becomes unnecessary.** Ultimately, the plan became unnecessary when Justice Owen Roberts changed his mind and voted to sustain important New Deal legislation. Whether his shift was in response to the pressure of the court-packing plan will always be in dispute; nonetheless, his change of mind will forever be known as "the switch in time that saved the nine."

B. **Court procedure.** The procedures followed in American courts have changed greatly over the past 200 years.

1. **English antecedents for the American system: courts of equity versus courts of law.** Initially, the American court system paralleled the English approach with two types of lower courts for civil litigation: courts of equity and courts of law. Courts of equity existed to grant court commands such as injunctions. Courts of law granted monetary relief. Parties had to decide which court system to use and could not seek relief in both. Procedures varied greatly in each type of court. For example, jury trials were available only in courts of law. Beginning in the mid-nineteenth century, courts of law and equity were combined and parties could seek both types of relief in a single court.

2. **Desire to simplify court procedures.** The trend throughout American history has been to simplify court procedure. Initially, American courts followed the English "writ" system in which every type of suit had its own procedural requirements, and even a small error by a party would lead to the permanent dismissal of the action. There were widespread complaints that too many cases were decided on procedural technicalities rather than the merits of the dispute.

   a. **Problems of procedural fairness.** Beginning in the mid-nineteenth century, states began to adopt codes of civil procedure to replace the writ system. This approach required plaintiffs to file detailed complaints alleging all of the facts supporting their action and allowed little discovery of additional information after the initiation of suit. Again, over time, there were objections that cases were decided on procedural technicalities. Some argued that it was unfair that plaintiffs were required to establish their case without any opportunity to learn information completely within the control of the defendant.

b. **Adoption of civil procedure rules.** In the mid-1930s, the Federal Rules of Civil Procedure were adopted. The core philosophy of these rules, which apply in all civil cases in federal court, is that plaintiffs should only be required to file a complaint with enough detail to provide fair notice to the defendant of the nature of the claim. Parties then are accorded broad rights to engage in discovery to learn all relevant facts from the other side. This system, termed "notice pleading," has also been adopted in most states.

II. **History of constitutional judicial review.** The use of constitutional judicial review has shifted dramatically over time.

A. **Early cases creating the authority for judicial review state decisions.** In the early nineteenth century, in cases such as *McCulloch v. Maryland* (1819) and *Cohens v. Virginia* (1821), the Supreme Court established its authority to review the actions of state governments and the decisions of state courts to assure their compliance with the United States Constitution.

B. **Use of judicial review before 1857.** After *Marbury v. Madison*, the Supreme Court did not declare unconstitutional another federal statute until *Dred Scott v. Sanford* in 1856-1857. In this infamous decision, the Supreme Court invalidated the Missouri Compromise, holding that slaves were property and not persons under the Constitution.

C. **Judicial review in the late nineteenth and early twentieth centuries: the "Lochner era."** Not until the late nineteenth century did the Supreme Court declare federal and state laws unconstitutional with any frequency. From then until 1937, a conservative Supreme Court, strongly committed to laissez-faire economics, invalidated federal and state economic regulations. This period of constitutional history is often referred to as the "Lochner era," taking its name from *Lochner v. New York* (1905) where the Supreme Court declared unconstitutional a state law prescribing maximum hours for bakers.

1. **Curtailment of congressional regulatory power.** The Court narrowly interpreted Congress's power to regulate commerce and invalidated federal laws protecting consumers and workers as an infringement of prerogatives left for exclusive state control.

2. **Workers left unprotected by freedom of contract rulings.** At the same time, the Court held that freedom of contract was a fundamental right protected under the "liberty" provision of the due process clause. State laws protecting workers, such as minimum wage and maximum hour laws, were declared unconstitutional as infringing freedom of contract.

D. **Shift in Court philosophy in 1937.** In 1937, the Court dramatically changed its approach and began to allow federal and state economic regulations. Within a few years, Roosevelt was able to replace the conservative Lochner era justices with individuals committed to his judicial philosophy. In 1942, in a famous footnote in *United States v. Carolene Products*, the Court articulated a philosophy of judicial review. The Court said that generally it would defer to government economic regulations and reserve aggressive judicial review for government actions which interfered with fundamental rights or discriminated against "discrete and insular minorities."

E. **The Warren Court and the expansion of rights and equality from 1954-1969.** The Warren Court ruled against racial segregation in the schools and other forms of racial discrimination. It also applied stricter standards to maintain separation of church and state and increased the rights of criminal defendants.

1. **Outlawing racial segregation in schools.** In the summer of 1953, then Chief Justice Fred Vinson died and was replaced by Earl Warren. In 1954, in *Brown v. Board of Education*, the Court declared unconstitutional state laws requiring segregation of public schools. In decisions that followed, the Court ruled impermissible laws segregating other aspects of life.

2. **Outlawing other forms of discrimination.** During the 1960's, under the leadership of Chief Justice Warren, the Court actively protected racial minorities and fundamental rights. For example, the Court protected the right for each person's vote to count equally in state elections by declaring the unequal apportionment of state

legislatures unconstitutional in *Baker v. Carr* (1962).

3. **Applying stricter standards of separation of church and state.** The Court applied a stricter standard toward the separation of church and state in invalidating prayer in public schools. In the same vein it denied the constitutionality of government aid to parochial schools.

4. **Further protection of rights of the criminally accused.** Most controversially, the Warren Court further protected the rights of criminal defendants by providing new remedies for their violation. Thus the Court required the exclusion of illegally obtained evidence and imposed requirements such as the famous *Miranda* warnings before questioning of suspects by police officers.

F. **The philosophical shift of the Supreme Court since 1969.** Since 1969, there have been nine vacancies to be filled on the Supreme Court. All have occurred during the terms of Republican presidents (Nixon, Ford, Reagan, and Bush). Jimmy Carter, the only Democratic president since 1969, did not have the opportunity to appoint a Supreme Court justice.

1. **Nixon Appointees.** In 1968, Richard Nixon campaigned for office by criticizing the Supreme Court and promising to appoint "strict constructionists" ("originalists"). The resignations of Chief Justice Warren in 1968 and of Justice Abe Fortas in 1969 provided President Nixon with two quick vacancies to fill. In 1971, the departure of Justices Hugo Black and John Harlan created two more vacancies.

   a. **Decline of "judicial activism."** The four Nixon appointees—Warren Burger, Harry Blackmun, William Rehnquist, and Lewis Powell—dramatically altered the Court's philosophy as "judicial activism" declined.

   b. **"Judicial activism" not entirely absent.** Nonetheless, "judicial activism" protecting individual rights was not completely over. Most notably, in 1973, the Supreme Court declared in *Roe v. Wade* that state laws prohibiting abortion during the first two trimesters of pregnancy are unconstitutional.

2. **Appointments during the 1980s.** Although no vacancies occurred on the Court during President Jimmy Carter's term, President Ronald Reagan appointed three members to the Court: Sandra Day O'Connor, Antonin Scalia, and Anthony Kennedy. George Bush appointed David Souter to the Court in 1990. These appointments solidified the Court's philosophical shift.

   a. **Recent trends in Supreme Court decisions.** The Supreme Court has indicated a reluctance to undertake "judicial activism" in order to protect individual or minority rights, which it leaves to legislation. The Court has also shown a much greater deference to laws alleged to violate rights or to discriminate.

   b. **Future trends.** The eventual replacement of the one liberal member of the Court—Harry Blackmun, over 80 years old in 1991—might solidify the trend against "judicial activism" even further.

Contemporary Perspective

I. **Court procedure.** Several circumstances combine to make questions concerning court procedure important contemporary issues.

A. **Increasing caseloads.** Courts in many parts of the country are overwhelmed by burgeoning caseloads. For example, the dramatic increase in drug prosecutions is straining judicial resources. Some federal courts are nearing the point at which they will not be able to hear civil cases because of the need to process criminal cases within the time limits set by the federal Speedy Trial Act. Will society provide the resources necessary for a judicial system to handle the volume of litigation now confronting the courts?

B. **Possible abuse of the system by attorneys.** There has been increasing concern that attorneys may be abusing the judicial system.

1. **Abuse of civil law procedures.** For example, the liberal rules of the notice pleading system and expansive discovery have led to the filing of some frivolous claims and abusive discovery practices. (Discovery is the legal process for obtaining certain information or evidence from the opposing side prior to trial.)

2. **New sanctions against attorney abuse—a double edged sword.** During the 1980s, the Federal Rules of Civil Procedure were amended to allow

for greater sanctioning of attorneys who act in a manner judged to be unreasonable. Most states are also expanding the use of sanctions for abuses.

a. **Benefits of sanctions against lawyers**. Benefits of sanctions against lawyers who abuse judicial facilities include providing a means of deterring undesirable lawyering practices.

b. **Costs of sanctions**. On the other hand, sanctions risk deterring not only undesirable actions but also creative litigation seeking to establish new rights. A key question for the future is whether it is possible to use sanctions to correct abuses without also penalizing and discouraging needed lawyering for the public interest.

C. **Alternative methods of settling disputes**. There is a trend towards greater reliance on alternative methods of resolving disputes, such as mediation and arbitration. These alternatives can lessen the burden on the courts and provide speedier resolution of disputes. They may also provide more access to the judicial system for the poor and the middle class.

1. **Disadvantages of alternative methods**. Alternative methods of resolving disputes may lack the procedural safeguards found in courts and may divert cases away from the courts that need judicial resolution. Alternative dispute resolution mechanisms may solve the controversy between the two parties, but they do not necessarily fully enforce the law or create the common law precedents needed for development of the law.

2. **The place of alternative methods in the American system: an unresolved question.** A central issue is the proper place for alternative dispute resolution mechanisms in the American system of justice. What types of cases should remain in the judicial system and which should be diverted to the alternative dispute resolution mechanisms is an unanswered question.

D. **The consequences of litigiousness for democracy.** A further problem for the American judicial system is a growing litigiousness of the population. Many different factors account for the rise in litigation. Many additional court suits are a result of federal and state statutes creating new causes of action, such as law prohibiting discrimination and protecting the environment. Also many people may be aware of their rights

and demand remedies rather than suffer without recourse. But at the same time, litigiousness might also be considered a symptom of social malaise and a significant weakening of social bonds. Sometimes frivolous matters are taken to court and sometimes people litigate rather than use more informal mechanisms for resolving disputes.

II. **Constitutional judicial review.** The future of judicial review at both state and federal levels is an important issue for the future.

A. **Judicial review of state law by state courts**. Increasingly, state courts are interpreting state constitutions to provide independent protection of constitutional rights. The nature and extent of such protections, however, is uncertain.

B. **The U.S. Supreme Court.** The role of the Supreme Court in protecting individual rights and minorities is uncertain in light of its increasing reluctance to engage in what it considers to be judicial activism. Whether the Court will continue to safeguard constitutional values from the excesses of the democratic process is uncertain.

III. **Selection of U.S. Supreme Court Justices.** The existence of a President of one party and a Senate controlled by another party creates the possibility for Senate rejection of Supreme Court nominations. Indeed, the defeat of Supreme Court nominee Robert Bork in 1987 because of his conservative views on constitutional questions has established a strong precedent for Senate scrutiny of nominees' views. Bork was rejected because of his criticism of Supreme Court decisions which protected individual rights or enhanced the rights of racial minorities. Historically, about 20% of presidential nominees have been rejected by the Senate, often because of their ideology. Two related questions emerge.

A. **Questioning during confirmation proceedings**. What questions is it appropriate to ask a nominee in the confirmation process? Should the confirmation process focus only on whether the individual is qualified for the position of justice solely on the basis of intelligence, knowledge, and experience? Or are the nominee's positions on particular constitutional issues important?

1. **Seeking explanations of a nominee's previously expressed views**. Rather than focusing on qualifications alone, should the senate require nominees to state their views on disputed constitutional questions? If nominees have taken posi-

tions in writings or speeches, should they be required to defend or explain them?

2. **Eliciting a nominee's views.** Conversely, if the nominee has not taken public positions, should the confirmation process attempt to elicit them? Whether the Senate should demand as a condition for confirmation that nominees answer specific questions about their views is a matter of dispute.

3. **Asking a nominee's position on unresolved legal questions.** The debate partly concerns whether it is proper for the Senate to ask questions about unresolved legal questions that might come before the Court.

B. **Disqualifying a nominee because of his or her views.** Closely related is the issue of what views should disqualify one from sitting on the Supreme Court. Is it appropriate for the Senate to reject a candidate because of his or her views on a single question, like the right to an abortion? Are there views about legal issues or the legal system that should disqualify a candidate for the Supreme Court?

4. STATE AND LOCAL GOVERNMENT

Each state retains its sovereignty, freedom, and independence, and every Power, Jurisdiction and right, which is not by this confederation expressly delegated to the United States, in Congress assembled.

Articles of Confederation (1781)

The proposed Constitution, so far from implying an abolition of the State Governments, makes them constituent parts of the national sovereignty by allowing them a direct representation in the Senate, and leaves in their possession certain exclusive and very important portions of sovereign power. This fully corresponds, in every rational import of the terms, with the idea of a Federal Government.

Alexander Hamilton (1787)

To study the Union before studying the state is to follow a path strewn with obstacles. The federal government was the last to take shape in the United States; the political principles on which it was based were spread throughout society before its time, existed independently of it, and only had to be modified to form the republic. Moreover...the federal government is something of an exception, whereas the government of each state is the normal authority....The great

political principles which now rule American society were born and grew up in the **state**; there is no room for doubt about that. So one must understand the state to gain the key to the rest.

Alexis de Tocqueville (1835)

In the Constitution, the term state most frequently expresses the combined idea...of people, territory, and government. A state, in the ordinary sense of the Constitution, is a political community of free citizens, occupying a territory of defined boundaries, and organized under a government sanctioned and limited by a written constitution, and established by the consent of the governed.... [T]he people of each State compose a State, having its own government, and endowed with all the functions essential to separate and independent existence, and...without the States in union, there could be no such political body as the United States.

Texas v. White (1869)

Municipal corporations owe their origin to, and derive their powers and rights wholly from, the legislature. It breathes into them the breath of life, without which they cannot exist. As it creates, so it may destroy. If it may destroy, it may abridge and control.

Chief Justice John F. Dillon, Iowa (1868)

[T]oday the question faces us whether the constituent States of the System can be saved for any useful purpose, and thereby saved as the vital cells that they have been heretofore of democratic sentiment, impulse, and action.

Edward S. Corwin (1950)

More and more, the states appear as administrative subdivisions of the nation, government survivals of another day which must be supported by grants-in-aid, supervised and coordinated by a growing federal bureaucracy, retained as training and proving grounds for political leadership on the national stage.

Carl J. Friedrich (1968)

Everything that can be run more effectively by state and local government we shall turn over to state and local government, along with the funding sources to pay for it. We are going to put an end to the money merry-go-round where our money becomes Washington's money, to be spent by states and cities only if they spend it exactly the way the federal bureaucrats tell them to.

Ronald Reagan (1980)

[T]he component parts of the Union look a lot better than the Union does.

Governor Anthony Earl, Wisconsin (1984)

Citizen advocates are fighting and winning battles at the state and local level—battles for clean indoor air, warnings on hazardous products, the disclosure of toxic hazards. But while they are winning on one front, their gains are too often eroded on another, "preempted" by [federal] laws that do little to accomplish their stated goals, but choke off effective regulation at the local levels of government.

Advocacy Institute and Public Citizens' Congress Watch (1990)

The American states are polities in their own right. They are complete political systems possessing substantial powers that affect every aspect of the lives of citizens from conception to death. At the same time, the states coexist in a federal union that both limits and enhances their powers and capabilities. If California were an independent nation, for example, it would be the sixth largest economic power in the world. But California would probably not have such a large economy if it did not enjoy the economic and political benefits of membership in the American federal union. Americans often show at best an incomplete grasp of the character of state and local government. Local governments actually provide most of the public services enjoyed by Americans. They also provide citizens with many opportunities to participate directly in government and politics on a face-to-face basis. Citizens need to grasp the role of state and local government in their own lives and in the life of their communities before they see how their participation matters and what avenues they might take to influence the actions and policies of state and local government.

OBJECTIVES

The citizen should be able to

1. explain how the states and their local governments are democratic political systems having principal responsibility for domestic functions in the United States.

2. describe the diversity in politics and government that exists among the fifty states and their local communities.

3. explain the institutions of state and local government and the principal changes that have occurred in state and local governance over the centuries.

4. take, defend, and evaluate positions on the leading political and governmental institutions and issues in state and local governance today.

FRAME OF REFERENCE
Conceptual Perspective

I. **The states as political systems.** Each state has a written constitution and bill of rights, democratically drafted and adopted by the citizens of the state; a complete set of government institutions (legislative, executive, and judicial) based on free elections; a complete set of political institutions (political parties, interest groups, and media); a substantial array of taxing, spending, and regulatory powers; and a diversity of local governments (counties, municipalities, townships, school districts, and special districts) based on free local elections and vested with varying degrees and types of powers.

A. **Union preceded by states.** The states evolved from the American colonies that began with the settlement of Jamestown, Virginia, in 1607. The colonies became both independent states and united states at the time of the Declaration of Independence in 1776. In 1781, the states delegated some of their powers to a confederal government under the Articles of Confederation. In 1788, the people of the states redelegated certain powers and delegated certain other of their powers to a new federal government under the U.S. Constitution.

B. **Constitutional setting.** The states were considered the essential parts of the Union at the time of ratification of the U.S. Constitution.

1. **Constitutional provisions.** Their place in the federal system is protected by the very structure of the Constitution and by such provisions as the guarantee that each state has two senators in the U.S. Senate and that no new state can be formed from the territory of an existing state without its consent.

2. **Reserved powers.** Also, the Tenth Amendment (1791) to the U.S. Constitution provides: "The powers not delegated to the United States by the Constitution, nor prohibited by it to the states, are reserved to the States respectively, or to the people."

C. **Advantages of states within the union.** Without the states, there would be no union. Within the union, the existence of the states provides six major advantages to the operation of American federal democracy.

1. **Participation.** State and local governments permit wider participation in governing than would otherwise be possible. Of the 497,697 elected officials in the United States, only 542 (0.1 percent) serve in the U.S. government compared to 18,134 (3.6 percent) in state government and 479,021 (96.2 percent) in local government.

2. **Experimentation.** States permit experimentation and variety in public policies. The states, as U.S. Supreme Court Justice **Louis Brandeis** (1856-1941) once said, are "laboratories of democracy."

3. **Equity.** States allow public policies and services to be developed in response to the needs and preferences of citizens living in different parts of the country.

    a. **Possibility of local control.** In this way, citizens are more likely to get and pay for the services they need or want, and to exercise control over those services.

    b. **Local adaptation.** States can also tailor and augment most federal policies to meet local needs and wants. For example, the federal government sets minimum national environmental protection standards. In most cases, states can set stricter standards, as many do, and regulate the environment where the federal government does not.

4. **Efficiency.** Because different public services have different area-wide costs and benefits, states (and their local governments) allow for the provision of cost-effective services based on appropriate territorial scope.

5. **Liberty.** Although, like the federal government, every state (and its local governments) has abused democracy and rights at some point in its history, states and localities help to protect liberty in two basic ways.

    a. **Countervailing powers.** They stand as countervailing powers to the potential tyranny of local officials and of a centralized national government—a role highlighted today by the struggles for state power in the USSR against centralized tyranny. At the same time, the federal government stands as a countervailing power to the tyranny that may arise in one or more states or localities.

    b. **Citizen choice.** State and local governments allow citizens to move from one jurisdiction to another in search of a polity more consistent with their preferences. The U.S. Constitution guarantees this mobility, as well as certain basic rights and services, across all states.

6. **Prosperity.** State and local governments help to promote prosperity by being able to attract, regulate, tax, and repel certain types of business and industry. To some extent, economic competition among the states complements economic competition in the general marketplace. Although there is significant national regulation of commerce to maintain a common and equitable market, there is no centralized economic planning, and state economies are affected by, but not dependent upon, decisions made by the federal government.

7. **Health and safety.** State and local governments have primary responsibility for public health and safety. As such, state and local governments not only provide services (e.g., police and public hospitals) but also regulate many activities, such as most of the nation's professional occupations (e.g., physicians, nurses, and beauticians). States also share regulatory authority with the federal government over some industries, such as banking and telecommunications. State bank regulators, for example, pioneered such practices as payment of interest on deposits and checking and NOW accounts.

D. **Policy importance.** The states and their local governments provide and pay for most domestic public policies, with occasional help from the federal government. The federal government has gradually increased its power over the states since 1789, but the states remain principally responsible for many policies. A leading example is public K-12 education, for which the federal government contributes less than 8 percent of the costs, leaving the rest to states and localities.

E. **Political culture.** The original states experienced more than a century and a half of social and political development prior to formation of the Union. Because they were settled by different ethnic and religious groups, and because they had different needs and conditions, the New England, Middle Atlantic, and Southern states developed distinctive political cultures. Political culture may be defined as the way in which a people looks at government and politics and the expectations they have of government. Slavery, for example, was a distinctive expression of southern political culture.

1. **Moralistic.** In the northern tier of states stretching from New England to Washington, a "moralistic" culture evolved, which emphasizes a commonwealth vision of political life. Widespread political participation is encouraged, issues are emphasized, and public officials are held to high standards. These states, for example, tended to pioneer strong merit systems for government employment, and they tend to have higher voter turnouts in elections.

2. **Individualistic.** In the middle states, a more individualistic political culture emerged, which stresses a marketplace view of politics. Politics is seen as a way to further the interests of specific groups; organized parties are important; government tends to be viewed as a business; and public officials are expected to derive some "profit" from government service. "Machine politics" was especially prevalent in these states.

3. **Traditionalistic.** In the southern states, a "traditionalist" political culture took root. This culture tends to confine political decision-making to a small elite and to be mostly concerned with maintaining the political status quo, as reflected in the South's clinging to slavery and then to racial segregation.

4. **Cultural mixes.** Although one cultural orientation predominates in many states, some states, such as California and Illinois, have regional cleavages arising from settlement in the state by groups representing all three of these cultural types. Furthermore, state political cultures change over time as they are affected by such factors as migration, reform, and economic development.

F. **State constitutions.** Each state has a constitution that sets forth the structure and responsibilities of state government. Unlike the U.S. Constitution, the primary purpose of state constitutions is to limit power. When the colonies became states in 1776, they acquired all the powers that had been exercised by the British government. The people quickly wrote constitutions for their states to limit the powers of state govern-

ment. The defense of liberty was a primary goal. Among other things, most of the early state constitutions contained bills of rights that guaranteed specific freedoms; they became a major basis for the Bill of Rights added to the U.S. Constitution in 1791. (In state constitutions, the declaration of rights comes first, not last.)

1. **Domestic governance.** In addition to legislative, executive, and judicial sections, state constitutions may contain provisions on suffrage and elections, taxation and finance, local government, civil service, public health, housing and social services, corporations and banking, labor, land, conservation and environmental protection, electoral apportionment, intergovernmental cooperation, and initiative, referendum, and recall.

2. **Cultural differences.** State constitutions reflect differences in the political cultures of the states, as well as other differences. For example:

   a. **New England constitutionalism.** In the New England states, which may be said to have a moralistic political culture, the constitutions are relatively short and concerned mainly with the essentials of government. Three of the New England states have preserved the constitution with which they entered the Union. In addition, Connecticut operated under its 1818 constitution until 1965; Rhode Island still operates under its 1842 constitution; and Vermont still has its 1793 constitution. This continuity suggests widespread agreement on political fundamentals.

   b. **Southern constitutionalism.** The southern states, which have a "traditionalistic" political culture, tend to have very long and detailed constitutions and to have had many constitutions, in part because of their secession during the Civil War. The record is held by Louisiana, which has had eleven constitutions since it entered the Union in 1812.

3. **Change and amendment.** State constitutions are easier to amend than is the U.S. Constitution. A common method of adding a state constitutional amendment is for the legislature to propose an amendment by a two-thirds majority in each chamber, and for the voters of the state to ratify

the amendment by a majority vote. Most state constitutions have many amendments, sometimes in the hundreds. As a result, state charters are more detailed, and often more restrictive of government powers, than the federal charter.

4. **Constitutions as statutes.** Because of the greater ease of adding amendments, state charters sometimes contain what many observers regard as statutory material. Interest groups that are effective in the legislature sometimes try to install their policy preferences into the state constitution because it is more difficult to alter than a statute.

G. **Municipal charters.** The states determine what types of local governments within their domain will have charters. Typically, municipalities have charters; in some states, counties operate under charters. When a locality is governed under a charter, it has fairly extensive powers, which are outlined in the charter. Charters provide for different levels of local government authority. A home-rule charter usually gives a municipality fairly extensive powers. Some other charters sharply limit local powers. Thus, there is variation in local powers within and between states. Localities such as townships and special districts do not usually have charters and have much more limited powers.

H. **State-local relations.** The primary feature of state-local relations is that, constitutionally, localities are creatures of the states. This feature is consistent with the states being formally unitary political systems. Unlike the states in the federal union, local governments have no petition or ratification authority in state constitutional change. A state may abolish local governments if it chooses. Connecticut and Rhode Island, for example, have abolished counties.

1. **Dillon's Rule.** A key element in state-local relations is the manner in which state courts interpret municipal charters. The general rule was set forth in 1868 by Judge **John Dillon** of the Iowa Supreme Court, in which he stated, "any doubt concerning the existence of power in a charter, and the power is denied." Dillon's Rule is the opposite of the implied powers doctrine, under which the U.S. Supreme Court interprets the U.S. Constitution's provisions relating to congressional power liberally or broadly.

2. **Home rule.** Under pressure from localities desiring more latitude to govern their own affairs,

the states have slowly relaxed the strictures imposed by Dillon's Rule. In 1875, Missouri was the first state to establish home rule as a part of its constitution. Under home rule, states provide localities with a general grant of power to enact local ordinances so long as they do not conflict with state or federal law.

II. **State politics and institutions.** Although the dynamics of state and local politics differ from one state or locality to another, certain features are common to most states.

A. **Political parties.** Each state has its own party system.

1. **State and national parties.** State parties are the bases of the national Democratic and Republican parties. State parties also play a role, through primary elections, caucuses, and voter mobilization, in electing the President. Each state has a number of electoral votes equal to its number of U.S. senators and representatives. The candidate who gets the most popular votes in a state gets all of that state's electoral votes. A candidate must get a majority of the votes in the electoral college to win the presidency.

2. **Party competition.** In the past, many states were dominated for long periods by one political party (e.g., Democrats in the South from the 1870s to the 1970s). Today, most states have two competitive parties.

3. **Parties and candidates.** In a majority of states, political parties are candidate-centered; that is, the outcome of elections depends more on the skills of the candidates than on the organizational strength of the parties. A major factor is the presence of the party primary, in which the party's voters determine the candidates who will run under the party label.

4. **Campaign finance.** Another factor weakening party organization is the rapidly increasing cost of political campaigns, which places a premium on a candidate's ability to raise large sums of money for contributors.

5. **Third parties.** States also are home to many third parties, such as socialists and libertarians, who periodically get elected to state and local offices. In 1990, Vermont elected a former socialist mayor to the U.S. House of Representatives.

6. **Nonpartisanship**. States are homes for nonpartisanship as well. In fact, because municipal officials in many states, and judges in some states, are elected on nonpartisan ballots, the majority of elected officials in the United States formally operate outside of the party system. State and county officials are still partisan, although Nebraska's unique unicameral legislature is officially nonpartisan.

B. **Interest groups**. Interest groups play a major role in state affairs, though probably not as great as in the past. Interest groups include private economic interests, issue groups such as environmentalists, and governmental groups such as town and city mayors. Business, teacher, and organized labor groups usually have the greatest influence today.

C. **Media**. Every state has a commercial and public media system that provides news and analysis of state and local government to citizens. Since the colonial era, newspapers have been the main source of local and state news. Today, television is also an important source of state and local news, although a few states are too small or inconveniently located (e.g., New Jersey) to have their own VHF network station. However, cable television is providing citizens in all states with new means of access to state and local government—if they choose to tune in.

D. **Voter participation**. Although citizen participation in elections varies among the states, voter turnout is generally lowest for local elections, highest for presidential elections, and in between for state elections.

1. **Apathy**. Some observers believe that low turnouts in state and local elections indicate that citizens are apathetic and perhaps even alienated from state and local government.

2. **Satisfaction**. Other observers believe that low turnouts indicate that citizens are basically satisfied with state and local government. When citizens do become disturbed about state and local government, turnout can be very high, even higher than in presidential elections.

3. **Publicity**. Some observers argue that low turnouts are mostly due to publicity. High turnouts occur in presidential elections because of the huge publicity. Turnout in all other elections, including off-year congressional elections and presidential primaries, is usually low. In addition, many state elections occur in non-presidential election years, and most local elections occur in the spring.

4. **Alternatives**. Some observers argue that many citizens do not feel an urgent need to participate in local elections especially, because they have many other "non-political" ways to participate in the public affairs of their local community.

E. **State legislatures**. State assemblies have generally been the most problem-afflicted branches of state government. The values that constitutional framers hoped would be realized through them, such as citizen governance, have sometimes been thwarted by incompetence, inefficiency, and corruption.

1. **Size**. State legislatures range in size from 49 members in Nebraska to 424 members in New Hampshire.

2. **Structure**. Forty-nine states have a bicameral (usually called House and Senate) legislature; Nebraska has a unicameral legislature (whose members are called senators).

3. **Functions**. State legislatures perform several key functions:

   a. **Representation**. The responsibility that state legislatures have performed most successfully has been to represent the interests of individual legislative districts, which in most states are fairly small areas, perhaps embracing several neighborhoods in a large city, or a few small communities.

      (1) **Voting**. One part of representation is voting. Legislators sometimes follow a "delegate" model, in which they closely follow the wishes of their constituents in voting on measures. Sometimes they adhere to a "trustee" model, in which they consider the overall interest of the state in their voting. In practice, most legislators are "politicos" who base their voting on a combination of constituent wishes and their own perception of state needs. (For a discussion of the "delegate" and "trustee" models of representation, see section on Morality and Politics in Civic Knowledge).

(2) **Casework**. Another part of representation is casework. Legislators help constituents who need assistance in dealing with state and federal agencies. For some legislators, this is the main part of their job. Occasionally, casework leads to new legislation, but for the most part, it involves a single individual (the legislator) resolving a problem for a constituent. The task can be performed well by a part-time official.

b. **Lawmaking**. Although state assemblies have always had the writing of statutes as their primary responsibility, their lawmaking has traditionally been strongly influenced by political groups outside of the legislature.

   (1) **Executive influence**. One group consists of executive departments and agencies. For most states, these agencies are composed of full-time employees, as contrasted with the usually part-time assemblies. The governor is often a dominant figure in a legislative session.

   (2) **Lobbyists**. Another major influence is interest groups. Lobbyists representing interest groups provide information that legislators need for lawmaking, bring public and financial pressure to bear on legislative decision-making, and provide support for election campaigns.

c. **Oversight of administration**. Legislatures have rarely performed this function well, largely because of the absence of the necessary staff. However, certain changes have occurred in recent years.

   (1) **Sunset laws**. About half of the states require a reauthorization of state administrative agencies; otherwise, the sun will "set" on them—they will go out of existence. Sunset laws have generally impelled greater scrutiny of executive departments.

   (2) **Legislative vetoes**. About half of the states provide for legislative oversight of the rules of administrative agencies. Depending on the state, a legislative committee or the full legislature may veto proposed rules if they are found to violate legislative intent.

   (3) **Budget control**. Legislatures have strengthened appropriation committees. These committees hold hearings on the governor's budget, and are less likely to rubber-stamp executive recommendations than in the past.

d. **Public education**. Legislators have the responsibility of informing their constituents about the issues before the legislature. This function has often been difficult to carry out well because of the low visibility of state politics, and the limited press coverage of the state capital. More recently, the rising importance of state affairs and the growth of television coverage have enhanced communication with constituents.

e. **Legislative institutionalization**. All state legislatures have become more professionalized and institutionalized in the past two decades. They are no longer the "sometime governments," as a 1971 report called them. They are much better staffed. Thirty-nine legislatures now meet in annual sessions; seven hold biennial sessions; and four are legally biennial but actually meet every year. While some assemblies still have large numbers of "citizen" legislators, more and more legislators are becoming career politicians.

F. **Governors**. The state chief executive, who serves a four-year term in 47 states and a two-year term in New Hampshire, Rhode Island, and Vermont, has several important roles and powers.

1. **Chief of state**. The governor is the chief of state. He or she represents the entire state, including all three branches of state government, in dealings with other states, with the federal government, and with foreign governments. The governor also plays a highly visible role as chief of state during a state emergency or natural disaster. The growth of television in covering state government has elevated the importance of the governor's role as chief of state.

   a. **Intergovernmental relations**. Governors spend considerable time on intergovernmental relations. They attend meetings of the

National Governors' Association and regional governors' associations, work with each other on common problems and interstate relations, appear before congressional committees, work with the federal bureaucracy, and meet with the president several times a year. About two-thirds of the states maintain full-time offices in Washington.

b. **Ambassadorial role.** Governors are increasingly building relationships with foreign countries to encourage economic development in their states. Most governors travel abroad once or twice a year on trade missions. Some 44 states have about 120 offices in foreign countries.

2. **Chief legislator.** The governor has traditionally been the source of many proposals written into law. As such, the governor has a leadership role in identifying public needs, promoting initiatives, establishing priorities, and building coalitions to support policies and legislative enactments. Governors have some specific powers in this regard.

a. **Item veto.** Governors in 43 states may veto items in legislation, such as specific appropriations in a large appropriation measure. This authority enhances the governor's bargaining power with legislators.

b. **Sessions.** Governors in all states can call special sessions of the legislature. In about one-quarter of the states, the governor alone can determine the agenda of the session. A considerable amount of the work of a biennial state legislature is accomplished in special session.

c. **Budget.** Governors in most states now have significant authority to prepare the proposed state budget. The document sent to the legislature bears the governor's imprimatur. The main debates in a session typically revolve around the proposed budget.

3. **Chief administrator.** The governor is in charge of the executive branch. Most governors can appoint the heads of executive departments, subject to confirmation by the state senate. Cabinet officers serve at the governor's pleasure. Governors also have some specific tools in directing the administrative branch:

a. **Personnel and fiscal controls.** The agencies that oversee personnel and financial affairs are normally under the governor's direct authority.

b. **Reorganization.** Governors in about half the states can shuffle bureaus and agencies among the executive departments without legislative approval.

c. **Executive orders.** A governor can order a department or agency to take almost any action that is not prohibited by law.

4. **Plural executives.** However, unlike the U.S. government, most states have a plural executive system. In addition to the governor, there are usually other independently elected officials, including an elected lieutenant governor (42 states), secretary of state (36 states), attorney general (43 states), treasurer (38 states), auditor (25 states), comptroller (10 states), education commissioner (16 states), agriculture commissioner (12 states), labor commissioner (4 states), and insurance commissioner (8 states). Only Maine, New Hampshire, New Jersey, and Tennessee have the governor as the sole elected executive official.

5. **Commander-in-chief.** The governor commands the state militia (i.e., National Guard) unless it is called into active-duty federal service by the president. National Guard units commonly assist communities during natural disasters and occasionally during riots. The governor is also in charge of the state police and state home guard, if these institutions have been established by the state.

6. **Chief of party.** The governor is normally the head of his or her state political party and relies on party teammates in the legislature to help enact his or her programs. Governors campaign for party members, help raise campaign funds, and provide direction for party policy.

G. **State Courts.** State courts (including county and municipal courts) handle more than 99 percent of all judicial business in the United States. About 98 million new cases were filed in state courts in 1989.

1. **Trial courts.** (Local courts are fully part of the state court system in most states, and are here treated as part of state courts.) To deal with

their workload, the states have two types of trial courts, in contrast to the federal courts, which use only one trial court.

a. **Trial courts of limited jurisdiction.** These courts (usually county and municipal) hear minor criminal and civil cases. As an example, they may take cases (misdemeanors) for which the maximum penalty is less than one year in jail. The volume of business in these courts is huge. In Maine, over 300,000 cases were disposed of in 1989, enough to have one of every four Mainers involved in a court action.

b. **Trial courts of general jurisdiction.** These courts can take any case, but usually hear the more serious cases, such as felonies, for which the maximum penalty normally exceeds one year in prison. These courts typically empanel trial juries (usually called petit juries).

2. **Intermediate appellate court.** Thirty-eight states now have an intermediate appeals court that hears first appeals from the trial courts of general jurisdiction. The losing party in a trial-court case always has at least one right of appeal.

3. **The state high court.** This court, usually called supreme court, is the final appeals court in a state. Seven state high courts have nine justices, 26 have seven justices, and 19 have five justices. (Oklahoma and Texas each have two high courts, one for criminal appeals and one for civil appeals.)

a. **Judicial review.** A state supreme court may void acts of the legislature or a local government as being in violation of the state constitution or U.S. Constitution. It may also declare a federal law unconstitutional, subject to review by the U.S. Supreme Court.

b. **Advisory opinions.** The state supreme court usually has a power to hand down advisory opinions, at the request of the legislature or the governor, on pending issues.

c. **Administration.** The state supreme court oversees the administration of justice in the state as well as settling appeals. For instance, it hears complaints about judicial conduct. Day-to-day administration is ordi-

narily carried out by a state court administrative office.

d. **Rights protection.** State supreme courts have in recent years focused new attention on the bills of rights that are part of state constitutions. In some states, they have extended those protections beyond the minimum level set by the U.S. Supreme Court. For instance, the California Supreme Court has extended the right of free speech to shopping malls, in contrast to the U.S. Supreme Court's holding that free speech is not protected in those areas because they are private property.

4. **Judicial selection.** Unlike federal judges, most state judges must face the voters. For example, the following selection procedures pertain to high court justices:

a. **Election.** In 25 states, justices are elected directly by the people on a partisan or nonpartisan ballot.

b. **Missouri plan.** In 14 states, justices are chosen by some form of the "Missouri plan." Under this plan, also called the "merit plan," a special commission proposes nominees to the governor, who then appoints a justice to the court from the list. The justice serves a fixed term (usually six years). At the end of the term, his or her name is placed on the ballot, and voters decide whether the justice is to be retained on the court. If retained, the justice is subject to a retention vote at the end of each fixed term.

c. **Gubernatorial appointment.** In seven states, the justices are appointed by the governor, subject to confirmation by the state senate or a special council.

d. **Legislative appointment.** In four states, the justices are selected by the legislature.

III. **Local governments.** The main types of local governments are counties, municipalities, townships, school districts, and special districts.

A. **Counties.** In all, the states contain some 3,042 counties. They are found in all states except Rhode Island and Connecticut. Rural counties maintain records, such as deeds and birth and marriage certificates, and handle law enforcement and road maintenance. Urban counties generally perform these functions, and often administer health, welfare, and recreation services as well. County officials are elected by the residents of their counties.

B. **Municipalities.** The nation's 19,205 municipalities (which include cities and, legally, some townships, boroughs, and villages) provide basic services—police, fire, streets, sewage, sanitation, housing, transportation, job training, economic development, and parks and recreation. About half of them administer health and welfare services and public education. In the case of the others, welfare is handled by state or county governments, and education is administered through an independent school district. Municipal officials are elected by the residents of their city.

C. **Townships.** There are 16,691 townships, located mostly in the northeast and north central states. These units are subdivisions of counties, with about the same responsibilities as counties or municipalities in some states. In some rural areas and Midwest states, townships perform few functions. Some are little more than road districts. Township officials are elected by the residents of their township.

D. **School districts.** The nation's 14,741 independent school districts provide primary and secondary education. Each is governed by a board elected by the residents of the district. School districts ordinarily levy a property tax to fund education, although a few states allow school districts to levy an income or payroll tax. The state provides additional funding, which, in some cases, amounts to three-quarters or more of a school district's budget.

E. **Special Districts.** The nation's 29,487 special districts are usually single-purpose governments established to provide a specific function, such as natural resources, mass transit, fire protection, sewage disposal, water supply, community colleges, or mosquito abatement, in a geographic area that may embrace several municipalities and even counties. Special districts are usually financed by user fees. Some districts, especially in metropolitan areas, also rely on property taxes (e.g., some sewer districts) and sales or income taxes (e.g., some mass transit districts). Some districts receive federal and state aid. A district is usually governed by a board appointed by the local governments within the district, although many are governed by a board elected directly by the residents of the district.

IV. **Structures of local government.** Two distinguishing features of local governments, as contrasted with the state and federal governments, are that many of them have weak or nonexistent executives, and lack a separation-of-powers arrangement.

A. **County commissions.** Counties have traditionally been "headless" or "hydra-headed" governments. Their typical form has been an elected board of commissioners or supervisors, which works with several other elected officials with specific functions, such as a sheriff and a recorder of deeds. Some urban counties now employ full-time managers with general executive responsibilities. The county board ordinarily exercises legislative and executive powers, and sometimes quasi-judicial powers.

B. **Municipal government.** Municipalities have four general types of government arrangements.

1. **Weak mayor/council.** This form predominates among smaller communities (less than 25,000 people). The mayor is weak in administrative power, and several other elected officials, such as a city treasurer and city clerk, share executive authority. The council is composed of citizens who usually remain in office for only one or two terms, and receive little or no compensation.

2. **Strong mayor/council.** This type is characteristic of larger cities; nearly all cities over 500,000 people use it. The mayor is in charge of the executive branch and has broad appointive power, much like a strong governor and the president. The council is likely to be composed of career politicians, but the mayor usually has a veto power.

3. **Council/manager.** This form began in Staunton, Virginia, in 1908. The elected council appoints a professional manager to head the executive branch. The manager serves at the council's pleasure. The mayor is usually weak. The arrangement is used in a majority of cities having between 25,000 and 250,000 people and is especially popular in suburbs and in growing communities. However, a few large cities, such as Dallas, Texas, and Phoenix, Arizona, have a council/manager system.

4. **Commission.** In this form, a group of elected commissioners acts as both the legislative body and the executive department of the city. The

fusion of legislative-executive functions in the hands of the same officials often impedes political accountability. The commission form, once popular, has undergone a long decline in usage. It is used in about 4 percent of municipalities.

C. **Municipal elections**. Many localities elect their executive and legislative officials under arrangements different from the election of state and federal officials.

   1. **Nonpartisanship**. About 70 percent of municipalities hold officially nonpartisan elections. This often shifts power away from the parties toward voter organizations, neighborhood groups, and private organizations, such as business associations.

   2. **Partisanship**. Party politics still remains in most large cities in the North and East. Communities with the mayor/council form are more likely to have partisan elections than those with the council/manager form, which is historically associated with nonpartisanship.

   3. **Electoral districting**. The most common method of election to city council is at-large; candidates are elected by the entire city. Ward election alone exists in only 13 percent of the nation's cities. Ward election tends to exist in cities with partisan elections and a mayor/council form. However, because racial and ethnic minorities tend not to do well in at-large elections, there has been growing pressure for ward elections, including pressure exerted under the U.S. Voting Rights Act. About one-quarter of cities elect some members of council by ward and others at large.

V. **Metropolitics**. Some of the major challenges of local government lie in the tensions between central cities and their suburbs.

A. **MSAs**. The U.S. Bureau of the Census defines a Metropolitan Statistical Area (MSA) as a city of 50,000 or more people together with adjacent counties closely tied, socio-economically, to the central city.

B. **Distribution**. In the mid-1980s, 31 percent of Americans lived in central cities; 45 percent in suburbs; and 24 percent in areas outside MSAs.

C. **Suburbs and central cities contrasted**. Suburban cities and unincorporated areas are increasing in population

at about twice the rate of central cities. Their proportion of black residents is about 5 percent, compared to 21 percent for cities. They have disproportionate numbers of white-collar employees and college graduates. Nearly three-quarters of suburban households own their own home, in comparison to about half of the households in central cities.

D. **Where differences are greatest**. Differences between central cities and suburbs are greatest in the Northeast. In the South and West, the contrasts are less sharp. Likewise, differences between cities and suburbs are greatest in the larger metropolitan areas, less so in smaller metropolitan areas.

E. **Finances**. Central cities often raise and spend more money per capita than suburbs, especially for such functions as police and welfare. However, suburbs tend to spend more on education.

VI. **State and local finance**. State and local governments finance most domestic functions in the United States, and their revenues have been growing faster than federal revenues. In 1988, state and local governments raised $767 billion in revenue; the federal government raised $1,012 billion. State and local governments spent $981 billion in 1988; the federal government spent $1,214 billion.

A. **Income tax**. Forty-one states have a broad-based personal income tax, and three states have a limited personal income tax. About 3,592 local governments in 11 states also levy a personal income tax. Forty-five states levy a corporate income tax.

B. **Sales tax**. Forty-five states have a general sales tax. Some 8,800 local governments in 31 states also levy a sales tax.

C. **Excise tax**. States levy excise taxes on such goods as motor fuels, cigarettes, and alcoholic beverages. (An excise tax is a tax on the manufacture, sale, or use of specific articles.)

D. **Property tax**. Property taxes are a major source of revenue for municipalities, counties, townships, and school districts.

E. **User charges**. User fees, such as those for automobiles, parks, and other services, are becoming a larger part of state and, especially, local revenues.

F. **Severance taxes**. Thirty-eight states levy severance taxes on such natural resources as oil, gas, coal, and timber. (A severance tax is a removal tax.)

G. **Budget limits**. Unlike the U.S. government, 49 states have a constitutional or statutory requirement to balance the state budget. Most state constitutions contain various provisions intended to impose fiscal discipline on state and local officials.

Historical Perspective

I. **Significant trends**. The origins of state and local government lie in the colonial era, during which time Americans asserted more and more rights of self-government and developed such key ideas as written constitutions, bills of rights, and the separation of powers. Prior to the 1930s, state and local governments raised some three-quarters of the nation's tax revenue and financed most government functions. Over the centuries, however, state and local governments have undergone some major changes. Stressed here are trends most relevant to the actions of these governments today.

A. **Constitutional change**. Thirty-one states have written more than one constitution. State constitutions reflect the historic time period in which they are prepared and adopted.

1. **Legislative dominance, 1776-1870**. Generally, state constitutions during this period stressed the pre-eminence of the legislature. The governor was very weak. In the first constitutions (1776-1790), governors in most cases were chosen by the legislature and served a one-year term.

   a. **Elected executives**. In the 1830s, as new executive officers were needed, the states made them subject in some cases to legislative election, but in most instances to popular election, which was an idea promoted by the Jacksonians. Currently, for example, 43 states elect their attorney general, a practice that dates from this period.

   b. **Decline of legislatures**. In the 1860s and 1870s, many legislatures became afflicted with corruption. Scandals erupted as industrialization and immigration led to efforts to win favors from legislatures. State voters began to curtail legislative authority.

2. **Boards and commissions, 1870-1920**. The general strategy was to restrict legislative authority by placing more power in independent boards and commissions.

   a. **Membership**. The typical board was filled by gubernatorial appointment, but board members had terms of office exceeding that of the governor.

   b. **Bipartisanship**. Most states required boards to have some members from each party.

   c. **Diffused power**. The effect of placing power in boards and commissions was that some states, such as New York, had 116 such units. State political power often became diffused and uncoordinated.

3. **Coordination and capacity, 1920-1990**. Constitutional reform in this most recent period has focused on strengthening the governor's office and state institutions generally, and on improving the ability of state agencies to respond to problems and provide modern services.

   a. **Gubernatorial strength**. Governors gained longer terms (i.e., four years), the ability to serve successive terms, executive budget power, more veto power, broad authority over executive appointments (leading to the formation of the governor's cabinet), more staff assistance, and more planning capabilities. Most states have also reduced the number of independently elected executive officials and independent boards and commissions.

   b. **Legislative reform**. Following the U.S. Supreme Court's reapportionment decision in *Baker v. Carr* (1962), constitutional provisions regulating legislatures were modified, mainly to reduce limitations on such matters as salary and length of sessions. Most states moved from biennial to annual legislative sessions. Other reforms have included larger and more professional staffs, more efficient legislative rules and procedures, better budget-review abilities, and tightened ethics rules.

   c. **Judicial reform**. State courts have generally been made more centralized and better coordinated, with fewer different types of courts. States have adopted court administrative offices to oversee court management, including personnel and fiscal operations. More emphasis has been placed on merit selection of judges, increased salaries and terms of office, better methods of disciplining judges, improved jury selection, supplying courts with modern technology, providing alternative means of dispute resolution, and state financing of local courts.

d. **Bureaucracy**. Civil service systems have been established in all states, although not all state employees have been brought under them, and emphasis has been placed on better pay and training for public employees. Furthermore, very recent U.S. Supreme Court decisions have restricted the ability of governors and mayors to hire and fire public employees for political purposes (i.e., patronage).

e. **Constitutional commissions**. Twelve states have adopted new constitutions since World War II. Many more states have used constitutional revision commissions, whose members are named by the governor and legislature. Commissions report to the legislature, except in Florida, where their recommendations, in certain cases, go directly to the voters. As a result, most states have substantially revised their constitutions.

B. **Fiscal and policy reform**. Generally, states have diversified their revenue sources, made their tax systems more progressive, and supplied more aid to local governments.

1. **Nineteenth century**. The early years found the states engaged in economic development, such as building roads and canals. However, most financial responsibilities were carried by localities, particularly toward the end of the century as urbanization took hold. In 1902, local governments spent five dollars for every one dollar expended by state governments.

2. **Intergovernmental aid**. State reform was partly assisted and stimulated by rising intergovernmental aid in this century. Federal fiscal aid to state and local governments grew from less than 2 percent of state and local expenditures in 1930 to about 10 percent in 1950, and to a high of 26.5 percent in 1978. State grants-in-aid to localities,

which comprised only 6 percent of local revenues in 1902, grew to a level of 55 percent of local revenues in 1988. State aid represented 42.9 percent of state spending from all state funds in 1990. Federal and state aid have generally been accompanied by policy requirements (mandates), some of which foster state and local reform.

3. **States as the stronger state-local partner**. The twentieth century has seen the states become the dominant fiscal partner in state-local relations. The main reason is the rise of broad-based taxes coming on top of the diversification of state economies. General sales taxes began in 1932 in Mississippi and are in use in 45 states; income taxes began in Hawaii in 1901 (as a territory) and Wisconsin in 1911, and are important revenue raisers in 41 states. Municipalities and counties continue to rely mainly on the property tax, mostly because their revenue-raising authority is limited by state law.

4. **State assumption of local functions**. The states have taken over many functions formerly handled locally, including welfare.

C. **Political reform**. State and local governments have experienced several waves of reform since 1789.

1. **Early democratization**. Most states gradually expanded voting rights during the early 19th century, especially during the Jacksonian era (1829-1837). By 1856, all of the original 13 states had abolished property qualifications for voting in general elections. Nearly everywhere, voting was confined to men, but statewide woman's suffrage began in Wyoming in 1869. Blacks were denied the right to vote as slaves and then as free persons in the South after Reconstruction, but were legally permitted to vote in most other states.

2. **Rise of the political parties**. The Jacksonian era produced an emphasis on popular voting, party competition, and patronage in government. The parties sought to win as many elective offices as possible, which often had the effect of fragmenting governmental power in states and localities. Executives were legally weak.

3. **Rise of political machines**. After the Civil War, many states and localities saw the rise of powerful party organizations led by a political "boss," who was not always an elected official. These

organizations, which took four forms, were developed, in part, to counteract the splintering of public power.

a. **Rings.** The early organizations were usually called "rings," and consisted of coalitions of public officials, patronage holders, and corporate interests. Essentially, they sought to raid public treasuries. A leading example was the Tweed Ring in New York City. In that case, **William ("Boss") Tweed** (1823-1878) and several city officials defrauded the city of at least $30 million.

b. **Urban "machines."** These party organizations became powerful in many big cities, mostly in the North and Midwest. Examples were the "Hague machine" in Jersey City, which lasted until 1949, and the "Daley machine" in Chicago, which lasted until 1976. The machines relied greatly on immigrant voters who supported machine candidates in return for jobs and other favors. Funds to provide services often came from businesses that wanted government franchises and contracts. Corruption was sometimes extreme. The New York City Courthouse, for example, was completed in 1871 at a cost of $8 million, although the estimate for the work was $350,000.

c. **Courthouse gangs.** These organizations emerged mainly in counties in the South, and consisted of local white elites, elected and non-elected, who ran county affairs and provided support for elite rule and white supremacy statewide.

d. **Corporate state parties.** Industrialization produced large and powerful corporations that often succeeded in dominating state governments, mainly through payoffs. Corporations focused on state governments because they were the principal regulators of commerce. Corporate dominance of state government often produced conflict between state government and local governments dominated by immigrant-based machines.

4. **Progressive period (1890-1925).** Many reforms that continue to shape state and local politics were instituted during this period. The Progressives generally emphasized governmental compe-tence, administrative neutrality, citizen participation, and government regulation of big business.

a. **The party primary.** The primary is used in all states to nominate candidates for public office, though its operation differs from state to state. Some states restrict participation to registered party members; others permit voters registered in different parties to participate in any party's primary.

b. **Initiative, referendum, recall.** These instruments were adopted, mostly in the West, to allow voters to legislate directly, and to remove officials from office under certain conditions.

c. **Business regulation.** State regulation of business, especially to protect employees and consumers, began in earnest during this period. However, the U.S. Supreme Court overturned many state initiatives.

d. **Municipal reform.** During this period, such urban reforms as council/manager government, nonpartisanship, at-large elections, and home rule began to spread throughout the country.

e. **Civil service.** Civil service reforms also began to be introduced into state and local governments, as well as the federal government.

5. **Post-World War II era.** The post-war era has been the single most concentrated period of state and local reform in American history. A distinguishing characteristic of this period has been the role of the federal government in promoting state and local reform. Given that many reforms of this period have been discussed above, we focus here on federally induced reforms and certain overall trends.

a. **Federally induced reforms.** The federal government helped to bring about certain key reforms in state institutions.

(1) **Legislative apportionment.** In *Baker v. Carr* (1962), the U.S. Supreme Court held that apportionment of state legislatures falls under the "equal protection" clause of the U.S. Constitution. In *Reynolds v. Sims* (1964), the Court

ordered legislative districts to be apportioned on a "one person, one vote" basis. States are now obliged to apportion their legislative bodies so that legislative districts have nearly equal populations.

(a) **Numerical changes.** Every state had to make some adjustments in its apportionment; in some cases, the changes were dramatic. For example, Vermont had assigned one House seat to every town. In 1960, 12 percent of the state's population could elect a majority of members of the Vermont House of Representatives. Under rules set out by the Supreme Court, no less than 45 percent of a state's population can elect a majority of either house of the state legislature.

(b) **Political impacts.** Reapportionment invigorated the politics of many states. Urban and suburban areas gained at the expense of rural districts. A larger number of younger, better educated legislators began to serve in state assemblies. States began to treat urban areas more fairly than in the past, when rural representatives were inordinately powerful.

(c) **Party balance.** Democrats gained some seats in northern legislatures because of the historic underrepresentation of cities. Republicans gained seats in southern legislatures as urban and suburban areas received more legislative seats. Neither party was decisively advantaged nationally because of reapportionment.

(2) **Federal civil rights policy.** Federal action to broaden the suffrage and to protect constitutional rights has significantly affected state affairs.

(a) **Constitutional amendments.** Amendments to the U.S. Constitution have broadened the electorates of the states. The Amendments include the Fifteenth (guaranteeing the right to vote to former slaves), the Nineteenth (providing for woman suffrage), and the Twenty-sixth (providing suffrage to persons 18 years of age). In each of these cases, however, a number of states or a majority of states had already provided for these voting rights.

(b) **The white primary.** The U.S. Supreme Court, in *Smith v. Allwright* (1944), opened the electoral process in the southern states by banning the white primary. Until that decision, Southern states permitted the Democratic party to prohibit blacks from voting in the party's primaries, which were tantamount to elections in one-party Democratic states. The Court has also prohibited apportionment arrangements that deny blacks "equal protection of the laws" by creating districts that inhibit the election of black legislators.

(c) **Desegregation.** In *Brown v. Board of Education* (1954), the U.S. Supreme Court held that segregated school systems violate the equal protection clause. That decision, and later congressional action in the 1960s, led to massive desegregation of schools in the southern states.

(d) **Voting rights.** In passing the Voting Rights Act of 1965, the Congress ended the practice of relying mostly on the courts to enforce voting rights. This measure concentrated on several states and areas in states where fewer than half of the adults had been registered for the 1964 election, and which required literacy or other tests for voting. The Act basically suspended such tests, and authorized federal officials to determine voter qualifications. Amendments in 1970 and 1975 extended the act's coverage to minority language groups and, thereby, to more states.

b. **Popularly induced reforms**. Although participation in state and local elections generally remains lower than in presidential elections, this period has seen a dramatic increase in voter use of initiatives and referendums to reform state and local governments. Where these tools are not available, there has been a dramatic increase in public interest-group activity and in the use of citizen commissions. Constitutional revision also has been driven substantially by voter pressure.

c. **Public employee unions**. Although labor unions are declining in the private sector, state and local public employee unions and related organizations have gained considerable strength in many parts of the country.

d. **Governmental activism**. Generally, policy activism now characterizes all state governments as well as many local governments. Counties, for example, which have traditionally been viewed as sleepy and nearly invisible governments, now provide many services; and some urban counties cover larger territories and have bigger budgets than some small states.

Contemporary Perspective

Having been overshadowed by the federal government for much of this century, the states have reemerged as strong and often innovative governments having generally positive public support. This resurgence is largely the product of a long period of reform stretching from World War II to the present. Similarly, most local governments have reemerged as strong and innovative governments. Although attention often focuses on the problems of large cities such as New York and Los Angeles, most of the nation's 38,938 counties, municipalities, and townships operate quite well. When asked in a 1989 national poll: Which level of government do you think spends your tax dollars most wisely? 36 percent of Americans named local government, 20 percent said state government, and 11 percent cited the federal government. Key questions facing Americans about state and local governments include the following:

I. **Trustworthiness of state and local governments**. The federal government came to overshadow state and local governments in the twentieth century in large part because Americans came to see the federal government during the Great Depression as being better able to raise revenue, solve major national problems, provide for public welfare, and protect rights. There is, therefore, some ambivalence about the resurgence of the states

because of fears that states and their local governments will roll back reforms of the past sixty-odd years. Such a reversal is unlikely, however, for several reasons:

A. **Federal floors**. Existing federal legislation and judicial decisions impose many requirements on state and local governments in such areas as public welfare and rights protection. These requirements, which did not exist in the past, will continue in the future and can only be rolled back by the federal government itself.

B. **Federal weaknesses**. At the same time, the problems of relying too greatly on the federal government, as opposed to a more balanced reliance on all governments in the federal system, began to become more evident by the early 1970s, as the Vietnam War and Watergate undermined confidence in the federal government; as stagflation in the 1970s and budget deficits in the 1980s raised questions about the federal government's ability to manage the economy and its own spending; and as the U.S. Supreme Court slowed the pace of federal rights protection.

C. **Continuing state and local reform**. What has often been called the "modernization" of state and local governments is likely to continue for several reasons.

1. **Standing reform**. In addition to federal requirements, existing state constitutional and statutory reform requirements are not likely to be reversed in any significant way.

2. **Reform focus**. State and local governments are the focus of many reform efforts by groups seeking to achieve objectives in those arenas that they cannot achieve in the federal arena. For example, as the American Civil Liberties Union has begun losing more than half of its appeals to the U.S. Supreme Court for the first time in more than 25 years, it has turned increasingly to state courts for rights protection.

3. **Professionalization**. Some states are now acknowledged to have better and more competent civil service systems and employees than the federal government. Generally, the professionalization of state governments and many local governments has made those governments more competent, innovative, and effective.

4. **Diversification**. Most importantly, the diversification of state and local political systems since the 1930s makes those governments much more responsive to diverse voices than in the past.

a. **Political**. White supremacy is nearly dead in the South, and only vestiges of machine politics survive in some northern cities. Two-party competition is more vigorous than in the past, and many new interest groups, such as labor, teacher organizations, consumer groups, and environmental organizations, have significant voices in state and local government. State and local government officials have more diverse backgrounds and higher levels of education than was true in the past.

b. **Economic**. State economies are much more diverse today. No longer can a single company dominate a state, as, for example, in the past ability of the Anaconda Copper Company to dominate Montana. Furthermore, though business groups remain powerful in state and local politics, they are themselves diverse and often divided on issues, thus weakening the strength of any particular business interest.

c. **Fiscal**. All states have diversified their revenue sources in order to raise more revenue and provide more protection for their budgets against fluctuations in the economy.

d. **Social**. The assimilation of older ethnic groups into American society, the arrival of new immigrants, and the various social revolutions of the past quarter-century have permeated every state's social system.

5. **Differences among states**. Of course, considerable differences exist among the 50 states and the nation's numerous local governments. Thus, some will live up to one's ideas of good government; others will not.

6. **Liberal and conservative ambivalence**. Generally, for liberals, ambivalence about state resurgence arises from fears that the states will never be as progressive as was the federal government during the New Deal and Great Society eras. Liberals point with concern to a state like Mississippi and a city like Yonkers, New York. Generally, for conservatives, ambivalence about state resurgence arises from fears that the states are becoming too much like the federal government was during the New Deal and Great Society eras. Conservatives

point with concern to a state like California and a city like New York City.

II. **Problems accompanying reform**. The resurgence of the states has had many benefits, but reforms also produce problems. For example:

A. **Rising costs**. As state and local governments provide more services and perform more functions, taxes and fees also increase. The public's expectation of performance, however, is often higher than its tolerance for taxation, thus producing periodic tax revolts and concern about waste in government.

B. **Legislative careerism**. As legislatures become more professionalized, with annual sessions, more staff, and higher salaries, more legislators become career politicians who, like the "Tuesday-Thursday club" in Congress, still legislate part time because they spend more time raising money and campaigning for reelection. Concern about careerism has, thus far, led voters in three states to impose term limits on legislators.

C. **Gubernatorial fund-raising**. As governors become more important and powerful, so too do the costs of gubernatorial elections, which now reach astronomical sums in large states.

D. **Bureaucracy**. As state and local governments perform more functions, the size and costs of their bureaucracies grow as well. Pension funds for state and local government employees, for example, total nearly $800 billion.

E. **Waste and corruption**. Growth in government creates opportunities for waste and corruption as public officials become less attentive to specific programs, come under pressure to fund more activities, and are approached by more interests that have big stakes in state and local government action. A zoning variance or tax abatement, for example, may be worth millions of dollars to a corporation. Recently, the federal government has become involved in prosecuting state and local officials for corruption.

III. **Financial costs of reform**. Virtually all states and most sizable local governments have the institutional capacity to be modern, full-service governments. Many, however, fall short on fiscal capacity. The single greatest pressure facing state and local governments is financial. This pressure stems from several factors:

A. **Economic downturns.** Most state and local revenue systems are more vulnerable to economic downturns than is the federal government's revenue system.

B. **No forward shifting.** Unlike the federal government, state and local governments cannot shift current service costs to future generations through deficit spending. State and local borrowing is generally limited to capital projects, such as roads and wastewater treatment plants, which can be financed equitably by borrowing because the projects benefit present and future generations. The federal government's debt in 1988 was some $2.7 trillion (53.6 percent of GNP); total state and local government debt was about $755 billion (15.5 percent of GNP).

C. **No upward shifting.** The federal government can shift costs to state and local governments through unfunded mandates. These are legislative and judicial requirements that state and local governments perform and pay for certain functions. State and local governments cannot shift costs to the federal government through mandates. State governments can, however, shift some costs to local governments through unfunded mandates. They can also pass some federal mandates on to local governments. These governments, however, cannot pass costs on to other governments through mandates, although local governments can sometimes shift costs onto the private sector.

D. **Rising mandates.** Unfunded and partially-funded federal mandates have increased significantly since the late 1960s.

E. **Declining federal aid.** Federal aid has declined from 26.5 percent to 18.2 percent of state and local spending since 1978.

F. **Expanding social welfare.** Most of the nation's major social welfare programs are funded by the federal and state governments. When the Congress expands these programs, the federal government often finances some of its share through deficit spending and unfunded mandates. States, however, must raise taxes and/or reduce services. Medicaid alone, for example, equalled 13.5 percent of state spending in 1990, and is growing rapidly. Because Medicaid is a federal-state program, states have only a limited ability to control costs; hence, states tend to reduce other services, such as education, which is mostly financed and controlled by state and local governments.

G. **Declining tax comity.** In the past, federal tax law made many concessions to state and local tax systems. Because of its financial problems, however, the federal government has curtailed these concessions (e.g., state and local sales-tax payments are no longer deductible from federal personal income-tax liability).

H. **Intergovernmental tax competition.** Increasingly, the federal, state, and local governments must compete for tax revenue.

I. **Interjurisdictional tax competition.** In various circumstances, state and local governments may find themselves in competition between and among themselves when they impose taxes.

1. **State and local taxes.** State and local taxes are constrained to some extent by competition between states and local governments. A city income tax, for example, may induce some residents to move elsewhere. If a state's sales-tax rate is higher than those of its neighbors, many residents will purchase goods in the neighboring states.

2. **Driving up taxes.** Competition, however, can also drive up state and local spending because governments must improve services, such as highways and schools, in order to be economically competitive.

J. **Differing economies.** Some states have strong, diverse economies; others have comparatively weak economies that rely greatly on one economic sector, such as agriculture.

K. **Tax revolts.** State and local governments tend to be more affected by citizen tax revolts than the federal government is, in part because state and local officials are closer at hand, state constitutional and statutory rules make it easier for citizens to effect tax changes, and many state and local levies—such as sales taxes, user fees, and property taxes—are very visible to citizens. Although the federal income tax and local property tax are the two taxes most disliked by Americans, citizens can usually restrain the property tax more easily.

L. **The fiscal squeeze.** In short, state and local governments experience many fiscal pressures quite unlike those of the federal government. These pressures require hard choices about tax and service levels, choices that frequently result in severe electoral punishment for governors and mayors.

IV. **Responsiveness of state and local reforms.** One of the classic arguments for state and local governance is that these governments are "closer to the people." This argument was hard to accept when many states were dominated by big corporations and many localities by courthouse gangs and political machines. Today, though, the classic argument may have new vitality.

A. **State and local providers.** Because state and local governments deliver nearly all domestic public services (e.g., police and fire protection) and administer most federal domestic programs, they are, in fact, closest to the people. For example, they must design the "workfare" programs required by the U.S. Family Support Act of 1988 and enroll welfare recipients in them.

B. **Policy success largely determined by state and local governments.** A policy idea that seems good on paper in Washington or in a state capital may not work in reality. In turn, states and localities do not always do a good job in implementing policy. Either way, state and local governments largely determine the success of most domestic policies. Therefore, they also tend to be criticized for policy failures, whether or not they originated the ideas.

C. **The limits of spending.** The prevailing view of recent generations that increasing public expenditures can eliminate social problems has been called into question by the persistence and sometimes aggravation of social problems despite higher spending. So long as this view prevailed, the federal government was asked to increase social spending. Although social programs certainly need money to operate, policy makers have become less sure about how much money is enough for particular programs, who should finance programs (i.e., public vs. private), and how money is best spent.

1. **Inflationary spending.** Sometimes public expenditures increase costs by spurring inflation and pushing up interest rates. For example, "infusions" of federal and state money into the health-care industry since 1965 have contributed to the higher-than-average inflation of medical costs.

2. **Beneficial spending.** At the same time, spending can reduce costs. A dollar well spent on education, for example, can produce a productive citizen who does not need public assistance or end up in prison.

D. **Behavioral alternatives to spending.** State and local governments are at the center of this debate because they spend the money for programs. Therefore, they are pressured to find alternatives to more spending that will give taxpayers "more bang for the buck." Several trends seem evident.

1. **Prevention.** Much like the way individuals exercise more and eat better to stay healthy, state and local governments are placing more emphasis on preventive programs, such as early childhood intervention.

2. **Regulation.** State and local governments are strengthening regulations to protect public health (e.g., anti-smoking ordinances), public safety (e.g., drunk-driver road checks), the environment (e.g., recycling laws), and so on. These measures have the added benefit of saving money in the long run.

3. **Fines and penalties.** State and local governments are increasing fines and penalties to discourage destructive behavior (e.g., drunk driving, highway speeding, and harmful waste disposal).

4. **User fees and charges.** State and local governments are imposing more user fees, not merely to raise revenue, but also to promote equity (by making those who benefit from a service pay for it) and to regulate behavior. For example, higher water and sewer fees pay for cleaner water and encourage citizens to conserve water. The major disadvantage of fees is that they fall more heavily on the poor. This is being counteracted to some extent by "lifeline" programs that subsidize services for the poor.

5. **Rationing.** A more draconian measure is service rationing. Oregon, for example, is rationing Medicaid services because health-care costs are outrunning the funds provided by the federal government and state taxpayers.

6. **Community alternatives.** State and local governments are experimenting with community alternatives to traditional institutionalization. For example, putting people in prison is more expensive than home confinement, halfway houses, and community service. The public, however, usually wants to "lock them up" and

"get them off the streets." With increasing drug crime and stiffer sentencing rules, corrections is one of the fastest growing areas of state spending.

7. **Institutional redesign**. State and local governments are experimenting with new institutional arrangements. In education, magnet schools, parental choice, vouchers, tuition tax-credits for private-school attendance, and home instruction are leading and controversial examples.

8. **Citizen involvement**. More emphasis also is being placed on citizen involvement because schools cannot work effectively without parent support; the environment cannot be adequately protected unless citizens change their behavior; and crime cannot be reduced effectively unless community residents perform watchdog services and cooperate with police.

V. **Possible alternatives to rising taxes or fees**. Most state and local governments still feel the ripple effects of the tax revolt of 1978 in which California voters initiated Proposition 13, a property-tax limitation measure. Hence, even though most state and local governments have raised taxes since 1978, they also have looked for less painful ways to raise revenue and cut costs. Three leading examples are economic development, privatization, and burden sharing.

A. **Economic development**. For most states and many local governments, economic development is their leading priority. An expanding economy gives a state or local government more revenue without raising taxes. By itself, though, growth does not always provide enough revenue to cover the costs of new or expanded services required by growth. One aspect of development today is global competition. In 1978, the same year as the California tax revolt and the high point of federal aid, the National Governors' Association created a standing committee on international trade, signaling the onset of aggressive state and local efforts to attract foreign investment and tourists, and to promote the export of products made in states.

B. **Privatization**. To reduce costs, many state and local governments are experimenting with the privatization of certain public services and with public-private partnerships. This trend is especially true of local governments because many local services (e.g., trash collection) are amenable to privatization. A frequently cited example is Scottsdale, Arizona, which contracts with a private company to provide the city's fire

protection. In other cases, both government and the private sector participate in an activity, such as construction and operation of a waste-water treatment plant.

1. **Residential community associations**. A little known example is that 9 to 12 percent of Americans live in largely self-financed private communities that are not public units of government. One is Reston, Virginia, with a population of more than 60,000. Residents of these communities pay the same federal, state, and local taxes as everyone else, but they also pay mandatory "dues" to their association, which then provides and pays for their streets, sidewalks, security, landscaping, recreation facilities, and the like.

2. **Shopping malls**. The business equivalent of residential associations are shopping malls and business parks. The rise of malls and business parks is privatizing "Main Street" America.

C. **Burden sharing**. In order to reduce or stabilize costs, local governments, especially, increasingly enter cooperative agreements with each other to provide services. At times, however, burden sharing becomes a "shell game" in which governments simply try to shift costs to other governments (e.g., from local government to state government.)

VI. **The intergovernmental context of state and local governance**. Because state and local governments are part of a network of 83,217 governments, their successes and failures depend to a great extent on intergovernmental relations.

A. **Federal-state relations less cooperative**. Relations between the federal and state governments have become less cooperative since the mid-1970s because of diminished federal aid and increased federal mandates and preemptions of state authority. Three basic issues are in contention here: (1) state policy-making autonomy; (2) state discretion in administering federal policies; and (3) federal-state cost sharing for domestic policies. However, given that annual interest payments on the federal government's debt have exceeded annual federal aid to state and local governments for a number of years, the prospects for improved cooperation in the near future are not bright.

B. **Decline in federal aid to states and localities**. Aid from the federal government to state and local government has been sharply curtailed since the mid-

1970s. Federal aid to local governments has experienced the greatest decline. Yet, costs continue to be shifted to local governments through mandates. For example, local governments will bear about 88 percent of the public costs of complying with federal environmental standards during the 1990s, with little federal financial assistance. Local governments have also lost some regulatory powers to the federal government. For example, when the Congress deregulated cable television in 1984, it prohibited local governments from regulating rates. Counties and municipalities have been trying to convince the Congress to return some of this power because citizens complain first to their county and municipal officials about rising cable television rates.

C. **State-local relations**. Relations between state and local governments have become very important, in part because of declining federal-local relations. Although state aid to local governments has increased, unfunded state mandates have increased too. Several issues are in contention here.

1. **Home rule**. Many observers believe that states should grant local governments, especially larger ones, more home-rule powers and, especially, more discretionary authority to raise revenue to finance themselves.

2. **Jurisdictional equity**. Another major issue is how best to distribute state aid equitably among local governments. A prominent and related issue is equity in school financing. Because schools rely heavily on the property tax, funding can vary greatly between rich and poor districts. Although the U.S. Supreme Court ruled in 1973 that education is not a fundamental right under the U.S. Constitution, a number of state high courts have ruled that education is a basic right under their state constitution, requiring among other things, more equalized funding of school districts across the state.

3. **Big cities**. State relations with large cities remain a sore point in many states because these cities believe that the state should provide much more financial assistance and flexibility for them to cope with their high concentrations of social, economic, and environmental problems.

4. **Rural communities**. Rural poverty and underdevelopment persist in nearly every state. Most of the nation's 3,042 counties, for example, are rural; and many have trouble coping with the financial

and technical requirements of modern government, such as environmental protection and health care.

D. **State-state relations**. These relations have improved considerably since the mid-1970s as states, especially within regions, have established more formal and informal relationships, and as state officials work through national associations, such as the Council of State Governments and National Conference of State Legislatures.

1. **Interstate compacts**. The states also engage in formal agreements, called interstate compacts, to deal with such problems as river-basin development, reciprocal education opportunities, low-level nuclear waste storage, and management of bridges over interstate rivers. Interstate compacts must be approved by the Congress.

2. **Interstate tensions**. There also are tensions and conflicts between states over such issues as waterway usage, law enforcement, pollution, waste disposal, and, occasionally, boundaries.

E. **Local-local relations**. These relations appear to have improved as well. About 77 percent of Americans live in urban areas, and about 50 percent live in the nation's 39 largest metropolitan areas, most of which have many local governments. The Chicago area, for example, has some 1,200 local governments.

1. **Consolidation**. Although many reformers have long urged consolidation of local governments in metropolitan areas into one or a few large municipal governments, citizens almost always vote against such plans. In Dallas, Miami, New York City, and several other large cities, there are neighborhoods or sections (e.g., Staten Island) that want to secede from their city.

2. **Cooperation**. Despite public resistance to consolidation, there has been a marked increase in voluntary inter-local cooperation through such mechanisms as regional councils of government; special districts to provide area-wide services (e.g., airports); metropolitan planning organizations; tax-base sharing; inter-local cost sharing of expensive services (e.g., a sophisticated crime lab); inter-local contracting to provide services (e.g., a suburb contracting with a neighboring suburb to provide police protection); and mutual assistance agreements, such as those that have long prevailed among fire fighters.

3. **Poverty and desegregation**. Inter-local cooperation will also be important for resolving problems of central-city poverty and racial segregation. Although suburbs are becoming more diverse in terms of race, class, and income, many poor and minority citizens remain "trapped" in central cities because of housing discrimination, too little affordable housing in suburbs, inadequate transportation to connect them to job opportunities, and other factors.

VII. **Civic virtue**. Many Americans believe that civic virtue is best cultivated locally where families and neighbors can work together. This may be one reason why Americans prefer to live in small and medium-size communities. Never in U.S. history have more than a third of Americans lived in communities having 100,000 or more people. Even in big cities, citizens often form neighborhood organizations to deal with their common concerns. In the past, of course, civic virtue has often fallen short of the ideal. Although Americans display a high level of civic virtue, especially in the time and money they spend voluntarily on community affairs, the resurgence of the states and the changes occurring in our federal system, which ultimately place more responsibilities on local governments, will put the idea of civic virtue to a supreme test in the twenty-first century.

B. INFORMAL INSTITUTIONS AND PROCESSES

In addition to constitutionally mandated institutions and processes of the American political system, informal institutions and processes which play a major role in the system have developed over the years. Among the most important are the following:

1. POLITICAL PARTIES AND ELECTIONS

To secure these rights, governments are instituted among men, deriving their just powers from the consent of the governed.

Declaration of Independence (1776)

Congress shall make no law...abridging the freedom of speech, or...the right of the people peaceably to assemble, and to petition the Government for a redress of grievances.

First Amendment, United States Constitution (1791)

The right to vote is the most basic right without which all others are meaningless....The vote is the most powerful instrument ever devised by man for breaking down injustice and destroying the terrible walls which imprison men because they are different from other men.

President Lyndon Johnson (1965)

[P]olitical parties created democracy and...modern democracy is unthinkable save in terms of parties....The most important distinction in modern political philosophy, the distinction between democracy and dictatorship, can be made best in terms of party politics.

E.E. Schattschneider (1942)

Democracy in practice is typified by the conduct of free and competitive elections. From the colonists' insistence on "no taxation without representation" to contemporary television debates, democratic citizenship at a minimum requires that citizens be able to choose the principal officials of the government. This hallmark of democracy is also evident elsewhere in the contemporary world. The dramatic events in Eastern Europe in 1989 centered on popular demands for free choice of government officials through competitive elections.

Effective elections, in turn, require competitive political parties. Historically, the rise of democracy was paralleled and stimulated by the growth of parties. Although party systems differ considerably from one nation or time period to another, multiple parties are always present in a democracy. Parties structure the vote for the electorate, present issues, link government to the citizenry, and organize the legislative and executive branches. These functions make them critical elements in American government.

OBJECTIVES

The citizen should be able to

1. explain the significance of elections and political parties in American democracy.

2. explain the formal rules and informal practices affecting the conduct of elections and the operation of political parties.

3. explain the differences among political parties on the basis of their history, programs, and group support.

4. explain the ways in which parties and elections can affect the policies of government.

5. take, defend, and evaluate proposals for the reform of the electoral process.

6. take, defend, and evaluate positions on the conduct and proposals of parties and candidates.

FRAME OF REFERENCE
Conceptual Perspective

I. **The significance of elections.** Free elections are the defining institutions of democratic government. The most basic meaning of democracy is that all people share in the decisions of government. In any modern community, the large number of people requires that government be conducted through representatives. Elections are the method of choosing these representatives.

   A. **Democracy and equality.** Because democracy assumes equality among individuals, all persons in a democracy must have an equal opportunity, within the same constituency, to choose their representatives.

      1. **Equal suffrage.** In recognition of equality, every citizen should be able to vote. The vote cannot be denied on the basis of race, religion, or sex. This principle has been recognized in the Constitution, its amendments, and federal law.

      2. **Equal voting.** Democracy also requires that all votes should count equally. It would be undemocratic, for example, if in state elections, rural voters had more influence than urban residents. Under the American federal system, however, in elections for the U.S. Senate the votes of states with smaller populations count disproportionately more than those from populous states. The reason is that all states, whether densely or sparsely populated, have two senators.

   B. **Democracy and political parties.** Democracy also requires organization, a means to make votes effective. The universal way in which the vote is now organized is through political parties. Parties carry on a number of important functions.

      1. **Parties manage the machinery of elections.** Political parties nominate candidates, canvass the electorate, conduct campaigns for many offices, and administer the voting process.

      2. **Parties organize opinion.** Parties present the voters a simple and understandable choice, usually only two principal candidates in any particular election. The party label on the ballot provides voters with a simple guide to the affiliations and beliefs of the candidates.

      3. **Parties link citizens to government.** By presenting alternative candidates, parties provide an effective means for voters to approve or disapprove of the past actions of government. By presenting programs, they allow the electorate an opportunity, sometimes limited in practice, to express its preferences on policy issues. By uniting voters under a common banner, they provide an opportunity for effective collective action.

      4. **Parties promote coordination in government.** Parties organize the legislative branches, provide a bridge between the separated institutions of the president and Congress, or the governor and state legislature, and promote interactions among the different levels of government in the federal system.

      5. **Parties promote emotional loyalties.** Through parties, citizens develop strong affective ties to other Americans. As they participate in politics, citizens also develop stronger loyalties to the governmental process.

II. **The conduct of American politics.** For the most part, American politics, elections, and parties reflect the federalist character of its political institutions. The two major parties battle each other vigorously but have virtually no competition from other, or "third" parties. A striking feature of American politics is the limited range of disagreement between the parties. Compared to other nations, ideology appears to be absent in the United States.

   A. **Federalism.** American politics is federalist politics. The states determine almost all voting qualifications, and there is no truly national election, even for president.

      1. **Constitutional limits of state voting requirements.** The national Constitution forbids states from discriminating among voters on the basis of race, religion, sex, or age over 18, or from imposing a poll tax. Otherwise, states can establish any voting requirement they wish.

      2. **Congressional districts established by states.** Members of the House of Representatives are selected from districts established by the states.

But these districts must contain equal numbers of residents, as counted in the decennial census. U.S. Senators are elected state-wide.

3. **Presidential elections and the electoral college.** The president is elected, in effect, by winning a series of state-wide elections, held on the same day. Each state chooses as many members of the "electoral college" as its total number of representatives and senators. These electoral votes are won as a bloc by the presidential candidate who gets the most popular votes in the state ("winner-take-all.") A candidate winning a majority of electoral votes becomes president. There are special constitutional provisions if nobody wins a majority.

4. **The "federal" makeup of parties.** The political parties are also federal in character. Each state party conducts its own affairs, although it is subject to some national rules against discrimination, and gets campaign help from the national party. It nominates its candidates in primary elections, which are governed by state laws. Federal laws prohibit discrimination in these primaries.

5. **Domination of primary elections in presidential nominations.** The presidential and vice-presidential nominations of each party are formally made in national conventions. In reality, however, the nominations are often decided by primary elections in different states held long before the convention.

B. **The two-party system.** The major parties, Republicans and Democrats, essentially monopolize American politics. They hold almost all the offices, receive virtually all the votes, and hold the loyalties of most voters.

1. **Party system not required by the Constitution.** Although the United States has a two-party system, this arrangement is not required by the theory of democracy or by the Constitution.

2. **Elections won by plurality encourage two-party system.** The American two-party system is strongly encouraged by the election structure. For most offices, only one person is elected in a single election, the winner being the person with the most votes, even if less than an absolute majority of all the votes cast.

3. **Presidency encourages two-party system.** The Presidency, as the most important single office in the country, is especially important in limiting competition to two parties—one favoring the actions of the president in office, the other in opposition.

4. **Political attitudes encourage two-party system.** American attitudes reinforce the dominant position of the two major parties. About two-thirds of the voters identify with either the Democrats or Republicans. The rest consider themselves Independents, but do not identify with any other specific party.

C. **Parties and issues.** On policy issues, the parties have overlapping views and show only limited differences, while disagreeing on some matters.

1. **Agreement by the two major parties on fundamental issues.** Both major parties support the capitalist form of economic organization, as well as the basic elements of social welfare. During the period after World War II, they also have agreed on the anti-communist foreign policy of the U.S. They continue to support the considerable involvement of the nation in international affairs.

2. **Issues debated in electoral campaigns.** In election campaigns, the debate between parties and candidates is often not on basic questions, such as what kind of economic system is preferable, but on the implementation of agreed goals, such as "peace and prosperity." Those in power may emphasize favorable economic news such as high employment or stable prices, for example, while their opponents may stress evidence of unemployment, high taxes, or inflation. While both parties support a large military involvement, lengthy and unsuccessful wars (such as the Vietnam war) usually hurt incumbent parties or candidates.

3. **Economic and social policy differences among parties.** The parties show some differences on matters of economic and social welfare policy.

   a. **Democrats and the poor.** Democrats tend to favor income redistribution, and therefore are more favorable to the interests of relatively poorer groups, blacks, and the working class.

b. **Republicans and business**. Republicans tend to favor capital formation, and therefore are more favorable to the interests of business corporations, and persons of higher income.

c. **Party divisions not hard and fast**. However, there are many exceptions, and individual legislators will place the interests of their own constituents above those of national groups.

4. **Recent party divisions over social issues**. Important differences between the parties are also evident in recent times on matters of social policy, and the regulation of individual life style. The issue of abortion has become particularly significant. Democrats tend to support a woman's "right to choice" on this issue; Republicans are more likely to support the "right to life" of the unborn fetus.

D. **Money and politics**. Electoral politics requires considerable financial resources. In the United States, except for presidential elections, these funds come principally from private sources.

1. **Necessity for candidates to raise funds**. The federal government pays part of the expenses of candidates seeking a party's presidential nomination and all of the expenses of the election contest after nominations are made, using funds designated on income tax returns. All other candidates, such as those for Congress, must raise their own funds, although there have been many proposals to change these arrangements.

2. **Sources of campaign funds and the question of equity**. Individual contributions and a congressional candidate's own funds are the chief sources of campaign finance other than PACs. This system raises questions about equity among persons running for public office. That is to say, those with private wealth have the advantage of having ready funds available for campaigns. They might also not need to spend as much time raising funds as their less wealthy opponents and therefore more time and energy for campaigning.

3. **Political Action Committees**. Political Action Committees (PACs) are groups set up by labor unions, business corporations, or special interest groups.

a. **What PACs do**. PACs collect money from individual members and contribute it to candidates or spend it on their behalf.

b. **Legal limits on PACs**. PACs must give money to at least five candidates in a federal election. They may not give more than $5,000 to a candidate in any one election, either a primary or a general contest.

c. **Incumbents' disproportionate receipt of PAC funds**. There is concern that PACs may improperly influence the actions of office-holders. In 1984, PACs gave $100 million to some three thousand candidates. A disproportionate share of the money went to incumbents. One reason for this is that all contributions of $100 or more must be made public; it would not be prudent for PACs to be seen contributing to a member's opponent, since most members are likely to be reelected. (In 1990 over 95% of congressional incumbents were reelected.)

4. **Aid to candidates by parties**. Political parties also aid candidates by providing advice, help in polling, assistance in the development of issues, and, to a lesser extent, funding. However, the parties' direct financial help to candidates is limited.

III. **The electorate's voting behavior**. Voting in the United States is affected by party loyalties, social groups, issues, and candidate qualities. In recent years, election campaigns have changed from "party-centered" to "candidate-centered" contests.

A. **Party loyalty**. Party identification is the single most significant influence on voting. Other things being equal, voters who identify themselves as party members will support their party's candidates.

1. **Democrats outnumber Republicans**. For the past fifty years, there have been more persons identified as Democrats. In recent years, however, Republicans have become almost as numerous.

2. **Weakening of party loyalty**. Party loyalty has weakened as an influence on voting. A third of the voters now consider themselves Independents. Even people who still identify as either Democrats or Republicans are increasingly ready to vote for the opposite party; historically,

Democrats have been more likely to do so than Republicans.

3. **Weakening of party loyalty by incumbency**. Incumbency is another important influence on voting, limiting the effect of party loyalty. The effect of incumbency is particularly important in congressional elections.

4. **Advantages of incumbency**. In recent elections, about 95% of the incumbents in the House of Representatives have won reelection.

   a. **Notoriety**. Incumbents are better known. They work assiduously in maintaining their notoriety through media coverage and public appearances.

   b. **Campaign fund receipts**. Incumbents receive the largest proportion of campaign contributions, particularly, as noted above, from PACs. The advantage in fund raising is especially significant, since experience shows that with few exceptions challengers must outspend incumbents to have a chance of unseating them.

   c. **Government resources**. Incumbents have access to government resources, enabling them to communicate with the voters, and to provide services to constituents. They have, for example, franking (postal) privileges allowing them free of charge to send constituents literature that places their job performance in a favorable light. They are also often able to influence government agencies to perform services for constituents, aiding their popularity.

B. **Voting among social groups**. Social groups show characteristic patterns of voting. These patterns are not absolute differences, however, and can change in particular elections or over longer time periods.

1. **Sources of Republican support**. Generally, as income levels increase, people are more likely to vote Republican. While George Bush received only one of every three votes from poor voters in 1988, he received better than two of every three votes from the wealthy. The same pattern is evident for education levels, but this occurs only because of the close relationship between income and education. At the highest levels of education, Democrats are more numerous.

2. **Sources of Democratic support**. Blacks vote overwhelmingly Democratic, at all income levels (eight-to-one in 1988). Whites are more evenly divided, while tending toward the Republicans, and voting better than five-to-four for Bush in 1988. Hispanics are also divided, although they voted three-to-two for the Democratic candidates in 1984 and 1988.

3. **Voting patterns among major religions**. Catholics are more Democratic than Protestants, although the historic difference has diminished. At present, Catholics are likely to show a 10-15% greater preference for Democratic candidates. Jews of all income levels tend to be Democrats.

4. **Voting among women**. In recent years, a "gender gap" has appeared in voting, with women somewhat more Democratic, and men somewhat more Republican. In 1988, a slight majority of women voted for Bush, while he won nearly three-to-two among men.

5. **Voting among old and young**. The oldest voters show the strongest identification with the Democrats, the youngest with the Republicans. These differences reflect the groups' historic experiences, since the oldest voters entered the electorate during the presidency of Franklin Roosevelt, and the youngest voters came of political age during the presidency of Ronald Reagan.

6. **Voting in the South**. The South is now the strongest Republican region, especially among white voters. This pattern reverses the historic Democratic loyalty of the "Solid South" after the Civil War, when white Southerners refused to vote for the party of Republican Abraham Lincoln.

C. **Issues and voting**. Issues affect electoral behavior because they underlie the party and group loyalties of the voters. Particular issues can also affect individual elections.

1. **Party identification along the political spectrum**. Democrats are more likely to consider themselves "liberals," and Republicans more likely to be "conservatives." However, there are many conservatives among Democrats, and a small number of liberals among Republicans. Moreover, most Americans of both parties call themselves "moderates."

2. **Broad labels less important than specific stands.** In most elections, these broad labels are less important than specific issues. The record of the incumbent candidate or party may be emphasized. For this reason, candidates attempt to take positions which are popular in their local constituencies.

3. **President's record as electoral factor.** Candidates for Congress also are affected by the record of the president.

    a. **The "coattail" effect in presidential elections.** In a presidential election year, legislative candidates may be brought into office on the "coattails" of a popular presidential candidate, but this effect has been less evident in recent years.

    b. **Effect of presidential popularity in off-year elections.** Even in off-year elections, when the president is not on the ballot, congressional candidates will still be affected by the president's record. Members of his party are more likely to win election when the president is personally popular and when the nation is in a period of economic prosperity. Conversely, members of his party are more likely to lose votes when the president is unpopular or the economy evidences rising unemployment or increased prices.

4. **Effects of "single-issue" voting.** Recent elections have seen an increase in single-issue voting, where people support or oppose a candidate only because of his or her stand on an isolated policy question, such as abortion. The presence of such voters may make candidates afraid to take positions on controversial issues, for fear that they will alienate enough voters to lose the election.

5. **Electoral victories lack specific mandates.** In most elections, there are many different issues, not just one. The multiplicity of issues makes it difficult to interpret an election result as a mandate for any particular program. The election does decide who governs. What the government then does depends on the workings of America's complex institutions.

D. **Individual candidates.** Candidates' personal qualities are increasingly important influences on voting patterns.

1. **Decline of party loyalty and role of television.** Party loyalty is less important because of the dominant role of the mass media, especially television, in contemporary election campaigns. Media techniques include paid commercials such as thirty-second "spots," televised debates, and staged "photo opportunities."

2. **The problem of "negative advertising."** Attacks on election opponents, known as "negative advertising," are common and appear to be increasing.

    a. **Negative effects.** These attacks are troublesome, because they discourage candidates from running for office, divert attention from the discussion of significant issues, and reduce voters' confidence in the political system.

    b. **Media analyses of negative advertising.** Some newspapers and television stations have begun to broadcast or publish careful analyses of negative advertising, testing their veracity. If such analyses become widespread, negative advertising may become less prone to questionable sensationalism or become less prevalent.

3. **Independence of candidates from their parties.** Candidates usually campaign independently from their party, emphasizing their individual qualities. This strategy reflects both the decline of party loyalty among voters, and the emphasis placed by mass media on individual characteristics of the candidates.

4. **Growing role of consultants in campaigns and the rise of impersonal politics.** Political consultants, media specialists, and experts in public opinion polls are important in campaigns. Their significant role is both a cause and an effect of the greater importance of the mass media in campaigns. Today, these specialists in impersonal communication have largely replaced the old-style, more personal, door-to-door party canvassers of the past.

5. **Factors shaping voter choice.** In judging candidates, voters use a variety of criteria.

    a. **Competence and honesty more important than appearance and personality.** Detailed research indicates that the most important factors are the candidates' perceived competence, experience, and honesty. Only a small proportion of voters knowingly rely on physical appearance or personality.

b. **Visual appearance in the Kennedy-Nixon debates**. In a very close contest, such as that exemplified by the television debates between John Kennedy and Richard Nixon in 1960, physical appearance might become a relevant factor. Even in that year, however, the voters emphasized the perceived competence and programs of the candidates.

E. **Voting participation**. A smaller percentage of Americans vote than in almost every other western democracy. In nations such as Britain or Germany, over three-fourths of the electorate participates. In the U.S., the largest turnout occurs in presidential elections, where slightly more than half the eligible adult population now participates, but turnout has decreased considerably (twelve percentage points) since 1960. Smaller proportions vote in congressional, state, and local elections. In these elections, turnout is frequently below forty percent of the adult population.

1. **Increased education and participation**. People with more years in school are more likely to vote. While only some two of five high-school dropouts vote, four of five college graduates go to the polls. However, even as education has risen in the United States, the level of voting has decreased.

2. **Increased income and participation**. Participation also increases with income; richer people are more likely to vote than poorer people. A third of the poorest Americans come to the polls, compared to three-fourths of those with family incomes above $50,000 a year. However, education has far more of an impact than income alone.

3. **Increased age and participation**. Electoral turnout increases with age. Despite their increased levels of education in America, young people are least likely to vote, with only one of three going to the polls. In contrast, close to three-fourths of senior citizens participate.

4. **Participation of African Americans and women**. Historic differences in voting participation have largely been eliminated. With the ending of discriminatory laws, blacks vote almost as frequently as whites of the same education and income. Women now vote in even larger proportions than men.

5. **Possible effect on voting of party decline**. Active parties increase turnout. The recent decline in voting may be related to the weakening of party activities.

6. **Difficulty of registration and voting levels**. Registration creates a significant burden on voting. In most states, a person must register personally before he or she can vote. In all other nations, this process is a governmental responsibility, and a person is placed on the voting books without personal effort. The burden of registration is especially significant for people who move, and therefore must register again from a new address, and for poor people, who are often unaware of registration procedures. Simple registration alone would probably increase voting turnout by ten percentage points.

7. **Partisan effect of higher electoral participation**. Higher turnout in the United States would probably not benefit either political party over the other. The best scholarly study estimates that the Democrats might gain no more than half a percentage point. Higher turnout would, however, probably mean that more attention would be paid to the interests of those who now do not vote.

Historical Perspective

After more than two hundred years, the United States is the world's oldest democracy, and its Democratic party is the world's oldest popular political party. The continuity of the nation's government is impressive, not only for its length but also for the stability of its political institutions. Within this continuity, there has also been important developmental change. The electoral franchise, once confined to white male property holders, has been equalized to include all adult citizens. A succession of party systems has adapted to the changing society and economy. The political parties themselves have changed both in name and in their basic character.a

I. **The democratization of American elections**. The Constitution established a republican form of government. It was also designed to limit popular involvement and electoral control of officials, which **James Madison** (1751-1836) feared as "the diseases most incident to republican government." Over the course of history, many of these barriers have fallen.

A. **Extensions of the vote**. Originally the vote was restricted to property holders, who presumably had a "stake in the country." Today the accepted principle is "one person, one vote."

   1. **Voting in the age of Jackson**. By the time of Andrew Jackson, almost all white males were enfranchised. Property qualifications were dropped in virtually every state, and a handful also allowed freed blacks to vote. Soon after, in 1848, the movement for woman suffrage was founded.

   2. **Extension of suffrage to freed slaves**. After the Civil War, the vote was constitutionally extended to the freed slaves. Through legal discrimination, intimidation, and economic domination, blacks were kept from actually voting in the South for decades. Black suffrage became a reality through the civil rights movement led by Rev. Martin Luther King, Jr., culminating in the Voting Rights Act of 1965.

   3. **Extension of suffrage to women and youth**. Later constitutional amendments extended the vote to women, in 1920, and to persons over the age of eighteen in 1971. Another amendment, in 1964, outlawed the poll tax, the last means by which wealth could be used to restrict voting.

   4. **Efforts to equalize votes**. The democratic principle is also evident in efforts to make votes equal to each other within the same constituency.

      a. **Redistricting with each census**. Under the Constitution, seats in the House of Representatives are redistributed every ten years to reflect the changing population of the states. In recent decades, this provision has meant a considerable shift of seats from areas of declining population in the Northeast and Midwest to areas of increasing population in the South and West.

      b. **Legal mandating of equal districts**. Under the Supreme Court's reapportionment decisions from 1962 to 1964, such as the landmark decision in *Baker v. Carr* (1962), both state and congressional legislative districts must have equal populations.

      c. **Direct election of the president**. Public opinion favors direct election of the president. Three-fourths of respondents in the Gallup Poll support this change.

      d. **Exceptions to equal voting**. Despite the general democratic principle of an equal vote for each citizen, the Constitution provides for two senators from each state, regardless of population. It is also possible for a president to be elected without a plurality of the popular vote. But this mathematical possibility is unlikely and has not occurred since 1888.

B. **Extensions of the democratic process**. As more people became able to vote, direct popular elections also came to play a larger role in the process of government.

   1. **Direct election of governors**. In most states, governors were originally selected by the legislature. In the nineteenth century, direct election was extended to the states' chief executive, and to other offices.

   2. **Direct election of U.S. senators**. United States senators were originally chosen by the state legislatures. As a result of the Seventeenth Amendment in 1913, senators are now elected by direct vote of the people.

   3. **Initiative, referendum, and recall**. The Progressive movement of the early twentieth century argued that "the cure for the ills of democracy is more democracy."

      a. **The Progressives' cure**. Suspicious of public officials and of organized interest groups, Progressives sought to give individual voters a more direct role in government. Under this principle, half the states have provided for direct legislation, through such procedures as the initiative and referendum. Some states also allow the recall of elected officials.

      b. **Criticism of the initiative and referendum**. Critics of these techniques believe they are sometimes manipulated by special interests through the cynical use of misleading advertising and other abuses.

4. **The direct primary election**. A lasting Progressive reform has been the direct primary for the nomination of party candidates for public office, now used for all offices except the presidency. In other nations, the nomination of candidates is left to the parties' own processes.

5. **Primary elections and selection of nomination convention delegates**. Primary elections have also become the dominant means of choosing delegates to the national party conventions that nominate presidential candidates.

   a. **Arguments favoring primary selection of delegates**. Those favoring this mechanism believe it is more democratic than negotiation among party leaders in "smoke-filled rooms."

   b. **Arguments against primary selection of delegates**. Critics argue that the turnout in primary elections is unrepresentative and that individualistic primary campaigns make it difficult for the party to achieve a coherent ticket and program.

II. **American party systems**. American history can be divided into periods of two-party competition, each of which has evidenced a distinct set of election results, issues, and group coalitions.

   A. **The first party system**. As party politics developed in the United States, it was based on the competition between Federalists and Republicans. This first party system originated in the 1796 presidential contest between John Adams and Thomas Jefferson.

   1. **Party politics from 1800 to 1824**. After the election of **Thomas Jefferson** (1741-1826) in 1800, the Republicans eventually became totally dominant, leading to a succession of Virginia presidents and the disappearance of the Federalists in the misnamed "Era of Good Feelings." The Republican party fractured in 1824, and no candidate received a majority of electoral votes. This election was the last in which a president was chosen by the House of Representatives.

   2. **Strength of central government the dominant issue**. The dominant issues in the 1790s and early 1800s turned on the implementation of the new Constitution. Federalists favored stronger central institutions, while the Republicans advocated states' rights.

   3. **Foreign and economic policies as party issues**. Specific issues also divided the parties. The Federalists favored stronger relations with Great Britain, while Republicans were supportive of the French Revolution. The policy leader of the Federalists was **Alexander Hamilton** (1755-1804), who sought to use the federal government to spur economic development through such measures as tariff protection of industry and full payment of the debts of the Revolution. Republicans supported economic policies favoring agricultural interests.

   4. **Regional support of parties**. The opposing group coalitions centered on Federalist strength among Eastern commercial interests, as opposed to Republican support among Southern agrarian interests.

   B. **The second party system**. From the time of the election of **Andrew Jackson** (1767-1845) in 1828 to the Civil War, the Democrats and Whigs were the dominant parties.

   1. **The age of Whigs and Democrats: 1828-1860**. This period was the most competitive in American electoral history. Both parties were active throughout the nation, and elections were close. **Martin Van Buren** (1782-1862) built an effective national party organization for the Democrats and Andrew Jackson, and succeeded him in the presidency. His own reelection bid failed when the Whigs nominated a war hero, **William Henry Harrison** (1773-1841) in 1840, and falsely pictured him as a common man, born in a log cabin. From then to the onset of the Civil War, the two parties alternated control of the White House.

   2. **Economic issues central**. The dominant political issues involved economic development. The Democrats supported economic decentralization and smaller entrepreneurs. The Whigs, unsuccessfully nominating **Henry Clay** (1777-1852) for the Presidency, supported his "American system" of sponsored economic development.

   3. **Democrats, Whigs, and the national bank**. The differences between the parties were exemplified by the issue of a national bank. When Jackson vetoed the bank bill in 1831, he followed the Democratic preference for decentralized economic development. In contrast, the Whigs favored such programs of national development as a

single banking system, subsidized transportation, and high tariffs.

4. **Social bases of party support**. The Democratic party found more support among small farmers, urban workers, Catholics, and westerners, while the Whigs were particularly strong in the East and among businessmen and southern planters.

5. **Whig decline; Republican rise**. The parties ultimately divided along regional lines as the slavery controversy proved insoluble by peaceful means. In 1856, the new Republican party replaced the Whigs as the second largest party. Four years later, with the Democrats split, **Abraham Lincoln** (1809-1865) was elected as a minority president with less than forty percent of the national vote.

C. **Parties after the Civil War**. As the post-Civil War Reconstruction came to an end in 1876, a new competitive third party system developed.

1. **Republican dominance in late nineteenth century**. Republicans won all but two presidential contests by the end of the nineteenth century, electing Presidents from **Ulysses S. Grant** (1822-1885) to **Benjamin Harrison** (1833-1901).

    a. **Close popular vote in presidential elections**. However, despite Republican victories, the popular results were always close. In 1876, Democrats won a majority of the popular vote, but disputed results in the electoral college brought **Rutherford Hayes** (1822-1893) to the White House by a margin of only one electoral vote. The next three elections saw razor-thin margins of victory (2,000 votes) for **James Garfield** (1831-1881) and **Grover Cleveland** (1837-1908) (27,000 votes), and the choice of Harrison with fewer votes than Cleveland, his Democratic opponent.

    b. **Regional basis of parties**. Despite their close competition nationally, the parties were regionally distinct, and did not contest in all states.

2. **Reconstruction and post-Reconstruction issues**. The issues that divided the parties after the Civil War changed once Reconstruction ended.

    a. **Reconstruction issues**. The parties differed in measures to deal with the consequences of the Civil War, with Republicans favoring strong central government power to protect the newly freed slaves, such as the Thirteenth to Fifteenth Amendments to the Constitution, while Democrats tried to restore the previous power of white slave holders.

    b. **Post-Reconstruction issues**. After 1876, Union troops were removed from the South, and the parties returned to economic and social issues, similar to those contested before the Civil War. Republicans favored high tariffs and national economic development, while Democrats endorsed low tariffs and states' rights. Republicans tended to be allied with such emerging moralistic movements as the prohibition of alcohol.

3. **Social bases of party support**. Republicans relied on the votes of farmers, Eastern businessmen, former soldiers of the Union army, and blacks. Democrats revived their former support in the northern states and controlled the region of the former Confederacy. After the removal of federal troops from the defeated South, black voting rights were suppressed in the region.

D. **Party realignment after 1896**. Politics was transformed in the election of 1896. The party system was realigned in that election, making the Republicans dominant until the 1930s, when the old populist appeal of **William Jennings Bryan** (1860-1925) reappeared under the leadership of Franklin D. Roosevelt and led to a new realignment of the party system.

1. **Republican domination of presidency, 1896-1932**. In 1896, the Democrats, led by William Jennings Bryan, adopted a program of monetary inflation, through the free coinage of silver. Bryan lost decisively to **William McKinley** (1843-1901), and the Republicans went on to win all but two of the succeeding eight elections. The only Democratic presidential victories came when Woodrow Wilson ran against a divided Republican party in 1912, and then won reelection as World War I approached.

2. **Issues arising from economic power and foreign policy**. New issue alignments developed from the emergence of the United States into a position of

world economic leadership and the growth of large corporations. The expansion of American power overseas after the Spanish-American War also brought foreign policy into electoral debate.

3. **Party policies on economic and foreign issues**. Republicans favored industrial development through tight money, the gold standard, and high tariffs, and an assertive foreign policy. Democrats sought the inflationary policy of unlimited coinage of silver, and opposed U.S. "imperialism" in Latin America and the Philippines. Major legislation to control corporations was initiated by presidents of both parties, particularly **Theodore Roosevelt** (1858-1919) and **Woodrow Wilson** (1856-1924).

4. **Regional voting patterns**. Voting patterns showed strong regional divisions, resulting in one-party Republican domination of the East and Midwest, with Democratic strength restricted to the South and some Western states.

E. **The New Deal Democratic party majority**. The great depression of 1929 and the ascendancy of **Franklin Delano Roosevelt** (1882-1945) (F.D.R) fundamentally changed U.S. politics.

1. **Domination of the Democratic party**. The Democratic majority won four successive victories for Roosevelt. The new Democratic majority continued after Roosevelt's death, leading to close presidential victories by **Harry Truman** (1884-1972) in 1948 and **John Kennedy** (1917-1963) in 1960. By 1964, when **Lyndon Johnson** (1908-1973) won the last convincing Democratic victory, the party's loyalists were an absolute majority of the nation's voters.

2. **New Deal era domestic and foreign policy**. Under F.D.R.'s New Deal of the 1930s, the United States created a modern welfare state, including programs of old-age pensions (social security), bank insurance, public housing, and agricultural subsidies. Roosevelt also reversed the traditional American foreign policy of international isolation, leading the U.S. into World War II and supporting the creation of the United Nations Organization. In the aftermath of the war and the invention of the atomic bomb, the United States became the world's leading military and economic power.

3. **Republican party policy**. Republicans opposed the New Deal and initially favored a more restricted role in international affairs. Eventually, however, Republicans came to accept these policies. The nomination and election of **Dwight D. Eisenhower** (1890-1969) in 1952 marked the party's acceptance of the welfare state and an internationalist foreign policy.

4. **Social and regional basis of party support**. The majority Democratic coalition combined urban residents, unionized manufacturing employees, Catholics, blacks and other ethnic minorities, and traditional Southern support. Republican votes came principally from higher-income voters, white Protestants, and the northern states.

F. **The contemporary parties**. Party alignments have become confused and shifting since the middle of the turbulent 1960s decade.

1. **Republican domination of presidential elections**. Republican candidates have won all but one Presidential election since 1964. Moreover, except in 1968, these Republican victories have been by convincingly large margins. At the same time, Democrats have dominated elections for state offices and for Congress, where the party has controlled the House of Representatives for all but four years in the past six decades.

2. **Decline of clearly defined party issues**. New issues have appeared, confusing political alignments. There is relatively little difference between the major parties on the issues of the Roosevelt period. Instead, political controversy has centered on such social issues as race and personal morality, or on foreign policy controversies, notably the Vietnam war.

3. **Social basis of contemporary parties**. Reflecting these political changes, social groups have altered their voting patterns. Except for blacks, most previously Democratic groups have weakened in their party loyalties. Republicans have gained new support among Catholics, white Southerners, and youth.

G. **Third parties**. Although American history has been dominated by two major parties, third parties have appeared regularly. While limited in their electoral success, they have had significant influence in raising policy issues.

1. **Free Soil party (1848)**. Before the Civil War, most third parties focused on the restriction or

abolition of slavery. The most important of these was the **Free Soil** party of 1848, which won ten percent of the vote for Martin Van Buren's presidential candidacy. Eventually, the Republican party absorbed most of the Free Soilers.

2. **People's party (1892)**. For the rest of the nineteenth century, third parties expressed the grievances of economically disadvantaged groups. The most important was the People's or Populist party of 1892, which won close to a tenth of the national vote. In the following election, its most prominent issue, the free coinage of silver, was adopted by the Democrats, absorbing the Populist protest.

3. **Early twentieth-century parties**. In the early twentieth century, economic discontents led to a number of significant minor parties.

   a. **Progressive party**. The most important third party was the Progressives. In 1912, led by Theodore Roosevelt, this party was second in the national balloting, winning over a quarter of the vote. By splitting the Republican vote, the Progressives helped to elect Wilson as President.

   b. **LaFollette's leadership.** In 1924, **Senator Robert LaFollette** (1855-1925) of Wisconsin, led the Progressives in a protest against the conservative candidates of both major parties. He won a sixth of the vote, but Republican **Calvin Coolidge** (1872-1933) was reelected with an absolute majority.

   c. **Socialist party**. On the Socialist ticket, **Eugene V. Debs** (1855-1926) won nearly a million votes in both 1912 and 1920, as did **Norman Thomas** (1884-1968) in 1932. After the economic reforms of the New Deal, the party's appeal diminished considerably.

4. **American Independent party**. In the past fifty years, the most important third party movements have come from the right side of the political spectrum. The largest of these movements was that of the American Independent party of 1968, led by **George Wallace** (b. 1919), which won a seventh of the national vote. His opposition to civil rights contributed to the growth of the Republican party in the south.

5. **Candidacy of John Anderson**. In 1980, Congressman **John Anderson** of Illinois mounted an independent campaign for president as a nonpartisan moderate. While the former Republican received considerable attention early in the race, he finally received less than seven percent of the vote.

III. **Political party development**. The parties have changed considerably over the course of American history.

A. **Party origins**. American parties began as personal and legislative factions in Congress and then reached out for broader support.

   1. **The Founding period**. Party factions first became evident after the adoption of the Constitution, in the controversies between Alexander Hamilton and Thomas Jefferson.

   2. **Formation of the Republican party**. Jefferson and Madison collaborated in forming the first party, the Republicans.

B. **Parties in the nineteenth century**. Fuller party development came in the nineteenth century, when politics was dominated by highly organized parties with strong voter loyalties.

   1. **"Machine" based parties**. "Machine" parties were based on strong state and local party organizations. In some areas, parties became "machines," which dominated politics through extensive material rewards. Patronage, appointments to public office for party service, was widespread.

   2. **Campaign activities.** Campaigns were conducted through the parties, which raised funds, controlled nominations, conducted emotive campaign rallies, canvassed the electorate personally, and usually succeeded in getting voters to choose a "straight ticket" of all party candidates.

   3. **Strong voter loyalty**. Voter loyalties to parties were very strong. The parties were at the center of community life, and provided many services to residents. Voters rarely defected from their party or split their tickets.

C. **The declining influence of modern parties**. The major American political parties evidence a continuing decline in their influence over voters during the course of the twentieth century.

1. **The rise of direct primaries and the decline of patronage**. Legal changes, such as the direct primary and the restriction of patronage, are a major cause of the weakening of parties. The direct primary has had not only the intended effect of weakening the parties, but also the unintended effects of increasing the importance of political contributors, incumbents, the mass media, and campaign consultants.

2. **Social changes and party decline**. Social changes have also contributed to this trend. The population is more mobile, wealthier and less dependent on party services, and more educated.

3. **Government takeover of party functions**. Government itself has taken over some of the earlier functions of parties. Social welfare through government, for example, makes voters less reliant on the favors of urban machines.

4. **Televised campaigning and party decline**. New means of communication also affect parties. Television favors individual, rather than party, campaigning. Candidates increasingly use such non-party techniques as direct mail, advertising, and polling. Election finance, similarly, flows to candidates rather than parties.

5. **Limited party revival**. Despite these general trends, there has been some recent revival of party organizations, both state and national. There is greater unity on policy issues among elected officials of the same party and greater services to candidates by the parties.

IV. **The problem of campaign finance**. Methods of raising money for campaigns have changed considerably since the nineteenth century.

A. **Early attempts to restrict sources of campaign finance**. Complaints about how campaign money was raised arose in the nineteenth century.

1. **Reform of soliciting civil servants for campaign contributions**. By the 1878 election, 75% of the money raised by the Republican Congressional Committee came from federal officeholders. The Civil Service Reform Act of 1883 ended this practice of soliciting campaign contributions from civil servants in Washington who owed their jobs to political appointments.

2. **Prohibiting corporate donations of money**. As early as the 1830s, corporate financing of campaigns was a political issue. The Act of 1907, in response to public criticism of the relationship between big business and the Republican party, prohibited corporations and national banks from making money "contributions" to candidates for federal office. Other types of political "contributions" were not prohibited.

3. **Requiring disclosure of contributions**. In 1910, Congress passed the first law requiring disclosure of campaign contributions in federal elections. A 1911 law required primary, convention, and preelection financial statements and limited the amounts that House and Senate candidates could spend. The Supreme Court overturned the regulation of primaries because the Constitution does not explicitly refer to the primary process.

4. **Ambiguity of "expenditure" in disclosure laws**. The Federal Corrupt Practices Act of 1925 codified existing laws and expanded the definition of "contribution" but left the term "expenditure" ambiguous.

5. **Attempts to regulate labor union campaign activities**. In response to public criticism of the relationship between labor and the Democratic Party, Congress passed the Smith-Connally War Labor Disputes Act of 1943, extending the scope of the Corrupt Practices Act to labor union activities. The Taft-Hartley Act of 1947 made Smith-Connally permanent and broadened its prohibition to include expenditures as well as contributions. This ensured that neither labor nor corporations could spend members' or stockholders' money for political purposes in connection with federal elections.

B. **Recent campaign finance**. Recent campaign finance legislation had significant results.

1. **The Federal Election Campaign Act of 1971**. The Federal Election Campaign Act of 1971 broadened the scope of congressional regulation beyond the general election to include primaries, caucuses, and conventions, bringing all campaigns for federal elective office under the control of Congress. This act provided the following:

a. **Disclosure requirements strengthened**. The act strengthened disclosure requirements for federal election campaigns and required the information to be made available to the public.

b. **Candidate expenditures limited**. The act initiated candidate spending limits and regulated expenditures on communications media advertising.

c. **Regulating corporate and union contributions**. The act codified rules regulating the use of corporate and union treasuries to establish separate funds (political action committees—PACs) to make campaign contributions. These rules permit corporations to collect "voluntary" contributions from their employees in order to advance partisan political views, thus officially recognizing the existence of PACs. The changes established equal treatment for corporations and labor organizations, but excluded entities with government contracts from establishing PACs.

2. **The 1974 amendments**. The 1974 Amendments to the Act were passed in reaction to the Watergate scandal. The amendments made a number of changes.

a. **Federal Elections Commission**. The amendments created the Federal Elections Commission (FEC) to administer revised disclosure provisions, new criminal code amendments and new tax law amendments that provide public campaign financing for presidential candidates. The FEC was empowered to compel campaign committees to report and to investigate suspected violations of law.

b. **Matching funds**. The amendments provided matching public funds for presidential primaries and full funding for general elections by means of the income tax check-off and further established subsidies for nominating conventions.

c. **Limiting individual contributions**. The amendments limited individual contributions to $1000 per election, with no more than $25,000 to all candidates combined per year.

d. **Limiting PAC contributions**. The amendments limited special interest group or PAC contributions to $5000 per candidate per election with no limit on total amount contributed.

e. **Limiting spending of federal candidates**. The amendments limited the permissible amount of overall campaign expenditures by candidates for federal office.

f. **Limiting spending of candidates' own money**. The amendments placed ceilings on what candidates could spend of their own money.

g. **Allowing more corporate PACs**. The amendments repealed a rule which had prohibited corporations with government contracts from creating PACs.

3. **Supreme court's ruling in *Buckley v. Valeo***. In *Buckley v. Valeo* (1976), the Supreme Court ruled in a case challenging the 1974 amendments on the grounds that limiting the use of money for political purposes was an unconstitutional restriction of speech, since all meaningful political communication requires the use of money. The Court:

a. **Contribution limitations upheld**. The Court upheld the constitutionality of all of the contribution limitations of the Campaign Act. The Court held that Congress's desire to address the actuality and appearance of corruption resulting from large individual financial contributions was sufficient to justify the "limited effect" which the contribution limitation had upon First Amendment freedoms.

b. **Expenditure limitations struck down.** The Court invalidated, on First Amendment grounds, both the independent expenditure ceiling and the limitation on a candidate's use of personal funds. Limitations on expenditure of personal funds, the Court said, was a restriction of free speech. The prevention of the appearance of corruption would be better served if the candidate did not have to depend on outside contributions. However, the expenditure ceiling imposed on candidates accepting federal matching funds was not affected.

4. **Amendments to the Act (1976)**. In the 1976 amendments to the Act, Congress undertook a major revision of the law concerning compliance and enforcement procedures, the issuance of advisory opinions, and the role of corporate and labor political action committees.

   a. **The FEC as an executive agency**. In response to the Court's stripping the FEC of virtually all its powers to administer, interpret, and enforce the law, Congress transformed the FEC into an executive agency and provided that all of its members be appointed by the President, subject to the approval of the Senate.

   b. **Expanding candidate expenditures**. The 1976 amendments expanded the general definition of candidate-controlled expenditures so as to include many of the "independent expenditures" struck down in *Buckley*.

   c. **Reform of corporate and labor contributing**. The 1976 amendments to the Act also repealed the basic prohibition against corporate and labor campaign contributions in connection with federal elections. However, the amendments substantially revised the rules relating to collection of contributions and administration of the collected funds by prohibiting the use of coercion in soliciting funds and requiring that persons solicited be informed of the political nature of the fund, that contributions were voluntary, and that there could be no reprisal for failure to contribute.

5. **Party-building encouraged**. The 1979 amendments to the Act also encouraged party-building activities by allowing local and state parties to purchase, in unlimited amounts, campaign materials to be used in connection with volunteer activities on behalf of a candidate, and to engage in voter registration and get-out-the-vote activities for their party's presidential and vice-presidential candidates.

Contemporary Perspective

Although the formal mechanisms of American politics still resemble the original constitutional system, they have changed greatly in their actual workings and effects. Further changes can be expected as the nation approaches the twenty-first century. These trends raise important questions for American citizens.

I. **Trends in American politics**. The nation is becoming more diverse in its population, more centralized in its economy, and less dominant in the international arena. The electoral system and the political parties must respond to these changes.

   A. **Social trends**. Fundamental social, economic, and political changes complicate the citizens' control of government through democratic elections.

      1. **Demographic diversity**. The nation is more diverse demographically. "Typical" Americans—white, Anglo-Saxon, and Protestant—are already a minority of the population. With higher birth rates and higher immigration among African Americans, Hispanics and Asians, ethnic "minorities" will constitute an increasing percentage of the nation, reaching nearly a third of the total U.S. population by the turn of the century.

      2. **Economic and international change and citizen control**. With a more complicated economy and a less secure international position, central government power and bureaucracy is likely to grow. Such problems as energy, education, arms control, space exploration, and international trade will probably require government action, even in the face of attempts to decentralize or deregulate. The ability of citizens to understand new and technical problems and to control government will be challenged.

      3. **The impersonal society**. A large population, and the dominance of impersonal means of communication through the mass media, make it more difficult for citizens to communicate with each other and to discuss politics.

   B. **Party changes**. The political parties, reflecting these social trends, are changing their character.

      1. **Lack of a majority party**. The traditional voting coalitions of the Democrats and Republicans are shifting, but neither major party has a clear majority. About a third of the electorate identifies with each major party.

      2. **Decline of party loyalty**. The strength of party loyalties has weakened, and more voters, about a

third of the total electorate, consider themselves independent.

3. **Strong central and weak local organizations.** The parties are more centralized and more bureaucratic in their organization. The national party organizations have taken on important responsibilities for fund raising, polling, training of candidates, and policy research. At the same time, the parties' grass roots bases have decayed. Parties and candidates communicate with voters largely through marketing techniques, not personally and face-to-face.

4. **The problem of campaign finance.** Contemporary politics involves spending large sums of money. As campaigns have become more expensive, questions arise about the sources and propriety of campaign contributions.

5. **Divided party control of federal government.** The parties are becoming more distinct from one another in their policy positions and more unified within government. At the same time, divided control of the Presidency and Congress is more common. This division may complicate cooperation between the executive and legislative branches of government.

II. **Issues for the democratic citizen.** In the coming years, citizens will need to make decisions not only about policy issues, but also about issues in the political process besides campaign finance.

A. **The electoral process.** Some issues that concern the citizen relate to the conduct of elections.

1. **The question of campaign finance.** Political Action Committees (PACs) are defended as a means of participation in elections, through financial contributions. They are also attacked as biasing the political system, because their money comes from wealthier persons, and because their contributions, given mostly to incumbent legislators, may give these committees undue advantages.

2. **Public finance of campaigns.** Another possible source of campaign financing is public funds, already provided for candidates and parties in a third of the states and for presidential candidates.

a. **Arguments for public finance.** Advocates see this system as a means of freeing candidates from the self-interested claims of contributors, while limiting the total amount of election spending.

b. **Arguments against public finance.** Critics are concerned that the limits on campaign expenditures will work to the advantage of incumbents, who are already better known and have other advantages of incumbency.

3. **Free television time and other proposals.** Other proposals for regulating campaign spending include fuller disclosure of contributions and expenditures, and providing free services for candidates, such as television time or subsidized mailings to voters.

4. **Proposals to increase voter turnout.** Can voting turnout be increased? One proposal now under consideration is that government take the responsibility for registering voters, for example, through the postal service or at the time of driver license renewals.

a. **Arguments for government registration of voters.** Giving government the responsibility of registering voters, advocates say, would remove the individual burdens involved in personal registration and bring the United States into line with other democracies.

b. **Arguments against government registration of voters.** Critics of the proposal respond that individuals should be willing to make this small effort if they want to vote and that personal registration is necessary to prevent election fraud.

5. **Proposals for direct presidential election.** The method of presidential election is regularly debated. Many plans would change the method of determining electoral votes. The most common proposal is to elect the president by direct, nation-wide popular vote.

a. **Arguments for direct presidential election.** Proponents of the idea of eliminating the electoral college by direct popular election of the president argue that the reform would make the most powerful office in the nation truly democratic.

b. **Arguments against direct presidential election.** Critics of the proposal see no reason to change a system that has worked well in almost every election and preserves some role for the states. They also fear that a direct election, if close, might encourage fraud and weaken the authority of presidents winning such elections.

6. **Proposals for increasing voter information.** How can citizens become better informed? Suggestions include more television debates, different formats for debates, free broadcast time for candidates and parties, and informational pamphlets sent to voters at public expense.

   a. **Arguments for increasing voter information.** Advocates of these and related changes believe that voters now lack sufficient relevant information.

   b. **Arguments against increasing voter information.** Critics emphasize the need not for a larger quantity of information, but for more balanced presentations, better analysis by media reporters, and better civic education to facilitate the voters' judgments.

7. **The problem of "negative advertising."** Negative advertising is generally condemned, but there is no clear means to control the practice. Legislation to curb negative advertising would be very difficult to draft, beginning with the problem of finding a clear definition. Furthermore, a restriction on advertising could easily become an infringement on rights of free speech. Since the conventional wisdom is that negative advertising works, most politicians will continue to use it until voters react against the practice.

B. **The role of the parties.** Citizens also need to consider the role of the political parties and how they might better serve the needs of a mass democracy.

   1. **Regulation of parties.** Should parties be as closely regulated as they have been in the past? Arguments are made for and against continued regulation of the parties.

      a. **Arguments in favor of regulating parties.** Those favoring regulation argue that parties are semi-official bodies, and that they must be watched to prevent the abuse of their power.

      b. **Arguments against regulating parties.** Critics see detailed regulations as hampering the parties in their competitive efforts to establish linkages with the voters. They also consider such regulation as restrictions on the parties' constitutional rights of freedom of speech and freedom of association.

   2. **The question of direct primary elections in the presidential nomination.** Should the nominating system be reformed? The direct primary was created to allow voters to overcome the power of party "bosses."

      a. **Arguments for retaining presidential primaries.** The system is still defended as an expression of democracy and a means to keep the parties open to new candidates and members.

      b. **Arguments against retaining presidential primaries.** Critics say that the system emphasizes individual candidates, undermines party coherence, and makes it difficult for voters to hold anyone responsible for the actions of government.

   3. **Proposals for national presidential primaries.** Has the extension of primaries in presidential nominations resulted in a politics lacking cohesion?

      a. **Arguments in favor of national presidential primaries.** To make the presidential selection process fully democratic, some argue that party conventions should be replaced by national presidential primaries.

      b. **Arguments against presidential primaries.** Others say that the nation would be better served if party leaders had more of a role, and could provide some "peer review" of the candidates' qualifications.

   4. **Proposals for increasing local party participation.** Do the present parties promote popular participation? Contemporary parties are becoming more efficient electoral organizations, but possibly at the cost of losing direct contacts with the voters.

      a. **Arguments for increasing local party power.** Some analysts think that local party members should be given more of a role in deciding party programs and in the selection of party officials. This would be an inducement for encouraging people to participate at the local level.

b. **Arguments against increasing local party power**. A different view is that local party activists tend to be relatively extreme in their policy views. If given more power within the party, say critics, their actions would make it more difficult to win elections.

C. **The challenge of American democracy**. The challenge of American democracy remains as stated by **Alexis de Tocqueville** (1805-1859) in 1835: "It is, indeed, difficult to conceive how men who have entirely given up the habit of self-government should succeed in making a proper choice of those by whom they are to be governed; and none will ever believe that a liberal, wise, and energetic government can spring from the suffrages of a subservient people."

2. INTEREST GROUPS

A landed interest, manufacturing interest, a mercantile interest, a moneyed interest, with many lesser interests, grow up of necessity in civilized nations, and divide them into different classes, actuated by various sentiments and views. The regulation of these various and interfering interests forms the principal task of modern legislation and involves the spirit of party and faction in the necessary and ordinary operations of government.

James Madison (1787)

INTRODUCTION

Americans like to believe there is strength in numbers. We believe that while one person acting alone may not be able to facilitate a change in government policy, a group of people acting in unison will. In a country with a population of over 250 million people, the idea of a group of citizens acting on behalf of the public interest is somewhat comforting—but how accurate an idea is that?

On the most basic level, interest groups are formal organizations that try to achieve their goals through influence on public policy. In order to understand interest groups, we should understand why people join both public interest and certain special interest groups. We also need to know that institutions such as business corporations form interest groups; and we should understand what interest groups can

reasonably expect to accomplish. If people join special interest groups for reasons other than a desire to affect public policy, or if the policies they advocate are not truly in the public interest, our understanding of interest groups must correspond to these realities.

Whatever our understanding of these groups might be, we must accept that interest groups are a fact of life in the modern American political system. Without them, our government would not exist in its current form, nor would many of our laws exist as they do. Whether the current role of some interest groups is a desirable part of our system or whether their present influence on public policy should continue are fundamental issues for the citizen to decide. To consider such issues, citizens must be well-grounded in the character and contemporary influence of interest groups.

OBJECTIVES

Citizens should be able to

1. explain what interest groups are and how they function.

2. distinguish public interest groups from special interest groups.

3. explain why interest groups are formed and why individuals join public interest and special interest groups.

4. describe historical examples of the influence of various types of interest groups.

5. explain and evaluate the tactics and techniques which both special interest and public interest groups use to influence policy making.

6. take, defend, and evaluate positions on the role of public and special interest groups in American society and suggest what reforms, if any, should be made.

FRAME OF REFERENCE
Conceptual Perspective

I. **A pluralist definition of interest groups**. Pluralism is the belief that democratic values can be preserved by a system in which (1) there are many competing interest groups, (2) public policy is determined through bargaining and compromise, and (3) voters can influence policy by choosing among parties and candidates. Interest groups may be defined as formal organizations that seek to influence public policy in democratic polities. Interest groups become sources of information and a means for taking action in a pluralist society like the United States.

A. **Interest groups' role in government**. Interest groups are indigenous to open societies. Their methods of organization, claims upon members' loyalties, techniques of asserting demands, and success in achieving goals, however, vary with the political culture in which they operate.

B. **Madison's view**. James Madison, in *The Federalist* No.10, gave a classic definition of one sort of interest group.

1. **Madison's definition of interest groups**. Madison described one kind of interest groups, which he called "factions," as "actuated by some common impulse of passion, or of interest, adverse to the rights of citizens, or to the permanent and aggregate interests of the community."

2. **The connection between freedom and interest groups**. At the same time, Madison believed that the impulse to form interest groups was a part of human nature acting in a free society. "Liberty is to faction," he wrote, "as air is to fire." Since he thought that interest groups opposed to the public good could only be eliminated by eliminating liberty, Madison sought to structure government in ways that control their influence and thereby prevent tyranny.

C. **A modern viewpoint**. In a large, complex society, a single individual has great difficulty being heard, much less affecting the governmental decision-making process. But, when many sharing a particular concern join together, their collective opinion can speak with more authority. Some of these groups are interest groups. They can become channels through which people can realize the democratic ideal of legitimate and satisfying interaction with government.

D. **Public interest versus special interest groups**. A basic difference between interest groups concerns their primary purposes.

1. **A definition of public interest groups**. Public interest groups are those that intend to further the benefit of the public as a whole, as opposed to a smaller section of society or their own membership. For example, a group promoting clean air legislation intends the good of everyone.

2. **A definition of special interest groups**. Special interest groups are those that intend to further the benefit of a section of society, including their own membership, rather than the whole. For example, a group advocating legislation for promoting the use of tobacco intends the good of only a section of society.

3. **Cover groups for special interests**. Special interest groups may seek to influence public policy by setting up groups claiming to be completely public-spirited. In fact, such groups are guided mainly or solely by special interests.

4. **Some special interests more benign than others**. Groups promoting a variety of benefits for sections of society are often regarded as benign and unobjectionable by most citizens. Groups promoting legislation to benefit disabled people are seldom accused of selfishness.

5. **"Public interest" groups not infallible**. It is also possible that bona fide public interest groups that intend the public good may be mistaken in their policies to achieve it. It is not clear, for example, that groups opposing all nuclear energy development in the name of the public good are entirely correct in their views. It is possible that some nuclear energy development is in the public interest. In other cases, some people may simply have a difference of opinion with public interest groups when the public good is uncertain.

E. **Interest groups composed either of institutions or individual members**. While one might assume that "interest groups" are made up of individual members, this is not necessarily the case. Two kinds of interest groups can be identified on the basis of its composition. (See Kay Lehman Schlozman and John T. Tierney, *The Mischiefs of Faction: Organized Interests in American Politics*, 1985.)

1. **Institutional groups**. Many interest groups, including many special interest groups, are composed of institutions. These may include interest groups representing businesses, educational institutions, state or local government, or other institutions.

2. **Membership groups.** A second kind of interest group is composed of individual members. Public interest or "citizen" groups fall into this category as well as some special interest groups. In the following section, membership groups are discussed.

II. **Group membership in pluralist thought.** Since policy choices ratified by public bodies are collective (everyone in the society is affected), people will benefit from an organized group's acquisition of a "good" or benefit regardless of whether or not they participated in the process by which it was obtained. If that is true, there must be some further reason for people to join interest groups than the acquisition of a public good, since that good would be acquired without joining the group.

A. **Why citizens might join interest groups.** People join interest groups for a variety of reasons.

1. **Basic assumptions.** There are several assumptions underlying the pluralist view of group membership.

   a. **The costs of group membership.** Group membership is **never** without a price for the individual, for example, financial costs and time commitments.

   b. **Benefits of joining as exceeding costs.** No rational person will incur the costs of joining unless two conditions are met.

      (1) **Benefits of joining as exceeding those of non-participation.** One condition is that the anticipated payoff resulting from such participation is appreciably higher than the probable payoff resulting from nonparticipation.

      (2) **Benefits of joining as exceeding membership costs.** A second condition is that the benefits gained from membership exceeds the costs of group membership. "Benefits" in this context may be tangible or intangible, altruistic or self-regarding.

   c. **Membership often temporary.** These arguments are consistent with what we know about people's interest in politics. Most people do not join a group simply because they wish to become part of a group organization or because incentives offered by the group. While there is an active strata of the politically active and aware, most people are often less interested in politics than they are in their everyday lives. When the two combine, political activity may occur temporarily, only to cease when the situation changes.

2. **Collective goods versus selective goods.** The dilemma of choosing between leading an "everyday" life only versus making a political commitment can be called choosing between "selective goods" and "collective goods."

   a. **What collective goods are.** Collective goods are benefits that **cannot be distributed selectively**—to some people but not to others. For example, under universal health insurance, no one could be denied the benefits of health care.

   b. **What selective goods are.** Selective goods are benefits **derived from membership in an organization** and thus **can be denied to non-members.** While under universal health insurance no one could be denied basic benefits, members of a retired person organization, for example, could deny non-members reduced rates on pharmaceutical, travel, and insurance (made available to members through mass purchasing arrangements). "Rational" retired persons would not join for benefits they can enjoy without membership. Such benefits, therefore, form an incentive for joining.

3. **Joining public interest groups to further the public good.** Some people join public interest groups for reasons other than securing benefits primarily for themselves. These individuals become members for such reasons as a desire to extend rights and benefits to other segments of society, the fulfillment of public spiritedness and civic duty, or for other altruistic purposes.

B. **Why people remain in interest groups.** The reasons for **renewing** membership may be dissimilar from the reasons for **joining** an organization. In deciding whether to renew membership, people usually have more knowledge of the particular group than they had when they originally joined. Generally, selective benefits become more important as membership is renewed, giving lobbyists more freedom to act without consulting rank-and-file members. And, since new members know less than veteran members about an organization's policy aspirations, they too are a weak source of constraint on the organization's lobbying efforts. Some people, on the other hand, may remain members of public interest groups without regard to selective benefits but rather because they continue to be public-spirited, feel membership part of their civic duty, or for similar reasons.

C. **Implications for governance**. The implications of personal motives for joining an organization are substantial.

   1. **Interest groups as poor links between the individual and government**. How can organizations be the link between members and government if people join to get selective benefits? If people join an association of retired people to get discounts on prescription medicine, can they be regarded as a political constituency when "their" lobbyists testify before Congress on a complex social security problem? If their lobbyist took a position contrary to that of most members, would they or could they instruct the lobbyist to stop? If the lobbyist did not act, would they resign from the organization? Unfortunately, there are no clear answers to any of these questions.

   2. **Gaining selective benefits as primary motive for joining**. Recent research has indicated that selective benefits are the primary reason for people joining many organizations, though not public interest organizations. In other cases, there is genuine political commitment. For example, doctors appear inclined to join the American Medical Association to receive selective benefits. On the other hand, women join the National Organization for Women because they wish to support its programs rather than for selective benefits.

   3. **Interest group representatives as speaking for their members**. If people join interest groups to receive selective goods, those who claim to represent them may not actually represent their views. Thus, the claims of these representatives may not be accurate.

III. **Alternative approaches to understanding interest groups**. While the United States government is considered by many students of politics to be a pluralist system, that proposition may not be correct or entirely correct. Recent research has questioned many of the assumptions made in classifying the United States as pluralist. If the United States is not a true pluralist system, our understanding of interest groups must correspondingly change.

A. **Why people join or fail to join interest groups**. The theory of pluralism accepts, without giving alternative possibilities much thought, the idea that people join groups to achieve public policy aspirations. This belief attributes more political interest to potential group members than is justified by the evidence.

   1. **Why people fail to join.** People do not join interest groups for a variety of reasons.

      a. **Apathy**. Most people have little more than a passing interest in politics until it directly affects their lives.

      b. **Lack of rational incentive**. The existence of shared interests or attitudes is often not a sufficient condition for "rational" people to form a group or to join an existing one. Many seem to believe that if others organize, the value added to the organization by their membership will be insignificant. They may wonder what one more voice adds to a group of thousands.

      c. **Ignorance**. People might wish to join public interest or other interest groups but fail to do so because they are unaware of those that further purposes they support.

   2. **Why people join public interest and special interest groups.** Perhaps the most significant aspect of the intense exploration of individual motives for joining or renewing membership is that single explanations for why people join groups are too simple. Some people join for a variety of reasons.

      a. **Civic-mindedness**. Some organizations such as citizens' groups attract those who are genuinely concerned with political, economic, environmental, or other reform.

      b. **Economic and other motives.** Other organizations, for example, trade associations, attract those with a more personalized vision. This does not mean that economic advancement or narrow self-interest always moves people to join special interest groups. They may fear social or economic insecurity, and they may be concerned that their legitimate interests will be attacked and wish to defend them.

B. **Problems for democracy raised by interest groups.** The pluralist view of society implies a political situation with a roughly equal distribution of opportunities to acquire political influence. But in the real world there is no assurance that the actual distribution of these resources is equal. Indeed, the unequal distribution of resources is one reason why some interest groups are formed. However, another understanding of the term "pluralism" is a system of multiple, competing interest groups that contributes to the shape of public policy through bargaining and compromise. In this sense, "pluralism" describes a political process in which interest groups organize, attempt to gain influence, and survive or disappear largely without the participation or encouragement of governmental bureaucracies.

1. **The question of elites.** One of the main problems with the modern pluralist theory of interest groups is the level of involvement of cohesive, formal or informal groups of the politically active—so-called "elites." Almost without exception, non-electoral political decisions are a result of bargaining and compromise among those who take an active role in politics and do not involve the general public.

   a. **The influence of elites not necessarily an evil.** One argument is that the influence of elites is not necessarily an evil. In any case, such elites are inevitable. Competition among elites helps to safeguard individual non-participants from governmental abuse, since no set of interests is likely to dominate indefinitely. A particular interest will win in some years, lose in others, win in some arenas, lose in others, win on some issues, lose on others.

   b. **The influence of elites as an evil.** On the other hand, some or most Americans might believe that grass roots, participatory democracy is ideal. In that case, the influence of elites may be regarded as an evil in so far as it detracts from the legitimate influence of ordinary citizens or the free deliberation of their representatives.

2. **Pressure groups or interest groups?** Elements of the theory of political pluralism are helpful for understanding the nature of interest groups. But perhaps these groups might better be described as "pressure" groups working outside a recognized role in government that raise serious problems in a democratic order.

   a. **Pluralism based on the rough equality of groups.** For the theory of pluralism to be accurate, there must be at least a rough equality of power of the major groups competing in the political system for power and influence.

   b. **Under pluralism, interest groups not controlled by government.** The system must be a loosely structured "free market" system. In this system, groups come into and leave the political arena with neither negative or positive sanctions from the government.

   c. **Interest groups best described as pressure groups?** Without a structurally recognized role in government, interest groups are more likely to use pressure from outside recognized institutions to achieve their policy goals. Some political scientists have taken to calling these organizations **pressure groups** rather than interest groups. The very term "pressure group" implies that American interest groups do not have the ease of access to decision making afforded by quasi-governmental status. Therefore, they must use "lobbying" tactics. Lobbying often means **pressure** as opposed to **bargaining**.

   d. **Pressure groups' operation by creating obligations and cashing in on them.** The term "pressure group" was first applied to politically active business associations. But the term better fits less privileged groups such as labor, consumer, and civil rights organizations. With freedom to organize and no guaranteed access to decision making, pressure groups gain their advantages by creating obligations and "cashing in" on them. Since the 1970s, the number of such groups—and their "Political Action Committees" (PACs)—has increased enormously. The focus is no longer on bargaining but on political pressure.

C. **The place of interest groups in American democracy: are they out of control?** The tremendous growth of PACs (the money-holding element of interest groups) has focused attention on the value of interest groups for democracy. Some argue that some interest groups have deviated so far from their initial purpose that they no longer function as a voice for citizen dissatisfaction. (This criticism would not seem to apply, however, to grass roots "citizen" groups.) The problem with interest groups has been viewed as a function of internal organization of the group itself, that is, whether the group reflects the views of its membership. The problem has also been viewed as a function of interest group participation in policy formation, that is, whether the public good is lost in the scramble for political influence.

1. **Question of interest groups' undemocratic internal organization.** With the free commerce in interest groups came doubts about whether interest groups further the interests of democracy. Critics of pluralism assert that the very organizations said to provide a linkage between rulers and ruled are themselves undemocratic.

    a. **Inactivity and inertia of most members.** Members in organizations other than grass roots citizen groups have little to say in policy positions taken by their group. Instead, largely as a result of receiving selective benefits available only to them, they do nothing to change their situation.

    b. **Actions of active members unchecked by majorities.** The politically active members who control interest groups are free to act, unchecked by the rank-and-file members, in whatever means they feel best serves the advantage of the group. Again, however, the lack of control by rank-and-file members may not be true of grass roots citizen groups.

2. **Interest groups and the public good.** Students of politics have been forced to reassess the political consequences of interest groups as a result of modern developments. The following considerations refer to groups seeking **selective benefits**, not to those seeking **collective benefits**.

    a. **Special interest groups as primarily distributors of selective benefits for members.** One political scientist has redefined special interest groups as "distributional coalitions," emphasizing the importance of distributing benefits for members as a principal function.

    b. **Special interest groups as restricting the country's attempt to make difficult choices.** The influence of organizations whose purpose is to defend its particular interests may constrain the ability of the nation to make difficult choices through its elected representatives.

c. **The reign of interest groups related to economic decline.** From this perspective, special interest groups may insure economic decline unless they are subordinated to a view that seeks the public good.

d. **Distribution of power versus the use of power.** The idea of pluralism does not refer to the distribution of power but rather to the use of power. Special interest groups are not all-encompassing either in their membership or in those who benefit from their activities. That is, they pursue their own—"special"—interest which may be opposed to the good of the polity as a whole.

e. **The relationship between interest groups and government.** The idea of interest groups as separated from government is often exaggerated.

    (1) **Government association with interest groups.** The federal government often seeks the advice of certain special interest and public interest groups in order to improve public involvement in policy formation or for political reasons.

    (2) **"Iron triangles."** In addition, "iron triangles"—coalitions of interest groups, executive branch bureaucracies, and congressional committees that promote a specific policy interest—provide preferential access to government. In the case of congressional committees, those making campaign contributions are usually assured of access. One result is that the voice of more than one interest can be heard. A second result is that the interests of those who are unorganized or who lack financial power may be and usually are unheard.

f. **The role of interest groups and the question of the public good.** When fragmented sectors of government, including bureaucracies, are tightly aligned with interest groups, policy formation is undoubtedly swayed. This raises the question of whether the public good is systematically undermined by such a system.

    (1) **The public good not necessarily undermined by interest groups.** Some critics

argue that the public good or interest is nothing else than the sum of all of the separate interests in society. Thus the problem with interest groups is that those who are unorganized, such as the poor, are under-represented. Nonetheless, at least in principle, a "free market" in which interest groups compete results in the closest possible approximation to the realization of the public good.

(2) **Interest groups as undermining the public good**. Other critics argue that the public good or interest does not magically emerge from the competition of interest groups. Special interest and private greed do not add up either in theory or in practice to the public good. For example, air pollution that injures health is obviously contrary to the public good. Yet special interests seek to minimize attempts to curb pollution. The public good does not automatically emerge, but must be vigorously represented. In many cases, interest groups seeking selective benefits for their constituents have been able to undermine the public good.

Historical Perspective
Part I. Citizen interest groups

I. **Populist Movement.** Among the ancestors of citizen interest groups of the late twentieth century was the nineteenth-century Populist movement.

A. **Problems, players, and goals**. The Populist Movement of 1877-1898 was largely made up of farmers attempting to forestall economic domination by industrialists.

1. **Growing industrial power**. In the 1880s, as national boundaries moved west and commerce expanded, the power of the federal government, northern industrialists, and bankers grew.

2. **Hardship for farmers**. Farmers, paying higher taxes to the government, higher freight costs to the railroads, and higher interest rates to the banks, were becoming tenants on land they once owned. Large landowners, often bankers, kept farmers in virtual serfdom through the crop-lien, or sharecropping system, in which crops were

exchanged for debt payments or goods with prices set by the creditors. Those farmers lucky enough to keep their land rarely made a profit.

3. **Populist goals**. The Populists attempted to reform the economic system in order to enable farmers to regain control of their lives and land. The Populists challenged the economic power of the bankers and industrialists and demanded that government be responsive to citizens rather than moneyed interests. The Populist Movement proposed innovative responses to an economic system increasingly run by bankers.

B. **Basis for claim**. The agrarian revolt of the late nineteenth century, better known as the Populist Movement, grew from the realization that policy makers in Washington and the state capitals failed to represent farmers' interests.

C. **Tactics**. Populist tactics included forming cooperatives, engaging in public education, and political organizing.

1. **Cooperatives**. In response to creditors and manufacturers who were profiting at their expense, farmers developed their own institutions to provide the services they needed. For example, they established economic cooperatives to sell crops and to buy seeds, farm merchandise, and groceries. These cooperative efforts were organized by various state and local "farmers alliances," the first of which was founded in 1877 in Texas.

2. **Public education**. "Alliance" leaders believed that spreading their ideas and movement would broaden their cause.

   a. **Lecture and organizing tours**. They embarked on lecture tours, educating farmers about the excessive power of banks and the crop-lien system. They organized the cooperative efforts that enabled farmers to become more economically independent.

   b. **Populist publications**. The Populists also published numerous books and pamphlets in an attempt to present history, economics, and law from the point of view of "the people." More than a thousand populist journals and magazines were circulated in the 1890s.

3. **Political organization**. By 1890, the Populist Movement had begun large-scale political organi-

zation as farmers began to recognize that government was failing to protect their interests in the emerging industrial society.

   a. **The Omaha Convention of 1892**. In 1892, farmers met in Omaha to establish formally a new political party, the People's Party, and to announce the platform that embodied the Populist economic vision.

   b. **The Omaha Platform**. The Omaha Platform advocated government ownership of communication and transportation industries, prohibition of alien land ownership, and the free and unlimited coinage of silver. It proposed United States Treasury notes ("greenbacks") as legal tender to replace national bank notes. It also proposed a more equitable system of taxing different social classes.

   c. **Growth of the People's Party**. Spreading their ideas through lectures and education drives, the People's Party grew rapidly, eventually numbering over two million citizens. Populist candidates won countless state and local elections, as well as two United States Senate and eleven House seats in the 1890s.

D. **Outcomes**. The results of the Populist Movement were mixed. The movement often benefitted members in the short term, but it was weakened by internal divisions.

  1. **Movement culture**. In addition to securing temporary economic benefits for their members, the farmers' alliances also generated a culture of mass democratic aspiration. Farmers and laborers who had previously felt alienated from the political process joined the Populist Movement because it affirmed their dignity as members of society and enabled them to believe in the viability of working collectively for individual liberty. The movement represented an attempt to create a democratic, egalitarian culture.

  2. **Shortcomings**. Internal problems of the movement ultimately led to its demise.

   a. **Internal divisions**. The Populist Movement was ultimately unable to overcome racial and geographical divisions within its membership. Political activity introduced new conflicts, and with the desire to win elections growing

after 1892, the original vision became blurred.

   b. **Candidates' misuse of Populist label**. Candidates, especially in the West, ran under the "Populist" label but held views that bore little resemblance to the Omaha Platform.

   c. **Merger of Populist party and final demise**. Although opposed by many, influential leaders decided to merge the Populist party with the Democratic party in a futile attempt to be on the winning side of the 1896 presidential election. When the Republican candidate, backed by substantial monetary support from big business, won by a landslide, the Populists were defeated and demoralized. In the merge with the Democrats, they had lost their autonomy.

II. **Suffrage**. Another historical antecedent of today's citizens' interest groups was the movement for woman suffrage. (See also, Gender Issues)

A. **Problems, players, and goals**. Shortly after the American Revolution, the right to vote was effectively extended to white, male landowners. State constitutions explicitly denied African Americans and women the right to vote.

  1. **Early advocates**. After 1848 a group of women fought to gain the rights and responsibilities of suffrage, the right to vote. These reformers included **Elizabeth Cady Stanton** (1815-1902), **Susan B. Anthony (1820-1906)**, and **Matilda Joslyn Gage** (1826-1891), who joined together to challenge the male-only political system.

  2. **Women not included under Fifteenth Amendment**. The Fifteenth Amendment, ratified in 1870, guaranteed black men the right to vote. The suffragists would have to convince legislators to amend the Constitution again before women would be granted the right to vote.

B. **Basis for claim**. Suffragists argued that there was no moral ground on which to deny women the right to vote.

C. **Tactics**. To press their campaign for the vote, women adopted a variety of tactics.

  1. **Petitions and donations**. Women went door-to-door gathering signatures for petitions supporting

woman's suffrage. They also collected donations to further the cause.

2. **Meetings, speeches, and conventions.** Women held mass meetings and national conventions to discuss their goals and strategies, and also to attract press attention. They wrote columns in newspapers, distributed pamphlets, and exchanged ideas with European women. They also made bold speeches on street corners in cities and towns throughout the country, using soapboxes as platforms.

3. **Lobbying.** Suffragists actively lobbied legislators to hold state referendums on the question of woman suffrage.

4. **Pressuring President Wilson.** During World War I, some of the more militant suffragists launched an attack on President Wilson's international reputation, seeking to embarrass him into giving his official support for woman suffrage.

   a. **Picketing the White House.** Suffragists picketed the White House with banners that proclaimed, "Democracy Should Begin at Home!" These protests attracted a great deal of attention, often drawing large and angry crowds.

   b. **Arrests and hunger strikes.** In a vain attempt to end the protests, police arrested picketers on flimsy charges of "obstructing sidewalk traffic," and a total of ninety-seven women were sent to jail. Many of them went on hunger strikes to protest the illegality of their arrests and were brutally force-fed.

D. **Outcomes.** The suffragists, although without the power to elect or reject the policy-makers they sought to influence, initiated a dramatic, fundamental change in American domestic policy. In 1920, the Nineteenth Amendment was ratified, and women were guaranteed the right to vote.

III. **Other public interest groups based on an idea or cause.** Although special interest groups based on economic and occupational concerns have had a prominent role in American political and social developments, there have also been numerous public interest groups organized around the promotion of a specific idea or cause advocated as part of the public interest. These early public interest groups generally focused on social reform.

A. **Temperance groups.** In the early 1800s, interest groups in the form of temperance organizations had a pervasive impact on American society. Groups such as the American Temperance Society (formed in 1826) and the Woman's Christian Temperance Union (1874) were vociferous champions of prohibition, and appealed to state governments to pass "local option laws" which would allow communities to forbid the selling, manufacture, and consumption of alcohol. As the result of political pressure from interest groups, sixteen states had adopted such laws prior to the Civil War. Another influential temperance group was the Anti-Saloon League, founded in Ohio in 1893. The League began as a social movement and quickly was transformed into a national organization which employed sophisticated political pressure tactics to advance its reformist agenda.

B. **Civil liberties and interest groups.** The American Civil Liberties Union founded in 1920, was created with the goal of promoting and protecting constitutional rights, often supporting unpopular causes in which issues of civil rights were in question.

C. **League of Women Voters of the United States.** This organization, founded in 1920 as an outgrowth of the woman suffrage movement, was formed with the intention of promoting political awareness and responsibility among citizens.

D. **Nature conservation groups.** The National Wildlife Federation, and the Sierra Club, founded in 1892 by **John Muir** (1838-1914), are public interest groups committed to environmental preservation, conservation, and protection.

IV. **Organizations promoting the welfare of social groups.** Some interest groups have been formed to promote the interests of specific social groups, such as racial minorities and veterans.

A. **The NAACP.** The National Association for the Advancement of Colored People (NAACP), established in 1909, is an interracial interest group that has promoted the elimination of racial discrimination and segregation, primarily through legal and political action. Attorneys representing the NAACP brought various cases concerning segregation before the U.S. Supreme Court in the 1950s, culminating in the historic decision in *Brown v. Board of Education of Topeka, Kansas* (May 17, 1957).

B. **Veterans' groups.** Other interest groups which promote the welfare of a specific social group include the American Legion (formed in 1919), an organization of veterans of World Wars I and II, and the Veterans of Foreign Wars (1913-14). Both of these groups attempt to promote the welfare of the nation's veterans through ensuring government provision for veterans' pensions and compensation, health care, disability, education, and other benefits.

V. **Desegregation of public facilities in the South**. From the 1950s to the 1970s, African Americans and their supporters waged a campaign against racial segregation.

   A. **Problems, players, and goals**. Racial segregation in schools, the work place, public facilities, and employment symbolized white oppression of blacks. Segregationist laws remained on the books in most southern states well into the 1960s.

   B. **Basis for claim**. Civil rights groups argued that segregation laws were immoral and unjust. They pointed out the inconsistencies between laws which treated blacks as second-class citizens and the guarantees of the U.S. Constitution.

   C. **Tactics**. Acts of civil disobedience led by the **Rev. Martin Luther King, Jr.** (1929-1968), including the bus boycotts sparked by Rosa Parks and the lunch-counter sit-ins, demonstrated the effectiveness of group activity. By using the foundation of preestablished community organizations—churches, student groups, labor unions, and other groups—blacks built a network of support for racial equality.

   D. **Outcomes**. Equal access to schools, public facilities and the polls is now legally protected. The African American community's mobilization led to national outrage which created a climate for significant legislative change as well as enforcement of other equal access protection.

VI. **Automobile safety regulation**. Efforts to improve automobile safety begun in the 1960s by consumer advocate **Ralph Nader** have resulted in substantial improvements in auto safety and a corresponding savings of lives and reduction of injuries.

   A. **Problems, players, and goals**. Consumer advocate Ralph Nader is best known for his battles for automobile safety.

      1. **Nader and auto safety problems**. Nader first came to public attention in the 1960s by exposing the safety problems of General Motor's Corvair automobile. He began his career as a "public citizen"

by uncovering evidence that automobile companies designed their cars for style, cost, performance, and calculated obsolescence, but not for safety. Safety was not a key feature in automobile design despite the five million reported accidents, nearly four hundred thousand fatalities, over one hundred thousand permanent disabilities and 1.5 million injuries yearly that had occurred.

      2. **Lack of producer incentive for auto safety**. The accident rate had no negative effect on the production and sale of automobiles. This circumstance created no economic incentive for making safety a priority. In 1964, General Motors (GM), which made $1.7 billion in profits, spent only $1 million on safety research. Seeing that industry did not spend more money on safety design voluntarily, Nader campaigned for federal regulations to require safety standards.

   B. **Basis for claim**. Nader maintained it is the government's responsibility to protect the safety of its citizens. He argued that the government should give safety a higher priority than corporate economic interests.

   C. **Tactics**. The tactic used to press the case for reform in automobile safety regulation was publicity.

      1. **Publication of** *Unsafe at any Speed*. Determined to inform the public of the blatant corporate negligence concerning auto safety, in 1965 Nader published *Unsafe at Any Speed: The Designed-in Dangers of the American Automobile*. In the book Nader described the dangerous defects of GM's Corvair automobile.

      2. **Reception of** *Unsafe at any Speed*. General Motors, threatened by this scathing report, hired detectives to follow Nader in an attempt to find or possibly fabricate information that might undermine his credibility. The plan backfired when exposed by a journalist; the ensuing publicity caused Nader's book to become a best seller.

   D. **Outcomes**. As a result of national attention to the issue, Nader was able to encourage Congress to hold hearings on automobile safety in 1966.

      1. **Creation of government watchdog agency**. The information revealed at the hearings led Congress to create the National Highway Traffic Safety Administration (NHTSA). This government

agency was invested with the power to set safety standards for motor vehicles and to place certain requirements on auto manufacturers.

2. **Implementation of safety standards.** In 1967, the first thirty safety standards were implemented. Most of them were designed to make automobile accidents less often fatal. Since then, NHTSA has adopted numerous other safety standards. In 1984, for example, consumer activists succeeded in winning a crash protection standard, which requires new cars to have either an air bag or automatic seat belts beginning in 1990.

3. **Reductions in fatalities and injuries.** Auto safety reforms have been estimated to have saved over two hundred thousand lives since 1966 and prevented millions of injuries. The efforts of Ralph Nader and other consumer advocates have encouraged citizens to pay more attention to auto safety, thus forcing the auto industry to make safety a higher priority.

VII. **Alinsky and redlining.** Techniques for community organizing were developed and taught by the late Saul Alinsky.

A. **Problems, players, and goals.** As a community organizer, **Saul Alinsky** (1909-1972) inspired groups of poor and disadvantaged citizens to organize against economic and political injustices, including the practice of "redlining," from the late 1930s to his death in 1972. Redlining refers to the practice of drawing a line around a particular community on a map and limiting the availability of bank loans for those residing within the redlined area, regardless of their qualifications. Minority neighborhoods have often been redlined.

B. **Basis for claim.** Community activists protested the practice because it singled out an entire group for unfair discrimination. Protesters believed that loan applicants should be judged on an individual basis.

C. **Tactics.** Upon discovering a bank's policy of redlining, the Alinsky activists organized hundreds of people to go to the bank and open up accounts for $20 for several days in a row. Then the protesters returned and closed their accounts, often repeating the process several times. This process tied up bank employees and money, pressuring the bank to change its discriminatory policy.

D. **Outcomes.** The banks Alinsky targeted often stopped redlining. Although redlining is still practiced, laws now exist to prevent banks engaging in redlining from opening new branches.

VIII. **The FTC Improvement Act.** Federal regulation of various business practices precipitated attempts to have them relaxed.

A. **Problems, players, and goals.** One principal player was the U.S. Chamber of Commerce. (For further discussion of the Chamber, see below, Part II. Special interest groups.)

1. **New federal regulations.** In the mid-1970s, the Chamber's constituency was threatened by a series of rules regulating various industries passed by the Federal Trade Commission (FTC), a government agency designed to protect consumers from misleading advertising and unfair pricing. The rules included those regulating credit practices, food advertising, prescription drugs, funeral practices, and "over-the-counter" drugs.

2. **Requirements of the rules.** The FTC required industries to deal honestly with their customers through means such as labeling packaging and providing price disclosures for services. For example, the Funeral Practices Rule required funeral directors to make itemized price lists available and to answer requests for price information over the phone. It also prohibited directors from requiring unnecessary caskets for cremations, and misleading consumers about legal requirements for funerals.

3. **Industry response to federal regulation.** While the Chamber had not been particularly active in the 1960s, these regulatory acts spurred interest in political action on behalf of business interests. From 1974 to 1980, the Chamber's membership doubled to 165,000 companies, and its annual budget tripled to $68 million.

B. **Basis for claim.** The Chamber's members maintained that increasing regulation would reduce profits and constrain the free market. The FTC argued that consumers deserved to be protected and that its measures would increase competition through price disclosures.

C. **Tactics.** The Chamber of Commerce formed Political Action Committees (PACs) to lobby Congress and make contributions to the campaigns of the members of Congress who supported their interests. The PACs also contacted members, alerting them to proposed legislation. The PACs encouraged Chamber members to send letters and mailgrams and to make telephone calls and visits to members of Congress to express opposition to the FTC rules.

D. **Outcomes**. The ultimate outcome favored limited relaxation of federal regulations. A bill was introduced in Congress that sought to restrict the FTC's regulatory powers. But the activities of public interest groups resulted in the FTC's retaining much of its regulatory power.

1. **Relaxation of federal consumer protection**. Because of the tactics adopted by Chamber of Commerce PACs, members of Congress perceived a huge outcry against regulation. Although polls showed a large majority of Americans approved of the specific regulations and even endorsed stronger ones, consumers were not as well organized as the Chamber of Commerce. Consumers were therefore not able to influence Congress, which, in the late 1970s, weakened most of the regulatory rules.

2. **The FTC Improvement Act**. In addition, the Senate Commerce Committee introduced the FTC Improvement Act in 1979, a complete revision of the original 1914 Act. The revision was designed to place severe limits on the FTC's power.

3. **Efforts to retain FTC powers.** Before Congress could vote on the proposed new act, however, a coalition of consumer and labor activists formed to lobby against it. The most visible and militant of the groups was the National Council of Senior Citizens (NCSC) and the American Association of Retired Persons (AARP), advocacy groups for older people. Members of AARP and NCSC wrote letters to the president and their representatives in Congress to express support for the FTC regulations.

4. **Retention of FTC powers**. This effort failed to stop the FTC Improvement Act, but it prompted the President to ask for a bill which retained some of the powers of the FTC. Such a measure passed the House and Senate overwhelmingly.

IX. **The Massachusetts bottle bill**. In the 1970s and 1980s, a New England public interest group organized a campaign to reduce environmental damage through recycling bottles.

A. **Problems, players, and goals**. The Massachusetts Public Interest Research Group (MASSPIRG), a student-run consumer and environmental group, hoping to promote recycling, advocated a law to implement a return deposit on bottles. Opponents of the proposed law included grocers and soft drink and liquor bottlers and distributors.

B. **Basis for claim**. MASSPIRG advocated bottle recycling as part of a long-term policy of decreasing volume in landfills and curbing the depletion of resources. But opponents maintained that the loss of income and jobs in the bottling industry made recycling too costly.

C. **Tactics**. In 1975, MASSPIRG gathered the one hundred thousand signatures needed to put a bottle recycling bill on the state ballot.

1. **Narrow defeat at the ballot box**. Opponents of the proposed law—grocers, soft drink and liquor bottlers, and distributors—spent over $2 million to lobby against it. The initiative was defeated at the polls by only eight-tenths of one percent.

2. **Further efforts for a "bottle bill."** MASSPIRG then went directly to the state legislature but faced the opposition of the powerful bottlers and distributors. MASSPIRG students held community meetings, spoke on radio programs, and campaigned door-to-door to let citizens know how successful the law had been in other states. By 1981, polls showed that seventy percent of Massachusetts residents supported the bottle bill. The legislature eventually passed the law, but then put the issue on a referendum to let the voters decide.

D. **Outcomes**. Despite the vast financial resources of the opposition, fifty-nine percent of the votes cast supported the bottle bill, which went into effect in 1983.

X. **Tobacco exports**. In the late 1980s, tobacco interests succeeded in pressuring the government into acting to increase tobacco exports.

A. **Problems, players, and goals**. The Tobacco Institute is a trade association of thirteen large tobacco manufacturers working primarily to limit regulation of their products. Facing trade barriers in nations that prohibit the import or advertising of tobacco products, tobacco industry lobbyists urged the White House to intervene. The American Public Health Association, representing thirty thousand professionals from all fields of public health, opposed any government effort to promote tobacco exports, pointing to the fact that 2.5 million people die annually from smoking-related diseases.

B. **Basis for claim**. U.S. tobacco farmers, who rely on expanding international markets to fuel demand for tobacco, viewed intervention on their behalf as an economic necessity. Tobacco manufacturers called on the White House to punish foreign countries that were violating the 1974 U.S. Trade Act, which prohibits discriminatory banning. But public health groups maintained that the U.S. government should not force foreign countries to accept the import of a dangerous product.

C. **Tactics**. Special interest groups representing the tobacco industry have consistently used PACs to lobby Congress to act on the industry's behalf. The Tobacco Institute's political action committee, TIPAC, contributed nearly $200,000 to members of Congress in 1988. And Philip Morris, a major U.S. tobacco manufacturer, ranked third among top corporate PACs in an eighteen month period during 1987 and 1988, contributing over $650,000. PAC spending helped secure congressional support for the tobacco industry.

D. **Outcomes**. The White House decided to invoke Section 301 of the U.S. Trade Act of 1974 to help tobacco companies develop new markets in the Third World. Section 301 gives the United States Trade Representative the authority to impose trade sanctions against any nation whose trade policies are "unjustifiable, unreasonable, or discriminatory." The United States threatened to impose strict trade sanctions on trading partners unless they opened up their markets to U.S. tobacco exports and allowed advertising of tobacco products. Under pressure, many Asian governments, including Thailand, lifted their restrictions on tobacco imports.

Part II. Special interest groups

I. **Economic interest groups in American history**. At various times in American history, special interest groups have been the motivating force behind important political and social issues. A number of the earliest special interest groups in the United States were based on economic interests, specifically business, labor, and agriculture. These economic and occupational interest groups were among the most effective early lobbyists.

II. **Economic interest groups and support for independence and constitutional reform**. Merchants, creditors, property owners, and others involved in commerce rallied in support of American independence and later were among those who advocated constitutional reform, culminating in the Philadelphia Convention of 1787.

III. **Business interest groups**. Since the founding of the republic, commercial interests have appealed to the government for the support of specific interests and attempted to influence government policy. Around the turn of the eighteenth century, for instance, American merchants banded together to promote and eventually attain protective tariffs.

A. **Early business associations**. Early business groups include the United States Brewers Association, founded in 1862 after the government levied a tax on beer. Others included the American Trucking Association, Inc. and the Association of American Railroads.

B. **Formation of the NAM**. In 1894 the **National Association of Manufacturers (NAM)**, one of the earliest and most powerful American business interest groups, was founded. The NAM represented the interests of larger industry on a national level, promoting the improvement of free enterprise.

C. **Foundation of the U.S. Chamber of Commerce.** Formed in 1912 at the suggestion of President **William Howard Taft** (1857-1930), the Chamber of Commerce of the United States is the world's largest federation of business companies and associations. The organization was formed with the intention of protecting and promoting the interests of smaller American businesses. It is the principal voice for the American business community. The Chamber's 180,000 members consist of local chambers of commerce, trade and professional associations, businesses, and individuals. The U.S. Chamber serves as a lobbying voice on Capitol Hill for its members.

IV. **The first labor interest groups in America**. Special interest groups representing organized labor also have an extensive history in American politics. Soon after American independence, craftsmen such as carpenters, shoemakers, printers, and masons organized groups in order to secure increased wages and better working conditions. The late eighteenth and early nineteenth centuries gave rise to numerous labor organizations which attempted to influence governmental policies.

A. **The Mechanics Union of Trade Associations**. Created in 1827, this organization was a combination of various craft unions and had political action as one of its primary objectives. It fought for the abolition of property restrictions on the right to vote as well as the guarantee of free education.

B. **The Knights of Labor**. Another early labor organization, the Noble Order of the Knights of Labor (formed in 1869), attempted to influence political decisions as well. In particular, the Knights of Labor lobbied for an eight hour work day and the abolishment of child labor.

C. **American Federation of Labor**. The American Federation of Labor (AFL) (initially the Federation of Organized Trades and Labor Unions of the United States and Canada, formed in 1881), was organized in 1886. Comprised of numerous separate unions, such as the International Association of Machinists, the United Shoe Workers, and the United Mine Workers, among others, by 1920 the AFL had become one of the most prominent interest groups in the country.

1. **Aims of the AFL**. Under the influence of its first president, **Samuel Gompers** (1850-1924), among other aims, the organization attempted to better working conditions, increase minimum wages and compensation for unemployment, and improve employee health care.

2. **Influence of the AFL**. Attempts to influence government policy by the AFL on government have continued for decades. For example, during World War II, the AFL promised not to strike in return for government assistance and support. When the AFL combined with the Congress of Industrial Organizations (CIO) in 1955, the organization became one of the most powerful special interest groups in the United States.

3. **Independent labor organizations**. Other influential independent labor organizations which separated from the AFL-CIO include the International Brotherhood of Teamsters, founded in 1899, and the United Mine Workers (UMW), established in 1890. Over the years, the UMW successfully lobbied for improved safety conditions, health care, pay, and pensions.

V. **Agricultural groups**. Agricultural groups became formally organized after the Civil War.

A. **The Grange**. The National Grange of the Patrons of Husbandry, established in 1867, is the oldest of the national farm special interest groups. Although the Grange (whose members were called "granges") initially emphasized social and cultural goals, the organization soon adopted a political agenda in order to represent the interests of farmers. By the 1870s, the Grange movement consisted of a coalition of farmers that opposed the grain transport monopolies by railroads and grain elevators, by applying political pressure on state government. The "Granger laws" were important because they established the constitutional principle of public regulation of private utilities.

B. **Other agricultural organizations.** Other large organizations promoting agricultural interests include the American Farm Bureau Federation founded in 1920, which at one time claimed 2.8 million farm-family members, and the National Farmer's Union. Over the decades, these organizations have promoted a variety of measures to benefit farmers, including programs regulating the production, price, and marketing of crops.

VI. **Professional groups**. Numerous professional interest groups have been organized since the mid-nineteenth century to protect and promote their members' welfare and interests. In general, these groups have had less influence on governmental policy than labor, business, and agricultural special interest groups. The earliest of such organizations include the American Medical Association (AMA), created in 1847; the American Bar Association (ABA), founded in 1878; and the National Education Association (NEA), formed in 1857. Today the NEA is the largest national professional organization in the world.

Contemporary Perspective
Part I. Public interest groups

Public interest groups and grass roots citizen movements in recent years have adopted a variety of tactics to further their goals. Citizens should know what these tactics are in order to judge which are legitimate and desirable means of furthering their goals.

I. **Direct action**. One particularly effective citizen technique is direct action including protests, boycotts, picketing, petition drives, and letter-writing campaigns.

A. **Civil disobedience**. Civil disobedience involves nonviolent refusal to obey an existing law or refusing to pay taxes in protest of a government law, activity, or policy. During the Civil Rights Movement, when blacks tried to register to vote in Selma, Alabama, the local governments passed ordinances against meetings of more than three people, a violation of the Constitutional right of assembly. Black activists disobeyed these laws by holding marches, mass meetings, and demonstrations for voting rights.

B. **Protests**. Protests, or public demonstrations, have long been an effective tool for change, particularly on college campuses, as evidenced by students seeking university divestment of investments in South Africa. At Columbia University in 1985, students demanding that the school end investments in corporations doing business in South Africa occupied the steps of an administration building for several weeks. Several months later, the administration agreed to the students' demands. Such protests have increased public awareness about a variety of issues and in some cases altered an institution's policy on South Africa. Often knowing that the community is informed and is willing to take further action is enough to jar policy makers into action.

C. **Boycotts**. A boycott is an attempt to force a business to change a policy by refusing to buy its products. Groups opposing McDonald's use of environmentally hazardous styrofoam and South American beef raised in the ravaged rain forests, have organized boycotts against McDonald's products. Citizens working against apartheid in South Africa boycott companies that do business there. After the Exxon Valdez oil spill, thousands of people boycotted Exxon products to express their outrage over Exxon's poor environmental record. Labor leaders have urged a public boycott of Eastern Airlines because of that company's treatment of its workers.

D. **Picketing**. Picketing at places of business or outside government offices has long been used as a method to demonstrate opposition to a policy. For example, a neighborhood group in New York picketed outside a local bakery in 1934 to demand lower bread prices.

E. **Petitions**. Another effective direct action technique is the petition drive. Petitions provide "hard proof," through the display of signatures, that the public supports a given position.

F. **Letter writing**. Letter writing shows more involvement with an issue than signing a petition because it takes more time and initiative. A large number of letters can have a tremendous impact. When then President Richard Nixon fired special prosecutor Archibald Cox in October 1973, the White House and Capitol Hill received 350,000 telegrams from concerned citizens.

Congressional leaders maintain that the telegrams played a major role in the congressional decision to start the impeachment process.

G. **Community organizing**. This tactic involves making the community aware of an issue and involving citizens in political activism by holding community meetings, campaigning door-to-door, and leafleting.

II. **Use of mass media**. Another important tactic for both public and special interest groups is effective use of the media.

A. **Radio and television talk shows**. Interest group leaders often appear on radio and television talk shows or other news programs to express their opinions to the public.

B. **Newspaper editorials**. Newspaper editorials can be an important factor in affecting public opinion. Interest groups often arrange meetings with editorial boards, asking that newspapers run supportive editorials or news articles.

C. **News releases and news conferences**. News releases and news conferences, generally reserved for important events such as launching a new project or releasing the results of a study, are effective ways to get a group's message to the press.

D. **Media events**. The Connecticut Citizen Action Group wrapped red paper tape around the doors to the Connecticut state legislature to dramatize the need for "cutting the red tape" in using the freedom of information law. In another case an Ohio senior citizen group, working to create a local consumer protection agency, interrupted a city council meeting by distributing white cowboy hats to supporters of the agency and black hats to those in opposition.

III. **Public education**. Many groups publish reports and fact sheets to let the public know about issues. One example, a voting profile, which rates legislators' voting records on issues important to a group, can help open government to greater citizen scrutiny. Environmental Action, a grassroots environmental group, publishes a "Dirty Dozen" list of twelve members of Congress who consistently vote against environmental preservation.

IV. **Watchdog activities**. Public interest groups often act as watchdogs, scrutinizing the actions of elected officials, regulatory agencies, and businesses, or exposing poor policy development or enforcement.

A. **Environmental monitoring**. Environmental groups spur government action by monitoring industry and government responses to pollution and waste disposal problems. For example, the New Jersey Public Interest Research Group (NJPIRG) exposed scores of industry violations of water pollution laws, sparking tougher enforcement of environmental laws.

B. **Use of the Freedom of Information Act**. Groups often obtain information on violations through the Freedom of Information Act (FOIA). Enacted in 1966, the FOIA gives any citizen the right to request and receive any document, file, or other record in the possession of any agency of the federal government, subject to nine exemptions.

V. **Lobbying**. Lobbying is the act of persuading legislators or other policy makers to change an existing law or policy, create a new one or reject a change under consideration. Persuasion tactics include providing information about an issue and demonstrating which segments of the population are aware of and support the position. Effective lobbying by public interest groups was illustrated in 1978 by the Connecticut Citizen Action Group, which garnered support through telephone networks and public hearings to persuade the Connecticut legislature to pass a bottle recycling law.

VI. **Litigation**. Taking an issue to court may be necessary if a law already in existence is not being enforced. Environmental groups have been successful in the courts in spurring action from lax regulatory agencies. But since lawsuits are time-consuming and costly, many interest groups use them only as a last resort.

VII. **Initiative**. Petition drives can play a formal role in the policy-making process by forcing a ballot initiative. An initiative, like that to reform the insurance industry in California, allows citizens to draft a proposed law, and, if they collect enough signatures, bring it to a vote of the public. In California, the consumer group Voter Revolt sponsored a successful ballot initiative, Proposition 103, designed to regulate the automobile insurance industry and mandate that insurance companies charge lower rates.

VIII. **Referendum**. Referendums are similar to initiatives. Citizen groups can, with a predetermined number of signatures, petition the legislature to present an issue to the voters. In some states, the legislature can act on the petition themselves, preventing it from going to the voters.

Part II. General considerations

I. **The contemporary relevance of interest groups**. Interest groups are likely to remain a permanent feature of American politics and therefore relevant to the citizen for the following reason.

A. **Interest groups as supplementing political representation**. Interest groups are voluntary associations that provide a supplement to **geographic** representation. The Constitution grants representation to people solely on the basis of where they live. It is unrealistic to believe that Virginians, say, will think alike, or even have the same political agenda.

B. **Functional vs. geographic representation**. Therefore, "functional representation" is often regarded as natural, possibly more so than geographic representation. In addition to being a Virginian, one is also a conservative or a liberal, a pharmacist or a plumber, and so on. Each of these functional identifications can attract an individual's adherence.

C. **The complexity of loyalties and interests**. However, one's combination of loyalties may be complementary or contradictory. Or one adherence may submerge the others. Often, the adherences are segmented and noncompetitive: one's personal self interest as a pharmacist may dictate membership in the National Association of Retail Druggists, while one's political ideology may suggest membership in the American Civil Liberties Union. These two group affiliations are sufficiently different that they will not usually impose cross-cutting demands.

D. **How some special interest groups retain membership**. Even so, a person has just so much time, money, and interest. Therefore, group membership is limited to one or two organizations in most cases. And active membership is uncommon. Often people are filled with a surge of enthusiasm for a group, but as the years go by the enthusiasm fades.

1. **Offering selective benefits**. Organizations, therefore, have come to rely upon selective incentives (goods and services available only to members) to keep membership stable. The American Association of Retired People is one of the most successful at providing selective incentives. From discount prescription drugs, to discount travel clubs, to low interest credit cards, to cooperative insurance arrangements, AARP offers an array of selective benefits that make the $5.00 annual membership fee appear trivial.

2. **Engaging in political action**. Interest groups may not be consistently political throughout their lives. At some point, however, the well being of the members requires political activity. The National Rifle Association was largely involved in providing marksmanship training and competition, until the spate of political assassinations in the 1960's generated demands for gun control. Now, the NRA is a vigorous lobbying organization.

II. **Interest groups and the American political system**. The American political system is uniquely suited to strong interest group activity.

A. **Divided authority**. Not only is authority divided between three branches of government, there are also 50 state governments, each with independent policy authority. Further, actual power in Congress is decentralized to Congressional committees and subcommittees. Thus, there are literally hundreds of "access points" for interest groups. Since American elected politicians are rarely disciplined by political parties, they are free to respond to group demands as they wish.

B. **Controversy over PACs**. The campaign finance reform legislation, creating Political Action Committees, as greatly enhanced the connection between interest groups and elected officials; PACs contribute more to their campaigns than do political parties. President Bush's 1991 State of the Union message called for the abolition of political action committees. The PACs responded by creating a combined public relations office to plead their case. They argue that their representative function is a valuable augmentation to regional representation.

C. **Interest groups not necessarily representative**. It is not entirely clear, however, how closely interest groups are "representative." The rules for nominating and electing representatives are clear. The rules for selecting leaders of interest groups vary substantially from organization to organization. Some hold elections, others do not. Some hold conventions, others do not. And the Washington staffs of not a few special interest groups are notorious for voicing views at odds with those of most of their members. Often, however, ordinary members are unaware that their view are not represented, or they are not organized to make their views effectively known.

D. **Special interests and the public good**. Another significant issue regarding special interest groups is that, in their zeal to protect their members, they lose sight of a larger "public interest" or public good.

1. **Special interest identification with the public good often spurious**. There is, obviously, a natural tendency for each group to identify its goals with a larger public interest, but such claims are often dubious. For example, in the 1990 taxing and spending legislation, cigars were exempted from the increase in tobacco taxes, largely because of effective lobbying rather than because of any inherent fiscal logic.

2. **Lobbying, budget deficits, and the public interest**. Each interest, like each person, tends to operate according to the saying, "Don't gore my ox," that is, "do not disturb the benefits we receive." The result of effective lobbying by special interests of every variety is chronic budget deficits, many of them extremely large. The effect of such deficits over time poses a threat to the national interest that neither legislators nor citizens can afford to ignore. Thoughtful citizens must consider that over time benefits and services must be either paid for or reduced. To believe otherwise may court social bankruptcy.

III. **Political liberty and the endurance of special interest groups**. Irrespective of the advantages and disadvantages of active interest groups, all free societies have them. As the American system is among the world's most open political systems, its interest groups are among the world's most active. Those that are well financed and organized are often effective in achieving their goals. The issues for citizens to contemplate and act upon is how to balance special interests—one or more of which most citizens may be identified with—with the public interest or good. The well being of American democracy depends in part on whether such a balance is achieved.

3. POLITICS AND THE ENVIRONMENT

In the first half of the twentieth century, conservationists in the United States were concerned with managing the land to ensure continued resources while preservationists were preoccupied with protecting the American wilderness and its delicate ecosystem. The technological changes which have occurred in the latter half of this century have created problems these early environmentalists could not have imagined. The widespread contamination of land, air, and water by chemical pollutants now constitutes a threat to human life and health too great to ignore. Responsible citizens need to be aware of the hazards of pollution and to be informed about the choices available to reduce environmental pollution while still utilizing the nation's resources. These environmental choices involve such issues as the use of existing timber forests, the protection of wilderness areas, and the need for clean water to drink, clean air to breathe, and safe food to eat.

OBJECTIVES

Citizens should be able to

1. describe the principal actors in the environmental policy making process, including government, business, environmental policy groups and grassroots environmental groups.

2. explain such conflicts in environmental policy making as short term versus long term goals; regulation versus prevention; and market-driven policies versus government regulation.

3. describe historical examples of environmental problems and the development of environmentalist philosophy.

4. identify and explain major environmental problems facing society today.

5. take, defend, and evaluate positions regarding the role of the citizen in solving environmental problems.

FRAME OF REFERENCE
Conceptual Perspective

I. **Principal actors in the environmental policy making process.** Principal actors in environmental policy making include a number of government agencies, private sector business organizations, and citizen groups concerned with environmental issues.

A. **Government.** Government policy toward the environment is based on a number of legislative enactments implemented by various government agencies.

1. **Major legislative actions.** The principal legislative enactments dealing with environmental policy are the following:

a. **Atomic Energy Act (1946).** The Atomic Energy Act gave the federal government a monopoly on operating nuclear power facilities but was amended in 1954 to allow licensing of private facilities.

b. **Wilderness Act (1964).** The Wilderness Act created the National Wilderness Preservation System which designates certain lands as wilderness areas and sharply curtails use of these lands with an exception for mineral use.

c. **National Environmental Policy Act (1969).** The National Environmental Policy Act (NEPA) imposes environmental responsibilities on all agencies of the federal government, including:

(1) **Federal programs to be environmentally sound.** The act makes it federal policy to use all practicable means to administer federal programs in the most environmentally sound fashion and requires each agency to consider the environmental consequences of its actions.

(2) **Environmental impact statements to be issued.** The act mandates that a study of the environmental consequences of any federal program, in the form of an "Environmental Impact" statement, be made available to government officials and agencies and to the public.

(3) **Council on Environmental Quality established.** The act established the Council on Environmental Quality to advise the President on environmental matters.

d. **Clean Air Act (1970)**. The Clean Air Act increased federal authority and responsibility over air quality.

   (1) **National pollution standards set**. The act required setting national standards for reducing air pollution and national standards for determining hazardous levels of air pollutants.

   (2) **States to attain air quality standards**. The act also required individual states to attain air quality of specified standards, within a specified period of time; it also required emission standards for new cars.

e. **Clean Water Act (1972)**. The Clean Water Act amends the Federal Water Pollution Control Act and establishes a system of standards, permits, and enforcement aimed at creating "fishable and swimmable" waters by 1983. According to the act, pollutant discharges into navigable waters were to be completely eliminated by 1985. The act also allowed the Environmental Protection Agency (EPA) to issue discharge permits and required the agency to publish a list of toxic pollutants and implement standards for reducing them that provide an "ample margin of safety."

f. **Costal Zone Management Act (1972)**. The Coastal Zone Management Act seeks to achieve a judicious use of coastal land and water resources by providing monetary assistance to states to develop and administer management programs.

g. **Endangered Species Act (1973)**. The Endangered Species Act was designed to protect more than 1,200 species of animals classified as threatened or endangered by the U.S. Fish and Wildlife Service of the Department of the Interior.

h. **Safe Drinking Water Act (1974)**. The Safe Drinking Water Act required EPA to set national standards for contaminants in public drinking water supplies adjusted to reflect economic and technological feasibility.

i. **Toxic Substances Control Act (1976)**. The Toxic Substances Control Act was the first comprehensive legislation governing toxic substances. The act requires data to be collected on the environmental effects of chemicals; and it recommends that the government have adequate authority to prevent unreasonable risks of injury to health or environment. The act also requires testing products for health risks prior to manufacture; and it requires manufacture to notify EPA before manufacturing new substances.

j. **The Federal Land Policy and Management Act (1976)**. The Federal Land Policy and Management Act mandates that the Secretary of the Interior shall take any action necessary to prevent unnecessary or undue degradation of federally-owned lands.

k. **Surface Mining Control Act (1977)**. The Surface Mining Control and Reclamation Act imposes a detailed series of regulatory restrictions on strip mining and requires restoration of the land to approximately its original state.

l. **Federal Insecticide Fungicide Rodenticide Act (FIFRA) (1978)**. The FIFRA requires "economic poisons" to be registered with the EPA before they may be distributed in interstate commerce. The act requires the EPA to review registration every five years and to consider restrictions on types or methods of use as an alternative to cancellation.

m. **Comprehensive Environmental Response Compensation and Liability Act (CERCLA) (Superfund) (1980)**. The CERCLA authorizes the President to require cleanup of toxic materials in accordance with a "national contingency plan." The act makes owners of facilities liable for government cleanup costs and for the destruction of natural resources owned by the government. It also establishes a fund, financed by a tax on production of toxic chemicals, to be used for payment of "response costs."

n. **Resource Conservation and Recovery Act (RCRA) (1984)**. The RCRA was passed in response to growing public awareness of serious problems relating to disposal of hazardous wastes.

(1) **Criteria for hazardous waste to be issued**. The act requires EPA to promulgate criteria for identifying hazardous wastes "taking into account toxicity, persistence and degradability in nature, potential for accumulation in tissues" and other hazardous traits.

(2) **Toxic storage and disposal standards set**. The act requires standards for generators, transporters, and disposal sites; and it requires standards for labeling, reporting, storage, disposal, and treatment methods for toxic materials. The act also sets forth criteria for the location, construction and operation of disposal sites.

o. **Emergency Planning and Community Right-To-Know Act (EPCRA) (1986)**. EPCRA requires facilities manufacturing hazardous chemicals to disclose the names and amounts of toxic materials they release into the environment. It also requires local officials to draft plans to respond to an emergency chemical accident in order to reduce the threat of catastrophic accidents.

2. **Federal executive organizations and agencies**. The following are federal agencies and departments with responsibilities for environmental issues.

a. **Environmental Protection Agency (EPA)**. The EPA, created in 1970, combines preexisting units from various federal departments. The agency is designed to protect and enhance the environment and to control and reduce pollution of air and water. EPA also regulates solid waste disposal and the use of pesticides, radiation, and toxic substances.

b. **Nuclear Regulatory Commission (NRC)**. Founded in 1974, NRC licenses and regulates uses of civilian nuclear energy, including operation of nuclear reactors, in order to protect public health and environment.

c. **Department of Agriculture (USDA)**. Founded in 1862, the USDA helps maintain natural resources such as soil, water and forests. The department regulates agricultural products and also operates the U.S. Forest Service.

d. **Department of the Interior**. The Department of the Interior, founded in 1849, directs the use and conservation of public lands and natural resources. The department prescribes the use of land and water resources, fish and wildlife, national parks, and mineral resources.

3. **Role of the courts**. The courts play an extremely important role in overseeing and enforcing existing environmental laws and regulations.

a. **Enforcement**. Environmental groups often sue polluters to force them to comply with existing regulations or regulatory agencies to ensure that they enforce the law properly.

b. **Defining priorities**. Since the EPA does not have the funds to do everything Congress has instructed it to do, a court case often serves to set policy by requiring EPA to revise its priorities.

c. **Affecting development**. Suits may stop or delay proposed construction or development projects, by challenging the validity of permits or the ability to comply with standards. Environmental groups are also often involved in court cases on the side of government regulators who are being sued by a company denied a permit.

B. **Private sector**. Corporations and other businesses of the private sector play active roles in shaping environmental policies that affect them.

1. **Campaign contributions**. Corporations exert an influence over the environmental policy-making process by offering financial support to political candidates who agree with their views on environmental matters. The ability of corporations to spend large amounts of money on political campaigns gives them an important advantage over environmental groups, which generally do not have the resources to make campaign contributions.

2. **Lobbyists**. Corporations hire lobbyists who attempt to persuade policy makers directly. Corporate resources enable them to exert significant influence in the policy making process.

a. **Strength of corporate lobbying.** Since 1981, for example, when the federal Clean Air Act was due for reauthorization, General Motors (GM) alone has had at least thirteen lobbyists working to oppose motor vehicle cleanup requirements in congressional clean air bills. GM has argued that proposed standards would result in excessive costs to manufacturers. GM reported paying lawyers and lobbyists more than $1.8 million to fight clean air legislation between 1981 and 1988.

b. **Weakness of environmentalists' lobbying.** By contrast, all the environmental groups in Washington combined have fewer than ten lobbyists advocating specific clean air measures opposed by hundreds of companies.

3. **Shaping public opinion.** Like environmentalist groups, businesses affected by environmental legislation try to shape public opinion, knowing that it helps shape public policy. By purchasing advertisements in newspapers and on television, maintaining large public relations offices, and promoting their products as "environmentally safe," companies attempt to communicate the message that they are responsibly addressing environmental problems. Frequently they argue that government intervention or regulation is unnecessary.

4. **Corporate policies.** Many of the corporations producing the goods and services consumed by U.S. citizens are also responsible for much of the nation's pollution and environmental degradation. An example of the way that corporate decisions can have a negative effect on the environment is illustrated by the production of styrofoam.

a. **Styrofoam production and the ozone layer.** In 1974 it was suggested that the production of chlorofluorocarbons (CFCs), an important component of styrofoam, have contributed to the depletion of the ozone layer, the protective atmospheric layer which prevents the sun's dangerous ultraviolet rays from reaching the earth. The main manufacturer of CFCs, the DuPont Corporation, refused to acknowledge the potential danger of CFCs and did not research alternatives throughout the 1970s and most of the 1980s.

b. **Insulation of corporate decision making.** In 1988, as a result of negative publicity,

DuPont agreed to gradually phase out its manufacture of CFCs. Environmentalists have charged that DuPont's phase out has been too slow and that the company is planning to use harmful alternatives. DuPont denies .such charges and environmentalists are unable to directly affect the company's decision-making process.

C. **Policy groups.** Examples of groups concerned with public policy include the following:

1. **Audubon Society.** Several national environmental groups, such as the Audubon Society, named after the American ornithologist and illustrator **James J. Audubon** (1785-1851), appeal to a broad constituency that favors nature conservation and wildlife preservation. Founded in 1886 and nationally incorporated in 1905, the Society has some 550,000 members.

a. **Issues addressed.** The society addresses such issues as preservation of old-growth forests, wetlands, arctic wildlife, and waterways such as the Platte River.

b. **Activities.** The Audubon Society publishes various magazines and journals, runs educational programs, and maintains numerous sanctuaries to protect natural habitats and wildlife. The society also lobbies Congress on legislation, initiates litigation, and supports research projects on various environmental issues.

2. **Natural Resources Defence Council.** Another major environmental organization involved in the policy making process is the Natural Resources Defense Council (NRDC), founded in 1970. In 1990 the Council's membership exceeded 130,000.

a. **Research and legal activities.** NRDC undertakes scientific and economic research on environmental issues. It combines these activities with legal action on environmental issues. As part of these legal activities, NRDC operates a Citizen Enforcement Program which sues companies it believes to be in violation of environmental statutes.

b. **Publication and lobbying activities.** NRDC publishes technical and consumer-oriented reports, including the

Amicus Journal on environmental thought and opinion. It also lobbies Congress and works on legislation with congressional staff.

D. **Grass roots organizations**. Examples of grassroots organizations that have nationwide membership include the following:

1. **Citizens Clearinghouse on Hazardous Waste (CCHW)**. CCHW was founded in 1980 by Lois Gibbs, a resident of the Love Canal area in New York, who was forced to leave her home because of hazardous waste contamination. CCHW provides assistance to over 6,000 local citizen groups working to promote responsible hazardous and solid waste management. The organization encourages citizen participation in waste management planning, permit distribution, and enforcement of regulations. CCHW publishes newsletters and action guides and initiates boycotts and other campaigns against targeted polluters.

2. **Greenpeace**. Greenpeace, an international organization founded in Canada, with membership in dozens of countries, attempts to oppose government and private sector actions it considers dangerous to the environment. For example, Greenpeace attempted to block French atomic testing in the South Pacific; Soviet atomic testing in the Arctic; whale hunting by Japanese whalers; and tuna fishing using nets that caused the drowning of thousands of porpoises.

II. **Conflicts in the environmental policy making process**. Examples of significant choices to be made in defining environmental policy include the following.

A. **Short term benefits versus long term costs**. Political demands for short-term economic gains that entail some form of environmental degradation or depletion often overshadow the need for long-term environmental planning and the calculation of long-term costs.

1. **Research ignored**. Research linking various toxic chemicals with chronic health problems or with long-term effect contamination of the environment is often overlooked in the interest of short-term economic benefit. For example, in 1907 the British government publicized the health effects of asbestos, and in 1918, asbestos workers in North America were denied life insurance. But it was not until 1975 that serious steps were taken to protect the health of asbestos workers.

2. **Technology ignored**. Technology exists to increase automobile fuel efficiency to forty-five miles per gallon (which would save 1.1 million barrels of oil per day by the year 2000). But the auto industry has resisted legislation requiring increased fuel efficiency, since such a policy would increase the price of automobiles, thus lowering sales. A 1988 poll of 1,000 people by the Analysis Group, however, found that 77% of Americans are willing to pay higher prices for automobiles in exchange for higher fuel efficiency.

B. **Free market versus government regulation**. A basic policy choice in dealing with environmental policy is whether market-driven policies or government regulation are to be preferred.

1. **Arguments for market-driven policies**. Some critics view environmental protection legislation involving government regulation as an unnecessary and undesirable intrusion on the free market. They argue that market-driven anti-pollution policies allocate resources through the efficient means of the market, rather than through government regulation, which, they maintain, promotes inefficiencies.

2. **Arguments for government regulation**. Other critics, including many environmentalists, argue that a market economy does not adequately protect the environment. These critics claim that the market rewards the polluter for engaging in the lowest-cost production process, but it does not force the polluter to pay for the consequent environmental degradation. They also assert that environmental costs are only beginning to be counted in the cost of doing business.

C. **Regulation versus prevention and reduction**. Many environmentalists argue that simply passing laws to control pollution has failed in the past and that prevention is a more sound alternative. For example, the Clean Air Act, passed by Congress in 1970, was designed to reduce pollution, not eliminate it. Consequently, the EPA developed "acceptable" pollution levels that still pose health risks through sustained exposure to "low" levels of pollutants. In the 1990s arguments continue on both sides.

a. **Arguments for banning pollutants**. Government emphasis on controlling air pollutants, rather than requiring an outright ban on pollutants, can be detrimental to the economy as well as the environment. For example, despite attempts to control acid rain, it still produces $5 billion in damage per year in the eastern United States alone.

b. **Arguments against total bans on pollutants.** Critics against total bans on pollutants argue that such bans would be ruinously expensive, driving many companies out of business. They argue that massive unemployment would result. Moreover, American companies doing international business would be left at a marked disadvantage against their international competitors, who operated under no such ban.

c. **Congressional exemption of some pollutants.** Congress has exempted certain industrial waste from RCRA regulations such as those from oil, gasoline, mining, and municipal incinerator ash. Such exemptions exemplify the government's practice of focusing on regulation of pollution production rather than promoting conservation and source reduction. Environmental critics argue that government regulation has been minimal.

Historical Perspective

I. **Development of environmentalist philosophy.** Environmentalist philosophy had its origins early in this century and developed conspicuously in the 1970s and 1980s.

A. **Early environmentalism.** Movements for the conservation and preservation of natural beauty were among early efforts to protect the environment.

1. **Conservationism.** Conservationism, the precursor to the modern environmental movement in the U.S., began largely with the concern for the aesthetic beauty of nature, including preservation of wildlife and conservation of natural resources. Conservationists tended to believe that nature was to be used by humans, but used wisely.

    a. **White House conference of 1908.** At a 1908 White House conference, President Theodore Roosevelt embraced the growing conservation movement by setting aside federal lands.

    b. **Purpose of conservation.** Roosevelt's primary concern was with conserving minerals and timber for future generations.

2. **Preservationism.** Preservationists, including **John Muir** (1838-1914), took the crusade further by urging preservation of the wilderness for its own sake. Several preservationists made considerable contributions to the study of ecology (the interrelationship between living things), which became the foundation for modern environmentalism.

3. **Preservationism versus conservationism.** The debate, which still exists today, between conserving resources to ensure continued economic growth and preservation as a means to protect the delicate ecosystem, was launched with the beginnings of the study of ecology. Ecologist **Aldo Leopold** in the 1940s and 1950s drew on Muir's political activism, showing the intricate connection between nature and humanity. For Leopold, preservation was essential to survival of the human race.

B. **Ecology movement.** The modern ecology movement was born after World War II and developed in the 1970s and 1980s.

1. **The new age of chemicals.** World War II spurred the development of thousands of new chemicals, compelling society to look at the environment not only for aesthetic reasons but also because of concerns about health and safety. Production of new chemical and nuclear technology resulted in new products, including synthetics and pesticides. Production of synthetic organic chemicals rose from 1.3 billion pounds in 1940 to 49 billion pounds in 1950. Total production reached 96.7 billion pounds in 1960 and rose again to 223.1 in 1970. By the end of the 1980s, industry was producing nearly 400 billion pounds of organic chemicals annually.

2. **Rachel Carson.** Rachel Carson (1907-1964) elaborated on earlier studies of ecology and was perhaps the most important voice for modern ecology. In her 1962 book, *Silent Spring*, Carson detailed the pervasiveness of chemical pesticides in the environment, showing how these chemicals accumulate at every level of the food chain.

3. **Earth Day 1970.** In 1969, Wisconsin Senator **Gaylord Nelson**, an early anti-pollution advocate, asked an ecologist to organize a nationwide teach-in on ecology issues on college campuses. The idea expanded into Earth Day 1970, a

nationwide day of protests and demonstrations to heighten awareness of environmental issues.

4. **Regulatory framework.** Growing public concern about the seriousness of environmental problems forced the government, in the early 1970s, to create a new regulatory system, including establishment of the EPA. As a result, significant gains were made in monitoring and controlling pollution.

C. **Deregulation in the 1980s.** Support for government regulation of industry became politically unfashionable in the 1980s. The result was large-scale deregulation.

1. **"Macho of technology."** Despite growing concern for health and environmental risks, many segments of society continued to respond to environmental threats with what author Ron Brownstein calls the "macho of technology." This term refers to the belief that technology will ultimately solve the numerous problems it creates.

2. **Budget reductions.** The philosophy of deregulation in the 1980s resulted in substantial cuts in the budgets of regulatory agencies. From 1981 to 1986, EPA's budget for air and water quality programs was cut by 42% and 62%, respectively. EPA's budget to control toxic substances was cut by 35%. Much of the regulatory framework was weakened and enforcement made more difficult due to budget constraints. The widespread conviction that the free market system, with little government regulation, would ameliorate environmental degradation was predominant during the decade.

D. **Modern environmental movement.** The modern environmental movement blossomed in the 1970s and 1980s.

1. **Re-regulation.** Many environmental groups advocate rebuilding and strengthening the regulatory framework partially dismantled in the 1980s.

2. **Beyond regulation, prevention and source reduction.** Some environmentalists, most notably Barry Commoner, advocate that environmental protection go beyond the regulatory approach.

a. **Arguments for eliminating pollutant production.** Commoner, measuring success in terms of reductions in pollutant levels in the atmosphere, land, and water, as well as in

the human body, believes that significant reductions occur only when production of a substance is eliminated rather than reduced.

b. **Rethinking consumption patterns.** Commoner asserts that the answer to environmental problems is source reduction and prevention. Part of this solution includes rethinking society's consumption patterns and employing alternatives to unlimited production such as recycling and organic gardening, a non-chemical approach to pest control that uses, for example, a parasitic wasp to control the walnut aphid.

3. **International environmentalism.** Several prominent organizations have issued warnings about threats to the environment.

a. **Smithsonian Institution report (1972).** A 1972 Smithsonian Institute report called "Limits to Growth" concluded that if the current growth trends in world population, food production, industrialization, pollution, and resource depletion continue unchanged, the limits to growth on earth would be reached sometime within the next one hundred years.

b. **Club of Rome report (1974).** The Club of Rome, a group of scientists and government leaders, was one of the first organizations to initiate action to save the environment on an international level. In 1974, the group issued a report called "Mankind at the Turning Point," which presented strategies for replacing uncontrolled growth with "organic growth."

c. **Council on Environmental Quality report (1980).** The 1980 Council on Environmental Quality's "Global 2000 Report" presented a bleak picture of the future, given continued population growth and increasing energy demands.

d. **Montreal Protocol (1987).** In 1987 representatives from twenty-four nations signed the Montreal Protocol, agreeing to reduce the release of ozone-depleting CFCs into the environment. Ninety-three nations are now participating.

e. **Emergence of "green politics."** The emergence of "green politics" in Europe and elsewhere in the world echoes the prevention and limited growth approach. Opposition is also growing to the practice of many industrialized countries of using less developed countries as dumping grounds for their waste products and as sites for polluting industries. These countries are experiencing the problems associated with economic development, without necessarily participating in its benefits.

II. **Case studies.** Local, state, national and international case studies illustrate the problems posed by environmental degradation.

A. **Local and state case studies.** The examples of chemical contamination at Love Canal, New York, and the accidental release of chemicals into the food chain in Michigan illustrate the damages of chemical environmental degradation.

1. **Love Canal.** The now-infamous story of hazardous waste contamination at Love Canal in Niagara Falls, New York eventually led to the creation of a $10.1 billion "Superfund" in 1980 to clean up similar problems nationwide.

a. **Development of the problem.** The Love Canal disaster dates back to 1942, when the Hooker Chemical and Plastics Corporation drained Love Canal and buried eighty-two different chemical substances there. Among these chemicals was an estimated 130 pounds of dioxin. A highly toxic poison, dioxin is so powerful that three ounces can kill more than a million people. Hooker later sold the land to the local Board of Education, which built a school on top of the dump. The land was "sold" for one dollar on the condition that the Hooker Corporation be free from any future liability.

b. **Emergence of the chemicals.** Over time, the buried wastes began surfacing, causing a number of problems, including chemical burns and noxious odors. In the mid-1970s, numerous residents near the canal found a black oily substance in their basements. The local newspaper, *The Niagara Gazette*, had the substance tested and found it contained fifteen organic chemicals, including three chlorinated hydrocarbons that are toxic by inhalation, ingestion, and skin absorption.

c. **Health problems.** Surveys of the first ring of homes around the canal found that 95% were contaminated. One survey concluded that "people living near the former dump site were experiencing as many as three and a half times the expected number of miscarriages, as well as a disproportionate number of birth defects and spontaneous abortions."

d. **Government action.** The city, the county, and the state abdicated responsibility for cleaning up the canal. Finally, two years after the health effects were made public and after aggressive citizen organizing, the state health commissioner intervened, declaring Love Canal an "official emergency." He advised children and pregnant women to move away.

e. **Community organization.** Ninety percent of the community's residents formed the Love Canal Homeowner's Association to demand aid.

(1) **Demands for federal aid.** After continued neglect by the federal government, Lois Gibbs, president of the Homeowner's Association, held hostage two officials of the Environmental Protection Agency and sent a telegram to President Carter seeking federal funding for the evacuation of the remaining Love Canal families.

(2) **Presidential declaration of emergency.** Carter declared a national emergency at Love Canal, and the first federal funds were issued for a human-made disaster. Nearly three hundred families were evacuated.

f. **Health problems continue.** Health problems continued even for families living outside the first ring of homes around the canal.

(1) **Study reveals spread of chemical toxicity.** A special study found widespread health problems among the families whose homes were situated above old stream beds or dried-up ponds. Rates of miscarriages and birth defects as well

as other illnesses were extremely high among families living in these areas. The survey hypothesized that the toxic chemicals were migrating through these previously wet areas of the canal. The Department of Health, however, did not take action.

(2) **Continued publicity of Love Canal problems**. As waste dumping in the river, an additional underground dump site, and the corresponding health effects were discovered, Lois Gibbs and the Homeowner's Association kept the issue in the public eye.

g. **Outcome**. In November 1979 the state of New York agreed to buy the homes of any remaining Love Canal residents who wished to leave. At the same time the governor announced plans to "revitalize" Love Canal by moving new families into the homes of those who had left. In 1988 Hooker Chemical was found liable for "justifiable governmental costs." Love Canal residents sued both Hooker and the city and settled for $20 million.

2. **PBBs in Michigan**. Contamination of animal feed in Michigan resulted in widespread human consumption of a toxic chemical, with unknown long-run consequences.

a. **Development of problem**. The contamination of beef and dairy products in Michigan with the chemical polybrominated biphenyl (PBB) alerted the public to the danger that careless handling of chemicals could taint their food supply for years. In 1973, Michigan Chemical Company, manufacturer of a feed additive called Nutrimaster, mistakenly shipped some bags of PBB, a fire retardant known to be toxic (with the trade name Firemaster), to a farm feed supplier in Battle Creek, Michigan. The two substances were improperly stored in similar bags, and employees, thinking they had received a normal shipment of feed additive, mixed it into the feed.

b. **Response**. Soon after, farmers began reporting illnesses and reduced milk production in their cows. The PBB was discovered, but officials incorrectly reported that only one type of feed was contaminated. Farmers continued to feed their cattle with the contaminated supply and

millions of people continued to consume products from the contaminated cows.

c. **Outcome**. Six years later, after the full extent of the contamination was revealed, the state of Michigan had 25,000 animals killed, while many more died from PBB poisoning. The state estimates the disaster has cost the taxpayers $59 million. The families of farmers who raised the PBB-tainted cattle have suffered from damaged immunological systems, damaged livers and impaired neurological functions. Researchers in 1979 reported that 90% of the population of Michigan had PBBs in their bodies.

B. **National case studies**. The energy situation in the U.S. has been the subject of increasing debate since 1973.

1. **Energy crisis**. The energy crises of 1973 and 1979 increased energy awareness. The public became aware of U.S. dependence on foreign oil and the dwindling supply of domestically produced fossil fuels. It also learned of the significant impact energy conservation could have on oil consumption. But critics argue that the government avoided long-term employment of conservation techniques, especially development of solar energy technology, partly on account of skillful lobbying by the oil industry.

2. **Nuclear power**. One proposed solution to the energy crisis was the promotion of nuclear power.

a. **Arguments against nuclear power**. Critics argued that the nuclear power industry's safety record was poor and demonstrated the enormous risks associated with this technology.

(1) **Release of radiation at Three Mile Island**. Critics of nuclear power pointed to the worst U.S. nuclear accident, which occurred in 1979 when the nuclear reactor at Three Mile Island (TMI) in Harrisburg, Pennsylvania, neared meltdown. Significant amounts of radiation were released.

(2) **Criminal conviction of reactor operator**. A year later, the Nuclear Regulatory Commission (NRC) illegally allowed the TMI reactor to open its vents, releasing

even more accident-generated radioactive gases. General Public Utility (GPU), the company responsible for the TMI accident, has been indicted and convicted of criminal misconduct.

   b. **Arguments in favor of nuclear power**. Other critics argue that new nuclear plant technologies are significantly safer than previously. They say that every large-scale form of energy that could be used in the near future has significant drawbacks. These critics point to the successful use of nuclear power in Western Europe, particularly in Germany and France. In this view, nuclear power is at least as good a choice as other forms of energy that could realistically be expected to replace fossil fuel sources.

C. **International and global case studies**. International environmental disasters as well as the global effects of fossil fuel burning underscore the growing importance of environmental issues in the world today.

   1. **Chemical accident at Bhopal, India**. The Bhopal disaster has brought attention to the special problems brought about by industrialized nations exporting their technology to the third world. In December 1984, forty-five tons of methyl isocyanate, a deadly chemical used to make pesticides, was released into the air through a faulty valve at a Union Carbide pesticide manufacturing plant on the outskirts of Bhopal, India. The toxic chemical floated toward Bhopal, passing over the heavily populated towns that surround the plant, and killed an estimated 10,000 people and injured many more.

   2. **Nuclear accident at Chernobyl, USSR**. The 1986 accident at Chernobyl, near Kiev, in the Soviet Ukraine, demonstrated the global danger of nuclear power.

      a. **Radiation spread**. Winds carried radiation emitted from Chernobyl to various places around the world, contaminating food supplies as far away as twelve hundred miles and irradiating tens of thousands of people.

      b. **Banning of New Zealand reindeer meat**. Because reindeer meat in Scandinavia was considered too dangerous for human consumption because of radiation contamination, fresh reindeer meat from New Zealand—which was not contaminated—was banned by the European Economic Community from import because it was feared that it would be mixed with the impure meat and sold to an unsuspecting public.

      c. **Long-term consequences of human irradiation**. The effects of radiation on human health, such as cancer or genetic damage, do not appear until long after exposure.

Contemporary Perspective

I. **Current environmental issues**. A host of environmental issues, ranging from global warming and energy policy to the use of public lands and solid waste disposal continue to occupy the attention of concerned citizens.

   A. **Energy**. Critics of fossil fuel consumption point to the potentially disastrous effects of the continued large-scale burning of such fuels. Other technologies are being considered as substitutes.

      1. **Fossil fuels**. Reliance for energy on fossil fuels—oil, coal and natural gas—is a major cause of air pollution, acid rain, and green-house gas emissions as well as land and water pollution via oil spills. In addition, oil companies continue to exploit pristine wilderness areas for oil development.

      2. **Nuclear energy**. Nuclear energy continues to be a controversial subject.

         a. **Safety of reactors**. Critics of nuclear power argue that nuclear reactors pose potential threats of enormous damage to both environment and health in the event of accidents such as those at Three Mile Island and Chernobyl.

         b. **Problem of waste disposal**. There is also the problem of disposing of nuclear waste. Between 1979 and 1986, more than 20,000 mishaps were recorded by the NRC at U.S. nuclear reactors. The 122 U.S. commercial nuclear reactors hold more than 15,000 metric tons of high-level waste in temporary storage pools at plant sites. This radioactive waste will continue to be harmful for 250,000 years.

3. **Renewable technologies and conservation.** The Center for Renewable Resources maintains that renewable energy technology can provide 20% of U.S. energy by the year 2000. Federal spending on research and development of renewable energy sources, however, was cut by 84% from 1980 to 1990.

   a. **Soft energy path.** Energy conservationist Amory Lovins' concept of a "Soft Energy Path" (SEP) advocates a combination of cleaner, renewable sources of energy, including solar power, to reduce consumption of fossil fuels. According to Lovins, energy consumption does not necessarily have to decrease or stabilize. Rather, using the concept of a SEP, the economy—and energy consumption—could continue to grow but in more environmentally sound ways.

   b. **Solar energy.** Another alternative to fossil fuels is solar power.

      (1) **Solar thermal plants.** Solar thermal plants incorporate large mirrors that focus the sun's energy on a liquid which is then used to produce steam or provide space heating directly. Seven thermal plants operating in California together produce over two hundred megawatts of power.

      (2) **Solar-powered cells.** Another solar technology involves the use of photovoltaic cells, which produce an electric current directly from the sun's rays. This technology is said to have tremendous potential as a future energy source and is already used in calculators. It will not, however, be cost-effective on a large scale until about the year 2000.

   c. **Wind.** Wind power is used on a limited scale in California, where 18,000 wind turbines generate electric power equivalent to 3 million barrels of oil, enough energy to power approximately 300,000 homes at a price competitive with conventional sources of power.

   d. **Hydroelectric power and biofuels.** The following are examples of the many types of renewable energy technologies:

      (1) **Hydroelectric power.** Hydroelectric power is currently the most popular, providing 10% to 14% of total electricity in recent years.

      (2) **Geothermal power.** Geothermal power, using the heat of the earth to spin turbines, is used in forty-four states.

      (3) **"Biofuels."** Biofuels, such as ethanol and methanol, provide liquid energy for transportation. Some biofuels are not much cleaner than gasoline; for example, methanol produces formaldehyde. But a corn-based ethanol has been tested as a gasoline additive to reduce harmful emissions. A much cleaner biofuel is hydrogen fuel, which could be produced using solar energy to split water particles.

   e. **Conservation.** The conservation efforts of the 1970s, in direct response to diminishing oil supplies, reduced oil imports by 60% or 2.4 million barrels of oil per day. Conservation efforts between 1975 and 1985 saved consumers an estimated $45 billion on heating bills. Investment in railroads and mass transit, equal to that invested in highways, could, it is argued, provide energy savings of 62% and significant additional employment opportunities for the work force.

B. **Public lands.** A continuing source of debate focuses on the ways the federal government should manage public lands to protect the environment. Principal agencies involved in this management include the National Park Service, the Forest Service, and the Bureau of Land Management.

   1. **Amount owned.** The federal government owns 730 million acres of land—almost a third of the entire United States—as well as a large area on the outer continental shelf. These public lands contain tremendous resources in the form of oil, natural gas, coal, minerals and timber.

   2. **Policies governing use.** The management of public lands has riven rise to a number of controversies concerning the environment.

      a. **Management in the public interest questioned.** Federal policy mandates that the public lands be retained and managed in the public interest. The federal government sells assets from the land, leases the land to private companies for the purpose of extracting resources, and honors mining claims. Environmentalists argue that these practices are not always consistent with the public interest.

b. **Multiple use and private mining policies.** Federal policy also mandates that public lands be managed for sustained long-term "multiple-use" of resources, including fishing and hunting, recreation, watershed functions, historical, natural and scenic value as well as mining and logging. An important exception is the policy on "hard rock minerals," including gold, silver, and copper, which gives anyone finding a hard rock mineral on federal land the right to mine the deposit, without paying a royalty to the government and without proper concern for degradation of the land.

3. **Timber.** The National Forest system, which covers 199 million acres, often allows private timber cutting in areas that lose money for the government and/or threaten other resources, in order to preserve the jobs and economic base provided by the industry in these areas. In the Tongass National Forest in Alaska, many environmentalists, fishermen, and natives who depend on the forest for subsistence have disputed with the Forest Service over its policy of allowing timber companies to cut the highest quality old-growth stands of trees. They argue that this practice damages fisheries, wildlife, and the ecosystem.

C. **Solid Waste Disposal.** An average U.S. citizen generates more than three pounds of trash every day. This adds up to 160 million tons of "municipal solid waste" every year. Eighty percent of this garbage gets buried in a dwindling number of landfills, 10% is incinerated, and only 10% is recycled.

1. **Landfills.** The amount of garbage Americans produce has increased rapidly in recent decades. As a result, EPA estimates that one-half of U.S. landfills will close by 1995.

a. **Costs.** Many cities and states are forced to export their waste to other states, at skyrocketing costs, because local landfill space is gone.

b. **Environmental hazards.** Solid waste landfills account for 20% of the sites on EPA's "superfund" list of the nation's worst toxic problems. Wastes seep underground, poison groundwater, and contaminate drinking water supplies.

2. **Incineration.** Many localities are opting for incineration to control the solid waste disposal problem. Incinerator facilities can burn as much as 4,000 tons of trash a day. Some are designed to generate electricity from the process.

a. **Environmental dangers.** Incineration creates a new source of pollution by increasing the concentration of toxic and carcinogenic chemicals in the air. By releasing oxides of nitrogen, incinerators become another source of acid rain. Incinerators do not totally eliminate the need for landfills because incinerator ash must be buried. Also, drinking water is susceptible to contamination if toxic ash seeps into groundwater.

b. **Dioxin.** A chemical commonly released from incineration is dioxin, one of the most deadly poisons known to science and the most toxic compound in Agent Orange (a chemical defoliant used in Vietnam). Scientists are not sure why incineration produces dioxin, and all attempts to eliminate its release during incineration have failed.

c. **Adding small-scale recycling for approval of large-scale incineration.** In order to make incineration more attractive, waste-management companies have developed a trade-off strategy by lobbying for small-scale recycling as a supplement to mass incineration. This effectively puts a limit on the amount of waste a community can recycle.

3. **Recycling.** Recycling reusable materials is a means of realizing considerable environmental benefits.

a. **Benefits.** Recycling cuts down on the amount of trash sent to landfills and slows down depletion of natural resources. Burning a ton of paper generates approximately fifteen hundred pounds of carbon dioxide. Recycling the same ton of paper is the equivalent of saving seventeen trees that absorb 250 pounds of carbon dioxide annually.

b. **Extent of recycling.** The U.S. recycles only 25% of its aluminum, 23% of paper, 9% of glass, and 1% of plastics. More than half of Europe's municipal waste and 93% of Japan's newspapers are recycled. At one time the U.S. was a leader in recycling. During World War II, for example, 35% of America's wood and fiber products, such as paper and cardboard, were recycled.

c. **Political barriers.** Political barriers have slowed America's transition to recycling. For example, glass manufacturers and bottlers lobby against legislation requiring recycling of bottles and cans because they believe recycling will add to their costs.

4. **Source reduction.** Source reduction involves designing, manufacturing and using products with the goal of lessening their quantity and toxicity in the waste stream. If waste is not created, it presents no disposal problem.

a. **Methods of source reduction.** This method requires reusing items whenever feasible; making products with fewer raw materials and with less toxic ones; producing durable goods or goods that are easier to repair; and making products that are easier to recycle.

b. **The problems of packaging and plastics.** Source reduction seeks to decrease the sheer volume of packaging, which accounts for half the volume of our trash and one-third of its weight. Much packaging is plastic, which is made from nonrenewable resources such as petroleum and natural gas. Techniques for recycling plastics are still in the early stages of development, so plastics remain more difficult and expensive to recycle than glass or metal containers.

D. **Global warming.** Many scientists agree that the emission of carbon dioxide and similar gases over the past century as a result of industrialization will have the effect of increasing the earth's temperature, with unknown, possibly disastrous, consequences.

1. **Definition.** By forming a gaseous chemical layer around the earth, carbon dioxide, a by-product of fossil fuel combustion and increased deforestation

(along with smaller concentrations of CFCs, methane and nitrous oxide) prevents the earth's normal rate of release of heat into space. Deforestation increases carbon dioxide in the atmosphere because plant life absorbs carbon dioxide and releases oxygen.

a. **Greenhouse effect.** Global warming, also known as the "greenhouse effect," threatens to increase the earth's temperature. No one knows how great this increase will be, but scientists have variously estimated that temperature rises over the next three to five decades will average 1.5 to 4.5 degrees centigrade (Celsius).

b. **The onset of global warming.** Recent studies of earth's temperature record over the last 120 years indicate that long-term global warming may already have begun. The level of "warming" chemicals are increasing at the alarming rate of 5% to 6% a year.

2. **Causes.** Much of the world, especially the developed economies, contributes to the emission of greenhouse gases.

a. **Emission of greenhouse gases by the industrialized world.** The industrialized world emits large amounts of carbon dioxide into the atmosphere. The U.S., for example, produces 27% of the world's carbon dioxide via automobile and industrial smokestack emissions.

b. **Emission of greenhouse gases by the developing** world. Forests in many developing nations are rapidly being destroyed, a process which releases carbon dioxide into the atmosphere. The largest single example of this process is the destruction of the rain forest of the Amazon basin in Brazil.

3. **Effects/Dangers.** The consequences of global warming are unknown. Scientists use computer models and other data to predict the possible damaging effects of these temperature rises, some of which are the following:

a. **Soil destruction.** Some scientists have predicted that if the practices resulting in the emission of green house gases are not halted, global warming may create torrential rainstorms which could produce soil run-off that would devastate the world's farmlands. As a result, many areas of the world could experience crop failure and ensuing famine.

b. **Effects of climate change**. Some scientists have argued that warm climates near the equator will expand to the traditionally colder climates near the Arctic and Antarctica. These shifting climates would create widespread extinction of those plants and animals unable to adapt to the warmer environment. If temperature rises caused the melting of polar ice caps, the resulting coastal flooding could destroy the land inhabited by millions of people.

E. **Ozone**. Ozone in the air people breathe is a health hazard. But ozone in the upper atmosphere has the opposite effect, protecting life below from the damaging effects of ultraviolet light.

1. **High-altitude ozone**. Ozone in the upper atmosphere is an important shield from ultraviolet light. Evidence shows that at various times a large "ozone hole" has appeared over Antarctica, raising fears of such holes appearing over inhabited parts of the earth.

a. **Dangers**. Although CFCs contribute to global warming, the primary danger attributed to them is the depletion of high-altitude ozone. Ozone forms a chemical layer on the outer edges of earth's atmosphere which deflects cancer-causing ultraviolet sunlight back to space. High-altitude ozone depletion and the resulting increase in the sun's ultraviolet light reaching earth threatens to increase the rate of skin cancer worldwide. EPA predicts 80 million new skin cancer cases over the next eighty years as a direct result of increased ultraviolet light exposure.

b. **Sources**. About 25% of all CFCs used in the U.S. are used as coolants for automobile air conditioners. The break-down of chemicals found in styrofoam plastics accounts for about 31% of CFCs. Other uses are in refrigerators, aerosol propellants, and new solvents for electronics manufacturing.

c. **Solutions**. Ninety-three nations agreed in 1990 to end CFC production by 1999, pledging their support for the development of safe and new chemical alternatives. Many envi-

ronmentalists, however, have called for stronger action, including an outright ban on these chemicals before the 1999 deadline.

2. **Ground-level ozone**. Gases in auto exhaust, gasoline fumes, and dry-cleaning fluids can cause ozone molecules to form in the air. At certain concentrations, ground-level ozone causes extensive crop damage and makes it difficult for humans to breathe by producing inflammation of the lungs. In 1989, the EPA reported that 101 areas in the United States, mostly cities, experienced ground-level ozone concentrations that exceeded recommended federal air quality standards.

F. **Population**. Environmentalists argue that population growth contributes notably to environmental degradation. As the world's population approaches an estimated five billion by the year 2000, increasing numbers of people will share the earth's already scarce natural resources. Problems posed by overpopulation, such as hunger, unemployment, and poverty seem destined to increase.

a. **Recent population growth**. Between 1950 and 1985, the world's population increased at an average rate of 66 million people each year. In this period, developing countries experienced an average population increase of 2.2% per year. Developed countries experienced an average population increase of nearly 1% per year.

b. **Reasons for population growth**. Population growth stems primarily from a combination of an absence of effective means of birth control and the desire or necessity in the third world for large families. Some studies have reported, however, that many women in developing countries desire means to reduce births.

c. **Efforts to reduce birth rates in the third world**. A variety of policies have been undertaken in the developing world to reduce birth rates.

(1) **Voluntary policies**. Some developing countries have offered such incentives to discourage pregnancies as paying individuals to be sterilized and paying them to use contraceptives. They have also provided development projects to communities that meet fertility goals, such as the use of contracep-

tion by a majority of a community's population.

(2) **Involuntary policies**. Coercive policies have sometimes been used in developing countries to reduce population growth. In India, forced sterilizations of men took place in the 1970s. In China, penalties were applied to those who did not comply with the policy of one child per couple.

(3) **Insufficient means to reduce population growth**. The most pressing problem in allowing developing countries to reduce population growth is the lack of contraceptives and insufficient education concerning family planning.

d. **Population growth and economic stability**. Population growth affects agricultural production and economic stability. As the world's population continues to grow, fields are farmed too frequently, producing soil erosion, poor crops, and increasing hunger.

G. **Toxins**. The use of toxic chemicals in agriculture and industry has resulted in health risks in affected workers as well as in the population as a whole.

1. **Production and use**. Chemical production and use are found throughout the economy. Some chemicals are toxic, others are not, and the effects on living organisms of still others is unknown.

a. **Chemical production**. Each year in the United States, 12,000 chemical manufacturing plants produce more than 70,000 chemicals, including 37,000 types of pesticides.

b. **Chemical use and disposition**. Chemicals are involved in a vast array of manufacturing processes. Some toxic chemicals are disposed of safely, but others are not. Those that are not safely disposed of eventually contaminate the air, soil, groundwater, rivers, lakes, and oceans as well as food and ultimately human bodies.

c. **Risks to workers**. Thousands of workers are exposed to the risks associated with various chemicals. In the U.S., between 1980 and 1985, there were an estimated 20,000 toxic-chemical accidents, killing an estimated four

hundred people and injuring some 4,500 others.

2. **Hazardous waste disposal**. The safe disposal of hazardous waste poses a serious health and environmental problem throughout much of the economy.

a. **Sources of hazardous waste**. American industry generates 250 million tons of toxic waste a year; more than one ton for every citizen. The federal government, including military installations, is also a major polluter, with 115 sites on the superfund list. In addition to industry byproducts, the hazardous waste stream is fed by a variety of sources, including auto repair shops, dry cleaners, and careless disposal of dangerous household products.

b. **Disposal problems**. Both the methods of disposing of toxic waste and the numbers of sites posing hazards are formidable problems.

(1) **Methods of disposal**. The major methods of disposal include illegal dumping; landfills fitted with liners that may eventually leak; above-ground storage in tanks or sheds; incineration; and underground injection.

(2) **Numbers of hazardous disposal sites**. EPA counts 29,000 waste sites that could qualify for the superfund cleanup program, which tackles only those toxic dumps that are considered the nation's worst. But other estimates put the number as high as 300,000. There are also 180,000 pits, ponds, and lagoons containing chemical poisons; an estimated 500 hazardous waste disposal facilities and 16,000 municipal and private landfills; and thousands of underground injection wells filled with liquid wastes.

(3) **Dangers posed to water supply**. According to the EPA, 15% to 20% of underground storage tanks are leaking; many leak into underground drinking water supplies that serve 120 million people, including 95% of rural Americans.

(4) **Widespread non-compliance with EPA regulations**. In 1987, Congress's General Accounting Office reported that non-compliance with EPA regulations concerning storage of hazardous waste was widespread due to inadequate EPA enforcement.

3. **Pesticides**. Many pesticides pose environmental and health hazards of great significance.

   a. **Contamination**. According to EPA estimates, pesticides have contaminated the groundwater in thirty-eight states, fouling the drinking water of half of all Americans. Of the 1.2 billion pounds of pesticides used each year, only an estimated 10% reaches the targeted organism. The rest ends up in food or seeps into the ground, possibly contaminating groundwater.

   b. **Health effects**. EPA estimates that some 6,000 cases of cancer a year are caused by just the one-third of the approved pesticides in use today that have been tested. Most of the 50,000 pesticides on the market have never been tested for long-term effects. Chemicals known to cause cancer, genetic mutations, and birth defects are legally and widely applied to vegetables and fruits. Workers are exposed to these chemicals during production, farm workers during application, and consumers when buying treated produce.

   c. **Alternatives**. Chemicals are not the only way to control insects and weeds. A small, but growing number of farmers are turning to "Integrated Pest Management" mechanisms that use natural methods, such as insect predators and different planting patterns, to produce their crops.

4. **Health effects**. Cancer rates in the United States are rising about 1% every year and rates of neurological disease, respiratory illness and birth defects are rising as well. There is no information on toxicity for 80% of the more than 48,500 chemicals listed by the EPA; less than one fifth have been tested for acute effects and less than one tenth for longer-term, carcinogenic or genetic impact.

5. **Minorities**. The effects of pollution and hazardous waste are more profound in minority and low-income communities, a phenomenon environmentalists call "environmental racism."

   a. **Urban areas**. Communities hardest hit by pollution tend to be in urban areas where, in the U.S., 71% of Blacks and 50% of Hispanics reside (only 34% of whites in the United States live in urban communities). In the United States, 15 million of the 26 million Blacks (or 58%) and over 8 million of the 15 million Hispanics (or 53%) live in communities with one or more uncontrolled toxic waste site.

   b. **Farm workers**. The life expectancy of migrant farm workers, exposed daily to harmful pesticides, is only forty-nine years. One study showed that 56% percent of migrant farm workers had abnormal liver and kidney functions and 78% percent had skin rashes potentially related to pesticide exposure.

   c. **Navajo Indians**. During the 1950s and 1960s, Navajo Indian miners produced uranium exclusively for the government without safety regulations. It is estimated that these miners now experience a cancer rate fourteen times higher than non-miners. One study showed that 72% of the male Navajo lung cancer victims in Arizona, Utah and New Mexico were uranium miners.

H. **Acid Rain**. Acid rain is a serious environmental hazard caused by mixing industrial wastes emitted into the atmosphere with rain.

   1. **Causes**. More than 30 million tons of the precursors of acid rain—sulfur dioxide and nitrogen oxides—pollute the eastern half of North America every year.

   2. **Effects**. In New York state, hundreds of lakes once filled with fish and other wildlife are now barren as a result of the damaging effects of acid rain. By neutralizing the chemicals vital for tree and plant survival, acid rain is retarding the growth of forests and destroying previously productive farmland. In New Hampshire's White Mountains, tree growth slowed by 18% between 1956 and 1965, a period of increased acidity in rainfall.

3. **Solutions**. The use of lime, "scrubbing" and other means are available to deal with the effects of acid rain. In addition, there are proposals to eliminate the causes of acid rain entirely.

   a. **Liming**. Scientists have sought to "control" acid rain by treating effected lakes and streams with lime, a compound which absorbs and neutralizes acids. The "liming" technique is still under review and scientists are uncertain about its cost and effectiveness.

   b. **Scrubbing/controls**. Other partial solutions include the application of "particular abatement technologies." Technologies such as "scrubbing" reduce but do not eliminate sulfur emissions into the atmosphere. This method could also impose an environmental hazard because it would require land filling toxic sulfur-rich sludge that accumulates during the desulfurization process. This problem would be ameliorated, but not solved, if the government required industry to switch from high-sulfur to low-sulfur coal.

   c. **Elimination**. Proposals like the Lovins' "Soft Energy Path" advocate moving away from the use of fossil fuels, including coal. If fully implemented, such a policy might eventually result in the elimination of acid rain. The economic feasibility of such a plan, however, remains the subject of debate.

I. **Third world issues**. Several environmental issues pose important hazards for third world countries in particular.

   1. **Pesticide export**. It is estimated that U.S. chemical corporations export at least 150 million pounds of pesticides each year that are totally prohibited, severely restricted or never registered for use in the United States.

      a. **Increase in pesticide poisoning**. Although the World Health Organization has reported that pesticide poisoning is increasing in developing nations, pesticide exports to developing nations have grown rapidly in the past twenty years.

      b. **Prospect of increased pesticide consumption**. As hunger increases, developing nations are more likely to seek pesticides for greater crop yields. Consequently, hunger may be replaced by pesticide-related illnesses.

   2. **Hazardous waste trade**. In addition, some industrialized countries are dumping their hazardous wastes in developing countries, which can rarely afford safe waste disposal. According to the environmental organization Greenpeace, more than 3 million tons of wastes were shipped from industrialized countries to less developed countries between 1986 and 1988.

II. **Opportunities for citizen participation**. Numerous avenues are available for citizens to participate in the amelioration of environmental problems and to influence public and private policy making.

   A. **Overview**. While individuals can make changes in their habits and lifestyles which will help to conserve resources and reduce pollutants, significant change will occur only if government and the private sector commit themselves to environmentally sound practices.

      1. **Power of individuals versus power of government**. Government institutions have resources and decision-making power not available to individual citizens. For example, an individual citizen can choose to buy the most fuel efficient car on the market, but only the federal government can raise fuel efficiency standards to force manufacturers to use already available technology to make cars more fuel efficient.

      2. **Individual behavior versus influence of public policy**. Individuals wishing to make a significant contribution to environmental issues not only must take individual action but must also attempt to influence the actions of government and the private sector.

   B. **Individual Action**. Individual action and lifestyle changes which promote a cleaner environment include the following:

      1. **Recycling**. Citizens can choose to recycle materials such as paper, glass, and plastics.

      2. **Efficient energy use**. Citizens can choose to conserve energy by using more energy-efficient products such as automobiles with high gas mileage and improved energy-efficient appliances. They can also moderate their use of energy in the home.

3. **Public transportation use**. Citizens can choose to use public transportation where feasible rather than private conveyance.

4. **Car pooling**. Citizens can choose to commute to their place of employment with others, thereby reducing gasoline consumption.

5. **Boycotts**. Citizens can choose to boycott environmentally unsound products.

6. **Product choice**. Citizens can choose to buy products with little or no packaging. They can also choose to buy products that are not made with chemicals that are harmful or potentially harmful. They may choose to buy organically-grown fruits and vegetables, for example.

C. **Effecting government and private sector change**. Effecting change involves becoming educated about specific environmental issues and then taking appropriate action at the local, state, national, and international levels.

1. **Awareness**. Awareness of environmental issues involves gathering information from a variety of sources and critically analyzing the accuracy of claims and counter claims.

   a. **Information sources**. Citizens can stay informed through newspapers, news magazines, and television programs as well as through environmental newsletters and journals.

   b. **Local responsibilities and interests**. Citizens can learn what environmental issues are important in their community and who the relevant decision makers are. For example, they can discover who is responsible for planning solid waste management or who may have an economic interest in various environmental policies.

2. **Local action**. A variety of opportunities for local action on environmental issues are available.

   a. **Attending to community needs**. Citizens can choose an issue based on the needs or problems of their community.

   b. **Joining or founding groups**. Citizens can join an existing group or start their own.

   c. **Influencing decision making**. Citizens can inform decision makers of their views and their willingness to act for change. Citizens can also attend community meetings and public hearings and make their views known.

   d. **Acting as watchdogs**. Citizens can act as watchdogs over local regulators or businesses to ensure that they comply with existing regulations.

   e. **Petitioning local business**. Citizens can directly confront business or industries by asking them to change policies which are environmentally unsound. For example, citizens might ask local markets and restaurants to discontinue styrofoam packaging.

3. **State, national and international action**. Citizens can take various kinds of actions at state, national, and international levels.

   a. **Voting**. Citizens can vote for and/or work to elect candidates who will best represent their views on environmental issues.

   b. **Direct action**. Citizens can join boycotts, sign petitions, write letters and participate in demonstrations to influence policy makers, legislators and corporations.

4. THE PRESS AND THE POLITICAL PROCESS

I fear three newspapers more than a hundred bayonets.

Napoleon Bonaparte (c. 1800)

Were it left to me to decide whether we should have a government without newspapers, or newspapers without a government, I should not hesitate a moment to prefer the latter. But I should mean that every man should receive those papers, and be capable of reading them.

Thomas Jefferson (c. 1790)

Whatever facilitates a general intercourse of sentiments, as good roads, domestic commerce, a free press, and particularly a circulation of newspapers through the entire body of people ...is favorable to liberty.

James Madison (1788)

There are Three Estates in Parliament; but in the Reporters' Gallery yonder, there sits a Fourth Estate more important far than they all.

Attributed to Edmund Burke (c. 1775)

The ability to present news objectively and to interpret it realistically is not a native instinct in the human species; it is a product of culture which comes with the knowledge of the past and acute awareness of how deceptive is our normal observation and how wishful our thinking.

Walter Lippmann (c. 1950)

There's a whole industry that dissects everything, every part of you every day, and you're measured against this media thing. Not against who you are or what you said.

Walter Mondale (1984)

Publicity is as essential to its (modern American government) orderly functioning as the power to levy taxes and pass laws.

Douglass Cater (1965)

Congress shall make no law...abridging the freedom of speech, or of the press.

The First Amendment (1791)

INTRODUCTION

The tradition of a free press is as old as the nation itself. The principles inherent in free speech and an unfettered flow of information have become a fundamental part of our national heritage, protected by the Constitution, and woven in the country's social and political fabric. From the early colonial era to the present, the American press has been recognized as a catalytic force in the affairs of the citizens and their governmental representatives.

Notably, during the last half century, American journalism has undergone a revolution, conceptually, stylistically and technologically, evolving into what has become popularly known as the mass media. These changes, far greater in depth and breadth than the evolutionary developments of the preceding five centuries—since **William Caxton** (1421-1491) constructed his printing press at Westminster, England, in 1476—have perceptibly altered the way governmental institutions function, the manner in which electoral politics is conducted and the perceptions society has of its political and cultural environment.

In a relatively brief interlude, traditional journalism—defined as a literary genre to inform, educate and entertain—has been vastly broadened. Television has emerged as a pervasive instrument in daily communications, and news is instantly relayed around the globe by space satellites. There is a prevailing sense that an event doesn't really happen—or at least isn't of much consequence—unless the media are there to observe and report it, as well as explain its significance.

Public opinion, shaped in a large measure by the interaction between the news media and government, has become a common arbiter among competing interests. One can hardly understand the way government and politics work unless he or she is sensitive to the contemporary role of the news media—for good or ill—as a marketplace of ideas and a conduit for information.

As the so-called "Fourth Branch of Government," the modern U.S. news media are not simply observers or instant chroniclers of events but rather are an integral (ex officio) part of the political and governing process, having an influential impact on public policy, governmental decisions and popular attitudes. Currently, people tend to follow the news on two levels: their interest is focused on (1) what is going on around them and throughout the world, and (2) how the media cover and interpret those events.

Notwithstanding the dynamic changes in mass communications over the last several decades, the fervent belief that a free flow of information is essential to the sustenance of a democratic society remains ever constant, and indeed is reinforced.

OBJECTIVES

The citizen should be able to

1. explain the importance of free speech and a free press in a democratic system.

2. describe the tradition, philosophical antecedents and historical background of the American press.

3. explain the differences among the various print and electronic news media and be familiar with their individual characteristics, including their style, political ideology (if any), and professional credibility.

4. explain the principal functions of the press as a disseminator of news and information, as an educational instrument, and as an interpreter of events and developments.

5. explain the interdependent relationship between government, electoral politics and the news media.

6. explain the constitutional latitude afforded the press, as well as its legal limitations and professional responsibilities.

7. explain how government officials and political candidates utilize the press and practice news management techniques.

8. use the news media to keep informed of current events and learn about contemporary issues, campaign developments and the political process.

9. evaluate the role and influence of the news media in political and governmental affairs.

10. distinguish between imagery and reality in news reports and political events.

11. explain the significance of public opinion in political affairs and in the making of government policy.

12. explain the position that strength of a free press is in its diversity, independence, and multiple voices.

13. take, defend, and evaluate positions on the strengths and weaknesses of the press as a source of information for the citizen and proposals for its improvement.

14. evaluate the utility for the citizen of supplementing the press with other sources of information in order to remedy its weaknesses.

15. take, defend, and evaluate positions regarding the proper scope and limits of a free press in American democracy.

FRAME OF REFERENCE
Conceptual Perspective

I. **The nature and functions of the press**. The press is one of the vital features of American democracy.

   A. **Power of the press and press responsibility**. Questions remain over whether they are mutually exclusive.

   1. **Power of the press to shape impressions**. Communications and information comprise the essence of governing in a democratic society. Accordingly, the power of the press is widely recognized, even if not clearly defined or measured. Above all, it is universally agreed that it is a major contributor in shaping perceptions and impressions about people, issues and events.

   2. **Freedom of the press implies obligations**. The responsibility of the press has long been a subject of debate. History suggests that while the Founders believed in press freedom, they also insisted on press responsibility. To them, press freedom was not an end in itself, but a means of securing certain higher values, such as individual rights and a viable representative government. Such concerns also imply substantial obligations—to search for the truth, and to be fair and unbiased in the presentation of news and commentary.

   3. **Obligations of the press unclear, perhaps nonexistent**. Many contemporary journalists, nonetheless, note that the First Amendment imposes no obligation that the press should act responsibly or with restraint—and that freedom of the press "includes the freedom to be wrong, even to be irresponsible," in the view of **Benjamin C. Bradlee**, executive editor of the *Washington Post*.

   4. **Freedom of the press may conflict with other freedoms**. In rebuttal, it is argued that the role of the press in society must be weighed against other legitimate interests. Following protests by the news media over the news blackout in the October 1983 Grenada invasion, Defense Secretary **Caspar Weinberger** declared, "The Founding Fathers did not proclaim freedom of the press and then resolutely stand aside. They expected government to put all constitutional rights as well as duties in a state of balance. Some [people] act as if they believe freedom of the press is the paramount freedom—so important that no other freedoms can exist without it. They seem to believe that any action required to produce a story is justified by the First Amendment. Unfortunately, such an attitude promotes the trampling of other, equally legitimate public interests—the national defense, an accused's right to a fair trial free from a jury influenced by news reports, the right of privacy and others."

   B. **The First Amendment and the intent of its authors**. The principle of a free press as stated in the Bill of Rights ensures protection against governmental control, including such potential interference as prior restraint, censorship and licensing. The press is the only private institution specifically protected by the Constitution, and for two centuries scholars, constitutional lawyers, and journalists have variously interpreted the intent of the Founders in drafting the provision.

1. **A free press has constitutional standing**. When the U.S. press comes under attack, its defenders invariably cite the First Amendment, which states in part, "Congress shall make no law...abridging the freedom of speech, or of the press." As such, those fourteen words confer formidable legal standing and shape the independent character of the American press.

2. **First Amendment a result of political expediency**. The Constitution, drafted in secret at the Federal Constitutional Convention in Philadelphia in 1787, made no mention of the press. Nor did any of the fifty-five delegates protest against the rule of secrecy. To ensure passage of the Constitution, the Federalists, who favored a strong national government, agreed to the appendage of a Bill of Rights to placate the anti-Federalists, equally determined to safeguard state's rights. Thus, the First Amendment, implemented in 1791 as part of the Bill of Rights, was the byproduct not of a libertarian ideal, but of political expediency.

3. **First Amendment almost the Third Amendment**. Notwithstanding its symbolic value, it was an accident of history that the First Amendment is in fact the first of the amendments making up the Bill of Rights. Two Amendments ahead of it on the list submitted to the states in 1789 were not adopted.

4. **Interpreting the meaning of the First Amendment an invitation to conjecture**. What the authors of the free speech/free press clause meant is open to conjecture; also, it is uncertain what impelled them to include it in the First Amendment. There was no crisis involving press or speech when the amendment was proposed and adopted. Nowhere is free speech or freedom of the press defined. Moreover, the provision carries no suggestion that the press should act responsibly or accept accountability.

   a. **Negatively stated**. Further muddling the mystery, the amendment is negative in thrust, stating, "Congress shall make no law...," thereby denying rather than granting powers to the federal legislative body. It was aimed explicitly at the federal government and was not addressed to the states.

   b. **The states for long exempted**. Not until the twentieth century did the U.S. Supreme Court, citing the Fourteenth Amendment, hold the states to the prohibitions of the First Amendment. Even so, the breadth of the protection conferred on the press by the First Amendment, remains less than clear.

5. **First Amendment guarantees people's right to know**. Constitutional scholar Leonard W. Levy has insisted that, "The First Amendment protected the freedom of the press, not the press" as a private enterprise. This strongly suggests that the amendment was intended to guarantee the people's right to know, rather than shield the press as a vested interest.

6. **Freedom of the press depends upon public support**. Regardless of their intent, as relatively cosmopolitan, learned men, many of whom were lawyers or students of the law, the framers of the Constitution were not unaware of the blossoming influence of the press in social and political affairs. **George Washington** acknowledged that the colonial press would play a significant role in whether the Constitution would be adopted by the states. He further supported favorable postal rates for newspapers. But inevitably, as **Alexander Hamilton** asserted in *The Federalist*, freedom of the press depends "on public opinion, and on the general spirit of the people and the government."

C. **The enigma of the press**. Communications is the transmission of information via a recognizable system of symbols, signs, sounds, and behavior to convey a common understanding.

   1. **Words can convey only a partial truth**. The printed and spoken word and visual reflections are the primary element in news communication. Words themselves are symbols, fraught with various meanings, shadings, nuances, and interpretations, which when built one upon another project images but seldom conform completely to reality. Journalists boast they are truth-seekers but, given the constraints of time and space, the most they can achieve is a semblance or approximation of the truth; they can submit **a** truth, but almost never the whole truth.

   2. **News as the distillation of the human experience**. However, news is more than simply the impression of events and developments as

reported in the newspapers and newsmagazines and broadcast over the air to satisfy people's interests or curiosity or provide amusement for them. News, in short, is the recorded distillation of the human experience. It also provides a chronology of the times in which we live and serves to reaffirm continuity in our lives. Our psychological reliance on news to inform and partially educate us about our physical, social and political environment is reflected in what people often say when meeting each other—"What's new?" "How're things?" "What d'you know?" "What's goin' on?"

3. **The definition of news**. News, as the term is popularly used, defies a common definition. By its very nature, it is both ephemeral and episodic, in the sense that it has a brief life span and is a separate and disjointed piece in the chronological history of humanity. Various definitions include: "News is anything you learned today, you didn't know yesterday," "Anything that makes the reader, viewer or listener say, 'Hey, I didn't know that!'" "That which is of interest to the greatest number of people at a particular moment," "Anything that will make people talk." In the main, news is the timely account of the unusual, the unexpected, the exceptional and the significant affecting a specific audience.

4. **The pre-television newspaper**. Prior to the advent of television, news was equated with fresh, fast-breaking incidents and developments that occurred yesterday at most or even within hours, prompting press runs of newspaper "extras" emblazoned with giant-sized headlines and sold on the streets by shouting newsboys. Minutes counted in hotly competitive urban areas and the first paper on the street with the hottest news reaped a financial windfall. It was a period when the "five Ws" reigned supreme—when the hard news story told the reader straight off in the lead sentence Who, What, When, Where, and perhaps Why. At such times, a newspaper's city room came alive with hectic activity, with editors bellowing orders and the tinny staccato of typewriters supplying a mechanical rhythm to the chaotic scene.

5. **The newspaper today**. Today, there is less of an aura of immediacy in newspaper city rooms since television skims the headlines first. "Extras" are extinct, a dimly-remembered relic of the past. The overriding responsibility of newspaper editors

and reporters is to provide analysis and explanation of why events occurred as they did, to fill in the background and stress the significance, and to describe the players and their roles. They must reach beyond and dig below the brief, rapid-fire news reports offered by television with its patina of entertainment.

6. **Print media and "soft" news**. Also, the print media have turned more to "soft" news or feature articles, often dealing with social and cultural trends. Many newspapers have adopted a magazine format by compartmentalizing service-oriented sections on topics such as health, science, home fashions, modern lifestyles, food, and business-economics. A reduction of columns from eight to six per page, larger print type, and the expansive use of color, maps, graphics and photographs lend an airy look to today's newspapers. And the incessantly humming, green-lettered VDTs (video display terminals) hovering like revered icons over every desk have forever changed the newsroom's ambience.

D. **A human, paradoxical institution**. The institutional character of the U.S. news media is dichotomous in nature.

1. **U.S. news media straddle public and private worlds**. News organizations are privately owned yet endowed with a public trust. To serve the public as independent purveyors of news, information and opinion, they must survive; and to survive, they must make a profit, mainly through commercial advertising. This potentially volatile mix between business and news, each with its own separate objectives, requires a sharp dividing line between them. In virtually all news organizations the two departments are separately operated as a protective measure against possible pressure by advertisers (who supply the bulk of the revenue) on the presentation of news.

2. **Journalists and their roles**. Many journalists maintain that they represent and serve as surrogates for the public. The counter-argument is that privately-owned newspapers, newsmagazines and radio-television outlets—many of which are part of billion dollar corporate conglomerates—represent no one except themselves and can speak for no one else. The press may act as a "watchdog" against injustice and official transgressions and can speak for an individual,

group or cause, but it cannot speak for any of them. To serve the public is not the same as to represent the public. Furthermore, the public is almost always divided on any given issue. Therefore, no single, outside entity can claim to be its spokesman.

3. **Difficulty of defining journalism**. A corresponding issue which has perennially bedeviled American journalism is the question of whether it is a profession, art, science or craft—or a combination of any or all.

   a. **As an art**. Journalism might be said to be an art because at its highest level of proficiency it demonstrates imagination, originality, and creativity.

   b. **As a science**. As in science, the value and credibility of journalism depend on accuracy and precision.

   c. **As a craft**. Journalism also meets the definition of a craft, in that it requires special skills and meticulous attention to provide a quality product.

   d. **As a profession**. Controversy over whether journalism is a profession provokes debate which neither the courts and the government nor its practitioners have been able to resolve. Unlike the medical, legal, and scientific professions, journalism has no educational requirements, or code of ethics applying to all of its members. Nor does it have a formal peer review structure authorized to oversee and enforce prescribed professional standards.

   e. **Objections to formal requirements**. Attempts to introduce any of these criteria have been met with vigorous objections from many major news organizations on the grounds they infringe upon First Amendment rights—and that furthermore, editors are employed to monitor standards and quality of work.

4. **Diversity of the press**. Despite a common misconception ("the media"), the press is not a monolithic institution. Rather, it is fragmented and diversified into innumerable parts—by ownership, format, editorial philosophy, style, approach, quality, political inclination, status, credibility, and audience.

5. **The press as a human institution**. One evident characteristic which marks the press as a whole is that it is a human institution. It is one of the few surviving institutions that uses modern technology but depends almost entirely on the mind, judgment, and morality of individuals in the pursuit of what legendary editor **Herbert Bayard Swope** called its "priestly mission."

   a. **Fallibility of the press**. The end product emanates from a concerted effort, but each person's contribution is visible and open to criticism and correction. Hence, journalism's almost total reliance on fallible humanity assures errors of commission and omission.

   b. **Relatively few inaccuracies**. What is perhaps surprising is not how many, but how relatively few flagrant factual mistakes there are in a newspaper, newsmagazine, or newscast. As **Stanley Walker**, onetime city editor of the New York Herald Tribune observed, "The newspaper is the best daily record we have of man's incredible meanness and magnificent courage."

E. **Expansion of the press's role**. The conceptual role of the press has been vastly expanded, largely because of advances in communications technology, the growing awareness of public opinion in politics, commerce, social affairs and governmental policy, and the artful refinement of techniques in dealing with the media.

1. **Functions of the press**. Most people perceive the media as a sort of transmission belt which merely moves news and information, which they can turn on or off as they wish. But to fully understand the role and function of the contemporary news media, they should think of it in broader, more substantive and even abstract terms. Other than merely acting as a conductor of information, the news media have several vital but less apparent functions. They serve as:

   a. **A platform or forum for public debate**. Almost all major issues, from abortion to health care to presidential elections, are largely explained, discussed and thrashed out in the media.

b. **An instrument to influence public opinion.** Leaders in government, the business community, the political arena, and the special interest field are keenly aware of the importance of the media in carrying their message and soliciting popular support.

c. **A catalyst for social, political and cultural movements.** New ideas and causes need to be defined, promoted, and publicized to be accepted and to gain recruits. The most effective method is through the news media. Civil rights leaders learned this in the late 1950s, followed later by advocates for women's rights, anti-war, consumer protection, environmental concerns, anti-nuclear and gay rights. In a sense, the press legitimizes such movements.

d. **A channel for diplomatic relations.** Heads of governments today often communicate with each other through the media. For example, in August, 1990, following the Iraqi invasion of Kuwait, **President Bush** asserted in remarks to reporters, "This will not stand. This will not stand, this aggression against Kuwait." In so saying, Bush was sending a warning to Iraqi President Saddam Hussein that the United States might use military force if diplomatic efforts and economic sanctions failed to produce a withdrawal of Iraqi occupation troops. At the same time, Bush was disclosing his position to the American people, as well as to the rest of the world.

e. **A vehicle by which U.S. government officials and agencies speak to one another.** Through the use of the media, government agencies are able to bypass tedious protocol, red tape, and time-consuming channels. Other than regular news announcements or releases, they may resort to unattributable "leaks" to the press to get their message across.

f. **Shaping impressions.** The media are a means by which public impressions are shaped of people, places, events, and issues.

F. **Perimeters of power.** The increased visibility of the press has raised the public's awareness regarding its influence and created a mystique about "the power of the press."

1. **Realities and perceptions concerning the strength of the press.** The common perception is that the press is powerful. Since perception is often construed as reality, it serves to enhance the power of the press in fact. Several questions persist, however, which should be considered.

   a. **What kind of power does the press exercise?** Seldom does the press initiate major newsworthy events. Instead, it mainly reacts to events and other stimuli, including public pressure and socio-cultural trends.

   b. **How does the press exert power?** For the most part, the power of the press is in its selectivity—in its ability to define what is news and in the manner in which it presents the news. Also, its power lies in its capacity to largely set the news agenda and in its freedom to make judgments and offer opinions about daily happenings and ongoing developments.

   c. **To what degree does the press exercise power.** Almost never is the impact of the press decisive by itself. More often, it is one of the elements or players in electoral politics and public affairs. In a notable example, notwithstanding its great contribution, the *Washington Post* was not solely responsible for exposing the Watergate scandal and bringing down President **Richard M. Nixon**. Congress, the courts, officials of several federal agencies, and television exposure played an equal role.

2. **Effect of the press on speeding up political decision making.** The impact and pervasiveness of the news media can have an inadvertent and at times unfortunate effect on official policy. Some observers contend that the ubiquitousness of the news media, particularly television with its dramatic appeal, creates anxieties and a sense of urgency, compelling government leaders to make hasty and often premature decisions without adequate consultation and mediation. "The most harmful effect of television news is its tendency to speed up the decision-making process on issues that television news is featuring and to slow down and interrupt the process of deciding other important issues that get less television attention," maintained Lloyd N. Cutler, former Carter White House counsel. Referring to what he calls the "doomsday clock," Cutler has said,

"If an ominous foreign event is featured on television news, the President and his advisers feel bound to make a response in time for the next evening news."

    a. **A presidential media response**. As an example, Cutler noted that promptly after the Soviet invasion of Afghanistan in 1979, President Carter went on television and announced a grain embargo, a decision which turned out to have an injurious effect on U.S. farm prices.

    b. **Media pressure and the hostage crisis**. Cutler also recalled that following the seizure of American hostages in Iran in November 1979, the television networks began a drumbeat, ticking off the number of days of captivity each evening, in effect serving as a form of oblique pressure which contributed to the decision leading to the tragic and unsuccessful effort to rescue the hostages.

  3. **Limits on press power**. All of this indicates that the power of the press is conditional rather than absolute, selective rather than collective, and causal rather than direct.

II. **Government, the electoral process, and the press**. A complex and intimate relationship exists between the operation of government, the electoral process, and the press.

  A. **The interrelationship between government and news media**. People must be informed if democracy is to work. Consequently, communications is such an essential element of the American political and governmental process that its use has become institutionalized.

    1. **Mutual dependence between press and government**. Historically, there has always been a symbiotic relationship between press and government. They need each other, they feed off each other, they are, to a large degree, mutually dependent. The press wants access and information; the government wants to get its message out in its own way and to solicit public support. Hence, the adversarial or perhaps love-hate relationship between them.

    2. **Public policy, popular opinion, and the press**. The connection between public policy and popular opinion is acknowledged by government officials,

who spend a large portion of their time and energy dealing with members of the news media and orchestrating public affairs campaigns. The difficulty for both the journalist and the public is distinguishing between the release of information which the people have a right to know, and flackery designed to polish the image of a president, an administration, an agency, or a program.

  3. **U.S. Government's public relations machine**. Government is the public's business; and to an immeasurable extent, the business of government involves public relations—that is, enhancing its goodwill and understanding with the governed.

    a. **Massive network of specialists**. Seeded throughout the federal government landscape, from the White House to the giant Cabinet departments to the mini-agencies cloistered in bureaucratic depths, is a massive, amorphous network of press, information, and public affairs specialists.

    b. **Functions of government publicists**. The chief function of a public relations machine is to retail, promote, package and, when it is in their interest, withhold information regarding Administration activities, policies, decisions, and personalities.

    c. **Wide range of activities**. Each day, the government's information arm spews out millions of words, pictures, books, statistics, pamphlets, magazines, and films. It arranges tours, sets up exhibits, sponsors aerial shows, schedules speakers, exhibits art works, offers press interviews and news briefings, transmits radio programs around the world in numerous languages, and bounces photos off airborne satellites. During the Persian Gulf War of 1991, it censored stories, photos, and video film sent from the battle area to ensure military security.

    d. **Number of government publicists large but unknown**. Because of ill-defined job titles, confusing budgetary practices, and misunderstanding over what constitutes government public relations (the preferred phrase in bureaucratic parlance is "public affairs" or "public information") the exact size, scope, and operations of this vast information machine is mostly hidden from public view. Although there are no reported figures, government personnel officials have estimated the number of federal employees engaged in some form of press-public relations at more than 20,000 and the cost in excess of $1 billion annually.

4. **Tension endemic between press and government.** A constant state of tension exists between the press and government. One side persistently seeks full disclosure, the other is equally determined to withhold information or put a golden gloss on that which is released. It is a loveless marriage of convenience, predominated by self-interest and the recognition that the relationship is mutually beneficial.

   a. **Government resources used to "manage the news."** Among the government's resources are regular press briefings, such as those held daily at the White House, State Department, and Pentagon. Announcements and comments made by press officials and other Administration executives largely set the day's news agenda. By so doing, the Administration is able to "manage the news."

   b. **Reporters dependent on government sources.** Reporters can and will seek out other views, but to a large degree, they are hostage to the process. In a widely-noted study, Leon V. Sigal reported that Washington correspondents are reliant on Administration sources and other official channels—such as press handouts, news conferences, interviews, hearings, backgrounders, and speeches—for more than 70 percent of their information. And political analyst Martin Linsky reported that a survey of high government officials showed that 42 percent admitted leaking information to the press, a figure which he termed "understated."

B. **The presidency and the press.** Modern presidents are compelled to be effective communicators. To lead the nation, deal with Congress, weigh the concerns of multitudinous interest groups and negotiate with foreign governments, presidents must be able to strike a popular chord and gain the endorsement of the electorate. In this pursuit, their principal means of reaching out to the public and the political sector and winning support is through the mass media. Basically, a president's authority is derived from three sources:

the Constitution, his role as a political leader, and his skill as a communicator.

1. **Mobilizing public opinion.** To be an effective leader, the president, among other things, must mobilize public opinion, define national problems, set priorities, and offer a vision for the future. This he must do by establishing a bond with the people. Hence, the importance of communications and media relations in the presidential realm. As students of the presidency have observed, the president's power is in his ability to persuade.

2. **Presidential style and the communications revolution.** As a result of the revolution in mass communications, presidents have altered their political styles and governing procedures. As a former White House aide observed, "Presidential power is communications power." Television, especially, has enhanced their ability to project their views and mobilize public sentiment.

3. **Presidents always in the public eye.** Today, an incumbent president is the subject of constant media exposure. His voice is the most distinct in public affairs, his face the most familiar. Each of his official acts and most of his personal activities are reported and photographed by the news media and disseminated around the world. No other celebrated figure can match him as a national attraction, thus ensuring that the public will listen and heed what he has to say.

4. **The presidential theater.** In a sense the presidency has evolved into a form of national theater in which the Chief Executive is the most visible actor on the American stage. Accordingly, the British scholar Harold Laski wrote, "Whatever voice is drowned amid the babel of tongues, his...can always be heard."

5. **The tug-of-war between the press and the president.** The news media, nonetheless, can do much for and to the president. In the antithetical embrace between the press and the presidency, the press will traditionally exhibit skepticism and excessive zeal. The president will attempt to impose the terms of public debate and seek to sculpt the shape of information. It is an unceasing contest in which there are only temporary victories by either side.

6. **The downside for the Chief Executive**. Predictably, presidents become frustrated in their dealings with the media. They sadly discover that while they can manage the news, they cannot control it. And while television serves as an unexcelled "bully pulpit," it correspondingly subjects a president to microscopic scrutiny and magnifies his flaws and defects, thereby diminishing some of the mystique and grandeur of the office.

7. **Political success, public opinion and the media**. It has long been recognized that political success, including that at the presidential level, rests almost wholly on favorable public opinion. "Public sentiment is everything," **Abraham Lincoln** declared. "With public sentiment nothing can fail, without it nothing can succeed."

8. **Shifts his public opinion**. Because presidents are constantly in the public eye and often at the mercy of events over which they have little or no control, they are vulnerable to the subtle and sometimes tempestuous shifts in the winds of public opinion.

9. **Style/personality and public opinion**. Since the institution of the presidency is an amalgamation of the man and the office, a president's style and personality have a deep effect on public opinion. Nixon's characteristic reserve, Ford's blandness, Carter's stiff moral righteousness, Reagan's cinematic charm, and Bush's "WASPish" demeanor have all figured one way or another in their presidential careers.

10. **Presidential power and access to news media**. Presidents possess numerous advantages and resources which serve to influence public opinion. Among them: the historical aura and mythology which shroud the presidency; the symbolic role of the president as the national spokesman and unifier; the majestic trappings of office; a huge corps of aides who supply him with information and intelligence, propose decision-making options, measure public opinion, and husband his time; an extensive press-public relations apparatus; and total and immediate access to the news media. This, and more, sets him apart in the eyes of the public.

11. **Size and scope of president's press-public relations operations**. About two-thirds of the White House Office staff, which fluctuates between 350 to 600 members, are involved in the task of promoting the president and his programs. In addition, some agencies under the umbrella of the Executive Office of the president, such as the Office of Management and Budget and the National Security Council, have their own press section.

12. **The White House as a communications center**. Few of these officials deal with decision-making or policy formulation, except in a peripheral sense. Rather, they are primarily concerned with seeing that the president and his policies, programs and decisions are perceived in the best possible light. They further are assigned to smooth the pathways between the White House and the press and the myriad political constituencies. In the view of one political scientist, "The whole of the White House is an institution for communicating on behalf of the president."

C. **The press and electoral politics**. The movement of the news media from the periphery to the center of politics and government is one of the most significant developments of the second half of the twentieth century. To a substantive degree, the mass media have redefined American politics.

1. **News media an ingredient of politics**. Today, it is commonly accepted that the news media are an active ingredient in electoral politics.

   a. **Sizing up candidates and issues**. With the decline of the political parties, the media play a major role in the assessment of candidates and the selection of issues—functions formerly handled by party leaders.

   b. **Media concerns**. Campaigns are designed with the media in mind. Candidates' speeches and appearances are planned for maximum media exposure. Generally, national candidates spend 50 percent or more of their campaign budgets on "paid media"—meaning political commercials, the vast portion on television.

   c. **Candidates need to master the media**. There is a sense among many candidates and their campaign advisers that if they cannot master the media, the media will ultimately master them. They are acutely aware that voters' impressions of the contestants' character and competence are mainly transmitted through the prism of the news media.

d. **News media and revolutionary changes in campaigning.** Critics contend that the news media, in their competitive zeal for drama and exclusive stories, are largely responsible for converting political campaigns into a form of burlesque in which style substitutes for substance and illusion for reality. Although politicians, political scientists, and journalists themselves are uncertain as to the extent of the news media's influence, there is no question that candidates would much prefer a "good press" to a critical press—or even worse, a press that ignores them.

2. **Television changes conduct of politics.** Television has not only changed how politics is covered, but how it is conducted. According to the late author-journalist Theodore H. White, "Television is...the playing field of politics."

a. **Television as complementary.** In a practical sense, television and politics complement each other: each revels in imagery and contrived scenarios and high-blown rhetoric.

b. **Television as producing a new breed of candidates.** Since modern candidates are less reliant on and less beholden to their party, they run virtually independent campaigns and are dependent on the news media to carry their candidacy to the voters. They are tutored on how to project on television, their speeches are tailored for a graphic sound bite which a television producer can easily fit into the evening newscast. The campaigns themselves have become less party-oriented and less issue-oriented, turning more on personality, style and symbolism.

c. **Made-for-television conventions.** National party conventions have evolved into synthetic, made-for-television productions, their outcome foreordained in the long-running state primaries. For the most part, they have become ceremonial investitures, a blend of politics and show business.

d. **Artificially created news.** In the pre-television era, **Woodrow Wilson** defined news as the atmosphere of events; today, news is artificially created for television. It is generally perceived as a "visual medium," but in reality television's reach goes beyond the limited scope of the camera.

3. **The impact of technology on campaigns.** Paralleling the advent of television, modern electoral campaigning has been restructured with refinements in the "packaging" of candidates, the scientific canvassing of popular attitudes, and the adoption of professional fund-raising techniques, including the use of direct-mail and the courting of PACs (political action committees).

a. **New dimension added by telecommunications advancements.** Included in the arsenal of wizardry available to contemporary candidates are satellite transmission services, cable television, videocassettes, teleconferences, electronic mailings, and video press releases. Using computers, campaign technicians can combine census data, postal zip codes, previous voting preferences, economic incomes and other information to define voter lifestyle profiles that can be used effectively to design political commercials, determine media buys in targeted markets, suggest the content of direct-mail and dictate the selection of campaign issues for the candidate to emphasize.

b. **Political consultants—a new elite.** The reliance of modern candidates on Madison Avenue-style campaign techniques and the emergence of technological innovations have produced a new type of political elite—the professional consultant.

c. **Consultants in high demand.** Today, it would be almost unthinkable to conduct a major campaign without calling on the services of specialists in organization, political strategy, media relations, polling, advertising, direct mail, issue research and analysis, telephone solicitation, and volunteer recruitment. Studies estimate that 75 percent of all state and federal candidates hire professional consultants.

d. **At the top of the campaign hierarchy.** Whereas they once loitered on the fringes of politics, political consultants now are perched among the top hierarchy of political campaigns.

e. **Butt of criticism**. Critics maintain that political consultants are responsible for adding significantly to campaign costs, for exploiting emotional and negative themes, and for encouraging candidates to bend with prevailing winds of popular opinion. In reply, the political consultants argue that they try to bring out the best in their clients and that they simply fill a void left by the erosion of the party structure. In any event, they appear to be permanently ensconced in the political establishment.

4. **Press coverage shapes political campaigns**. If, as is said, the contest shapes the coverage, it is equally true today that the coverage shapes the contest. Just as the political process has changed, so has the coverage of candidates and campaigns.

a. **Campaigns as a news showcase**. National news organizations view major campaigns as an opportunity to showcase their talent, creativity and professionalism. The television networks are keenly aware that their performance can affect their ratings—and thus their advertising revenues.

b. **Trends in campaign coverage**. From a journalistic perspective, there have been several new, if rather subtle, developments in campaign coverage. Editors now realize that accompanying the candidate on the campaign plane is only part of what's happening. They realize that stories of greater depth and significance can be gathered on the ground, including reports on crucial issues, on the mood and tilt of certain constituencies, and on the past record and performance of the contestants. They also stress the impact of economic developments and breaking international events on the campaign.

c. **Print news response to television**. There are also more analytical and thematic articles by the print press, which is at a disadvantage in competing with television in breaking daily news. The print press also publishes more background stories, profiles on the principal players, educational pieces explaining the political process, interpretive articles on relevant issues, and opinion-commentary pieces—all of which are intended to flesh out the full meaning and significance of the campaign and enhance the voter's understanding of it.

d. **Increased use of voter polls**. As an integral part of their political coverage, the news media have made significantly greater use of voter surveys. Many observers feel that they use them to an excess, since campaign polls, which essentially reflect a moment frozen in time, can quickly become outdated and thus present a distorted picture. Questions also arise over the validity of the surveys; whether, for example, the sample was adequately representative of the targeted audience, whether the questions were objectively posed, and whether the results and conclusions were properly and fairly presented.

e. **Media coverage of the media**. Another new dimension involves the increased coverage of the media, notably television, by the media. In such instances, assessments are made of the press's role and responsibility in the political process, and the authenticity of their reports. Critical evaluations are also offered of the professional propriety of certain stories.

f. **More attention paid to private matters**. In still another conspicuous change in political coverage, political reporters now focus more on the private lives, personal predilections, and family affairs of the candidates. Not too long ago, custom and a tacit understanding between the press and the candidates precluded the disclosure of intimate, private matters. But that invisible line drawn between public service and private behavior, which many journalists, rightly or wrongly, felt provided a measure of civility in their political coverage, has virtually been obliterated.

Historical Perspective

I. **The early history of the press**. The issue of freedom of the press arose in Europe early in the history of printing.

A. **A philosophy of free expression as predating the birth of the Republic.** The thinkers, statesmen and intellects of the Old and New World sensed the potential of free expression as a social and political force. **Thomas Jefferson** held that free speech was one of man's inalienable rights. But ordinary citizens of colonial America, not unnaturally, were more concerned with their individual liberties and well-being than with the nature of the press. Historically, the tradition of an independent press emerged incrementally, not in a straight line but in an uncharted trek through legal, moral and philosophical thickets.

1. **Philosophical antecedents.** The idea of freedom of expression in America had a number of European precursors.

   a. **Luther's praise of printing.** Although **Martin Luther** (1483-1546) assailed printers for their hunger for profits, he called printing "God's highest act of Grace."

   b. **Francis Bacon on the power of the press.** As far back as 1644, **Francis Bacon** (1561-1626) regarded the "force, effects and consequences" of the printing press as being on a par with gunpowder and the compass for having "changed the appearance and state of the world."

   c. **Milton's limited defense of a free press.** **John Milton** (1608-1674), in *Areopagitica* (1644), offered a narrow concept of a free press centering on the proposed termination of government licensing powers which, among other constrictions, required printers to submit manuscripts for official review in advance of publication. Milton, nonetheless, would still hold critics of the existing order accountable for material considered offensive to the government.

   d. **Blackstone's idea of freedom of the press.** **William Blackstone** (1723-1780), the great English jurist, conceived freedom of press to mean no prior censorship; but at the same time he charged that the press should be responsible for abusing its freedom.

   e. **Mill's defense of freedom of expression.** **John Stuart Mill** (1806-1873) maintained each individual is free to think and act as he chooses. He contended that as opinion is silenced, truth may be silenced as well, and that even a wrong opinion may contain an element of truth necessary to the discovery of the whole truth. Moreover, truth benefits—springs to life and becomes more sharply honed—in its clash with error.

2. **Freedom of the press in America; the Zenger case.** In 1735, **John Peter Zenger** (1697-1745) was charged with seditious libel for publishing articles critical of His Majesty's governor of New York, William Cosby. Zenger's attorney, **Andrew Hamilton** (1676?-1741), successfully argued that if the jury was convinced that the defendant had published the truth, justice required that he be acquitted.

   a. **Novelty of the truth as a defense against libel.** Hamilton's reliance on the truth was a bold stroke for that time. While standard legal procedure today, it should be recalled that the American colonies inherited their judicial system from the mother country.

   b. **Seventeenth century view.** In the seventeenth century, England's Star Chamber rationalized that a true statement regarding governmental misconduct might pose more of a danger than an easily rebuttable one.

3. **Limits on freedom of the press.** It is remembered that in proposing truth as a defense, Hamilton did not go so far as to claim that the press should be libel-proof.

   a. **The idea of libel upheld.** In a statement to the jury, Hamilton said, "Nothing ought to excuse a man who raises a false charge or accusation, even against a private person, and that no manner of allowance ought to be made to him who does so against a public magistrate." That basically reflected the sentiment of the colonial leaders, most of whom believed that the press should be free to publish without prior restraint but should not be immune from sanctions for printing false and malicious calumnies against the government.

   b. **Franklin on libeling officials.** Alluding to journalists guilty of libeling government officials, **Benjamin Franklin** (1706-1790), printer, publisher and patriot, declared, "We should, in moderation, content ourselves with tarring and feathering and tossing them in a blanket."

4. **Early colonial press and its audience**. Primitive by subsequent standards, the early colonial press was highly partisan. Newspapers mostly served as strident voices for particular factions, causes, parties, or individuals.

   a. **Started in port towns**. By the mid-eighteenth century, more than a dozen independent weekly newspapers, necessarily small because of poor transportation and the need to set type laboriously by hand, had been started, mostly in port towns.

   b. **Aimed at elite audiences**. Published mainly by printers and postmasters, the early colonial papers were directed at the educated, well-off urban classes and the political and commercial elites who could afford the relatively high subscription rates.

   c. **News content**. The "news" generally consisted of shipping and mercantile announcements, the promotion of special interests and information culled from old British newspapers brought in by ship. Personal attacks and biased information were common fare.

5. **The press on the eve of the revolution**. As the conflict between the Tories and Patriots became increasingly intense, the papers grew in numbers and circulation. They also assumed a more significant public role, some papers siding with the colonies and others with the crown.

   a. **Press freedom and the Stamp Act**. With rebellious fervor against British rule gathering momentum, many of the colonial papers, though divided on numerous issues, openly opposed stringent impositions by the crown, notably the 1765 Stamp Act. This act was intended to replenish the royal coffers depleted by the war against France. The act levied a penny tax per newspaper issue.

   b. **Opposition to the Stamp Act**. The colonial publishers angrily denounced the tax as an infringement on their freedom and an example of taxation without representation. Within a year the act was repealed by Parliament.

   c. **Press achieves new stature**. By the time of the Revolutionary War, publishers were recognized as influential figures and newspapers went to an estimated 40,000 colonial homes.

6. **Press freedom after independence**. Following the Revolutionary War, newspapers in the new nation transferred their partisan leanings to the debate and controversy over the powers of the central government, manifested in the struggle between the Federalists under the banner of Alexander Hamilton, Washington's chief lieutenant, and the anti-Federalists led by Thomas Jefferson.

   a. **Emergence of the "party press."** By now, the Founders were aware of the usefulness of the press and found expression for their views in the "party press"—newspapers and journals which sided with them and served their political purposes in mobilizing public opinion.

   b. **Papers established by Hamilton and Jefferson**. In his campaign to promote the Federalist cause, Alexander Hamilton established *The Gazette of the United States*. Not to be outdone, Thomas Jefferson recruited **Philip Freneau** (1752-1832), "The Poet of the Revolution," to ostensibly act as a paid "translator" at the State Department but in reality to publish an opposing newspaper, *The National Gazette*.

   c. **Performance exceeds promise**. It is highly unlikely that the Founding Fathers ever envisaged that the press would attain the lofty prominence that it has or that it would become the "Fourth Branch of Government." The struggle for press freedom in the early years of the Republic was part of a more ambitious struggle to form a constitutional government and to serve the political interests of the men who participated in the challenge.

7. **The press and the Sedition Act of 1798**. Notwithstanding earlier adoption of the First Amendment, Congress passed the Sedition Act of 1798, at a time when the political climate was tense because war with France appeared imminent.

   a. **Provisions of the act**. Endorsed by the Federalist Administration of John Adams, the legislation provided penalties of up to two years in prison and a fine of $2,000 for writing, printing or uttering "false, scandalous and malicious" statements against the government or Congress.

    b. **Jeffersonians' suspicions of political ploy.** To Jeffersonian Republicans, the act was an attempt by the Federalists to create a one-party press and a one-party government. Over the next two years, at least ten critics of government were convicted under the law, including two newspaper editors and a political writer.

    c. **Expiration of the law and consequences.** The law expired in 1801 when Jefferson assumed the presidency and pardoned all those prosecuted under its provisions. As it turned out, reconsideration of the act led to a broader legal definition of press freedom embodying principles for which libertarians had fought in cases involving seditious libel: the acceptance of truth as a defense, trial by jury, a requirement that criminal intent had to be demonstrated, and the need to distinguish between malicious libel and protected expressions of political opinion.

8. **Rise of "penny press."** With the birth of Jacksonian democracy in 1833, the "penny press," aimed at the mass of the American populace emerged. Its popularity—which coincided with the demise of the party press in America—resulted from a combination of factors:

    a. **High speed presses.** The development of high speed presses which enabled publishers to print thousands of copies of newspapers cheaply and quickly.

    b. **Increased literacy.** An increase in the level of literacy in the country provided an expanding pool of readers.

    c. **Growth of urbanization.** The rise of self-supporting urban workers enabled publishers to centralize their operations and design their papers to appeal to a specific audience.

    d. **Invention of the telegraph.** Also, the invention of the telegraph in 1844 meant that news could be transmitted almost immedi-

ately (in 1790 it took over ten days for news of an event in Boston to be published in Philadelphia).

9. **The popular press and its legendary editors.** Forerunner of the penny press was **Benjamin H. Day**'s(1810-1889) *New York Sun*, which cost one-cent compared to six-cents for most other dailies. It was soon followed by **James Gordon Bennett**'s (1795-1872) *New York Herald* and **Horace Greeley**'s (1811-1872) *New York Tribune*.

    a. **Format and appeal of the penny press.** As the country's first popular, commercialized newspapers, they played up human interest, crime and social injustice and enticed an untapped audience from among the middle levels of society.

    b. **Set precedent for U.S. press.** By cutting across social class and political party lines, the penny press attracted advertisers who relied on a broadly based clientele. The papers further expanded the scope and content of news, with first-hand accounts of national and foreign events, thus shaping a concept of the press that would endure.

    c. **Individualistic in style.** Aside from their common characteristics, each of the papers and their publishers were distinctly individualistic.

        (1) **The *Sun's* breezy style.** The *Sun* specialized in short, breezy items about local people and domestic occurrences.

        (2) **The *Herald's* innovations.** Bennett, who perceived himself as a reformer, pursued an aggressive editorial policy and broadened the *Herald* to include financial news and sports reporting.

        (3) **The *Tribune's* crusading zeal.** Greeley preferred to use the pages of his newspaper for crusades and causes. He called the *Tribune* "the great moral organ." As such, he exposed slum conditions in New York, advocated women's rights and opposed capital punishment, alcohol, and tobacco. Greeley's *Tribune* was the first major paper to endorse the abolition of slavery and the first to introduce a sepa-

rate editorial page. And as romanticized in legend, Greeley advocated the country's western expansion.

10. **Growth of the pre-Civil War press.** By the middle of the nineteenth century, the combined circulation of all U.S. dailies had climbed from 78,000 to an estimated 300,000. During this period, news reporting acquired special traits as a vocation. Interviewing became a common practice in news-gathering. Also, worldwide news agencies were established. The Associated Press (AP) was founded in 1848 and Reuters, the British wire service, the following year.

11. **The press and the Civil War.** Perhaps more than any other single event, the Civil War prompted sweeping changes in journalistic practices.

    a. **Hunger for news.** The overwhelming demand for news sent newspaper sales soaring and editors began to recognize the value of enterprising reporting in gaining exclusive news and offering up-to-the-moment developments to meet competition and satisfy a popular appetite for the latest war happenings.

    b. **Earlier war and foreign reporting erratic.** Reporting of wars and foreign affairs up to the mid-nineteenth century was on a haphazard basis. Editors simply plagiarized war news from foreign newspapers or relied on letters sent from the front by junior military officers, which more often than not were slanted and laden with self-aggrandizement.

    c. **Scope of Civil War reporting broadened.** Some 500 correspondents covered the war for the North alone. Many British and European newspapers devoted almost as much space to the war as the American press.

    d. **Mathew Brady and the advent of photography.** Modern photography also came into being during the Civil War. **Mathew Brady** (1823-1896) and his assistants followed the Northern armies and took thousands of photographs. Unfortunately, the daily newspapers were unable to publish them since they lacked the equipment and technique. Nonetheless, many of Brady's photos were published in special journals and displayed at exhibits. They offered a vivid visual account of the war and its horrible toll and served as an example for succeeding generations of photojournalists.

    e. **Civil War reporting uneven in quality.** Because of a confluence of factors—erratic mail service and interrupted telegraph transmissions, heavy-handed censorship, the inexperience of many reporters, and the unethical conduct of others—the reporting of the war, while highly professional in many instances, was often biased, inaccurate, sensationalist and propagandistic.

    f. **The rise of the war correspondent.** Yet, above all, the Civil War established war correspondence as a distinct brand of reporting and vastly expanded journalism's horizons. From then on, political leaders and military commanders would have to contend with the press and be ever aware of its influence on public opinion, for good or ill.

B. **The post-Civil War press.** The industrial revolution and the debut of the United States as a fledgling world power acted as a stimulant in the development of press and politics in the country.

1. **Rise of mass circulation newspapers.** The mass circulation newspapers of **William Randolph Hearst** (1863-1951) and **Joseph Pulitzer** (1847-1911), pandering to blatant sensationalism and jingoistic sentiments, flourished during the late nineteenth century and the early decades of the twentieth. Massive tides of immigrants were entering the United States. The newspapers of Hearst and Pulitzer catered to changing social conditions with glaring headlines, splashy "reform" crusades, circulation stunts and large doses of cheap melodrama and lurid tales of sin and sex—a formula popularly referred to as "yellow journalism."

2. **Entrance of quality journalism.** Ironically, this period of racy journalism also marked the beginning of the ascendancy of the *New York Times* as one of the premier newspapers in the world. Established in 1851, the paper gained a reputation for thoughtful, objective journalism under its legendary, early editor **Henry Raymond**. On the brink of bankruptcy in 1896, the *Times* was bought by **Adolph Ochs** (1858-1935), who

would launch a dynasty which would make the paper a social and political force and a model of journalistic excellence.

3. **The advent of muckraking journalism**. It was also during this turbulent era at the turn of the century that "muckraking" journalism—originally coined as a derogatory term by Theodore Roosevelt but adopted by its practitioners as a badge of honor—reached its zenith.

    a. **Opponents of social injustice and corruption**. Published mainly in national magazines of opinion, muckraking journalists specialized in essay-type, in-depth revelations of political corruption, social injustice, industrial abuse and other ills accompanying the meteoric economic and population growth of the nation.

    b. **Morally motivated**. In contrast to the sensation-seeking "yellow press," the muckrakers were motivated by a deep sense of morality and a rising social consciousness. Notable among them were: **Ida M. Tarbell** (1857-1944), who exposed the business practices of **John D. Rockefeller** (1839-1937) and the Standard Oil Company; **Lincoln Steffens** (1866-1936), who assailed corruption in city and state governments in a series labeled "The Shame of the Cities;" and **Upton Sinclair** (1878-1968), who disclosed unsanitary conditions and unfair labor practices in U.S. meat packing plants.

4. **The press after World War I**. The press underwent extensive growth and development in the decade after the end of the war.

    a. **The growth of tabloids**. With advances in newspaper photography and the bold use of editorial cartoons and illustrations, tabloids became the rage in New York during the jazz era of the 1920s. World War I had secured a prominent position for the U.S. in international affairs. The country was entering a decade of prosperity and its attention was captured by the movies, "flapper girls," airplanes, gangsters, sports heroes and Prohibition.

    b. **The New York tabloids**. In the forefront of the tabloids during the "Roaring Twenties" were the *Daily News*, *Daily Graphic*, and

Hearst's *Daily Mirror*. They offered their readers a pastiche of gossip, inside tidbits about the rich and famous, vivid crime stories, advice to the lovelorn, horoscopes, and sports. The writing was concise, lively, and explicit, and the smaller tabloid size made it easy for people to read while on the subway or bus.

5. **Newsmagazines and radio stake claims**. During this same period, new claims were staked on the American audience with the rising popularity of radio and the creation of *Time* magazine in 1923 by **Henry R. Luce** (1898-1968) and **Britton Hadden**, two young Yale graduates who felt there was a need to condense and provide focus to the news.

    a. **Magazines published since colonial era**. Magazines served as a supplemental form of information to newspapers since colonial times. In 1879, Congress lowered postal rates for periodicals and shortly afterwards, publishers ushered in a wave of mass-circulation magazines by restructuring editorial content to bring them in harmony with the popular tastes and interests of the rising American middle class.

    b. **Newsmagazines, 1900-1950**. Magazine sales boomed throughout the first half of the twentieth century. *Newsweek* and *U.S. News*, copying a format inaugurated by *Time*, appeared in 1933. In 1936, Henry Luce launched *Life*, a dazzling innovative pictorial magazine which was to revolutionize the visual media. Inspired by Life, *Look* magazine made its debut in 1937.

    c. **Decline of photo newsmagazines**. By the early 1970s both *Life* and *Look* would cease publication, killed by a medley of factors. Among them: high production costs, inroads by television, and the trend towards specialized magazines appealing to specific audiences—referred to as "niche journalism."

6. **The birth of radio**. The link of radio with politics was apparent from its inception.

    a. **Station KDKA and the advent of electronic news**. In 1920, Pittsburgh station KDKA went on the air to announce the election returns of the presidential race in which

Warren G. Harding (1865-1923) defeated James M. Cox. It marked the first radio newscast. Since that moment, the airwaves would serve as the foremost instant chronicler of events and rituals and forever change the way people perceive their local surroundings and the world beyond their immediate reach.

b. **FDR and fireside chats.** President **Franklin D. Roosevelt** (1882-1945) was one of the first politicians to realize radio's impact on public opinion. In 1933, he spoke directly to the American electorate in the first of his famous radio fireside chats.

c. **Radio during World War II.** During World War II, **Edward R. Murrow** (1908-1965) showed how radio news could be shifted from the studio to the scene of action and became a role model for succeeding generations of electronic newscasters.

7. **The arrival of television.** Television, the most glamorous medium, ironically lacks a rich early history to match its pervasive presence in American society.

a. **Network and station structure in place.** Following experimentation in the 1920s and 1930s, commercial television burst on the scene in the late 1940s. Radio provided an already established network and station structure, as well as news and entertainment formulae which television adopted. The star system had earlier been introduced by movies and radio. Advertisers, conditioned by radio, were lined up. Even the appropriate government regulatory agency, the Federal Communications Commission, was in place and prepared to deal with the new medium. Television's principal contribution was its technical magic.

b. **Television and public affairs.** The use of television in public affairs became evident for the first time in the 1954 Senate hearings centering on the U.S. Army and Red-baiting Senator **Joseph R. McCarthy** (1908-1957) of Wisconsin. In 1956, the major networks extensively covered the Eisenhower-Stevenson campaign. And in 1960, **John F. Kennedy** (1917-1963) and **Richard M. Nixon** engaged in the first television presidential debate.

c. **Television's visual impact.** As a visual medium, television stirs the imagination and provides a window on places and events. The unparalleled sensation of watching man walk on the moon, the poignant drama of President Kennedy's assassination and the heartsick anguish felt in viewing the Challenger space shuttle explosion remain indelible in the minds of millions of viewers. Television brought the Vietnam War, terrorism, the students' revolt in Beijing, and the fall of the Berlin wall into America's living rooms. The televised Watergate hearings of 1973 and the 1987 Iran arms sales/Contra-funding hearings served as a public education concerning shadowy government operations. And in January 1991, Americans watched transfixed as bombs fell at the start of the Persian Gulf War.

d. **The pervasiveness of television.** By the 1980s, an estimated 98 percent of all American homes had at least one television set, and nearly half had two or more sets. There were more television sets in the country than telephones or bathtubs. That alone suggests the extent that television has affected the lifestyles and perceptual socio-political views of contemporary Americans.

Contemporary Perspective

I. **The press and politics.** The press today—including its electronic branch—presents a number of issues to members of a democratic polity.

A. **Media's role in democratic system.** Today, it is widely accepted that an informed citizenry is a responsible citizenry. In discharging its public trust, the news media play a critical part in reaffirming that premise. Given advances in communications technology and the media's broadened conceptual role and increased visibility, the press is now recognized as both a mover and mirror of society.

1. **Adverse effects of media's enhanced role.** While the media's presence was being enhanced by the communications revolution, there were accompanying adverse effects. These include: the passage from traditional journalism to advocacy journal-

ism, the illusion of entertainment as news, the growth of media conglomerates, the phenomenon of journalists as celebrities, the split within the media over professional behavior and ethical standards, the sensationalization of news, the common lack of sensitivity, the blurring of the line between public office and private lives, the active participation of journalists in political and public policy activities, and the devaluation of objectivity as a journalistic ideal in favor of subjective interpretation and rampant speculation.

2. **Public has split view of the media**. Many Americans harbor an ambivalent attitude towards the news media. Studies have consistently indicated that the modern news media have lost credibility and the full confidence of readers, viewers and listeners. At the same time, even the media's most severe critics staunchly defend the free speech/free press clause in the First Amendment as an essential principle in a democratic society.

3. **The limits to freedom of expression**. For more than a century the legal boundaries of free expression were left virtually undisturbed.

   a. **"Clear and present danger" test**. In 1919, in *Schenck v. United States*, a case involving the so-called "clear and present danger" test, the defendants had been convicted of violating the Espionage Act by disseminating literature condemning U.S. entry into World War I and seeking to discourage prospective recruits from joining the military.

      (1) **Holmes' opinion**. Delivering the majority opinion upholding the conviction, Justice **Oliver Wendell Holmes, Jr.** (1841-1935) stated: "We admit that in many places and in ordinary times the defendants in saying all that was said in the circular would have been within their constitutional right. But the character of every act depends upon the circumstances in which it is done.... The most stringent protection of free speech should not protect a man in falsely shouting fire in a theater, and causing a panic."

      (2) **Freedom of speech not absolute**. The court, in essence, was saying that while the Constitution affords free speech considerable latitude, the right was not absolute in exceptional cases and had to be weighed against other rights, including those ensuring individual safety and the maintenance of peace.

   b. **Libel standard set**. In a landmark decision in 1964, the Supreme Court in *New York Times v. Sullivan* set a libel standard for public figures requiring proof of "actual malice," or "reckless disregard" of the truth on the part of the media.

      (1) **A boon for the press**. Legal experts generally agree that the law relaxes constraints on the press. Even so, the consensus seems to be that libel remains a murky area in U.S. jurisprudence.

      (2) **Difficulty of winning a libel suit**. To win a libel suit, the plaintiff must prove the actual intent of the news organization or demonstrate that it capriciously used available information when publishing or broadcasting a story. Statistics confirm that is an exceedingly difficult task for a plaintiff—but not an impossible one.

      (3) **Two celebrated cases**. Two of the most highly publicized cases—(former Israeli Defense Minister Ariel) *Sharon v. Time Magazine* and (Gen. William) *Westmoreland v. CBS*—ended in ambiguous stalemates in 1984-85, with neither of the plaintiffs being awarded damages.

      (4) **Cases often overturned on appeal**. Plaintiffs have learned that while they may win lower court libel suits heard by a jury, the vast majority of cases are reversed by appeals court judges. Although libel suits may have a "chilling effect" on small, less affluent news organizations which cannot afford exorbitant court costs, there is little evidence that they inhibit the rich and powerful among the media.

B. **Vietnam and Watergate—turning points in American press history.** The Vietnam War and the Watergate crisis of the early 1970s marked a turning point in the attitude and approach of the U.S. news media.

1. **Television's war coverage criticized**. The media, particularly television, which for the first time brought war into American homes, were widely cited for turning public opinion against the Vietnam conflict.

2. **The saga of Woodward and Bernstein**. In the Watergate affair, the press—with two young Washington Post reporters, **Carl Bernstein** and **Robert Woodward**, in the forefront—was largely responsible for disclosing abuse of office and attempted coverups at the highest levels of government, eventually leading to the resignation of President Nixon.

3. **Impact on media's role**. The media's role in each of these historical episodes served to underscore the inherent force of the news media. Previously, the ethic of the U.S. press was generally to observe and report in an objective, unchallenging manner. Afterwards, it became more adversarial and participatory—and in the view of media critics, more arrogant and prosecutorial. Investigative journalism became the vogue.

4. **The press and the political system**. Media coverage of political affairs and campaigns over the last several decades has been broadened in form and content.

   a. **Television prompts changes**. With the introduction of television, print coverage has become more penetrating and innovative; news organizations expend more money, manpower and resources on presidential and other major campaigns; and the competition has become more intense.

   b. **Press is part of the campaign**. The media's role has been expanded to the point where they have become part of the campaign, yet separate from it. Duke University's James David Barber refers to national political journalists as the "new kingmakers...the new powerbrokers." Stephen Hess, of The Brookings Institution, suggests that the nation is moving "from party democracy to media democracy." It is now recognized that, as in the physical sciences, merely observing an event changes it.

   c. **Expansion of coverage**. As the political process has changed so has the coverage. Content of coverage expanded. The media no longer simply focus on whether candidates are leading or trailing in a campaign. They have upgraded their coverage to include reports, analyses and assessments on the competence and leadership capabilities of candidates, their past public service performance, campaign strategy and tactics, and their advisory staff and consultants. The media additionally report on campaign contributors and financing techniques, media relations, political commercials, pertinent issues, personal background of key players, demographic breakdown of the electorate, trends in voter concerns and preferences, and on the electoral procedure itself.

   d. **Media coverage erratic**. Like the art of politics, media campaign coverage is disorderly, erratic, often spiced with hyperbole, and sometimes imprecise.

      (1) **Dole takes issue with media**. After dropping out of the 1988 Republican presidential race, Kansas Senator **Robert Dole** took the unusual step of occupying the floor of the chamber to upbraid the news media for what he referred to as their "issueless and negative" coverage of the contest. He indicted the press for "putting political gossip above information and titillation above education," as well as favoring Democratic candidates over Republican.

      (2) **Criticism of media not uncommon**. Such criticism has become endemic in the uneasy interrelationship between politics and the press. Among the commonly heard criticisms leveled at the news media: they begin their campaign coverage of presidential and other headline races too soon, fail to define and analyze the issues in-depth, tend to give heavier play to the early leaders than to the slow starters, magnify trivial incidents, and excessively focus on who is winning and losing, not unlike a horse race.

   e. **The press and private lives**. A vociferous, frequently voiced complaint against the media centers on their purported intrusion into the private lives of candidates in the pursuit of scandal and sensationalism.

    f. **The media's defense.** In their defense, media spokesmen argue that in running for national public office, candidates forfeit a part of their privacy. They further contend that an assessment of character is proper inasmuch as character is equated with leadership.

II. **New developments and old issues.** While the rise of "celebrity journalists," often practitioners of the "new journalism," raise novel questions, other issues, such as journalistic ethics and government's attempts to "manage" the news are perennial.

    A. **The "New Journalism."** The counter-revolution of the 1960s gave rise to what was popularly called the New Journalism.

        1. **Constrained by journalistic orthodoxy.** Proponents of the New Journalism felt constrained by journalistic orthodoxy and the demands of strict objectivity. This new breed—which included **Tom Wolfe, Hunter Thompson, Joan Didion, Jimmy Breslin, Gay Talese**, and **Norman Mailer**—was convinced that simply offering a litany of facts and relying on institutional sources failed to present the whole truth and needed to be put in a fuller context.

        2. **Blend of fact and fiction.** The practitioners of the "new" journalism discarded the sacred tenets of journalism—objectivity, fairness and balance—as quaint anachronisms which cloaked reality with vapid neutrality. They stretched the boundaries of traditional journalism by blending fact and fiction—by constructing imaginary scenarios, producing illusionary quotations and conjuring the inner thoughts of sources.

        3. **Influence on news reporting.** Emphasis was on writing style and description. While the genre provoked controversy within journalistic and literary circles, it nevertheless had an effect on standard news reporting to an uncertain extent.

    B. **The celebrity journalist and the decline of credibility.** Largely because of the exposure of television and the increased participatory role of journalism in public affairs, a new phenomenon has risen—the "celebrated journalist."

        1. **A distinct subculture.** Celebrated journalists mainly represent the major print and electronic organizations and comprise a distinct subculture within the journalistic community. They have virtually become part of the Establishment and many are better known to the public than their news sources. They are courted by high-level government and private sector officials; they wine and dine together and call each other by their first names.

        2. **Compresses "air space" between journalist and source.** This camaraderie goes against the journalistic tradition of maintaining an arms length (what **Walter Lippmann** (1889-1974) referred to as "air space") from news sources to ensure a semblance of objectivity. As might be expected, this high profile and a close association with news sources have diluted the credibility of American journalism as a whole.

        3. **Prototypical American journalist.** Overall, U.S. journalists are better educated, better paid, and more conscious of their status and impact than their predecessors.

            a. **Press perceived as liberal.** There has long existed a general sense that the press is predominately liberal in social and political attitudes.

                (1) **Supported by studies.** This view has been reinforced by studies which show that members of the national media are largely homogeneous in background. Typically, they are white males, primarily from the urban northeast corridor, graduates of highly-regarded schools, and products of upper-middle class homes. A large percentage possess a secular outlook on religious and social issues.

                (2) **Other factors noted.** It should be noted, however, that at least some of the perception of the "liberal press" stems from its challenging stance during the Vietnam War and its investigatory role in the Watergate affair.

                (3) **Initial motivation to go into journalism.** A liberal tilt within the bulk of the American press might also be attributed to the social consciousness which per-

suaded many of its members to go into journalism in the first place. Furthermore, they are trained and work in a culture which places a high premium on challenging authority and the governmental hierarchy.

(4) **Nature of news affects political stance**. The nature of contemporary news tends to pit liberal against conservatives on such issues as abortion, tax reform, environmental protection, consumer affairs, affirmative action, school busing, toxic waste disposal, and business deregulation. The critical question centers on whether the personal background and attitudes of journalists seep into their reporting.

b. **One side of argument**. On the one hand, it is said that journalists' personal perspectives on public policy have relevance to their work.

c. **The other side**. The counter-argument holds that if the press is liberal, why have so many liberal presidential candidates fared so poorly, notably George McGovern, Ted Kennedy, Walter Mondale and Michael Dukakis, as well as Jimmy Carter in his reelection bid.

C. **Ethical concerns and the press**. Paralleling the extension of the conceptual, behavioral, and attitudinal perimeters of the news media are the ethical concerns which cast a shadow over some current journalistic practices. Two categories of ethical issues may be identified. Mainly, questions of journalistic ethics fall into either of two categories—personal and institutional.

1. **Personal transgressions**. Within the personal category are: acceptance of gifts and other favors from news sources, reconstructing and otherwise distorting quotes, hyping or sensationalizing news stories, promoting personal political or ideological positions, moonlighting for government or other news sources, acceptance of extravagant speaking fees (honoraria) from corporate and other special interest groups, misrepresenting oneself to gain information.

2. **Institutional transgressions**. Among examples of controversial institutional practices are: invasion

of individual privacy, simulation or dramatization of events, purchasing news ("checkbook journalism"), employing ambush tactics to collar a source, using news columns for personal, political or revenue-enhancing purposes, withholding news for personal or political reasons, and slanting the news to enforce a particular point of view.

3. **Law beyond the law**. At issue is not the legality of such practices, but whether they are ethically defensible or professionally acceptable. As Chief Justice **Earl Warren** (1891-1974) once proclaimed, ethics are "a law beyond the law." Unfortunately, journalistic ethics are often morally ambiguous. They fall in a gray area in which right and wrong are not easily defined. As a result, the journalistic community is divided on the propriety of certain practices and is hesitant to impose an industry-wide code of conduct or agree on the creation of a monitoring and review board.

D. **Attempts to control free flow of information**. Governmental attempts to control information about what it is doing and why, often under the cloak of national security, has long been a cause of tension between it and the press.

1. **Resources and techniques**. Executive measures designed to regulate the flow of government information include: expanded use of secrecy classifications, lie detector tests to plug leaks from within the federal bureaucracy, signed pledges by non-elected officials binding them during their lifetime to submit to pre-publication review all articles and books they write for public consumption, and a tightening up of access under the Freedom of Information Act.

2. **The public's right to know**. Government news policies bring into play not only the issue of the public's right to know but the degree of trust between the people and their government.

Epilogue

Every American citizen should be cognizant that a democratic government can exist only when ideas and opinions are openly expressed, without fear or intimidation. As an extra-constitutional institution, the press serves as a purveyor of information and illuminator of social, political and cultural developments. Thus, it behooves each citizen to keep informed of issues and events in order to actively participate in public debate and the political system.

Currently available to Americans is a vast array of commercial news disseminators, diversified by political preference, style of presentation, format, and professional quality. They include 1,650 daily newspapers, about 10,000 weeklies, and more than 25,000 specialized periodicals. Americans can also tune in on some 10,000 radio stations and 1,800 television stations, as well as a multitude of television cable systems, presently received in about 60 percent of U.S. homes.

Americans should be mindful that the news media are an essential element in the political process, at both the electoral and governmental level. Aside from being actively engaged, every citizen can be heard in the political arena as a contributor to letters-to-the-editor and commentary sections of their local newspapers or as a participant in radio call-in public service programs.

In seeking news and information, U.S. citizens should be familiar with the role and functions of the press. They should be aware of the distinctive characteristics, targeted audiences and professional stature of the different news outlets and thereby know where they can find creditable reportage and substantive analyses from various perspectives.

5. TELEVISION AND POLITICS

After all we could get on very happily if aviation, wireless, television, and the like advanced no further than at present.
Edward Arthur Burroughs, Bishop of Ripon (1927)

From "No taxation without representation" to the concept of "one person one vote," discussions of democracy assume that free and informed voting is an important act of citizenship. At the ballot box, democratic theory proclaims, the people work their will. In the act of pulling the voting lever, government "of the people, by the people, for the people," which Lincoln celebrated at Gettysburg, becomes real. But how do we know for whom to vote? How accurate and reliable are our sources of information and the basis of our intuition?

In an electronic age, most citizens neither shake the hand of a major party candidate nor applaud or boo a stump speech. Instead, most of our political information about persons, parties, and positions is carried by television into the privacy of our living rooms. Much of it results from what academics call "inadvertent exposure." Between one program segment and another, the viewer watching a soap opera or a "sit-com" sees a brief political spot ad.

When television debates occur in presidential campaigns, they alone attract a large national audience. Debates in primaries, by contrast, attract small audiences of well-informed, often politically active, partisans. The audience that gathers political information from broadcast news is comparatively small; the audience that systematically garners political information from newspapers, even smaller.

All of this suggests that most Americans are not active seekers of political information. It does not suggest, however, that we are largely uninformed. With surprising regularity, Americans vote what political scientists see as their self-interest. They do this by factoring their personal well-being and that of their community into the voting equation. If the country is at peace and polls say that Americans perceive that they are better off than they were under the other party, the incumbent party is likely to be voted back in. The political advertisements, debates, and news coverage, the attacks and counter-attacks, the innuendo and name-calling that characterize political campaigns are not often decisive in determining the outcome of a national vote.

If informed voting is the outcome we seek, another factor comes into play. Most Americans don't vote in most elections. Some find it reassuring that those who are most informed are most likely to vote; studies of non-voters have found that their participation would not have altered most election outcomes anyway. But if voting is an act of personal investment in government and a means of helping set the national agenda, then the under-representation at the ballot box of the poor, certain minorities, and the homeless poses problems for democracy.

No one seriously argues, however, that a would-be voter is hurt by gaining access to accurate information about the candidates. Accordingly, this section will focus on the following questions: What do we need to know about those who dream about waking up in the Lincoln bedroom of the White House? Can and does the medium that brings us low-brow situation comedy tell us such things? If so, where, when, and with what limitations?

OBJECTIVES

Citizens should be able to

1. explain the basic characteristics of television and its role in the contemporary political process.

2. explain which kinds of issues are likely to be featured by candidates and which ignored.

3. explain which facets of character are likely to be of special concern to reporters in a given election.

4. evaluate the kinds of information available in televised news, advertisements, and debates, the limitations of each of these televised forms, and suggest means of compensating for these limitations.

5. evaluate candidates' use of television as a means of conveying information as opposed to the use of manipulative visual imagery.

6. take, defend, and evaluate positions on the strengths and weaknesses of television and its role in the political process.

FRAME OF REFERENCE
Conceptual Perspective

I. **Influence of television in changing politics**. Citizens report that they get most of their political information from television. Reliance on this medium has altered the way politics happens and the ways we respond to it in the United States.

   A. **Television as a means of direct access to candidates**. By giving the electorate direct access to the candidates, television diminishes the role of party in the selection of the major party nominees.

   B. **Television as a detraction from attention to issues**. By centering politics on the person of the candidate, television accelerates the electorate's focus on character rather than issues.

   C. **Effect of television on political communication**. Television has altered the forms of political communication.

   1. **Briefer messages**. The messages on which most of us rely are briefer than they once were. The stump speech of one-and-a-half to two hours that characterized nineteenth century political discourse has given way to the "thirty-second spot ad" and the "fifteen second sound bite" in broadcast news. The ninety-minute speeches of the Lincoln-Douglas debates have given way to one-and two-minute answers to reporters' questions in the 1988 presidential debates.

   2. **Electronic rather than live audiences**. Increasingly, the audience for speeches is not that standing in front of the politician but the viewing audience that will hear and see a snippet of the speech on the news. In these abbreviated forms, much of what constituted the traditional political discourse of earlier ages has been lost. In fifteen or thirty seconds, a speaker cannot establish the historical context that shaped the issue in question, cannot detail the probable causes of the problem, and cannot examine alterative proposals and argue that one is preferable to others. In snippets, politicians assert but do not argue.

   3. **Political style changed to suit television**. Because television is an intimate medium, speaking through it required a changed political style which is more conversational, personal, and visual than the old-style stump oratory.

   4. **Words dominated by image**. Our growing reliance on television means that our political world contains memorable pictures rather than memorable words. Also, words increasingly are spoken in places chosen to heighten their impact. "We have nothing to fear but fear itself" has given way to "Let them come to Berlin" and "Mr. Gorbachev, tear down this wall." Schools teach us to analyze words and print. But in a world in which politics is increasingly visual, informed citizenship requires a new set of skills.

   5. **Staging of "pseudo-events."** Recognizing the power of television's pictures, politicians craft televisual staged events, called "pseudo-events," designed to attract media coverage. Much of the political activity we see on television news has been crafted by politicians, their speech writers, and their public relations advisers for televised consumption. As a result, sound bites in news and answers to questions in debates increasingly sound like advertisements. Political managers, termed "handlers" in 1988, spend large amounts of time ensuring that their clients appear in visually compelling settings so that the pictures seen in the news will reinforce those seen in advertisements. In debates, candidates recall those staged "pseudo-events."

   D. **National changed to international politics by television**. Where the telegraph and then radio gave citizens a sense that politics was national, from Tiananmen Square to the crumbling Berlin Wall, satellite transmission of images has made it international.

E. **"Mainstreaming" viewers**. By focusing on mainstream values, television "mainstreams" its viewers. Heavy viewers of television differ from light viewers in some politically relevant ways.

1. **Heavy viewing and personal insecurity**. The likelihood that a character in a prime time program will be the victim of a crime is higher than it is in real life. Heavy viewers believe that they are more likely to be victims of crime than they actually are.

2. **Heavy viewing and response to crime**. Heavy viewers are also more conservative in their views about the socially appropriate response to crime. They are, for example, more likely than light viewers to favor heavy sentences and use of the death penalty. Heavy viewing conservatives and heavy viewing liberals are more likely to agree on how to respond to crime than are heavy and light viewing liberals.

3. **The homogenized views of heavy viewers**. Television's portrayal of crime seems to homogenize the views of television's heavy viewers. But where heavy viewing makes liberals more conservative on crime, television's valorization of governmental response to social problems, draws conservatives closer to a more liberal view of the value of government solutions to social problems.

II. **Changes in the character of televised information**. The quantity, quality, and audience for televised information about politics is changing.

A. **Increase of televised high-quality information**. Until the mid-1980s, those who sought extended political contact with candidates would have to give up their careers and become camp followers. Advertisements, news, and debates had all moved to highly abbreviated forms. In the mid-1980s, an increase in the quality of political programming was under way.

1. **PBS and C-SPAN (Cable) programming**. Change came with the increase in quality political programming on the Public Broadcasting System (PBS). In addition, C-SPAN, a twenty-four-hour-a-day public affairs channel, was created in 1980. The rise of cable television throughout the 1980s meant that the service was available to a wider audience. Thus the amount of substantive political information available on television increased.

2. **New programming available**. By 1988, any citizen with a television set could tune to PBS and hear ten-minute excerpts from candidate stump speeches on the *MacNeil-Lehrer News Hour*. They could watch the PBS news magazine *Frontline's* hour-long biographies on the two major party candidates by prize-winning author Garry Wills. Those with cable could attend to the complete stump speeches of the major candidates on C-SPAN. In short, by 1988 it was possible for an interested citizen to be more knowledgeable about the national race than at any time in the history of the United States.

B. **Direct address of specialized audiences by candidates**. The rise of cable television means that specialized audiences can now be addressed directly by candidates.

1. **Specialized audiences**. What had been a broadcast medium, reaching a large undifferentiated mass audience, has increasingly become a narrow-cast medium, reaching smaller, more homogeneous audiences. What was once true only of radio and direct mail became true of television in the mid-1980s. Spanish language cable reach Hispanics in large numbers; MTV (music videos) reach young viewers.

2. **Difficulty in monitoring and analyzing multiple political messages**. Where broadcasting dictated that political messages speak to concerns that transcended people's differences, the narrow casting of cable means that the special concerns of special segments of the audience can now be addressed. But where the limited number of broadcast channels meant that reporters could easily eavesdrop on and critique candidate advertising, the narrow-casting available on over one hundred cable channels makes this increasingly difficult.

III. **Electorate's lack of interest in becoming informed through television**. If the good news is that there is an unprecedented amount of available televised political information, the bad news is that the most educated electorate in human history is less disposed than ever to pay attention to it. Several examples give dramatic expressions of the statistical fact that viewership for political substance is steadily declining and has been for well over a decade. The trend has been clear for a considerable period.

A. **Decline in viewer interest in public affairs—1964 example**. In 1964 viewers faced an evening of television that offered three choices. On one channel was the predecessor of "Dallas" and "Dynasty"— "Peyton Place." On the second channel was "The Beverly Hillbillies." And on the third was a paid political program featuring former President Dwight David Eisenhower discussing the future of the world with Republican party nominee Barry Goldwater. The next morning Goldwater's opponent, incumbent president Lyndon Johnson eagerly called reporters' attention to the fact that the audience had overwhelmingly chosen Peyton Place and Beverly Hillbillies over Goldwater.

B. **Decline in viewer interest in public affairs—1980 example**. In 1980, a similar event occurred. On one network, a documentary on a famous member of the Senate by veteran newscaster Roger Mudd was shown. On another channel the movie "Jaws" was shown. Analysis of viewing showed that the movie eclipsed the political program by a wide margin.

C. **Decline in viewer interest in presidential speeches and debate**. Evidence of a decline in public interest in political programming can be seen by comparing other examples of audiences for presidential speeches and debates. Thus, more people watched the first Kennedy-Nixon debate of 1960 than watched the first Dukakis-Bush debate of 1988. In 1988 convention viewership was down as well from previous years. More people tuned in to the speeches of President Gerald Ford than to the speeches of President Jimmy Carter. A similar drop-off continued in the Reagan presidency.

D. **Lack of viewer interest in in-depth television news**. Further evidence of the lack of electorate interest in being informed about public affairs is the small audience for Public Broadcasting's week-night hour-long news program. On most evenings, *The MacNeil-Lehrer News Hour* attracts such a small audience that a percent does not appear in the ratings book.

IV. **Candidate image vs. stand on issues; candidate character vs. positions on issues**. Scholars have spent inordinate amounts of time trying to distinguish between messages that relate to candidate image and messages that relate to candidates' stands on issues.

A. **Ambiguity of division between candidate "image" and stand on issues**. Nearly every political message by a candidate says something that can be interpreted as an issue that tries to enhance the candidate's credibility, and therefore his or her image. It is more useful to recognize that stands on issues produce an image and that such "image" questions as trustworthiness and competence often are issues.

B. **Usefulness of distinction between candidate's character and stand on issues**. A more useful distinction separates the character or natural temperamental dispositions and biography of the candidate from the specific legislative action the candidate proposes. Thus candidates might demonstrate their compassion, a facet of character, by indicating their strong support for an appropriate policy position or stand on an issue.

C. **Increasing voter interest in character of candidates**. Since the early seventies, voters have been telling pollsters that the character of the candidates is more important to them than the candidates' policy positions or stands on issues.

V. **The comparative relevance of character and stands on issues**. In the past several decades there have been a number of discrepancies between what candidates say about the issues and what they do once in office. Judgment about a candidate's character has increasingly become a prominent issue.

A. **Candidates' stand on issues vs. performance in office**. In the 1960s and 1970s the electorate learned that judging a candidate on stands on issues was not a reliable predictor of his or her conduct in office.

1. **Actions against voter expectations**. Some candidates acted against voter expectations. Lyndon Johnson, elected in 1964 as the peace candidate, for example, escalated the war in Vietnam.

2. **Ability or inability to meet objectives**. Some presidents proved unable to meet many of their objectives.

   a. **John F. Kennedy**. John Kennedy did not succeed in translating his campaign promises into law; only after his death did his successor secure passage of some of Kennedy's key initiatives.

   b. **Jimmy Carter**. Jimmy Carter, elected to bring the budget into balance, and lower inflation and unemployment, had not accomplished any of these goals by the end of his term.

c. **Ronald Reagan**. In this period, one campaign stands out for accurately forecasting a president's positions and accomplishments. Ronald Reagan campaigned promising a defense build-up and tax cuts and produced both.

B. **Candidate's character increasingly judged important**. Meanwhile, the character of a candidate seems increasingly important in judging performance in office.

   1. **Trustworthiness**. Whether a person was truthful and trustworthy were focal concerns of those probing the failures of Johnson's handling of the Vietnam War and Nixon's handling of Watergate.

   2. **Competence**. Whether a person was competent was central to those probing the failures of the presidencies of Ford and Carter.

   3. **Honesty about health**. Whether a person was candid about his health was of concern to those who learned of Kennedy's Addison's Disease only after his death.

VI. **Capability of television to tell us about issues and the character of presidential candidates**. Television has the capacity to inform viewers about both political issues and candidates' character during presidential campaigns.

A. **Determining which issues are the likely focus of a campaign**. What is regarded as a peripheral issue in one campaign may be a primary one four years later. The general principles determining who will feature which issues, when, where, and how, can be specified.

   1. **Issues presented by candidates in broadcasts**. In their own advertisements, in debates, and in news clips, candidates reveal their popular past positions and conceal their unpopular ones. At the same time, candidates reveal the unpopular past positions of their opponents. Public opinion polls and focus-group tests (analysis of the response of small groups to various messages) help campaigns determine which issues will resonate with which voting group.

   2. **Issues presented by political action committee advertisements**. When an issue is controversial but nonetheless beneficial to one side or the other, that issue is more likely to be raised in the advertisements and news coverage of a political action committee (PAC) and not in the candidate's own messages. A PAC is a group of like-minded citizens, unaffiliated with a party or candidate, formed to advance a specific interest. A PAC contributes to candidacies and produces messages consistent with the self-interest of its members. Most major corporations have formed PACS, as have a number of ideological groups.

   3. **Some issues deliberately not presented**. When an issue hurts both candidates or both parties, as the savings and loan crisis did in 1988, it will be raised by neither candidate.

   4. **Party affiliation and stands on issues**. In general, at the presidential level the party affiliation of the contender has accurately predicted likely positions on certain issues. Republicans will, for example, favor less governmental intervention and less taxation but will support greater defense spending than will Democrats.

   5. **Major party candidates' issues generally focused upon**. In general, the issues on which news, advertising, and debates will focus are those advanced by major party nominees. Although in 1988 over one hundred citizens filed the appropriate papers to be considered bona fide presidential contenders, public discussion focuses, with few exceptions, on the Democratic and Republican parties' nominees and on the issues they consider important.

   6. **Specialized issues treated in specialized broadcasts or publications**. Issues of general concern will receive treatment in the mass media; issues of less national concern or highly specialized issues will be treated in specialty publications and broadcasts. For example, those interested in a candidate's monetary philosophy are more likely to find such information on *Wall Street Week in Review*, or in *The Wall Street Journal* than on the *NBC Nightly News* or in *USA Today*. Specific environmental policies are likely to be treated in magazines devoted to the subject.

   7. **Issues treated on television which lend themselves to visualization**. Since television is a visual medium, the messages produced on it are more likely to speak to issues that lend themselves to visualization. This means that crime and environmental pollution are more likely to be the subject of political advertisements and of news coverage than is the national debt or international liquidity.

B. **Determining which facets of character are the likely focus in a campaign**. The facets of character on which a campaign will focus differ from campaign to campaign. The general principles can be specified that determine whether a given audience will prize "competence," "honesty," "communicative ability," or some other feature of those who would be president.

1. **Character defects of most recent president**. The character defects of the most recent president are likely to shape the criteria by which the character of the candidates is judged. After Nixon's resignation, Carter won election campaigning as a candidate who would never lie and who would provide a government as good as its people.

2. **Societal norms**. Societal norms shape the criteria we set for candidate character. In the 1950s and '60s, a divorced candidate was weakened by that fact. During their presidential runs, it was raised as an issue against Stevenson and against Rockefeller. By the 1980s, being divorced no longer carried a social stigma and the country elected its first divorced president.

3. **Press and public as selecting facets of character**. The press and public are in the process of determining which facets of character are relevant to governance.

    a. **Youthful marijuana use**. In the 1988 primaries, we learned that having smoked marijuana in one's youth was not a disqualifier.

    b. **Consorting with prostitutes**. In the Texas gubernatorial campaign of 1990, we learned that the press and public consider it inappropriate for a candidate for governor to have purchased the services of prostitutes in his youth.

4. **Hypocrisy**. Any form of "hypocrisy," any discrepancy between private behavior and public statement of politics, is likely to be scrutinized by the press. In 1988 former Senator Gary Hart, pledging that they would find nothing, challenged the press to follow him. The press took him at his word and reported a weekend tryst with an aspiring actress that cost Hart his credibility as a presidential contender. The resulting press scrutiny of itself is instructive. The reporting was justified on two grounds: Hart's hypocrisy and reporters' contentions that Hart's behavior

showed a disposition toward risk taking unacceptable in one who would head the country.

C. **Treatment of issues and character in advertisements, news, and debates; counteracting television's limitations**. A number of factors limit the usefulness of political advertisements to the voter. But there are ways to counter these factors.

1. **Advertisements**. There is more issue content in many advertisements or "ads" than in broadcast news. The typical television viewer gets most of his or her political information from ads.

    a. **Factors that minimize the ability of ads to convey useful issue information**. Several factors minimize the ability of ads to convey useful information about issues.

        (1) **Conveying useful information not the goal of the advertising**. By stressing issues that will benefit them, candidates' ads attempt to set the issue agenda for the campaign.

        (2) **Partisan character of advertisements.** Because ads are partisan, paid sources of information, they are poor prime sources of political information.

            (a) **Suppression of unfavorable information**. Ads suppress information that would hurt their candidate.

            (b) **Evidence taken out of context**. Ads occasionally take evidence out of context.

            (c) **False inferences invited**. Ads occasionally invite false inferences.

        (3) **Political advertisements not tested for fairness or accuracy**. Political ads for bona fide candidates for federal office are not subject to tests of fairness or accuracy by those broadcasting them. The rules that do govern such ads are as follows:

            (a) **Several tests to be met**. A political ad for a bona fide candidate for federal office must meet four tests. First, it must have a discernible **disclaimer disclosing its sponsor**. Second, it must **fit the time purchased**. Third, it must meet the **technical standards** of the broadcast outlet. Fourth, it must **not be obscene**.

(b) **Advertising time available to opponents**. If a station has sold advertising time to one candidate in a race, it must make comparable time available for sale to all other bona fide candidates for that race.

(4) **Television ads as tending to be from wealthy candidates or from those able to raise money**. Since candidates must pay for most advertising time, we are more likely to see ads for those who are wealthy or able to raise more money than their opponents. At the presidential level, in the general election, this advantage is muted by equal federal financing of both major party candidates.

b. **Ways to compensate for or counter these limitations**. There are several means of compensating for or otherwise countering television's limitations.

(1) **Seeking alternative forms of information**. The best way to protect oneself from distortions in advertising is by seeking out alternative forms of information. The best informed voters are those who combine television viewing with newspaper and magazine reading. Since candidates often respond to the distortions of ads in press conferences, viewing news helps obtain the "other side."

(2) **Viewing debates attentively**. In debates, candidates are directly accountable to a press panel and to their opponents. Some questions of accuracy can be resolved by attentive debate viewing.

(3) **Proposals to regulate political ads**. Concern about the distortions in attack advertising has prompted calls for legislation. Opponents of these proposals argue that they violate the Constitution's protections of free speech. Proposals include the following:

(a) **Candidate to speak in person**. It has been proposed that candidates be required to make any attacks on an opposing candidate themselves, speaking in person in an ad.

(b) **Free response time for attacked candidate**. Another proposal is to provide free response time for a candidate attacked by a PAC ad.

(c) **Requiring press conference about advertisements**. It has been proposed that shortly after an ad begins airing, the sponsoring candidate be required to hold a press conference to respond to questions about it.

2. **The influence of broadcast network news**. Viewers tell pollsters that their voting choices are more influenced by print and broadcast news than by ads. This finding, however, may be the byproduct of our human tendency to report that we are influenced by approved sources and uninfluenced by presumably manipulative sources. No one disputes that when news coverage of a candidate is consistent with the candidate's ads and debate performance, the power of the candidate's message is magnified.

a. **Factors that minimize the ability of network news to communicate useful information on issues**. Several factors minimize the ability of network news to communicate useful information about political issues.

(1) **Broadcast focus on candidate's strategic intent not issues**. For over a decade, scholars have consistently found that broadcast and print journalism focus not on issue content of campaigns but on strategic intent of the candidates, the outcome of their strategies, and on who is "winning" or "losing." This focus on "horse race" and "game plan" displaces discussion of other matters.

(2) **Candidates' attempt to control the news agenda**. When they succeed, the news agenda and their ads are similarly focused, employ similar pictures, and repeat much of the same language.

(3) **Detraction from discussion of issues by news norms**. When the networks do focus on issues, some of their news norms minimize the impact of their discussion.

(a) **News as news only once**. Once a story on an issue has aired or been printed, it is unlikely to be re-aired. The problem occurs when a distorting ad repeatedly makes a false claim that is only corrected or contextualized a single time in the news. A problem occurs as well when the attention of parts of the public has not yet focused on the campaign at the time at which the "issue" is covered.

(b) **Issues covered as tending to be pre-selected by candidates, not reporters.** It is the job of reporters to cover the story, not to make it. Accordingly, reporters adopt a focus on the issues pre-selected by the candidates. However, reporters are willing to set the agenda for discussion of character and to probe any discrepancies between candidate character and accepted social norms.

b. **Ways to compensate for or counter the limitations of television news.** Means of overcoming the limitations of television news are the following:

(1) **Use of multiple sources and media.** To be well-informed, one must gather information from multiple news sources and multiple media.

(2) **Selection of relevant issues.** Another means of compensating for the deficiencies of television news is to determine what issues are relevant to oneself and to seek out forums in which those issues are likely to be addressed.

(3) **Paying attention early in primaries.** A further means of dealing with these deficiencies is to pay attention to news and debates in the early presidential primaries when news coverage is likely to treat emerging issues in depth.

(4) **Use of computer-based information.** Finally, computer-based retrieval in libraries or at home can retrieve early news stories of importance in putting candidate claims in their context. Often, newspapers carry careful studies of the biography and record of a candidate early in the primaries.

3. **The influence of debates.** In a national election, debates are the single most useful form of information available to voters. In debates, a large viewing audience has the opportunity to compare the candidates and their positions. Debates provide the only direct comparison available in most campaigns. The results are beneficial to every segment of the viewing audience from the least to the best educated. After each presidential debate, surveys have shown that viewers could more accurately identify and report the candidates' positions on the major debated issues.

a. **Factors that minimize the ability of debates to communicate useful information on issues.** A number of factors minimize the ability of debates to communicate useful information.

(1) **Candidates seeking of panelists and formats that protect them.** The candidates' desire to protect themselves from gaffes leads them to seek a panel of reporters that they expect will ask predictable questions. It leads them to negotiate a format that includes only short candidate answers, on the assumption that all possible questions can be anticipated and short answers prepared. And it leads them to negotiate a format that denies reporters the ability to follow-up their questions. They do this on the assumption that inconsistencies and inaccuracies are likely to be exposed in follow-up.

(2) **Tendency of voters' questions not to be asked.** The press panelists tend to ask questions of more interest to a knowledgeable reporter than to an information-seeking voter.

(3) **Reduction of debate to decisive moments.** Press coverage tends to reduce debates to a single decisive moment. This focus distracts from information about the candidates and their positions contained in the debate. These supposedly decisive moments include "There you go again." "Do you remember when you said 'there you go again'?" and "Senator, you are no John Kennedy."

(4) **Focus on strategic intent and who won.** The press focuses on strategic intent of candidates and on who won or lost the debate. There is no intelligent way to judge a "win" or "loss." More important is the fact that the focus on winning and losing displaces

other more useful discussions of what could be and should be learned from debates.

b. **Ways to compensate for these limitations**. Several means are available to counteract these limitations.

    (1) **Spotting errors and inconsistencies**. The well-informed voter will be able to spot errors and inconsistencies.

    (2) **Non-reliance on commentators**. The well-informed voter need not rely on commentators to determine what was and was not significant in the debate.

    (3) **Reliance on one's own judgment**. The well-informed viewer will not let debate coverage determine what is useful but will instead ask what issues and traits of character are important. The well-informed voter will systematically seek out such information.

Historical Perspective

During the four decades in which it has played a role in American politics, television has made it possible for the citizens of the United States to share some of the country's more memorable moments. The importance of television in American politics is well illustrated by recalling some of those moments.

I. **Television and the 1952 campaign**. Television first played a role in national politics in 1952 when both Adlai Stevenson and Dwight David Eisenhower touted their candidacies in political spot ads. However, the dominant form of political discourse in 1952 was the half-hour speech. The most famous speech of that year saved Richard Nixon's place on the Republican ticket and immortalized his cocker spaniel "Checkers." Charged with maintaining an illegal slush fund, Nixon responded by "baring his soul." The Republican National Committee in Washington was flooded with telegrams imploring "Ike" to keep Nixon on the ticket. The Republican team was elected in November.

II. **Television and the Army-McCarthy Hearings**. The power of television was demonstrated again in 1954 when the nationally televised "Army-McCarthy Hearings" examined the contending claims of the Army and Wisconsin Senator Joseph McCarthy. The Army claimed that McCarthy had tried to obtain special privileges for a young GI who had been on McCarthy's staff. McCarthy

charged that the Army had not been diligent in routing out subversives. The hearing effectively discredited McCarthy whose blustering style and insistent "points of order" could not camouflage the lack of substance in his claims.

III. **Television and the 1960 campaign**. Two events in the campaign of 1960 demonstrated the power of television.

A. **Kennedy's appearance before Baptist ministers**. In a televised exchange with the Baptist Houston ministers, John Kennedy decisively dispatched the presupposition that a person's Catholicity disqualified him from the presidency. A half-hour version of the exchange was then aired repeatedly by the Kennedy campaign to shore up his support among Catholics and to reassure skeptics.

B. **The first televised presidential debates**. The nation's first televised presidential debates also helped Kennedy. At the same time the telecast demonstrated the visual power of television. In the first debate, Nixon looked shifty-eyed and pale. Sweat formed on his lip and forehead. A recent illness had caused him to lose weight; as a result his suit did not fit well; and, as he stood behind the podium, he favored one leg. Where Kennedy's dark blue suit set him off from the background, Nixon's grey suit blended into the grey set. To "win" the debate, Kennedy only had to hold his own against his more experienced opponent. Kennedy accomplished his objective. In the close election that followed, some believe Nixon's poor appearance in the first debate cost him the election.

IV. **Television and the assassination of John F. Kennedy**. Word of the assassination of President John Kennedy transformed the nation into a community of television viewers. Citizens in twenty-two nations watched as well. For the first time in the nation's history, the networks canceled all other programming and commercials to permit the nation to share in mass-mediated visuals. The visual power of those four days is evident in the ability of those who saw it to recall the riderless horse, Kennedy's young son saluting, and the black-veiled widow standing in silent mourning in the funeral procession.

V. **The impeachment hearings of 1974**. In 1974 the nation watched as the House Judiciary Committee struggled to answer the question framed by Tennessee's Republican Senator Howard Baker, "What did the president know and when did he know it?" By conducting the hearings in a fair and impartial manner, the committee eased public acceptance of the resignation of the president. On August 8, 1974, after the House Committee had voted three articles of impeachment, Richard M. Nixon informed the country in a nationally televised address that on noon the next day he would officially resign.

VI. **The Space Shuttle disaster of 1986**. To some extent, the mission of the Space Shuttle Challenger was the creation of a telecast pseudo-event. For the first time in the history of the space program, the shuttle was to carry a teacher into space where she would conduct a science lesson for the nation's school children. After a highly publicized national search, the teacher was selected. On January 28, 1986, as the nation's school children watched in their classrooms, the shuttle containing the crew exploded. Instant replay made it possible for the networks to play and replay that tragic moment. A few hours after the explosion, President Ronald Reagan, in one of the most memorable speeches of his presidency, spoke words of consolation to the watching children and their parents.

VII. **The fall of communist regimes in 1989**. As communism was challenged and fell in Eastern Europe, an interesting pattern emerged. Where once embassies and military installations were the first target of the revolution, in the revolutions of the electronic age, the first military objective was taking and holding the main television station. The reason had been clear at least since the late 1960s when nightly newscasts' scenes of death in Vietnam eroded the credibility of political claims that the war was being won. In the 1980s, televised politics became international. Live by satellite, citizens from around the world watched as a young man stopped a tank in Tiananmen Square and as joyful crowds danced atop the Berlin Wall.

Contemporary Perspective

I. **Gathering and using available information**. The informed citizen is an active seeker of information who reads newspapers and watches PBS and C-SPAN as well as the other networks' news shows. By determining what information is relevant and then actively pursuing it, the informed citizen sets his or her own agenda. The informed citizen knows when advertising is distorted, discounts the distortions, and carefully weighs the question, "What does such distortion tell me about the sponsoring candidate?" The informed citizen asks of debates, "What are the habits of mind I see revealed by the candidates? How accurate is their self-portrayal and their portrayal of their opponent? What are the important similarities and differences between the candidates?"

II. **Forming judgments about political issues and candidates**. Finally, the informed citizen uses all available evidence to answer the question, "Under the leadership of which candidate am I better off and is the country better off?"

A. **Barriers to informed citizenship**. Answering that question is not necessarily easy. Candidates see little advantage in taking on controversial issues and offering programmatic specifics. The ideal of "informed citizenship" is complicated by media that abbreviate political messages, reducing complex ideas to sight and sound snippets. It is complicated as well by television's tendency to favor what we see over what is said and by the tendency of televised news to provide information of more use to would-be media consultants than to those aspiring to be educated voters.

B. **Separating relevant from irrelevant information**. If policy positions and information about candidate character are the wheat of politics, information about political strategy and projected outcomes is the chaff. Sorting one from the other is the challenge of the voter in a "media age."

6. PUBLIC OPINION

This public opinion strengthens or weakens all human institutions. Only fools, pure theorists or apprentices in moral philosophy, fail to take public opinion into account in their political undertakings.

Jacques Necker (1792)

The people, sir, is a great beast.

Alexander Hamilton (1791)

In proportion as the structure of a government gives force to public opinion, it is essential that public opinion should be enlightened.

George Washington (1797)

The obvious weakness of government by opinion is the difficulty of ascertaining it.

James Bryce (1888)

Whenever conditions are equal, public opinion brings immense weight to bear on every individual. It surrounds, directs, and oppresses him. The basic constitution of society has more to do with this than any political laws. The more alike men are, the weaker each feels in the face of all.

Alexis de Tocqueville (1835)

Democracy is predicated on the idea that the "will of the people" should be a powerful determinant of political life. Although this idea is a reality in many of the most industrialized countries—and a hope for people all over the globe—it is in many ways as confusing as it is attractive. Is the will of the people equivalent to public opinion? How should public opinion affect government decision making? While theorists debate over the meaning of public opinion and its proper role, the measurement of public opinion through surveys has become a powerful tool for politicians seeking to get elected, companies seeking to sell products, and news media seeking to attract an audience. As a result, Americans are surveyed about everything from their sex lives to their views on national security.

Although public opinion is being studied as never before, and the public is constantly bombarded with the results of these studies, surveys also show that many Americans believe that "no one cares what I think." And despite the fact that America has the most extensive communications system the world has ever known, leaders increasingly complain that public opinion is ill-informed and unstable. It is an increasingly difficult task to find an effective way of bringing a public voice into debates on the complex problems that face the country.

OBJECTIVES

The citizen should be able to

1. explain what public opinion is and how it is determined.

2. explain the ambivalence in western thought about the value of public opinion and how this ambivalence is part of our current thinking.

3. explain how American political institutions were in many ways designed as a compromise between opposing views on the role of public opinion in governance.

4. explain why and how public opinion surveys are conducted and evaluate the results of these surveys.

5. take, defend, and evaluate positions on the proper role of public opinion in the political process.

FRAME OF REFERENCE
Conceptual Perspective

I. **Definitions of public opinion.** Political theorists have struggled to come up with an adequate definition of public opinion, a task which political scientist V.O. Key once described as "not unlike coming to grips with the Holy Ghost."

A. **The notion of a "public."** Perhaps the simplest way to define a public is to describe it as a group of individuals who have some beliefs or attitudes in common. According to this definition, there are many different publics, created by regions (eg. Northwest USA), ideologies (conservatives), and membership in organizations (gun owners).

B. **Definitions of "opinion."** Opinion can be understood as some sort of expressed attitude or belief. Opinions can be expressed in a variety of ways, such as conversation, letters, speeches, or, today, through public opinion polls.

C. **Public opinion.** Some theorists have tried to restrict the definition of "public opinion" to include only those attitudes which are directly relevant to politics. In 1949, Hans Speier defined public opinion as "opinions on matters of concern to the nation freely and publicly expressed by men outside the government who claim a right that their opinions should influence or determine the actions, personnel, or structure of their government."

D. **Public opinion and polls.** With the growth of public opinion polls, however, there has been a tendency to move away from theoretical definitions such as the one given above and to think of public opinion as those attitudes which are measured, or could be measured, by surveys. Public opinion would thus be the aggregate of the private opinions of all the individuals in society and could range from views on important policy decisions to preferences for one product over another.

II. **Ambivalence about the role of public opinion.** Regardless of how it is defined, there is a deep ambivalence in American thinking about public opinion.

A. **An emphasis on the value of public opinion.** The democratic heritage of the United States places a high value on a government "of the people, by the people and for the people." What is distinctive about American political life is precisely that it values and respects the will of its citizens.

B. **A distrust of public opinion.** There is an equally deep American tradition that is suspicious of public opinion and sees a great danger in the "tyranny of the majority."

1. **Criticism of the public.** Leaders and experts frequently bemoan the fact that public opinion is often ill-informed and unstable. Magazines that cater to the most educated Americans gleefully point to signs of public ignorance, such as the fact that while the majority of Americans can correctly identify the judge on a popular television program, less than a tenth can correctly identify the Chief Justice of the Supreme Court.

2. **Criticism of leaders.** There is also great criticism of political leaders who seem to follow public opinion too closely; leadership is frequently taken to task for failing to take unpopular steps such as cutting middle class entitlement programs or raising taxes.

C. **A compromise on the role of public opinion.** This ambivalence about public opinion has deep roots in western culture and was an important factor in the founding of the American nation. The Founders themselves were divided on the value of public opinion, and the Constitution reflects this conflict.

1. **Mechanisms to insure a public voice.** Some of the institutions of American government were designed to insure that the public voice would be heard. The House of Representatives, for example, was designed to reflect the views of the majority.

2. **Checks on the majority.** The American government was also designed with checks and balances to limit the power of the majority. The Senate, for instance, with its longer term of office, was designed to counterbalance the House. Since all states have equal representation in the Senate, the less populous states would also have an equal voice with the more populous ones.

III. **Importance of public opinion.** Despite debate about the definition and proper role of public opinion, there is wide agreement about its importance in American governance.

A. **Elections.** One obvious area where public opinion is important is in elections. Although many factors influence election behavior, public opinion is clearly an important component. Politicians are increasingly willing to spend large amounts of money and energy to measure public opinion about themselves and the issues, to position themselves in ways that will gain

public support, and to use the media to influence public opinion.

B. **Policy making.** Some observers believe that one of the most important functions of public opinion is that it sets boundaries or permissions for policy makers. Public values and attitudes set broad guidelines for what leaders can and cannot do. As long as leaders stay within these boundaries they have somewhat of a free hand to do as they think best. But when policy decisions seem to violate these boundaries, leaders must either back off or at least take their case to the public.

C. **The impact of survey research.** Public opinion also has a tremendous impact on American life through the results of public opinion polling.

1. **A way for policy makers to pretest the impact of their decisions.** Public opinion surveys are now a standard tool for corporate and government leaders, many of whom keep a close watch on public opinion. The products that are available to Americans, the media programming they are exposed to, the decisions that are made by leaders, and the rhetoric used to defend these decisions are often shaped by complex and sophisticated methods for testing public opinion.

2. **An "iron triangle."** Many decisions are now made by an "iron triangle" consisting of a client (a corporation, candidate, special interest group, etc), a public opinion firm, and a communications firm (advertising or public relations). The public opinion researchers bring the public's perceptions to the client, media consultants help the client shape both actions and image in response to the public perception, and then design media campaigns to take the message back to the public. The public's perceptions can be measured again and the process starts all over again. This raises the question of the possibility of manipulating public opinion.

IV. **Public opinion surveys.** In the last sixty years, public opinion surveys have become a familiar feature of the American scene. But not all surveys are equally useful as a guide to public opinion. In order to have an understanding of how these surveys can be used and interpreted, it is necessary to have a sense of the mechanics of survey research. In evaluating the results of a survey, there are several questions that a citizen can profitably ask: Who did the survey? Why was it done? How were the interviewees selected? How many people were surveyed? What questions were asked? How were the questions interpreted?

A. **Who did the survey?** An important fact to know about surveys is who sponsors them.

1. **Sponsor-conducted surveys.** The most questionable surveys are those that are both paid for and conducted by an organization with a strong point of view on the subject and a vested interest in the results.

2. **Survey research firms.** There is more of a guarantee of reliability if the poll is conducted by an independent professional survey research firm that has been hired by a client who sponsors the survey. Clients may not choose to publish a study if the results do not support their interests, and researchers may have motives to interpret the results in ways that please the client; nonetheless, the independence and reputation of the survey organization gives greater confidence in the results.

B. **Why was it done?** Surveys of public opinion are done for a number of reasons.

1. **Market research.** Corporations hire research firms to find out how people feel about their products. Typically these surveys are not released to the public because the clients do not want their competitors to have access to this information. Sometimes isolated findings (often taken out of context) of such studies are used in advertising the product. Consumers are familiar with advertisements that say things like "Nine out of ten doctors preferred this medication." While market research has a tremendous impact on the products that are available, market research studies themselves are usually not a source of direct information for the citizen.

2. **Political surveying.** Political candidates take surveys to find out what potential voters think and how they are likely to vote. Once again, these findings are not usually released to the public, or are only released (or leaked) selectively as part of the campaign efforts of the candidate.

3. **News media surveys.** Many of the large news media conduct or commission public opinion surveys in order to generate news stories. These surveys sometimes deal with topics that are important and controversial and can be extremely valuable.

4. **Public relations surveys.** Often surveys are commissioned to build public relations for one cause or another. A widely publicized Gallup survey, for example, proved that large majorities of the public were opposed to the idea of phasing the penny out of the monetary circulation. However, the survey was funded by an organization that makes zinc (an important ingredient in the penny): the sponsor might have been less willing to publicize the results of the survey if it had found that Americans favored phasing out the penny.

5. **Non-profit surveys.** Some of the most detailed and interesting surveys are funded by foundations or are conducted by universities. Large corporations sometimes commission surveys as a public service, rather than as part of their strategic planning. These surveys are often the most in-depth and informative, and are usually publicized in the media.

C. **How were the interviewees selected?** One of the most important questions to ask about a survey is how the respondents were chosen. Although the number of people interviewed is also important, the selection of the sample is much more critical. A result that is based on the views of a correctly chosen small sample will be much more reliable than interviews with huge numbers of people who are not properly selected. Although there are a number of technical distinctions not discussed, the most important distinction is between non-random and random samples.

1. **Non-random samples.** Many surveys are based on the opinions of individuals who have **not** been randomly selected.

a. **Self-selected samples.** In some surveys, the respondents select themselves, rather than being selected by the researcher. For example, magazines frequently conduct surveys of their readers where the readers are invited to mail in responses; the responses are then tabulated and discussed in later issues of the magazine. It is not uncommon for such surveys to receive a much larger number of responses than would be gathered in a more traditional public opinion poll.

b.   **Problems with self-selected samples.** Because the respondents have selected themselves, the results cannot necessarily be projected to the population as a whole. It may be that those who responded did so because they felt particularly strongly about the issue being surveyed.

2.   **Random surveys.** The most useful surveys are those where the selection of those who will be interviewed is random.

a.   **Pure random surveys.** Suppose, for example, that the task is to survey voters in a certain area. Since the list of voters is public, the researcher could, perhaps, interview every 100th person on the list, or use some other means to select randomly a subgroup of the total population to interview. If this is done properly, the researcher can project the views of the entire voting population by talking to only a small number of individuals.

b.   **Nearly random surveys.** Other methods of drawing a sample give the research a group of respondents that is nearly random. Many surveys are conducted by telephone. Computers generate telephone numbers randomly within certain preselected areas, and researchers interview whoever answers the phone. There are problems here as well, since even today some groups are more likely to have a telephone, or more likely to be home when the researcher calls. Nonetheless, most of the professional survey research firms use methods that are very carefully developed and that give their researchers (and their clients) a great deal of confidence in the results.

D.   **How many people were surveyed?** Both common sense and the laws of statistics indicate that the more people interviewed, the more accurate the results of the survey will be. Past a certain point, however, increasing the number of people interviewed makes only a tiny difference in the accuracy of the results.

1.   **Margin of error.** Statisticians describe the reliability of a survey in terms of what they call the "margin of error." Many professional surveys interview approximately 1500 people. This sample size usually insures that the margin of error is something like plus or minus 4%. This means that in most cases, the results of the survey will be

within 4% (plus or minus) of the results that would have been obtained if the entire population had been interviewed.

2.   **Results that are less than the margin of error.** Differences that are less than the margin of error cannot be relied upon as accurate predictors of public attitudes. A Gallup survey in 1989 found that 71% of the public favored a constitutional amendment banning flag burning. When the same question was asked a year later, 69% of the public supported such an amendment. At first glance, the survey seems to show a small (2%) drop in support for the amendment. But since the margin of error for this survey was plus or minus 4%, the drop in numbers does not really demonstrate that support is diminishing.

3.   **Subgroups.** In many cases the most interesting part of a survey is the opinions held by smaller groups within the total group who were interviewed. In a survey on Social Security, for example, the most interesting finding might be the comparison of older people (who receive the benefits) with those of younger people (who pay for them). But as we look at smaller and smaller groups, the margin of error grows larger. Thus a researcher must be much more cautious in talking about the attitudes of a subgroup.

4.   **Oversampling.** If researchers are particularly interested in a certain subgroup, they sometimes interview a larger number of respondents in that group. This is called oversampling. A number of recent polls on racial issues, for example, interviewed more African American respondents than would normally be included in a general survey of public opinion. This allowed the researchers to contrast the opinions of African Americans with those of the rest of the population.

E.   **Sample size and margin of error.** Determining the margin of error for any given sample or subgroup is not easy, but the following table gives a rule of thumb.

F.   **What questions were asked?** The most important skill in designing survey questions is the use of common sense. Citizens who take the time to read the actual questions will often see the weaknesses of a survey, or come up with somewhat different interpretations of the findings.

Number of people in subgroup	Margin of error +/-
100	14%
200	10%
400	7%
800	5%
1000	4%
2000	3%

1. **Problematic questions.** Some questions do not work very well and do not give us useful information about public opinion.

    a. **Emotion-laden questions.** It is not difficult to design emotion-laden or simplistic questions that will elicit a predictable response. Such questions are frequently used by fund raisers, who disguise their fund-raising appeals as surveys.

    b. **Questions about unfamiliar subjects.** As a general rule, if a large percentage of the sample (25 percent or more) cannot answer the question, the results of those who did answer may not be too useful.

    c. **Different frameworks.** Another problem is caused by the fact that the researcher and the respondent often approach the issues from different perspectives or with different background information.

    d. **Questions that ask more than one thing.** Some questions actually raise two different questions. Suppose the question asks "Do you favor a tax increase to increase welfare benefits?" Some of those who disagree might do so because they are opposed to welfare altogether. Others might support welfare but feel that taxes are already too high. This second group might support the welfare increase if the money would come from some other program.

2. **Good questions.** Characteristics of well-constructed questions are the following:

    a. **Clear and simple questions.** Well-constructed questions are usually direct and simple, and are phrased in the interviewee's language, rather than the researcher's.

    b. **Posing trade-offs.** Most people answer survey questions quickly and straightforwardly, without taking a lot of time to think through the complexities of what they are saying. If the question is, "Would you approve or disapprove of a 10 percent cut in your real estate taxes?" many people will say, "I approve." It would be more interesting to ask, "Would you approve of a 10 percent cut in your real estate taxes even if it meant that the local schools would have to cut back many sports programs?" Good surveys, in other words, often try to probe beneath the superficial reactions to discover people's deeper priorities and values.

    c. **Multiple questions.** A good survey does not rest a major finding on the response to a single question. If a topic is complex and involves conflicting values, a single question can give an incomplete picture. Multiple-question findings give far more reliable answers.

    d. **Questions that show trends in public opinion.** One of the most important ways to measure trends and changes is by asking the same question at different periods of time. For example, in 1988, 33% of the population felt that America was the number one economic leader in the world. Only a year earlier, 47% had felt that America was number one. This is a very dramatic change for only one year. Seen as a trend, the statistics suggest that Americans are beginning to take note of the rapidly changing economic realities in the world.

    e. **Other factors in writing survey questions.** Good survey researchers have developed many other techniques for accurately measuring opinion. For example, if people are given a series of choices, they sometimes tend to choose the one in the middle. Researchers compensate for this by giving people two or four choices, rather than three or five.

G. **How were the questions interpreted?** Attentive readers of the newspaper often notice that there is a discrepancy between the eye-catching headlines and the story itself. This is particularly true with news stories about surveys.

1. **Different methods of reporting.** Reports of survey research findings often present summaries or interpretations of the results of the surveys rather than the raw numbers themselves. For example, during the Nixon administration, the Gallup polls consistently gave the President a higher approval rating than did the Harris polls. One reason for the difference was that Gallup merely asked people whether they approved or disapproved of the President's performance. The Harris polls gave the respondents four choices—"Excellent," "Good," "Only fair," and "Poor."

2. **Different frameworks yield different interpretations.** Sometimes the interpretations of survey results tell us more about the researcher's concerns than they do about the public's real values.

   a. **Does the public support press freedom?** The late **George Gallup** (1901-84) once conducted a survey for a convention of media people where he concluded that "the press in America is operating in an environment of public opinion that is increasingly indifferent—and to some extent hostile—to the cause of a free press in America." One of his key pieces of evidence was a finding that only 24 percent of the public could correctly identify the First Amendment to the Constitution, which guarantees freedom of the press.

   b. **Interpretations of Gallup's results.** Gallup's finding may reflect different perspectives, rather than different realities. Journalists live and work with the First Amendment. To them the idea that someone cannot correctly identify it suggests a lack of sympathy for constitutionally protected freedoms. As other studies show, the ability to correctly identify constitutional amendments is not a good test of whether or not people support the values associated with them. The fact that people cannot identify the First Amendment does not mean that they are hostile to press freedom, any more than the fact that they cannot identify the Eighth Amendment means that they believe that prisoners should be tortured.

H. **Criticisms of surveys.** There have been many criticisms both of polls and of pollsters.

1. **Inaccuracy.** Although a great deal of money and energy is spent on surveys, there have been some spectacular failures.

   a. **Examples of survey failures.** Some of the most famous failures, such as the mistaken predictions of the 1948 presidential election, were based on unscientific polling methods. There have also been massive failures in market research, such as the introduction of "New Coke" by the CocaCola Company.

   b. **Accuracy is based on freely given answers.** Some of the most significant failures have been in other parts of the world. Many observers believed that the Sandinistas in Nicaragua permitted the 1990 election that resulted in their ouster only because they believed in the public opinion polls predicting their victory. Of course, the whole idea of a public opinion poll assumes that people feel free to express their ideas. Public opinion polls in totalitarian or authoritarian states, when they are conducted at all, are usually highly unreliable.

2. **The "Bandwagon" effect.** Many people are concerned that surveys not only tell us what we do think, but also tell us what to think. The concern is that reading about public opinion polls will itself shape public opinion.

3. **Polls and elections.** Another area of concern is that polls have too much impact on political elections. In primary elections, even candidates with respectable showings are sometimes declared losers if they do not do as well as predicted by the media and the polls. In some cases, polls of citizens who have just voted are used to predict results of an election. If this information is released in one time zone, before the polls are closed in another time zone, it may discourage people in the later time zone from voting at all.

4. **Questionable uses of polling.** Questions have also been raised about some of the uses of polling. For example, some attorneys now use public opinion research techniques, testing their arguments with simulated juries whose responses are carefully evaluated. This data assists the attorneys both in shaping their arguments and in selecting juries who will be sympathetic to their point of view. Naturally this process benefits those clients who have the most money to spend.

5. **Kill the messenger.** Many public opinion researchers believe that people are hostile to polls because they do not like the results. Criticism of survey research is just another example of people who want to punish the bearer of bad news. In fact, professionally done polls are usually fairly accurate within their limits.

I. **Quantitative research.** Most of the reports of public opinion surveys that are described in the media are based upon what might be called quantitative surveys. In these studies, the interviewer has a fixed set of questions and the range of answers is predetermined (agree/disagree, etc). There is little opportunity for the respondent to qualify or explain the answer. While this type of research is highly reliable, it is also somewhat sterile. Within the margin of error, the researcher can predict how everyone in the population would answer a question phrased in precisely the same way. What it does not tell, unless further questions are asked, is why people answered as they did.

J. **Qualitative research.** In order to deal with some of the shortcomings of quantitative surveys many researchers are now supplementing traditional research with techniques that are more subjective and anecdotal. This is sometimes called "qualitative" research to distinguish it from more traditional quantitative methodologies. Such research is a more impressionistic or journalistic technique where the researcher asks open-ended questions to small groups of people.

1. **Focus groups.** One of the most common types of qualitative research is what is called the "focus group." In this technique, the research brings together a group of people (usually from 8 to 15) who are selected according to certain quotas. The respondents are paid for their time and participate in a guided but open-ended discussion of the topic. Frequently the clients for the study observe the session from behind a one-way mirror.

2. **Advantages of qualitative research.** Because the number of people interviewed is small, and because the respondents are not chosen randomly, these surveys do not permit the researcher to make definitive statements about how many people will support or oppose a given option. But what they lack in statistical validity, they make up in richness and insight. Focus groups can give clients a feel for what is behind the numbers. These insights and hypotheses can then be later tested by more quantitative methods.

3. **Uses of qualitative research.** Political consultants and advertisers made effective use of this technique in the 1988 presidential convention. Many researchers believe that many of the most devastating attacks on Governor Dukakis (such as his position on requiring the pledge, or on furloughs for prisoners) were originally developed in focus group interviews.

Historical Perspective

I. **A deep ambivalence about the role of public opinion.** Ambivalence about public opinion in Western culture has its origins in ancient Greece.

A. **Classical Greece.** The classical Greek philosophers were very concerned about the tension between the "one" (or the "few") and the "many." Their feelings about the status of opinion (in Greek, **doxa**) were related to how they resolved the larger tension between few and many.

1. **Plato.** One of the most influential Greek philosophers, Plato was hostile to democratic political structures. He advocated government by the few. He contrasted the opinions of the many with the knowledge of the elite few. As a result he had only contempt for opinion. For Plato, the many may be said in all cases to have opinions, but cannot be said to know any of the things they hold opinions about.

2. **Aristotle.** Other ancient philosophers were more sympathetic to the opinions of the many. Aristotle, for example, regarded the opinions of "the Many" as having some value. "There is this to be said for the Many. Each of them by himself may not be of a good quality; but when they all come together, it is possible that they may surpass—collectively and as a body, although not individually—the quality of the few best."

B. **Public Opinion in the early modern world.** Public opinion became much more important in Europe after the breakdown of feudalism and the emergence of the modern nation-state. In western Europe, public opinion first became a force during the English Civil War in the 1640s. (See in this Framework, The nature of the state.)

1. **Rousseau.** One of the first influential theorists to use the term "public opinion" was the French philosopher **Jean-Jacques Rousseau** (1712-1778)

who said, "Whoever makes it his business to give laws to a people must know how to sway opinions and through them govern the passions of men."

2. **Necker.** The popularity of the term, and much of our present thinking about public opinion, can be traced to **Jacques Necker** (1732-1804), a finance minister in pre-revolutionary France. Necker recognized the need for public confidence in fiscal policies and believed that the government should publish complete statements of its financial affairs. He popularized the term "public opinion" and stressed the importance of the support of public opinion to successful governance.

C. **Public opinion and the American founding.** Many of those who were most actively involved in the American founding were locked in a debate about the value of public opinion.

1. **Alexander Hamilton and James Madison.** Both **Alexander Hamilton** (1755-1804) and **James Madison** (1751-1836), for somewhat different reasons, shared some of Plato's concerns about the few and the many. At the Constitutional Convention in 1787, Hamilton remarked that "all communities divide themselves into the few and the many. The first are the rich and the well born, the other the masses of people. The voice of the people has been said to be the voice of God; and, however generally this maxim has been quoted and believed, it is not true in fact. The people are turbulent and changing; they seldom judge or determine right. Give therefore to the first class a distinct, permanent share in the government."

2. **Thomas Jefferson.** By contrast, **Thomas Jefferson** (1743-1826) was much more sympathetic to the public and felt that the United States offered unique opportunities to create and sustain an educated public, whose opinions would contribute to the wise governance of the country.

D. **De Tocqueville.** One of the most important and influential thinkers on public opinion in America was **Alexis de Tocqueville** (1805-1859), whose work *Democracy in America* is still regarded as one of the most insightful and informative works on American social and political life.

1. **An ambivalence about democracy.** De Tocqueville's perspectives about American

democracy were partially shaped by his own ambivalence about the role of the public. In one of his unpublished papers he wrote, "Intellectually I have an inclination for democratic institutions, but I am an aristocrat by instinct—that is to say, I despise and fear the masses."

2. **The tyranny of the majority.** One of de Tocqueville's main concerns about democracy was that it would lead to a new kind of tyranny, a "yoke heavier than any of those which have crushed mankind since the fall of the Roman empire." His concern was that individuals and ideas which disagreed with the majority would have no recourse and would be easily crushed.

3. **The role of public opinion.** De Tocqueville was concerned about the effects of public opinion on democratic institutions (such as the legislature and judges who were in some cases elected by the majority). But de Tocqueville was equally concerned about the role of public opinion on the people at large.

   a. **The importance of opinion.** De Tocqueville felt that in a democracy such as the United States, everyone was influenced by the beliefs and opinions of others. Public opinion is thus a powerful factor in shaping our own opinions.

   b. **The dangers to minority opinions.** In a democracy, however, the "bandwagon" effect becomes multiplied. When everyone is supposed to be equal, people have great confidence when their views reflect the views of the majority. But when individuals hold unpopular opinions, they are instantly overwhelmed by a sense of insignificance and weakness.

   c. **Public opinion in a democracy may breed conformity.** De Tocqueville's concern was that in a democracy public opinion itself was unduly powerful and would breed conformity and adherence to "ready-made opinions." People would feel relieved of the necessity to form opinions of their own.

   d. **Constitutional restraints as a remedy.** To control the dangerous effects of public opinion, de Tocqueville called for limitations on democratic government (such as an independent judiciary) that would allow democratic institutions to reflect the majority view without being "the slave of its passions."

II. **The history of public opinion measurement.** The first attempts to measure public opinion began in America in the early nineteenth century.

    A. **Straw votes.** The earliest efforts at polling in America were straw votes conducted by newspapers to predict elections. In 1824, for example, *The Harrisburg Pennsylvanian*, reported a straw vote of support for the various presidential candidates. Andrew Jackson, who had won the popular vote, led the balloting in the straw vote as well.

    B. **Market research.** Market research as such seems to have begun around the beginning of the twentieth century. One of the first major corporations to use market research techniques was E. I. du Pont de Nemours & Co. Early in the 1880s, du Pont began analyzing information from its customers and salespeople. By the 1920s, Market research was a growing discipline.

    C. **Predicting elections.** By the 1920s, there was also considerable interest in predicting the outcome of elections. The most famous examples of early polling were the surveys conducted by the magazine, the *Literary Digest*. Between 1916 and 1932, the *Digest* was remarkably accurate in predicting elections and referenda. The *Digest* predictions were also respected because they were based on massive numbers of respondents, numbering close to a quarter of a million.

    D. **The birth of scientific polling.** Despite its record of accuracy, the *Digest* was completely wrong about the 1936 presidential election. The *Digest* prediction of an overwhelming majority for Republican candidate Alf Landon was resoundingly contradicted by Franklin Roosevelt's 62% victory in the popular elections.

        1. **The problem with the *Digest* survey.** The problem with the *Digest* poll, of course, was that the size of the sample did not guarantee accuracy, especially since the *Digest* survey interviewed primarily the more wealthy respondents (likely to vote for Landon) and ignored the views of the mass of people who gave Roosevelt his majority.

        2. **The predictions of Gallup, Roper, and others.** The failure of the *Digest* survey not only discredited the old method, but also gave dramatic proof of the power of a different method. A new breed of pollsters (using samples that were more random) were able to predict the election itself and, by reduplicating the *Digest* sample, were able to predict just how mistaken the *Digest* results would be. The names of two of those who predicted the failure of the *Digest* survey—George Gallup and Elmo Roper—were eventually to become household words.

    E. **Contemporary survey research.** After their success in the 1936 election, the new public opinion surveyors established a new industry. However, they also had their own failures. George Gallup incorrectly predicted the very close 1948 election, which resulted in the famous picture of Harry Truman holding up a newspaper incorrectly announcing Dewey's victory. Despite this setback, scientific polling has become a permanent feature of the American political scene. Two of the most important individuals are the following:

        1. **Harris.** Louis Harris (b. 1921) achieved national recognition for his work with John F. Kennedy's successful bid for the presidency in 1960. He worked primarily with Democratic candidates and later moved into newspaper syndication.

        2. **Yankelovich.** While Harris and Gallup entered the survey research business from newspaper and political work, **Daniel Yankelovich** (b. 1924) has a more academic background. He entered the field via market research and is generally regarded as one of the most intellectually sophisticated students of public opinion today.

    F. **A major industry.** In the 1990s there are hundreds of polling organizations who work with corporations, political candidates, the media, and anyone else who wants to have a finger on the public pulse. Even foreign governments commission polls of American attitudes, as part of their effort to understand and shape their relationships with America.

Contemporary Perspective

I. **The growing importance of public opinion in resolving the issues that face the United States.** As the United States moves into the next century, the tension continues between a desire to be responsive to public opinion and a concern about the tyranny of the majority.

A. **Public opinion in the post-war period.** The role of public opinion in governance has changed subtly in the last two decades.

1. **Post-war growth.** In the first three decades after World War II, the United States experienced a remarkable period of economic growth. Driven by large gains in productivity, growth, and a stable world market, the standard of living rose dramatically making the American dream possible for millions of Americans.

2. **Sharing the gains.** Many of the political issues that the country faced had to do with how to distribute this wealth, as the country expanded entitlement programs, sent its youth to colleges, and spent its newfound wealth. In these areas, the government had little trouble gaining the support of public opinion.

3. **The slow-growth era.** Since the OPEC oil embargo in the early 1970s, however, the U.S. has suffered from lagging productivity growth and a much slower growth in its standard of living. After tax real income in 1990 is no higher than it was in 1970. Today the country faces a fiercely competitive and rapidly changing world market place, with a creaking industrial and educational infrastructure. This new condition has put real strains on the ability of the country to muster public opinion support for necessary policies.

4. **Sharing the pains.** The issues that face the country today are much more frequently problems of how to distribute sacrifices. As the country wrestles with massive federal deficits, trade imbalances, bills for the Savings and Loan crisis, skyrocketing health care costs, an aging population, and the costs of protecting the environment, the government struggles with issues of how to decide which groups will sacrifice first and most.

5. **The public holds the veto.** In resolving these sacrifice-sharing issues, public opinion has become much more important. In effect, public opinion has a veto power over any proposed solution. It is the average citizen who must save more, pay higher taxes or receive lower benefits, work harder for smaller pay increases in order to compete with new competitors, and be willing to pay more for health care (and perhaps receive less of it).

II. **Changing patterns of mass communications.** The character of mass communications has also changed in recent decades.

A. **Mass communications and public opinion.** There is obviously a close connection between the importance of public opinion to governance and the importance of the mass media that shape what the public thinks and feels.

B. **Need for more effective communication.** The fact that the big issues today involve sharing the pain rather than sharing the gain suggests that political leaders need to do a better job communicating with the public. The public needs to learn to think in the long term rather than in the short term.

C. **The shrinking sound bite.** Unfortunately, the trend seems to be toward more simplistic communications. The 1988 presidential campaign presented such an example. As the country struggled with massive problems such as reducing its deficits or rethinking its relationship to the Soviet Union, the campaign debated issues such as the pledge of allegiance to the flag and prison furloughs. Whereas in the 1968 presidential campaign, the average length of a candidate's appearance on the nightly television news was 48 seconds, by 1988 the average sound bit had shrunk to 9.8 seconds.

III. **Solutions.** While our national problems are growing more complex, our ways of talking about them seem to be growing more simplistic. Are there ways of reversing this trend? One of the most important thinkers in the field of public opinion, Daniel Yankelovich, has offered some creative solutions to this problem. These ideas have been explored both in Yankelovich's recent writings (especially his book, *Coming to Public Judgment*), and also through some experimental programs being conducted by several foundations.

A. **Two kinds of public opinion.** Yankelovich begins by distinguishing between two types of attitude:

1. **Mass opinion.** According to Yankelovich, most public opinion polls measure what might be called mass opinion. Mass opinion is the unreflective view of people who do not know very much about a subject and have not given it much thought. Because people have not thought much about these subjects, they are often likely to change their position when the implications of their opinions become apparent. Most voters, for example, initially favor high tariffs and economic

protectionism to protect American products and jobs, but they abandon this mass opinion when they realize that it will mean that foreign products will cost more. Mass opinion does not provide policy makers with a firm consensus for making difficult choices.

2. **Public judgment**. On other issues, however, a large proportion of the public has taken the time to think through their views and reach a more stable level of opinion that does reflect an awareness of costs and implications. Yankelovich calls this kind of attitude "public judgment." Public judgment is much more permanent than mass opinion. Since people have thought through the implications of their judgments, they will not abandon them easily.

B. **The need for public judgment**. In order to address the sharing problems that are on the national agenda, the public must reach this level of public judgment. Without a stable basis of public opinion, leaders will have no way to build consensus or compromise around the tough issues that need to be faced.

C. **The need for a new kind of communication**. Yankelovich believes, therefore, that public judgment can best be built by finding new ways of communicating with the public about important issues. Some of the most important factors are the following:

1. **Choices, not facts**. Much of current communications involves throwing more and more facts at the public. But the public is already overwhelmed with information to absorb. What people need is not more facts, but a new way of organizing these facts into choices. These choices need to be presented to people in ways that make their costs and implications clear.

2. **Values, not technicalities**. Experts and leaders frequently pose issues in terms of technical considerations. But the public thinks in terms of values. Choices need to be couched in ways that make clear what value issues are raised.

3. **Time, not instant results**. It takes time for public judgment to form. Sometimes experts who have wrestled with a subject for months expect that the public can understand it and accept it from a single speech. Instead, the choices need to be presented to people over time.

4. **Listening to the public**. People are much more likely to take an issue seriously if they know that someone cares what they think. If public judgment is to form, people need to be convinced that their views matter. Yankelovich's methodology combines communication campaigns with a citizen ballot at the end, where people have an incentive to think through the issue because they know their views will be heard and discussed.

D. **Practical implications**. The theory of public judgment has been put into practice in a number of different formats around the country. Two organizations, the Public Agenda Foundation and the Charles F. Kettering Foundation, have conducted a number of experiments in public judgment.

1. **The "Health Vote" campaign**. One of the first tests of the new method was the "Health Vote" campaign, conducted in Des Moines, Iowa, in 1982.

   a. **High health care costs**. Des Moines was selected because it was experiencing one of the highest rates of growth in medical expenses in the nation.

   b. **An incentive to participate**. The sponsors of the project developed a coalition of public leaders in Iowa, including representatives from state and federal government, major industry, hospitals, and insurance. All agreed to participate in the project and to give the results their attention.

   c. **Media campaign**. The next step was an extensive media campaign, where major health care choices were presented to the community through full-length television shows, brief radio and television announcements, newspaper articles, and town meetings over a period of several months.

   d. **Citizen ballot**. After the campaign, the *Des Moines Register* distributed a mail-in ballot on the choices. Over 30,000 people filled out the ballots (nearly 24% of those who received them). The write-in ballot was also supplemented by more traditional random sample surveys which were done both before and after the campaign to measure movement toward public judgment. The ballot and the surveys showed that the campaign created a significantly greater understanding of the options and their implications in the Des Moines area. The results were widely publicized and discussed by leadership.

e. **Slower growth in the rate of health care costs.** While direct causal links are impossible to show, the campaign was followed by a number of actions which resulted in markedly slower growth in health care expenses. Local leaders attributed much of the change to the success of the campaign.

2. **Other examples.** Various parts of this process have been duplicated in a number of other demonstration projects around the country on issues such as education, the environment, relations with the Soviet Union, and alternatives to incarceration. Fuller details are available from the Public Agenda Foundation in New York City. The Kettering Foundation in Dayton, Ohio, sponsors the National Issues Forum, which prepares materials for distribution to discussion groups around the country. Each year the Forum selects three different issues and sends materials to any groups who wish to participate; the materials use choices to help the participants move toward public judgment.

7. THE NATURE AND ROLE OF PROPAGANDA

I do not greatly care whether I have been right or wrong on any point, but I care a great deal about knowing which of the two I have been.

Samuel Butler (1903)

A liar begins with making falsehood appear like truth, and ends with making truth itself appear like falsehood.

William Stenstone (n.d.)

Two closely related convictions form the core of democratic theory. The first is the belief that ordinary citizens have the **right** to decide the course of public policy. The second is the claim that they have the **ability** to decide wisely. Of these, the second is clearly more fundamental: if the People cannot govern well, it is hard to see how they can demand the right to govern at all.

For citizens to choose wisely, they must be able both to understand the full range of available options and to see which one is best. These needs are served in American democracy by the constitutional guarantee of virtually unlimited freedom of speech and the press. The purpose of this guarantee is to encourage the kind of full and forceful confrontation among a diversity of views that reveals the nature and merits of each. This guarantee assumes, in the traditional formulation, that through open debate in the "free marketplace of ideas" the truth will emerge triumphant.

However comforting this notion of the inherent superiority of the truth might be, it must be recognized that its truth is by no means self-evident. To the contrary, both history and personal experience attest to the great power and persistence of error. At best, there may be some general tendency for truth to replace error over the course of time. But the process may span decades or centuries, and the outcome is neither certain nor final.

The problem is that a truly free marketplace must be open to many ideas, including some that are false or deceitful. Whether known by the ancient label of "sophistry" or the more modern term "propaganda," such views have always played a role in democratic debate. And there is no doubt that propaganda, often promulgated with great sophistication and tenacity, can overwhelm the limited intellectual defenses of individual citizens. Hence the widespread concern among both friends and foes of democracy that large segments of the public can be misled. Four fundamental changes in American society over the past two centuries have accentuated those fears.

The first change is the gradual expansion of the electorate. While the Bill of Rights guaranteed freedom of speech and the press to all citizens, the original Constitution left the right to determine voting qualifications to the several states. In practice, this meant that only a small minority of citizens—primarily free, adult men of property—were given the franchise. Whatever the shortcomings of these arrangements from the viewpoint of modern conceptions of equality and justice, they did serve an important practical function. Given the nature of American society at the time, they produced an electorate composed largely of those individuals with the highest levels of education, leisure for reflection, political knowledge and interest, and experience in the world of affairs. This group, of course, is the one presumably best able to resist the blandishments of sophists and demagogues.

Today the situation is dramatically different. A long stream of constitutional amendments, legislative acts, and court decisions, inspired by the egalitarian ideal of universal suffrage, has extended the franchise to nearly all adult citizens. Without questioning the substantial benefits of this change, it is important to note that one of its necessary costs is that the electorate now includes those individuals with the lowest levels of intellectual ability, education, knowledge, interest, and experience.

Mindful of the need to prepare these citizens for their civic duties, expansion of the electorate was accompanied by the gradual imposition of universal mandatory education designed in part to provide each American with the basic skills required for citizenship. But there is ample evidence that our education system has not been equal to this challenge, and the unpleasant truth is that millions of individuals who lack the ability to read a newspaper, count their change, or locate North America on a map of the world are now entrusted with the task of choosing wisely in elections and referendums. These new voters provide an especially vulnerable target for sophisticated propagandists.

The second change is grounded in the transformation of the United States from a quiet agricultural backwater to a modern superpower operating in a global society of interdependent nations. Faced with the exponential growth of knowledge, extreme intellectual specialization, the gradual expansion of government regulation and control to virtually all areas of human activity, and a vast increase in the range, complexity, and pace of problems that must be addressed, it is now difficult for even the most intelligent and motivated citizens to avoid being overwhelmed. This situation offers a fertile ground for the seductive distortions and simplifications of the propagandist.

The third change is the rapid evolution of American journalism. At the end of the Revolutionary War, the press consisted solely of a handful of print media: books, pamphlets and a scattering of small, local, and often highly partisan newspapers (35 in 1783, only one a daily). Today, the press encompasses a vast profusion of media, both print and broadcast, including almost 1,700 daily newspapers, 1,300 television stations, over 10,000 radio stations, and scores of thousands of books, magazines and other periodicals. More important, some media have achieved truly national scope in the sense that they can quickly disseminate information to a substantial fraction of either the entire population or the American policy-making elite. These "national media" include the television and radio networks, CNN, a few major newspapers (e.g., *The Wall Street Journal*, *USA Today*, *The New York Times* and *The Washington Post*) and news magazines (e.g., *Time*, *Newsweek* and *US News and World Report*), and the major wire services (especially AP and UPI).

Given these developments, it is clear that Americans now have available to them far more information at far greater speed and far less cost than at any time in the history of the country. But it is easy to exaggerate the significance of this fact. Regardless of the great amount and diversity of information, most people rely on only a few sources for their news of the world. More important, while there are thousands of local media in the United States, there are relatively few sources of original information about national and international affairs. Foremost among these are the handful of national media, on which nearly all local newspapers, television stations and radio stations depend for their national and international news. Thus, in reality, the majority of Americans get most of their information about nonlocal events from a small number of highly centralized sources.

The centralized character of the modern press has at least two important consequences. First, it means that any propagandist who gains access to the national media could have a major impact on public opinion because his message is disseminated so widely. Second, it gives immense power to the few thousand journalists who staff the national media. Members of a small, unitary and closed elite, they are the only individuals in contemporary society who can communicate directly to the American public on a daily basis. They also have the power to determine which other views will be heard in the marketplace of ideas. In particular, it is journalists in the national media who decide whether propagandists will be granted access to the public, and whether and by whom their views will be disputed.

The fourth important change is the development and widespread use of scientific opinion polls. First introduced in the 1930s, these surveys have become a mainstay of political discussion; few issues or policies escape extensive probing. In particular, it is now common for pollsters to report public reactions to events and initiatives within days or even hours of their occurrence. In the 1991 war against Iraq, for example, an ABC/*Washington Post* survey on President Bush's decision to begin hostilities was executed and reported within six hours of the initial attack. Results of these polls, many of them conducted or commissioned by the news media, are then often used by journalists to shape policy discussions and to demand accountability of political leaders.

While it is obviously valuable in a democracy to have accurate and timely information about public opinion on controversial issues, polling introduces certain serious problems as well. One problem is that poll results are often misinterpreted by both journalists and politicians. For example, it appears that the highly unpopular 1978 treaties which ceded control of the Panama Canal to Panama survived a closely contested ratification vote because several key senators mistakenly believed that the polls showed public opinion had shifted from opposition to support. More important, surveys are now often conducted before debate on an issue or policy is fully joined, and thus well before the merits of the various positions have been established. Because these polls reflect unstable first impressions rather than considered opinions, the effect is to greatly enhance the significance of the initial impact of propagandistic messages that have not yet been submitted to critical scrutiny.

Taken together, these considerations show that the study of propaganda is perhaps more important now than ever before. Clearly, if American democracy is to prosper, each citizen should learn how to avoid being manipulated and misled by propagandistic appeals. This suggests the following specific objectives.

OBJECTIVES

The citizen should be able to

1. explain the differences between propaganda and other forms of persuasive appeals;

2. identify and describe the most common propaganda techniques and explain in each case why their use is irrational and misleading;

3. explain the most common sources and goals of propaganda and relate the use of propaganda to prevailing political and journalistic structures and values;

4. explain the steps that are necessary to avoid being manipulated by propagandistic appeals.

FRAME OF REFERENCE
Conceptual Perspective

I. **Definitions of propaganda.** Like most terms in common usage for a period of centuries, the word "propaganda" has acquired a broad range of meanings and nuances. Most contemporary meanings, however, can be grouped under three general definitions.

    A. **Casual definition.** The most common and least precise definition of propaganda uses the term to denote messages that are consciously biased or tendentious. In this conception, the role of the propagandist is to build a case for a particular conclusion by arraying only those materials which lend it support. Other views and evidence are either ignored or considered only for purposes of refutation. Used in this sense, propaganda is interchangeable with other terms such as public relations, advertising or, more generally, persuasion.

    B. **Cultural definition.** The broadest and most recent definition of propaganda expands its meaning to encompass virtually all forms of tendentious communication in a technological society, including in particular messages that reflect unconscious biases. Thus, huge areas of social discourse, including much of education, popular entertainment, politics, journalism and the arts, can be considered propagandistic because they function to disseminate unexamined values and assumptions. For example, an elementary mathematics text that assigns problems dealing with the computation of interest payments can be seen as propaganda because it serves to reinforce a capitalistic view of economic and social relations. Derived from the influential writings of the French cultural critic **Jacques Ellul**, and broadly compatible with neomarxist analyses of hegemony and false consciousness, this view has dominated scholarly studies of propaganda since about 1970.

    C. **Rational definition.** The third view defines propaganda as persuasive communication that is not merely biased but rationally defective, in the sense that the propagandist uses falsehoods and distortions to mislead his audience. Thus, propaganda is always irrational; if the audience is intentionally misled, it is also unethical. Grounded in the ancient Aristotelian distinction between rhetoric and sophistry, this view dominated propaganda analysis and education for much of the twentieth century, and still provides the basis for most scholarly studies of fascist and communist propaganda.

II. **Choosing a definition.** Definitions are neither true nor false, only more or less useful. By this criterion, the best definition for present purposes is the third. This can be seen most clearly by examining the central distinction underlying each of the three basic definitions.

    A. **Conscious bias.** Defining propaganda as consciously biased communication is problematic because it fails to discriminate between very different activities. As noted above, this definition is quite broad, encompassing virtually all consciously persuasive messages. The term also typically connotes a negative evaluation. This definition implies that virtually all persuasive messages are somehow illicit or defective. But there is nothing inherently irrational or unethical about arraying materials in support of a particular claim. To the contrary, the American political and judicial systems both presuppose debate among precisely such messages. Problems arise when a message is not merely biased but misleading or deceitful. It is these messages that need to be singled out for critical evaluation by identifying them with a special label such as "propaganda." Defining propaganda as consciously biased communication not only fails to provide this identification but actually confuses the issue by suggesting that honest and deceitful persuasion are essentially similar. Numerous examples of this problem occurred during the 1991 war against Iraq when journalists and other commentators repeatedly characterized the statements of both American and Iraqi officials as "propaganda."

B. **Unconscious bias.** Expanding the definition of propaganda to include unconsciously biased messages simply compounds the problems noted above. In this view, even the most basic and settled truths of a society, such as "Democracy is the best form of government" or "Racism is evil," become "propaganda" if uttered unreflectively. Whatever its merits as a basis for radical critiques of existing societies and institutions, this definition so broadens the scope of the term as almost to empty it of meaning. Indeed, precisely because biases can be unconscious and unrecognized, it is impossible to know with certainty that any given message is **not** propagandistic.

C. **Defective proof.** The definition of propaganda as persuasive communication based on defective proof focuses specifically on the distinction between honest and misleading or deceitful persuasion. It is useful because almost everyone agrees that instances of flawed persuasion exist and that it is vital to identify them as such. The latter is especially true in democratic societies, which are guided in part by the judgments of ordinary citizens. If they are misled by sophistry, the state as a whole is weakened. The principal problem with this use of the term "propaganda" is that it is often misapplied as a mere epithet to dismiss disagreeable positions. This problem can be minimized through a more detailed analysis of this conception of propaganda.

III. **Defining characteristics of propaganda.** Propaganda may be formally defined as any conscious and open attempt to influence the beliefs of an individual or group, guided by a predetermined end and characterized by the systematic use of irrational and often unethical techniques of persuasion. Each term in the definition suggests a defining characteristic of propaganda and therefore merits separate discussion.

A. **Propaganda as deliberate and conscious.** The stipulation that propaganda is conscious means only that the propagandist deliberately seeks to influence his audience. It does not imply that he consciously

chooses to employ irrational and unethical techniques of persuasion. While this may often be the case, it is not invariably so.

B. **Openness of propaganda sources.** Propaganda is open in the sense that there is no attempt to hide the source of the propaganda message. This distinguishes propaganda from "disinformation," which may be defined as deceitful information spread by clandestine means such as forgery, blackmail, and the use of front groups and agents of influence, the latter including journalists who knowingly or unknowingly disseminate foreign or other hostile material without revealing its source. While the two are obviously related, propaganda analysis focuses primarily on message content while disinformation analysis tends to focus on message origin and the means employed in its distribution.

C. **Unsuccessful propaganda still propaganda.** The characterization of propaganda as an influence attempt means only that it can be identified independently of its effects. This contrasts with the view of some researchers in the broader field of persuasion who restrict the term "persuasion" to successful influence attempts.

D. **Propaganda's attempt to influence beliefs.** The stipulation that propaganda is an attempt to influence the beliefs of an audience in no way contradicts the common view that propaganda is typically intended to influence action. It does serve to remind that changes in belief are almost always a prerequisite for changes in external behavior, and that sometimes the purpose of propaganda is to inhibit action, not encourage it. It also suggests that the goals of propaganda are often more modest than is commonly thought. Specifically, there are three common goals of propaganda.

1. **Activation.** Here propagandists direct their messages to those already sympathetic to their views in an attempt to arouse them to active support. In the 1991 war against Iraq, for example, the Iraqi government disseminated its claims of massive, indiscriminate bombings of civilian areas through CNN and the other Western news media to the Arab world in hopes of stimulating widespread Arab opposition to the war.

2. **Conversion.** "Conversion" occurs when propagandists change hostile audiences from opposition to support of their views. Although obviously a desirable outcome, conversions are a rare and

difficult achievement, especially in campaigns conducted solely through the mass media. Thus conversion is seldom the explicit goal of experienced propagandists.

3. **Confusion**. The most common goal in a propaganda campaign directed at a hostile audience is not to convert the audience members but to modify the strength of their convictions. For example, the Soviet Union has long justified its destruction of KAL flight 007 on September 1, 1983, by asserting that the aircraft was spying for the United States. Because they have offered no positive proof for this claim, it appears that the Soviets are less concerned with convincing the American public that the aircraft actually was spying, than that it might have been, or at least that the Soviets were justified in thinking it was. By introducing doubt—however slight—about the true status of the aircraft, the Soviets can diminish condemnation of the act. Stated in general terms, a the propagandist who practices lying is successful to the extent that he reduces belief in the truth. Any reduction is useful, because it decreases the confidence with which an opponent will act. If the goal is to paralyze opposition, it is enough to instill the belief that a lie and the truth are equally probable, or that all parties to the discussion are lying. Thus propaganda can seek either action or inaction, conviction or doubt, and its efficacy should be judged accordingly.

E. **Directed at individuals or groups**. Saying that propaganda seeks to influence an individual or group implies that it can use either interpersonal or mediated channels of communication. This marks a break with the tradition that associates propaganda exclusively with the mass media. It is difficult to see the value of such a restriction. Propaganda existed before the invention of the modern high-speed media, and most if not all of the techniques of the craft can be used with equal facility in both mass and interpersonal settings. Further, many organized propaganda campaigns such as "grassroots" movements in the United States and "study" or "struggle" sessions in Marxist countries can be understood only if their major interpersonal components are considered. It must still be acknowledged, however, that most of the more dramatic, significant and readily documented examples of propaganda are found in the mass media.

F. **Predetermined end**. All propaganda is guided by some predetermined end. It is easy to make too much and

too little of this point. Nearly all communication is goal-directed, so in that sense propaganda is unexceptional. But the ends of propaganda have two somewhat special characteristics.

1. **Ends of propaganda are fixed**. In ordinary discussion, goals often fluctuate over the course of interaction. In propaganda, however, the ultimate goals are fixed and thus unresponsive to situational variations.

2. **Ends of propaganda are typically remote**. Unlike other communicators, the propagandist almost always seeks effects beyond the immediate occasion. These ends may be general or specific, hidden or open, sinister or benign, but they add a dimension of significance often missing from ordinary interaction.

G. **Use of irrational techniques**. The primary defining characteristic of propaganda is its reliance on irrational techniques of persuasion. There are, of course, many different views of rationality. For present purposes, a technique will be considered irrational if it serves to induce belief in an audience without providing adequate support for that belief. Put somewhat differently, a technique can be considered irrational if it produces a claim that cannot survive the unrestricted critical scrutiny of reasonable people. In one form or another, this critical (or "conflict") view of rationality underlies all Western democratic institutions and constitutes one of the proudest accomplishments of Western civilization. It therefore seems particularly appropriate as a standard for judging discourse in Western democratic societies.

H. **Systematic use of irrational techniques**. Given the normal human frailties of ignorance, error, laziness and inattention, careful examination will reveal that nearly all persuasive messages are marred by at least the occasional use of irrational techniques. It would serve little purpose to classify all of them as propaganda. Instead, the term should be reserved for those messages where the use of irrational techniques is systematic. Systematic use is indicated either by the frequent occurrence of those techniques or by their occasional occurrence at critical junctures of an argument. In the extreme case, a message could be considered propaganda if it contained a single, but absolutely crucial, error.

I. **Often unethical**. Propaganda is often, but not always, unethical. The determining factors include the ethical standard that is applied and the intent of the propagandist.

1. **Ethical behavior**. As with rationality, there are many opinions about the nature of ethical behavior. One widespread view centers on the idea of the present worth, dignity, and autonomy of the individual. Its primary assumption is that each person has a peculiarly authentic perspective which must be taken into account when dealing with that person. Thus individuals are seen as ends in themselves, uniquely qualified to judge what is in their own best interests, who must be fully consulted in matters affecting their fate.

2. **Ethical persuasion**. Applied to the realm of persuasion, this view sees any conscious attempt to manipulate the individual (e.g., by the use or threat of force, by offering defective proofs, or by arousing base emotions) as unethical, either because it uses the individual merely as means to another's end or because it denies him the opportunity to truly judge what is in his own individual best interest. Thus, any conscious use of irrational techniques of persuasion must also be unethical. This view of the individual is central to the Western conception of popular democracy and most of the rights it confers. It therefore seems particularly appropriate as a standard for ethical judgments of discourse in Western democratic societies.

3. **Ethical vs. unethical propaganda**. It is important to note that the crucial defining characteristic of propaganda is the systematic use of irrational techniques of persuasion. An irrational technique can be used consciously or unconsciously. If used consciously, the message is also unethical; if unconsciously (e.g., through ignorance or honest error), the message may very well be ethical. Thus unethicality is **not** a defining characteristic of propaganda.

J. **Techniques**. The last defining characteristic of propaganda is its reliance on characteristic techniques of reasoning and persuasion. Because propaganda can come from any source and deal with any subject matter, it is the use of these techniques in a message that provides the clearest possible proof of its propagandistic nature. Learning to recognize these techniques is therefore a crucial skill for those who want to avoid being manipulated by propagandists.

IV. **The techniques of propaganda**. Because the number of possible errors and fallacies is unlimited, the number of possible propaganda techniques is also unlimited. However, all can be placed into one of four general categories. Within each category, certain specific techniques can be identified because of their prominence in modern propaganda.

A. **Falsehoods and lies**. In a sense, all propagandistic claims are falsehoods. But it is useful to reserve this term to denote those claims, supported or unsupported, that are contradicted by logic or by verifiable facts. When a falsehood is uttered with full knowledge of its falsity, it becomes a lie. Falsehoods are merely irrational; lies are both irrational and unethical. Four kinds of lies are especially common in contemporary propaganda.

1. **The "Big Lie."** Usually associated with Nazi propaganda minister **Josef Goebbels** (1897-1945), the "Big Lie" is actually the oldest and simplest of all propaganda techniques. It consists of nothing more than an open, blatant falsehood that gains its force from constant and confident repetition. One recent example is the former Nicaraguan government's repeated and categorical denials, later retracted in the face of incontrovertible evidence from journalists at the scene, that its troops had entered Honduras in March of 1986 to attack Contra forces; another example is the Iraqi government's claims in early 1991 that it had destroyed hundreds of American aircraft and defeated coalition forces attempting to liberate Kuwait.

2. ***Tu quoque* response**. Latin for "thou too," the *tu quoque* response is a special case of the Big Lie. It consists of responding to an accuser with a mirror-image set of accusations. For example, on January 23, 1984, President Reagan charged the Soviet Union with specific, carefully documented violations of seven arms limitation treaties. The Soviet government responded immediately by accusing the United States of an almost identical set of specific violations, but offered no evidence to support them.

3. **Historical reconstruction**. All accounts of history involve a degree of selection and emphasis. But Marxist states are unique in the modern world for their systematic efforts to reconstruct or rewrite history through persistent and comprehensive modification of the historical record. Once a subject of considerable controversy, the

Soviet Union and several of its former East European satellites have recently acknowledged and repudiated this practice. It persists, however, in China and other unreformed Communist states. Two complementary procedures are used in such reconstructions.

a. **Elimination of records**. In this phase of reconstruction, evidence that conflicts with the official view of history is altered or destroyed. The classic instance of this practice concerns **Lavrenti Beria** (1899-1953), Stalin's head of internal security from 1938 to 1953. After his execution, Beria became a "non-person" and all public references to his existence were eliminated. For example, copies of the appropriate volume of the official *Great Soviet Encyclopedia* were recalled and the long and laudatory entry on him was physically removed. Similarly, historical photographs published in the official Chinese press in the 1980s had been retouched to remove all traces of the disgraced former leaders known as the "Gang of Four."

b. **Fabrication of records**. This involves the fabrication of evidence to support false claims included in the official version of history. For example, the Chinese government still uses filmed "confessions" extracted from captured American airmen to support its claim that the United States engaged in germ warfare attacks against China during the Korean War. Similarly, monuments erected by the Communist governments in Poland in 1985 and the Soviet Union in 1988 blamed, respectively, "Hitlerite fascism" and "fascists" for the massacre of thousands of captured Polish officers in the Katyn Forest of the Soviet Union during World War II. In fact, there is overwhelming evidence that the Soviet Union, not fascist Germany, was responsible for the massacre.

4. **Symbolic fictions**. A symbolic fiction is a falsehood that is endorsed by some supposedly disinterested and respectable party. For example, Soviet leaders have always claimed that the U.S.S.R. is a voluntary federation of fifteen sovereign republics. Few knowledgeable observers have ever taken this claim seriously, but the Soviet government demanded at the 1945 San Francisco Conference that all fifteen republics be given seats in the General Assembly of the proposed United Nations. The outcome was a "compromise" that gave full membership to the U.S.S.R., the Byelorussian S.S.R., and the Ukrainian S.S.R., and thus official United Nations endorsement of the falsehood.

B. **Omissions**. Every persuasive message must omit relevant material because no message can ever report all that is known about a subject. An omission is irrational, and therefore propagandistic, when the missing information is both available to the message source and highly damaging to his claims. For example, the Soviet Union and other Marxist countries have always claimed that the Korean War began when South Korea attacked North Korea. Thus, the historical summary of the Korean War provided under the entry "Korea" in the latest English-language translation of the official *Great Soviet Encyclopedia* begins with this claim and depicts the entire conflict as a war of aggression by South Korea, the United States, and unnamed "other countries" against the North. The overall thrust of the analysis is contradicted, however, by the indisputable fact that within a month of the outbreak of hostilities North Korean forces had seized approximately 85% of the total territory of South Korea. Omission of this information is therefore irrational and propagandistic.

C. **Distortions**. A distortion occurs whenever a message source draws an invalid or unjustifiable conclusion from the evidence he presents. Although the number of possible distortions is unlimited, several hundred of the most common have been named and described over the past 2,300 years. They can be found in any good logic text under the headings of formal and informal fallacies. The following distortions are especially common in contemporary propaganda.

1. **Misuse of quantified data**. A striking feature of contemporary public debate is the widespread reliance on quantified information, especially in the form of recurrent statistics, numerical estimates, and the quantified results of innumerable "studies." Unfortunately, much of this information is either intrinsically flawed or erroneously interpreted. One reason is that the vast majority of Americans—including a great many public figures such as journalists, political leaders, and media-designated experts—have little training in or understanding of quantitative methods. This ignorance is often evident in their use of data produced by those methods. In addition, much of the quantified information

reported in the news media has been artfully crafted by interested parties to advance particular agendas. Careful and objective examination of this information often reveals gross defects. In short, all claims involving quantified data are potentially erroneous and should be evaluated with the greatest of care.

2. **Selectivity biases**. Perhaps the most common form of inference is to generalize from information about a sample of instances to some broader conclusion. The conclusion will be accurate, however, only if the sample is representative of the whole. Representativeness is likely only if the sample is chosen by some formal probabilistic method, as it is in reputable opinion polls. All other methods of sampling are biased, and cannot support reliable generalizations. A very common propaganda technique is to "stack the deck" by carefully selecting an unrepresentative sample of instances. In this way it is possible to "prove" almost any claim whatsoever. Unfortunately, many of the most basic methods and values of journalism also encourage invalid generalization from biased samples. These include such hallowed practices as man-in-the-street interviews, selection of sources to give a "balanced" account of affairs, defining "news" to stress coverage of unusual and dramatic events, and the pressure to draw significant general conclusions from those events.

3. **Projections**. A product of the computer age, and a favorite device of those seeking to dramatize a perceived problem, projections involve using existing data to forecast future events and circumstances. Unfortunately, all projections are subject to three inherent weaknesses. First, any projection is only as good as the data and assumptions on which it is based. If these are flawed, the forecast will be flawed. Second, any attempt to forecast large-scale trends will necessarily involve the gross oversimplification of reality. It is simply not possible to include all potentially relevant variables—many of which are unknown—in a computer simulation. Third, a projection cannot predict the impact of creative responses to a problem, such as innovations in technology or substantial changes in human attitudes and behaviors. Yet such responses almost always occur as the severity of a problem increases. As a result of these weaknesses, nearly all widely publicized projections, especially in the areas of population growth, resource depletion

and environmental degradation and change, have turned out to be wildly inaccurate. Thus, in general, any projection that predicts catastrophic effects should be treated as highly suspect.

4. **Multiple assertions**. This consists of making contradictory claims to different audiences. For example, the Soviet government in the 1970s provided one account of the policy of detente to their own citizens and a contradictory account to foreign audiences in the United States and elsewhere. While it may be impossible in such cases to determine which of the accounts is false, they cannot both be true, thus revealing propagandistic intent.

5. **Multiple standards**. Common in both Marxist propaganda and American media coverage of foreign affairs, this technique involves using markedly different criteria to evaluate similar entities. For example, throughout the 1970s and 1980s many Marxists and some Western journalists tended to assess socialist countries according to their degree of progress since the evils and privations of prerevolutionary days, but judged capitalist societies on the basis of how far they had yet to go to realize their ideals. The contrasting reports on Cuba and Honduras broadcast on consecutive "60 Minutes" programs in January 1989 offer a particularly clear example of this practice. The segment on dictatorial Cuba stressed supposed gains in such areas as health care and education since the overthrow of the Batista regime in 1959, while the segment on Honduras focused on unresolved political and economic problems and suggested the elimination of U.S. aid on the grounds that it didn't benefit the Honduran people.

6. **Impossible certainty**. This fallacy consists of making a categorical assertion or inference about an issue on which certainty is impossible. It is most common in claims about the thoughts, feelings and intentions of individuals or groups, and in assertions about the causes of particular events. For example, journalists routinely offer "electoral explanations" in which the actions of political leaders are attributed solely to cynical calculations of the number of votes to be gained thereby. Similarly, reports on environmental problems often cite a particular environmental factor (e.g., toxic wastes, radioactive emissions) as the specific cause of individual cases of

illness or damage, even though other causes are at least equally possible.

D. **Suggestions**. The defining characteristic of a suggestion is that it presents information in such a way that the audience is likely to draw an invalid or unjustifiable conclusion. Unlike other forms of propaganda, the information provided may be either completely accurate or, in the case of definitions or labels, a matter of individual preference and therefore strictly speaking neither true nor false. Suggestion is a mainstay of advertising, especially when the goal is to create a particular image for a product. Three forms are especially common in political debate.

1. **Artful naming**. It has been recognized for millennia that the way a thing is treated is partly a result of what it is called. Thus finding the appropriate name for something is often a crucial issue in debate. Naming is irrational and propagandistic when a controversial or misleading label is used instead of proof to influence the reactions of an audience. Often the label is pejorative. For example, Senator Alan Simpson was widely criticized in February 1991 for calling CNN reporter Peter Arnett an Iraqi "sympathizer" without offering definitive proof of Arnett's sympathies. But propagandistic naming can also seek positive outcomes, as in the recent efforts by political progressives to modify attitudes and policies toward marginal groups by changing what they are called. For example, if someone is labeled a "homeless person" instead of, say, a "wino" or a "bum," it suggests a very different explanation for and solution to his problems. Or again, if the term "undocumented resident" is used instead of "illegal alien," it suggests very different conclusions about the relationship between the individual and American society (resident member vs. alien intruder) and the source of the alien's marginal status (lack of documents vs. illegal entry).

2. **Role referencing**. A positive variant of artful naming, role referencing is especially common in news reports of foreign affairs. It consists of describing an individual in terms of one of his marginal roles in hopes that the audience will falsely ascribe the stereotypical characteristics of that role to him. In particular, professional revolutionaries in the Third World are often described as poets, artists, teachers, writers, journalists, clergymen, social workers, or intellectuals. Similarly, a highly sympathetic 1984 story

on "60 Minutes" introduced Nicaraguan Deputy Foreign Minister Nora Astorga as "a national heroine, a lawyer, and a 35-year-old mother with five children," even though she had deserted her job and children in 1978 to join the Sandinista guerrillas in the field after luring a senior government official to his death in her bedroom with promises of sexual favors.

3. **Asymmetrical definition**. This technique occurs whenever a message source uses a word that has a substantially different meaning to the individual using the word than it does to his audience. Unless warned, audience members will naturally attribute their usual meaning to the word and thereby be misled.

    a. **Marxist asymmetries**. Historically, problems of asymmetrical definition have arisen most frequently in dealing with messages from Marxist sources, whose use of language differs dramatically from that of nonmarxists. Virtually all of the common terms of political discourse, including "peace," "freedom," "democracy," "majority," "truth," "consciousness," "reality," and hundreds of others, have acquired radically different meanings in the context of Marxist-Leninist dialectics. For example, as J.A.C. Brown has noted, in the typical Marxist lexicon "peace" refers to the state of affairs in a communist country because capitalist countries are seen to be in a state of open class warfare. Thus, if a Marxist leader says his country is committed to "world peace," it could mean his country is committed to establishing worldwide communism, because those are the only circumstances in some Marxist theory under which true "peace" is possible.

    b. **Academic asymmetries**. The dramatic transformation of American universities, which first came to public notice in the late 1980s, has also involved the use of radically different definitions for many key terms in the areas of education and social relations by some academics. These include: "equality," "diversity," "civility," "speech," "freedom," "education," "scholarship," "discrimination," "prejudice,", "oppression," "harassment," "bigotry," even "rape." Given the scope and intensity of the controversy engendered by these initiatives, the use of these and similar terms in academic discourse should be seen as potentially propagandistic, and their meanings examined with care.

Historical Perspective

I. **The classical tradition.** Although specific concerns about propaganda are largely a twentieth century phenomenon and are intimately linked with the development and spread of modern systems of mass communication, concerns about the influence of deceitful communication have been common since antiquity.

A. **Classical Greece and Aristotelian rhetoric.** The development of democratic government in Athens in the fifth and fourth centuries B.C. led quite naturally to an emphasis on the study of persuasion. The first systematic treatment of the subject was the *Rhetoric* by **Aristotle** (384-322 B.C.).

1. **The efficacy of truth.** In marked contrast to the pessimistic elitism of his mentor Plato, Aristotle adopted the more optimistic view of man and his ability to discern truth from error that later inspired American democracy. In the first chapter of the first book of the *Rhetoric*, he asserted that "things that are true and things that are just have a natural tendency to prevail over their opposites" and that "men have a sufficient natural instinct for what is true, and usually do arrive at the truth."

2. **Rhetoric vs. sophistic.** Aristotle's stated purpose in writing the *Rhetoric* was to rescue the subject from the "sophists," by whom he meant the class of itinerant teachers who offered, for a fee, instruction in certain tricks of reasoning and persuasion that could enable the student to prevail in public debate, especially before the courts. In Aristotle's view, the art of rhetoric is essentially amoral. What he produced, however, was a theory of rational and ethical persuasion that contrasted sharply with the fallacies and deceits of the sophists (which he attacked at length in the treatise *On Sophistical Refutations*). The result was a distinction, which has persisted to this day, between two fundamentally different forms of persuasion: rhetoric, which is both rational and ethical, and sophistry, which is neither.

B. **The rhetorical tradition.** This view of rhetoric as a noble form of persuasion persisted throughout antiquity. In particular, many of the leading intellectual figures of the Roman period, including **Cicero** (106 B.C.-43 B.C.), **Quintilian** (35 A.D.-95 A.D.), and **St. Augustine** (354 A.D.-430 A.D.), made seminal contributions to the subject. During the Middle Ages, the importance of rhetoric was indicated by its recognition as one of the seven liberal arts which formed the core of the educational curriculum. These were divided into the "higher," or more abstract, arts of the quadrivium (arithmetic, geometry, astronomy and music) and the "lower," or more practical arts of the trivium (grammar, rhetoric and logic).

II. **Catholicism and the origins of modern propaganda.** In 1622, Pope **Gregory XV** founded what was commonly called the *Sacra Congregatio de Propaganda Fide* (Congregation for the Propagation of the Faith). In part a response to the Protestant Reformation, the "Propaganda" provided centralized control and coordination of the missionary activities of the Church, including proselytizing in the New World and efforts to revitalize the faith in the Old. The word "propaganda" entered common usage from this source, first to denote any organization engaged in spreading a doctrine, then to describe either the doctrine itself or the techniques used in its propagation. In its original Catholic usage, propaganda was clearly a positive term. But as it entered common usage, it acquired sinister connotations, and by the mid-nineteenth century the English encyclopedist W.T. Brande could note its application as "a term of reproach to secret associations for the spread of opinions and principles which are viewed by most governments with horror and aversion."

III. **The first transformation of the press in America.** Although propaganda has existed throughout history, its impact has been greatly enhanced by the development of modern media of mass communication. In America, that development began in the nineteenth century.

A. **The penny press and the commercialization of the news.** For the first half-century of American democracy, newspapers tended to be expensive, small in size and circulation, and, because often subsidized by political parties or factions, highly opinionated. Seldom very profitable, these newspapers appealed mainly to the political and social elites. Beginning in 1833 with the publication of the *New York Sun*, however, they were rapidly replaced by the so-called "penny press." These newspapers, the first of the modern mass media, were essentially commercial ventures which depended on advertising revenues to turn a profit. These revenues, in turn, were determined by the newspaper's circulation. Circulation was maximized by reducing the cost of the newspaper to a penny and by gearing its content to the needs and interests of ordinary citizens. Commercialization also revolutionized the way in which the news was reported.

1. **First journalists.** At the time the Constitution was written, professional journalism did not exist. It arose in response to the demand by the new, fiercely competitive, mass circulation daily newspapers for a constant flow of interesting and timely information.

2. **The ideal of objectivity.** In the new world of commercial journalism, profit depended on advertising, advertising depended on circulation, and circulation depended in part on not alienating potential readers. Thus newspapers became markedly less partisan, and the ideal of journalistic objectivity was born. Although highly opinionated and even propagandistic reporting, including the excesses of "yellow journalism" and "muckraking," dominated coverage in the nineteenth century, the professionalization of journalism in the first decades of this century eventually established factual objectivity as the central value of the field.

B. **From a partisan to an informative press.** The commercialization of the press led to three important changes in American society. First, it provided an unprecedented wealth of information to the public, especially after the invention of the telegraph in 1844 and the formation of the first wire service in 1849 permitted timely reporting of events from throughout the nation and, eventually, the world. Second, the ideal of objectivity changed the role of the press in political discussion. Initially cast as partisan **participants** in the conflict of ideas, newspapers increasingly restricted themselves to **reproducing** the debate in their reports. Partisan participation, at least in theory, was relegated to the editorial pages. Third, journalists began to emerge as a powerful and privileged elite. It was they who decided which issues and policies would be allowed to participate fully in the conflict of ideas. And although freedom of the press remained a right of the individual citizen in theory, in practice its full and effective exercise was increasingly restricted to professional journalists. (For further discussion of the history of the American press, see the section devoted to the press in this Framework.)

IV. **World War I and the birth of modern propaganda.** The first widespread and systematic use of propaganda by governments occurred during the so-called Great War of 1914-18. It was also at this time that the term propaganda entered common usage in the United States.

A. **European propaganda.** World War I, the first "total war," was unprecedented in both scope and intensity. Accordingly, most of the European belligerents used state-sponsored propaganda in attempts to influence world opinion and, especially in the Western democracies, to sustain popular support in the face of awesome losses and privations. German propaganda—rigid, unimaginative and largely defensive—had little discernible impact. British and French propaganda, designed to place all blame for the war on the Central Powers and filled with lurid accounts of atrocities committed by the brutal and barbaric "Huns," was far more successful.

B. **American propaganda.** When America entered the war in April 1917, President **Woodrow Wilson** (1856-1924), who had won re-election five months earlier on the campaign slogan "He kept us out of war," faced the task of uniting a deeply divided country behind the war effort. He therefore established the Committee on Public Information (CPI), headed by progressive journalist **George Creel**, which blanketed the country with pro-war information (some of it fully propagandistic) disseminated through a wide range of mass and interpersonal channels of communication. Among its many activities, CPI distributed over 100 million pamphlets and posters; provided newspapers with a constant stream of articles, editorials, and editorial cartoons; fielded a force of 75,000 "Four Minute Men" to speak at public gatherings on weekly themes established by the Administration; and organized numerous Americanization Committees to instruct members of several dozen non-English ethnic minorities on views deemed appropriate in their new homeland.

C. **Postwar reaction.** The cessation of hostilities was followed in the United States (and Europe) by widespread criticism of government propaganda. This was fueled by revelations that many claims about responsibility for the war and German atrocities had been false, and by unease among intellectuals such as **John Dewey** (1859-1952) and **Walter Lippmann** (1889-1974) about government manipulation of information and public opinion. As a result, "propaganda" entered popular usage as a term for deceitful communication.

D. **Propaganda in advertising and public relations.** Professionals in advertising and the fledgling field of public relations took a diametrically opposite view of propaganda. Defining it in the traditional sense of persuasive communication, pioneering publicists such as **Ivy Lee** and **Edward Bernays** extolled its usefulness in a democratic society. For example, a 1926 article by **Bruce Bliven** was entitled "Let's Have More Propaganda." This served to perpetuate a second, more positive meaning of the term.

V. **Totalitarian propaganda and World War II**. Propaganda from 1920 until the end of the Second World War in 1945 was dominated by two important developments. The first was the introduction and rapid diffusion of radio. As the first instantaneous mass medium, its propaganda potential was widely feared (and exaggerated). The second was the growth of fascism and Marxism, both claiming to serve the interests of the masses and both relying on institutionalized propaganda as a principal instrument of political control.

A. **Fascist propaganda**. The fascist theory of propaganda is described most fully in Hitler's *Mein Kampf* and the diaries of Josef Goebbels. It is characterized by emotionalism (including both emotional message appeals and the use of pageantry and spectacle), extreme flexibility (including the simultaneous use of contradictory appeals designed for different audiences), pragmatic expediency (in the sense that the goal of propaganda is to serve the immediate needs of the Nazi Party, whatever those might be), and a primary focus on domestic audiences.

B. **Marxist propaganda**. The Marxist theory of propaganda, especially the dominant Marxist-Leninist variant developed in the Soviet Union, differs radically from the fascist view. It begins with the distinction made by the Marxist theoretician **Georgi Plekanov** (1857-1918) between propaganda, which "conveys many ideas to one or a few persons," and agitation, which "conveys only one or a few ideas, but to a great mass of people." It also distinguishes between communist propaganda, portrayed as wholly beneficial, and bourgeois propaganda, seen as inherently deceitful. Marxist propaganda differs from the fascist variety in three important respects.

1. **Logical basis**. Marxism is a highly elaborated, deductively ordered, and logically consistent ideology. Marxist propaganda is based on the application of this ideology to provide a theoretically correct interpretation of reality. It is therefore fully logical (or "scientific" in Marxist terms) and, because bound by the strictures of theory, both relatively inflexible and explicitly principled. The most basic tenet of Marxism and

Marxist propaganda is that "mere facts" have no inherent meaning and that truth is a matter of proper interpretation. For example, if a socialist country sends its troops to seize control of a neighboring country (as in the Korean War), it would be false to characterize this as an act of aggression because, by definition, all socialist countries are peace loving countries and, again by definition, no peace loving country attacks its neighbors. Thus, the seizure must be interpreted as a purely defensive reaction against actual or potential aggression by the neighboring country, and the fact that the seizure occurred can even be taken as proof of the neighboring country's aggressive intentions.

2. **International focus**. Because traditional Marxist states have sought to secure the inevitable triumph of communism in all countries of the world, Marxist (especially Soviet) propaganda has always focused on both domestic and international audiences. It has also been used traditionally in concert with the full range of covert disinformation techniques including forgeries, front groups, and agents of influence.

3. **Intellectual appeal**. In contrast to the relatively crude fascist propaganda designed principally to influence the masses, Marxist propaganda has often appealed to intellectual audiences as well. This was especially apparent in the 1930s, when many Western intellectuals either embraced Marxism or were sympathetic to its ideals. Some, including several prominent journalists, served as witting or unwitting propagandists for the Soviet Union. For example, *New York Times* correspondent **Walter Duranty**, who was stationed in Moscow from 1921 to 1933 and received a Pulitzer Prize in 1932 for his "dispassionate, interpretive reporting of the news from Russia," provided systematically distorted coverage, including repeated denials of the Ukrainian terror-famine of 1932-33 in which at least six million people perished as a direct result of deliberate Soviet policy. (See, Robert Conquest, *Harvest of Sorrow* [1986].)

C. **Propaganda in America**. Although remote from the massive ideological clashes of Europe, concerned interest in propaganda continued to grow in the United States throughout this period.

1. **Propaganda analysis**. As a direct outgrowth of the reaction against the use of propaganda in

World War I, a number of politically progressive scholars sought to educate the public about the dangers of propaganda throughout the 1920s and 1930s. An intellectual movement of considerable influence, propaganda analysis initially focused on exposing manipulations of news and information by powerful corporate and governmental interests in the United States, but expanded its focus to include Nazi (but seldom Soviet) propaganda as World War II approached. Highly successful in introducing antipropaganda training in the schools, the movement culminated in the founding of the Institute for Propaganda Analysis in 1937 under the leadership of Professor Clyde R. Miller of Columbia University.

2. **Propaganda in World War II.** American propaganda and persuasion activities during the war were coordinated by the Office of War Information (OWI). Among its major accomplishments were the commissioning and distribution of the seven *Why We Fight* films, designed to explain the causes and purposes of the war to all military personnel, and the creation of the Voice of America radio network. Reflecting the painful lessons of the First World War, OWI materials were generally truthful, but still highly and sometimes crudely tendentious.

3. **Propaganda research.** Systematic scientific research on the effects of persuasive appeals began in the 1930s. With the outbreak of war, many of the leading scientists in the field were brought together in the Research Branch of the War Department's Information and Educational Division to conduct large-scale studies of propaganda and persuasion. Their results, published after the war, formed the foundation for the subdiscipline of persuasion research.

VI. **Propaganda and the Cold War of 1945-89.** The defeat of fascism was followed by a protracted struggle between international communism, led by the Soviet Union, and liberal democracy, led by the United States; it ended with the collapse of communism in the late 1980s. The struggle progressed through two distinct periods, which also mark a dramatic shift in the role and conception of propaganda.

A. **The anticommunist consensus of 1945-65.** The rapid expansion of communism in Eastern Europe and Asia, the emergence of the Soviet Union as a nuclear superpower, and allegations (both true and false) of communist infiltration of American government,

education, and the communications and entertainment industries forged a broad popular and political consensus against communism that persisted without serious challenge until the mid-1960s. Throughout this period, sensitivity to Marxist propaganda was acute, in part because of popular fears produced by Chinese "brainwashing" techniques and the widespread collaboration of American prisoners of war during the Korean conflict, but primarily because of growing communist influence in the emerging nations of the Third World. To counter this influence, American information and aid programs were greatly expanded.

B. **Vietnam and its aftermath.** Aside from its inherent significance, the Vietnam conflict of 1964-73 served as a catalyst for a broad range of changes that have transformed American society and culture. Four changes are particularly important to the study of propaganda.

1. **Cultural alienation.** The experience of Vietnam, followed by the Watergate scandal and revelations of covert intelligence activities, produced widespread popular distrust of political leaders and institutions. As a result, some Americans have concluded that the American government is a principal source of propaganda. This attitude is especially common among members of the intellectual and artistic elite, many of whom have adopted an explicitly adversarial stance in relation to American culture and institutions.

2. **Interest group politics.** The success of the civil rights and antiwar movements introduced an era of popular activism in which organized interest groups sought to expand the rights of various social groups, including ethnic minorities, women, the poor, the elderly, the disabled, homosexuals, children, and animals, and to influence government policy on a wide range of issues, including consumer and foreign affairs, defense, and the environment. Often accorded extensive and uncritical treatment by the news media, these groups have emerged as a powerful and permanent force in American political and social debate. As discussed in more detail below, they are also at least a major potential source of propagandistic appeals.

3. **Cultural relativism.** Cultural relativism begins with the belief that truth is a product of cultural values and assumptions. Thus, different cultures will produce different truths and, because the

choice of values and assumptions is essentially arbitrary, the truths of one culture cannot be superior to those of any other culture. This view has devastating implications for propaganda analysis because it denies the validity of using the standards of one culture to evaluate the truth of messages from another culture. To impose such standards is to be guilty of the new sin of ethnocentrism. Although it has been strongly criticized on philosophical grounds, cultural relativism emerged as a dominant academic viewpoint in the Vietnam era and, as the basis of most "postmodernist" thinking, is now influential in many areas of American intellectual discourse. One consequence of the emphasis on cultural relativism was the virtual disappearance of scholarly studies of contemporary foreign (especially Marxist) propaganda after about 1970. Another consequence was a marked decrease in antipropaganda education.

4. **From an informative to a critical press.** The final change is a second fundamental transformation of the American press. It is the product of two related trends.

    a. **The rise of television news.** Since the mid-1960s, television has been rated as the principal source of news and information by more Americans than any other medium. Yet television news, because of its transience, visual impact, and inherent superficiality, is easily manipulated by propagandists.

    b. **Changing journalistic values.** Beginning with coverage of the Vietnam conflict, American journalists have gradually elevated the "watchdog" role of the press to a position of primacy. In this view, the role of the journalist is not merely to report the conflict of ideas but also to subject nearly all American policies, leaders, and institutions to systematic criticism. One result is extensive and often highly sympathetic coverage of the complaints of organized interest groups and other social critics. A second is the adoption by reporters of a stance of cultural neutrality in which the claims of hostile foreign governments are given the same status and credibility as those of American leaders. This practice, which began with reports from Hanoi during the Vietnam conflict, reached full fruition in many of the stories filed from Baghdad during the 1991 Iraq war. Both

results offer greatly expanded opportunities for domestic and foreign propagandists to relay their messages to the American public through the American news media.

Contemporary Perspective

I. **Recognizing propaganda in contemporary society.** Propaganda has always been a common feature in democratic societies. In the United States, a number of changes over the past two hundred years, especially changes in the structure and governing ideals of American journalism, have tended to favor increases in both the incidence and probable effectiveness of propaganda. Arguably, this process has accelerated since 1965. Thus American citizens must either learn to defend themselves against propaganda or accept being manipulated by others. The first line of defense is recognition of the major potential sources of propaganda in contemporary society, especially those that are seldom identified as such.

A. **Constraints on the effectiveness of propaganda.** Because it is based on defective proof, propaganda cannot survive critical analysis. It is also limited by the enforcement of significant penalties for its use. This suggests three major constraints on propaganda.

    1. **Awareness of persuasive intent.** Propaganda is less likely to be effective when it is directed to a skeptical audience. Audiences are most skeptical when they recognize that a message is intended to change their beliefs and behaviors, as in advertising and political appeals. Conversely, propaganda is more likely to be effective when it is perceived as simple information, education or entertainment.

    2. **Public scrutiny.** Propaganda is less likely to be effective when it is subjected to critical scrutiny in the same medium or forum in which it was disseminated. This occurs, for example, when the claims of politicians are challenged by their opponents or when journalists fulfill their watchdog role. Conversely, propaganda is more likely to be effective when it is relayed to an audience without comment or criticism, or when it is challenged only in a different medium or forum.

    3. **Accountability.** Propaganda is less likely to occur when communicators can be held responsible for the veracity of their claims. In contemporary

American society, for example, politicians and government officials are accountable to the electorate, and much commercial speech, including advertising, is subject to government regulation and judicial review. Conversely, propaganda is more likely to occur when the propagandist can operate with impunity.

B. **Well-constrained sources of propaganda.** In contemporary American society, the groups most commonly depicted as sources of propaganda are politicians, government agencies and officials, advertisers, businessmen and commercial corporations. But it is precisely these groups that are most often subjected to all three of the constraints enumerated above. As a result, both the incidence and effectiveness of propaganda from these groups are relatively low.

C. **Poorly constrained sources of propaganda.** The most important **potential** sources of propaganda in contemporary society are those which often engage in persuasive activity but are free of one or more of the three constraints listed above. There are at least five such sources.

1. **Nondemocratic societies.** Leaders and spokesmen of nondemocratic (especially Marxist) societies frequently make claims which are, by Western standards of rationality, clearly propagandistic. These claims can be made with impunity because their authors are not fully accountable to any free electorate. More important, they often gain credibility and effectiveness because of the way they are reported by the American news media. In a conflict between the United States and a nondemocratic nation, the claims of American spokesmen and leaders are (quite rightly) subjected to careful public scrutiny by journalists and others. The authors of these statements are also, of course, fully accountable to the American electorate and other democratic institutions such as Congress and the courts. In contrast, the claims of the opposing nation, even when blatantly mendacious, are typically relayed to the American public without journalistic comment or criticism as merely the "other side" of the controversy. At best, the claims of **both** sides are characterized as "public relations" or "propaganda." A product of the new journalistic value of cultural neutrality, these practices reached full fruition in the 1991 Gulf war, when all major American news media insisted on their right to report from within Iraq and several (including ABC, CBS, NBC, and, especially, CNN) explicitly equated American and Iraqi "propaganda."

2. **Interest groups.** Organized interest groups are among the most active participants in the contemporary conflict of ideas. Often characterized by passionate conviction, narrow and inflexible goals, and a reliance on tendentious amateur research, they are also a major potential source of propaganda. In some cases, this potential is greatly enhanced by the lack of effective constraints. For example, the efforts of groups which claim to serve altruistic or consensual goals such as aiding the disabled or improving the environment are often seen (and portrayed) as informative or educational rather than persuasive. These goals also make it difficult for any public figure to subject their messages to rigorous critical scrutiny. Similarly, the claims of many progressive and reformist groups are exempted from serious journalistic scrutiny, not only because their goals and values coincide with those of elite journalists but also because these groups assist the critical function of the press by providing dramatic (albeit often inaccurate or exaggerated) evidence of social problems and failures. Finally, it should be noted that interest groups are seldom accountable to anyone but their sponsors.

3. **Journalists.** Since the late 1970s, a large number of scholarly and popular studies have documented serious distortions and inaccuracies in national media (especially network television) coverage of a wide range of issues. Put bluntly, a substantial amount of coverage, including many investigative reports on complex or technical issues, could be characterized as propagandistic. Further, of all the potential sources of propaganda, journalists face the fewest effective constraints. The only group in society with direct and continuous access to the public, they have ample opportunity to portray their reporting as scrupulously fair and objective. In addition, critical scrutiny of the press is limited because journalists seldom allow trenchant critics access to the major media to air their complaints. Finally, the press is explicitly and uniquely shielded from outside control, and therefore from most forms of accountability. The press is accountable to the public in theory, but it is not at all clear how an aroused public might be able to call journalists to account.

4. **Educators**. In the traditional view, education and propaganda are depicted as polar opposites. In recent years, however, this distinction has been blurred, in part because of the use of education as an instrument of social reform but also because of the open and explicit politicization of some areas of the curriculum (especially the humanities and social sciences) by a small but active minority of faculty and administrators. The latter trend has stimulated widespread criticism since the late 1980s, much of it focused on perceived efforts to impose "politically correct" thinking in the classroom, and there are growing efforts to hold educators accountable for their discharge of the public trust. For the foreseeable future, however, education in the more readily politicized subjects should be seen as potentially propagandistic.

5. **Popular entertainment**. The propaganda potential of the entertainment media has been recognized since antiquity. This potential derives in large part from the audience's "willing suspension of disbelief" when attending to fictional material and is enhanced by failure to recognize its persuasive intent.

   a. **Television entertainment as persuasion**. In contemporary American society, the conscious use of popular entertainment for persuasive purposes, especially social criticism and reform, is widespread. For example, in a 1983 survey of 104 leading television writers, producers, and executives conducted by Linda Lichter, Robert Lichter, and Stanley Rothman, 66% of the respondents agreed that "TV should promote social reform." This view is clearly evident in television programming from *Sesame Street* to *Roseanne*, which is carefully crafted to challenge or negate pernicious "stereotypes" and frequently offers analyses of social problems and preferred solutions as well as instruction on the nature of enlightened attitudes and behaviors.

   b. **Elements of propaganda in films**. Similarly, numerous recent films have been designed to promote a specific (usually progressive) political viewpoint. Some, especially historical films, combine tendentiousness with falsification or distortion of key elements of the historical record.

   (1) *Born on the Fourth of July*. Several of the most important and dramatic scenes in Ron Kovic's biography *Born on the Fourth of July*, including his wounding in a Rambo-like exchange with the enemy, his failed speech at a Fourth of July celebration, his pilgrimage to Georgia to visit the family of soldier he had accidently killed, and his beating by police at a peaceful antiwar rally at Syracuse University, are neither mentioned in the book on which the film was based nor supported by the factual record. In the real world, Kovic was wounded while trying to rescue another Marine, never visited the family in Georgia, (and probably did not kill a comrade), never spoke at a Fourth of July celebration, and never attended the antiwar rally at Syracuse University (all of which began and ended peacefully, with no intervention by the police).

   (2) *Guilty by Suspicion*. Similarly, *Guilty by Suspicion*, tells the story of the fictitious David Merrill, a talented film maker whose career is destroyed during the anticommunist witch hunts of the McCarthy era solely because of his few casual contacts with communist front groups a decade earlier. In the film's climax, he wins a moral victory through his defiant testimony before the House Un-American Activities Committee (HUAC). In fact HUAC only subpoenaed witnesses from the film industry who had been identified as past or present **members** of the Communist party by two or more sources. It is doubtful that any of the 212 individuals on the notorious Hollywood "blacklist" could match the Merrill character's political innocence.

   (3) *Dances with Wolves*. Another example, the critically acclaimed *Dances with Wolves*, offers caricatures of godlike Sioux Indians and unrelievedly evil whites so gross that they recall the depictions of Aryans and Jews in Nazi propaganda of the 1930s.

II. **Defending against Propaganda**. In general, the best defense against propaganda is recognition of its existence by the individual citizen. The following suggestions will help to achieve this goal.

A. **Reasonable skepticism**. All messages should be treated as potentially propagandistic and examined with an attitude of reasoned skepticism. This is especially important in areas such as news, education, and entertainment where the persuasive intent of the message may not be immediately evident.

B. **Multiple sources**. The best way to identify propagandistic claims is to reproduce the conflict of ideas by monitoring a range of information sources from across the political spectrum. As a general rule in choosing these sources, print media are superior to broadcast media because they allow a more efficient use of time, provide a permanent record for study, and usually offer more complete, detailed, and rational coverage.

C. **Keeping score**. It is often difficult at the time a controversy occurs to determine with certainty which claims are true, especially when they involve predictions about the future. It is therefore crucial to monitor events after the controversy has been resolved or forgotten to see which views were accurate and which were not. In future controversies, claims from those organizations and individuals who have established a record of inaccuracy should be treated with special skepticism. Note that the press generally does **not** perform this function; some sources who have been consistently wrong in their assertions and predictions continue to be quoted as experts in the news media.

D. **Quantified research.** As noted above, current public policy debates often involve the use of quantified information that is either inherently flawed or erroneously interpreted. The only reliable way to avoid being misled by such data is to acquire a thorough knowledge of quantitative research methods, including the basics of statistical analysis. Failing that, the following general suggestions will be helpful in avoiding some of the most common errors.

1. **Credibility of the source**. Research reported in the news media comes from a wide range of sources. These sources, in turn, vary widely in their competence and integrity. As a general rule, the most reliable research appears in scholarly books and journals which employ a "peer review" process in which the study is evaluated anonymously by recognized experts in the field before being accepted for publication. Research generated by established "think tanks" such as the American Enterprise Institute or the Brookings Institution is also usually of high quality. Government research, including recurrent statistical measures, is generally accurate but sometimes highly politicized. Research from other sources should be treated with extreme caution, especially when the source is an interest group committed to advancing a particular set of interests or policies in a controversial area.

2. **Single studies**. Even the best studies sometimes produce aberrant findings that cannot be replicated in subsequent research. Thus it is unwise to draw firm conclusions from a single study, especially if it is based on a small number of cases or contradicts established wisdom.

3. **The meaning of quantified data**. Any time a message includes quantified information, the receiver should ask two questions. First, what is the meaning of the central term? For example, if a story claims that unemployment has risen to 6.5%, one should ask what exactly is meant by the term "unemployment." Second, how was the specific numerical quantity computed? One should ask, for instance, what method was used to arrive at the figure of "6.5%" unemployment. If the receiver is uncertain of the answer to either of these questions, then the quantified information is essentially ambiguous and of limited use in rational decision-making.

4. **Opinion polls**. Although surveys by reputable pollsters are generally quite accurate, their results are frequently misinterpreted, sometimes by the pollsters themselves. Most problems derive from the quality of the questions and response options provided to respondents.

a. **Good questions**. A good survey question should be simple, clear, precise and neutral (in the sense that it does not encourage the selection of a particular response).

b. **Informing respondents**. Some survey questions provide the respondents with substantial information about the issue being studied. Unfortunately, the responses to these questions are of little value in determining the views of members of the general public, who have not been informed about the issue by a pollster. It is also difficult to provide substantial information about an issue that does not bias responses. As a general rule, the greater the amount of information in a question, the more likely it is to violate all four of the criteria for a good question.

c. **Inferences from survey responses**. In general, respondents will answer **exactly** what they are asked. Even very slight changes in question wording can produce dramatically different responses. Thus it is dangerous to make **any** inferences about other opinions or behaviors from responses to a particular question. In addition, changes in public opinion can be validly demonstrated only when the different samples of respondents are provided with **identical** questions and response options.

d. **Reporting question wording**. Because survey results are so sensitive to the precise nature of the questions and response options provided, reports of survey findings should always include the complete text of the questions asked and the full range of possible responses. Without this information, the results are uninterpretable. (For further discussion about survey research, see the section on public opinion in this Framework).

E. **Critical thinking skills**. In the final analysis, the ability to identify and resist propagandistic appeals depends on the receiver's ability to rationally analyze and evaluate arguments. But these critical thinking skills seldom develop naturally; they must be consciously learned. Unfortunately, few Americans, even college graduates, receive any formal training in this area. For them, a course of self-study using any of the numerous popular books on reasoning, argument, or critical thinking is highly recommended.

8. INFORMAL PROCESSES OF WASHINGTON POLITICS

Congress shall make no law respecting...the right of the people peaceably to assemble, and to petition the government for a redress of grievances.

The First Amendment (1791)

Extend the sphere, and you take in a greater variety of parties and interests; you make it less probable that a majority of the whole will have a common motive to invade the rights of other citizens; or if such a common motive exists, it will be more difficult for all who feel it to discover their own strength, and to act in unison with each other.

James Madison (1787)

In Washington I frequently find myself believing that forty or fifty letters, six visits from professional politicians and lobbyists, and three editorials in Massachusetts newspapers constitute public opinion on a given issue. Yet in truth I rarely know how the great majority of the voters feel, or even how much they know of the issues that seem so burning in Washington.

Senator John F. Kennedy (c. 1958)

Better use has been made of association and this powerful instrument of action has been applied for more varied aims in America than anywhere else in the world.

Alexis de Tocqueville (1835)

The first three words of the Constitution are "We the People." If we were drafting this great document today, and if we were honest with ourselves, the first words would have to be—"We the special interests," or "We the big PAC contributors," or "We the international lobbyists," or "We the image makers, spin doctors, and sound bite specialists," or "We the arrogant White House staffers."

H. Ross Perot (1990)

INTRODUCTION

It is only natural to think of governing and policy making in terms of the formal institutions—the legislature, executive, and courts—designed and constituted to carry out those roles. But policies are made and implemented by **people** who occupy positions in formal institutions, who live in the communities where they make their decisions, and who interact with other people whose jobs involve working with them or for them, observing and studying them, feting them, trying to influence them, reporting on their activities for larger publics, working for common goals from the outside, and socializing with them.

The informal processes and politics that shape the daily lives of formal policy makers can shape their thinking and careers, alter their incentives, and influence their decisions just as much as the formal rules that govern their institutions. A quarter century ago, James Sterling Young's fascinating book,

The Washington Community, 1800-1828, described the society in the nation's capital in its formative years, noting, for example, the importance of boarding houses to social relationships and to political outcomes. While Washington has changed dramatically since the 1820s, the importance of the informal relationships and processes that link lawmakers and executives to other denizens of the capital has, if anything, intensified as government has grown larger and more complex.

The American political system is by definition complex and variegated. In a country as large and diverse as the United States there are countless voices to be heard, opinions to be registered, and interests at stake on a multitude of issues. Our open and fluid political system was designed to allow as many voices as possible to play a role in decision making by offering many ways to shape our formal institutions of governing—from elections to the right of citizens to petition the government for redress of grievances.

From the earliest stages of American democracy, informal mechanisms arose for organizing opinions and reaching and selecting policy makers: very early on, political parties, for example, formed, despite no mention of them in the Constitution. Structured interest groups took much longer to play a role in politics and governing, but even in the nineteenth century, de Tocqueville remarked on the greater importance of groups and informal associations in America's political system compared with those of Europe. And, from the time that Thomas Jefferson chose the Washington boarding house he would reside in as president, lawmakers, executives, and judges have coexisted and interrelated with journalists, financiers, merchants, lobbyists, civil servants, hostesses, and each other in a social atmosphere that has shaped their work.

In the twentieth century, the informal processes of governing, including political parties, interest groups, lobbies, and the press, have been studied by political scientists along with the formal institutions and processes such as Congress, the executive branch and the courts, as almost equally important and consequential elements of the American system. Indeed, one influential analyst some decades ago called the press "the fourth branch of government."

In the 1970s and 1980s, however, the nature of these informal processes changed, as Washington, D.C., the nation's capital, changed. More informal processes, including public relations, campaign consulting, and polling emerged; other institutions, including mass media, lawyers, think tanks, and public interest lobbies, sharply expanded their role, reach, and impact. Campaign technology changed, and campaign finance became a major area of controversy. At the same time, the formal processes of government changed too. Congress democratized and decentralized while expanding its staff, all creating new ways for outside groups, individuals, and other forces to gain access and entree. The courts became more involved as policy makers. The presidency, especially the Executive Office of the President, expanded as well and put more and more emphasis on mobilizing outside groups, using the media and employing other informal ways of influencing political and policy outcomes.

The importance and role of these informal processes have grown even as we have become more concerned about many aspects of them—the corrupting influence of campaign finance and PACs; the corrosive effect of negative advertising and politicians' reliance on polls; the overweening influence of lobbyists on public policy; the power and "slant" of the media; the "inside the Beltway" mentality of insularity in Washington, D.C., insensitive to broader currents of opinion in the country, fortified by all these informal forces.

Some of these criticisms of informal groups and processes are more on target and more justified than others; regardless, their impact on government and policy is significant for citizens across the nation. Citizens should be aware of these processes; a heightened awareness can contribute to greater participation, greater understanding of how and why our government operates the way it does, and greater appreciation of when and where reform is necessary (and where it might be counterproductive). All this ultimately can further the course of democracy in the country.

OBJECTIVES

The citizen should be able to

1. explain the importance of the informal processes of Washington politics in terms of their influence on the formal institutions of government.

2. identify those individuals and/or groups that play a significant role in the informal processes and explain how those players are able to influence politics and policy.

3. explain alternative means of participation in government, both direct and indirect, by which citizens can express their own opinions and advance their own interests.

4. explain the various ways in which groups and individuals active in the informal processes shape and influence federal policy.

5. explain the close ties which exist between the informal and the formal processes of government and evaluate these connections.

6. take, evaluate, and defend positions on the conflicts, that sometimes arise regarding informal processes of government, and on the arguments for and against reform efforts designed to "clean them up."

7. explain and evaluate the position that there is still a role for each citizen to play in the great debates on policy making, whether individually or through group association, despite the power and influence which the informal processes may wield over policy making.

FRAME OF REFERENCE
Conceptual Perspective

I. **A general description of the informal processes of Washington politics**. Theoretically, in a democracy every citizen can potentially influence the federal government, through direct participation, representation, or group affiliation. However, as our system has evolved, inevitably there have emerged some individuals who are able to exert greater influence than others. Those individuals with the greatest influence often play a pivotal role in the "informal processes" of Washington politics, often from more than one vantage point.

A. **Informal processes as affecting federal policy**. The individuals and organizations involved in the informal processes contribute to all stages of the policy-making process, from agenda setting to policy formulation to implementation. Their impact can be direct or indirect, short-term or long-term.

B. **Balancing competing demands as one of the critical functions of government**. As most important issues involve many competing and overlapping interests, the informal processes represent a means by which these competing interests are organized and expressed. The Framers expected these interests—called "factions" by Madison in *The Federalist* No. 10—to be actively pursuing their own narrow interests, while checking and balancing their counterparts, so that no individual or narrow faction would hold sway over the formal decision makers. Although the process does not always work as planned, ultimately decisions are, in fact, made and compromises reached, based in large part on the impact which the informal processes have on the formal processes of government.

C. **Most informal processes as taking place in Washington, D.C.** Politicians and policy makers live in Washington although, of course, members of Congress also have homes in their home districts.

1. **The significance of informal processes**. The people and organizations they interact with in the nation's capital, both in their workday lives and socially in the evenings and weekends, help shape their views and their actions. Most policy makers read the same newspapers and watch the same local and national television shows. Thus, what happens in Washington, outside the formal decision-making governmental institutions, may be key to their perceptions and behavior. Many average citizens are unaware of the presence of such influences, let alone the very real influence they have on politics and policy.

2. **Implications of informal power for representative democracy**. Those who are part of the informal processes do not represent a cross-section of America, yet they influence policy which affects the entire nation. This fact may have significant implications for our system of representative democracy. Some aspects of these informal processes have received a great deal of attention, including campaign finance (especially political action committees, or PACs) and lobbying (for example, the "Keating Five" of 1990-1991 in the Senate). They raise questions for citizens about where the legitimate links between constituents and representatives end and more pernicious or questionable ties begin—and raise additional questions about what, if anything, should be done about it.

II. **What the informal processes of Washington politics consist of**. There are various informal processes at work in Washington. They have an impact on politics and policy by affecting such areas as the campaign and election process, the legislative process, policy initiatives, congressional-executive relations, and judicial decision making. They can help to set the policy agenda—i.e., what items are actually being discussed, considered, and decided upon by the government; they can also help determine which items on the agenda are at the top of it. And they can shape the interpretation of outcomes: why one side won or lost; who the heroes and villains are; what the consequences might be. That interpretation can, in turn, shape behavior and outcomes in the future.

If, for example, the "conventional wisdom" emerges that the president "lost" the year's budget battle, his ability to exert policy leverage in the next policy fight might be lessened, as lawmakers become more resistant to his appeals for votes. On the other hand, if the conventional wisdom develops that the president wins **all** the close battles, he has more ability to sway the marginal votes in Congress the next time. Other careers can be advanced or hindered as the press, pundits, consultants, and politicians develop their own sense of who is up and who is down. H. Ross Perot was underscoring—and deploring—this process when he charged that "We the People" has been transformed into "We the image makers, spin doctors, and soundbite specialists." Recognizing this phenomenon, *Newsweek* magazine created its weekly "Conventional Wisdom Watch." *Newsweek*'s intent was in part to lampoon this process, believing that the conventional wisdom is often wrong. Right or wrong—and rightly or wrongly—it still has an impact on events, the agenda, and political power.

There are many different types of institutions, groups, and individuals involved in the informal processes in Washington. Some represent a specific interest or collection of interests; others represent (or claim to represent) the public interest; some are ideological while others have no strong policy point of view. Some exist to influence government directly; others, to influence it indirectly, by shaping or mobilizing public opinion. Others are in business to analyze and interpret what government does; yet others, to influence political races and campaigns.

A. **Interest groups and lobbyists**. These groups and individuals play a key role in the informal processes of Washington politics. Americans belong, through shared characteristics or individual choice, to countless groupings, many of which have no particular direct interest in what goes on in Washington. But thousands of groups do. They will pursue their interests in the nation's capital by participating in umbrella organizations, trade groups, coalitions, through individual Washington offices, or by hiring experts who lobby—i.e., make their point of view known to policy makers—on their behalf. Many of those experts are former members of Congress or former high executive branch officials. There is no formal count of lobbyists in Washington; an informed guess would be that there are upwards of 30,000 people in Washington whose jobs revolve around tracking and influencing public policy decisions.

1. **Varieties of lobbying groups**. The countless numbers of lobbying groups in Washington represent a multitude of interests including business, labor, professional associations, consumer interests, and the environment, to name just a few. There are single-interest groups, which focus on narrower, more specific interests, like abortion or gun control. There are also beneficiary groups, which are interested in protecting some benefit or form of support which they receive from the government, for example, the National Committee to Preserve Social Security and Medicare.

2. **Why groups wish to lobby**. Generally those groups whose existence is most directly connected to or dependent on government action have the most active lobbies in Washington. When federal legislation is likely to have a significant effect on some group, profession, or organization, it is safe to assume that they will make their voice heard. They will do all they can to either bring about some government action which they feel is beneficial or put a stop to some action which they feel is harmful. While intensity of feeling and the number of voters a group represents are important factors in the group's clout, its access to important decision makers—through friendships, expertise, political savvy, or campaign contributions—is critical.

3. **What lobbyists do**. What is it that these lobbying groups do to influence government? That depends, of course, on each group's particular interests and goals, but for the most part they attempt to establish and cultivate contacts within the decision-making bodies of government. They try to influence and even pressure legislators into making decisions which are in the group's best interests. They may collect data and marshall substantive arguments, presenting them to individual lawmakers or in testimony before congressional committees.

a. **The role of expertise, public relations, and membership involvement**. Expertise and credibility are important factors in a group's success. Interests may mobilize support from their group members and supporters, a tactic that is particularly potent if a group has large numbers of members spread across many congressional districts and states, and if the members are knowledgeable and passionate about the group's issues and positions. These factors have made the National Rifle Association (NRA) and the

American Association of Retired Persons (AARP) especially effective. And interests often try to use public relations to get broader public attention for their causes. Frequently it is lobbyists who bring constituents into the process by making individuals aware that some government action is going to have an impact on their lives.

b. **How an interest group reversed a Congressional act.** When the Catastrophic Health Insurance Act was enacted in 1987, the National Committee to Preserve Social Security and Medicare sent reams of letters and telegrams to elderly citizens, designed to alarm and jolt them, warning them that the law would add greatly to their taxes without providing them with any real additional benefits. They generated a huge response, with tens of thousands of the elderly writing their members of Congress and senators and appearing at town meetings to urge the law's repeal. Although the senior lawmakers who crafted the plan complained bitterly that the Committee had grossly distorted its effects, and the Bush Administration supported the law, Congress responded to the grass roots activity by reversing itself and repealing the law the next year.

c. **The role of money.** Oftentimes group pressure involves money, particularly in the form of campaign contributions, and especially through the organized contributions of political action committees, or PACs. This explains in part why traditionally lobbyists, especially Washington lobbyists, have had a somewhat negative image. Many people assume that there are conflicts of interest which pervade the system, that access is limited to those who have the money to buy it, and that often the public interest gets lost in the shuffle. And, of course, even if nearly all lobbying, and most relationships between lobbyists and lawmakers are legitimate and encouraged in our system of government, there continue to be those individuals, like savings and loan magnate Charles Keating, who use their political connections and money for their own personal benefit, adding to public disillusionment and skepticism.

d. **Lobbying through many channels.** Interests are not all simply represented by one individual, or one Washington office. Many groups will use multiple channels to advance their interests. For example, a large corporation may belong to general business organizations like the U.S. Chamber of Commerce and the Business Roundtable. A number of trade associations, like the American Petroleum Institute, the National Auto Dealers Association, or the Motion Picture Association of America maintain their own large Washington offices; hire groups that specialize in lobbying Congress or the White House, like Timmons and Company or Black, Manafort and Stone; hire "superlawyers" with influence in Washington from their service and experience in government and politics, William Coleman (former Secretary of Transportation,) or Stuart Eizenstat (former White House domestic policy advisor); and hire public relations firms, like Hill & Knowlton or Ogilvie and Mather, to get their messages across through television interviews, advertising campaigns, "op/ed" articles in newspapers, or other "p.r." techniques.

e. **The role of technology.** New technologies have been applied to group activities and pressure as well. The U.S. Chamber of Commerce and the labor movement have used television satellite "uplinks" or teleconferencing, tying live audiences in many cities together via television, to develop joint strategies for lobbying or campaign giving, or to mobilize grass roots support for an issue position. Many groups have used sophisticated computerized targeted direct mail techniques to raise money or to generate letters and phone calls to the Capitol.

f. **How lobbying has changed since the 1970s.** Both the number of lobbying groups in Washington and the way they operate has changed significantly in the past decade. The number of registered lobbyists more than doubled in the 1980s, due in part to the changes which have taken place in Congress over the last fifteen years or so. As the Congress has become more decentralized, with more committees handling more issues, more individual members having influence over policy areas, and more staff bringing greater expertise, more points of access have opened up to Congress—and groups have eagerly taken advantage. At the same time, and in part because more groups and more lawmakers have become active, legislative issues have become more varied and complex, and passage of legislation has become more difficult and problematic.

g. **Evaluating changes: more democracy or more special interests?** As the system has become more open and the issues more diverse, we have seen a greater emphasis on grass roots movements and constituent participation and awareness. Some have suggested that the process has become more democratic—more lobbyists means more groups, and thus more Americans, are seeing their interests represented in Washington and more checks and balances operate against any interest group or set of groups having too much clout. But others say that more groups and more lobbyists means, not checks and balances, but simply more special interests blocking the public interest—and, in any event, that money still talks and dominates the influence process in Washington, shutting out any role for the have-nots.

B. **Political consulting firms, public relations firms, and polling organizations.** These organizations have become important components of the informal processes of Washington politics. These groups sell their ability to maintain a finger on the public pulse, and they help politicians and candidates alike to shape their messages and their images in order to gain and maintain public support—and to gain and maintain public office.

1. **What political consultants do.** Consultants help politicians perceive trends in public opinion. They help them map out electoral, legislative, and leadership strategies. In essence they provide office holders and potential office holders with vital information, and they instruct them on how to use that information to enhance their public image or to govern effectively. Many of the most prominent consulting firms in Washington are associated with one of the two major political parties. They are often involved in developing party strategy. Some are associated with specific ideological movements within a party.

2. **The ubiquity of political consultants.** These consultants are employed by the administration, members of Congress, and state-level officials. Political consulting has become an extremely lucrative business, and as such there has been a substantial increase in the number of consultants, especially those located in Washington. Many of them are marketing their services abroad, in Western and Eastern Europe and in Latin America. Today almost all prominent politicians rely on the services of some type of consulting firm, including firms which do polling, media consulting, or both. These firms have a myriad of new technologies at their disposal which have enhanced their ability to reach voters, gauge public opinion, and "spruce up" a politician's image. Through the use of new media technologies, a politician's message can be both shaped to fit shifts in public opinion and targeted to reach a specific audience.

3. **The effects on politics of technology and consultants.** With regard to campaign politics, some contend that the new media technologies have shifted power away from the free media to candidate-centered media groups, thus creating more manipulation of political messages and campaigns. Furthermore, with satellite technology so readily available, candidates can create and control coverage of their own campaigns, diluting the influence of the mass media as a more objective recorder of campaign developments and messages. Many fear that the rise of political consulting has introduced a certain shallowness, a shortsightedness to politics. It has made it easier for some people to get elected, but perhaps more difficult for them to govern. And it has increased the focus on negative campaigning and electioneering, also increasing the cynicism voters have towards politics and politicians.

4. **Links between lobbyists and public relations firms.** It should be noted that politicians are not the only members of the Washington community who rely on the services of political consulting firms. For, in this day and age, in order to influence politicians and policy, it is often important first to influence the public. Therefore, we see lobbying groups and public relations firms teaming up and working together to influence the policy making process on behalf of their various clients and their respective interests. For example, some firms have a lobbying component and a campaign consulting compo-

nent; some of its members will advise candidates for office and even run their campaigns—then turn around and lobby them on behalf of their other clients. This practice has raised troubling questions about conflicts of interest (the lobbyists, after all, know the most intimate campaign secrets of the lawmakers they lobby). But there are no formal rules or laws to regulate these practices. The firm Black, Manafort and Stone was purchased by the giant international public relations firm Burson-Marstellar, continuing a trend in which public relations, advertising, and lobbying are becoming joined together as components of a broader strategy by groups to influence public policy.

5. **Links between lobbying and public relations firms**. Most of the groups which hire public relations and lobbying firms to shape policy outcomes are business corporations or trade associations. But not all are: in recent years the Roman Catholic Church hired one of the largest of such firms, which includes a prominent lobbying component, to manage a nationwide campaign to promote its pro-life and anti-abortion position. In addition, many foreign countries, political movements, or commercial interests also make use of these firms to get their messages across. Jonas Savimbi's Unita Movement in Angola, for example, hired a lobbying firm when Savimbi came to Washington to seek American support. The firm claimed that it was instrumental in securing an interview with Savimbi on *Sixty Minutes*, an invaluable showcase for his point of view, as well as meetings with prominent politicians, academics, and journalists.

C. **The media** are a central part of the informal processes of Washington politics. While the journalistic community likes to believe that it is merely an observer and recorder of events, there is no question that the Washington press corps is also an important **player** in the process of policy and public debate. The Washington press corps is unique within the more general category of the media. Many Washington journalists—particularly those who are columnists or commentators on television "talk shows"—have come from jobs in government and politics or are connected somehow with political causes. This explains, in part, why the objectivity of the Washington press is sometimes called into question.

1. **The rise of celebrity journalists**. With the expansion of public affairs television, including C-SPAN

and CNN, a number of journalists have become celebrities in their own right, reaching larger audiences more regularly than would have been the case with reporters or columnists in the past. As part of a larger "pundit class" that includes "think tank" and university experts, political consultants and pollsters, they interact daily with politicians and other government officials, sometimes advising them and then writing about or commenting on their performance, often moving between the reporting pages and the opinion pages of a newspaper. While respected journalists like David Broder can maintain the balance between objective reporting and expressing personal opinions, the line is not so clear for others, often leading to uneasy ethical questions for the press.

2. **The relationship between the media and government**. In a more general way, a symbiotic relationship exists between the press and the government in Washington. Washington media outlets often serve as messengers and/or "voice boxes" for governmental institutions. For many journalists their most valuable sources come from within the government. And for many government officials, using the media is often the most effective means of gaining support for their positions or initiating dialogue on some policy or issue. Much of what is said by prominent Washington journalists in their newspaper columns, weekly journals, and television news shows is closely followed by Washington decision makers. A poll taken of senior Congressional staffers by Fleishman-Hillard found, for example, that 92% read *The Washington Post* daily. This and other prominent media outlets not only provide a forum for current news makers, but the opinions of the media journalists themselves have become increasingly important and influential.

3. **The media, the electoral process, and office holders**. In addition to their role in policy debate, Washington journalists have become an integral part of campaign and electoral politics. The media now act as middle men between candidates and the electorate. They play a role in defining campaign issues and in evaluating candidates' positions and past performances. More and more, they are actively stepping in to criticize negative campaign commercials or define which campaign charges are "true" or "false." Prominent journalists in Washington

interact daily, often on intimate terms, with the policy-makers they cover. They are neighbors, friends and often confidants. Back in the early 1960s, *Newsweek* editor Ben Bradlee, who had been John F. Kennedy's next door neighbor, met with him regularly to discuss presidential decisions and even to offer advice, pledging to keep his role as presidential confidant separate from his role as journalist. This distinction, though, is hard to make; in Washington these kinds of relationships are tested daily, and the dilemmas they create are confronted.

D. **"Think tanks."** Research organizations ("think tanks") also play a significant role in the informal processes of Washington politics. Ronald Reagan's election in 1980 underscored the importance ideas could play in moving politics and policy; many of the ideas he stressed during his campaign for the presidency and in his first months in office, from deregulation to supply-side economic policy to his approaches to arms control, had been developed and honed in think tanks like the American Enterprise Institute (AEI) and the Hoover Institution at Stanford University. Many of the key people who occupied policy posts in his Administration came from these and other think tanks (just as many of the key players in the Carter Administration had come from the Brookings Institution and yet other think tanks.) Most of these organizations are devoted to public policy research. They serve as a home base for many scholars and experts engaged in various fields of research.

1. **The influence of "think tanks."** Unlike some of the other groups we have looked at, which clearly have specific interests and actively pursue policy initiatives, the work which takes place in think tanks has a more subtle influence. It is not always easy to identify a cause-and-effect process at work between scholarly output and legislative change. Nonetheless, the influence and impact of these research institutions, in the promulgation and advancement of ideas and in the impact of their various scholars and fellows, is clearly considerable. In addition, these scholars are responsible for a good deal of the literature which affects public and governmental debate. The ideas generated from their research and studies are sometimes catalysts for entire ideological movements which in turn affect policy and politics. And their links to the broader academic community, combined with their access to the policy community, enable them to translate the ideas of other academics from jargon into more easily understood language for the lay audience of policy makers. In the past we have seen shifts within political parties and new initiatives within presidential administrations which can be traced, directly or indirectly, to the work of individuals within these institutions.

2. **The political range of think tanks and their members.** These research organizations run the ideological spectrum. Some are clearly right of center, such as the Heritage Foundation and the Cato Institute; others pursue a left of center agenda, like the Institute for Policy Studies. Yet others are somewhere in between. Some institutions, like Brookings, the American Enterprise Institute, and the Urban Institute, have a great deal of variation in the viewpoints represented by their fellows. The scholars who inhabit these think tanks come from various backgrounds. Many have served official and unofficial roles in government. Many come from the world of academia. All have made their mark somehow in their fields of expertise. Aside from pursuing their own research projects, these scholars often engage in public speaking, testify before Congress, and informally advise and consult with members of Congress and the administration.

3. **The relationship between the media and think tank scholars.** Journalists often rely on these individuals for expert commentary and analysis. In addition, many write newspaper columns of their own, contribute Op-Ed pieces to widely read newspapers, and appear on television news and political talk shows. These are all ways in which members of thinks tanks contribute to and inform the public debate. Their presence in Washington is a major advantage for think tank scholars, giving them access to the media and to decision-makers that other scholars do not have; the resulting visibility adds to their access and credibility. In addition, think tank scholars put an emphasis on communicating their research findings to broader audiences, not just writing specialized papers for the academic community. When television networks mobilized in the immediate aftermath of the Gulf War, they all turned to a variety of "experts" on the Middle East, geopolitics, military affairs and weaponry, energy policy, and Islam for on-air analysis. Many, if not most, of these experts came from Washington think tanks like the Center for Strategic and International Studies (CSIS,) Brookings, AEI, and Heritage.

E. **Academics.** Academics in universities also take part in the informal processes of Washington politics. They are active in many areas of public policy, including economics, defense, foreign policy, law, health, welfare, and the environment. They frame debates; supply important information, research and statistics; and oftentimes provide rationales for and give legitimacy to new policy ideas and initiatives.

1. **The role of academics.** Academics have acted as advisors to the president or to cabinet members; they have consulted for federal agencies and worked for or testified before Congress. However, it must be noted that, in general, they are much less aggressive than some other participants in the informal processes of Washington politics in their pursuit of power and attempts at influence. But their influence can be significant. Some of the ideas that have been integrated into the policy debate on campaign finance, for example, came from academics like Larry Sabato of the University of Virginia and Herb Alexander of the University of Southern California (USC). The major legislation for expanding voter registration was generated by Professor Raymond Wolfinger of the University of California at Berkeley. Many elements of "Reaganomics" were promoted by Milton Friedman of Stanford University and Arthur Laffer of USC.

2. **The impact of academics.** The impact made by academics is often indirect and hard to measure. Sometimes it happens accidentally; other times it may be carefully calculated. Sometimes the students of academics bring their ideas to government or the public when they take jobs in Washington. Academics can have influence without being in Washington all of the time, but they must maintain a presence in order to become part of the policy debate.

3. **Barriers to the influence of academics.** Because they are ostensibly nonpolitical, academics' perspectives often clash with political realities and necessities; as a result, politicians cannot always do what academics may deem to be the right thing. And many academics are accustomed to communicating in jargon-filled prose to their colleagues, often finding it difficult to translate their research and ideas into forms that policy-makers and journalists can understand and use. But those who are able to overcome these difficulties can be central players in the policy arena.

F. **Lawyers.** Attorneys are a prominent feature of Washington life. There are more than 30,000 registered with the D.C. Bar in the nation's capital, a much higher per capita ratio than anywhere else in the world. Many of the lawyers in Washington actually work for the federal government, in the Justice Department, the Federal Trade Commission, on congressional staffs, or in other agencies or bureaus. Many, of course, practice law of the variety practiced anywhere else in America—divorces, civil suits, criminal actions, etc. But most of the law practiced in Washington is related in one way or another to the federal government. Much is practiced in front of regulatory bodies, like the Federal Communications Commission or the Food and Drug Administration, or by involvement in actions taken by federal agencies like the Department of Energy or the Department of Transportation.

1. **The role of Washington lawyers.** Clients may also use their lawyers to help them gain federal contracts, to prepare them to testify in front of Congress, or to pursue other agendas. For example, Robert Strauss was hired by MCA and Matsushita when the latter wanted to buy the former, to defuse congressional and administration opposition to the Japanese takeover of a prominent American entertainment firm. Congress or the executive may itself employ lawyers as special counsels or independent prosecutors. Brendan Sullivan became famous as the lawyer for Col. Oliver North when he testified in front of the Iran/Contra Committee. (Sullivan defended his active role by saying "I am not a potted plant.") Robert Bennett served as the special counsel to the Senate Ethics Committee investigating the Keating Five—even as other prominent Washington lawyers like James Hamilton (who had years earlier worked with the Watergate Committee) represented the five senators accused of impropriety.

2. **The revolving door between public office and private practice.** Prominent Washington lawyers like Lloyd Cutler, Joseph Califano, Elliot Richardson, and Clark Clifford have periodically left their law practices to serve in high positions in government—Cutler as Counsel to President Jimmy Carter; Califano as Secretary of Health, Education and Welfare under Carter; Richardson in several prominent Cabinet posts under presidents Nixon and Ford; Clifford as Secretary of Defense under Lyndon Johnson. Other top lawmakers and cabinet officers leave office and

join or create prominent Washington law firms. The "elder statesmen" of Washington—those named above, along with people like William Coleman, Sol Linowitz and Edmund Muskie—are nearly all using law practices as their vantage points to continue to have an impact on policy. Some are consulted informally by presidents or congressional leaders when crises arise; for example, President Reagan called Bob Strauss in for an informal chat to ask for advice during the Iran/Contra scandal. While Strauss is a prominent Democrat, Reagan valued him as an astute and honest observer of Washington politics and national affairs.

3. **Lawyers and lobbying.** Many lawyers find that practicing law in the nation's capital requires lobbying of Congress and the executive. Some law firms specialize in lobbying; others have created separate lobbying subsidiaries. Whether lawyering or lobbying, access to prominent public officials and intimate knowledge of the ins and outs of the policy process are required tools for much of the practice of law in Washington.

G. **Diplomats.** Ambassadors and other diplomats and foreign representatives can also be key figures in Washington politics and policy. The openness and permeability of Washington institutions, public and private, enable clever and resourceful foreign figures to be major spokesmen and players in governmental processes and in shaping public opinion.

1. **Using social skills and graces.** Some ambassadors develop stature and key contacts through their social skills. Former Ambassador Alejandro Orfila of Argentina and later the Organization of American States, and former Ambassador Ardeshir Zahedi of Iran developed reputations as lavish party givers, which disguised their skill at advancing the interests of their countries. Recently retired Ambassador Willem Wachmeister of Sweden used his skill as a top tennis player to cement contacts with top officials who also play tennis, like Senator Lloyd Bentsen of Texas, and President Bush.

2. **Working behind the scenes.** Other ambassadors work quietly behind the scenes, building contacts with top government officials and with the press, think tanks, and other denizens of the informal processes. For several years, Ambassador Tommy Koh of Singapore was one of the most effective players in Washington, despite the small size of

his country and his diplomatic staff. Prince Bandar of Saudi Arabia also used his personal stature, political savvy, and understanding of American politics to help assure congressional approval of arms sales to Saudi Arabia. Bandar also helped his cause by hiring Fred Dutton, another of the ubiquitous "Washington lawyers" and a former Kennedy Administration official, to help lobby Congress.

3. **Emerging as public figures.** Still other ambassadors become major public figures, increasing the publicity, and sometimes stature of their countries in the process. Alan Gottlieb of Canada was one such, whose visibility reminded Washingtonians of Canada's status as our largest trading partner and closest ally. This can be a dangerous strategy, however, if controversy emerges, as it did when Gottlieb's high profile wife, who wrote a column lampooning diplomacy in the *Washington Post*, slapped her social secretary at an embassy party, and when he hired former Reagan White House official Michael Deaver to exert influence on the Administration over the acid rain issue. Gottlieb's successor, Derek Burney, is in the Tommy Koh mold, and has proven to be especially effective.

4. **Starring as media figures.** Ambassadors can occasionally move well beyond their roles as diplomats and emissaries for their countries, and become major media figures—through events, and by virtue of the expansion of television as the universal medium of communication. When the Persian Gulf crisis broke, Iraq's Ambassador El-Mashat became an ever-present figure on American television, visiting Nightline, The MacNeil/Lehrer Newshour, the Today Show, Good Morning America, Face the Nation, Meet the Press, CNN, and every other major and minor public affairs show on a regular basis to explain and justify his country's actions. The ambassadors of Kuwait and Saudi Arabia played similar roles.

Historical Perspective

The informal processes of Washington politics have been in existence, in one form or another, since Washington was created out of the Potomac swamp. People have always been interested in the operations of government and the people running it, as government policy directly affects people's lives. Furthermore, since the United States Constitution guarantees citizens the right peaceably to assemble, associate, and petition the government, people have, since this nation was founded, attempted to protect their own individual and group interests. While organized interest groups did not set up shop in Washington in any serious numbers until the twentieth century, individual lobbyists were plying their trade by the early part of the nineteenth century. Of course, at the same time, journalists were covering Washington affairs; ambassadors were trying to influence policy; merchants, farmers, and industrialists were interacting with policy makers; and hostesses were vying to become the social center of the capital. As the nation and the federal government have grown and the world has become a more complicated place, the informal processes of politics have become more complex and more far-reaching in their impact on the formal processes of government.

I. **The Progressive Era and its effect on Washington politics.** In the 1880s and through the turn of the century, reformers began to focus on corruption in politics and the unfettered power of large "special interests" in the nation's economy.

   A. **Progressive reforms.** A number of reforms ensued, including ballot and other electoral reforms, civil service reform, and changes in governmental procedure. Especially under the leadership of activist progressive president Theodore Roosevelt, aggressive efforts to curb the trusts and regulate the economy were put in place, including antitrust laws and a number of federal regulatory agencies.

   B. **Organized special interests as a response to government regulation.** Ironically, this newly activist role for the federal government spurred business and other interests to focus more of their efforts in Washington. The Interstate Commerce Commission, the first independent regulatory commission, was founded in 1885; the National Association of Manufacturers, based in Washington to represent American industry, was founded in 1894. The first major enduring set of federal laws regulating American business, including Theodore Roosevelt's antitrust laws, were enacted in the first decade of the twentieth century; the U.S. Chamber of Commerce was created in 1912, at the behest of Roosevelt's successor, William H. Taft, to form a central organization to represent the position of American business.

II. **The New Deal Era.** Franklin Roosevelt's New Deal set in motion the rise of political liberalism and the creation of the welfare state.

   A. **The growth of government during the New Deal.** The federal government grew prodigiously. Federal programs, intended to help Americans survive difficult financial times and to insure that the U.S. would never again experience such a devastating economic crash, were initiated. The creation and persistence of these programs encouraged the proliferation of special interest groups, which suddenly saw a direct stake in the actions of the federal government (in, for example, Social Security) or in its increased regulatory capacity, over, for example, communications or energy, or in its increased ability to tax income and corporations directly.

   B. **Further growth of government during World War II.** The Second World War added its own layers to the federal government and to its power to regulate the nation's economy. Many of the agencies created to run the war stayed in place after the war's end, including but not limited to the vast new military bureaucracy. Scientists, economists, and other professionals also stayed on in Washington, leaving a much larger federal establishment in place for the Cold War era.

   C. **The expansion of Congress.** The expanded executive branch led to an expanded and professionalized Congress. 1946 and 1947, for example, brought the Employment Act, creating both the President's Council of Economic Advisors and the Congressional Joint Economic Committee; the National Security Act, creating the National Security Council; and the Legislative Reorganization Act, reforming the Congressional committee system, expanding the professional staffs of Congress, and creating a lobbying regulation law. As the federal government's size and reach grew, outside influences on it grew as well.

III. **The Vietnam Era.** The 1960s and 1970s saw an increased emphasis on social awareness; and therefore, new kinds of groups emerged to join the already established labor and business groups. These groups included environmentalists, consumer advocates, women's rights groups, and anti-war protesters, along with governmental reform groups like Common Cause.

   A. **From anti-war activists to public interest lobbies.** In some ways, the mid-1960s to early 1970s paralleled the late 1930s and early 1940s in that the federal government embarked on a multitude of new federally-funded and federally-regulated programs, and governmental reforms. Once again, people saw Washington as the place where all the action was, and individuals and informal groups gravitated there. The anti-Vietnam War movement created a whole group of young people schooled in the techniques of influencing the Congress and the executive; as the war itself waned, many of them simply shifted their expertise to other "public interest" pressure groups, ranging from environmental to anti-defense spending to consumer advocacy.

B. **Organized opposition a response to the success of public interest groups**. The new activists were able to create groups and keep them in place without large sums of money, or huge mass memberships, unlike the major business and labor groups that had dominated the Washington interest-group scene. Reforms that had democratized and decentralized power in Congress, opened up governmental decision-making processes, and added large numbers of staff, gave these groups access to lawmakers with influence that had not been possible in earlier eras. The result, through the early-to-mid-1970s, was a sharp increase in government regulation of business activity, from auto safety to pollution control to advertising. Business eventually reacted to the lobbying that caused this regulation by counter-lobbying—creating a much larger base of trade associations and firms setting up headquarters and offices in Washington itself.

IV. **Post-Watergate reforms and increased access to Congress**. The 1970s were a time of continuing change and reform in Washington.

A. **Reform and media vigilance**. Along with the Vietnam War-era reforms, there were additional significant institutional changes in the Congress and executive in the wake of the Watergate scandal. New campaign and ethics laws opened up the system, while curtailing traditional forms of campaign contributing, and creating and expanding political action committees (PACs) as a major source of campaign money. The increased media scrutiny of Washington politics that followed Watergate, and the enormous success of *Washington Post* reporters Bob Woodward and Carl Bernstein, meant congressmen and executive officials were more accountable to the public for their actions, and the public had greater access to government officials.

B. **The consequences of reform**. Reforms aimed at making Congress a more democratic body resulted in a more decentralized system. Power was spread out as more subcommittees were established and Congressional staff were increased dramatically. As a result there were more points of access for groups interested in influencing the system. Individual members and individual committees and subcommittees had more power and autonomy.

V. **The fragmented system of the 1980s and the growth of lobbying**. The results of all of these charges were seen in the 1980s, where a much more fragmented system was visible, with more and more people attempting to get a piece of the action and lawmakers faced with more and more conflicting pressures and demands.

A. **The new intensity of lobbying**. It seems that today lobbying breeds counter-lobbying, which in turn breeds counter-counter-lobbying. There is no doubt that policy-making action in Washington has become diffused and decentralized, with more players of more and more varieties.

B. **A nineteenth-century comparison**. In the early 1870s, Sam Ward was deemed the "King of the Lobby." Ward believed that the best way to a legislator's heart was through his stomach. He held extravagant dinner parties for congressmen, important members of the administration, and other prominent Washingtonians, serving the finest wines, sumptuous gourmet meals, and witty conversation. These people then did favors for him in return for his hospitality. Ward represented a variety of interests, both domestic and foreign. Ward was one of a kind.

C. **Today's lobbyists**. Today there are hundreds of would-be Sam Wards, trying to reach important policy-makers with social hospitality, political contributions, speech honorariums, weighty arguments, or the power of grass roots support. Those that represent a multitude of interests are joined by the representatives of hundreds or thousands of special interest and single-interest groups. What was an anomaly or anachronism has become a central part of the Washington policy scene.

Contemporary Perspective

When we look at Washington politics today, we see a complex and fragmented system. Legislation has become extremely complicated and detailed, as policy expertise on the part of congressmen and their staff has expanded sharply, in part to combat the expertise and resources available to the executive branch. But one consequence has been increasing difficulty in getting anything passed and enacted into law. The proliferation of interests which brings conflicting demands to bear on legislators and executive officials is both a cause and an effect of the complexity of the issues which face the world today and of the difficulty in getting action.

I. **"Informal" processes as integral parts of the political process**. Some policy struggles involve so many varied interests that it seems virtually impossible to bring about any acceptable compromise. Surely the founders of this nation intended for all people to have a voice and a right to petition the government, but it is unlikely that they ever envisioned a system of informal processes such as we have today—a system which is really an integral part of the political process, not just a detached influence on it. Some might suggest that the multiplicity of groups and interests which play an active role in policy making today are likely to undermine the national interest. There is no doubt that their presence and strength within the system make progress more difficult in areas such as federal budget reform, where there are a great many organized interests competing for limited funds.

II. **The case for today's informal processes: a more open system**. Others would argue that if the Framers did not envision anything like the contemporary Washington scene, they would be quite comfortable with it. Today's fragmented system may actually be more democratic, as it allows for many voices to be heard—for more checks and balances to be employed. When deadlock occurs or seems to occur, it reflects, it may be argued, not simply the clash of irreconcilable interests, but a public that is not ready or willing to take major action to solve a problem on which there is no consensus—it reflects, in other words, an acute sensitivity to the public mood. It may be the case, when it comes to informal influences on policy, that more is better. Not only are there more groups organized to represent their own interests, and the interests of the public, but they are more sophisticated. With the aid of modern technology, their techniques are more finely tuned. For example, public interest groups can now more readily inform the masses about important issues and initiatives by using computerized direct mail operations.

III. **The system today and proposals for reform**. Politicians have also capitalized on the new technologies at their disposal. Candidates and office-holders alike can now monitor voters' opinions on issues by using tracking polls and focus groups; they can then alter their positions accordingly. (For a discussion of polls and focus groups, see the section on Public Opinion above.) Along these same lines political advertising has become closely linked with polling. Using political advertising, candidates can respond to the latest shifts in opinion almost instantaneously.

A. **Proposals to reform campaign finance**. Many citizens and many politicians, of course, deplore ultrasensitivity to public opinion and public whim, and reliance on image makers and "spin doctors" to tailor positions to fit the public mood. And many believe, too, that the real sensitivity lawmakers show these days is to campaign contributors and other monied special interests who have corrupted the political process. They call for sweeping ethics reforms, conflict-of-interest rules and campaign finance reform to short-circuit the corrupting nature of today's informal processes of government. They certainly have a point. Lawmakers and their challengers scramble year-round to raise the huge amounts of money necessary these days to run for or stay in office. The money to do so has come increasingly from organized interests. And the close relationships between lobbyists and lawyers who were recently lawmakers or top government executives (and their staffs) with current lawmakers and regulators raises real questions about the power of the revolving door. (For further discussion on proposals for campaign finance, see the section on Political Parties and Elections, above.)

B. **Doubts about campaign finance reform proposals**. But many of the rules that now govern these relationships were forged by well-meaning reforms implemented to deal with these same problems just a decade or two ago; in some cases, they unintentionally created worse consequences. It is not at all clear that the reforms currently under consideration would reduce or eliminate special interest influence, make the campaign finance system less corrupting or money-oriented, and improve the quality of candidates running for office—or have the opposite effect. Some of the major proposals for campaign finance reform—for example, strict limits on campaign spending—are opposed by most political scientists who have carefully studied the matter as reducing competition in elections and increasing the obsession with money (by reducing supply but not demand).

C. **Term limitations and its limitations as reform**. At the same time, many concerned citizens have proposed limiting the terms of members of Congress to break their links with the informal forces around Washington, making them, these well-intentioned reformers believe, less dependent on special interests because they would not be seduced by Washington and the continuing need to be re-elected.

1. **A Congress without expertise**. But a Congress composed entirely of newer members would

mean a Congress where the expertise about policy, "where the bodies are buried," how to make things happen in committees, in federal agencies, and in all the myriad centers of influence; would be held by others— Congressional staffs, perhaps, along with permanent bureaucrats, lawyers, lobbyists, think tankers, and media people—in other words, just the people this reform is intended to defuse!

2. **Transfer of legislative expertise to lobbyists**. At the same time, by limiting lawmakers to eight or twelve years, a term limit would send more lawmakers every two years out to find jobs. Some would go back to their districts, as many do now. But many would become Washington lawyers, lobbyists, and other players in the informal scene. And many of those, knowing they had only a short time to serve in Congress, would begin immediately currying favor with interests to prepare for their next jobs, thus intensifying the relationships reformers are trying to block. While some change in the informal processes of Washington is clearly necessary, very careful thought is required before leaping to action.

CONCLUSION

There is, finally, a strange irony in today's informal political processes. As recently as three decades ago, only a few dozen interest groups were actually significant players in Washington. But there was still a great deal of pressure on the government from a multiplicity of outside forces. Citizens were more interested and more active in the public debate. This can be illustrated by looking at the civil rights and anti-war movements of the 1960s.

Today we see hundreds of interest groups, armed with organization, money, high technology, and expertise. However, there seems to be much less passion on the part of the citizenry, and in many cases, a real gap between the interests and issue positions of the Washington representatives of the groups, and the interests and drive of their memberships out in the country.

Herein lies the most important reason why citizens should be aware of and develop an understanding of the informal processes of Washington politics. To ensure that their own interests are heard and represented, citizens must be aware of the many ways in which they can become active participants in the political process, ways that are not—and should not be—limited to the informal processes discussed here.

The danger we face is that if the citizenry becomes too apathetic or too dependent on the professionals representing their group interests in Washington, the informal processes will establish a stranglehold on the entire system. If the informal processes become too closely tied with the formal processes of government, there may be no room for average citizens to take part in the great debates of policy making.

Citizens have a responsibility to understand how their system of government works; for they are ultimately responsible for protecting their own interests.

THE ROLE OF THE CITIZEN

American citizens have the right to determine what role, if any, they will play in the political process. In order to make intelligent decisions and as an aid in self-definition citizens should understand the differing traditions regarding the obligations of citizenship, alternative views of the rights and responsibilities of citizens, effective means of citizen participation, and current problems of citizenship.

TOPIC 1. RESPONSIBILITIES OF THE CITIZEN

As citizens of this democracy, you are the rulers and the ruled, the lawgivers and the law-abiding, the beginning and the end.

Adlai Stevenson (c. 1956)

OBJECTIVES

The citizen should be able to

1. analyze and evaluate different conceptions of citizenship.

2. take and defend a position on the responsibilities of citizenship.

3. explain what good government in a constitutional democracy requires of citizens.

FRAME OF REFERENCE
Conceptual Perspective

There are two principal and somewhat conflicting philosophical positions in the American tradition on the meaning of citizenship. They are as follows.

I. **Citizens have obligations (the classical republican tradition).** This view holds that citizenship necessarily implies certain responsibilities or duties to serve the common good. In this view, citizens ought to be motivated by a devotion to civic virtue, which places the common good before private interest. In one of its formulations, the republican view holds that citizenship is an office of government similar to any other office in that it involves certain responsibilities that flow from the nature of the office. In this view, a person fulfills the obligations of citizenship only by accepting the guidelines implicit in that concept of office.

II. **Citizens have rights (the liberal-democratic tradition).** This view holds that the rights of citizenship are important primarily because they enable citizens to protect themselves from the government and to advance individual liberty and interests. It emphasizes that whether or not one assumes some or all of the traditional obligations of citizenship is a matter of choice. Citizens have the right to choose the degree of involvement they wish to have in civic affairs and, therefore, have a right not to be involved at all, to be slightly involved, or to be fully active participants. Although participation is entirely voluntary, it would be imprudent for citizens not to keep watch through some degree of participation over those placed in office to safeguard their rights.

For the Historical and Contemporary Perspectives see Nature of the State and Civic Participation, respectively.

TOPIC 2. THE RIGHTS OF THE CITIZEN

[The people], it is true, have been much less successful than the great. They have seldom found either leisure or opportunity to form a union and exert their strength; ignorant as they were of arts and letters, they have seldom been able to frame and support a regular opposition. This, however, has been known by the great to be the temper of mankind; and they have accordingly labored in all ages to wrest from the populace, as they are contemptuously called, the knowledge of their rights and wrongs and the power to assert the former or redress the latter.

John Adams (1775)

It is essential for citizens to understand the nature of rights in general and their specific rights under the Constitution in order to be able to benefit from their exercise and to resist encroachments. It is also essential for the citizen to understand that there is a mutual relationship between rights and responsibilities, that certain rights give rise to responsibilities.

OBJECTIVES

The citizen should be able to

1. explain the different meanings given to the concept of "rights."

2. explain differences of opinion regarding the existence of certain rights, e.g., economic rights.

3. explain the constitutional rights of the American citizen.

4. take and defend positions on what should be considered the basic rights of citizens.

FRAME OF REFERENCE
Conceptual Perspective

I. **Meaning of "rights."** The phrase the "rights of the citizen" as a number of meanings which the citizen should understand in order to be able to participate in the formulation of public policy on such matters. They are as follows.

A. **Absence of prohibitions.** One meaning of the idea of "rights" is that people have a right to do anything that they are not prohibited from doing by ethical or legal restrictions. In this sense, other people may have no ethical or legal obligation to provide or respect such rights. The claim may be made, for example, that everyone has a right to a college education, but there may be no ethical or legal obligation to admit everyone to colleges and universities.

B. **Rights that imply duties.** A second meaning of rights is the idea of rights that entitle someone to something that others have an ethical or legal obligation to provide or to refrain from interfering with. Citizens, for example, may have a right to vote, to own property, or to some benefit such as medical care as provided by law. In this sense, the right of a person means that certain other people have a duty to provide or refrain from interfering with that right.

C. **Legal or moral rights.** Legal and moral rights can be distinguished from each other. Such rights can be only moral, only legal, or both moral and legal. A right that is only a moral right imposes only a moral duty on others not to infringe upon it. A legal right imposes a legal duty on others not to infringe upon it.

D. **Natural rights.** Some philosophers have argued that moral rights that impose duties on everyone exist "by nature" and that these natural rights overrule legal rights that contradict them. A form of this argument is found in the Declaration of Independence, where the idea of natural rights is used to defend the claim to a "right to revolution."

E. **Human rights.** Human rights are a set of ideals which societies are exhorted to fulfill and which no government is to impede or abolish. Human rights are said to apply to everyone—to all persons as persons, rather than as members of a politically organized society. Thus, human rights are distinguished from rights guaranteed by a legal system, such as civil rights under a constitution. Some rights often said to be human rights, such as the right to political and personal freedom, are also claimed to be natural rights; others, such as the right to social security listed in the UN Universal Declaration, are statements of aspirations for a decent life for everyone and cannot be said to bind governments or individuals without their consent.

II. **The legal rights of the American citizen.**

A. **Civil rights.** To protect rights fundamental to the preservation of a free society, the Constitution guarantees certain basic civil rights such as the right to political liberty. This right includes the rights of assembly, petition, voting, and running for public office. Civil rights also include the right to personal liberty which includes the rights of freedom of expression, association, worship, and security from unreasonable searches and seizures.

B. **Criminal rights.** To protect the individual from unfair and unreasonable treatment by the state, the Constitution guarantees certain procedural rights of the accused under criminal law such as the rights to counsel, trial by jury, and freedom from unreasonable search and seizure.

C. **Residual rights.** The rights explicitly stated in the Constitution do not exhaust those protected by it. The Ninth Amendment to the Constitution states that the "enumeration in the Constitution of certain rights, shall not be construed to deny or disparage others retained by the people."

For the Historical and Contemporary Perspectives see Individual Rights, below.

A. INDIVIDUAL RIGHTS

We hold these truths to be self-evident: That all Men...are endowed by their Creator with certain unalienable Rights, that among these are Life, Liberty, and the Pursuit of Happiness....

Thomas Jefferson (1776)

To secure the public good, and private rights [of individuals], against the danger of [an overbearing, majority] faction, and at the same time to preserve the spirit and the form of popular government, is then the great object to which our enquiries are directed....

James Madison (1787)

...[R]ecognition of the inherent dignity and of the equal and inalienable rights of all members of the human family is the foundation of freedom, justice and peace in the world.
United Nations Universal Declaration of Human Rights (1948)

The traditional purpose of American constitutional democracy is to secure individual rights. A constitution, however, is not self-enforcing. If citizens do not know, value, exercise, and protect their rights themselves, not even the most brilliantly conceived constitution will protect them. If citizens understand the origin and evolution of individual rights and the functions of those rights in society, they are more likely to respond intelligently and responsibly to current issues and events that concern these rights. Citizens who are to preserve individual rights for themselves and for posterity must assume responsibility for defending and advancing those rights against all sources of encroachment, including the potential tyranny of the majority against unpopular individuals in the minority, a persistent threat to individual rights in a democracy.

OBJECTIVES

The citizen should be able to

1. define and explain the importance of individual rights in a free society.

2. identify and interpret in historical context the fundamental primary documents on individual rights in the Anglo-American civic heritage.

3. explain the origin and evolution in Anglo-American history of individual rights in the current constitutional government of the United States.

4. identify developments and issues that involve individual rights, for example, the search of a home by police.

5. analyze and appraise situations in which individual rights are in conflict with each other and with other important values and interests, for example, the right to a fair trial versus freedom of the press.

6. take and defend positions on the proper scope and limits of individual rights in specific situations, for example, freedom of the press and the libel of an individual, or freedom of speech and national security.

7. analyze and appraise global issues which concern the rights of individuals.

FRAME OF REFERENCE
Conceptual Perspective

I. **A broad concept of individual rights in a liberal democratic society.** The modern idea of individual rights is that all persons, by virtue of their membership in the human species, have certain rights, such as "life, liberty, and the pursuit of happiness." Constitutional government is established to secure these individual rights, and the government may not unfairly or unreasonably restrict the exercise of them. A free government, a constitutional democracy, is distinguished by its capacity to provide both majority rule and protection of the rights of individuals. Three broad categories of individual rights—life, liberty, and the pursuit of happiness—are explained below.

II. **Life.** With a few narrowly defined exceptions, the individual's right to life is considered inviolable. The government may not have the capacity to totally control and dispose of the lives of its members, nor may private persons, except in certain cases of self-defense, jeopardize another person's life. Only in extreme circumstances, such as when certain criminal acts are being committed or in the case of capital punishment, may the state legally use deadly force. Citizens may be obligated to risk their lives in military service, but they are not obligated to intentionally give up or sacrifice their lives.

III. **Liberty.** In the American civic tradition, the right to liberty is an undisputed and central characteristic of the human condition. At the core of this concept of liberty is an understanding that the political obligations of parents or ancestors cannot be legitimately imposed upon either their descendants or others in the political order.

A. **Liberty, obligation, and consent of citizens.** The obligation of adults to live under a constitutional order or to accept the authority of private persons, such as employers or interest group leaders, is based upon personal consent, not upon force or inheritance. These obligations or responsibilities to authorities remain in force only so long as that consent continues. In the United States, individuals have liberty to resign from private associations and to join or form new ones.

They may freely emigrate and become part of another society willing to receive them.

1. **Constitutional consent and choice**. In the United States citizens have the constitutional means (Article V) to alter or reconstitute their frame of government through deliberation and choice. Furthermore, the American civic tradition as stated in the Declaration of Independence includes the responsibility and right of citizens to replace their political order and its governors if those governors have failed to secure individual rights or have persistently and flagrantly violated them.

2. **Responsibility for ordered liberty**. A generally accepted assumption is that unlicensed liberty leads inevitably to public disorder and then to despotism and therefore lies outside the civic tradition. The security of liberty for everyone in the civil society is a primary responsibility of the constitutional government and the citizenry.

B. **Personal liberty**. Amendment IV of the federal Bill of Rights provides that, "The right of the people to be secure in their persons, houses, papers, and effects, against unreasonable searches and seizures, shall not be violated...." The right to privacy is at the core of this concept of personal liberty. There is a private realm that public officials cannot legitimately invade. Within this private realm of society, individuals have certain liberties of thought, belief, and action, such as freedom of conscience in religious matters, freedom of association and expression, and the right to be let alone.

C. **Political liberty**. Amendment I of the federal Bill of Rights exemplifies the concept of political liberty: "Congress shall make no law...abridging the freedom of speech, or of the press; or the right of the people peaceably to assemble, and to petition the Government for a redress of grievances." Amendment I embodies the idea that the people of a free society have the right to participate freely in the political process, which requires the free flow of information and ideas, open debate, and the right of assembly. Elections occur at stated, agreed-upon intervals; political candidates and their supporters may not be subject to arbitrary arrest, harassment, or intimidation; and electoral corruption—such as buying votes and obstructing voters—and fraud, is not a significant part of the process.

D. **Economic liberty**. Amendment V of the federal Bill of Rights reflects the economic rights of individuals that are intertwined with political and personal liberties in the American civic tradition: "No person shall be...deprived of life, liberty, or property, without due process of law; nor shall private property be taken for public use, without just compensation." Central to the notion of economic liberty is the right of individuals to acquire, use, transfer, and dispose of private property without unreasonable governmental interference. In addition, economic freedom includes the right to seek employment where one pleases; to change employment at will; and to engage in any lawful economic activity either by oneself or in combination with others in units such as labor unions or business corporations.

IV. **The pursuit of happiness**. The "pursuit of happiness" is derived from the concept of liberty in a constitutional democracy. It includes the idea that while no government can guarantee the happiness of citizens, it is the right of citizens to attempt to attain—to "pursue"—happiness in their own way, so long as they do not infringe upon the rights of others. Government can contribute to this pursuit by establishing conditions of liberty and order that enable each individual to develop his or her personal capacities or potentialities to the fullest. In *The Federalist* No. 10 James Madison argued, "The protection of these faculties [capacities of individuals] is the first object of government." The "pursuit of happiness" supposes a fundamental human longing to seek fulfillment and establishes the right of individuals to conduct that search without unwarranted governmental interference.

V. **Constitutionalism and individual rights**. Security for individual rights is linked to constitutionalism, the doctrine that the power to govern is limited by organizations and procedures embodied in the fundamental written law or revered customs—the constitution—of a political order. The constitution is said to be the creation of the sovereign people, who grant limited power to government in order to establish conditions for both social order and secure individual rights. All persons in the society, including the major leaders, are obligated to abide by the supreme law of the constitution. Thus, limited government and the rule of law are means to protect the constitutional rights of individuals.

A. **Enforceable rights of individuals**. James Madison referred to declarations of rights, without means to enforce them, as mere "parchment barriers," which are insufficient to secure "the great rights of mankind."

1. **Necessity for government**. What is needed to ensure the availability and the authentic enjoyment of individual rights? An effective constitu-

tional government, one that functions according to limitations and procedures in a body of supreme law, is the instrument required to guarantee the rights of individuals living under its authority.

2. **Written constitutions.** In the United States, at the federal level, institutions for securing individual rights are embedded in a written constitution (for example, federalism, separation and sharing of powers among the branches of government, and powers granted and prohibited to government).

B. **Judicial protection for individual rights.** In the American system, a central role in protecting individual rights is played by the U.S. Supreme Court.

1. **Supreme Court's power of judicial review.** In the constitutional government of the United States, the Supreme Court has the special duty to guard individual rights through judicial review, its power to void government actions that violate the supreme law of the Constitution. "Without this [power], all the reservations of particular rights and privileges would amount to nothing," wrote Alexander Hamilton in *The Federalist* No. 78.

2. **Madison's view of the Court's role.** James Madison presciently observed in 1789 that "independent tribunals of justice will consider themselves in a peculiar manner the guardians of those rights; they will be an impenetrable bulwark against every assumption of power in the legislative or executive; they will be naturally led to resist every encroachment upon rights expressly stipulated for in the Constitution."

3. **The scope and operation of judicial review.** All courts in the United States, both federal and state, may exercise the power of judicial review to safeguard the constitutional rights of individuals. But the Supreme Court of the United States has the final decision on controversies about the meaning and application of constitutional law. A Supreme Court decision on the Constitution can be changed only by a change of opinions among a majority of members of the Court in a subsequent case or by the people's use of the process for amending the Constitution.

Historical Perspective

I. **Evolution of the concept of individual rights.** Although individuals had rights under law in the ancient world, the idea of individual natural rights is a modern idea that grew out of sixteenth-, seventeenth-, and eighteenth-century theories of natural law and political resistance to "illegitimate" ecclesiastical and secular power.

A. **The Hobbesian position on individual rights.** The first major writer to derive individual rights from the natural law tradition was an Englishman, **Thomas Hobbes**.

1. **Purpose of government to preserve life.** Hobbes argued in his *Leviathan* (1651) that government is founded on a mutual covenant among subjects who agree to obey a sovereign in order to preserve their lives, which are at risk in the anarchic state of nature from which they seek relief.

2. **Exchange of liberty for order and safety.** According to Hobbes, individuals freely agree to exchange their natural liberty for the absolute authority of a sovereign, who uses his legitimately acquired power to maintain order in a civil society, and thereby secure the individual's inalienable right to life.

3. **Authority derived from consent.** Although Hobbes argued the case for absolutism in government, he was the first modern philosopher to locate the source of political authority in the consent of the people. Thus, Hobbes is an ironic intellectual ancestor of later theorists who developed the case for political liberty, individual rights, and free government. (For Hobbes' theory, see also The nature of the state.)

B. **John Locke's *Second Treatise of Government*.** Another Englishman, **John Locke**, followed some of Hobbes's premises in developing his own ideas on individual rights to life, liberty, and property.

1. **Rights grounded in the "law of nature" and obligations in consent.** In his *Second Treatise* (1690), Locke held that each person is born with rights as part of the law of nature. Like Hobbes, Locke argued that our obligations to government in civil society, which limit the scope of one's natural freedom, arise only by our consent.

2. **Certain rights precede consent to authority.** He further tried to show that the individual's right to property is not derived from his consent to enter a civil society and its political order, but precedes it. Thus, a primary duty of government established by consent of the governed is protec-

tion of the person's natural right to property, along with the related rights to life and liberty, which in a civil society means freedom from the insecurity and oppression of arbitrary rule.

C. **The European Enlightenment**. The political ideas of Locke flowered among the **philosophers** of the eighteenth-century European Enlightenment. Political theorists such as **Voltaire** and **Montesquieu** (see following paragraph) built upon Locke's and others' ideas about natural individual rights and circulated them throughout Western Europe and North America, where they profoundly influenced political leaders and events. The political thought of the Enlightenment certainly was not uniform. Some currents of the Enlightenment proved more conducive than others to the realization of free government and individual rights. Enlightenment thinkers tended to believe, however, that the individual is not "owned" by the state; rather, each person has prior moral claims—eternal and immutable rights—which political authorities can never legitimately deny.

D. **Montesquieu's principles of republican government**. A Frenchman, **Charles Louis de Secondat, baron de la Brede et de Montesquieu** (1689-1755), was for Americans a leading Enlightenment theorist of free government and individual rights.

1. **Principles of *De l'esprit des lois* (1748)**. In *The Spirit of the Laws*, Montesquieu set forth principles of republicanism, federalism, separation of powers, and commercialism that profoundly influenced the founding period of the United States.

2. **Influence on American Framers**. He was referred to more frequently by the delegates to the Federal Convention than any other political thinker. Federalists and Anti-Federalists turned to his ideas to justify their positions. James Madison, in *The Federalist* No. 47, called him "the oracle who is always consulted and cited." And Madison used Montesquieu's conception of separated and shared powers in his model of a constitutional government designed to secure the rights of individuals against the abuse of power.

E. **Individual rights and the eighteenth-century revolutions**. The Enlightenment ideas about individual natural rights and free government influenced two great eighteenth-century political revolutions, the American and the French, which became pivotal events in the history of human liberty. These two revolutions generated political ideas, documents, and institutions that

have affected people and events around the world for more than two hundred years. Thomas Jefferson, for example, conveyed common ideas of the Enlightenment simply and compellingly in the Declaration of Independence, a document that has become a universal symbol of freedom and rights for individuals.

II. **Primary documents in the evolution of individual rights**. The revolutionary Enlightenment ideas about individual rights were institutionalized first in the United States. In 1792 James Madison stated how American practice reversed common European precedent: "In Europe charters of liberty have been granted by power. America has set the example and France has followed it of charters of power granted by liberty." This, he said, was "a revolution in the practice of the world." However, the Americans were not solely influenced by the Enlightenment in their thoughts about individual rights. They also heeded a long English legal tradition. Thus the origins of American ideas are also to be found in key documents of the Anglo-American heritage—from the English antecedents, through colonial era precedents, to the revolutionary establishment of a new nation, the United States of America, with its novel republican government.

A. **English antecedents**. Individual rights in the U.S. have roots in the constitutional history of England. These English antecedents are exemplified in three great charters of liberty: the Magna Carta (1215), the Petition of Right (1628), and the Bill of Rights (1689). In each of these documents, the English monarch acknowledged certain limitations upon the crown's power in behalf of individual rights of subjects. Thus, the three documents emanated from the authority of the crown in response to irresistible pressures from the monarch's subjects. The ultimate consequence in 1689, at the conclusion of the Glorious Revolution, was to make the monarch subservient to Parliament, which remained unlimited by any constitutional document. English antecedents of individual rights in America, and American deviations from these antecedents, can be found in the following documents:

1. **Magna Carta**. Magna Carta, or the Great Charter, exacted from King John by the feudal lords at Runnymede, England, is the first written statement of law that limits the power of the sovereign to abridge specified rights of certain individuals of the realm.

a. **Further application of Magna Carta's principles**. Although Magna Carta primarily protected feudal privileges of the English barons against abuses by the monarch, its most important provisions were set forth in broad terms. Therefore, generally applicable rights of individuals could develop from its principles. For example, the right to judgment by one's peers, the security of private property, and the right to due process of law in dealings with the government are all found in the document.

b. **Magna Carta as beginning of limited government**. Magna Carta, then, was the modest beginning of limited government and the rule of law as instruments for the protection of specified rights of individuals. According to **Winston S. Churchill** (1874-1965), "This reaffirmation of a supreme law and its expression in a general charter is the great work of Magna Carta, and this alone justifies the respect in which men have held it."

2. **Petition of Right (1628)**. After Magna Carta, the next great charter of English liberty is the Petition of Right, a statute that confirmed the idea of a law above the Crown, which even the monarch was obligated to obey. This document also asserted the right of the people to be taxed only with the consent of their representatives in government. Further, it provided protection against arbitrary imprisonment.

3. **Bill of Rights (1689)**. The English Bill of Rights, an act of Parliament, stated the basic rights of Englishmen against the Crown.

a. **The Bill as a summary of evolved rights**. For the most part, this statute reaffirmed and summarized rights of individuals that had evolved over five centuries. Thus, the power of the monarch was limited by law, but not the power of the Parliament.

b. **Examples of rights affirmed by the Bill**. Examples of these rights include the freedom of assembly and petition, freedom of speech for members of Parliament, prohibitions against excessive bail and fines and cruel and unusual punishments.

c. **The Bill as antithesis of American constitutional theory**. The failure of the Bill to limit the power of Parliament is the antithesis of the American concept of constitutional rights as legal limitations upon all branches of government and all public officials.

d. **The Bill as symbol of individual liberties**. Nonetheless, the English Bill of Rights was a significant symbol of individual liberties, which Americans used to justify their claims to the rights of Englishmen before and during their revolution against the British government.

B. **Anglo-American colonial precedents**. The political experience of the American colonies was even more important than the English antecedents in establishing precedents for the development of individual rights in the United States.

1. **Migration of legal ideas to America**. When people emigrated from England to America, they took their legal rights with them, embedded in the colonial charters that framed their local governments.

2. **Virginia Charter of 1606**. The Virginia Charter of 1606, for example, provided that the inhabitants possessed "all liberties, Franchises, and Immunities...to all Intents and Purposes, as if they had been abiding and born, within this our Realm of England."

3. **Individual rights guaranteed by many colonial charters**. This Virginia Charter was the first in a long series of Anglo-American colonial documents that provided precedents in these English colonies for individual rights included eventually in the constitutional government of the United States. These precedents are exemplified in the Massachusetts Body of Liberties, the Charter of Rhode Island, and the Pennsylvania Frame of Government.

a. **Massachusetts Body of Liberties (1641)**. This enactment of the colonial legislature of Massachusetts was the first American document to elaborate upon the rights of individuals. It became a model for similar colonial enactments, for example, the New York Charter of Liberties (1683) and the Pennsylvania Charter of Privileges (1701). Most of the fundamental rights later included in the federal Bill of Rights were included in the Massachusetts document, with the notable exception of the right to religious liberty. (Massachusetts had an established church until 1833.) Most important was a new American concept—legal rights enacted by the people's representatives for the people that would comprehensively limit government.

b. **Charter of Rhode Island (1663).** In 1635 Roger Williams brought the idea of religious liberty to his settlement in Providence, and this right to "liberty of conscience" was the basis for the Rhode Island colony. The colonial Charter of Rhode Island, therefore, became the first one to fully guarantee religious liberty to all inhabitants.

c. **Pennsylvania Frame of Government (1682). William Penn** (1644-1718) wrote this constitution for his colony of Pennsylvania. In the Preface to this document, Penn stated a basic American principle of free government and individual rights: "Any government is free to the people under it (whatever be the frame) where the laws rule and the people are a party to those laws." The purpose of the frame of government, wrote Penn, is to secure the rights of the people against potential abuses of power by their governors and to maintain the proper balance between authority and liberty. These ideas, of course, became the foundations of the U.S. Constitution.

C. **Documents of the American founding period**. By the time of their revolution against the British, Americans had arrived at a consensus about the individual rights that should be protected by law. These rights were formulated first in the constitutions and declarations of rights of the original thirteen states, from the Virginia Constitution and Declaration of Rights in 1776 to the Massachusetts and New Hampshire frames of government created in 1780 and 1783. These state documents were bases for the great federal charters of individual rights.

1. **The Virginia Declaration of Rights (1776).** This was the prototype of the modern American concept of constitutional rights—the first legal guarantee of individual rights to be included in a state institution created by elected representatives of the people.

a. **Rights as limits to legislative acts**. As such, the rights stipulated by the Declaration were part of a supreme law of the state and superseded any mere enactment of the legislative branch of the government.

b. **Similarity to Declaration of Independence**. The Virginia document included a statement about rights that was echoed several weeks later by the Declaration of Independence: "[A]ll men are by nature equally free and independent, and have certain inherent rights...the enjoyment of life and liberty, with the means of acquiring and possessing property, and pursuing and obtaining happiness and safety."

2. **The Northwest Ordinance (1787)**. This law of the Congress created by the Articles of Confederation set forth procedures and principles for governing the territory north and west of the Ohio River. It also contained the first bill of rights enacted at the federal level of government. The Northwest Ordinance guaranteed individual rights "as articles of compact between the original States and the people." These rights, modeled on the recently established bills of rights of the American states, presaged the federal Bill of Rights.

3. **The Constitution of the United States (1787)**. The Philadelphia Convention designed a Constitution that would protect individual rights by limiting government through structural devices, such as the distribution of powers among the branches of government and between the federal and state levels of the political system. A few explicit rights were also specified.

a. **Habeas corpus, ex post facto laws, and bills of attainder**. The privilege of the writ of habeas corpus and prohibitions of ex post facto laws and bills of attainder were provided in Article I, Section 9.

b. **Trial by jury**. Trial by jury in criminal cases was stipulated in Article III, Section 2.

c. **Religious tests for office**. Article VI prohibited any religious test as a condition for holding an office in the federal government.

d. **Narrow definition of treason**. Protection against politically motivated persecution of individuals was provided in Article III, Section 3, by a narrow definition of treason and rigorous requirements for establishing evidence of an act of treason.

4. **The federal Bill of Rights (1791)**. The immediate origin of the Bill of Rights was the ratification

debate that followed the framing of the Constitution, but the Bill's roots in American soil are deeper.

a. **Federalists' promise of a bill of rights**. During the state ratifying conventions of 1787-1788, opponents of the U.S. Constitution won a pledge from proponents ("Federalists") to amend the frame of government to include a bill of rights. The first federal Congress proposed twelve amendments in 1789, and the states ratified ten of them in 1791, adding them to the federal Constitution. The amendments became collectively known as the "Bill of Rights."

b. **Antecedents in state constitutions**. The Bill reflected the rights of individuals guaranteed in several of the state constitutions, for example, the Virginia Declaration of Rights (1776) and those of Maryland (1776), New York (1777), and Massachusetts (1780).

c. **The Bill's restrictions on federal government.** The rights guaranteed under the Bill, which are enforceable through the federal courts, were initially intended to restrict the power of all branches and officials of the federal government. (For the "nationalization" of the Bill's protections, see below under III. A.)

5. **Categories of rights in the Bill of Rights**. The ten amendments that comprise the Bill of Rights may be divided into three broad categories.

a. **The first four amendments**. Amendments I to IV guard certain liberties of individuals against infringement by the federal government, for example, freedom of speech, press, assembly, petition, and religion; the right to bear arms; protection against arbitrary quartering of troops in civilian homes; and protection of the privacy and security of one's home, person, and possessions.

b. **Amendments five to eight**. Amendments V to VIII define and protect specific rights of individuals accused of crimes or otherwise involved in the resolution of disputes under the law, for example, the right to due process of law; trial by jury in criminal and civil cases; confrontation of hostile witnesses; assistance of legal counsel; and protection against self-incrimination, double jeopardy, excessive bail or fines, and cruel and unusual punishments.

c. **Amendments nine and ten**. Amendments IX and X guarantee the retention of rights not stated in the Constitution and reserve to the states or the people powers not delegated to the federal government.

III. **Evolution of specific rights**. Individual rights in the U.S. Constitution of 1787 and Bill of Rights of 1791 were products of an evolutionary process that spanned more than five centuries. The evolution of constitution-based rights of individuals has continued from the U.S. founding period to the present. The origins and development of three basic rights—due process, habeas corpus, and free speech—are explained below as exemplifications of the evolution of the body of rights that Americans enjoy today.

A. **Due process of law**. The Fifth and Fourteenth Amendments to the Constitution provide that neither the life nor the liberty nor the property of an individual can be taken away without "due process of law"—including a fair hearing conducted according to all legal safeguards that protect the person against sanctions imposed by the state.

1. **English antecedents of due process of law**. The concept of legal procedural rights has been traced to King John's promise in the Magna Carta to obey the "law of the land." However, "due process of law" was first specified in an act of Parliament in 1354, which affirmed the Magna Carta and provided: "That no man...shall be put out of Land or Tenement, nor taken, nor imprisoned, nor disinherited, nor put to death, without being brought to Answer by due Process of Law." Procedural due process in criminal and civil cases was well established by the end of the seventeenth century in association with the fundamental concept of the sovereign's obligations to abide by the "law of the land."

2. **Anglo-American colonial precedents for the right to due process of law**. The English concept of due process was firmly established in colonial charters and statutes. The Massachusetts Body of Liberties (1641), for example, provided that a person could not be deprived of life, liberty, and property except by "some express law of the Country warranting the same, established by a general Court and sufficiently published." However, the first colonial American document to use

these words—"due process of law"—was a Massachusetts statute of 1682.

3. **Due process of law in the founding documents of the United States.** The specific wording—"due process of law"—is absent from the founding documents that preceded the federal Bill of Rights. All the original state constitutions, however, used the "law of the land" phrase to connote procedural due process. The Northwest Ordinance in its Second Article of Compact also used the phrase: "[N]o man shall be deprived of his liberty or property but by the judgment of his peers, or the law of the land."

4. **Development of due process of law in U.S. constitutional history.** During the twentieth century the U.S. Supreme Court has used the due process clauses of the Fifth and Fourteenth Amendments to reinforce and extend a wide range of individual rights. This has been done through development of "substantive due process" and the nationalization of the federal Bill of Rights through the "due process" clause of the Fourteenth Amendment.

    a. **Substantive due process.** The U.S. Supreme Court has developed the concept of "substantive due process" to prevent government from unfairly controlling or prohibiting certain actions of individuals. Traditional "procedural due process" involves adherence to the formal procedures of legal proceedings. But "substantive due process" concerns specific behaviors that government may not regulate, except under certain conditions. It must demonstrate that it cannot achieve a legitimate public end by less intrusive means. Thus, the Court has used substantive due process to invalidate hundreds of statutes pertaining to a wide variety of social and economic concerns, such as conditions of employment, sexual behavior, and other matters.

    b. **Nationalization of the federal Bill of Rights.** In the twentieth century, the U.S. Supreme Court has used the due process clause of the Fourteenth Amendment, which limits state governments, in concert with the Fifth Amendment's due process clause to protect individual rights against infringement by state and local governments. Most of the restrictions on federal government authority in the federal Bill of Rights have been extended to

all levels of government, thereby greatly expanding protections for individual rights to life, liberty, and property. The "nationalization" process, which has occurred gradually, is also known as "incorporation."

B. **Habeas corpus.** This Latin term means, "You shall/should have the body." Article I, Section 9 of the U.S. Constitution states: "The privilege of the writ of habeas corpus shall not be suspended, unless when in cases of rebellion or invasion the public safety may require it." A writ of habeas corpus requires officials to bring a person whom they have arrested before a judge in a court of law. If the judge finds their reasons for holding the prisoner unlawful, then the court frees the suspect. Thus, the writ of habeas corpus is a great guarantee of personal freedom against public officials who might detain individuals only because they belong to unpopular groups or criticize the government.

1. **English antecedents.** The writ of habeas corpus in English common law is older than the Magna Carta. It was used to secure the release of those unjustifiably detained not only in prison but also in hospitals or private custody. Parliament enacted a Habeas Corpus statute in 1640, but because it was not entirely effectual, an amendment act was passed in 1679. The Crown was thus prevented from unjustly holding individuals in prison for personal or political reasons. By the end of the seventeenth century this individual right was solidly established as the appropriate process for curbing illegal imprisonment.

2. **Anglo-American colonial precedents for habeas corpus.** The English Habeas Corpus Acts were not extended to the Anglo-American colonies. However, the writ was one of the widely recognized common law rights of individuals in the American colonies and was frequently invoked before the Revolution.

3. **Habeas corpus in founding documents of the United States.** The privilege of the writ of habeas corpus was included in several state constitutions enacted prior to the federal Constitution. The Second Article of Compact of the Northwest Ordinance of 1787 also protected this right.

4. **Development of habeas corpus in U.S. constitutional history.** The U.S. Supreme Court has consistently upheld the individual's habeas corpus right, even when this privilege has been suspend-

ed by the government to guard public safety and security.

a. **The Merryman case (1861).** In 1861, after the outbreak of the Civil War, President Lincoln suspended habeas corpus in parts of Maryland. This action was challenged in the *Ex parte Merryman* case. Chief Justice Taney, sitting as a circuit judge, ruled that only Congress had the right to suspend the writ, but Lincoln ignored the ruling.

b. *Ex parte Milligan* **(1866).** In *Ex parte Milligan* the Supreme Court decided that the writ could not be suspended in states (for example, Indiana), where public order and safety were not endangered by the Civil War.

c. **The writ as a fundamental protection of rights.** From the founding of the United States until the present era, Americans have believed the writ of habeas corpus to be a primary protection of their personal liberties. This belief was reflected in 1953 by Justice Felix Frankfurter, who wrote (*Brown v. Allen*) that the writ of habeas corpus is "[T]he best safeguard of freedom in the Anglo-American world."

C. **Freedom of Speech.** The right to free speech means that individuals may publicly express ideas and information—including expressions generally considered to be unwise, untenable, or unorthodox—without fear of punishment by the government. Thus, government officials may be criticized, and new ways of thinking and behaving may be advanced. Forms of free speech include the use of symbols, orderly public demonstrations, and radio and television broadcasts. Freedom of speech is an essential characteristic of a constitutional democracy, because through exercise of this right, individuals can communicate opinions both to others and to their representatives in the government. "It is only through free debate and exchange of ideas that government remains responsive to the will of the people," wrote Justice William O. Douglas.

1. **English antecedents.** The right to free speech stems from elements of the right to freedom of the press established in England during the seventeenth century. At that time, however, the right to free speech was specifically extended only to members of Parliament. All presses had to be licensed until 1694 when the law requiring licenses lapsed and was not renewed. But controls on

the press continued through prosecution for such offenses as treason and seditious libel.

2. **Anglo-American colonial precedents for free speech.** In the English colonies of North America, several colonial charters and constitutions explicitly protected freedom of the press, but the right to free speech, as in England, was guaranteed only to members of the legislative branch of government. In the American colonies, one legal case was particularly notable in the development of freedom of the press.

a. **The offensive journalism of Zenger.** John Peter Zenger (1697-1746) was a German-born journalist who published the *Weekly Journal* in New York in 1733. Zenger and the paper's backers vigorously attacked the policies of the governor of the colony, William Bradford. As a result, in 1734 he was charged with libel and imprisoned.

b. **Zenger's trial and acquittal.** The New York government disbarred all local attorneys who came forward to defend Zenger. As a result, in 1735 **Andrew Hamilton** (1676?-1741), a prominent Pennsylvania lawyer, was brought in for the trial. Hamilton provided a brilliant defense which established truth as a defense in libel cases. Zenger's acquittal helped to establish freedom of the press in America.

3. **Freedom of Speech in the founding documents of the United States.** Most constitutions of the original thirteen states protected freedom of the press, but the right of free speech was treated differently.

a. **Freedom of speech for legislators.** Freedom of speech in the colonies was typically extended only to members of the state legislature. An exception was the Pennsylvania Declaration of Rights (1776), which guaranteed freedom of the press and speech to the people.

b. **Proposals for a bill of rights include speech.** Proposals for a bill of rights in the U.S. Constitution, advanced in the first session of Congress by James Madison (June 8, 1789), included "freedom of speech." Thus, the First Amendment to the Constitution, ratified in 1791 with other provisions of the federal Bill of Rights, states: "Congress shall make no law...abridging the freedom of speech...."

4. **Development of the right to free speech in U.S. constitutional history**. The core issue on free speech in American history has been whether or not there should be any limitations on this basic political liberty; and if so, what they should be and why they are justified.

    a. **Remaining restrictions on speech**. During the twentieth century the Supreme Court has gradually expanded the right to free speech so that few restrictions remain. For example, speech that is obscene and words intended to and likely to provoke imminent physical attacks and thereby endanger public safety and order are not protected. And speech continues to be subject to reasonable limitations having to do with time, place, and manner of speaking.

    b. **Broad freedom of speech extends to states**. However, beyond these few restrictions, people have the right to say almost anything, including defamatory statements about their public officials. During the twentieth century, the Supreme Court has extended First Amendment freedoms to the states through the Fourteenth Amendment, which provides in part: "...nor shall any State deprive any person of...liberty [including free speech]... without due process of law."

Contemporary Perspective

I. **Ideas and issues on the meaning of individual rights**. There is widespread agreement in the world today that all people are entitled to certain rights, which many refer to as "human rights" to signify that these rights are derived from concrete ideas about what it means to be human. There is also much contention about the substance of rights and the means for their realization.

A. **Negative and positive conceptions of rights**. Two alternative conceptions about rights in the contemporary world are often labeled "negative" and "positive." These contending positions are based on different views of the role and responsibility of government in securing rights of the people.

1. **The negative conception**. The kinds of individual rights that are expressed in the U.S. Constitution and Bill of Rights are founded on the premise of a significant private sector of the civil society, which may not be violated by public officials. These political and personal rights are tied to traditional American constitutionalism: the notion that the higher law of the Constitution limits the power and authority of government to interfere with the private rights of individuals; and it maintains time-honored, public procedures (due process) for those instances when public officials enter the private realm on behalf of the common good. This traditional concept of individual rights is termed "negative" because it relies primarily on negation or limitation of the power and authority of government as the means to protect individual rights and liberties.

2. **The positive conception**. During the nineteenth and twentieth centuries, a new "positive" conception of individual rights has been advanced that emphasizes the duty of the government to provide for the economic security and the collective well-being of individuals in society. The right to employment, a minimum level of income, medical care, adequate housing, and social security in old age are examples of so-called new economic and social rights that require affirmative action or "positive" use of public power and resources for their realization.

B. **Conflict between negative and positive conceptions of rights**. The "positive" conception of economic and social rights has entered the constitutional government of the United States through legislation and decisions of the Supreme Court. However, the evolving alliance between the "older" negative rights and the "newer" positive rights has often been uneasy and tenuous, and raises challenging questions, conflicts, and other issues. Some of the issues raised by those who adopt the "positive" and "negative" concepts of rights concern the question of primacy or precedence of each set of rights.

1. **Positive rights as primary**. Some advocates of the positive view of rights claim that their conception takes precedence over the traditional view. They argue that bread is more important than freedom of speech, that the right to employment has priority over the right to privacy, and that the duties of government to provide for the people require enhancement of public power and authority to enter all areas of economic and social life to promote the common good.

2. **Negative rights as primary**. By contrast, proponents of the negative position express concern about the threats to traditional private rights of individuals posed by enormous increases of governmental power and authority required to provide collective rights of the people through large-scale public programs. Opponents of the primacy of positive rights argue that a potential consequence of the positive conception is the minimizing or elimination of the private sector of society and the private rights of individuals. Affirmative actions by government to advance the new economic and social rights could lead ultimately to a government so powerful that it could deprive individuals of their traditional and personal political liberties.

II. **Universality and particularity of individual rights**. During the second half of the twentieth century, individual rights, often called human rights, have become prominent items on the international political agenda, and their flagrant abuse anywhere in the world is likely to become a global issue. Most governments in the nation-states of today's world recognize the legitimacy of international interest in the inherent rights of everyone. And citizens of nation-states around the globe are more likely today than in the past to challenge violations of human rights both within and outside of their national political systems.

A. **United Nations documents on rights**. The United Nations has played an important part in advancing awareness and concern about rights around the world. Both the "older" political and personal rights and the "newer" economic and social rights were included in the United Nations Universal Declaration of Human Rights (1948). The introduction to the thirty Articles of this document is rooted in the older individual rights tradition of Western civilization, as are Articles 1 through 21. Articles 22 to 30 state newer economic, social, and cultural rights. The juxtaposition of the "new" and "old" rights has continued in the on-going formulation of what some have called an "International Bill of Rights"—a seemingly open-ended series of documents that proclaim the importance of rights to and for all people of the world.

B. **The claim and issue of universality**. The United Nations documents proclaim the universality of individual rights of humanity, as did the Enlightenment philosophers and the American constitution-makers. However, these claims to universality of human rights have been disputed by those who see them primarily as particular expressions of Western civilization rather than as global aspirations and standards. Those in the West, who invented the theories and practices of individual human rights, may have been speaking, writing, and acting only for themselves and their societies. However, they might also have been stating and practicing eternal and universal truths about human nature, human concerns, and human hopes for a better life.

C. **A global destiny for individual rights**. The global decline and demise of totalitarian and despotic political regimes during the latter part of the twentieth century (e.g., the communist regimes of Eastern Europe), and the subsequent rise of constitutional democracy symbolizes the broad appeal of individual political and personal rights among diverse peoples and cultures. It seems that people everywhere, if given a choice, will opt for free government and the individual rights it secures, as the surest political means to fulfillment of their needs and aspirations.

B. HUMAN RIGHTS

Now, therefore,
The General Assembly,
Proclaims this Universal Declaration of Human Rights as a common standard of achievement for all peoples and all nations, to the end that every individual and every organ of society, keeping this Declaration constantly in mind, shall strive by teaching and education to promote respect for these rights and freedoms and by progressive measures, national and international, to secure their universal and effective recognition and observance, both among the peoples of Member States themselves and among the peoples of territories under their jurisdiction.

United Nations General Assembly December 10, 1948

OBJECTIVES

The citizen should be able to

1. describe and analyze the meaning of the term "human rights" as it has come to be used in international affairs, especially in the twentieth century.

2. compare and contrast how different forms of government (constitutional and non-constitutional, democratic and dictatorial) treat the problems of human rights within their own borders as well as in their relations to other countries.

3. discuss critically major examples and causes of gross violations of the rights of racial, ethnic, and religious groups as well as of individuals in various countries and regions of the world.

4. discuss the positive role of governments, international agencies, and nongovernmental agencies in prohibiting or mitigating abuses of human rights.

5. take, explain, and defend positions regarding the responsibilities of citizens in a democratic society to promote the human rights of all persons at home and abroad.

FRAME OF REFERENCE
Conceptual Perspective

Although the United Nations Universal Declaration of Human Rights proclaims agreement on "a common standard of achievement for all peoples and all nations," there have been persistent and controversial distinctions made, in both international debate and practice, between two types of "rights."

I. **Civil and political rights.** There is broad agreement among adherents of liberal democracy on the desirable content of provisions for civil and political rights. These include provisions concerning:

A. **Freedom from arbitrary discrimination.** All human beings are born free and equal in dignity and are entitled to all the rights and freedoms of the Declaration without distinction as to race, color, sex, language, religion, political or other opinion, national or social origin, property, or birth.

B. **Freedom from slavery.** No one shall be held in slavery or involuntary servitude. Slavery and the slave trade are prohibited in all their forms.

C. **Freedom from torture and arbitrary detention.** No one shall be subjected to torture, cruel or inhuman punishment, or arbitrary arrest, detention, or exile.

D. **Right to equal justice and due process.** Everyone accused of a crime or other infraction of law has the right in full equality to a fair and public hearing by an independent and impartial tribunal and to due process of law.

E. **Right to privacy.** Everyone has the right to a personal realm into which it is not the business of government to enquire or intrude. Individuals shall not be subjected to arbitrary interference with their families, home, or correspondence, or their reputations subjected to attack.

F. **Right to nationality, movement, and asylum.** All individuals have the right to a nationality (not to be a stateless person), freedom of movement and residence in their own country, and to asylum in another country if they are fleeing political persecution.

G. **Right to marriage and property.** Everyone has the right to be legally allowed to marry and found a family; and to own property alone or in association with others.

H. **Right to freedom of thought and association.** Everyone has the right to freedom of thought, conscience, religion, expression, and opinion, and peaceful assembly and association.

II. **Right to free elections.** Everyone has the right to participate freely in his or her country's government, directly or indirectly through representatives, chosen in periodic and genuine elections, based on universal and equal suffrage, and secret ballots.

III. **Economic, social, and cultural rights.** A second class of rights in the U.N. Declaration is especially controversial in the United States. This second category of rights in the U.N. Declaration includes provisions regarding:

A. **Security of employment.** Everyone has the right to work, to a free choice of employment, to just and favorable conditions of employment, and protection against unemployment.

B. **Fair compensation.** Everyone has the right to fair remuneration for labor, and equal pay for equal work.

C. **Trade unionism.** Everyone has the right to form and join trade unions and to enjoy rest and leisure, including reasonable limitations on working hours and periodic holidays with pay.

D. **Social security.** All individuals have the right to a standard of living adequate for the health and well-being of themselves and their families, including food, clothing, and housing.

E. **Family.** Everyone has the right to protection of the family from abuse by government. Motherhood and childhood are entitled to special care and assistance. All children, whether born in or out of wedlock, shall enjoy the same social protection.

F. **Health.** Everyone has the right to the means necessary for maintaining physical and mental health and security.

G. **Education and culture.** Everyone has the right to a free elementary education, reasonable access to generally available technical and higher education, and participation in the cultural life of the community and its scientific progress.

H. **Peace.** Everyone has the right to a social and international order in which the rights and freedoms set forth in the Declaration can be realized.

Historical Perspective

The basic ideas of international human rights have roots in a variety of historical traditions.

I. **Roman law.** In the early Roman Republic the civil law applied only to Roman citizens, while foreigners had no rights and could be treated virtually as property. But by the third century B.C., the *jus gentium* (law of nations or peoples) was developed to apply to foreigners and eventually embraced all subjects governed by Rome as well as its citizens. By the third century A.D., when citizenship was granted throughout the Empire, the practice of applying a common law to all peoples provided a basis for the idea that all persons had certain natural rights.

II. **Judeo-Christian traditions.** The religious world view positing the sanctity of an immortal, supernatural soul contributed another facet to the idea that all human beings were endowed with certain spiritual potentials granted to them by a just, merciful, and all-powerful God. From the fifteenth century on, a universal Roman Catholic Church, as well as a variety of Protestant Christian churches, relied on religious authority combined with civil and military authority to carry this message to almost all parts of the inhabited world. (See also Political authority.)

III. **Natural rights.** From the seventeenth century on, a philosophy of inalienable natural rights nourished the English Bill of Rights, the early American state constitutions, the Declaration of Independence, the U.S. Constitution and Bill of Rights, and the French Declaration of the Rights of Man and the Citizen. (See also, The nature of the state and Individual rights)

IV. **Twentieth century gains and losses.** Twentieth century developments added to the idea of rights, including creation of the term "human rights." But the century also witnessed horrific examples of the negation of human rights.

A. **Statements on international human rights.** In the first half of the twentieth century, formal statements on international human rights were made by President Woodrow Wilson in his Fourteen Points for settlement of World War I (1918) and by President Franklin D. Roosevelt's Four Freedoms and their incorporation in the Atlantic Charter (1941) as goals to be achieved after the conclusion of World War II.

B. **Violations of human rights.** The strengthening of human rights in international law was overshadowed by the massive violations of these rights before, during, and after World War I and World War II. The massacres of Armenians by the Ottoman Empire during World War I, forced famine in the Ukraine and purges in Stalinist Russia in the 1930s, Nazi Germany's attempted genocide of Jews and massacres of Poles in the 1940s, the violent subjugation of Tibetans by Communist China in the 1950s and 1960s and mass killings of Cambodians by the Pol Pot regime in the 1970s are but the most heinous examples among many others.

C. **Human rights violations widespread**. Few countries have been immune from human rights violations in this century. In many cases European countries systematically disregarded such rights as colonial rulers in Africa and Asia. After independence many former colonies behaved as badly or worse toward their own citizens. Human rights violations during various periods of the century in a number of Central and South American countries have been well documented. Even the U.S. long sanctioned legal racial segregation as a residue of black slavery, forcibly removed Native Americans from their homelands in the nineteenth century, and enforced relocation and internment of Japanese-Americans during World War II.

V. **Post-World War II**. The victorious allies and the United Nations began to push harder for an international approach to safeguarding and promoting human rights.

A. **The Nuremberg trials.** The 1945-46 Nuremberg trials convicted officials of Nazi Germany of war crimes and established a new category of crimes known as "crimes against humanity," including murder, extermination, enslavement, deportation, imprisonment, torture, rape, or other inhumane acts committed against a civilian population.

B. **"An International Bill of Rights."** A significant breakthrough occurred when the Universal Declaration of Human Rights was formulated by a United Nations committee chaired by Eleanor Roosevelt and adopted by the General Assembly in 1948.

C. **Recent developments**. Since that time, various United Nations agencies have adopted more than one hundred other resolutions, covenants, conventions, and protocols elaborating on the Universal Declaration.

D. **The 1966 Covenants**. The most important of the post-1948 measures were two covenants adopted by the U.N. General Assembly in 1966: the Covenant on Civil and Political Rights and the Covenant on Economic, Social and Cultural Rights. When they came into force in 1976, President Jimmy Carter signed both and sent them to the Senate, which indefinitely delayed ratifying them. Some senators objected to them on the grounds that a meddling or hostile U.N. might interfere in domestic American policies dealing with social and economic affairs and the rights of the several states under the U.S. Constitution.

Contemporary Perspective

I. **Ambivalence of U.S. Foreign Policy**. American foreign policy has sometimes been ambivalent about the importance of human rights in its dealings with other countries.

A. **Ford and Carter administrations**. In 1975 the Congress and the Ford administration began to affirm that no U.S. foreign aid would go to nations that violated "universally recognized human rights." The Carter administration in 1976 made human rights a cornerstone of its foreign policy, but attention to the issue was weakened by the long stalemate and frustration over the American hostages taken by Iran.

B. **Reagan administration**. The Reagan administration began in 1981 by downgrading human rights as a major element in American foreign policy, but by 1986 had begun to change course by announcing that the U.S. would oppose tyranny in whatever form, whether of the left or the right.

C. **U.S. ratification of several conventions but not 1966 covenants**. The U.S. has not ratified the two 1966 comprehensive UN covenants on human rights. It has, however, ratified several specific UN conventions dealing with the abolition of slavery, rights of refugees, political rights of women, and the outlawing of genocide (the latter ratified in November 1988).

1. **Support for the 1966 covenants**. Supporters for the unratified conventions contend that rights listed in the covenants, such as health care, an adequate standard of living, and fair compensation for labor are indeed fundamental human rights. The conventions, they contend, should accordingly be ratified.

2. **Opposition to the covenants**. Opponents of ratification argue that many of the items in the covenants are little more than expressions of proponents' desires. They also argue that the covenants' implementation by public authority (as opposed to private agency and self-help) would require a large growth of government that would threaten basic civil and political rights and would cause economic ruin.

II. **Western and United Nations actions.** New developments on human rights proceeded in U.N and other forums.

A. **Prominence given to human rights**. Stepping up its concern for human rights in the 1980s, the U.N. Commission on Human Rights, the Council of Europe, the

European Commission and Court of Human Rights, and the Organization of American States all gave increasing legitimacy to human rights as a major factor in international relations.

B. **Continuing discussions**. The Helsinki Final Act of 1975 brought Eastern and Western European nations together, along with Canada and the U.S., into a continuing forum for discussion of human rights. The 34 nations of the Conference on Security and Cooperation in Europe (CSCE) promised to keep human rights on its agenda into the 1990s as it took on political and economic strength and declared the end of the Cold War in its Charter of Paris for a new Europe in 1990.

III. **Democratic Movements**. Further hope was aroused by stirrings of freedom in the Soviet Union's efforts at "openness" and other reforms as well as possible democratization. Hope was also aroused by democratic movements in Poland, Hungary, the Baltic states, Czechoslovakia, East Germany, Bulgaria, Romania, South Africa, and in various countries of Africa, Latin America, and Asia. (See Contemporary Perspective in the Nature of the State).

IV. **Continuing Violations**. Violations of human rights continue to occur on a massive scale. The following are examples:

A. **South Africa**. Despite efforts among important black and white leaders to create the conditions to negotiate the complete dismantling of apartheid, violence and repression continue in South Africa.

B. **Military dictatorships**. Human rights are routinely denied in military dictatorships of both right and left, in places such as Myanmar (formerly Burma), Cambodia, and Liberia.

C. **China**. China's crackdown on the student movement for democracy in 1989 led to continuing violation of the most basic human rights of civil and political liberty.

D. **Communal violence**. The disregard of human rights is endemic to the seemingly intractable violence among ethnic, nationalistic, and religious groups involving Muslims, Christians, Jews, Hindus, and Buddhists in various parts of the world, especially, for example, in the Middle East and in Central and South Asia.

V. **Terrorism and hostage taking**. Especially worrisome were the unpredictable onslaughts of terrorists taking hostages in Lebanon and murdering innocent victims on land, air, and sea. The murder of Israeli athletes at the Munich Olympics in 1972 and the bombing of an American airliner over Scotland in 1987 were but two among numerous crimes committed by terrorists.

VI. **Persian Gulf Crisis and War**. The Persian Gulf crisis of 1990-1991 presented the further spectacle of the blatant disregard of human rights.

A. **The invasion of Kuwait**. In August 1990, the United States, its allies, several Arab countries, and the U.N. itself were confronted with a terrible dilemma when Iraq invaded and annexed Kuwait in the struggle over oil and sovereignty in the Middle East. In several unprecedented unanimous decisions the U.N. Security Council denounced the action, established international embargoes, levied sanctions, and ordered Iraq to withdraw. As the Persian Gulf War drew to a close, the enormity of human rights violations suffered by Kuwaiti civilians at the hands of the Iraqi military began to be disclosed.

B. **The taking of hostages by Iraq**. A whole new dimension to the problem of international human rights arose when Iraq announced that all Western citizens—later amended to adult males—in Iraq and Kuwait would be detained and forcibly relocated to strategic military and industrial installations as "shields" against military attack on those installations.

C. **The escalation of human rights violations**. The official policy by a government to deny foreign nationals the freedom to leave its territory short of a declaration of war as a means of attempted blackmail of their governments was a sinister new violation of human rights as well as of international law. The policy of deliberately endangering these citizens' physical and emotional health and personal security as a weapon of international relations raised the issues of human rights to new heights, as did the plight of millions of Kurd and Shiite refugees following the war.

VII. **The uncertain future of human rights**. As the international pursuit of human rights entered a dangerous new stage, the gnawing questions for the world were these: will democracy, freedom, and human rights be gaining ground at the dawn of the next century? Or will humanity see the victory of repressive regimes as in the Napoleonic era of the early nineteenth century and in the war-plagued first half of the twentieth?

TOPIC 3. FORMS OF PARTICIPATION

The only thing necessary for the triumph of evil is for good men to do nothing.

(attributed to) **Edmund Burke** (c. 1780)

To be able to participate competently in the political process, the citizen should understand that political participation potentially includes many more forms than simply voting in periodic elections. These may include both participation as an individual and as a member of a group. Citizens should also be aware of the advantages and disadvantages of each form of participation in specific types of situations.

OBJECTIVES

The citizen should be able to

1. explain the various forms of political participation available to them.

2. identify the benefits and costs of alternative forms of participation in specific situations.

3. explain contemporary problems regarding participation.

FRAME OF REFERENCE
Conceptual Perspective

I. **Forms of individual participation.** Individuals may participate in formal as well as informal ways.

   A. **Formal means of participation.** Formal avenues of participation include, for example, voting for representatives or directly on legislation (referendums), holding electoral or appointive office, serving as an election official, and jury duty.

   B. **"Informal" means of participation.** Informal avenues of individual participation include, for example, engaging in civic writing, such as writing letters or articles; attending and speaking at public meetings; participating in public demonstrations; contributing to candidates, organizations, or causes; working in electoral campaigns; participating in community action and neighborhood governance organizations; and participating in initiative, referendum, and recall campaigns.

II. **Forms of participation through membership in a group.** A second form of participation is through membership at local, state, or national levels of such groups as political parties, interest groups, labor unions, and similar organizations. Such membership may include lobbying public officials directly or indirectly, engaging in various forms of civic writing, attending and speaking at meetings, recruiting new members, and soliciting contributions.

III. **Participation of citizens in foreign relations.** Citizens, individually and as members of groups, may play roles of varying importance in American relations with foreign countries and in world affairs generally.

   A. **Organizational membership.** The ordinary citizen plays varying roles in non-governmental international organizations. Organizations such as Amnesty International and the International Wildlife Fund can have an important impact on governments' domestic and foreign policies.

   B. **Unofficial ambassadors.** Individuals traveling abroad become citizen "ambassadors;" their behavior affects foreign perceptions of the United States.

   C. **Unofficial contacts.** Prominent American citizens often play unofficial but significant roles in direct contacts concerning economic and political issues with foreign governments.

For the Historical and Contemporary Perspectives see Part II, Civic Participation.

A. CIVIL DISOBEDIENCE IN DEMOCRATIC PERSPECTIVE

Our nation is founded on the principle that observance of the law is the eternal safeguard of liberty and defiance of the law is the surest road to tyranny....Americans are free to disagree with the law, but not to disobey it.

John F. Kennedy (c. 1962)

To break the law of the land is serious, but it is not always wrong.

Robert Bolt (1960)

The idea of civil disobedience arises from conflicts between organized society and individual conscience. In most religious and many ethical traditions, each individual is deemed personally responsible to an authority higher than the State. Yet these same traditions teach obedience to the law and civil authority as necessary "for without it, every man could swallow up his neighbor."

Some maintain that the idea of civil disobedience—openly and nonviolently breaking the law for reasons of conscience and accepting the law's punishment—can mediate between the values of law and conscience in a democratic society. Others believe acts of civil disobedience, however motivated, are coercive acts, not forms of moral or political persuasion, and that they pose a serious challenge to democratic processes and undermine the obligation to obey the law.

That charge is an especially weighty objection when the argument is about **organized**, as distinguished from **individual**, acts of civil disobedience. Explorations of the idea of civil disobedience take one deep into problems of law and conscience, the obligations of citizenship, and acceptable and unacceptable forms of democratic participation in projects for social change. This is especially true when the idea of civil disobedience is examined in the context of a democratic society.

Those willing to make the exploration soon encounter a range of confusions over what civil disobedience is and what it is not, disagreements over when it is or is not justified, and radically different estimates of its impact on the well-being of a democratic society. Still, there is a wide area of agreement over the conditions under which civil disobedience can serve not only conscience but society as a whole. Clarifying the confusions and disagreements is important, for acts of civil disobedience and civil disobedience campaigns **have** made significant contributions to the development of American democracy. Law and conscience can and have interacted in ways that serve the well-being of our society and helped realize the promise in the root values of the American constitutional system. But civil disobedience has also sometimes merged into efforts at insurrectionary violence, actions which arise not out of a deep commitment to democracy, but out of a profound disassociation from and hostility to our society.

Making the differences clear, given the complexity of the situations involved, is as difficult as it is significant. What is undertaken here is not a catechism of right answers, but an invitation to a thoughtful exploration of ideas and forms of action that involve fundamental judgments about the obligations and opportunities of citizenship in a democratic society.

Examination of the concept of civil disobedience in authoritarian or other non-democratic systems and of its role in moving such states toward more open democratic systems is a related exploration not undertaken here.

OBJECTIVES

The student should be able to

1. explain the essential features of civil disobedience in a democratic polity.

2. explain the major arguments in support of and in opposition to acts of civil disobedience which have those features.

3. explain how, in history and American experience, civil disobedience enables law and individual conscience to interact in ways that improve both.

4. explain how civil disobedience differs from other forms of law breaking and dissent.

5. explain the claim that a higher law offers criteria for moral judgment of the state's—even a democratic state's—law;

6. take, defend, and evaluate positions regarding whether participating in acts of civil disobedience will enhance or damage a democratic society.

FRAME OF REFERENCE
Conceptual Perspective

I. **Civil disobedience in a democratic perspective**. Civil disobedience may take place in more than one political context—under tyranny, under authoritarianism, and under constitutional democracy, for example. In this definition, however, we are concerned only with the context of constitutional democracy.

A. **What civil disobedience is**. Civil disobedience involves a deliberate, conscientious, open, nonviolent, public act which breaks the law. The act may be undertaken to preserve personal integrity or as part of an organized effort to achieve a change in that law or to protest other laws or government acts deemed unjust (to which the law broken may or may not be related). It is an act of **protest** undertaken in the name of a claimed higher principle. Because it is undertaken out of a commitment to the society and its system of law, it involves a **willingness to accept the punishment for law breaking**.

B. **Importance of the principal characteristics of civil disobedience**. Each of the terms above is

important; and each of the characteristics listed above are subjects of controversy. Citizens
contemplating civil disobedience will want to
explore them. In a time when various forms of
both **legal** dissent and acts of insurrectionary
violence are mistakenly called "civil disobedience," it is useful to begin with the above description of the elements of what most students
and practitioners have agreed clearly constitutes civil disobedience.

1. **The meaning of "*civil*."** An act is called "civil"
    disobedience because it breaks the civil, *i.e.*, the
    state's, law. It is also called civil because it is a
    civilized act, a peaceable attempt within the
    framework of established political authority to
    challenge that authority in some **specific** instance.

2. **Disobedience of law.** There is no statutory crime
    of "civil disobedience." What is disobeyed is a
    specific law, *e.g.*, the law that requires one to pay
    taxes, not to trespass, to register for the draft, to
    apply for a gun license, and so on.

3. **Protest of a public policy.** Where an act of civil
    disobedience is more than just a defense of per-
    sonal integrity, it always involves a protest of
    public policy judged to be unjust or wrong.

4. **Deliberate, conscientious action.** The act of civil
    disobedience is not undertaken casually. It is a
    conscious, reasoned act, undertaken after other
    means of dissent have been exhausted and usually
    as a last resort. It is conscientious in the sense
    that it expresses a moral judgment arrived at
    after serious reflection and consonant with the
    moral character of the actor.

5. **Open, public, nonviolent action.** An act of civil
    disobedience belongs and is intended to belong to
    the public life of the community. It is done open-
    ly, often after informing the authorities about the
    planned infraction. It differs from other criminal
    acts in that it respects the rights of others or
    goes to great lengths to justify their violation. It is
    intended as a contribution to the well-being of the
    society, or, if performed because of the dictates of
    private conscience, it is done without the inten-
    tion of damaging others or the society. It is, by
    definition, non-violent.

6. **Willing to accept penalty of the law.** The willing-
    ness to accept the law's penalty is a distinctive
    characteristic of civil disobedience in a demo-

cratic society. Because it does not seek to overthrow constituted authority or challenge the principle of lawfulness, it **serves** the law by willingly
and openly accepting its penalties. This characteristic is also a check on too lightly taken a
decision to commit a civilly disobedient act.

7. **Limits to action both by civil disobedients and by
    the state.** What the above characteristics imply is
    that those who practice civil disobedience accept
    the idea of **limits** to action. Violence is one key
    limit on the action of those who civilly disobey.
    By the same token, there are implied limits on
    part of the state's response to civil disobedience.
    Thus, both beating or other abuse of civil
    disobedients, quite apart from its illegality, is
    widely regarded as breaking an implicit under-
    standing that the limited character of the aims
    and tactics of those who disobey should be mir-
    rored by a limited response by authority. Handing
    down draconian sentences for civilly disobedient
    acts would also be regarded as out-of-bounds as
    a legitimate state response. The tacit agreement
    between those concerned—disobedients and
    authority—is a key feature of civil disobedience
    in a constitutional democracy.

II. **Some important distinctions.** Much of the argument about
civil disobedience involves discussion of the following:

A. **Moral/political; individual/socially organized.** One diffi-
    cult distinction is between civil disobedience that is
    primarily **moral** and action that, in intent and pur-
    pose, is **political.** The first is often the act of an **indi-
    vidual** who publicly proclaims his or her response to a
    direct conflict between his or her personal moral
    principle and the law: he or she cannot, in con-
    science, obey that law. By contrast, **political** civil
    disobedience is organized. It is essentially a method,
    a tactic designed to achieve a political goal. What
    guides such action is the desired result in public life,
    not the principle which required the individual to
    disobey. Moral civil disobedience may or may not have
    desired political effects. It proceeds, however, from a
    spirit of "I can do no other" rather than from a calcu-
    lation of consequences.

1. **The case of Sir Thomas More. Sir Thomas More**
    (1478-1535) did not agree with the act of Henry
    VIII's Parliament that required Englishmen to
    take an oath recognizing the King, not the Pope,
    as the head of the Church of England. But he did
    not resist until an attempt was made to force
    him **personally** to take that oath. His was an

individual moral act of civil disobedience, not an attempt to force political change.

2. **Two purposes of civil disobedience.** Both individual moral resistance and organized political efforts which meet the qualifications above may be described as civil disobedience. They may overlap, but they are different. Robert Bolt's drama, *A Man For All Seasons* (1960), explores this distinction in depth.

B. **Direct/indirect.** Civil disobedience can be direct or indirect.

1. **Direct civil disobedience.** Breaking the law which is itself the object of the protest involves one kind of civil disobedience. The law broken and the object of protest are identical. Thus, a person who refuses to cooperate with an order inducting him into the military, or, as a white, deliberately uses a "colored" waiting room in a state with legal segregation, breaks a law that is the object of his protest.

2. **Indirect civil disobedience.** But there are other forms of civil disobedience which involve breaking a law which is otherwise unobjectionable, because such a law can become the occasion for focusing attention on the real object of protest. Thus, blocking entrance to a draft board or to a segregated facility may be announced as civil disobedience and defended as such because the act is, at least symbolically, connected to the law which is being protested. Those undertaking such indirect acts may argue that there is no direct way for them to disassociate themselves from the law they believe to be immoral or unjust. Thus, Thoreau refused to pay his state taxes, not because he disapproved of them, but because he believed it necessary to separate himself from complicity in what he believed to be the unjust acts of his government. This kind of indirect civil disobedience is usually connected with political movements, not individual moral disobedience.

III. **What civil disobedience is not.** Some writings on civil disobedience have treated the original disobedience—Adam and Eve's—as the beginning of the story. This appears mistaken. Not every act of disobedience is civil disobedience. In the continuum that runs from legally permitted dissent to try to change the law on one side, to **revolution** on the other, civil disobedience occupies a middle position. Seriously interested citizens will want to reflect on the larger problems of **rebellion** and justifications for it.

Reflection is also called for on the history and theory of **nonviolent action**, the socially organized withdrawal of consent, as a way to force political change, and the forms of resistance used by pacifists in opposition to the military. All these are related to civil disobedience. In most cases, civil disobedience is a sub-head encountered when exploring these larger topics. It is important to understand both the relationships and the differences.

A. **Not revolutionary.** Civil disobedience—either as an act of an individual who refuses to obey a law in the name of a claimed higher principle or as an organized civic act undertaken by people in their capacity as citizens—must be sharply distinguished from efforts to overthrow legitimate authority. Such revolutionary acts may be conscientious or even warranted. But they are **not** civil disobedience, especially not in a democratic society.

B. **Not insurrectionary or legal protest.** Neither riots nor legal forms of protest qualify as civil disobedience. The former violently defies political authority, and the latter acts entirely within the boundaries of the law. While a **revolution** seeks to capture political authority, or a **rebellion** to demolish it, the **civil disobedient** (i.e., one who commits civil disobedience) only challenges that authority in some specific instance. What the three have in common in the case we suppose is an illegal challenge to the law of a democratic society. There is both an overlap and significant difference between **legal** forms of protest and civil disobedience.

C. **Not legal.** Civil disobedience is never a legal act. For instance, a conscientious objector is not a civil disobedient. Such a claim is **within** the law. It is only if a conscientious objector refuses to cooperate with the Selective Service System, or if his claim is rejected and he chooses to violate an induction order, that he may become civilly disobedient. Breaking a law to test its legality by appeal to a higher court is a related form of action, but it is not the same as civil disobedience, the central characteristic of which is the deliberate peaceful violation of a law with which one disagrees, not the claim that the law is "illegal" because it violates a higher law that takes precedence within the legal system, such as a law in conflict with the U.S. Constitution.

IV. **Sources, justifications, and challenges.** There are a number of sources and justifications used by those who commit civil disobedience.

A. **Higher law.** The essential ground for civil disobedience often lies in the assertion of a higher law that requires disobedience of man-made law. It is usually religious authority that is involved. But justification may take a different form such as "natural law," relating not to God's law but to the universe itself. This "natural law" claim is presented as being available to each human being by virtue of his or her reason or moral sense. Whatever the source, the claim is clear: there are universal moral laws which may sometimes justify deliberate violation of a state's—even a democratic state's—law.

B. **Conscience**. "Conscience" is the key term. It is the voice of the individual's sense of right and wrong. It provides a reason for action apart from fear and material gain. But different consciences are differently formed.

1. **Placing conscience above the law**. If one person asserts the right to put his or her conscience above the law, so may another. Thus, **Jeb Magruder**, a planner of the break-in to the Democratic Party's headquarters at the Watergate complex in Washington, D.C., in 1972, who was convicted of conspiracy to obstruct justice during the Nixon administration, testified that the dramatic civil disobedience during the Vietnam War of an admired former teacher, **William Sloan Coffin**, was the model for his own law breaking. Magruder acted, by his own account, out of conscience, to serve his idea of the public good.

2. **Challenges to placing conscience above the law**. The case for placing conscience above law has been challenged by many writers who point out that if the individual conscience—even the tested, informed, reflective conscience—is made absolute and is accordingly considered the final judge of what laws are to be obeyed or disobeyed, the result is an invitation to social chaos. Defenders of conscientious civil disobedience argue that there can be no **other** final judge. One may determine to obey or not to obey, but, in the final resort, each individual does make his own judgment. To this argument, critics might respond that it confuses the "ought" with the "is." That people do choose to place conscience above the law is not self-validating—perhaps they ought always to obey constitutionally-valid democratically created law. Perhaps they should follow the maxim endorsed by the philosopher **Immanuel Kant** (1724-1804) and "censure freely but obey punctually."

C. **Law**. The argument above does not speak to the original question, which is whether one can **justify** a deci-

sion to disobey. Different answers are given by those with different perspectives on the role of law in securing social order. For some, law and order are identical. Others argue that just as the law is not identical with justice—changes in the law can increase the measure of justice—so the current law can be regarded as an instrument for maintaining order, but not the **only** one. In this perspective, civil disobedience can be an instrument for achieving greater justice and, thus, helping guarantee order.

D. **Varieties of "civil disobedience."** As the examples above show, disentangling the justifications and challenges to the desirability and morality of civilly disobedient acts in a democracy is complex. There is a long list of theoretical and practical criticisms of civil disobedience: that it encourages interest groups to act coercively, seeking to prevail over the common good; that it undermines respect for the law and encourages individuals to take the law into their own hands; that it subverts the legal process by which we make and reform the law; that it leads to social chaos by undermining the core idea that our society is governed by laws, not men. Most of these criticisms are, however, most applicable to civil disobedience claims which do **not** have the features of civil disobedience listed above in I.A.

E. **The necessity for qualification in defining legitimate civil disobedience**. Each of the conceptual statements above can and has been challenged.

1. **Example of a possible exception to the elements of civil disobedience**. The claim, for example, that civil disobedience must be "open" runs up against situations like those faced in the 1850s by Abolitionists who violated the Fugitive Slave Act and smuggled slaves to free territory. In many cases, they acted in secret to protect not themselves, but the former slaves seeking freedom. Should their failure to be open disqualify their act as one of civil disobedience?

2. **Burden of proof for exceptions as being upon the civil disobedient**. What is suggested here is not a set of absolute conditions but a number of features which together constitute civil disobedience. The moral injunction that one should not tell a lie may be violated in the interest of saving a life without dissolving this moral standard. Similarly, there may be exceptions to the standards above for civil disobedience in a democracy, but the standards are our starting points from which each exception must justify its departure.

This is also the case with departures from the standards of the law itself. The burden of proof is on the civil disobedient, who must give good reasons why departures are morally and socially justified. But exceptions cannot include acts such as violent ones: whether or not violence is justified (which is a separate question) it is not civil disobedience.

Historical Perspective

Tracing civil disobedience in history can lead one into very long corridors. In the Book of Exodus, Pharaoh ordered the Hebrew midwives to kill all new-born males. The midwives, appealing to higher duty, refused, thus giving us one of the earliest known instances of civil disobedience. The major historical examples are found in religious history and in the actions of those expressing principled opposition to war.

But core elements of the idea of civil disobedience also appear in ancient philosophy, in literature, and throughout political history. They are interwoven with the development of both the theory and practice of resistance to tyranny and the growth of democratic government. Ideas of civil disobedience turn up in any study of nonviolent social organization for resistance or political change. They are present in the development of the idea of a free press, as found in the defiance by **John Milton** (1608-1674) in his *Areopagitica* of England's law requiring licensing of books by official censors (1644). They are even found in the history of science.

One may easily be led too far astray in studies of non-violence or pacifism or rebellion. Civil disobedience is a much narrower topic, sometimes a sub-head of these subjects. One may soon want to focus inquiry on an even more limited topic: civil disobedience in a democratic society. Still, the following historical mileposts can help illuminate the discussion:

I. *Antigone*. Sophocles' play, first performed in Athens in the fifth century B.C., tells the story of the conflict between Creon, King of Thebes, and Antigone. Creon has decreed that Antigone's brother, dead after leading an attack on the city, shall lie unburied outside the city gates, for he was guilty of treason. In that time, an unburied corpse was believed to find no rest. Antigone, out of piety and family loyalty, and appealing to a higher law than the law of the city, defies Creon's order, seeks to bury her brother, and is condemned to death. In this play, Creon's responsibility to enforce the law to preserve the integrity of the state comes into direct conflict with Antigone's refusal to obey: thus a classic confrontation between man-made law and an individual's conscience.

This play, the Greek prototype of civil disobedience, ends in tragedy for all concerned.

II. **Socrates.** In 399 B.C., in Athens, **Socrates** (469-399 B.C.) was tried and condemned to death for impiety and for "corrupting" the youth of Athens. He refused to stop teaching and comply with the law. Many today trace the idea of academic freedom back to his refusal. Socrates deliberately disobeyed, but believing the law under which he was accused to be a valid law of the state, he refused to evade punishment when friends urged him to escape from Athens. In the *Crito*, a Platonic dialogue, Socrates explains why. Having accepted the benefits of society, he felt a moral obligation to be a good citizen by demonstrating respect for the principle of lawfulness even as he disobeyed the law. He acknowledged the authority of the state even to the point of willingly giving up his life. However, Socrates asserted that there is one realm in which the claims of the state are void: the realm of conscience.

III. **Religious disobedience before Christ.** In the Old Testament Book of Daniel, Daniel's three friends disobey Nebuchadnezzar and refuse, under threat of death, to worship an idol. Thrown into the fiery furnace, they survive. The king frees them, recognizing that they must have a powerful god. The Old Testament is filled with such examples of individuals who openly and without violence refuse to obey an edict of the state, claiming devotion to God's law.

IV. **Early Christianity.** Christianity, in its first centuries, was one of the earliest widespread—and in the end, most successful—civil disobedience movements. The refusal of Christians of those days to enter Rome's army, following both Christ's teachings to shun violence and to avoid the idolatry of obeisance to Rome's gods, is often offered as an early example of civil disobedience.

V. **Boétie. Etienne de la Boétie**, a sixteenth-century writer, had a significant influence on both Thoreau and Tolstoy, and, through Tolstoy, on Gandhi. De la Boétie is one of the original theorists offering the socially organized nonviolent withdrawal of consent as a powerful political instrument to use against tyrants. In his essay "Voluntary Servitude," he called on people to deliver themselves from a tyrant by not obeying him. Thus, without violence, "a great Colossus whose base has been stolen [will] of his own weight sink [and] shatter."

VI. **Protestant sects.** The period of the Reformation in early sixteenth-century Germany, which saw both the rise of Protestantism and changes in the Roman Catholic church, produced a wide range of challenges to religious and state authority from the Reformation's radical wing. Similar challenges appeared during the English Civil War in 1642.

A. **The character of Protestant challenges to authority**. Protestant sects laid the essential ground for challenges to political and religious authority by finding the locus of final authority to be the individual soul in its relation to God. What was novel was the emphasis upon the directness of this relationship, unmediated by officers of the Church. Hence the term "the priesthood of all believers" to describe this central Protestant idea.

B. **Challenges to authority stemming from Protestant ideas**. Challenges from radical political and religious groups that directly or indirectly stem from Protestant ideas offer a variety of doctrines and practices, ranging from anarchism and withdrawal from society, to affirmations of individual conscience against the state by citizens loyal to political authority. The Historic Peace Churches in Germany (e.g., Mennonites, Brethren) and the Society of Friends (Quakers) in England and the United States provided many examples of conscientious non-violent challenges to state authority. Some, as in the case of the Anabaptist Mennonites, taught a religious removal from all affairs of state, yet their refusal to bear arms is a part of a broader history of civil disobedience. In the case of the Quakers, remarkable individuals like the Englishman **George Fox** (1724-1791) and the American **John Woolman** (1720-1772), one of the colonies' first opponents of slavery, as well as many ordinary believers, based their disobedience not on withdrawal, but on the primacy of an "inner light" representing "that of God" in every man, which sometimes dictated civil disobedience. Though varying in their rationale, religious pacifists' open refusal to obey laws that required participation in the military has played an important role in the development of a reasoned case for civil disobedience.

VII. **Thoreau**. The role of **Henry David Thoreau** (1817-1862) in giving visibility and support to concepts of civil disobedience is ironic. His essay (1848), explaining why he preferred jail to paying taxes to a state authority that warred against Mexico and helped enforce slavery, provides a most eloquent case for respecting "the right" rather than "the law."

A. **Thoreau as not advocating civil disobedience as it is known today**. But in this, the best known treatise on "civil disobedience," Thoreau nowhere uses the term. The essay was not given its present title, "On the Duty of Civil Disobedience," until after his death. The ideas presented in the essay do not match the previous description of the essential features of civil disobedience. Thoreau expresses no respect for any system of law and places the individual above the law. He "had no time" to pursue any legal channel for affecting change in the policies he protested. His original title was "On the Relation of the Individual to the State," and the essay is more of a contribution to anarchist thought than to the idea of civil disobedience in a democratic society.

B. **The influence of Thoreau's essay**. Thoreau's essay has nevertheless, for more than a century, been the first text many draw on when seeking to justify their action in refusing to obey a law deeply believed to be immoral. Its integrity and the quality of its challenge to passive compliance, as distinguished from conscientious disobedience, has earned the essay its reputation as a classic text of civil disobedience, despite its ambiguous relation to the concepts.

VIII. **Tolstoy.** Gandhi credited **Count Leo Tolstoy** (1828-1910) as one of the sources from which he concluded that it was the submissiveness and cooperation of the Indians that made British rule in India possible. Tolstoy, the nineteenth-century Russian novelist and social and religious theorist, condemned **forcible** resistance to authority, but as a Christian anarchist, he taught tax refusal and other forms of withholding cooperation with governmental authority as a way to carry out New Testament teachings.

IX. **Gandhi.** The influence of **Mohandas K. Gandhi** (1869-1948), known as the "Mahatma" ("Great Soul"), on the development and practice of civil disobedience is immense, but also ironic.

A. **Gandhi's civil disobedience not in a democratic context**. Though he challenged particular laws, Gandhi did so in the interest of fundamental change in governmental authority. His was a nonviolent **revolutionary** movement.

B. **The qualities of Gandhi's civil disobedience**. Despite the absence of a democratic context, the most distinctive elements of classic civil disobedience were prominent in Gandhi's teaching and practice. His openness, truthfulness, nonviolence, and willingness to accept the penalty of the law, even while breaking it, clarified civil disobedience concepts and enable us to distinguish them from other forms of law breaking. Yet these requirements flowed not from his respect for a legal system whose moral authority he denied, but from his attitude toward those he opposed. He insisted on respect for his opponents. He sought to form community out of differences. He appealed to that quality in men which could recognize injustice, and so change. These characteristics of Gandhian civil disobedience, even though set within an essentially insurrectionary movement, have been a deeply influential shaping force in establishing the spirit, purpose, and perspective of modern organized political civil disobedience which seeks to form community out of conflict.

C. **An example of a Gandhian civil disobedience campaign.** An example of a Gandhian campaign is as follows: In Vykom, India, in 1924, a group of Gandhians challenged the Maharajah's edict forbidding untouchables to use a road which passed a Brahmin temple. Despite beatings and arrests, for years, through storm and flood, the protesters nonviolently confronted the police cordon thrown across the road, until the state, with the support of Brahmin authorities, opened the road to all.

X. **Anarchists.** In the anarchist tradition, which rejects the state as a form of government, one nevertheless encounters some of the features of civil disobedience, *i.e.*, open, nonviolent disobedience to the state's edicts. The primacy of individual rights in the writings of **Pierre Joseph Proudhon** (1809-1865) and the case for gradual, nonviolent, reasoned elimination of political institutions in *An Inquiry Concerning Political Justice* (1793) by **William Godwin** (1756-1836) helped lay some of the theoretical groundwork for some forms of civil disobedience. One must not forget, however, the opposite current of Anarchist resistance to political authority through violent, secret organizations which engaged in assassination and other destruction and which recognized no moral or conventional restraint. The Russian **Sergei Netschaiev** (1848-1882) is an example of this extreme of anarchist thought and action.

XI. **Non-violent resistance to Nazis and Quislings.** In certain cases, nonviolent resistance was used against Nazis or Nazi-supported regimes. Two examples are the following.

A. **Norwegian teachers, 1943.** In Norway in 1942, between 8,000 and 10,000 teachers (out of a total of 12,000) refused to join the Nazi-sponsored teachers' organization and teach Nazi propaganda in the schools. They wrote the Department of Education announcing their refusal. One thousand teachers were arrested and sent to concentration camps in the far North, where they were kept under miserable conditions and threatened with death. The schools were closed. An outpouring of support from the public and continued non-violent resistance from teachers posed problems for the regime of the Nazi Quisling in power. Eight months after

their arrest, the teachers were released and the effort to organize a corporate state along fascist lines was abandoned in Norway.

B. **Danish resisters, 1943.** In Denmark in October 1943, Danish resisters acted non-violently against the law by preventing the arrest of Danish Jews. Some 6,500 of the 7,000 Danish Jews were successfully smuggled to Sweden. Again a caution: these examples of non-violent resistance to tyranny must be distinguished from disobedience which acknowledges governmental authority. A second caution is that there is no suggestion here that a general non-violent resistance either to the Nazis or anyone like them would be anything other than suicidal.

C. **The Nuremberg Trials.** Some have argued that the trials of Nazi war criminals after World War II provide justification and even protection for conduct in deliberate violation of state law as a protest against the illegal acts of a government. The trials held that individuals were legally and morally responsible for their participation in crimes of war (violations of the international law of war) and crimes against humanity (extermination and enslavement of civilian populations). For some writers, the outcome of the Nuremberg trials can be used to legally justify refusal to be drafted into a war deemed immoral. Others respond that the crimes punished at Nuremberg could be committed only by persons who had substantial freedom of choice, i.e., they were not applied to privates or non-commissioned or junior officers. Though the argument over the Nuremberg Trials covers some of the same ground surveyed in studies of civil disobedience, this argument is about legality, not about justified, clearly illegal, disobedience.

XII. **The American experience.** No richer history of experiments in civil disobedience can be found than the history of the use of these tactics in a wide range of movements for social change in America. The ideas and practice of civil disobedience have been a part of American history, from early Quaker resistance to policies calling for arming against the Indians, through the Abolitionists' response to the Fugitive Slave Act, and on to various labor, suffragette, and socialist or anarchist-led movements for social change. Moreover, civil disobedience ideas played major roles in youth revolts in the 1960s, in opposition to America's role in the Vietnam War, and most prominently in the theory and practice of the Civil Rights movement from 1955 until 1980. Two examples are given here. Both come closest to meeting the standards for civil disobedience in a democracy outlined above.

A. **Resisting nuclear tests in the Pacific.** In March 1958, four American pacifists, sponsored by the Committee for Non-Violent Action, attempted to sail their boat to the Marshall Islands in the Central Pacific at a time of scheduled nuclear bomb tests, in order to protest the development of nuclear weapons. The *Golden Rule* was halted at Honolulu, and the crew was imprisoned when they refused to abandon their plan. Though the voyage failed, this attempt to influence governmental policy by direct, open, non-violent sacrificial action outside the normal political processes was widely publicized and met all the standards for civil disobedience discussed above.

B. **Martin Luther King, Jr.** The **Rev. Martin Luther King, Jr.** (1929-1968) merged individual principled civil disobedience into a collective political movement which used protest marches and demonstrations, non-violent civil disobedience, and non-violent resistance to challenge state and local laws which denied black Americans equal access to schools, the voting booth, and public facilities.

1. **King as practicing classic civil disobedience.** From 1955, when he came to public notice as the leader of the Montgomery bus boycott, until his assassination in 1968, he embodied in his work all of the features of what we have called "classic civil disobedience". King urged people to disobey "unjust" laws and to do it openly, peacefully, and with a willingness to accept the penalty imposed by law for such conduct. He acknowledged his debt to Gandhi, and drew heavily on biblical themes (referring, for example, to Shadrach, Meshach, and Abednigo), and the fundamental values of an American society which affirmed the dignity of each human being, however inconsistently or hypocritically they were held at times.

2. **King's *Letter from Birmingham City Jail* as a civil disobedience classic.** King's *Letter from Birmingham City Jail* (1963), which distinguished between efforts to evade or defy the law and civil disobedience as practiced by those willing to follow his disciplines to affirm a higher moral law, is a classic of civil disobedience. In the *Letter*, King argued the case for direct non-violent action in the streets when long efforts at negotiations to change unjust laws failed. His work laid the groundwork for sweeping changes in American civil rights legislation.

Contemporary Perspective

Civil disobedience campaigns have played major roles in recent history in South Africa, Soviet-dominated Europe, and even in China. The revolutions of 1989 in Eastern Europe were largely non-violent, building on the example of the Solidarity movement in Poland, which also pioneered new forms of civil disobedience. In addition, civil disobedience concepts and campaigns are now significant parts of our own political culture, however obscure or peripheral they may have been in some periods of American history.

I. **Civil disobedience becoming more widespread.** In America, civil disobedience language and tactics now appear in almost every movement for social change, whatever its position on the political spectrum. It is now a regular tactic of groups opposed to American military programs—but a call to civil disobedience was also made by those far to their right on the political spectrum who have disobeyed the law and blocked entrances to abortion clinics. Parallel to the relationship of civil disobedience to civic law, a kind of para-civil disobedience is now visible in organized challenges to private authorities on campus, in churches, and in disputes over rent control. In California and the Northwest, environmental activists launched what were called widespread civil disobedience campaigns in American forests.

II. **Civil disobedience becoming more political.** Most current references to civil disobedience in news stories tell of organized coercive efforts to force change, rather than of individual efforts to bear witness to a higher law. The goal is rarely now an attempt at persuasion or reconciliation. Even those efforts which remain non-violent emphasize numbers of disobedients and efforts to organize a minority capable of preventing the normal functioning of society unless the protesters' goals are met. Whereas, for the most part, the term "civil disobedience" was previously used to designate expressions of principled resistance to political power, it is now often regarded as an instrument for exerting physical power.

III. **Civil disobedience becoming less disciplined.** In his "Letter from Birmingham City Jail," Martin Luther King, Jr. charted the steps to civil disobedience as requiring "self-purification" and extensive efforts at negotiation before undertaking, as a last resort, a civil disobedience campaign.

A. **"Direct action" and instances of pseudo-"civil disobedience."** Today the leader of a gun owners' club, defying a California law requiring the registration of semi-automatic guns, eschews efforts at negotiation and says, "If civil disobedience was good enough for Dr.

King, it's good enough for me." Only 6,000 of 300,000 expected registrants complied with the law. A leader of ACT-UP (AIDS Coalition to Unleash Power), offers rationales for violence while calling for "civil disobedience." Activists in the effort to save forests or stop animal experimentation drive spikes into trees (which can injure lumber mill workers) or bomb animal research centers.

B. **Unwillingness to tolerate civil disobedience.** Opponents of the sort of "direct action" just described have become less willing to tolerate civil disobedience in causes which involve complex weighing of consequences instead of clearly unjust laws. Civil disobedience campaigns against obvious injustice, such as the Civil Rights Movement of the 1960s, can draw on common values in the community to build support for their protest. That is not the case with many campaigns purporting to practice "civil disobedience" today.

C. **Use of civil disobedience as an attempt to enforce minority rule.** Civil disobedience has always been justified in utilitarian terms. It sought to form new agreements in the community. Today, instead of a way to provide the occasion for change which draws on common values, civil disobedience is often a means by which one part of the community seeks to impose its will, often a minority will, on others.

D. **The crisis of civil disobedience today.** The idea and practice of civil disobedience is now in crisis.

1. **Blurring the distinction between civil disobedience and insurrectionary violence.** The line between civil disobedience and insurrectionary violence has been blurred. In a time when governmental authority grows ever more intrusive, in which governmental leaders themselves offer defenses of extra-legal action based on "civil disobedience," one valuable instrument of democratic government is in jeopardy.

2. **The context of alienation from society.** Action set in an alienated context and conducted as an act of disassociation from, not commitment to, a society; action which seeks to evade, not accept, the law's penalty; or action which does not reject violence, but is instead consciously and publicly based on preparation for violence or designed to further a climate that will engender violence is not civil disobedience.

3. **Authentic civil disobedience as a service to society.** Civil disobedience which posits an authority superior to the state and presents to the individual and civic conscience imperatives by which the policies of the state are to be judged **serves** our society. It is needed in any democratic political theory adequate to the realities of twentieth-century mass societies. It should be an expected and essential part of the complex process by which a democratic polity fulfill its central values.

4. **The need for critical examination of what passes for "civil disobedience" today.** Given the recent misuse of the values and language of civil disobedience, it will take some hard work and some serious thought to restore that kind of civil disobedience to an honored place in our country.

B. CITIZENS AND THE POLICY PROCESS

At the end of the day, the American people are going to have to decide. No President can pursue a policy for very long without the support and the understanding of the Congress and the American people. That's been demonstrated over and over again.

Dean Rusk (1984)

For a long time this country of ours has lacked one of the instruments which freemen everywhere held fundamental. For a long time there have been no sufficient opportunities for counsel among the people; no place and method of talk, of exchange of opinion, of parley. We must learn, we freemen, to meet, as our fathers did, somehow, somewhere, for consultation. There must be discussion and debate, in which all freely participate....The whole purpose of democracy is that we may hold counsel with one another, so as not to depend upon the understanding of one man, but to depend upon the counsel of all. For only as men are brought into counsel, and state their own needs and interests, can the general interests of a great people be compounded into a policy suitable for all.

Woodrow Wilson (c.1912)

[T]he only title in our democracy superior to that of President, the title of citizen.

Jimmy Carter (1981)

I know of no safe depository of the ultimate powers of the society but the people themselves, and if we think them not enlightened enough to exercise their control with a wholesome discretion, the remedy is not to take it from them, but to inform their discretion.

Thomas Jefferson (1820)

INTRODUCTION

Throughout our nation's history, citizens—**individual Americans**—have been at the core of the policy process. Our representative democracy is based on the long-cherished idea that for democracy to work, citizens must engage in debate with one another on policy issues; public officials must come to learn about the views and concerns and hopes that citizens hold on these issues; and citizens, in various ways, must act on policy issues. It is central to this democratic tradition that the policy process takes the form of continuous public discourse. The role of citizens in the policy process has changed over the years. Among the factors that have led to changes in this relationship are the emergence of new conditions and challenges in technology, in our communities, and in the nature of politics itself. Indeed, at this juncture in the nation's history, this changing mix of factors is producing concern about the nation's political health—that the relationship of the public to the policy process is a state of disrepair. Because of these concerns, it is appropriate to explore the role of citizens in the process of creating public policy. Now, as in the past, that role remains essential to the working of American democracy.

OBJECTIVES

The citizen should be able to

1. explain why it is important for citizens to participate in the policy process.

2. discuss what it means to participate in the policy process.

3. discuss and assess the historical factors and trends that have come to affect the relationship between citizens and the policy process.

4. take, defend, and evaluate positions on the various ways to become involved in the policy process.

FRAME OF REFERENCE
Conceptual Perspective

I.   **The importance of citizens participating in the policy process.** We frequently take for granted that in a democratic society citizens will participate in the policy process. Yet, we often overlook just how essential citizen participation is to our nation's political and civic health. The importance of citizen involvement in America's policy process is illustrated by the following forms of civic participation.

A.   **Need for citizen input beyond the voting booth.** The policy process—indeed democracy—neither begins nor ends at the voting booth. Rather, democracy concerns primarily what happens between elections: how people come to form their opinions; whether, and how, they are able to express their considered thoughts as well as their hopes and dreams; and if, and how, we as a society decide on the ways in which to achieve our desired goals. Abraham Lincoln stated in his Gettysburg Address that America is to be a nation whose government is "of the people, by the people, and for the people." To fulfill the intent of this renowned description of democracy—that is, in order to have a vibrant and working democracy—citizens must participate in the policy process.

B.   **Necessity for decisions on various issues.** Our society faces many policy challenges. The homeless, drugs, AIDS, health care, defense, as well as a plethora of other issues are all on the public agenda today; undoubtedly, the specific issues on the agenda tomorrow will be different. Whatever issues ultimately stand before us, we are obliged to decide on whether, and how, we will act. What we decide will shape our quality of life; affect people both here and abroad; and reflect on the kind of society in which we choose to live and seek to create—for ourselves and for others.

C.   **Need for sustainable policies.** Effective action on many issues today requires ample resources over the short- and long-term. While these resources may be financial, they may include time and energy. For such policies to be developed, fundamental questions such as the following must be answered: What are our priorities? What do we value? What principles should guide our actions? Ultimately, in a democracy, only citizens can answer these questions.

D.   **Need to hear different perspectives.** Our increasingly diverse nation has given rise to correspondingly diverse perspectives on public issues. It is important, then, that citizens from all walks of life participate in the policy process; for only then can we, as a nation, hear and consider different perspectives, and find ways to balance them. Pursuing this path will make it more likely that the actions we take are effective and fair. Without broad citizen participation, policy decisions will be left to a handful of individuals who ultimately may represent only their own perspectives, potentially excluding the views and needs of many Americans.

E. **Need to create the political will to act**. Citizen participation in the policy process goes hand-in-hand with creating the political will to act. Whether citizens must write a check to finance new taxes for education or come together to rebuild a neighborhood park, a sense of political will must be present for effective and sustainable action. But political will is not easily created. Citizens must feel a sense of commitment to a desired end and a sense of common ownership and responsibility; they must also believe that change can occur. All of these factors which contribute to the political will to act may be distilled in the process of participation itself. Through the process of participation citizens can develop a sense of belonging to a community; indeed, a healthy civic life has broader implications for how people live together in their community.

II. **Ways in which citizens can participate in the policy process**. Generally, citizens engage in the policy process in two fundamental ways: through the civic life of their communities and through the governing process. Both are essential elements of a healthy policy process.

   A. **Citizen participation through the civic life of the community.** Much of the policy process in America today is informal. How citizens come to understand, consider, and act on policy issues often relates to activities outside the realm of government. For instance, citizens learn and think about issues by attending civic forums in their communities and, even more fundamentally, by talking with their neighbors. Citizens also belong to civic organizations like the local Parent Teachers Association, neighborhood associations, service organizations, ad hoc issue associations, and other groups. Through these and other activities citizens not only learn about policy issues but often find ways to address issues together.

   B. **Citizen participation in the governing process.** Citizens also take part in various facets of the formal process of governing. For instance, citizens attend public meetings and hearings sponsored by government agencies; they meet with or write to public officials to express their concerns; and citizens join organizations—such as trade groups, public interest organizations, and others—as a way of providing input into the policy process. Finally, of course, citizens vote in elections.

III. **Deliberation as the core of participating in the policy process.** Finding ways to effectively address the challenges before our society requires discussion, careful thought, and deliberation. Citizens must deliberate on issues if they are to play a constructive role in the formal and informal workings of the policy process. There are a number of important reasons for this.

   A. **Unreflective opinions as unreliable.** Citizens' unreflective opinions are often poor indicators of their considered views. Uninformed opinion is often beset by contradictions, mired by misperceptions, and easily changed by the introduction of new information. Making policy decisions on such views—which are often quite volatile—undercuts the ability of society to develop reasonable, informed policies.

   B. **Need for a sense of public judgment to develop policy.** To develop policies that reflect citizens' true values and attitudes, public thought must move from unreflective views to what has been called **public judgment**. Public judgment emerges only after people become informed about an issue and considered the costs of alternatives for dealing with it. Public judgment helps to create an environment for sound policy decisions and increases the likelihood for developing broadly-supported and sustainable policy.

   C. **Deliberation as part of public judgment.** The development of a considered judgment on policy issues requires that citizens deliberate—that they engage in careful thought and discussion.

       1. **Active, not passive participation.** Participating in the policy process should not be viewed as merely voting periodically and remaining inactive between elections. Rather, citizens, who are, after all, **members** of the body politic, play a part in the creation of public judgment on an issue only through action beyond the formalities of the electoral process.

       2. **Considered opinions as more likely to be taken seriously by office holders**. The deliberative process can contribute to reasoned views on policy issues that are more likely to influence public officials. Emotive demands, on the other hand, are more likely to be resisted by conscientious office holders or public servants.

IV. **What deliberation means.** Public deliberation on policy issues requires a number of critical components.

   A. **Need for a clear understanding of issues.** Deliberating on issues requires considering and wrestling with different aspects of public policy.

       1. **Understanding what is "at issue."** Participating in the policy process requires having a clear

sense of what is "at issue" in a particular situation.

a. **How debate can become obscured**. What is the debate about—what must be decided and why? It is not always easy to answer such questions: public debate can be obscured by lofty rhetoric, overwhelming amounts of information, and divisive discussion. Yet only by clarifying what is at issue can public judgment or individual action be effective.

b. **Finding the key issue**. The need to clarify issues is illustrated by the following example: suppose some school districts are seeking to implement a new "school-based management" committee structure where school administrators, teachers and parents collectively make decisions about running the school. Debate on the measure could become bogged down in deciding how many parents should sit on the school committee. The underlying issue is what role parents should play in the operation of their schools. But if this issue is sidestepped, the school district's new management committee may be unable to work effectively.

2. **Using basic facts as boundaries of debate**. Facts play an important role in policy discussions. They can help to focus debate and to define the issue at hand. Still, in too many debates the facts become the issue—indeed, at times policy discussions become mired in debate over the relevance and accuracy of particular facts. Instead, facts should be used to help elucidate positions in a debate—to help people tell their side of the story. The facts themselves should not become the issue. When facts do become the focus of the debate, larger, more basic issues may be at stake—such as opposing perspectives over how to define the issue or conflicting values concerning what lies at the root of the debate.

3. **Clarifying underlying values**. When one looks behind the facts in many policy debates, the core points at issue are often values: what is held to be important and how conflicting needs and desires can be balanced. Health care is a good example. The current debate on health care in many rural communities often revolves around the number of hospitals that will be forced to close and how affected communities will provide health care to their residents. Behind the "facts" of this situation are set of values which might include how people define "fairness" and "personal security"—that is, whether, and under what conditions, people will have access to health care. These values need to be understood and frequently discussed if the issue is to be resolved effectively. Once this discovery occurs, those debating **may** find the number of hospitals to be less important than ensuring the provision of quality care.

4. **Understanding trade-offs and consequences**. Thinking about policy issues requires weighing the trade-offs (the cost and benefits of alternatives) and consequences of various actions. Who will bear the economic, social or political costs of an action? What might have to be given up to act in one way rather than in another? What kinds of risks are acceptable? These questions become especially difficult to consider when emotions enter debate—when people perceive their vital concerns to be at stake—and especially when they may be willing to think about other points of view. Yet it is only by considering the cost and benefits of alternatives that people can make sensible choices among policy options; that they can recognize, understand, and accept the results of their decisions; and, ultimately, that lasting policies are developed.

B. **The need to see different perspectives.** Deliberating on issues requires an open-mind—the ability to see other people's points-of-view and the willingness to change one's own opinion.

1. **The importance of weighing different perspectives.** Citizens need to think about and weigh different perspectives on issues if they are to understand various issues and reach a considered judgment on what to do about them. For instance, there is much debate over what kind of health care services senior citizens should receive, who should pay for them, and what limits might exist. Yet, in this debate, senior citizens and younger individuals are not usually brought together to consider their different perspectives. One result is that people may not entertain another point of view.

2. **A willingness to rethink one's own point of view.** Essential to developing a reasoned view on an issue is open-mindedness—the willingness to listen to what others say and, when appropriate, alter one's thinking. Failure to adhere to this principle can undermine or even terminate the

process of deliberation. When people become entrenched in their own views, policy debates become gridlocked; it can become difficult to find common ground for action. Unaddressed problems can worsen.

C. **The need to make choices.** Making choices is an inherent part of the deliberating process on policy issues.

   1. **The act of making a choice.** The policy process is fundamentally about choosing between competing directions for action. On local issues, citizens may make these choices by participating in the civic life of their community. In the governing process, citizens—individually, as a whole, and through organizations they join—attempt to influence public officials who ultimately decide upon policy. Whether citizens are acting on their own or through the formal process of government, a key feature of the deliberative process is weighing options for action and **making choices**.

   2. **The need to accept consequences.** In their constructive deliberation, conscientious citizens strive to understand and **accept** the consequences of their choices. Few, if any, public decisions are without costs, whether political, economic, or social; and all involve the time and energy of individuals. Citizens need to recognize these costs and be prepared to bear them. For instance, most Americans want to reduce the federal budget deficit; but doing so requires reducing spending, raising revenues, or a combination of both. Each of these actions would have an effect on many if not most Americans. Yet, beyond rhetorical calls for deficit reduction, it is unclear what costs citizens are willing to bear. Here it must also be noted that there are often costs associated with **not** acting—with maintaining the status quo.

D. **Finding common ground.** Only through thinking about and openly discussing issues can common ground—those concerns and values that individuals hold in common—be found. Finding common ground does not necessarily mean that people have reached "consensus" on every aspect of an issue; rather, they may only have found broad areas of agreement so that they can move ahead. For instance, one might consider attempts to address youth issues: citizens in a community discussion place varying emphasis on different problem areas—such as teen pregnancy, drug and alcohol abuse, school drop-outs, and others. Seeking to reach a consensus would mean that everyone lists the same priorities or agrees on the exact nature of these

problems. But in many communities that is not possible. But finding common ground allows people to say, "Yes, my concerns are reflected in our discussion, even though we may not all agree on the absolute priorities or how we define every aspect of these problems. So let's move ahead before it's too late."

V. **Stages in the policy process where citizens can participate.** Even when citizens have the will and opportunity to deliberate on issues, there is the question of where in the policy process they can participate. There are various stages where this input **can** occur. And these stages are found in virtually all levels of the policy process—from local community, to state, to federal concerns.

A. **Giving and withholding consent.** In our democracy, citizens have always held the right to give or withhold consent on policy issues by raising their voices in public debate and, ultimately, by expressing their views through the ballot box. To some, giving or withholding consent is the most basic way to participate in the policy process. Yet, it must be noted that the citizen's contribution to the creation of public policy in this way is limited—sometimes having only a "yes" or "no" response on a particular measure, and not necessarily having a say on which issue is addressed and how.

B. **The naming and framing of the public agenda.** Perhaps the most critical step in the policy process is the naming and framing of the public agenda. It is here that decisions are made about what issues should be discussed and how they will be framed. For example, how does a community decide what are the most important issues to address? And, once it decides, how should a particular issue be framed? For instance, if the economy is identified as the most important issue, should it be discussed in terms of jobs and unemployment, economic growth, human capital, taxes, or other dimensions? Such decisions are made as part of the process of naming and framing the public agenda.

C. **Setting directions on issues.** Citizens can play an important role in providing input on the various directions that can be taken to act on an issue. This might include thinking about how to balance conflicting needs and values on policy choices: how as a society, for example, do we balance our desires to maintain the costs of health care and provide expanded care?

D. **Acting on policy issues.** After deliberating, citizens have the ability to act on policy issues in two fundamental ways.

1. **Informing public officials.** Some "actions" clearly are in the domain of the public official—voting in a legislative body or making an executive decision. In these cases, citizens can act in the policy process by providing informed input to public officials. This input can take many forms, including attending discussions between citizens and public officials, participating in demonstrations, writing letters, and participating in public opinion surveys and questionnaires.

2. **Acting alone and with others outside the formal structure of government.** In other areas in the policy process citizens can act **without** public officials. Citizens can work, individually or collectively, to tackle issues that do not require, or would not necessarily benefit from, a government response. For instance, neighbors can build a needed playground for local children or create tutorial programs to improve inadequate education and thus provide a citizen response to a community need. Traditionally, Americans have often acted for themselves without waiting for government, and the need for such voluntary action on many public problems continues.

VI. **The need to distinguish the roles of citizen and expert.** The policy process demands that citizens distinguish their roles from those of experts.

A. **The need for expert knowledge.** Many analysts believe that citizen participation in the policy process should not eliminate the role of experts. Citizens would be wise to maintain a perspective on their role and avoid making technical decisions. For instance, few will doubt that decisions involving engineering techniques should be left in the domain of experts since such decisions require technical knowledge and judgment. But less obvious cases may call for expert judgment, too. The public's role in deliberating on policy concerns discussing and weighing of ideas, values, conflicts, and directions—and not making technical decisions.

B. **Experts cannot be used as a proxy for citizen input.** Equally, however, experts and public officials should understand that their knowledge is no adequate substitute for constructive public input. Indeed, the nature of what citizens can offer in deciding upon policy cannot easily be replaced. For instance, finding common ground on an issue cannot be artificially constructed by public officials and experts. If values, concerns, and direction are not provided by the public at large, with depth and breadth of participation, then

public policy risks alienation from those it claims to serve and proceeds in a vacuum.

Historical Perspective

I. **Recent societal trends as continuously changing citizens' relationship to the policy process.** Over the last twenty to thirty years (the primary focus of this section) new pressures and trends have emerged in American society that have altered the policy process and our democracy itself. These trends have led to changes in the dynamics of how the policy process works and how citizens relate to it.

A. **The information explosion as a double-edged sword.** Now more than ever, Americans enjoy faster and broader access to information on the process of creating public policy and on policy issues. Changes in the amounts and kinds of information available has produced both benefits and challenges for the policy process.

1. **Greater access to information on the policy process.** For instance, citizens can now follow issues on nearly a moment-by-moment basis through relatively new television channels such as CNN and C-SPAN. They may watch policy debates and public forums as they occur on television and gain information on issues through vast databases and other sources. Similarly, they learn about issues and register their references through such avenues as electronic town-hall meetings or television call-in news polls whose results are available in a matter of hours or even minutes. And there are a plethora of magazines, newspapers, newsletters, and other materials that cover virtually every policy issue.

2. **Citizens and the "information paradox."** The onslaught of information has caused an "information paradox." Increasingly, information overload makes it difficult to understand what is relevant both to the policy process and to their daily lives.

B. **Positive and negative effects of the rise in technology.** New technologies, along with the broader application of existing technologies, has created both opportunities and challenges for the policy process.

1. **A greater use of technology provides more access to the policy process.** Citizens are now able to learn about policy-related events with greater speed and frequency because of technology.

a. **Role of television and radio.** Television and radio and other communication mediums allow the coverage of events around the world and at home. Citizens hear public officials and others discuss policy issues and their implications; radio and television talk shows impart timely information on public issues and encourage interaction between audience and guests, creating a national forum of sorts.

b. **Other information technologies.** Databases can be tapped by office and home computers, and facsimile (FAX) machines and other forms of technology place information at one's finger tips. All of these technologies allow for a greater and more rapid exchange of information; and they enable policy decisions to be made faster. But they also sometimes force policy decisions to be made precipitously, when a slower pace might yield more informed and effective action.

2. **Technology's capacity to create a false sense of deliberation and involvement.** Changes in technology do not always produce greater deliberation or involvement in the policy process; in fact, these changes can even undercut them. For instance, public officials can now walk into television studios and create programs for their districts. But the communication is only in one direction, without an exchange of views. Or, citizens may watch news programs that detail specific policy issues and accept such passive activity to suffice for their deliberation. But discussion with others is essential to exploring ideas and finding common ground. Again, electronic town hall meetings can be held; but such meetings, while they explore issues and provoke discussion, encompass a large audience of passive "participants." Witnessing the exchange of information is not a substitute for active and engaged deliberation.

C. **The consequences of greater social diversity.** During the post-World War II era, the Civil Rights and women's rights movements, for example, helped remove barriers for minorities and women to participate in the policy process. The result is that the tone and nature of our political debate has changed. Similarly, the increase in immigrants, most clearly evident in places such as California and New York City, has also changed the face of political debate. Various groups previously not involved in the policy process now find themselves an integral part of the process. Some may

have once been legally excluded from the full rights of citizenship; others may have had only a limited voice; or, being recent immigrants, they were simply not yet U.S. citizens and therefore not members of the sovereign body politic. Because of these recent historic changes, we must consider many more perspectives and interests in the policy process.

D. **The erosion in the sense of community.** The ever-changing nature of the communities in which we live has implications for the role of citizens in the policy process.

1. **Loss of central places.** Some analysts suggest that the process of "urbanization" began some 150 years ago. Then, after World War II, "suburbanization" began in earnest, and with this new trend, society became increasingly spread out. As neighborhoods and town centers were replaced by shopping malls and shopping strips, the sense of place and of community eroded. Of course, in many areas central places have been created where people can convene, but many others have not. The desire among the public for this sense of place is seen in recent building trends. In the 1980s and 1990s, some architects have attempted to restore a sense of community by building "new towns" where each house is within walking distance of a "town center."

2. **Increasing mobility.** Meanwhile, since World War II, Americans have become increasingly mobile, especially in the pursuit of employment. Seeking a job may have once meant staying close to home, but Americans may now shift from one coast to the other in search of employment. Such mobility was visible in the 1970s and early 1980s when job opportunities shifted significantly from the industrial East and Midwest, for instance, to the Sunbelt.

3. **Changes in a sense of belonging.** With changes in living patterns, many Americans have left their extended families and community roots behind. Many have fewer connections to the communities in which they live. They may not know their neighbors, may not have a sense of local public issues and their history, and may not feel comfortable participating in the policy process.

E. **The influence of mass communications on citizens' understanding of public issues.** Media coverage at all levels of public issues has changed as a result of trends in the mass communications industry. Information is now available almost instantly from a number of sources.

1. **Television as the primary news source**. Since the 1960s, television has become the primary source of information for most Americans; indeed, since the mid-1970s, the expansion of cable television has provided many more sources of information.

2. **Decline of hard news on television**. Yet a study of television news coverage reveals that, between 1975 and 1986, there was a 50 percent increase in human interest stories and a 37 percent decrease in stories on domestic policy issues.

3. **The shrinking soundbite**. A recent study by Harvard's Kennedy School of Government indicates that, in 1968, the average nightly news broadcast's "sound bite" (a unit of uninterrupted sound) of a presidential candidate was forty-five seconds while, in 1988, this average had fallen precipitously to a just under ten seconds.

4. **Distinction between news and entertainment blurred**. Moreover, some observers of broadcast communication suggest that, during the 1980s in particular, there was a growing blur between entertainment and hard news; it was sometimes difficult to know when a program was based on actual facts or was the creation of a television script.

5. **Newspaper readership declines**. While all of these changes were occurring in the broadcast media, newspaper readership declined. The response of some publications has been to use color, present more graphics, print shorter articles, and cover more human interest stories.

F. **"Segmentation" of the policy process**. Over the years Americans, along with various institutions, have come to view policy issues increasingly through the prism of narrow personal or special interests. Many observers of the policy process attribute this trend, at least in part, to government's more active role in society.

1. **Creating targets to be influenced in the executive branch**. In expanding its role, government created offices and agencies that could be targeted for influence by outside forces. Thus, between 1960 and 1977, twenty-six new federal agencies were created, including the Federal Highway Administration (1966), Environmental Protection Agency (1970) and Drug Enforcement Agency (1973).

2. **Decentralization of legislative power**. The legislative branch also became more segmented; over the last twenty to thirty years, fifty new congressional committees and over one hundred new subcommittees formed.

3. **The division of issues into single units**. The segmenting of the policy process has not been left exclusively to government: citizens have also segmented issues, typically focussing on issues that directly affect them. In addition, corporations have taken steps to focus public debate on their issues through funding political action committees (PACs), joining trade groups, and creating corporate public affairs offices. The results of this segmentation of the policy process are seen in a number of areas.

4. **Increase in "single issue" politics**. As the policy process and society generally has become segmented, American politics has become increasingly "single issue" oriented. Since the 1960s, there has been an explosion of "single issue" organizations around such areas as the environment, consumer rights, gun control, and abortion, among others. PACs expanded from 608 in 1974, to 4,157 in 1986—all representing a specific point of view. The result is that each interest actively pursues only its own agenda. Such pursuits are seen regularly during governmental budget battles where lobbyists line the hallways of Congress and other legislative bodies seeking to win victories for their respective interests and clients.

5. **Citizens join existing organizations to have their views heard**. Many Americans (as well as various public institutions and private concerns) now belong to "special" or "public" interest organizations to express their views on particular issues. Citizens may now belong to a plethora of trade associations, professional groups, and advocacy organizations. The increase in citizen membership in these groups is exemplified by the environmental movement, which tripled its membership in the 1960s and 1970s. Since the 1960s, many people have joined groups which focus on increasingly specialized issues. For instance, in 1970, 50 percent of all doctors belonged to the American Medical Association (AMA), while in 1980 only a third belonged. Yet during the same period, various organizations representing brain surgeons, pediatricians, and other medical specialties grew substantially.

6. **Citizens transferring civic duty to "surrogate" organizations.** By joining an existing organization, many Americans have opted to have the organization speak for them in the policy process. In a sense, many may find themselves participating in public debate by proxy: they may write a check to an organization as their primary means of participating. Even more, the targeted mail and calls that citizens receive from many organizations do not typically foster public discussion but, rather, advocate a position and seek support for it. The result may be that many citizens seldom take the opportunity to discuss issues among themselves; they are merely supporting organizations that may make decisions for citizens in absentia.

II. **The policy process as more like campaign politics.** While political campaigns and the policy process have never been entirely separate, they have never been as intertwined as they are today. The growing blur between the two has helped to reshape the policy process, how it works, and citizens' relationship to it.

A. **Advent of "specialists."** In the last twenty to thirty years, with the advent of professional campaign workers, political campaigns have become increasingly "specialized." In the 1980s, for instance, "spin doctors" emerged—media "handlers" (advisors) schooled in providing instant analysis of a political situation placing their candidate in the most positive light.

1. **The coming of specialists.** In the late 1960s and '70s, "get-out-the-vote" specialists, speech writers, and others came to dominate political campaigns. Some observers point to 1968 as a turning point in the use of campaign specialists, when out-of-state campaign workers, most of them amateurs, converged on New Hampshire and other states to work in the presidential primaries for Eugene McCarthy.

2. **The role of specialists today.** Now professional specialists are part of the policy process, advising not only public officials but also interest groups, corporations, and others, on interacting with the public on substantive policy matters. Indeed these specialists help to shape the nature of public discourse on policy issues: get-out-the-vote specialists devise "grass-roots" campaigns on behalf of their clients to drum up support for various policy initiatives; public relations gurus spell out what messages will "sell" to citizens and public officials; media people coach corporate executives in how to dress and how to answer questions for television interviews.

B. **Use of the media.** The use of the media now permeates all of politics and increasingly the policy process.

1. **The coming of media domination.** Greater use of the media in politics for such things as political advertisements and speeches took hold in the 1960s, when mass media technology, especially television, was further developed and refined. One memorable example was the advertisement shown by Lyndon Johnson's 1964 campaign showing a young girl picking the pedals from a daisy, with a mushroom cloud in the background and a voice-over suggesting fears of nuclear war should his opponent be returned to office.

2. **The application of media techniques today.** Now public officials, corporations, special interest organizations, and other interested parties are applying media-based campaign techniques. They hold staged events on issues they hope will be covered by the nightly news; they place paid "issue ads" in various media seeking to alter public opinion; and they use public relations campaigns for similar purposes.

3. **The creation of "issue campaigns."** Antecedents to "issue campaigns" occurred in the early 1970s, for instance, when the American Petroleum Institute sponsored television advertisements explaining the high cost of energy and the oil industry's response. More recent examples of attempts to mold public debate through media advertising include the dispute in the late 1980s over the Supreme Court nomination of Robert Bork; the National Rifle Association's bid to stop gun-control measures; and efforts by both pro-and- anti-abortion lobbyists.

C. **Application of technology.** Political campaigns increasingly have used technologies to manage political discourse and encourage political leanings.

1. **Using databases to target citizens.** Political campaigns increasingly use sophisticated databases to target mailings and political messages to citizens based on their proven political and consumer behaviors, such as the magazines they read, car models they drive, or the neighborhoods where they live. Thus, a 1988 book segmented the political views of Americans according to various cluster groups, down to their neighborhoods.

2. **Using computers to contact households.** In addition, technology is used to generate thousands of pre-recorded telephone messages directed to specific to American households. Public officials, special and public interest organizations, corporations and businesses, and others involved in the policy process have used these and other technologies. For instance, citizens identified by interest and issue now receive targeted, often unsolicited, mailings from certain groups on issues such as the environment, gun control, and abortion. While a message is sent to one house, neighbors believed to hold different views receive mailings from opposing groups. Or the same organization may send different messages on the same issue to each neighbor.

D. **Reliance on public opinion polls.** Political campaigns, the media, and others have used public opinion polling at least since the 1930s. Franklin Roosevelt's administration polled various targeted groups to test people's reactions to specific policies. Over the years, public officials, interest groups, corporations, and other groups have used opinion polls in an attempt to set public agendas and monitor public support. Thus, a company may survey residents of a state on various tax issues before commenting on a proposed tax initiative or offering its own alternative. And, since the mid 1970s, especially in the 1980s, polls were used by sitting U.S. presidents. Jimmy Carter was reportedly the first president to consult a full-time pollster; Carter's successor, Ronald Reagan, received weekly and sometimes daily readings of public opinion on specific issues.

III. **Citizens as less connected to the policy process.** As the policy process has changed over time, so too has the way that citizens view and participate in that process.

A. **Growth of citizens' mistrust of government.** Various events in recent years have caused a decline in Americans' trust in their government. Primary events that contributed to this sense of mistrust were the Vietnam War, the Watergate affair, the Abscam scandal, and the Iran-Contra arms deal. Other factors, such as seemingly uncontrollable campaign spending and the rising influence of special interest groups, have had a similar effect. Voter mistrust is illustrated by the recent term-limitation referendums in California, Colorado, and Oklahoma and by the fact that another twenty states may hold such referendums.

B. **Citizen sense of impotence of their role in the policy process.** Many citizens increasingly say that they to feel impotent in the policy process, believing that there is little room for individual citizens to play a role. A recent Kettering Foundation study of citizen attitudes on politics reveals that Americans believe that special interests, campaign financiers, the media, and other "power brokers" now control the policy process—that citizens have been either pushed out or left out of the political process. Observers such as Harry Boyte, author of a number of books on citizens and politics, suggest that the emphasis President Reagan placed on citizens as "individual consumers" helped to increase this feeling of powerlessness. He has written that "the Reagan years reinforced people's sense of themselves as spectators of the political process," rather than active and potent, contributing participants. (See above, "Civic and Community Action," in Part II, Participation).

C. **Citizens *seem* less willing to participate.** Voting is perhaps the easiest way to participate in the policy process in America. Yet, in many elections voting is at an all-time low. Sixty-five percent of the electorate participated in the 1904 presidential election; while in 1988, only about 53 percent voted. Moreover, in recent studies by the Kettering Foundation, both public officials and citizens report that Americans are less likely to participate in the policy process than in the past. Both groups say that citizens often do not take the time to learn about issues or participate in public forums because they believe that they cannot make a difference politically. Meanwhile, citizens are active in areas they call "community activities" and in traditional volunteerism—actions outside the formal processes of government policy formation. (For further discussion, see Rationale, Part II, Participation).

D. **Citizens *seem* interested primarily in issues that affecting them directly.** Some observers of the policy process suggest that Americans, now more than ever before, are willing to participate **only** when issues affect them directly. This tendency can be seen, in part, in the rise of ad hoc, issue-oriented groups. Examples include parents forming a coalition to improve their children's schools; neighbors creating a crime watch to protect their streets; or citizens protesting homelessness. But observers also point to parochialism—to "NIMBY" issues—"Not In My Backyard." These issues range from the placement of prisons or mental health facilities to the construction of utility plants. On NIMBY issues, citizens may vehemently oppose an action that they perceive will adversely affect their immediate neighborhood or area.

E. **There seem to be fewer central places for deliberative discussion.** Although deliberation is fundamental to the policy process, critics argue that there are too few opportunities for public discussion and deliberation. Some analysts believe that since the beginning of the century, public places formed by voluntary associations, coffee houses, clubs, and other places for political discussion have become scarce. Even public meetings today often result in citizens reacting to pre-determined policy solutions instead of engaging in true deliberation; and public officials typically say they face a lynch mob mentality by angry citizens. Indeed, both citizens and public officials say they lack the public space to engage in meaningful discussion that defines and explores public problems and the means to deal with them.

IV. **The historical tension over when and how citizens may be involved in the policy process.** There is an inherent, perhaps growing, tension in the formal (governmental) aspects of the American policy process which exists over how to balance the role of public officials and the role of citizens.

A. **A tension within representative democracy.** The American polity was founded on the idea of "representative" democracy where public officials, taking the public's views into account, make the ultimate decisions on policy and practice. Yet there has always been a tension between "trustee" forms of representation—where public officials generally decide what is in the best interest of the public—and public officials as "agents", where they more or less try to reflect the actual opinions of citizens. This tension persists today. (For a discussion of these two models of representation, see above in this Framework, "Morality and Politics.")

B. **Movement toward direct democracy through referendum.** Direct democracy was popular during the Progressive movement at the turn of the century in response to the corrupt activities of government officials. The trend waned until the 1970s when citizens sought to hold officials more fully accountable. In 1990, forty-three states and the District of Columbia used the referendum; California alone had twenty-eight propositions on its ballot.

1. **Advantages of referendum and initiative.** Some advocates of referendum and initiatives say that these measures offer citizens the chance to play a direct governing role. Moreover, the inability of government and society to act on certain issues has provided added importance to these measures:

they provide citizens with an opportunity "get action" on issues important to them.

2. **Disadvantages of referendum and initiative.** Opponents of these measures often say that citizens are generally not sufficiently informed to make direct decisions about policy and that people are forced to vote "yes" or "no," which only serves to polarize political debate. Indeed, referendums and initiatives serve to reinforce the "campaign" style of policy making—merely asking citizens to take sides, divide into pre-defined camps, with no attempt to find common ground.

V. **Indications of a policy process in crisis.** As a result of social, political, and other changes in the policy process, new trends are emerging that affect how the nation conducts its public business.

A. **De-emphasis on public discourse.** Many observers suggest that recent social changes have fundamentally altered the nature of the political process and the role of public discourse within it. Changes in the use of the media, technology, campaign specialists, and other tools of the modern professionalized policy process have all but replaced face-to-face discussion; they have been used to advocate one policy solution over another without ample discussion; and they have undermined the ability, and at times the desire, of citizens and public officials to hold public debate on critical policy issues. As we have seen, there also now seem to be fewer central places in American society in which such public discussion can occur.

B. **"Policy gridlock" seen as increasing.** Important policy discussions seem to be increasingly "gridlocked:" special interests collide, information overload paralyzes the ability to sort out issues, a search for common ground is often lacking, discussions of the cost and benefits of alternative policies fail to begin—all contributing to the inability of citizens (as well as public officials, corporations, and others) to move beyond their own particular perspective to one of shared interests and concerns.

1. **The budget deficit and policy gridlock.** The federal budget deficit, for instance, has been a clear example of this gridlock. Unable to find acceptable ways to reduce the deficit through either budget cuts or tax increases, Congress in 1985 passed the Gramm-Rudman-Hollings bill. The bill required Congress to reduce the deficit over five years, reaching a balanced budget by 1990. But,

thanks to policy gridlock, the budget is still not balanced.

2. **The consequences of budget imbalance.** The result is that, while badly needed social and economic programs went begging for lack of funds, in 1991 fully 6 percent of gross national product—a staggering sum—was paid in interest on the debt required to finance past deficits. In addition, investment funds badly needed to stimulate the economy and make the nation competitive with international rivals were siphoned off to service the debt.

C. **Sustainable policies as more difficult to find.** Because political debate is increasingly paralyzed, finding sustainable policies becomes all the more difficult.

1. **The absence of common ground.** Volatile opinions among citizens and leaders of various institutions undermine society's ability to identify and agree on policies that will earn broad-based, lasting support; and overcoming obstacles to understanding the values that underpin such opinion makes it even harder to create such sustainable policies.

2. **Examples of the public's veto of proposed policy.** Examples of these difficulties are not hard to find. In 1989, Congress passed catastrophic health care legislation in response to calls for an increase in health-care benefits for senior citizens; it was later rescinded as angry senior citizens rebelled against the plan. Health care issues remain on the critical list, but no movement is in sight toward resolving them. The reason for this inertia, according to some observers, is, in part, the difficulty of developing policies that reflect the values of Americans and that will earn their broad support. Another example of the public's veto occurred in 1989, when New Jersey's newly-elected governor announced sweeping changes in state taxes and education funding programs. Upon the swift and overwhelmingly negative public response to the changes, the governor found himself obliged to revise major sections of his initiative.

Contemporary Perspective

I. **Need to attack ills plaguing the policy process.** Successfully engaging citizens in the policy process requires changes in the process itself. Some of the areas, like those noted below, concern all of society—citizens, public officials, the media, and others—and require those in each component to act to address them effectively.

A. **Setting a place for citizens at the table of public debate.** Individual citizens must be viewed as integral parts of the policy process by public officials, the media, experts, and, of course, citizens themselves. Effecting change will require, among other things, that society find ways to balance the role of institutions—including government, interest groups, corporations, and others—with the role of citizens. A place at the table of public debate should be set for citizens. The nation must change the way it perceives the roles of various participants in the policy process play and how those participants interact.

B. **Enlarging the public's role beyond giving or withholding consent.** A basic role that citizens can play in the policy process is to give or withhold consent on policy issues; that occurs regularly in the voting booth, at public meetings, and in other ways. Still, the role of citizens often needs to go beyond merely giving or withholding consent: citizens need to play a role in the naming and the framing of the public agenda, deliberating on setting directions for action, and in acting on policy matters. It is in these stages that the substance of the policy process is set; by citizens assuming an active role in these areas, society can more effectively decide on a policy course that reflects the concerns and values of its citizens and that will be durable over time.

C. **Moving beyond public opinion polls as a substitute for citizen input.** Seeking citizens' participation in the creation of public policy clearly is important, but using public opinion surveys is by itself insufficient. While surveys can be helpful tools, they do not offer citizens the opportunity to deliberate, see others' perspectives, weigh options, and reach an informed and shared sense of what needs to be done. Neither can surveys reflect the decisions and choices people make as they work through a discussion. It is precisely because these characteristics of public discourse are neither engendered nor captured by surveys, that it is important to use means in addition to surveys to seek public input.

D. **Creating public places and processes for citizen participation.** Citizens must have access to the policy process if they are to participate. Thus government, civic organizations, and other institutions and individuals need to create public places—central places—where citizens can come together to exchange thoughts and discuss issues. It is also important to create the kinds of public processes—that is, what actually happens once people come together—that encourage citizens to openly and constructively discuss issues. Within these public processes, the needs of public officials also must be considered; public officials need to be able to gather information about public deliberation that will help them do their work.

E. **Improving the tone of the public debate.** The quality of policy debate rests in large measure on its tone. Political confrontation, mud-slinging in advertising, "name calling," demagoguery, and other negative aspects of today's political debate undermine the ability and desire of people to engage in honest, open, and rigorous discussion. No doubt the media must play a leadership role in improving the quality of coverage of the public debate; and public officials, interest groups, and other institutions must be held accountable for the type of information they disseminate. Still, expecting such action will not be enough; society as a whole must take the final responsibility for promoting constructive debate in the policy process.

II. **Need for citizens to become re-engaged in the policy process.** Fundamental to the health of the policy process is citizen participation. Yet, today, citizens need to become reengaged in political life if American democracy is to effectively address its challenges. This will require that citizens—**on their own**—take a number of important steps.

A. **Taking responsibility for deliberation on public issues.** The basic responsibility for being informed rests squarely upon citizens themselves.

1. **The role of public officials, media, and others.** Of course, public officials, the media, interest groups, and others play an important role in this process by providing information, clarifying issues, and offering a context for thinking about public debate. But they are not the primary actors. Instead, citizens must drive the process of becoming informed and deliberating.

2. **The potential role of National Issues Forums.** One way to do this is through the National Issues Forums which offer citizens a non-partisan setting to come together and inform themselves on issues, consider a broad range of policy choices, and identify concerns and values they hold in common. The Forums, held in communities across the nation, are sponsored by schools, libraries, community colleges, and citizens.

B. **Creation of public places for deliberation.** There is a need in our society to create "public places" where citizens can deliberate on issues. Based on the concept of the "town meeting" or "local pub," the agora of ancient Greece, the piazza or central square of many countries including early America, a public place is found virtually anywhere and everywhere citizens come together to talk. Today, such places might include public forums at a local school or at the work place; around the kitchen table of a private home; on a street corner; or any place where two or more people meet to think about and discuss policy issues. Creating public places for deliberation is clearly within the power of citizens. Here are some ideas to consider:

1. **The home.** One can invite neighbors into one's home one day or evening to discuss issues of common concern. These might include national issues or a topic important to the local community or neighborhood.

2. **Neighborhood and civic groups.** Citizens can become involved or approach an existing neighborhood association or a civic group (e.g., Parent Teachers Association, Knights of Columbus or Rotary Club) to sponsor forums on issues—to create a public place for citizen discussion of issues.

3. **Schools, libraries and other community institutions.** Various community institutions often provide a focal point for community activities; these institutions offer an opportunity to bring people together to discuss issues.

4. **The work place.** People often create their own sense of community around their work place—it is where they spend most of their day, where they may develop friendships, and where they interact regularly with others. Discussion groups can be formed after and before work or during lunch hours. Some employers may be willing to sponsor discussions during work hours.

C. **Emphasis upon shared interests.** As citizens deliberate on policy issues, it is essential that they seek to identify shared interests, not just their own private interests. Only by seeking shared interests can common concerns be determined and policies chosen that are likely to result in effective action. This quest requires wrestling with the ideas, hopes, and values of others. Through discussion, it is possible to understand others' points of view and find interests that are shared.

D. **Seeking a greater role in the policy process than voting alone.** Clearly citizens should fulfill their responsibility to vote in elections; but the policy process demands that citizens play a role that consists of more than just voting. Citizens must take the responsibility to interact with public officials through public hearings and meetings or through other avenues. The role of citizens in the policy process should be to continuously consider policy issues, express their views on them, and when appropriate, find ways to act on those views.

III. **Need to recapture a sense of community through civic duty.** Central to many of the issues discussed above is the need for citizens to develop a stake in the policy process, to feel a sense of political efficacy, and to see the need to move beyond personal interests to one of shared interests. Perhaps at the root of these concerns is the need to recapture a sense of community—a sense of connectedness. Central to this is tapping our sense of civic duty.

A. **The policy process as a means, not an end.** The policy process must be seen not as an end, but as a means to recapturing a sense of community in America. Through participating in the policy process, citizens will begin to interact directly with their neighbors, their colleagues, and others; their interaction will be focused on exchanging ideas and perhaps finding shared interests. Of course, this action might result in a new policy initiative or public program to address a policy challenge; but, perhaps more importantly, citizens can create something much greater than a single policy or program: they will develop a renewed sense of connection to others, a new sense of community. This will constitute a renewal of the deep civic tradition that extends back to the early days of the republic, and before that to colonial America.

B. **Connecting effective community action with a sense of political efficacy.** If citizens are to become engaged in the policy process, they must feel a sense of efficacy. That appears to be missing today. Although many Americans are actively involved in their communities seeking to address public problems, they do not seem to connect the formal policy process—and their ability to affect it—with those actions that they take on their own. Drawing connections between the two is essential to providing citizens with a sense of political potency: citizens must recognize their capacity to act effectively; and the nation must create the conditions that encourage citizen participation.

C. **Taking civic duty seriously.** Becoming engaged in the policy process, and in turn recapturing or extending a sense of community, can occur only if citizens take a serious view of their civic duty. A careful definition of civic duty is described elsewhere in these materials (see above, Civic Virtue); still, at its center, a sense of civic duty must include a commitment to deliberation; a commitment to the political and collective health of American society; and a commitment to pass on to others—especially children—the need to renew the tradition of civic duty. In acting within this tradition, citizens foster the sense of belonging and mutual recognition as they address the challenges before them.

INDEX

Burger, Chief Justice Warren E., 34, 463

Burke, Edmund, 538, 628; political ideas of, 129

Bush, President George, 34, 543

"Business cycle," 191

Butler, Benjamin, 66

Butts, R. Freeman, 5

Bynkershoek, Cornelius van, 355

Calhoun, John C., 406, 420

Calvin, John, 23, 101, 118, 363

Campaign finance, 498; reform of, in 1970s, 498-500; current reform proposals of, 609-10

Canada, 160; as U.S. neighbor, 323-26; geographical and demographic aspects of, 323; constitution of, 323; national character of, 323; linguistic and cultural bifurcation of, 323-24; regionalism, 324; political system of, 324-25; federalism of, compared with U.S., 324-25; 1982 constitution of, 325; trade between U.S. and, 325; constitution and crisis of, 326

Canon law, 338-39, 350

Capitalism, and liberal democracy, 130-31

Carlyle, Thomas, 130

Carson, Rachel, 525

Carter Administration, federalism and, 410-11

Carter, Jimmy, 287, 309, 544, 563, 637

Cassini family, 216

Castro, Fidel, 285

Categories of American law. See Law: categories of

Cater, Douglas, 538

Catt, Carrie Chapman, 265

Caxton, William, 538

Central America, and democracy, 157

Chamberlain, Houston, 150

Charlemagne, 100

Charles I (of England), 343

Charter of Paris (1990), 25

Charter of Rhode Island (1663), 618

Chavez, Caesar, 251

Checks and balances, 15

Chesapeake affair, 290

Chiang Kai-shek, 146, 299, 302

China: traditional view of the state of, 114; nineteenth century view of state, 114-15; modern state of, 146; founding of Chinese Communist Party (CCP), 146; communist state in, 146; and relations with USSR, 146; cultural revolution in, 146-47;

reform policies of, 147; challenges to, 147; Tiananmen Square massacre and, 147; early trade with U.S., 290; U.S. and Boxer Rebellion in, 294; U.S. post-war policy toward, 302; and Nixon Administration, 309; in the 1980s, 318

Chinese Communist Party (CCP). *See* China: founding of CCP

Christian law: history of, 338-42; contemporary issues of, 350

Christianity: and the state, 124; and divided loyalties, 124; contributions to western civilization of, 124; and the Middle Ages, 125

Churchill, Winston S., 297, 617

Cicero, 179, 278, 364; view of the state and the citizen of, 123

Cisneros, Henry G., 73

Citizen participation: civic and community action, 73-90; and the Congress, 436; and making of foreign policy, 328

Citizens: in ancient Greece, 120-22; in ancient Rome, 123; moral relationship of, with state, 124; and American role in world affairs, 288

Citizenship, 247; and early immigration policy, 244

Civic and community action: relations of, with politics, 74-6; and the voluntary tradition, 76-7; as problem solving patterns of, 75, 82; forms of, 77-8; and community politics today, 80-2; connecting community and public, 81

Civic commitments, 11

Civic dispositions, enumerated, 13-4

Civic education: importance of, 3-4; role of schools in, 4; role of family in, 5; and teaching politics to youth, 82; and democracy, 132; and public choice theory, 206

Civic humanism, 102. *See also* Atlantic community

Civic Participation. *See* Participation

Civic values, enumerated, 15-6

Civic virtue, 362; as an ultimate goal of civic education, 11; republican and liberal traditions of, 12; dispositions of, 12; commitments of, 14

Civil disobedience: definition of, 629; meaning of "civil" in, 630; characteristics of, 629-30; direct and indirect forms of, 631; what it is not, 631; sources of justification for, 631-33; varieties of, 633-34; qualification of defining legitimate forms of, 632-33; historical development of, 633-37;

major practitioners of, 633-35; and World War II, 635; in America, 635-36; current issues regarding, 636-37; crisis of, today, 637

Civil law, 338, 455; history of, 344-45; convergence with common law, 349-50

Civil rights: meaning of legal category of, 612; federal policy regarding, 479

Civil Society: and liberal democracy, 131-32; reemergence of in USSR, 145

Civil War, the press and, 552

Civilian control of the military, 15

Civility, as a civic disposition, 13

Clark, Septima, 81

Clark, William, 217

Clausewitz, Karl von, 279

Clay, Henry, 50, 51, 494

Clean Air Act, 521

Clean Water Act, 521

"Clear and present danger" test, 299-300

Cleveland, President Grover, 495

Climate change. *See* Global warming

Club of Rome Report, 526

Code Napoleon, 345

Coke, Edward, 127, 343

Cold War: out break of, in 1946, 299-300; decline of, in 1980s, 312; superpowers at the end of, 313

Columbus, Christopher, 215

Commission on the Status of Women, 269

Common history, as a bond among citizens, 257

Common good, 362. *See* also Public good

Common law, 333, 337-38, 455; history of, 342-44; convergence with civil law, 344

Common values and institutions, as bonds among citizens, 257

Communism: as a corruption of authority, 106; view of the state of, 140; in the twentieth century, 142; and Leninism, 142; and Stalinism, 143

Community action. *See* Civic and community action

Community service, 89

Compassion, as a civic disposition, 13

Comprehensive Enviromental Response Compensation and Liability Act, 521

Compromise, as a civic disposition, 13

Condorcet, Marquis de, 138

Conference on Security and Cooperation in Europe (CSCE), 25

Conflicts: among fundamental principles, 416-19; equality v. liberty,

The typeface used for CIVITAS is 10 point
Century Old Style Condensed, a modern
adaptation of the typeface invented by
Morris Fuller Benton in 1906. Known for its
legibility and called an American
masterpiece, the real forte of this typeface
lies in setting lengthy blocks of text.

Linotronic output by Graphic Connexions in
Cranbury, New Jersey.

Printing by Optic Graphics, Inc. in Glen
Burnie, Maryland.